BUSINESS ANALYSIS AND VALUATION

IFRS EDITION

SECOND EDITION

BUSINESS ANALYSIS AND VALUATION

IFRS EDITION   TEXT AND CASES

KRISHNA G. PALEPU

PAUL M. HEALY

ERIK PEEK

SOUTH-WESTERN
CENGAGE Learning

Australia • Brazil • Japan • Korea • Mexico • Singapore • Spain • United Kingdom • United States

SOUTH-WESTERN
CENGAGE Learning

Business Analysis and Valuation
IFRS edition: Text and Cases
Second Edition
Krishna G. Palepu, Paul M. Healy
and Erik Peek

Publishing Director: Linden Harris

Publisher: Brendan George

Development Editor: Anna Carter

Editorial Assistant: Helen Green

Content Project Editor: Lucy Arthy

Production Controller: Eyvett Davis

Marketing Manager: Amanda Cheung

Typesetter: KnowledgeWorks Global, India

Cover design: Adam Renvoize

Text design: Design Deluxe

For product information and technology assistance, contact **emea.info@cengage.com**.
For permission to use material from this text or product, and for permission queries, email **clsuk.permissions@cengage.com**.

The Author has asserted the right under the Copyright, Designs and Patents Act 1988 to be identified as Author of this Work.

This work is adapted from *Business Analysis and Valuation: Using Financial Statements*, published by South-Western, a division of Cengage Learning, Inc. © 2008.

British Library Cataloguing-in-Publication Data
A catalogue record for this book is available from the British Library.

ISBN: 978-1-4080-1749-4

Cengage Learning EMEA
Cheriton House, North Way, Andover, Hampshire. SP10 5BE.
United Kingdom

Cengage Learning products are represented in Canada by Nelson Education Ltd.

For your lifelong learning solutions, visit
www.cengage.co.uk

Purchase your next print book, e-book or e-chapter at
www.CengageBrain.com

Printed by R R Donnelley, China
1 2 3 4 5 6 7 8 9 10 – 12 11 10

CONTENTS

PART

4

ADDITIONAL CASES   567

PREFACE

Financial statements are the basis for a wide range of business analyses. Managers use them to monitor and judge their firms' performance relative to competitors, to communicate with external investors, to help judge what financial policies they should pursue, and to evaluate potential new businesses to acquire as part of their investment strategy. Securities analysts use financial statements to rate and value companies they recommend to clients. Bankers use them in deciding whether to extend a loan to a client and to determine the loan's terms. Investment bankers use them as a basis for valuing and analyzing prospective buyouts, mergers, and acquisitions. And consultants use them as a basis for competitive analysis for their clients. Not surprisingly, therefore, there is a strong demand among business students for a course that provides a framework for using financial statement data in a variety of business analysis and valuation contexts. The purpose of this book is to provide such a framework for business students and practitioners. This IFRS edition is the European adaptation of the authoritative US edition – authored by Krishna G. Palepu and Paul M. Healy – that has been used in Accounting and Finance departments in universities around the world. In 2007 we decided to write the first IFRS edition because of the European business environment's unique character and the introduction of mandatory IFRS reporting for public corporations in the European Union. This second IFRS edition is a thorough update of the successful first edition, incorporating new examples, cases, problems and exercises, elements from the fourth US edition, and regulatory updates.

THIS IFRS EDITION

Particular features of the IFRS edition are the following:

- A large number of examples support the discussion of business analysis and valuation throughout the chapters. The examples are from European companies that students will generally be familiar with, such as Alcatel, AstraZeneca, Bang & Olufsen, British American Tobacco, British Petroleum, Carlsberg, easyGroup, Finnair, GlaxoSmithKline, Loewe, Porsche, Royal Dutch Shell, and Volkswagen.

- The chapters dealing with accounting analysis (Chapters 3 and 4) prepare European students for the task of analyzing IFRS-based financial statements. All numerical examples of accounting adjustments in Chapter 4 describe adjustments to IFRS-based financial statements. Further, throughout the book we discuss various topics that are particularly relevant to understanding IFRS-based European financial reports, such as: the classification of expenses by nature and by function; a principles-based approach versus a rules-based approach to standard setting; the first-time adoption of IFRS; cross-country differences and similarities in external auditing and public enforcement, and cross-country differences in financing structures.

- The terminology that we use throughout the chapters is consistent with the terminology that is used in the IFRS.

- Throughout the chapters, we describe the average performance and growth ratios, the average time-series behavior of these ratios, and average financing policies of a sample of close to 8,000 firms that have been listed on European public exchanges between 1992 and 2008.

- This IFRS edition includes 15 cases about European companies. Twelve of these cases make use of IFRS-based financial statements. However, we also retained several popular cases from the US edition because they have proved to be very effective for many instructors.

   Colleagues and reviewers have made suggestions and comments that led us to incorporate the following changes in the second IFRS edition:

- Data, analyses, issues, and examples have been thoroughly updated in the second edition.
- The financial analysis and valuation chapters (Chapters 6–8) have been updated with a focus on firms in the consumer electronics sector, primarily Bang & Olufsen and Loewe.
- Chapter 6 on forecasting has been enhanced with an expanded discussion of business strategy analysis. Chapters 7 and 8 have been made more accessible without sacrificing the depth of coverage, through a slight change in structure, the addition of a comprehensive demonstration case, and the expansion of the discussion on cost of capital estimation.
- We have increased conciseness by incorporating key elements of the chapter in the first IFRS edition on debt financing into this edition's chapters on credit analysis (Chapter 10) and corporate governance (Chapter 12).
- Each chapter concludes with a summary of core concepts.
- We have included three new cases: Marks & Spencer's Accounting Choices (accompanying Chapter 4), Valuation at Novartis (Chapter 9) and Getronics' Debt Ratings (Chapter 10).
- Fourteen mini cases now accompany the first eight individual chapters. These real-life exercises help students to practice the techniques of business analysis and valuation. They complement the comprehensive end-of-chapter cases and, if desired, may serve as a time-efficient alternative.
- A set of lecture slides about each individual chapter is available on the book's companion website.

KEY FEATURES

This book differs from other texts in business and financial analysis in a number of important ways. We introduce and develop a framework for business analysis and valuation using financial statement data. We then show how this framework can be applied to a variety of decision contexts.

Framework for analysis

We begin the book with a discussion of the role of accounting information and intermediaries in the economy, and how financial analysis can create value in well-functioning markets (Chapter 1). We identify four key components, or steps, of effective financial statement analysis:

- Business strategy analysis
- Accounting analysis
- Financial analysis
- Prospective analysis

The first step, business strategy analysis (Chapter 2), involves developing an understanding of the business and competitive strategy of the firm being analyzed. Incorporating business strategy into financial statement analysis is one of the distinctive features of this book. Traditionally, this step has been ignored by other financial statement analysis books. However, we believe that it is critical to begin financial statement analysis with a company's strategy because it provides an important foundation for the subsequent analysis. The strategy analysis section discusses contemporary tools for analyzing a company's industry, its competitive position and sustainability within an industry, and the company's corporate strategy.

Accounting analysis (Chapters 3 and 4) involves examining how accounting rules and conventions represent a firm's business economics and strategy in its financial statements, and, if necessary, developing adjusted accounting measures of performance. In the accounting analysis section, we do not emphasize accounting rules. Instead we develop general approaches to analyzing assets, liabilities, entities, revenues, and expenses. We believe that such an approach enables students to effectively evaluate a company's accounting choices and accrual estimates, even if students have only a basic knowledge of accounting rules and standards. The material is also designed to allow students to make accounting adjustments rather than merely identify questionable accounting practices.

Financial analysis (Chapter 5) involves analyzing financial ratio and cash flow measures of the operating, financing, and investing performance of a company relative to either key competitors or historical performance. Our distinctive approach focuses on using financial analysis to evaluate the effectiveness of a company's strategy and to make sound financial forecasts.

Finally, under prospective analysis (Chapters 6–8) we show how to develop forecasted financial statements and how to use these to make estimates of a firm's value. Our discussion of valuation includes traditional discounted cash flow models as well as techniques that link value directly to accounting numbers. In discussing accounting-based valuation models, we integrate the latest academic research with traditional approaches such as earnings and book value multiples that are widely used in practice.

While we cover all four steps of business analysis and valuation in the book, we recognize that the extent of their use depends on the user's decision context. For example, bankers are likely to use business strategy analysis, accounting analysis, financial analysis, and the forecasting portion of prospective analysis. They are less likely to be interested in formally valuing a prospective client.

Application of the framework to decision contexts

The next section of the book shows how our business analysis and valuation framework can be applied to a variety of decision contexts:

- Securities analysis (Chapter 9)
- Credit analysis and distress prediction (Chapter 10)
- Merger and acquisition analysis (Chapter 11)
- Governance and communication analysis (Chapter 12)

For each of these topics we present an overview to provide a foundation for the class discussions. Where possible we discuss relevant institutional details and the results of academic research that are useful in applying the analysis concepts developed earlier in the book. For example, the chapter on credit analysis shows how banks and rating agencies use financial statement data to develop analysis for lending decisions and to rate public debt issues. This chapter also presents academic research on how to determine whether a company is financially distressed.

USING THE BOOK

We designed the book so that it is flexible for courses in financial statement analysis for a variety of student audiences – MBA students, Masters in Accounting students, Executive Program participants, and undergraduates in accounting or finance. Depending upon the audience, the instructor can vary the manner in which the conceptual materials in the chapters, end-of-chapter questions, and case examples are used. To get the most out of the book, students should have completed basic courses in financial accounting, finance, and either business strategy or business economics. The text provides a concise overview of some of these topics, primarily as background for preparing the cases. But it would probably be difficult for students with no prior knowledge in these fields to use the chapters as stand-alone coverage of them.

If the book is used for students with prior working experience or for executives, the instructor can use almost a pure case approach, adding relevant lecture sections as needed. When teaching students with little work experience, a lecture class can be presented first, followed by an appropriate case or other assignment material. It is also possible to use the book primarily for a lecture course and include some of the short or long cases as in-class illustrations of the concepts discussed in the book. Alternatively, lectures can be used as a follow-up to cases to more clearly lay out the conceptual issues raised in the case discussions. This may be appropriate when the book is used in undergraduate capstone courses. In such a context, cases can be used in course projects that can be assigned to student teams.

COMPANION WEBSITE

A companion website accompanies this book. This website contains the following valuable material for instructors and students:

- Instructions for how to easily produce standardized financial statements in Excel.
- Spreadsheets containing: (1) the reported and standardized financial statements of Bang & Olufsen (B&O) and Loewe; (2) calculations of B&O's and Loewe's ratios (presented in Chapter 5); (3) Loewe's forecasted financial statements (presented in Chapter 6); and (4) valuations of Loewe's shares (presented in Chapter 8). Using these spreadsheets students can easily replicate the analyses presented in Chapters 5 through 8 and perform "what-if" analyses – i.e., to find out how the reported numbers change as a result of changes to the standardized statements or forecasting assumptions.
- Spreadsheets containing case material.
- Answers to the discussion questions and case instructions (for instructors only).
- A complete set of lecture slides (for instructors only).

Accompanying teaching notes to the case studies can be found at www. harvardbusiness.org. Lecturers are able to register to access the teaching notes and other relevant information.

ACKNOWLEDGEMENTS

We thank the following colleagues who gave us feedback as we wrote this and the previous IFRS edition: Seraina Anagnostopoulou (Athens University of Economics and Business); Niclas Andrén (Lund University); Sanjay Bissessur (University of Amsterdam); Ignace De Beelde (Ghent University); Christina Dargenidou (University of Exeter Business School); Aditi Gupta (King's College London); Shifei Lisa Liu (The University of Liverpool Management School); Mark Mulcahy (University College Cork); Lakshmanan Shivakumar (London Business School); and Stephane Trebucq (Université Montesquieu Bordeaux IV). We are also very grateful to Pat Bond, James Clark, Anna Carter, and the rest of the publishing team at Cengage Learning for their help and assistance throughout the production of this edition.

AUTHORS

KRISHNA G. PALEPU is the Ross Graham Walker Professor of Business Administration and Senior Associate Dean for International Development at the Harvard Business School. During the past 20 years, Professor Palepu's research has focused on corporate strategy, governance, and disclosure. Professor Palepu is the winner of the American Accounting Association's Notable Contributions to Accounting Literature Award (in 1999) and the Wildman Award (in 1997).

PAUL HEALY is the James R. Williston Professor of Business Administration and Head of the Accounting and Management Unit at the Harvard Business School. Professor Healy's research has focused on corporate governance and disclosure, mergers and acquisitions, earnings management, and management compensation. He has previously worked at the MIT Sloan School of Management, ICI Ltd, and Arthur Young in New Zealand. Professor Healy has won the Notable Contributions to Accounting Literature Award (in 1990 and 1999) and the Wildman Award (in 1997) for contributions to practice.

ERIK PEEK is the Duff & Phelps Professor of Business Analysis and Valuation at the Rotterdam School of Management, Erasmus University, the Netherlands. Prior to joining RSM Erasmus University he has been an Associate Professor at Maastricht University and a Visiting Associate Professor at the Wharton School of the University of Pennsylvania. Professor Peek is a CFA charterholder and holds a PhD from the VU University Amsterdam. His research has focused on international accounting, financial analysis and valuation, and earnings management.

FRAMEWORK

A Framework for Business Analysis and Valuation Using Financial Statements

This chapter outlines a comprehensive framework for financial statement analysis. Because financial statements provide the most widely available data on public corporations' economic activities, investors and other stakeholders rely on financial reports to assess the plans and performance of firms and corporate managers.

A variety of questions can be addressed by business analysis using financial statements, as shown in the following examples:

- A security analyst may be interested in asking: "How well is the firm I am following performing? Did the firm meet my performance expectations? If not, why not? What is the value of the firm's stock given my assessment of the firm's current and future performance?"

- A loan officer may need to ask: "What is the credit risk involved in lending a certain amount of money to this firm? How well is the firm managing its liquidity and solvency? What is the firm's business risk? What is the additional risk created by the firm's financing and dividend policies?"

- A management consultant might ask: "What is the structure of the industry in which the firm is operating? What are the strategies pursued by various players in the industry? What is the relative performance of different firms in the industry?"

- A corporate manager may ask: "Is my firm properly valued by investors? Is our investor communication program adequate to facilitate this process?"

- A corporate manager could ask: "Is this firm a potential takeover target? How much value can be added if we acquire this firm? How can we finance the acquisition?"

- An independent auditor would want to ask: "Are the accounting policies and accrual estimates in this company's financial statements consistent with my understanding of this business and its recent performance? Do these financial reports communicate the current status and significant risks of the business?"

The industrial age has been dominated by two distinct and broad ideologies for channeling savings into business investments – capitalism and central planning. The capitalist market model broadly relies on the market mechanism to govern economic activity, and decisions regarding investments are made privately. Centrally planned economies have used central planning and government agencies to pool national savings and to direct investments in business enterprises. The failure of this model is evident from the fact that most of these economies have abandoned it in favor of the second model – the market model. In almost all countries in the world today, **capital markets** play an important role in channeling financial resources from savers to business enterprises that need capital.

Financial statement analysis is a valuable activity when managers have complete information on a firm's strategies, and a variety of institutional factors make it unlikely that they fully disclose this information. In this setting outside analysts attempt to create "inside information" from analyzing financial statement data, thereby gaining valuable insights about the firm's current performance and future prospects.

To understand the contribution that financial statement analysis can make, it is important to understand the role of financial reporting in the functioning of capital markets and the institutional forces that shape financial statements. Therefore we present first a brief description of these forces; then we discuss the steps that an analyst must perform to extract information from financial statements and provide valuable forecasts.

THE ROLE OF FINANCIAL REPORTING IN CAPITAL MARKETS

A critical challenge for any economy is the allocation of savings to investment opportunities. Economies that do this well can exploit new business ideas to spur innovation and create jobs and wealth at a rapid pace. In contrast, economies that manage this process poorly dissipate their wealth and fail to support business opportunities.

Figure 1.1 provides a schematic representation of how capital markets typically work. Savings in any economy are widely distributed among households. There are usually many new entrepreneurs and existing companies that would like to attract these savings to fund their business ideas. While both savers and entrepreneurs would like to do business with each other, matching savings to business investment opportunities is complicated for at least two reasons. First, entrepreneurs typically have better information than savers on the value of business investment opportunities. Second, communication by entrepreneurs to investors is not completely credible because investors know entrepreneurs have an incentive to inflate the value of their ideas. Third, savers generally lack the financial sophistication needed to analyze and differentiate between the various business opportunities.

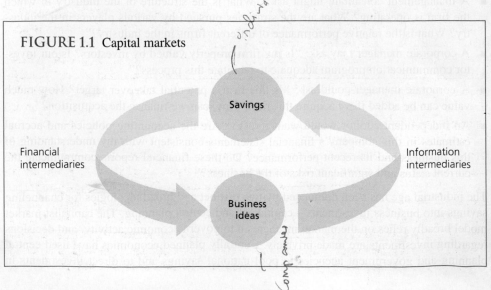

FIGURE 1.1 Capital markets

Savings

Financial intermediaries

Information intermediaries

Business ideas

The information and incentive issues lead to what economists call the lemons problem, which can potentially break down the functioning of the capital market.[1] It works like this. Consider a situation where half the business ideas are "good" and the other half are "bad." If investors cannot distinguish between the two types of business ideas, entrepreneurs with "bad" ideas will try to claim that their ideas are as valuable as the "good" ideas. Realizing this possibility, investors value both good and bad ideas at an average level. Unfortunately, this penalizes good ideas, and entrepreneurs with good ideas find the terms on which they can get financing to be unattractive. As these entrepreneurs leave the capital market, the proportion of bad ideas in the market increases. Over time, bad ideas "crowd out" good ideas, and investors lose confidence in this market.

The emergence of intermediaries can prevent such a market breakdown. Intermediaries are like a car mechanic who provides an independent certification of a used car's quality to help a buyer and seller agree on a price. There are two types of intermediaries in the capital markets. Financial intermediaries, such as venture capital firms, banks, collective investment funds, pension funds, and insurance companies, focus on aggregating funds from individual investors and analyzing different investment alternatives to make investment decisions. Information intermediaries, such as auditors, financial analysts, credit-rating agencies, and the financial press, focus on providing information to investors (and to financial intermediaries who represent them) on the quality of various business investment opportunities. Both these types of intermediaries add value by helping investors distinguish "good" investment opportunities from the "bad" ones.

The relative importance of financial intermediaries and information intermediaries varies from country to country for historical reasons. In countries where individual investors traditionally have had strong legal rights to discipline entrepreneurs who invest in "bad" business ideas, such as in the UK, individual investors have been more inclined to make their own investment decisions. In these countries, the funds that entrepreneurs attract may come from a widely dispersed group of individual investors and be channeled through public stock exchanges. Information intermediaries consequently play an important role in supplying individual investors with the information that they need to distinguish between "good" and "bad" business ideas. In contrast, in countries where individual investors traditionally have had weak legal rights to discipline entrepreneurs, such as in many Continental European countries, individual investors have been more inclined to rely on the help of financial intermediaries. In these countries, financial intermediaries, such as banks, tend to supply most of the funds to entrepreneurs and can get privileged access to entrepreneurs' private information.

Over the past decade, many countries in Europe have been moving towards a model of strong **legal protection of investors' rights** to discipline entrepreneurs and well-developed stock exchanges. In this model, financial reporting plays a critical role in the functioning of both the information intermediaries and financial intermediaries. Information intermediaries add value by either enhancing the credibility of financial reports (as auditors do), or by analyzing the information in the financial statements (as analysts and the rating agencies do). Financial intermediaries rely on the information in the financial statements to analyze investment opportunities, and supplement this information with other sources of information.

Ideally, the different intermediaries serve as a system of checks and balances to ensure the efficient functioning of the capital markets system. However, this is not always the case as on occasion the intermediaries tend to mutually reinforce rather than counterbalance each other. A number of problems can arise as a result of incentive issues, governance issues within the intermediary organizations themselves, and conflicts of interest, as evidenced by the spectacular failures of companies such as Enron and Parmalat. However, in general this market mechanism functions efficiently and prices reflect all available information on a particular investment. Despite this overall market efficiency, individual securities may still be mispriced, thereby justifying the need for financial statement analysis.

In the following section, we discuss key aspects of the financial reporting system design that enable it to play effectively this vital role in the functioning of the capital markets.

FROM BUSINESS ACTIVITIES TO FINANCIAL STATEMENTS

Corporate managers are responsible for acquiring physical and financial resources from the firm's environment and using them to create value for the firm's investors. Value is created when the firm earns a return on its investment in excess of the return required by its capital suppliers. Managers formulate business strategies to achieve this goal, and they implement them through business activities. A firm's business activities are influenced by its economic environment and its own business strategy. The economic environment includes the firm's industry, its input and output markets, and the regulations under which the firm operates. The firm's business strategy determines how the firm positions itself in its environment to achieve a competitive advantage.

As shown in Figure 1.2, a firm's **financial statements** summarize the economic consequences of its business activities. The firm's business activities in any time period are too numerous to be reported individually to outsiders. Further, some of the activities undertaken by the firm are proprietary in nature, and disclosing these activities in detail could

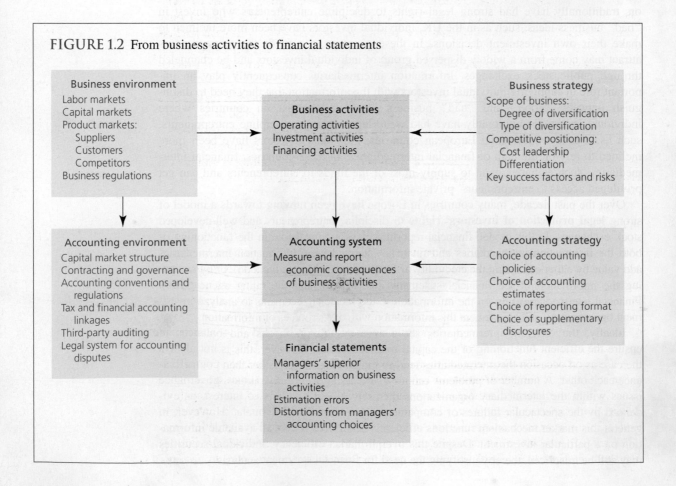

FIGURE 1.2 From business activities to financial statements

Business environment
Labor markets
Capital markets
Product markets:
 Suppliers
 Customers
 Competitors
Business regulations

Business activities
Operating activities
Investment activities
Financing activities

Business strategy
Scope of business:
 Degree of diversification
 Type of diversification
Competitive positioning:
 Cost leadership
 Differentiation
Key success factors and risks

Accounting environment
Capital market structure
Contracting and governance
Accounting conventions and
 regulations
Tax and financial accounting
 linkages
Third-party auditing
Legal system for accounting
 disputes

Accounting system
Measure and report
 economic consequences
 of business activities

Accounting strategy
Choice of accounting
 policies
Choice of accounting
 estimates
Choice of reporting format
Choice of supplementary
 disclosures

Financial statements
Managers' superior
 information on business
 activities
Estimation errors
Distortions from managers'
 accounting choices

be a detriment to the firm's competitive position. The firm's accounting system provides a mechanism through which business activities are selected, measured, and aggregated into financial statement data.

INFLUENCES OF THE ACCOUNTING SYSTEM ON INFORMATION QUALITY

Intermediaries using financial statement data to do business analysis have to be aware that financial reports are influenced both by the firm's business activities and by its accounting system. A key aspect of financial statement analysis, therefore, involves understanding the influence of the accounting system on the quality of the financial statement data being used in the analysis. The institutional features of accounting systems discussed next determine the extent of that influence.

Feature 1: Accrual accounting

One of the fundamental features of corporate financial reports is that they are prepared using accrual rather than cash accounting. Unlike cash accounting, **accrual accounting** distinguishes between the recording of costs and benefits associated with economic activities and the actual payment and receipt of cash. Net profit is the primary periodic performance index under accrual accounting. To compute net profit, the effects of economic transactions are recorded on the basis of *expected*, not necessarily *actual*, cash receipts and payments. Expected cash receipts from the delivery of products or services are recognized as revenues, and expected cash outflows associated with these revenues are recognized as expenses.

The need for accrual accounting arises from investors' demand for financial reports on a periodic basis. Because firms undertake economic transactions on a continual basis, the arbitrary closing of accounting books at the end of a reporting period leads to a fundamental measurement problem. Because cash accounting does not report the full economic consequence of the transactions undertaken in a given period, accrual accounting is designed to provide more complete information on a firm's periodic performance.

Feature 2: Accounting conventions and standards

The use of accrual accounting lies at the center of many important complexities in corporate financial reporting. Because accrual accounting deals with *expectations* of future cash consequences of current events, it is subjective and relies on a variety of assumptions. Who should be charged with the primary responsibility of making these assumptions? In the current system, a firm's managers are entrusted with the task of making the appropriate estimates and assumptions to prepare the financial statements because they have intimate knowledge of their firm's business.

The accounting discretion granted to managers is potentially valuable because it allows them to reflect inside information in reported financial statements. However, because investors view profits as a measure of managers' performance, managers have incentives to use their accounting discretion to distort reported profits by making biased assumptions. Further, the use of accounting numbers in contracts between the firm and outsiders provides another motivation for management manipulation of accounting numbers. Income management distorts financial accounting data, making them less valuable to external users of financial statements. Therefore, the delegation of financial reporting decisions to corporate managers has both costs and benefits.

A number of accounting conventions have evolved to ensure that managers use their accounting flexibility to summarize their knowledge of the firm's business activities, and not to disguise reality for self-serving purposes. For example, the measurability and conservatism conventions are accounting responses to concerns about distortions from managers' potentially optimistic bias. Both these conventions attempt to limit managers' optimistic bias by imposing their own pessimistic bias.

Accounting standards, such as International Financial Reporting Standards (IFRS), promulgated by the International Accounting Standards Board (IASB) and adopted by more than 70 countries worldwide, also limit potential distortions that managers can introduce into reported numbers.[2] Uniform accounting standards attempt to reduce managers' ability to record similar economic transactions in dissimilar ways, either over time or across firms.

Increased uniformity from accounting standards, however, comes at the expense of reduced flexibility for managers to reflect genuine business differences in their firm's financial statements. Rigid accounting standards work best for economic transactions whose accounting treatment is not predicated on managers' proprietary information. However, when there is significant business judgment involved in assessing a transaction's economic consequences, rigid standards that prevent managers from using their superior business knowledge would be dysfunctional. Further, if accounting standards are too rigid, they may induce managers to expend economic resources to restructure business transactions in order to achieve a desired accounting result.

Feature 3: Managers' reporting strategy

Because the mechanisms that limit managers' ability to distort accounting data add noise, it is not optimal to use accounting regulation to eliminate managerial flexibility completely. Therefore real-world accounting systems leave considerable room for managers to influence financial statement data. A firm's **reporting strategy** – that is, the manner in which managers use their accounting discretion – has an important influence on the firm's financial statements.

Corporate managers can choose accounting and disclosure policies that make it more or less difficult for external users of financial reports to understand the true economic picture of their businesses. Accounting rules often provide a broad set of alternatives from which managers can choose. Further, managers are entrusted with making a range of estimates in implementing these accounting policies. Accounting regulations usually prescribe *minimum* disclosure requirements, but they do not restrict managers from *voluntarily* providing additional disclosures.

A superior disclosure strategy will enable managers to communicate the underlying business reality to outside investors. One important constraint on a firm's disclosure strategy is the competitive dynamics in product markets. Disclosure of proprietary information about business strategies and their expected economic consequences may hurt the firm's competitive position. Subject to this constraint, managers can use financial statements to provide information useful to investors in assessing their firm's true economic performance.

Managers can also use financial reporting strategies to manipulate investors' perceptions. Using the discretion granted to them, managers can make it difficult for investors to identify poor performance on a timely basis. For example, managers can choose accounting policies and estimates to provide an optimistic assessment of the firm's true performance. They can also make it costly for investors to understand the true performance by controlling the extent of information that is disclosed voluntarily.

The extent to which financial statements are informative about the underlying business reality varies across firms and across time for a given firm. This variation in accounting quality provides both an important opportunity and a challenge in doing business analysis. The process through which analysts can separate noise from information in financial statements, and gain valuable business insights from financial statement analysis, is discussed in the following section.

Feature 4: Auditing

Auditing, broadly defined as a verification of the integrity of the reported financial statements by someone other than the preparer, ensures that managers use accounting rules and conventions consistently over time, and that their accounting estimates are reasonable. Therefore auditing improves the quality of accounting data.

Third-party auditing may also reduce the quality of financial reporting because it constrains the kind of accounting rules and conventions that evolve over time. For example, the IASB considers the views of auditors in the standard-setting process. Auditors are likely to argue against accounting standards producing numbers that are difficult to audit, even if the proposed rules produce relevant information for investors.

The legal environment in which accounting disputes between managers, auditors, and investors are adjudicated can also have a significant effect on the quality of reported numbers. The threats of lawsuits and resulting penalties, which vary greatly in strength across countries, have the beneficial effect of improving the accuracy of disclosure. However, the potential for a significant legal liability might also discourage managers and auditors from supporting accounting proposals requiring risky forecasts, such as forward-looking disclosures.

THE IMPACT OF EU DIRECTIVES ON FINANCIAL REPORTING AND AUDITING IN EUROPE

During the past decade, the European Commission has issued or revised a few Directives that significantly affect financial reporting and auditing practices in the European Union. The Revised Eighth Directive (8thD; effective since 2008) regulates the audit of financial statements. In addition, the Transparency Directive (TD; 2007) and Market Abuse Directives (MAD; 2004) regulate firms' periodic and ad-hoc disclosures, with the objective to improve the quality and timeliness of information provided to investors. Some of the highlights of these Directives include:

- Prescribing that firms issuing public debt or equity securities (public firms) publish their annual report no more than four months after the financial year-end. The annual report must contain the audited financial statements, a management report, and management's responsibility statement certifying that the financial statements give a true and fair view of the firm's performance and financial position (TD).

- Requiring that public firms publish semiannual financial reports, including condensed financial statements, an interim management report and a responsibility statement, within two months of the end of the first half of the fiscal year. The firms must also indicate whether the interim financial statements have been audited or reviewed by an auditor (TD).

- Enhancing interim reporting by requiring that public firms publish two interim management statements, describing the firms' financial position, material events and transactions (TD).

- Ensuring that each EU member state has a central filing and storage system for public financial reports (TD).

- Requiring that public firms immediately disclose any information that may have a material impact on their security price and prohibiting that insiders to the firm trade on such information before its disclosure (TD, MAD).

- Prohibiting that the external auditor provides any nonaudit services to the audited firm that may compromise his independence (8thD).

- Enhancing auditor independence by prescribing that the external auditor (the audit partner, not the audit firm) does not audit the same firm for more than seven consecutive years (8thD).

- Requiring that all audits are carried out in accordance with International Standards of Auditing (8thD).

- Requiring that all audit firms are subject to a system of external quality assurance and public oversight (8thD).

- Mandating that each public firm has an audit committee, which monitors the firm's financial reporting process, internal control system and statutory audit (8thD).

- Ensuring that each EU member state designates a competent authority responsible for supervising firms' compliance with the provisions of the Directives (8thD, TD, MAD).

Each EU member state must implement the Directives by introducing new or changing existing national legislation. Because the member states have some freedom in deciding how to comply with the Directives, some differences in financial reporting, disclosure and auditing regulation remain to exist. To illustrate, whereas public firms in most countries are required to publish their financial statements on a quarterly basis, public firms in, for example, the Netherlands and the UK comply with local interim reporting rules if they publish a semiannual financial statement and two interim management statements. The interim management statements typically do not include financial statements.

FROM FINANCIAL STATEMENTS TO BUSINESS ANALYSIS

Because managers' insider knowledge is a source both of value and distortion in accounting data, it is difficult for outside users of financial statements to separate true information from distortion and noise. Not being able to undo accounting distortions completely, investors "discount" a firm's reported accounting performance. In doing so, they make a probabilistic assessment of the extent to which a firm's reported numbers reflect economic reality. As a result, investors can have only an imprecise assessment of an individual firm's performance. **Financial and information intermediaries** can add value by improving investors' understanding of a firm's current performance and its future prospects.

Effective financial statement analysis is valuable because it attempts to get at managers' inside information from public financial statement data. Because intermediaries do not have direct or complete access to this information, they rely on their knowledge of the firm's industry and its competitive strategies to interpret financial statements. Successful intermediaries have at least as good an understanding of the industry economics as do the

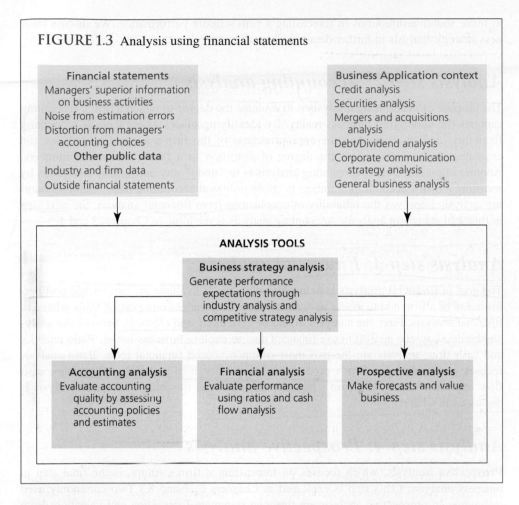

FIGURE 1.3 Analysis using financial statements

Financial statements
Managers' superior information on business activities
Noise from estimation errors
Distortion from managers' accounting choices

Other public data
Industry and firm data
Outside financial statements

Business Application context
Credit analysis
Securities analysis
Mergers and acquisitions analysis
Debt/Dividend analysis
Corporate communication strategy analysis
General business analysis

ANALYSIS TOOLS

Business strategy analysis
Generate performance expectations through industry analysis and competitive strategy analysis

Accounting analysis
Evaluate accounting quality by assessing accounting policies and estimates

Financial analysis
Evaluate performance using ratios and cash flow analysis

Prospective analysis
Make forecasts and value business

firm's managers, as well as a reasonably good understanding of the firm's competitive strategy. Although outside analysts have an information disadvantage relative to the firm's managers, they are more objective in evaluating the economic consequences of the firm's investment and operating decisions. Figure 1.3 provides a schematic overview of how business intermediaries use financial statements to accomplish four key steps:

1 Business strategy analysis.
2 Accounting analysis.
3 Financial analysis.
4 Prospective analysis.

Analysis step 1: Business strategy analysis

The purpose of **business strategy analysis** is to identify key profit drivers and business risks, and to assess the company's profit potential at a qualitative level. Business strategy analysis involves analyzing a firm's industry and its strategy to create a sustainable competitive advantage. This qualitative analysis is an essential first step because it enables the analyst to frame the subsequent accounting and financial analysis better. For example, identifying the key success factors and key business risks allows the identification of key accounting policies. Assessment of a firm's competitive strategy facilitates evaluating whether current profitability is sustainable. Finally, business analysis enables the analyst to make sound assumptions in forecasting a firm's future performance. We discuss business strategy analysis in further detail in Chapter 2.

Analysis step 2: Accounting analysis

The purpose of **accounting analysis** is to evaluate the degree to which a firm's accounting captures the underlying business reality. By identifying places where there is accounting flexibility, and by evaluating the appropriateness of the firm's accounting policies and estimates, analysts can assess the degree of distortion in a firm's accounting numbers. Another important step in accounting analysis is to "undo" any accounting distortions by recasting a firm's accounting numbers to create unbiased accounting data. Sound accounting analysis improves the reliability of conclusions from financial analysis, the next step in financial statement analysis. Accounting analysis is the topic in Chapters 3 and 4.

Analysis step 3: Financial analysis

The goal of **financial analysis** is to use financial data to evaluate the current and past performance of a firm and to assess its sustainability. There are two important skills related to financial analysis. First, the analysis should be systematic and efficient. Second, the analysis should allow the analyst to use financial data to explore business issues. Ratio analysis and cash flow analysis are the two most commonly used financial tools. Ratio analysis focuses on evaluating a firm's product market performance and financial policies; cash flow analysis focuses on a firm's liquidity and financial flexibility. Financial analysis is discussed in Chapter 5.

Analysis step 4: Prospective analysis

Prospective analysis, which focuses on forecasting a firm's future, is the final step in business analysis. (This step is explained in Chapters 6, 7 and 8.) Two commonly used techniques in prospective analysis are financial statement forecasting and valuation. Both these tools allow the synthesis of the insights from business analysis, accounting analysis, and financial analysis in order to make predictions about a firm's future.

While the intrinsic value of a firm is a function of its future cash flow performance, it is also possible to assess a firm's value based on the firm's current book value of equity, and its future return on equity (ROE) and growth. Strategy analysis, accounting analysis, and financial analysis, the first three steps in the framework discussed here, provide an excellent foundation for estimating a firm's intrinsic value. Strategy analysis, in addition to enabling sound accounting and financial analysis, also helps in assessing potential changes in a firm's competitive advantage and their implications for the firm's future ROE and growth. Accounting analysis provides an unbiased estimate of a firm's current book value and ROE. Financial analysis facilitates an in-depth understanding of what drives the firm's current ROE.

The predictions from a sound business analysis are useful to a variety of parties and can be applied in various contexts. The exact nature of the analysis will depend on the context. The contexts that we will examine include securities analysis, credit evaluation, mergers and acquisitions, evaluation of debt and dividend policies, and assessing corporate communication strategies. The four analytical steps described above are useful in each of these contexts. Appropriate use of these tools, however, requires a familiarity with the economic theories and institutional factors relevant to the context.

There are several ways in which financial statement analysis can add value, even when capital markets are reasonably efficient. First, there are many applications of financial statement analysis whose focus is outside the capital market context – credit analysis, competitive benchmarking, analysis of mergers and acquisitions, to name a few. Second, markets become efficient precisely because some market participants rely on analytical tools such as the ones we discuss in this book to analyze information and make investment decisions.

PUBLIC VERSUS PRIVATE CORPORATIONS

This book focuses primarily on public corporations. In some countries, financial statements of (unlisted) private corporations are also widely available. For example, the member states of the European Union (EU) require that privately held corporations prepare their financial statements under a common set of rules and make their financial statements publicly available. All corporations must prepare at least single company financial statements, while parent corporations of large groups must also prepare consolidated financial statements.[3] Consolidated financial statements are typically more appropriate for use in business analysis and valuation because these statements report the combined assets, liabilities, revenues, and expenses of the parent company and its subsidiaries. Single company financial statements report the assets, liabilities, revenues, and expenses of the parent company only and therefore provide little insight into the activities of subsidiaries.

EU law also requires that private corporations' financial statements be audited by an external auditor, although member states may exempt small corporations from this requirement.[4] The way in which private corporations in the EU make their financial statements available to the public is typically by filing these with a local public register that is maintained by agencies such as the companies register, the chamber of commerce, or the national bank.[5]

Private corporations' financial statements can be, and are being, used for business analysis and valuation. For example, venture capitalists, which provide equity funds to mostly private start-up companies, can use financial statements to evaluate potential investments. Nevertheless, although private corporations' financial statements are also subject to accounting standards, their usefulness in business analysis and valuation is less than that of public corporations' financial statements for the following reasons.[6] First, information and incentive problems are smaller in private corporations than in public corporations. Investors and managers of private corporations maintain close relationships and communicate their information through other means than public financial reports, such as personal communication or ad hoc reports. Because public reporting plays only a small role in communication, managers of private corporations have little incentive to make their public financial statements informative about the underlying business reality. Second, private corporations often produce one set of financial statements that meets the requirements of both tax rules and accounting rules. Tax rules grant managers less discretion in their assumptions than, for example, IFRS. Under tax rules, the recording of costs and benefits is also typically more associated with the payment and receipt of cash than with the underlying economic activities. Consequently, when private corporations' financial statements also comply with tax rules, they are less useful in assessing the corporations' true economic performance.[7]

SUMMARY

Financial statements provide the most widely available data on public corporations' economic activities; investors and other stakeholders rely on them to assess the plans and performance of firms and corporate managers. Accrual accounting data in financial statements are noisy, and unsophisticated investors can assess firms' performance only imprecisely. Financial analysts who understand managers' disclosure strategies have an opportunity to create inside information from public data, and they play a valuable role in enabling outside parties to evaluate a firm's current and prospective performance.

This chapter has outlined the framework for business analysis with financial statements, using the four key steps: business strategy analysis, accounting analysis, financial analysis, and prospective analysis. The remaining chapters in this book describe these steps in greater detail and discuss how they can be used in a variety of business contexts.

CORE CONCEPTS

Accounting analysis Second step of financial statement analysis, aimed at scrutinizing a firm's accounting policies and estimates and undoing the firm's financial statements from any accounting distortions.

Accounting standards Set of rules governing the determination of a company's revenues, profit and (change in) financial position under a system of accrual accounting.

Accrual accounting A system of accounting under which current net profit is derived from past and current as well as expected future cash flows arising from business transactions completed in the current period.

Auditing Certification of financial statements by an independent public accounting firm, aimed at improving the statements' credibility.

Business strategy analysis First step of financial statement analysis, aimed at identifying a firm's key profit drivers and business risks and qualitatively assessing the firm's profit potential.

Capital markets Markets where entrepreneurs raise funds to finance their business ideas in exchange for equity or debt securities.

Financial analysis Third step of financial statement analysis, which goal is to evaluate (the sustainability of) a firm's current and past financial performance using ratio and cash flow analysis.

Financial and information intermediaries Capital market participants who help to resolve problems of information asymmetry between entrepreneurs and investors and, consequently, prevent markets from breaking down. Information intermediaries such as auditors or financial analysts improve the (credibility of) information provided by the entrepreneur. Financial intermediaries such as banks and collective investment funds specialize in collecting, aggregating and investing funds from dispersed investors.

Financial statements Periodically disclosed set of statements showing a company's financial performance and change in financial position during a prespecified period. The statements typically include a balance sheet (financial position), an income statement and a cash flow statement (financial performance). One of the primary purposes of the financial statements is to inform current or potential investors about management's use of their funds, such that they can evaluate management's actions and value their current or potential claim on the firm.

Legal protection of investors' rights Laws and regulations aiming at providing investors the rights and mechanisms to discipline managers who control their funds. Examples of such rights and mechanisms are transparent disclosure requirements, the right to vote (by proxy) on important decisions or the right to appoint supervisory directors. In countries where small, minority investors lack such rights or mechanisms, financial intermediaries play an important role in channeling investments to entrepreneurs.

Lemons problem The problem that arises if entrepreneurs have better information about the quality of their business ideas than investors but are not able to credibly communicate this information. If this problem becomes severe enough, investors may no longer be willing to provide funds and capital markets could break down.

Prospective analysis Fourth and final step of financial statement analysis, which focuses on forecasting a firm's future financial performance and position. The forecasts can be used for various purposes, such as estimating firm value or assessing creditworthiness.

Reporting strategy Set of choices made by managers in using their reporting discretion, shaping the quality of their financial reports.

QUESTIONS, EXERCISES AND PROBLEMS

1 Matti, who has just completed his first finance course, is unsure whether he should take a course in business analysis and valuation using financial statements since he believes that financial analysis adds little value, given the efficiency of capital markets. Explain to Matti when financial analysis can add value, even if capital markets are efficient.

2 Accounting statements rarely report financial performance without error. List three types of errors that can arise in financial reporting.

3 Juan Perez argues that "learning how to do business analysis and valuation using financial statements is not very useful, unless you are interested in becoming a financial analyst." Comment.

4 Four steps for business analysis are discussed in the chapter (strategy analysis, accounting analysis, financial analysis, and prospective analysis). As a financial analyst, explain why each of these steps is a critical part of your job and how they relate to one another.

Problem 1 The Neuer Markt

Many economists believe that innovation is one of the main building blocks of economic growth and job creation. Not all economic infrastructures, however, are equally supportive of innovation. In 1995 venture capital investments in Europe amounted up to 4 percent of total Gross Domestic Product (GDP), compared to 6 percent of GDP in the US. During the second half of the 1990s European and US venture capital investments experienced an explosive but distinctively different level of growth. In fact, in 2000 venture capitalists invested an amount equal to 17 percent of European GDP in European companies, while investing 78 percent of US GDP in US companies.[8] The availability of venture capital can be crucial in the development of innovation. Venture capitalists serve an important role as intermediaries in capital markets because they separate good business ideas from bad ones and bestow their reputation on the start-ups that they finance. In addition to providing capital, venture capitalists offer their expertise in management and finance and let start-up companies benefit from their network of contacts. Their close involvement with start-ups' day-to-day operations and their ability to give finance in installments, conditional on start-ups' success, allows venture capitalists to invest in risky business ideas that public capital markets typically ignore.

To improve young, innovative and fast-growing companies' access to external finance, several European stock exchanges founded separate trading segments for this group of companies at the end of the 1990s. Examples of such trading segments were the Nuovo Mercato in Italy, the Nouveau Marché in France, the NMAX in the Netherlands, and the Neuer Markt in Germany. These new markets coordinated some of their activities under the EuroNM umbrella. For example, starting in 1999 the markets facilitated cross-border electronic trading to create a pan-European exchange. Another important way of cooperation was to harmonize the admission requirements for new listings.[9] These requirements were not easier to comply with than the admission requirements of the traditional, established trading segments of the European stock exchanges. On the contrary, the common idea was that a separate trading segment for innovative fast-growing companies needed stricter regulation than the established segments that targeted matured companies with proven track records. If this was true, having (some) common listing requirements across European new markets helped to prevent a race to the bottom in which companies would flee to markets with lenient listing requirements and markets start to compete with each other on the basis of their leniency.

The European new markets had also harmonized some of their disclosure requirements. All new markets required that companies produced quarterly reports of, at least, sales figures. Further, most of the new markets required that companies prepared their financial reports in accordance with either US GAAP or International Accounting Standards. Given the opportunities for electronic cross-border trading, strict disclosure requirements could help in broadening companies' investor base as well as improve investors' opportunities for diversifying their risky investments. However, because the new markets experienced difficulties in further harmonizing their admission and listing requirements and eventually came to realize that the small cap companies appealed primarily to local investors, their cooperative venture was dissolved in December 2000.

One of the European new markets was the Neuer Markt, a trading segment of the 'Deutsche Börse', the German stock exchange. The Neuer Markt's target companies were innovative companies that opened up new markets, used new processes in development, production, or marketing and sales, offered new products or services and were likely to achieve above-average growth in revenue and profit. On March 10, 1997, the initial public offering of Mobilcom AG started the existence of the exchange. The offering of Mobilcom's 640 thousand shares for an issue price of €31.95 was heavily oversubscribed, as 620 million additional shares could have been sold. Mobilcom's closing price at the end of the first trading day equaled €50.10, yielding an initial return of 56.8 percent. Other success stories followed. For example, on October 30, 1997, Entertainment München, better known as EM.TV, went public on the German Neuer Markt. The Munich-based producer and distributor of children's programs was able to place 600,000 of its common shares at a price set at the upper end of the bookbuilding range, collecting approximately €5.3 million in total. There was a strong demand for the company's shares. At the end of the first trading day, the share price closed at €9.72, up by 9.4 percent. At its peak, in February 2000, EM.TV's share price had increased from to €0.35 (split-adjusted) to slightly more than €120.

At the end of February 2000, being close to its three-year anniversary, the Neuer Markt comprised 229 companies with a total market capitalization of approximately €234 billion. However, in March 2000, the downfall began, in line with the plunge of the NASDAQ exchange. In September 2000, Gigabell AG, was the first company to file for insolvency. The total market capitalization of the growth segment of the Deutsche Börse declined further from €121 billion (339 firms) at the end of 2000 to €50 billion (327 firms) at the end of 2001. Because both the "going public" and the "being public" requirements were very strict compared to other segments and markets, several companies left the Neuer Markt, changing to the less regulated Geregelter Markt. During the first years of the 2000s, several Neuer Markt firms were found to have manipulated their financial statements. For example, in September 2000, EM.TV announced that it had overstated the sales and profit figures of its most recently acquired subsidiaries, the Jim Henson Company and Speed Investments, in the company's semiannual financial statements. Following this announcement, EM.TV's market capitalization declined by more than 30 percent. Other examples include computer games developer Phenomedia and Comrod, a provider of traffic information systems that was found to have falsified more than 90 percent of its 1998–2001 revenues.

On September 26, 2002, the Deutsche Börse announced that it would close its Neuer Markt trading segment in 2003. The remaining Neuer Markt companies could join the exchange's Prime Standard segment, which would adopt the Neuer Markt's strict listing requirements (i.e., quarterly reporting; IAS or US GAAP; at least one analyst conference per year; ad-hoc and ongoing disclosures in English), or its General Standard segment, with legal minimum transparency requirements. Approximately two-thirds of the remaining Neuer Markt firms decided to join the Prime Standard segment.

1 Do you think that exchange market segments such as the EuroNM markets can be a good alternative to venture capital? If not, what should be their function?

2 This chapter described four institutional features of accounting systems that affect the quality of financial statements. Which of these features may have been particularly important in reducing the quality of Neuer Markt companies' financial statements?

3 The decline of the Neuer Markt could be viewed as the result of a lemons problem. Can you think of some mechanisms that might have prevented the market's collapse?

4 What could have been the Deutsche Börse's objective of introducing two new segments and letting Neuer Markt firms choose and apply for admission to one of these segments? When is this strategy most likely to be effective?

NOTES

1. G. Akerlof, "The Market for 'Lemons': Quality Uncertainty and the Market Mechanism," *Quarterly Journal of Economics* (August 1970): 488–500. Akerlof recognized that the seller of a used car knew more about the car's value than the buyer. This meant that the buyer was likely to end up overpaying, since the seller would accept any offer that exceeded the car's true value and reject any lower offer. Car buyers recognized this problem and would respond by only making low-ball offers for used cars, leading sellers with high quality cars to exit the market. As a result, only the lowest quality cars (the "lemons") would remain in the market. Akerlof pointed out that qualified independent mechanics could correct this market breakdown by providing buyers with reliable information on a used car's true value.

2. Other countries have similar standard-setting bodies. For example, in the US, accounting standards are called Generally Accepted Accounting Principles (US GAAP) and are promulgated by the Financial Accounting Standards Board (FASB). The FASB and IASB cooperate to eliminate differences between US GAAP and IFRS and to develop new common standards.

3. The Seventh EU Company Law Directive, which governs the preparation of consolidated financial statements in the EU, defines large groups as those meeting at least two of the following three criteria in two consecutive years:

   1 Total assets above €17.5 million.
   2 Annual turnover above €35.0 million.
   3 More than 250 employees.

4. The Fourth EU Company Law Directive, which governs corporations' financial reporting in the EU, defines small corporations as those failing to meet two of the following three criteria in two consecutive years:

   1 Total assets above €4.4 million.

   2 Annual turnover above €8.8 million.

   3 More than 50 employees.

5. It should be noted that although the EU regulations have partly harmonized private corporations' accounting, the accessibility of public registers varies greatly and private corporations' financial statements are therefore in practice not equally available across the EU.

6. See R. Ball and L. Shivakumar, "Earnings Quality in UK Private Firms: Comparative Loss Recognition Timeliness," *Journal of Accounting and Economics* 39 (2005): 83–128, D. Burgstahler, L. Hail and C. Leuz, "The Importance of Reporting Incentives: Earnings Management in European Private and Public Firms," *The Accounting Review* 81 (2006): 983–1016, and E. Peek, R. Cuijpers and W. Buijink, "Creditors' and Shareholders' Reporting Demands in Public versus Private Firms: Evidence from Europe," *Contemporary Accounting Research* (2010), forthcoming.

7. The influence of tax rules is particularly strong on single company financial statements, which in many countries are the basis for tax computations. Although the influence of tax rules on consolidated financial statements is less direct, tax considerations may still affect the preparation of these statements. For example, companies may support their aggressive tax choices by having the consolidated statements conform to the single company statements.

8. See L. Bottazzi and M. Da Rin, "Venture Capital in Europe and the Financing of Innovative Companies," *Economic Policy*, April (2002): 231–269.

9. See L. Bottazzi and M. Da Rin, "Europe's 'New' Stock Markets," Working Paper, July 2002, and M. Goergen, A. Khurshed, J.A. McCahery and L. Renneboog, "The Rise and Fall of European New Markets: on the Short and Long-run Performance of High-tech Initial Public Offerings," Working Paper, European Corporate Governance Institute, September 2003. To be eligible for a listing on one of the two largest new markets, the Nouveau Marché and the Neuer Markt, companies had to meet all of the following admission requirements. First, companies' equity prior to the initial public offering (IPO) had to exceed €1.5 million. Second, companies had to issue more than 100,000 shares, which had to represent more than 20 percent of the companies' nominal capital, at an amount exceeding €5 million. Third, not more than 50 percent of the shares issued were allowed to come from existing shareholders; more than 50 percent of the issued shares had to come from a capital increase. Fourth, managers were not allowed to trade their shares during a six-month period following the IPO on the Neuer Markt. Managers of companies listed on the Nouveau Marché could not trade 80 percent of their shares for a period of 12 months. The other new markets had very similar admission requirements.

APPENDIX: DEFINING EUROPE

At various places in this book we refer to "Europe" and "European companies" without intending to imply that all European countries and companies are exactly alike. Because Europe's richness in diversity makes it impossible to describe the institutional details of each European country in detail, this book discusses primarily the commonalities between the countries that have chosen to harmonize the differences among their accounting systems. These countries are the 27 member states of the European Union as well as the three members of the European Economic Area (Iceland, Norway, and Liechtenstein), which are also committed to following EU accounting Directives. Of particular importance to the topic of this book is that, since 2005, companies from these 28 countries that have their shares publicly traded on a stock exchange are required to prepare their financial statements in accordance with IFRS. A special position is occupied by Switzerland, which is neither a member of the EU nor of the European Economic Area. Many of the issues that

TABLE 1.1 European stock exchanges

Countries	Stock exchange	Total market capitalization of domestic companies at December 2008 (in € billions)
Belgium, France, the Netherlands, Portugal	Euronext Brussels – Paris – Amsterdam – Lisbon	1,508.4
Denmark, Estonia, Finland, Iceland, Latvia, Lithuania, Norway, Sweden	OMX Exchanges Copenhagen – Tallinn – Helsinki – Reykjavik – Riga – Vilnius – Stockholm	404.1
Germany	Deutsche Börse	797.1
Italy	Borsa Italiana	374.7
Spain	Bolsa y Mercados Españoles (BME)	680.6
Switzerland	SWX Swiss Exchange	633.6
United Kingdom	London Stock Exchange	1,323.1

Source: World Federation of Exchanges. Euronext is a Pan-European exchange that was formed from the merger of the exchanges of Amsterdam, Brussels, Lisbon and Paris. OMX Exchanges includes the exchanges of Copenhagen, Helsinki, Stockholm, Tallinn, Riga, and Vilnius. The reported market capitalizations of the Euronext exchange and the OMX Exchanges represent the total sum of the sizes of the individual segments.

we address in this book also apply to a large group of Swiss listed companies, because Switzerland requires its listed companies with international operations to prepare IFRS-based financial statements.

In some of the chapters in this book we summarize the financial ratios, stock returns, and operational characteristics of a representative sample of listed European companies for illustrative purposes. This sample is composed of all domestic companies that were listed on one of the largest seven European stock exchanges (or their predecessors) between January 1992 (labeled the start of fiscal year 1992) and December 2008 (labeled the end of fiscal year 2008). Table 1.1 displays the seven largest European stock exchanges at the end of December 2008 and their countries of operation. The sample contains observations from 8,193 European companies operating in non-financial industries.

The role of capital market intermediaries in the dot-com crash of 2000

The rise and fall of the internet consultants

In the summer of 1999, a host of internet consulting firms made their debut on the Nasdaq. Scient Corporation, which had been founded less than two years earlier in March 1997, went public in May 1999 at an IPO price of $20 per share ($10 on a pre-split basis). Its close on the first day of trading was $32.63. Other internet consulting companies that went public that year included Viant Corporation, IXL Enterprises, and US Interactive (see Exhibit 1).

The main value proposition of these companies was that they would be able to usher in the new internet era by lending their information technology and web expertise to traditional "old economy" companies that wanted to gain Web-based technology, as well as to the emerging dot-com sector. Other companies like Sapient Corporation and Cambridge Technology Partners had been doing IT consulting for years, but this new breed of companies was able to capitalize on the burgeoning demand for internet expertise.

Over the following months, the stock prices of the internet consultants rose dramatically. Scient traded at a high of $133.75 in March 2000. However, this was after a 2–1 split, so each share was actually worth twice this amount on a pre-split basis. This stock level represented a 1238% increase from its IPO price and a valuation of 62 times the company's revenues for the fiscal year 2000. Similar performances were put in by the other companies in this group. However, these valuation levels proved to be unsustainable. The stock prices of web consulting firms dropped sharply in April 2000 along with many others in the internet sector, following what was afterwards seen as a general "correction" in the Nasdaq. The prices of the web consultants seemed to stabilize for a while, and many analysts continued to write favorably about their prospects and maintained buy ratings on their stocks. But starting early in September 2000, after some bad news from Viant Corporation and many subsequent analyst downgrades, the stocks went into a free-fall. All were trading in the single digits by February of 2001, representing a greater than 95% drop from their peak valuations (see Exhibit 2).

The dramatic rise and fall of the stock prices of the Web consultants, along with many others in the internet sector, caused industry observers to wonder how this could have happened in a relatively sophisticated capital market like that of the United States. Several well-respected venture capitalists, investment banks, accounting firms, financial analysts, and money management companies were involved in bringing these companies to market and rating and trading their shares (see Exhibit 3). Who, if anyone, caused the internet stock price bubble? What, if anything, could be done to avoid the recurrence of such stock market bubbles?

Gillian Elcock, MBA 2001, prepared this case from published sources under the supervision of Professor Krishna Palepu. HBS cases are developed solely as the basis for class discussion. Cases are not intended to serve as endorsements, sources of primary data, or illustrations of effective or ineffective management.

Context: The technology bull market

The 1980s and 1990s marked the beginning of a global technology revolution that started with the personal computer (PC) and led to the internet era. Companies like Apple, Microsoft, Intel, and Dell Computer were at the forefront of this new wave of technology that promised to enhance productivity and efficiency through the computerization and automation of many processes.

The capital markets recognized the value that was being created by these companies. Microsoft, which was founded in 1975, had a market capitalization of over $600 billion by the beginning of 2000, making it the world's most valuable company, and its founder, Bill Gates, one of the richest men in the world. High values were also given to many of the other blue-chip technology firms such as Intel and Dell (**Exhibit 4**).

The 1990s ushered in a new group of companies that were based on information networks. These included AOL, Netscape, and Cisco. Netscape was a visible symbol of the emerging importance of the internet: its browser gave regular users access to the World Wide Web, whereas previously the internet had been mostly the domain of academics and experts. In March 2000, Cisco Systems, which made the devices that routed information across the internet, overtook Microsoft as the world's most valuable company (based on market capitalization). This seemed further evidence of the value shift that was taking place from PC-focused technologies and companies to those that were based on the global information network.

It appeared obvious that the internet was going to profoundly change the world through greater computing power, ease of communication, and the host of technologies that could be built upon it. Opportunities to build new services and technologies were boundless, and they were global in scale. The benefits of the internet were expected to translate into greater economic productivity through the lowering of communication and transaction costs. It also seemed obvious that someone would be able to capitalize upon these market opportunities and that "the next Microsoft" would soon appear. No one who missed out on the original Microsoft wanted to do so the second time around.

A phrase that became popularized during this time was the "new economy." New economy companies, as opposed to old economy ones (exemplified by companies in traditional manufacturing, retail, and commodities), based their business models around exploiting the internet. They were usually small compared to their old economy counterparts, with little need for their real-world "bricks and mortar" structures, preferring to outsource much of the capital intensive parts of the business and concentrate on the higher value-added, information-intensive elements. Traditional companies, finding their market shares and business models attacked by a host of nimble, specialized dot-com start-ups, lived in danger of "being Amazoned." To many, the new economy was the future and old economy companies would become less and less relevant.

The capital markets seemed to think similarly. From July 1999 to February 2000, as the Nasdaq Composite Index (which was heavily weighted with technology and internet stocks) rose by 74.4%, the Dow Jones Industrial Average (which was composed mainly of old economy stocks) fell by 7.7%. Investors no longer seemed interested in anything that was not new economy.

Internet gurus and economists predicted the far-reaching effects of the internet. The following excerpts represent the mood of the time:

> Follow the personal computer and you can reach the pot of gold. Follow anything else and you will end up in a backwater. What the Model T was to the industrial era ... the PC is to the information age. Just as people who rode the wave of automobile technology—from tire makers to fast food franchisers—prevailed in the industrial

The role of capital market intermediaries in the dot-com crash of 2000

era, so the firms that prey on the passion and feed on the force of the computer community will predominate in the information era.[1]

—George Gilder, 1992

* * * * *

Due to technological advances in PC-based communications, a new medium—with the internet, the World Wide Web, and TCP/IP at its core—is emerging rapidly. The market for internet-related products and services appears to be growing more rapidly than the early emerging markets for print publishing, telephony, film, radio, recorded music, television, and personal computers. . . . Based on our market growth estimates, we are still at the very early stages of a powerful secular growth cycle.[2] *. . .*

—Mary Meeker, Morgan Stanley Dean Witter, February 1996

* * * * *

The easy availability of smart capital—the ability of entrepreneurs to launch potentially world-beating companies on a shoestring, and of investors to intelligently spread risk—may be the new economy's most devastating innovation. At the same time, onrushing technological change requires lumbering dinosaurs to turn themselves into clever mammals overnight. Some will. But for many others, the only thing left to talk about is the terms of surrender.[3]

—The Wall Street Journal, April 17, 2000

In the new economy, gaining market share was considered key because of the benefits of network effects. In addition, a large customer base was needed to cover the high fixed costs often associated with doing business. Profitability was of a secondary concern, and Netscape was one of the first of many internet companies to go public without positive earnings. Some companies deliberately operated at losses because it was essential to spend a lot early to gain market share, which would presumably translate at a later point into profitability. This meant that revenue growth was the true measure of success for many internet companies. Of course there were some dissenting voices, warning that this was just a period of irrational exuberance and the making of a classic stock market bubble. But for the most part, investors seemed to buy into the concept, as evidenced by the values given to several loss-making dot-coms (**Exhibit 5**).

Scient Corporation

The history of Scient, considered a leader in the internet consulting space, is representative of what happened to the entire industry. The firm was founded in November 1997. Its venture capital backers included several leading firms such as Sequioa Capital and Benchmark Capital **(see Exhibit 3)**

Scient described itself as "a leading provider of a new category of professional services called eBusiness systems innovation" that would "rapidly improve a client's competitive position through the development of innovative business strategies enabled by the integration

---

[1]Mary Meeker, Chris DePuy, "U.S. Investment Research, Technology/New Media, The internet Report (Excerpt from *Life After Television* by George Gilder, 1992)," *Morgan Stanley* (February 1996).

[2]Mary Meeker, Chris DePuy, "U.S. Investment Research, Technology/New Media, The internet Report," *Morgan Stanley* (February 1996).

[3]John Browning, Spencer Reiss, "For the New Economy, the End of the Beginning," *The Wall Street Journal* (Copyright 2000 Dow Jones & Company, Inc).

of emerging and existing technologies."[4] Its aim was to provide services in information technology and systems design as well as high-level strategy consulting, previously the domain of companies such as McKinsey and The Boston Consulting Group.

The company grew quickly to almost 2,000 people within 3 years, primarily organically. Its client list included AT&T, Chase Manhattan, Johnson & Johnson, and Homestore.com.[5] As with any consulting firm, its ability to attract and retain talented employees was crucial, since they were its main assets.

By the fiscal year ending in March 2000, Scient had a net loss of $16 million on revenues of $156 million (see financial statements in **Exhibit 6**). These revenues represented an increase of 653% over the previous year. Analysts wrote glowingly about the firm's prospects. In February 2000 when the stock was trading at around $87.25, a Deutsche Banc Alex Brown report stated:

> We have initiated research coverage of Scient with a BUY investment rating on the shares. In our view Scient possesses several key comparative advantages: (1) an outstanding management team; (2) a highly scalable and leverageable operating model; (3) a strong culture, which attracts the best and the brightest; (4) a private equity portfolio, which enhances long-term relationships and improves retention; and (5) an exclusive focus on the high-end systems innovation market with eBusiness and industry expertise, rapid time-to-market and an integrated approach. . . . Scient shares are currently trading at roughly 27x projected CY00 revenues, modestly ahead of pure play leaders like Viant (24x) and Proxicom (25x), and ahead of our interactive integrator peer group average of just over 16x. Our 12-month price target is $120. It is a stock we would want to own.[6]

And in March 2000, when the stock was at $77.75, Morgan Stanley, which had an "outperform" rating wrote:

> All said we believe Scient continue [sic] to effectively execute on what is a very aggressive business plan. . . . While shares of SCNT trade at a premium valuation to its peer group, we continue to believe that such level is warranted given the company's high-end market focus, short but impressive record of execution, and deep/experienced management team. As well, in our view there is a high probability of meaningful upward revisions to Scient's model.[7]

Scient's stock reached a high of $133.75 in March 2000 but fell to $44 by June as part of the overall drop in valuation of most of the technology sector. In September the company announced it had authorized a stock repurchase of $25 million. But in December 2000 it lowered its revenue and earnings expectations for the fourth quarter due to the slowdown in demand for internet consulting services. The company also announced plans to lay off 460 positions worldwide (over 20% of its workforce) as well as close two of its offices, and an associated $40–$45 million restructuring charge. By February 2001 the stock was trading at $2.94.

Most of the analysts that covered Scient had buy or strong buy ratings on the company as its stock rose to its peak and even after the Nasdaq correction in April 2000. Then in September, a warning by Viant Corporation of results that would come in below expectations due to a slowdown in e-business spending from large corporate clients, prompted

---

[4]Scient Corporation Prospectus, May 1999. Available from Edgar Online.

[5]Scient Corporation website, <http://www.scient.com/non/content/clients/client_list/index.asp>.

[6]F. Mark D'Annolfo, William S. Zinsmeister, Jeffrey A. Buchbinder, "Scient Corporation Premier Builder of eBusinesses," *Deutsche Banc Alex Brown* (February 14, 2000).

[7]Michael A. Sherrick, Mary Meeker, "Scient Corporation Quarter Update," *Morgan Stanley Dean Witter* (March 2, 2000).

many analysts to downgrade most of the companies in the sector, including Scient (**see Exhibit 7**). Several large mutual fund companies were holders of Scient as its stock rose, peaked, and fell (**see Exhibit 8**).

As the major technology indices continued their slump during late 2000 and early 2001, and the stock prices of the internet consulting firms floundered in the single digits, they received increasing attention from the press:

> *Examining the downfall of the eConsultants provides an excellent case study of failed business models. Rose-colored glasses, a lack of a sustainable competitive advantage, and a "me too" mentality are just some of the mistakes these companies made. . . . The eConsultants failed to do the one thing that they were supposed to be helping their clients do—build a sustainable business model . . . many eConsultants popped up and expected to be able to take on the McKinseys and Booz-Allens of the world. Now they are discovering that the relationships firmly established by these old economy consultants are integral to building a sustainable competitive advantage.*[8]

> *Seems like everything dot-com is being shunned by investors these days. But perhaps no other group has experienced quite the brutality that Web consultancies have. Once the sweethearts of Wall Street, their stocks are now high-tech whipping boys. Even financial analysts, who usually strive to be positive about companies they cover, seem to have given up on the sector. . . . Many of these firms were built on the back of the dot-com boom. Now these clients are gone. At the same time, pressure on bricks-and-mortar companies to build online businesses has lifted, leading to the cancellation or delay of Web projects.*[9]

The analysts who were formerly excited about Scient's prospects and had recommended the stock when it was trading at almost $80 per share now seemed much less enthusiastic. In January 2001, with the stock around $3.44, Morgan Stanley wrote:

> *We maintain our Neutral rating due to greater than anticipated market weakness, accelerating pricing pressure, the potential for increased turnover and management credibility issues. While shares of SCNT trade at a depressed valuation, we continute [sic] to believe that turnover and pricing pressure could prove greater than management's assumptions. While management indicated it would be "aggressive" to maintain its people, we still believe it will be difficult to maintain top-tier talent in the current market and company specific environment.*[10]

Performance of the Nasdaq

The performance of the stock prices of Scient and its peers mirrored that of many companies in the internet sector. So dramatic was the drop in valuation of these companies, that this period was subsequently often referred to as the "Dot-com crash."

In the months following the crash, the equity markets essentially closed their doors to the internet firms. Several once high-flying dot-coms, operating at losses and starved for cash, filed for bankruptcy or closed down their operations (**see Exhibit 9**).

The Nasdaq, which had reached a high of 5,132.52 in March of 2000 closed at 2470.52 in December 2000, a drop of 52% from its high. As of February 2001 it had not recovered, closing at 2151.83.

---

[8]Todd N. Lebor, "The Downfall of internet Consultants," *Fool's Den, Fool.com* (December 11, 2000).

[9]Amey Stone, "Streetwise—Who'll Help the Web Consultants?" *BusinessWeek Online* (New York , February 15, 2001). From www.businessweek.com.

[10]Michael A. Sherrick, Mary Meeker, Douglas Levine, "Scient Corporation. Outlook Remains Cloudy, Adjusting Forecasts," *Morgan Stanley Dean Witter* (January 18, 2001).

The role of intermediaries in a well-functioning market

In a capitalist economy, individuals and institutions have savings that they want to invest, and companies need capital to finance and grow their businesses. The capital markets provide a way for this to occur efficiently. Companies issue debt or equity to investors who are willing to part with their cash now because they expect to earn an adequate return in the future for the risk they are taking.

However, there is an information gap between investors and companies. Investors usually do not have enough information or expertise to determine the good investments from the bad ones. And companies do not usually have the infrastructure and know-how to directly receive capital from investors. Therefore, both parties rely on intermediaries to help them make these decisions. These intermediaries include accountants, lawyers, regulatory bodies (such as the SEC in the United States), investment banks, venture capitalists, money management firms, and even the media **(see Exhibit 10)**. The focus of this case is on the equity markets in the United States.

In a well-functioning system, with the incentives of intermediaries fully aligned in accordance with their fiduciary responsibility, public markets will correctly value companies such that investors earn a normal "required" rate of return. In particular, companies that go public will do so at a value which will give investors this fair rate of investment.

The public market valuation will have a trickle down effect on all intermediaries in the investment chain. Venture capitalists, who typically demand a very high return on investment, and usually exit their portfolio companies through an IPO, will do their best to ensure these companies have good management teams and a sustainable business model that will stand the test of time. Otherwise, the capital markets will put too low a value on the companies when they try to go public. Investment bankers will provide their expertise in helping companies to go public or to make subsequent offerings, and introducing them to investors.

On the other side of the process, portfolio managers, acting on behalf of investors will only buy companies that are fairly priced, and will sell companies if they become overvalued, since buying or holding an overvalued stock will inevitably result in a loss. Sell-side analysts, whose clients include portfolio managers and therefore investors, will objectively monitor the performance of public companies and determine whether or not their stocks are good or bad investment at any point in time. Accountants audit the financial statements of companies, ensuring that they comply with established standards and represent the true states of the firms. This gives investors and analysts the confidence to make decisions based on these financial documents.

The integrity of this process is critical in an economy because it gives investors the confidence they need to invest their money into the system. Without this confidence, they would not plough their money back into the economy, but instead keep it under the proverbial mattress.

What happened during the dot-com bubble?

Many observers believed that something went wrong with the system during the dot-com bubble. In April 2001, *BusinessWeek* wrote about "The Great internet Money Game. How America's top financial firms reaped billions from the Net boom, while investors got burned."[11] The following month, *Fortune* magazine's cover asked "Can we ever trust

[11]Peter Elstrom, "The Great internet Money Game. How America's top financial firms reaped billions from the Net boom while investors got burned," *BusinessWeek e.biz* (April 16, 2001).

The role of capital market intermediaries in the dot-com crash of 2000

Wall Street again?"[12] referring to the way in which, in some people's opinions, Wall Street firms had led investors and companies astray before and after the dot-com debacle.

The implications of the internet crash were far reaching. Many companies that needed to raise capital for investment found the capital markets suddenly shut to them. Millions of investors saw a large portion of their savings evaporate. This phenomenon was a likely contributor to the sharp drop in consumer confidence that took place in late 2000 and early 2001. In addition, the actual decrease in wealth threatened to dampen consumer spending. These factors, along with an overall slowing of the U.S. economy, threatened to put the United States into recession for the first time in over 10 years.

On a more macro level, the dot-coms used up valuable resources that could have been more efficiently allocated within the economy. The people who worked at failed internet firms could have spent their time and energy creating lasting value in other endeavors, and the capital that funded the dot-coms could have been ploughed into viable, lasting companies that would have benefited the overall economy. However, it could be argued that there were benefits as well, and that the large investment in the technology sector positioned the United States to be a world leader in the future.

Nevertheless, the question remained: how could the dot-com bubble occur in a sophisticated capital market system like that of the United States? Why did the market allow the valuations of many internet companies to go so high? What was the role of the intermediaries in the process that gave rise to the stock market bubble?

The intermediaries

One way to try to answer some of these questions is to look more closely at some of the key players in the investing chain. Much of the material in the following section is derived from interviews with representatives from each sector.

Venture capitalists

Venture capitalists (VCs) provided capital for companies in their early stages of development. They sought to provide a very high rate of return to their investors for the associated risk. This was typically accomplished by selling their stake in their portfolio companies either to the public through an IPO, or to another company in a trade sale.

The partners in a VC firm typically had a substantial percentage of their net worth tied up in their funds, which aligned their interests with their investors. Their main form of compensation was a large share of profits (typically 20%) in addition to a relatively low fee based on the assets under management.

A large part of a VC's job was to screen good business ideas and entrepreneurial teams from bad ones. Partners at a VC firm were typically very experienced, savvy business people who worked closely with their portfolio companies to both monitor and guide them to a point where they have turned a business idea into a well-managed, fully functional company that could stand on its own. In a sense, their role was to nurture the companies until they reached a point where they were ready to face the scrutiny of the public capital markets after an IPO. Typically, companies would not go public until they had shown profits for at least three quarters.[13]

After the dot-com crash, some investors and the media started pointing fingers at the venture capitalists that had invested in many of the failed dot-coms. They blamed them for

---

[12]*Fortune*, May 14, 2001.

[13]Peter Elstrom, "The Great internet Money Game. How America's top financial firms reaped billions from the Net boom while investors got burned," *BusinessWeek e.biz* (April 16, 2001).

being unduly influenced by the euphoria of the market, and knowingly investing in and bringing public companies with questionable business models, or that had not yet proven themselves operationally. Indeed, many of the dot-coms went public within record time of receiving VC funding—a study of venture-backed initial public offerings showed that companies averaged 5.4 years in age when they went public in 1999, compared with 8 years in 1995.[14]

Did the venture capital investing process change in a way that contributed to the internet bubble of 2000? According to a partner at a venture capital firm that invested in one of the internet consulting companies, the public markets had a tremendous impact on the way VCs invested during the late 1990s.[15] He felt that, because of expectations of high stock market valuations, VC firms invested in companies during late 1990s that they would not have invested in under ordinary circumstances. He also believed that the ready availability of money affected the business strategies and attitudes of the internet companies: "If the [management] team knows $50 million is available, it acts differently e.g. 'go for market share'."

The VC partner acknowledged that VCs took many internet companies public very early, but he felt that the responsibility of scrutinizing these companies lay largely with the investors that subscribed to the IPOs: "If a mutual find wants to invest in the IPO of a company that has no track record, profitability, etc. but sees it as a liquidity event, it has made a decision to become a VC. Lots of mutual funds thought 'VC is easy, I want a piece of it.'"

Investment bank underwriters

Entrepreneurs relied on investment banks (such as Goldman Sachs, Morgan Stanley Dean Witter and Credit Suisse First Boston) in the actual process of doing an initial public offering, or "going public." Investment banks provided advisory financial services, helped the companies price their offerings, underwrite the shares, and introduce them to investors, often in the form of a road show.

Investment banks were paid a commission based on the amount of money that the company manages to raise in its offering, typically on the order of 7%.[16] Several blue-chip firms were involved in the capital-raising process of the internet consultants (**see Exhibit 3**), and they also received a share of the blame for the dot-com crash in the months that followed it. In an article entitled *Just Who Brought Those Duds to Market?* the *New York Times* wrote:

> . . . *many Wall Street investment banks, from top-tier firms like Goldman, Sachs . . . to newer entrants like Thomas Weisel Partners . . . have reason to blush. In one blindingly fast riches-to-rags story, Pets.com filed for bankruptcy just nine months after Merrill Lynch took it public.*
>
> *Of course, investment banks that took these underperforming companies public may not care. They bagged enormous fees, a total of more than $600 million directly related to initial public offerings involving just the companies whose stocks are now under $1.*
>
> . . . *How did investment banks, paid for their expert advice, pick such lemons?*[17]

---

[14]Shawn Neidorf, "Venture-Backed IPOs Make a Comeback," *Venture Capital Journal* (Wellesley Hills, Aug 1, 1999).

[15]Limited partners are the investors in a venture capital fund; the venture capital firm itself usually serves as the general partner.

[16]Source: casewriter interview.

[17]Andrew Ross Sorkin, "Just Who Brought Those Duds to Market?" *NYTimes.com* (Copyright 2001 The New York Times Company).

The role of capital market intermediaries in the dot-com crash of 2000

Sell-side analysts

Sell-side analysts worked at investment banks and brokerage houses. One of their main functions was to publish research on public companies. Each analyst typically followed 15 to 30 companies in a particular industry, and his or her job involved forming relationships with and talking to the managements of the companies, following trends in the industry, and ultimately making buy or sell recommendations on the stocks. The recommendations analysts made could be very influential with investors. If a well-respected analyst downgraded a stock, the reaction from the market could be severe and swift, resulting in a same-day drop in the stock price. Sell-side analysts typically interacted with buy-side analysts and portfolio managers at money management companies (the buy-side) to market or "sell" their ideas. In addition, they usually provided support during a company's IPO process, providing research to the buy-side before the company actually went public. Sell-side analysts were usually partly compensated based on the amount of trading fees and investment banking revenue they help the firm to generate through their research.

In the months following the dot-com crash, sell-side technology and internet analysts found themselves the target of criticism for having buy ratings on companies that had subsequently fallen drastically in price. Financial cable TV channel CNBC ran a report called "Analyzing the Analysts," addressing the issue of whether or not they were to blame for their recommendations of tech stocks. A March 2001 article in *The Wall Street Journal* raised similar issues after it was reported that J.P. Morgan Chase's head of European research sent out a memo requiring all the company's analysts to show their stock recommendation changes to the company involved and to the investment banking division.[18] The previously mentioned issue of *Forbes* featured an article criticizing Mary Meeker, a prominent internet analyst.[19] And a *Financial Times* article entitled "Shoot all the analysts" made a sweeping criticism of their role in the market bubble:

> . . . *instead of forecasting earnings per share, they were now in the business of forecasting share prices themselves. And those prices were almost always very optimistic. Now, at last, they have had their comeuppance. Much of what many of them have done in the past several years has turned out to be worthless. High-flying stocks that a year ago were going to be cheap at twice the price have halved or worse—and some analysts have been putting out buy recommendations all the way down. . . . They should learn a little humility and get back to analysis.*[20]

Responding to the media criticism of financial analysts, Karl Keirstead, a Lehman Brothers analyst who followed internet consulting firms, stated:

> *It is too easy as they do on CNBC to slam the analysts for recommending stocks when they were very expensive. In the case of the internet consulting firms, looking back before the correction in April 2000, the fundamentals were "nothing short of pristine." The companies were growing at astronomical rates, and it looked as though they would continue to do so for quite a while. Under these assumptions, if you modeled out the financials for these companies and discounted them back at a reasonable rate, they did not seem all that highly valued.*[21]

---

[18]Wade Lambert, Jathon Sapsford, "J.P. Morgan Memo to Analysts Raises Eyebrows," *The Wall Street Journal* (Thursday, March 22, 2001).

[19]Peter Elkind, "Where Mary Meeker Went Wrong," *Fortune* (May 14, 2001).

[20]"Shoot all the analysts," *Financial Times* (Tuesday, March 20, 2001).

[21]Source: casewriter interview.

Keirstead also pointed out that there were times when it was legitimate to have a buy rating on a stock that was "overvalued" based on fundamentals:

The future price of a stock is not always tied to the discounted value of cash flow or earnings, it is equal to what someone is willing to pay. This is especially true in periods of tremendous market liquidity and huge interest in young companies with illiquid stocks and steep growth curves that are difficult to project. The valuation may seem too high, but if the fundamentals are improving and Street psychology and hype are building, the stock is likely to rally. Stock pickers must pay as much attention to these factors as the company and industry fundamentals.

When asked his view on why the buy-side institutions went along with the high valuations that these companies were trading for, Keirstead commented that, "A lot of buy-side analysts and portfolio managers became momentum investors in disguise. They claimed in their mutual fund prospectus that they made decisions based on fundamental analysis. Truth is, they played the momentum game as well."

Keirstead also commented on the criticism analysts had received for being too heavily influenced by the possibility of banking deals when making stock recommendations. He stated that this claim was "completely over-rated." Though there was some legitimacy to the argument and some of analysts' compensation did come from investment banking fees, it was a limited component. Analysts also got significant fees from the trading revenue they generated and the published rankings.[22] He pointed out that critics' arguments were ludicrous because if analysts only made decisions based on banking fees, it would jeopardize their rankings and credibility with their buy-side clients. However, he did note that the potential deal flow could have distorted the view of some technology analysts during the boom.

Finally, Keirstead described the bias that was present on the sell-side to be bullish:

To be negative when you are a sell-side analyst is to be a contrarian, to stick your neck out. You take a lot of heat, it's tough. And it would have been the wrong call for the last four years. Had I turned short in 1999 when these stocks seemed overvalued, I would have missed a 200% increase in the stocks. My view was: I can't be too valuation-sensitive. The stocks are likely to rise as long as the fundamentals hold and that's the position a lot of analysts took.

Consistent with this optimistic bias, there were very few sell recommendations from analysts during the peak of the internet stock bubble. According to financial information company First Call, more than 70% of the 27,000 plus recommendations outstanding on some 6,000 stocks in November 2000 were strong buys or buys, while fewer than 1% were sells or strong sells.[23]

Buy-side analysts and portfolio managers

The "buy-side" refers to institutions that do the actual buying and selling of public securities, such as mutual fund companies, insurance companies, hedge funds, and other asset managers.

There were two main roles on the buy side: analysts and portfolio managers. Buy-side analysts had some of the same duties as their sell-side counterparts. They were usually assigned to a group of companies within a certain industry and were responsible for doing industry research, talking to the companies' management teams, coming up with earning

---

[22]Several financial journals published analyst rankings. The most prominent ranking was by *Institutional Investor* magazine which published annual rankings of sell-side analysts by industry. These rankings were very influential in the analyst and investment community.

[23]Walter Updegrave, "The ratings game," *Money* (New York , January 2001).

The role of capital market intermediaries in the dot-com crash of 2000

estimates, doing valuation analysis, and ultimately rating the stock prices of the companies as either "buys" or "sells." The analyst's job was not yet complete, however. Though they did not publish their research, buy-side analysts needed to convince the portfolio managers within their company to follow their recommendations.

Portfolio managers were the ones who actually managed money, whether it was a retail mutual fund or an institutional account. Though they listened to the recommendations of the analysts, they were the ones who were ultimately responsible for buying or selling securities.

The compensation of the buy-side analysts was often linked to how well their stock recommendations do, and in the case of portfolio managers, compensation was determined by the performance of their funds relative to an appropriate benchmark return. These compensation schemes were designed to align the incentives of buy-side analysts and portfolio managers with the interests of investors.

Why then, did so may buy-side firms buy and hold on to the internet consulting firms during the market bubble? Did they really believe the companies were worth what they were trading for? Or did they know they were overvalued, but invest in them anyway for other reasons?

According to a former associate at a large mutual fund company, many people within his company knew that most of the internet companies were overvalued before the market correction, but they felt pressure to invest anyway:

> My previous employer is known as a value investor, growth at a reasonable price. At first the general impression in the firm was that a lot of the internet firms would blow up, that they didn't deserve these valuations. But articles were written about my company . . . that it was being left behind because it was not willing to invest in the internet companies. Some of the analysts at the firm began to recommend companies simply because they knew that the stock prices would go up, even though they were clearly overvalued. And portfolio managers felt that if they didn't buy the stocks, they would lag their benchmarks and their competitors—they are rewarded on a one-year term horizon and three-year horizon. It is very important to meet their benchmark, it makes up a material part of their compensation. In addition, they compare against the performance of their peers for marketing purposes.[24]

The role of information

The accounting profession

Independent accountants audited the financial statements of public companies to verify their accuracy and freedom from fraud. If they were reasonably satisfied, they provided an unqualified opinion statement which was attached to the company's public filings. If auditors were not fully satisfied, this is noted as well. Investors usually took heed of the auditor's opinion as it provided an additional level of assurance of the quality of the information they were receiving from companies.

In the year 2000, the accounting profession in the United States was dominated by five major accounting firms, collectively referred to as "The Big Five" (PriceWaterhouseCoopers, Deloitte & Touche, KPMG, Ernst & Young and Arthur Andersen.) The top 100 accounting firms had roughly a 50% share of the market and the Big Five account for about 84% of the revenues of the top 100.[25] However, the Big Five made up an even larger percentage of the auditing activity of internet IPOs. Of the 410 internet services and

---

[24]Source: casewriter interview.

[25]"Accounting Today Top 100 Survey Shows All is Well," *The CPA Journal* (May 1999).

software IPOs between January 1998 and December 2000, 373 of them, or 91% were audited by one of the Big Five accountants.[26]

During the aftermath of the dot-com crash, these firms came under some criticism for not adequately warning investors about the precarious financial position of some of the companies. The *Wall Street Journal* wrote an article addressing the fact that many dotcoms that went bankrupt were not given "going concern" clauses by their auditors. A going concern clause was included by an auditor if it had a substantial doubt that the company would be able to remain in operation for another 12 months:

> *In retrospect, critics say, there were early signs that the businesses weren't sustainable, including their reliance on external financing, rather than money generated by their own operations, to stay afloat. You wonder where some of the skepticism was . . . critics say many auditors appear to have presumed the capital markets would remain buoyant. For anybody to have assumed a continuation of those aberrant, irrational conditions was in itself irrational and unjustifiable whether it was an auditor, a board member or an investor. . . .[27]*

However, in the same article, accountants defended their actions by noting that going concern judgments were subjective, and that they were not able to predict the future any better than the capital markets.

Dr. Howard Schilit, founder and CEO of CFRA, an independent financial research organization,[28] believed that accountants certainly had to take a part of the blame for what happened. In his opinion, they "looked the other way when they could have been more rigorous in doing their work."[29] However, he noted that the outcome may not have been materially different even if they did.

One particular criticism he had was that many accountants didn't look closely enough at the substance of transactions and didn't do enough questioning of the circumstances surrounding sales contracts. His hope was that accountants "go back and learn what the basic rules are of when revenues should be booked. The rules haven't changed whether this is the new economy or old economy."

FASB—A regulator

The Financial Accounting Standards Boards (FASB) was an independent regulatory body in the United States whose mission was to "establish and improve standards of financial accounting and reporting for the guidance and education of the public, including issuers, auditors, and users of financial information."[30] FASB standards were recognized by the Securities and Exchange Commission (SEC), which regulates the financial reporting of public companies in the United States.

The accounting practices of some new economy firms posed challenges for auditors and investors, and though some observers felt that the accountants were not doing a good enough job, others thought that the accounting rules themselves were too ambiguous, and this fact lent itself to exploitation by the companies.

Specific examples included the treatment of barter revenues in the case of companies that exchanged on-line advertising space, the practice of booking gross rather than net revenues in commission-based businesses (e.g., Priceline.com), and the issue of when to

---

[26]Information extracted from IPO.com website http://www.ipo.com.

[27]Johnathan Weil, "'Going Concerns': Did Accountants Fail to Flag Problems at Dot-Com Casualties?" *The Wall Street Journal* (February 9, 2001).

[28]CFRA's mission is to warn investors and creditors about companies experiencing operational problems and particularly those that employ unusual or aggressive accounting practices to camouflage such problems.

[29]Source: casewriter interview.

[30]FASB website: http://accounting.rutgers.edu/raw/fasb/.

recognize revenues from long-term contracts (e.g., MicroStrategy Inc.) Given that the valuations of many internet firms were driven by how quickly they grew revenues, there was a lot of incentive to inflate this number. In fact, the accounting practices of dot-coms became so aggressive that the SEC had to step in:

> *The Securities & Exchange Commission's crackdown on the aggressive accounting practices that have taken off among many dot-com firms really began . . . when it quietly issued new guidelines to refocus corporate management and investors. . . . To rein in what it saw as an alarming trend in inflated revenue reports, the SEC required companies using lax accounting practices to restate financial results by the end of their next fiscal year's quarter. . . .*
>
> *The SEC has also directed the Financial Accounting Standards Board to review a range of internet company accounting practices that could boost revenues or reduce costs unfairly. Under the scrutiny, more companies are likely to issue restatements of financial results. . . .*[31]

In another spin on the issue, some questioned whether the accounting rules set out by the regulatory bodies had in fact become obsolete for the new economy. In July 2000, leaders in the accounting community told a Senate Banking subcommittee that the United States needed "a new accounting model for the New Economy." A major concern of theirs was that the current rules did not allow companies to report the value of intangible assets on their balance sheets, such as customers, employees, suppliers and organization.[32] Others argued that the accounting rules caused internet firms to appear unprofitable when they were actually making money. This was because old economy firms were allowed to capitalize their major investments such as factories, plants and equipment, whereas the rules did not allow capitalization of expenditures on R&D and marketing, which created value for many dot-com companies:

> *While internet stocks may not be worth what they are selling for, the movement in their prices may not be as crazy as it seems. Many of these companies reporting losses actually make money—lots of it. It all has to do with accounting. Old-economy companies get to capitalize their most important investments, while new economy ones do not. While Amazon.com announces a loss almost every quarter, when it capitalizes its investments in intangibles that loss turns into a $400-million profit.*[33]

Retail investors

The role of the general public in the dot-com craze cannot be ignored. In addition to the people who poured money into mutual funds, many retail investors began trading on their own, often electronically. A group of avid day traders grew up, some of whom quit their regular jobs to devote all their time and energy to trading stocks. Analysts estimated that they made up almost 18% of the trading volume of the NYSE and Nasdaq in 2000.[34] Sites such as Yahoo Finance grew in popularity, while chat rooms devoted to stocks and trading proliferated.

The number of accounts of internet stock brokers like Etrade and Ameritrade grew rapidly (Etrade grew from 544 thousand brokerage accounts in 1998 to 3 million in 2000 and Ameritrade grew from 98 thousand accounts in 1997 to 1.2 million in 2000) as they

---

[31]Catherine Yang, "Earth to Dot-Com Accountants," *BusinessWeek* (New York, April 3, 2000).

[32]Stephen Barlas, "New accounting model demanded," *Strategic Finance* (Montvale, September 2000).

[33]Geoffrey Colvin, "The Net's hidden profits," *Fortune* (New York, April 17, 2000).

[34]Amy S. Butte, "Day Trading and Beyond. A New Niche Is Emerging," *Bear Stearns Equity Research*, April 2000.

slashed their commissions, some to as low as $8/trade compared to the $50-$300[35] charged by traditional brokerage firms. These companies were dot-coms themselves and they were able to slash prices partly because they were operating at losses that they were not penalized for by the capital markets. This gave rise to an interesting positive feedback loop: the Etrades of the world, funded by the dot-com frenzied capital markets slashed their prices and therefore encouraged more trading, which continued to fuel the enthusiasm of investors for the markets.

The financial press also became increasingly visible during this period. Several publications like *Barrons* and *The Wall Street Journal* had always been very influential in the financial community. However, a host of other information sources, often on the web, sprang up to support the new demand for information. CNBC and CNNfn, major network channels devoted to the markets, often featured analysts and portfolio managers making stock recommendations or giving their views on the market.

Many of the retail investors did not know much about finance or valuation, and often didn't understand much about the companies whose shares they were buying. They were therefore likely to be heavily influenced by some of the intermediaries previously described, especially the financial press, and the sell-side analysts that publicly upgraded and downgraded companies.

These investors were pointed to by some as having had a large role in driving internet valuations to the levels they went to. The reasoning was that other more sophisticated buyers such as the institutional money managers, may have bought overvalued companies because they thought they could easily sell them later at even higher valuations to "dumb retail investors."

The companies themselves

The entrepreneurs who founded the internet consulting companies, and the management teams who ran them, could almost be described as bystanders to the process that took the stock prices of their companies to such lofty highs and then punishing lows. However, they were profoundly affected by these changes in almost every aspect of their businesses.

Obviously there were many benefits to having a high stock price. According to a managing director (MD) at one of the internet consultants, the company was facing a very competitive labor market while trying to grow organically, and having a stock that was doing well helped with recruiting people since the option part of the compensation package was attractive.[36] He also explained that people were proud to be a part of the firm, partly because the stock was doing so well.

As the stock price of the company continued to rise higher and higher, the MD admitted that he did become afraid that the market was overvaluing the company, and that this doubt probably went all the way up to the CEO. As he put it "we were trading at just absurd levels."

When asked about his thoughts on his firm's current stock price, the MD thought that the market had over-reacted and gone to the other extreme. He remarked that investors were worried that the internet consulting firms were facing renewed competition from companies like IBM, the Big Five accounting firms and the strategy consulting firms. Overall, though the rise and fall of the company's stock price was in many ways a painful experience, this MD thought that the market bubble presented a good opportunity that the company was able to capitalize upon. It was able to do a secondary offering at a high price and now had lots of cash on its balance sheet. His view was that "If you look at

[35]Lee Patterson, "If you can't beat 'em . . . ," *Forbes* (New York, August 23, 1999).
[36]Source: casewriter interview.

competitive sustainability [in this business], it could boil down to the company with the best balance sheet wins."

The blame game

In the aftermath of the dot-com crash, many tried to pinpoint whose fault it was that the whole bubble occurred in the first place. As mentioned previously, sell-side analysts, often the most visible group in the investment community, came under frequent attack in the media, as did, to some extent, venture capitalists, investment bankers, and even the accounting industry. Company insiders (including the founder of Scient) were also scrutinized for selling large blocks of shares when the stock prices of their companies were near their peaks.[37]

A *Wall Street Journal* article entitled "Investors, Entrepreneurs All Play the Blame Game," described how these various players were trying to blame each other for what happened:

> With the tech-heavy Nasdaq Composite Index dancing close to the 2,000 mark—down from over 5,000—internet entrepreneurs and venture capitalists have stepped up their finger-pointing about just who's at fault for the technology meltdown, which continues to topple businesses and once-cushy lifestyles. . . . Fingers pointed right and left—from entrepreneurs to venture capitalists, from analysts to day traders to shareholders—and back around again.[38]

The internet stock market bubble was certainly not the first one to occur. Other notables include the Tulip Craze of the seventeenth century and the Nifty Fifty boom of the 1970s. In all cases market valuations went to unsustainably high levels and ended with a sharp decrease in valuation that left many investors empty-handed.

But the question of what happened in this latest bubble remained: who, if anyone, could be blamed for the dot-com rise and crash? How did the various intermediaries described here affect or cause what happened? Was there really a misalignment of incentives in the system? If so, could it be fixed so that this sort of thing did not happen in the future? Or were market bubbles an inevitable part of the way the economy functioned?

Questions

1 What is the intended role of each of the institutions and intermediaries discussed in the case for the effective functioning of capital markets?

2 Are their incentives aligned properly with their intended role? Whose incentives are most misaligned?

3 Who, if anyone, was primarily responsible for the internet stock bubble?

4 What are the costs of such a stock market bubble? As a future business professional, what lessons do you draw from the bubble?

---

[37]Mark Maremont, John Hechinger, "If Only You'd Sold Some Stock Earlier—Say $100 Million Worth," *The Wall Street Journal* (March 22, 2001).

[38]Rebecca Buckman, "Investors, Entrepreneurs All Play the Blame Game," *The Wall Street Journal* (March 5, 2001).

EXHIBIT 1   **Timeline of the internet consultants—founding and IPO**

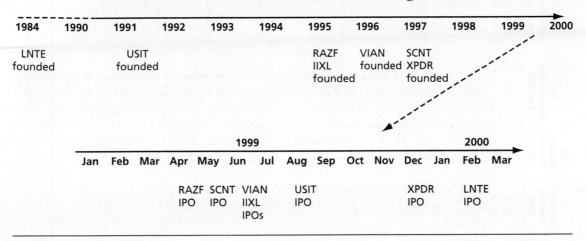

Source: Edgar Online, Marketguide.com

EXHIBIT 2   **Internet consultants—stock price highs and lows**

Company	IPO Price[a]	Peak Price	% Change IPO to Peak	Date of Peak	Price at End of Feb 2001	% Change from Peak
Scient	10	133.75	1,238%	10-Mar-00	2.94	−97.8%
Viant	8	63.56	695%	14-Dec-99	3.06	−95.2%
IXL Enterprises	12	58.75	390%	20-Jan-00	1.25	−97.9%
Lante	20	87.50	338%	29-Feb-00	1.81	−97.9%
Razorfish	8	56.94	612%	14-Feb-00	1.16	−98.0%
US Interactive	10	83.75	738%	4-Jan-00	0.56[b]	−99.3%
Xpedior	19	34.75	83%	10-Jan-00	0.69	−98.0%

[a]Split adjusted.

[b]Last trade on January 11, 2001. Filed for bankruptcy under Chapter 11 in January 2001.

Source: Bloomberg LP, The Center for Research in Security Prices (accessed via Wharton Research Database Services), Marketguide.com.

The role of capital market intermediaries in the dot-com crash of 2000

The role of capital market intermediaries in the dot-com crash of 2000

EXHIBIT 3   Intermediaries in the capital-raising process of the internet consultants

Company	Venture Capital Stage Investors	Investment Bank Underwriters	Auditors[a]	Analyst Coverage	Selected Institutional Holders	Venture Funding ($M)	IPO Amount Raised ($M)[b]	IPO Underwriting Fee ($M)	% Institutional Ownership[c]
Scient	Sequoia Capital, Benchmark Capital, Stanford Univ., Capital Research, Morgan Stanley Venture Partners, Amerindo Investment Advisors, Palantir Capital	Morgan Stanley Dean Witter, Hambrecht & Quist, Thomas Weisel Partners	PWC	Merrill Lynch, Morgan Stanley Dean Witter, CSFB, Lehman Brothers, UBS Warburg, SG Cowen, others	Capital Research, Putnam, Janus, Vanguard, Wellingon, State Street	31.2	60	4.2	34% (66% of float)
Viant	Kleiner Perkins Caufield & Byers, Mohr Davidow Ventures, Information Associates, Trident Capital, BancBoston Capital, General Motors, Technology Crossover Ventures	Goldman Sachs, Credit Suisse First Boston, WIT Capital Corporation	PWC	Goldman Sachs, Merrill Lynch, Lehman Brothers, CSFB, Wasserstein Perella, Bear Stearns, others	Fidelity, T Rowe Price, Putnam, Franklin, State Street, Vanguard, American Century, Goldman Sachs Asset Management	32.2	48	3.4	34% (67% of float)
IXL	Greylock Mgmt., Chase Capital Partners, Flatiron Partners, GE Capital, Kelso & Co., TTC Ventures, CB Capital, Portage Venture Partners, Transamerica Technology Finance	Merrill Lynch, BancBoston Robertson Stephens, DLJ, SG Cowen	PWC	Merrill Lynch, Robinson Humphrey, First Union Capital, others	Capital Research, State Street, Vanguard, Goldman Sachs Asset Management, GE Asset Management	91.0	72	5.0	29% (108% of float)
Lante	Frontenac Co., Dell Ventures, MSD Capital	Credit Suisse First Boston, Deutsche Bank Alex Brown, Thomas Weisel Partners	PWC	CSFB, Deutsche Bank, Thomas Weisel Partners, others	Fidelity, State Street, Vanguard, Goldman Sachs Asset Management	26.8	80	5.6	3% (21% of float)
Razorfish	N/A	Credit Suisse First Boston, BancBoston Robertson Stephens, BT Alex. Brown, Lehman Brothers	AA, PWC	CSFB, Lehman Brothers, SG Cowen, others	Janus, Capital Research, Fidelity, Vanguard, Goldman Sachs Asset Management	N/A	48	3.4	8% (14% of float)
US Interactive	Safeguard Scientific, Technology Leaders	Lehman Brothers, Hambrecht & Quist, Adams Harkness & Hill	KPMG	Lehman Brothers, Hambrecht & Quist, Deutsche Bank Alex Brown, others	T Rowe Price, Prudential, JP Morgan Investment Management, Credit Suisse Asset Mgmt.	N/A	46	2.0	4% (6% of float)
Xpedior	N/A	DLJ, First Union Securities, JP Morgan, The Robinson-Humphrey Group	E&Y	DLJ, First Union Securities, Robinson-Humphrey, others	Capital Research, T Rowe Price, Franklin, Vanguard, John Hancock	N/A	162	11.4	2% (10% of float)

[a]PW stands for PriceWaterhouseCoopers; AA for Arthur Anderson; E&Y for Ernst & Young.

[b]Includes underwriting fee.

[c]As of April 2001.

Sources: Compiled by casewriter.

EXHIBIT 4 **Market capitalization of major technology companies, January 2000**

Company	Market Capitalization ($ billions)[a]	Stock Price (January 3, 2000)
Microsoft	603	116.56
Intel	290	87.00
IBM	218	116.00
Dell Computer	131	50.88
Helwett Packard	117	117.44
Compaq Computer	53	31.00
Apple Computer	18	111.94

[a]Based on share price close on January 3, 2000 and reported shares outstanding.

Sources: Bloomberg LP, The Center for Research in Security Prices (accessed via Wharton Research Database Services), Edgar Online.

EXHIBIT 5 **Market valuations given to loss-making dot-coms**

Company	Net Income ('99/'00)[a] ($ millions)	Market Capitalization ($ billions)[b]	Stock Price (January 3, 2000)
Amazon.com	−720	30.8	89.38
DoubleClick	−56	30.1	268.00
Akamai Technologies	−58	29.7	321.25
VerticalNet	−53	12.4	172.63
Priceline.com	−1,055	8.4	51.25
E*Trade	−57	7.1	28.06
EarthLink	−174	5.2	44.75
Drugstore.com	−116	1.6	37.13

[a]As of end of 1999 or early 2000, depending on fiscal year end.

[b]Based on share price close on January 3, 2000 and reported shares outstanding.

Sources: Bloomberg LP, The Center for Research in Security Prices (accessed via Wharton Research Database Services), Edgar Online.

The role of capital market intermediaries in the dot-com crash of 2000

EXHIBIT 6   Scient—consolidated financial statements

INCOME STATEMENT (in thousands except per-share amounts)

	November 7, 1997 (inception) through March 31, 1998	Year Ended March 31	
		1999	2000
Revenues	$179	$20,675	$155,729
Operating expenses:			
Professional services	102	10,028	70,207
Selling, general and administrative	1,228	15,315	90,854
Stock compensation	64	7,679	15,636
Total operating expenses	1,394	22,022	176,697
Loss from operations	(1,215)	(12,347)	(20,968)
Interest income and other, net	56	646	4,953
Net loss	$(1,159)	$(11,701)	$(16,015)
Net loss per share:			
Basic and diluted	$(0.10)	$(0.89)	$(0.29)
Weighted average shares	11,894	13,198	54,590

EXHIBIT 6 **Scient—consolidated financial statements** *(continued)*

BALANCE SHEET (in thousands except per-share amounts)

	March 31	
	1999	**2000**
ASSETS		
Current Assets:		
Cash and cash equivalents	$11,261	$108,102
Short-term investments	16,868	121,046
Accounts receivable, net	5,876	56,021
Prepaid expenses	811	4,929
Other	318	4,228
Total Current Assets	35,134	294,326
Long-term investments	—	3,146
Property and equipment, net	3,410	16,063
Other	268	219
	$38,812	$313,754
LIABILITIES AND STOCKHOLDERS' EQUITY		
Current Liabilities:		
Bank borrowings, current	$413	$1,334
Accounts payable	832	5,023
Accrued compensation and benefits	2,554	33,976
Accrued expenses	2,078	9,265
Deferred revenue	524	6,579
Capital lease obligations, current	625	2,624
Total Current Liabilities	7,026	58,801
Capital lease obligations, long-term	680	2,052
	8,835	61,718
Commitments and contingencies (Note 5)		
Stockholders' equity:		
Convertible preferred stock; issuable in series, $.0001 par value; 10,000 shares authorized; 9,012 and no shares issued and outstanding, respectively	1	—
Common stock: $.0001 par value; 125,000 shares authorized; 33,134 and 72,491 shares issues and outstanding, respectively	3	7
Additional paid-in capital	70,055	297,735
Accumulated other comprehensive loss	—	(47)
Unearned compensation	(27,222)	(16,784)
Accumulated deficit	(12,860)	(28,875)
Total Stockholders' Equity	29,977	252,036
	$38,812	$313,754

Sources: Scient Corporation 10-K; Edgar Online http://www.freedgar.com (May 11, 2001).

The role of capital market intermediaries in the dot-com crash of 2000

EXHIBIT 7   **Analyst downgrades of the internet consultants**

Company	Number of Analysts that Downgraded during August 30–September 8, 2000
Viant	13
Scient	7
IXL Enterprises	7
US Interactive	5
Xpedior	3
Lante	1
Razorfish	0

ANALYST DOWNGRADES OF SCIENT CORPORATION, AUGUST 30–SEPTEMBER 8, 2000

Institution	Previous Recommendation	New Recommendation	Date of Downgrade
Merrill Lynch	LT Buy	LT Accumulate	1-Sep-2000
Lehman Brothers	Buy	Outperform	1-Sep-2000
ING Barings	Buy	Hold	1-Sep-2000
SG Cowen	Buy	Neutral	1-Sep-2000
Legg Mason	Buy	Market Perform	1-Sep-2000
BB&T Capital Markets	Hold	Source of Funds	1-Sep-2000
First Union Securities	Strong Buy	Buy	31-Aug-2000

Source: I/B/E/S (accessed via Wharton Research Database Services).

EXHIBIT 8   **Selected institutional holders of Scient Corporation, 1999–2000**

Institution	Quarter Ended:						
	June 1999	September 1999	December 1999	March 2000	June 2000	September 2000	December 2000
Capital Research	—	—	—	265	1,079,911	586,442	586,706
Putnam Investments	5,000	—	625,900	2,209,200	4,800,800	5,749,200	—
Wellington Management	—	—	—	—	—	—	803,000
State Street	—	12,450	38,167	52,867	89,667	180,668	672,352
Janus	267,300	273,915	483,730	775,085	1,359,700	4,382,250	—

Source: Edgar (SEC).

EXHIBIT 9   **Dot-coms that filed for bankruptcy or closed operations**

(Selected List)

August 2000
Auctions.com
Hardware.com
Living.com
SaviShopper.com
GreatCoffee

September 2000
Clickmango.com
Pop.com
FreeScholarships.com
RedLadder.com
DomainAuction.com
Gazoontite.com
Surfing2Cash.com
Affinia.com

October 2000
FreeInternet.com
Chipshot.com
Stockpower.com
The Dental Store
More.com
WebHouse
UrbanFetch.com
Boxman.com
RedGorilla.com
Eve.com
MyLackey.com
BigWords.com

Mortgage.com
MotherNature.com
Ivendor
TeliSmart.com

November 2000
Pets.com
Caredata.com
Streamline.com
Garden.com
Furniture.com
TheMan.com
Ibelieve.com
eSociety
UrbanDesign.com
HalfthePlanet.com
Productopia.com
BeautyJungle.com
ICanBuy.com
Bike.com
Mambo.com
Babystripes.com
Thirsty.com
Checkout.com

December 2000
Quepasa.com
Finance.com
BizBuyer.com
Desktop.com
E-pods.com
Clickabid.com

HeavenlyDoor.com
ShoppingList.com
Babygear.com
HotOffice.com
Goldsauction.com
AntEye.com
EZBid
Admart
I-US.com
Riffage.com

January 2000
MusicMaker.com
Mercata
Send.com
CompanyLeader.com
Zap.com
Savvio.com
News Digital Media
TravelNow.com
Foodline.com
LetsBuyIt.com
e7th.cm
CountryCool.com
Ibetcha.com
Fibermarket.com
Dotcomix
New Digital Media
GreatEntertaining.com
AndysGarage.com
Lucy.com
US Interactive

Sources: Johnathan Weil, "'Going Concerns': Did Accountants Fail to Flag Problems at Dot-Com Casualties?" *Wall Street Journal*, February 2001; Jim Battey, "Dot-com details: The numbers behind the year's e-commerce shake-out," *Infoworld*, March 2001.

The role of capital market intermediaries in the dot-com crash of 2000

The role of capital market intermediaries in the dot-com crash of 2000

EXHIBIT 10 **Capital flows from investors to companies**

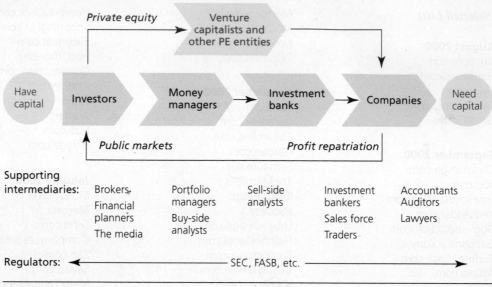

Supporting
intermediaries:

| Brokers,
Financial
planners
The media | Portfolio
managers
Buy-side
analysts | Sell-side
analysts | Investment
bankers
Sales force
Traders | Accountants
Auditors
Lawyers |

Regulators: ◄————————————————— SEC, FASB, etc. —————————————————►

Source: Created by casewriter.

BUSINESS ANALYSIS AND VALUATION TOOLS

Strategy Analysis

S trategy analysis is an important starting point for the analysis of financial statements. Strategy analysis allows the analyst to probe the economics of a firm at a qualitative level so that the subsequent accounting and financial analysis is grounded in business reality. Strategy analysis also allows the identification of the firm's profit drivers and key risks. This in turn enables the analyst to assess the sustainability of the firm's current performance and make realistic forecasts of future performance.

A firm's value is determined by its ability to earn a return on its capital in excess of the cost of capital. What determines whether or not a firm is able to accomplish this goal? While a firm's cost of capital is determined by the capital markets, its profit potential is determined by its own strategic choices:

1 The choice of an industry or a set of industries in which the firm operates (industry choice).

2 The manner in which the firm intends to compete with other firms in its chosen industry or industries (competitive positioning).

3 The way in which the firm expects to create and exploit synergies across the range of businesses in which it operates (corporate strategy).

Strategy analysis, therefore, involves industry analysis, competitive strategy analysis, and corporate strategy analysis.[1] In this chapter, we will briefly discuss these three steps and use the European airline industry, IKEA and the easyGroup, respectively, to illustrate the application of the steps.

INDUSTRY ANALYSIS

In analyzing a firm's profit potential, an analyst has to first assess the profit potential of each of the industries in which the firm is competing because the profitability of various industries differs systematically and predictably over time. For example, the ratio of earnings before interest and taxes to the book value of assets for European listed companies between 1992 and 2008 was 5.4 percent. However, the average returns varied widely across specific industries: for the household furniture industry, the profitability ratio was 6 percentage points greater than the population average, and for the gold and silver ore mining industry it was 15 percentage points less than the population average.[2] What causes these profitability differences?

There is a vast body of research in industrial organization on the influence of industry structure on profitability.[3] Relying on this research, strategy literature suggests that the

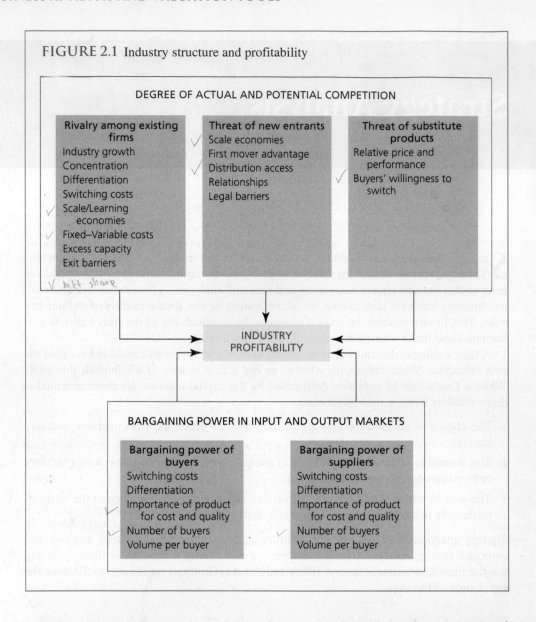

FIGURE 2.1 Industry structure and profitability

average profitability of an industry is influenced by the "five forces" shown in Figure 2.1.[4] According to this framework, the intensity of competition determines the potential for creating abnormal profits by the firms in an industry. Whether or not the potential profits are kept by the industry is determined by the relative **bargaining power** of the firms in the industry and their customers and suppliers. We will discuss each of these industry profit drivers in more detail below.

Degree of actual and potential competition

At the most basic level, the profits in an industry are a function of the maximum price that customers are willing to pay for the industry's product or service. One of the key determinants of the price is the degree to which there is **competition** among suppliers of the same or similar products. At one extreme, if there is a state of perfect competition in the industry, micro-economic theory predicts that prices will be equal to marginal cost, and there will be few opportunities to earn supernormal profits. At the other extreme, if the industry is dominated by a single firm, there will be potential to earn monopoly profits. In reality, the degree of competition in most industries is somewhere in between perfect competition and monopoly.

There are three potential sources of competition in an industry:

1 Rivalry between existing firms.
2 Threat of entry of new firms.
3 Threat of substitute products or services.

We will discuss each of these **competitive forces** in the following paragraphs.

Competitive force 1: Rivalry among existing firms

In most industries the average level of profitability is primarily influenced by the nature of rivalry among existing firms in the industry. In some industries firms compete aggressively, pushing prices close to (and sometimes below) the marginal cost. In other industries firms do not compete aggressively on price. Instead, they find ways to coordinate their pricing, or compete on nonprice dimensions such as innovation or brand image. Several factors determine the intensity of competition between existing players in an industry:

Industry growth rate If an industry is growing very rapidly, incumbent firms need not grab market share from each other to grow. In contrast, in stagnant industries the only way existing firms can grow is by taking share away from the other players. In this situation one can expect price wars among firms in the industry.

Concentration and balance of competitors The number of firms in an industry and their relative sizes determine the degree of concentration in an industry.[5] The degree of concentration influences the extent to which firms in an industry can coordinate their pricing and other competitive moves. For example, if there is one dominant firm in an industry (such as Microsoft in the operating systems industry in the 1990s), it can set and enforce the rules of competition. Similarly, if there are only two or three equal-sized players (such as Boeing and Airbus in the large commercial aircraft industry), they can implicitly cooperate with each other to avoid destructive price competition. If an industry is fragmented, price competition is likely to be severe.

Degree of differentiation and switching costs The extent to which firms in an industry can avoid head-on competition depends on the extent to which they can differentiate their products and services. If the products in an industry are very similar, customers are ready to switch from one competitor to another purely on the basis of price. Switching costs also determine customers' propensity to move from one product to another. When switching costs are low, there is a greater incentive for firms in an industry to engage in price competition. The PC industry, where the standardization of the software and microprocessor has led to relatively low switching costs, is extremely price competitive.

Scale/learning economies and the ratio of fixed to variable costs If there is a steep learning curve or there are other types of scale economies in an industry, size becomes an important factor for firms in the industry. In such situations, there are incentives to engage in aggressive competition for market share. Similarly, if the ratio of fixed to variable costs is high, firms have an incentive to reduce prices to utilize installed capacity. The airline industry, where price wars are quite common, is an example of this type of situation.

Excess capacity and exit barriers If capacity in an industry is larger than customer demand, there is a strong incentive for firms to cut prices to fill capacity. The problem of excess capacity is likely to be exacerbated if there are significant barriers for firms to exit the industry. Exit barriers are high when the assets are specialized or if there are regulations that make exit costly. The competitive dynamics of the steel industry demonstrates these forces at play.

Competitive force 2: Threat of new entrants

The potential for earning abnormal profits will attract new entrants to an industry. The very threat of new firms entering an industry potentially constrains the pricing of existing firms within it. Therefore the ease with which new firms can enter an industry is a key determinant of its profitability. Several factors determine the height of barriers to entry in an industry:

ebay

Economies of scale When there are large economies of scale, new entrants face the choice of having either to invest in a large capacity which might not be utilized right away or to enter with less than the optimum capacity. Either way, new entrants will at least initially suffer from a cost disadvantage in competing with existing firms. Economies of scale might arise from large investments in research and development (the pharmaceutical or jet engine industries), in brand advertising (sportswear industry), or in physical plant and equipment (telecommunications industry).

First mover advantage Early entrants in an industry may deter future entrants if there are first mover advantages. For example, first movers might be able to set industry standards, or enter into exclusive arrangements with suppliers of cheap raw materials. They may also acquire scarce government licenses to operate in regulated industries. Finally, if there are learning economies, early firms will have an absolute cost advantage over new entrants. First mover advantages are also likely to be large when there are significant switching costs for customers once they start using existing products. For example, switching costs faced by the users of Microsoft's Windows operating system make it difficult for software companies to market a new operating system.

Access to channels of distribution and relationships Limited capacity in the existing distribution channels and high costs of developing new channels can act as powerful barriers to entry. For example, a new entrant into the auto industry is likely to face formidable barriers because of the difficulty of developing a dealer network. Similarly, new consumer goods manufacturers find it difficult to obtain supermarket shelf space for their products. Existing relationships between firms and customers in an industry also make it difficult for new firms to enter an industry. Industry examples of this include auditing, investment banking, and advertising.

Legal barriers There are many industries in which legal barriers such as patents and copyrights in research-intensive industries limit entry. Similarly, licensing regulations limit entry into taxi services, medical services, broadcasting, and telecommunications industries.

Competitive force 3: Threat of substitute products

The third dimension of competition in an industry is the threat of substitute products or services. Relevant substitutes are not necessarily those that have the same form as the existing products but those that perform the same function. For example, airlines and high-speed rail systems might be substitutes for each other when it comes to travel over short distances. Similarly, plastic bottles and metal cans substitute for each other as packaging in the beverage industry. In some cases, threat of substitution comes not from customers' switching to another product but from utilizing technologies that allow them to do without, or use less of, the existing products. For example, energy-conserving technologies allow customers to reduce their consumption of electricity and fossil fuels.

The threat of substitutes depends on the relative price and performance of the competing products or services and on customers' willingness to substitute. Customers' perception of whether two products are substitutes depends to some extent on whether they perform the same function for a similar price. If two products perform an identical function, then it would be difficult for them to differ from each other in price. However, customers' willingness to switch is often the critical factor in making this competitive dynamic work. For example, even when tap water and bottled water serve the same function, many customers may be unwilling to substitute the former for the latter, enabling bottlers to charge a price premium. Similarly, designer label clothing commands a price premium even if it is not superior in terms of basic functionality because customers place a value on the image offered by designer labels.

Bargaining power in input and output markets

While the degree of competition in an industry determines whether there is *potential* to earn abnormal profits, the *actual profits* are influenced by the industry's bargaining power with its suppliers and customers. On the input side, firms enter into transactions with suppliers of labor, raw materials and components, and finances. On the output side, firms either sell directly to the final customers or enter into contracts with intermediaries in the distribution chain. In all these transactions, the relative economic power of the two sides is important to the overall profitability of the industry firms.

Competitive force 4: Bargaining power of buyers

Two factors determine the power of buyers: price sensitivity and relative bargaining power. Price sensitivity determines the extent to which buyers care to bargain on price; relative bargaining power determines the extent to which they will succeed in forcing the price down.[6]

Price sensitivity Buyers are more price sensitive when the product is undifferentiated and there are few switching costs. The sensitivity of buyers to price also depends on the importance of the product to their own cost structure. When the product represents a large fraction of the buyers' cost (for example, the packaging material for soft-drink producers), the buyer is likely to expend the resources necessary to shop for a lower-cost alternative. In contrast, if the product is a small fraction of the buyers' cost (for example, windshield wipers for automobile manufacturers), it may not pay to expend resources to search for lower-cost alternatives. Further, the importance of the product to the buyers' own product quality also determines whether or not price becomes the most important determinant of the buying decision.

Relative bargaining power Even if buyers are price sensitive, they may not be able to achieve low prices unless they have a strong bargaining position. Relative bargaining power in a transaction depends, ultimately, on the cost to each party of not doing business with the other party. The buyers' bargaining power is determined by the number of buyers relative to the number of suppliers, volume of purchases by a single buyer, number of alternative products available to the buyer, buyers' costs of switching from one product to another, and the threat of backward integration by the buyers. For example, in the automobile industry, car manufacturers have considerable power over component manufacturers because auto companies are large buyers with several alternative suppliers to choose from, and switching costs are relatively low. In contrast, in the personal computer industry, computer makers have low bargaining power relative to the operating system software producers because of high switching costs.

Competitive force 5: Bargaining power of suppliers

The analysis of the relative power of suppliers is a mirror image of the analysis of the buyers' power in an industry. Suppliers are powerful when there are only a few companies and few substitutes available to their customers. For example, in the soft-drink industry, Coke and Pepsi are very powerful relative to the bottlers. In contrast, metal can suppliers to the soft-drink industry are not very powerful because of intense competition among can producers and the threat of substitution of cans by plastic bottles. Suppliers also have a lot of power over buyers when the suppliers' product or service is critical to buyers' business. For example, airline pilots have a strong bargaining power in the airline industry. Suppliers also tend to be powerful when they pose a credible threat of forward integration. For example, insurance companies are powerful relative to insurance intermediaries because of their own presence in the insurance-selling business.

APPLYING INDUSTRY ANALYSIS: THE EUROPEAN AIRLINE INDUSTRY

Let us consider the above concepts of industry analysis in the context of the European airline industry. In the early 1980s, the European airline industry was highly regulated. Bilateral agreements between European governments severely restricted competition by determining which airlines could operate which routes at what fares. During the ten years from 1987 to 1997, the European Union (EU) gradually liberalized the industry, and reduced government intervention. The industry exhibited steady growth. While the four largest European airlines carried 54 million passengers in 1980, the same airlines carried 147 million passengers in 2000.[7] Despite the steady growth in passenger traffic, however, many of the large European airlines, such as Alitalia, British Airways, KLM, Lufthansa, and SAS, reported poor performance in the early 2000s and were forced to undergo internal restructuring. Other national carriers, such as Sabena and Swissair, went bankrupt. What accounted for this low profitability? What was the effect of liberalization on competition? What was the European airline industry's future profit potential?

Competition in the European airline industry

The competition was very intense for a number of reasons:

- Rivalry – industry growth. Between 1995 and 2004, the average annual industry growth was a moderate 5 percent. The industry growth was negative, at minus 5 percent, in the year immediately following the September 11 2001 terrorist attacks, compared with a range from 7 to 10 percent in the years before 2001.[8]
- Rivalry – concentration. The industry was fragmented. While several new airlines had entered the industry after the liberalization period, inefficient and loss-making national carriers, which were often state owned or state controlled, did not leave the industry because they were kept from bankruptcy through state subsidies and loans.
- Rivalry – differentiation and switching costs. Services delivered by different airlines on short-haul flights, within Europe, were virtually identical, and, with the possible

exception of frequent flyer programs, there were few opportunities to differentiate the products. Switching costs across different airlines were also low because in some areas airports were geographically close and code-sharing agreements increased the number of alternatives that passengers could consider.

- Rivalry – excess capacity. The European airlines had a structural excess capacity problem. Between 1995 and 2004, the average annual passenger load factor, which measures the percentage of passenger seats filled, was 72 percent. Because airlines lacked the opportunity to differentiate, they engaged in price competition in an attempt to fill the empty seats.

- Threat of new entrants – access to distribution channels/legal barriers. The system that most of the large European airports used to allocate their time slots among the airlines could have created barriers to entry. Slots are the rights to land at, or take off from, an airport at a particular date and time. In the twice-yearly allocation of time slots, priority was given to airlines that had slots in the previous season. After 1993, however, EU regulation promoted the entry of new airlines to the European market by requiring that at least 50 percent of the slots that became available were allocated to new entrants. New airlines also successfully managed to enter the European market by using alternative, smaller airports in the vicinity of those used by the established airlines. Most of these new entrants focused on offering low-fare, no-frills flights. Early new entrants were low-cost carriers easyJet and Ryanair, which experienced explosive growth and forced the incumbent airlines to start competing on price. In fact, the number of weekly passengers that new entrants in the low-fare, no-frills segment carried during the summer season increased from about 300,000 passengers in 1999 to 2.6 million passengers in 2005.

- Threat of new entrants. New entrants had easy access to capital. Purchased aircraft served to securitize loans, or aircraft could be leased. Further, second-hand aircraft became cheap during industry downturns, when troubled airlines disposed of excess capacity.

- Threat of new entrants – legal barriers. After 1997, European airlines faced no legal barriers to enter European markets outside their domestic market. Measures taken by the EU to deregulate the industry made it possible for the airlines to freely operate on any route within the EU, instead of having to conform to bilateral agreements between countries.

- Threat of substitute products. High-speed rail networks were being expanded and provided a potential, not yet fully exploited, substitute for air travel over shorter distances.

The power of suppliers and buyers

Suppliers and buyers had significant power over firms in the industry for these reasons:

- Suppliers' bargaining power. Airlines' primary costs for operating passenger flights were airport fees and handling charges, aircraft depreciation and maintenance, fuel, and labor. Ninety percent of the aircraft that European airlines had acquired or leased came from two commercial aircraft manufacturers, Airbus and Boeing. The strong dependence of European airlines on only two aircraft suppliers impaired airlines' bargaining power. Further, during the 1990s, ground handling agents at several European airports were monopolist and charged higher handling fees than agents at airports with competition. Liberalization measures taken by the EU promoted competition among ground handling agents, but in the early 2000s, still very few airports had more than two competing agents. In addition, although competition among jet fuel suppliers helped to ensure that the fuel prices that suppliers charged to the airlines did not deviate much from market prices, the fluctuations in fuel market prices were beyond airlines' control. Finally, European airline employees had significant power over their employers since their job security tended to be well-protected and the threat of a strike was an efficient bargaining tool in labor negotiations.

■ Buyers' bargaining power. Buyers gained more power because of the development of web booking systems, which made market prices transparent. Buyers were price sensitive since they increasingly viewed air travel as a commodity. Being able to easily compare prices across different airlines substantially increased their bargaining power.

As a result of the intense rivalry and low barriers to entry in the European airline industry, there was severe price competition among different airlines. Further, government interference kept the national carriers from entering into mergers. Instead, they created alliances that did not sufficiently reduce or reallocate capacity. These factors led to a low profit potential in the industry. The power of suppliers and buyers reduced the profit potential further.

There were some indications of change in the basic structure of the European airline industry. First, most of the established airlines cut capacity in 2002, which led to an overall improvement in the passenger load factor (75 percent, on average, compared to less than 70 percent in the 1990s). Second, in 2003, the merger between two established airlines, Air France and KLM, was one of the first signs of consolidation in the industry. Third, the EU was mandated to negotiate an "open skies" agreement with the US, which should substitute for all the bilateral agreements between European governments and the US, and open up a new market for European airlines. As a result, the profitability of the European airline industry may improve in the near future.

Limitations of industry analysis

A potential limitation of the industry analysis framework discussed in this chapter is the assumption that industries have clear boundaries. In reality, it is often not easy to clearly demarcate industry boundaries. For example, in analyzing the European airline industry, should one focus on the short-haul flight segment or the airline industry as a whole? Should one include charter flights and cargo transport in the industry definition? Should one consider only the airlines domiciled in Europe or also the airlines from other continents that operate flights to Europe? Inappropriate industry definition will result in incomplete analysis and inaccurate forecasts.

COMPETITIVE STRATEGY ANALYSIS

The profitability of a firm is influenced not only by its industry structure but also by the strategic choices it makes in positioning itself in the industry. While there are many ways to characterize a firm's business strategy, as Figure 2.2 shows, there are two generic competitive strategies: (1) **cost leadership** and (2) **differentiation**.[9] Both these strategies can potentially allow a firm to build a sustainable competitive advantage. Strategy researchers have traditionally viewed cost leadership and differentiation as mutually exclusive strategies. Firms that straddle the two strategies are considered to be "stuck in the middle" and are expected to earn low profitability.[10] These firms run the risk of not being able to attract price conscious customers because their costs are too high; they are also unable to provide adequate differentiation to attract premium price customers.

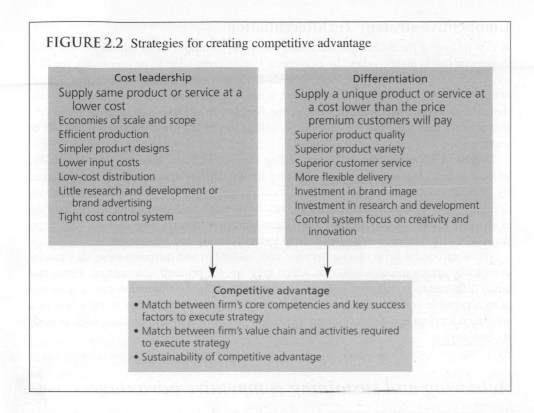

FIGURE 2.2 Strategies for creating competitive advantage

Cost leadership
Supply same product or service at a lower cost
Economies of scale and scope
Efficient production
Simpler product designs
Lower input costs
Low-cost distribution
Little research and development or brand advertising
Tight cost control system

Differentiation
Supply a unique product or service at a cost lower than the price premium customers will pay
Superior product quality
Superior product variety
Superior customer service
More flexible delivery
Investment in brand image
Investment in research and development
Control system focus on creativity and innovation

Competitive advantage
- Match between firm's core competencies and key success factors to execute strategy
- Match between firm's value chain and activities required to execute strategy
- Sustainability of competitive advantage

Sources of competitive advantage

Cost leadership enables a firm to supply the same product or service offered by its competitors at a lower cost. Differentiation strategy involves providing a product or service that is distinct in some important respect valued by the customer. As an example in food retailing, UK-based Sainsbury's competes on the basis of differentiation by emphasizing the high quality of its food and service, and by operating an online grocery store. In contrast, Germany-based Aldi and Lidl are discount retailers competing purely on a low-cost basis.

Competitive strategy 1: Cost leadership

Cost leadership is often the clearest way to achieve competitive advantage. In industries where the basic product or service is a commodity, cost leadership might be the only way to achieve superior performance. There are many ways to achieve cost leadership, including economies of scale and scope, economies of learning, efficient production, simpler product design, lower input costs, and efficient organizational processes. If a firm can achieve cost leadership, then it will be able to earn above-average profitability by merely charging the same price as its rivals. Conversely, a cost leader can force its competitors to cut prices and accept lower returns, or to exit the industry. For example, the entrance of low-cost carriers to the European airline industry at the end of the 1990s forced the incumbent airlines to change their strategy and focus more on competing through price.

Firms that achieve cost leadership focus on tight cost controls. They make investments in efficient scale plants, focus on product designs that reduce manufacturing costs, minimize overhead costs, make little investment in risky research and development, and avoid serving marginal customers. They have organizational structures and control systems that focus on cost control.

Competitive strategy 2: Differentiation

A firm following the differentiation strategy seeks to be unique in its industry along some dimension that is highly valued by customers. For differentiation to be successful, the firm has to accomplish three things. First, it needs to identify one or more attributes of a product or service that customers value. Second, it has to position itself to meet the chosen customer need in a unique manner. Finally, the firm has to achieve differentiation at a cost that is lower than the price the customer is willing to pay for the differentiated product or service.

Drivers of differentiation include providing superior intrinsic value via product quality, product variety, bundled services, or delivery timing. Differentiation can also be achieved by investing in signals of value such as brand image, product appearance, or reputation. Differentiated strategies require investments in research and development, engineering skills, and marketing capabilities. The organizational structures and control systems in firms with differentiation strategies need to foster creativity and innovation.

While successful firms choose between cost leadership and differentiation, they cannot completely ignore the dimension on which they are not primarily competing. Firms that target differentiation still need to focus on costs so that the differentiation can be achieved at an acceptable cost. Similarly, cost leaders cannot compete unless they achieve at least a minimum level on key dimensions on which competitors might differentiate, such as quality and service.

Achieving and sustaining competitive advantage

The choice of competitive strategy does not automatically lead to the achievement of competitive advantage. To achieve competitive advantage, the firm has to have the capabilities needed to implement and sustain the chosen strategy. Both cost leadership and differentiation strategy require that the firm makes the necessary commitments to acquire the core competencies needed, and structures its value chain in an appropriate way. Core competencies are the economic assets that the firm possesses, whereas the value chain is the set of activities that the firm performs to convert inputs into outputs. The uniqueness of a firm's core competencies and its value chain and the extent to which it is difficult for competitors to imitate them determines the sustainability of a firm's competitive advantage.[11]

To evaluate whether a firm is likely to achieve its intended competitive advantage, the analyst should ask the following questions:

- What are the key success factors and risks associated with the firm's chosen competitive strategy?

- Does the firm currently have the resources and capabilities to deal with the key success factors and risks?

- Has the firm made irreversible commitments to bridge the gap between its current capabilities and the requirements to achieve its competitive advantage?

- Has the firm structured its activities (such as research and development, design, manufacturing, marketing and distribution, and support activities) in a way that is consistent with its competitive strategy?

- Is the company's competitive advantage sustainable? Are there any barriers that make imitation of the firm's strategy difficult?

- Are there any potential changes in the firm's industry structure (such as new technologies, foreign competition, changes in regulation, changes in customer requirements) that might dissipate the firm's competitive advantage? Is the company flexible enough to address these changes?

Applying competitive strategy analysis

Let us consider the concepts of competitive strategy analysis in the context of IKEA. In 2008, Sweden-based IKEA was the world's largest furniture retailer. The company, founded by Ingvar Kamprad as a mail-order company, bought its first furniture factory and showroom in 1953. During the 1960s, IKEA started to develop the operating concept that the company is still renowned for: selling flat-packed furniture through large warehouse stores. In those years, IKEA also started to expand internationally.

While continuously expanding its worldwide store base, IKEA firmly established itself in the furniture retailing industry by following a low-cost strategy. For the fiscal year ending August 31 2008, IKEA achieved €22.2 billion in revenues. IKEA's average annual growth rate during the nine years between 1999 and 2008 was approximately 11 percent. Although the company did not reveal its profit margin because of its private status, industry analysts estimated this at 10 percent.[12] This margin was well above those of some of IKEA's larger competitors, such as US-based Target (7–8 percent). IKEA was one of the most successful and, presumably, one of the most profitable furniture retailers in the industry. How did IKEA achieve such performance?

IKEA's superior performance was based on a low-cost competitive strategy that consisted of the following key elements:[13]

- Global strategy. IKEA followed a purely global strategy. In each of the 36 countries where the retailer operated its stores, it targeted the same customer group – young families and young couples – and offered virtually the same selection of furniture. This strategy of strong economic integration and low responsiveness to national cultures helped the company to achieve economies of scale.

- Sourcing of production. IKEA did not own any production facilities other than Swedwood, which supplied 10 percent of its furniture. Instead, the company outsourced its production to manufacturers located throughout the world. Because IKEA had developed a network of 1,300 suppliers in 54 countries, the company could choose among a large number of manufacturers. Often, the company was a manufacturer's sole customer. Consequently, IKEA had substantial bargaining power in its dealings with its suppliers, which kept input costs to a minimum.

- Economic designs. Although IKEA outsourced its production, the company kept tight control of the design of its furniture. Its designers worked two to three years ahead of production to have sufficient time to find the most economic design solutions and review potential suppliers.

- Logistics. IKEA incorporated logistics into its strategy. The company operated large warehouse stores on relatively cheap locations outside the city centers. These warehouse stores sold furniture in flat-pack format that customers assembled at home. The integration of stores and warehouses and the use of flat-packs helped IKEA to economize on costs for storage and transportation.

- Sales. IKEA stores were able to employ a lower amount of sales staff than other stores because customers needed little assistance. All warehouse stores were designed such that customers, after having made their choice, picked the flat-packs from the shelves and paid for their purchases at a central location in the store. IKEA also provided its customers with limited after-sales service. Through this strategy, the company was able to keep personnel expenses to a minimum.

As a result of the above strategy, IKEA achieved a significant cost advantage over its competitors in the furniture retailing industry. Consequently, IKEA was able to continuously cut prices and maintain the price difference with its competitors. Because, over the years, the company had made large investments in knowledge of low-cost furniture design, store design, and logistics, the business model was difficult to replicate, making its competitive advantage sustainable. Although IKEA's brand image varied greatly across countries, in some countries it had become a cult brand. In 2008, Interbrand Corp. estimated the value of the IKEA brand at €8.5 billion. This value was similar to the values of brands such as Dell, Budweiser and Philips. The strength of the retailer's brand name, the diversity in its assortment, and the distinctiveness of its designs illustrate that IKEA's strategy also exhibited some characteristics of a differentiation strategy.[14] However, the company's continuous focus on cost control was most likely the main driver of success. IKEA's success inspired some local competitors, such as France-based Fly, to attempt to replicate parts of its strategy. However no competitor to date has been able to replicate the business model on a similar scale.

CORPORATE STRATEGY ANALYSIS

So far in this chapter we have focused on the strategies at the individual business level. While some companies focus on only one business, many companies operate in multiple businesses. For example, of all companies that were listed on the seven largest European exchanges at the end of 2008, 46 percent operated in more than two business segments.[15] In the 1990s and 2000s, there has been an attempt by US and western European companies to reduce the diversity of their operations and focus on a relatively few "core" businesses. However, multi-business organizations continue to dominate the economic activity in many countries in the world.

When analyzing a multi-business organization, an analyst has to not only evaluate the industries and strategies of the individual business units but also the economic consequences – either positive or negative – of managing all the different businesses under one corporate umbrella. For example, General Electric has been very successful in creating significant value by managing a highly diversified set of businesses ranging from aircraft engines to light bulbs. In contrast, during the first half of the 2000s, shareholders of several German conglomerates, such as MAN and Siemens, pressured their companies to improve profitability by spinning off their "noncore" divisions.

Sources of value creation at the corporate level

Economists and strategy researchers have identified several factors that influence an organization's ability to create value through a broad corporate scope. Economic theory suggests that the optimal activity scope of a firm depends on the relative transaction cost of performing a set of activities inside the firm versus using the market mechanism.[16] Transaction cost economics implies that the multiproduct firm is an efficient choice of organizational form when coordination among independent, focused firms is costly due to market transaction costs.

Transaction costs can arise out of several sources. They may arise if the production process involves specialized assets such as human capital skills, proprietary technology, or other organizational know-how that is not easily available in the marketplace. Transaction costs also may arise from market imperfections such as information and incentive problems. If buyers and sellers cannot solve these problems through standard mechanisms such as enforceable contracts, it will be costly to conduct transactions through market mechanisms.

For example, as discussed in Chapter 1, public capital markets may not work well when there are significant information and incentive problems, making it difficult for entrepreneurs to raise capital from investors. Similarly, if buyers cannot ascertain the quality of products being sold because of lack of information, or cannot enforce warranties because of poor legal infrastructure, entrepreneurs will find it difficult to break into new markets. Finally, if employers cannot assess the quality of applicants for new positions, they will have to rely more on internal promotions rather than external recruiting to fill higher positions in an organization. Emerging economies often suffer from these types of transaction costs because of poorly developed intermediation infrastructure.[17] Even in many advanced economies, examples of high transaction costs can be found. For example, in many countries other than the US and western European nations, the venture capital industry is not highly developed, making it costly for new businesses in high technology industries to attract financing. Even in Europe and the US, transaction costs may vary across economic sectors. For example, until recently electronic commerce was hampered by consumer concerns regarding the security of credit card information sent over the internet.

Transactions inside an organization may be less costly than market-based transactions for several reasons. First, communication costs inside an organization are reduced because confidentiality can be protected and credibility can be assured through internal mechanisms. Second, the headquarters office can play a critical role in reducing costs of enforcing agreements between organizational subunits. Third, organizational subunits can share valuable nontradable assets (such as organizational skills, systems, and processes) or nondivisible assets (such as brand names, distribution channels, and reputation).

There are also forces that increase transaction costs inside organizations. Top management of an organization may lack the specialized information and skills necessary to manage businesses across several different industries. This lack of expertise reduces the possibility of actually realizing economies of scope, even when there is potential for such economies. This problem can be remedied by creating a decentralized organization, hiring specialist managers to run each business unit, and providing these managers with proper incentives. However, decentralization will also potentially decrease goal congruence among subunit managers, making it difficult to realize economies of scope.

Whether or not a multi-business organization creates more value than a comparable collection of focused firms is, therefore, context dependent.[18] Analysts should ask the following questions to assess whether an organization's corporate strategy has the potential to create value:

■ Are there significant imperfections in the product, labor, or financial markets in the industries (or countries) in which a company is operating? Is it likely that transaction costs in these markets are higher than the costs of similar activities inside a well-managed organization?

■ Does the organization have special resources such as brand names, proprietary know-how, access to scarce distribution channels, and special organizational processes that have the potential to create economies of scope?

■ Is there a good fit between the company's specialized resources and the portfolio of businesses in which the company is operating?

■ Does the company allocate decision rights between the headquarters office and the business units optimally to realize all the potential economies of scope?

■ Does the company have internal measurement, information, and incentive systems to reduce agency costs and increase coordination across business units?

Empirical evidence suggests that creating value through a multi-business corporate strategy is hard in practice. Several researchers have documented that diversified companies trade at a discount in the stock market relative to a comparable portfolio of focused companies.[19] Studies also show that acquisitions of one company by another, especially when the two are in unrelated businesses, often fail to create value for the acquiring companies.[20] Finally, there is considerable evidence that value is created when multi-business companies increase corporate focus through divisional spin-offs and asset sales.[21]

There are several potential explanations for the above diversification discount. First, managers' decisions to diversify and expand are frequently driven by a desire to maximize the size of their organization rather than to maximize shareholder value. Second, diversified companies often suffer from incentive misalignment problems leading to suboptimal investment decisions and poor operating performance. Third, capital markets find it difficult to monitor and value multi-business organizations because of inadequate disclosure about the performance of individual business segments.

In summary, while companies can theoretically create value through innovative corporate strategies, there are many ways in which this potential fails to get realized in practice. Therefore, it pays to be skeptical when evaluating companies' corporate strategies.

Applying corporate strategy analysis

Let us apply the concepts of corporate strategy analysis to easyGroup, a privately-owned company that licenses the "easy" brand name to, and holds shares in, various no-frills, low-cost businesses. EasyGroup's first and primary holding, easyJet, started operations as a low-fare short-haul airline company in 1995 and five years later placed 28 percent of its shares on the London Stock Exchange at an amount of £224 million. The company grew rapidly and began to pose a serious threat in the short-haul segment to the dominance of leading European airlines like Air France, British Airways, and Lufthansa. EasyJet's revenues increased from £46 million in 1997 to £1,341 million in 2005.

Flush with his success in selling cheap short-haul flights, Stelios Haji-Ioannou, the founder of easyJet and private owner of easyGroup, stretched the "easy" brand name to other industries. The new ventures that easyGroup started had a few common characteristics. They primarily sold services with high fixed costs and exploited the fact that the demand for a service could be highly elastic to its price. In fact, when demand was low, the ventures sold their services at often drastically reduced prices. Because the easyGroup ventures consistently offered their services through the internet and rewarded customers for booking in advance, they were able to flexibly adjust prices to demand. Further, because of the no-frills character of services and the bypassing of intermediaries in industries such as the travel industry, the ventures were able to keep tight control over their costs. Following this strategy, easyGroup expanded into car rental, pizza delivery, bus transport, cruise travel, cinemas, and hotels. In an interview, Haji-Ioannou emphasized his unique position: "Brand extension is very tricky. It's like starting another company, all the time. This is the privilege of entrepreneurs spending their own money."[22]

EasyGroup's diversification into unrelated businesses was not without risks. Haji-Ioannou claimed that easyGroup could create value through its broad corporate focus for the following reasons:[23]

- Through easyJet's rapid growth, its marketing strategy, and the innovations that the airline company had brought to the European airline industry, Haji-Ioannou had gained much exposure for his "easy" brand throughout Europe. Making use of easyJet's valuable brand name and its established reputation in offering no-frills services at low prices, Haji-Ioannou could economize on transaction costs in his new ventures. Customers are likely to have greater trust in new businesses that operate under a familiar brand name. Further, brand-stretching can help to economize on advertising. In fact, Haji-Ioannou admitted on occasions that, without the airline, the other businesses were not likely to survive.

- EasyGroup had been able to acquire critical expertise in flexible pricing and online selling. This is a general competency that can be exploited in many industries.

- EasyGroup's revenues came from licensing the "easy" brand and holding financial stakes in easyJet and the new ventures. Haji-Ioannou planned to take a venture public when it had proven to be successful, as he had done with easyJet. Because the easyGroup did not produce the services itself, the company shared the risks of production with the ventures' other stakeholders.

There were also signs that easyGroup was expanding too rapidly and that its diversification beyond air travel was likely to fail. Very few of the easyGroup's new business ventures were profitable during their first years of operation. For example, at the end of 2003, the losses incurred by easyGroup's internet café chain added up to an estimated £100 million. In many of the industries that easyGroup entered, incumbent companies also had valuable brand names, execution capabilities, and customer loyalty. Therefore these companies were likely to offer formidable competition to easyGroup's individual business lines. EasyGroup's critics also pointed out that expanding rapidly into so many different areas is likely to confuse customers, dilute easyGroup's brand value, and increase the chance of poor execution.

An interesting question to examine is whether there are systematic reasons to believe that a company such as easyGroup can succeed in pursuing a wide focus because its business model – online selling of no-frills services under one common brand – somehow allows it to manage this diversity in a fundamentally different manner than a traditional company would be able to. EasyGroup's poor financial performance during the early 2000s cast doubts on whether it can succeed as a diversified company.

SUMMARY

Strategy analysis is an important starting point for the analysis of financial statements because it allows the analyst to probe the economics of the firm at a qualitative level. Strategy analysis also allows the identification of the firm's profit drivers and key risks, enabling the analyst to assess the sustainability of the firm's performance and make realistic forecasts of future performance.

Whether a firm is able to earn a return on its capital in excess of its cost of capital is determined by its own strategic choices:

1 The choice of an industry or a set of industries in which the firm operates (industry choice).
2 The manner in which the firm intends to compete with other firms in its chosen industry or industries (competitive positioning).
3 The way in which the firm expects to create and exploit synergies across the range of businesses in which it operates (corporate strategy). Strategy analysis involves analyzing all three choices.

Industry analysis consists of identifying the economic factors that drive the industry profitability. In general, an industry's average profit potential is influenced by the degree of rivalry among existing competitors, the ease with which new firms can enter the industry, the availability of substitute products, the power of buyers, and the power of suppliers. To perform industry analysis, the analyst has to assess the current strength of each of these forces in an industry and make forecasts of any likely future changes.

Competitive strategy analysis involves identifying the basis on which the firm intends to compete in its industry. In general, there are two potential strategies that could provide a firm with a competitive advantage: cost leadership and differentiation. Cost leadership involves offering at a lower cost the same product or service that other firms offer. Differentiation involves satisfying a chosen dimension of customer need better than the competition, at an incremental cost that is less than the price premium that customers are willing to pay. To perform strategy analysis, the analyst has to identify the firm's intended strategy, assess whether the firm possesses the competencies required to execute the strategy, and recognize the key risks that the firm has to guard against. The analyst also has to evaluate the sustainability of the firm's strategy.

Corporate strategy analysis involves examining whether a company is able to create value by being in multiple businesses at the same time. A well-crafted corporate strategy reduces costs or increases revenues from running several businesses in one firm relative to the same businesses operating independently and transacting with each other in the marketplace. These cost savings or revenue increases come from specialized resources that the firm has that help it to exploit synergies across these businesses. For these resources to be valuable, they must be nontradable, not easily imitated by competition, and nondivisible. Even when a firm has such resources, it can create value through a multi-business organization only when it is managed so that the information and agency costs inside the organization are smaller than the market transaction costs.

The insights gained from strategy analysis can be useful in performing the remainder of the financial statement analysis. In accounting analysis the analyst can examine whether a firm's accounting policies and estimates are consistent with its stated strategy. For example, a firm's choice of functional currency in accounting for its international operations should be consistent with the level of integration between domestic and international operations that the business strategy calls for. Similarly, a firm that mainly sells housing to low-income customers should have higher than average bad debt expenses.

Strategy analysis is also useful in guiding financial analysis. For example, in a cross-sectional analysis the analyst should expect firms with cost leadership strategy to have lower gross margins and higher asset turnover than firms that follow differentiated strategies. In a time series analysis, the analyst should closely monitor any increases in expense ratios and asset turnover ratios for low-cost firms, and any decreases in investments critical to differentiation for firms that follow differentiation strategy.

Business strategy analysis also helps in prospective analysis and valuation. First, it allows the analyst to assess whether, and for how long, differences between the firm's performance and its industry (or industries) performance are likely to persist. Second, strategy analysis facilitates forecasting investment outlays the firm has to make to maintain its competitive advantage.

CORE CONCEPTS

Bargaining power in input and output markets One of the two main drivers of an industry's profit potential. The greater the bargaining power of buyers and suppliers, the lower is the industry's profit potential.

Competitive forces Five forces that together determine an industry's profit potential through their influence on the degree of actual and potential competition with the industry or the bargaining power in input and output markets.

Competitive strategy analysis Analysis of the strategic choices that a firm has made to position itself in the industry. Firms typically choose between to mutually exclusive strategies: (1) cost leadership or (2) differentiation. The competitive strategy that a firm has chosen and the industry's profit potential together affect the firm's profitability.

Corporate strategy analysis Analysis of a firm's business structure and processes to establish whether and how the firm has minimized or can potentially minimize its transaction costs.

Cost leadership Strategy in which a firm achieves a competitive advantage by producing and delivering its products or services at a lower cost than its competitors.

Differentiation Strategy in which a firm achieves a competitive advantage by producing and delivering products or services with unique features at premium prices.

Industry analysis Analysis of an industry's profit potential.

Industry competition One of the two main drivers of an industry's profit potential. The degree of actual and potential competition is determined by three competitive forces: (1) the rivalry among existing firms in the industry; (2) the threat of new entrants to the industry; and (3) the threat of substitute products.

QUESTIONS, EXERCISES AND PROBLEMS

1 Judith, an accounting student, states, "Strategy analysis seems to be an unnecessary detour in doing financial statement analysis. Why can't we just get straight to the accounting issues?" Explain to Judith why she might be wrong.

2 What are the critical drivers of industry profitability?

3 One of the fastest growing industries in the last 20 years is the memory chip industry, which supplies memory chips for personal computers and other electronic devices. Yet the average profitability for this industry has been very low. Using the industry analysis framework, list all the potential factors that might explain this apparent contradiction.

4 Joe argues, "Your analysis of the five forces that affect industry profitability is incomplete. For example, in the banking industry, I can think of at least three other factors that are also important; namely, government regulation, demographic trends, and cultural factors." His classmate Jane disagrees and says, "These three factors are important only to the extent that they influence one of the five forces." Explain how, if at all, the three factors discussed by Joe affect the five forces in the banking industry.

5 Examples of European firms that operate in the pharmaceutical industry are Glaxo-SmithKline and Bayer. Examples of European firms that operate in the tour operating industry are Thomas Cook and TUI. Rate the pharmaceutical and tour operating industries as high, medium, or low on the following dimensions of industry structure:

   1 Rivalry.
   2 Threat of new entrants.
   3 Threat of substitute products.
   4 Bargaining power of suppliers.
   5 Bargaining power of buyers.

   Given your ratings, which industry would you expect to earn the highest returns?

6 In 2005, Puma was a very profitable sportswear company. Puma did not produce most of the shoes, apparel and accessories that it sold. Instead, the company entered into contracts with independent manufacturers, primarily in Asia. Puma also licensed independent companies throughout the world to design, develop, produce and distribute a selected range of products under its brand name. Use the five-forces framework and your knowledge of the sportswear industry to explain Puma's high profitability in 2005.

7 In response to the deregulation of the European airline industry during the 1980s and 1990s, European airlines followed their US peers in starting frequent flyer programs as a way to differentiate themselves from others. Industry analysts, however, believe that frequent flyer programs had only mixed success. Use the competitive advantage concepts to explain why.

8 What are the ways that a firm can create barriers to entry to deter competition in its business? What factors determine whether these barriers are likely to be enduring?

9 Explain why you agree or disagree with each of the following statements:

a It's better to be a differentiator than a cost leader, since you can then charge premium prices.

b It's more profitable to be in a high technology than a low technology industry.

c The reason why industries with large investments have high barriers to entry is because it is costly to raise capital.

10 There are very few companies that are able to be both cost leaders and differentiators. Why? Can you think of a company that has been successful at both?

11 Many consultants are advising diversified companies in emerging markets such as India, Korea, Mexico, and Turkey to adopt corporate strategies proven to be of value in advanced economies like the US and Western Europe. What are the pros and cons of this advice?

Problem 1 The European airline industry

The Association of European Airlines (AEA) is an association of 34 established European airlines, mostly national flag carriers such as Air France, Lufthansa, Finair and SAS but also some cargo specialists such as TNT and Cargolux. The AEA continuously surveys its members and publishes reports and statistics about its members' passenger and cargo traffic and capacity, and operating performance. Although the members of the AEA do not represent the whole European airline industry, the AEA statistics are a useful source of information about the state of the industry. Following is a selection of statistics illustrating the developments in the industry during the years 2002–2007.

Revenue passenger kilometers (RPK) is the number of passengers transported times the average number of kilometers flown. Cargo tonne kilometers (CTK) is the amount of cargo transported (in tonne) times the number of kilometers flown. Load factors are defined as the ratio of realized RPKs (or CTKs) and available seat kilometers (tonne kilometers). Note that the description of the European Airline Industry in this chapter covered the period 1995–2004. Use the above information to answer the following questions about whether and how competition in the European airline industry has changed after 2004:

1 Evaluate how the rivalry among existing firms has developed after 2004.

2 Evaluate the influence of rising fuel prices on the AEA airlines' profitability between 2003 and 2006. If fuel prices had not increased after 2003, what would have been the pre-interest breakeven load factor in 2006 (assuming all other factors constant)?

3 During the period examined, some airlines started to charge fuel surcharges to their customers. For example, late 2007 KLM charged its customers €27 on European flights and €80 on intercontinental flights. Other airlines had similar surcharges. How do such practices affect your answer to question 2?

4 The operating margins of the AEA airlines became positive, on average, in 2004 and gradually improved thereafter. What do you think are the most important drivers behind this development? (Also consider your answers to questions 2 and 3.)

TABLE 2.1

		2002	2003	2004	2005	2006	2007
AEA market share of the . . .							
. . . 4 largest AEA airlines	%	58.9%	58.8%	58.5%	58.2%	57.6%	56.5%
. . . 8 largest AEA airlines	%	79.8%	79.3%	79.4%	79.1%	78.3%	77.1%
Revenue passenger kilometers	mn.	589,575	598,454	656,677	699,515	741,608	781,165
RPK growth	%	−4.9%	1.5%	9.7%	6.5%	6.0%	5.3%
Cargo tonne kilometers	mn.	31,499	32,548	36,009	36,004	37,418	38,635
CTK growth	%	−0.3%	3.3%	10.6%	0.0%	3.9%	3.3%
Available seat kilometers	mn.	801,370	815,998	880,085	922,077	970,717	1,015,004
ASK growth	%	−8.8%	1.8%	7.9%	4.8%	5.3%	4.6%
Available tonne kilometers	mn.	87,371	88,952	97,869	102,398	107,568	112,477
ATK growth	%	−3.3%	1.8%	10.0%	4.6%	5.0%	4.6%
Passenger load factor	%	73.6%	73.3%	74.6%	75.9%	76.4%	77.0%
Cargo load factor	%	36.1%	36.6%	36.8%	35.2%	34.8%	34.3%
Overall load factor	%		68.6%	68.4%	68.9%	69.7%	
Revenue per kilometer	€c		79.1	80.0	82.2	84.5	
Cost per kilometer	€c		54.0	54.2	55.5	56.9	
Fuel cost to total cost	%		12.10%	15.20%		22.80%	
Pre-interest breakeven load factor	%		68.3%	67.8%	67.5%	67.3%	
Average AEA operating margins (before interest)	%	1.6%	−0.3%	2.0%	2.3%	3.4%	5.2%
Average AEA operating margins (after interest)	%	−1.2%	−2.1%	0.5%	1.1%	2.5%	4.6%
Millions weekly seats of low-cost carriers (non-AEA members)	mn.	0.9	1.5	1.9	2.6	3.1	3.9
Low-cost carriers growth	%	50.0%	66.7%	26.7%	36.8%	19.2%	25.8%

Source: Association of European Airlines

NOTES

1. The discussion presented here is intended to provide a basic background in strategy analysis. For a more complete discussion of the strategy concepts, see, for example, *Contemporary Strategy Analysis* by Robert M. Grant (Oxford: Blackwell Publishers, 2005); *Economics of Strategy* by David Besanko, David Dranove, and Mark Shanley (New York: John Wiley & Sons, 2004); *Strategy and the Business Landscape* by Pankaj Ghemawat (London: Pearson Education, 2005); and *Corporate Strategy: Resources and the Scope of the Firm* by David J. Collis and Cynthia Montgomery (Burr Ridge, IL: Irwin/McGraw-Hill, 1997).

2. The data to calculate these statistics come from Thomson Financial's Worldscope database. The statistics apply to all companies that were listed between January 1992 and December 2008 on one of the seven largest European stock exchanges (see the Appendix to Chapter 1 for more details about the sample of European companies).

3. For a summary of this research, see *Industrial Market Structure and Economic Performance*, second edition, by F. M. Scherer (Chicago: Rand McNally College Publishing Co., 1980).

4. See *Competitive Strategy* by Michael E. Porter (New York: The Free Press, 1980).

5. The four-firm concentration ratio is a commonly used measure of industry concentration; it refers to the market share of the four largest firms in an industry.

6. While the discussion here uses the buyer to connote industrial buyers, the same concepts also apply to buyers of consumer products. Throughout this chapter we use the terms buyers and customers interchangeably.

7. The industry statistics in this section are drawn from the Association of European Airlines (AEA) yearbooks and STAR database.

8. The growth rates represent the annual growth rates in passenger-kilometers (cumulative number of kilometers traveled by all passengers). These data come from the Association of European Airlines (AEA). Because the AEA collects data only from its members, which are primarily the established airlines, the growth rates may not reflect the growth that new entrants experienced.

9. For a more detailed discussion of these two sources of competitive advantage, see Michael E. Porter, *Competitive Advantage: Creating and Sustaining Superior Performance* (New York: The Free Press, 1985).

10. Ibid.

11. See *Competing for the Future* by Gary Hammel and C. K. Prahalad (Boston: Harvard Business School Press, 1994) for a more detailed discussion of the concept of core competencies and their critical role in corporate strategy.

12. Kenny Capell, "IKEA, How the Swedish Retailer Became a Global Cult Brand," *Business Week*, November 14 2005.

13. See K. Kling and I. Goteman, "IKEA CEO Anders Dahlvig on International Growth and IKEA's Unique Corporate Culture and Brand Identity," *Academy of Management Executive* (2003): 31–37; R. Normann and R. Ramirez, "From Value Chain to Value Constellation: Designing Interactive Strategy," *Harvard Business Review* 71 (1993): 65–77; Capell, op. cit.

14. One of the strategic challenges faced by corporations is having to deal with competitors who achieve differentiation with low cost. For example, Japanese auto manufacturers have successfully demonstrated that there is no necessary trade-off between quality and cost. The example of IKEA also suggests that combining low cost and differentiation strategies is possible when a firm introduces a significant technical or business innovation. However, such cost advantage and differentiation will be sustainable only if there are significant barriers to imitation by competitors.

15. Business segment data come from Thomson Financial's Worldscope database.

16. The following works are seminal to transaction cost economics: Ronald Coase, "The Nature of the Firm," *Economica* 4 (1937): 386–405; *Markets and Hierarchies: Analysis and Antitrust Implications* by Oliver Williamson (New York: The Free Press, 1975); David Teece, "Toward an Economic Theory of the Multi-product Firm," *Journal of Economic Behavior and Organization* 3 (1982): 39–63.

17. For a more complete discussion of these issues, see Krishna Palepu and Tarun Khanna, "Building Institutional Infrastructure in Emerging Markets," *Brown Journal of World Affairs*, Winter/Spring 1998, and Tarun Khanna and Krishna Palepu, "Why Focused Strategies May Be Wrong for Emerging Markets," *Harvard Business Review*, July/August 1997.

18. For an empirical study that illustrates this point, see Tarun Khanna and Krishna Palepu, "Is Group Affiliation Profitable in Emerging Markets? An Analysis of Diversified Indian Business Groups," *Journal of Finance* (April 2000): 867–891.

19. See Larry Lang and Rene Stulz, "Tobin's q, diversification, and firm performance," *Journal of Political Economy* 102 (1994): 1248–1280, and Phillip Berger and Eli Ofek, "Diversification's Effect on Firm Value," *Journal of Financial Economics* 37 (1994): 39–65.

20. See Paul Healy, Krishna Palepu, and Richard Ruback, "Which Takeovers Are Profitable: Strategic or Financial?" *Sloan Management Review* 38 (Summer 1997): 45–57.

21. See Katherine Schipper and Abbie Smith, "Effects of Recontracting on Shareholder Wealth: The Case of Voluntary Spinoffs," *Journal of Financial Economics* 12 (December 1983): 437–467; L. Lang, A. Poulsen and R. Stulz, "Asset Sales, Firm Performance, and the Agency Costs of Managerial Discretion," *Journal of Financial Economics* 37 (January 1995): 3–37.

22. "Stelios on Painting the World Orange," *Brand Strategy* (February 2005): 18–19.

23. Ibid.

Haier: Taking a Chinese company global

Only by entering the international market can we know what our competition is doing, can we raise our competitive edge. Otherwise, we'll lose the China market to foreigners.

—Zhang Ruimin, 1996[1]

All success relies on one thing in overseas markets—creating a localized brand name. We have to make Americans feel that Haier is a localized U.S. brand instead of an imported Chinese brand.

—Zhang Ruimin, 2003[2]

On December 26, 2004, Haier Group, ranked China's number-one company by the *Asian Wall Street Journal*,[3] celebrated its 20th anniversary with annual sales topping RMB 100 billion.[a] (See **Exhibit 1** for Haier revenue growth.) Starting with a defunct refrigerator factory in Qingdao, Shandong province, founder and CEO Zhang Ruimin built Haier into China's largest home appliance maker.[b] Globally, Haier ranked third in white goods revenues, and was the second-largest refrigerator manufacturer (with about 6% of the global market) behind Whirlpool and ahead of Electrolux, Kenmore, and GE.[4] Zhang pledged to make Haier the world's best-selling refrigerator brand by 2006. (See **Exhibit 2** for global appliance market shares.)

Haier held about a 30% share of China's RMB 129 billion white goods market,[5] and had a growing presence in "black goods" sectors such as televisions and personal computers, but margins on domestic sales were shrinking. The Haier Group's Shanghai-listed arm, Qingdao Haier, saw 2004 profit margins drop to 2.6%, from a high of 9.4% just five

Professors Krishna Palepu and Tarun Khanna and Senior Researcher Ingrid Vargas, Global Research Group, prepared this case. HBS cases are developed solely as the basis for class discussion. Cases are not intended to serve as endorsements, sources of primary data, or illustrations of effective or ineffective management.

[a]At the time, 8.26 RMB = 1 US$.

[b]Haier, derived from the Chinese word for "sea," was pronounced "high–R," and Qingdao, "ching-dow." In Chinese, given names followed the family name. The family name Zhang was pronounced "Jong."

[1]Zhang Ruimin quoted in Pamela Yatsko, "To Serve and Profit: A Chinese Fridge-Maker Wows Customers with Service," *Far Eastern Economic Review,* October 17, 1996, available from Factiva, http://www.factiva.com, accessed November 1, 2004.

[2]Zhang Ruimin quoted in Yibing Wu, "China's Refrigerator Magnate," *The McKinsey Quarterly* No. 3, 2003, available at http://www.mckinseyquarterly.com, accessed February 23, 2005.

[3]"The Asian Wall Street Journal 200 (A Special Report): How Asia's National Champion's Stack U ___ he *Asian Wall Street Journal*, February 21, 2005, available from Factiva, http://www.factiva.com, accessed March 10, 2005.

[4]"Business in China—The Next Stage," *Asia Pulse*, March 17, 2005 and "Haier Ranks Second in Global Refrigerator Markets," *China Daily*, January 12, 2002, available from Factiva, http://www.factiva.com, accessed November 1, 2004.

[5]Access Asia Limited, "Refrigerators and Freezers in China: A Market Analysis," April 2005, available from ISI Emerging Markets, http://www.securities.com, accessed May 25, 2005.

years earlier. (See **Exhibit 3** for Qingdao Haier financials and **Exhibit 4** for revenues by product.) Industry observers attributed the decline to increased competition from local firms and foreign multinationals in China. National overcapacity was estimated at 30% in televisions, washing machines, refrigerators, and other major appliances. Manufacturers were cutting prices at 10% to 15% annually.[6] In this environment, Haier was betting its future on global sales. Haier's 2004 export revenues were nearly double the previous year's, and the company was targeting $1 billion in sales to the United States alone for 2005. Could Haier become China's first true multinational brand? In the process, would Haier be able to defend its dominant position in China against growing competition from Western and Asian multinationals?

Haier's first 20 years

Company origins[7]

Haier originated in 1984 when Zhang took over a failing refrigerator factory in the Chinese port city of Qingdao. At the time, Zhang was vice general manager of the household appliance division of Qingdao's municipal government, and became convinced of the latent demand for refrigerators by the sight of customers standing in line to pay cash for second-rate refrigerators as they came off the production line at Qingdao General Refrigerator Factory. The local government wanted to appoint Zhang director of the nearly bankrupt company which had to borrow from neighboring villages to pay salaries to its 800 employees, and Zhang reluctantly accepted the challenge.

The factory was a collective enterprise whose ultimate authority was the municipal government, although the workers collectively held ownership of its assets and shared any profits after the payment of local and national taxes and appropriate reinvestment in the company. Unlike the government's authority over state-owned enterprises, it did not own or have any claim—other than taxes—on a collective enterprise's assets or profits. The government could influence senior staffing and major business decisions, however. Poor performance, labor disputes, or mismanagement of funds were all grounds for the dismissal of senior managers by the local authorities.

In 1984 there were about 300 refrigerator manufacturers in China, most producing poor-quality products. Zhang believed that Chinese consumers would be willing to pay more for higher-quality products and reliable service. Inspired by the workmanship of German products that he saw during a 1984 trip to Germany, Zhang remarked "Our people aren't more stupid than Germans. Why can't we do the same as them?" and promptly entered into a technology licensing agreement with German refrigerator manufacturer Liebherr.[8] Haier later imported freezer and air conditioner production lines from Derby of Denmark and Sanyo of Japan. Joint ventures (JVs) with companies such as Japan's Mitsubishi and Italy's Merloni infused Haier with more foreign technology and designs. "First we observe and digest," Zhang explained. "Then we imitate. In the end, we understand it well enough to design it independently."[9]

One of Zhang's biggest hurdles was getting workers to understand that Haier's commitment to quality was unlike that seen at other Chinese companies. To get his message across, Zhang once pulled 76 refrigerators off the line, some for minor flaws such as scratches, and ordered staff to smash them to bits. "That got their attention," laughed

[6]Dexter Roberts et al., "China's Power Brands: Bold Entrepreneurs are Producing the Mainland's Hot Consumer Products," *BusinessWeek*, November 8, 2004, available from Factiva, http://www.factiva.com, accessed March 10, 2005.

[7]This section is largely based on Lynn Sharp Paine, "The Haier Group (A)," HBS Case No. 398-101, rev. July 27, 2001, Harvard Business School Publishing, 2001.

[8]Pamela Yatsko, "To Serve and Profit."

[9]Zhang Ruimin quoted in Lynn Sharp Paine, "The Haier Group (A)," p. 7.

Zhang. "They finally understood that I wasn't going to sell just anything, like my competitors would. It had to be the best."[10] Haier promoted personal accountability by having poorly performing workers stand on a pair of yellow painted feet on the factory floor at the end of the workday to explain their failings to assembled colleagues.

Haier made a profit of RMB 1 million in its second year, when its refrigerators sold in three major Chinese cities. Despite overwhelming market demand and soaring prices for refrigerators, Haier resisted mass production, focusing on quality and brand-building instead. In 1988, Haier won a gold medal for quality in a national refrigerator competition. In 1989 China's refrigerator market faced oversupply, but rather than cut prices as its competitors had, Haier raised them. Zhang discovered that the Haier brand commanded a 15% premium, even during a price war.[11]

By the early 1990s, oversupply was no longer an issue. "At that time, demand outstripped supply, and we didn't have a big-scale operation. So we were focused on the China market. We didn't think about building our brand in the international market yet," explained Yang Mianmian, Zhang's right hand since 1984 and later named group president. "Our target is to become a first-class brand. We need to have a fairly large scale in order to achieve this," added a Haier marketing executive. "If this brand is not of large scale, it will not be successful."

Growth and diversification

By 1991, Haier had become China's leading refrigerator manufacturer. "Now we could let our reputation precede our new products," said Zhang. "It was time to diversify."[12] Haier found two candidates: the Qingdao Air Conditioner Factory, and the Qingdao General Freezer Factory, both stumbling due to poor management. Haier took on the debt of each firm and retained most of their employees. Introducing a new air conditioner type at the former and Haier worker discipline at the latter, within one year the new divisions had transformed a deficit of RMB 15 million into profits.

The newly expanded refrigerator, freezer, and air conditioner manufacturer was renamed Haier Group in 1992. The same year Haier acquired 500 acres of Qingdao land for a new industrial park to house corporate headquarters and the bulk of the firm's factories and subsidiaries. The land cost RMB 80 million and construction costs were estimated to exceed RMB 1 billion, while Haier's 1992 profits were just RMB 51 million.

To finance such a large capital investment, Haier was counting on promised bank loans of RMB 1.6 billion, but within a month of the land purchase, the Chinese central government tightened credit nationally in an effort to halt real estate speculation.[13] Finding no other option, Haier turned to China's nascent stock market, listing 43.7% of its refrigerator division on the Shanghai Stock Exchange in November 1993. The IPO of A shares (limited to investors from mainland China) raised RMB 369 million. "It was the first time Haier had done such a risky thing," recalled Zhang. "If we had not been successful with our IPO, Haier would have disappeared. We'd never done anything like this, and that should be the only time we do it."[14]

Acquisitions continued throughout the 1990s, sometimes under government pressure to take over poorly performing firms.[15] In 1995, the Qingdao Municipal Government pushed

[10]Ibid., p. 6.

[11]Jeannie J. Yi and Shawn X. Ye, *The Haier Way: The Making of a Chinese Business Leader and a Global Brand* (Dumont, New Jersey: Homa & Sekey Books, 2003), pp. 30 and 65.

[12]Zhang Ruimin quoted in Lynn Sharp Paine, "The Haier Group (A)," p. 7.

[13]Jeannie J. Yi and Shawn X. Ye, *The Haier Way,* p. 65.

[14]Jeannie J. Yi and Shawn X. Ye, *The Haier Way,* pp. 65–66. Zhang eventually secured 240 RMB in bank loans, which together with the IPO revenue and Haier's own funds, paid for the industrial park by 1996.

[15]"Haier Group Buys Up Ailing State Firms," *South China Morning Post,* September 14, 1997, available from Factiva, http://www.factiva.com, accessed November 1, 2004.

Haier: Taking a Chinese company global

the nearly bankrupt Red Star washing machine company onto Haier with the obligation to take on the firm's employees and RMB 132 million in debt, the equivalent of Haier's 1993 profits.[16] Within 18 months, however, Haier had turned Red Star into the top-ranked washing machine manufacturer in China.[17] Haier added televisions and telecommunications equipment to its product mix with the 1997 acquisition of Yellow Mountain Electronics located in Anhui province. By 1997, Haier had taken over 15 companies in accordance with Haier's acquisition strategy. "We buy only those firms that have markets and good products but bad management," Zhang said. "Then we introduce our own management and quality control to turn them around."[18]

Operational restructuring

By 1998, Haier's annual revenues had reached RMB 16.8 billion and the firm's domestic market shares for refrigerators, washing machines, and air conditioners each exceeded 30%. Haier had much to celebrate, but the long period of extraordinary growth of consumer demand in China was showing signs of slowing. Retail consumption for 1997 had grown 11.6% over the previous year, the lowest increase since 1990. Industry optimists pointed to growing income levels among rural Chinese who accounted for 72% of population, but only about 10% of rural households owned a refrigerator and 20% had a washing machine in 1998.[19] (See **Exhibit 5**.)

Haier had exported appliances on an "original equipment manufacturer" (OEM) basis since the early 1990s, and by the mid-1990s had established several overseas JVs in Asia. (See *Haier in International Markets* on p. 75.) Haier was anxious to focus on overseas markets, but after a decade of adding factories, the company first reorganized to achieve greater efficiency and position itself to compete effectively with multinationals both at home and abroad. Haier's many manufacturing facilities were restructured into seven product divisions: Refrigerator, Air Conditioner, Washing Machine, IT Products, Kitchen & Bath, Technology Equipment, and Direct Affiliates (including communications, housing, and biological engineering).

Before 1998, most of the acquired businesses operated independent R&D, procurement, production, and sales departments. Haier replaced the numerous service departments with four new Group-wide "Development Divisions"—Capital Flow (Finance), Commerce Flow (Sales), Material Flow (Logistics), and Overseas (Global Operations)—whose heads reported directly to the Haier Group president. These new businesses operated as independent profit centers that competed with third-party service providers for Haier's business and could sell services to external clients as well.[20] Human Resources, R&D, and Customer Relations were also joined into group-wide business centers and sold their services on a fee basis to Haier Divisions. Similarly, Total Planning Management, Total Quality Management, and Total Equipment Management centers were formed by combining these functions across divisions. In 2000, Haier added an e-commerce company serving businesses and individual customers.

---

[16]"China and the Chaebol," *The Economist*, December 20, 1997, available from ProQuest, ABI/Inform, http://www.proquest.com, accessed April 10, 2005; and Jeannie J. Yi and Shawn X. Ye, *The Haier Way*, pp. 66–67.

[17]Lynn Sharp Paine, "The Haier Group (C)," HBS Case No. 398-162, rev. July 27, 2001, Harvard Business School Publishing, 2001, p. 2.

[18]"Haier Group Buys Up Ailing State Firms," *South China Morning Post*, September 14, 1997, available from Factiva, http://www.factiva.com, accessed November 1, 2004.

[19]"End of Golden Age Brings Painful Change," *South China Morning Post*, March 12, 1998, available from Factiva, http://www.factiva.com, accessed November 1, 2004.

[20]This section is based largely on Jeannie J. Yi and Shawn X. Ye, *The Haier Way*, pp. 149–162.

Haier in Chinese markets

By 2004, Haier had overtaken domestic rivals and defended its ground against encroaching multinationals to become the number-one appliance company in China. While several firms held a top-three position in a particular market such as washing machines or air conditioners, Haier was the only company with leading shares across white goods sectors (**Exhibit 6**). Haier was dominant in the RMB 48 billion refrigerator and freezer market, which accounted for about 38% of all white goods sales in China. In 2002, Haier's share of the country's refrigerator market was 27% by volume and 52% by revenue, and analysts estimated that the company accounted for 61% of industry profits.[21]

National competitors

From over 100 refrigerator producers in 1989, by 1996 China had just 20 major producers remaining, with the 10 largest accounting for 80% of the market, up from 50% four years earlier. According to a Chinese industry association, refrigerator manufacturers needed to produce more than one million units annually to be profitable.[22] Only three Chinese manufacturers, together accounting for about 60% of the market, fell into this category in 1996, Haier among them.

In the 1980s, Haier's commitment to quality had been enough to distinguish it from competitors, but as the weakest Chinese firms failed or were acquired, Haier faced more formidable Chinese competitors, many specializing in just one or two product lines. Chronic price wars, especially in the refrigerator sector, hurt all of the leading players, with some selling stock at or below cost to clear inventories. According to an industry analyst, "the leading domestic players failed to reach their growth potential due to the numerous money-losing small competitors, which were being sustained in part by regional governments' budgets."[23] But Haier cited its more diversified holdings, its differentiated products, and its export strategy as protective factors that ensured continued profits.

Among Haier's domestic rivals, only Guangdon Kelon, which had once held the top position in China's white goods market, offered a full line of home appliances. Like Haier, Kelon started out as a refrigerator manufacturer in the early 1980s. In 1998, Kelon merged with a leading Chinese air conditioner manufacturer. The company listed on the Hong Kong and Shenzhen stock exchanges in the late 1990s, and Whirlpool chose Kelon to manufacture washing machines in China. In contrast to Haier's single-brand approach, Kelon followed a multibrand strategy in China. High-end appliances carried the Kelon name; the Ronshen brand was used for mid-level models; and low-cost refrigerators and air conditioners sold under the Combine brand. Because Kelon sold refrigerators and air conditioners under all three brands, each with its own assembly lines and marketing campaigns, the company cited the attainment of scale efficiency as its biggest challenge.[24]

Blaming intense competition in China's refrigerator market, Kelon reported significant losses in 2000 and 2001. An accounting scandal revealed that the listed firm and its parent group had routinely shared credit facilities and paid each other's operating expenses.[25] Another Chinese refrigeration firm, Greencool Enterprises, acquired a majority shareholding

[21]Access Asia Limited, "Refrigerators and Freezers in China: A Market Analysis."

[22]Scott Stevens, "Don't Blink: Household Electrical Appliances '96 Exhibition in Beijing, China," *Appliance* 39 Vol. 53, No. 10, October 1, 1996; and Li Yan, "Fridge Firms Face Tough Competition from Abroad," *Business Weekly*, February 16, 1997, both available from Factiva, http://www.factiva.com, accessed November 1, 2004.

[23]Winston Yau, "Haier's Earnings Defy Domestic Price War," *South China Morning Post*, March 30, 2002, available from Factiva, http://www.factiva.com, accessed November 1, 2004.

[24]"Online Extra: Kelon: 'We are a Multibrand Company,'" *BusinessWeek Online*, November 8, 2004, http://www.businessweekasia.com, accessed May 17, 2005.

[25]Ben Paul, "Stalking the Dragon," *The Edge* (Singapore), September 16, 2002, available from Factiva, http://www.factiva.com, accessed November 1, 2004.

in Kelon in late 2001. Kelon's new management introduced a strategy of targeting China's rural population, selling nearly a million units of a new lower-priced brand in the first year.[26] Haier already had a strong presence in the rural markets, but had not specifically targeted this segment with specially priced products. "The future lies in the second-line and third-line markets, which is the rural population in counties and townships," said Kelon's chief executive.[27] In 2003, about 23% of rural Chinese households owned a refrigerator.[28] Kelon posted a modest profit in 2003, but reported a loss of RMB 44.7 million in 2004, citing weak sales.[29]

Foreign entrants

China's entry into the World Trade Organization in December 2001 added pressure on Haier. "Before, our competitors were domestic brands," said Gao. "But now after China's ascension into the WTO, our competitors are Siemens, Electrolux, Samsung, LG, Matsushita, Sony, GE, and Whirlpool." Some foreign consumer appliance brands were in China even earlier. Whirlpool formed a JV with a Chinese manufacturer to produce refrigerators in a plant near Beijing as early as 1994.[30] By 1996, Zhang noted that a second generation of competition had hit the Chinese white goods market. He observed: "The Chinese market has become part of the international appliance marketplace."[31]

Most multinationals realized that penetrating the Chinese market would not be easy. "Normally, people think it's a market of 1.2 billion people and that it's going to explode," said a Siemens executive. "But in terms of saturation levels, urban areas in China are quite well equipped. The big gap is in the rural areas and smaller towns, where saturation levels are below 10%."[32] Many multinationals were banking on the emergence of a replacement market in the large cities where they targeted the high-end market. "Setting up a sales and marketing network is a big challenge," added the Siemens executive. "It is tied closely to local conditions. . . . The key point is to build an effective sales and marketing organization that can also follow changes in distribution."[33]

The media noted that multinationals tended to underestimate the Chinese manufacturers, expecting competition to come from other newly arrived foreign firms. Instead, they found themselves competing with Haier and Kelon. "Their technology was nearly as good as Whirlpool's, their prices were lower, and their styling and distribution were better suited to China," wrote *The Economist*.[34] Thinking that the China market was not ready for the latest technology, Whirlpool produced Freon refrigerators with its JV partner in 1995. Meanwhile, Chinese manufacturers began to respond to consumer demand for Freon-free units. In 1996, the Whirlpool JV sold less than 60% of its newly manufactured Freon refrigerators, resulting in a loss of nearly $11 million. Realizing its mistake,

[26]"China's Kelon Cuts Refrigerator Prices," *Xinhua Financial Network*, March 2, 2004, available from Factiva, http://www.factiva.com, accessed November 1, 2004.

[27]Liu Congmeng quoted in Lee Chyen Yee, "China's Guangdon Kelon Turns Inward for Growth," *Reuters News*, March 4, 2003, available from Factiva, http://www.factiva.com, accessed November 1, 2004.

[28]"Konka to Concentrate on Refrigerator," *SinoCast China IT Watch*, 26 November 2003, available from Factiva, http://www.factiva.com, accessed November 1, 2004.

[29]"HK Guangdong Kelon Electrical Hldgs FY Loss CNY44.7M," *Dow Jones Chinese Financial Wire*, April 28, 2005, available from Factiva, http://www.factiva.com, accessed May 6, 2005.

[30]"Whirlpool to Make Refrigerators in China," *Reuters News*, December 5, 1994, available from Factiva, http://www.factiva.com, accessed November 1, 2004.

[31]Zhang Ruimin quoted in Scott Stevens, "Don't Blink."

[32]Scott Stevens, "Don't Blink."

[33]Ibid.

[34]"Infatuation's End," *The Economist*, September 25, 1999, available from Factiva, http://www.factiva.com, accessed March 15, 2005.

Whirlpool invested in a Freon-free production line in China, but by the time it was ready 18 months later, the market was nearly saturated.[35] Whirlpool invested in refrigerator, air conditioner, washing machine, and microwave factories in the mid-1990s, and accumulated losses of over $100 million in China by 1997. The U.S. company sold most of its holdings, saving the microwave factory by focusing it on exports, and devoting its washing machine factory to production for Kelon, which marketed the washers in China under its own brand.[36] But in 2001, Whirlpool began a comeback, launching 30 new products and setting up two global research and development centers and a large production facility in China.[37]

Foreign brands were taking market share away from Chinese brands at alarming rates. Multinational-brand refrigerator unit sales represented 31% of the Chinese market in 2002, up from 26% the previous year. Foreign brands were especially strong in the automatic washing machine sector where they accounted for 38% of sales in 2002, up from 31% in 2001. Nevertheless, Yang believed that Haier would preserve its local knowledge advantage over foreign firms:

> *Haier is much closer to China's consumers, so we have a grasp on their changing tastes. We design according to Chinese consumers. And we have paid a lot of attention to developing human resources in the areas of marketing and design. Foreign companies design products for China based on foreign approaches. They are not in tune with Chinese culture and values.*

Retail channels

Before 2000, Haier's customers were mostly state-owned department stores, but by 2004 appliance sales had moved out of the department stores and into individual specialized shops and private retail chains. In 2004, domestic chains such as GOME accounted for about 30% of Haier's sales. GOME was China's largest home appliance seller with over 100 outlets in 22 of China's largest cities. International chains like Wal-Mart, in China only a few years, accounted for no more than 5% of Haier's domestic revenue. In second- and third-tier cities, Haier had set up networks of licensed dealers that accounted for another 30% of sales. Independent retail shops and government purchases accounted for about 15% each, with online and telephone sales making up the rest.

The shift in retail channels since 2000 affected how Haier managed its customer relations. As Gao explained:

> *A few years ago Chinese white goods customers were not very picky and it was easy for large shops to make sales. At that time all we had to do to get their orders and keep our great market share was to maintain a good relationship with these large shops and give them the goods on time. Now our distributors are the major domestic chains as well as international retailers like Wal-Mart and Carrefour. These private retailers put more emphasis on the bottom line. The old concept of sales as managing the distributor relationship through "wine and dine" is not applicable in the current market. Retailers are no longer focused on how much you can drink together, but on how much money you can make for them.*

The introduction of Western retail models to China's major cities coincided with the arrival of foreign multinational appliance brands like Siemens and GE which were very

[35] "China—Whirlpool Misunderstood China Market Experts Say," ChinaOnline, March 19, 2002, available from LexisNexis Academic, http://web.lexis-nexis.com, accessed June 8, 2005.

[36] "Infatuation's End."

[37] "Whirlpool Steps up China Comeback," *Dow Jones International News*, October 28, 2001; and "Whirlpool Relaunching Stratagem in China," *AsiaPort Daily News*, March 29, 2002; both available from Factiva, http://www.factiva.com, accessed March 15, 2005.

Haier: Taking a Chinese company global

familiar with these channels. The WTO-mandated opening of the rest of China to foreign retailers by the end of 2004 threatened to erase domestic firm advantages beyond the first-tier cities. However, Gao did not believe that knowledge and experience of dealing with large multinational retail chains would give foreign white goods firms enough of an edge to displace Haier. "The multinational brands together account for less than 10% of China's white goods market, so they don't have much clout with retail chains, whether domestic or international," he said. Foreign brands would fare even worse in second- and third-tier cities and in rural areas, according to Gao. He explained:

> Many foreign brands, including American ones like GE and Whirlpool, have a hard time adapting to the Chinese population and vastness. Their tried and tested sales approaches work on a more uniform population. But the diversity in geography and buying preferences in China are huge. In the rural areas, it's mostly small private enterprises that sell appliances. In one county, there may be only two or three such shops that monopolize the whole area. There are no domestic or international hyper-markets in China's rural regions.

Haier's market advantages

Haier executives cited the reputation of the brand and the company's creativity as the firm's main strengths for competing inside China. "Consumers recognize Haier as the number-one brand in China," said Gao. "Our prices are 20% more than our competitors', but we still have the most sales." The brand was supported by investing 5% to 7% of revenue into R&D each year. "This means we have new products each year. Our products are not made obsolete by our competitors, but by our own new products," Gao added. Haier executives would not claim any definitive operational superiority, but there were at least three areas in which Haier consistently won praise: innovative and rapid market response, superior after-sales service, and efficient distribution.

Market responsiveness

"We have been successful in China because we are focused on meeting customer needs," said Zhang. "We are organized to understand what customers want and to meet those needs, which are sometimes quite differentiated."[38] Haier's 42 distribution centers throughout China operated as independent "sales companies" that needed to be responsive to the needs of customers to remain profitable.

When a customer in China's rural Sichuan province complained to Haier that his washing machine was breaking down, service technicians found the plumbing clogged with mud. Rural Chinese were using the Haier machines, meant to wash clothing, to clean sweet potatoes and other vegetables. Haier engineers modified the washer design to accommodate peasant needs. Since then, Haier washing machines sold in Sichuan were labeled, "Mainly for washing clothes, sweet potatoes and peanuts."[39]

To accommodate summer lifestyles requiring frequent changes of clothing, Haier created a tiny washing machine that cleaned a single change of clothes. The model saved on electricity and water usage, making it an instant hit in Shanghai. It was later successfully introduced to Europe. Other innovations included a washer that cleaned clothes without detergent, and a model that could wash and dry clothes in a single machine, also popular in cities where space and time were at a premium.

Haier's strategy of meeting localized market demand at home and abroad with innovative models (for example, a refrigerator with a compartment for pickling Korean kimchee

[38]Zhang Ruimin, quoted in Yibing Wu, "China's Refrigerator Magnate."
[39]Andrew Browne, "Haier Group Never Says 'No'," *Reuters News*, December 9, 1997, available from Factiva, http://www.factiva.com, accessed March 15, 2005.

cabbage) had resulted in about 96 product categories and 15,100 specifications. Haier executives maintained that these kinds of feature innovations were inexpensive to produce, but highly valued by customers. "To manage the costs of manufacturing our many different product models, our products are based on modules of components and subsystems, and on basic platforms that we can vary," said Zhang. "Periodically, we will add some new features, but the basic model is there. We don't change them randomly."[40]

Service

In 1990, Haier had set up a service center in Qingdao that used a computerized system to track tens of thousands of customers. The effort soon paid off, as customers throughout China, accustomed to expecting little or no after-sales service, began to recognize Haier as a new breed of company. Stories like that of taxi driver Chu Xiaoming and his 10-year-old Haier refrigerator were repeated throughout China. In 1996, Chu half-heartedly called Haier's customer hotline, not expecting to get much help for a broken-down appliance purchased a decade earlier. One industry observer noted:

> *To Chu's surprise, a uniformed serviceman showed up on his doorstep the very next day. He took the fridge back to the factory and lent Chu another for the interim. Two weeks later, Chu's old refrigerator was once again chilling his family's meats and vegetables. And best of all, the service didn't cost an arm and a leg. "They only charged me 200–300 renminbi ($24–$36) for the repairs," he said. "I'm very satisfied."[41]*

By 2004, Haier had a service network of 5,500 independent contractors, one for each sales outlet. Some of these service contractors were exclusive to Haier; others serviced both Haier and competing products. Haier product owners could call a nationwide hotline to arrange for a house call by a service agent. If the appliance needed to be removed from the home for servicing, Haier provided a temporary replacement free of charge. Haier's warranty periods covering full repair costs either met or exceeded Chinese government regulations. According to Gao, customer appreciation of Haier service was one of the company's greatest competitive advantages. "In the country's ranking of service levels and after-sales service, Haier always ranks number one," he said. "Whether in quality of service or in volume, no one is able to compare to Haier at the moment."

Distribution

Haier Logistics, an independently operated company created in 1999 as part of Haier's reorganization, had become a national pioneer in the field, offering "just in time" (JIT) purchasing, raw materials delivery, and product distribution. Between 1998 and 2004, Haier had reduced the size of its main raw materials warehouse from 200,000 square meters with an inventory cycle of over 30 days, to a 20,000-square-meter distribution center with a seven-day inventory cycle. In 2004 Haier's JIT order-execution center purchased about 300,000 different components for the group's production lines from about 1000 suppliers in China and overseas, down from 2,300 suppliers before the reorganization. Logistics delivered raw materials to the production sites every two hours, on average, with inventory updates and inter-company payments made automatically using bar code scanning. Factory production usually began as soon as an order was received and took one or two days, depending on the product.

Haier required full payment in cash before completing delivery on purchase orders. Once payment had been received, Logistics delivered the goods to one of 42 Haier distribution centers located throughout China. Substantial government investments in transportation infrastructure since the late 1980s allowed Haier to take advantage of China's

[40]Zhang Ruimin, quoted in Yibing Wu, "China's Refrigerator Magnate."
[41]Pamela Yatsko, "To Serve and Profit."

Haier: Taking a Chinese company global

growing highway network. Working with over 300 transport companies which used about 16,000 vehicles across every region of China except Tibet, the network moved over 100,000 products each day, not counting small items like cellular telephones and vacuum cleaners. Haier delivered very large orders directly to retailer warehouses. Each distribution center dealt with an average of 200 customers, some with multiple retail outlets. The entire process, from initial order to final delivery of the products, took about 10 days, down from 36 days before the reorganization and introduction of information systems.

The main differentiator between Haier Logistics and domestic competitors was that Haier had reorganized logistics into a single company serving the entire group. Other Chinese companies like Midea and TCL had separate logistics operations for each product line. "Haier has very broad product lines, and Logistics makes deliveries for the entire group and for other brands besides Haier group," said logistics information center executive Zhan Li. "When transporting a refrigerator, we can also deliver a microwave, a water heater, and other products. Other companies don't really do this. This kind of scale and volume probably gives us one of the lowest logistics costs." Zhan also saw Haier's advantage over multinational companies:

> In China, there are still regulations limiting multinationals in the area of Logistics, so they have entered China on a JV basis. Multinationals have more experience than us, having gained knowledge of different approaches and practices through their worldwide operations. But in terms of logistics cost or network, they have no competitive advantage. Their staff costs must be higher than ours and they don't have a network in China. So I don't think they are very competitive in the China domestic market.

Establishing a logistics network in China was a complicated matter, requiring coverage of a vast territory, navigating widely divergent terrains, and negotiating with numerous local governments. Regulations affecting transportation could vary from location to location—for example, weight limits for trucks, making logistics a more onerous production than in developed countries. Obstacles to creating a highly integrated warehousing system like Haier's were also numerous. In large cities like Shanghai, it was difficult to find warehouse space large enough to accommodate the huge trucks required for white goods. In the most remote areas it was a challenge to connect warehouses to a company's information network. "Setting up a warehouse and delivering goods to surrounding areas in Inner Mongolia or Xinjiang Autonomous Region is difficult and expensive," said Zhan. "It's not something you can build overnight. It involves a lot of infrastructure."

Foreign multinationals could contract with one of the many independent Chinese logistics companies to handle distribution, but costs would likely be higher and coverage areas were usually limited to particular regions. "Foreign companies tend to cluster in the more developed costal areas and there are many independent logistics companies based there. These companies don't have extensive penetration of internal regions of the country, but the volume of business is not that great in those regions," explained Zhan. Multinationals that wanted China-wide coverage would have to patch together a national network using several different logistics companies. Still, many foreign companies, such as Samsung, successfully outsourced logistics to Chinese service providers. Foreign multinationals that tried to run their own distribution networks generally failed. The *China Economic Times* attributed Whirlpool's losses in the washing machine market to the multinational company's neglect of its Chinese JV partner's existing distribution network. Whirlpool tried to establish its own sales team and distribution channels, leading to high operating costs for its Chinese JV.[42]

---

[42]"China—Whirlpool Misunderstood China Market Experts Say," ChinaOnline, March 19, 2002, available from LexisNexis Academic, http://web.lexis-nexis.com, accessed June 8, 2005.

Some Haier executives were cautious about relying on their strengths in the distribution and service networks, or even on superior knowledge of the domestic market. Gao believed that foreign companies entering China could access similar resources through third parties and become more competitive if they adapted to local market needs. He elaborated:

> *They can spend money buying people who understand the China market, and they can buy the sales channels and service as well. Electrolux came into China with nothing, and they took people from Haier and quickly established a brand in China. So I don't think these are the core strengths for Haier. I think these tangible strengths are temporary. If we just sit on these strengths, sooner or later GE will catch up. I think GE and Whirlpool are great companies with a long history of over 100 years. They haven't done very well in China because they have not been very localized. If they get localized, I am sure they would do very well.*

Haier in international markets

Haier developed a formal global expansion strategy beginning in 1997 when Zhang announced his "three thirds" goal of having Haier's revenue derive in equal parts from sales of goods in three categories: one-third from goods produced and sold in China, one-third produced in China and sold overseas, and one-third produced and sold overseas. Overseas sales for 1998, largely to Europe and the United States, amounted to just over $62 million, or about 3% of total Group sales.[43] The creation of Haier's Overseas Promotion Division in 1999 signaled the beginning of rapid growth in international sales through exports and overseas production, bringing the combined figure to nearly 17% of total revenue in 2004. (See **Exhibit 1b**.)

Haier had started to venture into overseas markets as a contract manufacturer for multinational brands in the early 1990s, first exporting to the United Kingdom and Germany, and then to France and Italy. Haier also used JVs to explore foreign markets. In 1994, Mitsubishi invested $30 million for a 55% stake in a JV with Haier to set up China's largest air conditioner plant. The Qingdao factory would produce five of Mitsubishi's latest models for export to Japan.[44] In 1995, Haier became one of the first Chinese companies to engage in foreign direct investment, setting up a refrigerator and air conditioner plant in Indonesia as the majority partner in a JV with a local firm.[45] In 1997 Haier launched its first European manufacturing base, producing air conditioners in Belgrade through a JV with a Yugoslav company.[46]

Haier refrigerators sold particularly well in Germany, where they were marketed by the German appliance firm Liebherr under the "Blue Line" brand. When a blind quality test by a German magazine gave Haier's Blue Line refrigerators eight top rankings, beating Liebherr's seven, Haier decided it was time to market its own brand overseas. In 1997, Germany became the first export market for Haier-branded refrigerators. The same year, Haier formed a JV with the Philippine electronics company LKG to manufacture Haier-branded freezers, air conditioners, and washing machines in the Philippines for sale to local and regional markets.[47]

---

[43]Gao Wei, "Haier Plans Overseas Expansion," *Business Weekly*, July 4, 1999, available from Factiva, http://www.factiva.com, accessed March 15, 2005.
[44]"Zhang's Qingdao Masterpiece," *Business Weekly*, June 19, 1994, available from Factiva, http://www.factiva.com, accessed November 1, 2004.
[45]James Hardin, "China's Future Dragons—Successful Companies are Emerging," *Financial Times*, August 14, 1997, p. 17, available from Factiva, http://www.factiva.com, accessed November 1, 2004.
[46]Jeannie J. Yi and Shawn X. Ye, *The Haier Way*, p. 199.
[47]Ibid., p. 191.

Haier continued OEM production for foreign multinationals and actively sought new OEM clients, but after 1999 the company was focused on selling Haier-branded products in overseas markets. "The objective of most Chinese enterprises is to export products and earn foreign currency. This is their only purpose," said Zhang. "Our purpose in exporting is to establish a brand reputation overseas."[48]

Typically, Chinese manufacturers exported products under an OEM client brand. For example, Kelon, Haier's largest domestic rival, had overseas sales amounting to 12.5% of total revenue in 2003,[49] but did not market its own brand overseas. At one time, Kelon-made refrigerators carrying the Magic Chef brand sold alongside Haier-branded refrigerators at U.S. Wal-Mart stores.[50] Because of the low-quality image associated with Chinese-manufactured products, said Kelon's chairman, the company preferred to manufacture products for multinational OEMs.[51]

Haier, on the other hand, was willing to bear the early costs of establishing the firm as an independent player overseas. "I predict that overseas profit growth will be a little slower than the overall company's profit growth," said Zhang. "In some mature markets we will make profits, but in entering new markets we may also at first lose money."[52]

In pursuing expansion of its brand to international markets, Haier was emulating the strategies of successful Japanese and Korean firms such as Sony, Samsung, and LG. LG Electronics, with total 2004 revenues of $24 billion (about 25% from white goods sales), was perhaps the most likely model for Haier. LG produced the first Korean refrigerator in the 1950s, and expanded into other home appliances and electronics. In the 1990s, following a makeover of its budget Lucky-Goldstar brand into the higher-end LG brand, the company began its global expansion into strategic markets selected primarily on the basis of market size and expected growth, openness to foreign businesses, and intensity of competition.[53]

LG decided to focus international expansion on China and Southeast Asia. The company also established regional headquarters for Eastern Europe, Latin America, the Middle East, and Africa, which were considered secondary but high-potential markets. Seeing no competitive advantage in pursuing the developed markets of the United States, Japan, and Western Europe, LG initially maintained only a modest presence in those regions.[54] Aided by the fall of the Korean currency during the late-1990s Asian financial crisis, LG's overseas sales soared from 30% of appliance revenues before the crisis to 70% in 2001. By 2004, LG's overseas appliance sales reached about US $4 billion, and the company had made significant inroads in the U.S. market. However, while 82% of the firm's appliance sales were LG-branded, branded products accounted for just 55% of LG's U.S. sales.[55]

International strategies

Focus on difficult markets first

Shunning conventional wisdom, Haier determined to focus on the "difficult" developed markets first, and only after proving itself in those, to go after the relatively "easy"

[48]Zhang Ruimin, quoted in Yibing Wu, "China's Refrigerator Magnate."

[49]Guangdon Kelon's chairman, Gu Chujun, reported 2003 revenues of $4 billion and overseas sales of revenue of $500 in "Online Extra: Kelon: 'We are a Multibrand Company.'"

[50]"Chinese Brands Out of the Shadows," *The Economist*, August 28, 1999, available from Factiva, http://www.factiva.com, accessed November 1, 2004.

[51]"Online Extra: Kelon: 'We are a Multibrand Company.'"

[52]Zhang Ruimin, quoted in "Online Extra: Haier: 'Local Resources' are Key Overseas," *BusinessWeek Online*, November 8, 2004, http://www.businessweekasia.com, accessed May 17, 2005.

[53]J. Stewart Black, Allen J. Morrison and Young Chul Chang, "LG Group: Developing Tomorrow's Global Leaders," IVEY Case No. 9A98G009, January 22, 1999, Ivey Management Services, 1998, p. 12.

[54]Ibid.

[55]Moon Ihlwan, "White-Hot Goods: LG Electronics is Ringing Up Huge Overseas Sales," *BusinessWeek*, September 30, 2002, available from Factiva, http://www.factiva.com, accessed May 16, 2005.

emerging markets. In 2004, about 70% of Haier's overseas sales came from the developed markets of Europe, the United States, and Japan. Zhang explained the strategy:

> *Many Chinese enterprises will first export to Southeast Asia, for instance, which has competitive markets but where there are no strong, dominant competitors. . . . We go to easier markets after we first penetrate difficult markets such as the United States and Europe. These are much bigger markets. They are also the home markets of our largest global competitors, and we believe that if we can succeed there, we can succeed in easier markets.*[56]

Haier also saw going into developed markets as a way to challenge itself to meet the highest quality standards. "We chose the developed countries first because the requirements of both customers and retailers are very tough and not easy to meet," said Li Pan, Haier's brand manager for overseas markets. "For example, by entering the U.S. market, we learn the UL requirements and the difference between the U.S. customers and the Chinese customers. We learn a lot of things that we could not know if we just got into the Southeast Asian market or other developing markets."

The prestige of having a brand that sold in Europe or the United States was such that Haier could arrive in emerging markets with a ready-made reputation, thought Haier Overseas Division executives. "Customers in India or the Middle East already know our brand because when they travel they have seen our advertisements in Paris or Tokyo," said one executive. Haier also used its U.S. and European experience to convince emerging market retailers to carry Haier products. Haier found that even having a few successful products in the developed markets opened the door to introducing the full line of Haier products to developing markets, including high-end models, from the beginning.

"If we can effectively compete in the mature markets with such brand names as GE, Matsushita, and Philips, we can surely take the markets in the developing countries without much effort," reasoned Zhang. "It is just like what we did with the domestic market. After Haier refrigerators had taken Beijing and Shanghai, we met no difficulties getting into medium and small cities."[57]

Begin with niche products

Haier typically entered developed markets with just a few models to test the waters and steer clear of major competitors. "When we entered the U.S. market, we found that nobody was making competitive refrigerators for students or for offices. So we offered what the U.S. manufacturers did not make because for them the volume and prices were too low, and within three years we had over 30% market share in compact refrigerators," said Overseas Division executive Diao Yunfeng. With minimal competition, the niche products brought in high margins, added Diao. When others began to imitate, Haier added new features such as mini-fridges that doubled as computer desks, aimed at college students living in dorms.

Having a very successful product like compact refrigerators or wine cellars in the U.S. allowed Haier to get the attention of the major retail chains like Wal-Mart and Best Buy. Having developed a relationship with them, Haier was in a stronger position to get the major chains to consider Haier's major appliances. "After we were successful in the niche products, then we started to introduce regular products to the U.S. like the standard refrigerators, the apartment refrigerators, air conditioners, washing machines, and other products," said Diao.

---

[56]Zhang Ruimin, quoted in Yibing Wu, "China's Refrigerator Magnate."
[57]Zhang Ruimin, quoted in Jeannie J. Yi and Shawn X. Ye, *The Haier Way*, p. 188.

Staff with locals

When entering a new market, "the first stage is to use the right people to establish the structure," said Li. "If we use local people, we can expand very quickly because local people know the local market very well. If we use Haier, we don't have enough human resources, especially people with an international perspective, to expand worldwide." Haier would begin by identifying a local person with experience, preferably in a leading white goods firm, to head the country operation. That person would hire a local team and develop sales and distribution channels.

"Our strategy is not just export; we want to use local people and local thinking to satisfy the needs of the customer," said Yang. "Compared to other foreign brands, we have an advantage in that we have gathered experienced people who have worked for top brands to join us." This is not the same as what multinationals entering China have done, explained Yang. "When top foreign companies come to China, they also use local Chinese, but these Chinese have not worked with major brands before. So if they are using Chinese people with no brand experience to build their brand in China, then they are in trouble."

Li believed that in time Haier would have to place its own people in key positions overseas to get better market intelligence. "We want to get more involved in the details ourselves. We have to know the information at the end terminal. You have to have your own people who will report from the field," said Li. "People are our eyes, noses, and ears. If you don't have the people, you don't know what is happening in the market. The country CEO cannot report on everything."

Yang preferred to continue sending only temporary technical support teams from China while relying on local partners to operate the business. Yang believed that U.S. consumers saw Haier as an American brand, "because Haier is produced and sold by Americans," she said. "We hope to have Haier in each country be the Haier that *they* created. For example, in the United States, we hope that it is Americans who build up Haier America," said Yang. "If Americans can create GE and Whirlpool and Electrolux, they can create Haier."

International divisions

Haier organized overseas sales into five large regional markets: The Americas, Europe, the Middle East, Southeast Asia and East Asia. The Americas region, dominated by U.S. sales, accounted for about 30% of overseas revenue, Europe for another 30%, and the remaining regions combined made up the remaining 40%. Haier-branded products, about 80% in white goods, sold globally through 62 distributors and over 30,000 retail outlets. About 59,000 sales agents and 12,000 service personnel supported sales operations. Haier operated 18 design institutes, 13 overseas factories, and 11 industrial complexes (eight in China and one each in the U.S., Pakistan, and Jordan).[58]

Haier's formal International Divisions included JVs on five continents. Usually Haier was the majority shareholder. In some cases, such as in the Middle East, Haier held a minority share in JVs. Launched in Dubai, United Arab Emirates in 1999, Haier Middle East developed a network of dealerships and service centers throughout the region. In 2002, Haier began manufacturing locally through JVs with firms in Iran and Algeria that produced refrigerators, washing machines, and air conditioners.[59] Haier Industrial Park in Pakistan began production in 2002. The JV with the Pakistani R Group, the country's largest dealer of household appliances, took advantage of Pakistan's largest marketing and

---

[58]"Haier Group," *Euromonitor International*, January 2005, available from http://www.euromonitor.com, accessed March 28, 2005.
[59]Jeannie J. Yi and Shawn X. Ye, *The Haier Way*, p. 191.

sales network for white goods.[60] In 2001 Haier formed a JV with a Nigerian firm, Nigeria Haier Company, and in 2002 Haier New Zealand launched. As of early 2005, Haier's largest overseas operations were in Europe and the United States, with the recently launched India operation poised for rapid growth.

Haier America

Haier's entry into the U.S. market began in 1994 when Michael Jemal, a partner in a New York-based import company, Welbilt Appliances, approached the Qingdao manufacturer. At the time, just three Haier compact refrigerator models met U.S. energy and safety standards, and Jemal purchased 150,000 units to be sold in the U.S. All 150,000 sold under the Welbilt name within the year, capturing 10% of the U.S. market for compact refrigerators.

Following the success of the Welbilt line of mini-refrigerators, in 1999 Haier and Jemal formed a JV called "Haier America" to market a broader selection of products under the Haier brand. Haier America launched with rented office space in Manhattan, 17 staff people, and a $50 million sales target for the first year of operations. Jemal compared the new Haier operation to Sony's 1960 startup in a similarly dilapidated New York building. The difference was that Sony had brought 13 people from Japan to staff the new business; the Haier team was all American, except for the accountant who was sent from Qingdao.[61] Haier America later moved its headquarters into a landmark building on Broadway, which Haier purchased in 2001 for $14.5 million.

Haier established a $40 million industrial park and refrigerator factory in South Carolina. "Of course, labor costs are much higher in the United States than they are in China. They can be 10 times higher," said Zhang. "But our strategy in the U.S. market is not to manufacture cheap products, take them out of the factory, and push them into the market. We intend to manufacture quality products that we can sell at a premium."[62] Haier's U.S. factory had production capacity for 400,000 units per year. In 2002 Haier sold 80,000 full-size refrigerators in the U.S., accounting for about 2% of the market. Haier's U.S. factory, even after a planned expansion, did not have capacity for producing Haier's 10% target market share, so Haier planned to supplement with exports from China.[63]

Jemal focused on getting Haier products into the large chain retailers such as Home Depot, Best Buy, and Office Depot. (See **Exhibit 7** for U.S. distribution channels.) The most difficult one to break into was Wal-Mart, recalled Jemal. "It took us a whole year just to get an appointment." Wal-Mart finally agreed to look at Haier's room air conditioners, and after testing different products for quality and visiting Haier's manufacturing facilities in Qingdao, placed an order for 50,000 units. The next year, Wal-Mart doubled its order. In 2002, Haier sold 400,000 units of compact refrigerators, washing machines, and air conditioners to the giant retailer. In March 2005, Wal-Mart's online site listed 44 different Haier products, most targeted to the college student market. The best-sellers were a $140 compact refrigerator, a 125-can beverage center for $165, and a $200 portable clothes washer. Topping Wal-Mart's list of Haier products was a half-keg beer dispenser selling for $675.[64]

The focus on niche markets enabled Haier to avoid head-on competition with the likes of GE, Whirlpool, Maytag, and Frigidaire, which together accounted for 98% of U.S. sales of full-size refrigerators. "We don't look to compete with them, because they are much bigger than we are," said Jemal. "We believe we have our separate position in the market, and they have theirs. They can step on us anytime they want, because we are so small compared

---

[60]Ibid.

[61]Ibid., pp. 205–225.

[62]Zhang Ruimin quoted in Yibing Wu, "China's Refrigerator Magnate."

[63]Yibing Wu, "China's Refrigerator Magnate."

[64]Wal-Mart website, http://www.walmart.com, accessed March 17, 2005.

to them in the United States."[65] (See **Exhibit 8 and 9** for U.S. appliance market shares.) In 2005 *Euromonitor* reported that Haier had a 26% share for compact refrigerators, over 50% of the wine cellar market, and 17% of air conditioner sales in the United States.[66]

Haier Europe

In 2000 Haier Europe, headquartered in Varese, Italy, near the Swiss border, began coordinating sales and marketing of Haier products in 13 European countries, growing to 17 markets by 2004. Product lines included refrigerators, freezers, washing machines, dishwashers, microwave ovens, and small appliances, all designed specifically for the European market. Haier chose a former sales executive of Italy's Merloni, Europe's third-largest appliance maker, to head its European operations. The Italian executive had started his own trading company, selling GE, Whirlpool, and Siemens products, before joining Haier.[67]

In 2001, Haier invested $8 million to acquire a refrigerator plant in Padova, Italy, from Meneghetti SpA, one of Italy's largest manufacturers of built-in appliances made to match kitchen cabinetry. The new Haier plant manufactured built-in refrigerators and freezers for the expanding built-in sector, popular in the European market. In 2002, a new Italy-based company, Haier A/C Trading, began distributing Haier air conditioners in the local market.[68] By 2004 Haier had an estimated 10% share of European air conditioner sales.[69] Haier's European HQ in Varese coordinated logistics through four distribution centers in Italy, Spain, the United Kingdom, and the Netherlands.

The European appliance market was similar to the U.S. market in size and degree of development, but significant differences in distribution channels and consumer preferences across countries made it difficult for manufacturers to establish scale economies. For example, most Europeans favored front-loading washers, but in France, one of the largest markets, consumers preferred top-loaders. Independent appliance retailers dominated in Germany and Italy, while chain stores were common in France and the United Kingdom. There were few pan-European appliance retailers, and national and independent stores often favored domestic manufacturers. As a result, multinational appliance manufacturers had often found themselves at a disadvantage to local national players that tended to dominate in individual countries.[70]

Haier India

Haier earmarked India as a potential high-growth market, and invested heavily in building up production, distribution, and sales capacities in the country. In 1999 Haier formed an alliance with Indian appliance firm Fedder Lloyd Corp. to jointly produce and market refrigerators nationally. In January 2004 Haier launched a broad range of products in the Indian market, with the goal of becoming one of the top three white goods firms in India within five to seven years. A few months later, Haier announced a $200 million investment in India over four years to establish a refrigerator factory and research and development center that would serve as a production site for Southeast Asian and African markets. In June 2004, Haier India formed an alliance with Whirlpool and Voltas to manufacture refrigerators and air conditioners for the Indian market.[71]

[65]Jeannie J. Yi and Shawn X. Ye, *The Haier Way*, p. 214.

[66]"Haier Group," *Euromonitor International*, January 2005, available from http://www.euromonitor.com, accessed March 28, 2005.

[67]Jeannie J. Yi and Shawn X. Ye, *The Haier Way*, p. 199.

[68]Ibid., p. 201.

[69]"Haier Group," *Euromonitor International*.

[70]Charles W.F. Baden-Fuller and John M. Stopford, "Globalization Frustrated: The Case of White Goods," *Strategic Management Journal* 12, October 1991, pp. 493–507, available from ProQuest, ABI/Inform, http://www.proquest.com, accessed June 8, 2005; and U. Srinivasa Rangan and Jonathan Roche, "Whirlpool Corporation, 2002," Babson College case number BAB048, November 6, 2003.

[71]"Haier Group," *Euromonitor International*.

In India, Haier discovered that the "easy" emerging markets were not so easy. The biggest challenges for Haier in India were "the environment, the economy, and especially the channels," said Li. "In the United States you can easily find the top 10 chain stores. But in India, you cannot find them." Haier found that emerging markets required an even greater reliance on locals. Haier employed a former Whirlpool India executive to head Haier India. "This key person explains the whole market to us, including how to develop the channels and how to do the marketing, and we just provide the product. He chooses the products and proposes modifications for the local market," said Li. "He also helped us to find the right factory, find the best way to assemble the product, and get it to the distributor. In India we used local human resources to help us establish the whole business."

Competing abroad

Zhang explained his two-pronged strategy for competing with local brands on Haier's home turf:

> *Consumers in the United States are used to popular brands like GE and Whirlpool, so they'll wonder why they should choose a brand they've never heard of. But large companies are established and slow moving, and we see an opportunity to compete against them in their home markets by being more customer-focused than they are. To win over those consumers we have two approaches: speed and differentiation.*[72]

Product differentiation

Just as in China, Haier paid close attention to consumer needs in overseas markets and was willing to make small product modifications to please customers. "Our strategy for selling large refrigerators is the same as for compact refrigerators," said Zhang. "We send our R&D people to the United States to talk directly with our customers, or even with the salespeople in chain stores, to find out their specific needs."[73] Haier's market research resulted in simple innovations such as a freezer with a separate compartment to keep ice cream at a slightly warmer temperature, making it softer and easier to serve. "Consumers like the features we provide," said Zhang. "Large manufacturers aren't paying attention to such minor details."[74]

Response speed

Haier's 18 design centers, some in foreign markets, facilitated rapid product development. Ideas from the field could be quickly tested and made into prototypes. For example, having noted that American customers did not like deep-box freezers because items at the bottom were difficult to reach, during a visit to Qingdao, Jemal suggested to Zhang a two-level model with a drawer on the bottom. Seventeen hours later, Jemal was presented with a working model of his design. Haier executives also credited the firm's flat structure with aiding speed. Salespeople would provide market intelligence directly to model managers who, in competition with each other, would quickly assess the feasibility and profitability of a design before mobilizing resources to produce it.

The next 20 years

Haier faced a number of challenges in the coming years, including moving beyond niche markets in the United States to its goal of introducing a full line of products. While Haier had done well on a small scale, some industry observers doubted whether a Chinese

Haier: Taking a Chinese company global

---

[72]Zhang Ruimin, quoted in Yibing Wu, "China's Refrigerator Magnate."
[73]Ibid.
[74]Ibid.

company could break into the major leagues. "As a brand, Haier doesn't work," said a U.S. industry analyst. "People may buy a dorm refrigerator from Haier, but I don't think they'll spend a lot of money on an appliance from a company they've never heard of."[75] A Whirlpool executive believed that "one of the steps that many of the Asian companies have missed is the huge investment that's required to build brand equity."[76] But in 2005, Haier was spending about 10% of revenues on global branding and marketing, more than double the industry average.[77]

Haier would also continue to be challenged at home. Whirlpool and Electrolux had invested millions of dollars on factories and distribution in China. According to *Euromonitor*, "These companies believe that going head–to-head with Haier Group in its domestic market will prevent it from gaining the profits it might otherwise use to support its advance in the U.S."[78]

Haier's leadership was most concerned with securing the human resources needed to maintain rapid growth, especially to manage foreign markets. Haier also needed talent to develop the next generation of products. The company planned to combine its expertise in white goods with information technology, a relatively new area for Haier, to produce "intelligent" home appliances.

But above all, Haier kept its eye on developing the brand. "We are number three in the world for white goods," said Yang. "We want to be number one." Haier planned to get there one step at a time, securing market leadership at home in each sector, and then taking that product line into the global market. "In the international market, we want to get a 10% share to begin with. After that, we can expand more." Haier's long-term goal was to achieve Zhang's vision of one-third domestic sales, one-third exports, and one-third produced and sold abroad, said Yang. "Exports are about 20% now, and overseas made are at less than 10%—so the potential is great."

[75]Michael Arndt, "Can Haier Freeze Out Whirlpool and GE?" *BusinessWeek Online*, April 11, 2002, available from Factiva, http://www.factiva.com, accessed March 15, 2005.

[76]David L. Swift, executive vice president of Whirlpool Corp.'s North American region, quoted in Dexter Roberts et al., "China's Power Brands."

[77]Ben Uglow, Paloma Danjuan, and Martin Wilkie, Morgan Stanley Equity Research Europe, "Asia: Notes from Our Trip," *Capital Goods Industry Research*, January 10, 2005, p. 8, available from Thomson Research/Investext, http://research.thomsonib.com, accessed March 10, 2005.

[78]"Haier Group," *Euromonitor International*.

EXHIBIT 1A **Haier Group approximate revenue and net profit (in RMB billions)**

RMB bil	1994	1995	1996	1997	1998	1999	2000	2001	2002	2003	2004
Revenue	2.6	4.3	6.2	10.8	16.8	26.9	40.6	60.2	72.0	80.0	100.0
YoY growth	72%	69%	42%	75%	56%	60%	51%	48%	20%	11%	25%
Net profit							1.4	2.0	2.7	1.6	1.9
Net margin							3.4	3.3	3.8	2.0	1.9

Note: Profit data for 1994–1999 were not available. Haier attributed the 2003 decline in profit to price wars in the domestic market and to increased investments in overseas markets.
Source: Company documents.

EXHIBIT 1B **Haier Group approximate revenue breakdown (in US$ millions)**

US$ millions	1998	1999	2000	2001	2002	2003	2004
Domestic sales	1,971	3,112	4,633	6,861	7,868	8,648	10,100
as % of total revenue	97.0	95.8	94.3	94.2	90.3	89.3	83.4
Exports from China	62	138	280	424	444	532	1,000
as % of total revenue	3.0	4.2	5.7	5.8	5.1	5.5	8.3
Overseas made & sold	<1	<1	<1	<1	400	500	1,000
as % of total revenue	na	na	na	na	4.6	5.2	8.3
Total revenue	2,033	3,250	4,913	7,284	8,712	9,680	12,100

Source: Company documents.

EXHIBIT 2A **Manufacturer global market shares for large kitchen appliances[a] (retail volume)**

Manufacturer	Base Country	2001 Volume %	2002 Volume %
Whirlpool Corp	United States	7.9	7.9
Electrolux AB	Sweden	7.3	7.1
Bosch-Siemens Hausgerate	Germany	5.8	5.7
General Electric (GE)	United States	5.3	5.4
Haier Group	China	3.2	3.8
Matsushita Ltd	Japan	3.1	3.2
Maytag Corp	United States	3.0	3.1
LG Group	Korea	2.4	2.6
Sharp Electronics	Japan	2.6	2.6
Merloni Elettrodomestici	Italy	2.3	2.5
Samsung Electronics Co	Korea	1.8	2.0
Wuxi Little Swan Co	China	1.5	2.0
Others		53.8	52.1
Total		100.0	100.0

Haier: Taking a Chinese company global

EXHIBIT 2B **Brand global market shares for large kitchen appliances[a] (retail volume)**

Brand	Manufacturer	2001 Volume %	2002 Volume %
Whirlpool	Whirlpool Corp	5.2	5.2
GE	General Electric (GE)	3.7	3.8
Haier	Haier Group	3.2	3.8
Bosch	Bosch-Siemens Hausgerate	2.8	2.8
Sharp	Sharp Electronics	2.6	2.6
LG	LG Group	2.2	2.5
Maytag	Maytag Corp	1.9	2.0
Samsung	Samsung Electronics Co	1.8	2.0
Little Swan	Wuxi Little Swan Co	1.5	2.0
National	Matsushita Ltd	1.8	1.9
Siemens	Bosch-Siemens Hausgerate	1.7	1.6
Electrolux	Electrolux AB	1.5	1.6
Others		70.1	68.2
Total		100.0	100.0

[a]Large kitchen appliances included refrigerators, freezers, stoves, ovens, washers, dryers, microwave ovens, and dishwashers.

Note: Manufacturers with more than one major brand may have a high manufacturer market share and lower brand shares.

Source: Euromonitor International, "The World Market for Domestic Electrical Appliances," February 2004, available from Global Market Information Database, http://www.euromonitor.com, accessed May 24, 2005.

Haier: Taking a Chinese company global

EXHIBIT 3A Qingdao Haier financials in RMB millions, 2000–2004

Year ended December 31	2000	2001	2002	2003	2004
Income Statement					
Sales revenue	4,828	11,442	11,554	11,688	15,299
Operating costs	6,135	11,098	11,548	11,570	14,892
Taxes	48	201	108	100	113
Net profit	424	618	397	369	369
Balance Sheet					
Current assets	2,263	3,445	3,494	4,020	3,958
Total assets	3,934	6,942	7,324	7,373	7,107
Current liabilities	828	1,613	1,664	1,392	783
Long term debt	NA	NA	0	138	138
Total liabilities	1,123	2,010	2,065	1,984	1,389
Total equity	2,810	4,932	5,259	5,389	5,719
Cash Flows					
Operating activities	478	702	391	424	738
Investing activities	−461	−2,365	−658	206	−149
Financing activities	−126	1,914	218	−363	−704
Net change in cash	−109	250	−50	267	−115
Cash beginning balance	491	382	632	582	830
Cash ending balance	382	632	582	849	715

EXHIBIT 3B Qingdao Haier financial ratios, 2000–2004

Year ended December 31	2000	2001	2002	2003	2004
Liquidity Ratios					
Current ratio	2.7	2.1	2.1	2.9	5.1
Quick ratio	2.3	1.8	1.5	2.5	4.0
Working capital (US$ mil)	173.4	221.3	221.1	317.5	383.5
Operating Ratios					
Asset turnover	1.3	2.1	1.6	1.6	2.1
Inventory turnover	9.1	20.1	16.5	16.5	18.3
Receivables turnover	7.3	15.4	15.6	18.9	19.5
Profitability Ratios (%)					
Gross margin	18.0	16.6	12.9	14.5	13.1
Operating margin	7.7	8.6	5.6	5.2	4.1
EBITDA margin	9.7	10.1	7.2	6.8	5.5
Profit margin	8.9	5.4	3.4	3.2	2.4
Return on equity	15.7	16.0	7.8	6.9	6.7
Return on assets	11.0	11.4	5.6	5.0	5.1
SG&A expense/sales	10.4	8.2	7.6	9.5	9.1

Source: Company documents.

Haier: Taking a Chinese company global

EXHIBIT 4 **Qingdao Haier 2003 revenues by product**

Product category	Revenues (as % of RMB 11.7 billion total)
Air conditioners	52
Refrigerators	28
Freezers	7
Small electrical appliances	4
Other	9

Source: Adapted from "Qingdao Haier," *China Securities Research*, November 8, 2004, available from Thomson Research/Investext, http://research.thomsonib.com, accessed April 9, 2005.

EXHIBIT 5 **China's household penetration rates for consumer goods**

	1985	1990	1995	2000	2001	2002
Refrigerators						
Urban	6.6	42.7	66.2	80.1	81.9	87.4
Rural			5.2	12.3	13.6	14.8
Air Conditioners						
Urban		1.4	8.1	30.8	35.8	51.1
Rural			0.2	1.3	1.7	na
Washing Machines						
Urban	48.3	78.4	89.0	90.5	92.2	92.9
Rural			16.9	28.6	29.9	31.8
Color Televisions						
Urban	17.2	59.0	89.8	116.6	120.5	126.4
Rural			16.9	48.7	54.4	48.1

Source: Graham Ormerod, "Guangdong Kelon: A White Good Comeback Play," *G.K. Goh Research*, August 29, 2003, available from Thomson Research/Investext, http://research.thomsonib.com, accessed April 9, 2005.

EXHIBIT 6A **Refrigerator market shares in China (retail volume)**

Company	Leading Brands	2002 (%)	2003 (%)	2004 (%)
Haier Group	Haier	26.7	26.2	28.2
Guangdon Kelon	Kelon, Ronshen, Combine	13.4	12.4	10.8
Henan Xinfei	Xinfei	8.5	8.5	8.9
Wuxi Bosch-Siemens	Siemens	8.4	8.4	8.5
Changsha Zhongyi Group	Electrolux	10.1	7.7	6.9
Nanjing LG Panda Appliance	LG	4.9	7.0	6.6
Hefi Meiling Group	Meiling	8.4	7.8	6.1
Suzhou Samsung	Samsung	4.2	3.9	4.4
Hefei Rongshida Group	Rongshida	2.6	3.6	4.1
Panasonic China	Panasonic	1.7	2.3	2.9
Others		11.1	12.1	12.8

EXHIBIT 6B **Washing machine market shares in China (retail volume)**

Company	Leading Brands	2002 (%)	2003 (%)	2004 (%)
Haier Group	Haier	25.8	25.7	30.4
Wuxi Little Swan	Little Swan	20.7	18.8	16.5
Hefei Rongshida Group	Rongshida	10.6	10.0	10.6
Nanjing LG Panda Appliance	LG	5.0	6.7	7.0
Matsushita Electric China	National	6.1	6.0	6.3
Shanghai Whirlpool	Whirlpool	4.0	4.2	4.0
Wuxi Bosch-Siemens	Siemens	3.5	3.6	3.6
Suzhou Samsung	Samsung	2.7	3.1	2.8
Hefei Royalstar	Sanyo	2.4	2.4	2.6
Jiangmen Jinling	Jinling	3.4	2.2	1.9
Others		16.0	17.4	14.2

EXHIBIT 6C **Air conditioner market shares in China (retail volume)**

Company	Leading Brands	2002 (%)	2003 (%)	2004 (%)
Haier Group	Haier	16.3	16.6	17.5
GD Midea Holding	Midea	10.9	10.9	11.4
Chuhai Gree	Gree	7.4	9.1	10.0
LG Electronics (Tianjin)	LG	5.5	6.4	6.4
Ningbo O	Ningbo	4.0	6.5	6.1
Qingdao Hisense	Hisense	6.2	5.7	5.6
Guangdon Kelon	Kelon, Ronshen, Combine	5.6	5.8	5.7
Chunlan Group	Chunlan	2.6	2.5	4.0
Guangdong Chigo	Chigo	1.0	1.5	3.2
TCL	TCL	1.6	1.9	3.0
Others		38.8	33.0	27.0

Source: Provided by Haier, based on data from Chinese State Statistic Bureau, China Market Monitor Company, Ltd.

Haier: Taking a Chinese company global

EXHIBIT 7   **United States white goods sales ($ millions) and distribution channels (%), 2003–2004**

	2003	2004
Refrigerators	$5,649.4	$6,149.4
Sears	38.5	40.0
Mass merchandisers & clubs	7.5	9.0
Appliance stores	28.5	28.0
Home improvement centers	22.5	20.0
Others	3.0	3.0
Laundry appliances	$5,325.8	$5,946.2
Sears	40	42
Mass merchandisers & clubs	8	8
Appliance stores	28	27
Home improvement centers	20	18
Others	4	5
Room air conditioners	$1,655.6	$1,392.4
Sears	17	17
Mass merchandisers & clubs	31	39
Appliance stores	14	15
Home improvement centers	28	23
Others	10	6
Cooking appliances	$2,998.4	$3,276.2
Sears	36	36
Mass merchandisers & clubs	6	6
Appliance stores	32	34
Home improvement centers	23	19
Others	3	5

Source: Adapted from Gerry Beatty, "Most White Goods Rose in 2004," *HFN*, February 28, 2005, p. 44, available from Factiva, www.factiva.com, accessed March 11, 2005.

EXHIBIT 8 **U.S. large household appliance market shares (%)**

Company	1998	1999	2000	2001	2002	2003
Whirlpool	35.7	35.6	33.1	33.0	33.7	33.3
General Electric	28.5	28.5	26.6	28.5	28.5	26.1
Maytag	17.0	18.2	17.9	19.0	16.4	14.3
Electrolux (Frigidaire)	11.9	11.8	16.6	16.7	17.7	19.7
Goodman (Amana)[a]	4.7	3.9	2.5			
Others[b]	2.2	2.0	3.3	2.8	3.7	6.6
Total	100.0	100.0	100.0	100.0	100.0	100.0

[a]Amana was acquired by Maytag in 2001.

[b]"Others" included Asian competitors such as Haier, LG, and Samsung which together accounted for much of the 2003 share increase.

Source: Laura A. Champine and Anand Krishnan, Morgan Keegan Equity Research, "Whirlpool Corporation," March 14, 2005, available from Thomson Research/Investext, http://research.thomsonib.com, accessed April 28, 2005.

EXHIBIT 9 **Asian manufacturers in U.S. appliance market, 2003**

Company	Market Share	Price Range	Major Products	Other Products	Major Prod Distributor	Other Product Distributors
LG (Korean)	1.9 %	mid to high	refrigerators, washers, dryers	microwaves, A/Cs, vacuum cleaners, compact refrigerators, dehumidifiers, toasters	Best Buy	Sears, Best Buy
Samsung (Korean)	1.6 %	high	refrigerators, washers, dishwashers	microwaves, A/Cs, vacuum cleaners, dehumidifiers	Best Buy	Sears
Haier (Chinese)	1.0 %	low	refrigerators, freezers, washers, ranges	microwaves, A/Cs, compact refrigerators, wine coolers, compact dishwashers	Best Buy	Wal-Mart, Lowe's, Sears, Home Depot, Target
Daewoo (Korean)	.5%	low	None	microwaves, A/Cs, compact refrigerators	n/a	Best Buy, Home Depot

Source: Michael Rehaut, Jonathan F. Barlow, JP Morgan North American Equity Research, "Appliance Industry: Imports, Distribution Shift Drives Negative Outlook," January 8, 2004, available from Thomson Research/Investext, http://research.thomsonib.com, accessed April 28, 2005.

Overview of Accounting Analysis

The purpose of accounting analysis is to evaluate the degree to which a firm's accounting captures its underlying business reality.[1] By identifying places where there is accounting flexibility, and by evaluating the appropriateness of the firm's accounting policies and estimates, analysts can assess the degree of distortion in a firm's accounting numbers. Another important skill is adjusting a firm's accounting numbers using cash flow information and information from the notes to the financial statements to "undo" any accounting distortions. Sound accounting analysis improves the reliability of conclusions from financial analysis, the next step in financial statement analysis.

THE INSTITUTIONAL FRAMEWORK FOR FINANCIAL REPORTING

There is typically a separation between ownership and management in public corporations. Financial statements serve as the vehicle through which owners keep track of their firms' financial situation. On a periodic basis, firms typically produce four financial reports:

1. An income statement that describes the operating performance during a time period.
2. A balance sheet that states the firm's assets and how they are financed.
3. A cash flow statement that summarizes the cash flows of the firm.
4. A statement of comprehensive income that outlines the sources of non-owner changes in equity during the period between two consecutive balance sheets.[2]

These statements are accompanied by notes that provide additional details on the financial statement line items, as well as by management's narrative discussion of the firm's performance in the Management Report section.[3]

To evaluate effectively the quality of a firm's financial statement data, the analyst needs to first understand the basic features of financial reporting and the **institutional framework** that governs them, as discussed in the following sections.

Accrual accounting

One of the fundamental features of corporate financial reports is that they are prepared using accrual rather than cash accounting. Unlike cash accounting, **accrual accounting** distinguishes between the recording of costs and benefits associated with economic activities and the actual payment and receipt of cash. Net profit is the primary periodic performance index under accrual accounting. To compute net profit, the effects of economic transactions are recorded on the basis of *expected*, not necessarily *actual*, cash receipts and payments. Expected cash receipts from the delivery of products or services are recognized as revenues, and expected cash outflows associated with these revenues are recognized as expenses.

While there are many rules and conventions that govern a firm's preparation of financial statements, there are only a few conceptual building blocks that form the foundation of accrual accounting. The following definitions are critical to the income statement, which summarizes a firm's revenues and expenses:[4]

- **Revenues** are economic resources earned during a time period. Revenue recognition is governed by the realization principle, which proposes that revenues should be recognized when (a) the firm has provided all, or substantially all, the goods or services to be delivered to the customer and (b) the customer has paid cash or is expected to pay cash with a reasonable degree of certainty.

- **Expenses** are economic resources used up in a time period. Expense recognition is governed by the matching and the conservatism principles. Under these principles, expenses are (a) costs directly associated with revenues recognized in the same period, or (b) costs associated with benefits that are consumed in this time period, or (c) resources whose future benefits are not reasonably certain.

- **Profit/loss** is the difference between a firm's revenues and expenses in a time period.[5] The following fundamental relationship is therefore reflected in a firm's income statement:

$$Profit = Revenues - Expenses$$

In contrast, the balance sheet is a summary at one point in time. The principles that define a firm's **assets**, **liabilities**, equities, **revenues**, and **expenses** are as follows:

- **Assets** are economic resources owned by a firm that are (a) likely to produce future economic benefits and (b) measurable with a reasonable degree of certainty.

- **Liabilities** are economic obligations of a firm arising from benefits received in the past that (a) are required to be met with a reasonable degree of certainty and (b) whose timing is reasonably well defined.

- **Equity** is the difference between a firm's assets and its liabilities.

The definitions of assets, liabilities, and equity lead to the fundamental relationship that governs a firm's balance sheet:

$$Assets = Liabilities + Equity$$

Delegation of reporting to management

While the basic definitions of the elements of a firm's financial statements are simple, their application in practice often involves complex judgments. For example, how should revenues be recognized when a firm sells land to customers and also provides customer financing? If revenue is recognized before cash is collected, how should potential defaults be estimated? Are the outlays associated with research and development activities, whose payoffs are uncertain, assets or expenses when incurred? Are contractual commitments under lease arrangements or post-employment plans liabilities? If so, how should they be valued?

Because corporate managers have intimate knowledge of their firms' businesses, they are entrusted with the primary task of making the appropriate judgments in portraying myriad business transactions using the basic accrual accounting framework. The accounting discretion granted to managers is potentially valuable because it allows them to reflect inside information in reported financial statements. However, since investors view profits as a measure of managers' performance, managers have an incentive to use their accounting discretion to distort reported profits by making biased assumptions. Further, the use of accounting numbers in contracts between the firm and outsiders provides a motivation for management manipulation of accounting numbers.

This earnings management distorts financial accounting data, making it less valuable to external users of financial statements. Therefore, the delegation of financial reporting decisions to managers has both costs and benefits. Accounting rules and auditing are mechanisms designed to reduce the cost and preserve the benefit of delegating financial reporting to corporate managers. The legal system is used to adjudicate disputes between managers, auditors, and investors.

International Financial Reporting Standards

Given that it is difficult for outside investors to determine whether managers have used accounting flexibility to signal their proprietary information or merely to disguise reality, a number of accounting concepts and conventions have evolved to mitigate the problem. For example, in most countries financial statements are prepared using the concept of prudence, where caution is taken to ensure that assets are not recorded at values above their fair values and liabilities are not recorded at values below their fair values. This reduces managers' ability to overstate the value of the net assets that they have acquired or developed. Of course, the prudence concept also limits the information that is available to investors about the potential of the firm's assets, because many firms record their assets at historical exchange prices below the assets' fair values or values in use.

Accounting standards and rules also limit management's ability to misuse accounting judgment by regulating how particular types of transactions are recorded. For example, accounting standards for leases stipulate how firms are to record contractual arrangements to lease resources. Similarly, post-employment benefit standards describe how firms are to record commitments to provide pensions and other post-employment benefits for employees. These accounting standards, which are designed to convey quantitative information on a firm's performance, are complemented by a set of disclosure principles. The disclosure principles guide the amount and kinds of information that is disclosed and require a firm to provide qualitative information related to assumptions, policies, and uncertainties that underlie the quantitative data presented.

More than 85 countries have delegated the task of setting accounting standards to the International Accounting Standards Board (IASB). For example, since 2005 EU companies that have their shares traded on a public exchange must prepare their consolidated financial statements in accordance with International Financial Reporting Standards (IFRS) as promulgated by the IASB and endorsed by the European Union. Most EU countries, however, also have their own national accounting standard-setting bodies. These bodies may, for example, set accounting standards for private companies and for single entity financial statements of public companies.[6] Another of their tasks is to comment on the IASB's drafts of new or modified standards. There are similar private sector or public sector accounting standard-setting bodies in many other countries. For example, in the US the Securities and Exchange Commission (SEC) has the legal authority to set accounting standards. Since 1973 the SEC has relied on the Financial Accounting Standards Board (FASB), a private sector accounting body, to undertake this task.

Uniform accounting standards attempt to reduce managers' ability to record similar economic transactions in dissimilar ways either over time or across firms. Thus they create a uniform accounting language and increase the credibility of financial statements by limiting a firm's ability to distort them. Increased uniformity from accounting standards, however, comes at the expense of reduced flexibility for managers to reflect genuine business differences in a firm's accounting decisions. Rigid accounting standards work best for economic transactions whose accounting treatment is not predicated on managers' proprietary information. However, when there is significant business judgment involved in assessing a transaction's economic consequences, rigid standards are likely to be dysfunctional for some companies because they prevent managers from using their superior business knowledge to determine how best to report the economics of key business events. Further, if accounting standards are too rigid, they may induce managers to expend economic resources to restructure business transactions to achieve a desired accounting result or forego transactions that may be difficult to report on.

As a solution to the adverse effects of rigid accounting rules, the IASB often defines standards that are based more on broadly stated principles than on detailed rules. For example, most accountants agree that when a company leases an asset but nevertheless carries substantially all the risk of value loss, the asset is essentially owned by the company and should be recorded as such on the balance sheet. In its standard for leases, the IASB takes this basic principle as a standard and leaves much responsibility to the managers and auditors to decide which leased assets are economically owned by the company. In contrast, the US accounting standard for leases issued by the FASB sets out four numerical criteria that managers and auditors must use to classify leased assets. The US standard thus leaves managers much less room for interpretation than the international standard. However, because the US standard provides explicit guidance, it is also easier for managers to circumvent the intention of the standard, even though they may technically comply with it.

The leasing example illustrates what many see as an important difference in the approaches that the IASB and the FASB are taking to standard-setting. Proponents of the principles-based approach claim that reporting in accordance with principles, instead of technical rules, ensures that the financial statements reflect the economic substance of firms' transactions, instead of their legal form. However, because principles-based standards provide less technical guidance than rules-based standards, they demand more professionalism from auditors in exercising their duties and are more difficult to enforce. Proponents of the rules-based approach therefore claim that using rules-based standards increases the verifiability of the information included in the financial statements, reduces managers' misuse of their reporting discretion, and increases the comparability of financial statements across firms. The FASB, however, is currently turning toward a principles-based approach, which suggests that during the coming years global standard-setting will become more and more principles-based.[7]

External auditing

Broadly defined as a verification of the integrity of the reported financial statements by someone other than the preparer, external auditing ensures that managers use accounting rules and conventions consistently over time, and that their accounting estimates are reasonable. In Europe, the US and most other countries, all listed companies are required to have their financial statements audited by an independent public accountant. The standards and procedures to be followed by independent auditors are set by various institutions. By means of the Eighth Company Law Directive, the EU has set minimum standards for public audits that are performed on companies from its member countries. These standards prescribe, for example, that the external auditor does not provide any nonaudit services to the audited company that may compromise his independence. To maintain independence, the auditor (the person, not the firm) must also not audit the same company for more than seven consecutive years. Further, all audits must be carried out in accordance with the International Auditing Standards (ISA), as promulgated by the International Auditing and Assurance Standards Board (IAASB) and endorsed by the EU.

In the US, independent auditors must follow Generally Accepted Auditing Standards (GAAS), a set of standards comparable to the ISA. All US public accounting firms are also required to register with the Public Company Accounting Oversight Board (PCAOB), a regulatory body that has the power to inspect and investigate audit work, and if needed discipline auditors. Like the Eighth Company Law Directive in the EU, the US Sarbanes

Oxley Act specifies the relationship between a company and its external auditor, for example, requiring auditors to report to, and be overseen by, a company's audit committee rather than its management. In addition, this Act also prohibits public accounting firms from providing non-audit services to a company that it audits and mandates periodic rotation of audit firms.

While auditors issue an opinion on published financial statements, it is important to remember that the primary responsibility for the statements still rests with corporate managers. Auditing improves the quality and credibility of accounting data by limiting a firm's ability to distort financial statements to suit its own purposes. However, as audit failures at companies such as Ahold, Enron, and Parmalat show, auditing is imperfect. Audits cannot review all of a firm's transactions. They can also fail because of lapses in quality, or because of lapses in judgment by auditors who fail to challenge management for fear of losing future business.

Third-party auditing may also reduce the quality of financial reporting because it constrains the kind of accounting rules and conventions that evolve over time. For example, the IASB considers the views of auditors – in addition to other interest groups – in the process of setting IFRS. To illustrate, at least one-third of the IASB board members have a background as practicing auditor. Further, the IASB is advised by the Standards Advisory Committee, which contains several practicing auditors. Finally, the IASB invites auditors to comment on its policies and proposed standards. Auditors are likely to argue against accounting standards that produce numbers that are difficult to audit, even if the proposed rules produce relevant information for investors.

Legal liability

The legal environment in which accounting disputes between managers, auditors, and investors are adjudicated can also have a significant effect on the quality of reported numbers. The threat of lawsuits and resulting penalties have the beneficial effect of improving the accuracy of disclosure. In the EU, the Transparency Directive requires that every Member State has established a statutory civil liability regime for misstatements that managers make in their periodic disclosures to investors. However, legal liability regimes vary in strictness across countries, both within and outside Europe. Under strict regimes, such as that found in the US, investors can hold managers liable for their investment losses if they prove that the firm's disclosures were misleading, that they relied on the misleading disclosures, and that their losses were caused by the misleading disclosures. Under less strict regimes, such as those found in Germany and the UK, investors must additionally prove that managers were (grossly) negligent in their reporting or even had the intent to harm investors (i.e., committed fraud).[8] Further, in some countries only misstatements in annual and interim financial reports are subject to liability, whereas in other countries investors can hold managers liable also for misleading ad hoc disclosures.

The potential for significant legal liability might also discourage managers and auditors from supporting accounting proposals requiring risky forecasts – for example, forward-looking disclosures. This type of concern has motivated several European countries to adopt a less strict liability regime.[9]

Public enforcement

Several countries adhere to the idea that strong accounting standards, external auditing, and the threat of legal liability do not suffice to ensure that financial statements provide a truthful picture of economic reality. As a final guarantee on reporting quality, these countries have public enforcement bodies that either proactively or on a complaint basis initiate reviews of companies' compliance with accounting standards and take actions to correct noncompliance. In the US, the Securities and Exchange Commission (SEC) performs such reviews and frequently disciplines companies for violations of US GAAP. In recent years, several European countries have also set up proactive enforcement agencies that should enforce listed companies' compliance with IFRS. Examples of such agencies are the French AMF (Autorité des Marchés Financiers), the German DPR (Deutsche Prüfstelle für Rechnungslegung), the Italian CONSOB (Commissione Nazionale per le Società e la Borsa), and the UK Financial Reporting Review Panel. Because each European country maintains control of domestic enforcement, there is a risk that the enforcement of IFRS exhibits differences in strictness and focus across Europe. To coordinate enforcement activities, however, most European enforcement agencies cooperate in the Committee of European Securities Regulators (CESR). One of the CESR's tasks is to develop mechanisms that lead to consistent enforcement across Europe. For example, the Committee promotes that national enforcement agencies have access to and take notice of each other's enforcement decisions. The coming years will show whether a decentralized system of enforcement can consistently assure that European companies comply with IFRS.

Public enforcement bodies cannot ensure full compliance of all listed companies. In fact, most proactive enforcement bodies conduct their investigations on a sampling basis. For example, the UK Financial Reporting Review Panel periodically selects industry sectors on which it focuses its enforcement activities. Within these sectors, the Review Panel then selects individual companies either at random or on the basis of company characteristics such as poor governance. The set of variables that European enforcers most commonly use to select companies includes market capitalization or trading volume (both measuring the company's economic relevance), share price volatility, the likelihood of new equity issues and the inclusion of the company in an index.[10]

Strict public enforcement can also reduce the quality of financial reporting because, in their attempt to avoid an accounting credibility crisis on public capital markets, enforcement bodies may pressure companies to exercise excessive prudence in their accounting choices.

PUBLIC ENFORCEMENT PRACTICES

The fact that most countries have a public enforcement agency does not, of course, imply that all countries have equally developed and effective enforcement systems. One measure of the development of public enforcement is how much a country spends on enforcement. A recent study has shown that there still is significant variation worldwide in enforcement agencies' staff and budget size. For example, in 2006 agencies in Italy, the Netherlands, the UK and the US spent more than twice as much as their peers in France, Germany, Spain and Sweden.[11] Although public enforcement has important preventive effects – it deters violations of accounting rules just through its presence – another measure of its development is an enforcement agency's activity, potentially measured by the number of investigations held and the number of actions taken against public companies. Most agencies disclose annual reports summarizing their activities. So far, these reports illustrate that most actions taken by (non-US) enforcement agencies are recommendations to firms on how to improve their reporting and better comply with IFRS in the future. In a few cases the agencies took corrective actions. Following are a two examples of such actions:

■ In the year ending in March 2008, the UK Financial Reporting Review Panel reviewed 224 annual reports, 157 on its own initiative and 67 in response to complaints or referrals. In only a few cases a firm had to either restate its current financial statements or adjust the prior period figures in its next financial statements. For example, in its 2006/2007 balance sheet, The Investment Company plc classified its participating preference shares as equity rather than a combination of debt and equity, as prescribed by IAS 32. As a consequence, The Investment Company's equity was overstated and the firm was asked to make a prior period adjustment in its 2007/2008 financial statements.

■ In March 2008 the Finish Financial Supervisory Authority issued a public warning – an administrative sanction – to Cencorp Corporation. The Authority disclosed that Cencorp should not have recognized a deferred tax asset for the carryforward of tax losses in its 2005 and 2006 financial statements because the company lacked convincing evidence that it could utilize the carryforward in future years. In its 2007 financial statement Cencorp restated its comparative figures for 2005 and 2006.

FACTORS INFLUENCING ACCOUNTING QUALITY

Because the mechanisms that limit managers' ability to distort accounting data themselves add noise, it is not optimal to use accounting regulation to eliminate managerial flexibility completely. Therefore, real-world accounting systems leave considerable room for managers to influence financial statement data. The net result is that information in corporate financial reports is noisy and biased, even in the presence of accounting regulation and external auditing.[12] The objective of **accounting analysis** is to evaluate the degree to which a firm's accounting captures its underlying business reality and to "undo" any accounting distortions. When potential distortions are large, accounting analysis can add considerable value.[13]

There are three potential **sources of noise and bias** in accounting data:

1 That introduced by rigidity in accounting rules.
2 Random forecast errors.
3 Systematic reporting choices made by corporate managers to achieve specific objectives.

Each of these factors is discussed below.

Noise from accounting rules

Accounting rules introduce noise and bias because it is often difficult to restrict management discretion without reducing the information content of accounting data. For example, International Accounting Standard (IAS) 38 issued by the IASB requires firms to recognize assets for development outlays when these are likely to produce future economic benefits, but requires firms to expense the preceding research outlays when they are incurred. Development expenditures are those incurred for the actual design of a new product. In contrast, research expenditures are not directly associated with a product. Clearly, some research expenditures have future value while others do not. However, because IAS 38 does not allow firms to distinguish between the two types of expenditures in the early stages of research, it leads to a systematic distortion of reported accounting numbers. Broadly speaking, the degree of distortion introduced by accounting standards depends on how well uniform accounting standards capture the nature of a firm's transactions.

Forecast errors

Another source of noise in accounting data arises from pure forecast error, because managers cannot predict future consequences of current transactions perfectly. For example, when a firm sells products on credit, accrual accounting requires managers to make a judgment about the probability of collecting payments from customers. If payments are deemed "reasonably certain," the firm treats the transactions as sales, creating trade receivables on its balance sheet. Managers then make an estimate of the proportion of receivables that will not be collected. Because managers do not have perfect foresight, actual defaults are likely to be different from estimated customer defaults, leading to a forecast error. The extent of errors in managers' accounting forecasts depends on a variety of factors, including the complexity of the business transactions, the predictability of the firm's environment, and unforeseen economy-wide changes.

Managers' accounting choices

Corporate managers also introduce noise and bias into accounting data through their own accounting decisions. Managers have a variety of incentives to exercise their accounting discretion to achieve certain objectives:[14]

■ Accounting-based debt covenants. Managers may make accounting decisions to meet certain contractual obligations in their debt covenants. For example, firms' lending agreements with banks and other debt holders require them to meet covenants related to interest coverage, working capital ratios, and net worth, all defined in terms of accounting numbers. Violation of these agreements may be costly because lenders can trigger penalties including demanding immediate payment of their loans. Managers of firms close to violating debt covenants have an incentive to select accounting policies and estimates to reduce the probability of covenant violation. The debt covenant motivation for managers' accounting decisions has been analyzed by a number of accounting researchers.[15]

■ Management compensation. Another motivation for managers' accounting choice comes from the fact that their compensation and job security are often tied to reported profits. For example, many top managers receive bonus compensation if they exceed certain prespecified profit targets. This provides motivation for managers to choose accounting policies and estimates to maximize their expected compensation.[16] Stock option awards can also potentially induce managers to manage earnings. Options provide managers with incentives to understate earnings prior to option grants to lower the firm's current share price and hence the option exercise price, and to inflate earnings and share prices at the time of the option exercise.[17]

■ Corporate control contests. In corporate control contests, such as hostile takeovers, competing management groups attempt to win over the firm's shareholders. Accounting numbers are used extensively in debating managers' performance in these contests. Therefore, managers may make accounting decisions to influence investor perceptions in corporate control contests. Also, when takeovers are not necessarily hostile but structured as a share-for-share merger, the acquiring firm may overstate its performance to boost its share price and by this reduce the share exchange ratio.[18]

■ Tax considerations. Managers may also make reporting choices to trade off between financial reporting and tax considerations. For example, US firms are required to use LIFO inventory accounting for shareholder reporting in order to use it for tax reporting. Under LIFO, when prices are rising, firms report lower profits, thereby reducing tax payments. Some firms may forgo the tax reduction in order to report higher profits in their financial statements. In countries where such a direct link between financial reporting and tax reporting does not exist, tax considerations may still indirectly affect managers' reporting decisions. For example, firms that recognize losses aggressively in their tax statements may support their aggressive tax choices by having the financial reporting treatment of these losses conform to their tax treatment. Having no divergence between the tax treatment and the financial reporting treatment could increase the probability that tax authorities allow the tax treatment.[19]

- Regulatory considerations. Since accounting numbers are used by regulators in a variety of contexts, managers of some firms may make accounting decisions to influence regulatory outcomes. Examples of regulatory situations where accounting numbers are used include actions to end or prevent infringements of competition laws, import tariffs to protect domestic industries, and tax policies.[20]

- Capital market considerations. Managers may make accounting decisions to influence the perceptions of capital markets. When there are information asymmetries between managers and outsiders, this strategy may succeed in influencing investor perceptions, at least temporarily.[21]

- Stakeholder considerations. Managers may also make accounting decisions to influence the perception of important stakeholders in the firm. For example, since labor unions can use healthy profits as a basis for demanding wage increases, managers may make accounting decisions to decrease profit when they are facing union contract negotiations. In countries like Germany, where labor unions are strong, these considerations appear to play an important role in firms' accounting policy. Other important stakeholders that firms may wish to influence through their financial reports include suppliers and customers.[22]

- Competitive considerations. The dynamics of competition in an industry might also influence a firm's reporting choices. For example, a firm's segment disclosure decisions may be influenced by its concern that disaggregated disclosure may help competitors in their business decisions. Similarly, firms may not disclose data on their margins by product line for fear of giving away proprietary information. Finally, firms may discourage new entrants by making profit-decreasing accounting choices.

In addition to accounting policy choices and estimates, the level of disclosure is also an important determinant of a firm's accounting quality. Corporate managers can choose disclosure policies that make it more or less costly for external users of financial reports to understand the true economic picture of their businesses. Accounting regulations usually prescribe minimum disclosure requirements, but they do not restrict managers from voluntarily providing additional disclosures. Managers can use various parts of the financial reports, including the Management Report and notes, to describe the company's strategy, its accounting policies, and its current performance. There is wide variation across firms in how managers use their disclosure flexibility.[23]

STEPS IN ACCOUNTING ANALYSIS

In this section we discuss a series of steps an analyst can follow to evaluate a firm's accounting quality.

Step 1: Identify key accounting policies

As discussed in the chapter on business strategy analysis, a firm's industry characteristics and its own competitive strategy determine its key success factors and risks. One of the goals of financial statement analysis is to evaluate how well these success factors and risks are being managed by the firm. In accounting analysis, therefore, the analyst should identify and evaluate the policies and the estimates the firm uses to measure its critical factors and risks.

Key success factors in the banking industry include interest and credit risk management; in the retail industry, inventory management is a key success factor; and for a manufacturer competing on product quality and innovation, research and development and product defects after the sale are key areas of concern. A significant success factor in the leasing business is to make accurate forecasts of residual values of the leased equipment at the end of the lease terms. In each of these cases, the analyst has to identify the accounting measures the firm uses to capture these business constructs, the policies that determine how the measures are implemented, and the key estimates embedded in these policies. For example, the accounting measure a bank uses to capture credit risk is its loan loss reserves, and the accounting measure that captures product quality for a manufacturer is its warranty expenses and reserves. For a firm in the equipment leasing industry, one of the most important accounting policies is the way residual values are recorded. Residual values influence the company's reported profits and its asset base. If residual values are overestimated, the firm runs the risk of having to take large write-offs in the future.

CRITICAL ACCOUNTING ESTIMATES

When identifying a firm's key accounting policies, it is helpful that the IFRS mandate firms to explicitly identify the accounting methods and estimates that require most judgment and are of critical importance to the usefulness of their accounting information. For example, in its 2008 financial statements cruise company Carnival Corporation & plc reported that ". . . our most significant assets are our ships and ships under construction, which represent 76% of our total assets. We make several critical accounting estimates dealing with our ship accounting. First, we compute our ships' depreciation expense, which represented approximately 10% of our cruise costs and expenses in fiscal 2008 and which requires us to estimate the average useful life of each of our ships as well as their residual values. Secondly, we account for ship improvement costs by capitalizing those costs which we believe will add value to our ships and depreciate those improvements over their estimated useful lives, while expensing repairs and maintenance and minor improvement costs as they are incurred. Finally, when we record the retirement of a ship component that is included within the ship's cost basis, we may have to estimate its net book value." Other areas of significant judgment identified by Carnival were: (1) the determination of fair values of ships and trademarks for which no active market exists (in impairment tests) and (2) the valuation of potential liabilities related to lawsuits, environmental claims, guest and crew claims and tax matters.

Step 2: Assess accounting flexibility

Not all firms have equal flexibility in choosing their key accounting policies and estimates. Some firms' accounting choice is severely constrained by accounting standards and conventions. For example, even though research and development is a key success factor for biotechnology companies, managers have no accounting discretion in reporting on research activities and, in practice, often make no distinction between development and research because the future benefits of development outlays are too difficult to assess. Similarly, even though marketing and brand building are key to the success of consumer goods firms, they are required to expense all their marketing outlays. In contrast, managing credit risk is one of the critical success factors for banks, and bank managers have the freedom to estimate expected defaults on their loans. Similarly, shipbuilding companies can adequately show the profitability status of their long-term projects because they have the flexibility to recognize proportions of the project revenues during the life of the project.

If managers have little flexibility in choosing accounting policies and estimates related to their key success factors (as in the case of biotechnology firms), accounting data are likely to be less informative for understanding the firm's economics. In contrast, if managers have considerable flexibility in choosing the policies and estimates (as in the case of banks), accounting numbers have the potential to be informative, depending upon how managers exercise this flexibility.

Regardless of the degree of accounting flexibility a firm's managers have in measuring their key success factors and risks, they will have some flexibility with respect to several other accounting policies. For example, all firms have to make choices with respect to depreciation policy (straight-line or accelerated methods), inventory accounting policy (FIFO or average cost), policy for amortizing intangible assets other than goodwill (write-off over 20 years or less), and policies regarding the estimation of pension and other post-employment benefits (expected return on plan assets, discount rate for liabilities, and rate of increase in wages and healthcare costs). Since all these policy choices can have a significant impact on the reported performance of a firm, they offer an opportunity for the firm to manage its reported numbers.

ACCOUNTING FLEXIBILITY

Carnival calculates the average useful life and residual value of its ships as the weighted average of the useful lives and residual values of the ships' major components, such as cabins and engines. Management's estimate of the average useful life of its ships is 30 years; the residual value is set at 15 percent of the ships' initial cost. In the notes to the financial statements, management illustrates its accounting flexibility as follows: ". . . if we change our assumptions in making our determinations as to whether improvements to a ship add value, the amounts we expend each year as repair and maintenance costs could increase, which would be partially offset by a decrease in depreciation expense, resulting from a reduction in capitalized costs. Our fiscal 2008 ship depreciation expense would have increased by approximately $30 million for every year we reduced our estimated average 30 year ship useful life. In addition, if our ships were estimated to have no residual value, our fiscal 2008 depreciation expense would have increased by approximately $150 million." In 2008, $30 million was equivalent to roughly 1 percent of the company's operating income.

Step 3: Evaluate accounting strategy

When managers have accounting flexibility, they can use it either to communicate their firm's economic situation or to hide true performance. Some of the strategy questions one could ask in examining how managers exercise their accounting flexibility include the following:

■ How do the firm's accounting policies compare to the norms in the industry? If they are dissimilar, is it because the firm's competitive strategy is unique? For example, consider a firm that reports a lower provision for warranty costs than the industry average. One explanation is that the firm competes on the basis of high quality and has invested considerable resources to reduce the rate of product failure. An alternative explanation is that the firm is merely understating its warranty provision.

■ Do managers face strong incentives to use accounting discretion to manage earnings? For example, is the firm close to violating bond covenants? Or are the managers having difficulty meeting accounting-based bonus targets? Does management own a significant amount of shares? Is the firm in the middle of a takeover battle or union negotiations? Managers may also make accounting decisions to reduce tax payments or to influence the perceptions of the firm's competitors.

■ Has the firm changed any of its policies or estimates? What is the justification? What is the impact of these changes? For example, if warranty expenses decreased, is it because the firm made significant investments to improve quality?

■ Have the company's policies and estimates been realistic in the past? For example, firms may overstate their revenues and understate their expenses during the year by manipulating quarterly or semiannual reports, which arc not subject to a full-blown external audit. However, the auditing process at the end of the fiscal year forces such companies to make large year-end adjustments, providing an opportunity for the analyst to assess the quality of the firm's interim reporting. Similarly, firms that depreciate fixed assets too slowly will be forced to take a large write-off later. A history of write-offs may be, therefore, a sign of prior earnings management.

■ Does the firm structure any significant business transactions so that it can achieve certain accounting objectives? For example, leasing firms can alter lease terms (the length of the lease or the bargain purchase option at the end of the lease term) so that the transactions qualify as sales-type leases for the lessors. Enron structured acquisitions of joint venture interests and hedging transactions with special purpose entities to avoid having to show joint venture liabilities, and to avoid reporting investment losses in its financial statements.[24] Such behavior may suggest that the firm's managers are willing to expend economic resources merely to achieve an accounting objective.

Step 4: Evaluate the quality of disclosure — financial analyst

Managers can make it more or less easy for an analyst to assess the firm's accounting quality and to use its financial statements to understand business reality. While accounting rules require a certain amount of minimum disclosure, managers have considerable choice in the matter. Disclosure quality, therefore, is an important dimension of a firm's accounting quality.

In assessing a firm's disclosure quality, an analyst could ask the following questions:

■ Does the company provide adequate disclosures to assess the firm's business strategy and its economic consequences? For example, some firms use management's narrative report in their financial statements to clearly lay out the firm's industry conditions, its competitive position, and management's plans for the future. Others use the report to puff up the firm's financial performance and gloss over any competitive difficulties the firm might be facing.

■ Do the notes to the financial statements adequately explain the key accounting policies and assumptions and their logic? For example, if a firm's revenue and expense recognition policies differ from industry norms, the firm can explain its choices in a note. Similarly, when there are significant changes in a firm's policies, notes can be used to disclose the reasons.

■ Does the firm adequately explain its current performance? The Management Report section of the annual report provides an opportunity to help analysts understand the reasons behind a firm's performance changes. Some firms use this section to link financial performance to business conditions. For example, if profit margins went down in a period, was it because of price competition or because of increases in manufacturing costs? If the selling and general administrative expenses went up, was it because the firm is investing in a differentiation strategy, or because unproductive overhead expenses were creeping up?

■ If accounting rules and conventions restrict the firm from measuring its key success factors appropriately, does the firm provide adequate additional disclosure to help outsiders understand how these factors are being managed? For example, if a firm invests in product quality and customer service, accounting rules do not allow the management to capitalize these outlays, even when the future benefits are certain. The firm's review of its operations can be used to highlight how these outlays are being managed and their performance consequences. For example, the firm can disclose physical indexes of defect rates and customer satisfaction so that outsiders can assess the progress being made in these areas and the future cash flow consequences of these actions.

- If a firm is in multiple business segments, what is the quality of segment disclosure? Some firms provide excellent discussion of their performance by product segments and geographic segments. Others lump many different businesses into one broad segment. The level of competition in an industry and management's willingness to share desegregated performance data influence a firm's quality of segment disclosure.

- How forthcoming is the management with respect to bad news? A firm's disclosure quality is most clearly revealed by the way management deals with bad news. Does it adequately explain the reasons for poor performance? Does the company clearly articulate its strategy, if any, to address the company's performance problems?

- How good is the firm's investor relations program? Does the firm provide fact books with detailed data on the firm's business and performance? Is the management accessible to analysts?

Step 5: Identify potential red flags

In addition to the preceding steps, a common approach to accounting quality analysis is to look for "red flags" pointing to questionable accounting quality. These indicators suggest that the analyst should examine certain items more closely or gather more information on them. Some common red flags are the following:

- Unexplained changes in accounting, especially when performance is poor. This may suggest that managers are using their accounting discretion to "dress up" their financial statements.[25]

- Unexplained transactions that boost profits. For example, firms might undertake balance sheet transactions, such as asset sales or debt-for-equity swaps, to realize gains in periods when operating performance is poor.[26]

- Unusual increases in trade receivables in relation to sales increases. This may suggest that the company is relaxing its credit policies or artificially loading up its distribution channels to record revenues during the current period. If credit policies are relaxed unduly, the firm may face receivable write-offs in subsequent periods as a result of customer defaults. If the firm accelerates shipments to its distributors, it may either face product returns or reduced shipments in subsequent periods.

- Unusual increases in inventories in relation to sales increases. If the inventory buildup is due to an increase in finished goods inventory, it could be a sign that demand for the firm's products is slowing down, suggesting that the firm may be forced to cut prices (and hence earn lower margins) or write down its inventory. A build-up in work-in-progress inventory tends to be good news on average, probably signaling that managers expect an increase in sales. If the build-up is in raw materials, it could suggest manufacturing or procurement inefficiencies, leading to an increase in cost of sales (and hence lower margins).[27]

- An increasing gap between a firm's reported profit and its cash flow from operating activities. While it is legitimate for accrual accounting numbers to differ from cash flows, there is usually a steady relationship between the two if the company's accounting policies remain the same. Therefore, any *change* in the relationship between reported profits and operating cash flows might indicate subtle changes in the firm's accrual estimates. For example, a firm undertaking large construction contracts might use the percentage-of-completion method to record revenues. While earnings and operating cash flows are likely to differ for such a firm, they should bear a steady relationship to each other. Now suppose the firm increases revenues in a period through an aggressive application of the percentage-of-completion method. Then its earnings will go up, but its cash flow remains unaffected. This change in the firm's accounting quality will be manifested by a *change* in the relationship between the firm's earnings and cash flows.

- An increasing gap between a firm's reported profit and its tax profit. Once again, it is quite legitimate for a firm to follow different accounting policies for financial reporting and tax accounting as long as the tax law allows it. However, the relationship between a firm's book and tax accounting is likely to remain constant over time, unless there are significant changes in tax rules or accounting standards. Thus, an *increasing* gap between a firm's reported profit and its tax profit may indicate that financial reporting to shareholders has become more aggressive. For example, warranty expenses are estimated on an accrual basis for financial reporting, but they are recorded on a cash basis for tax reporting. Unless there is a big change in the firm's product quality, these two numbers bear a consistent relationship to each other. Therefore, a change in this relationship can be an indication either that product quality is changing significantly or that financial reporting estimates are changing.

- A tendency to use financing mechanisms like research and development partnerships, special purpose entities, and the sale of receivables with recourse. While these arrangements may have a sound business logic, they can also provide management with an opportunity to understate the firm's liabilities and/or overstate its assets.[28]

- Unexpected large asset write-offs. This may suggest that management is slow to incorporate changing business circumstances into its accounting estimates. Asset write-offs may also be a result of unexpected changes in business circumstances.[29]

- Large year-end adjustments. A firm's annual reports are audited by the external auditors, but its interim financial statements are usually only reviewed. If a firm's management is reluctant to make appropriate accounting estimates (such as provisions for uncollectible receivables) in its interim statements, it could be forced to make adjustments at the end of the year as a result of pressure from its external auditors. A consistent pattern of year-end adjustments, therefore, may indicate aggressive management of interim reporting.[30]

- Qualified audit opinions or changes in independent auditors that are not well justified. These may indicate a firm's aggressive attitude or a tendency to "opinion shop."

- Poor internal governance mechanisms. Internal governance agents, such as independent directors or supervisors, audit committees, and internal auditors, are responsible for assuring the flow of credible information to external parties. When a firm's supervising directors or audit committee lack independence from management or its internal control system has deficiencies, accounting may be of questionable quality.[31] A lack of independence can be the result of, for example, family bonds, economic relationships, or prior working relationships. We discuss the role of governance in more detail in Chapter 12.

- Related-party transactions or transactions between related entities. These transactions may lack the objectivity of the marketplace, and managers' accounting estimates related to these transactions are likely to be more subjective and potentially self-serving.[32]

While the preceding list provides a number of red flags for potentially poor accounting quality, it is important to do further analysis before reaching final conclusions. Each of the red flags has multiple interpretations; some interpretations are based on sound business reasons, and others indicate questionable accounting. It is, therefore, best to use the red flag analysis as a starting point for further probing, not as an end point in itself.[33]

Step 6: Undo accounting distortions

If the accounting analysis suggests that the firm's reported numbers are misleading, analysts should attempt to restate the reported numbers to reduce the distortion to the extent possible. It is, of course, virtually impossible to perfectly undo the distortion using outside information alone. However, some progress can be made in this direction by using the cash flow statement and the notes to the financial statements.

A firm's cash flow statement provides a reconciliation of its performance based on accrual accounting and cash accounting. If the analyst is unsure of the quality of the firm's accrual accounting, the cash flow statement provides an alternative benchmark of its performance. The cash flow statement also provides information on how individual line items in the income statement diverge from the underlying cash flows. For example, if an analyst is concerned that the firm is aggressively capitalizing certain costs that should be expensed, the information in the cash flow statement provides a basis to make the necessary adjustment.

The notes to the financial statements also provide information that is potentially useful in restating reported accounting numbers. For example, when a firm changes its accounting policies, it provides a note indicating the effect of that change if it is material. Similarly, some firms provide information on the details of accrual estimates such as the provision for doubtful receivables. The tax note usually provides information on the differences between a firm's accounting policies for shareholder reporting and tax reporting. Since tax reporting is often more conservative than shareholder reporting, the information in the tax note can be used to estimate what the earnings reported to shareholders would be under more conservative policies.

In Chapter 4, we show how to make accounting adjustments for some of the most common types of accounting distortions.

ACCOUNTING ANALYSIS PITFALLS

There are several potential pitfalls and common misconceptions in accounting analysis that an analyst should avoid.

Conservative accounting is not "good" accounting

Some firms take the approach that it pays to be conservative in financial reporting and to set aside as much as possible for contingencies. This logic is commonly used to justify the expensing of research and advertising, and the rapid write-down of intangible assets other than goodwill. It is also used to support large loss reserves for insurance companies, for merger expenses, and for restructuring charges.

From the standpoint of a financial statement user, it is important to recognize that conservative accounting is not the same as "good" accounting. Financial statement users want to evaluate how well a firm's accounting captures business reality in an unbiased manner, and conservative accounting can be as misleading as aggressive accounting in this respect.

It is certainly true that it can be difficult to estimate the economic benefits from many intangibles. However, the intangible nature of some assets does not mean that they do not have value. Indeed, for many firms these types of assets are their most valued. For example, Swiss-based pharmaceutical Novartis' two most valued assets are its research capabilities that permit it to generate new drugs, and its sales force that enables it to sell those drugs to doctors. Yet neither is recorded on Novartis' balance sheet. From the investors' point of view, accountants' reluctance to value intangible assets does not diminish their importance. If they are not included in financial statements, investors have to look to alternative sources of information on these assets.

Further, conservative accounting often provides managers with opportunities for reducing the volatility of reported earnings, typically referred to as "earnings smoothing," which may prevent analysts from recognizing poor performance in a timely fashion. Finally, over time investors are likely to figure out which firms are conservative and may discount their management's disclosures and communications.

Not all unusual accounting is questionable

It is easy to confuse unusual accounting with questionable accounting. While unusual accounting choices might make a firm's performance difficult to compare with other firms' performance, such an accounting choice might be justified if the company's business is unusual. For example, firms that follow differentiated strategies or firms that structure their business in an innovative manner to take advantage of particular market situations may make unusual accounting choices to properly reflect their business. Therefore it is important to evaluate a company's accounting choices in the context of its business strategy.

Similarly, it is important not to necessarily attribute all *changes* in a firm's accounting policies and accruals to earnings management motives.[34] Accounting changes might be merely reflecting changed business circumstances. For example, as already discussed, a firm that shows unusual increases in its inventory might be preparing for a new product introduction. Similarly, unusual increases in receivables might merely be due to changes in a firm's sales strategy. Unusual decreases in the allowance for uncollectible receivables might be reflecting a firm's changed customer focus. It is therefore important for an analyst to consider all possible explanations for accounting changes and investigate them using the qualitative information available in a firm's financial statements.

Common accounting standards are not the same as common accounting practices

Listed firms in the EU and elsewhere prepare their consolidated financial statements under a common set of accounting standards, IFRS. The adoption of IFRS makes financial statements more comparable across countries and lowers the barriers to cross-border investment analysis. It is important, however, not to confuse the adoption of common accounting *standards* such as IFRS with the introduction of common accounting *practices*.[35]

In this chapter we have discussed some international differences that have remained in place after the adoption of IFRS. For example, although the EU sets minimum standards for external auditing, it remains up to the member countries to implement and enforce such rules. Further, IFRS may not be similarly enforced throughout Europe because all European countries have their own public enforcement bodies. Finally, the role of financial reports in communication between managers and investors differs across firms and countries. In Chapter 1 we discussed the reporting differences between private corporations and public corporations. Similar, potentially smaller differences exist between widely held and closely held listed firms. The analyst should therefore carefully consider these aspects of a firm's reporting environment.

VALUE OF ACCOUNTING DATA AND ACCOUNTING ANALYSIS

What is the value of accounting information and accounting analysis? Given the incentives and opportunities for managers to affect their firms' reported accounting numbers, some have argued that accounting data and accounting analysis are not likely to be useful for investors.

Researchers have examined the value of earnings and return on equity (ROE) by comparing stock returns that could be earned by an investor who has perfect foresight of firms' earnings, return on equity (ROE), and cash flows for the following year.[36] To assess the importance of earnings, the hypothetical investor is assumed to buy shares of firms with subsequent earnings decreases. If this strategy is followed each year during the period 1964 to 1996, the hypothetical investor would have earned an average return of 37.5 percent. If a similar investment strategy is followed using ROE, buying shares with subsequent increases in ROE and selling shares with ROE decreases, an even higher annual return, 43 percent, would be earned. In contrast, cash flow data appear to be considerably less valuable than earnings or ROE information. Annual returns generated from buying shares with increased subsequent cash flow from operations and selling shares with cash flow decreases would be only 9 percent. This suggests that next period's earnings and ROE performance are more relevant information for investors than cash flow performance.

Overall, this research suggests that the institutional arrangements and conventions created to mitigate potential misuse of accounting by managers are effective in providing assurance to investors. The research indicates that investors do not view earnings management as so pervasive as to make earnings data unreliable.

A number of research studies have examined whether superior accounting analysis is a valuable activity. By and large, this evidence indicates that there are opportunities for superior analysts to earn positive stock returns. Studies show that companies criticized in the financial press for misleading financial reporting subsequently suffered an average share price drop of 8 percent.[37] Firms where managers appeared to inflate reported earnings prior to an equity issue and subsequently reported poor earnings performance had more negative share price performance after the offer than firms with no apparent earnings management.[38] Finally, US firms subject to SEC investigation for earnings management showed an average share price decline of 9 percent when the earnings management was first announced and continued to have poor share price performance for up to two years.[39]

These findings imply that analysts who are able to identify firms with misleading accounting are able to create value for investors. The findings also indicate that the stock market ultimately sees through earnings management. For all of these cases, earnings management is eventually uncovered and the share price responds negatively to evidence that firms have inflated prior earnings through misleading accounting.

SUMMARY

In summary, accounting analysis is an important step in the process of analyzing corporate financial reports. The purpose of accounting analysis is to evaluate the degree to which a firm's accounting captures the underlying business reality. Sound accounting analysis improves the reliability of conclusions from financial analysis, the next step in financial statement analysis.

There are six key steps in accounting analysis. The analyst begins by identifying the key accounting policies and estimates, given the firm's industry and its business strategy. The second step is to evaluate the degree of flexibility available to managers, given the accounting rules and conventions. Next, the analyst has to evaluate how managers exercise their accounting flexibility and the likely motivations behind managers' accounting strategy. The fourth step involves assessing the depth and quality of a firm's disclosures. The analyst should next identify any red flags needing further investigation. The final accounting analysis step is to restate accounting numbers to remove any noise and bias introduced by the accounting rules and management decisions.

The next chapter discusses how to implement these concepts and shows how to make some of the most common types of adjustments.

CORE CONCEPTS

Accounting analysis Evaluation of the potential accounting flexibility that management has and the actual accounting choices that it makes, focusing on the firm's key accounting policies. The accounting analysis consists of the following six steps:

1 Identification of the firm's key accounting policies.

2 Assessment of management's accounting flexibility.

3 Evaluation of management's reporting strategy.

4 Evaluation of the quality of management's disclosures.

5 Identification of potential red flags or indicators of questionable accounting quality.

6 Correction of accounting distortions.

Accrual accounting A system of accounting under which current net profit is derived from past and current as well as expected future cash flows arising from business transactions completed in the current period.

Assets Economic resources owned by a firm that are (a) likely to produce future economic benefits and (b) measurable with a reasonable degree of uncertainty. Examples of economic resources are inventories and property, plan and equipment.

Expenses Economic resources (e.g., finished goods inventories) used up in a time period.

Institutional framework for financial reporting Institutions that govern public corporations' financial reporting. These institutions include:

a Accounting standards set by public or private sector accounting standard-setting bodies, which limit management's accounting flexibility. In the EU, public corporations report under International Financial Reporting Standards, set by the International Accounting Standards Board.

b Mandatory external auditing of the financial statements by public accountants. In the EU, the Eight Company Law Directive has set minimum standards for external audits.

c Legal liability of management for misleading disclosures. The Transparency Directive requires that each EU Member State has a statutory civil liability regime.

d Public enforcement of accounting standards. Enforcement activities of individual European public enforcement bodies are coordinated by the Committee of European Securities Regulators.

Liabilities Economic obligations of a firm arising from benefits received in the past that (a) are required to be met with a reasonable degree of certainty and (b) whose timing is reasonably well defined. Examples of economic obligations are bank loans and product warranties.

Revenues Economic resources (e.g., cash and receivables) earned during a time period.

Sources of noise and bias in accounting data Three potential sources of noise and bias in accounting data are:

a Rigid accounting standards.

b Management's forecast errors.

c Management's reporting strategy (accounting choices).

QUESTIONS, EXERCISES AND PROBLEMS

1 A finance student states, "I don't understand why anyone pays any attention to accounting earnings numbers, given that a "clean" number like cash from operations is readily available." Do you agree? Why or why not?

2 Fred argues, "The standards that I like most are the ones that eliminate all management discretion in reporting – that way I get uniform numbers across all companies and don't have to worry about doing accounting analysis." Do you agree? Why or why not?

3 Bill Simon says, "We should get rid of the IASB, IFRS, and EU Company Law Directives, since free market forces will make sure that companies report reliable information." Do you agree? Why or why not?

4 Many firms recognize revenues at the point of shipment. This provides an incentive to accelerate revenues by shipping goods at the end of the quarter. Consider two companies, one of which ships its product evenly throughout the quarter, and the second of which ships all its products in the last two weeks of the quarter. Each company's customers pay 30 days after receiving shipment. Using accounting ratios, how can you distinguish these companies?

5 a If management reports truthfully, what economic events are likely to prompt the following accounting changes?

   ■ Increase in the estimated life of depreciable assets.

   ■ Decrease in the allowance for doubtful accounts as a percentage of gross trade receivables.

   ■ Recognition of revenues at the point of delivery rather than at the point cash is received.

   ■ Capitalization of a higher proportion of research expenditures costs.

   b What features of accounting, if any, would make it costly for dishonest managers to make the same changes without any corresponding economic changes?

6 The conservatism (or prudence) principle arises because of concerns about management's incentives to overstate the firm's performance. Joe Banks argues, "We could get rid of conservatism and make accounting numbers more useful if we delegated financial reporting to independent auditors rather than to corporate managers." Do you agree? Why or why not?

7 A fund manager states, "I refuse to buy any company that makes a voluntary accounting change, since it's certainly a case of management trying to hide bad news." Can you think of any alternative interpretation?

Problem 1 Fair value accounting for financial instruments

One of the key accounting policies of banks and other financial institutions is how they recognize (changes in) the fair value of the securities that they hold in the balance sheet and income statement. The international rules on the recognition and measurement of financial instruments require a firm to recognize financial securities (other than loans and receivables) at their fair values if the firm does not intend to hold these assets to their maturities (labeled held-for-trading instruments). Changes in the securities' fair values must be recognized as gains or losses in the income statement. Financial securities that a firm initially intended to hold to their maturities but that are currently available for sale must also be recognized at their fair values. However, changes in the fair value of these available-for-sale securities are temporarily recorded in equity and recognized in the income statement once the securities get sold. If the firm intends to hold the financial instruments to their maturities (held-to-maturity instruments), they must be recognized at (amortized) historical cost.

How should the fair values of financial instruments be determined? The rules require that they be derived from quoted market prices if an active market for the assets exists (typically referred to as marking to market). If quoted market prices are not available, firms can use their own valuation technique to determine the assets' fair values (referred to as marking to model); however, their valuation should be based on assumptions that outside market participants would reasonably make, not management's own assumptions.

Complications may arise if quoted market prices are available but, at least in the eyes of some, unreliable. For example, the credit crisis of 2008 led to a substantial increase in the uncertainty about the quality and value of asset-backed securities, such as mortgage-backed loans. As a result of the heightened uncertainty, investors fled asset-backed securities and the market for such securities became highly illiquid. Observable prices from infrequent transactions remained available; however, managers of financial institutions owning asset-backed securities claimed that these prices did not properly reflect the values of the securities if one had the option to hold on to the securities until the crisis was over or the securities matured. In response to these claims, the IASB provided additional guidance and reemphasized that in declining, illiquid markets, managers had the option to use their own valuations to determine fair values. Consequently, many financial institutions choose to move away from marking to market towards adjusting market prices or marking to model.

Prior to the credit market crisis of 2008, an important detail of the international accounting rules for financial instruments was that instruments could not be reclassified between categories (with the exception, of course, of reclassifications from held-to-maturity to available-for-sale). The crisis, however, led some bank managers to change their minds about which securities were actually held for trading purposes and which securities were better held to their maturities. Under great political pressure of the EU the IASB amended this rule in October 2008.[40] The amendment allowed firms to reclassify securities out of the held-for-trading category in rare circumstances, such as those created by the crisis, if management decided not to sell the securities in the foreseeable future. A survey carried out by the CESR revealed that 48 out of 100 European financial institutions reclassified one or more financial instruments in their financial statements for the third quarter of 2008.

1   Discuss how the changes in the reclassification rules affect the balance between noise introduced in accounting data by rigidity in accounting rules and bias introduced in accounting data by managers' systematic accounting choices.

2   The move from marking to market to marking to model during the credit crisis increased managers' accounting flexibility. Managers of financial institutions may have incentives to bias their valuations of financial instruments. Summarize the main incentives that may affect these managers' accounting choices.

3   Some politicians argued that fair value accounting needed to be suspended and replaced by historical cost accounting. What is the risk of allowing financial institutions to report their financial securities such as asset-backed securities at historical cost?

Problem 2 *Key accounting policies*

Consider the following companies.

Juventus F.C. S.p.A. is an Italian publicly listed football club. The club's primary sources of revenue are:

a   Season and single ticket sales.

b   Television, radio and media rights.

c   Sponsorship and advertising contracts.

d   The disposal of players' registration rights.

Players' registration rights are recognized on the balance sheet at cost and amortized over the players' contract terms. The club leases its stadium Stadio Delle Alpi under an operating lease arrangement; however, it has started the construction of a new stadium, which is cofinanced by an outside sponsor in exchange of exclusive naming rights.

Spyker Cars N.V. is a Netherlands-based publicly listed designer and manufacturer of exclusive sports cars. In 2008, the company's revenues amounted to €7,852 thousand, of which €5,772 thousand was related to car sales and €1,752 thousand was income from GT racing activities. In that year, Spyker produced 30 new cars and sold 37 cars. It held 42 cars in stock at the end of the year. Further, the company spent close to €6 million on development and €378,000 on research. Spyker had been loss-making since its initial public offering in 2004. At the end of 2008, the car manufacturer had €76 in tax-deductible carry forward losses.

J Sainsbury plc is a UK-based publicly listed retailer that operates 502 supermarkets and 290 convenience stores and has an estimated 17 percent market share in the UK During the period 2004–2008, the company's net profit margins ranged from 1.5 to 3.7 percent. At the end of March 2008, the net book value of Sainsbury's land and buildings was £5.9 billion. A part of the company's supermarket properties was pledged as security for long-term borrowings. In 2008 Sainsbury had 151,000 employees (98,600 full-time equivalents); many of them participated in one of the retailer's defined-benefit pension plans.

1   Identify the key accounting policies for each of these companies.

2   What are these companies' primary areas of accounting flexibility? (Focus on the key accounting policies.)

Problem 3 Euro Disney and the first five steps of accounting analysis

Euro Disney S.C.A. is a holding company, holding 82 percent of the shares of Euro Disney Associés S.C.A., which operates, amongst others, the Disneyland Park, Disneyland Hotel, and Davy Crockett Ranch in Paris and holds 99.99 percent of the shares of EDL Hotels S.C.A. EDL Hotels operates all of the Disney Hotels in Paris (except for the Disneyland Hotel and Davy Crockett Ranch).

Euro Disney Associés leases the Disneyland Park (including land) under a finance lease from Euro Disneyland S.N.C., which is owned by (1) a syndicate of banks and financial institutions (83 percent participation) and (2) a wholly-owned subsidiary of US-based The Walt Disney Company (17 percent participation). EDL Hotels S.C.A. rents land to a group of six special-purpose financing companies, who, in turn, own the hotels on the land and lease these hotels back to EDL Hotels. All special-purpose financing companies are fully consolidated in Euro Disney's financial statements, despite the absence of ownership in some cases. This is because, as the company reports in its 2008 annual report, "the substance of the relationship is between the group and these financing companies is such that they are effectively controlled by the group." In fact, all special-purpose financing companies are managed by management companies that are directly or indirectly owned by The Walt Disney Company or Euro Disney Associés.

Euro Disney's primary sources of revenue are its two theme parks (entrance fees, merchandise, food and beverage, special events), its seven hotels and Disney Village (room rental, merchandise, food and beverage, dinner shows, convention revenues). Disney

Village offers themed dining, entertainment and shopping facilities. The company has, on average, 13,500 employees annually. The company and its subsidiaries are considered as one French economic and labor unit, regulated by the National Collective Bargaining Agreement signed in 2001 with six out of seven trade union represented in the unit. The majority of the company's employees (about 90 percent) have a permanent contract. To cope with the seasonal nature of the business, Euro Disney is able to move employees from its theme parks to its hotels and vice versa. Approximately 5 percent of total person-nel expenses consist of training costs.

In 2005, after a period of poor performance, Euro Disney began renegotiations with its lenders and The Walt Disney Company, obtained waivers for certain debt covenants and agreed to restructure its financial obligations. As part of the restructuring, the company would issue new share capital, obtain the option to defer certain payments to The Walt Disney Company, and receive authorization for a new investment plan. Further, the company would change its organizational structure to the one described above. Since the restructur-ing Euro Disney's debt agreements include debt covenants requiring the company to main-tain minimum ratios of adjusted operating income (before depreciation and amortization) to total debt service obligations. The adjusted operating income figure is also used to deter-mine the amount of interest on the company's Walt Disney Studio Park loans and the roy-alties and management fees payable to The Walt Disney Company. In particular, if actual performance is less than the contractually agreed benchmark, the company can defer the payments of interest, royalties and management fees. The debt covenants also limit the amount of new debt capital that Euro Disney can attract to €50 million.

Euro Disney S.C.A. is publicly listed on the Euronext Paris stock exchange. By the end of 2008, 39.8 percent of its shares were owned by The Walt Disney Company, 10 percent were owned by Prince Alwaleed and 50.2 percent were in the hands of dispersed shareholders. The company has a Supervisory Board with nine independent members, two of which are representatives of The Walt Disney Company, an audit committee and a nominations committee. Euro Disney S.C.A. as well as both operating companies of Euro Disney S.C.A., i.e., Euro Disney Associés and Euro Disney Hotels, are managed by management company Euro Disney S.A.S. (referred to as the *Gérant*), an indirect wholly-owned subsidiary of The Walt Disney Company. At the end of fiscal year 2008, the CEO of the *Gérant* (Euro Disney S.A.S.) was Philippe Gas, who replaced Karl Holz on September 1, 2008. For the management services provided to the holding and operat-ing companies, the *Gérant* receives management fees. The aggregate compensation for the seven independent Supervisory Board members was €286,421 in 2008. The two rep-resentative of The Walt Disney Company received an annual fixed salary, a bonus, restricted stocks, and stock options from The Walt Disney Company. Philippe Gas' employment contract promised him:

1   An annual salary of €368,650.

2   A discretionary annual bonus based on individual performance relative to the object-ives of the company and The Walt Disney Company Parks & Resorts operating segment.

3   Discretionary grants of the company's stock options, The Walt Disney Company's stock options, and The Walt Disney Company's restricted stock.

4   The Use of a company car.

In addition to Philippe Gas, the Executive Committee of the *Gérant* consisted of five senior vice presidents and six vice presidents.

Euro Disney reported net losses in 2006 and 2007 and a small profit (€1.7 million) in 2008. Whereas the company's total revenues increased by 9 percent to €1,330 million in 2008, direct operating costs, marketing and sales expenses, and general and administrative expenses increased by 6, 2.8 and 10.3 percent, respectively. Euro Disney's operating cash flows amounted to €151.9, €191.1 and €178.2 million in 2006, 2007 and 2008, respectively. In all three years, the cash flows used in investing activities were less than the operating cash flows. In 2008 Euro Disney used part of the surplus of operating over investment cash flows to repay some of its borrowings, thereby reducing the non-current debt to equity ratio from 5.7 to 5.6. The company's trade receivables to sales ratio increased from 7.1 percent in 2007 to 7.5 percent in 2008. Liabilities for deferred revenues as a percent of sales decreased from 10.1 percent in 2007 to 9.0 percent in 2008. The allowance for uncollectible receivables increased from 1.6 percent (of gross trade receivables) in 2007 to 2.2 percent in 2008; the allowance for inventories obsolescence decreased from 8.2 percent (of gross inventories) in 2007 to 6.7 percent in 2008. During fiscal year 2008, Euro Disney did not make any voluntary change in its accounting methods and did not recognize any asset write-offs. Related party transactions consisted primarily of the payment of royalties and management fees to the *Gérant* as well as payments to the *Gérant* to reimburse the direct and indirect costs of the technical and administrative services provided. Euro Disney's tax expense was zero in 2006, 2007 and 2008. At the end of fiscal year 2008, the company's unused tax loss carry forwards amounted to €1.3 billion and could be carried forward indefinitely. The company's 2008 financial statements received an unqualified audit opinion.

At the end of 2008, Euro Disney's share price was €3.60. The company's average share return since December 31, 2005 had been −31 percent (annually).

1   Identify the key accounting policies (step 1) and primary areas of accounting flexibility (step 2) for Euro Disney.

2   What incentives may influence management's reporting strategy (step 3)?

3   What disclosures would you consider an essential part of the company's annual report, given its key success factors and key accounting policies (step 4)?

4   What potential red flags can you identify (step 5)?

NOTES

1. Accounting analysis is sometimes also called quality of earnings analysis. We prefer to use the term accounting analysis because we are discussing a broader concept than merely a firm's earnings quality.

2. Firms are allowed to combine the income statement, which describes the composition of net profit, and the statement of comprehensive income, which describes net profit and all other non-owner changes in equity, into one statement. Further, since 2009 the IFRSs refer to the balance sheet as a "statement of financial position," to the cash flow statement as a "statement of cash flows," and to the statement of comprehensive income as a "statement of total recognized income and expense." However, firms are free to choose other titles. Throughout this book we will refer to these statements as the balance sheet, the cash flow statement, and the statement of comprehensive income, which is how they traditionally have been – and still are – titled by most firms.

3. At the time of writing there is no globally accepted name for management's narrative discussion of the firm's performance, nor has the IASB set detailed standards on what firms should report in this section. Throughout this book we will refer to this section as the Management Report section and assume that it typically contains at least a Letter to the Shareholders and a review of the firm's financial performance during the fiscal year and its financial position at the end of the year.

4. These definitions paraphrase those of the IASB, "Framework for the Preparation and Presentation of Financial Statements" (also referred to as the "Conceptual Framework"). Our intent is to present the definitions at a conceptual, not technical, level. For more complete discussion of these and related concepts, see the IASB's Conceptual Framework.

5. Strictly speaking, the comprehensive net income of a firm also includes gains and losses from increases and decreases in equity from nonoperating activities or exceptional items.

6. The EU has given its individual member states the option to permit or require private companies to use IFRS for the preparation of their single entity and/or consolidated financial statements. Similarly, member states may permit or require public companies to prepare their single entity financial statements in accordance with IFRS.

7. See "Study Pursuant to Section 108(d) of the Sarbanes-Oxley Act of 2002 on the Adoption by the United States Financial Reporting System of a Principles-Based Accounting System" by the US Securities and Exchange Commission (2003) and "FASB Response to SEC Study on the Adoption of a Principles-Based Accounting System" by the Financial Accounting Standards Board (2004).

8. For a description of international differences in managers' legal liability for the information that they provide in prospectuses, see R. La Porta, F. Lopez-de-Silanes, and A. Shleifer, "What Works in Securities Laws?" *The Journal of Finance* 61 (2006): 1–32.

9. See, for example, the UK HM Treasury's report (July 2008) on the "Extension of the Statutory Regime for Issuer Liability," describing motivations for making managers subject to civil liability for fraudulent misstatements only.

10. For a description of how European agencies enforced IFRS in 2006 see the results of a CESR survey described in "CESR's review of the implementation and enforcement of IFRS in the EU" (November 2007).

11. See H.E. Jackson and M.J. Roe, "Public and Private Enforcement of Securities Laws: Resource-Based Evidence," Working Paper (2009).

12. Thus, although accrual accounting is theoretically superior to cash accounting in measuring a firm's periodic performance, the distortions it introduces can make accounting data less valuable to users. If these distortions are large enough, current cash flows may measure a firm's periodic performance better than accounting profits. The relative usefulness of cash flows and accounting profits in measuring performance, therefore, varies from firm to firm. For empirical evidence on this issue, see P. Dechow, "Accounting Earnings and Cash Flows as Measures of Firm Performance: The Role of Accounting Accruals," *Journal of Accounting and Economics* 18 (July 1994): 3–42, and A. Charitou, C. Clubb, and A. Andreou, "The Effect of Earnings Permanence, Growth and Firm Size on the Usefulness of Cash Flows and Earnings in Explaining Security Returns: Empirical Evidence for the UK," *Journal of Business Finance and Accounting* 28 (June/July 2001): 563–594.

13. For example, Abraham Briloff wrote a series of accounting analyses of public companies in *Barron's* over several years. On average, the share prices of the analyzed companies changed by about 8 percent on the day these articles were published, indicating the potential value of performing such analysis. For a more complete discussion of this evidence, see G. Foster, "Briloff and the Capital Market," *Journal of Accounting Research* 17 (Spring 1979): 262–274.

14. For a complete discussion of these motivations, see *Positive Accounting Theory*, by R. Watts and J. Zimmerman (Englewood Cliffs, NJ: Prentice-Hall, 1986). A summary of this research is provided by T. Fields, T. Lys and L. Vincent in "Empirical Research on Accounting Choice," *Journal of Accounting and Economics* 31 (September 2001): 255–307.

15. The most convincing evidence supporting the covenant hypothesis is reported in a study of the accounting decisions by firms in financial distress: A. Sweeney, "Debt-Covenant Violations and Managers' Accounting Responses," *Journal of Accounting and Economics* 17 (May 1994): 281–308.

16. Studies that examine the bonus hypothesis generally report evidence supporting the view that managers' accounting decisions are influenced by compensation considerations. See, for example, P. Healy, "The Effect of Bonus Schemes on Accounting Decisions," *Journal of Accounting and Economics* 7 (April 1985): 85–107; R. Holthausen, D. Larcker and R. Sloan, "Annual Bonus Schemes and the Manipulation of Earnings," *Journal of Accounting and Economics* 19 (February 1995): 29–74; and F. Guidry, A. Leone and S. Rock, "Earnings-Based Bonus Plans and Earnings Management by Business Unit Managers," *Journal of Accounting and Economics* 26 (January 1999): 113–142.

17. For empirical evidence that CEOs of firms with scheduled awards make opportunistic voluntary disclosures to maximize stock award compensation, see D. Aboody and R. Kasznik, "CEO Stock Option Awards and the Timing of Corporate Voluntary Disclosures," *Journal of Accounting and Economics* 29 (February 2000): 73–100.

18. L. DeAngelo, "Managerial Competition, Information Costs, and Corporate Governance: The Use of Accounting Performance Measures in Proxy Contests," *Journal of Accounting and Economics* 10 (January 1988): 3–36 and M. Erickson and S. Wang, "Earnings Management by Acquiring Firms in Stock for Stock Mergers," *Journal of Accounting and Economics* 27 (1999): 149–176.

19. The trade-off between taxes and financial reporting in the context of managers' accounting decisions is discussed in detail in *Taxes and Business Strategy* by M. Scholes and M. Wolfson (Englewood Cliffs, NJ: Prentice-Hall, 1992). Many empirical studies have examined firms' LIFO/FIFO choices.

20. Several researchers have documented that firms affected by such situations have a motivation to influence regulators' perceptions through accounting decisions. For example, J. Jones documents that firms seeking import protections make profit-decreasing accounting decisions in "Earnings Management During Import Relief Investigations," *Journal of Accounting Research* 29, No. 2 (Autumn 1991): 193–228. Similarly, W. Beekes finds that UK water and electricity companies make profit-decreasing accounting choices in years of regulatory price reviews in "Earnings Management in Response to Regulatory Price Review. A Case Study of the Political Cost Hypothesis in the Water and Electricity Sectors in England and Wales," Working paper, Lancaster University, 2003. A number of studies find that banks that are close to minimum capital requirements overstate loan loss provisions, understate loan write-offs, and recognize abnormal realized gains on securities portfolios (see S. Moyer, "Capital Adequacy Ratio Regulations and Accounting Choices in Commercial Banks," *Journal of Accounting and Economics* 12 (1990): 123–154; M. Scholes, G. P. Wilson, and M. Wolfson, "Tax Planning, Regulatory Capital Planning, and Financial Reporting Strategy for Commercial Banks," *Review of Financial Studies* 3 (1990): 625–650; A. Beatty, S. Chamberlain, and J. Magliolo, "Managing Financial Reports of Commercial Banks: The Influence of Taxes, Regulatory Capital and Earnings," *Journal of Accounting Research* 33, No. 2 (1995): 231–261; and J. Collins, D. Shackelford, and J. Wahlen, "Bank Differences in the Coordination of Regulatory Capital, Earnings and Taxes," *Journal of Accounting Research* 33, No. 2 (Autumn 1995): 263–291). Finally, Petroni finds that financially weak property-casualty insurers that risk regulatory attention understate claim loss reserves: K. Petroni, "Optimistic Reporting in the Property Casualty Insurance Industry," *Journal of Accounting and Economics* 15 (December 1992): 485–508.

21. P. Healy and K. Palepu, "The Effect of Firms' Financial Disclosure Strategies on Stock Prices," *Accounting Horizons* 7 (March 1993): 1–11. For a summary of the empirical evidence, see P. Healy and J. Wahlen, "A Review of the Earnings Management Literature and Its Implications for Standard Setting," *Accounting Horizons* 13 (December 1999): 365–384.

22. R. Bowen, L. DuCharme, and D. Shores, "Stakeholders' Implicit Claims and Accounting Method Choice," *Journal of Accounting and Economics* 20 (December 1995): 255–295, argue that, based on theory and anecdotal evidence, managers choose long-run income-increasing accounting methods as a result of ongoing implicit claims between a firm and its customers, suppliers, employees, and short-term creditors.

23. Financial analysts pay close attention to managers' disclosure strategies; Standard and Poor's publishes scores that rate the disclosure of companies from around the world. For a discussion of these ratings, see, for example, T. Khanna, K. Palepu, and S. Srinivasan, "Disclosure Practices of Foreign Companies Interacting with US Markets," *Journal of Accounting Research* 42 (May 2004): 475–508.

24. See P. Healy and K. Palepu, "The Fall of Enron," *Journal of Economic Perspectives* 17, No. 2 (Spring 2003): 3–26.

25. For detailed analyses of companies that made such changes, see R. Schattke and R. Vergoossen, "Barriers to Interpretation: A Case Study of Philips Electronics NV," *Accounting and Business Research* 27 (1996): 72–84, and K. Palepu, "Anatomy of an Accounting Change," in *Accounting and Management: Field Study Perspectives*, edited by W. Bruns, Jr. and R. Kaplan (Boston: Harvard Business School Press, 1987).

26. Examples of this type of behavior are documented by J. Hand in his study, "Did Firms Undertake Debt-Equity Swaps for an Accounting Paper Profit or True Financial Gain?" *The Accounting Review* 64 (October 1989): 587–623, and by E. Black, K. Sellers, and T. Manley in "Earnings Management Using Asset Sales: An International Study of Countries Allowing Noncurrent Asset Revaluation," *Journal of Business Finance and Accounting* 25 (November/December 1998): 1287–1317.

27. For an empirical analysis of inventory build-ups, see V. Bernard and J. Noel, "Do Inventory Disclosures Predict Sales and Earnings?" *Journal of Accounting, Auditing, and Finance* (Fall 1991).

28. For research on accounting and economic incentives in the formation of R&D partnerships, see A. Beatty, P. Berger, and J. Magliolo, "Motives for Forming Research and Development Financing Organizations," *Journal of Accounting and Economics* 19 (April 1995): 411–442. An overview of Enron's use of special purpose entities to manage earnings and window-dress its balance is provided by P. Healy and K. Palepu, "The Fall of Enron," *Journal of Economic Perspectives* 17, No. 2 (Spring 2003): 3–26.

29. For an empirical examination of asset write-offs, see J. Elliott and W. Shaw, "Write-offs as Accounting Procedures to Manage Perceptions," *Journal of Accounting Research* 26 (1988): 91–119.

30. R. Mendenhall and W. Nichols report evidence consistent with managers taking advantage of their discretion to postpone reporting bad news until the year-end. See R. Mendenhall and W. Nichols, "Bad News and Differential Market Reactions to Announcements of Earlier-Quarter versus Fourth-Quarter Earnings," *Journal of Accounting Research*, Supplement (1988): 63–86.

31. K. Peasnell, P. Pope, and S. Young report evidence that independent outside directors prevent earnings management. See K. Peasnell, P. Pope, and S. Young, "Board Monitoring and Earnings Management: Do Outside Directors Influence Abnormal Accruals?," *Journal of Business Finance and Accounting* 32 (September 2005): 1311–1346.

32. The role of insider transactions in the collapse of Enron are discussed by P. Healy and K. Palepu, "The Fall of Enron," *Journal of Economic Perspectives* 17, No. 2 (Spring 2003): 3–26.

33. This type of analysis is presented in the context of provisions for bad debts by M. McNichols and P. Wilson in their study, "Evidence of Earnings Management From the Provisions for Bad Debts," *Journal of Accounting Research,* Supplement (1988): 1–31.

34. This point has been made by several accounting researchers. For a summary of research on earnings management, see K. Schipper, "Earnings Management," *Accounting Horizons* (December 1989): 91–102.

35. See H. Daske, L. Hail, C. Leuz, and R. Verdi, "Mandatory IFRS Reporting around the World: Early Evidence on the Economic Consequences," *Journal of Accounting Research* 46 (2008): 1085–1142.

36. See J. Chang, "The Decline in Value Relevance of Earnings and Book Values," unpublished dissertation, Harvard University, 1998. Evidence is also reported by J. Francis and K. Schipper, "Have Financial Statements Lost Their Relevance?," *Journal of Accounting Research* 37, No. 2 (Autumn 1999): 319–352; and W. E. Collins, E. Maydew, and I. Weiss, "Changes in the Value-Relevance of Earnings and Book Value over the Past Forty Years," *Journal of Accounting and Economics* 24 (1997): 39–67.

37. See G. Foster, "Briloff and the Capital Market," *Journal of Accounting Research* 17, No. 1 (Spring 1979): 262–274.

38. See S. H. Teoh, I. Welch, and T. J. Wong, "Earnings Management and the Long-Run Market Performance of Initial Public Offerings," *Journal of Finance* 53 (December 1998a): 1935–1974; S. H. Teoh, I. Welch and T. J. Wong, "Earnings Management and the Post-Issue Underperformance of Seasoned Equity Offerings," *Journal of Financial Economics* 50 (October 1998): 63–99; and S. Teoh, T. Wong, and G. Rao, "Are Accruals During Initial Public Offerings Opportunistic?," *Review of Accounting Studies* 3, No. 1–2 (1998): 175–208.

39. See P. Dechow, R. Sloan, and A. Sweeney, "Causes and Consequences of Earnings Manipulation: An Analysis of Firms Subject to Enforcement Actions by the SEC," *Contemporary Accounting Research* 13, No. 1 (1996): 1–36, and M. D. Beneish, "Detecting GAAP Violation: Implications for Assessing Earnings Management among Firms with Extreme Financial Performance," *Journal of Accounting and Public Policy* 16 (1997): 271–309.

40. For an illustration of the circumstances surrounding the IASB's decision to amend the reclassification rules, see P. André, A. Cazavan-Jeny, W. Dick, C. Richard and P. Walton, "Fair Value Accounting and the Banking Crisis in 2008: Shooting the Messenger," *Accounting in Europe* 6 (2009): 3–24.

Fiat Group's first-time adoption of IFRS

In June 2002, the Council of the European Union adopted new regulations that required companies listed in the EU to prepare their consolidated financial statements in accordance with International Financial Reporting Standards (IFRS). According to the new rules, companies must apply IFRS no later than in the fiscal year starting in 2005. Member states of the EU could, however, allow companies that were listed outside the EU and prepared their statements in accordance with U.S. Generally Accepted Accounting Principles (U.S. GAAP) to apply IFRS in either 2006 or 2007.

The decision of the European Council also affected Italy-based car manufacturer Fiat, which had its shares traded on the Italian Stock Exchange and reported its financial statements in accordance with Italian accounting standards (henceforth Italian GAAP). The Fiat Group decided not to apply IFRS earlier than required and reported its first IFRS-based annual report in fiscal year 2005.

Business description and financial performance[1]

In 2005 the Italy-based Fiat Group generated its revenues primarily from the production and sales of passenger vehicles, tractors, agricultural equipment, and light commercial vehicles. Its portfolio of passenger car brands included large-volume brands such as Fiat, Alfa Romeo, and Lancia (generating €19.5 billion in revenues), as well as luxury, high-margin brands such as Maserati and Ferrari (generating €1.8 billion in revenues). In addition to these activities, the Fiat Group produced components and production systems, provided administrative and financial services to its group companies, published a daily newspaper (*La Stampa*), and sold advertising space for multimedia customers. Total revenues amounted to €46.5 billion in 2005. The company's pretax profit was €1 billion.

The Fiat Group had its ordinary shares traded on the Italian Stock Exchange and had American Depository Receipts (ADRs) traded on the New York Stock Exchange. About one quarter of the group's ordinary shares were widely held, 45 percent were in the hands of banks and other institutional investors, and 30 percent were held by Fiat's primary shareholder, IFIL investments, which was controlled by the Agnelli family. Through IFIL Investments and several other investment vehicles, the Agnelli family, who were the founders of Fiat, held a substantial voting block in the group. Fiat Group's board of directors consisted of three executive directors and 12 non-executive directors, of which eight were considered "independent" from the company and its major shareholder. The company's chairman of the board of directors was Luca Cordero di Montezemolo, former protégé of Fiat's long-time boss Gianni Agnelli, chief executive officer (CEO) of Fiat's subsidiary Ferrari, and chairman of Italy's employers association Confindustria. Vice-chairman was John Elkann, who was a member of the Agnelli family, and CEO was Sergio Marchionne.

The first half of the 2000s had not been a successful period for the Fiat Group. Italian GAAP-based revenues had been declining from €57.5 billion in 2000 to €46.7 billion in 2004. Possible causes for the group's underperformance were the economic slowdown in Europe,

Professor Erik Peek prepared this case. The case is intended solely as the basis for class discussion and is not intended to serve as an endorsement, source of primary data, or illustration of effective or ineffective management.

[1]This section is primarily based on the Fiat Group's 2005 Annual Report and Report on Corporate Governance.

the group's continued diversification into unrelated industries, and its lack of innovation and development of new car models. In fiscal 2005, however, the company reported a slight increase in (IFRS-based) revenues of 2 percent and its first net profit since 2000, inducing management to designate the year 2005 as a "turning point" for Fiat. In spring 2006, analysts expected the Fiat Group's revenues to grow from €46.5 billion in 2005 to approximately €50.5 billion in 2006 and €52.2 billion in 2007. They also expected the Fiat Group to remain profitable in the next two years. Estimated pretax profits for 2006 and 2007 were €1.2 billion and €1.7 billion, respectively.[2] **Exhibit 1** shows the Fiat Group's stock price and accounting performance during the first half of the 2000s as well as its debt ratings in January 2006. In the first half of 2006 the Fiat Group made two Eurobond issues, each for €1 billion.

First-time adoption of IFRS

The general rule

In June 2003, the International Accounting Standards Board (IASB) issued IFRS 1 on firms' first-time adoption of IFRS. The objective of this new standard was to ensure that all firms preparing their financial statements for the first time in accordance with the IFRSs, (1) execute the transition to new reporting principles in a consistent manner and (2) provide sufficient additional disclosures to help the users of their statements understand the effects of the transition. IFRS 1 requires that a first-time adopter applies *retrospectively* the IFRSs that are *effective at the reporting date* of its first IFRS-based statements. Retrospective application of current IFRSs means that the firm recognizes all its assets and liabilities not only as if it has always applied IFRS but also as if the current IFRS version has always been effective and prior IFRS versions have never existed.[3] This illustrates that IFRS 1 aimed especially to improve comparability across first-time adopters, as opposed to improving comparability between first-time adopters and current users of IFRS, whose assets and liabilities are often affected by prior IFRS versions.

As well as the *reporting date* of the first IFRS statements, the *transition date* is important for the application of IFRS 1. The transition date is the beginning of the earliest fiscal year for which the first-time adopter prepares full IFRS-based comparative statements. Every first-time adopter is required to prepare an opening balance sheet at the transition date, although it is not required to publicly disclose this opening balance sheet. The accounting policies that a first-time adopter must use to prepare its opening balance sheet are the same policies that it uses to prepare its first IFRS-based financial statements (including the comparative statements).

Retrospective application of the IFRSs does not imply that on the transition date the first-time adopter can revise the estimates that it made for the same date under previous reporting standards. For example, if a first-time adopter receives information after the transition date that suggests that the economic life of one of its assets is three years instead of the previously assumed two years, the IFRS-based opening balance sheet on the transition date must reflect the "old" economic life assumption of two years. Hence, IFRS 1 explicitly forbids the first-time adopter modifying its prior financial statements with hindsight.

Exemptions

Retrospective application of current IFRSs may carry costs that exceed the benefits of the information that it produces. The IASB acknowledged the importance of a cost–benefit trade-off and included several exemptions from full retrospective application:

[2]Source: Reuters consensus estimates.

[3]IFRS 1 allows first-time adopters to apply new IFRSs that will become effective on a date after the reporting date but that permit earlier application.

- The international standard on business combinations (IFRS 3) requires firms to recognize their acquisitions of other firms using purchase accounting. Under purchase accounting, a firm separately discloses on its balance sheet the fair value of the acquired assets as well as the excess of the purchase price over this amount (labeled goodwill). Under a few other accounting regimes, such as in the UK, firms can – or could – record some of their acquisitions using pooling accounting, whereby the acquirer recorded only the historical cost of the acquired assets on its balance sheet. Retrospective application would require a firm to restate all past business combinations that it recorded using the pooling method. IFRS 1 allows first-time adopters not to restate business combinations that occurred prior to the transition date. If a firm nevertheless chooses to restate a business combination that occurred on a date prior to the transition date, it must also restate all other business combinations that occurred after this particular date.

- When a firm records its property, plant and equipment, intangible assets, and investment property at their (depreciated) historical cost, IFRS 1 allows it to assume that these assets' fair values at the transition date are the assets' historical cost. IFRS 1 refers to this assumed value as the assets' "deemed cost." Alternatively, if the firm has revalued any of these assets prior to the adoption of IFRS and the revalued amount is broadly comparable to fair value under IFRS, it can use the revalued amount as deemed cost.

- A first-time adopter may choose to immediately recognize (into equity) the cumulative actuarial gains and losses on all its pension plans. By doing so, the first-time adopter avoids splitting the cumulative gains and losses that have arisen since the inception of the plans into a recognized and an unrecognized portion, which may be a difficult exercise when the firm uses the "corridor approach" for recognizing actuarial gains and losses.[4]

- A firm that consolidates the translated values of subsidiaries' foreign currency-denominated assets on its balance sheet, recognizes the cumulative translation difference, which arises because exchange rates fluctuate over the years, as a separate component in equity. Because separately reporting restated cumulative translation differences generates little additional information, a first-time adopter can choose to add the cumulative translation differences to equity and reset the line item to zero upon adoption.

- International accounting rules require a firm to separate the debt from the equity component of convertible debentures – or similar compound financial instruments – and account for these separately. Consequently, the equity component of compound financial instruments may remain on the firm's balance sheet after the debt component is no longer outstanding. IFRS 1 allows a first-time adopter not to separate the debt and equity components of compound financial instruments if the debt component is no longer outstanding on the transition date.

- A subsidiary that becomes a first-time adopter later than its parent can choose between reporting its assets and liabilities in accordance with IFRS 1 – using its own transition date – or reporting its assets and liabilities in accordance with the reporting principles used by its parent – using its parent's transition date. A parent that becomes a first-time adopter later than its subsidiary must report its subsidiary's assets and liabilities in its

---

[4]Unrecognized actuarial losses arise, for example, when a change in a firm's actuarial assumptions increases its pension obligation, but the resulting change in the obligation is not recognized as a pension expense. Under the "corridor approach," the firm annually compares the cumulative unrecognized actuarial gains and losses to the greater of 10 percent of the pension obligation or 10 percent of the fair value of the pension plan assets. When the cumulative unrecognized actuarial gains and losses exceed their benchmark, the firm amortizes the difference over the remaining working lives of the active employees.

consolidated financial statements as they are reported in the subsidiary's financial statements.

■ International rules require firms to report stock options using the fair value method, under which they record an expense for stock option compensation when the options are issued. The value of the options issued is estimated using a recognized option valuation model and is then expensed over the vesting period. A first-time adopter is, however, not required to use this method for options that it issued prior to November 7, 2002 or that vested before the later of (1) the transition date and (2) January 1, 2005.

This list of optional exemptions is nonexhaustive because every time that the IASB issues a new reporting standard, it may decide to exempt a first-time adopter from retrospective application of the new standard. In addition to these optional exemptions, IFRS 1 includes a few mandatory exemptions. For example, a first-time adopter cannot rerecognize assets and liabilities that it derecognized prior to January 1, 2004, under its previous accounting principles.

Required disclosures

According to IFRS 1, a first-time adopter needs to disclose at least the following information in its first-time IFRS-based financial statements:

■ At least one year of comparative information under IFRSs. The comparative information of firms that adopted IFRS before January 1, 2006, such as the Fiat Group and most other listed firms in the E.U., need not comply with the international standards on financial instruments (IAS 32 and IAS 39) and on insurance contracts (IFRS 4). However, these firms must disclose the nature of the adjustments that would make the comparative information comply with these three reporting standards.

■ A reconciliation of equity under IFRS and equity under previous reporting standards at the transition date and at the end of the latest fiscal year prior to the first-time adoption of IFRS.

■ A reconciliation of the profit or loss under IFRS and under previous reporting standards in the latest fiscal year prior to the first-time adoption of IFRS.

■ The additional disclosures required by the international standard on the impairment of assets (IAS 36) if the firm recognized or reversed an impairment loss in its opening IFRS balance sheet.[5]

■ An explanation of the material adjustments made to the cash flow statement.

■ The aggregate adjustments that the firm made to the carrying amounts of the assets for which it uses the fair values as deemed cost.

The Fiat Group's first-time adoption of IFRS

For the Fiat Group the reporting date of its first IFRS statements was December 31, 2005. The company's transition date was January 1, 2004. Despite not being required to do so, the Fiat Group publicized its opening balance sheet for January 1, 2004 on May 11, 2005 in an appendix to the company's interim report for the first quarter of 2005. In addition to the 2004 opening balance sheet, the first-quarter report included an IFRS-based 2004

Fiat Group's first-time adoption of IFRS

---

[5]These disclosures are, for example, the amount of impairment, with an indication of the income statement item under which the impairment was categorized; the events that gave rise to the impairment (reversal); the nature of the impaired asset or cash generating unit, and the discount rate used to determine the value in use or the basis for determining the net selling price.

closing balance sheet, an IFRS-based 2004 income statement, and a reconciliation of IFRS-based and Italian GAAP-based opening and closing equity for fiscal 2004.

Exhibit 4 reports excerpts from appendix 1 to the 2005 financial statements of the Fiat Group. In this appendix, the group outlined the effects of the transition to IFRS on its balance sheet and income statement.

Questions

1   What are Fiat's key accounting policies? Which of Fiat's key accounting policies are affected by the adoption of IFRS?

2   Summarize the differences between Fiat's key accounting methods under Italian GAAP and those under IFRS. What characterizes the differences between the two sets of methods? From the perspective of a minority investor in the company's shares, which methods provide better information about the economic performance of Fiat?

3   Summarize the main factors that affect management's reporting incentives and strategy in fiscal year 2005. Which factors might reduce management's incentive to fully comply with the IFRSs?

EXHIBIT 1   **Market performance and accounting performance for the Fiat Group**

Fiat's stock price and the MSCI World Automobiles Price Index from January 2000 to December 2005

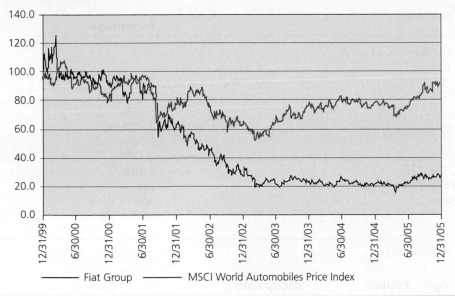

Source: Thomson Datastream.

Fiat's Accounting Performance from 2000 to 2005

(in € millions)	2005 (IFRS)	2004 (Italian GAAP)	2003 (Italian GAAP)	2002 (Italian GAAP)	2001 (Italian GAAP)	2000 (Italian GAAP)
Consolidated revenues	46,544	46,703	47,271	55,649	58,006	57,555
Operating result	2,215	−833	−510	−762	318	855
Group interest in net result	1,331	−1,586	−1,900	−3,948	−455	644
Group interest in stockholders' equity	8,681	5,099	6,793	7,641	12,170	13,320
Return on equity (in %)	15.3%	−26.7%	−26.3%	−39.9%	−3.5%	5.1%
Cash flow from operations	3,716	−358	−1,947	1,053	2,435	N.A.

Source: Annual reports of the Fiat Group.

Fiat's Debt Ratings in January 2006

Rating agency	Rating (long-term senior unsecured)	Date of rating	Rating (short-term senior unsecured)	Date of rating
Standard and Poor's	BB−	8/1/2005	B	8/2/2005
Fitch	BB−	1/20/2006	B	1/20/2006
Moody's	Ba3	1/31/2006		

Source: Reuters.

EXHIBIT 2   Fiat Group's shareholders and directors

On December 31, 2005, the Fiat Group had 1,092,246,316 ordinary shares, 103,292,310 preference shares and 79,912,800 savings shares outstanding and trading on public exchanges. All shares had a par value of €5. Holders of ordinary shares had voting rights but holders of preference shares and savings shares had limited or no voting rights. The ordinary shares were held by the following investors or investor groups:

Investor (group)	Percentage
IFIL Investments S.p.A. (controlled by IFI S.p.A., in turn controlled by Giovanni Agnelli & C. S.A.p.A.)	30.46%
Banca Intesa	6.08%
Unicredito	5.58%
Capitalia	3.80%
BNL	2.73%
Generali	2.38%
Libyan Arab Foreign Inv. Co.	2.28%
International Institutional Investors	approx. 12.5%
Italian Institutional Investors	approx. 10%
Other stockholders	approx. 24%

Source: Annual reports of the Fiat Group.

Director	Age	Position	Background
Luca Cordero di Montezemolo	59	Chairman of the Board[3]	Chairman and CEO of Ferrari S.p.A. since 1991; Director of La Stampa, Pinault-Printemps-Redoute S.A., Tod's, Indesit Company; Chairman of Bologna Fiere; President of Confindustria (the Federation of Italian Industries).
Andrea Agnelli	31	Director	Past positions at Iveco, Piaggio S.p.A., Auchan S.A., Juventus F.C. S.p.A., Ferrari S.p.A. and Philip Morris International Inc.
Roland Berger	68	Director[3]	Chairman of the Supervisory Board of Roland Berger Strategy Consultants, Munich.
Tiberto Brandolini d'Adda	58	Director	Chairman and CEO of Sequana Capital (formerly Worms & Cie); General Partner of Giovanni Agnelli & C.; Vice Chairman and Member of the Executive Committee of IFIL S.p.A.
John Philip Elkann	30	Vice Chairman of the Board[1,3]	Chairman of Itedi S.p.A., IFIL S.p.A. and Giovanni Agnelli & C. S.a.p.a.z.; Member of the Boards of Exor Group SA, IFI S.p.A. and RCS Media Group.
Luca Garavoglia	31	Director[1]	Chairman of Davide Campari-Milano S.p.A., parent company of the Campari Group.
Gian Maria Gros-Pietro	64	Director[1]	President of Federtrasporto (Italian association of transportation companies); Member of the Directive Committee and General Council of Assonime (Italian listed companies association), the Board of the Union of Industrialists of Rome, Confindustria's General Council, the Board of Edison S.p.A., the Board of SEAT Pagine Gialle S.p.A,, the Executive Committee and the General Council of the Aspen Institute Italia, the International Business Council of the World Economic Forum and the Supervisory Board of Sofipa Equity Fund; Chairman of Autostrade S.p.A.; Vice President of I.G.I. (Istituto Grandi Infrastrutture); Senior Advisor for Italy of Société Générale Corporate & Investment Banking.

(continued)

Director	Age	Position	Background
Hermann-Josef Lamberti	50	Director[2]	Chief Operating Officer and Member of the Board of Managing at Deutsche Bank AG; Chairman of the Supervisory Board of Deutsche Bank Privat und Geschaftskunden AG; Member of the Supervisory Board of Carl Zeiss AG and Deutsche Börse AG; Non-executive Director of Euroclear plc and Euroclear Bank SA.
Sergio Marchionne	54	CEO[3]	CEO of Fiat S.p.A., Fiat Auto Holding B.V. and Fiat Auto S.p.A..; Chairman of the Board of Directors of Lonza Group Ltd.; Director of Serono Ltd.; Member of the Supervisory Board of Hochtief; Chairman of Société Générale de Surveillance Holding SA, Banca Unione di Credito, CNH (Case New Holland) and ACEA (European Automobile Manufacturers Association); Member of the General Councils of Confindustria and Assonime (the Association of listed Italian companies); Permanent member of the Fondazione Giovanni Agnelli.
Virgilio Marrone	60	Director	General Manager and CEO of IFI S.p.A.; Member of the boards of SanPaolo IMI S.p.A. and the Exor Group.
Vittorio Mincato	70	Director[2]	Past CEO of Eni S.p.A; Chairman of Poste Italiane S.p.A.; Member of CNEL (the Italian National Committee for Economy and Labor); Chairman of Assonime, the Executive Board of Confindustria and the Boards of Directors of Parmalat S.p.A., the Teatro alla Scala Foundation, the Accademia Nazionale di Santa Cecilia, and the Accademia Olimpica; Vice President of the Union of Industrialists of Rome.
Pasquale Pistorio	70	Director[3]	Past President and CEO and Current Honory Chairman of SGS-THOMSON Microelectronics (STMicroelectronics); Member of numerous organizations, including the Internal Advisory Council of the Government of Singapore, the ICT Task Force of the United Nations, the International Business Council of the World Economic Forum, and the Boards of Telecom Italia S.p.A. and Chartered Semiconductor Manufacturing; Chairman of ENIAC, the technological platform for nanoelectronics of the EU; Vice President of Confindustria for innovation and research.
Carlo Sant'Albano	42	Director	Managing Director and General Manager of IFIL S.p.A; Member of the Boards of Sequana Capital, Juventus F.C. and Alpitour.
Ratan Tata	68	Director	Chairman of Tata Sons Limited, the holding company of the Tata Group; Chairman of the major Tata companies including Tata Steel, Tata Motors, Tata Power, Tata Consultancy Services, Tata Tea, Tata Chemicals, Indian Hotels and Tata Teleservices Limited; Associated with a number of important business and philanthropic organizations in India and abroad.
Mario Zibetti	67	Director[2]	Past senior partner at Arthur Andersen S.p.A.; Member of the Board of Directors of Ersel Finanziaria S.p.A., Comital – Cofresco S.p.A. and Fabio Perini S.p.A.

[1] Member of the Nominating and Compensation Committee
[2] Member of the Internal Control Committee
[3] Member of the Strategic Committee
Source: Form 20-F 2005 of the Fiat Group.

Fiat Group's first-time adoption of IFRS

EXHIBIT 3 **Letter from the chairman and the chief executive officer, December 2005**

2005 marked a turning point for Fiat. We delivered on our commitments, we met all of our targets and we even exceeded a number of them. We had promised that 2004 would be Fiat's final year of net losses – and we achieved net income of over 1.4 billion euros in 2005. We had committed to a drastic cut in net industrial debt – and it was reduced by two-thirds. We had decided to focus on the relaunch of our Automobile activities, and in the last quarter of 2005 Fiat Auto posted a trading profit of 21 million euros after 17 consecutive quarters of losses. This has contributed to restoring Fiat's credibility, not only in Italy, but internationally, as evidenced by the improvement in our debt ratings and our ability to attract a large number of institutional investors in our debt raising activities. Our reputation has also benefited from the launch of new models across all brands that have been received extremely well by the public for their creativity, style, technology, and innovation, qualities that have distinguished the best Fiat cars since the firm was founded.

These breakthroughs, as well as all the other operational and financial improvements highlighted in this annual report, could not have been achieved without the strenuous efforts of the entire Fiat community, each and every one of whose members contributed to the relaunch of the Group with dedication and discipline. To do so, the Fiat people had to endorse fundamental changes in attitude, to assume greater responsibility and accountability, and to show their determination to deliver. We would like to express our sincere thanks to all of them.

During 2005, we also built a strong base for more effective and profitable operations in the future. First of all, we successfully resolved all pending strategic and financial issues: we settled our outstanding matters with General Motors and received a 1.56 billion euro cash payment; the Italenergia Bis transaction led to a 1.8 billion euro reduction in net industrial debt; and finally, conversion of the Mandatory Convertible Facility resulted in a 3 billion euro debt reduction and a sharp improvement in Group equity.

Fiat's business governance structure, especially in Automobiles, was right-sized to match realistic demand and market conditions. In Autos we have put in place a fully market-oriented organization, unbundling the brands: Fiat, Lancia and Alfa Romeo now face the customer on their own, while sharing key functions such as manufacturing, quality and safety.

Everything is driven by the brands and for the brands. Similarly, in Agricultural and Construction Equipment, Case New Holland was reorganized along four brands rather than regions. And we have begun to aggressively streamline processes throughout the organization. The Company will reap the benefits of these structural improvements in 2006 and beyond.

Last year, we made other important decisions that will shape the Group's future, in the form of targeted industrial alliances with major international partners. Seven such agreements were struck in the Automobile Sector – with Pars Industrial Development Foundation (PDIF), PSA-Tofas, Zastava, Suzuki, Ford, Severstal Auto and Tata Motors – while another partnership was established in commercial vehicles and industrial engines, between Iveco and SAIC.

Though much was done in 2005 to set the Company on course towards a real, lasting rebirth of our Group, the process is far from over and much remains to be done. Nonetheless, today's Fiat is a much different company from what it was just a year ago. The Group improved all key financial indicators. Our cash position – about 7 billion euros at 2005 year end – is strong. The financial markets are showing increased confidence in our prospects, as demonstrated by the steady appreciation of the Fiat share price. We have nearly completed the process of making our Internal Control System fully Sarbanes Oxley compliant, a move that will further enhance confidence in the Group at the international level. The Fiat we are talking about is a Group with a reinvigorated managerial structure, a leaner organization, a solid financial structure and stronger market positions thanks to new products. This new Fiat can achieve new, challenging targets in 2006.

At Group level, we aim to deliver positive cash flow from operations, a trading profit between 1.6 and 1.8 billion euros, and net income of about 700 million euros. While we do not expect market conditions for our operating Sectors to change materially this year, we have set high trading margin targets (trading profit as a percentage of revenues) for all of them: 7% to 7.5% at CNH, 5.5% to 6% at Iveco, and 3.5% to 4% in Components and Production Systems. The Automobile Sector should also turn in a positive performance, with a trading margin of 0.5% to 1%. This result will be supported by the full-year contribution of new models already rolled out. These will be joined in coming months by other new models, as we implement our aggressive product renewal plan calling for the launch of 20 new cars and the restyling of 23 current models between 2005 and 2008.

We made a clean break with the past, while respecting all commitments made to stakeholders. We are clearly within reach of recovering our position as a competitive automotive Group. This is why we are keeping up the pressure that has enabled us to get this far, demanding much from ourselves and from all the men and women of the Fiat community. We have no intention of lessening the momentum that has allowed Fiat to generate a series of steady improvements, quarter after quarter, throughout 2005. We will remain focused on reducing costs in non-essential areas, while continuing to invest in innovation. We will complement our advanced technological resources with better commercial organization and more efficient services. Finally, we will continue to seek new international opportunities, implementing our strategy of targeted alliances with key partners who will help us reduce capital commitments, and share investments and risks.

It is for all these reasons that we feel confident about our future.

Turin, February 28, 2006
Luca Cordero di Montezemolo – Chairman
Sergio Marchionne – Chief Executive Officer

EXHIBIT 4   **Excerpts from appendix 1 of Fiat's 2005 financial statements: Transition to international financial reporting standards**

Following the coming into force of European Regulation No. 1606 dated July 19, 2002, starting from January 1, 2005, the Fiat Group adopted International Financial Reporting Standards (IFRS) issued by the International Accounting Standards Board (IASB). This Appendix provides the IFRS reconciliations of balance sheet data as of January 1 and December 31, 2004, and of income statement data for the year ended December 31, 2004 as required by IFRS 1 – First-time Adoption of IFRS, together with the related explanatory notes. This information has been prepared as part of the Group's conversion to IFRS and in connection with the preparation of its 2005 consolidated financial statements in accordance with IFRS, as adopted by the European Union.

Reconciliations required by IFRS 1

As required by IFRS 1, this note describes the policies adopted in preparing the IFRS opening consolidated balance sheet at January 1, 2004, the main differences in relation to Italian GAAP used to prepare the consolidated financial statements until December 31, 2004, as well as the consequent reconciliations between the figures already published, prepared in accordance with Italian GAAP, and the corresponding figures remeasured in accordance with IFRS. The 2004 restated IFRS consolidated balance sheet and income statement have been prepared in accordance with IFRS 1 – First-time Adoption of IFRS. In particular, the IFRS applicable from January 1, 2005, as published as of December 31, 2004, have been adopted, including the following:

- IAS 39 – Financial Instruments: Recognition and Measurement, in its entirety. In particular, the Group adopted derecognition requirements retrospectively from the date on which financial assets and financial liabilities had been derecognized under Italian GAAP.
- IFRS 2 – Share-based Payment, which was published by the IASB on February 19, 2004 and adopted by the European Commission on February 7, 2005.

Description of main differences between Italian GAAP and IFRS

The following paragraphs provide a description of the main differences between Italian GAAP and IFRS that have had effects on Fiat's consolidated balance sheet

and income statement. Amounts are shown pre-tax and the related tax effects are separately summarized in the item R. Accounting for deferred income taxes.

A. Development costs

Under Italian GAAP applied research and development costs may alternatively be capitalised or charged to operations when incurred. Fiat Group has mainly expensed R&D costs when incurred. IAS 38 – Intangible Assets requires that research costs be expensed, whereas development costs that meet the criteria for capitalisation must be capitalised and then amortized from the start of production over the economic life of the related products.

Under IFRS, the Group has capitalised development costs in the Fiat Auto, Ferrari-Maserati, Agricultural and Construction Equipment, Commercial Vehicle and Components Sectors, using the retrospective approach in compliance with IFRS 1.

The positive impact of 1,876 million euros on the opening IFRS stockholders' equity at January 1, 2004, corresponds to the cumulative amount of qualifying development expenditures incurred in prior years by the Group, net of accumulated amortization. Consistently, intangible assets show an increase of 2,090 million euros and of 2,499 million euros at January 1, 2004 and at December 31, 2004, respectively.

The 2004 net result was positively impacted by 436 million euros in the year, reflecting the combined effect of the capitalisation of development costs incurred in the period that had been expensed under Italian GAAP, and the amortization of the amount that had been capitalised in the opening IFRS balance sheet at January 1, 2004. This positive impact has been accounted for in Research and development costs.

In accordance with IAS 36 – Impairment of Assets, development costs capitalised as intangible assets shall be tested for impairment and an impairment loss shall be recognized if the recoverable amount of an asset is less than its carrying amount, as further described in the paragraph I. Impairment of assets.

B. Employee benefits

The Group sponsors funded and unfunded defined benefit pension plans, as well as other long term benefits to employees.

Under Italian GAAP, these benefits, with the exception of the Reserve for Employee Severance Indemnities ("TFR") that is accounted for in compliance with a specific Italian law, are mainly recorded in accordance with IAS 19 – Employee Benefits, applying the corridor approach, which consists of amortizing over the remaining service lives of active employees only the portion of net cumulative actuarial gains and losses that exceeds the greater of 10% of either the defined benefit obligation or the fair value of the plan assets, while the portion included in the 10% remains unrecognized.

With the adoption of IFRS, TFR is considered a defined benefit obligation to be accounted for in accordance with IAS 19 and consequently has been recalculated applying the Projected Unit Credit Method. Furthermore, as mentioned in the paragraph "Optional exemptions", the Group elected to recognize all cumulative actuarial gains and losses that existed at January 1, 2004, with a negative impact on opening stockholders' equity at that date of 1,247 million euros.

Consequently pension and other post-employment benefit costs recorded in the 2004 IFRS income statement do not include any amortization of unrecognized actuarial gains and losses deferred in previous years in the IFRS financial statements under the corridor approach, and recognized in the 2004 income statement under Italian GAAP, resulting in a benefit of 94 million euros.

The Group has elected to use the corridor approach for actuarial gains and losses arising after January 1, 2004.

Furthermore, the Group elected to state the expense related to the reversal of discounting on defined benefit plans without plan assets separately as Financial expenses, with a corresponding increase in Financial expenses of 127 million euros in 2004.

C. Business combinations

As mentioned above, the Group elected not to apply IFRS 3 – Business Combinations retrospectively to business combinations that occurred before the date of transition to IFRS.

As prescribed in IFRS 3, starting from January 1, 2004, the IFRS income statement no longer includes goodwill amortization charges, resulting in a positive impact on Other operating income and expense of 162 million euros in 2004.

D. Revenue recognition—sales with a buy-back commitment

Under Italian GAAP, the Group recognized revenues from sales of products at the time title passed to the customer, which was generally at the time of shipment. For contracts for vehicle sales with a buy-back commitment at a specified price, a specific reserve for future risks and charges was set aside based on the difference between the guaranteed residual value and the estimated realizable value of vehicles, taking into account the probability that such option would be exercised. This reserve was set up at the time of the initial sale and adjusted periodically over the period of the contract. The costs of refurbishing the vehicles, to be incurred when the buy-back option is exercised, were reasonably estimated and accrued at the time of the initial sale.

Under IAS 18 – Revenue, new vehicle sales with a buy-back commitment do not meet criteria for revenue recognition, because the significant risks and rewards of ownership of the goods are not necessarily transferred to the buyer. Consequently, this kind of contract is treated in a manner similar to an operating lease transaction. More specifically, vehicles sold with a buy-back commitment are accounted for as Inventory if they regard the Fiat Auto business (agreements with normally a short-term buy-back commitment) and as Property, plant and equipment if they regard the Commercial Vehicles business (agreements with normally a long-term buy-back commitment). The difference between the carrying value (corresponding to the manufacturing cost) and the estimated resale value (net of refurbishing costs) at the end of the buy-back period, is depreciated on a straight-line basis over the duration of the contract. The initial sale price received is accounted for as a liability. The difference between the initial sale price and the buy-back price is recognized as rental revenue on a straight-line basis over the duration of the contract.

Opening IFRS stockholders' equity at January 1, 2004 includes a negative impact of 180 million euros mainly representing the portion of the margin accounted for under Italian GAAP on vehicles sold with a buy-back commitment prior to January 1, 2004, that will be recognized under IFRS over the remaining buy-back period, net of the effects due to the adjustments to the provisions for vehicle sales with a buy-back commitment recognized under Italian GAAP.

Fiat Group's first-time adoption of IFRS

This accounting treatment results in increases in the tangible assets reported in the balance sheet (1,001 million euros at January 1, 2004 and 1,106 million euros at December 31, 2004), in inventory (608 million euros at January 1, 2004 and 695 million euros at December 31, 2004), in advances from customers (equal to the operating lease rentals prepaid at the date of initial sale and recognized in the item Other payables), as well as in Trade payables, for the amount of the buy-back price, payable to the customer when the vehicle is bought back. In the income statement, a significant impact is generated on revenues (reduced by 1,103 million euros in 2004) and on cost of sales (reduced by 1,090 million euros in 2004), while no significant impact is generated on the net operating result; furthermore, the amount of these impacts in future years will depend on the changes in the volume and characteristics of these contracts year-over-year. Notwithstanding this, these changes are not expected to have a particularly significant impact on Group reported earnings in the coming years.

E. Revenue recognition—Other

Under Italian GAAP the recognition of disposals is based primarily on legal and contractual form (transfer of legal title).

Under IFRS, when risks and rewards are not substantially transferred to the buyer and the seller maintains a continuous involvement in the operations or assets being sold, the transaction is not recognized as a sale.

Consequently, certain disposal transactions, such as the disposal of the 14% interest in Italenergia Bis and certain minor real estate transactions, have been reversed retrospectively: the related asset has been recognized in the IFRS balance sheet, the initial gain recorded under Italian GAAP has been reversed and the cash received at the moment of the sale has been accounted for as a financial liability.

In particular, in 2001 the Group acquired a 38.6% shareholding in Italenergia S.p.A., now Italenergia Bis S.p.A. ("Italenergia"), a company formed between Fiat, Electricité de France ("EDF") and certain financial investors for the purpose of acquiring control of the Montedison – Edison ("Edison") group through tender offers. Italenergia assumed effective control of Edison at the end of the third quarter of that year and consolidated Edison from October 1, 2001. In 2002 the shareholders of Italenergia entered into agreements which resulted, among other things, in the transfer of a 14% interest in Italenergia from Fiat to other shareholders (with a put option that would require Fiat to repurchase the shares transferred in certain circumstances) and the assignment to Fiat of a put option to sell its shares in Italenergia to EDF in 2005, based on market values at that date, but subject to a contractually agreed minimum price in excess of book value.

Under Italian GAAP, Fiat accounted for its investments in Italenergia under the equity method, based on a 38.6% shareholding through September 30, 2002 and a 24.6% shareholding from October 1, 2002; in addition it recorded a gain of 189 million euros before taxes on the sale of its 14% interest in the investee to other shareholders effective September 30, 2002.

Under IFRS, the transfer of the 14% interest in Italenergia to the other shareholders was not considered to meet the requirements for revenue recognition set out in IAS 18, mainly due to the existence of the put options granted to the transferees and de facto constraints on the transferees' ability to pledge or exchange the transferred assets in the period from the sale through 2005. Accordingly, the gain recorded in 2002 for the sale was reversed, and the results of applying the equity method of accounting to the investment in Italenergia was recomputed to reflect a 38.6% interest in the net results and stockholders' equity of the investee, as adjusted for the differences between Italian GAAP and IFRS applicable to Italenergia.

This adjustment decreased the stockholders' equity at January 1, 2004 and at December 31, 2004 by an amount of 153 million euros and 237 million euros, respectively. Furthermore this adjustment increased the investment for an amount of 291 million euros at January 1, 2004 and of 341 million euros at December 31, 2004 and financial debt for amounts of 572 million euros at January 1, 2004 and of 593 million euros at December 31, 2004, as a consequence of the non-recognition of the transfer of the 14% interest in Italenergia.

F. Scope of consolidation

Under Italian GAAP, the subsidiary B.U.C. – Banca Unione di Credito – as required by law, was excluded from the scope of consolidation as it had dissimilar activities, and was accounted for using the equity method.

IFRS does not permit this kind of exclusion: consequently, B.U.C. is included in the IFRS scope of consolidation. Furthermore, under Italian GAAP investments that are not controlled on a legal basis or a de facto basis determined considering voting rights were excluded from the scope of consolidation.

Under IFRS, in accordance with SIC 12 – Consolidation – Special Purpose Entities, a Special Purpose Entity ("SPE") shall be consolidated when the substance of the relationship between an entity and the SPE indicates that the SPE is controlled by that entity.

This standard has been applied to all receivables securitisation transactions entered into by the Group (see the paragraph Q. Sales of receivables below), to a real estate securitisation transaction entered into in 1998 and to the sale of the Fiat Auto Spare Parts business to "Società di Commercializzazione e Distribuzione Ricambi S.p.A." ("SCDR") in 2001.

In particular, in 1998 the Group entered in a real estate securitisation and, under Italian GAAP, the related revenue was recognized at the date of the legal transfer of the assets involved. In the IFRS balance sheet at January 1, 2004, these assets have been written back at their historical cost, net of revaluations accounted before the sale, if any. Cash received at the time of the transaction has been accounted for in financial debt for an amount of 188 million euros at January 1, 2004.

The IFRS stockholders' equity at January 1, 2004 was negatively impacted for 105 million euros by the cumulative effect of the reversal of the capital gain on the initial disposal and of the revaluation previously recognized under Italian GAAP, net of the related effect of asset depreciation, as well as the recognition of financial charges on related debt, net of the reversal of rental fees paid, if any. The impact on the 2004 net result is not material.

Furthermore, in 2001 the Group participated with a specialist logistics operator and other financial investors in the formation of "Società di Commercializzazione e Distribuzione Ricambi S.p.A." ("SCDR"), a company whose principal activity is the purchase of spare parts from Fiat Auto for resale to end customers. At that date Fiat Auto and its subsidiaries sold their spare parts inventory to SCDR recording a gain of 300 million euros. The Group's investment in SCDR represents 19% of SCDR's stock capital and was accounted for under the equity method for Italian GAAP.

Under IFRS, SCDR qualifies as a Special Purpose Entity (SPE) as defined by SIC 12 due to the continuing involvement of Fiat Auto in SCDR operations. Consequently, SCDR has been consolidated on a line by line basis in the IFRS consolidated financial statements, with a consequent increase in financial debt of 237 million euros and of 471 million euros at January 1, 2004 and at December 31, 2004, respectively. Opening stockholders' equity at January 1, 2004 was reduced by 266 million euros by the amount corresponding to the unrealized intercompany profit in inventory

held by SCDR on that date; this amount did not change significantly at the end of 2004.

G. Property, plant and equipment

Under Italian GAAP and IFRS, assets included in Property, Plant and Equipment were generally recorded at cost, corresponding to the purchase price plus the direct attributable cost of bringing the assets to their working condition.

Under Italian GAAP, Fiat revalued certain Property, Plant and Equipment to amounts in excess of historical cost, as permitted or required by specific laws of the countries in which the assets were located. These revaluations were credited to stockholders' equity and the revalued assets were depreciated over their remaining useful lives.

Furthermore, under Italian GAAP, the land directly related to buildings included in Property, Plant and Equipment was depreciated together with the related building depreciation.

The revaluations and land depreciation are not permitted under IFRS. Therefore IFRS stockholders' equity at January 1, 2004 reflects a negative impact of 164 million euros, related to the effect of the elimination of the asset revaluation recognized in the balance sheet, partially offset by the reversal of the land depreciation charged to prior period income statements.

In the 2004 IFRS income statement, the abovementioned adjustments had a positive impact of 14 million euros in 2004 due to the reversal of the depreciation of revalued assets, net of adjustments on gains and losses, if any, on disposal of the related assets, and to the reversal of land depreciation.

H. Write-off of deferred costs

Under Italian GAAP, the Group deferred and amortized certain costs (mainly start-up and related charges). IFRS require these to be expensed when incurred.

In addition, costs incurred in connection with share capital increases, which are also deferred and amortized under Italian GAAP, are deducted directly from the proceeds of the increase and debited to stockholders' equity under IFRS.

I. Impairment of assets

Under Italian GAAP, the Group tested its intangible assets with indefinite useful lives (mainly goodwill) for impairment annually by comparing their carrying amount with their recoverable amount in terms of the value in use of the asset itself (or group of assets). In determining the value in use the Group estimated the future cash inflows and outflows of the asset (or group of assets) to be derived from the continuing use of the asset and from its ultimate disposal, and discounted those future cash flows. If the recoverable amount was lower than the carrying value, an impairment loss was recognized for the difference.

With reference to tangible fixed assets, under Italian GAAP the Group accounted for specific write-offs when the asset was no longer to be used. Furthermore, in the presence of impairment indicators, the Group tested tangible fixed assets for impairment using the undiscounted cash flow method in determining the recoverable amount of homogeneous group of assets. If the recoverable amount thus determined was lower than the carrying value, an impairment loss was recognized for the difference. Under IFRS, intangible assets with indefinite useful lives are tested for impairment annually by a methodology substantially similar to the one required by Italian GAAP. Furthermore, development costs, capitalised under IFRS and expensed under Italian GAAP, are attributed to the related cash generating unit and tested for impairment together with the related tangible assets, applying the discounted cash flow method in determining their recoverable amount.

Consequently, the reconciliation between Italian GAAP and IFRS reflects adjustments due to both impairment losses on development costs previously capitalised for IFRS purposes, and the effect of discounting on the determination of the recoverable amount of tangible fixed assets.

L. Reserves for risks and charges

Differences between Italian GAAP and IFRS refer mainly to the following items:

- Restructuring reserve: the Group provided restructuring reserves based upon management's best estimate of the costs to be incurred in connection with each of its restructuring programs at the time such programs were formally decided. Under IFRS the requirements to recognize a constructive obligation in the financial statements are more restrictive, and some restructuring reserves recorded under Italian GAAP have been eliminated.

- Reserve for vehicle sales incentives: under Italian GAAP Fiat Auto accounted for certain incentives at the time at which a legal obligation to pay the

incentives arose, which may have been in periods subsequent to that in which the initial sale to the dealer network was made. Under IAS 37 companies are required to make provision not only for legal, but also for constructive, obligations based on an established pattern of past practice. In the context of the IFRS restatement exercise, Fiat has reviewed its practice in the area of vehicle sales incentives and has determined that for certain forms of incentives a constructive obligation exists which should be provided under IFRS at the date of sale.

M. Recognition and measurement of derivatives

Beginning in 2001 the Fiat Group adopted – to the extent that it is consistent and not in contrast with general principles set forth in the Italian law governing financial statements – IAS 39 Financial Instruments: Recognition and Measurement. In particular, taking into account the restrictions under Italian law, the Group maintained that IAS 39 was applicable only in part and only in reference to the designation of derivative financial instruments as "hedging" or "non-hedging instruments" and with respect to the symmetrical accounting of the result of the valuation of the hedging instruments and the result attributable to the hedged items ("hedge accounting"). The transactions which, according to the Group's policy for risk management, were able to meet the conditions stated by the accounting principle for hedge accounting treatment, were designated as hedging transactions; the others, although set up for the purpose of managing risk exposure (inasmuch as the Group's policy does not permit speculative transactions), were designated as "trading". The main differences between Italian GAAP and IFRS may be summarized as follows:

- Instruments designated as "hedging instruments" – under Italian GAAP, the instrument was valued symmetrically with the underlying hedged item. Therefore, where the hedged item was not adjusted to fair value in the financial statements, the hedging instrument was also not adjusted. Similarly, where the hedged item had not yet been recorded in the financial statements (hedging of future flows), the valuation of the hedging instrument at fair value was deferred. Under IFRS:

  - In the case of a fair value hedge, the gains or losses from remeasuring the hedging instrument at fair value shall be recognized in the income statement and the gains or losses on the hedged item attributable to the hedge risk shall adjust the carrying amount of the hedged item and be recognized in the income statement. Consequently, no impact arises on net income (except for the ineffective portion of the hedge, if any) and on net equity, while adjustments impact the carrying values of hedging instruments and hedged items.

■ In the case of a cash flow hedge (hedging of future flows), the portion of gains or losses on the hedging instrument that is determined to be an effective hedge shall be recognized directly in equity through the statement of changes in equity; the ineffective portion of the gains or losses shall be recognized in the income statement. Consequently, with reference to the effective portion, only a difference in net equity arises between Italian GAAP and IFRS.

■ Instruments designated as "non-hedging instruments" (except for foreign currency derivative instruments) – under Italian GAAP, these instruments were valued at market value and the differential, if negative compared to the contractual value, was recorded in the income statement, in accordance with the concept of prudence. Under IAS 39 the positive differential should also be recorded. With reference to foreign currency derivative instruments, instead, the accounting treatment adopted under Italian GAAP was in compliance with IAS 39.

In this context, as mentioned in the consolidated financial statements as of December 31, 2003, Fiat was party to a Total Return Equity Swap contract on General Motors shares, in order to hedge the risk implicit in the Exchangeable Bond on General Motors shares. Although this equity swap was entered into for hedging purposes it does not qualify for hedge accounting and accordingly it was defined as a non-hedging instrument. Consequently, the positive fair value of the instrument as of December 31, 2003, amounting to 450 million euros, had not been recorded under Italian GAAP. During 2004 Fiat terminated the contract, realizing a gain of 300 million euros.

In the IFRS restatement, the above mentioned positive fair value at December 31, 2003 has been recognized in opening equity, while, following the unwinding of the swap, a negative adjustment of the same amount has been recorded in the 2004 income statement.

N. Treasury stock

In accordance with Italian GAAP, the Group accounted for treasury stock as an asset and recorded related

valuation adjustments and gains or losses on disposal in the income statement.

Under IFRS, treasury stock is deducted from stockholders' equity and all movements in treasury stock are recognized in stockholders' equity rather than in the income statement.

O. Stock options

Under Italian GAAP, with reference to share-based payment transactions, no obligations or compensation expenses were recognized.

In accordance with IFRS 2 – Share-based Payment, the full amount fair value of stock options on the date of grant must be expensed. Changes in fair value after the grant date have no impact on the initial measurement. The compensation expense corresponding to the option's fair value is recognized in payroll costs on a straight-line basis over the period from the grant date to the vesting date, with the offsetting credit recognized directly in equity.

The Group applied the transitional provision provided by IFRS 2 and therefore applied this standard to all stock options granted after November 7, 2002 and not yet vested at the effective date of IFRS 2 (January 1, 2005). No compensation expense is required to be recognized for stock options granted prior to November 7, 2002, in accordance with transitional provision of IFRS 2.

P. Adjustments to the valuation of investments in associates

These items represent the effect of the IFRS adjustments on the Group portion of the net equity of associates accounted for using the equity method.

Q. Sales of receivables

The Fiat Group sells a significant part of its finance, trade and tax receivables through either securitisation programs or factoring transactions.

A securitisation transaction entails the sale without recourse of a portfolio of receivables to a securitisation vehicle (special purpose entity). This special purpose entity finances the purchase of the receivables by issuing asset-backed securities (i.e. securities whose repayment and interest flow depend upon the cash flow generated by the portfolio). Asset-backed securities are divided into classes according to their degree of seniority and rating: the most senior classes are placed with investors on the market; the junior class, whose repayment is subordinated to the senior classes, is normally subscribed for by the seller. The residual interest in the receivables retained by the seller is therefore limited to the junior securities it has subscribed for.

Factoring transactions may be with or without recourse on the seller; certain factoring agreements without recourse include deferred purchase price clauses (i.e. the payment of a minority portion of the purchase price is conditional upon the full collection of the receivables), require a first loss guarantee of the seller up to a limited amount or imply a continuing significant exposure to the receivables cash flow.

Under Italian GAAP, all receivables sold through either securitisation or factoring transactions (both with and without recourse) had been derecognized. Furthermore, with specific reference to the securitisation of retail loans and leases originated by the financial services companies, the net present value of the interest flow implicit in the instalments, net of related costs, had been recognized in the income statement.

Under IFRS:

■ As mentioned above, SIC 12 – Consolidation – Special Purpose Entities states that an SPE shall be consolidated when the substance of the relationship between the entity and the SPE indicates that the SPE is controlled by that entity; therefore all securitisation transactions have been reversed.

■ IAS 39 allows for the derecognition of a financial asset when, and only when, the risks and rewards of the ownership of the assets are substantially transferred: consequently, all portfolios sold with

recourse, and the majority of those sold without recourse, have been reinstated in the IFRS balance sheet.

The impact of such adjustments on stockholders' equity and on net income is not material. In particular, it refers mainly to the reversal of the gains arising from the related securitisation transactions on the retail portfolio of receivables of financial service companies, realized under Italian GAAP and not yet realized under IFRS.

With regards to financial structure, the reinstatement in the balance sheet of the receivables and payables involved in these sales transactions causes a significant increase in trade and financial receivables and in financial debt balances, and a worsening in net debt. In particular, in consequence of these reinstatements, trade receivables increase by 3,563 million euros and 2,134 euros at January 1, 2004 and at December 31, 2004, respectively; at the same dates, financial receivables increase by 6,127 million euros and 6,997 euros, and financial debt increased by 10,581 million euros and 10,174 million euros, respectively.

R. Accounting for deferred income taxes

This item includes the combined effect of the net deferred tax effects, after allowance, on the above mentioned IFRS adjustments, as well as other minor differences between Italian GAAP and IFRS on the recognition of tax assets and liabilities.

Effects of transition to IFRS on the consolidated balance sheet at January 1, 2004

(in € millions)	Italian GAAP	Reclassifi-cations	Adjust-ments	IAS/IFRS	
Intangible assets, of which:	3,724		1,774	5,498	Intangible assets, of which:
Goodwill	2,402			2,402	Goodwill
Other intangible fixed assets	1,322		1,774	3,096	Other intangible fixed assets
Property, plant and equipment, of which:	9,675	(945)	817	9,547	Property, plant and equipment
Property, plant and equipment	8,761	(31)			
Operating leases	914	(914)			
		31		31	Investment property
Financial fixed assets	3,950	70	(121)	3,899	Investment and other financial assets
Financial receivables held as fixed assets	29	(29)			
		914	(50)	864	Leased assets
Deferred tax assets	1,879		266	2,145	Deferred tax assets
Total Non-Current assets	**19,257**	**41**	**2,686**	**21,984**	**Non-current assets**
Net inventories	6,484		1,113	7,597	Inventories
Trade receivables	4,553	(682)	2,678	6,549	Trade receivables
		12,890	7,937	20,827	Receivables from financing activities
Other receivables	3,081	(148)	541	3,474	Other receivables
		407	10	417	Accrued income and prepaid expenses
				2,129	Current financial assets, of which:
		32		32	Current equity investments
		515	260	775	Current securities
		430	892	1,322	Other financial assets
Financial assets not held as fixed assets	120	(120)			
Financial lease contracts receivable	1,797	(1,797)			
Financial receivables	10,750	(10,750)			
Securities	3,789	(3,789)			
Cash	3,211	3,214	420	6,845	Cash and cash equivalents
Total Current assets	**33,785**	**202**	**13,851**	**47,838**	**Current assets**
Trade accruals and deferrals	407	(407)			
Financial accruals and deferrals	386	(386)			
			21	21	Assets held for sale
TOTAL ASSETS	**53,835**	**(550)**	**16,558**	**69,843**	**TOTAL ASSETS**
Stockholders' equity	**7,494**	**(934)**		**6,560**	**Stockholders' equity**
				7,455	Provisions, of which:
Reserves for employee severance indemnities	1,313	1,503	1,224	4,040	Employee benefits
Reserves for risks and charges	5,168	(1,550)	(203)	3,415	Other provisions
Deferred income tax reserves	211	(211)			
Long-term financial payables	15,418	6,501	14,790	36,709	Debt, of which:
				10,581	Asset-backed financing
				26,128	Other debt
Total Non-current liabilities	**22,110**	**6,243**			

(continued)

Fiat Group's first-time adoption of IFRS

Effects of transition to IFRS on the Consolidated Balance Sheet at January 1, 2004

(in € millions)	Italian GAAP	Reclassifi-cations	Adjust-ments	IAS/IFRS	
		568	(223)	345	Other financial liabilities
Trade payables	12,588		(297)	12,291	Trade payables
Others payables	2,742		1,948	4,690	Other payables
Short-term financial payables	6,616	(6,616)			
Total Current liabilities	**21,946**	**(6,048)**			
		211	274	485	Deferred tax liabilities
Trade accruals and deferrals	1,329		(21)	1,308	Accrued expenses and deferred income
Financial accruals and deferrals	956	(956)			
					Liabilities held for sale
TOTAL LIABILITIES AND STOCKHOLDERS' EQUITY	**53,835**	**(550)**	**(934)**	**69,843**	**TOTAL STOCKHOLDERS' EQUITY AND LIABILITIES**

Effects of transition to IFRS on the income statement for the year ended December 31, 2004

(in € millions)	Italian GAAP	Reclassifi-cations	Adjust-ments	IAS/IFRS	
Net revenues	46,703		(1,066)	45,637	Net revenues
Cost of sales	39,623	675	(1,177)	39,121	Cost of sales
Gross operating result	**7,080**				
Overhead	4,629	51	21	4,701	Selling, general and administrative costs
Research and development	1,810	1	(461)	1,350	Research and development costs
Other operating income (expenses)	(619)	346	(142)	(415)	Other income (expenses)
Operating result	**22**	**(381)**	**409**	**50**	**Trading profit**
		154	(4)	150	Gains (losses) on the disposal of equity investments
		496	46	542	Restructuring costs
		(243)		(243)	Other unusual income (expenses)
		(966)	**359**	**(585)**	**Operating result**
		(641)	(538)	(1,179)	Financial income
Result from equity investments	8		127	135	Result from equity investments
Non-operating income (expenses)	(863)	863			
EBIT	**(833)**				
Financial income (expenses)	(744)	744			
Income (loss) before taxes	**(1,577)**		**(52)**	**(1,629)**	**Result before taxes**
Income taxes	(29)		(21)	(50)	Income taxes
Net result of normal operations	**(1,548)**		**(31)**	**(1,579)**	**Net result of normal operations**
Result from discontinued operations					Result from discontinued operations
Net result before minority interest	**(1,548)**		**(31)**	**(1,579)**	**Net result before minority interest**

Fiat Group's first-time adoption of IFRS

Implementing Accounting Analysis

We learned in Chapter 3 that accounting analysis requires the analyst to adjust a firm's accounting numbers using cash flow information and information from the notes to the financial statements to "undo" any accounting distortions. This entails recasting a firm's financial statements using standard reporting nomenclature and formats. Firms frequently use somewhat different formats and terminology for presenting their financial results. **Recasting the financial statements** using a standard template, therefore, helps ensure that performance metrics used for financial analysis are calculated using comparable definitions across companies and over time.

Once the financial statements have been standardized, the analyst is ready to identify any distortions in financial statements. The analyst's primary focus should be on those accounting estimates and methods that the firm uses to measure its key success factors and risks. If there are differences in these estimates and/or methods between firms or for the same firm over time, the analyst's job is to assess whether they reflect legitimate business differences and therefore require no adjustment, or whether they reflect differences in managerial judgment or bias and require adjustment. In addition, even if accounting rules are adhered to consistently, accounting distortions can arise because accounting rules themselves do a poor job of capturing firm economics, creating opportunities for the analyst to adjust a firm's financials in a way that presents a more realistic picture of its performance.

This chapter shows how to recast the firm's financial statements into a template that uses standard terminology and classifications, discusses the most common types of accounting distortions that can arise, and shows how to make adjustments to the standardized financial statements to undo these distortions.

A balance sheet approach is used to identify whether there have been any distortions to assets, liabilities, or shareholders' equity. Once any asset and liability misstatements have been identified, the analyst can make adjustments to the balance sheet at the beginning and/or end of the current year, as well as any needed adjustments to revenues and expenses in the latest income statement. This approach ensures that the most recent financial ratios used to evaluate a firm's performance and forecast its future results are based on financial data that appropriately reflect its business economics.

In some instances, information taken from a firm's notes to the financial statements, cash flow statement, and statement of comprehensive income enables the analyst to make a precise adjustment for an accounting distortion. However, for many types of accounting adjustments the company does not disclose all of the information needed to perfectly undo the distortion, requiring the analyst to make an approximate adjustment to the financial statements.

RECASTING FINANCIAL STATEMENTS

Firms sometimes use different nomenclature and formats to present their financial results. For example, the asset goodwill can be reported separately using such titles as Goodwill, "Excess of cost over net assets of acquired companies," and "Cost in excess of fair value," or it can be included in the line item Other Intangible Assets. Interest Income can be reported as a subcategory of Revenues, shown lower down the income statement as part of Other Income and Expenses, or it is sometimes reported as Interest Expense, Net of Interest Income.

These differences in financial statement terminology, classifications, and formats can make it difficult to compare performance across firms, and sometimes to compare performance for the same firm over time. The first task for the analyst in accounting analysis is, therefore, to recast the financial statements into a common format. This involves designing a template for the balance sheet, income statement, cash flow statement, and statement of comprehensive income that can be used to standardize financial statements for any company.

One particular obstacle that the analyst must overcome in recasting IFRS-based income statements is that the international standards allow firms to classify their operating expenses in two ways: by nature or by function. The classification by nature defines categories with reference to the cause of operating expenses. Firms using this classification typically distinguish between the cost of materials, the cost of personnel, and the cost of non-current assets (depreciation and amortization). In contrast, the classification by function defines categories with reference to the purpose of operating expenses. Under this classification, firms typically differentiate between costs that are incurred for the purpose of producing the products or services sold – labeled Cost of Sales – and costs for overhead activities such as administrative work and marketing – labeled Selling, General and Administrative Expenses (SG&A). Only income statements that are prepared using the latter classification include the line item "**Gross Profit**," which is defined as the difference between Sales and Cost of Sales and measures the efficiency of a firm's production activities.

Although the **classification of operating expenses by function** potentially provides better information about the efficiency and profitability of a firm's operating activities, some analysts prefer the **classification of expenses by nature** because this classification is less arbitrary and requires less judgment from the firm. The coexistence of two classifications generally will not cause problems as long as the choice for a particular classification is industry-related. For example, firms that operate in the airline industry are more likely to classify their expenses by nature, whereas manufacturing firms are more likely to classify their expenses by function. Firms that operate in similar industries may, however, prefer different classifications.

A further complication may be that firms use similar terminology under different approaches. For example, in 2007 Hennes & Mauritz (H&M) reported that its Gross Profit was 61 percent of Sales, while Inditex, owner of brands such as Zara and Massimo Dutti and one of H&M's main competitors, reported that its Gross Profit was 57 percent of Sales. Because the two firms classified their expenses differently, however, these amounts were not comparable. Inditex's (mislabeled) Gross Profit was calculated by subtracting the nature-based cost of merchandise from sales, whereas H&M's Gross Profit reflected the difference between Sales and the function-based Cost of Sales, which included depreciation and the cost of procurement personnel. Fortunately, the IFRSs require that when firms classify their expenses by function, they should also report a classification of expenses by nature in the notes to the financial statements. Hence, the analyst can always recast H&M's income statement into the format that Inditex used.

Tables 4.1, 4.2, 4.3, 4.4, and 4.5 present the format used throughout the book to standardize the income statement, balance sheet, cash flow statement, and statement of comprehensive income, respectively.

To create standardized financials for a company, the analyst classifies each line item in that firm's financial statements using the appropriate account name from the templates set out in the tables. This may require using information from the notes to the financial statements to ensure that accounts are classified appropriately. An example,

TABLE 4.1 Standardized income statement format (classification of operating expenses by function)

Standard income statement accounts	Sample line items classified in account
Sales	Revenue(s)
	Turnover
	Membership fees
	Commissions
	Licenses
Cost of Sales (by function)	Cost of merchandise sold
	Cost of products sold
	Cost of revenues
	Cost of services
	Depreciation on manufacturing facilities
SG&A (by function)	General and administrative
	Marketing and sales
	Distribution expenses
	Servicing and maintenance
	Depreciation on selling and administrative facilities
Other Operating Income, Net of Other Operating Expense (by function)	Amortization of intangibles
	Research and development
	Start-up costs
	Special charges
	Gains/Losses on sale of investments/non-current assets
	Foreign exchange gains/losses
	Asset impairments
	Restructuring charges
Net Interest Expense (Income) Interest Income Interest Expense	Net finance cost
	Interest charge on non-current provisions
	Interest earned
Investment Income	Result from associate companies
	Equity income from associates
	Dividend income
	Rental income
Minority Interest	
Tax Expense	Provision for taxes
Net Profit/Loss	Net income

TABLE 4.2 Standardized income statement format (classification of operating expenses by nature)

Standard income statement accounts	Sample line items classified in account
Sales	Revenue(s)
	Turnover
	Membership fees
	Commissions
	Licenses
Cost of Materials (by nature)	Cost of outsourced work and services received
	Raw materials and work subcontracted
	Cost of components
	Changes in inventories and own work capitalized (correction)
Personnel Expense (by nature)	Salaries and wages
	Social security
	Post-employment/Pension benefits
	Share-based payments
Depreciation and Amortization (by nature)	
Other Operating Income, Net of Other Operating Expense (by nature)	Transport and distribution costs
	Operating lease installments
	Insurance premiums
	Reversal of provisions
	Gains/Losses on sale of investments/non-current assets
	Foreign exchange gains/losses
	Asset impairments
	Restructuring charges
Net Interest Expense (Income) Interest Income Interest Expense	Net finance cost
	Interest charge on non-current provisions
	Interest earned
Investment Income	Result from associate companies
	Equity income from associates
	Dividend income
	Rental income
Minority Interest	
Tax Expense	Provision for taxes
Net Profit/Loss	Net income

applying the templates to standardize the 2008 financial statements for audio and video equipment manufacturer Bang & Olufsen a/s, is shown in the Appendix at the end of this chapter.

Once the financials have been standardized, the analyst can evaluate whether accounting adjustments are needed to correct for any **distortions in assets, liabilities, or equity**.

TABLE 4.3 Standardized balance sheet format

Standard balance sheet accounts	Sample line items classified in account	Standard balance sheet accounts	Sample line items classified in account
Assets		Liabilities and equity	
Cash and Marketable Securities	Cash and cash equivalents Short-term investments Time deposits	*Current Debt*	Current borrowings Notes payable Bank overdrafts Current portion of non-current borrowings Current portion of finance lease obligation
Trade Receivables	Accounts receivable Trade debtors	*Trade Payables*	Accounts payable Trade creditors
Inventories	Inventory Finished goods Raw materials Work-in-progress Stocks	*Other Current Liabilities*	Accrued expenses Amounts due to related parties Income tax liabilities Social security and payroll taxes Dividends payable Current deferred (unearned) revenue Current provisions
Other Current Assets	Prepaid expenses Claims for tax refunds Current assets classified as held for sale Current derivative financial instruments Amounts due from affiliates Amounts due from employees	*Non-Current Debt*	Long-term borrowings/financial liabilities Subordinated debentures Finance lease obligations Convertible debentures Provision for post-employment benefits Provision for decommissioning costs Other non-current provisions
Non-Current Tangible Assets	Property, plant and equipment Land and buildings Non-current assets classified as held for sale	*Deferred Tax Liability*	
Non-Current Intangible Assets	Goodwill Software/product development costs Deferred financing costs Deferred subscriber acquisition costs Deferred catalog costs Deferred charges Trademarks and licenses	*Other Non-Current Liabilities (non-interest bearing)*	Non-current deferred (unearned) revenues Other non-current liabilities
Deferred Tax Asset *Other Non-Current Assets*	Investments accounted for using the equity method	*Minority Interest* *Preference Shares*	Preference shares Convertible preference shares

(continued)

TABLE 4.3 Standardized balance sheet format (*Continued*)

Standard balance sheet accounts	Sample line items classified in account	Standard balance sheet accounts	Sample line items classified in account
	Investments in associates Finance lease receivables Investment property Biological assets Non-current derivative financial instruments		
		Ordinary Shareholders' Equity	Share capital Share premium Retained earnings Treasury shares/Own shares purchased but not canceled Other reserves

TABLE 4.4 Standardized cash flow statement format

Standard cash flow statement accounts	Sample line items classified in account
Net Profit or Profit minus Taxes Paid	
Non-Operating Gains (Losses)	Gain (loss) on disposal of investments/non-current assets Cumulative effect of accounting changes Gain (loss) on foreign exchange
Non-Current Operating Accruals	Depreciation and amortization Deferred revenues/costs Deferred taxes Impairment of non-current assets Other non-cash charges to operations Equity earnings of affiliates/unconsolidated subs, net of cash received Minority interest Stock bonus awards
Net (Investments in) or Liquidation of Operating Working Capital	Changes in: Trade receivables Other receivables Prepaid expenses Trade payables Accrued expenses (liabilities) Due from affiliates Accounts payable and accrued expenses Refundable/payable income taxes Inventories Provision for doubtful accounts Other current liabilities (excluding current debt) Other current assets

(continued)

TABLE 4.4 Standardized cash flow statement format (*Continued*)

Standard cash flow statement accounts	Sample line items classified in account
Net (Investment in) or Liquidation of Non-Current Operating Assets	Purchase/disposal of non-current assets
	Acquisition of research and development
	Acquisition/sale of business
	Capital expenditures
	Acquisition of subsidiaries and equity investments
	Capitalization of development costs
	Cost in excess of the fair value of net assets acquired
	Investment in financing leases
Net Debt (Repayment) or Issuance	Principal payments on debt
	Borrowings (repayments) under credit facility
	Issuance (repayment) of long-term debt
	Net increase (decrease) in short-term borrowings
	Notes payable
Dividend (Payments)	Cash dividends paid on ordinary shares/preference shares
	Distributions
Net Share (Repurchase) or Issuance	Proceeds from issuance of ordinary shares
	Issue of ordinary share for services
	Issue (redemption) of preferred securities
	Issue of subsidiary equity
	Purchase (issue) of treasury shares
	Capital contributions

TABLE 4.5 Standardized statement of comprehensive income format

Standard statement of comprehensive income accounts	Sample line items classified in account
Net Profit	Net profit (income) for the period
Unrealized Revaluations, Net of Transfers to Income	Effect of change in fair value of available-for-sale securities
Recognized Actuarial Gains/Losses	Actuarial gains/losses on defined benefit schemes
Gains/Losses on Cash Flow Hedges	Change in fair value of derivatives
Foreign Exchange Gains/Losses	Exchange rate differences
	Foreign currency translation adjustment
Other Non-Owner Changes in Equity	Change in accounting policy
Comprehensive Income	Total recognized income and expense

EXTENSIBLE BUSINESS REPORTING LANGUAGE

An increasing number of firms worldwide prepare and report their financial statements using the Extensible Business Reporting Language (XBRL). These XBRL statements typically complement the traditional financial statements, but in future years XBRL reporting may start to replace the traditional way of financial reporting. XBRL is a language that supports the internet-based communication of financial information. The basic idea underlying this language is that it provides a "tag" for every individual item in a company's financial statements, including the notes, which describes the main characteristics of the item. Tags contain information about, for example, the accounting standards that the company uses to prepare the item as well as the fiscal year and the broader category of items to which the item belongs. The data items including their tags are reported in an XBRL instance document, which the company makes publicly available through the internet. By using the appropriate software that recognizes the tags, an analyst can then extract only the needed information from the instance document and ignore irrelevant items. One advantage of XBRL reporting is therefore that it substantially reduces the time that the analyst needs to collect and summarize financial statement information.

The process of tagging data items is somewhat similar to the process of recasting financial statements. Because companies use accepted taxonomies to categorize their financial statement items, they take over some of the analyst's work of standardizing the financial statements. The IASC Foundation XBRL Team has developed the IFRS taxonomy, which classifies all possible data items that may appear in an IFRS-based financial statement and defines the relationships among them. The use of the IFRS taxonomy for XBRL reporting by listed European companies may therefore eventually reduce the importance of recasting IFRS-based financial statements.

FIRST-TIME ADOPTION OF IFRS

The widespread use of **IFRS** to prepare financial statements is a fairly recent phenomenon. By the end of 2004, around 1,000 firms worldwide prepared their financial statements in conformity with IFRS. Since the mandated introduction of IFRS-based reporting in, amongst other countries, the EU, Australia (2005), New Zealand, and China (2007), however, the number of IFRS users has grown explosively to over 10,000 firms. In 2008 the US Securities and Exchange Commission proposed a roadmap that could lead to the adoption of IFRS in the US and a further explosion in the number of IFRS users around the mid-2010s. Although the worldwide move to using one common set of accounting rules yields many advantages for the analyst, the switch from local to international accounting rules also complicates the accounting analysis a little.

In the first year that a firm applies IFRS, it is required to provide the current year's IFRS-based financial figures as well as restate prior year's balance sheet and income statement for comparative purposes. This means that the firm traces back every historical event and assumption that is relevant to a particular line item on the opening balance sheet of the prior year, recalculates the impact of these events and assumptions on the items, and essentially produces its first IFRS-based opening balance sheet as if it had applied IFRS all along (though applying current IFRSs). The firm then records all the events during the prior year and the current year in accordance with IFRS. To avoid the misuse of hindsight, when preparing its opening IFRS-based balance sheet the first-time IFRS adopter cannot use information that it received after the balance sheet date.

In their first IFRS-based financial statements firms have to disclose at least the following information to illustrate the effects of IFRS adoption on their financial figures:

- A description of the sources of differences between equity reported under previous accounting standards and under IFRS as well as the effects of these differences in quantitative terms. The firm must provide such reconciliations for equity in both its opening and its closing comparative balance sheets.

■ A reconciliation of net profit reported under previous accounting standards and under IFRS for the prior year.

Some firms also voluntarily disclose the opening IFRS-based balance sheet of the prior year, improving the analyst's dataset, but they are not required to do so.

Unfortunately, it is practically difficult for a first-time IFRS adopter to trace back every relevant historical event because it may not have collected or stored all the necessary data in the past. Further, the informational benefits of recalculating and restating certain line items may not outweigh the associated costs. For example, firms that consolidate the translated values of subsidiaries' foreign currency-denominated assets on their balance sheets, recognize the cumulative translation difference, which arises because exchange rates fluctuate over the years, as a separate component in equity. When these firms adopt IFRS they would face the tedious task of recalculating all cumulative translation differences on their subsidiaries. Because separately reporting restated cumulative translation differences generates little additional information, however, first-time IFRS adopters can choose to add the cumulative translation differences to equity and reset the line item to zero upon adoption. To facilitate the first-time preparation of an IFRS-based opening balance sheet, the rules on the first-time IFRS application allow more of these exemptions and even prohibit some restatements. At various places throughout this chapter, we address some of these exemptions and prohibitions.

RECOGNITION OF ASSETS

Accountants define assets as resources that a firm owns or controls as a result of past business transactions, and which are expected to produce future economic benefits that can be measured with a reasonable degree of certainty. Assets can take a variety of forms, including cash, marketable securities, receivables from customers, inventories, fixed assets, noncurrent investments in other companies and intangibles.

Distortions in asset values generally arise because there is ambiguity about whether:

■ The firm owns or controls the economic resources in question.

■ The economic resources are likely to provide future economic benefits that can be measured with reasonable certainty.

■ The fair value of assets fall below their book values.

■ Fair value estimates are accurate.

Who owns or controls resources?

For most resources used by a firm, ownership or control is relatively straightforward: the firm using the resource owns the asset. However, some types of transactions make it difficult to assess who owns a resource. For example, who owns or controls a resource that has been leased? Is it the lessor or the lessee? Or consider a firm that discounts a customer receivable with a bank. If the bank has recourse against the firm should the customer default, is the real owner of the receivable the bank or the company? Or consider a firm owning 49 percent of another firm's ordinary shares. Does the firm control all of the investment's assets or only the net investment it legally owns?

Accounting rules often leave some discretion to managers and auditors in deciding whether their company owns or controls an asset. Leaving discretion to managers and auditors can be preferred over imposing detailed and mechanical rules if the latter solution causes managers to structure their transactions such that they avoid recognizing an asset. Following this idea, the IASB frequently takes a principles-based approach to setting accounting standards, thereby granting managers greater reporting discretion than under a rules-based approach. For example, the international standard for preparing consolidated financial statements (IAS 27) requires that firm A reports all the assets of firm B on its balance sheet when firm A has the power to govern the financial and operating policies of firm B. This broadly defined principle anticipates situations where firm A owns less than half of firm B's voting shares but has other ways to influence firm B's decisions, such as through board memberships or contractual agreements. Similarly, the international standard on lease accounting (IAS 17) relies on the basic principle that when a lessee carries substantially all the risks of a leased asset, the asset is essentially owned by the lessee and must be reported on its balance sheet. This standard leaves much responsibility to managers and auditors to decide which leased assets are economically owned by the company.[1]

While reporting discretion is necessary to benefit from managers' insider knowledge about the economic substance of their company's transactions, it also permits managers to misrepresent transactions and satisfy their own financial reporting objectives. Accounting analysis, therefore, involves assessing whether a firm's reported assets adequately reflect the key resources that are under its control, and whether adjustments are required to compare its performance with that of competitors. Although firms are generally inclined to understate the assets that they control, thereby inflating the return on capital invested, they may sometimes pretend to control subsidiaries for the sake of inflating asset and revenue growth. For example, in the period from 1999 to 2001, Dutch food retailer Royal Ahold fraudulently reported the assets, liabilities, revenues, and operating profits of jointly controlled joint ventures in its financial statements as if the company fully controlled the joint ventures. The correct accounting treatment would have been to report only half of the joint ventures' assets and liabilities on Ahold's balance sheet and only half of the joint ventures' revenues, expenses, and operating profits in Ahold's income statement. By fully consolidating the joint ventures, Royal Ahold overstated its revenues by a total amount of €27.6 billion and its annual sales growth by an average of 24 percent. Analyzing the accounting of a firm that follows a strategy of growing through acquisitions, such as Ahold, thus would include identifying subsidiaries that are fully consolidated but not fully owned and assessing their impact on the firm's net assets, revenues, and growth figures.

In situations where standard setters or auditors impose rigid and mechanical accounting rules on managers to reduce reporting discretion, accounting analysis is nevertheless also important because these detailed rules permit managers to "groom" transactions to satisfy their own reporting objectives. For example, mechanical US rules on lease accounting permit two lease transactions with essentially the same but slightly different contract terms to be structured so that one is reported as an asset by the lessee, and the other is shown as an asset by the lessor. The analyst may attempt to correct for this distortion by adjusting the way in which the lessee and the lessor report these transactions.

Although a principles-based approach to standard setting may discourage the structuring of transactions, it cannot fully prevent it. In applying broadly defined reporting principles managers and auditors need guidance about, for example, the meaning of "carrying substantially all risks." When standard setters or standard interpretations committees, such as the International Financial Reporting Interpretations Committee (IFRIC), provide such guidance, they are bound to introduce some mechanical rules that auditors and public enforcers may hang on to. For example, the international standard for lease accounting includes several qualitative criteria for assessing whether the lessee is the economic owner of a leased asset. One example of a qualitative lease classification criterion is that leased assets are normally assumed to be owned by the lessee when the lease term covers the major part of the asset's economic useful life. Following the detailed US rules on lease accounting, auditors and public enforcers may themselves attach quantitative values to the term "major part," such as "greater than 75 percent." This practice of quantifying principles-based accounting standards could again encourage managers to structure transactions.

Asset ownership issues also arise indirectly from the application of rules for revenue recognition. Firms are permitted to recognize revenues only when their product has been shipped or their service has been provided to the customer. Revenues are then considered "earned," and the customer has a legal commitment to pay for the product or service. As a result, for the seller, recognition of revenue frequently coincides with "ownership" of a receivable that is shown as an asset on its balance sheet. Accounting analysis that raises questions about whether or not revenues have been earned therefore often affects the valuation of assets.

Ambiguity over whether a company owns an asset creates a number of opportunities for accounting analysis:

- Despite management's best intentions, financial statements sometimes do a poor job of reflecting the firm's economic assets because it is difficult for accounting rules to capture all of the subtleties associated with ownership and control.

- Accounting rules on ownership and control are the result of a trade-off between granting reporting discretion, which opens opportunities for earnings management, and imposing mechanical, rigid reporting criteria, which opens opportunities for the structuring of transactions. Because finding the perfect balance between discretion and rigidity is a virtually impossible task for standard setters, accounting rules cannot always prevent important assets being omitted from the balance sheet even though the firm bears many of the economic risks of ownership.

- There may be legitimate differences in opinion between managers and analysts over residual ownership risks borne by the company, leading to differences in opinion over reporting for these assets.

- Aggressive revenue recognition, which boosts reported earnings, is also likely to affect asset values.

Can economic benefits be measured with reasonable certainty?

It is almost always difficult to accurately forecast the future benefits associated with capital outlays because the world is uncertain. A company does not know whether a competitor will offer a new product or service that makes its own obsolete. It does not know whether the products manufactured at a new plant will be the type that customers want to buy. A company does not know whether changes in oil prices will make the oil drilling equipment that it manufactures less valuable.

Accounting rules deal with these challenges by stipulating which types of resources can be recorded as assets and which cannot. For example, the economic benefits from research and development are generally considered highly uncertain: research projects may never deliver promised new products, the products they generate may not be economically viable, or products may be made obsolete by competitors' research. International rules (IAS 38), therefore, require that research outlays be expensed and development outlays only be capitalized if they meet stringent criteria of technical and economic feasibility (which they rarely do in industries such as the pharmaceutical industry). In contrast, the economic benefits from plant acquisitions are considered less uncertain and are required to be capitalized.

Rules that require the immediate expensing of outlays for some key resources may be good accounting, but they create a challenge for the analyst – namely, they lead to less timely financial statements. For example, if all firms expense R&D, financial statements will reflect differences in R&D success only when new products are commercialized rather than during the development process. The analyst may attempt to correct for this distortion by capitalizing key R&D outlays and adjusting the value of the intangible asset based on R&D updates.[2]

Have fair values of assets declined below book value?

An asset is impaired when its fair value falls below its book value. In most countries accounting rules require that a loss be recorded for permanent asset impairments. International rules (IAS 36) specify that an impairment loss be recognized on a non-current asset when its book value exceeds the greater of its net selling price and the discounted cash flows expected to be generated from future use. If this condition is satisfied, the firm is required to report a loss for the difference between the asset's fair value and its book value.

Of course markets for many non-current operating assets are illiquid and incomplete, making it highly subjective to infer their fair values. Further, if the cash flows of an individual asset cannot be identified, IAS 36 requires that the impairment test be carried out for the smallest possible *group* of assets, called the cash generating unit, that has identifiable cash flows. Consequently, considerable management judgment is involved in defining the boundaries of cash generating units, deciding whether an asset is impaired and determining the value of any impairment loss.

For the analyst, this raises the possibility that asset values are misstated. International accounting rules themselves permit a certain amount of asset overstatement since the test for asset impairment is typically applied to the cash-generating unit. This can create situations where no financial statement loss is reported for an individual asset that is economically impaired but whose impairment is concealed in the group.

Are fair value estimates accurate?

Managers estimate fair values of assets not only for asset impairment testing. One other use of fair value estimates is to adjust the book value of assets when firms use the revaluation method instead of the historical cost method. The international accounting rules for non-current assets (IAS 16) allow firms to record their non-current assets at fair value instead of their historical cost prices. When doing so, firms must regularly assess whether the reported book values deviate too much from the assets' fair values and, if necessary make adjustments. Although revaluation adjustments are recorded in the statement of comprehensive income (not in the income statement), revaluations do affect earnings through the depreciation expense because, under this method, depreciation is determined by reference to the assets' fair value.

Fair value estimates are also needed to calculate goodwill in business combinations. Specifically, the amount by which the acquisition cost exceeds the fair value of the acquired net assets is recorded on the balance sheet as goodwill. The international standard for business combinations (IFRS 3) requires that the amount of goodwill is not amortized but regularly tested for impairment. This may create the incentive for managers to understate the fair value of acquired net assets and, consequently, overstate goodwill.

Finally, the international rules on the recognition and measurement of financial instruments (IAS 39) require a firm to recognize financial assets other than loans and receivables, such as investments in asset-backed securities, at their fair values if the firm does not intend to hold these assets to their maturities. Financial assets that a firm initially intended to hold to their maturities but that are currently available for sale must also be recognized at their fair values. Changes in the fair value of the second category of assets, other than impairment, are temporarily recorded in equity and later recognized in the income statement, once the assets get sold. All changes in the fair value of the first category of assets are immediately recognized in profit or loss.

The task of determining fair values is delegated to management, with oversight by the firm's auditors, potentially leaving opportunities for management bias in valuing assets and for legitimate differences in opinion between managers and analysts over asset valuations. In most cases, management bias will lead to overstated assets since managers will prefer not to recognize an impairment or prefer to overstate nonamortized goodwill in business combinations. However, managers can also bias asset values downward by "taking a bath," reducing future expenses and increasing future earnings.

To reduce management's discretion in determining the fair value of financial assets, their values must be derived from quoted market prices if an active market for the assets exists (typically referred to as marking to market). If quoted market prices are not available, firms can use their own valuation technique to determine the assets' fair values (referred to as marking to model); however, their valuation should be based on assumptions that outside market participants would reasonably make, not management's own assumptions. During the credit market crisis of 2008 trading in asset-backed securities came to a halt because of the high uncertainty surrounding the value of these securities. As fewer transactions in asset-backed securities took place at increasingly volatile prices, financial institutions owning such securities argued that market prices could no longer be reliably used to determine the securities' fair values. Following the guidance of the IASB, many financial institutions started to adjust market prices or use their own valuations to assess fair value. Of course, this move away from using observable market prices increases managers' accounting flexibility and increases the importance as well as the difficulty of establishing whether financial institutions' fair value estimates are reliable.

In summary, distortions in assets are likely to arise when there is ambiguity about whether the firm owns or controls a resource, when there is a high degree of uncertainty about the value of the economic benefits to be derived from the resource, and when there are differences in opinion about the value of asset impairments. Opportunities for accounting adjustments can arise in these situations if:

- Accounting rules do not do a good job of capturing the firm's economics.
- Managers use their discretion to distort the firm's performance.
- There are legitimate differences in opinion between managers and analysts about economic uncertainties facing the firm that are reflected in asset values.

FIRST-TIME ADOPTION: FAIR VALUE AS DEEMED COST

The international rules on the first-time application of IFRS (IFRS 1) suggest one additional use of fair value estimates. When a firm who uses the historical cost method applies IFRS for the first time in its financial statements, it can choose to consider the fair value of its non-current assets, such as property, plant and equipment, and investment property, as the "deemed cost" of its assets. Deemed cost is the assumed cost price of an asset at which it will initially be recorded in the firm's balance sheet. The firm then calculates depreciation on its non-current assets in reference to the deemed cost. First-time IFRS adopters thus have a one-time opportunity to exercise additional discretion over the book values of their non-current assets.

ASSET DISTORTIONS

Asset overstatements are likely to arise when managers have incentives to increase reported earnings. Thus, adjustments to assets also typically require adjustments to the income statement in the form of either increased expenses or reduced revenues. Asset understatements typically arise when managers have incentives to deflate reported earnings. This may occur when the firm is performing exceptionally well and managers decide to store away some of the current strong earnings for a rainy day. Income smoothing, as it has come to be known, can be implemented by overstating current period expenses (and understating the value of assets) during good times. Asset (and expense) understatements can also arise in a particularly bad year, when managers decide to "take a bath" by understating current period earnings to create the appearance of a turnaround in following years.

Accounting rules themselves can also lead to the understatement of assets. In many countries accounting standards require firms to expense outlays for research and advertising because, even though they may create future value for owners, their outcomes are highly uncertain. Also, until recently some acquisitions were accounted for using the pooling method, whereby the acquirer recorded the target's assets at their book value rather than their actual (higher) purchase price. In these cases the analyst may want to make adjustments to the balance sheet and income statement to ensure that they reflect the economic reality of the transactions.

Finally, asset understatements can arise when managers have incentives to understate liabilities. For example, if a firm records lease transactions as operating leases or if it discounts receivables with recourse, neither the assets nor the accompanying obligations are shown on its balance sheet. Yet in some instances this accounting treatment does not reflect the underlying economics of the transactions – the lessee may effectively own the leased assets, and the firm that sells receivables may still bear all of the risks associated with ownership. The analyst may then want to adjust the balance sheet (and also the income statement) for these effects.

Accounting analysis involves judging whether managers have understated or overstated assets (and also earnings) and, if necessary, adjusting the balance sheet and income statement accordingly. The most common items that can lead to overstatement or understatement of assets (and earnings) are the following:

- Depreciation and amortization on non-current assets.
- Impairment of non-current assets.
- Leased assets.
- Intangible assets.
- The timing of revenue (and receivables) recognition.
- Allowances (e.g., allowances for doubtful accounts or loan losses).
- Write-downs of current assets.
- Discounted receivables.

DEFERRED TAXES ON ADJUSTMENTS

Most firms use different accounting rules for business reporting and tax reporting. As a consequence, the assets and liabilities that firms report in their financial statements may differ in value from the assets and liabilities that they report in their tax statements. Consider a firm whose property, plant, and equipment have a book value of €300 in its financial statements but a tax base of €100 in its tax statements. Ignoring future investments, the firm will record a total amount of €300 in depreciation in its future financial statements, whereas it can only record an amount of €100 in tax-deductible depreciation in its future tax statements. Because the firm's tax statements are not publicly available, the analyst must estimate the firm's future tax deductions based on the book value of property, plant, and equipment as reported in the financial statements. This book value, however, overstates the firm's future tax deductions by an amount of €200 (€300 – €100). The IFRSs, therefore, require that the firm discloses the amount of overstatement of future tax deductions in its current financial statements. To do this, the firm recognizes a deferred tax liability on its balance sheet. Given a tax rate of 35 percent, the deferred tax liability equals €70 ([€300 – €100] × €0.35). This liability essentially represents the tax amount that the firm must pay in future years, in excess of the tax expense that the firm will report in its future financial statements. It also represents the tax amount that the firm would have to pay immediately were the firm to sell the asset for its current carrying amount. All additions to (reductions in) the deferred tax liability are accompanied by the recognition of a deferred tax expense (income) in the firm's income statement. Assets whose book values in the financial statements are below the tax bases recorded in the tax statements create a deferred tax asset.

When the analyst makes adjustments to the firm's assets or liabilities to undo any distortions, the deferred tax liability (or asset) is also affected. This is because the adjustments do not affect the tax statements and, consequently, change the difference between book values and tax bases. For example, when the analyst reduces the book value of property, plant, and equipment by €50, the deferred tax liability is reduced by an amount of €17.50 (€50 × €0.35) to €52.50 ([€250 – €100] × € 0.35).

The international accounting standard for income taxes requires that deferred taxes be recognized on any difference between book values and tax bases with the exception of a few differences, such as those related to:

- Nondeductible assets and nontaxable liabilities.
- Nondeductible goodwill and nontaxable negative goodwill.

Examples of asset understatement

We illustrate below some of the types of distortions that understate assets, and show corrections that the analyst can make to ensure that assets are reflected appropriately.

Overstated depreciation for non-current assets

Because non-current assets such as manufacturing equipment decrease in value over time, accounting rules require that firms systematically depreciate the book values of these assets. The reduction in the book value of the assets must be recognized as depreciation or amortization expense in the income statement. Managers make estimates of asset lives, salvage values, and amortization schedules for depreciable non-current assets. If these estimates are optimistic, non-current assets and earnings will be overstated. This issue is likely to be most pertinent for firms in heavy asset businesses (e.g., airlines, utilities), whose earnings contain large depreciation components. Firms that use tax depreciation estimates of asset lives, salvage values, or amortization rates are likely to amortize assets more rapidly than justifiable given the assets' economic usefulness, leading to non-current asset understatements.

In 2008 Lufthansa, the German national airline, reported that it depreciated its aircraft over 12 years on a straight-line basis, with an estimated residual value of 15 percent of initial cost. These assumptions imply that Lufthansa's annual depreciation expense was, on average, 7.1 percent ([1 – 0.15]/12) of the initial cost of its aircraft. In contrast, British Airways (BA), the UK national carrier, reported that its aircraft depreciation was also estimated using the straight-line method but assuming an average annual depreciation percentage of 4.4 percent of initial cost.

For the analyst these differences raise several questions. Do Lufthansa and BA fly different types of routes, potentially explaining the differences in their depreciation policies? Alternatively, do they have different asset management strategies? For example, does Lufthansa use newer planes to attract more business travelers, to lower maintenance costs, or to lower fuel costs? If there do not appear to be operating differences that explain the differences in the two firms' depreciation rates, the analyst may well decide that it is necessary to adjust the depreciation rates for one or both firms to ensure that their performance is comparable.

The difference in depreciation assumptions for BA and Lufthansa could at least partially reflect Lufthansa's decision to use similar depreciation rates for financial and tax reporting purposes, whereas BA uses different rates for these purposes. To evaluate this explanation, the analyst could examine the airlines' deferred tax liabilities. Recall that the deferred tax liability measures the difference between the book value and the tax base of a firm's net assets. In 2008 Lufthansa's deferred tax liability for depreciation and amortization was €619 million. Based on its tax percentage of 25 percent, this implies that the differences between Lufthansa's tax depreciation (and amortization) and its reported depreciation had accumulated to an amount of €2,476 million (619/0.25). This amount is equal to 18.0 percent (2,476/13,755) of accumulated depreciation on Lufthansa's non-current assets, which suggests that, on average, tax depreciation was 18.0 percent greater than reported depreciation. In the same year, BA's deferred tax liability of £1,105 million and accumulated depreciation on its non-current assets of £6,613 million implied that its accumulated differences between tax depreciation and reported depreciation were 55.7 percent ([1,105/0.30]/6,613) of accumulated depreciation. Hence, the difference between BA's depreciation rates for financial and tax reporting purposes appears to be substantially greater than the difference between Lufthansa's tax and reported depreciation rates.

To adjust for this effect, the analyst could decrease Lufthansa's depreciation rates to match those of BA's. The following financial statement adjustments would then be required in Lufthansa's financial statements:

1 Increase the book value of the fleet at the beginning of the year to adjust for the relatively high depreciation rates that had been used in the past. The necessary adjustment is equal to the following amount: original minus adjusted depreciation rate × average asset age × initial asset cost. At the beginning of 2008, Lufthansa reported in the notes to its financial statements that its fleet of aircraft had originally cost €17,066 million, and that accumulated depreciation was €9,893 million. This implies that the average age of Lufthansa's fleet was 8.2 years, calculated as follows:

€ (millions unless otherwise noted)

Aircraft cost, 1/1/2008	€17,066	Reported
Depreciable cost	€14,506.1	Cost × (1 − 0.15)
Accumulated depreciation, 1/1/2008	€9,893	Reported
Accumulated depreciation/Depreciable cost	68.20%	
Depreciable life	12 years	Reported
Average age of aircraft	8.184 years	12 × 0.6820 years

If Lufthansa used the same life and salvage estimates as BA, the annual depreciation rate would have been 4.4 percent, implying that given the average age of its fleet, accumulated depreciation would have been €6,145 (8.184 × 0.044 × 17,066) versus the reported €9,893. Consequently, the company's Non-Current Tangible Assets would have increased by €3,748 (9,893 − 6,145).

2 Calculate the offsetting increase in equity (retained earnings) and in the deferred tax liability. Given the 25 percent marginal tax rate, the adjustment to Non-Current Tangible Assets would have required offsetting adjustments of €937 (.25 × 3,748) to the Deferred Tax Liability and €2,811 (0.75 × 3,748) to Shareholders' Equity.

3 Reduce the depreciation expense (and increase the book value of the fleet) to reflect the lower depreciation for the current year. Assuming that €1,154 million net new aircraft purchased in 2008 were acquired throughout the year, and therefore require only half a year of depreciation, the depreciation expense for 2008 (included in Cost of Sales) would have been €776 million {0.044 × [17,066 + (1,154/2)]} versus the €1,250 {(0.85/12) × [17,066 + (1,154/2)]} million reported by the company. Thus Cost of Sales would decline by €474 million.

4 Increase the tax expense, net profit, and the balance sheet values of equity and the deferred tax liability. Given the 25 percent tax rate for 2008, the Tax Expense for the year would increase by €119 million. On the balance sheet, these changes would increase Non-Current Tangible Assets by €474 million, increase Deferred Tax Liability by €119 million, and increase Shareholders' Equity by €355 million.

Note that these changes are designed to show Lufthansa's results as if it had always used the same depreciation assumptions as BA rather than to reflect a change in the assumptions for the current year going forward. This enables the analyst to be able to compare ratios that use assets (e.g., return on assets) for the two companies. By making the adjustments, the analyst substantially improves the comparability of Lufthansa's and BA's financial statements.

In summary, if Lufthansa were using the same depreciation method as BA, its financial statements for the years ended December 31, 2007 and 2008 would have to be modified as follows (references to the above described steps are reported in brackets):

€ (millions)	Adjustments December 31, 2007		Adjustments December 31, 2008	
	Assets	Liabilities	Assets	Liabilities
Balance sheet				
Non-Current Tangible Assets	+3,748 (1)		+3,748 (1)	
			+474 (3)	
Deferred Tax Liability		+937 (2)		+937 (2)
				+119 (4)
Shareholders' Equity		+2,811 (2)		+2,811 (2)
				+355 (4)
Income statement				
Cost of Sales				−474 (3)
Tax Expense				+119 (4)
Net Profit				+355 (4)

Leased assets off balance sheet

One of the objectives of the balance sheet is to report the assets for which a firm receives the rewards and bears the risks. These can also be assets the firm does not legally own but leases from another firm. There are two ways in which a firm can record its leased assets. Under the operating method, the firm recognizes the lease payment as an expense in the period in which it occurs, keeping the leased asset off its balance sheet. In contrast, under the finance method, the firm records the asset and an offsetting lease liability on its balance sheet. During the lease period, the firm then recognizes depreciation on the asset as well as interest on the lease liability.

Assessing whether a lease arrangement should be considered a rental contract (and hence recorded using the operating method) or equivalent to a purchase (and hence shown as a finance lease) is subjective. It depends on whether the lessee has effectively accepted most of the risks of ownership, such as obsolescence and physical deterioration. To guide the reporting of lease transactions, the international accounting rules include criteria for distinguishing between the two types. IAS 17 explains that a firm would normally consider a lease transaction equivalent to an asset purchase if any of the following conditions hold:

1 Ownership of the asset is transferred to the lessee at the end of the lease term.

2 The lessee has the option to purchase the asset for a bargain price at the end of the lease term.

3 The lease term is for the major part of the asset's expected useful life.

4 The present value of the lease payments is equal to substantially all of the fair value of the asset.

5 The asset cannot be used by other than the lessee without major modifications.

However, because the criteria for reporting leases are broadly defined and inconclusive, they create opportunities for management to circumvent the spirit of the distinction between capital and operating leases, potentially leading to the understatement of lease assets. This is likely to be an important issue for the analysis of heavy asset industries where there are options for leasing (e.g., airlines).[3] Debt rating analysts tend to consider the distinction between operating leases and finance leases as artificial and capitalize the present value of future operating lease payments before analyzing a firm's financial position. An example of how to capitalize operating lease commitments follows.[4]

Finnair, the Finnish airline company, accounts for part of its rented flight equipment using the operating method. These rented resources are therefore excluded from Finnair's balance sheet, making it difficult for an analyst to compare Finnair's financial performance with other airlines that have a different mixture of finance and operating leases. To correct this accounting, the analyst can use the information on noncancelable lease commitments presented in Finnair's lease note to estimate the value of the assets and liabilities that are omitted from the balance sheet. The leased equipment is then depreciated over the life of the lease, and the lease payments are treated as interest and debt repayment.

On December 31, 2007 and 2008, Finnair reports the following minimum future rental payments:

(€ millions)	December 31, 2008	December 31, 2007
Less than 1 year	76.1	75.3
1–2 years	54.8	68.5
2–3 years	49.0	49.9
3–4 years	40.5	45.2
4–5 years	24.4	37.0
More than 5 years	41.1	48.9
Total	285.9	324.8

Because Finnair does not show the present value of its operating lease commitments, the analyst must decide how to allocate the lump sum values of €41.1 and €48.9 over year six and beyond, and estimate a suitable interest rate on the lease debt. It is then possible to compute the present value of the lease payments.

Finnair indicates that its annual interest rate on outstanding interest-bearing debt is 4.7 percent and the lease expense reported in 2008 is €82.6 million. Assume that the annual rental payments in the sixth is equal to the rental payment in the fifth year (€24.4 and €37.0) and the remainder of the lump sum values (€16.7 and €11.9) is due in the seventh year. With a discount rate of 4.7 percent, the present values of the minimum rental payments for the years ended December 31, 2007 and 2008 are as follows:

(€ millions)	December 31, 2008	December 31, 2007
Within one year	72.7	71.9
Over one year	176.4	209.7
Total	249.1	281.6

Given this information, the analyst can make the following adjustments to Finnair's beginning and ending balance sheets, and to its income statement for the year ended December 31, 2008:

1 Capitalize the present value of the lease commitments for December 31, 2007, increasing Non-Current Tangible Assets and Non-Current Debt by €281.6.

2 Calculate the value of any change in lease assets and lease liabilities during the year from new lease transactions. On December 31, 2007, Finnair's liability for lease commitments in 2009 and beyond was €209.7. If there had been no changes in these commitments, one year later (on December 31, 2008), they would have been valued at €219.6 (209.7 × 1.047). Yet Finnair's actual lease commitment on December 31, 2008 was €249.1. Further, Finnair's actual lease expense in 2008 was €82.6, instead of the "anticipated" amount of €75.3 (see the table above showing the minimum future rental payments, third column). The unanticipated lease expense reflects an increase in Finnair's lease commitments of €7.3 ([82.6 − 75.3]) which is paid in the same year as it occurs. In total, these differences indicate that the company increased its leased aircraft capacity by €36.8 ([249.1 − 219.6] + [82.6 − 75.3]). Finnair's Non-Current Tangible Assets and Non-Current Debt therefore increased by €36.8 during 2008.

3 Reflect the change in lease asset value and expense from the depreciation during the year. The depreciation expense for 2008 (included in Cost of Sales) is the depreciation rate (1/7) multiplied by the beginning cost of leased equipment (€281.6) plus depreciation on the increase in leased equipment for 2008 (€36.8), prorated throughout the year. The depreciation expense for 2008 is therefore €42.9 (281.6/7 + 0.5 × [36.8/7]).

4 Add back the operating lease expense in the income statement, included in Cost of Sales. As previously mentioned, the operating lease expense, which is equal to the lease payment that Finnair made to its lessors, is €82.6. When lease liabilities are recorded on the balance sheet, as under the finance method, the lease payment must be treated as the sum of interest and debt repayment (see next item), instead of being recorded as an expense.

5 Apportion the lease payment between Interest Expense and repayment of Non-Current Debt. The portion of this that is shown as Interest Expense is the interest rate (4.7 percent) multiplied by the beginning lease liability (€281.6) plus interest on the increase in the leased liability for 2008 (€36.8), prorated throughout the year. The interest

expense for 2008 is therefore €14.1 (0.047 × 281.6 + 0.5 × 0.047 × 36.8). The Non-Current Debt repayment portion is then the remainder of the total lease payment, €68.5 (82.6 − 14.1).

6 Make any needed changes to the Deferred Tax Liability to reflect differences in earnings under the finance and operating lease methods. Finnair's expenses under the finance lease method are €57.0 (€42.9 depreciation expense plus €14.1 interest expense) versus €82.6 under the operating lease method. Finnair will not change its tax books, but for financial reporting purposes it will show higher earnings before tax and thus a higher Tax Expense through deferred taxes. Given its 26 percent tax rate, the Tax Expense will increase by €6.7 (0.26 × [82.6 − 57.0]) and the Deferred Tax Liability will increase by the same amount.

In summary, the adjustments to Finnair's financial statements on December 31, 2007 and 2008, are as follows:

€(millions)	Adjustments December 31, 2007		Adjustments December 31, 2008	
	Assets	Liabilities	Assets	Liabilities
Balance sheet				
Non-Current Tangible Assets:				
Beginning capitalization	+281.6 (1)	+281.6 (1)	+281.6 (1)	
New leases			+36.8 (2)	
Annual depreciation			−42.9 (3)	
Non-Current Debt:				
Beginning debt				+281.6 (1)
New leases				+36.8 (2)
Debt repayment				−68.5 (5)
Deferred Tax Liability				+6.7 (6)
Shareholders' Equity				+18.9 (6)
Income statement				
Cost of Sales:				
Lease expense				−82.6 (4)
Depreciation expense				+42.9 (3)
Interest Expense				+14.1 (5)
Tax Expense				+6.7 (6)
Net Profit				+18.9 (6)

These adjustments increase Finnair's fixed assets by 13 percent in 2007 and 2008, reducing the company's asset turnover (sales/assets) from the reported value of 102 percent to 90 percent in 2007, and from 109 percent to 97 percent in 2008. There is also a difference in earnings, since the lease expense is replaced with the depreciation and interest expenses. This leads to an increase in operating earnings (before interest). As a result, the company's return on operating assets for 2008 actually increases from the reported value of −5.0 percent to −1.1 percent.

Key intangible assets off balance sheet

Some firms' most important assets are excluded from the balance sheet. Examples include investments in R&D, software development outlays, and brands and membership bases that are created through advertising and promotions. Accounting rules in most countries specifically prohibit the capitalization of research outlays, primarily because it is believed that the benefits associated with such outlays are too uncertain. New products or software may never reach the market due to technological infeasibility or to the introduction of superior products by competitors. Expensing the cost of intangibles has two implications for analysts. First, the omission of intangible assets from the balance sheet inflates measured rates of return on capital (either return on assets or return on equity).[5] For firms with key omitted intangible assets, this has important implications for forecasting long-term performance; unlike firms with no intangibles, competitive forces will not cause their rates of return to fully revert to the cost of capital over time. For example, pharmaceutical firms have shown very high rates of return over many decades, in part because of the impact of R&D accounting. A second effect of expensing outlays for intangibles is that it makes it more difficult for the analyst to assess whether the firm's business model works. Under the matching concept, operating profit is a meaningful indicator of the success of a firm's business model since it compares revenues and the expenses required to generate them. Immediately expensing outlays for intangible assets runs counter to matching and, therefore, makes it more difficult to judge a firm's operating performance. Consistent with this, research shows that investors view R&D and advertising outlays as assets rather than expenses.[6] Understated intangible assets are likely to be important for firms in pharmaceutical, software, branded consumer products, and subscription businesses.

How should the analyst approach the omission of intangibles? One way is to leave the accounting as is, but to recognize that forecasts of long-term rates of return will have to reflect the inherent biases that arise from this accounting method. A second approach is to capitalize intangibles and amortize them over their expected lives.

For example, consider the case of AstraZeneca, one of the largest pharmaceutical companies in the world. AstraZeneca does not capitalize most of its R&D costs because regulatory uncertainties surrounding the development and marketing of new products mean that the recognition criteria for research expenditures are rarely met. What adjustment would be required if the analyst decided to capitalize all of AstraZeneca's R&D and to amortize the intangible asset using the straight-line method over the expected life of R&D investments? Assume for simplicity that R&D spending occurs evenly throughout the year, that only half a year's amortization is taken on the latest year's spending, and that the average expected life of R&D investments is approximately five years. Given R&D outlays for the years 2003 to 2007, the R&D asset at the end of 2007 is $10.5 billion, calculated as follows:

Year	R&D Outlay	Proportion Capitalized 31/12/07	Asset 31/12/07	Proportion Capitalized 31/12/08	Asset 31/12/08
2008	$5.2b			$(1 - 0.2/2)$	$ 4.7b
2007	5.2	$(1 - 0.2/2)$	$ 4.7b	$(1 - 0.2/2 - 0.2)$	3.6
2006	3.9	$(1 - 0.2/2 - 0.2)$	2.7	$(1 - 0.2/2 - 0.4)$	2.0
2005	3.4	$(1 - 0.2/2 - 0.4)$	1.7	$(1 - 0.2/2 - 0.6)$	1.0
2004	3.5	$(1 - 0.2/2 - 0.6)$	1.1	$(1 - 0.2/2 - 0.8)$	0.4
2003	3.0	$(1 - 0.2/2 - 0.8)$	0.3		
Total			$10.5		$11.6

The R&D amortization expense (included in Other Operating Expenses) for 2007 and 2008 are $3.6 billion and $4.0 billion, respectively, and are calculated as follows:

Year	R&D Outlay	Proportion Amortized 31/12/07	Expense 31/12/07	Proportion Amortized 31/12/08	Expense 31/12/08
2008	$5.2b			0.2/2	$0.5b
2007	5.2	0.2/2	$0.5b	0.2	1.0
2006	3.9	0.2	0.8	0.2	0.8
2005	3.4	0.2	0.7	0.2	0.7
2004	3.5	0.2	0.7	0.2	0.7
2003	3.0	0.2	0.6	0.2/2	0.3
2002	3.1	0.2/2	0.3		
Total			$3.6		$4.0

Since AstraZeneca will continue to expense software R&D immediately for tax purposes, the change in reporting method will give rise to a Deferred Tax Liability. Given a marginal tax rate of 28 percent, this liability will equal 28 percent of the value of the Intangible Asset reported, with the balance increasing Shareholders' Equity.

In summary, the adjustments required to capitalize software R&D for AstraZeneca for the years 2007 and 2008 are as follows:

($ billions)	Adjustments December 31, 2007		Adjustments December 31, 2008	
	Assets	Liabilities	Assets	Liabilities
Balance sheet				
Non-Current Intangible Assets	+10.5		+11.6	
Deferred Tax Liability		+2.9		+3.2
Shareholders' Equity		+7.5		+8.4
Income statement				
Other Operating Expenses		−5.2		−5.2
Other Operating Expenses		+3.6		+4.0
Tax Expense		+0.4		+0.3
Net Profit		+1.2		+0.9

Discounted receivables

To improve liquidity a firm may sometimes decide to sell part of its receivables to a financial institution, after which the financial institution services the collection of the receivables. Once the receivables have been sold, the seller must decide whether it accounts for the transaction as a sale or as a received loan collateralized by receivables. Under current international accounting rules (IAS 39 and its implementation guidance), receivables that are discounted with a financial institution are considered "sold" if the "seller" cedes control over the receivables to the financier. Control is surrendered if the receivables are beyond the reach of the seller's creditors should the seller file for bankruptcy, if the financier (and not the seller) has the right to pledge or sell its interest in the receivables, and if the seller has no legal right or commitment to repurchase the receivables. Also, when the seller continues to service the receivables, control is surrendered if the seller has the contractual obligation to transfer any collections to the financier without material delay. The seller can then record the discount transaction as an asset sale. Otherwise it is viewed as a financing transaction that generates a liability for the "seller."

Just because a firm has "sold" receivables for financial reporting purposes does not necessarily mean that it is off the hook for credit risks. Financial institutions that discount receivables often have recourse against the "seller," requiring the seller to continue to estimate bad debt losses and record a recourse liability for the amount of losses that it guarantees. In this event, international accounting rules permit the transaction to be reported as an asset sale only when the seller satisfies the above conditions for surrendering control of the receivables and the financier assumes all risks other than the credit risk. In extreme cases, where there is significant uncertainty about the value of the recourse liability, the analyst has to decide whether to restate the firm's financial statements by returning the "sold" receivables to the balance sheet. This will also increase the firm's liabilities, and it will affect its income statement since any gains and losses on the sale need to be excluded, and interest income on the notes receivables and interest expense on the loan need to be recorded each year.

Sweden-based car manufacturer Volvo regularly discounts a proportion of its customer finance receivables. In 2005 Volvo reported in the notes to its first IFRS-based financial statements that its discounted receivables did not meet the IAS 39 requirements for asset derecognition. In contrast, in Volvo's prior period financial statements, which were prepared in accordance with Swedish GAAP, discounted receivables with similar characteristics were considered "sold" and derecognized from the balance sheet. Because Volvo chose to apply IAS 39 only to the fiscal years starting after January 1, 2005, the receivables that were discounted during 2004 remained off the 2004 balance sheet that Volvo reported in its 2005 financial statements (for comparative purposes), rendering the assets and liabilities for the years 2004 and 2005 not comparable.

In 2004 Volvo reported a contingent liability (off balance) of SEK2,471 million for receivables that had been discounted with recourse. This contingent liability represents the maximum amount for which Volvo is liable if the receivables cannot be collected. The amount that Volvo received from the financier in exchange for the receivables is, however, less than SEK2,471 because the financier must be compensated for taking on the collection of receivables. One way for the analyst to make the 2004 balance sheet comparable to the 2005 balance sheet is to reverse the sale by recording an asset for the full SEK2,471 million, recording a liability for less than SEK2,471 million, and reversing the loss on the transaction (equal to the difference between SEK2,471 and the liability). This would require the following adjustments:

1 Volvo's Other Long-Term Assets would be increased by the receivable commitment (SEK2,471 million). In turn, Long-Term Debt would be recorded to reflect the value of the cash advanced to Volvo under the discount transaction. Assuming that Volvo charges its customers an annual interest rate of roughly 9 percent, customers repay the receivables in equal monthly installments over the next four years, and the financier charges a 10 percent interest rate, the receivable loan would be valued at SEK2,428 million. Note that the interest rate differential compensates the financier for collecting the receivables. The value of the loan can be calculated as follows. The annual interest rates of 9 and 10 percent correspond with monthly interest rates of 0.721 and 0.797 percent ($1.09^{1/12} - 1$ and $1.1^{1/12} - 1$). The present value of an annuity of SEK1 per month for 48 months is SEK40.45 (SEK39.76) for a monthly interest rate of 0.721 (0.797) percent. Hence, the receivable of SEK2,471 million corresponds with monthly installments of SEK61.08 million (2,471/40.45). Given an annual interest rate of 10 percent

and a monthly interest rate of 0.797 percent, these installments have a present value of SEK2,428 million (61.08 × 39.76).

2 The after-tax difference between the face value of the receivables and the loan, which would have been shown as a loss on sale under the reported accounting, needs to be reversed, increasing equity. Given the above assumptions and Volvo's 28 percent marginal tax rate, the adjustment would increase Shareholders' Equity by SEK31 million [43 × (1 – 0.28)].

3 The impact of the tax deduction from reporting a loss on sale, which would have reduced the Deferred Tax Liability, needs to be reversed. For Volvo, this amount would have resulted in a roughly SEK12 million (43 × 0.28) increase in the Deferred Tax Liability.

4 During the year ended December 31, 2005, customers are scheduled to make 12 monthly payments of SEK61.08 million on the discounted receivables, reducing the value of notes receivable under the adjusted accounting. Customers total payment in 2005 amounts to SEK733.0 million (12 × 61.08). At the end of 2005, the remaining duration of the receivables is 36 months and the value of the receivables would reduce to SEK1,930.7 million (which is the present value of 36 monthly installments of 61.08 at 9 percent). For Volvo, customers' total payment of SEK733.0 can be split up into the receivable repayment of SEK540.3 million (2,471.0 – 1,930.7) and Interest Income of SEK192.7 million (733.0 – 540.3).

5 The present value of the loan would be SEK1,904.8 (the present value of 36 monthly installments of 61.08 at 10 percent) at the end of 2005, reflecting the loan repayment of SEK523.2 million (2,428 – 1,904.8). For 2005, Volvo's income statement would include Interest Expense from the loan of SEK209.8 million (733.0 – 523.2) along with any tax effects. The loan would decline by a smaller amount than the receivables, since SEK17.1 million of the receivable repayments are allocated to covering the higher interest charged on the loan (exactly offsetting the wedge between the Interest Income and the Interest Expense for the year). In other words, the value of the loan declines by the value of receivable repayments by customers (SEK540.3 million) net of the portion of the repayment that represents incremental interest charged by the bank relative to the rate Volvo charged its customers (SEK17.1 million, or SEK209.8 million – SEK192.7 million).

6 The net effect of the income statement adjustments on pretax profit is minus SEK17.1 million in 2005. The Tax Expense would therefore have to be decreased by SEK4.8 million (17.1 × 0.28) and Net Profit by SEK12.3 million (17.1 × [1 – 0.28]).

The overall effect of these adjustments on Volvo's financial statements would, therefore, be as follows:

SEK (millions)	Adjustments December 31, 2004		Adjustments December 31, 2005	
	Assets	Liabilities	Assets	Liabilities
Balance sheet				
Other Non-Current Assets	+2,471.0 (1)		+2,471.0 (1)	
			−540.3 (4)	
Non-Current Debt		+2,428.0 (1)		+2,428.0 (1)
				−523.2 (5)
Deferred Tax Liability		+12.0 (3)		+12.0 (3)
				−4.8 (6)

(Continued)

	Adjustments December 31, 2004		Adjustments December 31, 2005	
SEK (millions)	Assets	Liabilities	Assets	Liabilities
Shareholders' Equity		+31.0 (2)		+31.0 (2)
				−12.3 (6)
Income statement				
Other Operating Income				
Interest Income				+192.7 (4)
Interest Expense				+209.8 (5)
Tax Expense				−4.8 (6)
Net Profit				−12.3 (6)

FIRST-TIME ADOPTION: APPLYING THE CURRENT VERSION OF IFRS

Because the IASB regularly revises its set of standards, the international rules on the first-time application of IFRS explicitly mention that a first-time IFRS adopter must apply the rules that are effective at the reporting date, being the fiscal year-end date of the current year. It is possible that a new or revised standard became effective during the year of first-time IFRS adoption. In this situation, a first-time adopter must also apply the new or revised standard to the prior year balance sheet and income statement that it reports for comparative purposes.

The above example provides an illustration of an exception to this general rule. Firms that adopt IFRS for the first time are not allowed to recognize previously de-recognized assets in their comparative balance sheets if the assets have been derecognized prior to January 2004. Further, firms that adopted IFRS prior to January 2006, as most European first-time adopters did, were not required to comply with the international accounting rules for financial instruments (IAS 32 and 39), which include the asset de-recognition rules, when preparing their first-time IFRS comparative balance sheet. Volvo therefore used different treatments for its discounted receivables in 2004 and 2005. Fortunately, pre-January 2006 adopters of IFRS must disclose the effects of IAS 32 and 39 adoptions on the opening balance sheet of the current year, which helps the analyst to make the necessary adjustments to the comparative statements.

Examples of asset overstatement

We illustrate below some of the types of distortions that overstate assets, and show corrections that the analyst can make to ensure that assets are reflected appropriately. Note that some of the accounting methods that we describe can also be used by managers to understate assets. For example, managers may overstate allowances, which would lead to understatement of assets. The corrections that we describe can of course be easily modified to undo the effects of asset overstatement.

Accelerated recognition of revenues

Managers typically have the best information on the uncertainties governing revenue recognition – whether a product or service has been provided to customers and whether cash collection is reasonably likely. However, managers may also have incentives to accelerate the recognition of revenues, boosting reported earnings for the period. Trade receivables and earnings will then be overstated. During the 1990s and the early 2000s, aggressive revenue recognition is one of the most popular forms of earnings management cited by the US public enforcer, the SEC.

In November 1999 and January 2000, analysts at the Center for Financial Research and Analysis (CFRA) raised questions about the propriety of revenue recognition for MicroStrategy, a US-based software company. MicroStrategy recognized revenues from the sale of licenses "after execution of a licensing agreement and shipment of the product, provided that no significant Company obligations remain and the resulting receivable is deemed collectible by management."[7] While MicroStrategy prepared its financial statements in accordance with US GAAP, its accounting principle for the recognition of license revenues was also in accordance with the international standard on revenue recognition (IAS 18). CFRA analysts were concerned about MicroStrategy's booking two contracts worth $27 million as quarterly revenues when the contracts were not announced until several days after the quarter's end. If the analysts decided to adjust for these distortions, the following changes would have to be made to Micro Strategy's financial reports:

1 In the quarter that the contracts were booked, Sales and Trade Receivables would both decline by $27 million.

2 Cost of Sales would decline and Inventory would increase to reflect the reduction in sales. The value of the Cost of Sales/Inventory adjustment can be estimated by multiplying the sales adjustment by the ratio of cost of sales to sales. For MicroStrategy, cost of license revenues is only 3 percent of license revenues, indicating that the adjustment would be modest ($0.8m). Also, since MicroStrategy does not have any inventory, the balance sheet adjustment would be to prepaid expenses, which are included in Other Current Assets on the standardized balance sheet.

3 The decline in pretax profit would result in a lower Tax Expense in the company's financial reporting books (but presumably not in its tax books). Consequently, the Deferred Tax Liability would have to be reduced. MicroStrategy's marginal tax rate was 35 percent, implying that the decline in the Tax Expense and Deferred Tax Liability was $9.2 million [($27 − 0.8) × .35].

The full effect of the adjustment on the quarterly financial statements would therefore be as follows:

($ millions)	Adjustments	
	Assets	**Liabilities and Equity**
Balance sheet		
Trade Receivables	−27.0 (1)	
Other Current Assets	+0.8 (2)	
Deferred Tax Liability		−9.2 (3)
Shareholders' Equity		−17.0 (3)
Income statement		
Sales		−27.0 (1)
Cost of Sales		−0.8 (2)
Tax Expense		−9.2 (3)
Net Profit		−17.0 (3)

Of course, provided the contracts were legitimate transactions, the above adjustments imply that forecasts of the next quarter's revenues should include the $27 million worth of contracts.

In March 2000 MicroStrategy confirmed that the CFRA analysts' suspicions about aggressive revenue recognition were founded. The company announced that it had "recorded revenue on certain contracts in one reporting period where customer signature and delivery had been completed, but where the contract may not have been fully executed by the Company in that reporting period."[8] After reviewing all licensing contracts near the end of the prior three years, MicroStrategy was forced to restate its financial statements to correct for the improprieties. The outcome was that trade receivables for 1999 were reduced from $61.1 million to $37.6 million, leading to a dramatic drop in the company's stock price.

Delayed write-downs of non-current assets

Deteriorating industry or firm economic conditions can affect the value of non-current assets as well as current assets. When the fair value of an asset falls below its book value, the asset is "impaired." Firms are required to recognize impairments in the values of non-current assets when they arise. However, since second-hand markets for non-current assets are typically illiquid and incomplete, estimates of asset valuations and impairment are inherently subjective. This is particularly true for intangible assets such as goodwill, which is the amount by which the cost of business acquisitions exceeds the fair value of the acquired assets. As a result, managers can use their reporting judgment to delay write-downs on the balance sheet and avoid showing impairment charges in the income statement.[9] This issue is likely to be particularly critical for heavily asset-intensive firms in volatile markets (e.g., airlines) or for firms that follow a strategy of aggressive growth through acquisitions and report substantial amounts of goodwill.[10] Warning signs of impairments in non-current assets include declining non-current asset turnover, declines in return on assets to levels lower than the weighted average cost of capital, write-downs by other firms in the same industry that have also suffered deteriorating asset use, and overpayment for or unsuccessful integration of key acquisitions. Managers may sometimes also have incentives to overstate asset impairment. Overly pessimistic management estimates of non-current asset impairments reduce current period earnings and boost earnings in future periods.

Consider discount airliner easyJet's acquisition of GB Airways. In January 2008 easyJet acquired all shares of GB Airways for an amount of £129.4 million. The airline estimated the fair value of GB's net assets (assets minus liabilities) at £79.2 million and, consequently, recorded £50.2 million (129.4 − 79.2) of goodwill in its balance sheet for the year ended September 30, 2008. The fair value estimate included fair value adjustments of £72.4 million for GB's landing rights at Gatwick airport and £30.0 million for GB's landing rights at Heathrow airport. It also included the fair value of GB's seven A321 Airbus aircraft, amounting to £83.4 million. In its 2008 financial statements easyJet reported that it would periodically test the amount of goodwill for impairment, together with its other assets, which easyJet considered all part of one cash generating unit.

On November 18, 2008, easyJet's non-executive director and primary shareholder Stelios Haji-Ioannou issued a press release stating that he could not approve easyJet's 2008 financial statements for several reasons. In particular, the director/shareholder argued that:

- The Gatwick landing rights have a zero fair value because the airport was not capacity constrained.
- Given that these landing rights have no value, goodwill on the GB acquisition amounts to £122.6 million (50.2 + 72.4). This amount should be tested for impairment separate

from the other assets of easyJet because, like competitor Ryanair, easyJet could consider its routes as separate cash generating units.

■ EasyJet needed to write down the value of the seven A321 Airbus aircraft that it had acquired.

The airline was trying to sell the seven aircraft but experienced some difficulty finding potential buyers during the economic downturn. On November 20, 2008, easyJet announced, however, that it had been able to sell two aircraft for a price that was in line with management's prior expectations. Although this announcement helped to ease outsiders' concerns about the fair value of the aircraft, an analyst might still decide that the landing rights are likely to have a zero fair value and need to be written down (rather than reclassified as goodwill). To record an additional write-down of £72.4 million in the September 2008 financials, it would be necessary to make the following balance sheet adjustments:

1   Reduce Non-Current Intangible Assets and increase Other Expenses by £72.4 million.

2   Reduce the Deferred Tax Liability and the Tax Expense for the tax effect of the write-down. Assuming a 28 percent tax rate, this amounts to £20.3 million.

3   Reduce Shareholders' Equity and Net Profit for the after-tax effect of the write-down (£52.1 million).

(£ millions)	Adjustment	
	Assets	**Liabilities and Equity**
Balance sheet		
Non-Current Intangible Assets	−72.4 (1)	
Deferred Tax Liability		−20.3 (2)
Shareholders' Equity		−52.1 (3)
Income statement		
Other Expenses		+72.4 (1)
Tax Expense		−20.3 (2)
Net Profit		−52.1 (3)

Note that the write-down of depreciable assets at the beginning of the year will require the analyst to also estimate the write-down's impact on depreciation and amortization expense for the year.

Delayed write-downs of current assets

If current assets become impaired – that is, their book values fall below their realizable values – accounting rules generally require that they be written down to their fair values. Current asset impairments also affect earnings since write-offs are charged directly to earnings. Deferring current asset write-downs is, therefore, one way for managers to boost reported profits.[11] Analysts that cover firms where management of inventories and receivables is a key success factor (e.g., the retail and manufacturing industries) need to be particularly cognizant of this of earnings management. If managers over-buy or over-produce in the current period, they are likely to have to offer customers discounts to get rid of surplus inventories. In addition, providing customers with credit carries risks of default. Warning signs for delays in current asset write-downs include growing days' inventory and days' receivable, write-downs by competitors, and business downturns for a firm's major customers.

Managers potentially have an incentive to overstate current asset write-downs during years of exceptionally strong performance, or when the firm is financially distressed. By overstating current asset impairments and overstating expenses in the current period, managers can show lower future expenses, boosting earnings in years of sub-par performance or when a turnaround is needed. Overstated current asset write-downs can also arise when managers are less optimistic about the firm's future prospects than the analyst.

Underestimated allowances

Managers make estimates of expected customer defaults on trade receivables and loans. If managers underestimate the value of these allowances, assets and earnings will be overstated. Warning signs of inadequate allowances include growing days receivable, business downturns for a firm's major clients, and growing loan delinquencies. If managers overestimate allowances for doubtful accounts or loan losses, trade receivables and loans will be understated.

Consider the allowances for doubtful accounts reported by Luxemburg-based Metro International S.A. in the years 2002–2007. In these years, Metro International derived most of its revenues from selling advertisements in its international newspaper Metro, which it distributed free in more than 20 countries. To illustrate the low collection risk on its trade receivables, Metro reported in the notes to its financial statements that its receivables came "from a large number of customers, in different industries and geographical areas, none of which in itself is material in size." At the end of 2007, about 93 percent of Metro's receivables were less than 120 days old. From 2002 to 2007, Metro reported the following values for its gross trade receivables and allowances:

Year	Gross trade receivables	Allowances for doubtful accounts	Allowances / Gross receivables (%)
2002	$39,093k	$3,129k	8.0 %
2003	54,025	5,447	10.1 %
2004	70,817	7,073	10.0 %
2005	76,014	9,748	12.8 %
2006	103,225	12,593	12.2 %
2007	112,250	13,385	11.9 %

During these six years, the actual write-offs on Metro's receivables varied from 0.5 to 3 percent of the beginning balances of trade receivables (in both years), which was much less than the 8–13 percent that Metro added to its allowance. Given the low collection risk on the company's receivables, Metro could be overstating its allowances. If the analyst decided that allowances were indeed overstated, adjustments would have to be made to Trade Receivables and to Equity for the after-tax cost of the overstated provision for doubtful accounts.

On December 31, 2007, Metro reported the following values for its allowances and write-offs:

($ thousands)	December 31, 2007	December 31, 2006	December 31,2005
Allowances for doubtful accounts			
Balance at beginning of year	12,593	9,748	7,073
Provision for bad debts	3,147	4,218	3,070
Write-offs	(2,355)	(1,373)	(395)
Balance at end of year	13,385	12,593	9,748

If the analyst decided that receivable allowances for Metro in 2007 and 2006 should be 5 percent rather than 12 percent, the following adjustments would have to be made:

1 Increase Trade Receivables on December 31, 2006 and 2007 by $7,432 thousand ([0.122 − 0.050] × 103,225) to reflect the adjustment to the allowance.

2 Given the company's marginal tax rate of 28 percent, increase Shareholders' Equity for 2006 by $5,351 thousand ([1 − 0.28] × 7,432), and increase the Deferred Tax Liability for 2006 by $2,081 thousand (0.28 × 7,432).

3 After adjustment, the beginning and ending balances of the allowance for 2007 are $5,161 thousand (12,593 − 7,432) and $5,640 thousand (13,385 − [0.119 − 0.050] × 112,250), respectively. Whereas the actual write-off on receivables for 2007 remains unchanged ($2,355 thousand), the adjusted provision for bad debts is 2,834 (5,640 − 5,161 + 2,355). Because the unadjusted provision for 2007 was $3,147 thousand, increase Trade Receivables and decrease Cost of Sales for 2007 by $313 thousand (3,147 − 2,834).

4 Increase the tax expense, net profit, and the balance sheet values of equity and the deferred tax liability. Given the tax rate of 28 percent, the Tax Expense and Deferred Tax Liability for 2007 would increase by $88 thousand (0.28 × 313), whereas Net Profit and Shareholders' Equity would increase by $225 thousand ([1 − 0.28] × 313).

The adjustment to the December 31, 2006 and 2007, financial statements would, therefore, be as follows:

€ (millions)	Adjustments December 31, 2006		Adjustments December 31, 2007	
	Assets	Liabilities	Assets	Liabilities
Balance sheet				
Trade Receivables	+7,432 (1)		+7,432 (3) +313 (3)	
Deferred Tax Liability		+2,081 (2)		+2,081 (2) +88 (4)
Shareholders' Equity		+5,351 (2)		+5,351 (2) +225 (4)
Income statement				
Cost of Sales				−313 (3)
Tax Expense				+88 (4)
Net Profit				+225 (4)

Unfortunately, not all firms that report under IFRS separately disclose the allowances for doubtful accounts (or inventory obsolescence). This makes it sometimes difficult for the analyst to identify the overstatement or understatement of allowances.

Understated allowances are also a point of attention when analyzing the financial statements of loss-making firms. When a firm reports a loss in its tax statements, it does not receive an immediate tax refund but becomes the holder of a claim against the tax authorities, called a tax loss carryforward, which can be offset against future taxable profits. The period over which the firm can exercise this claim differs across tax jurisdictions. The international accounting standard for income taxes requires that firms record a deferred tax asset for a tax loss carryforward that is probable of being realized. Because changes in this deferred tax asset affect earnings through the tax expense, managers can manage earnings upwards by overstating the probability of realization.

During its first five years of operations, from 2001 to 2005, the Dutch manufacturer of exclusive cars Spyker Cars N.V. had been loss making. In December 2005 and December 2004, when Spyker reported net losses of €1.9 million and €5.0 million, respectively, the company reported the following losses carried forward and deferred tax assets:

(€ millions)	December 31, 2005	December 31, 2004
Total loss carried forward	19.822	15.687
× Tax rate	29.6%	34.5%
Calculated deferred tax	5.867	5.412
Allowance	(1.467)	(3.058)
Recognized deferred tax asset	4.400	2.354

Spyker deducted an allowance from its calculated deferred tax assets because management deemed it not probable that the tax loss carryforwards could be fully realized in future years. The allowance, however, was substantially lower in 2005 than in 2004 because management expected an increase in Spyker's future profitability, justifying a decrease in the allowance from 56.5 percent of the deferred tax asset to 25 percent.

Any increase (decrease) in the deferred tax asset is offset by a decrease (increase) in the tax expense. If the analyst believed that management's optimism in 2005 was unwarranted and decided to increase the allowance to 56.5 percent, it would be necessary to reduce the Deferred Tax Asset, Shareholders' Equity, and Net Profit by €1.848 million ([0.565 − 0.250] × 5.867) and increase the Tax Expense by the same amount.

	Adjustments	
(€ millions)	Assets	Liabilities and Equity
Balance sheet		
Deferred Tax Asset	−1.848	
Shareholders' Equity		−1.848
Income statement		
Tax Expense		+1.848
Net Profit		−1.848

In the years 2006–2008, Spyker kept reporting pre-tax losses. At the end of 2007, Spyker's management decided to deduct an allowance of 100 percent from its deferred tax asset, thereby removing the asset from its balance sheet in full.

KEY ANALYSIS QUESTIONS

The following are some of the questions an analyst can probe when analyzing whether a firm's assets exhibit distortions:

- *Depreciation and amortization.* Are the firm's depreciation and amortization rates in line with industry practices? If not, is the firm aggressive or conservative in its estimates of the assets' useful lives? What does the deferred tax liability for depreciation and amortization suggest about the relationship between reported depreciation and tax depreciation?

- *Asset impairment.* Have industry or firm economic conditions deteriorated such that non-current assets' fair values could have fallen below their book values? Have industry peers recently recognized asset impairments? Does the firm have a history of regular write-downs, suggesting a tendency to delay?

- *Leased assets.* Does the firm have a material amount of off-balance sheet lease commitments? Is there a large variation in the proportion of operating leases to finance leases across industry peers?

- *Intangible assets.* Does the firm make material investments in non-current intangible assets, such as research and development, that are omitted from the balance sheet? If so, are these investments likely to yield future economic benefits? Does the immediate expensing of these investments lead to artificially permanent abnormal earnings?

- *Revenue recognition.* Are trade receivables abnormally high (relative to sales), suggesting aggressive revenue recognition?

- *Allowances.* Did the firm make unexplained changes in its allowance for doubtful accounts (or loan losses)? Is the size of the allowance in line with industry practices? Did the characteristics of the firm's receivables (e.g., concentration of credit risk) change such that the firm should adjust its allowance? Are the allowances that the firm recognizes systematically smaller or greater than its write-offs? Is it likely that the firm's deferred tax assets for losses carried forward can be realized?

- *Discounted receivables.* Is the recourse liability sufficiently large to cover the amount of collection losses that the firm guarantees? Is the value of the recourse liability so uncertain that it is better to return the discounted receivables to the balance sheet?

RECOGNITION OF LIABILITIES

Liabilities are defined as economic obligations arising from benefits received in the past, and for which the amount and timing is known with reasonable certainty. Liabilities include obligations to customers that have paid in advance for products or services; commitments to public and private providers of debt financing; obligations to federal and local governments for taxes; commitments to employees for unpaid wages and post-employment benefits; and obligations from court or government fines or environmental clean-up orders.

Distortions in liabilities generally arise because there is ambiguity about whether (1) an obligation has really been incurred and/or (2) the obligation can be measured.

Has an obligation been incurred?

For most liabilities there is little ambiguity about whether an obligation has been incurred. For example, when a firm buys supplies on credit, it has incurred an obligation to the supplier. However, for some transactions it is more difficult to decide whether there is any such obligation. For example, if a firm announces a plan to restructure its business by laying off employees, has it made a commitment that would justify recording a liability? Or, if a software firm receives cash from its customers for a five-year software license, should the firm report the full cash inflow as revenues, or should some of it represent the ongoing commitment to the customer for servicing and supporting the license agreement?

Can the obligation be measured?

Many liabilities specify the amount and timing of obligations precisely. For example, a 20-year €100 million bond issue with an 8 percent coupon payable semiannually specifies that the issuer will pay the holders €100 million in 20 years, and it will pay out interest of €4 million every six months for the duration of the loan. However, for some liabilities it is difficult to estimate the amount of the obligation. For example, a firm that is responsible for an environmental clean-up clearly has incurred an obligation, but the amount is highly uncertain.[12] Similarly, firms that provide post-employment benefits for employees have incurred commitments that depend on uncertain future events, such as employee mortality rates, and on future inflation rates, making valuation of the obligation subjective. Future warranty and insurance claim obligations fall into the same category – the commitment is clear but the amount depends on uncertain future events.

Accounting rules frequently specify when a commitment has been incurred and how to measure the amount of the commitment. However, as discussed earlier, accounting rules are imperfect – they cannot cover all contractual possibilities and reflect all of the complexities of a firm's business relationships. They also require managers to make subjective estimates of future events to value the firm's commitments. Thus the analyst may decide that some important obligations are omitted from the financial statements or, if included, are understated, either because of management bias or because there are legitimate differences in opinion between managers and analysts over future risks and commitments. As a result, analysis of liabilities is usually with an eye to assessing whether the firm's financial commitments and risks are understated and/or its earnings overstated.

LIABILITY DISTORTIONS

Liabilities are likely to be understated when the firm has key commitments that are difficult to value and therefore not considered liabilities for financial reporting purposes. Understatements are also likely to occur when managers have strong incentives to overstate the soundness of the firm's financial position, or to boost reported earnings. By understating leverage, managers present investors with a rosy picture of the firm's financial risks. Earnings management also understates liabilities (namely deferred or unearned revenues) when revenues are recognized upon receipt of cash, even though not all services have been provided.

Accounting analysis involves judging whether managers have understated liabilities and, if necessary, adjusting the balance sheet and income statement accordingly. The most common forms of liability understatement arise when the following conditions exist:

- Unearned revenues are understated through aggressive revenue recognition.
- Provisions are understated.
- Loans from discounted receivables are off-balance sheet.
- Non-current liabilities for leases are off-balance sheet.
- Post-employment obligations, such as pension obligations, are not fully recorded.

Examples of liability understatement

Unearned revenues understated

If cash has already been received but the product or service has yet to be provided, a liability (called unearned or deferred revenues) is created. This liability reflects the company's commitment to provide the service or product to the customer and is extinguished once that is accomplished. Firms that recognize revenues prematurely, after the receipt of cash but prior to fulfilling their product or service commitments to customers, understate deferred revenue liabilities and overstate earnings. Firms that bundle service contracts with the sale of a product are particularly prone to deferred revenue liability understatement since separating the price of the product from the price of the service is subjective.

Consider the case of MicroStrategy, the software company discussed earlier, which bundles customer support and software updates with its initial licensing agreements. This raises questions about how much of the contract price should be allocated to the initial license versus the company's future commitments. In March 2000 MicroStrategy conceded that it had incorrectly overstated revenues on contracts that involved significant future customization and consulting by $54.5 million. As a result, it would have to restate its financial statements for 1999 as well as for several earlier years. To undo the distortion to 1999 financials, the following adjustments would have to be made:

1 In the quarter that the contracts were booked by the company, Sales would decline and unearned revenues (included in Other Current Liabilities) would increase by $54.5 million.

2 Cost of Sales would decline and prepaid expenses (inventory for product companies) would increase to reflect the lower sales. As noted earlier, MicroStrategy's cost of license revenues is only 3 percent of license revenues, implying that the adjustment to prepaid expenses (included in Other Current Assets) and Cost of Sales is modest ($1.6 million).

3 The decline in pretax profit would result in a lower Tax Expense in the company's financial reporting books (but presumably not in its tax books). Given MicroStrategy's marginal tax rate of 35 percent, the decline in the Tax Expense as well as in the Deferred Tax Liability is $18.5 million [($54.5 − 1.6) × 0.35].

The full effect of the adjustment on the quarterly financial statements would, therefore, be as follows:

	Adjustments	
(€ millions)	Assets	Liabilities and Equity
Balance sheet		
Other Current Assets	+1.6 (2)	
Other Current Liabilities		+54.5 (1)
Deferred Tax Liability		−18.5 (3)
Shareholders' Equity		−34.4
Income statement		
Sales		−54.5 (1)
Cost of Sales		−1.6 (2)
Tax Expense		−18.5 (3)
Net Profit		−34.4

MicroStrategy's March 10 announcement that it had overstated revenues prompted the SEC to investigate the company. In the period when it announced its overstatements, MicroStrategy's stock price plummeted 94 percent, compared to the 37 percent drop by the NASDAQ in the same period.

Provisions understated

Many firms have obligations that are likely to result in a future outflow of cash or other resources but for which the exact amount is hard to establish. Examples of such uncertain liabilities are liabilities that arise from obligations to clean up polluted production sites or to provide warranty coverage for products sold. International accounting rules prescribe that a firm recognizes a provision – or nonfinancial liability – on its balance sheet for such uncertain liabilities when:

1 It is probable that the obligation will lead to a future outflow of cash.

2 The firm has no or little discretion to avoid the obligation.

3 The firm can make a reliable estimate of amount of the obligation.

When an uncertain liability does not meet these requirements for recognition, the firm discloses the liability only in the notes to the financial statements, as a "contingent liability." The international rules for the recognition of provisions may result in the understatement of a firm's liabilities. Because of the uncertainty surrounding the obligations, managers have much discretion in deciding whether obligations are probable as well as in estimating the amount of the obligation. Further, the use of a probability threshold below which uncertain liabilities are not recognized may lead to situations in which obligations with a relatively low probability but with a high expected value remain off-balance. An analyst may therefore decide that some of a firm's contingent liabilities are less uncertain than management asserts and undo the distortion by recognizing the liability on-balance as a provision. Additionally, the analyst may be of the opinion that low-probability obligations that nevertheless expose the firm to substantial risks because of their high expected value must also be recognized on the balance sheet.

At the end of the fiscal year 2008, British American Tobacco plc (BAT) – through some of its subsidiaries – was defendant in 3,251 US product liability cases, some of which involved amounts of hundreds of millions of US dollars. The company reported that in several cases that went to trial before the balance sheet date, judges had awarded substantial damages against BAT. Nevertheless, the company chose not to recognize a provision for potential damages because it considered it improbable that individual cases would result in an outflow of resources, even though in the aggregate the cases could have a material effect on the company's cash flow.

Assume that an analyst estimates the present value of future damages and settlements, discounted at BAT's incremental borrowing rate of 7 percent, to be £1 billion. In this particular situation, the analyst could base such an estimate on the historical probability that a tobacco company would lose a product liability case times the average damages awarded. Sometimes a firm's notes on contingent liabilities provide an indication of the size of the liability. For BAT, the following adjustments would have to be made to recognize the liability of £1 billion:

1 At the end of fiscal year 2007, the liability of £1 billion would be recognized as Non-Current Debt. Shareholders' Equity would decline by £0.7 billion (1.0 billion × [1 − 0.30]) and the Deferred Tax Liability would decline by £0.3 billion (1.0 billion × 0.30).

2 Because the non-current provision is a discounted liability, the provision increases as interest accrues. In 2008 BAT's income statement would include additional Interest Expense for an amount of £70 million (1.0 billion × 0.07). Tax Expense and the Deferred Tax Liability would decline by £21 million (70 million × 0.30) and Net Profit and Shareholders' Equity would decline by £49 million (70 million × [1 − 0.30]). The additional Interest Expense would result in an increase in Non-Current Debt.

The full effect of the adjustments would be as follows:

£ (millions)	Adjustments December 31, 2007		Adjustments December 31, 2008	
	Assets	Liabilities	Assets	Liabilities
Balance sheet				
Non-Current Debt		+1,000 (1)		+1,000 (1)
				+70 (2)
				(*Continued*)

£ (millions)	Adjustments December 31, 2007		Adjustments December 31, 2008	
	Assets	Liabilities	Assets	Liabilities
Deferred Tax Liability		−300 (1)		−300 (1)
				−21 (2)
Shareholders' Equity		−700 (1)		−700 (1)
				−49 (2)
Income statement				
Interest Expense				+70 (2)
Tax Expense				−21 (2)
Net Profit				−49 (2)

Discounted receivables off balance sheet

As discussed earlier, receivables that are discounted with a financial institution are considered "sold" if the "seller" cedes control over the receivables to the financier. Yet if the sale permits the buyer to have recourse against the seller in the event of default, the seller continues to face collection risk. Given the management judgment involved in forecasting default and refinancing costs, as well as the incentives faced by managers to keep debt off the balance sheet, it will be important for the analyst to evaluate the firm's estimates for default as well as the inherent commitments that it has for discounted receivables. Are the firm's estimates reasonable? Is it straightforward to forecast the costs of the default and prepayment risks? If not, does the analyst need to increase the value of the recourse liability? Or, in the extreme, does the analyst need to undo the sale and recognize a loan from the financial institution for the discounted value of the receivables.

Non-current liabilities for leases are off balance sheet

As discussed earlier in the chapter, key lease assets and liabilities can be excluded from the balance sheet if the company structures lease transactions to fit the accounting definition of an operating lease. Firms that groom transactions to avoid showing lease assets and obligations will have very different balance sheets from firms with virtually identical economics that either use finance leases or borrow from the bank to actually purchase the equivalent resources. For firms that choose to structure lease transactions to fit the definition of an operating lease, the analyst can restate the leases as finance leases, as discussed in the "Asset distortions" section. This will ensure that the firm's true financial commitments and risks will be reflected on its balance sheet, enabling comparison with peer firms.

Post-employment benefit obligations not fully recorded

Many firms make commitments to provide pension benefits and other post-employment benefits, such as healthcare, to their employees. International accounting rules require managers to estimate and report the present value of the commitments that have been earned by employees over their years of working for the firm. This obligation is offset by any assets that the firm has committed to post-employment plans to fund future plan benefits. If the funds set aside in the post-employment plan are greater (less) than the plan commitments, the plan is overfunded (underfunded). Several important issues arise for analyzing post-employment benefit obligations. First, estimating the obligations themselves is subjective – managers have to make forecasts of future wage and benefit rates, worker attrition rates, the expected lives of retirees, and the discount rate.[13] If these forecasts are too low, the firm's benefit obligations (as well as the annual expenses for benefits reported in the income statement) will be understated.[14] Second, the accounting rules allow that incremental bene-fit commitments that arise from changes to a plan, and changes in plan funding status that arise from abnormal investment returns on plan assets, are smoothed over time rather than reflected immediately. As a result, for labor-intensive firms that offer attractive post-employment benefits to employees, it is important that the analyst assesses whether reported post-employment plan liabilities reflect the firms' true commitments.

International accounting rules require that firms estimate the value of post-employment commitments, called the post-employment benefit obligation, as the present value of future expected payouts under the plans. The obligation under pension plans is the present value of plan commitments factoring in the impact of future increases in wage rates and salary scales on projected payouts. For other post-employment plans, such as post-employment healthcare or life insurance, the firm's obligation is calculated as the present value of expected future benefits for employees and their beneficiaries.

Each year the firm's post-employment obligations are adjusted to reflect the following factors:

- Current service cost. Defined benefit plans typically provide higher benefits for each additional year of service with the company. For example, a company may promise its employees pension benefits in the amount of 2 percent of their career-average pay for every year worked. The value of incremental benefits earned from another year of serv-ice is called the current service cost, and increases the firm's obligation each year.

- Interest cost. The passage of time increases the present value of the firm's obligation. The interest cost recognizes this effect, and it is calculated by multiplying the obliga-tion at the beginning of the year by the discount rate.

- Actuarial gains and losses. Each year the actuarial assumptions used to estimate the firm's commitments are reviewed and, if appropriate, changes are made. The effect of these changes is shown as Actuarial Gains and Losses.

- Past service cost. Occasionally companies may decide to amend their post-employment plans. For example, during recent years some companies have switched from linking pension benefits to employees' career-end pay to linking pension benefits to employ-ees' career-average pay. Because these amendments affect the future payouts under the plans, they also affect the current post-employment benefit obligation. The effect of these amendments is shown as Past Service Cost (or Benefit).

- Benefits paid. The plan commitments are reduced as the plan makes payments to re-tirees each year.

- Other. The post-employment obligations can change because of changes in foreign exchange rates, plan curtailments, and plan settlements.

For example, in the notes to its financial statements, brewing company Carlsberg pro-vided the following information on its post-employment benefit obligation for the years ended December 31, 2008 and 2007:

DKK (millions)	December 31, 2008	December 31, 2007
Benefit obligation at beginning of year	8,151	8,134
Current service cost	139	162
Interest cost	340	323
Actuarial (gains) / losses	(462)	345
Benefits paid	(433)	(426)
Other	(699)	(387)
Benefit obligation at end of year	7,036	8,151

Carlsberg's obligation at the end of 2008 was DKK7.0 billion, a 13.7 percent decrease over the prior year.

To meet their commitments under post-employment plans, firms make contributions to the plans. These contributions are then invested in equities, debt, and other assets. Plan assets, therefore, are increased each year by new company (and employee) contributions. They are also increased or decreased by the returns generated each year from plan investments. Finally, plan assets decline when the plan pays out benefits to retirees. For the years ended December 31, 2008 and 2007, Carlsberg reported the following assets for post-employment plans:

DKK (millions)	December 31, 2008	December 31, 2007
Fair value of plan assets at beginning of year	6,234	6,334
Actual return on plan assets	(517)	235
Contributions to plans	273	318
Benefits paid	(347)	(333)
Other	(398)	(320)
Fair value of plan assets at end of year	5,245	6,234

Carlsberg had expected to earn a return of 4.94 percent on its beginning plan assets in 2008. The company's plan assets decreased because they generated an unexpected loss of DKK825 million ($-517 - [0.0494 \times 6,234]$) during the year. The difference between Carlsberg's post-employment plan obligations and the plan assets, DKK1.79 billion (7.036 − 5.245), represents the company's unfunded obligation to employees under the plan.

Of course, estimating post-employment obligations is highly subjective. It requires managers to forecast the future payouts under the plans, which in turn involves making projections of employees' service with the firm, retirement ages, and life expectancies, as well as future wage rates. It also requires managers to select an interest rate to estimate the present value of the future benefits. For example, Carlsberg projected that future salaries would grow at 2.6 percent per year, on average. It also assumed that the appropriate discount rate was 4.6 percent. Under the simplified assumption that Carlsberg's retired workforce size remains constant throughout the next 30 years and then gradually decreases to zero over a period of 30 years, a 0.1 percent decrease in the discount rate (or a 0.1 percent increase in salary growth) would increase the post-employment benefit obligation by close to DKK116 million.[15] Given the management judgment involved in making these forecasts and assumptions, analysts should question whether reported obligations adequately reflect the firm's true commitments.

So, given Carlsberg's unfunded post-employment benefit obligation of DKK1.79 billion, it is reasonable that the company reports a liability on its balance sheet for a similar amount. Unfortunately, not all companies follow the same practice. International accounting rules allow that firms smooth out shocks to plan obligations that occur because of actuarial gains or losses. If the value of plan assets increases or decreases unexpectedly in a given year, or there needs to be adjustment in the actuarial assumptions made to estimate the obligation, the financial statement impact can be reflected gradually rather than immediately. For example, consider the post-employment plans of one of Carlsberg's competitors, brewing company Heineken. Even though the actual gap between Heineken's post-employment obligation and plan assets in 2008 is €732 million, this is not the value of the liability recorded on its balance sheet. Heineken provides a separate disclosure that reconciles the actual and the reported obligation:

€ (millions)	December 31, 2008	December 31, 2007
Benefit obligation at end of year	4,963	2,858
Fair value of plan assets at end of year	(4,231)	(2,535)
Funded status	732	323
Unrecognized actuarial (loss) / gain	(143)	171
Recognized liability for post-employment obligations	€ 589	€ 494

The unrecognized actuarial loss (gain) arises because Heineken's earlier actuarial assumptions about parameters such as future salaries, retirement rates, and assumed rates of return on plan assets have proven to be too optimistic (pessimistic). International rules on post-employment accounting allow companies to choose between fully and immediately recognizing current actuarial gains and losses in the statement of comprehensive income (outside the income statement) or recognizing the cumulative actuarial gains and losses over time (in the income statement) rather than right away. In contrast with Carlsberg, Heineken has opted for gradual recognition over time.[16] Consequently, Heineken's reported post-employment liability understates its real commitment by €143 million (3 percent of Heineken's equity).[17]

There is an additional reason why the recognized post-employment liability is not necessarily equal to the unfunded post-employment benefit obligation. International accounting rules require that past service cost be recognized in the income statement on a straight-line basis over the period until the employees become entitled to the additional benefits from the plan amendments (i.e., until the benefits become "vested"). This treatment of past service cost results in the delayed recognition of the effect of pension plan amendments on the post-employment benefit obligation.

What does post-employment accounting imply for financial analysis? It is reasonable for the analyst to raise several questions about a firm's post-employment obligations, particularly for firms in labor-intensive industries.

1 Are the assumptions made by the firm to estimate its post-employment obligations realistic? These include assumptions about the discount rate, which is supposed to represent the current market interest rate for benefits, as well as assumptions about increases in wage and benefit costs. If these assumptions are optimistic, the obligations recorded on the books understate the firm's real economic commitment. As discussed above, the analyst may estimate that a 0.1 percent increase in expected salary growth increases Carlsberg's obligation by DKK116 million and use this information to adjust for any optimism in management's assumptions. For example, if the analyst decided that Carlsberg's forecasts of future salaries were too low and needed to increase by 0.1 percent, the post-employment obligation would have to be increased by DKK116 million, with offsetting declines to equity (for the after-tax effect) and to the deferred tax liability. The adjustment to Carlsberg's 2008 balance sheet, assuming a 25 percent tax rate, would be as follows:

	Adjustment	
DKK (millions)	**Assets**	**Liabilities and Equity**
Balance sheet		
Long-Term Debt		+116
Deferred Tax Liability		−29
Shareholders' Equity		−87

2 Does the off-balance sheet post-employment obligation need to be brought on the balance sheet? The process of smoothing differences between actual and forecasted parameters for post-employment plans may understate the obligations for post-employment benefits. For some companies this understatement because of cumulative actuarial gains and losses is substantial. As noted above, Heineken reports a liability for post-employment benefits that is €143 million less than the actual unfunded obligations. The analyst can adjust for this distortion by increasing the firm's Long-Term Debt, and making offsetting adjustments to the Deferred Tax Liability (since the change would not affect the company's taxable profit) and Shareholders' Equity. Assuming a 25.5 percent tax rate, the adjustment to Heineken's 2008 balance sheet would be as follows:

	Adjustment	
€ (millions)	Assets	Liabilities and Equity
Balance sheet		
Long-Term Debt		+143
Deferred Tax Liability		−36.5
Shareholders' Equity		−106.5

3 What effect do post-employment assumptions play in the income statement? The post-employment cost each year comprises

a Service cost, plus.

b Interest cost, plus.

c Amortization of any past service costs, plus or minus.

d Amortization of actuarial gains and losses, minus.

e Expected return on plan assets (the expected long-term return multiplied by beginning assets under management).

For example, Carlsberg and Heineken show that their post-employment expenses for 2008 and 2007 are as follows:

	Carlsberg		Heineken	
(millions)	2008	2007	2008	2007
Income statement				
Service cost	DKK139	DKK162	€75	€71
Interest cost	340	323	258	133
Expected return on plan assets	(308)	(321)	(241)	(129)
Amortization of past service cost	0	0	5	1
Amortization of cumulative actuarial				
losses/(gains)	0	0	(1)	2
Other	(49)	(4)	(18)	4
Net expense	122	160	78	82
Statement of comprehensive income				
Recognized net actuarial (loss) / gain	(363)	(431)	0	0

This expense reflects the effect of smoothing actual asset returns and revisions in actuarial assumptions discussed earlier. Conceptually, the post-employment expense should equal the change in the post-employment obligation minus the change in the fair value of plan assets. However, neither Carlsberg nor Heineken fully and immediately recognize the obligations from changes in actuarial assumptions in their income statements. Carlsberg recognizes such changes in the statement of comprehensive income, whereas Heineken delays the recognition to future periods. Further, to calculate the post-employment expense companies subtract the expected return on plan assets – instead of the actual return on plan assets – from the interest and service costs. The difference between the expected return and the annual return is added to and treated similarly as the other actuarial gains and losses.

In 2008 Heineken's current period actuarial loss, calculated as the increase in the unrecognized cumulative actuarial losses, was €315 million (disclosed in the notes to the financial statements), while Carlsberg's current period actuarial loss was DKK363 million (recognized in the statement of comprehensive income). If the analyst used the current period actuarial losses to undo the earnings effects of smoothing unexpected returns and changes in actuarial assumptions, an additional €315 million and DKK363 million in post-employment expenses, included in personnel expenses, would be required. These adjustments would also lower the firms' tax expenses. The full income statement adjustment would therefore be as follows:

| (millions) | Adjustment | |
	Carlsberg	Heineken
Income statement		
Personnel Expense	+DKK363	+€315
Tax Expense	−90.8	−80.3
Net Profit	−DKK272.2	−€234.7

If desired, similar adjustments can be made to undo the earnings effects of smoothing past-period service costs (if present).

FIRST-TIME ADOPTION: ACTUARIAL GAINS AND LOSSES

Rules on the first-time adoption of IFRS allow companies to recognize all cumulative actuarial gains and losses in the opening IFRS balance sheet at the first time of adoption. Immediate recognition of cumulative gains (losses) would result in a decrease (increase) in the on-balance post-employment liability and an offsetting increase (decrease) in opening equity. Firms can choose to do so irrespective of the method they use for recognizing the actuarial gains and losses that occur after the date of the opening IFRS balance sheet. Consequently, the amount of unrecognized cumulative actuarial gains and losses is likely to be small for companies that have recently adopted IFRS.

KEY ANALYSIS QUESTIONS

The following are some of the questions an analyst can probe when analyzing whether a firm's liabilities exhibit distortions:

- *Unearned revenues*. Has the firm recognized revenues for services or products that have yet to be provided?

- *Provisions*. Did the firm disclose contingent liabilities that expose the firm to material risks? If so, can the expected value of such liabilities be estimated and recognized on the balance sheet? Did the firm make unexplained changes in its provisions? Is the size of the provisions in line with industry practices?

- *Post-employment benefits*. Are the assumptions made by the firm to estimate its post-employment obligations realistic? What is the effect of smoothing differences between actual and forecasted parameters for post-employment benefits on the off-balance sheet post-employment obligation? Does the analyst need to adjust long-term debt for the off-balance sheet post-employment obligation?

EQUITY DISTORTIONS

Accounting treats stockholders' equity as a residual claim on the firm's assets, after paying off the other claimholders. Consequently, equity distortions arise primarily from distortions in assets and liabilities. For example, distortions in assets or liabilities that affect earnings also lead to **distortions in equity**. However, there are forms of equity distortions that would not typically arise in asset and liability analyses. One particular issue is how firms account for contingent claims on their net assets that they sometimes provide to outside stakeholders. Two examples of such contingent claims are employee stock options and conversion options on convertible debentures.

Contingent claims

A stock option gives the holder the right to purchase a certain number of shares at a predetermined price, called the exercise or strike price, for a specified period of time, termed the exercise period. In the 1990s, stock options became the most significant component of compensation for many corporate executives. Proponents of options argue that they provide managers with incentives to maximize shareholder value and make it easier to attract talented managers. Convertible debentures also contain a stock option component. Holders of these debentures have the right to purchase a certain number of shares in exchange for their fixed claim. When deciding on how to account for these contingent claims in a firm's financial statements, the following two factors are important to consider:

- Although providing a contingent claim does not involve a cash outflow for the firm, the claim is by no means costless to the firm's shareholders. The potential exercise of the option dilutes current shareholders' equity and as such imposes an economic cost on the firm's shareholders. To improve current net profit as a measure of the firm's current economic performance the economic cost of contingent claims should therefore be included in the income statement in the same period in which the firm receives the benefits from these claims.

- The contingent claims are valuable to those who receive them. Employees are willing to provide services to the firm in exchange for employee stock options. Convertible debenture holders are willing to charge a lower interest rate to the firm in exchange for the conversion option. If, in future years, the firm wishes to receive similar services or similar low interest rates without providing contingent claims on its net assets, it must be willing to give up other resources. To improve current net profit as a predictor of the firm's future net profit the income statement should therefore include an expense that reflects the value of the contingent claims to the recipients.

These two factors underline the importance of accurately recording the cost of options in a firm's income statement. International rules require firms to report stock options using the fair value method (discussed in IFRS 2). The fair value method requires firms to record an expense for stock option compensation when the options are issued. The value of the options issued is estimated using a recognized valuation model, such as the Black-Scholes model, and is then expensed over the vesting period.[18] Prior to the European adoption of IFRS, the local accounting rules in most European countries permitted firms to report stock options using the intrinsic value method. Under the intrinsic value method, no compensation expense is reported at the grant date for the vast majority of stock options awarded, where the exercise price is equal to the firm's current stock price. If the options are subsequently exercised, there is also no expense recorded, and the new stock that is issued is valued at the exercise price rather than its higher market value.

Although there is no question that Black-Scholes valuations present a more accurate reflection of the economic cost of stock option awards to the firm's shareholders than the zero cost reported under the intrinsic value method, these valuations can be highly sensitive to management's assumptions about its share price characteristics. For example, when using the Black-Scholes model to value options, managers can understate the stock option expense by understating the expected future share price volatility or overstating the expected future dividend yield. One task of the analyst is therefore to assess the adequacy of management's valuation assumptions. Additionally, research suggests that employees attach much lower values than the Black-Scholes values to the nonmarketable options that they receive. This implies that when a firm plans to replace its stock option awards with cash-based forms of compensation, the analyst should assess whether a decrease in the compensation expense can be expected.

International accounting rules also require a firm to separate the debt from the equity component of convertible debentures. To do so, the firm first estimates what the fair value of the debentures would have been if the conversion option had not been attached to the debentures. This fair value is equal to the present value of the future fixed payments on the debentures, discounted at the firm's effective interest rate on nonconvertible debentures. The value of the equity component is then set equal to the proceeds of the debenture issue minus the fair value of the debt component. The economic cost of the conversion option is included in the income statement by calculating the interest expense on the debentures on the basis of the effective interest rate on nonconvertible debentures. Under these rules, firms may have the incentive to understate the effective interest rate on nonconvertible debentures, thereby understating the convertible debentures' equity component and effective interest expense.

Recycling of gains and losses

In accordance with the international accounting rules on the measurement of financial instruments (IAS 39), firms typically record securities held available for sale at fair value and include any (unrealized) fair value gains or losses directly in the statement of comprehensive income. In the period in which these instruments are eventually sold, the cumulative unrealized gains and losses are taken from equity and recognized in the income statement. As a result, gains and losses that were previously included in comprehensive income (statement of comprehensive income) are "recycled" and re-included in net profit.

A disadvantage of recycling unrealized gains or losses on financial instruments held available for sale is that the discretionary timing of a firm's securities sales determines in which period gains or losses become realized. This contrasts, for example, with the way in which a firm treats unrealized gains and losses on securities that are held for short-term trading purposes. The difference between securities classified as available for sale and those held for short-term trading is that the former type of securities were originally designated by the firm as long-term investments. Consequently, international accounting rules require that only revaluation gains and losses on securities held for short-term trading be considered as profit from operating activities and directly included in the income statement. The analyst can, however, use the information from the statement of comprehensive income to incorporate unrealized gains and losses on financial instruments held available for sale in profits and undo the financial statements from any distortions caused by a firm's discretionary timing of securities sales.

In its statements of comprehensive income for the fiscal years 2007 and 2008, Spain-based Banco Bilbao Vizcaya Argentaria (BBVA) disclosed the following amounts related to its securities held available for sale:

€ (millions)	2007	2008
Revaluation gains (losses) on securities held available for sale	1,857	(2,065)
Revaluation (gains) losses transferred to the income statement	(1,537)	(1,722)
Income tax on the net amount of current unrealized revaluation gains/losses and transfers to the income statement (estimate)	(104)	1,136
Net effect on shareholders' equity	216	(2,651)

To transfer current year's unrealized revaluation gains and losses (net of current realizations) to net income, the following adjustments would have to be made:

€ (millions)	2007	2008
Statement of comprehensive income		
Unrealized Revaluations, Net of Transfers to Income	−216	+2,651
Net Profit	+216	−2,651
Income statement		
Other Operating Income, Net of Other Operating Expense	+320	−3,787
Tax Expense	+104	−1,136
Net Profit	+216	−2,651

These adjustments would increase BBVA's net profit by 3.0 percent in 2007 and decrease its net profit by 43.1 percent in 2008. The bank's return on beginning-of-year equity would increase by 0.8 percentage points in 2007 and decrease by 11.9 percentage points in 2008.

SUMMARY

To implement accounting analysis, the analyst must first recast the financial statements into a common format so that financial statement terminology and formatting is comparable between firms and across time. A standard template for recasting the financials, presented in this chapter, is used throughout the remainder of the book.

Once the financial statements are standardized, the analyst can determine what accounting distortions exist in the firm's assets, liabilities, and equity. Common distortions that overstate assets include delays in recognizing asset impairments, underestimated allowances, aggressive revenue recognition leading to overstated receivables, and optimistic assumptions on long-term asset depreciation. Asset understatements can arise if managers overstate asset write-offs, use operating leases to keep assets off the balance sheet, or make conservative assumptions for asset depreciation. They can also arise because accounting rules require outlays for key assets (e.g., research outlays and brands) to be immediately expensed.

For liabilities, the primary concern for the analyst is whether the firm understates its real commitments. This can arise from off-balance liabilities (e.g., operating lease obligations), from understated provisions, from questionable management judgment and limitations in accounting rules for estimating post-employment liabilities, and from aggressive revenue recognition that understates unearned revenue obligations. Equity distortions frequently arise when there are distortions in assets and liabilities. However, they can also arise if understated expenses are reported for stock option compensation, or for the issuance of compound financial instruments such as convertible debentures.

Adjustments for distortions can, therefore, arise because accounting standards, although applied appropriately, do not reflect a firm's economic reality. They can also arise if the analyst has a different point of view than management about the estimates and assumptions made in preparing the financial statements. Once distortions have been identified, the analyst can use cash flow statement information and information from the notes to the financial statements to make adjustments to the balance sheet at the beginning and/or end of the current year, as well as any needed adjustments to revenues and expenses in the latest income statement. This ensures that the most recent financial ratios used to evaluate a firm's performance and to forecast its future results are based on financial data that appropriately reflect its business economics.

Several points are worth remembering when undertaking accounting analysis. First, the bulk of the analyst's time and energy should be focused on evaluating and adjusting accounting policies and estimates that describe the firm's key strategic value drivers. Of course this does not mean that management bias is not reflected in other accounting estimates and policies, and the analyst should certainly examine these. But given the importance of evaluating how the firm is managing its key success factors and risks, the bulk of the accounting analysis should be spent examining those policies that describe these factors and risks. Similarly, the analyst should focus on adjustments that have a material effect on the firm's liabilities, equity, or earnings. Immaterial adjustments cost time and energy but are unlikely to affect the analyst's financial and prospective analysis.

It is also important to recognize that many accounting adjustments can only be approximations rather than precise calculations, because much of the information necessary for making precise adjustments is not disclosed. The analyst should, therefore, try to avoid worrying about being overly precise in making accounting adjustments. By making even crude adjustments, it is usually possible to mitigate some of the limitations of accounting standards and problems of management bias in financial reporting.

CORE CONCEPTS

Classification of operating expenses by function Classification in which firms distinguish categories of operating expense with reference to the *purpose* of the expense. This classification typically distinguishes (at least) the following categories of expenses: (a) Cost of Sales and (b) Selling, General and Administrative Expenses.

Classification of operating expenses by nature Classification in which firms distinguish categories of operating expense with reference to the *cause* of the expense. This classification typically distinguishes the following categories of expenses: (a) Cost of Materials, (b) Personnel Expense and (c) Depreciation and Amortization.

Examples of asset value distortions Examples of asset value distortions are:

a Non-current asset understatement resulting from overstated depreciation or amortization.

b Non-current asset understatement resulting from off-balance sheet operating leases.

c Non-current asset understatement resulting from the immediate expensing of investments in intangible assets (such as research).

d Current asset (receivables) understatement resulting from the sales of receivables.

e Current asset (receivables) overstatement resulting from accelerated revenue recognition.

f Non-current or current asset overstatement resulting from delayed write-downs, and

g Current asset overstatement resulting from underestimated allowances (e.g., for doubtful receivables or inventories obsolescence).

Examples of liability distortions Examples of liability distortions are:

a Liability understatement resulting from understated unearned revenues (e.g., revenues from long-term service contracts).

b Liability understatement resulting from understated provisions.

c Liability understatement resulting from the sales of receivables (with recourse).

d Non-current liability understatement resulting from off-balance sheet operating leases.

e Liability understatement resulting from post-employment obligations that are (partly) kept off-balance.

Gross profit Difference between Sales and Cost of Sales.

IFRS 1 International Financial Reporting Standard governing the first-time adoption of IFRS. This standard requires first-time adopters to produce their first IFRS-based opening balance sheet as if they have applied IFRS all along. The standard, however, also allows some exceptions to this rule in situations where retrospective adoption is complicated.

Recasting of financial statements Process of standardizing the formats and nomenclature of firms' financial statements (income statement, balance sheet, cash flow statement, comprehensive income statement).

Sources of asset value distortions Managers may strategically bias or accounting rules may force them to bias the book values of assets if there is uncertainty about:

a Who the economic resources that potentially give rise to the assets.

b Whether the economic resources will provide future economic benefits that can be reliably measured.

c What the fair value of the assets is.

d Whether the fair value of the asset is less than its book value.

Sources of liability distortions Managers may strategically bias or accounting rules may force them to bias the book values of liabilities if there is uncertainty about:

a Whether an obligation has been occurred.

b Whether the obligation can be reliably measured.

Sources and examples of equity distortions Distortions in assets and liabilities can lead to equity distortions. However, (a) contingent claims such as employee stock options or convertible debentures as well as (b) the recycling of unrealized fair value gains and losses can directly cause distortions in equity.

QUESTIONS, EXERCISES AND PROBLEMS

1 On the companion website to this book there is a spreadsheet containing the financial statements of:

a Cadbury plc for the fiscal year ended December 31, 2008.

b The Unilever Group for the fiscal year ended December 31, 2008.

c Audi AG for the fiscal year ended December 31, 2008.

   Use the templates shown in Tables 4.1, 4.2, 4.3, and 4.4 to recast these companies' financial statements.

2 Refer to the Lufthansa example on asset depreciation estimates in this chapter. What adjustments would be required if Lufthansa's aircraft depreciation was computed using an average life of 25 years and salvage value of 5 percent (instead of the reported values of 12 years and 15 percent)? Show the adjustments to the 2007 and 2008 balance sheets, and to the 2008 income statement.

3 At the beginning of 2008, the Rolls-Royce Group reported in its footnotes that its plant and equipment had an original cost of £2,110 million and that accumulated depreciation was £1,146. Rolls-Royce depreciates its plant and equipment on a straight-line basis under the assumption that the assets have an average useful life of 14 years (assume a 10 percent salvage value). Rolls-Royce's tax rate equals 28.5%. What adjustments should be made to Rolls-Royce's (i) balance sheet at the beginning of 2008; and (ii) income statement for the year 2008, if you assume that the plant and equipment has an average useful life of 10 years (and a 10 percent salvage value)?

4 Car manufacturers Volvo and Fiat disclosed the following information in their 2008 financial statements:

	Volvo	Fiat
Property, plant and equipment (PP&E) at cost	SEK 119,089m	€ 36,239m
Accumulated depreciation on PP&E	SEK 61,819m	€ 23,632m
Deferred tax liability for depreciation of PP&E	SEK 3,885m	€ 679m
Statutory tax rate	28%	27.5%

   Purely based on the companies' deferred tax liabilities, which of the two companies appears to be most conservative in its depreciation policy?

5 Dutch Food retailer Royal Ahold provides the following information on its finance leases in its financial statements for the fiscal year ended December 28, 2008:

   Finance lease liabilities are principally for buildings. Terms range from 10 to 25 years and include renewal options if it is reasonably certain, at the inception of the lease, that they will be exercised. At the time of entering into finance lease agreements, the commitments are recorded at their present value using the interest rate implicit in the lease, if this is practicable to determine; if not the interest rate applicable for long-term borrowings is used.

The aggregate amounts of minimum lease liabilities to third parties, under noncancelable finance lease contracts for the next five years and thereafter are as follows:

(€ millions)	Future minimum lease payments	Present value of minimum lease payments
Within one year	€ 143	€ 50
Between one and five years	537	214
After five years	1,236	811
Total	1,916	1,075
Current portion of finance lease liabilities		50
Non-current portion of finance lease liabilities		1,025

What interest rate does Ahold use to capitalize its finance leases?

6 On December 28, 2008, Royal Ahold disclosed the following information about its operating lease commitments:

(€ millions)	2007	2008
Within one year	€ 456	€ 454
Between one and five years	1,539	1,557
After five years	2,933	2,845
Total	4,928	4,856

Ahold's operating lease expense in 2008 amounted to €551 million. Assume that Ahold records its finance lease liabilities at an interest rate of 8 percent. Use this rate to capitalize Ahold's operating leases at December 31, 2007 and 2008.

a Record the adjustment to Ahold's balance sheet at the end of 2007 to reflect the capitalization of operating leases.

b How would this reporting change affect Ahold's income statement in 2008?

7 When bringing operating lease commitments to the balance sheet, some analysts assume that in each year of the lease term depreciation on the operating lease assets is exactly equal to the difference between (a) the operating lease payment and (b) the estimated interest expense on the operating lease obligation.

a Explain how this simplifies the adjustments.

b Do you agree that this is a valid assumption?

8 Refer to the AstraZeneca example on intangibles in this chapter. What would be the value of AstraZeneca's R&D asset at the end of fiscal years 2007 and 2008 if the average expected life of AstraZeneca's R&D investments is only three years?

9 What approaches would you use to estimate the value of brands? What assumptions underlie these approaches? As a financial analyst, what would you use to assess whether the brand value of £1.6 billion reported by confectionary company Cadbury

plc in 2008 for its candy and gum brands Halls, Trident and Dentyne was a reasonable reflection of the future benefits from these brands? What questions would you raise with the firm's CFO about the firm's brand assets?

10 Refer to the Volvo example on discounted receivables in this chapter. What adjustments would be necessary if the interest rate that Volvo charges its customers equals the interest rate that the bank charges Volvo, i.e., 10 percent?

11 In early 2003 Bristol-Myers Squibb announced that it would have to restate its financial statements as a result of stuffing as much as $3.35 billion worth of products into wholesalers' warehouses from 1999 through 2001. The company's sales and cost of sales during this period were as follows:

(millions)	2001	2000	1999
Net sales	$18,139	$17,695	$16,502
Cost of products sold	$ 5,454	$ 4,729	$ 4,458

The company's marginal tax rate during the three years was 35 percent. What adjustments are required to correct Bristol-Myers Squibb's balance sheet for December 31, 2001? What assumptions underlie your adjustments? How would you expect the adjustments to affect Bristol-Myers Squibb's performance in the coming few years?

12 As the CFO of a company, what indicators would you look at to assess whether your firm's non-current assets were impaired? What approaches could be used, either by management or an independent valuation firm, to assess the value of any asset impairment? As a financial analyst, what indicators would you look at to assess whether a firm's non-current assets were impaired? What questions would you raise with the firm's CFO about any charges taken for asset impairment?

13 On March 31, 2006, Germany's largest retailer Metro AG reported in its quarterly financial statements that it held inventories for 54 days' sales. The inventories had a book value of €6,345 million.

   a How much excess inventory do you estimate Metro is holding in March 2006 if the firm's optimal Days' Inventories is 45 days?

   b Calculate the inventory impairment charge for Metro if 50 percent of this excess inventory is deemed worthless? Record the changes to Metro's financial statements from adjusting for this impairment.

14 On December 31, 2007 and 2008 Deutsche Telekom AG had net trade receivables in the amount of €7,530 million and €7,224 million, respectively. The following proportion of the receivables was past due on the reporting date:

	2007	2008
Not past due on the reporting date	(53.6%) 4,039	(55.8%) 4,029
Past due on the reporting date	(46.4%) 3,491	(44.2%) 3,195
Total	(100.0%) 7,530	(100.0%) 7,224

The changes in Deutsche Telekom's allowance for doubtful receivables were as follows:

Item	2007	2008
Allowance on January 1	1,148	1,071
Currency translation adjustments	(8)	(7)
Additions (allowance recognized as expense)	662	547
Use	(510)	(437)
Reversal	(221)	(151)
Allowance on December 31	1,071	1,023

Assume that Deutsche Telekom's statutory tax rate was 30.5 percent in 2007 and 2008. Further assume that an analyst wishes to recognize an additional allowance for 20 percent of the receivables that are past due on the reporting date.

a What adjustments should the analyst make to Deutsche Telekom's balance sheet at the end of 2007?

b What adjustments should the analyst make to Deutsche Telekom's 2008 income statement?

15 Refer to the British American Tobacco example on provisions in this chapter. The cigarette industry is subject to litigation for health hazards posed by its products. In the US, the industry has been negotiating a settlement of these claims with state and federal governments. As the CFO for UK-based British American Tobacco (BAT), which is affected through its US subsidiaries, what information would you report to investors in the annual report on the firm's litigation risks? How would you assess whether the firm should record a provision for this risk, and if so, how would you assess the value of this provision? As a financial analyst following BAT, what questions would you raise with the CFO over the firm's litigation provision?

16 Refer to the Carlsberg – Heineken example on post-employment benefits in this chapter.

a Discuss the components of the pension expense. In your opinion, which of these components should be excluded from earnings?

b Carlsberg and Heineken use different methods to account for their actuarial gains and losses. Which of these two methods is, from an analyst's point of view, preferable?

17 Some argue that (1) because estimating the value of a contingent claims (such as executive stock options) is surrounded with uncertainty and (2) the claims do not represent a cash outlay, the value of these claims should not be included in the income statement as an expense. Do you agree with these arguments?

Problem 1 Merger accounting

International rules for merger accounting (IFRS 3) require that firms report mergers using the purchase method. Under this method the cost of the merger for the acquirer is the actual value of the consideration paid for the target firm's shares. The identifiable assets and liabilities of the target are then recorded on the acquirer's books at their fair values. If the value of the consideration paid for the target exceeds the fair value of its identifiable assets and liabilities, the excess is reported as goodwill on the acquirer's balance sheet. For example, when company A acquires company B for an amount of €1 billion (paid out in shares) and company B's net assets have a book value of €0.5 billion and a fair value of €0.7 billion, company A would record company B's net assets on its balance sheet for an amount of €0.7 billion and recognize €0.3 billion (1.0 − 0.7) of goodwill. The new rules require goodwill assets to be written off only if they become impaired in the future. However, as recently as 2003 some large acquisitions were reported using the pooling method. Under pooling accounting, the purchase of a target firm's shares is recorded at their historical book value rather than at their market value, so that no goodwill is recorded. For example, in the above example, company A would record company B's net assets on its balance sheet for an amount of €0.5 billion, ignoring the net assets' fair value and the amount of goodwill on the acquisition. This is likely to be a consideration for the analyst in evaluating the performance of serial share-for-share acquirers.

In December 2000 the pharmaceutical companies SmithKline Beecham and Glaxo Wellcome merged their activities to form UK-based GlaxoSmithKline. GlaxoSmithKline reported under UK Generally Accepted Accounting Principles (UK GAAP) and recorded the merger transaction using the pooling method. After the merger, the former shareholders of Glaxo Wellcome held close to 59 percent of GlaxoSmithKline's ordinary shares. Because GlaxoSmithKline's shares were listed on the New York Stock Exchange, the company also had to prepare a reconciliation of its UK GAAP statements with US GAAP. The US accounting rules did not, however, consider the transaction a merger of equals but an acquisition of SmithKline Beecham by Glaxo Wellcome. These rules did not permit, therefore, the use of the pooling method to record the transaction.

The additional disclosures that GlaxoSmithKline made as part of its reconciliation to US GAAP provide the analyst with much of the information that is needed to adjust for the distortion from using pooling accounting. Under the terms of the deal, the acquisition price of SmithKline Beecham was £43.9 billion. At the time of the acquisition, the book value of SmithKline Beecham's net assets was £2.7 billion and the fair value adjustments to SmithKline Beecham's net assets amounted up to £25.0 billion. The amount of goodwill thus equaled £16.2 billion (43.9 − 2.7 − 25.0). At the end of the fiscal year 2005, GlaxoSmithKline reported in its first IFRS-based financial statements that its goodwill on the acquisition of SmithKline Beecham had a remaining value of £15.9 billion, while fair value adjustments for acquired product rights were valued at £12.1 billion. The company did not, however, record these amounts on its balance sheet. The international rules on the first-time application of IFRS allow first-time adopters not to restate the accounting for business combinations (mergers and acquisitions) that took place prior to the start of the previous year because such restatements are complex and may require previously uncollected information. Like most first-time adopters, GlaxoSmithKline chose to apply this exemption. Pooling accounting therefore remained to affect GlaxoSmithKline's (and many other) IFRS-based financial statements.

1 Discuss why, from an analyst's point of view, purchase accounting is preferable over pooling accounting.

2 What adjustments should an analyst make to GlaxoSmithKline's 2006 beginning balance sheet to correct for the distortions from using pooling accounting? (Assume that GlaxoSmithKline's marginal tax rate is 30 percent. Note that the international accounting rules for income taxes prohibit the recognition of deferred taxes on nondeductible goodwill.)

3 What adjustments should an analyst make to GlaxoSmithKline's 2006 income statement?

Problem 2 Impairment of non-current assets

Consider the acquisitions by Germany-based media company EM.TV & Merchandising AG of the Jim Henson Company, creator of The Muppet Show, and Speed Investments Ltd., co-owner of the commercial rights to Formula One motor racing. At the end of the 1990s, EM.TV pursued a strategy of aggressive growth through the acquisitions of TV and marketing rights for well-known cartoon characters, such as the Flintstones, and popular sporting events. After its initial public offering on the Neuer Markt segment of the German Stock Exchange in October 1997, EM.TV's share price soared from €0.35 (split-adjusted) to a high of just above €120 in February 2000. Its high share price helped EM.TV to finance several acquisitions through a secondary stock offering and the issuance of convertible debt. In March and May 2000, respectively, the company made its two largest acquisitions with the intention of expanding its international reputation. The company acquired the Jim Henson Company for €699 million and Speed Investment for €1.55 billion. At the time of the acquisition, Speed Investment's book value of equity was negative and the amount of goodwill that EM.TV recognized on the investment was €2.07 billion. The rationale of capitalizing this amount of goodwill on EM.TV's balance sheet is that it could truly represent the future economic benefits that EM.TV expects to receive from its investment but that are not directly attributable to the investment's recorded assets and liabilities. However, the analyst should consider the possibility that EM.TV has overpaid for its new investments, especially in times where its managers are flush with free cash flow.

At the end of the fiscal year, when EM.TV's share price had already declined to €5.49, the company was forced to admit that it had overpaid for its latest acquisitions. Goodwill impairment charges for the year ending in December 2000 amounted to €340 million for the Jim Henson Company and €600 million for Speed Investment. In its annual report, EM.TV commented that "the salient factor for the write-offs was that, at the time of the acquisitions, the expert valuation was determined by the positive expectations of the capital markets. This was particularly expressed through the use of corresponding multiples." Despite the large write-offs, a considerable amount of goodwill, related to the acquisition of Speed Investment, remained part of EM.TV's assets. This amount of €1.41 billion was equal to 170 percent of EM.TV's book value of equity.

Given the questionable financial health of Speed Investment, did the initial €2.07 billion of goodwill ever represent a true economic asset? Was it reasonable to expect to receive €2.07 billion in future economic benefits from a firm that had not been able to earn profits in the past? If not, was the €600 million write-down adequate?

1 What balance sheet adjustments should an analyst make if she decided to record an additional write-down of €1.41 billion in the December 2000 financials?

2 What effect would this additional write-down have on EM.TV's depreciation expense in 2001? (Assume that the adjustments to EM.TV's balance sheet are in conformity with current IFRSs.)

Problem 3 Philips Electronics' US GAAP and IFRS statements

In 2008 Royal Philips Electronics NV disclosed two sets of financial statements: one set prepared in accordance with US Generally Accepted Accounting Principles and one set in accordance with IFRS. The methods that Philips used to account for research and development investments and post-retirement benefit obligations differed under the two sets of standards. Following is a short summary of these methods.

Development expenditures Under IFRS firms can capitalize development outlays, whereas under US GAAP such outlays must be expensed as incurred. In its 2008 IFRS-based financial statements, Philips Electronics recognized a development asset of €357 million (€518 million in 2007). The company's development expenditures amounted to €233, €259, €295, €233 and €154 million in 2004, 2005, 2006, 2007 and 2008, respectively. In these years, total R&D expenditures were €1,615, €1,602, €1,659, €1,629 and €1,622 million, respectively.

Post-retirement benefit obligations In the notes to its financial statement, Philips describes its methods for post-retirement benefits as follows:

US GAAP	IFRS
The net pension asset or liability recognized in the balance sheet in respect of defined-benefit postemployment plans is the fair value of plan assets less the present value of the projected defined-benefit obligation at the balance sheet date, together with adjustments for projected unrecognized past service costs. [. . .] Pension costs in respect of defined-benefit postemployment plans primarily represent the increase of actuarial present value of the obligation for postemployment benefits based on employee service during the year and the interest on this obligation in respect of employee service in previous years, net of the expected return on plan assets. Actuarial gains and losses arise mainly from changes in actuarial assumptions and differences between actuarial assumptions and what has actually occurred.	
They are recognized in the income statement, over the expected average remaining service periods of the employees, only to the extent that their net cumulative amount exceeds 10% of the greater of the present value of the obligation or of the fair value of plan assets at the end of the previous year (the corridor). Unrecognized gains and losses in the Netherlands, France and Thailand are amortized using the straight-line method over the expected average remaining service period without applying the corridor.	The Company recognizes all actuarial gains and losses directly in equity through the statement of recognized income and expense.
Unrecognized prior-service costs related to pension plans and postretirement benefits other than pensions are being amortized by assigning a proportional amount to the statements of income of a number of years, reflecting the average remaining service period of the active employees.	To the extent that postemployment benefits vest immediately following the introduction of a change to a defined-benefit plan, the resulting past service costs are recognized immediately.
The funded status of the Company's defined-benefit pension plans and postretirement benefits other than pensions is reflected on the balance sheet [. . .]. Actuarial gains and losses, prior service costs or credits [. . .] that are not yet recognized as components of net periodic benefit costs are recognized net of tax, as a component of accumulated other comprehensive income. Amounts recognized in accumulated other comprehensive income are adjusted as they are subsequently recognized as components of net periodic pension cost.	Recognized assets are limited to the present value of any reductions in future contributions or any future refunds, in accordance with IFRIC Interpretation 14 'The Limit on a Defined Benefit Asset, Minimum Funding Requirements and their Interaction.' (p. 197: '' . . . the amount of net assets recognized is limited to the available future benefits from the plan. The future benefits is determined as the present value of the estimated future service costs in each year less the estimated minimum funding contributions required [. . .] in each year.'')

Obligations for contributions to defined-contribution pension plans are recognized as an expense in the income statement as incurred.

At the beginning of 2008, the present value of Philips' projected benefit obligation in the Netherlands was €11,260 million; the fair value of its Dutch plan assets was €13,771 million. In the other countries, the projected benefit obligation was €7,419 million and the fair value of plan assets was €6,429 million. The amounts recognized in accumulated other comprehensive income (before tax) were:

	Netherlands		Other Countries	
	2007	**2008**	**2007**	**2008**
Net actuarial loss	105	273	1,083	1,447
Prior service cost (credit)	(421)	(378)	36	26

Make the following simplifying assumptions: (1) in all years Philips' statutory tax rate is 25.5 percent; (2) the weighted average remaining service period of Philips' employees is 10 years (in all countries); (3) Philips use the corridor approach for its actuarial gains and losses in all countries other than the Netherlands.

1 Estimate the average expected life of Philips' investments in development at the end of 2008.

2 Using the estimate derived under 1, what adjustments should an analyst make to the 2008 beginning balance sheet and 2008 income statement to immediately expense all development outlays and derecognize the development asset?

3 What adjustments should be made to the 2008 beginning balance sheet and 2008 income statement to recognize an asset for both research and development investments? Assume that the average expected life of Philips' investments in research at the end of 2007 and 2008 is equal to that of Philips' development investments at the end of 2008.

4 Summarize the main differences between Philips' treatment of postemployment benefits under US GAAP and their treatment under IFRS. If all differences other than those in postemployment benefit accounting would be eliminated, would you expect Philips' equity to be higher under US GAAP or under IFRS?

5 What do you estimate is the effect of the US GAAP treatment of actuarial gains and losses and prior service costs on Philips' net income in 2008?

Problem 4 H&M and Burberry's non-current assets

Hennes & Mauritz AB (H&M) and Burberry Group plc (Burberry) are publicly listed apparel retailers. The following information is taken from their financial statements for the fiscal years ending on November 30, 2007 and March 31, 2008, respectively (hereafter referred to as fiscal 2007):

	H&M fiscal 2007	**Burberry fiscal 2007**
Land and buildings book value at the beginning of the year	SEK 420m	£58.2m
Book value of land, buildings, and equipment leased under finance leases at the beginning of the year	SEK 222m	£0.0m
Equipment at cost at the beginning of the year	SEK 13,605m	£192.8m
Equipment book value at the beginning of the year	SEK 7,134m	£99.2m

(Continued)

	H&M fiscal 2007	Burberry fiscal 2007
Cost of equipment acquired during the year	SEK 3,466m	£38.3m
Buildings depreciation expense	SEK 14m	£1.9m
Equipment depreciation expense	SEK 1,750m	£27.0m
Sales	SEK 78,346m	£995.4m

Both retailers had non-cancellable operating leases related to land, buildings and equipment. Under the operating lease agreements, the companies were committed to paying the following amounts:

	H&M		Burberry	
Due in ...	fiscal 2007	fiscal 2006	fiscal 2007	fiscal 2006
Year 1	SEK 6,801m	SEK 6,169m	£39.1m	£31.5m
Years 2–5	SEK 19,732m	SEK 17,689m	£112.9m	£86.0m
After year 5	SEK 12,478m	SEK 11,593m	£167.5m	£103.8m
Actual lease payment made during the year	SEK 7,810m	SEK 7,030m	£43.0m	£31.0m

The incremental borrowing rate of H&M in fiscal years 2006 and 2007 was 4.4 percent; the incremental borrowing rate of Burberry in fiscal years 2006 and 2007 was 5.4 percent. The statutory tax rates of H&M and Burberry were 28 and 30 percent, respectively.

Assume that all land, buildings and equipment have zero residual values. Further assume that both retailers recognize half a year of depreciation on assets acquired during the year.

1 Two measures of the efficiency of a firm's investment policy are (a) the ratio of land, buildings and equipment to sales and (b) the ratio of depreciation to sales. Calculate both ratios for H&M and Burberry based on the reported information. Which of the two companies appears to be relatively more efficient in its investment policy?

2 Calculate the depreciation rates that H&M and Burberry use for their equipment.

3 What adjustments to (a) the beginning book value of H&M's equipment and (b) the equipment depreciation expense would be required if you would assume that H&M uses the Burberry's depreciation rate?

4 What adjustments to (a) the beginning book value of H&M's and Burberry's land, buildings and equipment and (b) H&M's and Burberry's depreciation expense would be required if you would capitalize the retailers' operating leases?

5 Recalculate the investment efficiency measures using the adjusted data. Do the adjustments affect your assessment of the retailers' investment efficiency?

NOTES

1. At the time of writing the IASB was discussing to revise its accounting standard for leases (IAS 17). The Board proposed to abandon the distinction between economically owned and other leases and require firms to record all rights to use leased assets and all obligations to make lease payments on their balance sheet. This revision, which would become effective not before 2012, would substantially reduce management's discretion in reporting leased assets.

2. See P. Healy, S. Myers, and C. Howe, "R&D Accounting and the Tradeoff Between Relevance and Objectivity," *Journal of Accounting Research* 40 (June 2002): 677–711, for analysis of the value of capitalizing R&D and then annually assessing impairment.

3. V. Beattie, K. Edwards, and A. Goodacre show that adjustments to capitalize operating leases have a significant impact on leverage and other key financial ratios of UK firms. See "The Impact of Constructive Operating Lease Capitalisation on Key Accounting Ratios," *Accounting and Business Research* 28 (Autumn 1998): 233–254.

4. Some research suggests that the distinction between finance and operating lease obligation is not fully arbitrary. In their study "Recognition Versus Disclosure: An Investigation of the Impact on Equity Risk Using UK Operating Lease Disclosures," *Journal of Business Finance and Accounting* 27 (November/December 2000): 1185–1224, V. Beattie, A. Goodacre, and S. Thomson find that UK investors interpret the operating lease obligation as an obligation that increases a firm's equity risk but less so than ordinary debt.

5. P. Healy, S. Myers, and C. Howe, "R&D Accounting and the Tradeoff Between Relevance and Objectivity," *Journal of Accounting Research* 40 (June 2002): 677–711, show that the magnitude of this bias is sizable.

6. See e.g., B. Bublitz and M. Ettredge, "The Information in Discretionary Outlays: Advertising, Research and Development," *The Accounting Review* 64 (1989): 108–124; M. Hirschey and J. Weygandt, "Amortization Policy for Advertising and Research and Development Expenditures," *Journal of Accounting Research* 23 (1985): 326–335; B. Lev and T. Sougiannis, "The Capitalization, Amortization, and Value-Relevance of R&D," *Journal of Accounting and Economics* 21 (1996): 107–138; P. Green, A. Stark, and H. Thomas, "UK Evidence on the Market Valuation of Research and Development Expenditures," *Journal of Business Finance and Accounting* 23 (March 1996): 191–216; D. Aboody and B. Lev, "The Value-Relevance of Intangibles: The Case of Software Capitalization," *Journal of Accounting Research* 36 (1998): 161–191; and M. Ballester, M. Garcia-Ayuso, and J. Livnat, "The Economic Value of the R&D Intangible Asset," *European Accounting Review* 12 (2003): 605–633.

7. MicroStrategy 1998 10-K, Note 1.

8. Ibid.

9. J. Francis, D. Hanna, and L. Vincent find that management is more likely to exercise judgment in its self-interest for goodwill write-offs and restructuring charges than for inventory or PP&E write-offs. See "Causes and Effects of Discretionary Asset Write-Offs," *Journal of Accounting Research* 34, Supplement, 1996.

10. P. Healy, K. Palepu, and R. Ruback find that acquisitions add value for only one-third of the 50 largest acquisitions during the early 1980s, suggesting that acquirers frequently do not recover goodwill. See "Which Takeovers Are Profitable – Strategic or Financial?" *Sloan Management Review,* Summer 1997. Studying a sample of 519 UK acquirers between 1983 and 1995, S. Sudarsanam and A. Mahate find in their study "Glamour Acquirers, Method of Payment and Post-acquisition Performance: The UK Evidence," *Journal of Business Finance and Accounting* 30 (January 2003): 299–341, that the risk of not recovering goodwill is especially large for glamour acquirers, who have experienced a large share price run-up prior to the acquisition.

11. J. Elliott and D. Hanna find that the market anticipates large write-downs by about one quarter, consistent with managers being reluctant to take write-downs on a timely basis. See "Repeated Accounting Write-Offs and the Information Content of Earnings," *Journal of Accounting Research* 34, Supplement, 1996.

12. Mary E. Barth and Maureen McNichols discuss ways for investors to estimate the value of environmental liabilities. See "Estimation and Market Valuation of Environmental Liabilities Relating to Superfund Sites," *Journal of Accounting Research* 32, Supplement, 1994.

13. Defined contribution plans, where companies agree to contribute fixed amounts today to cover future benefits, require very little forecasting to estimate their annual cost since the firm's obligation is limited to its annual obligation to contribute to the employees' pension funds.

14. E. Amir and E. Gordon show that firms with larger post-retirement benefit obligations and more leverage tend to make more aggressive estimates of post-retirement obligation parameters. See "A Firm's Choice of Estimation Parameters: Empirical Evidence from SFAS No. 106," *Journal of Accounting, Auditing and Finance* 11, No. 3, Summer 1996.

15. The annuity of a €1 payout that grows at rate g_a during n_a years and then gradually declines to zero over a period of n_b years can be calculated as follows:

$$\text{Annuity} = \frac{1 - ([1 + g_a]/[1 + r])^{n_a}}{(r - g_a)} + \left(\frac{1 - ([1 - 1/n_b]/[1 + r])^{n_b}}{(r + 1/n_b)} \right) \left(\frac{1}{(1 + r)^{n_a}} \right).$$

Given a discount rate (r) of 4.6 percent, g_a equal to 2.6 percent, and n_a and n_b equal to 30 years, the annuity is equal to €24.95. Decreasing the discount rate from 4.6 percent to 4.5 percent increases the annuity by €0.41, or 1.65 percent. 1.65 percent of Carlsberg's post-employment obligation of DKK 7.036 billion is approximately DKK116 million.

16. Gradual recognition implies that if the cumulative actuarial gains and losses exceed an amount of 10 percent of the post-employment benefit obligation (or the fair value of plan assets, if greater), the company amortizes the difference over the average expected remaining working lives of the current workforce.

17. M. Barth finds that investors regard these disclosures in the notes to the financial statements as more useful than the liability reported on the balance sheet. See "Relative Measurement Errors Among Alternative Pension Asset and Liability Measures," *The Accounting Review* 66, No. 3, 1991.

18. The Black-Scholes option pricing model estimates the value of an option as a nonlinear function of the exercise price, the remaining time to expiration, the estimated variance of the underlying stock, and the risk-free interest rate. Studies of the valuation of executive stock options include T. Hemmer, S. Matsunaga, and T. Shevlin, "Optimal Exercise and the Cost of Granting Employee Stock Options with a Reload Provision," *Journal of Accounting Research* 36, No. 2, 1998; C. Cuny and P. Jorion, "Valuing Executive Stock Options with Endogenous Departure," *Journal of Accounting and Economics* 20 (September 1995): 193–206; and S. Huddart, "Employee Stock Options," *Journal of Accounting and Economics* 18 (September 1994): 207–232.

APPENDIX: RECASTING FINANCIAL STATEMENTS INTO STANDARDIZED TEMPLATES

The following tables show the financial statements for Bang & Olufsen a/s for the year ended May 31, 2008. The first column in each statement presents the recast financial statement classifications that are used for each line item. Note that the classifications are not applied to subtotal lines such as Total current assets or Net profit. The recast financial statements for Bang & Olufsen are prepared by simply totaling the balances of line items with the same standard classifications. For example, on the recast balance sheet there are four line items classified as Other Current Assets: receivables from associates, income tax receivables, other receivables, and prepayments.

Bang & Olufsen reported balance sheet (DKK millions)

Classifications	Fiscal year ended May 31	2008
	ASSETS	
Non-Current Intangible Assets	Goodwill	44.8
Non-Current Intangible Assets	Acquired rights	41.1
Non-Current Intangible Assets	Completed development projects	218.8
Non-Current Intangible Assets	Development projects in progress	112.5
Non-Current Tangible Assets	Land and Buildings	274.4
Non-Current Tangible Assets	Plant and machinery	221.8
Non-Current Tangible Assets	Other equipment	50.0
Non-Current Tangible Assets	Leasehold improvements	28.7
Non-Current Tangible Assets	Tangible assets in progress and prepayments for tangible assets	80.8
Other Non-Current Assets	Investment property	52.8
Other Non-Current Assets	Investments in associates	6.3
Other Non-Current Assets	Other financial receivables	52.0
Deferred Taxes – Non-Current Asset	Deferred tax assets	22.7
	Total non-current assets	**1,206.7**

(Continued)

Bang & Olufsen reported balance sheet (DKK millions) (*Continued*)

Classifications	Fiscal year ended May 31	2008
Inventories	Inventories	801.4
Trade Receivables	Trade receivables	593.0
Other Current Assets	Receivables from associates	0.0
Other Current Assets	Income tax receivables	39.7
Other Current Assets	Other receivables	38.9
Other Current Assets	Prepayments	30.5
Cash and Marketable Securities	Cash	107.1
	Total current assets	**1,610.6**
Other Non-Current Assets	**Non-current assets classified as held for sale**	**0.0**
Total Assets	**TOTAL ASSETS**	**2,817.3**
	LIABILITIES AND SHAREHOLDERS' EQUITY	
Ordinary Shareholders' Equity	Share capital	120.8
Ordinary Shareholders' Equity	Share premium	14.6
Ordinary Shareholders' Equity	Translation reserve	(42.9)
Ordinary Shareholders' Equity	Reserve for cash flow hedges	0.0
Ordinary Shareholders' Equity	Retained earnings	1,379.2
	Equity attributable to shareholders of the parent company	**1,471.7**
Minority Interest	Minority interests	12.1
	Total equity	**1,483.8**
Non-Current Debt	Pensions	9.5
Deferred Taxes – Non-Current Liability	Deferred tax	64.2
Non-Current Debt	Provisions	77.3
Non-Current Debt	Mortgage Loans	235.7
Non-Current Debt	Loans from banks etc.	101.1
Other Non-Current Liabilities (non-interest bearing)	Other non-current liabilities	6.6
	Non-current liabilities	**494.4**
Current Debt	Mortgage loans, short term part	8.5
Current Debt	Loans from banks etc., short term part	42.9
Current Debt	Other loans from banks	53.7
Other Current Liabilities	Provisions	46.0
Trade Payables	Trade Payables	216.0
Other Current Liabilities	Payables to associates	1.8
Other Current Liabilities	Income tax	66.3
Other Current Liabilities	Other payables	320.0
Other Current Liabilities	Deferred income	83.9
	Total current liabilities	**839.1**
Total Liabilities and Shareholders' Equity	**TOTAL EQUITY AND LIABILITIES**	**2,817.3**

Bang & Olufsen reported income statement (DKK millions)

Classifications	Fiscal year ended May 31	2008
Sales	**Net turnover**	**4,092.0**
Cost of Sales (function)	Production costs	(2,199.6)
	Gross profit	**1,892.4**
Other Operating Income, Net of Other Operating Expenses (function)	Development costs	(545.5)
SG&A (function)	Distribution and marketing costs	(1,003.5)
SG&A (function)	Administration costs	(148.7)
	Operating profit	**194.7**
Investment Income	Result of investments in associates after tax	(11.2)
Investment Income	Gain on sale of shares in subsidiary	0.0
Other Operating Income, Net of Other Operating Expenses (function)	Exchange rate gains (losses)	(12.3)
Net Interest Expense or Income	Interest and other financial income	20.0
Net Interest Expense or Income	Interest and other financial costs	(37.5)
	Result before tax	**153.7**
Tax Expense	Tax on result for the year	(41.4)
	Group profit	**112.3**
Minority Interest	Minority interests	(7.6)
Net Profit/Loss	**Profit attributable to shareholders of Bang & Olufsen**	**104.7**
	INCOME STATEMENT ITEMS BY NATURE	
Cost of Materials (nature)	Cost of materials	(1,743.4)
Other Operating Income, Net of Other Operating Expenses (nature)	Amortization of development costs	(151.7)
Depreciation and Amortization (nature)	Amortization of other intangible non-current assets	(2.0)
Other Operating Income, Net of Other Operating Expenses (nature)	Impairment losses on intangible non-current assets	(2.4)
Depreciation and Amortization (nature)	Depreciation of tangible non-current assets	(139.5)
Other Operating Income, Net of Other Operating Expenses (nature)	Impairment on tangible non-current assets	0.0
Depreciation and Amortization (nature)	Depreciation of investment property	(3.6)
Personnel Expenses (nature)	Remuneration to the Board of Directors	(3.6)
Personnel Expenses (nature)	Remuneration to the Board of Management	(16.0)
Personnel Expenses (nature)	Share-based payment	(20.6)
Personnel Expenses (nature)	Wages, salaries and fees	(835.6)
Personnel Expenses (nature)	Pensions	(39.5)
Personnel Expenses (nature)	Other statutory contributions	(36.4)

Bang & Olufsen reported cash flow statement (DKK millions)

Classifications	Fiscal year ended May 31	2008
	OPERATING ACTIVITIES	
Profit Before Tax	Result for the year	112.3
	Adjustment for:	
Non-Current Operating Accruals	Depreciations, amortizations and impairment losses	299.2
Non-Current Operating Accruals	Change in liabilities	(6.7)
Profit Before Tax	Financial income	(20.0)
Profit Before Tax	Financial costs	49.8
Profit Before Tax	Share of associates' result after tax	11.2
Non-Operating Gains (Losses)	Gain on sale of non-current assets	0.0
Non-Operating Gains (Losses)	Gain on disposal of activities	0.0
Profit Before Tax	Tax on result for the year	41.4
Non-Current Operating Accruals	Various adjustments	16.9
Net (Investments in) or Liquidation of Operating Working Capital	Change in receivables	131.9
Net (Investments in) or Liquidation of Operating Working Capital	Change in inventories	(107.1)
Net (Investments in) or Liquidation of Operating Working Capital	Change in accounts payables etc.	(47.0)
Profit Before Tax	Interest received	20.0
Profit Before Tax	Interest paid	(49.8)
Taxes Paid	Income tax paid	(120.3)
	Cash flow from operating activities	**331.8**
	INVESTMENT ACTIVITIES	
Net (Investments in) or Liquidation of Operating Non-Current Assets	Purchase of intangible non-current assets	(124.9)
Net (Investments in) or Liquidation of Operating Non-Current Assets	Purchase of tangible non-current assets	(190.4)
Net (Investments in) or Liquidation of Operating Non-Current Assets	Sale of intangible non-current assets	1.5
Net (Investments in) or Liquidation of Operating Non-Current Assets	Sale of tangible non-current assets	23.3
Net (Investments in) or Liquidation of Operating Non-Current Assets	Disposals (acquisitions) of activities	0.0
Net (Investments in) or Liquidation of Operating Non-Current Assets	Change in financial receivables	36.2
	Cash flow from investment activities	**(254.3)**
	FINANCING ACTIVITIES	
Net Debt (Repayment) or Issuance	Proceeds from long-term loans	200.0
Net Debt (Repayment) or Issuance	Repayment of long-term loans	(48.7)
Net Debt (Repayment) or Issuance	Other bank loans	14.2
Dividend (Payments)	Dividend paid	(247.7)
Net Share (Repurchase) or Issuance	Dividend, own shares	14.0
Net Share (Repurchase) or Issuance	Repurchase of own shares	(100.2)

(Continued)

Bang & Olufsen reported cash flow statement (DKK millions) (Continued)

Classifications	Fiscal year ended May 31	2008
Net Share (Repurchase) or Issuance	Subscription of employee shares	0.0
Net Share (Repurchase) or Issuance	Sale of own shares	1.6
	Cash flow from financing activities	**(166.8)**
	Change in cash and cash equivalents	**(89.3)**
	Cash and cash equivalents 1 June	196.4
	Cash and cash equivalents 31 May	**107.1**

The standardized financial statements for Bang & Olufsen a/s are as follows:

Bang & Olufsen standardized balance sheet (DKK millions)

Fiscal year ending May 31	2008
Assets	
Cash and marketable securities	107.1
Trade receivables	593.0
Inventories	801.4
Other current assets	109.1
Total current assets	**1,610.6**
Non-current tangible assets	655.7
Non-current intangible assets	417.2
Deferred taxes	22.7
Other non-current assets	111.1
Total non-current assets	**1,206.7**
Total assets	**2,817.3**
Liabilities	
Trade payables	105.1
Current debt	216.0
Other current liabilities	518.0
Total current liabilities	**839.1**
Non-current debt	423.6
Deferred taxes	64.2
Other non-current liabilities (non-interest-bearing)	6.6
Total non-current liabilities	**494.4**
Total liabilities	**1,333.5**
Minority interest	12.1
Shareholders' equity	
Preference shares	0.0
Ordinary shareholders' equity	1,471.7
Total shareholders' equity	**1,471.7**
Total liabilities and shareholders' equity	**2,817.3**

Bang & Olufsen standardized income statement (DKK millions)

Fiscal year ending May 31	2008
Sales	**4,092.0**
Cost of sales	(2,199.6)
Gross profit	**1,892.4**
SG&A	(1,152.2)
Other operating income, net of other operating expense	(557.8)
Operating profit	**182.4**
Investment income	(11.2)
Net interest expense (income)	(17.5)
Profit before tax	**153.7**
Tax expense	(41.4)
Profit after tax	**112.3**
Minority interest	(7.6)
Net profit	**104.7**
Income statement items by nature	
Cost of materials	(1,743.4)
Personnel expenses	(951.7)
Depreciation and amortization	(145.1)

Bang & Olufsen standardized cash flow statement (DKK millions)

Fiscal year ending May 31	2008
Profit before tax	**153.7**
Taxes paid	(120.3)
After-tax net interest expense (income)	12.8
Non-operating losses (gains)	0.0
Non-current operating accruals	320.6
Operating cash flow before working capital investments	**366.8**
Net (investments in) or liquidation of operating working capital	(22.2)
Operating cash flow before investment in non-current assets	**344.6**
Net (investment in) or liquidation of operating non-current assets	(254.3)
Free cash flow available to debt and equity	**90.3**
After-tax net interest expense (income)	(12.8)
Net debt (repayment) or issuance	165.5
Free cash flow available to equity	**243.0**
Dividend (payments)	(247.7)
Net stock (repurchase) or issuance	(84.6)
Net increase (decrease) in cash balance	**(89.3)**

Marks and Spencer's accounting choices

On March 2, 2009, Credit Suisse analyst Tony Shiret issued a new research report about clothing retailer Marks and Spencer Group plc (M&S), setting a target price of 160 pence—which was substantially less than the company's share price of 265 pence—and reiterating his sell recommendation. The more than one hundred pages long report sharply criticized the strategic choices of M&S's management during the past year, claimed that the company's recent performance was not as good it appeared, and called upon management to change the company's course. In addition, Shiret and his team critically analyzed management's reporting strategy and showed how past discretionary accounting choices might have helped management to overstate M&S's accounting performance. The report explicitly discussed the company's accounting for pension liabilities, intangible assets and depreciation.

Marks and Spencer's current chief executive officer and chairman of the board, Sir Stuart Rose, had been appointed in May 2004. During Rose's tenure, M&S had reported steadily increasing sales and net profits, positive abnormal profits, and consistently positive cash flows from operations. Rose joined Marks and Spencer after a period in which the company's share price had underperformed. In the year of his appointment, the new chairman implemented a new strategic plan aimed at modernizing the company's stores, tightening cost control and improving the efficiency of inventory management and procurement. The new plan led to a significant improvement in operating margins.

In addition to questioning some of M&S's accounting practices in his report, analyst Tony Shiret argued that since Rose's appointment M&S had made limited performance improvements and that the company was still too reliant on older customers. On the day that Shiret issued his research report, M&S's share price dropped by 4 percent.

On May 19, 2009, M&S published its financial statements for the fiscal year ending on March 31, 2009 (hereafter referred to as fiscal year 2009/2008). The retailer's profitability had declined since the prior year, primarily due to the economic downturn, forcing management to cut the company's dividend. M&S had been able to keep its leverage ratio relatively constant, but only because of a somewhat unusual transaction that helped the company to reclassify one of its liabilities as equity. This liability had been the result of a transaction in January 2007, when the company sold (and leased back) £1.1 million of its property portfolio to a new partnership that it jointly owned with its pension fund. Part of the transaction was that the partnership promised to pay £50m annually (financed through the annual rental payments made by M&S) to M&S's pension fund during a period of 15 years. Because M&S had full control over the financing and operating decisions of the partnership, it had to consolidate the partnership in its financial statement, thus recognizing the liability to the pension fund. The transaction helped the pension fund to increase its pension plan assets and reduce M&S's pension deficit. In fiscal years 2009/2008 and 2008/2007, M&S also changed the terms of its defined benefit plans to recognize an exceptional pension credit and further reduce the pension deficit.

Professor Erik Peek prepared this case. The case is intended solely as the basis for class discussion and is not intended to serve as an endorsement, source of primary data, or illustration of effective or ineffective management.

Three days after the publication date, Shiret and his team issued a new report, increasing the target price to 195 pence but keeping the sell recommendation unchanged. In this report as well as another report following a few weeks later, the analyst repeated his concerns about some of M&S's accounting choices. Adding to these concerns was the reclassification as equity of a liability that Shiret continued to see as debt.

Questions

1   **Exhibits 1 and 2** report the income statements and excerpts from the notes to Marks and Spencer's financial statements for the fiscal years ending between March 31, 2005 and March 31, 2009. Critically analyze M&S's accounting choices. What choices may have helped the company to overstate its net profits between 2005 and 2009?

2   **Exhibit 3** provides information about the liability that Marks and Spencer reclassified as equity. Do you agree with the decision to reclassify? What will be the effect of this decision on future financial statements?

EXHIBIT 1 Marks and Spencer Group—(comprehensive) income statements

(£ millions)	2009/2008	2008/2007	2007/2006	2006/2005	2005/2004
Revenue	**9,062.1**	**9,022.0**	**8,588.1**	**7,797.7**	**7,490.5**
Cost of sales	(5,690.2)	(5,535.2)	(5,246.9)	(4,812.1)	(4,884.3)
Gross profit	**3,371.9**	**3,486.8**	**3,341.2**	**2,985.6**	**2,606.2**
Selling and marketing expenses	(2,074.4)	(1,912.7)	(1,779.2)	(1,625.7)	(1,493.0)
Administrative expenses	(570.1)	(534.5)	(584.1)	(522.7)	(476.8)
Other operating income	41.5	49.7	66.1	18.6	12.7
Profit on property disposals	6.4	27.0	1.9	(5.7)	30.7
Exceptional costs (strategic restructure)	(135.9)	0.0	0.0	0.0	(81.7)
Exceptional pension credit	231.3	95.0	0.0	0.0	0.0
Operating profit	**870.7**	**1,211.3**	**1,045.9**	**850.1**	**598.1**
Finance income	50.0	64.4	33.8	30.5	27.9
Finance costs	(214.5)	(146.6)	(112.6)	(134.9)	(120.9)
Exceptional finance costs	0.0	0.0	(30.4)	0.0	0.0
Profit on ordinary activities before taxation	**706.2**	**1,129.1**	**936.7**	**745.7**	**505.1**
Income tax expense	(199.4)	(308.1)	(277.5)	(225.1)	(150.1)
Profit for the year	**506.8**	**821.0**	**659.2**	**520.6**	**355.0**
Taxation:					
Current tax	(121.8)	(117.4)	(179.5)	(153.6)	(103.7)
Deferred tax from					
– fixed assets temporary differences	(2.0)	13.7	4.4	(2.7)	1.9
– accelerated capital allowances	17.3	(41.4)	(18.2)	(10.7)	0.8
– pension temporary differences	(87.0)	(150.5)	(71.4)	(42.4)	(48.3)
– other short-term temporary differences	(5.7)	(12.9)	(12.5)	(14.9)	(4.1)
– overseas deferred tax	(0.2)	0.4	(0.3)	(0.8)	0.3
Other information:					
Net cash flow from operating activities	1,290.6	1,069.8	1,292.5	1,096.0	1,435.1
Inventories	536.0	488.9	416.3	374.3	338.9
Trade and other receivables (including prepayments and accrued income)	285.2	307.6	196.7	210.5	213.8
Total assets	7,258.1	7,161.0	5,381.0	5,210.5	4,867.3
Total equity	2,100.6	1,964.0	1,648.2	1,155.3	909.2
Comprehensive income statement:					
Profit for the year	**506.8**	**821.0**	**659.9**	**523.1**	**586.2**
Foreign currency translation difference	33.1	21.3	(14.0)	11.1	0.0
Actuarial (losses)/gains on retirement benefit schemes	(927.1)	605.4	(8.6)	(169.3)	(78.1)
Cash flow and net investment hedges					
– fair value movements in equity	304.8	(33.5)	(7.4)	(3.1)	0.0
– recycled and reported in net profit	(206.8)	1.3	10.7	(1.4)	0.0
– amount recognized in inventories	(8.6)	2.4	2.1	(3.8)	0.0
Tax on items taken directly to equity	225.8	(185.7)	24.5	80.7	24.9
Net (losses)/gains not recognized in the income statement	**(578.8)**	**411.2**	**7.3**	**(85.8)**	**(53.2)**
Total recognized income and expense for the year	**(72.0)**	**1,232.2**	**667.2**	**437.3**	**533.0**

Source: 2009/2008 – 2005/2004 annual reports of Marks and Spencer.

Marks and Spencer's accounting choices

EXHIBIT 2   **Marks and Spencer Group—excerpts from the notes to the financial statements (2009/2008 – 2005/2004)**

Property, plant and equipment

The Group's policy is to state property, plant and equipment at cost less accumulated depreciation and any recognized impairment loss. Assets in the course of construction are held at cost less any recognized impairment loss.

Depreciation is provided to write off the cost of tangible non-current assets (including investment properties), less estimated residual values, by equal annual installments as follows:

■ freehold land – not depreciated.

■ freehold and leasehold buildings with a remaining lease term over 50 years – depreciated to their

residual value over their estimated remaining economic lives.

■ leasehold buildings with a remaining lease term of less than 50 years – over the remaining period of the lease.

■ fixtures, fittings and equipment – 3 to 25 years according to the estimated life of the asset.

Residual values and useful economic lives are reviewed annually. Depreciation is charged on all additions to, or disposals of, depreciating assets in the year of purchase or disposal. Any impairment in value is charged to the income statement.

(£ millions)	2009/2008	2008/2007	2007/2006	2006/2005	2005/2004
Land and buildings:					
Cost at year-end	2,566.6	2,525.2	2,468.2	2,392.2	2,412.0
Accumulated depreciation at year-end	(108.6)	(103.8)	(95.3)	(82.2)	(82.7)
Net book value at year-end	2,458.0	2,421.4	2,372.9	2,310.0	2,329.3
Additions (other than acquisitions)	45.7	82.6	63.9	34.7	
Disposals	58.4	73.8	6.4	34.1	
Depreciation charge	9.2	8.5	13.9	10.7	
Other changes in the net book value (exchange differences, acquisitions, etc.)	58.5	48.2	19.3	(9.2)	
Fixtures, fittings & equipment:					
Cost at year-end	4,811.9	4,473.3	3,653.3	3,287.1	3,162.1
Accumulated depreciation at year-end	(2,546.4)	(2,377.0)	(2,089.2)	(2,061.8)	(1,926.8)
Net book value at year-end	2,265.5	2,096.3	1,564.1	1,225.3	1,235.3
Additions (other than acquisitions)	395.2	692.8	578.7	251.8	
Disposals	17.3	5.2	10.7	6.2	
Depreciation charge	372.5	287.8	254.9	256.9	
Other changes in the net book value (exchange differences, acquisitions, etc.)	163.8	132.4	25.7	1.3	
Deferred tax assets/(liabilities) for tangible assets:					
Deferred tax asset/(liability) at year-end	(78.9)	(76.9)	(90.6)	(95.0)	(97.3)
Credited/(charged) to the income statement during the year	(2.0)	13.7	4.4	(2.7)	
Statutory tax rate	28.0%	28.0%	30.0%	30.0%	

Intangible assets

Software intangibles: Where computer software is not an integral part of a related item of computer

hardware, the software is treated as an intangible asset. Capitalised software costs include external direct costs of material and services and the payroll and payrollrelated costs for employees who are directly associated with the project.

Capitalised software development costs are amortized on a straight-line basis over their expected economic lives, normally between three to five years.

Computer software under development is held at cost less any recognized impairment loss.

(£ millions)	2009/2008	2008/2007	2007/2006	2006/2005	2005/2004
Goodwill:					
Cost at year-end	119.2	117.9	69.5	69.5	69.5
Accumulated depreciation at year-end	0.0	0.0	0.0	0.0	0.0
Net book value at year-end	119.2	117.9	69.5	69.5	69.5
Additions (other than acquisitions)	1.3	48.4	0.0	0.0	
Disposals	0.0	0.0	0.0	0.0	
Depreciation charge	0.0	0.0	0.0	0.0	
Other changes in the net book value (exchange differences, acquisitions, etc.)	(0.0)	0.0	0.0	0.0	
Computer software:					
Cost at year-end	102.9	82.9	51.2	42.3	32.8
Accumulated depreciation at year-end	(56.6)	(34.6)	(18.7)	(27.0)	(19.8)
Net book value at year-end	46.3	48.3	32.5	15.3	13.0
Additions (other than acquisitions)	1.9	18.6		0.2	
Transfers (from computer software under development)	18.0	12.5		9.5	
Depreciation charge	22.0	15.9		7.4	
Other changes in the net book value (exchange differences, acquisitions, etc.)	0.1	0.6	17.2	0.0	
Computer software under development:					
Cost at year-end	178.8	78.0	25.4	6.7	5.6
Accumulated depreciation at year-end	0.0	0.0	0.0	0.0	0.0
Net book value at year-end	178.8	78.0	25.4	6.7	5.6
Additions (other than acquisitions)	118.8	65.1	46.2	10.7	
Transfers (to computer software)	18.0	12.5	25.9	9.5	
Depreciation charge	0.0	0.0	0.0	0.0	
Other changes in the net book value (disposals etc.)	0.0	0.0	(1.6)	(0.1)	

Leases

(£ millions)	2009/2008	2008/2007	2007/2006	2006/2005	2005/2004
Finance leases:					
Minimum lease payments, not later than one year	18.3	11.6	7.1	4.8	5.5
Minimum lease payments, later than one year but not later than five years	51.3	45.4	19.5	9.8	13.6
Minimum lease payments, later than five years	209.4	214.9	196.0	197.7	201.2
Total minimum lease payments	279.0	271.9	222.6	212.3	220.3

(continued)

Marks and Spencer's accounting choices

(£ millions)	2009/2008	2008/2007	2007/2006	2006/2005	2005/2004
Present value of finance lease obligations:					
– current	13.7	6.2	4.4	2.7	4.4
– non-current	88.2	77.3	57.2	47.5	49.5
Operating leases:					
Minimum lease payments, not later than one year	44.0	17.9	10.6	10.2	13.3
Minimum lease payments, later than one year but not later than five years	178.5	90.4	57.4	49.9	62.1
Minimum lease payments, later than five years but not later than 25 years	2,464.4	2,223.6	1,778.3	1,724.4	1,658.1
Minimum lease payments, later than 25 years	1,488.0	1,551.1	1,527.6	1,515.4	1,554.7
Total minimum lease payments	**4,174.9**	**3,883.0**	**3,373.9**	**3,299.9**	**3,288.2**

Post-retirement benefits

(£ millions)	2009/2008	2008/2007	2007/2006	2006/2005	2005/2004
A. Pensions and other post-retirement assets/liabilities:					
Total market value of assets	3,977.0	5,045.5	5,227.5	4,606.2	3,956.8
Present value of scheme liabilities	(4,112.4)	(4,542.3)	(5,487.0)	(5,381.3)	(4,611.0)
Net funded pension plan (deficit)/asset	**(135.4)**	**503.2**	**(259.5)**	**(775.1)**	**(654.2)**
Unfunded retirement benefits	(1.0)	(1.3)	(1.2)	(1.7)	(2.5)
Postretirement healthcare	(15.8)	(18.4)	(22.6)	(18.1)	(19.3)
Net retirement benefit (deficit)/asset	**(152.2)**	**483.5**	**(283.3)**	**(794.9)**	**(676.0)**
B. Pensions and other post-retirement benefits/expenses:					
Current service cost	72.2	106.1	113.9	109.9	113.8
Curtailment gain	(5.0)	(3.0)	(2.0)	(13.0)	(14.0)
Exceptional pension credit	(231.3)	(95.0)	0.0	0.0	0.0
Operating cost	**(164.1)**	**8.1**	**111.9**	**96.9**	**99.8**
Expected return on plan assets	(334.6)	(342.7)	(282.0)	(265.5)	(248.3)
Interest on scheme liabilities	299.2	283.8	261.2	248.0	236.9
Finance cost	**(35.4)**	**(58.9)**	**(20.8)**	**(17.5)**	**(11.4)**
Service cost and finance cost of discontinued operations	0.0	0.0	0.0	1.3	3.4
Curtailment gain on disposal of Financial Services	0.0	0.0	0.0	0.0	(7.0)
Total (operating + finance cost)	**(199.5)**	**(50.8)**	**91.1**	**80.7**	**84.8**
C. Assumptions:					
Rate of increase in salaries	1.0%	3.1 – 4.5%	3.7%	3.7%	3.7%
Discount rate	6.8%	6.8%	5.3%	4.9%	5.5%
Inflation rate	2.9%	3.5%	3.0%	2.9%	2.9%
Long-term healthcare cost increase	7.9%	8.5%	8.0%	7.9%	7.9%

(continued)

Marks and Spencer's accounting choices

(£ millions)	2009/2008	2008/2007	2007/2006	2006/2005	2005/2004
D. Pension plan assets and expected rates of return					
Property partnership interest	13.3%	10.0%	9.5%	0%	0%
	(7.1%)	(6.0%)	(5.5%)	(–)	(–)
UK equities	12.1%	15.6%	15.8%	17%	26%
	(8.0%)	(8.3%)	(8.4%)	(8.0%)	(8.1%)
Overseas equities	16.2%	22.0%	26.5%	30%	27%
	(8.0%)	(8.3%)	(8.4%)	(8.0%)	(8.4%)
Government bonds	3.2%	9.6%	6.9%	16%	31%
	(4.2%)	(4.6%)	(4.7%)	(4.3%)	(4.8%)
Corporate bonds	57.3%	40.6%	41.2%	27%	13%
	(6.8%)	(6.0%)	(5.3%)	(4.9%)	(5.5%)
Cash and other	2.1%	2.1%	0.1%	10%	3%
	(4.2%)	(5.0%)	(5.5%)	(4.5%)	(3.8%)
	100%	**100%**	**100%**	**100%**	**100%**
	(7.2%)	**(6.7%)**	**(6.6%)**	**(6.2%)**	**(6.7%)**
E. Other information:					
Participants: active members	21000	24000	27000	31000	35000
Participants: deferred members	57000	58000	57000	57000	56000
Participants: pensioners	42000	39000	37000	38000	36000
Employer contributions	92.1	111.1	611.3	130.2	156.4
Employee contributions	2.0	1.0	0.0	0.0	0.0
Benefits paid	226.5	220.4	191.8	164.2	160.1
Actual return on plan assets	(945.7)	(79.9)	201.6	720.2	326.3
Cumulative actuarial (gains) and losses recognized in equity at year end	(1,257.3)	(330.2)	(935.6)	(927.0)	(757.7)

Marks and Spencer's accounting choices

EXHIBIT 3   Marks and Spencer Group—notes about the partnership liability

Note 22 Partnership liability to the Marks & Spencer UK Pension Scheme (2007/2006 financial statements)

The partnership liability to the Marks & Spencer UK Pension Scheme of £496.9m (last year £nil) relates to the amortizing liability in respect of the obligations of the Marks and Spencer Scottish Limited Partnership to the Marks & Spencer UK Pension Scheme. The Group has agreed a plan with the Pension Scheme Trustee to address the majority of the deficit by transferring properties with a current market value of £1.1bn into a partnership established by the Group. A limited interest in this partnership was contributed to the Pension Scheme on 13 March 2007. The Group retains control over these properties, including the flexibility to substitute alternative properties. The properties held in the partnership have been leased back to Marks and Spencer plc. The pension scheme is entitled to a distribution from the profits of the partnership of £50m per annum for 15 years from July 2008. The Group has the right to buy out the Trustee's partnership interest at any point for an amount equal to the net present value of the remaining annual distributions due to the pension scheme.

Each year the obligation will reduce as payments are made to the pension scheme by the partnership and an interest charge will be taken to the income statement representing the unwinding of the discounted obligation at an implied interest rate of 5.32%. The fair value of this liability was £495.3m (last year £nil).

Note 21 Partnership liability to the Marks & Spencer UK Pension Scheme (2009/2008 financial statements)

Last year the partnership liability of £723.2m related to an amortizing liability in respect of obligations of the Marks and Spencer Scottish Limited Partnership to the Marks & Spencer UK Pension Scheme. During the year an interest charge of £38.0m was taken to the income statement representing the unwinding of the discount included in this obligation at an implied average interest rate of 5.7% (last year 5.7%).

On 25 March 2009 the terms of the Scottish Limited Partnership agreement were amended to make the payment by the Scottish Limited Partnership of annual distributions to the Pension Scheme discretionary at the instance of Marks and Spencer plc in relation to financial years 2010/11 onwards. This discretion is exercisable if the Group does not pay a dividend or make any other form of return to its shareholders. As a result, the distributions to the Pension Scheme in 2009 and 2010 remain as financial liabilities, while the remaining financial instrument is now an equity instrument (see note 26).

The agreement includes a clause such that, following a default event (including the appointment of an administrator, liquidator, receiver or similar officer in respect of Marks and Spencer plc or Marks and Spencer Group plc and the winding up or dissolution of Marks and Spencer plc or Marks and Spencer Group plc) or on a relevant change of law, the net present value of the outstanding distributions becomes payable to the Pension Scheme by the Scottish Limited Partnership at the option of the Pension Scheme. On the basis of the expected cash flows associated with such an event, the related financial liability has been fair valued at nil.

Financial Analysis

The goal of financial analysis is to assess the performance of a firm in the context of its stated goals and strategy. There are two principal tools of financial analysis: ratio analysis and cash flow analysis. **Ratio analysis** involves assessing how various line items in a firm's financial statements relate to one another. Cash flow analysis allows the analyst to examine the firm's liquidity, and how the firm is managing its operating, investment, and financing cash flows.

Financial analysis is used in a variety of contexts. Ratio analysis of a company's present and past performance provides the foundation for making forecasts of future performance. As we will discuss in later chapters, financial forecasting is useful in company valuation, credit evaluation, financial distress prediction, security analysis, mergers and acquisitions analysis, and corporate financial policy analysis.

RATIO ANALYSIS

The value of a firm is determined by its profitability and growth. As shown in Figure 5.1, the firm's growth and profitability are influenced by its product market and financial market strategies. The product market strategy is implemented through the firm's competitive strategy, operating policies, and investment decisions. Financial market strategies are implemented through financing and dividend policies.

Thus the four levers managers can use to achieve their growth and profit targets are:

1 Operating management.
2 Investment management.
3 Financing strategy.
4 Dividend policies.

The objective of ratio analysis is to evaluate the effectiveness of the firm's policies in each of these areas. Effective ratio analysis involves relating the financial numbers to the underlying business factors in as much detail as possible. While ratio analysis may not give all the answers to an analyst regarding the firm's performance, it will help the analyst frame questions for further probing.

In ratio analysis, the analyst can:

1 Compare ratios for a firm over several years (a time-series comparison).
2 Compare ratios for the firm and other firms in the industry (cross-sectional comparison).
3 Compare ratios to some absolute benchmark.

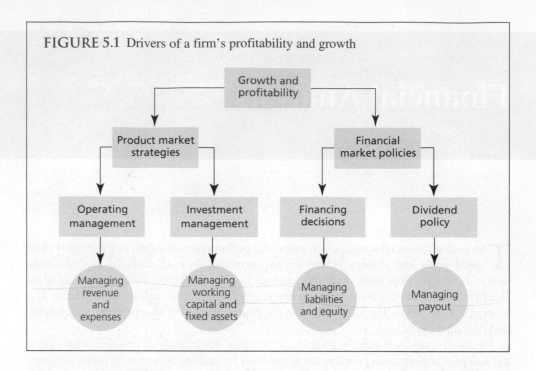

FIGURE 5.1 Drivers of a firm's profitability and growth

In a **time-series comparison**, the analyst can hold firm-specific factors constant and examine the effectiveness of a firm's strategy over time. **Cross-sectional comparison** facilitates examining the relative performance of a firm within its industry, holding industry-level factors constant. For most ratios there are no absolute benchmarks. The exceptions are measures of rates of return, which can be compared to the cost of the capital associated with the investment. For example, subject to distortions caused by accounting, the rate of return on equity (ROE) can be compared to the cost of equity capital.

In the discussion below, we will illustrate these approaches using the example of Bang & Olufsen a/s, a renowned Danish manufacturer of audio and video equipment. We will compare Bang & Olufsen's ratios for the fiscal year ending May 31, 2008, with its own ratios for the fiscal year ending May 31, 2007, and with the ratios for Loewe AG, a German competitor, for the fiscal years ending December 31, 2007 and 2008.[1]

After seeing years of moderate growth, Bang & Olufsen's sales have fallen 6 percent due to unfavorable market conditions in 2008. Analyzing the company's performance over time therefore allows us to assess how a slowdown in sales growth affects financial performance. Comparison of Bang & Olufsen with Loewe allows us to see the impact of different strategies on financial ratios. While pursuing slightly different competitive strategies, Bang & Olufsen and Loewe also follow different investment and financing strategies. Loewe uses more debt financing than Bang & Olufsen. Further, Bang & Olufsen invests substantially more in product development and property, plant and equipment than Loewe. We will illustrate how these differences between the two companies affect their ratios. We will also try to see which strategy is delivering better performance for shareholders.

In order to facilitate replication of the ratio calculations presented below, we present in the appendix to this chapter three versions of the financial statements of both these companies. The first version is the one reported by the two companies in their annual reports. The second set of financial statements is presented in the standardized format described in Chapter 4. These "standardized and adjusted financial statements" not only put both companies' financials in one standard format to facilitate direct comparison but also have been adjusted for two forms of asset/liability understatement: the omission from the balance sheet of (1) operating lease assets and liabilities and (2) research and development assets. We also present the two companies' financial statements in a third format in the appendixes. These statements, labeled "Condensed Financial Statements," are essentially a recasting of the standardized and adjusted financial statements to facilitate the calculation of several ratios discussed in the chapter. We will discuss later in the chapter how this recasting process works.[2]

BACKGROUND INFORMATION ON BANG & OLUFSEN AND LOEWE

General informationx

Denmark-based Bang & Olufsen a/s (occasionally referred to as B&O) is a manufacturer of luxurious audio and video systems. During the fiscal year ended May 31, 2008 (labeled fiscal 2008), the company employed close to 2,500 employees, primarily in Denmark and the Czech Republic. In 2008 B&O derived 82 percent of its total revenues from selling audio and video equipment within Europe. Sales in the US and Asia accounted for 6 and 9 percent of total sales, respectively.

Loewe AG is one of B&O's primary competitors. The Germany-based company is smaller than B&O, having close to 1,000 employees. Loewe's product portfolio includes LCD flat-screen televisions, DVD recorders, and audio components such as speakers, making the company a specialist in home cinema solutions. However, the company derives most of its revenues from the sales of televisions (87 percent). Loewe's primary geographical markets are Germany (23 percent of sales), Austria (13 percent), Switzerland (9 percent), and the Benelux (6 percent).

The industry

B&O and Loewe primarily operate in the household audio and video segment of the consumer electronics industry. The consumer electronics industry is a cyclical industry, implying that the demand for consumer electronics typically varies with economic cycles. Technological innovations in the industry or one of its segments can, however, make the industry grow at a (much) faster rate than the economy. For example, the introduction of the flat panel screen technology significantly boosted sales in the segment for televisions during the five years after 2003.

Despite its (technology-driven) above-average growth, the consumer electronics industry is highly competitive. Within most of its segments, including the household audio and video segment, the number of competitors is relatively large. While many of these competitors make high fixed investments in manufacturing capacity, R&D and product innovation, new products tend to become commodities shortly after their introduction. This tendency reduces the opportunities for differentiation and increases the intensity of price competition in the industry. To illustrate, the average selling price of a 40 inch LCD television in Europe decreased from about €2,800 to slightly more than €1,000 in three years time (2006–2008). The profit potential in the industry tends to be further reduced by the fact that large consumer electronics retailers like Mediamarkt and Euronics have significant bargaining power over the electronics manufacturers.

The strategy

Both B&O and Loewe pursue a differentiation strategy, competing on design, technology and quality rather than price. However, Loewe started to focus on differentiation more recently and is still developing its image and reputation as a luxury brand. Other mechanisms that both companies use to improve their profitability relative to the industry average are to (1) outsource part of their R&D and component production activities, such as the production of LCD panels, to suppliers over which they have significant bargaining power and (2) bypass powerful electronics retailers by selling products through single-brand dealerships or shop-in-shop outlets.

B&O has been following a differentiation strategy since the end of the 1960s. In the 1980s, when the company's profitability came under pressure, the company changed from distributing its products via multi-brand stores to (mostly) independent single-brand dealerships. Later, the company also developed a shop-in-shops concept, allowing multi-brand stores to sell B&O products in a separate section of their store. In 2008, 822 B1 outlets, of which 55 were directly owned by B&O, accounted for 81 percent of B&O's sales to consumers; 400 shop-in-shop outlets accounted for the remaining 19 percent. To control the quality of its distribution, B&O organizes training sessions and has set up an e-learning portal, allowing the company to train close to 2,700 sales persons and 1,100 technicians each year.

Although Loewe has always had the reputation of a high-quality brand in its home market, Germany, the company started to fully develop its image as an international luxury brand after its initial public offering in 1998. Especially after its restructuring in 2003, Loewe stepped up its marketing efforts and opened single-brand stores ("galleries") in major international cities to elevate customers' brand awareness worldwide, thereby gradually moving in the direction of Bang & Olufsen.

Both Bang & Olufsen and Loewe invest in R&D. In 2008 B&O's development expenditures amounted to DKK 530 million, or 13 percent of sales. Approximately 500 engineers and technicians, 20 percent of B&O's workforce, were involved in development activities. Their primary target was to launch between three and five new products each year. In the same year Loewe spent substantially less on R&D than B&O: 2 percent of sales (€7.2 million). The company had 140 employees, or 14 percent of its workforce, working at its R&D department.

Measuring overall profitability

The starting point for a systematic analysis of a firm's performance is its return on equity (ROE), defined as

$$\text{ROE} = \frac{\text{Net profit}}{\text{Shareholders' equity}}$$

ROE is a comprehensive indicator of a firm's performance because it provides an indication of how well managers are employing the funds invested by the firm's shareholders to generate returns. On average over long periods, large publicly traded firms in Europe generate ROEs in the range of 10 to 12 percent.

In the long run, the value of the firm's equity is determined by the relationship between its ROE and its cost of equity capital.[3] That is, those firms that are expected over the long run to generate ROEs in excess of the cost of equity capital should have market values in excess of book value, and vice versa. (We will return to this point in more detail in Chapter 7 on valuation.)

A comparison of ROE with the cost of capital is useful not only for contemplating the value of the firm but also in considering the path of future profitability. The generation of consistent supernormal profitability will, absent significant barriers to entry, attract competition. For that reason, ROEs tend over time to be driven by competitive forces toward a "normal" level – the cost of equity capital. Thus one can think of the cost of equity capital as establishing a benchmark for the ROE that would be observed in a long-run competitive equilibrium. Deviations from this level arise for two general reasons. One is the industry conditions and competitive strategy that cause a firm to generate supernormal (or subnormal) economic profits, at least over the short run. The second is distortions due to accounting.

Table 5.1 shows the ROE based on reported earnings for Bang & Olufsen and Loewe.

Bang & Olufsen's ROE declined from 19.4 to 8.6 percent between 2007 and 2008, indicating that the unfavorable market conditions affected the company's performance disproportionately compared to its sales. It is not uncommon that earnings decline at a faster rate than sales. Because some of a firm's costs are fixed in the short run, cost changes exhibit stickiness and do not proportionally follow sales changes when sales declines. An example of costs that tend to be sticky are Bang & Olufsen's R&D expenditures. We will take a closer look at these expenditures in a later section. Compared to historical trends of ROE in the economy, Bang & Olufsen's earnings performance in 2008 can be viewed as being below average. Further, its ROE in 2008 is not adequate to cover reasonable estimates of its cost of equity capital.[4]

In 2008 Bang & Olufsen's performance was far behind Loewe's ROE, which showed an improvement from 13.1 to 27.3 percent. At that performance Loewe was earning excess returns relative to both the historical trends in ROE in the European economy, as well as to its own cost of equity. Loewe's superior performance relative to Bang & Olufsen is reflected in the difference in the two companies' ratio of market value of equity to book value. As we will discuss in Chapter 7, ROE is a key determinant of a company's market to book ratio. As of May 31, 2008, Bang & Olufsen's market value to book value ratio was 1.4, while the same ratio for Loewe was 2.0.

Decomposing profitability: Traditional approach

A company's ROE is affected by two factors: how profitably it employs its assets and how big the firm's asset base is relative to shareholders' investment. To understand the effect of these two factors, ROE can be decomposed into return on assets (ROA) and a measure of financial leverage, as follows:

$$ROE = ROA \times \text{Financial leverage}$$
$$= \frac{\text{Net profit}}{\text{Assets}} \times \frac{\text{Assets}}{\text{Shareholders' equity}}$$

ROA tells us how much profit a company is able to generate for each euro of assets invested. Financial leverage indicates how many euros of assets the firm is able to deploy for each euro invested by its shareholders.

TABLE 5.1 Return on equity for Bang & Olufsen and Loewe

Ratio	B & O 2008	B & O 2007	Loewe 2008	Loewe 2007
Return on equity	8.6%	19.4%	27.3%	13.1%

The ROA itself can be decomposed as a product of two factors:

$$\text{ROA} = \frac{\text{Net profit}}{\text{Sales}} \times \frac{\text{Sales}}{\text{Assets}}$$

The ratio of net profit to sales is called net **profit margin** or return on sales (ROS); the ratio of sales to assets is known as **asset turnover**. The profit margin ratio indicates how much the company is able to keep as profits for each euro of sales it makes. Asset turnover indicates how many sales euros the firm is able to generate for each euro of its assets.

Table 5.2 displays the three drivers of ROE for our electronics manufacturers: net profit margins, asset turnover, and **financial leverage**. In 2008 Bang & Olufsen's decrease in ROE is largely driven by decreases in its net profit margin and in its asset turnover. In fact, its financial leverage slightly increased, which weakly helped to cushion its deteriorating operating performance. Loewe's performance seems to be superior on every dimension. The company has superior operating performance, as indicated by its high ROA relative to Bang & Olufsen's ROA. On top of this, Loewe's superior operating performance is leveraged by its more aggressive financial management relative to Bang & Olufsen.

Decomposing profitability: Alternative approach

Even though the above approach is popularly used to decompose a firm's ROE, it has several limitations. In the computation of ROA, the denominator includes the assets claimed by all providers of capital to the firm, but the numerator includes only the earnings available to equity holders. The assets themselves include both operating assets and financial assets such as cash and short-term investments. Further, net profit includes profit from operating activities, as well as interest income and expense, which are consequences of financing decisions. Often it is useful to distinguish between these two sources of performance. Finally, the financial leverage ratio used above does not recognize the fact that a firm's cash and short-term investments are in essence "negative debt" because they can be used to pay down the debt on the company's balance sheet.[5] These issues are addressed by an alternative approach to decomposing ROE discussed below.[6]

Before discussing this alternative ROE decomposition approach, we need to define some terminology (see Table 5.3) used in this section as well as in the rest of this chapter.

We use the terms defined in Table 5.3 to recast the financial statements of Bang & Olufsen and Loewe. These recast financial statements, which are shown in the appendixes to this chapter, are used to decompose ROE in the following manner:

TABLE 5.2 Traditional decomposition of ROE

Ratio	B & O 2008	B & O 2007	Loewe 2008	Loewe 2007
Net profit margin (ROS)	4.5%	9.6%	5.3%	2.3%
× Asset turnover	1.06	1.15	1.64	1.66
= Return on assets (ROA)	4.8%	11.1%	8.7%	3.8%
× Financial leverage	1.80	1.75	3.13	3.46
= Return on equity (ROE)	8.6%	19.4%	27.3%	13.1%

TABLE 5.3 Definitions of accounting items used in ratio analysis

Item	Definition
Net interest expense after tax	(Interest expense − Interest income) × (1 − Tax rate)[a]
Net operating profit after taxes (NOPAT)	Net profit + Net interest expense after tax
Operating working capital	(Current assets − Cash and marketable securities) −(Current liabilities − Current debt and current portion of non-current debt)
Net non-current assets	Total non-current assets − Non-interest-bearing non-current liabilities
Net debt	Total interest-bearing non-current liabilities + Current debt and current portion of non-current debt − Cash and marketable securities
Net assets	Operating working capital + Net non-current assets
Net capital	Net debt + Shareholders' equity

a. The calculation of net interest expense treats interest expense and interest income as absolute values, independent of how these figures are reported in the income statement.

$$\text{ROE} = \frac{\text{NOPAT}}{\text{Equity}} - \frac{\text{Net interest expense after tax}}{\text{Equity}}$$

$$= \frac{\text{NOPAT}}{\text{Net assets}} \times \frac{\text{Net assets}}{\text{Equity}} - \frac{\text{Net interest expense after tax}}{\text{Net debt}} \times \frac{\text{Net debt}}{\text{Equity}}$$

$$= \frac{\text{NOPAT}}{\text{Net assets}} \left(1 + \frac{\text{Net debt}}{\text{Equity}} \right) - \frac{\text{Net interest expense after tax}}{\text{Net debt}} \times \frac{\text{Net debt}}{\text{Equity}}$$

$$= \text{Operating ROA} + (\text{Operating ROA} - \text{Effective interest rate after tax})$$
$$\times \text{Net financial leverage}$$

$$= \text{Operating ROA} + (\text{Spread} \times \text{Net financial leverage})$$

Operating ROA is a measure of how profitably a company is able to deploy its operating assets to generate operating profits. This would be a company's ROE if it were financed with all equity. Spread is the incremental economic effect from introducing debt into the capital structure. This economic effect of borrowing is positive as long as the return on operating assets is greater than the cost of borrowing. Firms that do not earn adequate operating returns to pay for interest cost reduce their ROE by borrowing. Both the positive and negative effect is magnified by the extent to which a firm borrows relative to its equity base. The ratio of net debt to equity provides a measure of this net financial leverage. A firm's spread times its net financial leverage, therefore, provides a measure of the financial leverage gain to the shareholders.

Operating ROA can be further decomposed into NOPAT margin and operating asset turnover as follows:

$$\text{Operating ROA} = \frac{\text{NOPAT}}{\text{Sales}} \times \frac{\text{Sales}}{\text{Net assets}}$$

NOPAT margin is a measure of how profitable a company's sales are from an operating perspective. Operating asset turnover measures the extent to which a company is able to use its operating assets to generate sales.

Table 5.4 presents the decomposition of ROE for Bang & Olufsen and Loewe. The ratios in this table show that there is a significant difference between Bang & Olufsen's ROA and its operating ROA. In 2008, for example, Bang & Olufsen's ROA was 4.8 percent, while its operating ROA was 7.8 percent. This difference between Bang & Olufsen's operating ROA and ROA can be partly attributed the company's large cash holdings and (non-interest-bearing) deferred tax liabilities.

The difference in ROA and operating ROA is even more remarkable for Loewe: its ROA in 2008 was 8.7 percent whereas the operating ROA was 15.3 percent. One of the reasons that Loewe's operating ROA is dramatically larger than its ROA is that the company makes intensive use of trade payables and other current liabilities to finance its operations. This shows that, for at least some firms, it is important to adjust the simple ROA to take into account interest expense, interest income, and financial structure.

The appropriate benchmark for evaluating operating ROA is the weighted average cost of debt and equity capital, or WACC. In the long run, the value of the firm's assets is determined by where operating ROA stands relative to this norm. Moreover, over the long run and absent some barrier to competitive forces, operating ROA will tend to be pushed toward the weighted average cost of capital. Since the WACC is lower than the cost of equity capital, operating ROA tends to be pushed to a level lower than that to which ROE tends.

The average operating ROA for large firms in Europe, over long periods of time, is in the range of 7 to 9 percent. Bang & Olufsen's operating ROA in 2008 is within this range, indicating that its operating performance is about average. At 15.3 percent, Loewe's operating ROA is far larger than Bang & Olufsen's and also the European industrial average and any reasonable estimates of Loewe's weighted average cost of capital. This superior operating performance of Loewe would have been obscured by using the simple ROA measure.[7]

Although Loewe dominates Bang & Olufsen in terms of both operating drivers of ROE in 2008, one year earlier Bang & Olufsen still had a substantially better NOPAT margin than Loewe. Bang & Olufsen's higher NOPAT margin is primarily a result of its strategy of focusing on the high-end segment of the consumer electronics market and asking higher premium prices than Loewe, which is still developing its image and reputation as a luxury brand. Loewe's higher operating asset turnover shows that the company is able to utilize its operating assets efficiently enough to compensate for the lower margins on its sales.

Loewe is also able to create shareholder value through its financing strategy. In 2007 the spread between Loewe's operating ROA and its after-tax interest cost was 5.9 percent; its net debt as a percent of its equity was 93 percent. Both these factors contributed to a

TABLE 5.4 Distinguishing operating and financing components in ROE decomposition

Ratio	B & O 2008	B & O 2007	Loewe 2008	Loewe 2007
Net operating profit margin	4.9%	9.9%	5.5%	2.5%
× Net operating asset turnover	1.59	1.89	2.78	2.99
= Operating ROA	7.8%	18.6%	15.3%	7.6%
Spread	3.6%	11.1%	14.1%	5.9%
× Net financial leverage	0.20	0.07	0.85	0.93
= Financial leverage gain	0.7%	0.8%	12.0%	5.5%
ROE = Operating ROA + Financial leverage gain	8.6%	19.4%	27.3%	13.1%

net increment of 5.5 percent to its ROE. Thus, while Loewe's operating ROA in 2004 was 7.6 percent, its ROE was 13.1 percent. In 2008 Loewe's spread increased to 14.1 percent, its net financial leverage went down to 85 percent, leading to a 12.0 percent net increment to ROE due to its debt policy. With an operating ROA of 15.3 percent in that year, its ROE went up to 27.3 percent.

Bang & Olufsen had low leverage in 2007, to the tune of 7 percent. As a result, even though Bang & Olufsen had a positive spread of 11.1 percent, it had a modest financial leverage gain of only 0.8 percent. This financial leverage gain helped to produce a high ROE of 19.4 percent. With a higher level of leverage, Bang & Olufsen could have exploited its spread to produce an even higher ROE. In the following year, fiscal year 2008, Bang & Olufsen's net financial leverage did increase, partly because the company repurchased its own shares. However, the increase in leverage was offset by a decrease in the spread, causing the financial leverage gain to decrease from 0.8 to 0.7 percent.

Assessing operating management: Decomposing net profit margins

A firm's net profit margin or ROS shows the profitability of the company's operating activities. Further decomposition of a firm's ROS allows an analyst to assess the efficiency of the firm's operating management. A popular tool used in this analysis is the common-sized income statement in which all the line items are expressed as a ratio of sales revenues. This type of analysis is also referred to as vertical analysis.

Common-sized income statements make it possible to compare trends in income statement relationships over time for the firm, and trends across different firms in the industry. Income statement analysis allows the analyst to ask the following types of questions:

1 Are the company's margins consistent with its stated competitive strategy? For example, a differentiation strategy should usually lead to higher gross margins than a low-cost strategy.

2 Are the company's margins changing? Why? What are the underlying business causes-changes in competition, changes in input costs, or poor overhead cost management?

3 Is the company managing its overhead and administrative costs well? What are the business activities driving these costs? Are these activities necessary?

To illustrate how the income statement analysis can be used, common-sized income statements for Bang & Olufsen and Loewe are shown in Table 5.5. The table also shows some commonly used profitability ratios. We will use the information in Table 5.5 to investigate why Bang & Olufsen had a net profit margin (or return on sales) of 4.5 percent in 2008 and 9.6 percent in 2007, while Loewe had a net margin of 5.3 percent in 2008 and 2.3 percent in 2007. Bang & Olufsen and Loewe classify their expenses by function in the income statement and disclose a classification of their expenses by nature in the notes to the financial statements. Consequently, we can decompose the companies' net profit margins both by function and by nature.

Decomposition by function

Although not required to do so by the international accounting rules, some firms classify their operating expensing according to function. The decomposition of operating expenses by function is potentially more informative than the decomposition by nature. This is because the functional decomposition requires the firm to use judgment in dividing total operating expenses into expenses that are directly associated with products sold or services

TABLE 5.5 Common-sized income statement and profitability ratios

Ratio	B & O 2008	B & O 2007	Loewe 2008	Loewe 2007
Line items as a percent of sales				
Sales	100.0%	100.0%	100.0%	100.0%
Cost of materials	(42.6%)	(43.9%)	(55.4%)	(60.3%)
Personnel expense	(23.3%)	(21.7%)	(17.9%)	(16.0%)
Depreciation and amortization	(4.8%)	(4.2%)	(4.0%)	(3.5%)
Other operating expense	(21.9%)	(16.4%)	(14.7%)	(14.0%)
Net interest expense/income	(0.6%)	(0.4%)	(0.3%)	(0.6%)
Tax expense	(1.8%)	(4.0%)	(2.4%)	(3.2%)
Profit from discontinued operations	0.0%	0.0%	0.0%	0.0%
Net profit	4.5%	9.6%	5.3%	2.3%
Operating expense line items as a percent of sales (by function)				
Cost of sales	(53.1%)	(52.9%)	(68.0%)	(71.6%)
Selling, general, and admin. expense	(28.2%)	(24.0%)	(22.9%)	(20.9%)
Other operating income/expense	(11.3%)	(9.3%)	(1.1%)	(1.4%)
Key profitability ratios				
Gross profit margin	46.9%	47.1%	32.0%	28.4%
EBITDA margin	12.2%	18.0%	12.1%	9.7%
NOPAT margin	4.9%	9.9%	5.5%	2.5%
Net profit margin	4.5%	9.6%	5.3%	2.3%

delivered (cost of sales) and expenses that are incurred to manage operations (selling, general, and administrative expense).

The difference between a firm's sales and cost of sales is gross profit. Gross profit margin is an indication of the extent to which revenues exceed direct costs associated with sales, and it is computed as

$$\text{Gross profit margin} = \frac{\text{Sales} - \text{Cost of Sales}}{\text{Sales}}$$

Gross margin is influenced by two factors: (1) the price premium that a firm's products or services command in the marketplace and (2) the efficiency of the firm's procurement and production process. The price premium a firm's products or services can command is influenced by the degree of competition and the extent to which its products are unique. The firm's cost of sales can be low when it can purchase its inputs at a lower cost than competitors and/or run its production processes more efficiently. This is generally the case when a firm has a low-cost strategy.

Table 5.5 indicates that B&O's gross margin in 2008 decreased only marginally to 46.9 percent, reflecting steadiness in the company's price premium. This suggests that, assuming constant operational efficiency, the company has not changed the price markup on its products despite the decline in consumers' demand. Not surprisingly so, given that maintaining a steady price premium is crucial to the success of differentiating companies such as B&O. Loewe's gross margin is significantly lower than that of B&O, reflecting that Loewe's current market positioning does not yet allow the company to set its price premium as high as that of its competitor. In contrast to B&O, however, Loewe managed to increase its gross margin from 28.4 to 31.0 percent. A probable reason for this is that

Loewe has been further developing its differentiation strategy, allowing the company to increase its price premium. In addition, a worldwide slowdown in the demand for components helped Loewe to increase its bargaining power over component suppliers and force them to cut their prices. Finally, the depreciation of the US dollar by 6 percent (on average) also reduced Loewe's procurement costs, given that the company does most of its procurement in dollars.

A company's selling, general, and administrative (SG&A) expenses are influenced by the operating activities it has to undertake to implement its competitive strategy. As discussed in Chapter 2, firms with differentiation strategies have to undertake activities to achieve differentiation. A company competing on the basis of quality and rapid introduction of new products is likely to have higher R&D costs relative to a company competing purely on a cost basis. Similarly, a company that attempts to build a brand image, distribute its products through full-service retailers, and provide significant customer service is likely to have higher selling and administration costs relative to a company that sells through warehouse retailers or direct mail and does not provide much customer support.

A company's SG&A expenses are also influenced by the efficiency with which it manages its overhead activities. The control of operating expenses is likely to be especially important for firms competing on the basis of low cost. However, even for differentiators, it is important to assess whether the cost of differentiation is commensurate with the price premium earned in the marketplace.

Several ratios in Table 5.5 allow us to evaluate the effectiveness with which Bang & Olufsen and Loewe managed their SG&A expenses. First, the ratio of SG&A expense to sales shows how much a company is spending to generate each euro of sales. Loewe definitely had the edge in terms of a cost management strategy as demonstrated by its lower ratio of SG&A to sales. In 2008 Loewe's SG&A expenses as a percent of sales was 22.9 percent compared to 28.2 percent for Bang & Olufsen. In addition, Bang & Olufsen's other operating expense to sales, which primarily includes research and development, exceeded Loewe's other operating expense by close to 10 percent. Note that this difference in the other operating expense to sales ratio cannot be explained by differences in the companies' accounting treatments of R&D outlays because we adjusted the financial statements for such differences before calculating the ratios. It illustrates that Bang & Olufsen invests substantially more in research and development than Loewe and is relatively less successful in bringing newly developed products to the market.

It is interesting to note that Bang & Olufsen showed significant increases in some of its cost to sales ratios from 2007 to 2008. In periods of sales decline, changes in selling, administration and R&D expenditures typically lag behind sales changes, thus increasing the ratio of these costs to sales. This is because it is costly to firms to temporarily cut capacity in down periods and bring back capacity when sales recover. For example, in many countries labor regulations make it difficult to lay off personnel. Also, temporarily cutting back on R&D could harm a firm's competitive position in the long run. Note that a firm's expenditures on production can be just as sticky as, for example, selling or research expenditures. However, production costs that are allocated to unsold products end up on the firm's balance sheet as part of inventories. The temporary capitalization of these costs dampens the positive effect of sales declines on the cost of sales to sales ratio, though it leads to an increase in the inventories to sales ratio. We will get back to this issue in the section on asset turnover.

Decomposition by nature

The international accounting rules require that all firms reporting under IFRS classify and disclose their operating expenses by nature, either in the income statement or in the notes to the financial statements. Like most firms, Bang & Olufsen and Loewe distinguish four expense categories:

1 Cost of materials.
2 Personnel expense.
3 Depreciation and amortization.
4 Other operating expenses.

Table 5.5 indicates that Bang & Olufsen experienced an increase in personnel expense in 2008. As argued earlier, this is possibly because personnel expenses tend to exhibit stickiness in the presence of a sales decline, given that it is costly to lay off personnel and often difficult to cut salaries. The increase in personnel costs worsened the operating margin by 1.6 percent. An advantage of classifying operating expenses by nature is that these expenses can be more easily related to their main driver, such as the number of employees. This helps us to further analyze the development in Bang & Olufsen personnel expenses.

In 2008 Bang & Olufsen's average workforce grew by 5.7 percent to 2,541 employees, which given the decline in sales, led to a reduction in employee productivity. In particular, sales per employee decreased by 8.3 percent to DKK1.67 million (or €224 thousand). Although Bang & Olufsen was able to reduce its personnel cost per employee by 1.9 percent to DKK388 thousand per employee (which is equal to €52 thousand per employee), this reduction was not sufficient to offset the decrease in employee productivity. In 2008 Loewe spent on average €66,500 per employee, up 11 percent from €59,900 per employee in 2007, which illustrates that the company had a more expensive workforce. However, because Loewe was able to earn €371 thousand in sales per employee, its personnel expense to sales ratio was still significantly lower than Bang & Olufsen's. The increase in Loewe's per-employee wage expense was partly due to a catch up in wage increases which were foregone during prior years under the company's collective wage agreement as well as to a one-time bonus payment to the company's employees in 2008.

Both Bang & Olufsen and Loewe experienced a small increase in their depreciation and amortization expense of roughly 0.5 percent. When we compare Bang & Olufsen's with Loewe's cost of materials, we see that Bang & Olufsen's cost of materials as a percent of sales is substantially lower. This difference in margin between sales and cost of materials is consistent with Bang & Olufsen having a greater price markup on its products. Both companies were able to improve their cost of materials to sales ratio, possibly because of a decrease in the costs of components. For Loewe, an increase in price markup may also have contributed to the improvement of the ratio. Finally, note that cost of materials to sales decreased more than cost of sales to sales, both for Bang & Olufsen and Loewe. This suggests that production costs other than the cost of materials, such as the costs of production personnel, increased during 2008.

NOPAT margin and EBITDA margin

Given that Bang & Olufsen and Loewe are pursuing different pricing, distribution, and R&D strategies, it is not surprising that they have different cost structures. As a percentage of sales, Bang & Olufsen's cost of materials and cost of sales are lower, and its personnel expense, SG&A expense and other operating expense are higher. The question is, when these costs are netted out, which company is performing better? Two ratios provide useful signals here: net operating profit margin (NOPAT margin) and EBITDA margin:

$$\text{NOPAT margin} = \frac{\text{NOPAT}}{\text{Sales}}$$

$$\text{EBITDA margin} = \frac{\text{Earnings before interest, taxes, depreciation and amortization}}{\text{Sales}}$$

NOPAT margin provides a comprehensive indication of the operating performance of a company because it reflects all operating policies and eliminates the effects of debt policy. EBITDA margin provides similar information, except that it excludes depreciation and amortization expense, a significant noncash operating expense. Some analysts prefer to use EBITDA margin because they believe that it focuses on "cash" operating items. While this is to some extent true, it can be potentially misleading for two reasons. EBITDA is not a strictly cash concept because sales, cost of sales, and SG&A expenses often include noncash items. Also, depreciation is a real operating expense, and it reflects to some extent the consumption of resources. Therefore, ignoring it can be misleading.

From Table 5.5 we see that Bang & Olufsen's NOPAT margin and EBITDA margin worsened between 2007 and 2008. Because of this development, in 2008 the company is able to retain only 4.9 cents in net operating profits for each euro of sales, whereas Loewe is able to retain 5.5 cents. Loewe and Bang & Olufsen have a similar EBITDA margin.

Recall that in Table 5.3 we define NOPAT as net profit plus net interest expense. Therefore, NOPAT is influenced by any nonoperating income (expense) items included in net profit. We can calculate a "recurring" NOPAT margin by eliminating these items. For Bang & Olufsen, recurring NOPAT margin was 5.4 percent in 2008 and 9.9 percent in 2007. The 2008 margin is higher than the NOPAT margin number we discussed above, suggesting that a portion of the company's NOPAT is derived from sources other than its core operations. These sources include investment, impairment and foreign exchange rate losses that Bang & Olufsen reported in its financial statements. Recurring NOPAT may be a better benchmark to use when one is extrapolating current performance into the future because it reflects margins from the core business activities of a firm.

Tax expense

Taxes are an important element of firms' total expenses. Through a wide variety of tax planning techniques, firms can attempt to reduce their tax expenses.[8] There are two measures one can use to evaluate a firm's tax expense. One is the ratio of tax expense to sales, and the other is the ratio of tax expense to earnings before taxes (also known as the average tax rate). The firm's tax note provides a detailed account of why its average tax rate differs from the statutory tax rate.

When evaluating a firm's tax planning, the analyst should ask two questions: (1) Are the company's tax policies sustainable, or is the current tax rate influenced by one-time tax credits? (2) Do the firm's tax planning strategies lead to other business costs? For example, if the operations are located in tax havens, how does this affect the company's profit margins and asset utilization? Are the benefits of tax planning strategies (reduced taxes) greater than the increased business costs?

Table 5.5 shows that Bang & Olufsen's tax rate decreased significantly between 2007 and 2008. Bang & Olufsen's taxes as a percent of sales were also lower than Loewe's. One reason for this is that Loewe's pretax profits as a percent of sales were higher. In addition, a 3 percent reduction in the Danish statutory tax rate had a negative one-time effect of 0.5 percent on Bang & Olufsen's taxes-to-sales ratio in 2008. Similarly, Loewe's taxes as a percent of sales decreased because the company's tax expense in 2007 was temporarily inflated by the one-time effect of a tax rate change in Germany. Without this effect, Loewe's taxes-to-sales ratio would have increased from 1.9 percent in 2007 to 2.4 percent in 2008.

In summary, we conclude that Bang & Olufsen's reduction in return on sales is primarily driven by an increase in the SG&A-to-sales and other operating expenses-to-sales ratios – most likely as a result of selling, administration and R&D costs' sticky behavior in the presence of a sales decline. The company was able to reduce its cost of materials. In comparison with Loewe, Bang & Olufsen has a higher gross profit margin, consistent with the higher price markup on its products, but a lower NOPAT margin, resulting from the company's high expenditures on SG&A and R&D.

Evaluating investment management: Decomposing asset turnover

Asset turnover is the second driver of a company's return on equity. Since firms invest considerable resources in their assets, using them productively is critical to overall profitability. A detailed analysis of asset turnover allows the analyst to evaluate the effectiveness of a firm's investment management.

There are two primary areas of asset management: (1) working capital management and (2) management of non-current assets. Working capital is defined as the difference between a firm's current assets and current liabilities. However, this definition does not distinguish between operating components (such as trade receivables, inventories, and trade payables) and the financing components (such as cash, marketable securities, and notes payable). An alternative measure that makes this distinction is operating working capital, as defined in Table 5.3:

Operating working capital = (Current assets − Cash and marketable securities)

− (Current liabilities − Current debt and current portion of non-current debt)

Working capital management

The components of operating working capital that analysts primarily focus on are trade receivables, inventories, and trade payables. A certain amount of investment in working capital is necessary for the firm to run its normal operations. For example, a firm's credit policies and distribution policies determine its optimal level of trade receivables. The nature of the production process and the need for buffer stocks determine the optimal level of inventories. Finally, trade payables are a routine source of financing for the firm's working capital, and payment practices in an industry determine the normal level of trade payables.

The following ratios are useful in analyzing a firm's working capital management: operating working capital as a percent of sales, operating working capital turnover, trade receivables turnover, inventories turnover, and trade payables turnover. The turnover ratios can also be expressed in number of days of activity that the operating working capital (and its components) can support. The definitions of these ratios are as follows:

$$\text{Operating working capital to sales ratio} = \frac{\text{Operating working capital}}{\text{Sales}}$$

$$\text{Operating working capital to sales turnover} = \frac{\text{Sales}}{\text{Operating working capital}}$$

$$\text{Trade receivables turnover} = \frac{\text{Sales}}{\text{Trade receivables}}$$

$$\text{Inventories turnover} = \frac{\text{Cost of sales}}{\text{Inventories}} \quad \text{or} \quad \frac{\text{Cost of materials}}{\text{Inventories}}$$

$$\text{Trade payables turnover} = \frac{\text{Purchases}}{\text{Trade payables}} \quad \text{or} \quad \frac{\text{Cost of sales}}{\text{Trade payables}} \quad \text{or} \quad \frac{\text{Cost of materials}}{\text{Trade payables}}$$

$$\text{Days' receivables} = \frac{\text{Trade receivables}}{\text{Average sales per day}}$$

$$\text{Days' inventories} = \frac{\text{Inventories}}{\text{Average cost of sales per day}} \quad \text{or} \quad \frac{\text{Inventories}}{\text{Average cost of materials per day}}$$

$$\text{Days' payables} = \frac{\text{Trade payables}}{\text{Average purchases per day}} \quad \text{or} \quad \frac{\text{Trade payables}}{\text{Average cost of sales per day}}$$

$$\text{or} \quad \frac{\text{Trade payables}}{\text{Average cost of materials per day}}$$

Operating working capital turnover indicates how many euros of sales a firm is able to generate for each euro invested in its operating working capital. Trade receivables turnover, inventories turnover, and trade payables turnover allow the analyst to examine how productively the three principal components of working capital are being used. Days' receivables, days' inventories, and days' payables are another way to evaluate the efficiency of a firm's working capital management.[9]

Non-current assets management

Another area of investment management concerns the utilization of a firm's non-current assets. It is useful to define a firm's investment in non-current assets as follows:

$$\text{Net non-current assets} = (\text{Total non-current assets}$$
$$- \text{Non-interest-bearing non-current liabilities})$$

Non-current assets generally consist of net property, plant, and equipment (PP&E), intangible assets such as goodwill, and other assets. Non-interest-bearing non-current liabilities include such items as deferred taxes. We define net non-current assets and net working capital in such a way that their sum, net operating assets, is equal to the sum of net debt and equity, or net capital. This is consistent with the way we defined operating ROA earlier in the chapter.

The efficiency with which a firm uses its net non-current assets is measured by the following two ratios: net non-current assets as a percent of sales and net non-current asset turnover. Net non-current asset turnover is defined as:

$$\text{Net non-current asset turnover} = \frac{\text{Sales}}{\text{Net non-current assets}}$$

PP&E is the most important non-current asset in a firm's balance sheet. The efficiency with which a firm's PP&E is used is measured by the ratio of PP&E to sales, or by the PP&E turnover ratio:

$$\text{PP \& E turnover} = \frac{\text{Sales}}{\text{Net property, plant and equipment}}$$

The ratios listed above allow the analyst to explore a number of business questions in four general areas:

1 How well does the company manage its inventories? Does the company use modern manufacturing techniques? Does it have good vendor and logistics management systems? If inventories ratios are changing, what is the underlying business reason? Are new products being planned? Is there a mismatch between the demand forecasts and actual sales?

2 How well does the company manage its credit policies? Are these policies consistent with its marketing strategy? Is the company artificially increasing sales by loading the distribution channels?

3 Is the company taking advantage of trade credit? Is it relying too much on trade credit? If so, what are the implicit costs?

4 Are the company's investment in plant and equipment consistent with its competitive strategy? Does the company have a sound policy of acquisitions and divestitures?

Table 5.6 shows the asset turnover ratios for Bang & Olufsen and Loewe. Between 2007 and 2008 Bang & Olufsen became less efficient in its working capital management, as can be seen from the increase in operating working capital as a percent of sales and the decrease in operating working capital turnover. Working capital management worsened because of decreases in both trade receivables turnover and inventories turnover. These decreases were partly offset by an increase in days' payables, which favorably impacted the company's working capital management ratios. The decrease in inventories turnover could be the result of Bang and Olufsen experiencing difficulty in selling its products and thus capitalizing a larger proportion of its production costs (i.e., the proportion related to unsold products) on its balance sheet. In addition to the decrease in working capital turnover, Bang & Olufsen's non-current asset utilization significantly worsened in 2008: its net non-current asset turnover decreased, while PP&E turnover remained constant.

Bang & Olufsen and Loewe had fairly similar working capital utilization ratios in 2008. Although Loewe took better advantage of trade credit from its vendors, Bang & Olufsen was able to collect its receivables in 65 days, in contrast to Loewe's 94 receivable days. Loewe was able to improve its working capital to sales ratio relative to Bang & Olufsen's by managing its inventories more efficiently than its competitor. Finally, consistent with the difference in strategies, Loewe achieved better non-current asset utilization ratios in 2008 relative to Bang & Olufsen. The difference between Bang & Olufsen's net non-current asset turnover and Loewe's is explained by the fact that Bang & Olufsen had a much larger amount of capitalized product development costs than Loewe. Bang & Olufsen has also invested a substantially larger amount in property, plant and equipment than Loewe: 21.2 percent of sales versus 12.5 percent of sales.

Evaluating financial management: Financial leverage

Financial leverage enables a firm to have an asset base larger than its equity. The firm can augment its equity through borrowing and the creation of other liabilities like trade

TABLE 5.6 Asset management ratios

Ratio	B & O 2008	B & O 2007	Loewe 2008	Loewe 2007
Operating working capital/Sales	16.9%	13.7%	17.3%	14.2%
Net non-current assets/Sales	52.9%	45.1%	19.1%	19.7%
PP&E/Sales	21.2%	21.4%	12.5%	11.2%
Operating working capital turnover	5.90	7.33	5.78	7.03
Net non-current asset turnover	1.89	2.22	5.23	5.07
PP&E turnover	4.72	4.67	8.03	8.92
Trade receivables turnover	5.58	6.68	3.81	4.55
Days' receivables	64.6	53.9	94.4	79.1
Inventories turnover	2.51	3.38	3.96	3.75
Days' inventories	143.4	106.4	90.9	96.1
Trade payables turnover	8.16	9.78	6.93	6.56
Days' payables	44.1	36.8	51.9	54.8

payables, provisions, and deferred taxes. Financial leverage increases a firm's ROE as long as the cost of the liabilities is less than the return from investing these funds. In this respect it is important to distinguish between interest-bearing liabilities such as notes payable, other forms of current debt and non-current debt that carry an explicit interest charge, and other forms of liabilities. Some of these other forms of liability, such as trade payables or deferred taxes, do not carry any interest charge at all. Other liabilities, such as finance lease obligations or pension obligations, carry an implicit interest charge. Finally, some firms carry large cash balances or investments in marketable securities. These balances reduce a firm's net debt because conceptually the firm can pay down its debt using its cash and short-term investments.

While financial leverage can potentially benefit a firm's shareholders, it can also increase their risk. Unlike equity, liabilities have predefined payment terms, and the firm faces risk of financial distress if it fails to meet these commitments. There are a number of ratios to evaluate the degree of risk arising from a firm's financial leverage.

Current liabilities and short-term liquidity

The following ratios are useful in evaluating the risk related to a firm's current liabilities:

$$\text{Current ratio} = \frac{\text{Current assets}}{\text{Current liabilities}}$$

$$\text{Quick ratio} = \frac{\text{Cash and marketable securities} + \text{Trade receivables (net)}}{\text{Current liabilities}}$$

$$\text{Cash ratio} = \frac{\text{Cash and marketable securities}}{\text{Current liabilities}}$$

$$\text{Operating cash flow ratio} = \frac{\text{Cash flow from operations}}{\text{Current liabilities}}$$

All these ratios attempt to measure the firm's ability to repay its current liabilities. The first three compare a firm's current liabilities with its current assets that can be used to repay those liabilities. The fourth ratio focuses on the ability of the firm's operations to generate the resources needed to repay its current liabilities.

Since both current assets and current liabilities have comparable duration, the current ratio is a key index of a firm's short-term liquidity. Analysts view a current ratio of more than one to be an indication that the firm can cover its current liabilities from the cash realized from its current assets. However, the firm can face a short-term liquidity problem even with a current ratio exceeding one when some of its current assets are not easy to liquidate. Further, firms whose current assets have high turnover rates, such as food retailers, can afford to have current ratios below one. Quick ratio and cash ratio capture the firm's ability to cover its current liabilities from liquid assets. Quick ratio assumes that the firm's trade receivables are liquid. This is true in industries where the creditworthiness of the customers is beyond dispute, or when receivables are collected in a very short period. When these conditions do not prevail, cash ratio, which considers only cash and marketable securities, is a better indication of a firm's ability to cover its current liabilities in an emergency. Operating cash flow is another measure of the firm's ability to cover its current liabilities from cash generated from operations of the firm.

The liquidity ratios for Bang & Olufsen and Loewe are shown in Table 5.7. Bang & Olufsen's liquidity situation in 2007 was comfortable, thanks to its large cash balance and a sound operating cash flow. All of Bang & Olufsen's liquidity ratios worsened in 2008 but remained at acceptable levels. Loewe's current and quick ratios were comparable to

TABLE 5.7 Liquidity ratios

Ratio	B & O 2008	B & O 2007	Loewe 2008	Loewe 2007
Current ratio	1.88	2.38	1.74	1.55
Quick ratio	1.02	1.51	1.14	0.91
Cash ratio	0.22	0.66	0.04	0.07
Operating cash flow ratio	0.38	0.69	0.72	0.27

those of Bang & Olufsen in 2008. The company saw its current, quick and operating cash flow ratios improve and reached a comfortable liquidity position.

Debt and long-term solvency

A company's financial leverage is also influenced by its debt financing policy. There are several potential benefits from debt financing. First, debt is typically cheaper than equity because the firm promises predefined payment terms to debt holders. Second, in most countries, interest on debt financing is tax deductible whereas dividends to shareholders are not tax deductible. Third, debt financing can impose discipline on the firm's management and motivate it to reduce wasteful expenditures. Fourth, it is often easier for management to communicate their proprietary information on the firm's strategies and prospects to private lenders than to public capital markets. Such communication can potentially reduce a firm's cost of capital. For all these reasons, it is optimal for firms to use at least some debt in their capital structure. Too much reliance on debt financing, however, is potentially costly to the firm's shareholders. The firm will face financial distress if it defaults on the interest and principal payments. Debt holders also impose covenants on the firm, restricting the firm's operating, investment, and financing decisions.

The optimal capital structure for a firm is determined primarily by its business risk. A firm's cash flows are highly predictable when there is little competition or there is little threat of technological changes. Such firms have low business risk and hence they can rely heavily on debt financing. In contrast, if a firm's operating cash flows are highly volatile and its capital expenditure needs are unpredictable, it may have to rely primarily on equity financing. Managers' attitude toward risk and financial flexibility also often determine a firm's debt policies.

There are a number of ratios that help the analyst in this area. To evaluate the mix of debt and equity in a firm's capital structure, the following ratios are useful:

$$\text{Liabilities-to-equity ratio} = \frac{\text{Total liabilities}}{\text{Shareholders' equity}}$$

$$\text{Debt-to-equity ratio} = \frac{\text{Current debt} + \text{Non-current debt}}{\text{Shareholders' equity}}$$

$$\text{Net debt-to-equity ratio} = \frac{\text{Current debt} + \text{Non-current debt} - \text{Cash and marketable securities}}{\text{Shareholders' equity}}$$

$$\text{Debt-to-equity ratio} = \frac{\text{Current debt} + \text{Non-current debt}}{\text{Current debt} + \text{Non-current debt} + \text{Shareholders' equity}}$$

Net debt-to-net capital ratio =

$$\frac{\text{Interest bearning liabilities } - \text{ Cash and marketable securities}}{\text{Interest bearning liabilities } - \text{ Cash and marketable securities } + \text{ Shareholders' equity}}$$

The first ratio restates the assets-to-equity ratio (one of the three primary ratios underlying ROE) by subtracting one from it. The second ratio provides an indication of how many euros of debt financing the firm is using for each euro invested by its shareholders. The third ratio uses net debt, which is total debt minus cash and marketable securities, as the measure of a firm's borrowings. The fourth and fifth ratios measure debt as a proportion of total capital. In calculating all the above ratios, it is important to include all interest-bearing obligations, whether the interest charge is explicit or implicit. Recall that examples of line items that carry an implicit interest charge include capital lease obligations and pension obligations. Analysts sometimes include any potential off-balance sheet obligations that a firm may have, such as noncancelable operating leases, in the definition of a firm's debt.

The ease with which a firm can meet its interest payments is an indication of the degree of risk associated with its debt policy. The interest coverage ratio provides a measure of this construct:

$$\text{Interest coverage (earning basis)} = \frac{\text{Net profit} + \text{Interest expense} + \text{Tax expense}}{\text{Interest expense}}$$

Interest coverage (cash flow basis) =

$$\frac{\text{Cash flow from operations} + \text{Interest expense} + \text{Taxes paid}}{\text{Interest expense}}$$

One can also calculate coverage ratios that measure a firm's ability to measure all fixed financial obligations, such as interest payments, lease payments, and debt repayments, by appropriately redefining the numerator and denominator in the above ratios. In doing so it is important to remember that while some fixed charge payments, such as interest and lease rentals, are paid with pretax euros, others, such as debt repayments, are made with after-tax euros.

The earnings-based coverage ratio indicates the euros of earnings available for each euro of required interest payment; the cash flow-based coverage ratio indicates the euros of cash generated by operations for each euro of required interest payment. In both these ratios, the denominator is the interest expense. In the numerator we add taxes back because taxes are computed only after interest expense is deducted. A coverage ratio of one implies that the firm is barely covering its interest expense through its operating activities, which is a very risky situation. The larger the coverage ratio, the greater the cushion the firm has to meet interest obligations.

KEY ANALYSIS QUESTIONS

Some of the business questions to ask when the analyst is examining a firm's debt policies are:

- Does the company have enough debt? Is it exploiting the potential benefits of debt – interest tax shields, management discipline, and easier communication?
- Does the company have too much debt given its business risk? What type of debt covenant restrictions does the firm face? Is it bearing the costs of too much debt, risking potential financial distress and reduced business flexibility?
- What is the company doing with the borrowed funds? Investing in working capital? Investing in fixed assets? Are these investments profitable?
- Is the company borrowing money to pay dividends? If so, what is the justification?

TABLE 5.8 Debt and coverage ratios

Ratio	B & O 2008	B & O 2007	Loewe 2008	Loewe 2007
Liabilities-to-equity	0.80	0.75	2.13	2.46
Debt-to-equity	0.29	0.31	0.91	1.03
Net debt-to-equity	0.20	0.07	0.85	0.93
Debt-to-capital	0.22	0.23	0.48	0.51
Net debt-to-net capital	0.16	0.07	0.46	0.48
Interest coverage (earnings based)	11.54	36.86	26.98	9.76
Interest coverage (cash flow based)	9.55	16.30	62.47	13.70

We show debt and coverage ratios for Bang & Olufsen and Loewe in Table 5.8. Bang & Olufsen recorded an increase in its liabilities-to-equity and net debt-to-net capital ratios. The company's interest coverage decreased substantially but remained at comfortable levels. Loewe's debt ratios confirm that it has been following a more aggressive debt policy than Bang & Olufsen. Its interest coverage ratios increased in 2008, however, and are far above Bang & Olufsen's ratios. The interest coverage ratios illustrate that both companies' current earnings and cash flows are more than sufficient to cover their interest expenses.

Ratios of disaggregated data

So far we have discussed how to compute ratios using information in the financial statements. Analysts often probe these ratios further by using disaggregated financial and physical data. For example, for a multi-business company, one could analyze the information by individual business segments. Such an analysis can reveal potential differences in the performance of each business unit, allowing the analyst to pinpoint areas where a company's strategy is working and where it is not. It is also possible to probe financial ratios further by computing ratios of physical data pertaining to a company's operations. The appropriate physical data to look at varies from industry to industry. As an example in retailing, one could compute productivity statistics such as sales per store, sales per square meter, customer transactions per store, and amount of sales per customer transaction; in the hotel industry, room occupancy rates provide important information; in the cellular telephone industry, acquisition cost per new subscriber and subscriber retention rate are important. These disaggregated ratios are particularly useful for young firms and young industries such as internet firms, where accounting data may not fully capture the business economics due to conservative accounting rules.

Putting it all together: Assessing sustainable growth rate

Analysts often use the concept of sustainable growth as a way to evaluate a firm's ratios in a comprehensive manner. A firm's **sustainable growth rate** is defined as:

$$\text{Sustainable growth rate} = \text{ROE} \times (1 - \text{Dividend payout ratio})$$

We already discussed the analysis of ROE in the previous four sections. The dividend payout ratio is defined as:

$$\text{Dividend payout ratio} = \frac{\text{Cash dividends paid}}{\text{Net profit}}$$

A firm's dividend payout ratio is a measure of its dividend policy. Firms pay dividends for several reasons. They provide a way for the firm to return to its shareholders any cash generated in excess of its operating and investment needs. When there are information asymmetries between a firm's managers and its shareholders, dividend payments can serve as a signal to shareholders about managers' expectation of the firm's future prospects. Firms may also pay dividends to attract a certain type of shareholder base.

Sustainable growth rate is the rate at which a firm can grow while keeping its profitability and financial policies unchanged. A firm's return on equity and its dividend payout policy determine the pool of funds available for growth. Of course the firm can grow at a rate different from its sustainable growth rate if its profitability, payout policy, or financial leverage changes. Therefore, the sustainable growth rate provides a benchmark against which a firm's growth plans can be evaluated. Figure 5.2 shows how a firm's sustainable growth rate can be linked to all the ratios discussed in this chapter. These linkages allow an analyst to examine the drivers of a firm's current sustainable growth rate. If the firm intends to grow at a higher rate than its sustainable growth rate, one could assess which of the ratios are likely to change in the process. This analysis can lead to asking business questions such as these: Where is the change going to take place? Is management expecting profitability to increase? Or asset productivity to improve? Are these expectations realistic? Is the firm planning for these changes? If the profitability is not likely to go up, will the firm increase its financial leverage or cut dividends? What is the likely impact of these financial policy changes?

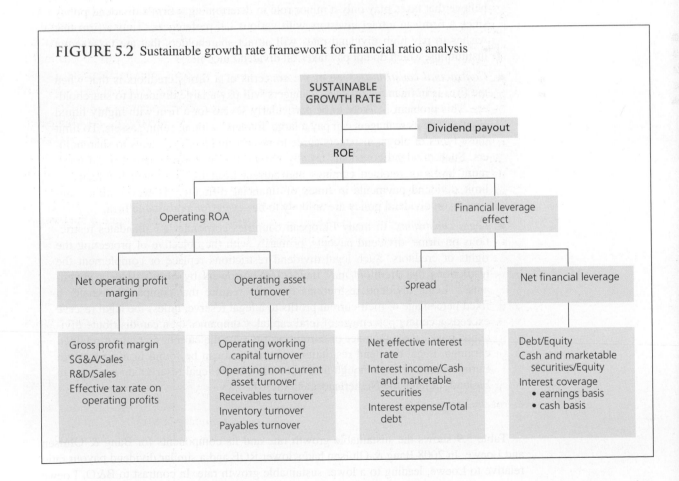

FIGURE 5.2 Sustainable growth rate framework for financial ratio analysis

Conflicts of interest between managers and shareholders can also have implications for dividend policy decisions. Shareholders of a firm with high profits and free cash flows and few profitable investment opportunities want managers to adopt a dividend policy with high payouts, thus reducing the sustainable growth rate. This will deter managers from growing the firm by investing in new projects that are not valued by shareholders or from spending the free cash flows on management perks. If a firm's sustainable growth rate is much higher than warranted by the firm's growth opportunities, one could evaluate the possible reasons for why management has not changed its dividend policy: Is management expecting profitability to decrease? If profitability is not expected to decline, has the firm reduced or will it reduce leverage? Are there contractual or legal constraints preventing the firm from paying higher dividends?

CONSTRAINTS ON DIVIDEND POLICIES

A firm's dividend policy affects its sustainable growth, financing decisions and conflicts with its shareholders. The following factors impose some constraints on dividend policy:

- *Tax costs of dividends.* Classical models of the tax effects of dividends predict that if the capital gains tax rate is less than the rate on dividend income, investors will prefer that the firm either pays no dividends, so that they subsequently take gains as capital accumulation, or that the firm undertakes a share repurchase, which qualifies as a capital distribution. Today many practitioners and theorists believe that taxes play only a minor role in determining a firm's dividend policy since a firm can attract investors with various tax preferences. Thus a firm that wishes to pay high dividend rates will attract shareholders that are tax-exempt institutions, which do not pay taxes on dividend income.

- *Contractual constraints.* One of the concerns of a firm's creditors is that when the firm is in financial distress, managers will pay a large dividend to shareholders. This problem is likely to be particularly severe for a firm with highly liquid assets, since its managers can pay a large dividend without selling assets. To limit these types of ploys, managers agree to restrict dividend payments to shareholders. Such dividend covenants usually require the firm to maintain certain minimum levels of retained earnings and current asset balances, which effectively limit dividend payments in times of financial difficulty. However these constraints on dividend policy are unlikely to be severe for a profitable firm.

- *Legal constraints.* In many European countries corporate law mandates restrictions on firms' dividend payouts, primarily with the objective of protecting the rights of creditors. Such legal dividend restrictions replace or complement the restrictions that creditors may impose on borrowers by means of debt covenants.[10] Legal dividend restrictions typically require that companies transfer a fixed percentage of their current profits to a legal reserve, unless the legal reserve exceeds a certain percentage of total capital. Companies then can distribute dividends out of the remainder of current profits plus the current amount of retained earnings. Legal dividend restrictions of this kind can be found in most western European countries, although mandated transfers to legal reserves do not exist in Finland, Ireland, the Netherlands, and the UK.

Table 5.9 shows the sustainable growth rate and its components for Bang & Olufsen and Loewe. In 2008 Bang & Olufsen had a lower ROE and a similar dividend payout ratio relative to Loewe, leading to a lower sustainable growth rate. In contrast to B&O, Loewe

TABLE 5.9 Sustainable growth rate

Ratio	B & O 2008	B & O 2007	Loewe 2008	Loewe 2007
ROE	8.6%	19.4%	27.3%	13.1%
Dividend payout ratio	34.6%	67.4%	34.5%	49.0%
Sustainable growth rate	5.6%	6.3%	17.9%	6.7%

improved its sustainable growth rate because of its improved ROE and a decline in its payout ratio.

Bang & Olufsen's sustainable growth rates in 2007 and 2008 are close to the economy-wide average sustainable growth rate and slightly above the company's average growth rate during the past ten years of 4.5 percent. In contrast, Loewe's sustainable growth rate in 2008 significantly exceeds Loewe's historical growth rates as well as reasonable expectations of Loewe's future growth. This observation raises the question of whether Loewe's shareholders would have been better off had management increased the dividend payments. One reason for management not to raise dividends, and thus bring the sustainable growth rate in line with expected growth, is that it expects that the current increase in profitability will not persist and wants to avoid cutting dividends in the future.

Historical patterns of ratios for European firms

To provide a benchmark for analysis, Table 5.10 reports historical values of the key ratios discussed in this chapter. These ratios are calculated using financial statement data for our sample of 8,193 publicly listed European companies. The table shows the median values of ROE, its key components, and the sustainable growth rate for each of the years 1992 to 2008, and the average for this 17-year period. The data in the table show that the average ROE during this period has been 10.2 percent, average operating ROA has been 7.5 percent, and the average spread between operating ROA and net borrowing costs after tax has been 3.5 percent. The average sustainable growth rate for European companies during this period has been 5.7 percent. Of course an individual company's ratios might depart from these economy-wide averages for a number of reasons, including industry effects, company strategies, and management effectiveness. Nonetheless, the average values in the table serve as useful benchmarks in financial analysis.

CASH FLOW ANALYSIS

The ratio analysis discussion focused on analyzing a firm's income statement (net profit margin analysis) or its balance sheet (asset turnover and financial leverage). The analyst can get further insights into the firm's operating, investing, and financing policies by examining its cash flows. Cash flow analysis also provides an indication of the quality of the information in the firm's income statement and balance sheet. As before, we will illustrate the concepts discussed in this section using Bang & Olufsen's and Loewe's cash flows.

Cash flow and funds flow statements

All companies reporting in conformity with IFRSs are required to include a statement of cash flows in their financial statements under IAS 7. In the reported cash flow statement,

TABLE 5.10 Historical values of key financial ratios

Year	ROE	NOPAT margin	Operating asset turnover	Operating ROA	Spread	Net financial leverage	Sustainable growth rate
1992	8.1%	3.3%	1.88	6.4%	1.3%	0.68	3.9%
1993	8.6%	3.5%	1.84	6.5%	1.8%	0.69	4.1%
1994	11.0%	4.0%	1.96	7.7%	3.6%	0.61	6.2%
1995	11.9%	4.3%	2.06	8.6%	4.2%	0.54	6.7%
1996	12.0%	4.3%	2.05	8.4%	4.3%	0.54	6.7%
1997	13.9%	4.7%	2.14	9.6%	5.7%	0.49	8.2%
1998	13.7%	4.5%	2.20	9.5%	5.5%	0.47	8.4%
1999	12.7%	4.2%	2.11	8.6%	4.9%	0.46	7.5%
2000	11.1%	3.7%	2.07	7.6%	3.9%	0.44	6.5%
2001	6.1%	2.7%	1.78	5.2%	1.2%	0.40	3.0%
2002	4.5%	2.2%	1.65	4.1%	0.6%	0.42	1.7%
2003	6.2%	2.6%	1.74	4.9%	1.7%	0.42	2.5%
2004	9.3%	3.5%	1.86	6.8%	3.6%	0.38	5.0%
2005	11.4%	4.2%	1.97	8.5%	4.9%	0.32	6.7%
2006	12.1%	4.5%	1.90	9.0%	5.2%	0.27	7.6%
2007	12.0%	4.8%	1.81	9.2%	5.0%	0.26	7.2%
2008	8.5%	4.1%	1.66	7.4%	2.8%	0.31	5.1%
Average	10.2%	3.8%	1.92	7.5%	3.5%	0.45	5.7%

Source: Financial statement data for all nonfinancial companies publicly listed on one of the seven major European exchanges (Thomson Financial's Worldscope database).

firms classify their cash flows into three categories: cash flow from operations, cash flow related to investments, and cash flow related to financing activities. Cash flow from operations is the cash generated by the firm from the sale of goods and services after paying for the cost of inputs and operations. Cash flow related to investment activities shows the cash paid for capital expenditures, intercorporate investments, acquisitions, and cash received from the sales of non-current assets. Cash flow related to financing activities shows the cash raised from (or paid to) the firm's shareholders and debt holders.

Firms use two cash flow statement formats: the direct format and the indirect format. The key difference between the two formats is the way they report cash flow from operating activities. In the direct cash flow format, which is used by only a small number of firms in practice, operating cash receipts and disbursements are reported directly. In the indirect format, firms derive their operating cash flows by making adjustments to net profit. Because the indirect format links the cash flow statement with the firm's income statement and balance sheet, many analysts and managers find this format more useful.

You may recall from Chapter 3 that net profit differs from operating cash flows because revenues and expenses are measured on an accrual basis. There are two types of accruals embedded in net profit. First, there are current accruals like credit sales and unpaid expenses. Current accruals result in changes in a firm's current assets (such as trade receivables, inventories, and prepaid expenses) and current liabilities (such as trade payables and current provisions). The second type of accruals included in the income statement is non-current accruals such as depreciation, deferred taxes, and equity income from unconsolidated subsidiaries. To derive cash flow from operations from net profit, adjustments have to be made for both these types of accruals. In addition, adjustments have to be made for non-operating gains included in net profit such as profits from asset sales.

As an alternative, some firms report a funds flow statement rather than a cash flow statement of the type described above. Funds flow statements show working capital flows, not cash flows. It is useful for analysts to know how to convert a funds flow statement into a cash flow statement.

Funds flow statements typically provide information on a firm's working capital from operations, defined as net profit adjusted for non-current accruals, and gains from the sale of non-current assets. As discussed above, cash flow from operations essentially involves a third adjustment, the adjustment for current accruals. Thus it is relatively straightforward to convert working capital from operations to cash flow from operations by making the relevant adjustments for current accruals related to operations.

Information on current accruals can be obtained by examining changes in a firm's current assets and current liabilities. Typically, operating accruals represent changes in all the current asset accounts other than cash and cash equivalents, and changes in all the current liabilities other than notes payable and the current portion of non-current debt.[11] Cash from operations can be calculated as follows:

Working capital from operations

− Increase (or + decrease) in trade receivables

− Increase (or + decrease) in inventories

− Increase (or + decrease) in other current assets excluding cash and cash equivalents

+ Increase (or − decrease) in trade payables

+ Increase (or − decrease) in other current liabilities excluding debt.

Funds flow statements often do not classify investment and financing flows. In such a case, the analyst has to classify the line items in the funds flow statement into these two categories by evaluating the nature of the business transactions that give rise to the flow represented by the line items.

Analyzing cash flow information

Cash flow analysis can be used to address a variety of questions regarding a firm's cash flow dynamics:

- How strong is the firm's internal cash flow generation? Is the cash flow from operations positive or negative? If it is negative, why? Is it because the company is growing? Is it because its operations are unprofitable? Or is it having difficulty managing its working capital properly?

- Does the company have the ability to meet its short-term financial obligations, such as interest payments, from its operating cash flow? Can it continue to meet these obligations without reducing its operating flexibility?

- How much cash did the company invest in growth? Are these investments consistent with its business strategy? Did the company use internal cash flow to finance growth, or did it rely on external financing?

- Did the company pay dividends from internal free cash flow, or did it have to rely on external financing? If the company had to fund its dividends from external sources, is the company's dividend policy sustainable?

- What type of external financing does the company rely on? Equity, current debt, or non-current debt? Is the financing consistent with the company's overall business risk?

- Does the company have excess cash flow after making capital investments? Is it a long-term trend? What plans does management have to deploy the free cash flow?

While the information in reported cash flow statements can be used to answer the above questions directly in the case of some firms, it may not be easy to do so always for a number of reasons. First, even though IAS 7 provides broad guidelines on the format of a cash flow statement, there is still significant variation across firms in how cash flow data are disclosed. Therefore, to facilitate a systematic analysis and comparison across firms, analysts often recast the information in the cash flow statement using their own cash flow model. Second, firms may choose to include interest expense and interest income in computing their cash flow from operating activities. However, these two items are not strictly related to a firm's operations. Interest expense is a function of financial leverage, and interest income is derived from financial assets rather than operating assets. Therefore it is useful to restate the cash flow statement to take this into account.

Analysts use a number of different approaches to restate the cash flow data. One such model is shown in Table 5.11. This presents cash flow from operations in two stages. The first step computes cash flow from operations before operating working capital investments. In computing this cash flow, the model excludes interest expense and interest income. To compute this number starting with a firm's net profit, an analyst adds back three types of items:

1 After-tax net interest expense because this is a financing item that will be considered later.

2 Non-operating gains or losses typically arising out of asset disposals or asset write-offs because these items are investment related and will be considered later.

3 Non-current operating accruals such as depreciation and deferred taxes because these are noncash operating charges.

TABLE 5.11 Cash flow analysis

Line item (DDK or € millions)	B & O 2008	B & O 2007	Loewe 2008	Loewe 2007
Profit before taxes minus taxes paid	147.1	493.9	27.2	18.5
After-tax net interest expense (income)	17.8	11.7	0.8	1.0
Non-operating losses (gains)	0.0	(11.5)	(1.7)	(1.7)
Non-current operating accruals	704.2	594.3	26.0	24.4
Operating cash flow before working capital investments	869.1	1,088.4	52.3	42.1
Net (investments in) or liquidation of operating working capital	(22.2)	(142.2)	15.7	(13.0)
Operating cash flow before investment in non-current assets	846.9	946.2	68.0	29.1
Net (investment in) or liquidation of non-current operating assets	(728.7)	(694.1)	(26.7)	(24.3)
Free cash flow available to debt and equity	118.3	252.1	41.3	4.9
After-tax net interest expense (income)	(17.8)	(11.7)	(0.8)	(1.0)
Net debt (repayment) or issuance	142.5	(104.8)	(1.6)	(3.0)
Free cash flow available to equity	243.0	135.6	38.9	0.9
Dividend (payments)	(247.7)	(200.2)	(3.5)	0.0
Net share (repurchase) or issuance	(84.6)	(241.5)	0.0	(0.8)
Net increase (decrease) in cash balance	(89.3)	(306.1)	35.4	0.1

Several factors affect a firm's ability to generate positive cash flow from operations. Healthy firms that are in a steady state should generate more cash from their customers than they spend on operating expenses. In contrast, growing firms – especially those investing cash in research and development, advertising and marketing, or building an organization to sustain future growth – may experience negative operating cash flow. Firms' working capital management also affects whether they generate positive cash flow from operations. Firms in the growing stage typically invest some cash flow in operating working capital items like accounts receivable, inventories, and accounts payable. Net investments in working capital are a function of firms' credit policies (trade receivables), payment policies (trade payables, prepaid expenses, and provisions), and expected growth in sales (inventories). Thus, in interpreting firms' cash flow from operations after working capital, it is important to keep in mind their growth strategy, industry characteristics, and credit policies.

The cash flow analysis model next focuses on cash flows related to long-term investments. These investments take the form of capital expenditures, intercorporate investments, and mergers and acquisitions. Any positive operating cash flow after making operating working capital investments allows the firm to pursue long-term growth opportunities. If the firm's operating cash flows after working capital investments are not sufficient to finance its long-term investments, it has to rely on external financing to fund its growth. Such firms have less flexibility to pursue long-term investments than those that can fund their growth internally. There are both costs and benefits from being able to fund growth internally. The cost is that managers can use the internally generated free cash flow to fund unprofitable investments. Such wasteful capital expenditures are less likely if managers are forced to rely on external capital suppliers. Reliance on external capital markets may make it difficult for managers to undertake long-term risky investments if it is not easy to communicate to the capital markets the benefits from such investments.

Any excess cash flow after these long-term investments is free cash flow that is available for both debt holders and equity holders. Payments to debt holders include interest payments and principal payments. Firms with negative free cash flow have to borrow additional funds to meet their interest and debt repayment obligations, or cut some of their investments in working capital or long-term investments, or issue additional equity. This situation is clearly financially risky for the firm.

Cash flow after payments to debt holders is free cash flow available to equity holders. Payments to equity holders consist of dividend payments and share repurchases. If firms pay dividends despite negative free cash flow to equity holders, they are borrowing money to pay dividends. While this may be feasible in the short-term, it is not prudent for a firm to pay dividends to equity holders unless it has a positive free cash flow on a sustained basis. On the other hand, firms that have a large free cash flow after debt payments run the risk of wasting that money on unproductive investments to pursue growth for its own sake. An analyst, therefore, should carefully examine the investment plans of such firms.

The model in Table 5.11 suggests that the analyst should focus on a number of cash flow measures:

1 Cash flow from operations before investment in working capital and interest payments, to examine whether or not the firm is able to generate a cash surplus from its operations.

2 Cash flow from operations after investment in working capital, to assess how the firm's working capital is being managed and whether or not it has the flexibility to invest in non-current assets for future growth.

3 Free cash flow available to debt and equity holders, to assess a firm's ability to meet its interest and principal payments.

4 Free cash flow available to equity holders, to assess the firm's financial ability to sustain its dividend policy and to identify potential agency problems from excess free cash flow.

These measures have to be evaluated in the context of the company's business, its growth strategy, and its financial policies. Further, changes in these measures from year to year provide valuable information on the stability of the cash flow dynamics of the firm.

KEY ANALYSIS QUESTIONS

The cash flow model in Table 5.11 can also be used to assess a firm's earnings quality, as discussed in Chapter 3. The reconciliation of a firm's net profit with its cash flow from operations facilitates this exercise. The following are some of the questions an analyst can probe in this respect:

- Are there significant differences between a firm's net profit and its operating cash flow? Is it possible to clearly identify the sources of this difference? Which accounting policies contribute to this difference? Are there any onetime events contributing to this difference?

- Is the relationship between cash flow and net profit changing over time? Why? Is it because of changes in business conditions or because of changes in the firm's accounting policies and estimates?

- What is the time lag between the recognition of revenues and expenses and the receipt and disbursement of cash flows? What type of uncertainties need to be resolved in between?

- Are the changes in receivables, inventories, and payables normal? If not, is there adequate explanation for the changes?

Finally, as we will discuss in Chapter 7, free cash flow available to debt and equity and free cash flow available to equity are critical inputs into the cash flow-based valuation of firms' assets and equity, respectively.

Analysis of Bang & Olufsen's and Loewe's cash flow

Bang & Olufsen and Loewe reported their cash flows using the indirect cash flow statement. Table 5.11 recasts these statements using the approach discussed above so that we can analyze the two companies' cash flow dynamics.

Cash flow analysis presented in Table 5.11 shows Bang & Olufsen had an operating cash flow before working capital investments of DKK846.9 million in 2008, a decrease from DKK946.2 million in 2007. The difference between earnings and these cash flows is primarily attributable to the depreciation and amortization charge included in the company's income statement. Bang & Olufsen's decrease in operating cash flow is moderate compared to the decrease in profitability. As a result of the sales decrease, and possibly in anticipation of a further slowdown, the company reduced its investments in trade receivables and inventories, while at the same time increasing its reliance on vendor financing (i.e., increasing receivables). The resulting reduction in working capital investment positively contributed to the company's operating cash flow. In addition, Bang & Olufsen's decrease in net profit was partly due to an increase in the depreciation and amortization charge, which is a non-current operating accrual.

Loewe also reduced its investment in operating working capital. Whereas the company made a net investment in working capital of €13.0 million in 2007, it managed to squeeze an additional €15.7 million from its working capital by decreasing trade receivables and inventories and increasing trade payables, like Bang & Olufsen. Loewe's non-current operating accruals remained stable from 2007 to 2008. Consequently, the percentage increase in Loewe's operating cash flow exceeded the percentage increase in the company's net profit.

Both Bang & Olufsen generated more than adequate cash flow from operations to meet their total investments in non-current assets. Consequently, in 2008 Bang & Olufsen had DKK118.3 million of free cash flow available to debt and equity holders; Loewe's free cash flow to debt and equity holders was €41.3 million.

In 2008 Bang & Olufsen was a net borrower, increasing the free cash flow available to equity holders. The company utilized this free cash flow not only to pay regular dividends but also to repurchase shares in 2007 and 2008. As a result, distributions to equity holders exceeded the free cash flow in both years and Bang & Olufsen gradually drew down its cash balance from its extraordinarily high level at the beginning of these years. Doing so helped the company also to gradually increase leverage and will improve its financial leverage gain when profitability recovers.

Loewe paid €0.8 million in interest (net of taxes) and was a net repayer of debt, leaving it with €38.9 million in free cash flow available to equity holders. The company distributed a small amount of cash to its shareholders – €3.5 million in dividends – leaving a cash increase of about €35.4 million. As noted earlier, this observation raises the question as to whether a higher dividend payout or the initiation of a share repurchase would have been warranted, especially given the lack of growth opportunities in the near term.

SUMMARY

This chapter presents two key tools of financial analysis: ratio analysis and cash flow analysis. Both these tools allow the analyst to examine a firm's performance and its financial condition, given its strategy and goals. Ratio analysis involves assessing the firm's income statement and balance sheet data. Cash flow analysis relies on the firm's cash flow statement.

The starting point for ratio analysis is the company's ROE. The next step is to evaluate the three drivers of ROE, which are net profit margin, asset turnover, and financial leverage. Net profit margin reflects a firm's operating management, asset turnover reflects its investment management, and financial leverage reflects its liability management. Each of these areas can be further probed by examining a number of ratios. For example, common-sized income statement analysis allows a detailed examination of a firm's net margins. Similarly, turnover of key working capital accounts like accounts receivable, inventories, and accounts payable, and turnover of the firm's fixed assets allow further examination of a firm's asset turnover. Finally, short-term liquidity ratios, debt policy ratios, and coverage ratios provide a means of examining a firm's financial leverage.

A firm's sustainable growth rate – the rate at which it can grow without altering its operating, investment, and financing policies – is determined by its ROE and its dividend policy. The concept of sustainable growth provides a way to integrate the ratio analysis and to evaluate whether or not a firm's growth strategy is sustainable. If a firm's plans call for growing at a rate above its current sustainable rate, then the analyst can examine which of the firm's ratios is likely to change in the future.

Cash flow analysis supplements ratio analysis in examining a firm's operating activities, investment management, and financial risks. Firms reporting in conformity with IFRSs are currently required to report a cash flow statement summarizing their operating, investment, and financing cash flows. Since there are wide variations across firms in the way cash flow data are reported, analysts often use a standard format to recast cash flow data. We discussed in this chapter one such cash flow model. This model allows the analyst to assess whether a firm's operations generate cash flow before investments in operating working capital, and how much cash is being invested in the firm's working capital. It also enables the analyst to calculate the firm's free cash flow after making long-term investments, which is an indication of the firm's ability to meet its debt and dividend payments. Finally, the cash flow analysis shows how the firm is financing itself, and whether its financing patterns are too risky.

The insights gained from analyzing a firm's financial ratios and its cash flows are valuable in forecasts of the firm's future prospects.

CORE CONCEPTS

Alternative approach to ROE decomposition Decomposition of return on equity into NOPAT margin, asset turnover, financial spread and net financial leverage. Operating return on assets is the product of NOPAT margin and asset turnover. The financial leverage gain is the product of financial spread and net financial leverage.

$$ROE = \frac{NOPAT}{Sales} \times \frac{Sales}{Net\ assets} + Spread \times \frac{Net\ debt}{Shareholders'\ equity}$$

$$= Operating\ ROA + Spread \times \frac{Net\ debt}{Shareholders'\ equity}$$

where

$$Spread = Operating\ ROA - \frac{Net\ interest\ expense\ after\ tax}{Net\ debt}$$

Asset turnover analysis Decomposition of asset turnover into its components, with the objective of identifying the drivers of (changes in) a firm's asset turnover and assessing the efficiency of a firm's investment management. The asset turnover analysis typically distinguishes between working capital turnover (receivables, inventories and payables) and non-current assets turnover (PP&E and intangible assets).

Cross-sectional comparison Comparison of the ratios of one firm to those of one or more other firms from the same industry.

Financial leverage analysis Analysis of the risk related to a firm's current liabilities and mix of non-current debt and equity. The primary considerations in the analysis of financial leverage are whether the financing strategy (1) matches the firm's business risk and (2) optimally balances the risks (e.g., financial distress risk) and benefits (e.g., tax shields, management discipline).

Profit margin analysis Decomposition of the profit margin into its components, typically using common-sized income statements. The objective of profit margin analysis is to identify the drivers of (changes in) a firm's margins and assess the efficiency of a firm's operating management. The operating expenses that impact the profit margin can be decomposed by function (e.g., cost of sales, SG&A) or by nature (e.g., cost of materials, personnel expense, depreciation and amortization).

Ratio analysis Analysis of financial statement ratios to evaluate the four drivers of firm performance:

1 Operating policies.
2 Investment policies.
3 Financing policies.
4 Dividend policies.

Sustainable growth rate The rate at which a firm can grow while keeping its profitability and financial policies unchanged.

$$\text{Sustainable growth rate} = \text{ROE} \times \left(1 - \frac{\text{Cash dividends paid}}{\text{Net profit}}\right)$$

Time-series comparison Comparison of the ratios of one firm over time.

Traditional approach to ROE decomposition Decomposition of return on equity into profit margin, asset turnover and financial leverage:

$$\text{ROE} = \frac{\text{Net profit}}{\text{Sales}} \times \frac{\text{Sales}}{\text{Assets}} \times \frac{\text{Assets}}{\text{Shareholders' equity}}$$

QUESTIONS, EXERCISES AND PROBLEMS

1 Which of the following types of firms do you expect to have particularly high or low asset turnover? Explain why.
   ■ A supermarket.
   ■ A pharmaceutical company.
   ■ A jewelry retailer.
   ■ A steel company.

2 Which of the following types of firms do you expect to have high or low sales margins? Why?
   ■ A supermarket.
   ■ A pharmaceutical company.
   ■ A jewelry retailer.
   ■ A software company.

3 Sven Broker, an analyst with an established brokerage firm, comments: "The critical number I look at for any company is operating cash flow. If cash flows are less than earnings, I consider a company to be a poor performer and a poor investment prospect." Do you agree with this assessment? Why or why not?

4 In 2005 France-based food retailer Groupe Carrefour had a return on equity of 19 percent, whereas France-based Groupe Casino's return was only 6 percent. Use the decomposed ROE framework to provide possible reasons for this difference.

5 Joe Investor asserts, "A company cannot grow faster than its sustainable growth rate." True or false? Explain why.

6 What are the reasons for a firm having lower cash from operations than working capital from operations? What are the possible interpretations of these reasons?

7 ABC Company recognizes revenue at the point of shipment. Management decides to increase sales for the current quarter by filling all customer orders. Explain what impact this decision will have on:
   ■ Days' receivable for the current quarter.
   ■ Days' receivable for the next quarter.

- Sales growth for the current quarter.
- Sales growth for the next quarter.
- Return on sales for the current quarter.
- Return on sales for the next quarter.

8 What ratios would you use to evaluate operating leverage for a firm?

9 What are the potential benchmarks that you could use to compare a company's financial ratios? What are the pros and cons of these alternatives?

10 In a period of rising prices, how would the following ratios be affected by the accounting decision to select LIFO, rather than FIFO, for inventory valuation?

- Gross margin.
- Current ratio.
- Asset turnover.
- Debt-to-equity ratio.
- Average tax rate.

Problem 1 ROE decomposition

Inditex S.A. is the Spain-based parent company of a large number of clothing design, manufacturing and retail subsidiaries. The company's brands include Zara, Pull & Bear, and Massimo Dutti. At the end of the fiscal year ending on January 31, 2009 (fiscal year 2008), the subsidiaries of Inditex operated 4,359 stores across 73 countries, making Inditex one of the three largest clothing retailers in the world.

The following tables show the standardized and adjusted income statements and balance sheets for Inditex, for the years ended January 31, 2007 and 2008. Operating lease obligations have been capitalized and the operating lease expense has been replaced with depreciation and interest expense, following the procedure described in Chapter 4:

Standardized and adjusted income statement

(€ millions)	2008	2007
Sales	**10,407**	**9,435**
Cost of materials	(4,493)	(4,086)
Personnel expense	(1,703)	(1,473)
Depreciation and amortization	(910)	(803)
Other operating income, net of other operating expense	(1,168)	(1,039)
Operating profit	**2,133**	**2,033**
Investment income	0	(9)
Net interest expense	(84)	(72)
Profit before taxes	**2,050**	**1,953**
Tax expense	(455)	(474)
Profit after taxes	**1,595**	**1,479**
Minority interest	(8)	(7)
Net profit	**1,587**	**1,471**

Standardized and adjusted balance sheet
(€ millions)

	2008	2007
Non-Current Tangible Assets	6,325	6,000
Non-Current Intangible Assets	148	139
Deferred Tax Asset	203	133
Other Non-Current Assets	188	165
Total non-current assets	**6,863**	**6,437**
Trade Receivables	585	464
Inventories	1,055	1,007
Other Current Assets	158	45
Cash and Marketable Securities	1,466	1,466
Total current assets	**3,264**	**2,982**
TOTAL ASSETS	**10,127**	**9,418**
Shareholders' equity	**5,055**	**4,414**
Minority Interest	**27**	**24**
Non-Current Debt	2,003	2,095
Deferred Tax Liability	343	197
Other Non-Current Liabilities (non interest bearing)	308	229
Total non-current liabilities	**2,655**	**2,522**
Current Debt	234	371
Trade Payables	2,073	1,975
Other Current Liabilities	84	112
Total current liabilities	**2,391**	**2,458**
TOTAL LIABILITIES AND SHAREHOLDERS' EQUITY	**10,127**	**9,418**

1 Calculate Inditex's net operating profit after taxes, operating working capital, net non-current assets, net debt and net assets in 2007 and 2008. (Use the effective tax rate [tax expense/profit before taxes] to calculate NOPAT.)

2 Decompose Inditex's return on equity in 2007 and 2008 using the traditional approach.

3 Decompose Inditex's return on equity in 2007 and 2008 using the alternative approach. What explains the difference between Inditex's return on assets and its operating return on assets?

4 Analyze the underlying drivers of the change in Inditex's return on equity. What explains the decrease in return on equity? How strongly appears Inditex to be affected by the economic crisis of 2008? (In your answer, make sure to address issues of store productivity, cost control, pricing and leverage.)

Problem 2 Ratio analysis and acquisitions

TomTom is a Netherlands-based designer and manufacturer of portable GPS car navigation systems that it sells across the world. The company's initial public offering in 2005 helped boost the company's revenues from €192 million in 2004 to €1,364 million in 2006. In the fourth quarter of 2007, TomTom acquired 29.9 percent of the shares of Tele Atlas, a provider of digital maps. The company completed the acquisition in 2008. The following tables show the components of return on equity and balance sheet items as a percent of sales for TomTom N.V. for 2006, 2007 and 2008. The ratios have been calculated after removing the margin effect of a one-time impairment charge in 2008:

Ratio	2008	2007	2006
Net operating profit margin	12.6%	17.5%	15.9%
× Net operating asset turnover	1.03	1.87	11.11
= Operating ROA	12.9%	32.6%	176.7%
Spread	9.7%	29.2%	175.4%
× Net financial leverage	2.21	−0.31	−0.78
= Financial leverage gain	21.5%	−9.1%	−136.4%
ROE = Operating ROA + Financial leverage gain	34.5%	23.5%	40.3%

Ratio	2008	2007	2006
Operating working capital/Sales	5.9%	8.2%	10.6%
Net non-current assets/Sales	91.5%	45.4%	−1.6%
Non-current intangible assets/Sales	111.5%	3.2%	2.9%
...... of which Goodwill/Sales	51.1%	0.0%	0.0%
Non-current financial assets/Sales	0.3%	47.0%	0.0%
PP&E/Sales	3.2%	1.0%	0.6%
Days' accounts receivable	62.4	83.5	70.2
Days' inventory	58.6	48.4	56.4
Days' accounts payable	61.3	56.2	30.6

1   Summarize the main factors behind the decrease in TomTom's ROE in 2007 and the increase in the company's ROE in 2008.

2   What effect did the acquisition of a 29.9 stake in Tele Atlas have on the components of TomTom's ROE in 2007?

3   What effect did the acquisition of a majority stake in Tele Atlas have on the components of TomTom's ROE in 2008?

Problem 3 Ratios of Volkswagen and Porsche

Germany-based Volkswagen AG is a leading car manufacturer, offering a wide variety of car brands, such as Audi, Bentley, Bugatti, Lamborghini, SEAT, Skoda and Volkswagen. Germany-based Dr. Ing. h.c.F. Porsche AG is one of its industry peers, focusing on the manufacturing of exclusive sports cars and multipurpose SUVs, such as the Porsche 911, the Porsche Boxster, and the Porsche Cayenne. In 2004 Volkswagen's earnings performance suffered from the slow economic growth in Germany as well as in the other eurozone countries. At the same time the strong euro harmed the company's exports to its primary markets outside the eurozone, such as the US and Asia. Price competition, stimulated by car manufacturers' overcapacity, forced Volkswagen to lower the price premium it had traditionally asked for its products and to launch a cost savings program, called ForMotion, in March 2004. The program focused on cutting product costs, one-time investments and development outlays, and overhead costs.

Porsche's sales were also negatively affected by the slowdown in economic growth in the eurozone, the strong euro, and rising petroleum prices. However, because of the company's focus on the top segment of the passenger car market, it was able to maintain its price premium and stay out of the price wars that were harming Volkswagen's sales. In September 2005 Porsche acquired an 18.5 percent interest in Volkswagen AG, financed by cash, with the intention of becoming Volkswagen's largest single shareholder.

The following tables show the components of return on equity, common-size income statements, asset turnover ratios, and leverage ratios for Volkswagen and Porsche:

ROE Decomposition	Volkswagen 2005	Volkswagen 2004	Porsche 2005
Net operating profit margin	1.9%	1.3%	11.7%
× Net operating asset turnover	1.08	1.07	1.69
= Operating ROA	2.1%	1.4%	19.7%
Spread	1.0%	0.6%	20.5%
× Net financial leverage	2.70	2.51	0.34
= Financial leverage gain	2.6%	1.5%	6.9%
ROE = Operating ROA + Financial leverage gain	4.7%	2.8%	26.6%

Income statement line items as a percent of sales	Volkswagen 2005	Volkswagen 2004	Porsche 2005
Sales	100.0%	100.0%	100.0%
Cost of materials	(65.7%)	(66.5%)	(43.7%)
Personnel expense	(15.4%)	(15.8%)	(14.7%)
Depreciation and amortization	(9.1%)	(9.6%)	(7.8%)
Other operating expense	(6.9%)	(6.2%)	(15.3%)
Net interest expense/income	(1.2%)	(0.8%)	0.2%
Tax expense	(0.6%)	(0.4%)	(7.0%)
Net profit	1.2%	0.8%	11.8%
Cost of sales	(86.5%)	(88.2%)	N.A.
Selling, general, and admin. expense	(11.8%)	(11.8%)	N.A.
Other operating income/expense	1.3%	1.8%	N.A.

Asset turnover ratios	Volkswagen 2005	Volkswagen 2004	Porsche 2005
Operating working capital/Sales	23.6%	23.6%	11.4%
Net non-current assets/Sales	69.1%	70.2%	47.9%
PP&E/Sales	33.9%	36.3%	30.9%
Operating working capital turnover	4.2	4.2	8.8
Net non-current asset turnover	1.4	1.4	2.1
PP&E turnover	3.0	2.8	3.2
Trade receivables turnover	3.6	3.7	8.3
Days' receivables	100.0	97.2	43.3
Inventories turnover	5.5	5.1	4.6
Days' inventories	65.8	71.0	78.3
Trade payables turnover	8.4	7.6	7.6
Days' payables	42.7	47.6	47.2

Ratio	Volkswagen 2005	Volkswagen 2004	Porsche 2005
Liabilities-to-equity	4.32	3.97	2.05
Debt-to-equity	3.25	2.96	1.39
Net debt-to-equity	2.70	2.51	0.34

(continued)

Ratio	Volkswagen 2005	Volkswagen 2004	Porsche 2005
Debt-to-capital	0.76	0.75	0.58
Net debt-to-net capital	0.65	0.61	0.06
Interest coverage (earnings based)	2.53	2.41	not relevant
Interest coverage (cash flow based)	10.95	16.32	not relevant

1   Analyze the effect of the cost savings program on Volkswagen's ROE using all available information about ROE's components.

2   Compare the ratios of Volkswagen and Porsche. In particular:

  a Discuss how differences in the two companies' product strategies can explain some of differences in their ratios.

  b Analyze the efficiency of the car manufacturers' working capital management. Are the manufacturers equally efficient?

  c Although Volkswagen and Porsche's PP&E turnover ratios are fairly similar in 2005, their net non-current assets turnover ratios are substantially different. What may explain this difference?

  d Discuss how Volkswagen's and Porsche's financial strategies differ. What effect do these strategic differences have on return on equity? (Also explain why Porsche's financial spread exceeds its operating return on assets.)

Problem 4 The Fiat Group in 2008

In 2009, following the worldwide credit crisis, several US-based car manufacturers, such as Chrysler and General Motors, approached bankruptcy and needed to be bailed out by the US government and private investors. Italy-based Fiat Group S.p.A. decided to help rescue Chrysler by acquiring 20 to 35 percent of the car manufacturer's shares. In exchange, Fiat would get access to Chrysler's vehicle platforms and manufacturing facilities, which could eventually help the Italian manufacturer to re-enter the US market. Following the initial rumors about private negotiations between Fiat and Chrysler and Fiat's (coinciding) announcement that it would not pay a dividend for 2008, Fiat's share price dropped by more than 25 percent in one week's time. The question arose whether Fiat's performance was really stronger than Chrysler's.

The following tables show the financial statements of the Fiat Group S.p.A. for the fiscal years 2006–2008. In all three years, Fiat earned a return on equity in excess of 12 percent. Decompose Fiat's return on equity and evaluate the drivers of the company's performance during the period 2006–2008. What trends can you identify in the company's performance? What has likely been the effect of the credit crisis on Fiat?

Income statement (€ millions)	2008	2007	2006
Net revenues	59,380	58,529	51832
Cost of sales	(49,423)	(48,924)	(43,888)
Selling, general and administrative costs	(5,075)	(4,924)	(4,697)
Research and development costs	(1,497)	(1,536)	(1,401)
Other income (expenses)	(23)	88	105
Trading profit	**3,362**	**3,233**	**1,951**

(continued)

Income statement (€ millions)	2008	2007	2006
Gains (losses) on the disposal of investments	20	190	607
Restructuring costs	(165)	(105)	(450)
Other unusual income (expenses)	(245)	(166)	(47)
Operating profit/(loss)	**2,972**	**3,152**	**2,061**
Financial income (expenses)	(947)	(564)	(576)
Result from investments	162	185	156
Profit before taxes	**2,187**	**2,773**	**1,641**
Income taxes	(466)	(719)	(490)
Profit from continuing operations	**1,721**	**2,054**	**1,151**
Profit from discontinued operations	0	0	0
Net profit/(loss)	**1,721**	**2,054**	**1,151**

Balance sheet (€ millions)	2008	2007	2006
Intangible assets	7,048	6,523	6,421
Property, plant and equipment	12,607	11,246	10,540
Investment property	0	10	19
Investments and other financial assets	2,177	2,214	2,280
Leased assets	505	396	247
Defined benefit plan assets	120	31	11
Deferred tax assets	2,386	1,892	1,860
Total non-current assets	**24,843**	**22,312**	**21,378**
Inventories	11,346	9,990	8,548
Trade receivables	4,390	4,384	4,944
Receivables from financing activities	13,136	12,268	11,743
Current tax receivables	770	1,153	808
Other current assets	2,600	2,291	2,278
Current financial assets	967	1,016	637
Cash and cash equivalents	3,683	6,639	7,736
Total current assets	**36,892**	**37,741**	**36,694**
Assets held for sale	37	83	332
TOTAL ASSETS	**61,772**	**60,136**	**58,404**
Shareholders' equity	10,354	10,606	9,362
Minority interest	747	673	674
Employee benefits	3,366	3,597	3,761
Other provisions	4,778	4,965	4,850
Asset-backed financing	6,663	6,820	8,344
Other debt	14,716	11,131	11,844
Other financial liabilities	1,202	188	105
Trade payables	13,258	14,725	12,603
Current tax payables	331	631	311
Deferred tax liabilities	170	193	263
Other current liabilities	6,185	6,572	5,978
Liabilities held for sale	2	35	309
TOTAL SHAREHOLDERS' EQUITY AND LIABILITIES	**61,772**	**60,136**	**58,404**

Cash flow statement (€ millions)	2008	2007	2006
Net profit/(loss)	1,721	2,054	1,151
Amortization and depreciation (net of vehicles sold under buy-back commitments)	2,901	2,738	2,969
(Gains) losses on disposal	(50)	(297)	(575)
Other non-cash items	253	(138)	7
Dividends received	84	81	69
Change in provisions	(161)	6	229
Change in deferred taxes	(490)	(157)	(26)
Change in items due to buy-back commitments	(88)	34	(18
Change in working capital	(3,786)	1,588	812
Cash flows from (used in) operating activities	**384**	**5,909**	**4,618**
Cash flows from (used in) investment activities	**(6,310)**	**(4,601)**	**(1,390)**
Cash flows from (used in) financing activities	**3,127**	**(2,375)**	**(1,731)**
Translation exchange differences	(159)	(33)	(173)
Total change in cash and cash equivalents	**(2,958)**	**(1,100)**	**(1,324)**

NOTES

1. For Bang & Olufsen, we will call the fiscal year ending May 2008 as the year 2008, and the fiscal year ending May 2007 as the year 2007.
2. A spreadsheet containing the three versions of the financial statements of Bang & Olufsen and Loewe as well as all ratios described throughout this chapter is available on the companion website of this book. This spreadsheet also shows how we capitalized omitted operating lease assets and research and development assets on Bang & Olufsen's and Loewe's balance sheet before calculating all ratios.
3. In computing ROE, one can either use the beginning equity, ending equity, or an average of the two. Conceptually, the average equity is appropriate, particularly for rapidly growing companies. However, for most companies, this computational choice makes little difference as long as the analyst is consistent. Therefore, in practice most analysts use ending balances for simplicity. This comment applies to all ratios discussed in this chapter where one of the items in the ratio is a flow variable (items in the income statement or cash flow statement) and the other item is a stock variable (items in the balance sheet). Throughout this chapter we use the beginning balances of the stock variables.
4. We discuss in greater detail in Chapter 8 how to estimate a company's cost of equity capital. The equity beta for both Bang & Olufsen and Loewe was close to 1.4 in 2008, and the yield on long-term treasury bonds was approximately 4 percent. If one assumes a risk premium of 5 percent, the two firms' cost of equity is 11 percent; if the risk premium is assumed to be 7 percent, then their cost of equity is 13.8 percent. Lower assumed risk premium will, of course, lead to lower estimates of equity capital.
5. Strictly speaking, part of a cash balance is needed to run the firm's operations, so only the excess cash balance should be viewed as negative debt. However, firms do not provide information on excess cash, so we subtract all cash balance in our definitions and computations below. An alternative possibility is to subtract only short-term investments and ignore the cash balance completely.
6. See Doron Nissim and Stephen Penman, "Ratio Analysis and Valuation: From Research to Practice," *Review of Accounting Studies* 6 (2001): 109–154, for a more detailed description of this approach.
7. Both Bang & Olufsen have a solid financial position and a relatively low cost of debt. Given the level of leverage, the weighted average cost of capital will be lower than the cost of equity. We will discuss in Chapter 8 how to estimate a company's weighted average cost of capital.

8. See *Taxes and Business Strategy* by Myron Scholes and Mark Wolfson (Englewood Cliffs, NJ: Prentice-Hall, 1992).
9. Average sales (or average cost of sales) is calculated as annual sales (or annual cost of sales) divided by the number of days in the year. There are a number of issues related to the calculation of turnover ratios in practice. First, in calculating all the turnover ratios, the assets used in the calculations can either be beginning of the year values, year-end values or an average of the beginning and ending balances in a year. We use the average values in our calculations. Second, strictly speaking, one should use credit sales to calculate trade receivables turnover and days' receivables. But since it is usually difficult to obtain data on credit sales, total sales are used instead. Similarly, in calculating trade payables turnover or days' payables, cost of sales (or cost of materials) is substituted for purchases for data availability reasons. Third, the ratios for income statements classified by function differ from those for income statements classified by nature. Turnover ratios for the two types of statements are therefore not perfectly comparable.
10. See Christian Leuz, Dominic Deller, and Michael Stubenrath, "An International Comparison of Accounting-Based Payout Restrictions in the United States, United Kingdom and Germany," *Accounting and Business Research* 28 (1998): 111–129.
11. Changes in cash and marketable securities are excluded because this is the amount being explained by the cash flow statement. Changes in current debt and the current portion of non-current debt are excluded because these accounts represent financing flows, not operating flows.

APPENDIX A: BANG & OLUFSEN A/S FINANCIAL STATEMENTS

CONSOLIDATED STATEMENTS OF EARNINGS (DDK MILLIONS)

Fiscal year ended May 31	2008	2007	2006
Net turnover	4,092.0	4,375.7	4,225.2
Production costs	(2,199.6)	(2,338.0)	(2,281.1)
Gross profit	1,892.4	2,037.7	1,944.1
Development costs	(545.5)	(458.8)	(442.9)
Distribution and marketing costs	(1,003.5)	(910.2)	(920.3)
Administration costs	(148.7)	(138.7)	(142.0)
Operating profit	194.7	530.0	438.9
Result of investments in associates after tax	(11.2)	(1.1)	(1.0)
Gain on sale of shares in subsidiary	0.0	11.5	0.0
Exchange rate gains (losses)	(12.3)	(7.6)	(9.5)
Interest and other financial income	20.0	15.7	17.7
Interest and other financial costs	(37.5)	(24.1)	(15.4)
Result before tax	153.7	524.4	430.7
Tax on result for the year	(41.4)	(151.9)	(134.7)
Group profit	112.3	372.5	296.0
Minority interests	(7.6)	(5.1)	(2.0)
Group profit attributable to shareholders of B&O	104.7	367.4	294.0

Source: 2008 and 2007 Annual Report, Bang & Olufsen a/s.

CONSOLIDATED BALANCE SHEETS (DKK millions)

Fiscal year ended May 31	2008	2007	2006
ASSETS			
Goodwill	44.8	44.8	18.0
Acquired rights	41.1	44.4	12.1
Completed development projects	218.8	244.6	216.3
Development projects in progress	112.5	116.2	109.8
Land and Buildings	274.4	252.1	332.8
Plant and machinery	221.8	203.8	200.7
Other equipment	50.0	70.7	58.2
Leasehold improvements	28.7	29.1	26.6
Tangible assets in progress and prepayments for tangible assets	80.8	62.2	49.1
Investment property	52.8	56.4	0.7
Investments in associates	6.3	15.8	6.0
Other financial receivables	52.0	88.2	28.8
Deferred tax assets	22.7	21.2	36.4
Total non-current assets	**1,206.7**	**1,249.5**	**1,095.5**
Inventories	801.4	694.3	567.4
Trade receivables	593.0	733.8	655.1
Receivables from associates	0.0	8.5	0.0
Income tax receivables	39.7	27.0	16.6
Other receivables	38.9	30.0	51.4
Prepayments	30.5	22.8	25.5
Cash	107.1	196.4	502.5
Total current assets	**1,610.6**	**1,712.8**	**1,818.5**
Non-current assets classified as held for sale	**0.0**	**0.0**	**1.1**
TOTAL ASSETS	**2,817.3**	**2,962.3**	**2,915.1**
LIABILITIES AND SHAREHOLDERS' EQUITY			
Share capital	120.8	120.8	124.5
Share premium	14.6	14.6	14.6
Translation reserve	(42.9)	(17.3)	(4.7)
Reserve for cash flow hedges	0.0	0.1	0.0
Retained earnings	1,379.2	1,557.7	1,603.6
Equity attributable to shareholders of the parent company	1,471.7	1,675.9	1,738.0
Minority interests	12.1	6.0	4.1
Total equity	**1,483.8**	**1,681.9**	**1,742.1**
Pensions	9.5	9.7	15.5
Deferred tax	64.2	67.8	63.7
Provisions	77.3	97.0	91.9
Mortgage Loans	235.7	93.4	107.2
Loans from banks etc.	101.1	97.1	129.7
Other non-current liabilities	6.6	6.1	0.0
Non-current liabilities	**494.4**	**371.1**	**408.0**
Mortgage loans, short term part	8.5	14.0	13.8
Loans from banks etc., short term part	42.9	32.4	32.5
Other loans from banks	53.7	39.5	0.0

(continued)

CONSOLIDATED BALANCE SHEETS (DKK millions) *(Continued)*

Fiscal year ended May 31	2008	2007	2006
Provisions	46.0	33.3	31.1
Trade Payables	216.0	213.7	196.3
Payables to associates	1.8	0.0	0.0
Income tax	66.3	122.3	78.3
Other payables	320.0	356.2	361.4
Deferred income	83.9	97.9	51.6
Total current liabilities	**839.1**	**909.3**	**765.0**
TOTAL EQUITY AND LIABILITIES	**2,817.3**	**2,962.3**	**2,915.1**

Source: 2008 and 2007 Annual Report, Bang & Olufsen a/s.

CONSOLIDATED STATEMENTS OF CASH FLOWS (DKK millions)

Fiscal year ended December 31	2008	2007	2006
OPERATING ACTIVITIES			
Result for the year	112.3	372.5	296.0
Adjustment for:			
Depreciations, amortizations and impairment losses	299.2	248.9	232.3
Change in liabilities	(6.7)	4.5	10.2
Financial income	(20.0)	(15.7)	(17.7)
Financial costs	49.8	31.7	24.9
Share of associates' result after tax	11.2	1.1	1.0
Gain on sale of non-current assets	0.0	0.0	3.3
Gain on disposal of activities	0.0	(11.5)	0.0
Tax on result for the year	41.4	151.9	134.7
Various adjustments	16.9	0.6	5.7
Change in receivables	131.9	(93.2)	(122.0)
Change in inventories	(107.1)	(131.4)	(112.8)
Change in accounts payables etc.	(47.0)	82.4	46.6
Interest received	20.0	15.7	17.7
Interest paid	(49.8)	(31.7)	(24.9)
Income tax paid	(120.3)	(105.0)	(100.4)
Cash flow from operating activities	**331.8**	**520.8**	**394.6**
INVESTING ACTIVITIES			
Purchase of intangible non-current assets	(124.9)	(210.1)	(171.4)
Purchase of tangible non-current assets	(190.4)	(157.6)	(185.2)
Sale of intangible non-current assets	1.5	0.7	0.0
Sale of tangible non-current assets	23.3	9.8	13.5
Disposals (acquisitions) of activities	0.0	32.7	(27.7)
Change in financial receivables	36.2	(53.9)	(7.7)
Cash flow from investment activities	**(254.3)**	**(378.4)**	**(378.5)**
FINANCING ACTIVITIES			
Proceeds from long-term loans	200.0	0.0	74.6
Repayment of long-term loans	(48.7)	(46.3)	(38.8)

(continued)

CONSOLIDATED STATEMENTS OF CASH FLOWS (DKK millions) *(Continued)*

Fiscal year ended December 31	2008	2007	2006
Other bank loans	14.2	39.5	0.0
Dividend paid	(247.7)	(200.2)	(149.0)
Dividend, own shares	14.0	11.3	5.7
Repurchase of own shares	(100.2)	(271.3)	(148.9)
Subscription of employee shares	0.0	0.0	5.6
Sale of own shares	1.6	18.5	5.3
Cash flow from financing activities	**(166.8)**	**(448.5)**	**(245.5)**
Change in cash and cash equivalents	**(89.3)**	**(306.1)**	**(229.4)**
Cash and cash equivalents 1 June	196.4	502.5	731.9
CASH AND CASH EQUIVALENTS 31 MAY	**107.1**	**196.4**	**502.5**

Source: 2008 and 2007 Annual Report, Bang & Olufsen a/s.

STANDARDIZED AND ADJUSTED STATEMENTS OF EARNINGS (DKK millions)

Fiscal year ended May 31	2008	2007	2006
Sales	**4,092.0**	**4,375.7**	**4,225.2**
Cost of sales	(2,172.6)	(2,314.6)	(2,281.1)
Gross profit	**1,919.4**	**2,061.1**	**1,944.1**
SG&A	(1,152.2)	(1,048.9)	(1,062.3)
Other operating income, net of other operating expense	(463.9)	(407.1)	(452.4)
Operating profit	**303.3**	**605.1**	**429.4**
Investment income	(11.2)	10.4	(1.0)
Net interest expense (income)	(24.6)	(16.6)	2.3
Profit before tax	**267.4**	**598.9**	**430.7**
Tax expense	(75.5)	(174.3)	(134.7)
Profit after tax	**191.9**	**424.7**	**296.0**
Minority interest	(7.6)	(5.1)	(2.0)
Net profit	**184.3**	**419.6**	**294.0**

Source: Authors' calculations.

STANDARDIZED AND ADJUSTED BALANCE SHEETS (DKK millions)

Fiscal year ending May 31	2008	2007	2006
ASSETS			
Non-current tangible assets	957.9	867.2	937.0
Non-current intangible assets	1,176.7	1,115.6	962.5
Deferred taxes – Non-current asset	22.7	21.2	36.4
Other non-current assets	111.1	160.4	36.6
Total non-current assets	**2,268.4**	**2,164.4**	**1,972.5**
Trade receivables	593.0	733.8	655.1
Inventories	801.4	694.3	567.4

(continued)

STANDARDIZED AND ADJUSTED BALANCE SHEETS (DKK millions) *(Continued)*

Fiscal year ending May 31	2008	2007	2006
Other current assets	109.1	88.3	93.5
Cash and marketable securities	107.1	196.4	502.5
Total current assets	**1,610.6**	**1,712.8**	**1,818.5**
TOTAL ASSETS	**3,879.0**	**3,877.2**	**3,791.0**
LIABILITIES AND SHAREHOLDERS' EQUITY			
Preference shares	0.0	0.0	0.0
Ordinary shareholders' equity	2,017.2	2,152.5	2,162.4
Total shareholders' equity	**2,017.2**	**2,152.5**	**2,162.4**
Minority Interest	**12.1**	**6.0**	**4.1**
Non-current debt	706.0	531.2	613.9
Deferred tax liability	298.0	272.1	245.6
Other non-current liabilities (non interest-bearing)	6.6	6.1	0.0
Total non-current liabilities	**1,010.6**	**809.3**	**859.5**
Current debt	105.1	85.9	46.3
Trade payables	216.0	213.7	196.3
Other current liabilities	518.0	609.7	522.4
Total current liabilities	**839.1**	**909.3**	**765.0**
TOTAL LIABILITIES AND SHAREHOLDERS' EQUITY	**3,879.0**	**3,877.2**	**3,791.0**

Source: Authors' calculations.

STANDARDIZED AND ADJUSTED STATEMENTS OF CASH FLOWS (DKK millions)

Fiscal year ended May 31	2008	2007	2006
Profit before tax	**267.4**	**598.9**	**430.7**
Taxes paid	(120.3)	(105.0)	(100.4)
After-tax net interest expense (income)	17.8	11.7	(1.6)
Non-operating losses (gains)	0.0	(11.5)	3.3
Non-current operating accruals	704.2	594.3	249.2
Operating cash flow before working capital investments	**869.1**	**1,088.4**	**581.2**
Net (investments in) or liquidation of operating working capital	(22.2)	(142.2)	(188.2)
Operating cash flow before investment in non-current assets	**846.9**	**946.2**	**393.0**
Net (investment in) or liquidation of non-current operating assets	(728.7)	(694.1)	(378.5)
Free cash flow available to debt and equity	**118.3**	**252.1**	**14.5**
After-tax net interest expense (income)	(17.8)	(11.7)	1.6
Net debt (repayment) or issuance	142.5	(104.8)	35.8
Free cash flow available to equity	**243.0**	**135.6**	**51.9**

(continued)

STANDARDIZED AND ADJUSTED STATEMENTS OF CASH FLOWS (DKK millions)
(Continued)

Fiscal year ended May 31	2008	2007	2006
Dividend (payments)	(247.7)	(200.2)	(149.0)
Net share (repurchase) or issuance	(84.6)	(241.5)	(132.3)
Net increase (decrease) in cash balance	**(89.3)**	**(306.1)**	**(229.4)**

Source: Authors' calculations.

CONDENSED STATEMENTS OF EARNINGS (DKK millions)

Fiscal year ended May 31	2008	2007	2006
Sales	**4,092.0**	**4,375.7**	**4,225.2**
Net operating profit after tax	**202.0**	**431.3**	**292.4**
Net profit	184.3	419.6	294.0
+ Net interest expense after tax	17.7	11.7	(1.6)
= **Net operating profit after tax**	**202.0**	**431.3**	**292.4**
− **Net interest expense after tax**	**17.7**	**11.7**	**(1.6)**
= Net interest expense (income)	24.6	16.6	(2.3)
× (1 − Tax expense/Profit before tax)	71.8%	70.9%	68.7%
= **Net interest expense after tax**	**17.7**	**11.7**	**(1.6)**
= **Net profit**	**184.3**	**419.6**	**294.0**

Source: Authors' calculations.

CONDENSED BALANCE SHEETS (DKK millions)

Fiscal year ended May 31	2008	2007	2006
Net working capital			
Trade receivables	593.0	733.8	655.1
+ Inventories	801.4	694.3	567.4
+ Other current assets	109.1	88.3	93.5
− Trade payables	216.0	213.7	196.3
− Other current liabilities	518.0	609.7	522.4
= **Net working capital**	**769.5**	**693.0**	**597.3**
+ **Net non-current assets**			
Non-current tangible assets	957.9	867.2	937.0
+ Non-current intangible assets	1,176.7	1,115.6	962.5
+ Other non-current assets	111.1	160.4	36.6
− Minority interest	12.1	6.0	4.1
− Deferred taxes	275.3	250.9	209.2
− Other non-current liabilities (non-interest-bearing)	6.6	6.1	0.0
= **Net non-current assets**	**1,951.7**	**1,880.2**	**1,722.8**
= **Total assets**	**2,721.2**	**2,573.2**	**2,320.1**

(continued)

CONDENSED BALANCE SHEETS (DKK millions) (*Continued*)

Fiscal year ended May 31	2008	2007	2006
Net debt			
Current debt	105.1	85.9	46.3
+ Non-current debt	706.0	531.2	613.9
− Cash	107.1	196.4	502.5
= **Net debt**	**704.0**	**420.7**	**157.7**
+ **Ordinary shareholders' equity**	**2,017.2**	**2,152.5**	**2,162.4**
= **Total net capital**	**2,721.2**	**2,573.2**	**2,320.1**

Source: Authors' calculations.

APPENDIX B: LOEWE AG FINANCIAL STATEMENTS

CONSOLIDATED STATEMENTS OF EARNINGS (€ millions)

Fiscal year ended December 31	2008	2007	2006
Sales	**374.0**	**372.5**	**341.9**
Cost of sales	(255.7)	(268.2)	(255.7)
Gross margin	**118.3**	**104.3**	**86.2**
Amortization of capitalized development costs	(6.7)	(7.1)	(6.7)
Selling expenses	(75.9)	(68.3)	(56.5)
General and administrative expenses	(9.5)	(9.4)	(8.9)
Other operating income	9.0	8.9	13.9
Other operating expenses	(6.6)	(7.4)	(14.9)
Income from investments	0.0	0.0	0.1
EBIT	**28.5**	**21.1**	**13.2**
Interest and similar income	1.8	0.5	0.2
Interest and similar expense	(2.8)	(2.7)	(2.9)
Profit from ordinary activities (EBT)	**27.5**	**18.9**	**10.5**
Income tax expense	(8.5)	(11.5)	(3.6)
Net income before minority interests	**19.0**	**7.4**	**6.9**
Minority interest	(0.2)	(0.2)	(0.3)
Net income	**18.9**	**7.2**	**6.5**

Source: 2008 and 2007 Annual Report, Loewe AG.

CONSOLIDATED BALANCE SHEETS (€ millions)

Fiscal year ended December 31	2008	2007	2006
ASSETS			
Intangible assets	5.9	6.0	5.5
Property, plant and equipment	42.6	39.6	36.3
Financial assets	1.1	0.8	0.7

(continued)

CONSOLIDATED BALANCE SHEETS (€ millions) (*Continued*)

Fiscal year ended December 31	2008	2007	2006
Income tax assets	0.3	0.4	0.0
Miscellaneous non-current assets	0.3	0.4	1.0
Deferred taxes	11.3	16.6	24.1
Total non-current assets	**61.6**	**63.7**	**67.6**
Inventories	51.1	52.3	59.9
Trade accounts receivable	88.8	98.1	81.9
Income tax assets	0.2	0.2	0.0
Miscellaneous current financial assets	3.9	1.7	2.2
Cash and cash equivalents	37.2	3.9	6.5
Total current assets	**181.2**	**156.2**	**150.4**
TOTAL ASSETS	**242.8**	**219.9**	**218.0**
LIABILITIES AND SHAREHOLDERS' EQUITY			
Subscribed capital	13.0	13.0	13.0
Capital reserve	47.0	47.0	47.0
Retained earnings	13.5	3.6	0.0
Other reserve	1.5	−0.5	0.0
Accumulated profit	13.5	8.0	4.4
Minority interests	1.2	1.1	1.7
Shareholders' equity	**89.7**	**72.2**	**66.1**
Provisions for pensions and similar obligations	41.0	39.4	37.9
Other non-current provisions	17.0	15.2	13.1
Non-current financial liabilities	2.3	3.3	4.2
Non-current liabilities	**60.3**	**57.9**	**55.2**
Income tax provisions	4.4	4.1	4.0
Other current provisions	49.2	45.7	46.0
Current financial liabilities	1.0	2.3	5.8
Trade accounts payable	29.0	29.9	34.2
Miscellaneous current financial liabilities	9.3	7.8	6.8
Total current liabilities	**92.8**	**89.8**	**96.7**
TOTAL EQUITY AND LIABILITIES	**242.8**	**219.9**	**218.0**

Source: 2008 and 2007 Annual Report, Loewe AG.

CONSOLIDATED STATEMENTS OF CASH FLOWS (€ millions)

Fiscal year ended December 31	2008	2007	2006
OPERATING ACTIVITIES			
EBIT	28.5	21.1	13.23
Adjustment for:			
Interest paid	(0.9)	(1.0)	(1.3)
Interest received	1.8	0.5	0.2
Depreciation and amortization of non-current assets	20.4	19.1	17.6
Other non-cash items	(1.7)	(1.7)	(1.6)
Decrease (+) of non-current receivables	0.0	0.2	0.0
Increase (+) in pension provisions	1.5	1.5	1.1

(continued)

CONSOLIDATED STATEMENTS OF CASH FLOWS (€ millions) *(Continued)*

Fiscal year ended December 31	2008	2007	2006
Increase (+)/decrease (-) of other non-current provisions	1.8	2.0	(2.1)
Income taxes paid	(3.6)	(3.9)	(2.4)
Decrease (+) in inventories	1.2	7.7	(20.5)
Decrease (+)/increase (-) in trade accounts receivable and other assets	10.0	(17.8)	9.4
Increase (+) in other current provisions	3.4	(0.1)	11.1
Increase (+)/decrease (-) in trade accounts payable and other liabilities	1.1	(2.7)	(10.5)
Net cash from operations	**63.7**	**24.9**	**14.2**
INVESTING ACTIVITIES			
Payments for purchases of intangible assets and property, plant and equipment	(23.6)	(23.1)	(18.5)
Payments for purchases of financial assets	(0.4)	(0.1)	(0.0)
Proceeds from disposals of intangible assets and property, plant and equipment	0.1	0.1	0.1
Net cash from investing activities	**(23.8)**	**(23.1)**	**(18.4)**
FINANCING ACTIVITIES			
Decline in minority interest	0.0	(0.8)	0.0
Dividend payment	(3.5)	0.0	(0.0)
Repayment (−) of loans	(0.9)	(0.9)	(5.3)
Net cash from financing activities	**(4.5)**	**(1.7)**	**(5.3)**
Cash-effective change in liquidity	**35.4**	**0.1**	**(9.6)**

Source: 2008 and 2007 Annual Report, Loewe AG.

STANDARDIZED AND ADJUSTED STATEMENTS OF EARNINGS (€ millions)

Fiscal year ended December 31	2008	2007	2006
Sales	**374.0**	**372.5**	**341.9**
Cost of sales	(254.4)	(266.8)	(255.7)
Gross profit	**119.6**	**105.8**	**86.2**
SG&A	(85.5)	(77.7)	(65.4)
Other operating income, net of other operating expense	(4.1)	(5.1)	(7.7)
Operating profit	**30.0**	**23.0**	**13.1**
Investment income	0.0	0.0	0.1
Net interest expense (income)	(1.1)	(2.3)	(2.7)
Profit before tax	**28.9**	**20.7**	**10.5**
Tax expense	(8.9)	(12.0)	(3.6)
Profit after tax	**20.0**	**8.7**	**6.9**
Minority interest	(0.2)	(0.2)	(0.3)
Net profit	**19.8**	**8.5**	**6.5**

Source: Authors' calculations.

STANDARDIZED AND ADJUSTED BALANCE SHEETS (€ millions)

Fiscal year ending December 31	2008	2007	2006
ASSETS			
Non-current tangible assets	51.0	46.6	41.8
Non-current intangible assets	7.0	6.8	5.8
Deferred taxes – Non-current asset	11.3	16.6	24.1
Other non-current assets	1.8	1.5	1.7
Total non-current assets	**71.1**	**71.5**	**73.4**
Trade receivables	88.8	98.1	81.9
Inventories	51.1	52.3	59.9
Other current assets	4.1	1.9	2.2
Cash and marketable securities	37.2	3.9	6.5
Total current assets	**181.2**	**156.2**	**150.4**
TOTAL ASSETS	**252.4**	**227.7**	**223.9**
LIABILITIES AND SHAREHOLDERS' EQUITY			
Preference shares	0.0	0.0	0.0
Ordinary shareholders' equity	90.0	72.7	64.7
Total shareholders' equity	**90.0**	**72.7**	**64.7**
Minority Interest	**1.2**	**1.1**	**1.7**
Non-current debt	67.7	63.6	60.7
Deferred tax liability	0.6	0.6	0.1
Other non-current liabilities (non interest-bearing)	0.0	0.0	0.0
Total non-current liabilities	**68.3**	**64.2**	**60.8**
Current debt	1.0	2.3	5.8
Trade payables	29.0	29.9	34.2
Other current liabilities	62.8	57.7	56.8
Total current liabilities	**92.8**	**89.8**	**96.7**
TOTAL LIABILITIES AND SHAREHOLDERS' EQUITY	**252.4**	**227.7**	**223.9**

Source: Authors' calculations.

STANDARDIZED AND ADJUSTED STATEMENTS OF CASH FLOWS (€ millions)

Fiscal year ended December 31	2008	2007	2006
Profit before tax	**30.8**	**22.4**	**12.1**
Taxes paid	(3.6)	(3.9)	(2.4)
After-tax net interest expense (income)	0.8	1.0	1.8
Non-operating losses (gains)	(1.7)	(1.7)	(1.6)
Non-current operating accruals	26.0	24.4	16.6
Operating cash flow before working capital investments	**52.3**	**42.1**	**26.5**
Net (investments in) or liquidation of operating working capital	(22.2)	(142.2)	(188.2)
Operating cash flow before investment in non-current assets	**846.9**	**946.2**	**393.0**
Net (investment in) or liquidation of non-current operating assets	(728.7)	(694.1)	(378.5)
Free cash flow available to debt and equity	**118.3**	**252.1**	**14.5**

(continued)

STANDARDIZED AND ADJUSTED STATEMENTS OF CASH FLOWS (€ millions)
(Continued)

Fiscal year ended December 31	2008	2007	2006
After-tax net interest expense (income)	(17.8)	(11.7)	1.6
Net debt (repayment) or issuance	142.5	(104.8)	35.8
Free cash flow available to equity	**243.0**	**135.6**	**51.9**
Dividend (payments)	(247.7)	(200.2)	(149.0)
Net share (repurchase) or issuance	(84.6)	(241.5)	(132.3)
Net increase (decrease) in cash balance	**(89.3)**	**(306.1)**	**(229.4)**

Source: Authors' calculations.

CONDENSED STATEMENTS OF EARNINGS (€ millions)

Fiscal year ended December 31	2008	2007	2006
Sales	**374.0**	**372.5**	**341.9**
Net operating profit after tax	**20.6**	**9.5**	**8.3**
Net profit	19.8	8.5	6.5
+ Net interest expense after tax	0.8	1.0	1.8
= Net operating profit after tax	**20.6**	**9.5**	**8.3**
− Net interest expense after tax	**0.8**	**1.0**	**1.8**
= Net interest expense (income)	1.1	2.3	2.7
× (1 − Tax expense/Profit before tax)	69.2%	41.9%	65.4%
= Net interest expense after tax	**0.8**	**1.0**	**1.8**
= Net profit	**19.8**	**8.5**	**6.5**

Source: Authors' calculations.

CONDENSED BALANCE SHEETS (€ millions)

Fiscal year ended December 31	2008	2007	2006
Net working capital			
Trade receivables	88.8	98.1	81.9
+ Inventories	51.1	52.3	59.9
+ Other current assets	4.1	1.9	2.2
− Trade payables	29.0	29.9	34.2
− Other current liabilities	62.8	57.7	56.8
= Net working capital	**52.1**	**64.8**	**53.0**
+ Net non-current assets			
Non-current tangible assets	51.0	46.6	41.8
+ Non-current intangible assets	7.0	6.8	5.8
+ Other non-current assets	1.8	1.5	1.7
− Minority interest	1.2	1.1	1.7
− Deferred taxes	(10.7)	(16.0)	(24.0)
− Other non-current liabilities (non-interest-bearing)	0.0	0.0	0.0
= Net non-current assets	**69.3**	**69.9**	**71.7**
= Total assets	**121.4**	**134.6**	**124.7**

(continued)

CONDENSED BALANCE SHEETS (€ millions) (*Continued*)

Fiscal year ended December 31	2008	2007	2006
Net debt			
Current debt	1.0	2.3	5.8
+ Non-current debt	67.7	63.6	60.7
− Cash	37.2	3.9	6.5
= **Net debt**	**31.4**	**61.9**	**60.0**
+ **Ordinary shareholders' equity**	**90.0**	**72.7**	**64.7**
= **Total net capital**	**121.4**	**134.6**	**124.7**

Source: Authors' calculations.

Carrefour S.A.

Analyst Chrystelle Moreau of Leblanc Investissements, a small Paris-based investment firm, glanced through the annual report of Groupe Carrefour for the fiscal year 2005 that she had just received. The past year had been a turbulent year for Carrefour's shareholders and the analyst wondered what had caused the turbulence and whether a turn-around could be expected. In February 2005, Daniel Bernard had stepped down as Carrefour's President and Chief Executive Officer (CEO). Bernard had been succeeded as CEO by Jose Luis Duran, Carrefour's former Chief Financial Officer. Luc Vandevelde – protégé of Carrefour's principal shareholder, the Halley family, and former CEO of Promodès and Marks and Spencer – had become President of the company's Supervisory Board.[1] Following the departure of Daniel Bernard, three other members of the Management Board had also resigned from their positions.

When publicly announcing Bernard's resignation, the company's Board acknowledged Bernard's achievements by reporting that:

> . . . in 13 years Carrefour has gone from the number 1 in the French market to a strong world number 2 in retail and an uncontested European number 1 that masters the four formats of modern commerce. In Asia, Latin America as in Europe, the group has become the leading player. Over this time, revenue has grown more than four-fold and net profit, at end 2003, has increased eight-fold corresponding to a 19 percent annual growth rate. Over this period, the share price has been multiplied by 4, one of the three best world-wide performances of the sector and the 11th of the CAC40.

Yet rumors suggested that Carrefour's largest shareholder had become unhappy with Daniel Bernard's performance and Carrefour's share price responded positively to the announcement of Bernard's resignation.[2]

During the 1990s, Carrefour had been one of Moreau's favorite shares. The company had created a great reputation for its broad assortment and low prices, and had shown an outstanding share price performance. During the first half of the 2000s, however, Carrefour's share price had fallen from about €80 to €40, despite the fact that the company had consistently earned returns on equity in excess of 17 percent. At the beginning of 2005, investors speculated that Carrefour would be taken over by its US rival Wal-Mart. Moreau's investment firm had not sold its Carrefour holdings following Carrefour's merger with Promodès in 1999 and, consequently, had incurred substantial losses on its investment. Moreau was preparing herself for Carrefour's upcoming shareholders' meeting. In particular, she wanted to get a better understanding of what had caused Carrefour's share price decline during the past years as well as the company's current financial position, before voting on any proposals that Carrefour's new management would make during the meeting.

Professor Erik Peek prepared this case. The case is intended solely as the basis for class discussion and is not intended to serve as an endorsement, source of primary data, or illustration of effective or ineffective management.

[1]Concurrent with Carrefour's management change, the company switched from having a one-tier board structure to having a two-tier board structure. That is, the company split its Board of Directors into a Management Board and a Supervisory Board.

[2]See "Changing shopkeepers," *The Economist*, February 3, 2005.

Company background

France-based food retailer Carrefour was established in 1959 by the Fournier and Defforey families and opened it first hypermarket in Sainte-Geneviève-de-Bois in 1963. The hypermarket concept was the store concept that Carrefour would eventually become most famous for. The typical characteristic of such hypermarkets is that they offer a wide assortment of food as well as nonfood products at economic prices and are of a much greater size than the traditional supermarkets. Specifically, the size of hypermarkets can range from 5,000 to 20,000 square meters. In comparison, Carrefour's regular supermarkets, which operate under the names Champion, GB, Globi, GS, and Gima, have an average size of between 1,000 and 2,000 square meters.

In 1979 Carrefour opened its first hard discount stores under the "Ed" banner in France and under the "Dia" banner in Spain. The hard discount stores sell a much smaller variety of products than the hypermarkets (on average 800 products versus 20,000 to 80,000) on a much smaller store space (between 200 and 800 square meters) at discount prices. Some of the discount products are sold under own brand names, such as the Dia brand name. In 1985 Carrefour also started to sell products under its own brand name in its other, non-discount stores.

During the 1970s and 1980s, Carrefour expanded across the oceans and established hypermarkets in, for example, Brazil (1975), Argentina (1982), and Taiwan (1989). The international and intercontinental expansion of Carrefour took off especially in the 1990s when Carrefour opened a large number of hypermarkets in southern Europe (Greece, Italy, and Turkey), eastern Europe (Poland), Asia (China, Hong Kong, Korea, Malaysia, Singapore, and Thailand), and Latin America (Mexico, Chile, and Colombia). **Exhibit 1** provides information about Carrefour's operations by geographic segment and by store format. The exhibit also illustrates that intercontinental expansion primarily occurred through the opening of hypermarkets. Most of Carrefour's smaller supermarkets were located throughout Europe.

In addition to its traditional food and nonfood retailing activities, the company soon offered traveling, financial, and insurance services to its customers in Brazil, France, and Spain. For example, Carrefour has its own payment card, the "Pass" card, which it introduced in the early 1980s. In the beginning, the Pass card offered customers priority at store check-outs and allowed them to pay their bills in installments. Later, the card became linked to a Visa credit card and customers could borrow money for out-of-store purchases. By the end of 2005, Carrefour's financial services unit had €3.5 billion in credit outstanding throughout the world.

One of the key events in Carrefour's history took place in 1999, when it merged with Promodès, a large French food retailer that owned the Champion supermarket chain. At the time of the merger, Carrefour and Promodès were, respectively, the sixth and ninth largest retailers in the world and held market shares of around 18 and 12 percent in France. After the merger, the combined company, which continued under the name Carrefour, became Europe's largest retailer, the world's second largest retailer, and the world's most international supermarket chain. An important trigger for the merger was that in the late 1990s, US-based Wal-Mart, the world's largest retailer, was expanding its operations to Europe and posed a potential threat to the French retailer's strong position in their home market. As a result of the merger, the Halley family, who had founded Promodès and had always been its controlling shareholder, became the principal shareholder of Carrefour, holding a 13 percent stake in Carrefour by the end of 2005.

The integration of the operations of Promodès and Carrefour went slowly and the merger of the two retailers was the start of a difficult period. Immediately following the merger, Carrefour acquired a few other supermarket chains, such as Norte in Argentina, GS in Italy, and GB in Belgium, emphasizing its desire to aggressively expand its operations and become the leading international retailer. However, over the years, competition in the food retailing industry substantially increased and all retailers came under pressure to cut prices. The need to lower prices became even stronger when the European economy slowed down in 2001. Carrefour's sales growth in its home market suffered from the competition of France-based Leclerc and Auchan, which focused their strategy on cutting prices and gaining market share. Although Carrefour did join its French rivals in cutting prices, the company aimed much more at improving its margins than increasing sales volumes. Only in 2003, when Carrefour's sales growth in France approached zero, did the company start to put more emphasis on competing on price, gaining market share, and stimulating customer loyalty. In April 2004, Carrefour launched a new customer loyalty program. The customer loyalty card helped the company to create a database that registers the purchasing habits of its customers and helps it respond more promptly to changes in customer preferences. By that time, Carrefour's sales growth in its home market had come to a halt and the company started to lose market share. Analysts worried that this could hinder Carrefour's international expansion. One analyst stated:[3]

We are seeing that there is a lack of growth and a decline in the market share in the main businesses, which are the hypermarkets in France. Without the contribution of the hypermarkets in France, we don't have enough resources to fuel the growth outside France.

Carrefour had been listed on the Paris Stock Exchange (Euronext) since 1970. The company's stock price performance during the first half of the 2000s is summarized in **Exhibit 2**.

Carrefour after its management change

After having replaced Daniel Bernard, Jose Luis Duran announced in Carrefour's 2004 Annual Report that one of his primary goals was to make Carrefour a growth company. He commented on his plans as follows:

In 2004, the growth in our sales, neglecting the effects of exchange rates, was about 4%, of which 3% were attributable to the increase in sales floor area and 1% to growth on a like for like basis. In the future, we must record a growth in sales as close as possible to double digits. To do this, the contribution from new openings should be on the order of 3% to 5%, from like for like sales of 1% to 3% and from tactical acquisitions of 1% to 2%.

Although his focus was to improve growth, the new CEO planned to put an end to Carrefour's over-aggressive expansion abroad and its incoherent pricing strategy in France.[4] Carrefour's new strategy was to withdraw from poorly performing markets and increase its capital expenditures in successful markets. In addition, the company intended to focus less on margins, but more on increasing sales volume and cost savings. In its home market, the company hoped to regain market share from its French competitors, Leclerc and Auchan, as well as from deep-discounters such as Aldi and Lidl. To regain price competitiveness, Carrefour frequently surveyed its hypermarket customers and quickly adjusted its prices on the basis of the survey outcomes. Finally, Carrefour planned to broaden its product assortment and lengthen the opening hours of its stores. To achieve the latter goal, Carrefour needed to increase its staff.

[3]See "Sign of the Times for Carrefour," BBC News website, February 3, 2005.
[4]See "Carrefour at Crossroads," *The Economist*, October 20, 2005.

For 2006, Carrefour expected to open about 1.5 million square meters of new store space (worldwide), of which 425,000 square meters was to be through acquisitions, and achieve sales growth above its growth rate in 2005. In 2005, Carrefour had spent €1.8 billion on store openings and enlargements. Total capital expenditure would increase from €2.5 billion in 2004 and €3.1 billion in 2005 to €10 billion in the 2006–2008 period. The company would, however, remain engaged in price wars in many of its markets, including France, albeit possibly to a lesser extent. Carrefour's leading positions in China and Europe would also remain under attack from US retailer Wal-Mart. One way in which it could relieve some of the pressure on its margins was to negotiate with its suppliers on pricing. In 2004 and 2005, Carrefour had managed to come to an agreement with its key suppliers of branded consumer goods that they would cut or only moderately increase their prices. However, suppliers were planning to raise their prices by 4–6 percent in 2006. In addition, the new French Dutreil law that took effect on January 1, 2006, ruled that supplier discounts in excess of 20 percent must be passed on to retailers' customers in the form of lower prices. Given these developments, Carrefour's price cuts in 2006 would likely focus on its private labels. In 2005, Carrefour had relaunched its private labels on prominent display and the company expected its Carrefour product range to include 11,000 products by the end of 2006.

Tesco

In 2005 one of Carrefour's European industry peers was UK-based Tesco, the world's third largest retailer, after Carrefour and Wal-Mart. The company had been founded in 1919 and had become the leading retailer in its domestic market in 1995.

The strategies of Carrefour and Tesco exhibited some similarities. Particularly, both retailers strived for international expansion and reserved a substantial amount of store space for nonfood products. Tesco's operations were less international than Carrefour's. In 2005, 70 percent of Carrefour's store space was outside France, whereas 56 percent of Tesco's store space was located outside the UK Tesco operated primarily in eastern Europe (Czech Republic, Hungary, Poland, and Slovakia) and Asia (e.g., China, Japan, South Korea, and Thailand).

The company had four different store formats, which all operated under the Tesco banner. Tesco Express and Metro stores were the smallest type of stores (with up to 5,000 square meters) and focused on selling food products. Tesco's Superstores occupied between 7,000 and 16,000 square meters and offered both food and nonfood products. Since 1997, Tesco also operated Extra stores, which offered a wide range of food and nonfood lines, including electrical equipment, clothing, and health and pharmaceutical products. These stores had store spaces of approximately 20,000 square meters. Tesco's Superstores and Extra stores were thus comparable, at least in size and assortment, to Carrefour's Hypermarkets. Illustrative of the similarity between the two retailer's operations is that in September 2005 the companies swapped stores. Tesco received 15 Carrefour stores in the Czech Republic and Slovakia in return for six Tesco stores in Taiwan.

Although Tesco seemed to follow the example of Carrefour in terms of the international expansion and the adoption of a multiformat approach, the UK retailer had set an example for creating customer loyalty in the 1990s. The problem of a declining market share that Carrefour experienced in its domestic market in 2005 was fairly similar to the problem that Tesco had experienced in the early 1990s. In those years, Tesco suffered from slowing sales growth and lower margins, primarily because it was stuck between two strategies: the strategy of deep-discounters such as Asda and the strategy of high-quality retailers such as Sainsbury's. In response to the problems, Tesco lowered its prices, introduced its private brand label, which became highly successful, expanded its nonfood operations, and introduced a loyalty card that helped the retailer to observe the shopping patterns of its customers. These actions boosted Tesco's sales growth and profits and helped the company to become the market leader in the UK.

In 2005 Tesco's sales of nonfood products grew twice as fast as its sales of food products. Like Carrefour, Tesco offered financial services, such as banking and insurance services, to its customers. Unlike Carrefour, Tesco operated a very successful online grocery store in the UK, which had 170,000 registered customers. In the fiscal year ending on February 25, 2006, Tesco's return on equity of 16.7 percent was comparable to Carrefour's ROE in 2005 of 17.1 percent. **Exhibit 5** shows a summary of Tesco's financial performance in 2005. Tesco's market performance in the first half of the 2000s had been significantly better than Carrefour's. Between January 1, 2000 and February 25, 2006, Tesco's share price increased by 82 percent. This total return corresponded to an average annual return of slightly above 10 percent.

Concurrent with the presentation of its results for fiscal 2005, Tesco announced that it planned to sell and lease back close to £5 billion of property over the next five years. During 2005, the company had already sold and leased back close to £0.4 billion of property. Approximately £1.5 billion of the proceeds from these sale and leaseback transactions would be used to return cash to Tesco's shareholders and reduce the company's investment base.

Carrefour S.A.

EXHIBIT 1 Carrefour's operations by geographic segment and store format

Fiscal year	France	Rest of Europe	Latin America	Asia	Hyper-market	Super-market	Hard discount	Other
Net sales (in € millions)								
2005	35,577	27,102	5,075	5,744	43,802	13,239	6,441	11,015
2004	35,723	27,123	4,721	5,101	42,147	13,080	5,813	11,627
2003	35,704	25,527	4,619	4,637	41,587	12,688	4,934	11,278
2002	35,101	23,608	5,382	4,639	40,551	12,371	5,498	10,310
2001	34,335	22,144	8,440	4,567	40,997	13,897	4,864	9,728
Earnings before interest and taxes (in € millions)								
2005	1,713	1,145	133	185				
2004	1,965	1,070	50	149				
2003	2,144	952	13	143				
2002	2,065	796	23	141				
2001	1,905	733	53	134				
Capital expenditures (in € millions)								
2005	791	1,192	248	381				
2004	874	1,008	231	336				
2003	818	1,169	295	436				
2002	609	1,224	276	355				
2001	776	1,438	370	318				
Sales area of consolidated stores (in square meters, thousands)								
2005	3,245	4,596	1,621	1,618	7,087	2,319	1,674	
2004	3,056	4,265	1,854	1,496	6,885	2,321	1,466	
2003	2,919	3,994	1,902	1,228	6,510	2,277	1,255	
2002	2,781	4,142	1,792	1,051	6,180	2,132	1,093	
2001	2,716	3,752	1,783	899	5,674	2,177	997	

EXHIBIT 2   **Carrefour's stock price and the MSCI world retailing price index from December 1995 to February 2006 (price on December 29, 1995 = 100)**

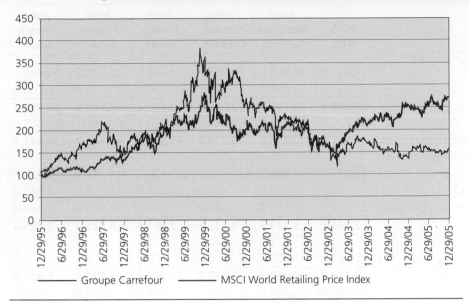

Source: Thomson Datastream.

Carrefour S.A.

EXHIBIT 3   **Carrefour's consolidated income statements, balance sheets, and cash flow statements, 2001 to 2005 (in € millions)**

Consolidated Income Statements

	2005 IFRS	2004 Restated to IFRS[a]	2004 French GAAP	2003 French GAAP	2002 French GAAP	2001 French GAAP
Net sales	74,496.8	72,668.0	72,668.0	70,486.2	68,728.8	69,486.1
Other income	1,011.3	1,038.6	0.0	0.0	0.0	0.0
Total income	**75,508.1**	**73,706.6**	**72,668.0**	**70,486.2**	**68,728.8**	**69,486.1**
Cost of sales	(58,626.5)	(57,052.8)	(56,554.2)	(54,630.4)	(53,182.1)	(53,875.0)
Gross margin from current operations	**16,881.6**	**16,653.8**	**16,113.8**	**15,855.8**	**15,546.7**	**15,611.1**
Sales, general, and administrative expenses	(12,232.7)	(11,888.2)	(11,792.9)	(11,478.4)	(11,419.2)	(11,728.7)
Other income and expenses	0.0	0.0	596.2	493.6	547.5	645.2
Depreciation, amortization, and provisions	(1,474.2)	(1,652.3)	(1,683.4)	(1,619.6)	(1,649.6)	(1,702.0)
Activity contribution	**3,174.7**	**3,113.3**	**3,233.8**	**3,251.4**	**3,025.4**	**2,825.6**
Nonrecurring income	264.6	229.5	0.0	0.0	0.0	0.0
Nonrecurring expenses	(285.0)	(305.5)	0.0	0.0	0.0	0.0
EBIT	**3,154.2**	**3,037.3**	**3,233.8**	**3,251.4**	**3,025.4**	**2,825.6**
Interest income, of which	(454.6)	(484.5)	(424.1)	(463.7)	(526.9)	(646.2)
Net debt expense	(395.9)	(401.9)	(493.8)	(548.3)	(669.5)	(778.6)
Other financial income and expenses	(58.7)	(82.6)	69.7	84.6	142.6	132.4
Earnings before taxes	**2,699.6**	**2,552.8**	**2,809.7**	**2,787.7**	**2,498.5**	**2,179.4**
Income tax	(793.9)	(762.7)	(836.4)	(846.2)	(736.4)	(585.7)
Net income from recurring operations of consolidated companies	**1,905.7**	**1,790.2**	**1,905.7**	**1,941.5**	**1,762.1**	**1,593.7**
Net income from companies consolidated by the equity method	50.6	40.7	101.4	107.2	107.4	127.0
Net income before from recurring operations	**1,956.3**	**1,830.9**	**2,074.7**	**2,048.7**	**1,869.5**	**1,720.7**
Goodwill amortization	0.0	0.0	(319.3)	(318.0)	(309.7)	(368.5)
Nonrecurring income	0.0	0.0	(246.2)	9.1	(14.9)	59.2
Net income from discontinued operations	(374.2)	(85.5)	0.0	0.0	0.0	0.0
Minority interest	(146.1)	(154.2)	(122.4)	(110.7)	(170.8)	(145.6)
Total net income, Group share	**1,436.0**	**1,591.1**	**1,386.8**	**1,629.1**	**1,374.1**	**1,265.8**
Net earnings per share (€)	2.05	2.28	1.99	2.27	1.93	1.78
Net earnings per share (€) – diluted	2.05	2.28	1.99	2.24	1.87	1.72
Weighted average shares outstanding	699,470	697,161	697,161	716,142.4	711,164.0	711,147.1
Weighted average shares outstanding, diluted	699,471	697,161	697,161	728,070.1	734,303.5	734,295.7
Pro forma: Labor costs	(7,115.1)	(6,579.5)	(6,877.2)	(6,519.9)	(6,308.8)	(6,447.7)

[a]In 2005, Carrefour changed its depreciation period for buildings (from 20 years to 40 years). The column "2004 Restated to IFRS" reports IFRS-based income statement figures after restating buildings depreciation. The income statement figures in column "2004 French GAAP" are based on the original buildings depreciation period of 20 years.

Consolidated Balance Sheets

	2005 IFRS	2004 Restated to IFRS	2004 French GAAP	2003 French GAAP	2002 French GAAP	2001 French GAAP
Goodwill	10,235.0	9,329.0	8,851.0	9,131.5	9,302.0	9,813.9
Other intangible assets	862.0	730.0	1,046.0	1,066.3	998.5	987.7
Tangible fixed assets	13,401.0	12,617.0	12,897.0	12,255.0	12,384.5	13,630.7
Financial assets	1,175.0	1,141.0	1,014.0	825.2	889.9	996.5
Investment in companies accounted for by the equity method	467.0	247.0	551.0	630.5	607.0	542.7
Deferred tax assets	1,029.0	1,066.0	1,049.0	633.4	576.3	589.1
Investment properties	463.0	481.0	0.0	0.0	0.0	0.0
Consumer credit from financial companies	1,398.0	1,594.0	0.0	0.0	0.0	0.0
Non-current assets	**29,030.0**	**27,205.0**	**25,406.0**	**24,541.9**	**24,758.2**	**26,560.6**
Inventories	6,110.0	5,621.0	6,243.0	5,690.7	5,722.8	5,909.4
Commercial receivables	3,451.0	3,147.0	3,059.0	3,182.2	3,154.6	2,945.6
Consumer credit from financial companies short-term	2,357.0	1,627.0	0.0	0.0	0.0	0.0
Tax receivables	598.0	423.0	411.0	764.4	607.5	542.9
Other assets	813.0	900.0	928.0	1,463.7	1,652.7	2,715.0
Cash and cash equivalents	3,733.0	3,203.0	2,930.0	3,420.4	3,028.5	4,796.9
Assets held for sale	158.0	0.0	0.0	0.0	0.0	0.0
Current assets	**17,220.0**	**14,921.0**	**13,571.0**	**14,521.4**	**14,166.1**	**16,909.8**
Total assets	**46,250.0**	**42,126.0**	**38,977.0**	**39,063.3**	**38,924.3**	**43,470.4**
Shareholders' equity, group share	8,385.0	6,947.0	7,549.0	7,089.3	6,623.3	7,377.4
Shareholders' equity, minority interest	1,001.0	929.0	780.0	891.0	922.7	1,294.0
Shareholders' equity	**9,386.0**	**7,876.0**	**8,329.0**	**7,980.3**	**7,546.0**	**8,671.4**
Borrowings	7,628.0	7,340.0	7,126.7	7,231.4	8,330.6	10,304.1
Provisions	2,325.0	1,954.0	1,274.0	1,165.1	1,157.5	1,310.1
Deferred tax liabilities	226.0	353.0	471.0	483.8	516.8	716.4
Consumer credit refinancing	264.0	255.0	0.0	0.0	0.0	0.0
Non-current liabilities	**10,443.0**	**9,902.0**	**8,871.7**	**8,880.3**	**10,004.9**	**12,330.6**
Borrowings – under 1 year	2,895.0	2,632.0	2,597.3	4,080.9	3,718.6	3,167.2
Trade payables	16,025.0	14,721.0	14,362.0	13,660.4	13,278.2	12,996.7
Consumer credit refinancing short-term	3,199.0	2,654.0	0.0	0.0	0.0	0.0
Tax payables	1,241.0	1,388.0	1,368.0	0.0	0.0	0.0
Other liabilities	3,022.0	2,952.0	3,448.0	4,461.4	4,376.6	6,304.5
Liabilities held for sale	38.0	0.0	0.0	0.0	0.0	0.0
Current liabilities	**26,420.0**	**24,347.0**	**21,775.3**	**22,202.7**	**21,373.4**	**22,468.4**
Total liabilities and shareholders' equity	**46,250.0**	**42,126.0**	**38,977.0**	**39,063.3**	**38,924.3**	**43,470.4**

Carrefour S.A.

Carrefour S.A.

Consolidated Cash Flow Statements

	2005 IFRS	2004 Restated to IFRS	2004 French GAAP	2003 French GAAP	2002 French GAAP	2001 French GAAP
Net income			1,509.1	1,737.6	1,539.4	1438.5
Income before tax	2,700.0	2,553.0				
Tax	(757.0)	(830.0)				
Provision for amortization	1,564.0	1,939.0	2,102.2	2,066.0	1,950.0	2,537.8
Capital gains and losses on sales of assets	(160.0)	(56.0)	(69.9)	(190.5)	(266.1)	(1,106.5)
Changes in provisions	300.0	(127.0)	(87.0)	(118.4)	(119.0)	(82.2)
Dividends on companies accounted for by the equity method	6.0	(47.0)	(48.0)	(63.2)	(78.5)	(87.4)
Impact of discontinued activities	(71.0)	0.0	0.0	0.0	0.0	0.0
Cash flow from operations	**3,582.0**	**3,432.0**	**3,406.4**	**3,431.6**	**3,025.8**	**2,700.3**
Change in working capital	175.0	875.0	841.2	323.0	(149.0)	837.9
Impact of discontinued activities	19.0	0.0	0.0	0.0	0.0	0.0
Change in cash flow from operating activities (excluding financial companies)	**3,775.0**	**4,307.0**	**4,247.6**	**3,754.5**	**2,876.8**	**3,538.2**
Acquisition of tangible and intangible fixed assets	(3,026.0)	(2,570.0)	(2,563.7)	(2,717.3)	(2,423.0)	(3,397.8)
Acquisition of financial assets	(51.0)	(123.0)				
Acquisition of subsidiaries	(775.0)	(315.0)	(438.6)	(349.9)	(582.0)	(951.3)
Disposals of subsidiaries	565.0	19.0				
Disposals of fixed assets	707.0	546.0	545.8	883.2	704.7	1,952.4
Disposals of investments	26.0	375.0	394.3	302.7	245.5	1,705.6
Other uses	(126.0)	(80.0)	(84.4)	(84.9)	(1,108.9)	(314.5)
Impact of discontinued activities	63.0	0.0	0.0	0.0	0.0	0.0
Net cash from investing activities	**(2,617.0)**	**(2,148.0)**	**(2,146.6)**	**(1,966.1)**	**(3,163.7)**	**(1,005. 6)**
Proceeds on issue of shares	88.0	(368.0)	(367.6)	17.3	300.4	183.7
Dividends paid by Carrefour (parent company)	(656.0)	(525.0)	(608.9)	(522.5)	(475.5)	(424.6)
Dividends paid by consolidated companies to minority interests	(102.0)	(152.0)				
Change in borrowings	128.0	(1,596.0)	(1,588.0)	(737.0)	(1,422.1)	(477.2)
Net cash from financing activities	**(542.0)**	**(2,641.0)**	**(2,564.5)**	**(1,242.2)**	**(1,597.3)**	**(718.0)**
Impact of currency fluctuations	(59.0)	(27.0)	(26.6)	(154.5)	115.7	41.3
Net change in cash and cash equivalents	**531.0**	**(514.0)**	**(490.1)**	**391.8**	**(1,768.4)**	**1,855.9**
Cash and cash equivalents at beginning of year	3,202.0	3,717.0	3,420.6	3,028.6	4,797.0	2,941.1
Cash and cash equivalents at end of year	**3,733.0**	**3,202.0**	**2,930.4**	**3,420.5**	**3,028.6**	**4,797.0**

EXHIBIT 4   **Excerpts from Carrefour's annual report for the fiscal year ending December 31, 2005**

A. Interview with the Chairman of the Management Board

José Luis Duran, with the publication of the 2005 Annual Report, what is your overall assessment of the year 2005?

2005 represents a crucial turning point in the Carrefour group's strategy. We confronted this crucial period against a difficult background of intensified competition, weaker consumer spending in Europe and a rapidly changing regulatory environment in France. In the light of this situation, we not only rethought our economic model and our strategy, but above all our ambitions. By tracing out the most direct route from the existing situation to our objectives, we dared to break a number of taboos. In particular, we broke with a policy of short-term results, which favoured margin growth to the detriment of growth in sales and long-term results. Our objective is to be among the three leading players in the retail distribution sector in each of our markets. And the first results are already in:

- We have found the way back to growth, with the opening of more than a million square meters of new sales floor area through organic growth, in addition to 425,000 square meters from tactical acquisitions, whilst the average pace of growth over the last five years never exceeded one million square meters.

- Our sales increased by 6.1% on a like-for-like basis and by 4.3% worldwide at constant exchange rates, and by 28% in Latin America, 20.5% in Asia, 6.1% in Europe (excluding France) and 1.2% in France.

- We have recaptured market share in grocery retailing as a result of our determined pricing policy, particularly in France. In this market, our entire range of banners gained market share of 0.6 points in grocery retailing in 2005 and, as a result of their pricing offensive, Carrefour hypermarkets in France increased their market share by 0.3 points. This shows the exceptional vitality of the hypermarket format when we offer customers the best product range at the best price.

Thanks to the efforts made in 2005, the Carrefour Group has built a firm foundation for stronger and more sustainable growth in 2006. That is also why we withdrew from four countries (Japan, Mexico, the Czech Republic and Slovakia) and why we disposed of two of our activities (catering outlets in France and the cash & carry business in Spain) where the Group was no longer in a position to maintain its leadership position. From now on, we are concentrating all our resources on our strategic assets (i.e. those that show a potential for profitability and strong growth). Today, the course is clear for us and our teams.

What is your outlook for 2006–2008?

The strategy begun in 2005 is a fundamental strategy designed for the medium term (through to 2008), and we are pursuing it with determination. We are controlling costs in all regions. Our average net debt is improving, in spite of rising investments and dividends. Our financial expenses are down by 6%. Our net income per share from recurring operations is stable overall and our healthy net cash flow ensures that we have the resources we need to carry out our strategic plan. Although I remain cautious, I am optimistic: the Group has a high potential for growth. Over the 2006–2008 period, we will open on average twice as many hypermarkets throughout the world as between 2001 and 2004. In fact, we plan to add 1.5 million square meters annually through organic growth and we will take advantage of the best opportunities for tactical acquisitions. Naturally, we will pay scrupulous attention to the allocation of capital and to the profitability of all these investments.

How do you intend to build loyalty among your customers?

Our customers are at the heart of the Carrefour Group's strategy. The best proof that we have regained the trust of our customers is an increase in sales and in our grocery market share in France. The new pricing strategy in France that I have already mentioned was a necessary prerequisite, and we plan to maintain our competitiveness in 2006. And we are going even further, by strengthening our initiatives in the area of customer relations. To that end, we still need to increase our understanding of current trends in our customers' purchasing behaviours, customs and lifestyles. This can be accomplished by making better use of our databases. On the basis of this improved understanding of the attitudes of our customers and by more clearly anticipating their expectations, we can adapt our product range accordingly by implementing a more targeted price strategy and by further developing our product mix and services. In 2005, we launched some major strategic programmes to prepare for these changes. This involves an in-depth change in our approach to developing goods and services.

What are the priorities and time frames for these projects?

These programmes will be implemented over the entire duration of the plan. They naturally imply a profound change in our management methods and tools. In practice, this project must enable us to win market share in all sectors, and not only in the grocery and fresh produce sector where we are already the leader, but in non-food segments as well. All our teams are mobilized to offer the best range of products and services. Market testing carried out in Spain in 2005, with small Carrefour hypermarkets and the MaxiDia stores, shows that we are continually getting closer to our customers and their expectations and that innovation in this sphere tends to pay off.

How is this strategy put into practice by employees?

A strategy can only succeed if the idea is transformed into action, and then the action is transformed into results. The best guarantee of the successful implementation of our strategy is therefore the exceptional know-how and energy of our 436,000 employees. Their daily commitment to customer service is without a doubt our best asset. A number of teams participated directly in the preparation of the strategic plan through participating in task forces that brought together people from all store formats and all geographical areas, possessing the full range of functional and operational skills. It is this direct upstream involvement that facilitates implementation and guarantees that these programmes can be made fully operational. Based on the success of these task forces, we decided to modify the organization of the Group by simplifying our structures and reinforcing the teams in direct contact with the customer. This simplification and the reallocation of resources have allowed us to strengthen our in-store teams. In France, we recruited and trained some 15,000 employees, which puts the Carrefour Group, once again, at the top of the list of national recruiters.

What are your priorities in terms of sustainable development?

Our customers also think and act as citizens. We have fully incorporated sustainable development into our new strategy. All of the Group's employees are developing projects that respond in concrete terms to the concerns and expectations of the populations that we serve throughout the world, in areas such as food safety, nutrition and social responsibility. For instance, in Colombia, Carrefour was one of the main industry leaders involved in the production and sale of substitute products to replace the cultivation of crops for illicit use. For its efforts in this area, Carrefour Colombia was awarded the United Nations Vienna prize. In Thailand, Carrefour has initiated an aquaculture project at Baan Nam Kem to help the fishermen of southern Thailand reconstruct the aquaculture facilities destroyed by the tsunami of December 2004. At a time when the overexploitation of marine resources is becoming a cause for alarm, the Carrefour Group is marketing four frozen fish items in France and Belgium under its own brand name which are the product of responsible, environmentally friendly fishing practices. These are just a few examples that illustrate our commitment to sustainable development.

In conclusion, would you say that the Carrefour Group is once again a growth company?

Trust cannot be imposed; it must be earned. Carrefour is an extraordinarily modern and proactive retail distribution enterprise turned resolutely towards the future; it is the second largest such enterprise in the world, and certainly the most international in scope. I believe in our teams' ability to make the Carrefour Group a lasting vehicle for international growth, and I am totally committed to that objective, as is the entire management team.

B. Excerpts from the notes to the consolidated financial statements

Note 1: Accounting principles

Under the terms of European regulation 1606/2002 of July 19, 2002 on international standards, the Carrefour Group's consolidated financial statements for the fiscal year 2005 have been drawn up for the first time in accordance with IFRS international accounting standards applicable as from January 1, 2005, as approved by the European Union. The consolidated financial statements have been drawn up on the basis of historic cost, with the exception of certain assets and liabilities subject to IFRS standards. The asset and liability categories concerned are described, where applicable, in the corresponding notes below. Non-current assets and groups of assets held for sale are valued at their book value or the fair value minus sale costs, whichever is the lower.

The main estimates made by management when preparing the financial statements concern the valuations and useful lives of current and non-current operating assets and goodwill, the amount of provisions for risks and other provisions relating to the business, as well as assumptions made for the calculation of retirement pension commitments or deferred taxes. Details of the main assumptions retained by the Group are provided in each of the paragraphs in the Appendix devoted to the financial statements. The specific rules for initial adoption, as defined in IFRS1 "Initial adoption of international financial information standards", have been applied. We have opted to present the income statement by type. The other options selected, where applicable, are indicated in the following sections. IAS 32 and IAS 39 relating to financial instruments have been applied as from January 1, 2005. IFRS 5 relating to non-current assets held for sale and discontinued operations was applied as of January 1, 2004.

Change in estimate

In 2005, the Group decided to make a change in estimate as to the duration of the depreciation of its buildings, increasing it from 20 to 40 years. The change in estimate, reflected in a change in the duration of depreciation retroactive to January 1, 2005, can be justified by the fact that the contribution values of the stores, as determined by expert assessors within the context of the project for the creation of the European property company, Carrefour Property, in 2005, have proved that buildings still have significant market value after 20 years. Following the creation of Carrefour Property, the Group decided to engage in an overall review of the useful economic life of its assets. AFREXIM (association of property experts) has thus conducted a sectoral study of the economic life span of a building. The property expert's report concluded in 2005 that the economic life span of a building within the Group is 40 years. An income statement and balance sheet restated under this change in estimate were communicated for the purpose of comparison with 2004 in December 2004. This information was prepared on the basis of the "published" IFRS financial statements drawn up on December 31, 2004.

Groups of companies

The Group has chosen the option offered by IFRS 1, which does not restate company groupings prior to January 1, 2004 in accordance with IFRS 3. As from January 1, 2004, all company groupings are entered in the accounts by the acquisition method. The difference between the acquisition cost, which includes expenses directly attributable to the acquisition, and the fair value of assets, net of liabilities and any liabilities accepted as part of the business composition, is shown as goodwill. Negative goodwill resulting from the acquisition is immediately entered in the income statement. For companies acquired during the course of the fiscal year and increases in investments, only the income for the period after the acquisition date is shown in the consolidated income statement. For companies disposed of during the course of the fiscal year and dilutions, only the income for the period prior to the disposal date is shown in the consolidated income statement.

Conversion rate for foreign companies

In accordance with the option offered under IFRS 1, the Group has chosen to restate the translation adjustments accumulated at January 1, 2004 under "consolidated reserves". This option has no impact on the Group's total shareholders' equity; it involves a reclassification within shareholders' equity from the entry "Translation adjustments" to the entry "Other reserves" totaling 3,236 million euros.

Fixed assets

2 – Goodwill

In accordance with IFRS 3, goodwill has not been amortized since January 1, 2004. Instead, goodwill is subject to an impairment test during the second half of each year. IAS 36, "Depreciation of assets", states that this impairment test should be conducted either at the level of each Cash Flow Generating Unit (CFGU) to which goodwill has been allocated or at business group level within a business sector or geographic sector in which the return on investment of acquisitions is evaluated. The level of analysis at which Carrefour evaluates the current value of goodwill generally corresponds to countries or to operations by country.

Carrefour S.A.

Carrefour S.A.

The need to record a loss in value is evaluated by comparing the book value of CFGU or CFGU group assets and liabilities and their recoverable value. The recoverable value is the market value or useful value, whichever is the higher. The useful value is estimated by discounting future cash flows over a period of 4 years with determination of a final value calculated on the basis of the discounting of the fourth year figures at the perpetual rate of growth to infinity and the use of a discount rate specific to each country. The specific discounting rate for each country takes into consideration the specific risk to a country determined by a grid containing the five weighted indicators below: monetary risk; political and regulatory situation; competition; Carrefour's experience curve in the country; potential for growth in the market.

These discounting rates are validated by the Group's Management Committee and were between 5.7% and 11.6% for the fiscal year 2005, depending on the country. The market value is assessed with regard to recent transactions or professional practices.

3 – Intangible fixed assets

Other intangible fixed assets basically correspond to software programs that are depreciated over between one and five years.

4 – Tangible fixed assets

In accordance with IAS 16 "Tangible fixed assets", land, buildings and equipment, fixtures and fittings are evaluated at their cost price at acquisition or the cost of sales, less depreciation and loss in value. [...] Tangible fixed assets are depreciated on a straight line basis according to the following average useful lives:

- Construction: buildings 40 years, grounds 10 years, car parks 62/3 years
- Equipment, fixtures and fittings and installations 62/3 years to 8 years
- Other fixed assets 4 to 10 years

Customer receivables outstanding: Refinancing to financial service companies

Customer receivables due to financial service companies refer primarily to consumer credit granted to customers of companies within the Group's scope of consolidation. These loans, together with the amounts outstanding from refinancing that back them, are considered to be assets and liabilities, held until their maturity date and are classified on the basis of their maturity date as current or non-current assets and liabilities.

Employee benefits

The Group's employees enjoy short-term benefits (paid leave, sick leave, profit-sharing), long-term benefits (long-service medals, seniority bonus etc.) and post-employment advantages on the basis of specific contributions/benefits (retirement benefit).

b – Schemes with defined benefits and long-term advantages

The Carrefour Group makes provision for the various defined benefit schemes dependent on the accumulated years of service within the Group that are not totally pre-financed. This commitment is calculated annually on the basis of the method of projected units of credit, on an actuarial basis, taking into consideration factors such as salary increases, age of departure, mortality, personnel rotation and discount rates. The Group has decided to apply the "corridor" method, whereby the effect of variations in actuarial terms is not recognized on the income statement, as long as the former remain within a range of 10%. Thus actuarial differences exceeding 10% between the value of the commitment and the value of the hedging assets – whichever is the higher – on the income statement are spread over the expected average working life of employees benefiting from this scheme.

In accordance with the option offered by IFRS 1, the Group has chosen to record all its actuarial losses and gains in its pension commitments that have not yet been recognized in the French financial statements at December 31, 2003, directly, corresponding to shareholders' equity at January 1, 2004.

c – Share-based compensation

In accordance with the option offered by IFRS 1, the Group has decided to limit the application of IFRS 2 to stock option plans paid in shares, allocated after November 7, 2002, the rights to which had not yet been acquired at January 1, 2004. This application had no effect on total shareholders' equity at January 1, 2004. Three plans granted between 2003 and 2005 fall within the scope of IFRS2 "Share-based compensation". These are subscription or purchase options reserved for employees with no special acquisition conditions, aside from effective presence at the end of the period of the vesting period.

The benefits granted that are remunerated by these schemes are posted as expenses, which corresponds to an increase in shareholders' equity over the vesting period. The accounting expense for each period corresponds to the fair value of the assets and services received on the basis of the "Black & Scholes" formula on the date on which these were granted and spread over the vesting period.

The restricted stock plans granted by the Group are recognized as an expense spread over the period of acquisition of the rights. The plans granted in 2004 and 2005 are dependent on the achievement of non-market objectives; since, however, it is thought to be unlikely that these objectives will be achieved, no expense has been recognized for the allocation of free shares in 2005. Details of share allocation plans are provided in the management report.

Financial debt and financial instruments

d – Derecognition of financial assets

In December 2002, the Group contracted into a programme for securitizing receivables. This programme only partially transfers the risks and advantages of the variation in value discounted by future cash flows from receivables. As a result, part of these securitized receivables have been recognized as financial debt.

Other revenues

Other revenues (financial and travel services, rental income, franchise fees etc.) are recorded on a separate line called "other revenues" and recorded underneath the "net sales" line in the income statement. Some expenses, such as the cost of payments made by customers in several installments and of loyalty schemes not funded by suppliers, are recorded net of other revenues. This entry includes fees received by finance companies from debit cards, traditional credit applications or revolving credit applications. Fees are spread across the duration of the contract.

Note 4: Net sales

(€ millions)	31/12/2005	31/12/2004 published restated Dep/40 yrs	% Var	31/12/2004 IFRS
Sales	74,496.8	72,668.0	2.5%	70,284.2

At constant exchange rates, net sales would have been 73,325 million euros. The impact of exchange rate fluctuations represented 1,172 million euros at December 31, 2005, of which 655 million euros in the Latin America region, 339 million euros in the Europe region (mainly Turkey and Poland) and 178 million euros in the Asia region. Excluding the sale of Japan, the Czech Republic, Slovakia, Mexico, Prodirest, supermarkets in Brazil and in Spain, and PuntoCash, sales would have risen by 6% at current exchange rates and 4.3% at constant exchange rates.

Note 12: Net income from discontinued operations

(€ millions)	31/12/2005	31/12/2004 published restated Dep/40 yrs	31/12/2004 IFRS
Discontinued operations, group share	(371.5)	(84.8)	(154.9)
Discontinued operations, minority share	(2.7)	(0.7)	11.6
Total	(374.2)	(85.5)	(143.3)

In December 2005, net income from discontinued operations were accounted for by:

- the impact of the sale of Japan for 1 million euros, a provision for depreciation of 90 million euros having been recorded at December 31, 2004;
- the impact of the sale of Mexico for (29) million euros, corresponding for the most part to capital losses, since income for the period was not significant;
- net income for the period and net income from the sale of the food service activity in France, amounting to (22) million euros;
- losses for the year in the Czech Republic and Slovakia amounting to (63) million euros;
- losses for the year from Cash & Carry in Spain (Puntocash) amounting to (2) million euros;
- the impact of the closure of the Brazilian supermarkets in 2005 amounting to (196) million euros;
- the impact of the closure of the Spanish supermarkets in 2005 amounting to (63) million euros.

In December 2004, net income from discontinued operations resulted from (published financial statements):

- latent losses of 90 million euros in Japan,
- gains from the disposal of securities (Modelo Continente, Optique in the Czech Republic), amounting to 10.6 million euros,
- other items for a net expense of 5.4 million euros.

Note 14: Intangible fixed assets

(€ millions)	31/12/2005	31/12/2004 published
Net goodwill	10,235	9,329
Other net intangible fixed assets	657	623
Intangible fixed assets in progress	205	106
Net intangible fixed assets	11,097	10,059

Carrefour S.A.

(€ millions)	Net goodwill end 2004 IFRS	Acquisitions 2005	Impairments 2005	Foreign currency translation adjustments 2005	Net goodwill end 2005
France	3,340	281			3,621
Italy	2,971	140			3,111
Belgium	925	3			928
Spain	1,213	9	(4)		1,218
Brazil	273	53	(92)	85	319
Argentina	184			25	209
Other countries	423	390		17	830
Total	9,329	876	(96)	127	10,235

At December 31, 2005, goodwill in France consisted of Comptoirs Modernes and Euromarché, in Italy GS, in Belgium GB, in Spain Continente and the buyback of the shares of minority shareholders in Centros Comerciales Carrefour, in Brazil the Sonae stores and in Argentina Norte.

The main acquisitions in the year were Hyparlo and Pennymarket in France, the buyback of 2% of GS Spa in Italy, the acquisition of 10 Sonae hypermarkets in Brazil and for the "other countries" of the Group Hypernova (Poland), Gima and Endi (Turkey). An impairment was recorded in Brazil for the supermarkets sold off in 2005.

Change to intangible fixed assets

(€ millions)	Gross	Depreciation	Net
At January 1, 2005	13,719	(3,660)	10,059
Acquisitions	428	(251)	177
Disposals	(21)		(21)
Foreign currency adjustments	103	51	154
Changes in consolidation scope and transfer	867	(140)	727
At December 31, 2005	15,097	(4,000)	11,097

Note 15: Tangible fixed assets

(€ millions)	31/12/2005	31/12/04 published restated Dep/40yrs	31/12/2004 published
Land	3,110	3,117	3,117
Buildings	8,031	7,330	7,330
Equipment, fixtures & fittings and installations	12,064	10,987	10,987
Other fixed assets	1,108	1,077	1,077
Fixed assets in progress	1,055	844	844
Leased land	144	145	145
Leased buildings	1,268	1,217	1,217
Leased equipment, fixtures & fittings and installations	134	99	99
Other leased fixed assets	32	1	1
Gross tangible fixed assets	26,947	24,816	24,816
Depreciation	(12,319)	(10,974)	(11,132)
Depreciation of leased fixed assets	(944)	(843)	(843)
Impairment	(283)	(223)	(223)
Net tangible fixed assets	13,401	12,775	12,617

The Carrefour Group has carried out a review of all its property leasing agreements. Agreements considered to be as financial leasing agreements have been recapitalized in the opening balance, whereas other agreements have been considered as operating lease agreements.

Leased fixed assets (€ millions)	Total	Less than 1 year	1 to 5 years	More than 5 years
Financing lease agreements				
Minimum rents to be paid	805	52	196	557
Discounted value	372	34	123	215
Total sub-leasing income receivable	13			
Minimum rents paid during the year	171	NA	NA	NA
Conditional rents	NA	NA	NA	NA
Sub-leasing income	3			
Simple lease agreements				
Minimum rents to pay	5,202	751	1,780	2,670
Total minimum income to be received from sub-leasing	77	NA	NA	NA
Minimum rents paid during the year	860	NA	NA	NA
Conditional rents	31	NA	NA	NA

Note 20: Commercial receivables

(€ millions)	31/12/2005	31/12/2004 published
Trade receivables	1,246	1,236
Depreciation on bad debts	(143)	(150)
Net receivables from customers	1,103	1,137
Supplier receivables	2,348	2,011
Total	3,451	3,147

Trade receivables are primarily those due from Group franchisees. Supplier receivables correspond to rebates owed by the Group's suppliers.

Carrefour S.A.

Note 26: Borrowings

Breakdown of debt (€ millions)	31/12/2005	31/12/2004 published [2]
Bonds	7,737	7,280
Derivatives – liabilities	294	
Other borrowings	1,329	1,459
Other LT debts	188	186
Commercial paper	520	577
Leasing	455	470
Total borrowings[1]	10,523	9,972
Total restatement of borrowings	10,497	9,972

(1) Amount of borrowing restated to include the derivatives shown as assets in the balance sheet.

(2) IAS 32 and IAS 39 relating to financial instruments were applied as from January 1, 2005. Only the financial statements to December 31, 2005 are affected by the application of these standards, which explains why the fair value of the derivatives in the balance sheet was zero at December 31, 2004.

Based on equivalent accounting principles (by applying IAS 32 and IAS 39 to the 2004 financial statements), the Group's net debt would have been 7,546 million euros at the end of 2004.

At December 31, 2005, the Group had no bank covenants.

Carrefour S.A.

Carrefour S.A.

Main adjustments

Main adjustments to the income statement at December 31, 2004, drawn up in accordance with French standards, with the income statement at December 31, 2004 drawn up in accordance with IFRS

(€ millions)	Adjustments	Ending of goodwill amortization	Financial leasing (IAS 17)	Employee benefits (IAS 19)	Valuation of inventories (IAS 2)	Stock options (IFRS 2)	Other adjustments	Reclassifications
Net sales								1,038.6
Other income								1,038.6
Cost of sales	(84.2)				(84.2)			(414.4)
Gross margin from current operations	**(84.2)**				**(84.2)**			**624.2**
Sales, general and administrative expenses	(6.3)		18.5	(9.0)	(0.5)		(15.3)	(89.0)
Other income and expenses	13.8			13.8				(610.0)
Depreciation, amortization and provisions	0.4		(11.2)				11.6	30.7
Activity contribution	**(76.3)**		**7.3**	**4.8**	**(84.7)**		**(3.7)**	**(44.1)**
Non-recurring income and expenses	(37.9)		0.0	0.0	0.0	(30.6)	(7.3)	(38.1)
EBIT	**(114.2)**		**7.3**	**4.8**	**(84.7)**	**30.6**	**(11.0)**	**(82.2)**
Interest income	(48.7)		(14.1)	(32.7)	(0.6)		(1.3)	(11.7)
Income before tax	**(162.9)**		**(6.8)**	**(27.9)**	**(85.3)**	**(30.6)**	**(12.3)**	**(93.9)**
Income tax	39.8		1.9	2.8	25.2	10.7	(0.8)	(33.9)
Share of net income of accounted for by the equity method								(60.7)
Net income from recurring operations	**(123.1)**		**(4.9)**	**(25.1)**	**(60.1)**	**(19.9)**		**(120.7)**
Net income from recurring operations, Group share	(109.7)		(3.9)	(25.1)	(55.1)	(19.9)	(5.7)	(195.4)
Goodwill amortization	319.3	319.3						
Non-recurring income								246.2
Impact of discontinued operations, group share	(5.8)						(5.8)	(79.0)
Total net income, Group share	**203.8**	**319.3**	**(3.9)**	**(25.1)**	**(55.1)**	**(19.9)**	**(11.5)**	**0.0**

Main adjustments to the balance sheet at December 31, 2004, drawn up in accordance with French standards, with the balance sheet at December 31, 2004 drawn up in accordance with IFRS

(€ millions)	Consolidation of finance companies (IAS 27)	Ending of goodwill	Employee benefits (IAS 19)	Financial leasing (IAS 17)	Inventories (IAS 2)	Preopening costs and rebates	Deferred tax (IAS 12)	Other adjustments	Total adjustments	Reclassifications
Goodwill		319							319	159
Other intangible fixed assets								(10)	(10)	(306)
Tangible fixed assets	3			226				(36)	193	(473)
Financial assets	19			(3)			2		18	109
Investments in companies accounted for by the equity method	(304)								(304)	0
Deferred tax assets				(16)			(96)		(112)	131
Investment properties									0	481
Consumer credit from financial companies	1,594								1,594	0
Non-current assets	**1,312**	**319**		**207**			**(94)**	**(46)**	**1,698**	**101**
Inventories					(635)				(635)	13
Commercial receivables									0	89
Consumer credit from financial companies – short-term	1,617								1,617	10
Tax receivables									0	12
Other assets	57					(26)			31	(59)
Cash and equivalents	306								306	(34)
Current assets	**1,980**				**(635)**	**(26)**			**1,319**	**31**
Total assets	**3,292**	**319**		**207**	**(635)**	**(26)**			**3,017**	**132**
Shareholders' equity, Group share	2	319	(318)	(37)	(418)	(22)			(602)	0
Shareholders' equity, non-Group share	209		(2)	(6)	(36)	(4)			149	0
Shareholders' equity	**211**	**319**	**(320)**	**(43)**	**(454)**	**(26)**			**(453)**	**0**
Borrowings	211								0	7,340
Provisions	81		531						612	148
Deferred tax liabilities					(181)				(181)	(17)
Bank loan refinancing	255								255	70
Non-current liabilities	**547**		**211**	**(43)**	**(181)**				**233**	**(7,337)**
Borrowings – less than 1 year				245					245	359
Trade payables									0	0
Consumer credit from financial companies – short-term	2,654								2,654	0
Tax payables			(211)						0	20
Other liabilities	91			5					(115)	(380)
Current liabilities	**2,745**		**(211)**	**250**					**2,784**	**(7,338)**
Total liabilities and shareholders' equity	**3,292**	**319**	**0**	**207**	**(635)**	**(26)**			**3,017**	**132**

Carrefour S.A.

EXHIBIT 5   Summary of Tesco's IFRS-based accounting performance in the fiscal years ending February 26, 2005 and February 25, 2006[a]

	2006 (IFRS)	2005 (IFRS)
Sales	**100.0%**	**100.0%**
Cost of materials / Sales	(75.1%)	(74.6%)
Personnel expenses / Sales	(10.8%)	(10.9%)
Depreciation and amortization / Sales	(2.1%)	(2.2%)
Other operating income / Sales	0.2%	0.1%
Other operating expenses / Sales	(6.4%)	(6.7%)
Net interest expense or income / Sales	(0.3%)	(0.4%)
Investment income / Sales	0.2%	0.2%
Tax expense / Sales	(1.6%)	(1.6%)
Net profit margin	**4.0%**	**4.0%**
Net interest expense after tax / Sales	0.2%	0.2%
Net operating profit margin	4.2%	4.2%
× Net operating asset turnover	2.69	2.56
= Operating ROA	11.3%	10.9%
Spread	9.6%	8.8%
× Financial leverage	0.56	0.54
= Financial leverage gain	5.4%	4.8%
ROE = Operating ROA + Financial leverage gain	**16.7%**	**15.6%**
Operating working capital / Sales	(8.3%)	(9.2%)
Net long-term assets / Sales	45.5%	48.3%
PP&E / Sales	40.3%	42.9%
Operating working capital turnover	(12.0)	(10.9)
Net long-term asset turnover	2.2	2.1
PP&E turnover	2.5	2.3
Accounts receivable turnover	44.2	44.0
Inventory turnover	20.2	19.3
Accounts payable turnover	3.2	2.9
Days' accounts receivable	8.1	8.2
Days' inventory	17.8	18.6
Days' accounts payable	113.9	122.6

[a]The ratios in this table are based on balance sheet items' ending balances. The results for the year ended 25 February 2006 include 52 weeks for the UK and Ireland and 14 months for the majority of the remaining International Business.

Carrefour S.A.

Prospective Analysis: Forecasting

Most financial statement analysis tasks are undertaken with a forward-looking decision in mind – and, much of the time, it is useful to summarize the view developed in the analysis with an explicit forecast. Managers need forecasts to formulate business plans and provide performance targets; analysts need forecasts to help communicate their views of the firm's prospects to investors; and bankers and debt market participants need forecasts to assess the likelihood of loan repayment. Moreover, there are a variety of contexts (including but not limited to security analysis) where the forecast is usefully summarized in the form of an estimate of the firm's value. This estimate can be viewed as an attempt to best reflect in a single summary statistic the manager's or analyst's view of the firm's prospects.

Prospective analysis includes two tasks – forecasting and valuation – that together represent approaches to explicitly summarizing the analyst's forward-looking views. In this chapter we focus on forecasting; valuation is the topic of the next two chapters. Forecasting is not so much a separate analysis as it is a way of summarizing what has been learned through business strategy analysis, accounting analysis, and financial analysis. However, there are certain techniques and knowledge that can help a manager or analyst to structure the best possible forecast, conditional on what has been learned in the previous steps. Below we summarize an approach to structuring the forecast, offer information useful in getting started, explore the relationship between the other analytical steps and forecasting, and give detailed steps to forecast earnings, balance sheet data, and cash flows. The key concepts discussed in this chapter are illustrated using a forecast for Loewe, the manufacturer of luxury audio and video systems examined in Chapter 5.

THE OVERALL STRUCTURE OF THE FORECAST

The best way to forecast future performance is to do it comprehensively – producing not only an earnings forecast, but also a forecast of cash flows and the balance sheet. A **comprehensive forecasting approach** is useful, even in cases where one might be interested primarily in a single facet of performance, because it guards against unrealistic implicit assumptions. For example, if an analyst forecasts growth in sales and earnings for several years without explicitly considering the required increases in working capital and plant assets and the associated financing, the forecast might possibly imbed unreasonable assumptions about asset turnover, leverage, or equity capital infusions.

A comprehensive approach involves many forecasts, but in most cases they are all linked to the behavior of a few key "drivers." The drivers vary according to the type of business involved, but for businesses outside the financial services sector, the sales forecast is nearly always one of the key drivers; profit margin is another. When asset turnover is expected to remain stable – often a realistic assumption – working capital accounts and investment in plant should track the growth in sales closely. Most major expenses also track sales, subject to expected shifts in profit margins. By linking forecasts of such amounts to the sales forecast, one can avoid internal inconsistencies and unrealistic implicit assumptions.

In some contexts the manager or analyst is interested ultimately in a forecast of cash flows, not earnings per se. Nevertheless, even forecasts of cash flows tend to be grounded in practice on forecasts of accounting numbers, including sales, earnings, assets, and liabilities. Of course it would be possible in principle to move *directly* to forecasts of cash flows – inflows from customers, outflows to suppliers and laborers, and so forth – and in some businesses this is a convenient way to proceed. In most cases, however, the growth prospects, profitability, and investment and financing needs of the firm are more readily framed in terms of accrual-based sales, operating earnings, assets, and liabilities. These amounts can then be converted to cash flow measures by adjusting for the effects of non-cash expenses and expenditures for working capital and plant.

A practical framework for forecasting

The most practical approach to forecasting a company's financial statements is to focus on projecting **"condensed" financial statements**, as used in the ratio analysis in Chapter 5, rather than attempting to project detailed financial statements that the company reports. There are several reasons for this recommendation. First, this approach involves making a relatively small set of assumptions about the future of the firm, so the analyst will have more ability to think about each of the assumptions carefully. A detailed line item forecast is likely to be very tedious, and an analyst may not have a good basis to make all the assumptions necessary for such forecasts. Further, for most purposes condensed financial statements are all that are needed for analysis and decision making. We therefore approach the task of financial forecasting with this framework.

Recall that the condensed income statement that we used in Chapter 5 consists of the following elements: sales, net operating profits after tax (NOPAT), net interest expense after tax, taxes, and net profit. The condensed balance sheet consists of: net operating working capital, net non-current assets, net debt, and equity. Also recall that we start with a balance sheet at the beginning of the forecasting period. Assumptions about how we use the beginning balance sheet and run the firm's operations will lead to the income statement for the forecasting period; assumptions about investment in working capital and non-current assets, and how we finance these assets, results in a balance sheet at the end of the forecasting period.

To forecast the condensed income statement, one needs to begin with an assumption about next-period sales. Beyond that, assumptions about NOPAT margin, interest rate on beginning debt, and tax rate are all that are needed to prepare the condensed income statement for the period.

To forecast the condensed balance sheet for the end of the period (or the equivalent, the beginning of the next period), we need to make the following additional assumptions:

1 The ratio of operating working capital to sales to estimate the level of working capital needed to support those sales.

2 The ratio of net operating non-current assets to the following year's sales to calculate the expected level of net operating non-current assets.

3 The ratio of net debt to capital to estimate the levels of debt and equity needed to finance the estimated amount of assets in the balance sheet.

Once we have the condensed income statement and balance sheet, it is relatively straightforward to compute the condensed cash flow statement, including cash flow from operations before working capital investments, cash flow from operations after working capital investments, free cash flow available to debt and equity, and free cash flow available to equity.

Below we discuss how best to make the necessary assumptions to forecast the condensed income statement, balance sheet, and cash flow statements below.

PERFORMANCE BEHAVIOR: A STARTING POINT

Every forecast has, at least implicitly, an initial "benchmark" or point of departure – some notion of how a particular amount, such as sales or earnings, would be expected to behave in the absence of detailed information. For example, in starting to contemplate fiscal 2009 profitability for Loewe, one must begin somewhere. A possibility is to begin with the 2008 performance. Another starting point might be 2008 performance adjusted for recent trends. A third possibility that might seem reasonable – but one that generally turns out not to be very useful – is the average performance over several prior years.

By the time one has completed a business strategy analysis, an accounting analysis, and a detailed financial analysis, the resulting forecast might differ significantly from the original point of departure. Nevertheless, simply for purposes of having a starting point that can help anchor the detailed analysis, it is useful to know how certain key financial statistics behave "on average" for all firms.

In the case of some key statistics, such as earnings, a point of departure based only on prior behavior of the number is more powerful than one might expect. Research demonstrates that some such benchmarks for earnings are almost as accurate as the forecasts of professional security analysts, who have access to a rich information set (we return to this point in more detail below). Thus the benchmark is often not only a good starting point but also close to the amount forecast after detailed analysis. Large departures from the benchmark could be justified only in cases where the firm's situation is demonstrably unusual.

Reasonable points of departure for forecasts of key accounting numbers can be based on the evidence summarized below. Such evidence may also be useful for checking the reasonableness of a completed forecast.

Sales growth behavior

Sales growth rates tend to be "mean-reverting": firms with above-average or below-average rates of sales growth tend to revert over time to a "normal" level (historically in the range of 6 to 10 percent for European firms) within three to ten years. Figure 6.1 documents this effect for 1992 through 2008 for all the publicly traded European (nonfinancial) firms covered by Thomson Financial's Worldscope database. All firms are ranked in terms of their sales growth in 1992 (year 1) and formed into five portfolios based on the relative ranking of their sales growth in that year. Firms in portfolio 1 are in the top 20 percent of rankings in terms of their sales growth in 1992, those in portfolio 2 fall into the next 20 percent, while those in portfolio 5 are in the bottom 20 percent when ranked by sales growth. The sales growth rates of firms in each of these five portfolios are traced from 1992 through the subsequent nine years (years 2 to 10). The same experiment is repeated with every year between 1993 and 1999 as the base year (year 1). The results are averaged over the eight experiments and the resulting sales growth rates of each of the five portfolios for years 1 through 10 are plotted in the figure.

The figure shows that the group of firms with the highest growth initially – sales growth rates of just over 65 percent – experience a decline to about 23 percent growth rate

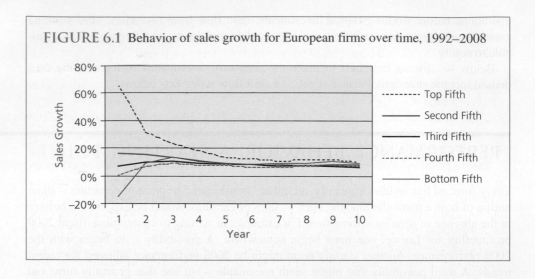

FIGURE 6.1 Behavior of sales growth for European firms over time, 1992–2008

within two years and are never above 23 percent in the next seven years. Those with the lowest initial sales growth rates, minus 15 percent, experience an increase to about a 13 percent growth rate by year 3, and average about 9 percent annual growth in years 4 through 10. One explanation for the pattern of sales growth seen in Figure 6.1 is that as industries and companies mature, their growth rate slows down due to demand saturation and intraindustry competition. Therefore, even when a firm is growing rapidly at present, it is generally unrealistic to extrapolate the current high growth indefinitely. Of course, how quickly a firm's growth rate reverts to the average depends on the characteristics of its industry and its own competitive position within an industry.

Earnings behavior

Earnings have been shown on average to follow a process that can be approximated by a "random walk" or "random walk with drift." Thus the prior year's earnings figure is a good starting point in considering future earnings potential. As will be explained, it is reasonable to adjust this simple benchmark for the earnings changes of the most recent quarter (that is, changes relative to the comparable quarter of the prior year after controlling for the long-run trend in the series). Even a simple random walk forecast – one that predicts next year's earnings will be equal to last year's earnings – is surprisingly useful. One study documents that professional analysts' year-ahead forecasts are only 22 percent more accurate, on average, than a simple random walk forecast.[1] Thus a final earnings forecast will *usually* not differ dramatically from a random walk benchmark.

The implication of the evidence is that, in beginning to contemplate future earnings possibilities, a useful number to start with is last year's earnings; the average level of earnings over several prior years is not useful. Long-term trends in earnings tend to be sustained on average, and so they are also worthy of consideration. If quarterly or semiannual data are also included, then some consideration should usually be given to any departures from the long-run trend that occurred in the most recent quarter or half year. For most firms, these most recent changes tend to be partially repeated in subsequent quarters or half years.[2]

Returns on equity behavior

Given that prior earnings serves as a useful benchmark for future earnings, one might expect the same to be true of rates of return on investment, like ROE. That, however, is not the case for two reasons. First, even though the *average* firm tends to sustain the current earnings level, this is not true of firms with unusual levels of ROE. Firms with abnormally high (low) ROE tend to experience earnings declines (increases).[3]

Second, firms with higher ROEs tend to expand their investment bases more quickly than others, which causes the denominator of the ROE to increase. Of course, if firms could earn returns on the new investments that match the returns on the old ones, then the level of ROE would be maintained. However, firms have difficulty pulling that off. Firms with higher ROEs tend to find that, as time goes by, their earnings growth does not keep pace with growth in their investment base, and ROE ultimately falls.

The resulting behavior of ROE and other measures of return on investment is characterized as "mean-reverting": firms with above-average or below-average rates of return tend to revert over time to a "normal" level (for ROE, historically in the range of 8 to 12 percent for European firms) within no more than ten years.[4] Figure 6.2 documents this effect for European firms from 1992 through 2008. All firms are ranked in terms of their ROE in 1992 (year 1) and formed into five portfolios. Firms in portfolio 1 have the top 20 percent ROE rankings in 1992, those in portfolio 2 fall into the next 20 percent, and those in portfolio 5 have the bottom 20 percent. The average ROE of firms in each of these five portfolios is then traced through nine subsequent years (years 2 to 10). The same experiment is repeated with every year between 1993 and 1999 as the base year (year 1), and the subsequent years as years +2 to +10. Figure 6.2 plots the average ROE of each of the five portfolios in years 1 to 10 averaged across these eight experiments.

Though the five portfolios start out in year 1 with a wide range of ROEs (−29 percent to +48 percent), by year 10 the pattern of **mean-reversion** is clear. The most profitable group of firms initially – with average ROEs of 48 percent – experience a decline to 18 percent within three years. By year 10 this group of firms has an ROE of 13 percent. Those with the lowest initial ROEs (−24 percent) experience a dramatic increase in ROE and then level off at 2 percent in year 10.

The pattern in Figure 6.2 is not a coincidence; it is exactly what the economics of competition would predict. The tendency of high ROEs to fall is a reflection of high profitability attracting competition; the tendency of low ROEs to rise reflects the mobility of capital away from unproductive ventures toward more profitable ones.

Despite the general tendencies documented in Figure 6.2, there are some firms whose ROEs may remain above or below normal levels for long periods of time. In some cases the phenomenon reflects the strength of a sustainable competitive advantage (e.g., Wal-Mart), but in other cases it is purely an artifact of conservative accounting methods.

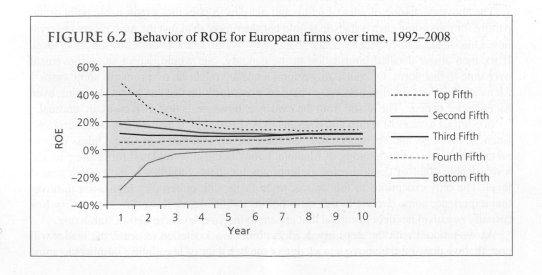

FIGURE 6.2 Behavior of ROE for European firms over time, 1992–2008

A good example of the latter phenomenon is pharmaceutical firms, whose major economic asset, the intangible value of research and development, is not recorded on the balance sheet and is therefore excluded from the denominator of ROE. For those firms, one could reasonably expect high ROEs – in excess of 20 percent – over the long run, even in the face of strong competitive forces.

The behavior of components of ROE

The behavior of rates of return on equity can be analyzed further by looking at the behavior of its key components. Recall from Chapter 5 that ROEs and profit margins are linked as follows:

$$\text{ROE} = \text{Operating ROA} + (\text{Operating ROA} - \text{Net interest rate after tax})$$
$$\times \text{Net financial leverage}$$
$$= (\text{NOPAT margin} \times \text{Operating asset turnover}) +$$
$$(\text{Spread} \times \text{Net financial leverage})$$

The time-series behavior of the components of ROE for European companies for 1992 through 2008 are shown in a series of figures in the appendix to this chapter. Some major conclusions can be drawn from these figures:

1 Operating asset turnover tends to be rather stable, in part because it is so much a function of the technology of the industry. The only exception to this is the set of firms with very high asset turnover, which tends to decline somewhat over time before stabilizing.

2 Net financial leverage also tends to be stable, simply because management policies on capital structure aren't often changed.

3 NOPAT margin and spread stand out as the most variable component of ROE; if the forces of competition drive abnormal ROEs toward more normal levels, the change is most likely to arrive in the form of changes in profit margins and the spread. The change in spread is itself driven by changes in NOPAT margin, because the cost of borrowing is likely to remain stable if leverage remains stable.

To summarize, profit margins, like ROEs, tend to be driven by competition to "normal" levels over time. What constitutes normal varies widely according to the technology employed within an industry and the corporate strategy pursued by the firm, both of which influence turnover and leverage.[5] In a fully competitive equilibrium, profit margins should remain high for firms that must operate with a low turnover, and vice versa.

The above discussion of rates of return and margins implies that a reasonable point of departure for forecasting such a statistic should consider more than just the most recent observation. One should also consider whether that rate or margin is above or below a normal level. If so, then absent detailed information to the contrary, one would expect some movement over time to that norm. Of course this central tendency might be overcome in some cases – for example, where the firm has erected barriers to competition that can protect margins, even for extended periods. The lesson from the evidence, however, is that such cases are unusual.

In contrast to rates of return and margins, it is reasonable to assume that asset turnover, financial leverage, and net interest rate remain relatively constant over time. Unless there is an explicit change in technology or financial policy being contemplated for future periods, a reasonable point of departure for assumptions for these variables is the current period level. The only exceptions to this appear to be firms with either very high asset turnover that experience some decline in this ratio before stabilizing, or those firms with very low (usually negative) net debt to capital that appear to increase leverage before stabilizing.

As we proceed with the steps involved in producing a detailed forecast, the reader will note that we draw on the above knowledge of the behavior of accounting numbers to some extent. However, it is important to keep in mind that a knowledge of *average* behavior will not fit all firms well. The art of financial statements analysis requires not only knowing what the "normal" patterns are but also having expertise in identifying those firms that will *not* follow the norm.

RELATIONSHIP OF FORECASTING TO THE OTHER ANALYSES

In general, the mean-reverting behavior of sales growth and return on equity that is demonstrated by the broader market should hold true. The starting point for any forecast should therefore be the time-series behavior of the various measures of firm performance, as discussed. However, the three levels of analysis that precede prospective analysis – strategy, accounting, and financial performance – can also lead to informed decisions by an analyst about expected performance, especially in the short and medium term.

We use the example of Loewe, the manufacturer of luxury audio and video systems discussed in Chapter 5, to illustrate the strategic analysis that informs the forecast as well as the mechanics of forecasting. A projection of the future performance of Loewe for the year 2009 must be grounded in an understanding of questions such as these:

■ From business strategy analysis. Has Loewe been able to create a brand reputation and a retailing infrastructure that will allow it to continue to dominate the market for luxury audio and video systems in Germany, Austria, Switzerland and the Benelux? Will Loewe be able to replicate this market dominance outside these countries? Will Loewe's shift in focus towards Bang & Olufsen's target customer group eventually force the company to raise its R&D spending to the levels of its competitor? Will Loewe's bargaining power over its component suppliers decrease as they cut excess capacity and/or demand recovers? How will major sporting events, such as the FIFA World Cup 2010, affect consumers' demand for large screen flat panel televisions? Will Loewe's short-term sales growth and gross margins come under pressure as the economic downturn continues, possibly because customers become more price sensitive?

■ From accounting analysis. Are there any aspects of Loewe's accounting that suggest past earnings and assets are misstated, or expenses or liabilities are misstated? If so, what are the implications for future accounting statements?

■ From financial analysis. What are the sources of Loewe's superior performance in 2008? Is this performance sustainable? Is there any discernable pattern in Loewe's past performance? If so, are there any reasons why this trend is likely to continue or change?

The key challenge in building a forecast, therefore, is to predict whether Loewe will be able to grow its sales, both in the short-term and the long-term, and maintain its margins and superior turnover or whether competition, the continuing economic downturn, or the company's further development of its differentiation strategy will force Loewe to follow the general mean-reverting trends discussed above.

Macroeconomic and industry factors

In the first half of 2009, the European economy was in a period of recession. Although the financial crisis found its origin in the US – where loans and mortgages of dubious quality had been securitized and sold on to investors—it strongly affected the European economy through at least two channels. First, European banks had also heavily invested in

TABLE 6.1 Realized and expected economic growth rates

	2006	2007	2008	2009e	2010e
European Union	4.7%	4.4%	3.9%	−1.0%	0.9%
Germany	2.8%	1.9%	2.7%	−0.2%	0.0%
Weighted average of Loewe's European markets	3.7%	3.1%	3.4%	−0.6%	0.4%

securitized financial assets. Because the value of these assets plunged as the crisis intensified, banks' financial strength deteriorated significantly in 2008. This led the European banks, like their worldwide peers, to freeze interbank lending, which in turn reduced the availability of commercial credit and halted economic growth. Second, a drastic slowdown in international trade significantly affected the growth of European countries whose economy depended strongly on exports, such as Germany, Ireland and the Netherlands. During the last quarter of 2008, the average nominal growth in Private Consumption – an aggregate measure of households' purchases – in the European Union was −0.8 percent, compared to 1.3 percent one year earlier. Early 2009 the Directorate-General for Economic and Financial Affairs of the European Commission forecast that annual Private Consumption growth in the EU for 2009 and 2010 would be −1.0 and 0.9 percent, respectively. Table 6.1 shows the realized and predicted Private Consumption growth rates for the EU, Loewe's primary market Germany, and a set of European countries where Loewe operates. These growth rates illustrate that while economy-wide growth was around 3–4 percent during the period 2006–2008, a standstill in economic growth was expected for the next two years.

The consumer electronics industry is a cyclical industry. Because consumers tend to delay their purchases of durable goods such as televisions during periods of economic uncertainty, consumer electronics sales typically vary with economic cycles. However, technological innovations can cause the industry to grow at a faster rate than the economy, on average. For example, the introduction of plat panel televisions boosted the growth of television sales in Europe at the end of the mid-2000s as more and more consumers started to replace their old CRT televisions with plat panels. At the end of 2008, CRT replacement still constituted a significant proportion of all television sales, given that 53 percent of all European households did not yet own a plat panel television. Future technological developments that could further boost European television sales in 2009 and beyond were the increasing availability of high definition broadcasting and the introduction of ultra slim televisions.

The growth rates in the televisions industry are greatly relevant to Loewe because 87 percent of the company's revenues come from the sales of televisions. Table 6.2 displays the realized and predicted growth rates in the European television and flat panel television markets. The industry growth rates are higher than the economy-wide growth rates but clearly fluctuate with the economic cycle. The question immediately arises of why Loewe, with realized sales growth rates of 7.1, 8.9 and 0.4 percent in 2006, 2007 and 2008, respectively, has not been able to keep up with the growth of the market. One obvious explanation is that during the past few years the company's increasing focus on differentiation forced it to forego sales growth to benefit its brand image and profit margins. In fact, whereas during the years 2006 to 2008 the average price of a 40 inch LCD television decreased from €2.8 thousand to €1 thousand, Loewe kept its price of such a television almost constant at about €3.9 thousand. Although this decision might have kept Loewe from improving sales volumes, it helped the company to preserve its image as a premium brand and improve its gross margin from 25 percent in 2006 to 32 percent in 2008.

TABLE 6.2 Realized and expected industry growth rates

	2006	2007	2008	2009e	2010e
European TV market	30.5%	11.2%	0.9%	0.0%	10.9%
European LCD TV market	95.5%	40.4%	10.3%	7.5%	16.2%

Next to economy-wide and industry growth, Loewe's performance is sensitive to changes in foreign exchange rates. In particular, because Loewe makes purchases of LCD panels in US dollars, an appreciation (depreciation) of the dollar can negatively (positively) impact the company's profit margin. In 2008 the dollar-euro exchange rate fluctuated strongly, reaching a high of €1.60 per dollar versus a low of €1.23 per dollar. While Loewe hedged approximately fifty percent of its exposure to the US dollar, the net effect of the exchange rate fluctuations was to reduce the company's manufacturing costs.

Future exchange rates strongly depend on future developments in economic growth, inflation rates, trade balances, interest rates, investment flows and other economic factors, making the prediction of exchange rates a complicated task. In the first half of 2009, the exchange rate of the dollar to the euro was still volatile and it was uncertain in which direction the exchange rate would move in the near future. For the purpose of forecasting Loewe's near term financial performance, a prudent assumption is that the exchange rate will remain around its current level.

Sales growth

A good starting point for developing a forecast of short-term sales growth is management's outlook. Management typically provides guidance about future sales and margins in the Management Report section of the annual report but sometimes also in interim reports, press releases or analyst conferences. The analyst's task is to critically challenge the assumptions underlying management's expectations, using information about macroeconomic, industry and firm-specific factors.

In the 2008 annual report Loewe's management expressed the expectation that the company's sales would grow in 2009, primarily due to the replacements of ordinary CRT televisions with LCD televisions, technological innovations, and consumers' increased awareness of the Loewe brand. There are, however, several reasons to expect that near-term sales growth, if at all positive, is moderate:

- Although replacement sales and technological innovations seem to be important drivers of growth in the consumer electronics industry, they are less so during an economic downturn. This is because consumers tend to delay the purchase of luxury goods in times of economic uncertainty.

- Major sporting events, such as the Olympics or the FIFA World Cup, typically trigger consumers to purchase innovative technological products and, in particular, replace their old CRT television with a flat-panel display. In contrast to 2008 – the year of the China Summer Olympics and the European UEFA Cup in Austria and Switzerland – there will be no important sporting events in 2009.

- Historically Loewe has grown at a slower rate than the European LCD televisions market. Two of the factors driving this growth discrepancy – the company's move towards a purer differentiation strategy and its presence in lower growth segments such as the audio systems segment – remain present, especially in the near term.

Some of the same factors that dampen Loewe's growth prospects in the near term may help to boost the company's growth in the longer term. First, the delay of purchases in 2009 will likely amplify consumer demand in 2010 and the years beyond, when the economy recovers. Second, events such as the Winter Olympics and the FIFA World Cup in 2010 will stimulate television sales, starting in late 2009 and going forward into 2010.

New technological innovations will keep contributing to sales growth in the years after 2009. In the shorter term, Germany's full switch to HD television broadcasting in 2010 is expected to boost consumers' replacement sales in Loewe's home market. In the longer term, slim-display LCD televisions are expected to replace the current generation of flat-panel displays. Years of experience and a strong reputation in the top segment of the European LCD televisions market could help Loewe to also become one of the primary European suppliers of ultra slim large-screen televisions and, consequently, benefit from this growth impetus.

A potential new growth driver for Loewe in the longer term is the expansion into new geographical markets such as Scandinavia, Eastern Europe and Russia. Although the company has long focused on a few concentrated markets, management has expressed its desire to upgrade its operations in Italy, France and the UK and to expand into new markets. Part of the company's international growth strategy is to open flagship stores, which management refers to as galleries, in large metropolitan areas such as Paris, Hong Kong, Istanbul and Riyadh. Loewe's expansion plans foresee an increase in the number of galleries by 73, or 40 percent, in 2009. These galleries should further increase consumers' brand awareness and support long-term sales growth outside the company's current markets.

Loewe's international operations present an interesting forecasting challenge. In the past few years the company's operations in markets such as Italy and the UK have not been invariably successful. Growth in these markets has typically lagged behind home growth. Loewe's ability to replicate its home market success in foreign growth markets thus remains to be seen.

Overall, the projections in Table 6.3 show a recession-driven standstill in 2009 and a steep improvement in the growth of television sales during the years 2010 to 2012, when the economic recovery, sporting events, technological innovations and Loewe's international expansion provide an impetus to the company's growth. While long-term trends in the television market are uncertain, it is reasonable to assume that Loewe will not be immune to the long-run forces of competition and mean reversion. Consequently, television sales growth forecast after 2012 gradually revert the average growth rate of the European economy.

In 2008, 13 percent of Loewe's revenues came from the sales of DVD and audio systems to consumers and electronic components to other manufacturers. Because growth in these other revenues has typically lagged behind growth in television sales, growth forecasts for these revenues follow the expected growth rates of the European economy. The overall sales growth rate is the weighted average of the television sales growth rate and the other sales growth rate.

TABLE 6.3 Forecasted sales growth for loewe

Forecast year	2009	2010	2011	2012	2013	2014	2015	2016	2017	2018
TV sales	0.0%	5.0%	10.0%	12.0%	10.5%	9.0%	7.5%	6.0%	4.5%	4.0%
Other sales	−1.0%	0.9%	3.0%	4.0%	4.0%	4.0%	4.0%	4.0%	4.0%	4.0%
Overall Sales Growth	−0.1%	4.5%	9.1%	11.0%	9.8%	8.5%	7.1%	5.8%	4.5%	4.0%

NOPAT MARGINS

During the past few years Loewe has worked towards positioning itself as a premium brand. It is therefore unlikely that the economic climate in 2009 will persuade the company to temporarily cut sales prices, thereby reducing its gross margin, as such actions would put the company's carefully developed brand image at risk. The following two opposing forces will be relevant drivers of the company's future gross margins:

- Suppliers of electronic components have been cutting capacity to cope with the economic decline. The reduction in suppliers' overcapacity may weaken Loewe's bargaining position and, consequently, increase its material costs.

- Although Loewe has been moving in the direction of Bang & Olufsen's pure differentiation strategy, the company's gross margin of 32 percent in 2008 was still substantially lower than B&O's gross margin of 47 percent. Consumers' increasing awareness of Loewe as a premium brand should allow to company to gradually increase its price premium.

Whereas the first factor will put pressure on Loewe's gross margin in the short term, the second factor will stimulate a gradual improvement in gross margin by several percentage points in the medium term. In the long run, however, it is not unlikely that Loewe's gross margin will come down a little as more competitors enter the premium segment. In particular, the declining growth in replacement sales may stimulate large electronics manufacturers operating in the commodity segment to divert their attention to the top end of the televisions market.

The shift in strategy, of course, also requires investments in marketing, sales, and development. Loewe's current spending on sales and administration (23 percent of total sales) is already close to that of its rival Bang & Olufsen (24-25 percent of total sales pre-2008), making it less likely that the selling, general and administrative expense to sales ratio will rise much in the future. In contrast, however, it is not unthinkable that Loewe's strategy will force the company to step up its research and development activities because differentiation in the consumer electronics market requires continuous innovation. As the example of Bang & Olufsen shows, greater reliance on in-house R&D exposes Loewe to the risk of declining R&D productivity or a drying R&D pipeline, potentially leading to an explosion in R&D expenses as a percent of sales. However, if Loewe carefully plans and monitors its R&D expansion, the company should be able to limit the increase in the development (amortization) expense to sales ratio to a few percentage points.

Under the assumptions that:

1 The gross margin will gradually increase because of an increasing price premium, though less strongly in earlier years because of increasing material costs.
2 The SG&A expense to sales ratio will only moderately increase.
3 The R&D (amortization) expense to sales ratio will increase by a few percentage points.
4 The effective tax rate will remain stable.

Loewe's future NOPAT margin will follow the pattern depicted in Table 6.4.

Working capital to sales

During the past two years Loewe's has made similar net investments in working capital as its competitor Bang & Olufsen (i.e., 14-17 percent of sales). The composition of these

TABLE 6.4 Forecasted sales growth for Loewe

Forecast year	2009	2010	2011	2012	2013	2014	2015	2016	2017	2018
Gross margin	32.0%	33.0%	34.0%	35.0%	36.0%	37.0%	37.0%	36.5%	36.0%	35.5%
SG&A expenses	−23.0%	−23.3%	−23.6%	−23.9%	−24.2%	−24.5%	−24.8%	−24.8%	−24.8%	−24.8%
Other expenses	−1.5%	−2.0%	−2.5%	−3.0%	−3.5%	−4.0%	−4.5%	−4.5%	−4.5%	−4.5%
Tax expense (net of interest tax shield)	−2.3%	−2.4%	−2.5%	−2.5%	−2.6%	−2.6%	−2.3%	−2.1%	−2.0%	−1.8%
NOPAT margin	5.2%	5.3%	5.4%	5.6%	5.7%	5.9%	5.3%	4.9%	4.6%	4.2%

investments differed slightly, possibly because of differences in the companies' distribution strategies. In particular, Loewe kept inventory levels at a minimum by storing all finished goods in one central warehouse in Germany and shipping directly to its customers. In several countries the company also used independent distributors. A potential flip side of this strategy is that Loewe needs to extend more short-term credit to its customers and distributors, thereby making its trade receivables to sales ratio higher than that of Bang & Olufsen. At the beginning of 2009, there were no signs that Loewe had any intention of changing this distribution strategy.

In 2008 Loewe experienced a decline in working capital turnover. This decline was, however, primarily caused by an above-normal amount of beginning trade receivables that the company recognized on its opening balance sheet after a very successful fourth quarter in 2007. Therefore, it is reasonable to expect that Loewe's net working capital to sales ratio will revert to its pre-2008 level.

Non-current assets to sales

The above-described expected increase in development outlays will automatically lead to an increase in Loewe's net non-current assets to sales ratio because their temporary capitalization creates a non-current asset on the company's balance sheet. In particular, under the assumption that the expected economic useful life of Loewe's marginal investments in development is three years, a 1 percent (of sales) increase in development expenditures causes a 1.5 percent (of sales) increase in net non-current assets (in the long run).[6]

Loewe should be able to realize its future expansion plan and further development of the differentiation strategy with minimal other changes to its non-current assets to sales ratio. The company's distribution network consists of independent retailers. The planned worldwide expansion of Loewe's network of galleries, which operate under franchise agreements, thus requires limited capital expenditure. Similarly, outsourcing the production of electronic components, such as flat-panel displays, helps the company to minimize its investments in production facilities. A possible source of moderate changes to Loewe's non-current assets to sales ratio is the required additional investments in presentation systems for retailers that need to be made as the company replaces more of its shop-in-shop outlets with galleries.

Capital structure

At the end of fiscal year 2008 Loewe had a substantial amount of excess cash. Assuming that the company needs a cash balance of 2 percent of sales to finance its daily operations, excess cash amounted to almost 12 percent of net assets. It is uncertain which actions the company will undertake to dispose of its excess cash. Two likely options are that Loewe will use the amount to finance the expansion of its gallery network or redistribute the amount to its shareholders, either through share repurchases or a special dividend. Under both scenarios, the company's net debt to net capital ratio will increase by up to 12 percentage points. Given the financial strength of the firm, such a change in leverage should not have any impact on the cost of debt.

MAKING FORECASTS

The analysis of Loewe's performance in Chapter 5, and the preceding discussions about general market behavior and Loewe's strategic positioning, leads to the conclusion that while the economic slowdown may stall Loewe's growth in 2009, in the medium-term it is likely that the company can defy the forces of competition and, at least temporarily, earn substantial abnormal profits.

Table 6.5 shows the forecasting assumptions for years 2009 to 2018. Table 6.6 shows the forecasted income statements for these same fiscal years, and beginning of the year balance sheets for years 2010 to 2019. Recall that the balance sheet at the beginning of fiscal 2009 is the same as the balance sheet reported by the company for the year ending December 31, 2008. We have chosen a ten-year forecasting period because we believe that the firm should reach such a steady state of performance by the end of the period that a few simplifying assumptions about its subsequent performance are sufficient to estimate firm value (discussed in further detail in Chapter 8). For example, as we will discuss in Chapter 8, a reasonable assumption for the period following the forecasting period is that a portion of the firm's abnormal profits will be competed away and the performance of the firm will revert towards the mean, as has been the general trend that we have seen earlier in the chapter.

We discuss below the forecasting assumptions, which are based on the foregoing discussion of the various elements that comprise the forecast.

The overall one year ahead forecast

As mentioned above, we have the actual balance sheet for the beginning of 2009, so there is no need to forecast this. Making a short-term income statement forecast, such as a one

TABLE 6.5 Forecasting assumptions for Loewe

Forecast year	2009	2010	2011	2012	2013	2014	2015	2016	2017	2018
Sales growth rate	−0.1%	4.5%	9.1%	11.0%	9.8%	8.5%	7.1%	5.8%	4.5%	4.0%
NOPAT margin	5.2%	5.3%	5.4%	5.6%	5.7%	5.9%	5.3%	4.9%	4.6%	4.2%
Beginning net working capital/sales	14.0%	14.0%	14.0%	14.0%	14.0%	14.0%	14.0%	14.0%	14.0%	14.0%
Beginning net non-current assets/sales	18.5%	19.5%	20.5%	22.0%	22.5%	23.0%	23.5%	24.0%	24.5%	25.0%
Beginning net debt to net capital	25.9%	37.9%	37.9%	37.9%	37.9%	37.9%	37.9%	37.9%	37.9%	37.9%
After tax cost of net debt	2.6%	2.6%	2.6%	2.6%	2.6%	2.6%	2.6%	2.6%	2.6%	2.6%

Note: In addition to these assumptions, we also assume that sales will continue to grow at 4.0 percent in 2019 and all the balance sheet ratios remain constant, to compute the beginning balance sheet for 2019 and cash flows for 2018.

year ahead forecast, is usually a straightforward extrapolation of recent performance. This is a particularly valid approach for an established company for several reasons. First, the company is unlikely to effect major changes to its operating and financing policies in the short-term unless it is in the middle of a restructuring program. Second, the beginning of the year balance sheet for any given year will put constraints on operating activities during that fiscal year. For example, inventories at the beginning of the year will determine to some extent the sales activities during the year; stores or production facilities in operation at the beginning of the year also determine to some extent the level of sales achievable during the year. To put it another way, since our discussion above shows that asset turns for a company do not usually change significantly in a short time, sales in any period are to some extent constrained by the beginning of the period assets in place in the company's balance sheet. As discussed earlier, the economic crisis complicates the short-term income statement forecast a little as it may temporarily distort sales growth and profit margins.

Our strategic analysis led to an expectation of slowing growth in both of Loewe's product segments, primarily because of the overall slowdown in the growth of the European economy. As shown in Table 6.5, we assume that sales will decline at −0.1 percent, which is marginally lower than the 0.4 percent sales growth that the company achieved in 2008. This growth rate leads to an expected sales level in 2008 of €373.5 million, down from €374.0 million in 2008 as Table 6.6 shows.

The next key assumption to be made about Loewe's performance in 2009 is its NOPAT margin. We expect that Loewe's margin decreases from 5.5 percent in 2008 to 5.2 percent in 2009. Although Loewe's suppliers may raise their selling prices, the company's premium strategy should help it to maintain its gross margin of 32 percent from the previous year. Loewe's SG&A and other expense to sales ratios will slightly increase because of the company's increased investment in marketing, distribution and development.

The next two forecast items – net operating working capital to sales and net operating non-current assets to sales – have already been determined by the balance sheet position at December 31, 2008. Therefore, we are starting with a given level of assets to work with. So we can either make an assumption about sales growth rate and check the implied ratio of beginning net assets to sales for reasonableness, or make an assumption of the beginning net assets to sales ratio for the year and check for the reasonableness of the implied sales growth rate. In other words, we are free to make only one of the two assumptions – either sales growth or net asset turns. In subsequent years in the forecast horizon, we relax this constraint because we can build up both a desired beginning balance sheet and income statement for the following years.

The third assumption we make to forecast Loewe's income statement for 2008 relates to the after-tax cost of debt. The company's beginning level of debt and its beginning debt to capital ratio for 2008 are determined by its actual balance sheet at the start of the fiscal year. Although the firm temporarily has excess cash, the effect on leverage is not likely to affect its cost of debt (adjusting for any changes in overall market interest rates). As a result, it is reasonable to assume that the firm's relative cost of debt will be similar to its cost of borrowing in prior years as reflected in the net interest expense to net debt ratio. Given stable interest rates, the cost of borrowing is expected to remain stable at 3.8 percent, or 2.6 percent on an after-tax basis.

These assumptions together lead to a projected €18.5 million net income in fiscal year 2009 compared with a reported net income of €19.8 million in 2008.

Overall forecasts for years two to ten

In making longer-term forecasts, in this instance for years two to ten, we have relied on our analysis of the firm and its prospects as well as the time-series behavior of various performance ratios discussed earlier. Given our assumptions of increased growth in the European market for LCD televisions, we assume that Loewe will be able to gradually increase its sales growth rate to 11 percent in years two to four. Thereafter, sales growth will gradually decline as the European LCD TV adoption rate increases, Loewe finds fewer locations outside its current markets in which to profitably expand, and the intensity of competition gets stronger in Loewe's premium segment.

We assume a pattern of steadily increasing and then declining NOPAT margins over time. The assumption that the NOPAT margin increases in the medium-term is consistent with our assessment of effects of Loewe's differentiation strategy. The assumed time-series trend for the second half of the forecasting period is consistent with that documented earlier in the chapter for firms with initially high NOPAT and with our assessment of the competitive response of the other players in Loewe's industry. While Loewe clearly has a significant competitive advantage over its rivals, it is prudent to assume, given the history of European firms, that this advantage will decline over time. Overall, we assume that the company's NOPAT margin reaches its peak of 5.9 percent in year 6 and then declines to reach a value of 4.2 percent by year 10.

Loewe currently has a beginning net working capital to sales ratio of 17.3 percent. Based on the sales growth assumption for year one, this ratio is projected to decline to 14.0 percent. The forecast assumes that a ratio of 14.0 percent is maintained throughout the forecast horizon. As discussed, as Loewe steps up its investments in product development, non-current asset turns should slightly deteriorate. Consequently, the ratio of net non-current assets to sales is expected to increase from 19.5 percent in year two to 25.0 by year 10.

After Loewe disposes of its excess cash, amounting to approximately 12 percent of sales, the company's net debt to net assets ratio will increase from 25.9 to 37.9 percent in year two. After year two, the company's capital structure should remain relatively unchanged. As a result, the ratio of net debt to book value of net capital of 37.9 percent is maintained for the duration of the forecast horizon. This assumption of a constant capital structure policy is consistent with the general pattern observed in the historical data discussed earlier in the chapter. Consequently, the forecast assumes that Loewe's cost of (net) debt remains at 3.8 percent, or an after-tax cost of 2.6 percent.

Having made this set of key assumptions, it is a straightforward task to derive the forecasted income statements and beginning balance sheets for years 2009 through 2018 as shown in Table 6.6. Under these forecasts, Loewe's sales will grow to €692.7 million, a little less than double the level in 2008. By 2018, the firm will have a net operating asset base of €270.2 million and shareholders' equity of €167.9 million. Consistent with market-wide patterns of mean-reversion in returns, Loewe's return on equity will decline from 24.0 percent in 2014 to 15.9 percent by 2018, and operating return on assets will show a similar pattern.

Cash flow forecasts

Once we have forecasted income statements and balance sheets, we can derive cash flows for the years 2009 through 2018. Note that we need to forecast the beginning balance sheet for 2019 to compute the cash flows for 2018. This balance sheet is not shown in Table 6.6. For the purpose of illustration, we assume that all the sales growth and the balance sheet ratios remain the same in 2019 as in 2018. Based on this, we project a beginning balance sheet for 2019 and compute the cash flows for 2018. Cash flow to capital is equal to NOPAT minus increases in net working capital and net non-current assets. Cash flow to equity is cash flow to capital minus net interest after tax plus increase in net debt. These two sets of forecasted cash flows are presented in Table 6.6. As the table shows, the free

TABLE 6.6 Forecasted financial statements for Loewe

Fiscal year	2009	2010	2011	2012	2013	2014	2015	2016	2017	2018
Beginning balance sheet (€ millions)										
Beginning net working capital	52.1	54.5	59.4	66.0	72.4	78.5	84.1	89.0	93.0	96.7
+ Beginning net non-current assets	69.3	76.3	87.5	104.2	117.0	129.7	141.9	153.3	163.5	173.5
= Net operating assets	121.4	130.7	146.9	170.2	189.4	208.2	226.1	242.4	256.5	270.2
Net debt	31.4	49.5	55.6	64.4	71.7	78.8	85.6	91.7	97.1	102.3
+ Shareholders' equity	90.0	81.2	91.3	105.8	117.7	129.4	140.5	150.6	159.4	167.9
= Net capital	121.4	130.7	146.9	170.2	189.4	208.2	226.1	242.4	256.5	270.2
Income statement (€ millions)										
Sales	373.5	390.1	425.6	472.6	518.7	562.5	602.7	637.6	666.0	692.7
Net operating profits after tax	19.3	20.7	23.2	26.4	29.7	33.1	32.0	31.6	30.6	29.3
– Net interest expense after tax	0.8	1.3	1.4	1.7	1.9	2.0	2.2	2.4	2.5	2.7
= Net profit	18.5	19.4	21.7	24.7	27.9	31.0	29.8	29.2	28.0	26.7
Operating ROA	15.9%	15.8%	15.8%	15.5%	15.7%	15.9%	14.1%	13.0%	11.9%	10.9%
ROE	20.5%	23.9%	23.8%	23.4%	23.7%	24.0%	21.2%	19.4%	17.6%	15.9%
BV of assets growth rate	–9.8%	7.7%	12.4%	15.9%	11.3%	9.9%	8.6%	7.2%	5.8%	5.4%
BV of equity growth rate	23.9%	–9.8%	12.4%	15.9%	11.3%	9.9%	8.6%	7.2%	5.8%	5.4%
Net operating asset turnover	3.1	3.0	2.9	2.8	2.7	2.7	2.7	2.6	2.6	2.6
Net profit	18.5	19.4	21.7	24.7	27.9	31.0	29.8	29.2	28.0	26.7
– Change in net working capital	–2.3	–5.0	–6.6	–6.4	–6.1	–5.6	–4.9	–4.0	–3.7	–3.9
– Change in net non-current assets	–7.0	–11.2	–16.7	–12.8	–12.7	–12.3	–11.4	–10.2	–10.0	–6.9
+ Change in net debt	18.1	6.1	8.8	7.3	7.1	6.8	6.2	5.3	5.2	4.1
= Free cash flow to equity	27.3	9.4	7.3	12.8	16.2	19.9	19.6	20.4	19.5	19.9
Net operating profit after tax	19.3	20.7	23.2	26.4	29.7	33.1	32.0	31.6	30.6	29.3
– Change in net working capital	–2.3	–5.0	–6.6	–6.4	–6.1	–5.6	–4.9	–4.0	–3.7	–3.9
– Change in net non-current assets	–7.0	–11.2	–16.7	–12.8	–12.7	–12.3	–11.4	–10.2	–10.0	–6.9
= Free cash flow to capital	10.0	4.6	–0.1	7.2	10.9	15.2	15.7	17.4	16.9	18.5

Note: We do not show the beginning balance sheet forecasted for 2019 here, but it is implicit in the calculation of cash flows for 2018. As stated in Table 6.5, we assume that sales continue to grow in 2019 and that all the balance sheet ratios continue to be the same, to derive the beginning balance sheet for 2018.

cash flow to all providers of capital increases from €10.0 million to €18.5 million by 2018, after an initial decrease to −€0.1 million in 2011. In addition, the firm is expected to increase the free cash flow it generates to its equity holders from €9.4 million in 2010 to €19.9 million by 2018.

SENSITIVITY ANALYSIS

The projections discussed thus far represent nothing more than an estimation of a most likely scenario for Bang & Olufsen. Managers and analysts are typically interested in a broader range of possibilities. For example, an analyst estimating the value of Bang & Olufsen might consider the sensitivity of the projections to the key assumptions about sales growth, profit margins, and asset utilization. What if Loewe's focus on creating brand awareness in its current and new markets leads to a substantial increase in marketing costs? Alternatively, what if Loewe is able to capture a greater share of consumers' replacement purchases and grow sales at a faster rate than assumed in the above forecasts? It is wise to also generate projections based on a variety of assumptions to determine the sensitivity of the forecasts to these assumptions.

There is no limit to the number of possible scenarios that can be considered. One systematic approach to **sensitivity analysis** is to start with the key assumptions underlying a set of forecasts and then examine the sensitivity to the assumptions with greatest uncertainty in a given situation. For example, if a company has experienced a variable pattern of gross margins in the past, it is important to make projections using a range of margins. Alternatively, if a company has announced a significant change in its expansion strategy, asset utilization assumptions might be more uncertain. In determining where to invest one's time in performing sensitivity analysis, it is therefore important to consider historical patterns of performance, changes in industry conditions, and changes in a company's competitive strategy.

In the case of Loewe, two likely alternatives to the forecast can be readily envisioned. The forecast presented above expects that Loewe's sales growth will be less than the expected growth of the LCD televisions market. An upside case for Loewe would have the firm capture a greater market share and grow at least in line with the market as a whole. On the downside, the projected marginal increase in Loewe's selling expense could turn out to be too optimistic, flattening the improvement in the company's NOPAT margin.

Seasonality and interim forecasts

Thus far we have concerned ourselves with annual forecasts. However, traditionally for security analysts in the US and increasingly for security analysts in Europe, forecasting is very much a quarterly exercise. Forecasting quarter by quarter raises a new set of questions. How important is seasonality? What is a useful point of departure for **interim forecasts** – the most recent quarter's performance? The comparable quarter of the prior year? Some combination of the two? How should quarterly data be used in producing an annual forecast? Does the item-by-item approach to forecasting used for annual data apply equally well to quarterly data? Full consideration of these questions lies outside the scope of this chapter, but we can begin to answer some of them.

Seasonality is a more important phenomenon in sales and earnings behavior than one might guess. It is present for more than just the retail sector firms that benefit from holiday sales. Seasonality also results from weather-related phenomena (e.g., for electric and gas utilities, construction firms, and motorcycle manufacturers), new product introduction patterns (e.g., for the automobile industry), and other factors. Analysis of the time-series behavior of earnings for US firms suggests that at least some seasonality is present in nearly every major industry.

The implication for forecasting is that one cannot focus only on performance of the most recent quarter as a point of departure. In fact the evidence suggests that, in forecasting earnings, if one had to choose only one quarter's performance as a point of departure, it would be the comparable quarter of the prior year, not the most recent quarter. Note how this finding is consistent with the reports of analysts or the financial press; when they discuss a quarterly earnings announcement, it is nearly always evaluated relative to the performance of the comparable quarter of the prior year, not the most recent quarter.

Research has produced models that forecast sales, earnings, or EPS based solely on prior quarters' observations. Such models are not used by many analysts, because analysts have access to much more information than such simple models contain. However, the models are useful for helping those unfamiliar with the behavior of earnings data to understand how it tends to evolve through time. Such an understanding can provide useful general background, a point of departure in forecasting that can be adjusted to reflect details not revealed in the history of earnings, or a "reasonableness" check on a detailed forecast.

One model of the earnings process that fits well across a variety of industries is the so-called Foster model.[7] Using Q_t to denote earnings (or EPS) for quarter t, and $E(Q_t)$ as its expected value, the Foster model predicts that:

$$E(Q_t) = Q_{t-4} + \delta + \varphi(Q_{t-1} - Q_{t-5})$$

Foster shows that a model of the same form also works well with quarterly sales data.

The form of the Foster model confirms the importance of seasonality because it shows that the starting point for a forecast for quarter t is the earnings four quarters ago, Q_{t-4}. It states that, when constrained to using only prior earnings data, a reasonable forecast of earnings for quarter t includes the following elements:

- The earnings of the comparable quarter of the prior year (Q_{t-4}).

- A long-run trend in year-to-year quarterly earnings increases (δ).

- A fraction (φ) of the year-to-year increase in quarterly earnings experienced most recently ($Q_{t-1} - Q_{t-5}$).

The parameters δ and φ can easily be estimated for a given firm with a simple linear regression model available in most spreadsheet software.[8] For most firms the parameter φ tends to be in the range of 0.25 to 0.50, indicating that 25 to 50 percent of an increase in quarterly earnings tends to persist in the form of another increase in the subsequent quarter. The parameter δ reflects in part the average year-to-year change in quarterly earnings over past years, and it varies considerably from firm to firm.

Research indicates that the Foster model produces one-quarter-ahead forecasts that are off by $.30 to $.35 per share, on average.[9] Such a degree of accuracy stacks up surprisingly well with that of security analysts, who obviously have access to much information ignored in the model. As one would expect, most of the evidence supports analysts being more accurate, but the models are good enough to be "in the ball park" in most circumstances. While it would certainly be unwise to rely completely on such a naïve model, an understanding of the typical earnings behavior reflected by the model is useful.

SUMMARY

Forecasting represents the first step of prospective analysis and serves to summarize the forward-looking view that emanates from business strategy analysis, accounting analysis, and financial analysis. Although not every financial statement analysis is accompanied by such an explicit summarization of a view of the future, forecasting is still a key tool for managers, consultants, security analysts, investment bankers, commercial bankers and other credit analysts, among others.

The best approach to forecasting future performance is to do it comprehensively – producing not only an earnings forecast but a forecast of cash flows and the balance sheet as well. Such a comprehensive approach provides a guard against internal inconsistencies and unrealistic implicit assumptions. The approach described here involves line-by-line analysis, so as to recognize that different items on the income statement and balance sheet are influenced by different drivers. Nevertheless, it remains the case that a few key projections – such as sales growth and profit margin – usually drive most of the projected numbers.

The forecasting process should be embedded in an understanding of how various financial statistics tend to behave on average, and what might cause a firm to deviate from that average. Absent detailed information to the contrary, one would expect sales and earnings numbers to persist at their current levels, adjusted for overall trends of recent years. However, rates of return on investment (ROEs) tend, over several years, to move from abnormal to normal levels – close to the cost of equity capital – as the forces of competition come into play. Profit margins also tend to shift to normal levels, but for this statistic "normal" varies widely across firms and industries, depending on the levels of asset turnover and leverage. Some firms are capable of creating barriers to entry that enable them to fight these tendencies toward normal returns, even for many years, but such firms are the unusual cases.

Forecasting should be preceded by a comprehensive business strategy, accounting, and financial analysis. It is important to understand the dynamics of the industry in which the firm operates and its competitive positioning within that industry. Therefore, while general market trends provide a useful benchmark, it is critical that the analyst incorporates the views developed about the firm's prospects to guide the forecasting process.

For some purposes, including short-term planning and security analysis, forecasts for quarterly periods are desirable. One important feature of quarterly data is seasonality; at least some seasonality exists in the sales and earnings data of nearly every industry. An understanding of a firm's intra-year peaks and valleys is a necessary ingredient of a good forecast of performance on a quarterly basis.

Forecasts provide the input for estimating a firm's value, which can be viewed as the best attempt to reflect in a single summary statistics the manager's or analyst's view of the firm's prospects. The process of converting a forecast into a value estimate is labeled valuation and is discussed next.

CORE CONCEPTS

Comprehensive forecasting approach Forecasting of the (condensed) income statement, balance sheet and cash flow statement to make sure that the performance forecast does not imbed unreasonable assumptions about future asset turnover, leverage, or equity changes.

Condensed financial statements Recommended focus of the forecasting task. The condensed financial statements consist of the following elements:

1 Income statement: Sales, net operating profit after tax, net interest expense after tax, net profit.

2 Balance sheet: Net working capital, net non-current assets, net operating assets, net debt, shareholders' equity, net capital.

3 Cash flow statement: Net profit (net operating profit after taxes), change in net working capital, change in net non-current assets, change in net debt.

Interim forecasts Forecasts of quarterly performance. A key issue in interim forecasting is the seasonality of performance, i.e., the tendency of quarterly performance to exhibit within-year time-series patterns that repeat themselves across years.

Mean-reversion Tendency of financial ratios to revert to the industry or economy average over time. Financial ratios or indicators that tend to revert to the mean are: sales growth, return on equity, return on assets and financial spread. Financial ratios that have a low tendency to revert to the mean are: operating asset turnover and net financial leverage.

Prospective analysis Fourth and final step of financial statement analysis, which focuses on forecasting a firm's future financial performance and position. The forecasts can be used for various purposes, such as estimating firm value or assessing creditworthiness.

Sensitivity analysis Analysis of how sensitive performance forecasts are to (realistic) changes in the key assumptions made to produce the forecast. In a sensitivity analysis, the analyst typically produces forecasts under various scenarios.

QUESTIONS, EXERCISES AND PROBLEMS

1 GlaxoSmithKline is one of the largest pharmaceutical firms in the world, and over an extended period of time in the recent past it consistently earned higher ROEs than the pharmaceutical industry as a whole. As a pharmaceutical analyst, what factors would you consider to be important in making projections of future ROEs for GlaxoSmith-Kline? In particular, what factors would lead you to expect GlaxoSmithKline to continue to be a superior performer in its industry, and what factors would lead you to expect GlaxoSmithKline's future performance to revert to that of the industry as a whole?

2 An analyst claims, "It is not worth my time to develop detailed forecasts of sales growth, profit margins, etcetera, to make earnings projections. I can be almost as accurate, at virtually no cost, using the random walk model to forecast earnings." What is the random walk model? Do you agree or disagree with the analyst's forecast strategy? Why or why not?

3 Which of the following types of businesses do you expect to show a high degree of seasonality in quarterly earnings? Explain why.

■ A supermarket.

■ A pharmaceutical company.

■ A software company.

■ An auto manufacturer.

■ A clothing retailer.

4 What factors are likely to drive a firm's outlays for new capital (such as plant, property, and equipment) and for working capital (such as receivables and inventory)? What ratios would you use to help generate forecasts of these outlays?

5   How would the following events (reported this year) affect your forecasts of a firm's future net profit?

■   An asset write-down.

■   A merger or acquisition.

■   The sale of a major division.

■   The initiation of dividend payments.

6   Consider the following two earnings forecasting models:

$$\text{Model 1}: E_t\,(EPS_{t+1}) = EPS_t$$

$$\text{Model 2}: E_t\,(EPS_{t+1}) = \frac{1}{5}\sum_{t=1}^{5} EPS_t$$

$E_t(EPS)$ is the expected forecast of earnings per share for year $t+1$, given information available at t. Model 1 is usually called a random walk model for earnings, whereas Model 2 is called a mean-reverting model. The earnings per share for Telefónica for the period 2000 to 2004 are as follows:

Year	1	2	3	4	5
EPS	€0.61	€0.43	€(1.08)	€0.40	€0.58

a   What would be the year 6 forecast for earnings per share for each model?

b   Actual earnings per share for Telefónica in 6 were €0.91. Given this information, what would be the year 7 forecast for earnings per share for each model? Why do the two models generate quite different forecasts? Which do you think would better describe earnings per share patterns? Why?

7   An investment banker states, "It is not worth my while to worry about detailed long-term forecasts. Instead, I use the following approach when forecasting cash flows beyond three years. I assume that sales grow at the rate of inflation, capital expenditures are equal to depreciation, and that net profit margins and working capital to sales ratios stay constant." What pattern of return on equity is implied by these assumptions? Is this reasonable?

Problem 1   Predicting Tesco's 2009/2010 earnings

On April 21, 2009, UK-based retailer Tesco plc presented its preliminary financial statements for the fiscal year ending on March 31, 2009. The following tables show a selection of Tesco's financial figures for the fiscal years 2007/2008 and 2008/2009 (i.e., the fiscal years ending on March 31, 2008 and 2009, respectively):

Income statement (£ millions)	2008/2009	2007/2008
Sales	54,327	47,298
Operating expenses	(51,121)	(44,507)
Net Interest Expense or Income	(284)	(112)
Investment Income	32	124
Tax expense	(788)	(673)
Net profit	**2,166**	**2,130**

Balance sheet (£ millions)	2008/2009	2007/2008
Net working capital	**(4,912)**	**(3,885)**
Non-current tangible assets	23,152	19,787
Non-current intangible assets	4,027	2,336
Other Non-current assets	3,469	1,725
Non-interest bearing liabilities	(888)	(954)
Net non-current assets	**29,760**	**22,894**
Net debt	11,910	7,194
Equity	12,938	11,815
Net assets = net capital	**24,848**	**19,009**

Other information (£ millions)	2008/2009	2007/2008
Depreciation of non-current tangible assets	1,036	876
Amortization of non-current intangible assets	153	116
Non-current tangible assets at cost	29,844	25,550
Non-current intangible assets at cost	4,790	2,944
Dividends paid	883	792

In addition to disclosing the financial statements, Tesco's management also provided guidance about future investment plans, financing strategies, and performance expectations. In particular, the following information became available to investors and analysts on the publication date:

- In 2008/2009, Tesco opened 9 million square feet of new store space. The retailer plans to open 8 million square feet of new store space in 2009/2010.

- Revenues in 2008/2009 were the revenues of 53 weeks. The fiscal year 2009/2010 will include 52 weeks.

- Group capital expenditure during 2008/2009 was GBP 4.7 billion, a little more than planned (GBP 4.5b) due to currency movements. Tesco's management indicates that capital expenditures in 2009/2010 will be around GBP 3.5 billion. One reason for why capital expenditures can be reduced is that in the current economic downturn, Tesco can buy more new store space for less.

- Tesco's effective tax rate in 2008/2009 was 26.7 percent versus 24.0 percent in 2007/2008. The increase in tax rate was primarily the result of one-time tax benefits in 2007/2008. Management expects the effective tax rate for 2009/2010 to be around 27 percent.

- In 2008/2009, Tesco was able to realize cost saving of close to GBP 550 million through its Step-Change program. Management expects these cost savings to persist.

- In 2008/2009, Tesco's net finance cost, including the company's return on pension assets, was GBP 284 million. The underlying interest charge was GBP 309 million, up from GBP 159 million in 2007/2008. The weighted average coupon rate of Tesco's debt was 5.6 percent.

- Tesco's net debt rose substantially during 2008/2009 as a result of:

    1 1, increased capital expenditures.

    2 An increased pension deficit (GBP 0.65 billion increase).

    3 The significant depreciation in the sterling-dollar/euro exchange rates (with a debt impact of approximately GBP 1 billion).

If exchange rates remain stable, management intends to bring down net debt by approximately GBP 1 billion during 2009/2010. Further, management disclosed the following information about realized and planned store openings:

(£ millions)	UK	Rest of Europe	Asia	US
2008/2009 (Realized):				
Revenues	38,191	8,862	7,068	206
Operating profit	2,540	479	343	(156)
Square feet store space (× 1,000):				
Beginning-of-year	29,549	22,517	23,363	530
Openings, extensions, adjustments	1,773	3,502	3,006	620
Acquisitions	239	3,015	0	0
Closures/disposals	(276)	(196)	(190)	0
End-of-year	31,285	28,838	26,179	1,150
2009/2010 (Expected):				
Square feet store space (× 1,000):				
Beginning-of-year	31,285	28,838	26,179	1,150
Openings, extensions, adjustments	1,897	2,697	2,733	600
Acquisitions	98	0	0	0
Closures/disposals	(225)	0	(63)	0
End-of-year	33,055	31,535	28,849	1,750

1   Predict Tesco's 2009/2010 sales using the information about the company's store space and revenues (per geographical segment).

2   Predict the 2009/2010 book values of Tesco's non-current assets and working capital using the information about the company's investment plans. Make simplifying assumptions where necessary.

3   During fiscal year 2008/2009, at least two factors influenced Tesco's operating expenses: (a) the increase in depreciation and (b) the cost savings of approximately GBP 550 million. Assume that all other changes in the company's operating profit margin were caused by the economic downturn.

   a   What was the net effect of the downturn on Tesco's operating margins?

   b   Estimate Tesco's 2009/2010 operating expense under the assumption that the effect of the economic downturn fully persists in 2009/2010. (Estimate the company's depreciation and amortization expense separately from the other operating expenses.)

4   Estimate Tesco's 2009/2010 interest expense and net debt-to-equity ratio under the assumption that the company reduces its net debt in 2009/2010, as planned.

5   What do the above estimates (and your estimate of Tesco's 2009/2010 tax expense) imply for the company's free cash flow to equity holders in 2009/2010? How likely is it that Tesco will be able to reduce its net debt in 2009/2010?

NOTES

1. See Patricia O'Brien, "Analysts' Forecasts as Earnings Expectations," *Journal of Accounting and Economics* (January 1988): 53–83.

2. See George Foster, "Quarterly Accounting Data: Time Series Properties and Predictive Ability Results," *The Accounting Review* (January 1977): 1–21.

3. See Robert Freeman, James Ohlson, and Stephen Penman, "Book Rate-of-Return and Prediction of Earnings Changes: An Empirical Investigation," *Journal of Accounting Research* (Autumn 1982): 639–653.

4. See Stephen H. Penman, "An Evaluation of Accounting Rate-of-Return," *Journal of Accounting, Auditing, and Finance* (Spring 1991): 233–256; Eugene Fama and Kenneth French, "Size and Book-to-Market Factors in Earnings and Returns," *Journal of Finance* (March 1995): 131–156; and Victor Bernard, "Accounting-Based Valuation Methods: Evidence on the Market-to-Book Anomaly and Implications for Financial Statements Analysis," University of Michigan, working paper (1994). Ignoring the effects of accounting artifacts, ROEs should be driven in a competitive equilibrium to a level approximating the cost of equity capital.

5. A "normal" profit margin is that which, when multiplied by the turnover achievable within an industry and with a viable corporate strategy, yields a return on investment that just covers the cost of capital. However, as mentioned above, accounting artifacts can cause returns on investment to deviate from the cost of capital for long periods, even in a competitive equilibrium.

6. Recall the example on off-balance sheet intangible assets in Chapter 4. With a three-year amortization period, the proportion of outlays during the years t through t+2 that remains capitalized at the end of year t+2 equals 1.5 ([1 − .33/2] + [1 − .33/2 − .33] + [1 − .33/2 − .67]).

7. See Foster, op. cit. A somewhat more accurate model is furnished by Brown and Rozeff, but it requires interactive statistical techniques for estimation – Lawrence D. Brown and Michael Rozeff, "Univariate Time Series Models of Quarterly Accounting Earnings per Share," *Journal of Accounting Research* (Spring 1979): 179–189.

8. To estimate the model, we write in terms of realized earnings (as opposed to expected earnings) and move Q_{t-4} to the left-hand side:

$$Q_t - Q_{t-4} = \delta + \varphi(Q_{t-1} - Q_{t-5}) + e_t$$

We now have a regression where $(Q_t - Q_{t-4})$ is the dependent variable, and its lagged value – $(Q_{t-1} - Q_{t-5})$ – is the independent variable. Thus, to estimate the equation, prior earnings data must first be expressed in terms of year-to-year changes; the change for one quarter is then regressed against the change for the most recent quarter. The intercept provides an estimate of δ, and the slope is an estimate of φ. The equation is typically estimated using 24 to 40 quarters of prior earnings data.

9. See O'Brien, op. cit.

APPENDIX: THE BEHAVIOR OF COMPONENTS OF ROE

In Figure 6A we show that ROEs tend to be mean-reverting. In this appendix we show the behavior of the key components of ROE – operating ROA, operating margin, operating asset turnover, spread, and net financial leverage. These ratios are computed using the same portfolio approach described in the chapter, based on the data for all European firms for the time period 1992 through 2008.

FIGURE 6A.1 Behavior of operating ROA for European firms over time, 1992–2008

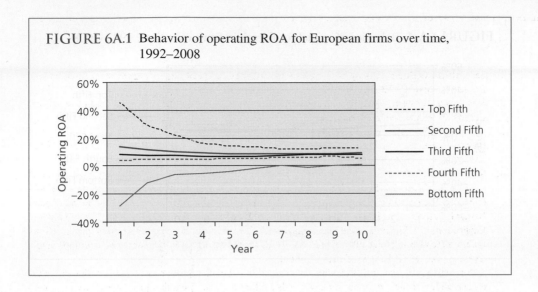

FIGURE 6A.2 Behavior of NOPAT margin for European firms over time, 1992–2008

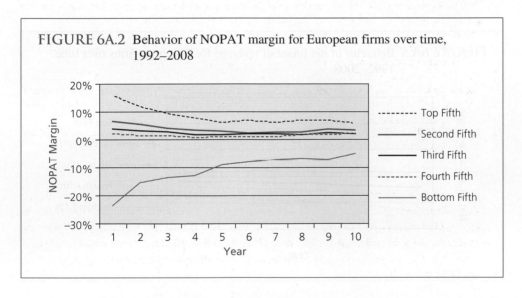

FIGURE 6A.3 Behavior of operating asset turnover for European firms over time, 1992–2008

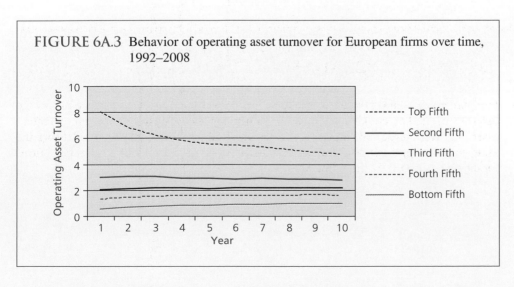

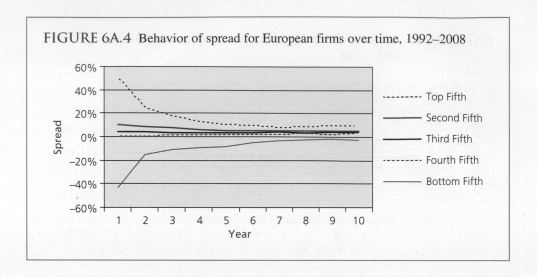

FIGURE 6A.4 Behavior of spread for European firms over time, 1992–2008

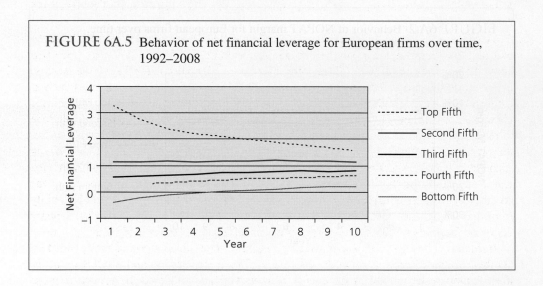

FIGURE 6A.5 Behavior of net financial leverage for European firms over time, 1992–2008

Forecasting earnings and earnings growth in the European oil and gas industry

Industry overview

In 2005 the largest companies operating in the European oil exploration and production industry all tended to operate on a global scale. They were typically categorized as "price takers" because they had little control over the prices that they could ask from their customers. One reason for this small influence on prices was that the 11 oil-producing developing countries that coordinated their production activities through the OPEC organization had a strong influence on the worldwide oil supply and crude oil prices. Although the OPEC countries possessed close to 75 percent of the worldwide proved oil reserves, they supplied only 40 percent of the worldwide oil production to stabilize prices at higher levels. National taxes also influenced local prices and demand for oil. For example, in Europe fuel prices were, on average, four times as large as fuel prices in the US, tempering the demand in Europe.

During the first half of the 2000s, crude oil prices soared to record levels. While at the end of 1999 the price for a barrel of crude oil was close to $25, the crude oil price was above $55 by the end of 2005. There were several potential reasons for this strong increase in the crude oil price.[1] The increasing demand for oil from emerging economies such as China had led to a situation in which the amount of oil demanded had approached the maximum production capacity. While the OPEC countries had increased their production to record levels, they had invested insufficiently in new capacity and were unable to further increase oil supply. Oil supply had also come under pressure because of the close to 12 percent reduction in the US oil production capacity after the devastations of Hurricane Katrina in 2005. Further, oil prices were strongly affected by speculative trading in the commodity markets in response to the crisis in the Middle East and the political instability in oil-producing African countries. **Exhibit 1** shows the crude oil price between January 2000 and December 2005 as well as the prices of oil futures at the end of 2005.

Because oil and gas companies were price takers, their success critically depended on (1) their ability to grow and (2) the efficiency of their exploration and production activities. Although the growth of the energy markets typically followed the growth in gross domestic product, oil and gas companies could grow at a faster or slower rate than the economy average for the following reasons. First, some companies were able to open up new markets, primarily in the emerging countries. The most important emerging market at the end of 2005 was China, which contributed almost one-third to the total worldwide increase in oil consumption. Second, although the demand for energy tended to follow the growth of the economy, the supply of oil and gas was limited by the natural availability of the energy sources. By the end of 2005, many industry analysts feared that oil and gas companies' proved developed oil and gas reserves would reduce in the near future. Third, companies could diversify into other segments of the energy market. For example oil and natural gas companies produced or started to produce coal, nuclear energy, or hydroelectric energy.

Professor Erik Peek prepared this case. The case is intended solely as the basis for class discussion and is not intended to serve as an endorsement, source of primary data, or illustration of effective or ineffective management.

[1]See "The Structure of the Oil Market and Causes of High Prices" by Pelin Berkmen, Sam Ouliaris, and Hossein Samiei, *International Monetary Fund, 2005.*

The increasing oil price tended to have a positive impact on oil and gas companies' profits in the first half of the 2000s. Nonetheless, various other developments put pressure on the companies' profit margins. First, because oil was traded in US dollars, the weak dollar implied that it was expensive for oil companies to buy resources in other currencies. Second, steel prices were also rising, making oil and gas companies' capital investments more expensive. Third, and most importantly, during the first half of the 2000s exploration costs per barrel of oil equivalent (BOE) had risen sharply.[2]

Oil and gas companies that had operations in developing countries were also subject to a substantial degree of country risk. Many companies were extending their operations to developing countries in, for example, West Africa or around the Caspian Sea, because they were running out of reserves in the developed countries. Operations in such developing countries could, however, be disrupted by political crises, acts of war, and expropriation or nationalization of reserves and production facilities by governments. For example, in 2006 Bolivia announced plans to nationalize its oil and gas fields, which were then owned by several international oil and gas producers.

Oil and gas companies' accounting and disclosure

As argued, because oil and gas companies are price takers, their future profitability depends primarily on (1) the quantity and quality of their current oil and gas reserves, (2) their ability to efficiently extract and produce oil and gas, and (3) their ability to replace extracted reserves. Some inherent characteristics of oil and gas companies' exploration and development activities, however, make accounting for these activities a difficult exercise. Particularly, because the future economic benefits of current exploration and development expenditures are hard to establish, deciding on which expenditures must be capitalized as assets and which expenditures must be categorized as "unsuccessful" and immediately written-off can be problematic.

Most oil and gas companies use the "successful efforts method" of accounting for exploration and development activities. Under this method, the key financial reporting estimate is for proved oil and gas reserves. Accounting standards consider oil and gas reserves to be proved when the company has government and regulatory approval for the extraction of reserves and is able to bring the reserves quickly to the market in a commercially viable manner. Companies make these estimates using geological information about each reservoir, reservoir production histories, and reservoir pressure histories. The distinction between proved and unproved reserves is important because only exploration expenditures that are associated with proved reserves are capitalized as assets. Specifically, under the successful efforts method, companies capitalize their exploration expenditures for a short period, after which they choose between continued capitalization and immediate amortization based on whether the exploration has successfully led to the booking of proved reserves. In addition, oil companies' depreciation, depletion, and amortization of production plants are typically calculated using the unit-of-production method, where the expected production capacity is derived from the proved reserves. The following paragraphs from British Petroleum's (BP's) 2005 Annual Report describe how BP accounts for exploration and development expenditures and illustrates the basic idea underlying the successful efforts method:

> *Exploration and property leasehold acquisition costs are capitalized within intangible fixed assets and amortized on a straight-line basis over the estimated period of exploration. Each property is reviewed on an annual basis to confirm that drilling activity is planned and it is not impaired. If no future activity is planned, the*

---

[2]See "Oil Companies' Profits: Not Exactly What They Seem to Be," *The Economist*, October 28, 2004.

remaining balance of the licence and property acquisition costs is written off. Upon determination of economically recoverable reserves ("proved reserves" or "commercial reserves"), amortization ceases and the remaining costs are aggregated with exploration expenditure and held on a field-by-field basis as proved properties awaiting approval within other intangible assets. When development is approved internally, the relevant expenditure is transferred to property, plant and equipment.

Geological and geophysical exploration costs are charged against income as incurred. Costs directly associated with an exploration well are capitalized as an intangible asset until the drilling of the well is complete and the results have been evaluated. These costs include employee remuneration, materials and fuel used, rig costs, delay rentals and payments made to contractors. If hydrocarbons are not found, the exploration expenditure is written off as a dry hole. If hydrocarbons are found and, subject to further appraisal activity, which may include the drilling of further wells (exploration or exploratory-type stratigraphic test wells), are likely to be capable of commercial development, the costs continue to be carried as an asset. All such carried costs are subject to technical, commercial and management review at least once a year to confirm the continued intent to develop or otherwise extract value from the discovery. When this is no longer the case, the costs are written off. When proved reserves of oil and natural gas are determined and development is sanctioned, the relevant expenditure is transferred to property, plant and equipment.

Expenditure on the construction, installation or completion of infrastructure facilities such as platforms, pipelines and the drilling of development wells, including unsuccessful development or delineation wells, is capitalized within property, plant and equipment.

The method that BP uses to account for its exploration and development expenditures is similar to the method used by many other oil and gas companies, including Repsol YPF and Royal Dutch Shell. Most oil and gas companies also provide supplemental disclosures about their oil and gas reserves. These disclosures typically show (1) the exploration and development costs that the company incurred during the year, (2) the exploration and development costs that the company capitalized over the years, (3) the results of the company's oil and gas exploration and development activities, and (4) the movements in the company's proved and unproved oil and gas reserves during the year. **Exhibit 2** summarizes the supplemental information that BP, Repsol YPF, and Royal Dutch Shell provided in annual reports for the fiscal year ended on December 31, 2005.

A description of three European oil and gas companies

Following are the descriptions of three European companies that operated in the oil and gas industry in 2005: British Petroleum, Repsol YPF, and Royal Dutch Shell.

British Petroleum

At the end of the second half of the 2000s, British Petroleum (BP) was the world's largest oil and gas company in terms of revenues. The company operated in more than 100 countries, in which it employed approximately 96,000 people. Between 2001 and 2005, BP's return on assets gradually increased from 5 percent to 12 percent. In that period – between December 31, 2000 and December 31, 2005 – BP's share price increased by 14.6 percent, yielding an average annual return of 2.8 percent. By the end of 2005, BP's market value was £127.9 billion.

BP's shares were widely held. In 2005, the company's largest shareholder owned less than 4 percent of BP's ordinary shares outstanding. Like many other oil and gas companies, BP had excess cash that it returned to its shareholders through share repurchases and dividends. In 2005, the company repurchased ordinary shares for an amount of £6.7 billion and paid out £4.0 billion in dividends. BP was a financially healthy company. Standard and Poor's had rated BP's public debt at AA.

Although BP's primary activities were the exploration, development, and production of oil and natural gas, the company also operated in other product segments. However, in 2005 less than 10 percent of the company's revenues and less than 5 percent of its net profits came from the marketing and trading of liquefied natural gas, solar energy, and renewables. BP's primary geographical segment was Europe, where it generated 43 percent of its revenues, followed by the US (40 percent of its revenues).

Fiscal year 2005 had been a year of contrasts for BP. Whereas the company's profitability improved because of rising oil prices, its performance was negatively affected by several events that impaired production and distribution: an explosion at the company's Texas City refinery, the Asian tsunami, and hurricanes in the Gulf of Mexico. BP's income statement for fiscal 2005 included a charge of $700 million for fatality and personal injury claims resulting from the explosion at the Texas City refinery. The company reported that the Texas City incident and extreme weather conditions had resulted in an approximate total loss of $2 billion because of forgone production and repair costs.

BP's capital expenditures in the exploration and production segment totaled $10.1 billion in 2005.[3] The company's proved developed and undeveloped reserves increased by 1 billion barrels of oil equivalent (BOE) because of discoveries and improvements in recovery techniques. BP's daily production in 2005 was approximately 4 million BOEs.

Repsol YPF

Of the three described European oil and gas companies – BP, Royal Dutch Shell and Repsol YPF – Repsol was a smallest, although the company was one of the ten largest oil producers in the world. In 2005, the company operated in more than 20 countries, primarily in Europe and Latin America, employing approximately 36,000 people. Between 2001 and 2005, Repsol's return on assets gradually increased from 4.5 to 8.5 percent. During these years, the company's share price had increased by an average of 7.7 percent, to reach a market value of €30.1 billion on December 31, 2005. Repsol had a few large shareholders, who were primarily banks and pension funds. These shareholders held in total close to 45 percent of the company's ordinary share capital. Repsol's dividends totaled €732 million in 2005. In that year the company had not repurchased ordinary shares, but it had announced plans to do so in the near future.

Excess cash was also used to reduce the company's net debt and improve its financial strength. In 2005, Standard and Poor's rated Repsol's public debt at BB.

Repsol's operating activities were strongly focused on exploring for, producing, and retailing oil and natural gas. The company generated a small fraction of its revenues – less than 5 percent – from electricity generation. In addition, Repsol was active in researching and testing bio-fuels. The company had most of its operations located in Europe and Latin America and was less geographically diversified than BP and Royal Dutch Shell. Its primary markets were Spain and Argentina, Bolivia, and Brazil, where it made 44 percent (Spain) and 16 percent (ABB) of its sales, respectively.

Fiscal year 2005 had been one Repsol's most successful years in its history. The company's profitability had benefited from the economic growth in its primary markets, the

---

[3]Note that BP's reporting currency was US dollars, whereas the company's shares were traded in British pounds.

rising oil prices, and improved refining margins. At the end of 2005, however, Repsol announced that it had downwardly revised its estimates of proved reserves. In particular, estimated reserves were adjusted by 659 million BOEs in Bolivia, 509 million BOEs in Argentina, and 86 million BOEs in the rest of the world. The adjustments to the Bolivian reserves were primarily made because of the political uncertainty in that country. However, adjustments in the other countries were the result of "a better knowledge of the field data." Repsol's daily production in 2005 was approximately 1.1 million BOEs.

For the years 2005–2009, Repsol's management targeted double-digit growth. In 2005, the company made capital expenditures of €1.9 billion in the exploration and production segment and was expanding its operations to other geographical areas, such as North Africa, Russia, and Central Asia. In its 2005 Annual Report, the company identified as one of its most important tasks for the near future to increase its reserves replacement rate.

Royal Dutch Shell

By the beginning of 2006, Royal Dutch Shell Plc was the world's third largest energy and petrochemical group. The company employed more than 110,000 people in 140 countries. Prior to 2005, Royal Dutch Shell was the umbrella name for a group of operating companies that were owned by two exchange-listed companies with separate management boards: Netherlands-based Royal Dutch Petroleum Company and UK-based Shell Transport and Trading Company. Royal Dutch held a 60 percent stake in the operating companies, while Shell Transport and Trading held a 40 percent stake. Because the complex ownership structure inhibited effective decision making and governance, however, in July 2005 the two exchange-listed companies unified under a single parent company – Royal Dutch Shell Plc. The shares of Royal Dutch Shell were widely held. The company's largest shareholder held less than 7 percent of the company's ordinary share capital.

Royal Dutch Shell's core activities were the production, development, and retailing of oil and natural gas. Almost 90 percent of its revenues came from these activities; the remainder came from the production of petrochemical products. Forty percent of Royal Dutch Shell's revenues in 2005 came from its European operations, 33 percent of its revenues came from its US operations, and 20 percent of its sales was made in non-European countries from the eastern hemisphere.

In the period from 2000 to 2002, the Royal Dutch Shell group reported gradually declining returns on its assets of between 20 percent and 14 percent. Both exchange-listed holding companies experienced share price declines of about 30 and 20 percent, respectively, reaching a combined market capitalization of €148.6 billion. In 2003, Royal Dutch Shell's return on assets increased to 17 percent but its (combined) market value remained almost unchanged.

On January 9, 2004, Royal Dutch Shell surprised investors with the announcement that its proved oil and gas reserves were about 20 percent smaller than it had previously disclosed. Specifically, the company reclassified 2.7 billion barrels of oil and natural gas liquids as well as 7.2 trillion standard cubic feet of natural gas as "probable but not proved." The estimated value of the reclassified reserves was close to €6 billion. The market value of Royal Dutch Shell decreased by 7.5 percent, or €10.6 billion, in response to the announcement. In February and March, two exchange regulators, the US Securities and Exchange Commission (SEC) and the UK Financial Services Authority (FSA), started their investigations into the matter. On April 30, 2004, the company's market value had decreased by 8.9 percent (adjusted for changes in the FTSE All-World Oil & Gas Price Index), or €12.6 billion since the day before the announcement. By that time, rating agency Standard and Poor's had also downgraded Royal Dutch Shell's debt from AAA to AA.

To restore credibility after the restatements of its oil and gas reserves, Royal Dutch Shell undertook several steps. The company improved its internal control systems, replaced some of its directors, abandoned its practice of evaluating business unit's performance and calculating managers' bonuses based on reserve bookings, and unified Royal Dutch Petroleum and Shell Transport and Trading under a single parent company. On April 29, 2004, Royal Dutch Shell also announced that it would immediately relaunch its share repurchase program. The company would return close to €1.4 billion to its shareholders in 2004 and €3.6 billion in 2005.

In 2005, Royal Dutch Shell reported a return on assets of 11.5 percent. In that year, the company's share price increased by close to 17 percent, to reach a market value of €176 billion. Royal Dutch Shell's capital expenditures in the exploration and production segments were $10.8 billion in 2005, when its daily oil and gas production level had declined from 3.7 million to 3.4 million BOEs.

Questions

1　What are the European oil and gas companies' drivers of profitability? What are their key risks?

2　Using the supplemental information summarized in **Exhibit 2**, analysts can produce several ratios that provide insight into the efficiency of the companies' exploration, development, and production activities as well as their growth opportunities. Develop a set of ratios that provide such insights. How efficient are the three oil and gas companies in exploration and production?

3　**Exhibit 3** summarizes analysts' one-year-horizon (2006), two-year-horizon (2007), and three-year-horizon (2008) forecasts of sales growth and profit margins. For each of the three oil and gas companies, provide arguments justifying the most pessimistic scenarios as well as arguments justifying the most optimistic scenarios.

4　Given your answers to the previous questions, what are your forecasts of the oil and gas companies' net profits for fiscal year 2006? What are your expectations about each of the companies' long-term earnings growth (i.e., growth in 2007 and 2008)?

EXHIBIT 1   **Crude Brent oil prices**

Crude Brent oil price from December 1999 to December 2005

Source: Thomson Datastream.

Crude Brent oil futures prices on December 31, 2005

Crude Brent oil futures for delivery in	Price in US$ per barrel
December 2006	62.27
December 2007	62.05
December 2008	60.47
December 2009	59.01
December 2010	57.97
December 2011	57.45

Source: Thomson Datastream.

Forecasting earnings and earnings growth in the European oil and gas industry

EXHIBIT 2   **Supplementary information about BP's, Repsol YPF's, and Royal Dutch Shell's oil and natural gas reserves**

	British Petroleum (in US$ millions)		Repsol YPF (in €millions)		Royal Dutch Shell (in US$ millions)	
	2005	2004	2005	2004	2005	2004
Gross capitalized costs of oil and natural gas exploration and development						
Proved properties	109,223	102,819	26,066	22,099	102,373	99,090
Unproved properties	4,661	4,311	1,217	728	4,382	4,307
Auxiliary equipment and facilities	N.A.	N.A.	1,756	1,149	3,988	3,868
Accumulated depreciation and impairment losses	(57,907)	(53,671)	(17,025)	(13,943)	(62,592)	(59,307)
Net capitalized costs	55,977	53,459	11,954	10,033	48,151	47,958
Costs of oil and natural gas exploration and development incurred during the year						
Acquisition of properties						
Proved	0	0	166	209	37	19
Unproved	63	78	650	118	262	2
Exploration and appraisal costs	1,266	1,039	1,417	1,164	413	317
Development costs	7,678	7,270	9,159	8,414	1,448	1,013
Total costs	9,007	8,387	11,392	9,905	2,159	1,351
Results of oil and natural gas exploration, development, and production activities						
Sales and other operating revenues						
To third parties	12,695	9,472	2,359	1,861	10,936	9,400
To group companies	29,119	22,264	4,398	3,961	31,579	24,807
Other income	N.A.	N.A.	731	399	N.A.	N.A.
Total sales	41,814	31,736	7,488	6,221	42,515	34,207
Exploration expenditure	(684)	(637)	(275)	(309)	(1,158)	(1,102)
Production costs	(4,391)	(3,577)				
Production taxes	(2,999)	(2,087)				
Production costs (including taxes)			(2,356)	(1,895)	(7,349)	(6,497)
Other operating costs	(6,857)	(3,764)	(404)	(287)	(1,639)	(1,983)
Depreciation, depletion and amortization	(5,628)	(5,157)	(1,280)	(1,239)	(8,381)	(7,797)
Impairment and (gains) losses on sale of business and fixed assets	893	(469)	N.A.	N.A.	N.A.	N.A.
Profit before taxation	22,148	16,045	3,173	2,491	23,988	16,828
Taxes	(7,950)	(5,327)	(1,960)	(1,376)	(14,523)	(9,769)
Results of operations	14,198	10,718	1,213	1,115	9,465	7,059

(continued)

EXHIBIT 2 **Supplementary information about BP's, Repsol YPF's, and Royal Dutch Shell's oil and natural gas reserves** (*continued*)

	British Petroleum (in US$ millions)		Repsol YPF (in €millions)		Royal Dutch Shell (in US$ millions)	
	2005	**2004**	**2005**	**2004**	**2005**	**2004**
Proved developed and undeveloped reserves of crude oil and natural gas liquids (in million barrels)						
Reserves at the beginning of the year						
Developed reserves	6,084	5,872	1,311	1,412	3,234	3,858
Undeveloped reserves	4,646	4,444	373	469	1,654	1,955
Total reserves	10,730	10,316	1,683	1,882	4,888	5,813
Revision of previous estimates	107	517	(370)	(42)	92	(195)
Increase due to improvements in recovery techniques	335	210	7	19	6	50
Extensions and discoveries	220	371	17	26	380	110
Purchases of reserves-in-place	2	252	38	11	14	0
Sales of reserves-in-place	(75)	(37)	(14)	(5)	(15)	(95)
Production	(912)	(899)	(194)	(208)	(729)	(795)
Reserves at the end of the year						
Developed reserves	5,532	6,084	875	1,311	2,898	3,234
Undeveloped reserves	4,875	4,646	291	373	1,738	1,654
Total reserves	10,407	10,730	1,167	1,683	4,636	4,888
Proved developed and undeveloped reserves of natural gas (in billion cubic feet)						
Reserves at the beginning of the year						
Developed reserves	21,004	22,698	12,077	10,182	21,352	20,869
Undeveloped reserves	24,546	23,831	6,130	9,759	19,215	20,690
Total reserves	45,550	46,529	18,207	19,942	40,567	41,559
Revision of previous estimates	2,046	(2,189)	(4,960)	(1,014)	(612)	(113)
Increase due to improvements in recovery techniques	2,017	1,173	0	2	2	58
Extensions and discoveries	567	3,876	129	523	2,577	2,970
Purchases of reserves-in-place	68	5	34	29	135	9
Sales of reserves-in-place	(1,491)	(643)	(27)	(45)	(21)	(708)
Production	(3,148)	(3,201)	(1,247)	(1,230)	(3,032)	(3,208)
Reserves at the end of the year						
Developed reserves	20,750	21,004	7,160	12,077	20,999	21,352
Undeveloped reserves	24,859	24,546	4,977	6,130	18,617	19,215
Total reserves	45,609	45,550	12,137	18,207	39,616	40,567
Conversion rate: × billion cubic feet of gas = 1 million barrel of oil equivalents	5.80	5.80	5.80	5.80	5.80	5.80

Source: Annual Reports for the fiscal year ended on December 31, 2005 of British Petroleum, Repsol YPF, and Royal Dutch Shell.

Forecasting earnings and earnings growth in the European oil and gas industry

EXHIBIT 3 **Analysts' forecasts for fiscal years 2006, 2007, and 2008 at the beginning of 2006**

Forecasts of sales growth

Fiscal year 2006 relative to fiscal year 2005	Most pessimistic forecast	Consensus forecast	Most optimistic forecast
British Petroleum	3.0%	19.5%	47.3%
Repsol YPF	−7.8%	9.6%	28.6%
Royal Dutch Shell	−5.1%	6.5%	18.2%

Fiscal year 2007 relative to fiscal year 2005	Most pessimistic forecast	Consensus forecast	Most optimistic forecast
British Petroleum	−5.4%	17.2%	41.9%
Repsol YPF	−8.5%	7.3%	15.4%
Royal Dutch Shell	−14.0%	0.4%	11.7%

Fiscal year 2008 relative to fiscal year 2005	Most pessimistic forecast	Consensus forecast	Most optimistic forecast
British Petroleum	−9.8%	9.2%	25.6%
Repsol YPF	0.4%	5.5%	13.1%
Royal Dutch Shell	−17.2%	−4.7%	10.0%

Forecasts of net profit margins

Fiscal year 2006 relative to fiscal year 2005	Most pessimistic forecast	Consensus forecast	Most optimistic forecast
British Petroleum	6.7%	7.8%	8.8%
Repsol YPF	5.7%	6.5%	7.2%
Royal Dutch Shell	6.5%	7.6%	8.8%

Fiscal year 2007 relative to fiscal year 2005	Most pessimistic forecast	Consensus forecast	Most optimistic forecast
British Petroleum	6.5%	7.9%	8.9%
Repsol YPF	5.5%	6.3%	7.0%
Royal Dutch Shell	6.6%	7.4%	8.2%

Fiscal year 2008 relative to fiscal year 2005	Most pessimistic forecast	Consensus forecast	Most optimistic forecast
British Petroleum	7.2%	8.2%	9.0%
Repsol YPF	5.7%	6.2%	6.9%
Royal Dutch Shell	6.6%	7.3%	8.8%

Source: Reuters Estimates.

EXHIBIT 4 Financial statements of British Petroleum, Royal Dutch Shell, and Repsol YPF for the fiscal year ended December 31, 2005

CONSOLIDATED INCOME STATEMENTS – BRITISH PETROLEUM ($ millions)

Fiscal year ended December 31,	2005	2004
Sales and other operating revenues	249,465	199,876
Earnings from jointly controlled entities – after interest and tax	3,083	1,818
Earnings from associates – after interest and tax	460	462
Interest and other revenues	613	615
Total revenues	**253,621**	**202,771**
Gains on sale of businesses and fixed assets	1,538	1,685
Total revenues and other income	**255,159**	**204,456**
Purchases	(172,699)	(135,907)
Production and manufacturing expenses	(21,092)	(17,330)
Production and similar taxes	(3,010)	(2,149)
Depreciation, depletion and amortization	(8,771)	(8,529)
Impairment and losses on sale of businesses and fixed assets	(468)	(1,390)
Exploration expense	(684)	(637)
Distribution and administration expenses	(13,706)	(12,768)
Fair value (gain) loss on embedded derivatives	(2,047)	0
Profit before interest and taxation from continuing operations	**32,682**	**25,746**
Finance costs	(616)	(440)
Other finance expense	(145)	(340)
Profit before taxation from continuing operations	**31,921**	**24,966**
Taxation	(9,473)	(7,082)
Profit from continuing operations	**22,448**	**17,884**
Profit (loss) from Innovene operations	184	(622)
Minority interest	(291)	(187)
Profit for the year	**22,341**	**17,075**

CONSOLIDATED BALANCE SHEETS – BRITISH PETROLEUM ($ millions)

Fiscal year ended December 31,	2005	2004
Property, plant, and equipment	85,947	93,092
Goodwill	10,371	10,857
Intangible assets	4,772	4,205
Investments in jointly controlled entities	13,556	14,556
Investments in associates	6,217	5,486
Other investments	967	394
Fixed assets	**121,830**	**128,590**
Loans	821	811
Other receivables	770	429
Derivative financial instruments	3,652	898
Prepayments and accrued income	1,269	354
Defined benefit pension plan surplus	3,282	2,105
Total non-current assets	**131,624**	**133,187**
Loans	132	193
Inventories	19,760	15,645
Trade and other receivables	40,902	37,099

(continued)

Forecasting earnings and earnings growth in the European oil and gas industry

CONSOLIDATED BALANCE SHEETS – BRITISH PETROLEUM ($ millions) (cont.)

Fiscal year ended December 31,	2005	2004
Derivative financial instruments	9,726	5,317
Prepayments and accrued income	1,598	1,671
Current tax receivable	212	159
Cash and cash equivalents	2,960	1,359
Total current assets	**75,290**	**61,443**
TOTAL ASSETS	**206,914**	**194,630**
Trade and other payables	42,136	38,540
Derivative financial instruments	9,083	5,074
Accruals and deferred income	5,970	4,482
Finance debt	8,932	10,184
Current tax payable	4,274	4,131
Provisions	1,102	715
Total current liabilities	**71,497**	**63,126**
Other payables	1,935	3,581
Derivative financial instruments	3,696	158
Accruals and deferred income	3,164	699
Finance debt	10,230	12,907
Deferred tax liabilities	16,443	16,701
Provisions	9,954	8,884
Defined benefit pension plan and other post-retirement benefit plan deficits	9,230	10,339
Total non-current liabilities	**54,652**	**53,269**
Share capital	5,185	5,403
Reserves	74,791	71,489
BP shareholders' equity	**79,976**	**76,892**
Minority interest	789	1,343
TOTAL LIABILITIES AND SHAREHOLDERS' EQUITY	**206,914**	**194,630**

CONSOLIDATED INCOME STATEMENTS – REPSOL YPF (€ millions)

Fiscal year ended December 31,	2005	2004
Sales	**48,024**	**38,273**
Other income	**3,021**	**2,019**
Material used	(32,512)	(24,920)
Staff costs	(1,542)	(1,330)
Depreciation and amortization charge	(2,450)	(2,368)
Other expenses	(8,380)	(6,988)
Profit from continuing operations before finance costs	**6,161**	**4,686**
Finance costs	(722)	(624)
Income tax	(2,332)	(1,627)
Share of results of companies accounted for using the equity method	117	131
Profit for the year	**3,224**	**2,566**
Minority interests	(104)	(152)
Net income	**3,120**	**2,414**

CONSOLIDATED BALANCE SHEETS – REPSOL YPF (€ millions)

Fiscal year ended December 31,	2005	2004
Property, plant, and equipment	23,304	20,303
Investment property	54	52
Goodwill	3,773	3,204
Other intangible assets	1,003	693
Available-for-sale financial assets	1	83
Investments accounted for using the equity method	399	449
Financial assets	1,746	2,030
Deferred tax assets	1,197	1,099
Total non-current assets	**31,477**	**27,913**
Inventories	3,730	2,638
Trade and other receivables	6,841	5,277
Income tax receivables	586	270
Current financial assets	501	267
Cash and cash equivalents	2,647	3,328
Total current assets	**14,305**	**11,780**
TOTAL ASSETS	**45,782**	**39,693**
Equity attributable to shareholders of the Parent	16,262	12,806
Minority interests	528	424
Total equity	**16,790**	**13,230**
Preference shares	3,485	3,386
Non-current bank borrowings and other financial liabilities	6,236	7,333
Deferred tax liabilities	3,380	2,960
Non-current provisions for contingencies and expenses	2,878	1,996
Other non-current liabilities	1,704	1,618
Total non-current liabilities	**17,683**	**17,293**
Current bank borrowings and other financial liabilities	2,701	3,142
Trade and other payables	7,783	5,550
Income tax payable	635	445
Current provisions for contingencies and expenses	190	33
Total current liabilities	**11,309**	**9,170**
TOTAL EQUITY AND LIABILITIES	**45,782**	**39,693**

CONSOLIDATED INCOME STATEMENTS – ROYAL DUTCH SHELL ($ millions)

Fiscal year ended December 31,	2005	2004
Revenue	**306,731**	**266,386**
Cost of sales	(252,622)	(223,259)
Gross profit	**54,109**	**43,127**
Selling, distribution and administrative expenses	(15,482)	(15,098)
Exploration	(1,286)	(1,809)
Share of profit of equity accounted investments	7,123	5,015
Interest and other income	1,171	1,483
Interest expense	(1,068)	(1,059)
Income before taxation	**44,567**	**31,659**
Taxation	17,999	12,168
Income from continuing operations	**26,568**	**19,491**
Income/(loss) from discontinued operations	(307)	(234)
Income attributable to minority interest	(950)	(717)
Income for the period	**25,311**	**18,540**

Forecasting earnings and earnings growth in the European oil and gas industry

CONSOLIDATED BALANCE SHEETS – ROYAL DUTCH SHELL ($ millions)

Fiscal year ended December 31,	2005	2004
Intangible assets	4,350	4,528
Property, plant and equipment	87,558	87,918
Investments:		
Equity accounted investments	16,905	19,190
Financial assets	3,672	2,700
Deferred tax	2,562	2,789
Prepaid pension costs	2,486	2,479
Other	4,091	5,793
Total non-current assets	**121,624**	**125,397**
Inventories	19,776	15,375
Accounts receivable	66,386	37,473
Cash and cash equivalents	11,730	9,201
Total current assets	**97,892**	**62,049**
TOTAL ASSETS	**219,516**	**187,446**
Debt	7,578	8,858
Deferred tax	10,763	12,930
Retirement benefit obligations	5,807	6,795
Other provisions	7,385	6,828
Other	5,095	5,800
Total non-current liabilities	**36,628**	**41,211**
Debt	5,338	5,734
Accounts payable and accrued liabilities	69,013	37,909
Taxes payable	8,782	9,058
Retirement benefit obligations	282	339
Other provisions	1,549	1,812
Total current liabilities	**84,964**	**54,852**
Ordinary share capital	571	584
Preference share capital	0	20
Treasury shares	(3,809)	(4,187)
Other reserves	3,584	8,865
Retained earnings	90,578	80,788
Minority interest	7,000	5,313
Total equity	**97,924**	**91,383**
TOTAL LIABILITIES AND SHAREHOLDERS' EQUITY	**219,516**	**187,446**

Prospective Analysis: Valuation Theory and Concepts

The previous chapter introduced forecasting, the first stage of prospective analysis. In this and the following chapter we describe valuation, the second and final stage of prospective analysis. This chapter focuses on valuation theory and concepts, and the following chapter discusses implementation issues.

Valuation is the process of converting a forecast into an estimate of the value of the firm's assets or equity. At some level, nearly every business decision involves valuation, at least implicitly. Within the firm, capital budgeting involves consideration of how a particular project will affect firm value. Strategic planning focuses on how value is influenced by larger sets of actions. Outside the firm, security analysts conduct valuation to support their buy/sell decisions, and potential acquirers (often with the assistance of investment bankers) estimate the value of target firms and the synergies they might offer. Even credit analysts, who typically do not explicitly estimate firm value, must at least implicitly consider the value of the firm's equity "cushion" if they are to maintain a complete view of the risk associated with lending activity.

In practice, a wide variety of valuation approaches are employed. For example, in evaluating the fairness of a takeover bid, investment bankers commonly use five to ten different methods of valuation. Among the available methods are the following:

- Discounted dividends. This approach expresses the value of the firm's equity as the present value of forecasted future dividends.

- Discounted cash flow (DCF) analysis. This approach involves the production of detailed, multiple-year forecasts of cash flows. The forecasts are then discounted at the firm's estimated cost of capital to arrive at an estimated present value.

- Discounted abnormal earnings. Under this approach the value of the firm's equity is expressed as the sum of its book value and the present value of forecasted **abnormal earnings**.

- Discounted abnormal earnings growth. This approach defines the value of the firm's equity as the sum of its capitalized next-period earnings forecast and the present value of forecasted **abnormal earnings growth** beyond the next period.

- Valuation based on price multiples. Under this approach a current measure of performance or single forecast of performance is converted into a value by applying an appropriate price multiple derived from the value of comparable firms. For example, firm value can be estimated by applying a price-to-earnings ratio to a forecast of the firm's earnings for the coming year. Other commonly used multiples include price-to-book ratios and price-to-sales ratios.

These methods are developed throughout the chapter, and their pros and cons discussed. All of the above approaches can be structured in two ways. The first is to directly value the equity of the firm, since this is usually the variable the analyst is directly interested in estimating. The second is to value the assets of the firm, that is, the claims of equity and net debt, and then to deduct the value of net debt to arrive at the final equity estimate. Theoretically, both approaches should generate the same values. However, as we will see in the next chapter, there are implementation issues in reconciling the approaches. In this chapter we illustrate valuation using an all-equity firm to simplify the discussion. A brief discussion of the theoretical issues in valuing a firm's assets is included in Appendix A.

DEFINING VALUE FOR SHAREHOLDERS

How should shareholders think about the value of their equity claims on a firm? Finance theory holds that the value of any financial claim is simply the present value of the cash payoffs that its claimholders receive. Since shareholders receive cash payoffs from a company in the form of dividends, the value of their equity is the present value of future dividends (including any liquidating dividend).[1]

$$\text{Equity value} = \text{PV of expected future dividends}$$

If we denote r_e as the cost of equity capital (the relevant discount rate), the **equity value** is as follows:

$$\text{Equity value} = \frac{\text{Dividend}_1}{(1 + r_e)} + \frac{\text{Dividend}_2}{(1 + r_e)^2} + \frac{\text{Dividend}_3}{(1 + r_e)^3} + \ldots$$

Notice that the valuation formula views a firm as having an indefinite life. But in reality firms can go bankrupt or get taken over. In these situations shareholders effectively receive a terminating dividend on their shares.

If a firm had a constant dividend growth rate (g^{div}) indefinitely, its value would simplify to the following formula:

$$\text{Equity value} = \frac{\text{Dividend}_1}{r_e - g^{div}}$$

To better understand how the discounted dividend approach works, consider the following example. At the beginning of year 1, Down Under Company raises €60 million of equity and uses the proceeds to buy a fixed asset. Operating profits before depreciation (all received in cash) and dividends for the company are expected to be €40 million in year 1, €50 million in year 2, and €60 million in year 3, at which point the company terminates. The firm pays no taxes. If the cost of equity capital for this firm is 10 percent, the value of the firm's equity is computed as follows:

Year	Dividend	PV factor	PV of dividend
	(a)	(b)	(a) × (b)
1	€40m	0.9091	€ 36.4m
2	50	0.8264	41.3
3	60	0.7513	45.1
Equity value			€122.8m

The above valuation formula is called the dividend discount model. It forms the basis for most of the popular theoretical approaches for equity valuation. Despite its theoretical importance, the dividend discount model is not a very useful valuation model in practice. This is because equity value is created primarily through the investment and operating activities of a firm. Dividend payments tend to be a by product of such activities and their timing and amount depends strongly on the firm's investment opportunities. Within a period of five to ten years, which tends to be the focus of most prospective analyses, dividends may therefore reveal very little about the firm's equity value. For example, high-growth start-up firms tend not to pay out dividends until later into their life cycle but they nonetheless have value when they start their operations. Predicting long-run dividends for these firms is a tedious, virtually impossible task. As the first stage of the prospective analysis, as discussed in Chapter 6, typically produces comprehensive, detailed forecasts for the near term but unavoidably makes simplifying assumptions for the longer term, useful valuation models value near-term profitability and growth directly rather than indirectly through long run dividends. The remainder of the chapter discusses how the dividend discount model can be recast to generate such useful models. The models that we discuss are the discounted cash flow, discounted abnormal earnings, discounted abnormal earnings growth, and price multiple models of value.

THE DISCOUNTED CASH FLOW MODEL

As we described in the previous section, the value of an asset or investment is the present value of the net cash payoffs that the asset generates. The **discounted cash flow** valuation model clearly reflects this basic principle of finance. The model defines the value of a firm's net assets as the present value of cash flows generated by these assets (OCF) minus the investments made in new assets (Investment), or, alternatively stated, as the sum of the **free cash flows to debt and equity** holders discounted at the weighted average cost of debt and equity (WACC).

$$\text{Asset value} = \text{PV of free cash flows to debt and equity claim holders}$$
$$= \frac{\text{OCF}_1 - \text{Investment}_1}{(1 + \text{WACC})} + \frac{\text{OCF}_2 - \text{Investment}_2}{(1 + \text{WACC})^2} + \cdots$$

Note that in this equation OCF excludes interest payments (unlike the operating cash flows reported in IFRS-based cash flow statements), as these are distributions to debt holders.

The cash flows that are available to equity holders are the cash flows generated by the firm's net assets minus capital outlays, adjusted for cash flows from and to debt holders, such as interest payments, debt repayments and debts issues. As discussed in Chapter 5, operating cash flows to equity holders are simply net profit plus depreciation less changes in working capital. Capital outlays are capital expenditures less asset sales. Finally, net cash flows from debt owners are issues of new debt less retirements less the after-tax cost of interest. By rearranging these terms, the free cash flows to equity can be written as follows:

$$\text{Free cash flows to equity} = \text{Net profit} - \Delta\text{BVA} + \Delta\text{BVND}$$

where ΔBVA is the change in book value of operating net assets (changes in working capital plus capital expenditures less depreciation expense), and ΔBVND is the change in book value of net debt (interest-bearing debt less excess cash). Using the discounted cash flow model, equity value is thus estimated as follows:

$$\text{Equity value} = \text{PV of free cash flows to equityclaim holders}$$
$$= \frac{\text{Net profit}_1 - \Delta BVA_1 + \Delta BVND_1}{(1 + r_e)}$$
$$+ \frac{\text{Net profit}_2 - \Delta BVA_2 + \Delta BVND_2}{(1 + r_e)^2} + \ldots$$

Valuation under this method therefore involves the following three steps:

Step 1: Forecast free cash flows available to equity holders over a finite forecast horizon (usually 5 to 10 years).

Step 2: Forecast free cash flows beyond the terminal year based on some simplifying assumption.

Step 3: Discount free cash flows to equity holders at the cost of equity. The discounted amount represents the estimated value of free cash flows available to equity.

Returning to the Down Under Company example, there is no debt, so that the free cash flows to owners are simply the operating profits before depreciation. Since the company's cost of equity is assumed to be 10 percent, the present value of the free cash flows is as follows:

Year	Net profit	Change in book value of net assets	Change in book value of net debt	Free cash flows to equity	PV factor	PV of free cash flows
	(a)	(b)	(c)	(d) = (a) – (b) + (c)	(e)	(d) × (e)
1	€20m	−€20m	€0m	€40m	0.9091	€ 36.4m
2	30	−20	0	50	0.8264	41.3
3	40	−20	0	60	0.7513	45.1
Equity value						€122.8m

Earlier we indicated that the discounted cash flow model can be obtained by recasting the dividend discount model. To see how this works, recall our formulation of the free cash flows to equity holders in terms of net profit, the change in the book value of net assets (ΔBVA) and the change in the book value of net debt (ΔBVA). In the recast financial statements, which we described in Chapter 5 and use throughout this book, the change in the book value of net assets minus the change in the book value of net debt is equal to the change in the book value of equity (ΔBVE). The free cash flows to equity can therefore be written as:

$$\text{Free cash flows to equity} = \text{Net profit} - \Delta BVA + \Delta BVND$$
$$= \text{Net profit} - \Delta BVE$$
$$= \text{Dividends}$$

which illustrates the relationship between free cash flows to equity and dividends.[2]

As discussed in Chapter 6, the key ingredient to an accurate prediction of future free cash flows is a full set of predicted future (condensed) income statements and balance sheets. Given the prominence of earnings forecasts in most prospective analyses, models have been developed that express equity value directly in terms of expected earnings, book values of equity and cost of equity, thus further sharpening the focus of the valuation exercise. The following sections describe two of these accounting-based valuation models: the **discounted abnormal earnings model** and the **discounted abnormal earnings growth model**. In a later section, we also show that these accounting-based valuation model can help in better understanding the rationale underlying valuation based on price multiples.

THE DISCOUNTED ABNORMAL EARNINGS VALUATION METHOD

As discussed in Chapter 3, there is a link between dividends, earnings and equity. At the end of each accounting period net profit for the period is added to retained earnings, a component of equity. Dividends are taken out of retained earnings. Stated differently, if all equity effects (other than capital transactions) flow through the income statement,[3] the expected book value of equity for existing shareholders at the end of year 1 (BVE_1) is simply the book value at the beginning of the year (BVE_0) plus expected net profit (Net profit$_1$) less expected dividends (Dividend$_1$).[4] This relation can be written as follows:

$$\text{Dividend}_1 = \text{Net profit}_1 + BVE_0 - BVE_1$$

By substituting this identity for dividends into the dividend discount formula and rearranging the terms, equity value can be rewritten as follows:[5]

Equity value = Book value of equity + PV of expected future abnormal earnings

Abnormal earnings are net profit adjusted for a capital charge, which is computed as the discount rate multiplied by the beginning book value of equity. Abnormal earnings incorporate an adjustment to reflect the fact that accountants do not recognize any opportunity cost for equity funds used. Thus, the discounted abnormal earnings valuation formula is

$$\text{Equity value} = BVE_0 + \frac{\text{Net profit}_1 - r_e \cdot BVE_0}{(1 + r_e)} + \frac{\text{Net profit}_2 - r_e \cdot BVE_1}{(1 + r_e)^2} + \ldots$$

The earnings-based formulation has intuitive appeal. If a firm can earn only a normal rate of return on its book value, then investors should be willing to pay no more than book value for its shares. Investors should pay more or less than book value if earnings are above or below this normal level. Thus, the deviation of a firm's market value from book value depends on its ability to generate "abnormal earnings." The formulation also implies that a firm's equity value reflects the cost of its existing net assets (that is, its book equity) plus the net present value of future growth options (represented by cumulative abnormal earnings).

To illustrate the earnings-based valuation approach, let's return to the Down Under Company example. Assuming the company depreciates its fixed assets using the straight-line method, its accounting-based earnings will be €20 million lower than dividends in each of the three years. Further, the book value of equity at the beginning of years 2 and 3 equals prior year's beginning book value plus prior year's earnings minus prior year's dividends. The firm's beginning book equity, earnings, abnormal earnings, and valuation will be as follows:

Year	Beginning book value	Earnings	Capital charge	Abnormal earnings	PV factor	PV of abnormal earnings
	(a)	(b)	(c) = r_e × (a)	(d) = (b) − (c)	(e)	(d) × (e)
1	€60m	€20m	€6m	€14m	0.9091	€ 12.7m
2	40	30	4	26	0.8264	21.5
3	20	40	2	38	0.7513	28.6
Cumulative PV of abnormal earnings						62.8
+ Beginning book value						60.0
= Equity value						€122.8m

Notice that the value of Down Under's equity is exactly the same as that estimated using the discounted cash flow method. This should not be surprising. Both methods are derived from the dividend discount model. And in estimating value under the two approaches, we have used the same underlying assumptions to forecast earnings and cash flows.

KEY ANALYSIS QUESTIONS

Valuation of equity under the discounted abnormal earnings method requires the analyst to answer the following questions:

- What are expected future net profit and book values of equity (and therefore abnormal earnings) over a finite forecast horizon (usually five to ten years) given the firm's industry competitiveness and the firm's positioning?

- What is expected future abnormal net profit beyond the final year of the forecast horizon (called the "terminal year") based on some simplifying assumption? If abnormal returns are expected to persist, what are the barriers to entry that deter competition?

- What is the firm's cost of equity used to compute the present value of abnormal earnings?

Accounting methods and discounted abnormal earnings

One question that arises when valuation is based directly on earnings and book values is how the estimate is affected by managers' choice of accounting methods and accrual estimates. Would estimates of value differ for two otherwise identical firms if one used more conservative accounting methods than the other? We will see that, provided that analysts recognize the impact of differences in accounting methods on future earnings (and hence their earnings forecasts), the accounting effects per se should have no influence on their value estimates. There are two reasons for this. First, accounting choices that affect a firm's current earnings also affect its book value, and therefore they affect the capital charges used to estimate future abnormal earnings. For example, conservative accounting not only lowers a firm's current earnings and book equity but also reduces future capital charges and inflates its future abnormal earnings. Second, double-entry bookkeeping is by nature self-correcting. Inflated earnings for one period have to be ultimately reversed in subsequent periods.

To understand how these two effects undo the effect of differences in accounting methods or accrual estimates, let's return to Down Under Company and see what happens if its managers choose to be conservative and expense some unusual costs that could have been capitalized as inventory in year 1. This accounting decisions causes earnings and ending book value to be lower by €10 million. The inventory is then sold in year 2. For the time being, let's say the accounting choice has no influence on the analyst's view of the firm's real performance.

Managers' choice reduces abnormal earnings in year 1 and book value at the beginning of year 2 by €10 million. However, future earnings will be higher, for two reasons. First, future earnings will be higher (by €10 million) when the inventory is sold in year 2 at a lower cost of sales. Second, the benchmark for normal earnings (based on book value of equity) will be lower by €10 million. The €10 million decline in abnormal earnings in year 1 is perfectly offset (on a present value basis) by the €11 million higher abnormal earnings in year 2. As a result, the value of Down Under Company under conservative reporting is identical to the value under the earlier accounting method (€122.8 million).

Year	Beginning book value	Earnings	Capital charge	Abnormal earnings	PV factor	PV of abnormal earnings
	(a)	(b)	(c) = $r_e \times$ (a)	(d) = (b) – (c)	(e)	(d) × (e)
1	€60m	€10m	€6m	€4m	0.9091	€ 3.6m
2	30	40	3	37	0.8264	30.6
3	20	40	2	38	0.7513	28.6
Cumulative PV of abnormal earnings						62.8
+ Beginning book value						60.0
= Equity value						€122.8m

Provided the analyst is aware of biases in accounting data that arise from managers' using aggressive or conservative accounting choices, abnormal earnings-based valuations are unaffected by the variation in accounting decisions. This shows that strategic and accounting analyses are critical precursors to abnormal earnings valuation. The strategic and accounting analysis tools help the analyst to identify whether abnormal earnings arise from sustainable competitive advantage or from unsustainable accounting manipulations. For example, consider the implications of failing to understand the reasons for a decline in earnings from a change in inventory policy for Down Under Company. If the analyst mistakenly interpreted the decline as indicating that the firm was having difficulty moving its inventory, rather than that it had used conservative accounting, she might reduce expectations of future earnings. The estimated value of the firm would then be lower than that reported in our example. To avoid such mistakes, the analyst would be wise to go through all steps of the accounting analysis, including step 6 (undo accounting distortions), and then perform the financial and prospective analyses using the restated financial statements.

THE DISCOUNTED ABNORMAL EARNINGS GROWTH VALUATION METHOD

As discussed above, abnormal earnings are the amount of earnings that a firm generates in excess of the opportunity cost for equity funds used. The annual change in abnormal earnings is generally referred to as abnormal earnings growth and can be rewritten as follows:

$$\text{Abnormal earnings growth} = \text{change in abnormal earnings}$$
$$= (\text{Net profit}_2 - r_e \cdot \text{BVE}_1) - (\text{Net profit}_1 - r_e \cdot \text{BVE}_0)$$
$$= (\text{Net profit}_2 - r_e \cdot [\text{BVE}_0 + \text{Net profit}_1 - \text{Dividend}_1])$$
$$\quad - (\text{Net profit}_1 - r_e \cdot \text{BVE}_0)$$
$$= \text{Net profit}_2 + r_e \cdot \text{Dividend}_1 - (1 + r_e) \cdot \text{Net profit}_1$$
$$= \Delta \text{Net profit}_2 - r_e \cdot (\text{Net profit}_1 - \text{Dividend}_1)$$
$$(= \text{abnormal change in earnings})$$

This formula shows that abnormal earnings growth is actual earnings growth benchmarked against normal earnings growth. Normal earnings growth is calculated as the portion of prior period earnings that is retained in the firm times a normal rate of return. When abnormal earnings growth is zero, the firm functions like a savings account. In this particular case, the firm earns an abnormal return on its existing investment but is only able to earn a normal rate of return on the additional investments that it finances from its retained earnings. Consequently, an investor would be indifferent between reinvesting earnings in the firm and receiving all earnings in dividends.

The discounted dividend model can also be recast to generate a valuation model that defines equity value as the capitalized sum of (1) next-period earnings and (2) the discounted value of abnormal earnings growth beyond the next period. The **discounted abnormal earnings** growth valuation formula is:[6]

$$\text{Equity value} = \frac{\text{Net profit}_1}{r_e} + \frac{1}{r_e}\left[\frac{\Delta\text{Net profit}_2 - r_e \cdot (\text{Net profit}_1 - \text{Dividend}_1)}{(1 + r_e)}\right.$$

$$\left. + \frac{\Delta\text{Net profit}_3 - r_e \cdot (\text{Net profit}_2 - \text{Dividend}_2)}{(1 + r_e)^2} + \cdots\right]$$

This approach, under which valuation starts with capitalizing next-period earnings, has practical appeal because investment analysts spend much time and effort on estimating near-term earnings as the starting point of their analysis. The valuation formula shows that differences between equity value and capitalized next-period earnings are explained by abnormal changes in earnings – or changes in abnormal earnings – beyond the next period.

Notice that this formula also views the firm as having an indefinite life. However, the formula can be easily used for the valuation of a finite-life investment by extending the investment's life by one year and setting earnings and dividends equal to zero in the last year. For example, consider the earnings and dividends of the Down Under Company during its three years of existence. Capitalized year 1 earnings are equal to €200.0 million (20.0/.1). Abnormal earnings growth equals €12.0 million in year 2 (30.0 + 40.0 × .1 – 20.0 × 1.1) and €12.0 million in year 3 (40.0 + 50.0 × .1 –30.0 × 1.1). In year 4, when earnings and dividends are zero, abnormal earnings growth is –€38.0 million (0.0 + 60.0 × .1 – 40.0 × 1.1). The total value of the firm's equity is computed as follows:

Year	Earnings	Retained earnings	Normal earnings growth	Abnormal earnings growth	PV factor	PV of abnormal earnings growth
	(a)	(b) = (a) − Dividends	(c) = $r_e \times$ (b)$_{t-1}$	(d) = Δ(a) − (c)	(e)	(d) × (e)
1	€20m	−€20m				
2	30	−20	−€2m	€12m	0.9091	€ 10.91m
3	40	−20	−2	12	0.8264	9.92
4	0	0	−2	−38	0.7513	−28.55
Cumulative PV of abnormal earnings growth						−7.72
+ Earnings in year 1						20.00
=						€ 12.28m
× 1/r_e						10.00
= Equity value						€ 122.8m

Note that the Down Under Company gradually reduces its investment because the annual dividend payments exceed annual earnings. Consequently, normal earnings growth is negative and the firm's abnormal earnings growth is greater than its actual earnings growth in every year.

Like the abnormal earnings method, the value estimate from the abnormal earnings growth model is not affected by the firm's accounting choices. For example, recall the situation where the Down Under Company reports conservatively and expenses unusual costs that could have been capitalized in year 1, thereby reducing earnings by €10.0 million. Under conservative accounting, the value of capitalized year 1 earnings decreases from €200.0 million to €100.0 million. This reduction, however, is exactly offset by an increase in the discounted value of abnormal earnings growth, as shown in the following table:

Year	Earnings	Retained earnings	Normal earnings growth	Abnormal earnings growth	PV factor	PV of abnormal earnings growth
	(a)	(b) = (a) − Dividends	(c) = $r_e \times (b)_{t-1}$	(d) = Δ(a) − (c)	(e)	(d) × (e)
1	€10m	−€30m				
2	40	−10	−€3m	€33m	0.9091	€ 30.00m
3	40	−20	−1	1	0.8264	0.83
4	0	0	−2	−38	0.7513	−28.55
Cumulative PV of abnormal earnings growth						2.28
+ Earnings in year 1						10.00
=						€ 12.28m
× $1/r_e$						10.00
= Equity value						€ 122.8m

This value is again identical to the value estimated under the discounted dividends and abnormal earnings approaches.

DEMONSTRATION CASE: LOEWE AG

During the first few weeks following the fiscal year ended on December 31, 2008, seven analysts disclosed their forecasts of Loewe's 2009 and 2010 sales, EBIT, and net profit. Under the simplifying assumption that Loewe's effective tax rate in 2009 and 2010 will be 30.0 percent (compared to 30.8 percent in 2008), analysts' average expectations of Loewe's future net interest expense can be easily imputed from these forecasts:

	2008 realized	2009 expected	2010 expected
Sales	€374.0m	€364.5m	€368.7m
EBIT	30.0	25.2	26.0
Net interest expense	(1.1)	(1.0)	(0.4)
Pre-tax profit	28.9	24.2	25.6
Tax expense (30%)	(8.9)	(7.3)	(7.6)
Net profit	19.8	16.9	18.0

Required:

1 These forecasts are not sufficient to estimate the value of Loewe's equity. Forecast Loewe's ending net working capital, net non-current assets, net debt and shareholders' equity under the simplifying assumption that the future growth in these items follows sales growth. Also calculate NOPAT.

2 Assume that Loewe's cost of equity is 10 percent. Calculate:

   a Dividends in 2009 and 2010.

   b Abnormal earnings in 2009 and 2010.

   c Abnormal earnings growth in 2010.

   d Free cash flows to equity in 2009 and 2010.

3 To estimate Loewe's equity value, we need to make an assumption about what will happen to Loewe's profits, dividends, equity, debt and assets after 2010. In the next chapter we will discuss several assumptions that the analyst can make. For now, we assume that in 2011 Loewe liquidates all its assets at their book values, uses the proceeds to pay off debt and pays out the remainder to its equity holders. What does this assumption imply about:

  a The book value of Loewe's assets and liabilities at the end of 2011?

  b Loewe's net profit in 2011?

  c Loewe's final dividend payment in 2011?

  d Loewe's free cash flow to equity holders in 2011?

  e Loewe's abnormal earnings growth in 2011 and 2012 (!)?

4 Estimate Loewe's equity value at the end of 2008 using:

  a The discounted dividends model and the discounted cash flow model.

  b The discounted abnormal earnings model.

  c The discounted abnormal earning growth model.

Answers:

1 Expected sales growth in 2009 and 2010 is −2.5 percent (9.5/374.0) and 1.2 percent (4.2/364.5), respectively. The values of the four balance sheet items at the end of 2008 are known. Based on the expected sales growth rates, the expected values at the end of 2009 and 2010 are:

Ending ...	2008 realized	2009 expected	2010 expected
Net working capital	€ 52.1m	€ 50.8m	€ 51.4m
Net non-current assets	69.3	67.5	68.3
Net debt	31.4	30.6	30.9
Shareholders' equity	90.0	87.7	88.8
Net assets / capital	121.4	118.3	119.7

2 Calculations:

  a $\text{Dividends}_{2009} = \text{Equity}_{2008} + \text{Profit}_{2009} - \text{Equity}_{2009} = 90.0 + 16.9 - 87.7 = 19.2$.
  $\text{Dividends}_{2010} = \text{Equity}_{2009} + \text{Profit}_{2010} - \text{Equity}_{2010} = 87.7 + 18.0 - 88.8 = 16.9$.

  b $\text{Abnormal Earnings}_{2009} = \text{Profit}_{2009} - r_e \times \text{Equity}_{2008} = 16.9 - 10\% \times 90.0 = 7.9$.
  $\text{Abnormal Earnings}_{2010} = \text{Profit}_{2010} - r_e \times \text{Equity}_{2009} = 18.0 - 10\% \times 87.7 = 9.2$.

  c $\text{Abnormal Earnings growth}_{2010} = \Delta\text{Profit}_{2010} - r_e \times (\text{Profit}_{2009} - \text{Dividends}_{2009}) = 1.1 - 10\% \times (16.9 - 19.2) = 1.3$.

  (Check that Abnormal earnings growth = ΔAbnormal earnings (see b).)

  d $\text{FCF to Equity}_{2009} = \text{Profit}_{2009} - \Delta\text{Net Assets}_{2009} + \Delta\text{Net Debt}_{2009} = 16.9 - (-3.1) + (-0.8) = 19.2$.
  $\text{FCF to Equity}_{2010} = \text{Profit}_{2010} - \Delta\text{Net Assets}_{2010} + \Delta\text{Net Debt}_{2010} = 18.0 - 1.4 + 0.3 = 16.9$.

  (Note that the free cash flows to equity holders is equal to the dividends paid out to equity holders.)

3 Calculations:

a Loewe's assets and liabilities will have book values of zero at the end of 2011.

b Loewe's net profit will be zero in 2011 because all assets have been sold at their book values (i.e., profit on the sale = 0).

c The final dividend payment in 2011 will be equal to the ending book value in 2010: $\text{Dividends}_{2011} = \text{Equity}_{2010} + \text{Profit}_{2011} - \text{Equity}_{2011} = 88.8 + 0 - 0 = 88.8$.

d $\text{FCF to Equity}_{2011} = \text{Profit}_{2011} - \Delta\text{Net Assets}_{2011} + \Delta\text{Net Debt}_{2011} = 0 - (-119.7) + (-30.9) = 88.8$ (Note that the final free cash flows to equity holders is equal to the final dividend.).

e $\text{Abnormal Earnings}_{2011} = \text{Profit}_{2011} - r_e \times \text{Equity}_{2010} = 0 - 10\% \times 88.8 = -8.9$.

f $\text{Abnormal Earnings growth}_{2011} = \Delta\text{Profit}_{2011} - r_e \times (\text{Profit}_{2010} - \text{Dividends}_{2010}) = -18.0 - 10\% \times (18.0 - 16.9) = -18.1$.
$\text{Abnormal Earnings growth}_{2012} = \Delta\text{Profit}_{2012} - r_e \times (\text{Profit}_{2011} - \text{Dividends}_{2011}) = 0 - 10\% \times (0 - 88.8) = 8.9$.

(Check that Abnormal earnings growth = ΔAbnormal earnings (see e and 2b).)

4 Calculations:

a Note that Loewe's expected dividends are exactly equal to its free cash flows to equity holders. Using the discounted dividends (DIV) model (or discounted cash flow model), Loewe's equity value is calculated as follows:

$$\text{Equity value}_{\text{end 2008}} = \frac{\text{DIV}_{2009}}{(1 + r_e)} + \frac{\text{DIV}_{2010}}{(1 + r_e)^2} + \frac{\text{DIV}_{2011}}{(1 + r_e)^3}$$

$$= \frac{19.2}{(1.1)} + \frac{16.9}{(1.1)^2} + \frac{88.8}{(1.1)^3} = 98.1$$

b Using the discounted abnormal earnings (AE) model, Loewe's equity value is calculated as follows:

$$\text{Equity value}_{\text{end 2008}} = \text{BVE}_{\text{end 2008}} + \frac{\text{AE}_{2009}}{(1 + r_e)} + \frac{\text{AE}_{2010}}{(1 + r_e)^2} + \frac{\text{AE}_{2011}}{(1 + r_e)^3}$$

$$= 90 + \frac{7.9}{(1.1)} + \frac{9.2}{(1.1)^2} + \frac{-8.9}{(1.1)^3} = 98.1$$

c Using the discounted abnormal earnings growth (AE) model, Loewe's equity value is calculated as follows:

$$\text{Equity value}_{\text{end 2008}} = \frac{\text{Profit}_{2009}}{r_e} + \frac{1}{r_e}\left[\frac{\text{AEG}_{2010}}{(1 + r_e)} + \frac{\text{AEG}_{2011}}{(1 + r_e)^2} + \frac{\text{AEG}_{2012}}{(1 + r_e)^3}\right]$$

$$= \frac{16.9}{0.1} + \frac{1}{0.1}\left[\frac{1.3}{(1.1)} + \frac{-18.1}{(1.1)^2} + \frac{8.9}{(1.1)^3}\right] = 98.1$$

At the end of 2008, Loewe had 13 million shares outstanding. The equity value estimate of €98.1 million thus corresponds with an estimate of €7.55 per share. On January 28, 2009, one day after Loewe's preliminary annual earnings announcement, the company's closing share price was €6.95.

VALUATION USING PRICE MULTIPLES

Valuations based on price multiples are widely used by analysts. The primary reason for the popularity of this method is its simplicity. Unlike the discounted dividend, discounted abnormal earnings (growth), and discounted cash flow methods, **multiple-based valuations** do not require detailed multiyear forecasts of a number of parameters such as growth, profitability, and cost of capital.

Valuation using multiples involves the following three steps:

Step 1: Select a measure of performance or value (e.g., earnings, sales, cash flows, book equity, book assets) as the basis for multiple calculations. The two most commonly used metrics are based on earnings and book equity.

Step 2: Calculate price multiples for comparable firms, i.e., the ratio of the market value to the selected measure of performance or value.

Step 3: Apply the comparable firm multiple to the performance or value measure of the firm being analyzed.

Under this approach, the analyst relies on the market to undertake the difficult task of considering the short- and long-term prospects for growth and profitability and their implications for the values of the comparable firms. Then the analyst assumes that the pricing of those other firms is applicable to the firm at hand.

Main issues with multiple-based valuation

On the surface, using multiples seems straightforward. Unfortunately, in practice it is not as simple as it would appear. Identification of "comparable" firms is often quite difficult. There are also some choices to be made concerning how multiples will be calculated. Finally, understanding why multiples vary across firms, and how applicable another firm's multiple is to the one at hand, requires a sound knowledge of the determinants of each multiple.

Selecting comparable firms

Ideally, price multiples used in a comparable firm analysis are those for firms with similar operating and financial characteristics. Firms within the same industry are the most obvious candidates. But even within narrowly defined industries, it is often difficult to identify comparable firms. Many firms are in multiple industries, making it difficult to identify representative benchmarks. In addition, firms within the same industry frequently have different strategies, growth opportunities, and profitability, creating selection problems.

One way of dealing with these issues is to average across *all* firms in the industry. The analyst implicitly hopes that the various sources of noncomparability cancel each other out, so that the firm being valued is comparable to a "typical" industry member. Another approach is to focus on only those firms within the industry that are most similar.

For example, consider using multiples to value Bang & Olufsen (B&O). Business and financial databases such as Thomson One classify the company in the Household Audio and Video industry. Its competitors, with equity values above €300 million, include Grundig, Harman International, Philips, Loewe, Panasonic, Sharp, Sony, TCL, and Videocon. The average price-earnings ratio for a profitable subset of these direct competitors was 10.6 and the average price-to-book ratio was 1.0. However, it is unclear whether these multiples are useful benchmarks for valuing B&O. Many of these competitors have a wider product offering than B&O and operate on a significantly larger scale, both in terms of revenue and geographic reach. In addition, not all competitors are as sensitive to the economic downturn as B&O.

A potential problem of choosing comparable firms from different countries is that a variety of factors that influence multiples may differ across countries. For example, the cost of equity, which is inversely related to the price-earnings multiple, is affected by the risk-free interest rate. Consequently, international differences in risk-free interest rates lead to international differences in price-earnings multiples. In addition, international differences in accounting standards may lead to systematic international differences in net profits, which is the denominator in price-earnings multiples. The most obvious way to get around this problem is to choose comparable firms from one country. This is, however, often not feasible in smaller equity markets. The alternative solution is to explicitly take into account the country factors that affect multiples. For example, when using the multiples of the above group of competitors, it is important to realize that at the time that the multiples were calculated, risk-free interest rates in the European (Monetary) Union were higher than the risk-free interest rate in Japan (domicile of Panasonic, Sharp and Sony). This may have caused the average price-earnings multiple of B&O's Japanese competitors to be relatively high: 14.8.

Multiples for firms with poor performance

Price multiples can be affected when the denominator variable is performing poorly. This is especially common when the denominator is a flow measure, such as earnings or cash-flows. For example, several competitors of B&O, such as Grundig, Philips, and TCL reported losses in 2008, making the price-earnings ratios negative. Because negative price-earnings ratios have no sensible meaning, these were ignored in the calculation of the average price-earnings ratio.

What are analysts' options for handling the problems for multiples created by transitory shocks to the denominator? One option is to simply exclude firms with large transitory effects from the set of comparable firms, as we did above. If poor performance is due to a one-time write down or special item, analysts can simply exclude that effect from their computation of the comparable multiple. For example, in 2008 Philips recorded a loss of €0.18 per share, including close to €0.60 per share (after tax) in impairment and restructuring charges. If these charges were excluded, Philips' net profit would be €0.42 per share and its price-earnings ratio would change from negative to positive (26.4). This change shows the sensitivity of price-earnings multiples to transitory shocks. Finally, analysts can reduce the effect on multiples of temporary problems in past performance by using a denominator that is a forecast of future performance rather than the past measure itself. Multiples based on forecasts are termed *leading* multiples, whereas those based on historical data are called *trailing* multiples. Leading multiples are less likely to include one-time gains and losses in the denominator, simply because such items are difficult to anticipate.

Adjusting multiples for leverage

Price multiples should be calculated in a way that preserves consistency between the numerator and denominator. Consistency is an issue for those ratios where the denominator reflects performance *before* servicing debt. Examples include the price-to-sales multiple and any multiple of operating earnings or operating cash flows. When calculating these multiples, the numerator should include not just the market value of equity but the value of debt as well.

Determinants of value-to-book and value-earnings multiples

Even across relatively closely related firms, price multiples can vary considerably. The abnormal earnings valuation method provides insight into factors that lead to differences in value-to-book multiples across firms. Similarly, the abnormal earnings growth valuation method helps to explain why value-to-earnings multiples vary across firms.

If the abnormal earnings formula is scaled by book value, the left-hand side becomes the equity value-to-book ratio as opposed to the equity value itself. The right-hand side variables now reflect three multiple drivers: (1) earnings deflated by book value, or our old friend return on equity (ROE), discussed in Chapter 5, (2) the growth in equity book value over time, and (3) the firm's cost of equity. The actual valuation formula is as follows:

$$\text{Equity value-to-book ratio} = 1 + \frac{\text{ROE}_1 - r_e}{(1 + r_e)} + \frac{(\text{ROE}_2 - r_e)\left(1 + g_1^{\text{equity}}\right)}{(1 + r_e)^2}$$

$$+ \frac{(\text{ROE}_3 - r_e)\left(1 + g_1^{\text{equity}}\right)\left(1 + g_2^{\text{equity}}\right)}{(1 + r_e)^3} + \ldots$$

where g_t^{equity} = growth in book value of equity (BVE) from year t–1 to year t or:

$$\frac{\text{BVE}_t - \text{BVE}_{t-1}}{\text{BVE}_{t-1}}$$

A firm's value-to-book ratio is largely driven by the magnitude of its future abnormal ROEs, defined as ROE less the cost of equity capital (ROE − r_e). Firms with positive abnormal ROE are able to invest their net assets to create value for shareholders and will have price-to-book ratios greater than one. In contrast, firms with negative abnormal ROEs are unable to invest shareholder funds at a rate greater than their cost of capital and have ratios below one.

The magnitude of a firm's value-to-book multiple also depends on the amount of growth in book value. Firms can grow their equity base by issuing new equity or by reinvesting profits. If this new equity is invested in positive valued projects for shareholders – that is, projects with ROEs that exceed the cost of capital – the firm will boost its equity value-to-book multiple. Conversely, for firms with ROEs that are less than the cost of capital, equity growth further lowers the multiple.

The valuation task can now be framed in terms of two key questions about the firm's "value drivers":

- Will the firm be able to generate ROEs that exceed its cost of equity capital? If so, for how long?
- How quickly will the firm's investment base (book value) grow?

If desired, the equation can be rewritten so that future ROEs are expressed as the product of their components: profit margins, sales turnover, and leverage. Thus the approach permits us to build directly on projections of the same accounting numbers utilized in financial analysis (see Chapter 5) without the need to convert projections of those numbers into cash flows. Yet in the end, the estimate of value should be the same as that from the dividend discount model.[7]

Returning to the Down Under Company example, the implied equity value-to-book multiple can be estimated as follows:

	Year 1	Year 2	Year 3
Beginning book value	€60m	€40m	€20m
Earnings	€20m	€30m	€40m
ROE	0.33	0.75	2.00
− Cost of capital	0.10	0.10	0.10

(continued)

	Year 1	Year 2	Year 3
= Abnormal ROE	0.23	0.65	1.90
× (1+ cumulative book value growth)	1.00	0.67	0.33
= Abnormal ROE scaled by book value growth	0.23	0.43	0.63
× PV factor	0.909	0.826	0.751
= PV of abnormal ROE scaled by book value growth	0.212	0.358	0.476
Cumulative PV of abnormal ROE scaled by book value growth	1.046		
+ 1.00	1.000		
= Equity value-to-book multiple	2.046		

The equity value-to-book multiple for Down Under is therefore 2.046, and the implied equity value is €122.8 (€60 times 2.046), once again identical to the dividend discount model value.

The equity value-to-book formulation can also be used to construct the equity value-earnings multiple as follows:

$$\text{Equity value-to-earnings multiple} = \text{Equity value-to-book multiple} \times \frac{\text{Book value of equity}}{\text{Earnings}}$$

$$= \frac{\text{Equity value-to-book multiple}}{\text{ROE}}$$

In other words, the same factors that drive a firm's equity value-to-book multiple also explain its equity value-earnings multiple. The key difference between the two multiples is that the value-earnings multiple is affected by the firm's current level of ROE performance, whereas the value-to-book multiple is not. Firms with low current ROEs therefore have very high value-earnings multiples and vice versa. If a firm has a zero or negative ROE, its PE multiple is not defined. Value-earnings multiples are therefore more volatile than value-to-book multiples.

The following data for a subset of firms in the Household Audio and Video industry illustrate the relation between ROE, the price-to-book ratio, and the price-earnings ratio:

Company	ROE	Price-to-book ratio	Price-earnings ratio
Videocon	14.49%	0.42	3.65
Harman International	10.95%	2.16	19.69
Loewe	21.32%	1.15	6.41

Both the price-to-book and price-earnings ratios are high for Harman. Investors therefore expect that in the future Harman will generate higher ROEs than its current level (11.0 percent). In contrast, Loewe has a price-to-book ratio greater than one (1.15) but a low price-earnings ratio (6.41). This indicates that investors expect that Loewe will continue to generate positive abnormal ROEs but that the current level of ROE (21.3 percent) is not sustainable. Finally, Videocon has a relatively low price-to-book ratio, 0.42, and a low price-earnings multiple. Investors apparently do not expect Videocon to sustain its good performance.

The effect of future growth in net profit on the price-earnings multiple can also be seen from the model that arises when we scale the abnormal earnings growth valuation formula by next-period net profit. The valuation formula then becomes:

Leading equity value-to-earnings ratio =

$$\frac{1}{r_e} + \frac{1}{r_e}\left[\frac{g_2^{profit} + (d_1 - 1)r_e}{(1 + r_e)} + \frac{\left(1 + g_2^{profit}\right)\left[g_3^{profit} + (d_2 - 1)r_e\right]}{(1 + r_e)^2} \ldots\right]$$

where d_t = dividend payout ratio in year t

g_t^{profit} = growth in net profit (NP) from year t − 1 to year t or

$$\frac{NP_t - NP_{t-1}}{NP_{t-1}}$$

In this formula, future earnings growth rates and dividend payouts are the basis for estimating price-earnings multiples.[8] Consider the earnings growth rates and dividend payout ratios of the Down Under Company. The earnings growth rates (g_t^{profit}) are 50, 33, and −100 percent in years 2, 3, and 4, respectively. Dividend payouts are 200 percent, 167 percent, and 150 percent in years 1, 2, and 3, respectively. Substituting these percentages in the leading price-earnings formula yields:

Leading equity value-to-earnings ratio =

$$\frac{1}{r_e} + \frac{1}{r_e}\left[\frac{g_2^{profit} + (d_1 - 1)r_e}{(1 + r_e)} + \frac{\left(1 + g_2^{profit}\right)\left[g_3^{profit} + (d_2 - 1)r_e\right]}{(1 + r_e)^2}\right.$$
$$\left. + \frac{\left(1 + g_2^{profit}\right)\left(1 + g_3^{profit}\right)\left[g_4^{profit} + (d_3 - 1)r_e\right]}{(1 + r_e)^3}\right]$$
$$= \frac{1}{.1} + \frac{1}{.1}\left[\frac{.5 + .1}{1.1} + \frac{1.5 \times [.33 + 0.067]}{1.1^2} + \frac{1.5 \times 1.33 \times [-1 + .05]}{1.1^3}\right] = 6.14$$

The price-earnings multiple of 6.14 is consistent with a value of equity of €122.8 (6.14 × €20).

KEY ANALYSIS QUESTIONS

To value a firm using multiples, an analyst must assess the quality of the variable used as the multiple basis and determine the appropriate peer firms to include in the benchmark multiple. Analysts are therefore likely to be interested in answering the following questions:

- How well does the denominator used in the multiple reflect the firm's performance? For example, if earnings or book equity are used as the denominator, has the firm made conservative or aggressive accounting choices that are likely to unwind in the coming years? Is the firm likely to show strong growth in earnings or book equity? If earnings are the denominator, does the firm have temporarily poor or strong performance?

- What is the sustainability of the firm's growth and ROE based on the competitive dynamics of the firm's industry and product market and its own competitive position?

- Which are the most suitable peer companies to include in the benchmark multiple computation? Have these firms had growth (earnings or book values), profitability, and quality of earnings comparable to the firm being analyzed? Do they have the same risk characteristics?

SHORTCUT FORMS OF EARNINGS-BASED VALUATION

The discounted abnormal earnings valuation formula can be simplified by making assumptions about the relation between a firm's current and future abnormal earnings. Similarly, the equity value-to-book formula can be simplified by making assumptions about long-term ROEs and growth.

Abnormal earnings (growth) simplification

Several assumptions about the relation between current and future abnormal earnings are popular for simplifying the abnormal earnings model and the abnormal earnings growth model. First, abnormal earnings are assumed to follow a random walk. The random walk model for abnormal earnings implies that an analyst's best guess about future expected abnormal earnings are current abnormal earnings. The model assumes that past shocks to abnormal earnings persist forever, but that future shocks are random or unpredictable. The random walk model can be written as follows:

$$\text{Forecasted AE}_1 = \text{AE}_0$$

Forecasted AE_1 is the forecast of next year's abnormal earnings and AE_0 is current period abnormal earnings. Under the model, forecasted abnormal earnings for two years ahead are simply abnormal earnings in year one, or once again current abnormal earnings. In other words, the best guess of abnormal earnings in any future year is just current abnormal earnings. It is also possible to include a drift term in the model, allowing earnings to grow by a constant amount, or at a constant rate in each period.

How does the above assumption about future abnormal earnings simplify the discounted abnormal earnings valuation model? If abnormal earnings follow a random walk, all future forecasts of abnormal earnings are simply current abnormal earnings. Consequently, the present value of future abnormal earnings can be calculated by valuing the current level of abnormal earnings as a perpetuity. It is then possible to rewrite value as follows:

$$\text{Equity value} = \text{BVE}_0 + \frac{\text{AE}_0}{r_e}$$

Equity value is the book value of equity at the end of the year plus current abnormal earnings divided by the cost of capital. The perpetuity formula can be adjusted to incorporate expectations of constant growth in future abnormal earnings.

A logical consequence of the above assumption is also that future abnormal earnings growth equals zero. When abnormal earnings growth in any future year is zero, the abnormal earnings growth valuation model can be rewritten as follows:

$$\text{Equity value} = \frac{\text{Net profit}_1}{r_e}$$

Equity value is then set equal to the capitalized value of next-period net profit.

In reality, shocks to abnormal earnings are unlikely to persist forever. Firms that have positive shocks are likely to attract competitors that will reduce opportunities for future abnormal performance. Firms with negative abnormal earnings shocks are likely to fail or to be acquired by other firms that can manage their resources more effectively. The persistence of abnormal performance will therefore depend on strategic factors such as barriers to entry and switching costs, discussed in Chapter 2. To reflect this, analysts frequently assume that current shocks to abnormal earnings decay over time. Under this assumption, abnormal earnings are said to follow an autoregressive model. Forecasted abnormal earnings are then:

$$\text{Forecasted } AE_1 = \beta AE_0$$

β is a parameter that captures the speed with which abnormal earnings decay over time. If there is no decay, β is one and abnormal earnings follow a random walk. If β is zero, abnormal earnings decay completely within one year. Estimates of β using actual company data indicate that for a typical firm, β is approximately 0.6. However, it varies by industry, and is smaller for firms with large accruals and onetime accounting charges.[9]

Note that if the rate of decay in abnormal earnings, β, is constant, the perpetual growth rate in abnormal earnings equals $\beta - 1$. The autoregressive model therefore implies that equity values can again be written as a function of current abnormal earnings and book values:[10]

$$\text{Equity value} = BVE_0 + \frac{\beta AE_0}{r_e - (\beta - 1)}$$

This formulation implies that equity values are simply the sum of current book value plus current abnormal earnings weighted by the cost of equity capital and persistence in abnormal earnings.

Under the assumption that abnormal earnings follow an autoregressive model, abnormal earnings growth, or the change in abnormal earnings, in year 1 can be rewritten as $(\beta - 1)AE_0$ and the abnormal earnings growth model simplifies to:

$$\text{Equity value} = \frac{\text{Net profit}_1}{r_e} + \frac{(1 + r_e)}{r_e} \left[\frac{(\beta - 1)AE_1}{r_e - (\beta - 1)} \right]$$

This formula illustrates that equity values can be expressed as the sum of capitalized next-period earnings plus next-period abnormal earnings weighted by the cost of equity capital and persistence in abnormal earnings.

An advantage of the abnormal earnings growth model over the abnormal earnings model is that the former model can be simplified by making assumptions about the change in abnormal earnings. This can be useful in situations where the analyst believes, for example, that a firm has a sustainable competitive advantage but expects that the growth in abnormal earnings will gradually decay over time. Under the assumption that:

$$\text{Forecasted } (AE_2 - AE_1) = \beta(AE_1 - AE_0)$$

the abnormal earnings growth model simplifies to:

$$\text{Equity value} = \frac{\text{Net profit}_1}{r_e} + \frac{(1 + r_e)}{r_e} \left[\frac{\beta(AE_1 - AE_0)}{r_e - (\beta - 1)} \right]$$

ROE and growth simplifications

It is also possible to make simplifications about long-term ROEs and equity growth to reduce forecast horizons for estimating the equity value-to-book multiple. Firms' long-term ROEs are affected by such factors as barriers to entry in their industries, change in production or delivery technologies, and quality of management. As discussed in Chapter 6, these factors tend to force abnormal ROEs to decay over time. One way to model this decay is to assume that ROEs revert to the mean. Forecasted ROE after one period then takes the following form:

$$\text{Forecasted } ROE_1 = ROE_0 + \beta \left(ROE_0 - \overline{ROE} \right)$$

$\overline{ROE}$ is the steady state ROE (either the firm's cost of capital or the long-term industry ROE) and β is a "speed of adjustment factor" that reflects how quickly it takes the ROE to revert to its steady state.[11]

Growth rates in the book value of equity are driven by several factors. First, the size of the firm is important. Small firms can sustain very high growth rates for an extended period, whereas large firms find it more difficult to do so. Second, firms with high rates of growth are likely to attract competitors, which reduces their growth rates. As a result, steady-state rates of growth in book equity are likely to be similar to rates of growth in the overall economy, which have averaged 2–4 percent per year.

The long-term patterns in ROE and book equity growth rates imply that for most companies there is limited value in making forecasts for valuation beyond a relatively short horizon, generally five to ten years. Powerful economic forces tend to lead firms with superior or inferior performance early in the forecast horizon to revert to a level that is comparable to that of other firms in the industry or the economy. For a firm in steady state, that is, expected to have a stable ROE and book equity growth rate (g^{equity}), the value-to-book multiple formula simplifies to the following:

$$\text{Equity value-to-book multiple} = 1 + \frac{ROE_0 - r_e}{r_e - g^{equity}}$$

Of course, analysts can make a variety of simplifying assumptions about a firm's ROE and growth. For example, they can assume that they decay slowly or rapidly to the cost of capital and the growth rate for the economy. They can assume that the rates decay to the industry or economy average ROEs and book value growth rates. The valuation formula can easily be modified to accommodate these assumptions.

COMPARING VALUATION METHODS

We have discussed four methods of valuation derived from the dividend discount model: discounted dividends, discounted abnormal earnings (or abnormal ROEs), discounted abnormal earnings growth, and discounted cash flows. Since the methods are all derived from the same underlying model, no one version can be considered superior to the others. As long as analysts make the same assumptions about firm fundamentals, value estimates under all four methods will be identical. However, we discuss below important differences between the models.

Focus on different issues

The methods frame the valuation task differently and can in practice focus the analyst's attention on different issues. The earnings-based approaches frame the issues in terms of accounting data such as earnings and book values. Analysts spend considerable time analyzing historical income statements and balance sheets, and their primary forecasts are typically for these variables.

Defining values in terms of ROEs has the added advantage that it focuses analysts' attention on ROE, the same key measure of performance that is decomposed in a standard financial analysis. Furthermore, because ROEs control for firm scale, it is likely to be easier for analysts to evaluate the reasonableness of their forecasts by benchmarking them with ROEs of other firms in the industry and the economy. This type of benchmarking is more challenging for free cash flows and abnormal earnings.

Differences in required structure

The methods differ in the amount of analysis and structure required for valuation. The discounted abnormal earnings and ROE methods require analysts to construct both pro forma income statements and balance sheets to forecast future earnings and book values. In contrast, the discounted abnormal earnings growth model requires analysts to forecast future earnings and dividends. The discounted cash flow method requires analysts to forecast income statements and changes in working capital and long-term assets to generate free cash flows. Finally, the discounted dividend method requires analysts to forecast dividends.

The discounted abnormal earnings (growth), ROE, and free cash flow models all require more structure for analysis than the discounted dividend approach. They therefore help analysts to avoid structural inconsistencies in their forecasts of future dividends by specifically allowing for firms' future performance and investment opportunities. Similarly, the discounted abnormal earnings/ROE method requires more structure and work than the discounted cash flow method and the discounted abnormal earnings growth method to build full pro forma balance sheets. This permits analysts to avoid inconsistencies in the firm's financial structure.

Differences in terminal value implications

A third difference between the methods is in the effort required for estimating terminal values. Terminal value estimates for the abnormal earnings, abnormal earnings growth, and ROE methods tend to represent a much smaller fraction of total value than under the discounted cash flow or dividend methods. On the surface, this would appear to mitigate concerns about the aspect of valuation that leaves the analyst most uncomfortable. Is this apparent advantage real? As explained below, the answer turns on how well value is already reflected in the accountant's book value.

The abnormal earnings and abnormal earnings growth valuations do not eliminate the discounted cash flow terminal value problem, but they do reframe it. Discounted cash flow terminal values include the present value of *all* expected cash flows beyond the forecast horizon. Under abnormal earnings valuation, that value is broken into two parts: the present values of *normal* earnings and *abnormal* earnings beyond the terminal year. The terminal value in the abnormal earnings technique includes only the *abnormal* earnings. The present value of *normal* earnings is already reflected in the original book value. Similarly, under the abnormal earnings growth approach the present value of near-term abnormal earnings is already reflected in next-period earnings or the growth in earnings over the forecast horizon. The terminal value includes only the *changes in abnormal* earnings that are expected to occur in the years beyond the terminal year.

The abnormal earnings and abnormal earnings growth approaches, then, recognize that current book value and earnings over the forecast horizon already reflect many of the cash flows expected to arrive after the forecast horizon. The approaches build directly on accrual accounting. For example, under accrual accounting book equity can be thought of as the minimum recoverable future benefits attributable to the firm's net assets. In addition, revenues are typically realized when earned, not when cash is received. The discounted cash flow approach, on the other hand, "unravels" all of the accruals, spreads the resulting cash flows over longer horizons, and then reconstructs its own "accruals" in the form of discounted expectations of future cash flows. The essential difference between the two approaches is that abnormal earnings (growth) valuation recognizes that the accrual process may already have performed a portion of the valuation task, whereas the discounted cash flow approach ultimately moves back to the primitive cash flows underlying the accruals.

The usefulness of the accounting-based perspective thus hinges on how well the accrual process reflects future cash flows. The approach is most convenient when the accrual process is "unbiased," so that earnings can be abnormal only as the result of economic rents and not as a product of accounting itself.[12] The forecast horizon then extends to the point where the firm is expected to approach a competitive equilibrium and earn only normal earnings on its projects. Subsequent abnormal earnings would be zero, and the terminal value at that point would be zero. In this extreme case, *all* of the firm's value is reflected in the book value and earnings projected over the forecast horizon.

Of course accounting rarely works so well. For example, many firms expense research and development costs, and book values fail to reflect any research and development assets. As a result, firms that spend heavily on research and development – such as pharmaceuticals – tend on average to generate abnormally high earnings even in the face of stiff competition. Purely as an artifact of research and development accounting, abnormal earnings would be expected to remain positive indefinitely for such firms, and, under the abnormal earnings approach, the terminal value could represent a substantial fraction of total value.

If desired, the analyst can alter the accounting approach used by the firm in his or her own projections. "Better" accounting would be viewed as that which reflects a larger fraction of the firm's value in book values and earnings over the forecast horizon.[13] This same view underlies analysts' attempts to "normalize" earnings; the adjusted numbers are intended to provide better indications of value, even though they reflect performance only over a short horizon.

Research has focused on the performance of abnormal earnings-based valuation relative to discounted cash flow and discounted dividend methods. The findings indicate that over relatively short forecast horizons (ten years or less), valuation estimates using the abnormal earnings approach generate more precise estimates of value than either the discounted dividend or discounted cash flow models. This advantage for the abnormal earnings-based approach persists for firms with conservative or aggressive accounting, indicating that accrual accounting does a reasonably good job of reflecting future cash flows.[14] The performance of the abnormal earnings growth valuation model has not yet been extensively studied. However, the model's close relationship to the abnormal earnings model makes it subject to many of the same practical advantages.

Research also indicates that abnormal earnings estimates of value outperform traditional multiples, such as price-earnings ratios, price-to-book ratios, and dividend yields, for predicting future share price movements.[15] Firms that have high abnormal earnings model estimates of value relative to current price show positive abnormal future stock returns, whereas firms with low estimated value-to-price ratios have negative abnormal share price performance.

KEY ANALYSIS QUESTIONS

The above discussion on the trade-offs between different methods of valuing a company raises several questions for analysts about how to compare methods and to consider which is likely to be most reliable for their analysis:

■ What are the key performance parameters that the analyst forecasts? Is more attention given to forecasting accounting variables, such as earnings and book values, or to forecasting cash flow variables?

■ Has the analyst linked forecasted income statements and balance sheets? If not, is there any inconsistency between the two statements, or in the implications of the assumptions for future performance? If so, what is the source of this inconsistency and does it affect discounted earnings-based and discounted cash flow methods similarly?

■ How well does the firm's accounting capture its underlying assets and obligations? Does it do a good enough job that we can rely on book values as the basis for long-term forecasts? Alternatively, does the firm rely heavily on off-balance sheet assets, such as R&D, which make book values a poor lower bound on long-term performance?

■ Has the analyst made very different assumptions about long-term performance in the terminal value computations under the different valuation methods? If so, which set of assumptions is more plausible given the firm's industry and its competitive positioning?

SUMMARY

Valuation is the process by which forecasts of performance are converted into estimates of price. A variety of valuation techniques are employed in practice, and there is no single method that clearly dominates others. In fact, since each technique involves different advantages and disadvantages, there are gains to considering several approaches simultaneously.

For shareholders, a firm's equity value is the present value of future dividends. This chapter described four valuation techniques directly based on this dividend discount definition of value: discounted dividends, discounted abnormal earnings/ROEs, discounted abnormal earnings growth, and discounted free cash flows. The discounted dividend method attempts to forecast dividends directly. The abnormal earnings approach expresses the value of a firm's equity as book value plus discounted expectations of future abnormal earnings. The abnormal earnings growth approach defines equity value as capitalized next-period earnings plus the present value of future changes in abnormal earnings. Finally, the discounted cash flow method represents a firm's equity value by expected future free cash flows discounted at the cost of capital.

Although these four methods were derived from the same dividend discount model, they frame the valuation task differently. In practice they focus the analyst's attention on different issues and require different levels of structure in developing forecasts of the underlying primitive, future dividends.

Price multiple valuation methods were also discussed. Under these approaches, analysts estimate ratios of current price to historical or forecasted measures of performance for comparable firms. The benchmarks are then used to value the performance of the firm being analyzed. Multiples have traditionally been popular, primarily because they do not require analysts to make multiyear forecasts of performance. However, it can be difficult to identify comparable firms to use as benchmarks. Even across highly related firms, there are differences in performance that are likely to affect their multiples.

The chapter discussed the relation between two popular multiples, value-to-book and value-earnings ratios, and the discounted abnormal earnings valuation. The resulting formulations indicate that value-to-book multiples are a function of future abnormal ROEs, book value growth, and the firm's cost of equity. The value-earnings multiple is a function of the same factors and also the current ROE.

CORE CONCEPTS

Abnormal earnings Difference between net profit and a capital charge. The capital charge is calculated as the cost of equity times the beginning of the period book value of equity.

Abnormal earnings growth Change in abnormal earnings. The change in abnormal earnings can be rewritten as the abnormal change in earnings, which is calculated as the difference between the actual period change in net profit and the expected change in net profit. The expected change in net profit is calculated as the cost of equity times prior period's retained net profit:

$$\text{Abnormal earnings growth (AEG)} = \Delta\text{Net profit}_2 - r_e \cdot (\text{Net profit}_1 - \text{Dividend}_1)$$

Discounted abnormal earnings growth model Model expressing equity value as a function of next-period net profit and the present value of abnormal earnings growth (AEG) beyond the next period:

$$\text{Equity value} = \frac{\text{Net profit}_1}{r_e} + \frac{1}{r_e}\left[\frac{\text{AEG}_2}{(1+r_e)} + \frac{\text{AEG}_3}{(1+r_e)^2} + \ldots\right]$$

Discounted abnormal earnings model Model expressing equity value as the sum of the beginning book value of equity and the present value of future abnormal earnings (AE):

$$\text{Equity value} = \text{BVE}_0 + \frac{\text{AE}_1}{(1+r_e)} + \frac{\text{AE}_1}{(1+r_e)^2} + \ldots$$

Discounted cash flow model Model expressing equity value as the present value of future free cash flows to equity (FCFE):

$$\text{Equity value} = \frac{\text{FCFE}_1}{(1+r_e)} + \frac{\text{FCFE}_2}{(1+r_e)^2} + \ldots$$

Equity value Present value of expected future dividends (DIV):

$$\text{Equity value} = \frac{\text{DIV}_1}{(1+r_e)} + \frac{\text{DIV}_2}{(1+r_e)^2} + \frac{\text{DIV}_3}{(1+r_e)^3} + \ldots$$

This dividend-discount model can be recast to generate the discounted abnormal earnings model, the discounted abnormal earnings growth model, and the discounted free cash flow model.

Free cash flow to debt and equity Cash flow available for distribution to creditors and shareholders. The free cash flow to debt and equity is equal to: net profit + after-tax net interest expense – change in net working capital – change in net non-current assets.

Free cash flow to equity Cash flow available for distribution to shareholders. The free cash flow to equity is equal to: net profit – change in net working capital – change in net non-current assets + change in net debt.

Multiple-based valuation Use of price multiples – ratios of market value to a measure of firm performance (e.g., net profit) or value (e.g., book value of equity) – of comparable firms to value equity.

SUMMARY OF NOTATIONS USED IN THIS CHAPTER

AE	Abnormal earnings
AEG	Abnormal earnings growth
BVA	Book value of operating net assets
BVE	Book value of equity
BVND	Book value of net debt
DIV	Dividends
EBIT	Earnings before interest and taxes
g^{div}	Dividend growth rate
g^{equity}	Growth rate in the book value of equity
g^{profit}	Growth rate in net profit
NP	Net profit
OCF	Operating cash flow
PV	Present value
r_e	Cost of equity
WACC	Weighted average cost of capital (debt and equity)

QUESTIONS, EXERCISES AND PROBLEMS

1 Jonas Borg, an analyst at EMH Securities, states: "I don't know why anyone would ever try to value earnings. Obviously, the market knows that earnings can be manipulated and only values cash flows." Discuss.

2 Explain why terminal values in accounting-based valuation are significantly less than those for DCF valuation.

3 Manufactured Earnings is a "darling" of European analysts. Its current market price is €15 per share, and its book value is €5 per share. Analysts forecast that the firm's book value will grow by 10 percent per year indefinitely, and the cost of equity is 15 percent. Given these facts, what is the market's expectation of the firm's long-term average ROE?

4 Given the information in question 3, what will be Manufactured Earnings' share price if the market revises its expectations of long-term average ROE to 20 percent?

5 Analysts reassess Manufactured Earnings' future performance as follows: growth in book value increases to 12 percent per year, but the ROE of the incremental book value is only 15 percent. What is the impact on the market-to-book ratio?

6 How can a company with a high ROE have a low PE ratio?

7 What types of companies have:

   a A high PE and a low market-to-book ratio?

   b A high PE ratio and a high market-to-book ratio?

   c A low PE and a high market-to-book ratio?

   d A low PE and a low market-to-book ratio?

8 Free cash flows (FCF) used in DCF valuations discussed in the chapter are defined as follows:

     FCF to debt and equity = Earnings before interest and taxes × (1 − tax rate) +

                    Depreciation and deferred taxes − Capital

                    expenditures − / + Increase/decrease

                    in working capital

           FCF to equity = Net profit + Depreciation and deferred taxes −

                    Capital expenditures − / + Increase/decrease

                    in working capital + / − Increase/decrease in debt

   Which of the following items affect free cash flows to debt and equity holders? Which affect free cash flows to equity alone? Explain why and how.

   ■ An increase in trade receivables.

   ■ A decrease in gross margins.

   ■ An increase in property, plant, and equipment.

   ■ An increase in inventories.

   ■ Interest expense.

   ■ An increase in prepaid expenses.

   ■ An increase in notes payable to the bank.

9 Starite Company is valued at €20 per share. Analysts expect that it will generate free cash flows to equity of €4 per share for the foreseeable future. What is the firm's implied cost of equity capital?

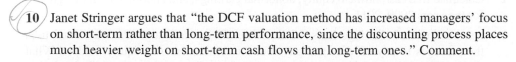

10 Janet Stringer argues that "the DCF valuation method has increased managers' focus on short-term rather than long-term performance, since the discounting process places much heavier weight on short-term cash flows than long-term ones." Comment.

Problem 1 Estimating Hugo Boss's equity value

Hugo Boss AG is a German designer, manufacturer and distributor of men's and women's clothing, operating in the higher end of the clothing retail industry. During the period 2001–2008, the company consistently earned returns on equity in excess of 18 percent, grew its book value of equity (before special dividends) by 5.5 percent per year, on average, and paid out 65–70 percent of its net profit as dividends. In 2008, the company paid out a special dividend of €345.1 million. Consequently, the company's book value of equity decreased from €546.8 million in 2007 to €199.0 million in 2008.

   On April 1, 2009, one month before the publication of the first-quarter results, when Hugo Boss's 70.4 million common shares trade at about €11 per share, an analyst produces the following forecasts for Hugo Boss.

Income statement (€ millions)		2009E	2010E	2011E
Sales		1548.1	1493.9	1561.2
Gross profit		897.9	875.1	923.7
EBIT		179.6	176.9	196.2
Net interest expense		(45)	(40)	(35)
EBT		134.6	136.9	161.2
Tax expense		(36.3)	(37)	(43.5)
Net profit		98.3	99.9	117.7

Balance sheet (€ millions)	2008R	2009E	2010E	2011E
Total non-current assets	459.2	480.8	499.1	512
Inventories	381.4	325.1	304.3	305.3
Trade receivables	201	175.4	160.8	156.1
Cash & cash equivalents	24.6	33.5	32.5	47.2
Other current assets	95.4	136.5	172.5	203.2
Total current assets	702.4	670.5	670.1	711.8
Shareholders' equity	199	200.2	221.6	259
Non-current provisions	27.9	25.6	24.7	25.8
Non-current debt	588.5	576.7	565.2	553.9
Other non-current liabilities (non-interest bearing)	26.7	24.5	23.6	24.8
Deferred tax liabilities	17.9	18.3	18.7	19
Total non-current liabilities	661	645.1	632.2	623.5
Current provisions	59.3	59.3	59.3	59.3
Current debt	40.2	40.2	40.2	40.2
Other current liabilities	202.1	206.5	215.9	241.8
Total current liabilities	301.6	306	315.4	341.3
TOTAL EQUITY AND LIABILITIES	1161.6	1151.3	1169.2	1223.8

Assume that Hugo Boss's cost of equity equals 12 percent.

1   Calculate free cash flows to equity, abnormal earnings, and abnormal earnings growth for the years 2009–2011.

2   Assume that in 2012 Hugo Boss AG liquidates all its assets at their book values, uses the proceeds to pay off debt and pays out the remainder to its equity holders. What does this assumption imply about the company's:

   a Free cash flow to equity holders in 2012 and beyond?

   b Abnormal earnings in 2012 and beyond?

   c Abnormal earnings growth in 2012 and beyond?

3   Estimate the value of Hugo Boss's equity on April 1, 2009 using the above forecasts and assumptions. Check that the discounted cash flow model, the abnormal earnings model and the abnormal earnings growth model yield the same outcome.

4   The analyst estimates a target price of €20 per share. What is the expected value of Hugo Boss's equity at the end of 2011 that is implicit in the analysts' forecasts and target price?

5   Under the assumption that the historical trends in the company's ROE (i.e., approximately 18 percent), payout ratio (70 percent) and book value growth

(5.5 percent) continue in the future, what would be your estimate of Hugo Boss's equity value-to-book ratio *before the company paid out its special dividend*? How does the special dividend payment change your estimate of the equity value-to-book ratio?

Problem 2   Estimating Adidas's equity value

Germany-based Adidas is one of the world's largest producers of sportswear. During 2008, Adidas showed strong operational performance but saw its equity value decrease by 47 percent to €5,252 million as a result of the overall decline of international stock markets. On April 1, 2009, one month before the publication of the first-quarter results, an analyst produces the following forecasts of Adidas's 2009–2011 performance and financial position:

Income statement (€ millions)		2009E	2010E	2011E
Sales		10428.0	10617.0	11143.0
Gross profit		4771.8	5005.3	5277.3
EBIT		771.0	903.3	970.9
Net interest expense		−141.0	−115.6	−113.9
Profit before tax		630.0	787.7	857.0
Tax expense		−181.2	−226.5	−246.5
Group profit		448.8	561.2	610.5
Minority interest		−2.5	−3.3	−3.5
Net profit		446.3	557.9	607.0

Balance sheet (€ millions)	2008R	2009E	2010E	2011E
Fixed assets	4630.0	4737.8	4850.4	4958.1
Non-cash current assets	4518.0	4332.1	4400.0	4596.0
Cash	385.0	338.2	312.0	547.6
Total assets	9533.0	9408.1	9562.4	10101.7
Shareholders' equity	3386.0	3735.5	4181.2	4666.3
Minority interest	14.0	7.0	3.5	−1.3
Non-current provisions	1526.0	1480.6	1509.7	1576.7
Non-current and current debt	2625.0	2300.0	2000.0	1900.0
Other non-current liabilities	764.0	738.1	721.0	757.0
Current liabilities	1218.0	1147.0	1147.0	1203.0
Total equity and liabilities	9533.0	9408.1	9562.4	10101.7

Other estimates	2008R	2009E	2010E	2011E
Dividends		96.8	112.2	121.9

Assume that Adidas's cost of equity equals 12 percent.

1   Check whether all changes in the book value of equity that the analyst predicts can be fully explained through earnings and dividends. Why is this an important property of the analyst's equity estimates?

2   When using these forecasts to estimate the value of equity, the analyst can deal with minority interests in the following ways:

a (1) Classify minority interests on the balance sheet as a non-interest-bearing liability (and hence as a negative operating asset) and (2) exclude income from minority interests from earnings (i.e., focus on net profit).

b (1) Classify minority interests on the balance sheet as (group) equity, (2) include income from minority interests in earnings (i.e., focus on group profit), and (3) subtract the book value of minority interests from the estimated value of group equity to arrive at the value of shareholders' equity.

These approaches may yield different values. Discuss potential drawbacks of both approaches.

3 Based on a market value of €4,849 million on March 31, 2009 and the analyst's estimates, Adidas's leading market value-to-earnings ratio is 10.9. What does this ratio suggest about the analyst's expectations about future abnormal earnings growth?

4 Calculate abnormal earnings for the years 2009–2011.

5 Assume that abnormal earnings in 2012 and beyond are zero. Estimate the value of Adidas's group equity (group equity is the sum of shareholders' equity and minority interests). What might explain the difference between your equity value estimate and Adidas's actual market value (of €4,849 million)?

NOTES

1. From a theoretical perspective, it is preferred to express equity *per share* as a function of dividends *per share*. This is because only the discounted dividends *per share* model accurately accounts for the wealth transfer from new shareholders to the current shareholders that occurs when a firm offers shares to new shareholders in future years at a price that is not equal to the prevailing market price. To simplify the discussion of the other valuation models, however, we describe all models on a "total equity value basis," thereby implicitly assuming that future capital transactions do not affect the firm's current equity value per share – i.e., are value neutral.

2. In practice, firms do not have to pay out all of their free cash flows as dividends; they can retain surplus cash in the business. The conditions under which a firm's dividend decision affects its value are discussed by M. H. Miller and F. Modigliani in "Dividend Policy, Growth and the Valuation of Shares," *Journal of Business* 34 (October 1961): 411–433.

3. The incorporation of all nonowner changes in equity into profit is called clean surplus accounting. It is analogous to "recognized income and expense," the concept defined in IAS 1.

4. Changes in book value also include new capital contributions. However the dividend discount model assumes that new capital is issued at fair value. As a result, any incremental book value from capital issues is exactly offset by the discounted value of future dividends to new shareholders. Capital transactions therefore do not affect firm valuation.

5. The appendix to this chapter provides a simple proof of the earnings-based valuation formula.

6. The abnormal earnings growth model and its properties are extensively discussed in the following articles: J. A. Ohlson and B. E. Juettner-Nauroth, "Expected EPS and EPS Growth as Determinants of Value," *Review of Accounting Studies* (2005): 349–365; J. A. Ohlson, "On Accounting-Based Valuation Formulae," *Review of Accounting Studies* (2005): 323–347; S. H. Penman, "Discussion of 'On Accounting Based Valuation Formulae' and 'Expected EPS and EPS Growth as Determinants of Value'," *Review of Accounting Studies* (2005): 367–378.

7. It may seem surprising that one can estimate value with no explicit attention to two of the cash flow streams considered in DCF analysis – investments in working capital and capital expenditures. The accounting-based technique recognizes that these investments cannot possibly contribute to value without impacting abnormal earnings, and that therefore only their earnings impacts need be considered. For example, the benefit of an increase in inventory turnover surfaces in terms of its impact on ROE (and thus, abnormal earnings), without the need to consider explicitly the cash flow impacts involved.

8. This model must not be confused with the PEG ratio. The PEG ratio, which is defined as the price-earnings ratio divided by the short-term earnings growth rate, is a rule-of-thumb used by some analysts to determine whether a share is overpriced. The rule suggests that shares whose PEG ratio is above one are overpriced. Valuation using the PEG ratio has, however, no clear theoretical basis.

9. See P. M. Dechow, A. P. Hutton, and R. G. Sloan, "An Empirical Assessment of the Residual Income Valuation Model," *Journal of Accounting and Economics* 23 (January 1999).

10. This formulation is a variant of a model proposed by James Ohlson, "Earnings, Book Values, and Dividends in Security Valuation," *Contemporary Accounting Research* 11 (Spring 1995). Ohlson includes in his forecasts of future abnormal earnings a variable that reflects relevant information other than current abnormal earnings. This variable then also appears in the equity valuation formula. Empirical research by Dechow, Hutton, and Sloan, "An Empirical Assessment of the Residual Income Valuation Model," *Journal of Accounting and Economics* 23 (January 1999), indicates that financial analysts' forecasts of abnormal earnings do reflect considerable information other than current abnormal earnings, and that this information is useful for valuation.

11. This specification is similar to the model for dividends developed by J. Lintner, "Distribution of Incomes of Corporations Among Dividends, Retained Earnings, and Taxes," *American Economic Review* 46 (May 1956): 97–113.

12. Unbiased accounting is that which, in a competitive equilibrium, produces an expected ROE equal to the cost of capital. The actual ROE thus reveals the presence of economic rents. Market value accounting is a special case of unbiased accounting that produces an expected ROE equal to the cost of capital, even when the firm is *not* in a competitive equilibrium. That is, market value accounting reflects the present value of future economic rents in book value, driving the expected ROEs to a normal level. For a discussion of unbiased and biased accounting, see G. Feltham and J. Ohlson, "Valuation and Clean Surplus Accounting for Operating and Financial Activities," *Contemporary Accounting Research* 11, No. 2 (Spring 1995): 689–731.

13. In Bennett Stewart's book on EVA valuation, *The Quest for Value* (New York: HarperBusiness, 1999), he recommends a number of accounting adjustments, including the capitalization of research and development.

14. S. Penman and T. Sougiannis, "A Comparison of Dividend, Cash Flow, and Earnings Approaches to Equity Valuation," *Contemporary Accounting Research* (Fall 1998): 343–383, compares the valuation methods using actual realizations of earnings, cash flows, and dividends to estimate prices. J. Francis, P. Olsson, and D. Oswald, "Comparing Accuracy and Explainability of Dividend, Free Cash Flow and Abnormal Earnings Equity Valuation Models," *Journal of Accounting Research* 38 (Spring 2000): 45–70, estimates values using *Value Line* forecasts.

15. See C. Lee and J. Myers, "What is the Intrinsic Value of the Dow?" *The Journal of Finance* 54 (October 1999): 1693–1741.

APPENDIX A: ASSET VALUATION METHODOLOGIES

All of the valuation approaches discussed in this chapter can also be structured to estimate the value of a firm's assets (or the combined debt and equity) rather than its equity. Switching from equity valuation to asset valuation is often as simple as substituting financial measures related to equity for financial measures related to the entire firm. For example, in the earnings-based valuation model, net income (the earnings flow to equity) is replaced by NOPAT (the earnings available for debt and equity), and book values of assets replace the book value of equity. Value multiples are based on ROEs for the equity formulation and on ROAs for valuing asset multiples. And the discount rate for equity models is the cost of equity compared to the weighted average cost of capital (or WACC) for asset valuation models.

The formulas used for asset valuation under the various approaches are presented below.

Abnormal earnings valuation

Under the earnings-based approach, the value of the assets is

$$\text{Asset value} = \text{BVA}_0 + \frac{\text{NOPAT}_1 - \text{WACC} \cdot \text{BVA}_0}{(1 + \text{WACC})} + \frac{\text{NOPAT}_2 - \text{WACC} \cdot \text{BVA}_1}{(1 + \text{WACC})^2} + \cdots$$

BVA is the book value of the firm's assets, NOPAT is net operating profit (before interest) after tax, and WACC is the firm's weighted-average cost of debt and equity. From this asset value the analyst can deduct the market value of net debt to generate an estimate of the value of equity.

Valuation using price multiples

The multiple valuation can be structured as the debt plus equity value-to-book assets ratio by scaling the abnormal NOPAT formula by book value of net operating assets. The valuation formula then becomes:

$$
\begin{aligned}
\text{Debt plus equity value-to-book ratio} = 1 &+ \frac{\text{ROA}_1 - \text{WACC}}{(1 + \text{WACC})} \\
&+ \frac{(\text{ROA}_2 - \text{WACC})(1 + g_1^{\text{assets}})}{(1 + \text{WACC})^2} \\
&+ \frac{(\text{ROA}_3 - \text{WACC})(1 + g_1^{\text{assets}})(1 + g_2^{\text{assets}})}{(1 + \text{WACC})^3} + \cdots
\end{aligned}
$$

where

ROA = operating return on assets = NOPAT/(Operating working capital + Net non-current assets)

WACC = weighted average cost of debt and equity

g_t^{assets} = growth in book value of assets (*BVA*) from year t − 1 to year t or

$$\frac{\text{BVA}_t - \text{BVA}_{t-1}}{\text{BVA}_{t-1}}$$

The value of a firm's debt and equity to net operating assets multiple therefore depends on its ability to generate asset returns that exceed its WACC, and on its ability to grow its asset base. The value of equity under this approach is then the estimated multiple times the current book value of assets less the market value of debt.

Discounted cash flow model

The free cash flow formulation can be structured by estimating the value of claims to net debt and equity and then deducting the market value of net debt. The value of debt plus equity is computed as follows:

Debt plus equity value = PV of free cash flows to net debt and equity claim holders

$$= \frac{\text{NOPAT}_1 - \Delta\text{BVA}_1}{(1 + \text{WACC})} + \frac{\text{NOPAT}_2 - \Delta\text{BVA}_2}{(1 + \text{WACC})^2} + \cdots$$

The firm's asset valuation therefore depends on the expected free cash flows to debt and equity holders during the forecast horizon, the forecasted terminal value of the free cash flows, and the weighted average cost of capital.

APPENDIX B: RECONCILING THE DISCOUNTED DIVIDENDS, DISCOUNTED ABNORMAL EARNINGS, AND DISCOUNTED ABNORMAL EARNINGS GROWTH MODELS

To derive the abnormal earnings model from the dividend discount model, consider the following two-period valuation:

$$\text{Equity value} = \frac{\text{Dividend}_1}{(1 + r_e)} + \frac{\text{Dividend}_2}{(1 + r_e)^2}$$

With clean surplus accounting, dividends (*DIV*) can be expressed as a function of net profit (*NP*) and the book value of equity (*BVE*):

$$\text{Dividend}_t = \text{Net profit}_t + BVE_{t-1} - BVE_t$$

Substituting this expression into the dividend discount model yields the following:

$$\text{Equity value} = \frac{\text{Net profit}_1 + BVE_0 - BVE_1}{(1 + r_e)} + \frac{\text{Net profit}_2 + BVE_1 - BVE_2}{(1 + r_e)^2}$$

This can be rewritten as follows:

$$\text{Equity value} = \frac{\text{Net profit}_1 - r_e BVE_0 + (1 + r_e)BVE_0 - BVE_1}{(1 + r_e)}$$
$$+ \frac{\text{Net profit}_2 - r_e BVE_1 + (1 + r_e)BVE_1 - BVE_2}{(1 + r_e)^2}$$
$$= BVE_0 + \frac{\text{Net profit}_1 - r_e BVE_0}{(1 + r_e)} + \frac{\text{Net profit}_2 - r_e BVE_1}{(1 + r_e)^2} - \frac{BVE_2}{(1 + r_e)^2}$$

The value of equity is therefore the current book value plus the present value of future abnormal earnings. As the forecast horizon expands, the final term (the present value of liquidating book value) becomes inconsequential under the assumption that the long-term growth in the book value of equity is less than the cost of equity. A simple and appealing condition under which this assumption holds is when the firm has a constant dividend pay-out ratio.[1]

To derive the abnormal earnings growth model from the dividend discount model consider the same two-period dividend model and express dividends in the second (and final) period as a function of net profit and first-period dividends:

$$\text{Dividend}_2 = \text{Net profit}_2 + \text{Net profit}_1 - \text{Dividend}_1$$

Substituting this expression into the dividend discount model yields the following:

$$\text{Equity value} = \frac{\text{Net profit}_1 + \text{Dividend}_1 - \text{Net profit}_1}{(1 + r_e)} + \frac{\text{Net profit}_1 + \text{Net profit}_2 - \text{Dividend}_1}{(1 + r_e)^2}$$

1. R. P. Brief, J. O'Hanlon, and K. V. Peasnell explain under which conditions the equality between the discounted abnormal earnings (growth) model and the discounted dividends model holds in the following study: "Error in Constant Growth Accounting Valuation Models," New York University and Lancaster University, working paper, 2005.

This can be rewritten as follows:

$$\text{Equity value} = \frac{\text{Net profit}_1}{(1+r_e)} + \frac{\text{Net profit}_1}{(1+r_e)^2} - \frac{(\text{Net profit}_1 - \text{Dividend}_1)(1+r_e)}{(1+r_e)^2}$$

$$+ \frac{(\text{Net profit}_2 - \text{Dividend}_1)}{(1+r_e)^2}$$

$$= \frac{\text{Net profit}_1}{(1+r_e)} + \frac{\text{Net profit}_1}{(1+r_e)^2} + \frac{\text{Net profit}_2 + r_e\text{Dividend}_1 - (1+r_e)\text{Net profit}_1}{(1+r_e)^2}$$

The value of equity is therefore the capitalized value of first-period earnings plus the present value of second-period abnormal earnings growth. Note that in contrast to the abnormal earnings model, the abnormal earnings growth model does not assume clean surplus accounting.

Puma AG Rudolf Dassler Sport

D uring the second half of the 1990s and the first half of the 2000s one of the success
stories of the Deutsche Börse, the German stock exchange, was athletic shoe and
apparel manufacturer Puma AG Rudolf Dassler Sport. Between its initial public offering
in 1986 and 1993, Puma AG had been making losses. After 1993, however, the company
managed to successfully restructure its operations, started to report profits again, and
became one of the most profitable investments on the German exchange. Investors who
had been wise enough to invest in Puma's shares at the beginning of 1994 earned an average annual return on their investment of 33 percent during the next 12 years.

Puma AG[1]

The history of Puma AG started in 1924 when the two brothers Rudolf Dassler and Adolf
Dassler founded the "Gebrüder Dassler Shuhfabrik" (Dassler Brothers Shoe Company) in
Herzogenaurach, Germany. After a difference of opinion with his brother, Rudolf Dassler
left the family business and founded the "Puma Shuhfabrik Rudolph Dassler" in 1948.
Adolf Dassler also started his own sports shoe company under the name Adidas, which
would become one of Puma's principal competitors.

During the first four decades of operations, Puma grew to become one of the world's
premier athletic shoe and apparel manufacturers. Various famous athletes achieved their
successes in Puma sports shoes. In football, Pelé wore Puma shoes while winning the
World Cup with the Brazilian national team in 1958, 1962, and 1970. In tennis, Boris
Becker won Wimbledon wearing Puma shoes in 1985. In athletics, Jim Hines was the
first man to finish the 100 meters sprint within 10 seconds, wearing Puma shoes, in
1968.

In the early 1990s Puma's European market share came under increasing pressure when
US-based athletic shoe manufacturers Nike and Reebok penetrated the European market
for athletic shoes and apparel. Puma lost its position as the second largest European athletic shoe seller and became fourth largest, after Adidas, Nike and Reebok. By that time
Puma had already suffered a series of losses and had accumulated a substantial amount of
debt. Primary reasons for its losses were that the company's marketing activities were
unfocused, the company failed to innovate, its production costs were too high, and its
product range was too broad.[2] Puma's weak financial health also made it difficult for the
company to compete in marketing with its two U.S. competitors. The company especially
failed to compete successfully outside its primary segments, soccer and track and field, in
growth segments such as basketball.

The year 1993, however, became Puma's turnaround year. In an attempt to reverse the
situation, Puma appointed the then 30-year-old Jochen Zeitz as the company's Chief Executive Officer (CEO). Under the leadership of Zeitz the company began to implement a

---

Professor Erik Peek prepared this case. The case is intended solely as the basis for class discussion and is not
intended to serve as an endorsement, source of primary data, or illustration of effective or ineffective
management.

[1]Material in this section is drawn from Puma's 2005 Annual Report and its corporate website.
[2]See "Where Nike and Reebok Have Plenty of Running Room," *Business Week*, March 11, 1991.

long-term worldwide restructuring program. To improve transparency toward its investors, Puma also started to report its financial statements in accordance with International Accounting Standards (IAS), thereby being one of the first companies worldwide to adopt these standards.

Puma's long-term business plan

Puma's worldwide business plan consisted of four different phases. The first phase of restructuring started in fiscal 1993 and ended in fiscal 1997. During this phase, the company restructured its worldwide organization, closed inefficient production plants, and streamlined its product range to increase profitability and reduce indebtedness. The restructuring led to the first success of CEO Jochen Zeitz in 1994, when Puma reported its first net profit since its initial public offering on the German stock exchange in 1986.

The second phase of the plan was aimed at reinforcing Puma's brand image. In this phase Puma invested extensively in marketing and product development, effectively increasing its marketing and R&D outlays by 2–4 percent and 10–15 percent, respectively. The brand image that Puma built was that of one of the most desirable "Sportlifestyle" brands, a brand with distinctive designs that combined style and function. Some steps that Puma took to create this image were to (1) enter into contracts with major designers such as Jill Sander, Marc Jacobs, and Philippe Starck, (2) reduce the number of shops selling its products, (3) start targeted marketing campaigns, for example, by using product placements in movies and TV shows, (4) connect to its customers through famous spokespersons such as tennis player Serena Williams and athlete Wilson Kipketer, and (5) engage in co-branding arrangements with, for example, Porsche.[3]

The third phase, which followed the second phase in 2002, had the objectives to further strengthen Puma's brand image, consistently achieve double-digit sales growth, and reach a sales level of €2 billion by the end of 2006. To improve sales growth Puma invested in product innovation and started to develop its own retail business. In 2002, Puma opened concept retail stores in Frankfurt, London, Rome, Milan, Melbourne, Tokyo, Boston, and Seattle. In 2003, further stores were opened in the cities of Amsterdam, Stockholm, Sydney, Osaka, Philadelphia, and Las Vegas. Puma targeted generating 10 percent of its corporate sales from retail. The company achieved this target in fiscal 2004.

Puma launched the fourth phase of its business plan in 2006. This phase focused on the expansion of Puma to achieve a target sales level of €3.5 billion. Puma planned to expand its product categories in existing business segments as well as in previously unexplored segments. For example, in March 2006 Puma licensed the Japan-based Charmant Group to sell Puma branded eyewear. The management of Puma believed such an expansion into fashion to be a necessary step in creating a company that was truly "Sportlifestyle" based.

Puma realized its geographic expansion plans, in particular by acquiring firms in so-called license markets, where in prior years independent distributors sold Puma branded products under license. Target firms were very often the licensees of these markets. For example, in 2005 Puma agreed to acquire the Argentinean licensee Unisol, the Japanese licensee for apparel Hit Union, and Hong-Kong-based Swire Pacific, which was the company's licensee in Hong Kong and China.

Puma also planned to expand its non-Puma brands. One of Puma's primary non-Puma brands was the Tretorn brand, which Puma had purchased in 2001. To expand its non-Puma brands, Puma repositioned the Tretorn brand by expanding the brand's product range. In addition to the repositioning of the Tretorn brand, Puma had plans to acquire more non-Puma brands in subsequent years.

[3]See "Stay Cool: Apple Shines and Puma Sprints Ahead as the Two Brands Capture the 'cool factor'," *Marketing Management*, September/October 2005.

Sales and production

Puma made use of two different approaches to selling its products. One approach was to let Puma subsidiaries distribute Puma branded products to its customers. The other approach was to license independent companies to produce and distribute Puma branded products. Under a licensing contract, the licensee typically provides a minimum guarantee of sales, either paid in advance or in installments. Further, the licensor typically charges the licensee additional royalties based on the number of products sold. In the early 1990s, the sports licensing business was highly competitive and several licensing companies went bankrupt. By 2006, however, the licensing industry had gone through a process of consolidation and licensees had become financially healthier.

Puma outsourced much of its production to independent factories, mostly located in low-wage countries. In 2004, 81 percent of Puma's production came from the Far East/Asia. The remainder was produced in Europe and America. The companies to which Puma sourced its production were by no means small, powerless production companies. For example, one of Puma's suppliers was Hong-Kong-based Yue Yuen. This supplier employed 252,000 people, had production plants in China, Vietnam, and Indonesia with, in total, 3.4 million square meters of floor space, and produced 167.2 million pairs of shoes per year for most of the larger athletic shoe sellers.

The development and design of new products took place in Puma's product development centers in Herzogenaurauch, London, Taiwan, and Boston. Puma invested an increasing amount of money and resources in product development. Between 2000 and 2005, product development expenses had increased from €18.2 million to €42 million. In percentage terms this increase in product development outlays was, however, smaller than the increase in Puma's consolidated sales.

Puma's financial performance

Exhibit 1 summarizes Puma's financial performance between 1993 and 2005. During these years Puma reported its financial statements in accordance with International Accounting Standards (IAS/IFRS). Hence, all reported figures were prepared under one set of standards. The exhibit shows that Puma increased its consolidated sales from €210 million in 1993 to close to €1.8 billion in 2005. The company remained profitable in each year after 1993, although operating asset turnover and NOPAT margins came under pressure during the implementation of the second phase of Puma's long-term business plan between 1998 and 2002. While accessories made up 4 percent of sales in 1993, the segment generated 11 percent of consolidated sales in 2005, which illustrates Puma's change in strategy.

Questions

1   Puma's profit margin decreased from 16.8 to 16.1 percent in 2005. Consensus earnings forecasts for fiscal 2006 (see **Exhibit 1**) indicate that analysts expect a further decline in Puma's profit margin to 11.1 percent. On which factors do Puma's future profit margins critically depend? Do you expect these factors to change over the coming years? Do you agree with analysts' assessment of Puma's next year's profitability?

2   Assume that investors had perfect foresight of one-year-ahead earnings at the end of each fiscal year between 1993 and 2004. Which long-term growth rate assumptions are consistent with the observed end-of-year share prices between 1993 and 2004? When are investors typically positive about long-term growth in earnings?

3   Given your expectations about one-year-ahead earnings and long-term earnings growth, what is your assessment of the value of Puma's shares at the end of fiscal 2005?

Puma AG Rudolf Dassler Sport

Puma AG Rudolf Dassler Sport

EXHIBIT 1 Puma's historical and expected performance, 1993–2007

(€ millions)	2007E	2006E	2005	2004	2003	2002	2001	2000	1999	1998	1997	1996	1995	1994	1993
Brand sales			2,387.0	2,016.6	1,691.5	1,380.0	1,011.7	831.1	714.9	647.4	622.5	594.0	577.2	554.2	541.3
Percentage growth in brand sales			18.4%	19.2%	22.6%	36.4%	21.7%	16.3%	10.4%	4.0%	4.8%	2.9%	4.2%	2.4%	
Consolidated sales	2,747.0	2,386.0	1,777.5	1,530.3	1,274.0	909.8	598.1	462.4	372.7	302.5	279.7	250.5	211.5	199.5	210.0
Percentage growth in consolidated sales	15.1%	34.2%	16.2%	20.1%	40.0%	52.1%	29.3%	24.1%	23.2%	8.2%	11.7%	18.4%	6.0%	−5.0%	
Footwear			1,175.0	1,011.4	859.3	613.0	384.1	270.9	209.0	202.5	193.8	176.2	154.4	143.5	141.9
Apparel			473.9	416.0	337.0	238.5	169.5	163.5	139.0	85.8	73.1	64.4	50.3	49.9	59.8
Accessories			128.6	102.9	77.7	58.3	44.5	28.0	24.7	14.2	12.9	9.9	6.8	6.2	8.4
Gross profit	1,395.5	1,214.5	929.8	794.0	620.0	396.9	250.6	176.4	141.7	108.2	102.3	94.0	79.0	69.5	62.8
Profit from operations	463.0	378.0	397.7	360.0	263.2	125.0	59.0	22.8	16.3	4.7	36.3	33.3	31.0	23.1	−26.1
Earnings before taxes	474.0	388.0	404.1	365.7	264.1	124.4	57.4	21.2	14.4	3.4	37.4	33.2	26.5	17.3	−35.4
Net earnings	322.0	265.0	285.8	257.3	179.3	84.9	39.7	17.6	9.5	4.0	34.6	42.8	24.6	14.9	−36.9
Dividends			31.9	16.1	11.2	8.8	4.6	1.6	1.6	1.6	1.6	1.6	0.0	0.0	0.0
Royalty and commission income			55.7	43.7	40.4	44.9	37.2	28.9	23.9	24.5	25.9	25.5	26.0	27.1	21.4
Marketing and retail expenses			272.0	214.6	163.9	125.1	86.9	67.0	61.0	47.9	29.0	N.A.	N.A.	N.A.	N.A.
Product development and design expenses			42.0	36.9	29.9	24.2	19.9	18.2	15.2	15.2	7.3	N.A.	N.A.	N.A.	N.A.
Personnel expenses			199.4	157.5	126.6	103.0	81.1	64.4	51.5	41.3	35.2	N.A.	N.A.	N.A.	N.A.
End-of-year order backlog			1,069.0	822.6	722.0	531.1	360.1	232.1	187.2	133.5	130.8	111.4	90.9	94.4	85.2
Operating working capital			234.6	65.9	92.0	73.4	109.1	78.2	64.1	50.1	70.0	21.2	17.8	6.6	34.1
Net non-current assets			217.4	129.7	131.3	100.0	87.9	64.0	60.5	45.4	18.3	24.9	24.0	26.5	32.1
Net assets			452.0	195.6	223.3	173.4	197.0	142.2	124.7	95.5	88.3	46.2	41.7	33.1	66.2
Equity			870.9	535.8	383.0	252.2	176.7	131.3	112.2	97.7	96.7	61.6	−13.6	−38.1	−53.0
Net debt			−419.0	−340.3	−159.7	−78.8	20.3	10.9	12.5	6.2	−8.4	−15.5	55.3	71.3	119.2

Profit margin	11.7%	11.1%	16.1%	16.8%	14.1%	9.3%	6.6%	3.8%	2.5%	1.3%	12.4%	17.1%	11.6%	7.5%	−17.6%
ROE (end-of-year equity)			32.8%	48.0%	46.8%	33.7%	22.5%	13.4%	8.5%	4.1%	35.8%	69.4%	N.A.	N.A.	N.A.
ROE (beginning-of-year equity)		30.4%	53.3%	67.2%	71.1%	48.0%	30.2%	15.7%	9.7%	4.1%	56.1%	N.A.	N.A.	N.A.	N.A.
NOPAT			281.3	253.3	178.7	85.3	40.8	18.9	10.6	3.8	33.6	42.9	28.8	19.9	−27.2
NOPAT margin			15.8%	16.6%	14.0%	9.4%	6.8%	4.1%	2.8%	1.3%	12.0%	17.1%	13.6%	10.0%	−13.0%
Operating asset turnover			3.9	7.8	5.7	5.2	3.0	3.3	3.0	3.2	3.2	5.4	5.1	6.0	3.2
Operating ROA			62.2%	129.5%	80.0%	49.2%	20.7%	13.3%	8.5%	4.0%	38.0%	93.0%	69.0%	60.1%	−41.1%
Net financial leverage			−0.48	−0.64	−0.42	−0.31	0.11	0.08	0.11	0.06	−0.09	−0.25	N.A.	N.A.	N.A.
Spread			61.1%	128.3%	79.6%	49.7%	13.3%	−1.1%	−6.1%	−21.9%	25.2%	93.7%	N.A.	N.A.	N.A.
Financial leverage effect			−29.4%	−81.5%	−33.2%	−15.5%	1.5%	−0.1%	−0.7%	−1.4%	−2.2%	−23.5%	N.A.	N.A.	N.A.
Weighted average shares outstanding	15,672	15,898	16,066	16,025	15,932	15,611	15,392	15,390	15,390	15,390	15,390	15,390	14,000	14,000	14,000
Net earnings per share	20.55	16.67	17.79	16.06	11.25	5.44	2.58	1.14	0.62	0.26	2.25	2.78	1.76	1.06	−2.64
End-of-year equity per share			54.21	33.44	24.04	16.16	11.48	8.53	7.29	6.35	6.28	4.00	−0.97	−2.72	−3.79
End-of-year share price			246.70	202.30	140.00	65.03	34.05	12.70	17.20	11.25	18.61	26.69	18.41	14.93	7.75

Source: Puma's annual reports and corporate website.

EXHIBIT 2   Management's outlook for fiscal year 2006

Outlook

For the year 2006 PUMA again expects a very successful year. The Soccer World Cup offers PUMA an ideal platform for heightening the brand presence while also impressively highlighting its product capabilities. With a total of 12 teams and numerous individual players, PUMA has the largest World Cup portfolio and is therefore the leading outfitter of this tournament. In addition to the three-time World Champion, Italy, eleven more teams will contribute to a strengthening of the brand presence. Through the use of new technologies, innovative designs and creative concepts as well as the biggest advertising campaign in the company's history, PUMA will set strong accents at the Soccer World Cup with the aim to further consolidate its position as one of the leading soccer brands worldwide.

Further expansion of the global economy in 2006

According to a report of the "Kiel Institute for the World Economy" (Institut für Weltwirtschaft an der Universität Kiel) under the present general political and economic conditions and assuming that oil prices and exchange rates will remain largely constant, global economic expansion will continue in the year 2006, although at a somewhat slower pace than in the first half of 2005. In the oil-importing industrial and emerging nations, the oil price will continue to have a dampening effect for some time. However, the world economy should remain highly dynamic since the stimulating factors will also remain effective.

Overall economic demand could expand more gradually in the USA. Private consumption is expected to flatten out, since the stabilization of real estate prices tends to encourage saving. In Japan, where the adjustment processes could bear fruit in the corporate and banking sector, the overall economy should continue on an upward course. Due to growing demand, a slight economic recovery is expected in the Euro zone. In particular, the progress in the restructuring of the corporate sector will result in a more pronounced increase in investment activity. The mood in the overall economy is expected to remain cautious, however.

The world economic forecasts should also make themselves felt in the sporting goods sector since global economic development can significantly influence general consumer behaviour. Particularly in the year of the World Soccer Championships, an upswing in the sporting goods industry is to be expected in Europe.

In the 2006 Word Soccer Championships year, PUMA will present new product innovations in typical PUMA style. The products will have an authentic brand design, high functionality and unmistakable marketing. The year 2006 will also see the largest marketing campaign in the company's history.

The aim is to achieve a high market presence through the soccer products and the global marketing campaigns, and therefore to strengthen the brand image even further.

Management raises sales forecast to new record-high for the first year of Phase IV

Due to a significant improvement in the orders position for the EMEA region, a stronger than expected orders volume in America and the accelerated integration of six license markets into the group, as early as at the beginning of the year, management raised the original sales target for the first year of Phase IV. On a currency neutral basis, a growth of approximately 30% on consolidated sales, and thus a new record high of approximately €2.3 billion is expected.

Sales increases in all regions

The planned sales growth will extend throughout all regions. Due to the takeovers of individual license markets, the regional distribution of sales will improve as planned. The share of Asia/Pacific should grow from 11% to 20% of consolidated sales. America will continue to yield 27%, while the EMEA region is expected to decline from 62% to approximately 53% according to plan.

Operating profit raised to €350 million

As already announced in the publication of Phase IV measures, the regional change will impact the average gross profit margin. Overall, the gross profit margin in 2006 is expected to fluctuate within the range of 50% and 51%. The takeover of six license markets into the consolidated business will lead to a corresponding reduction in royalty and commission income. Selling, general and administrative expenses will be impacted in particular by disproportionately high marketing expenses for the World Cup and other PUMA campaigns, as well as by planned expansion of the group's retail operations and higher expenses for product development, design and distribution. Overall, however, due to the higher sales expectations, operating expenses will rise to only approximately 35% of sales, compared to the expected 37%. The operating margin is expected to decrease to approximately 15% as a result of brand-building investments in 2006 and conversion of the license businesses into consolidated business. Based on the very positive orders position and the rapid implementation of Phase IV measures, management now expects operating profit of at least €350 million, compared to the original expectation of between €300 million and €330 million. The tax rate is expected to be in the 31%–33% range.

Despite the planned strategic expenditure, consolidated earnings are expected to fall only 10%–15% below the previous year's level, compared to the announced level of 20%. Thus, in absolute figures consolidated earnings are expected to significantly exceed the original expectations.

Expansion of the consolidation group in 2006

Beginning in financial year 2006, the consolidated group will be expanded by companies in Japan, Taiwan, China, Hong Kong, Argentina and Canada. The effects on the net assets, financial position, and results of operations are presented in the Notes. The structuring of contracts with some joint venture companies is such that a disclosure of minority interests is not required since, in economic terms, these companies are fully allocable to PUMA as of January 1, 2006.

Capital expenditures

The investment planning for 2006 provides for capital expenditure of between €130 million and €150 million.

Investments in intangible assets will be necessary, primarily for continued expansion of the group's own retail operations. Capital expenditure of approximately €70 million for the acquisition of new subsidiaries and joint venture companies is included in this calculation.

The targeted investments at the start of Phase IV of the long-term corporate development will lead to introduction of the steps required to strengthen PUMA's position as one of the three leading companies in the sporting goods industry, with the long-term objective of becoming the most desirable Sportlifestyle company.

Management is optimistic

Management is optimistic that the PUMA brand will take yet another large and successful leap in international competition in the year of the Soccer World Cup and during the first year of Phase IV. New sales records are expected for the year 2006. The high level of planned investment activity and an associated increase in the cost ratio at the start of Phase IV should impact profits to a significantly lesser extent than originally expected. Therefore, the operating profit in the current year is expected to be at the high level of €350 million, despite the large amount of investments planned. Beginning from 2007, the cost ratio is expected to decline, and management is confident that yet another record high result can be achieved in addition to continuing record sales. This positive development should lead to at least full exploitation of the calculated sales potential of €3.5 billion in Phase IV of the long-term oriented business plan.

Herzogenaurach, January 25, 2006
The Board of Management

EXHIBIT 3　Puma AG Rudolf Dassler Sport: Selected notes to the financial statements

1. General remarks

Under the "PUMA" brand name, PUMA Aktiengesell-schaft Rudolf Dassler Sport (hereinafter "PUMA AG") and its subsidiaries are engaged in the development and sales of a broad range of sport and sportlifestyle articles that includes footwear, apparel and accessories. The company is a joint stock company under German law and has its registered head office in Herzogenaurach, Federal Republic of Germany; its responsible court of registration is at Fürth (Bavaria, Germany).

The consolidated financial statements of PUMA AG and its subsidiaries (hereinafter the "Company" or "PUMA"), were prepared in accordance with the "International Financial Reporting Standards (IFRS)" issued by the International Accounting Standards Board (IASB) and the supplementary provisions to be applied in accordance with Section 315a (1) of the German Commercial Code (HGB). All IASB standards and interpretations as adopted by the EU that are obligatory for financial years as from January 1, 2005 have been applied. In August 2005, the IASB published IFRS 7 "Financial Instruments: Disclosures"; this standard will lead to a fundamental change in disclosing requirements concerning financial instruments. In accordance with IFRS 7, companies are required to provide more detailed information on the type and extent of risks associated with financial instruments, in addition to the disclosure requirements relating to the reporting, disclosure and valuation requirements for financial instruments that are already in place. The standard will come into force on January 1, 2007 and is not applied prior to that date.

The consolidated financial statements of PUMA AG are prepared in euro currency (EUR or €). Disclosures in million euros may lead to rounding-off differences since the calculation of individual items is based on figures presented in thousands.

In accordance with IFRS 2, the figures from 2004 were correspondingly restated. In addition, a claim for a tax return in the USA leads to an adjustment of the previous year's figures. The adjustments were explained in the respective disclosures in the notes to the consolidated financial statements ("Notes") where necessary.

Also, in 2005, other operating income was directly netted with the respective administration and general expenses. The previous year's figure was adjusted accordingly.

2. Significant accounting and valuation principles [selection]

Recognition of sales

Sales are recognized and included in profits at the time of the passage of risks. Sales are disclosed net of returned purchases, discounts, rebates, and sales-dependent advertising costs.

Royalty and commission income

Royalty income is treated as income in accordance with the statements to be presented by the licensees. In certain cases, values must be assessed in order to permit accounting on an accrual basis. Commission income is invoiced to the extent that the underlying purchase transaction is deemed realized.

Advertising and promotion expenses

The company recognizes advertising expenses at the time of origin. Generally, promotion expenditure is spread over the contract term as an expense on an accrual basis.

Product development

The company is continuously engaged in developing new products in order to comply with market requirements or market changes. The costs are recorded as an expense at the date of origin; they are not capitalized since the criteria specified in IAS 38 are not fulfilled.

3. Corporate acquisitions

The corporate acquisitions described under "Consolidated Group" had no significant impact on the company's results of operations in 2005.

The goodwill acquired in the financial year is as follows:

(€ millions)	2005
Total purchase prices – of which paid (€17.9 million)	35.6
Fair value of acquired net assets	11.0
Goodwill	24.6

Transactions from acquisition impacted the net assets and financial position in fiscal year 2005 as follows:

(€ millions)	2005
Inventories	11.1
Receivables	30.2
Goodwill	24.6
Other assets	22.1
Bank debt	−14.8
Other liabilities	−38.1
Purchase price	35.6

€18 million from the total purchase price amounting to €36 million were already paid in 2005. The remaining amount of €18 million is classified as liabilities from acquisitions. The liabilities from acquisitions include the amount of €7 million, which is due within one year, and €11 million due in 5 years.

The position "Other assets" includes prepayments from acquisitions amounting to €10 million (please see paragraph 7 of these Notes).

5. Inventories

Inventories are divided into the following main categories:

(€ millions)	2005	2004
Raw materials and supplies	0.5	0.5
Finished goods and merchandise		
Footwear	114.2	106.9
Apparel	86.5	71.9
Accessories/Others	19.5	18.2
Goods in transit	76.1	54.1
Inventories, gross	296.8	251.6
Value adjustments	−58.5	−50.5
Inventories, net	238.3	201.1

Of the total amount of reported inventories, the amount of €64 million (previous year: €58 million) is stated at net realizable value.

6. Trade receivables

(€ millions)	2005	2004
Trade receivables, gross	303.3	188.2
Value adjustments	−25.8	−20.1
Trade receivables, net	277.5	168.1

Advance payments on acquisitions relate to majority shares acquired in companies in Taiwan and China/ Hong Kong in 2006. The item is reclassified to shares in affiliated companies upon transfer of the shares and eliminated within the scope of consolidation.

Other current assets are due within one year. The fair value represents the book value. As of tax reclaims relating to the management incentive program the last year's figures were restated amounting to €13 million.

25. Management of the currency risk

The company is exposed to currency risks which result from an imbalance in the global cashflow. This imbalance is largely due to the high level of sourcing on a US Dollar basis in the Far East. Sales are invoiced in other currencies to a great extent; in addition, the company earns royalty income mainly in Japanese YEN (JPY) and USD. The resulting assets and liabilities are subject to exchange-rate fluctuations from the date of their origin up to realization.

The PUMA Group uses derivative and primary hedging instruments to minimize the currency risk arising from currency fluctuations. Derivative transactions are concluded if a hedging requirement arises from future transactions or after netting existing foreign currency receivables and liabilities. In accordance with the Group's treasury principles, no derivative financial instruments are held for trading purposes. As a general rule, derivatives are combined with the associated underlying transactions to valuation units (hedge accounting) and, to this extent do not impact the net income/net loss for the year.

The company hedges its net demand or net surplus of the respective currencies on a rolling basis 24 months in advance, thus hedging the planning period for the years 2006 and 2007 against currency fluctuations.

The net demand or net surplus results from the demand for a certain currency, net of expected income in the same currency. Forward exchange deals are used to hedge exchange rate risks.

For accounting purposes, hedging transactions are clearly linked to certain parts of the overall risk position. As of the balance sheet date, forward exchange deals related almost exclusively to the purchase of USD and EUR, and the sale of JPY and USD concluded with international renowned financial institutions only. The credit risk is therefore assessed as being very low or unlikely. At present, the terms of the derivatives are up to 24 months. The contracts are used exclusively to hedge contracts already concluded, or where conclusion is expected.

The nominal amounts and market values of open rate-hedging transactions, largely related to cashflow hedging, are structured as follows:

Puma AG Rudolf Dassler Sport

(€ millions)	Nominal amount 2005	Nominal amount 2004	Market value 2005	Market value 2004
Total forward exchange transactions	616.1	724.6	27.6	−59.6

The nominal amount corresponds to the amounts of the respective hedging transactions as agreed upon between the parties involved. The market value is the amount at which the financial instrument would be traded between interested parties on the balance sheet date. As a general rule, the market values are determined on the basis of the market values communicated by the respective banks. The market value is reported under Other Financial Assets or Other Liabilities in accordance with IAS 39, and offset against equity with neutral effects on profits in as much as the hedging transaction relates to future transactions.

The underlying and hedging transactions will probably impact the revenue results within the next 24 months. In the financial year, the amount of €22 million was reclassified from equity as inventory acquisition costs (IAS 32.59). Management does not expect any adverse influences on the Group's financial position from the use of derivative financial instruments.

29. Other financial obligations

The company's other financial obligations relate to license, promotion and advertising contracts. In addition, the company leases and rents offices, warehouses, facilities, a car park and also sales premises for its own retail business. The residual term of the lease contract for the logistics centre in Germany (operative leasing) is 6 years. The term of rental contracts concerning the retail business is between 5 and 15 years. The terms of all other rental and lease contracts are between 1 and 5 years.

As of the balance sheet date, the company's financial obligations were as follows:

(€ millions)	2005	2004
From license, promotion and advertising contracts:		
2006 (2005)	47.4	33.4
2007–2010 (2006–2009)	170.5	53.4
From rental and lease contracts:		
2006 (2007)	46.6	29.5
2007–2010 (2006–2009)	153.3	90.8
As from 2001 (as from 2010)	81.3	48.4

32. Events after the balance sheet date

In the context of its long-term corporate development plan (Phase IV) published in July 2005, PUMA will acquire the majority share or 100% respectively, in the following companies in January 2006. These companies will then be responsible for the sales & marketing of PUMA products in the respective countries with immediate effect. In accordance with the agreements concluded with minority shareholders with a view to acquisition after expiry of the term of the agreement, the companies in Japan and Taiwan are to be allocated to the PUMA Group at 100% in economic terms with effect from January 1, 2006. The other companies are purely joint ventures which are recognized through taking the respective minority interest into account. The following companies were founded – or a majority interest was acquired – and they were included in consolidation with effect from January 1, 2006.

Asia Pacific	America
PUMA Apparel Japan K.K., Japan	Unisol S.A., Argentina
PUMA Taiwan Sports Ltd., Taiwan	ATA Inc., Canada
Liberty China Holding Ltd., British Virgin Islands	
Liberty Sports Marketing Ltd., Hong Kong	
Liberty Shanghai Ltd., China	

The change in the consolidated group is expected to impact net assets and the financial position as of the time of initial consolidation (January 1, 2006) as follows.

(€ millions)	Asia/Pacific	America	Total
Total purchase price	73.6	42.4	115.9
Fair value of the net assets acquired	25.5	20.9	46.4
Goodwill	48.0	21.5	69.5

€10 million from the total purchase price amounting to €116 million were already paid in 2005 (please see paragraph 7 of these Notes).

Prospective Analysis: Valuation Implementation

To move from the valuation theory discussed in the previous chapter to the actual task of valuing a company, we have to deal with two key issues. First, we have to estimate the cost of capital to discount our forecasts. And second, we have to make forecasts of financial performance stated in terms of abnormal earnings and book values, or free cash flows, over the life of the firm. The forecasting task itself is divided into two subcomponents: (1) detailed forecasts over a finite number of years and (2) a forecast of terminal value, which represents a summary forecast of performance beyond the period of detailed forecasts.

This chapter builds on the forecast developed in Chapter 6 and provides guidance on calculating cost of capital, computing a terminal value, and synthesizing the different pieces of the analytical process to estimate firm or equity value.

COMPUTING A DISCOUNT RATE

To value a company's equity, the analyst discounts abnormal earnings (growth), abnormal ROE, or cash flows available to equity holders. The proper discount rate to use is the cost of equity.

Estimating the cost of equity

Estimating the **cost of equity** (r_e) can be difficult, and a full discussion of the topic lies beyond the scope of this chapter. In any case, even an extended discussion would not supply answers to all the questions that might be raised in this area because the field of finance is in a state of flux over what constitutes an appropriate measure of the cost of equity.

The capital asset pricing model

One common approach to estimating the cost of equity is to use the **capital asset pricing model** (CAPM). The main idea of the CAPM is that investors holding a portfolio of investments (only) care about – and thus want to be compensated for – the risk that an asset contributes to the portfolio. This type of risk, labeled beta or systematic risk, is the risk created by the correlation between the asset's return and the returns of the other investments in the portfolio. The CAPM therefore expresses the cost of equity as the sum of a required return on riskless assets plus a premium for beta or systematic risk:

$$r_e = r_f + \beta [E(r_m) - r_f]$$

[handwritten annotations: "risk free rate" pointing to r_f; "systematic risk" pointing to β; "Market risk premium" pointing to $E(r_m) - r_f$]

357

where r_f is the riskless rate; $[E(r_m) - r_f]$ is the risk premium expected for the market as a whole, expressed as the excess of the expected return on the market index over the riskless rate; and β is the systematic risk of the equity.

To compute r_e one must estimate three parameters: the riskless rate, r_f, the market risk premium $[E(r_m) - r_f]$, and systematic risk, β. To estimate the required return on riskless assets, analysts often use the rate on intermediate-term government bonds, based on the observation that it is cash flows beyond the short-term that are being discounted.[1] Theory calls for the use of a short-term rate, but if that rate is used here, a difficult practical question arises: how does one reflect the premium required for expected inflation over long horizons? While the premium could, in principle, be treated as a portion of the term $[E(r_m) - r_f]$, it is probably easier to use an intermediate- or long-term riskless rate that presumably reflects expected inflation.

The systematic or beta risk (β) of a share reflects the sensitivity of its cash flows and earnings (and hence stock price) to economy-wide market movements.[2] A firm whose performance increases or decreases at the same rate as changes in the economy as a whole will have a beta of one. Firms whose performance is highly sensitive to economy-wide changes, such as luxury goods producers, capital goods manufacturers, and construction firms, will have beta risks that exceed one. And firms whose earnings and cash flows are less sensitive to economic changes, such as regulated utilities or supermarkets, will have betas that are lower than one. Financial services firms, such as Standard & Poor's and Thomson Financial, provide estimates of beta for publicly-listed companies that are based on the historical relation between the firm's stock returns and the returns on the market index. These estimates provide a useful way to assess publicly-traded firms' beta risks. For firms that are not publicly-traded, analysts can use betas for publicly-traded firms in the same industries, adjusting for any differences in financial leverage, as an indicator of the likely beta risk.

LOEWE'S BETA

One way to estimate systematic risk is to regress the firm's stock returns over some recent time period against the returns on the market index. In this regression the slope coefficient on the market index represents an estimate of a company's (historical) β. Using monthly returns on the MSCI Europe index as the measure for market returns, the estimated relationship between Loewe's monthly stock returns and the market index between January 2004 and December 2008 is as follows:

Monthly return Loewe $= 0.01 + 1.66 \times$ Monthly market return ($R^2 = 29\%$)

This equation indicates that Loewe's historical beta estimate is 1.66. When changing the length of the estimation period from 60 months to (the most recent) 48, 36, or 24 months, the beta estimate remains relatively stable and ranges from 1.53 to 1.66. Based on these results, we assume that the best estimate of Loewe's future beta is 1.6.

Finally, the market risk premium is the amount that investors demand as additional return for bearing beta risk. It is the excess of the expected return on the market index over the riskless rate r_f. When r_f is measured the rate on intermediate-term government bonds, then average worldwide common stock returns (based on the returns to a 16-country, common-currency equity index) have exceeded that rate by 4.9 percent over the 1900–2002 period.[3] This excess return constitutes an estimate of the market risk premium $[E(r_m) - r_f]$. Based on the risk premium's historical means and variances between 1900 and 2002, one study reports that plausible estimates of future market risk premiums for the "world market," the UK, and the US are somewhere around 5.0, 5.5, and 5.5 percent, respectively. However, it is important to realize that the market risk premium has varied substantially across countries and will likely continue to do so, albeit to a lesser degree when worldwide stock markets will further integrate and worldwide disclosure and securities regulation will be further harmonized.[4] In addition, while the historical risk premium has been calculated over a long time period, the premium is likely to change over time because of, for example, the changing risk preferences of investors.

LOEWE'S RISK PREMIUM

At the end of 2008, the yield on ten-year government bonds in the euro area was close to 4 percent, approximately equal to its average in the period 2004–2008 (Source: Eurostat). Using the 2008 ending value of the yield as a measure for the risk-free rate and assuming that the market risk premium equals 5 percent, the CAPM-based estimate of Loewe's cost of equity equals,

$$\text{Cost of equity} = 4.0 \text{ percent } (r_f) + 1.6(\beta) \times 5.0 \text{ percent } (E(r_m) - r_f) = 12 \text{ percent}$$

The firm size effect

Although the above CAPM is often used to estimate the cost of capital, the evidence indicates that the model is incomplete. Assuming stocks are priced competitively, stock returns should be expected just to compensate investors for the cost of their capital. Thus long-run average returns should be close to the cost of capital and should (according to the CAPM) vary across stocks according to their systematic risk. However, factors beyond just systematic risk seem to play some role in explaining variation in long-run average returns. The most important such factor is labeled the "size effect": smaller firms (as measured by market capitalization) tend to generate higher returns in subsequent periods. Why this is so is unclear. It could mean either that smaller firms are riskier than indicated by the CAPM or that they are underpriced at the point their market capitalization is measured, or some combination of both.

Average stock returns for European firms (from the 17 European countries described in Chapter 1) varied across size deciles from 1992 to 2008 as shown in Table 8.1. The table shows that, historically, investors in firms in the top two deciles of the size distribution have realized returns of, on average, 11.2 to 12.5 percent. In contrast, firms in the smallest two size deciles have realized significantly higher returns of, on average 13.8 to 21.5 percent. Note, however, that if we use firm size as an indicator of the cost of capital, we are implicitly assuming that large size is indicative of lower risk. Yet finance theorists have not developed a well-accepted explanation for why that should be the case.

One method for combining the cost of capital estimates is based on the CAPM and the "size effect." The approach calls for adjustment of the CAPM-based cost of capital, based on the difference between the average return on the market index used in the CAPM and the average return on firms of size comparable to the firm being evaluated. The resulting cost of capital is

$$r_e = r_f + \beta[E(r_m) - r_f] + r_{SIZE}$$

In light of the continuing debate on how to measure the cost of capital, it is not surprising that managers and analysts often consider a range of estimates. In addition to the question about whether or not the historical risk premium of about 5 percent is valid today,[5] there is debate over whether beta is a relevant measure of risk, and whether other metrics such as

TABLE 8.1 European firms' stock returns and firm size

Size deciles	Market value of largest company in decile, in 2008 (€ millions)	Average annual stock return 1992–2008 (%)	Fraction of total market capitalization represented by decile (in 2008, %)
1-small	6.8	21.5%	0.02
2	16.3	13.8%	0.06
3	32.2	11.9%	0.14
4	54.4	10.3%	0.25
5	91.4	11.5%	0.42
6	163.7	10.1%	0.73
7	307.1	10.1%	1.33
8	668.8	11.2%	2.72
9	2,149.3	12.5%	6.97
10-large	158,448.0	11.2%	87.36

Source: Thomson Datastream. Annual stock returns are based on compounded monthly returns. The returns come from all European companies that were listed on one of the seven major European stock exchanges between 1992 and 2008 (see Chapter 1 for details).

size should be reflected in cost of capital estimates. Since these debates are still unresolved, it is prudent for analysts to use a range of risk premium estimates in computing a firm's cost of capital.

LOEWE'S SIZE PREMIUM

At the end of 2008, the market value of Loewe's shares was approximately €112 million, down from €204 million in 2007 due to the overall market decline. Although the equity value that we estimate for Loewe may deviate from its market price, this value is not likely to fall within the bottom three size deciles of the European market. Consequently, it is unnecessary to adjust Loewe's cost of equity estimate for a size effect.

Adjusting the cost equity for changes in leverage

The beta risk of a firm's equity changes as a function of its leverage. As the leverage increases, the sensitivity of the firm's equity performance to economy-wide changes also increases. To see this, recall from Chapter 5 that return on equity (ROE) can be decomposed in the following manner:

$$ROE = Operating\ ROA + (Operating\ ROA - Effective\ interest\ rate\ after\ tax)$$
$$\times\ \frac{Net\ debt}{Equity}$$

This equation shows that if net debt equals equity, a 2 percent increase in operating return on assets (ROA) after an economy-wide recovery will increase ROE by 4 percent, all else equal. In contrast, if net debt is two times equity, the same increase in operating ROA will increase ROE by 6 percent. Hence, the equity beta of a firm does not only reflect the sensitivity of its assets' performance to economy-wide movements (labeled **asset beta**) but also the net financial leverage effect on its equity performance. If an analyst is contemplating changing capital structure during the forecasting period relative to the historical capital structure of the firm, or changing the capital structure over time during the forecasting period, it is important to re-estimate the equity beta and to take these changes into account. We describe below a simple approach to this task.

We begin with the observation that the beta of a portfolio of assets is the weighted average of the assets' individual betas. Similarly, the beta of a firm's assets is equal to the weighted average of its debt and equity betas, weighted by the proportion of debt and equity in its capital structure, taking into account the tax shield on debt:

$$\beta_{\text{ASSET}} = \frac{(1 - \text{Tax rate}) \times \text{Net debt}}{(1 - \text{Tax rate}) \times \text{Net debt} + \text{Equity}} \beta_{\text{DEBT}}$$

$$+ \frac{\text{Equity}}{(1 - \text{tax rate}) \times \text{Net debt} + \text{Equity}} \beta_{\text{EQUITY}}$$

A firm's equity beta can be estimated directly using its stock returns and the capital asset pricing model. Its debt beta can be inferred from the capital asset pricing model if we have information on its current interest rate and the risk-free rate, using the CAPM formula. From these estimated equity and debt betas at the current capital structure, we can infer the firm's asset beta.

When the firm's capital structure changes, its equity and debt betas will change, but its asset beta remains the same. We can take advantage of this fact to estimate the expected equity beta for the new capital structure. We first have to get an estimate of the interest rate on debt at the new capital structure level. Once we have this information, we can estimate the implied debt beta using the capital asset pricing model and the risk-free rate. Now we can estimate the equity beta for the new capital structure using the identity that the new equity beta and the new debt beta, weighted by the new capital structure weights, have to add up to the asset beta estimated earlier.

For many firms that have a low probability of bankruptcy, the current interest rate will be close to the risk-free rate and the debt beta will be close to zero. To simplify the calculation of leverage-adjusted betas, many analysts thus assume that the debt beta equals zero. Under this assumption, the equity and asset betas have the following relationship:

$$\beta_{\text{EQUITY}} = \left[1 + (1 - \text{Tax rate}) \times \frac{\text{Net debt}}{\text{Equity}} \right] \times \beta_{\text{ASSET}}$$

Note that in this equation, debt and equity are measured in terms of economic values rather than book values. We will later discuss some of the complications involved in obtaining these economic values

LOEWE'S ASSET BETA

During the years 2006–2008, the ratio of Loewe's after-tax book value of debt to market value of equity ranged from 0.24 to 0.19 and averaged at 0.21.

	2008	2007	2006
Book/market value of net debt	€ 31.4m	€ 61.9m	€ 60.0m
× (1 − Tax rate)	69.2%	67.0%	65.4%
After-tax value of net debt	€ 21.7m	€ 41.5m	€ 39.3m

	2008	**2007**	**2006**
Market value of equity	€112.0m	€203.6m	€162.6m
Leverage ratio	19.4%	20.4%	24.1%

Given Loewe's low leverage and high creditworthiness, it is safe to assume that the market value of the company's debt is close to its book value. Footnote disclosures in the company's financial statements, made in accordance with international accounting standard IFRS 7, also confirm this. Using the average after-tax leverage ratio of 0.21 and our previous equity beta estimate of 1.6, Loewe's asset beta can be easily derived:

$$\beta_{ASSET} = \frac{1}{[1 + 0.21]} \times \beta_{EQUITY} = \frac{1}{1.21} \times 1.6 = 1.32$$

To illustrate the importance of knowing a company's asset beta, consider what would happen if Loewe decides to double its leverage (ratio). This decision would increase the company's equity beta from 1.6 to close to 1.9 ($[1 + 2 \times 0.21] \times 1.32 = 1.87$) and, in turn, increase its cost of equity from 12 percent to close to 13.5 percent ($4 + 1.87 \times 5 = 13.35$).

In our forecasts we assume that Loewe's leverage ratio will increase by approximately 46 percent ($0.379/0.259 - 1$). Consequently, we assume that Loewe's beta will increase to $1.7([1 + 1.46 \times 0.21] \times 1.32)$, thereby raising its cost of equity capital to 12.5 percent ($4.0 + 1.7 \times 5.0$).

Estimating the weighted average cost of capital

To value a company's assets, the analyst discounts abnormal NOPAT (growth), abnormal operating ROA, or cash flows available to both debt and equity holders. The proper discount rate to use is therefore the **weighted average cost of capital (WACC)**. The WACC is calculated by weighting the costs of debt and equity capital according to their respective market values:

$$WACC = \frac{Net\,debt}{Net\,debt + Equity}\,(1 - Tax\,rate) \times Cost\,of\,debt + \frac{Equity}{Net\,debt + Equity}\,Cost\,of\,equity$$

Estimating the cost of debt

The cost of debt is the interest rate on the debt. If the assumed capital structure in future periods is the same as the historical structure, then the current interest rate on debt will be a good proxy for this. However, if the analyst assumes a change in capital structure, then it is important to estimate the expected interest rate given the new level of debt ratio. One approach to this would be to estimate the expected credit rating of the company at the new level of debt and use the appropriate interest rates for that credit category. We discuss the estimation of credit ratings in further detail in Chapter 10.

It is also worth noting that the cost of debt will change over time if market interest rates are expected to change. This can arise if investors expect inflation to increase or decrease over the forecast horizon. Since we typically discount nominal earnings or cash flows, the cost of debt is a nominal rate, and will change over time to reflect changes in inflation. This can be handled by scaling the cost of debt up or down over time to reflect expected changes in interest rates each year. If interest rates are projected to rise by 3 percent as a result of expected inflation, the cost of debt for the firm we are analyzing should also increase by 3 percent. The yield curve, which shows how investors expect interest rates to change over time can be used to assess whether time-varying interest rates are likely to be important in the analysis.

Finally, the cost of debt should be expressed on a net-of-tax basis because it is after-tax cash flows that are being discounted. In most settings the market rate of interest can be converted to a net-of-tax basis by multiplying it by one minus the marginal corporate tax rate.

Weighting the costs of debt and equity

The weights assigned to debt and equity represent their respective fractions of total capital provided, measured in terms of economic values. Computing an economic value for debt should not be difficult. International accounting standards (IFRS 7) require that firms disclose the economic value of their liabilities in the notes to the financial statements. Further, if interest rates have not changed significantly since the time the debt was issued, it is reasonable to use book values rather than economic values in the WACC calculation. If interest rates have changed and economic value information is not available from the financial statements, the value of the debt can be estimated by discounting the future payouts at current market rates of interest applicable to the firm.

What is included in debt? Should short-term as well as long-term debt be included? Should payables and accruals be included? The answer is revealed by recalling that abnormal NOPAT and free cash flows to debt and equity are the earnings and cash flows *before* servicing short-term and long-term debt – indicating that both short-term and long-term debt should be considered a part of capital when computing the WACC. Servicing of other liabilities, such as trade payables or accruals, should already have been considered as we computed abnormal NOPAT or free cash flows. Thus internal consistency requires that operating liabilities not be considered a part of capital when computing the WACC.

The tricky problem we face is assigning an economic value to equity. That is the very amount we are trying to estimate in the first place! How can the analyst possibly assign a market value to equity at this intermediate stage, given that the estimate will not be known until all steps in the valuation analysis are completed? One common approach to the problem is to insert at this point "target" ratios of debt to capital and equity to capital. For example, one might expect that a firm will, over the long run, maintain a capital structure that is 40 percent debt and 60 percent equity. The long-run focus is reasonable because we are discounting cash flows over the long horizon.

Another way around the problem is to start with book value of equity as a weight for purposes of calculating an initial estimate of the WACC, which in turn can be used in the discounting process to generate an initial estimate of the value of equity. That initial estimate can then be used in place of the guess to arrive at a new WACC, and a second estimate of the value of equity can be produced. This process can be repeated until the value used to calculate the WACC and the final estimated value converge.

WACC and changes in leverage

At first sight, the weighted average cost of capital estimate seems highly sensitive to expected changes in leverage. In reality, it might be less so than the cost of equity capital. An increase in leverage results in two partly offsetting effects. On the one hand, it increases the weight on the cost of debt. On the other hand, it increases the levered equity beta, thereby increasing the cost of equity capital, as illustrated above.

Because future interest payments on debt create a valuable tax shield, increases in leverage do have a (moderately) reducing effect on the WACC. Just like using a constant cost of equity, using a constant WACC if the firm's economic leverage is expected to change over time thus introduces noise into the value estimate. As a consequence, if the forecasts imply that economic leverage changes over time but the cost of equity and WACC estimates are based on beginning economic leverage, the indirect estimate of equity value, being the estimated value of the company's assets minus the value of debt, will not be equal to the direct estimate of equity value.

Comparing the direct and indirect estimate of equity value can help to detect future changes in economic leverage. In particular, if the direct equity value estimate exceeds the indirect estimate, this suggests that the predicted change in economic leverage exceeds the change that is implicit in the cost of equity and WACC estimates. We therefore recommend comparing the two estimates to check whether the economic leverage assumptions that are implicit in the cost of equity and WACC calculations are consistent with the performance and balance sheet forecasts.

LOEWE'S WEIGHTED AVERAGE COST OF CAPITAL

To estimate the weighted average cost of capital for Loewe, we start with the assumption that its after-tax cost of debt is 2.6 percent, based on the ratio of the net interest expense after tax to beginning net debt in fiscal 2008. The company's cost of equity was calculated to be 12.5 percent. Clearly this estimate is only a starting point, and the analyst can change the estimate by changing the assumed market risk premium or by adjusting for the size effect.

Loewe's equity market values at the end of 2006, 2007, and 2008 were €162.6, €203.6, and €112.0 million, respectively; at the end of these years, the book (market) value of its net debt was €60.0, €61.9, and €31.4 million, respectively. Using these numbers we can calculate the (historical) average "market value" weights of debt and equity in the company's capital structure as 24 percent and 76 percent respectively. As indicated, our forecasts imply that the net debt to capital ratio increase by 46 percent, changing the weights of debt and equity to 32 and 68 percent, respectively. Based on these weights and the above estimates of costs of equity and debt, our estimate of Loewe's weighted average cost of capital (WACC) in August 2006 is 9.3 percent.

DETAILED FORECASTS OF PERFORMANCE

The horizon over which detailed forecasts are to be made is itself a choice variable. We will discuss later in this chapter how the analyst might make this choice. Once it is made, the next step is to consider the set of assumptions regarding a firm's performance that are needed to arrive at the forecasts. We described in Chapter 6 the general framework of financial forecasting and illustrated the approach using Loewe.

The key to sound forecasts is that the underlying assumptions are grounded in a company's business reality. Strategy analysis provides a critical understanding of a company's value proposition, and whether current performance is likely to be sustainable in future. Accounting analysis and ratio analysis provide a deep understanding of a company's current performance, and whether the ratios themselves are reliable indicators of performance. It is, therefore, important to see the valuation forecasts as a continuation of the earlier steps in business analysis rather than as a discreet exercise not connected from the rest of the analysis.

Since valuation involves forecasting over a long time horizon, it is not practical to forecast all the line items in a company's financial statements. Instead, the analyst has to focus on the key elements of a firm's performance. Specifically, we forecasted Loewe's condensed income statement, beginning balance sheet, and free cash flows for a period of ten years starting in fiscal year 2009 (year beginning in January 2009). We will use these same forecasting assumptions and financial forecasts, which are repeated here in Tables 8.2 and 8.3, as a starting point to value Loewe as of January 1, 2009. A spreadsheet containing Loewe's actual and forecasted financial statements as well as the valuation described in this chapter is available on the companion website of this book.

Making performance forecasts for valuing loewe

As discussed in Chapter 7, the forecasts required to convert the financial forecasts shown above into estimates of value differ depending on whether we wish to value a firm's equity or its assets. To value equity, the essential inputs are:

- **Abnormal earnings:** net profit less shareholders' equity at the beginning of the year times cost of equity.
- **Abnormal ROE:** the difference between ROE and the cost of equity.
- **Abnormal earnings growth:** the change in net profit less the cost of equity times prior period's change in equity (or the change in abnormal earnings).
- **Free cash flow to equity:** net income less the increase in operating working capital less the increase in net non-current assets plus the increase in net debt.

Alternatively, to value a company's assets, the significant performance forecasts would be:

- **Abnormal NOPAT:** NOPAT less total net capital at the beginning of the year times the weighted average cost of capital.
- **Abnormal operating ROA:** the difference between operating ROA and the weighted average cost of capital.
- **Abnormal NOPAT growth:** the change in NOPAT less the weighted average cost of capital times prior period's change in net operating assets (or the change in abnormal NOPAT).
- **Free cash flow to capital:** NOPAT less the increase in operating working capital less the increase in net non-current assets.

TABLE 8.2 Forecasting assumptions for Loewe

Forecast year	2009	2010	2011	2012	2013	2014	2015	2016	2017	2018
Sales growth rate	−0.1%	4.5%	9.1%	11.0%	9.8%	8.5%	7.1%	5.8%	4.5%	4.0%
NOPAT margin	5.2%	5.3%	5.4%	5.6%	5.7%	5.9%	5.3%	4.9%	4.6%	4.2%
Beginning net working capital/sales	14.0%	14.0%	14.0%	14.0%	14.0%	14.0%	14.0%	14.0%	14.0%	14.0%
Beginning net non-current assets/sales	18.5%	19.5%	20.5%	22.0%	22.5%	23.0%	23.5%	24.0%	24.5%	25.0%
Beginning net debt to net capital	25.9%	37.9%	37.9%	37.9%	37.9%	37.9%	37.9%	37.9%	37.9%	37.9%
After tax cost of net debt	2.6%	2.6%	2.6%	2.6%	2.6%	2.6%	2.6%	2.6%	2.6%	2.6%

TABLE 8.3 Forecasted financial statements for Loewe

Fiscal year	2009	2010	2011	2012	2013	2014	2015	2016	2017	2018
Beginning balance sheet (€ millions)										
Beginning net working capital	52.1	54.5	59.4	66.0	72.4	78.5	84.1	89.0	93.0	96.7
+ Beginning net non-current assets	69.3	76.3	87.5	104.2	117.0	129.7	141.9	153.3	163.5	173.5
= Net operating assets	**121.4**	**130.7**	**146.9**	**170.2**	**189.4**	**208.2**	**226.1**	**242.4**	**256.5**	**270.2**
Net debt	31.4	49.5	55.6	64.4	71.7	78.8	85.6	91.7	97.1	102.3
+ Shareholders' equity	90.0	81.2	91.3	105.8	117.7	129.4	140.5	150.6	159.4	167.9
= Net capital	**121.4**	**130.7**	**146.9**	**170.2**	**189.4**	**208.2**	**226.1**	**242.4**	**256.5**	**270.2**
Income statement (€ millions)										
Sales	373.5	390.1	425.6	472.6	518.7	562.5	602.7	637.6	666.0	692.7
Net operating profits after tax	19.3	20.7	23.2	26.4	29.7	33.1	32.0	31.6	30.6	29.3
- Net interest expense after tax	0.8	1.3	1.4	1.7	1.9	2.0	2.2	2.4	2.5	2.7
= Net profit	**18.5**	**19.4**	**21.7**	**24.7**	**27.9**	**31.0**	**29.8**	**29.2**	**28.0**	**26.7**
Operating ROA	15.9%	15.8%	15.8%	15.5%	15.7%	15.9%	14.1%	13.0%	11.9%	10.9%
ROE	20.5%	23.9%	23.8%	23.4%	23.7%	24.0%	21.2%	19.4%	17.6%	15.9%
BV of assets growth rate	−9.8%	7.7%	12.4%	15.9%	11.3%	9.9%	8.6%	7.2%	5.8%	5.4%
BV of equity growth rate	23.9%	−9.8%	12.4%	15.9%	11.3%	9.9%	8.6%	7.2%	5.8%	5.4%
Net operating asset turnover	3.1	3.0	2.9	2.8	2.7	2.7	2.7	2.6	2.6	2.6
Net profit	18.5	19.4	21.7	24.7	27.9	31.0	29.8	29.2	28.0	26.7
- Change in net working capital	−2.3	−5.0	−6.6	−6.4	−6.1	−5.6	−4.9	−4.0	−3.7	−3.9
- Change in net non-current assets	−7.0	−11.2	−16.7	−12.8	−12.7	−12.3	−11.4	−10.2	−10.0	−6.9
+ Change in net debt	18.1	6.1	8.8	7.3	7.1	6.8	6.2	5.3	5.2	4.1
= Free cash flow to equity	**27.3**	**9.4**	**7.3**	**12.8**	**16.2**	**19.9**	**19.6**	**20.4**	**19.5**	**19.9**
Net operating profit after tax	19.3	20.7	23.2	26.4	29.7	33.1	32.0	31.6	30.6	29.3
- Change in net working capital	−2.3	−5.0	−6.6	−6.4	−6.1	−5.6	−4.9	−4.0	−3.7	−3.9
- Change in net non-current assets	−7.0	−11.2	−16.7	−12.8	−12.7	−12.3	−11.4	−10.2	−10.0	−6.9
= Free cash flow to capital	**10.0**	**4.6**	**−0.1**	**7.2**	**10.9**	**15.2**	**15.7**	**17.4**	**16.9**	**18.5**

Table 8.4 shows Loewe's performance forecasts for all eight of these financial statement variables for the ten-year period 2009–2018.

As discussed earlier, to derive cash flows in 2018, we need to make assumptions about the sales growth rate and balance sheet ratios in 2019. The cash flow forecasts shown in Table 8.4 are based on the simple assumption that the sales growth and beginning balance sheet ratios in 2019 remain the same as in 2018. We discuss the sensitivity of this assumption and the terminal value assumption later in the chapter.

Loewe's projected abnormal ROE increases from 8.0 percent in 2008 to 11.5 percent in 2014 and then declines again due to the forces of competition. Abnormal operating ROA, abnormal NOPAT, and abnormal earnings show a similar trend. A slightly different pattern is shown for cash flow to equity and cash flow to debt. First, projected cash flow to equity for 2009 is high because we expect to bring leverage back to its pre-2008 level and hence increase net debt. Second, the decline in cash flows to debt and equity is moderate relative to the decline in, for example, abnormal ROE. This pattern arises because Loewe is expected to gradually reduce its investments in working capital and net non-current assets after 2012, when sales growth starts to slow.

TABLE 8.4 Performance forecasts for Loewe

Fiscal year	2009	2010	2011	2012	2013	2014	2015	2016	2017	2018
Equity valuation (€ millions)										
Abnormal earnings	7.2	9.3	10.3	11.5	13.2	14.8	12.2	10.3	8.1	5.7
Abnormal ROE	8.0%	11.4%	11.3%	10.9%	11.2%	11.5%	8.7%	6.9%	5.1%	3.4%
Free cash flow to equity	27.3	9.4	7.3	12.8	16.2	19.9	19.6	20.4	19.5	19.9
Abnormal earnings growth		2.0	1.1	1.2	1.6	1.7	−2.7	−1.9	−2.2	−2.5
Asset valuation (€ millions)										
Abnormal NOPAT	8.0	8.5	9.5	10.6	12.1	13.7	11.0	9.0	6.7	4.2
Abnormal ROA	6.6%	6.5%	6.5%	6.2%	6.4%	6.6%	4.8%	3.7%	2.6%	1.6%
Free cash flow to capital	10.0	4.6	−0.1	7.2	10.9	15.2	15.7	17.4	16.9	18.5
Abnormal NOPAT growth		0.6	1.0	1.1	1.5	1.6	−2.7	−1.9	−2.3	−2.5
Discount rates:										
Equity	0.889	0.790	0.702	0.624	0.555	0.493	0.438	0.390	0.346	0.308
Assets	0.915	0.837	0.766	0.701	0.641	0.587	0.537	0.491	0.449	0.411
Growth factors:[a]										
Equity	1.00	0.90	1.01	1.17	1.31	1.44	1.56	1.67	1.77	1.87
Assets	1.00	1.08	1.21	1.40	1.56	1.71	1.86	2.00	2.11	2.23

a. The growth factor is relevant only for calculating the present value for abnormal ROA and ROE.

TERMINAL VALUES

Explicit forecasts of the various elements of a firm's performance generally extend for a period of five to ten years. The final year of this forecast period is labeled the *terminal year* (selection of an appropriate terminal year is discussed later in this section). **Terminal value** is then the present value of either abnormal earnings or free cash flows occurring beyond the terminal year. Since this involves forecasting performance over the remainder of the firm's life, the analyst must adopt some assumption that simplifies the process of forecasting. A key question is whether it is reasonable to assume a continuation of the terminal year performance or whether some other pattern is expected.

Clearly, the continuation of a sales growth that is significantly greater than the average growth rate of the economy is unrealistic over a very long horizon. That rate would likely outstrip inflation in the euro and the real growth rate of the world economy. Over many years, it would imply that the firm would grow to a size greater than that of all the other firms in the world combined. But what would be a suitable alternative assumption? Should we expect the firm's sales growth rate to ultimately settle down to the rate of inflation? Or to a higher rate, such as the nominal GDP growth rate? And perhaps equally important, will a firm that earns abnormal profits continue to do so by maintaining its profit margins on a growing, or even existing, base of sales?

To answer these questions, we must consider how much longer the rate of growth in industry sales can outstrip overall economic growth, and how long a firm's competitive advantages can be sustained. Clearly, looking 11 or more years into the future, any forecast is likely to be subject to considerable error. Below we discuss a variety of alternative approaches to the task of calculating a terminal value.

Terminal values with the competitive equilibrium assumption

Fortunately, in many if not most situations, how we deal with the seemingly imponderable questions about long-range growth in sales simply *does not matter very much!* In fact, under plausible economic assumptions, there is no practical need to consider sales growth beyond the terminal year. Such growth may be *irrelevant*, so far as the firm's current value is concerned!

How can long-range growth in sales *not* matter? The reasoning revolves around the forces of competition. One impact of competition is that it tends to constrain a firm's ability to identify, on a consistent basis, growth opportunities that generate supernormal profits. The other dimension that competition tends to impact is a firm's margins. Ultimately, we would expect high profits to attract enough competition to drive down a firm's margins, and therefore its returns, to a normal level. At this point, the firm will earn its cost of capital, with no abnormal returns or terminal value. (Recall the evidence in Chapter 6 concerning the reversion of ROEs to normal levels over horizons of five to ten years.)

Certainly a firm may at a point in time maintain a competitive advantage that permits it to achieve returns in excess of the cost of capital. When that advantage is protected with patents or a strong brand name, the firm may even be able to maintain it for many years, perhaps indefinitely. With hindsight, we know that some such firms – like Coca-Cola – were able not only to maintain their competitive edge but to expand it across dramatically increasing investment bases. However, with a few exceptions, it is reasonable to assume that the terminal value of the firm will be zero under the **competitive equilibrium assumption**, obviating the need to make assumptions about long-term growth rates.

Competitive equilibrium assumption only on incremental sales

An alternative version of the competitive equilibrium assumption is to assume that a firm will continue to earn abnormal earnings forever on the sales it had in the terminal year, but there will be no abnormal earnings on any incremental sales beyond that level. If we invoke the competitive equilibrium assumption on incremental sales for years beyond the terminal year, then it does not matter what sales growth rate we use beyond that year, and we may as well simplify our arithmetic by treating sales *as if* they will be constant at the terminal year level. Then operating ROA, ROE, NOPAT, net profit, free cash flow to debt and equity, and free cash flow to equity will all remain constant at the terminal year level.

For example, by treating Loewe as if its competitive advantage can be maintained only on the nominal sales level achieved in the year 2018, we will be assuming that in *real* terms its competitive advantage will shrink. Under this scenario, it is simple to estimate the terminal value by dividing the 2018 level of each of the variables by the appropriate discount rate. Under the abnormal earnings (NOPAT) growth valuation method, Loewe's abnormal earnings (NOPAT) growth beyond 2018 and its terminal value will be zero. As one would expect, terminal values in this scenario will be higher than those with no abnormal returns on all sales in years 2019 and beyond. This is entirely due to the fact that we are now assuming that Loewe can retain indefinitely its superior performance on its existing base of sales.

Terminal value with persistent abnormal performance and growth

Each of the approaches described above appeals in some way to the "competitive equilibrium assumption." However, there are circumstances where the analyst is willing to assume that the firm may defy competitive forces and earn abnormal rates of return on new projects for many years. If the analyst believes supernormal profitability can be extended to larger markets for many years, it can be accommodated within the context of valuation analysis.

One possibility is to project earnings and cash flows over a longer horizon, i.e., until the competitive equilibrium assumption can reasonably be invoked. In the case of Loewe, for example, we could assume that the supernormal profitability will continue for five years beyond 2018 (for a total forecasting horizon of 15 years from the beginning of the forecasting period), but after that period, the firm's ROE and operating ROA will be equal to its cost of equity and its weighted average cost of capital.

Another possibility is to project growth in abnormal earnings or cash flows at some constant rate. For instance, one could expect Loewe to maintain its advantage on a sales base that remains constant in *real* terms, implying that sales grow beyond terminal year 2018 at the expected long-run European inflation rate of between 2 and 4 percent. Beyond our terminal year, 2018, as the sales growth rate remains constant at the inflation rate, abnormal earnings (growth), free cash flows, and book values of assets and equity also grow at the constant inflation rate. This is simply because we held all other performance ratios constant in this period. As a result, abnormal operating ROA and abnormal ROE remain constant at the same level as in the terminal year.

This approach is more aggressive than the preceding assumptions about terminal value, but it may be more realistic. After all, there is no obvious reason why the *real* size of the investment base on which Loewe earns abnormal returns should depend on inflation rates. The approach, however, still relies to some extent on the competitive equilibrium assumption. The assumption is now invoked to suggest that supernormal profitability can be extended only to an investment base that remains constant in real terms. In rare situations, if the company has established a market dominance that the analyst believes is immune to the threat of competition, the terminal value can be based on both positive real sales growth and abnormal profits.

When we assume that the abnormal performance persists at the same level as in the terminal year, projecting abnormal earnings (growth) and free cash flows is a simple matter of growing them at the assumed sales growth rate. Since the rate of abnormal earnings and cash flows growth is constant starting in the year after the terminal year, it is also straightforward to discount those flows. The present value of the flow stream is the flow at the end of the first year (after the terminal year) divided by the difference between the discount rate and steady-state growth rate, provided that the discount rate exceeds the growth rate. There is nothing about this valuation method that requires reliance on the competitive equilibrium assumption, so it could be used with *any* rate of growth in sales. The question is not whether the arithmetic is available to handle such an approach but rather how realistic it is.

Terminal value based on a price multiple

A popular approach to terminal value calculation is to apply a multiple to abnormal earnings, cash flows, or book values of the terminal period. The approach is not as ad hoc as it might at first appear. Note that under the assumption of no sales growth, abnormal earnings or cash flows beyond the terminal year remain constant. Capitalizing these flows in perpetuity by dividing by the cost of capital is equivalent to multiplying them by the inverse of the cost of capital. For example, in the case of Loewe, capitalizing free cash flows to equity at its cost of equity of 12.5 percent is equivalent to assuming a terminal cash flow multiple of 8. Thus applying a multiple in this range to Loewe is similar to discounting all free cash flows beyond 2018 while invoking the competitive equilibrium assumption on incremental sales.

The mistake to avoid here is to capitalize the future abnormal earnings or cash flows using a multiple that is too high. The earnings or cash flow multiples might be high currently because the market anticipates abnormally profitable growth. However, once that growth is realized, the price-earnings multiple should fall to a normal level. It is that normal price-earnings ratio, applicable to a stable firm or one that can grow only through zero net present value projects, that should be used in the terminal value calculation. Thus multiples in the range of 7 to 12 – close to the reciprocal of cost of equity and WACC – should be used here. Higher multiples are justifiable only when the terminal year is closer and there are still abnormally profitable growth opportunities beyond that point. A similar logic applies to the estimation of terminal values using book value multiples.

Selecting the terminal year

A critical question posed by the above discussion is how long to make the detailed forecast horizon. When the competitive equilibrium assumption is used, the answer is whatever time is required for the firm's returns on incremental investment projects to reach that equilibrium – an issue that turns on the sustainability of the firm's competitive advantage. As indicated in Chapter 6, historical evidence indicates that most firms in Europe should expect ROEs to revert to normal levels within five to ten years. But for the typical firm, we can justify ending the forecast horizon even earlier – note that the return on *incremental* investment can be normal even while the return on *total* investment (and therefore ROE) remains abnormal. Thus a five- to ten-year forecast horizon should be more than sufficient for most firms. Exceptions would include firms so well insulated from competition (perhaps due to the power of a brand name) that they can extend their investment base to new markets for many years and still expect to generate supernormal returns.

Estimates of loewe's terminal value

Choosing terminal year

In the case of Loewe, the terminal year used is ten years beyond the current one. Table 8.3 shows that the ROE (and operating ROA) is forecasted to decline at the end of these ten years, from the unusually high 24.0 percent in 2014 to 15.9 percent by 2018. At this level the company will earn an abnormal return on equity of 3.4 percent, since its cost of equity is estimated to be 12.5 percent.

Based on the foregoing strategic assessment of Loewe, we believe that the firm has created a competitive advantage that should be sustainable in the long term. Consequently, we assume that the firm will have reached a steady state of performance in 2018 and extending the forecast horizon will not lead to further insights into how market dynamics will impact Loewe's performance. The overall projection, therefore, expects that while Loewe's current level of abnormal performance is not sustainable and that growth will slow and margins will get squeezed, the firm has created a market position that will allow it to make some level of abnormal earnings in the long-term. Based on this logic, we will fix 2018 as the terminal year for Loewe and attempt to estimate its terminal value at that time.

Terminal value under varying assumptions

Table 8.5 shows Loewe's terminal value under the various theoretical approaches we discussed above. Scenario 1 of this table shows the terminal value if we assume that Loewe will continue to grow its sales at 4.0 percent beyond fiscal year 2018, and that it will continue to earn the same level of abnormal returns as in 2018 (that is, we assume that all the other forecasting assumptions will be the same as in 2018). Under this scenario, terminal values in the abnormal earnings model (TV_{AE}), the abnormal earnings growth model (TV_{AEG}), and the free cash flow model (TV_{FCF}) are as follows:

TABLE 8.5 Terminal values for Loewe under various assumptions (using abnormal earnings methodology)

Scenario number	Approach	Scenario	Terminal sales growth	Terminal NOPAT margin	Value beyond the forecast horizon (AE terminal value)
1	Persistent abnormal performance	Sales growth and margins based on detailed analysis and forecast	4.0%	4.2%	€21.37
2	Abnormal returns on constant sales (real terms)	Sales grow at the rate of inflation, margins maintained	2.0%	4.2%	€16.96
3	Abnormal returns on constant sales (nominal terms)	Essentially zero sales growth, margins maintained	0.0%	4.2%	€13.97
4	Competitive equilibrium	Margins reduced so no abnormal earnings	4.0%	3.4%	€ 0.0

$$TV_{AE} = \frac{1.04 \times AE_{2018}}{(0.125 - 0.04) \times (1.125)^{10}}$$

$$TV_{AEG} = \frac{1}{0.125} \times \frac{0.04 \times AE_{2018}}{(0.125 - 0.04) \times (1.125)^9}$$

$$TV_{FCF} = \frac{1.04 \times FCFE_{2018}}{(0.125 - 0.04) \times (1.125)^{10}}$$

where AE_{2018} and $FCFE_{2018}$ are expected abnormal earnings and free cash flow to equity for fiscal 2018, respectively. Using the abnormal earnings methodology this scenario leads to a terminal value of €21.37 million.

Scenario 2 calculates the terminal value assuming that Loewe will maintain its margins only on sales that grow at the long-run expected rate of inflation, assumed to be 2 percent, dropping the terminal value in the abnormal earnings model to €16.96 million. Scenario 3 shows the terminal value if we assume that the company's competitive advantage can be maintained only on the nominal sales level achieved in 2018. As a result, sales growth beyond the terminal year is assumed to be zero, which is equivalent to assuming that incremental sales do not produce any abnormal returns. The terminal value under this scenario drops to €13.97 million.

The final scenario invokes the competitive equilibrium assumption, i.e., margins will be eroded such that the firm will have no abnormal returns irrespective of the rate of sales growth, leading to no terminal value in the abnormal earnings model. For the sake of illustration, the expected sales growth of 4.0 percent is maintained. To portray the competitive equilibrium, margins are lowered to eliminate any competitive advantage that Loewe will have. In this final scenario, the terminal values are as follows:

$$TV_{AE} = 0$$

$$TV_{AEG} = \frac{1}{0.125} \times \frac{-1 \times AE_{2018}}{(1.125)^{10}}$$

$$TV_{FCF} = \frac{BVE_{2018}}{(1.125)^{10}}$$

where BVE_{2018} is Loewe's end-of-year book value of equity in fiscal 2018.

COMPUTING ESTIMATED VALUES

Table 8.6 shows the estimated value of Loewe's assets and equity, each using four different methods discussed in Chapter 7. The value of assets is estimated using abnormal operating ROA, abnormal NOPAT, abnormal NOPAT growth, and free cash flows to debt and equity. The value of equity is estimated using operating ROE, abnormal earnings, abnormal earnings growth, and free cash flow to equity. These values are computed using the financial forecasts in Table 8.4 and the terminal value forecast using the persistent abnormal performance scenario.

In Table 8.6, present values of abnormal NOPAT (growth) and free cash flow to capital are computed using a WACC of 9.3 percent; present values of abnormal earnings (growth) and free cash flow to equity are computed using a cost of equity of 12.5 percent. Note that under the abnormal earnings (NOPAT) growth valuation approach, abnormal earnings

TABLE 8.6 Valuation summary for Loewe using various methodologies

	Beginning book value	Value from forecast period 2009–2018	Value beyond forecast horizon (terminal value)	Total value	Value per share (€)
Equity value (€ millions)					
Abnormal earnings	90.03	56.74	21.37	168.14	12.92
Abnormal ROE	90.03	56.74	21.37	168.14	12.92
Abnormal earnings growth	N.A.	160.75	7.40	168.14	12.92
Free cash flows to equity	N.A.	93.00	75.14	168.14	12.92
Asset value (€ millions)					
Abnormal NOPAT	121.42	60.04	33.80	215.26	N.A.
Abnormal ROA	121.42	60.04	33.80	215.26	N.A.
Abnormal NOPAT growth	N.A.	199.98	15.28	215.26	N.A.
Free cash flows to capital	N.A.	65.98	149.28	215.26	N.A.

(NOPAT) growth values in year t are multiplied by the corresponding discount factors in year t − 1. To calculate the present values of abnormal operating ROA and abnormal ROE, the values for each year are first multiplied by the corresponding growth factor, as shown in the formulae in Chapter 7, and then they are discounted using the WACC and cost of equity, respectively. Under the assumptions and forecasts we have made, Loewe's estimated value per share is €12.92 and the total firm value is €215.26 million.

Value estimates presented in each scenario show that the abnormal returns method, abnormal earnings method, abnormal earnings growth method, and the free cash flow method result in the same value, as claimed in Chapter 7. Note also that Loewe's terminal value represents a significantly larger fraction of the total value of assets and equity under the free cash flow method relative to the other methods. As discussed in Chapter 7, this is due to the fact that the abnormal returns and earnings methods rely on a company's book value of assets and equity, so the terminal value estimates are estimates of incremental values over book values. Similarly, under the abnormal earnings growth method, the terminal value estimates reflect only the changes in abnormal earnings that are expected to occur beyond the terminal year. In contrast, the free cash flow approach ignores the book values, so the terminal value forecasts are estimates of total value during this period.

The primary calculations in the above estimates treat all flows as if they arrive at the end of the year. Of course, they are likely to arrive throughout the year. If we assume for the sake of simplicity that cash flows will arrive mid-year, then we should adjust our value estimates upward by the amount $[1 + (r/2)]$, where r is the discount rate.

Finally, it is worth noting that the asset valuation (€215.26) and the equity valuation (€168.14) imply that the value of debt should be €47.12, which is close to the economic value of €49.50 (at the end of 2009) that we used in the cost of capital calculations. Under the competitive equilibrium scenario, the implied value of debt decreases to €34.69. This arises because although Loewe's book leverage remains constant, under this scenario its economic leverage increases over the forecast horizon. The estimated cost of equity and WACC used to compute equity and asset valuations do not correctly capture these changes.

Value estimates versus market values

As the discussion above shows, valuation involves a substantial number of assumptions by analysts. Therefore the estimates of value will vary from one analyst to another. The only way to ensure that one's estimates are reliable is to make sure that the assumptions are grounded in the economics of the business being valued. It is also useful to check the assumptions against the time-series trends for performance ratios discussed in Chapter 6. While it is quite legitimate to make assumptions that differ markedly from these trends in any given case, it is important for the analyst to be able to articulate the business and strategy reasons for making such assumptions.

When a company being valued is publicly traded, it is possible to compare one's own estimated value with the market value of a company. When an estimated value differs substantially from a company's market value, it is useful for the analyst to understand why such differences arise. A way to do this is to redo the valuation exercise and figure out what valuation assumptions are needed to arrive at the observed stock price. One can then examine whether the market's assumptions are more or less valid relative to one's own assumptions. As we discuss in the next chapter, such an analysis can be invaluable in using valuation to make buy or sell decisions in the security analysis context.

In the case of Loewe, our estimated value of the firm's equity per share (€12.92) is above the observed value, of €7.04, at the end of January 2009, when the market had assimilated the announced results for the quarter and fiscal year ended December 31, 2008. In the months following the announcement, Loewe's share price fluctuated between €6.95 and €9.70. Analysts' target prices ranged from €8 to €17. Clearly the market was making less optimistic assumptions than our own. Although part of the discrepancy can surely be attributed to the uncertainty in stock markets at the beginning of 2009, the differences in the two sets of assumptions might also be related to growth rates, NOPAT margins, or asset turns. One could run different scenarios regarding each of these variables and test the sensitivity of the estimated value to these assumptions.

Sensitivity analysis

Recall that in Chapter 6, we developed what we believed to be a reasonable assessment of Loewe's expected future performance. The resulting valuation seems to be more optimistic the market's expectations, as the imputed value per share exceeded the traded value per share at the time. However, we acknowledged that the company's future could play out in multiple ways and proposed two alternative scenarios. As shown in Table 8.7, if Loewe is able to capture a greater market share and grow in line with the market as a whole (7.5

TABLE 8.7 Equity valuation under various scenarios using abnormal earnings

Scenario	Beginning book value	Value from forecast period 2009–2018	Value beyond forecast horizon (terminal value)	Total value	Value per share (€)
Slower growth in LCD sales than the market, moderate increase in SG&A expense	90.03	56.76	21.37	168.14	12.92
LCD sales growth in 2009–2010 follows market growth, moderate increase in SG&A expense	90.03	71.26	30.32	191.62	14.73
Slower growth in LCD sales than the market, excessive increase in SG&A expense	90.03	42.34	−1.03	131.35	10.10

percent growth in LCD sales in 2009; 16.2 percent in 2010), its value per share would be €14.73. If, on the other hand, its differentiation strategy results in excessive selling expenditures, resulting in an increase of its SG&A expense to, say, 26 percent by 2015, its shares would be worth only €10.10 per share. The changes in equity value in these scenarios are driven primarily by changes in sales growth and margins, performance measures that are most strongly affected by the forces of competition.

SOME PRACTICAL ISSUES IN VALUATION

The above discussion provides a blueprint for doing valuation. In practice, the analyst has to deal with a number of other issues that have an important effect on the valuation task. We discuss below three frequently encountered complications – accounting distortions, negative book values, and excess cash.

Dealing with accounting distortions

We know from the discussion in Chapter 7 that accounting methods per se should have no influence on firm value (except as those choices influence the analyst's view of future real performance). Yet the abnormal returns and earnings valuation approaches used here are based on numbers that vary with accounting method choices.

Since accounting choices must affect both earnings *and* book value, and because of the self-correcting nature of double-entry bookkeeping (all "distortions" of accounting must ultimately reverse), estimated values will not be affected by accounting choices, *as long as the analyst recognizes the accounting distortions.*[6]

If accounting reliability is a concern, the analyst has to expend resources on accounting adjustments. When a company uses "biased" accounting – either conservative or aggressive – the analyst needs to recognize the bias to ensure that value estimates are not biased. If a thorough analysis is not performed, a firm's accounting choices can influence analysts' perceptions of the real performance of the firm and hence the forecasts of future performance. Accounting choice would affect expectations of future earnings and cash flows, and distort the valuation, regardless of whether the valuation is based on DCF or discounted abnormal earnings. For example, if a firm overstates current revenue growth through aggressive revenue recognition, failure to appreciate the effect is likely to lead the analyst to overstate future revenues, affecting both earnings and cash flow forecasts.

An analyst who encounters biased accounting has two choices – either to adjust current earnings and book values to eliminate managers' accounting biases, or to recognize these biases and adjust future forecasts accordingly. Whereas both approaches lead to the same estimated firm value, the choice will have an important impact on what fraction of the firm's value is captured within the forecast horizon, and what remains in the terminal value. Holding forecasting horizon and future growth opportunities constant, higher accounting quality allows a higher fraction of a firm's value to be captured by the current book value, earnings, and the abnormal earnings within the forecasting horizon.

Dealing with negative book values

A number of firms have negative earnings and book values of book equity. Firms in the start-up phase have negative equity, as do those in high technology industries. These firms incur large investments whose payoff is uncertain. Accountants write off these investments as a matter of conservatism, leading to negative book equity. Examples of firms in this situation include biotechnology firms, internet firms, telecommunication firms, and other high technology firms. A second category of firms with negative book equity are those that are performing poorly, resulting in cumulative losses exceeding the original investment by the shareholders.

Negative book equity and negative earnings make it difficult to use the accounting-based approach to value a firm's equity. There are several possible ways to get around this problem. The first approach is to value the firm's assets (using, for example, abnormal operating ROA or abnormal NOPAT) rather than equity. Then, based on an estimate of the value of the firm's debt, one can estimate the equity value. Another alternative is to "undo" accountants' conservatism by capitalizing the investment expenditures written off. This is possible if the analyst is able to establish that these expenditures are value creating. A third alternative, feasible for publicly traded firms, is to start from the observed share price and work backwards. Using reasonable estimates of cost of equity and steady-state growth rate, the analyst can calculate the average long-term level of abnormal earnings or abnormal earnings growth needed to justify the observed share price. Then the analytical task can be framed in terms of examining the feasibility of achieving this abnormal earnings (growth) "target."

It is important to note that the value of firms with negative book equity often consists of a significant option value. For example, the value of high tech firms is not only driven by the expected earnings from their current technologies but also the payoff from technology options embedded in their research and development efforts. Similarly, the value of troubled companies is driven to some extent by the "abandonment option" – shareholders with limited liability can put the firm to debt holders and creditors. One can use the options theory framework to estimate the value of these "real options."[7]

Dealing with excess cash and excess cash flow

Firms with excess cash balances, or large free cash flows, also pose a valuation challenge. In our projections in Table 8.3, we implicitly assumed that cash beyond the level required to finance a company's operations will be paid out to the firm's shareholders. Excess cash flows are assumed to be paid out to shareholders either in the form of dividends or share repurchases. Notice that these cash flows are already incorporated into the valuation process when they are earned, so there is no need to take them into account when they are paid out.

It is important to recognize that both the accounting-based valuations and the discounted cash flow valuation assume a dividend payout that can potentially vary from period to period. This dividend policy assumption is required as long as one wishes to assume a constant level of financial leverage, a constant cost of equity, and a constant level of weighted average cost of capital used in the valuation calculations. As discussed in a later chapter, firms rarely have such a variable dividend policy in practice. However, this in itself does not make the valuation approaches invalid, as long as a firm's dividend policy does not affect its value. That is, the valuation approaches assume that the well known Modigliani-Miller theorem regarding the irrelevance of dividends holds.

A firm's dividend policy can affect its value if managers do not invest free cash flows optimally. For example, if a firm's managers are likely to use excess cash to undertake value-destroying acquisitions, then our approach overestimates the firm's value. If the analyst has these types of concerns about a firm, one approach is to first estimate the firm according to the approach described earlier and then adjust the estimated value for whatever agency costs the firm's managers may impose on its investors. One approach to evaluating whether or not a firm suffers from severe agency costs is to examine how effective its corporate governance processes are.

SUMMARY

We illustrate in this chapter how to apply the valuation theory discussed in Chapter 7. The chapter explains the set of business and financial assumptions one needs to make to conduct the valuation exercise. It also illustrates the mechanics of making detailed valuation forecasts and terminal values of earnings, free cash flows, and accounting rates of return. We also discuss how to compute cost of equity and the weighted average cost of capital. Using a detailed example, we show how a firm's equity values and asset values can be computed using earnings, cash flows, and rates of return. The sensitivity of equity and firm value to the assumptions, both during the forecast horizon and for the terminal value, are highlighted. Finally, we offer ways to deal with some commonly encountered practical issues, including accounting distortions, negative book values, and excess cash balances.

CORE CONCEPTS

Asset beta Sensitivity of a firm's assets' performance to economy-wide movements. The asset beta can be derived from the firm's equity beta, its debt to equity ratio and its tax rate:

$$\beta_{ASSET} = \frac{(1 - \text{Tax rate}) \times \text{Net debt}}{(1 - \text{Tax rate}) \times \text{Net debt} + \text{Equity}} \beta_{DEBT}$$
$$+ \frac{\text{Equity}}{(1 - \text{tax rate}) \times \text{Net debt} + \text{Equity}} \beta_{EQUITY}$$

The asset beta remains constant if leverage changes and can be used to calculate the effect of a change in leverage on the equity beta.

Capital asset pricing model Model expressing the cost of equity as a function of (1) the risk-free rate (r_f) and (2) a risk premium for systematic risk ($[E(r_m) - r_f]$):

$$r_e = r_f + \beta[E(r_m) - r_f]$$

The risk-free rate is typically the rate of return on intermediate-term government bonds. Systematic or beta risk (β) is the risk from correlation of the firm's return and the market return.

Competitive equilibrium assumption Assumption that competitive forces will drive down a firm's abnormal earnings until it reaches an equilibrium stage in which the firm's return on equity equals it cost of equity. If it is assumed that the firm reaches this equilibrium stage in or before the terminal year, the terminal value is equal to zero in the abnormal earnings (growth) model and is equal to the discounted terminal-year book value of equity in the free cash flow model.

Cost of equity Rate of return that equity investors demand on their investment and discount rate in the equity valuation model. One way to estimate the cost of equity is to use the capital asset pricing model. Firm size may also affect the cost of equity: small firms tend to have higher (required) rates of return.

Terminal value Present value of abnormal earnings (growth) or free cash flows occurring beyond the last year of the forecasting period (labeled terminal year).

Weighted average cost of capital (WACC) Rate of return that equity and debt investors demand on their investment and discount rate in the asset valuation model. The WACC is the weighted average of the *after-tax* cost of debt and the cost of equity:

$$WACC = \frac{Net\ debt}{Net\ debt + Equity} r_{DEBT} + \frac{Equity}{Net\ debt + Equity} r_{EQUITY}$$

The weights must be calculated using the market values of debt and equity.

QUESTIONS, EXERCISES AND PROBLEMS

1 A spreadsheet containing Loewe's actual and forecasted financial statements as well as the valuation described in this chapter is available on the companion website of this book. How will the forecasts in Table 8.3 for Loewe change if the assumed growth rate in sales from 2009 to 2018 remains at 5 percent (and all the other assumptions are kept unchanged)?

2 Recalculate the forecasts in Table 8.3 assuming that the NOPAT profit margin declines by 0.1 percentage points per year between fiscal 2009 and 2018 (keeping all the other assumptions unchanged).

3 Recalculate the forecasts in Table 8.4 assuming that the ratio of net operating working capital to sales is 10 percent, and the ratio of net non-current assets to sales is 25 percent for all the years from fiscal 2009 to fiscal 2018. Keep all the other assumptions unchanged.

4 Calculate Loewe's cash payouts to its shareholders in the years 2009–2018 that are implicitly assumed in the projections in Table 8.3.

5 How will the abnormal earnings calculations in Table 8.4 change if the cost of equity assumption is changed to 10 percent?

6 How will the terminal values in Table 8.6 change if the sales growth in years 2019 and beyond is 5 percent, and the company keeps forever its abnormal returns at the same level as in fiscal 2018 (keeping all the other assumptions in the table unchanged)?

7 Calculate the proportion of terminal values to total estimated values of equity under the abnormal earnings method, the abnormal earnings growth method, and the discounted cash flow method. Why are these proportions different?

8 Under the competitive equilibrium assumption the terminal value in the discounted cash flow model is the present value of the end-of-year book value of equity in the terminal year. Explain.

Under the competitive equilibrium assumption the terminal value in the discounted abnormal earnings growth model is the present value of abnormal earnings in the terminal year times minus one, capitalized at the cost of equity. Explain.

What will be Loewe's cost of equity if the equity market risk premium is 6 percent?

11 Assume that Loewe changes its capital structure so that its market value weight of debt to capital increases to 45 percent, and its after-tax interest rate on debt at this new leverage level is 4 percent. Assume that the equity market risk premium is 7 percent. What will be the cost of equity at the new debt level? What will be the weighted average cost of capital?

12 Nancy Smith says she is uncomfortable making the assumption that Loewe's dividend payout will vary from year to year. If she makes a constant dividend payout assumption, what changes does she have to make in her other valuation assumptions to make them internally consistent with each other?

Problem 1 Hugo Boss's and Adidas's terminal values

Refer to Problem 1 in Chapter 7 (see p. 339).

1 The analyst following Hugo Boss estimates a target price of €20 per share. Under the assumption that the company's profit margins, asset turnover, and capital structure remain constant after 2011, what is the terminal growth rate that is implicit in the analysts' forecasts and target price?

2 Using the analyst's forecasts, estimate Hugo Boss's equity value under the following three scenarios:

   a Hugo Boss enters into a competitive equilibrium in 2012.

   b After 2011, Hugo Boss's competitive advantage can only be maintained on the nominal sales level achieved in 2011.

   c After 2011, Hugo Boss's competitive advantage can be maintained on a sales base that remains constant in real terms.

3 Using the analyst's forecasts, estimate Hugo Boss's equity value under the assumption that the company's profitability gradually reverts to its required level (i.e., $AE_t = 0.75 \times AE_{t-1}$) after the terminal year.

   Refer to Problem 2 in Chapter 7.

4 Using the analyst's forecasts, estimate Adidas's terminal values in the discounted cash flow and the abnormal earnings growth models under the assumption that the company enters into a competitive equilibrium in 2012.

Problem 2 Anheuser-Busch InBev S.A.

In November 2008, the Belgian InBev S.A. completed the acquisition of US-based Anheuser-Busch. The brewer acquired Anheuser-Busch for close to €40 billion, of which it classified approximately €25 billion as goodwill. At the end of the fiscal year ending on December 31, 2008, Anheuser-Busch InBev's (AB InBev) net assets amounted to €61,357 million, consisting of €64,183 million in non-current assets and –€2,826 million in working capital. The company's book value of equity amounted to €16,126 million.

Early May, 2009, when AB Inbev's 1,593 million common shares trade at about €24 per share, an analyst produces the following forecasts for the company and issues an "overweight" (buy) recommendation.

Forecasts (€ millions)	2009	2010	2011	2012	2013	2014	2015	2016	2017	2018
Sales	28,475	26,688	27,909	29,047	30,086	31,011	31,810	32,470	32,311	32,658
NOPAT	6,169	6,294	6,729	7,003	7,254	7,476	7,669	7,828	7,790	7,874
Depreciation and amortization	2,297	2,158	2,228	2,318	2,402	2,475	2,539	2,592	2,579	2,607
Investment in non-current assets	−1,526	−1,441	−1,549	−1,743	−1,805	−1,860	−1,909	−1,948	−1,939	−1,959
Investment in working capital	485	580	669	435	451	465	477	487	485	490
Free cash flow to debt and equity	**7,425**	**7,590**	**8,077**	**8,014**	**8,301**	**8,556**	**8,777**	**8,958**	**8,915**	**9,011**

1   The analyst estimates that AB InBev's weighted average cost of capital is 9 percent and assumes that the free cash flow to debt and equity grows indefinitely at a rate of 1 percent after 2018. Show that under these assumptions, the equity value per share estimate exceeds AB InBev's share price.

2   Calculate AB InBev's expected abnormal NOPATs between 2009 and 2018 based on the above information. How does the implied trend in abnormal NOPAT compare with the general trends in the economy?

3   Estimate AB InBev's equity value using the abnormal NOPAT model (under the assumption that the WACC is 9 percent and the terminal growth rate is 1 percent). Why do the discounted cash flow model and the abnormal NOPAT model yield different outcomes?

4   What adjustments to the forecasts are needed to make the two valuation models consistent?

NOTES

1. See T. Copeland, T. Koller, and J. Murrin, *Valuation: Measuring and Managing the Value of Companies*, 2nd edition (New York: John Wiley & Sons, 1994).
2. One way to estimate systematic risk is to regress the firm's stock returns over some recent time period against the returns on the market index. The slope coefficient represents an estimate of β. More fundamentally, systematic risk depends on how sensitive the firm's operating profits are to shifts in economy-wide activity, and the firm's degree of leverage. Financial analysis that assesses these operating and financial risks should be useful in arriving at reasonable estimates of β.
3. The average return reported here is the arithmetic mean as opposed to the geometric mean. Ibbotson and Associates explain why this estimate is appropriate in this context (see *Stocks, Bonds, Bills, and Inflation*, 2002 Yearbook, Chicago). This estimate of the worldwide equity risk premium comes from E. Dimson, P. Marsh, and M. Staunton, "Global Evidence on the Equity Risk Premium," *Journal of Applied Corporate Finance* 15, No. 4 (2003): 8–19.
4. E. Dimson, P. Marsh, and M. Staunton (2003), op. cit., argue that when estimating future equity risk premiums, it is preferred to take a global approach than a country-by-country approach. Reasons for taking a global approach are, for example, that many country-specific events that affected historical risk premiums are nonrecurring and that worldwide capital markets have integrated significantly. In their study "International Differences in the Cost of Equity Capital: Do Legal Institutions and Securities Matter," *Journal of Accounting Research* 44, No. 3 (2006): 485–531, L. Hail and C. Leuz provide evidence that international differences in the strictness of disclosure and securities regulation and enforcement also create international differences in firms' cost of equity. Harmonization of such regulations within, for example, the European Union may therefore also reduce the country variations in risk premiums.

5. See William R. Gebhardt, Charles M. C. Lee, and Bhaskaran Swaminathan, "Toward an Ex-Ante Cost of Capital," *Journal of Accounting Research* 39 (2001): 135–176; and James Claus and Jacob Thomas, "Equity Premia as Low as Three Percent? Evidence from Analysts' Earnings Forecasts for Domestic and International Stock Markets," *The Journal of Finance* 56 (October 2001): 1629–1666.

6. Valuation based on discounted abnormal earnings does require one property of the forecasts: that they be consistent with "clean surplus accounting." Such accounting requires the following relation:

$$\text{End-of-period book value} = \text{Beginning book value} + \text{earnings} - \text{dividends}$$
$$\pm \text{ capital contributions/withdrawals}$$

Clean surplus accounting rules out situations where some gain or loss is excluded from earnings but is still used to adjust the book value of equity. For example, under IFRS, gains and losses on foreign currency translations are handled this way. In applying the valuation technique described here, the analyst would need to deviate from IFRS in producing forecasts and treat such gains/losses as a part of earnings. However, the technique does *not* require that clean surplus accounting has been applied *in the past* – so the existing book value, based on IFRS or any other set of principles, can still serve as the starting point. All the analyst needs to do is apply clean surplus accounting in his/her forecasts. That much is not only easy but is usually the natural thing to do anyway.

7. If negative earnings are likely to be transitory, this may be a reason to extend the forecast horizon. P. Joos and G. Plesko find that the probability of losses being transitory is negatively related to the size of the loss and positively related to the size of the firm, sales growth, whether or not the loss is the first loss, and whether or not the firm pays out dividends. If a loss is likely to be permanent, the value of the firm is driven by the value of the abandonment option. See P. Joos and G. Plesko, "Valuing Loss Firms," *The Accounting Review* 80 (2005): 847–870.

Ryanair Holdings plc

R yanair is a low-cost, low-fare airline headquartered in Dublin, Ireland, operating over 200 routes in 20 countries. The company has directly challenged the largest airlines in Europe and has built a 20-year-plus track record of incredibly strong passenger growth while progressively reducing fares. It is not unusual for one-way tickets (exclusive of taxes) to sell on Ryanair's website for less than €1.00. See **Exhibit 1** for an excerpt of Ryanair's website, where fares between London and Stockholm, for example, are available for 19 pence (approximately US$0.33). CEO Michael O'Leary, formerly an accountant at KPMG, described the airline as follows: "Ryanair is doing in the airline industry in Europe what Ikea has done. We pile it high and sell it cheap. . . . For years flying has been the preserve of rich [people]. Now everyone can afford to fly."[1] Having created profitable operations in the difficult airline industry, Ryanair, as did industry analysts, likened itself to U.S. carrier Southwest Airlines, and its common stock has attracted the attention of investors in Europe and abroad.

Low-fare airlines

Historically the airline industry has been a notoriously difficult business in which to make consistent profits. Over the past several decades, low-fare airlines have been launched in an attempt to operate with lower costs, but with few exceptions, most have gone bankrupt or been swallowed up by larger carriers (see **Exhibit 2** for a list of failed airlines). Given the excess capacity in the global aircraft market in more recent years, barriers to entry in the commercial airline space have never been so low. Price competition in the U.S. and Europe, along with rising fuel costs, has had a deleterious affect on both profits and margins at most carriers. The current state of the industry can be described for most carriers as, at best, tumultuous.

The introduction of the low-fare sector in the United States predated its arrival in Europe. An open-skies policy was introduced through the Airline Deregulation Act of 1978, which removed controls of routes, fares, and schedules from the control of the Civil Aeronautics Board.[2] This spurred 22 new airlines to be formed between 1978 and 1982, each hoping to stake its claim in the newly deregulated market.[3] These airlines maximized their scheduling efficiencies, which, in combination with lower staff-to-plane ratios and a

Professor Mark T. Bradshaw prepared this case with the assistance of Fergal Naugton and Jonathan O'Grady (MBAs 2005). This case was prepared from published sources. HBS cases are developed solely as the basis for class discussion. Cases are not intended to serve as endorsements, sources of primary data, or illustrations of effective or ineffective management.

[1]G. Bowley, "How Low Can You Go?" FT.com website, June 20, 2003.

[2]U.S. Centennial of Flight Commission report, www.centennialofflight.gov/essay/Commercial_Aviation/Dereg/Tran8.htm.

[3]N. Donohue and P. Ghemawat, "The US Airline Industry, 1978–1988 (A)," HBS No. 390-025.

more straightforward service offering, gave them a huge cost advantage over the big airlines. This led to the current two-tier industry structure, with the low-fare airlines waging fare wars with the larger established carriers.

This was, however, a challenging time for the start-ups. First, the Federal Reserve raised the funds rate from 7.93% in 1978 to 12.26% in 1982. This had a dramatic effect on the financing costs for the start-up airlines, making financing of capital expenditures excessively costly. In addition, at this time the incumbent airlines were generally in relatively strong financial positions. Their deep pockets made it possible for them to run at a loss on certain routes in order to undercut the start-ups where necessary. As a result, many of the new companies failed.

One notable exception, however, was Southwest Airlines. By focusing on secondary airports, lightning-fast turnarounds, information technology, and a strong firm culture, it managed to gain passenger share and profitability. Within a decade, ticket prices in the U.S. had fallen by 33%, and the volume of passengers had more than doubled.[4]

In Europe, it was not until 1992, with the signing of the Maastricht Treaty, that years of protectionism by the governments of the so-called flag carriers began to be dismantled. In 1993, European Union (EU) national carriers were for the first time permitted to offer international services from other EU countries. By 1997, this was broadened to include domestic destinations and opened to any certified EU airline. Open skies had arrived in Europe.

Even before then, start-up airlines had begun to enter the European space. These companies would typically negotiate with their country's flag carrier for the right to fly to secondary airports only. Ticket sales were handled by agents, and the resulting cost structure forced the start-ups to compete with the incumbents primarily on service. Because they were not competing to provide traffic for the major hubs but rather targeting customers who had not previously considered flights for travel, they were in effect growing the market and were thus not seen as a major threat to the legacy carriers. However, with the Maastricht Treaty, the number of new airlines entering the industry greatly increased, and these start-ups were now free to compete solely on cost, looking across the Atlantic to the Southwest model.

Subsequently, as the new entrants vied for market space, prices fell, encouraging previously untapped demand. European passenger volumes had a strong upward trajectory (5%-plus compound annual growth rate between 1998 and 2003). However, while low-cost passenger numbers soared, the long-haul operators faced reduced traffic and higher fuel costs due to events such as the SARS virus and the September 11 attacks. The flag carriers, now financially constrained, were forced to renegotiate, and even cancel, contracts for the delivery of new aircraft from Airbus and Boeing. The two aerospace giants were left with significant numbers of planes for which the start-ups proved to be welcome customers.

Unlike the arrangements legacy carriers negotiated with major airports, start-up airlines negotiated dramatically lower landing and facility charges with secondary airports. They argued that, because they were bringing a significant number of passengers through these airports on a regular basis, the airports would be able to substantially increase the rents they received from concession stands and other retailers. As the low-fare airlines had no particular loyalty to one airport over another, the threat that they could simply stop flying to a particular airport was real.

Ryanair Holdings plc

---

[4]"Freedom in the Air," *The Economist*, April 3, 1997.

Ryanair

Ryanair was Europe's first low-fare carrier, with an initial route between Waterford, Ireland and London. The initial cabin crew had to be no taller than 5' 2" because the aircraft being deployed were among the smallest being flown on commercial routes. The company immediately challenged incumbents Aer Lingus and British Airways and obtained approval for a Dublin-London (Luton) route, charging less than half of what the large carriers were charging. A price war ensued, but over the next decade Ryanair eventually overtook Aer Lingus and British Airways on this route, the largest international route in Europe at that time.[5] (See **Exhibit 3** for Ryanair's remarkable passenger growth from 1985 through 2004.)

The company went public on May 9, 1997, and shortly thereafter was voted "Airline of the Year" by the Irish Air Transport Users Committee, "Best Managed National Airline" in the world by *International Aviation Week* magazine, "Best Value Airline" by the U.K.'s *Which* consumer magazine, and most popular airline on the Web by Google. Relative to that of other airlines, Ryanair's common stock has performed reasonably well since the company went public, despite negative events such as the Iraq war and significant increases in fuel prices. The company emphasizes that it defines customer service by low airfares and safety, rather than by the quality of food, pleasantness of staff, and other peripheral items.

See **Exhibit 4** for the stock price performance of Ryanair and selected European airlines since Ryanair's initial public offering. Additionally, see **Exhibits 5–7** for Ryanair's 2004 financial statements and supplemental revenue and cost information. The financial statements were prepared under Irish and U.K. accounting standards. Because the company has shares trading on the NASDAQ in the U.S., they also provide a reconciliation of major line items from Irish and U.K. accounting standards to U.S. accounting standards (see **Exhibit 8**).

Ryanair's objectives, as set forth in its 2004 annual report, include:

- Increasing passenger traffic by 20% each year.
- Reducing fares by 5% each year.
- Reducing costs by 5% each year.
- Realizing a profit margin of 20% or more.

To date, there are numerous factors that have contributed to the company's profitability, including the following:

1 *Cut-price deals.* Ryanair will frequently sell a large number of seats in advance for a nominal fee, for example, €1.00 or less. Indeed, currently approximately 25% of passenger tickets are free, and Mr. O'Leary has a goal of eventually bringing this figure to 50% by 2010. This attracts immense publicity as customers scramble to log in and purchase seats. For each seat purchased, tax and duties must also be paid, which typically amount to €30–€40. The tickets are sold on a nonrefundable basis. Because they are so cheap, many buy multiple seats to gain flexibility, and the "no show" rate is therefore much higher for these types of tickets. Average fares reflect these cut-price deals as well as higher fares that travelers pay to secure seats on routes in higher demand.

2 *Point-to-point flights.* Each route is a mini-business unit. Capacity is tailored to fit demand according to computer-simulated models. If a route is unprofitable, it can simply be cut from the schedule. Passengers may not buy connecting flights so must check in for each Ryanair flight individually. This reduces the firm's liability in the event of a delay and reduces instances of lost baggage.

[5]Company website.

3 *Flights to secondary airports.* By avoiding the large hubs, Ryanair is able to negotiate reduced landing charges. There is the added benefit of lower congestion at such airports. This allows the aircraft to complete the journey in the shortest possible time. The downside to passengers is that sometimes these airports are located in locations far from the intended destination. For example, the company flies to Frankfurt-Hahn, not Frankfurt, which is 100 kilometers away. As O'Leary states, "For the price-sensitive customers, distance is no problem."[6]

4 *Quick turnaround.* Ryanair aircraft are expected to land and take off again from an airport inside 25 minutes. This is only possible because they fly into secondary airports. This allows the firm to maximize the number of flights per day.

5 *No overnighting of staff.* By flying point to point, a Ryanair plane ends the day where it started. This means that crew can return to their homes, and expensive hotel bills and per diems are avoided.

6 *Internet bookings.* The firm sells over 97% of its tickets via the internet at its website, www.ryanair.com, which is now the most popular European travel site. This cuts out travel agent commission costs (averaging approximately 10% of the ticket cost) and gives the airline maximum control over scheduling and capacity. Moreover, it funnels customers towards other services such as car hire and rail tickets, for which Ryanair collects a commission itself. O'Leary is not bashful about this substantial source of cost savings and revenues, having stated, "Screw the travel agent. Take the [agents] out and shoot them. What have they done for passengers over the years?"[7]

7 *One class.* Ryanair does not offer passengers the choice of business and economy class, eliminating the requirement for food to be delivered to the aircraft when it lands, thus facilitating low turnaround times. Moreover, offering only one class of service furthers the goal of providing low fares, which the company believes is the ultimate in customer service. According to its passenger service and lowest fares charter, "Ryanair believes that any passenger service commitment must involve a commitment on pricing and punctuality, and should not be confined to less important aspects of 'service' which is the usual excuse the high fare airlines use for charging high air fares."[8]

8 *One aircraft type.* The company flies Boeing 737 planes exclusively. This reduces maintenance training costs and allows for bulk buying of spare parts. The strong financial position of the company allowed it to purchase many of the aircraft that had been canceled by incumbent airlines. These new airplanes are more fuel efficient and have a higher passenger capacity. As of the end of fiscal 2004, the company had fully hedged fuel costs through September 2004, but were largely unhedged thereafter. Subsequently, the company hedged its fuel through the end of fiscal 2006 at US$49 per barrel, while market values topped US$70 per barrel. Additionally, the company has ordered winglets that will be retrofitted on all aircraft, which will reduce fuel burn by approximately 2.5%, which translates into savings of approximately US$10,000–14,000 per aircraft per month.

9 *Personnel costs and incentives.* Because the aircraft that Ryanair pilots fly are new, the firm claims that their pilots' experience is of value to the competition. Therefore, it charges pilots for training, the cost of which is earned back by the pilots through years of service. Pilots have financial incentives for smooth landings, not so much for passenger comfort but for reduced maintenance costs. Additionally, the airline does not provide food or beverages for free but does offer items for sale on each flight. Flight attendants are paid a commission based on the total of beverage and other sales in flight.

[6]G. Bowley, "How Low Can You Go?"
[7]Ibid.
[8]Company website.

Ryanair Holdings plc

Ryanair Holdings plc

Ryanair has an entrepreneurial culture and takes great pride in breaking with old conventions. This spirit is disseminated from the top by the swashbuckling manner of CEO O'Leary. Irish business folklore has it that when he first decided to employ the internet to sell seats, O'Leary did not hire a firm of IT consultants and Web designers. He instead visited a local technical college and offered the project as a challenge to the eager students in the computer lab. They learned by doing, and O'Leary got a website with the necessary functionality at a fraction of list price. He is also known for wild publicity stunts, such as driving a tank to easyJet's headquarters in England and broadcasting the theme to the television show "The A-Team." He taunts the competition even with the painting of aircraft. One of Ryanair's airplanes is painted with the message, "Arrivederci Alitalia."[9]

O'Leary is not bashful of his company's achievements, and has a unique demeanor for a company CEO, often charmingly foul-mouthed and offensive. In a recent interview, he stated "I don't give a [*&%#] if nobody likes me. I am not a cloud bunny, I am not an aerosexual. I don't like aeroplanes. I never wanted to be a pilot like those other platoons of goons who populate the air industry."[10] Attacking competitors is not out of the question either, as he recently said of Jurgen Weber, CEO of Lufthansa, "Weber says Germans don't like low fares. How the [*&%#] does he know? He never offered them any."[11]

He positions the airline as a champion against inefficiencies and monopolies, and his manner has been described as arrogant and dismissive. Even in financial reports for investors, he often leads off with tirades against airports that charge too much or other issues that adversely affect Ryanair. For example, the 2005 road show included several slides titled "Stansted Airport: The Rip-Off," which highlighted costs of a cross-subsidization plan across airports run by the British Airport Authority. Similarly, in discussing 2005 financial results, the company report stated:

> *In Ireland, the situation at Dublin Airport has descended into a farce. The Dublin Airport Authority which is responsible for this third world facility is to be rewarded for its incompetence by being allowed to build the second terminal. This facility will not be available until 2009 at the earliest and in the mean time passengers at Dublin will be forced to endure long queues and intolerable overcrowding while the Government protects this failed monopoly by blocking competition. . . . The [prime minister] recently demonstrated how hopelessly out of touch he is by claiming that the present overcrowded terminal has the capacity for 6 million more passengers per annum. It would appear that there aren't any queues at the VIP escort to the Government jet. . . . Had the Government heeded Ryanair's calls for a competing second terminal seven years ago, this current embarrassment for Irish tourism would have been avoided. As always in Ireland the ordinary passengers suffer, while the politicians fudge.[12]*

Turbulence in 2004

Just after reporting third-quarter profit increases of 10% (quarter ended December 31, 2003), Ryanair issued a profit warning in January 2004 for the company's upcoming full-year results for the fiscal year ending March 31, 2004. O'Leary stated, "While we now expect after-tax profits for the current year to dip slightly, our annualized profit margin will still be in excess of 20%, and Ryanair will continue to be the world's most profitable airline by margin." Ryanair's share price dropped 30% on the news (see **Exhibit 9**). The

---

[9]G. Bowley, "How Low Can You Go?"

[10]A. Clark, "The Guardian profile: Michael O'Leary," *The Guardian*, June 24, 2005.

[11]M. Ridley, "The World's Favourite 'Despot'," *Daily Express*, June 1, 2005.

[12]Company press release, May 31, 2005.

expected fall in profits for the fourth quarter was attributed to lower yields (i.e., average passenger fares) and lower load factors (i.e., seats with paying passengers as a fraction of total seats available). According to O'Leary, the lower yields were due to Ryanair's strategy of steadily lowering fares as part of its battle plan. He argued, "This is not due to overcapacity. It's the result of the ongoing fare wars under way across Europe, and we're winning them. It's like Southwest in the U.S. When they first went into California, their stock price fell by 40% to 50% due to fare wars with the likes of the United [Airlines] shuttle and other California carriers. Ten years later, Southwest owned California."[13]

More bad news followed immediately after the profit warning, when Ryanair received an unfavorable ruling from the European Commission (EC) regarding $18 million in financial incentives it had received from Charleroi Airport in Belgium between 2001 and 2003. The commissioners indicated that the ruling was an attempt to encourage economic growth while simultaneously ending state subsidies that have been declared illegal under the EU. The ruling put additional pressure on Ryanair's stock price. In response, O'Leary explained, "Any share price jumps up and down, and ours is no exception. But as long as the basic business model is sound and you're executing it properly, nothing will stop you—certainly not a bunch of EU commissioners who think everyone should pay higher fares."[14]

Financial performance

Prior to the profit warnings in early 2004, Ryanair had been profitable every quarter and reported annual increases in sales, operating profit, and net income in every year (see **Exhibit 10**). As forewarned in January 2004, despite an increase in sales for fiscal 2004, net income declined for the fiscal year ended March 31, 2004 relative to the fiscal 2003 level. This was the first reported year-over-year downturn in profits since the company went public.

Nevertheless, Ryanair continued to add capacity in 2004, increasing available seat kilometers by 64%. The overall load factor for 2004 exceeded 80%, relative to a break-even level of 59%. The company's fleet of planes had 189 seats, implying that, on average, 111 seats had to be filled for the company to break even. Ryanair has the lowest cost structure of any comparable airline, as seen in **Exhibit 11**. The company is obsessive about low costs, down to details such as making employees provide their own pens and not allowing the charging of cell phones in corporate facilities. Low costs permit Ryanair to charge lower fares and still provide a high return on investment. See **Exhibit 12** for average revenue per passenger, return on equity (ROE), and other financial metrics for 15 airlines. Ryanair's average revenue per passenger (in US$) is just $49. The only other airlines with similarly low fares include U.K.-based easyJet (US$77 per passenger) and Southwest Airlines (US$89). Nearly half of the airlines listed (all U.S.-based incumbent carriers) report losses and/or have meaningless ROE because the denominator of the calculation (i.e., book value of equity) is negative. For 2004, Ryanair reports the highest ROE, 17%. The only other airline with profitability approaching that of Ryanair is Japan Airlines, but the duPont decomposition of ROE indicates that this is largely driven by Japan Airlines' use of significant leverage, relative to limited leverage at Ryanair. Even with the relatively strong profitability, the stock market values Ryanair at just a modest level relative to other airlines, trading at a price-to-earnings ratio of 20.8 relative to 50.5 for newcomer JetBlue Airways and 40.7 for veteran low-fare airline Southwest.

Ryanair Holdings plc

[13]"Airing Ryanair's Beef with the EC," *BusinessWeek Online*, February 16, 2004.
[14]Ibid.

Valuation

Following the series of bad news announcements in early 2004, the investor community split into two camps: those that saw the downturn in profits and cash flows as the end of Ryanair's strong performance run versus those that believed the stock price drop to be an overreaction to a company that retained strong fundamentals. **Exhibit 13** provides an analysis of Ryanair's profitability and operating, investment, and financing activities over the most recent three years. The overall picture is that of a financially healthy company with strong sales growth, high profitability, and negative net debt (i.e., interest-bearing liabilities less than cash and liquid resources).

Exhibit 14 summarizes equity analyst reports released during the first six months of 2004 that encompass the profit warnings in January, the EU decision in February, and the announcement of earnings in June. The recommendations span the range from sell, with target prices below the current trading price (e.g., target price of €4.40 when the current stock price was €4.65), to buy, with target prices at lofty levels up to 35% above the current trading price (e.g., target price of €6.00 when the current stock price was €4.41).

Clearly, discrepancies in valuations reflect divergent opinions on numerous issues that plague the airline sector, such as fare competition, cost containment, regulation, and macroeconomic vulnerability. Perhaps not surprisingly, in contrast to many market observers in the airline industry, Ryanair continues to have a bullish outlook, signing purchase agreements for an additional 140 Boeing 737 aircraft in February 2005. Each aircraft will have an approximate cost of US$51 million. With the addition of these aircraft to the 91 in service already, the company expects to grow annual passenger traffic to 70 million by 2012, almost triple the number in 2004.

Ryanair Holdings plc

EXHIBIT 1   **Ryanair website**

Ryanair Holdings plc

Source: www.ryanair.com, July 8, 2005.

EXHIBIT 2   Failed airlines in the U.S. and Europe

U.S.	People's Express	Italy	Volare
	Frontier Airlines		Agent Air
	Texas Air		Air Freedom
	New York Air		Free Airways
			Windjet
Great Britain	Duo		
	Now	Poland	Air Polonia
			DreamAir
Ireland	Fresh Aer		GetJet
	JetMagic		Silesian Air
	JetGreen		White Eagle
	Skynet		
		Finland	Flying Finn
Germany	Berlinjet		
	Low Fare Jet	Norway	Goodjet
	V-Bird		
		Bosnia	Air Bosnia
France	Aeris		
	Air Littoral	Spain	Air Cataluyna
	Airlib Express		
	Fly Eco		

Source: Merrion Stockbrokers Irish Equity Research report, January 21, 2005.

Ryanair Holdings plc

EXHIBIT 3   **Annual Ryanair passenger traffic (number of passengers), 1985–2006 (estimated)**

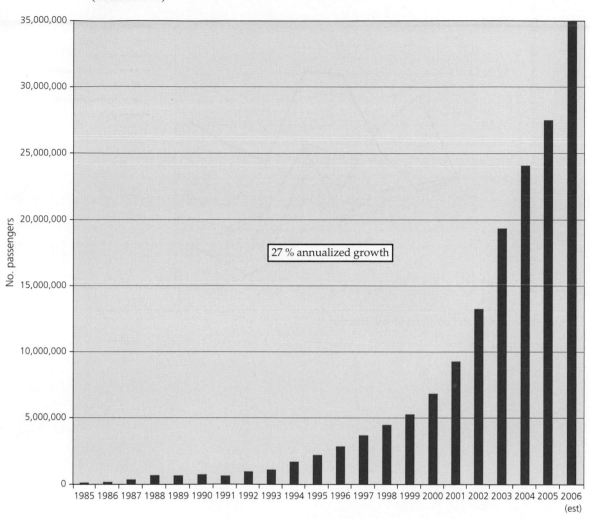

27 % annualized growth

Ryanair Holdings plc

Source: Ryanair investor relations website.

EXHIBIT 4   **Relative stock price performance of selected European and U.S. airlines: 1997–2003**

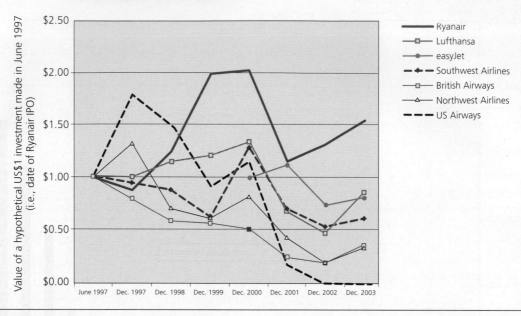

Source: Standard & Poor's Compustat Global database.

Ryanair Holdings plc

EXHIBIT 5   **Financial statements**

Consolidated Profit and Loss Account
(all amounts in €000, except per share and share amounts)

	2004	2003	2002
Operating revenue			
Scheduled revenues	924,566	731,951	550,991
Ancillary revenues	149,658	110,557	73,059
Total operating revenue – continuing operations	1,074,224	842,508	624,050
Operating expenses			
Staff costs	(123,624)	(93,073)	(78,240)
Depreciation and amortization	(101,391)	(76,865)	(59,010)
Other operating expenses	(597,922)	(409,096)	(323,867)
Total operating expenses excluding goodwill	(822,937)	(579,034)	(461,117)
Operating profit – continuing operations before amortization of goodwill	251,287	263,474	162,933
Amortization of goodwill	(2,342)	—	—
Operating profit – continuing operations after amortization of goodwill	248,945	263,474	162,933
Other (expenses)/income			
Foreign exchange gains	3,217	628	975
(Loss) on disposal of fixed assets	(9)	(29)	527
Interest receivable and similar income	23,891	31,363	27,548
Interest payable and similar charges	(47,564)	(30,886)	(19,609)
Total other (expenses)/income	(20,465)	1,076	9,441
Profit on ordinary activities before tax	228,480	264,550	172,374
Tax on profit on ordinary activities	(21,869)	(25,152)	(21,999)
Profit for the financial year	206,611	239,398	150,375
Earnings per ordinary share (€ cents)			
Basic	27.28	31.71	20.64
Diluted	27.00	31.24	20.32
Weighted average number of ordinary shares (000's)			
Basic	757,447	755,055	728,726
Diluted	759,300	766,279	739,961

Ryanair Holdings plc

EXHIBIT 5   Financial statements *(continued)*

Consolidated Balance Sheet (all amounts in €000)

	2004	2003
Fixed assets		
Intangible assets	44,499	0
Tangible assets	1,576,526	1,352,361
Total fixed assets	1,621,025	1,352,361
Current assets		
Cash and liquid resources	1,257,350	1,060,218
Accounts receivable	14,932	14,970
Other assets	19,251	16,370
Inventories	26,440	22,788
Total current assets	1,317,973	1,114,346
Total assets	2,938,998	2,466,707
Current liabilities		
Accounts payable	67,936	61,604
Accrued expenses and other liabilities	338,208	251,328
Current maturities of long term debt	80,337	63,291
Short term borrowings	345	1,316
Total current liabilities	486,826	377,539
Other liabilities		
Provisions for liabilities and charges	94,192	67,833
Accounts payable due after one year	30,047	5,673
Long term debt	872,645	773,934
Total other liabilities	996,884	847,440
Shareholders' funds-equity		
Called-up share capital	9,643	9,588
Share premium account	560,406	553,512
Profit and loss account	885,239	678,628
Total shareholders' funds-equity	1,455,288	1,241,728
Total liabilities and shareholders' funds	2,938,998	2,466,707

EXHIBIT 5 Financial statements *(continued)*

Consolidated Cash Flow Statement (all amounts in €000)

	2004	2003	2002
Net cash inflow from operating activities	462,062	351,003	309,109
Return on investments and servicing of finance			
Interest received	26,292	30,171	30,193
Interest paid	(46,605)	(29,563)	(19,833)
Net cash (outflow)/inflow from return on investments and servicing of finance	(20,313)	608	10,360
Taxation			
Corporation tax paid	(2,056)	(3,410)	(5,071)
Capital expenditure			
Purchase of tangible fixed assets	(331,603)	(469,878)	(372,587)
Sale of tangible fixed assets	4	31	563
Net cash (outflow) from capital expenditure	(331,599)	(469,847)	(372,024)
Acquisitions			
Purchase consideration	(20,795)	—	—
Onerous lease payments	(11,901)	—	—
Net cash (outflow) from acquisition of subsidiary undertakings	(32,696)	—	—
Net cash inflow/(outflow) before financing and management of liquid resources	75,398	(121,646)	(57,626)
Financing			
Loans raised	187,035	331,502	175,746
Loans repaid	(71,278)	(44,779)	(27,886)
Issue of share capital	6,948	56	188,331
Share issue costs	—	—	(6,330)
Capital element of finance leases	—	(1)	(107)
Net cash inflow from financing	122,705	286,778	329,754
Management of liquid resources			
(Increase) in liquid resources	(249,220)	(166,329)	(251,241)
Net cash (outflow)/inflow from financing and management of liquid resources	(126,515)	120,449	78,513
Increase (decrease) in cash	(51,117)	(1,197)	20,887

Ryanair Holdings plc

EXHIBIT 5   Financial statements *(continued)*

Consolidated Statement of Changes in Shareholders' Funds-equity (all amounts in €000)

	Called-up share capital	Share premium account	Profit and loss account	Total
Balance at March 31, 2002	9,587	553,457	439,230	1,002,274
Issue of ordinary equity shares (net of issue costs)	1	55	—	56
Profit for the financial year	—	—	239,398	239,398
Balance at March 31, 2003	9,588	553,512	678,628	1,241,728
Issue of ordinary equity shares	55	6,894	—	6,949
Profit for the financial year	—	—	206,611	206,611
Balance at March 31, 2004	9,643	560,406	885,239	1,455,288

Source: 2004 and 2003 Ryanair annual reports.

EXHIBIT 6   Supplemental revenue information (€000)

Ancillary revenues comprise:	**2004**	**2003**
Nonflight scheduled	66,616	35,291
Car Hire	35,110	27,615
Inflight	30,100	23,142
Internet income	17,721	12,159
Charter	111	12,350
	149,658	110,557

All of the group's operating profit arises from airline-related activities. Nonflight-scheduled revenue arises from the sale of rail and bus tickets, hotel reservations and other revenues. Inflight revenues reflect sales of refreshments (e.g., peanuts, drinks) and other items (e.g., duty-free sales, etc.). Internet income comprises revenue generated from Ryanair.com excluding internet car hire revenue which is included under the heading 'Car Hire.'

Ancillary revenue increased by 35% to €149.7 million and reflects strong growth in nonflight scheduled revenue, car hire and hotel revenue, offset, by the cessation of the charter program as Ryanair replaced charter capacity with scheduled services. Ancillary revenues were also negatively impacted by the strengthening of the euro versus sterling in the year, as 65% of ancillary revenues are denominated in sterling. Ancillary revenue, excluding charters increased by 52%, higher than the growth in passenger numbers, and accounted for 14% of total revenues compared to 13% in the year ended March 31, 2003.

Source: 2004 Ryanair annual report.

Ryanair Holdings plc

EXHIBIT 7 **Supplemental cost information (€000)**

STAFF NUMBER AND COSTS

Average weekly number of employees, including the executive director, during the year, analyzed by category:	2004	2003
Flight and cabin crew	1,530	983
Sales, operations and administration	758	763
	2,288	1,746

Aggregate payroll costs of these persons:	2004	2003
Wages, salaries and related costs	112,258	82,633
Social welfare costs	9,660	7,835
Other pension costs	1,706	2,605
	123,624	93,073

OTHER OPERATING EXPENSES

Other operating expenses comprise:	2004	2003
Fuel and oil	174,991	128,842
Airport and handling charges	147,221	107,994
Route charges	110,271	68,406
Maintenance, materials and repairs	43,420	29,709
Marketing and distribution costs	16,141	14,623
Aircraft rentals	11,541	—
Other costs	78,034	59,522
	582,619	409,096
Exceptional costs		
Aircraft rentals	13,291	—
Buzz reorganization	3,012	—
	16,303	—
	597,922	409,096

Other costs include, among other things, certain direct costs of providing inflight service, car hire costs and other non-flight scheduled costs.

Exceptional items are those items that are material items which derive from events or transactions that fall within the ordinary activities of the group but which need to be disclosed by virtue of their size or incidence. The exceptional costs relate to the closure of Buzz for one month post acquisition to restructure the business and integrate it into Ryanair and the exceptional lease costs associated with the early permanent retirement of 6 Boeing 737-200 aircraft which are no longer operated due to scratch marks which occurred during an aircraft painting program. The costs are treated as exceptional as they are material to the results for the year.

Source: 2004 Ryanair annual report.

Ryanair Holdings plc

EXHIBIT 8   **Summary of differences between Irish/United Kingdom and U.S. GAAP (€000)**

Ryanair Holdings plc

	2004	2003	2002
Profit for financial year as reported in the consolidated profit and loss account and in accordance with Irish and U.K. GAAP	206,611	239,398	150,375
Adjustments			
Pensions	89	697	751
Derivative financial instruments (net of tax)	—	(4,189)	—
Amortization of goodwill	2,342	—	—
Employment grants	—	469	464
Capitalised interest regarding aircraft acquisition programme	7,213	5,262	5,027
Darley Investments Limited	88	88	88
Taxation – effect of above adjustments	(913)	85	(1,156)
Net income in accordance with U.S. GAAP	215,430	241,810	155,549
Total assets as reported in the consolidated balance sheets and in accordance with Irish and U.K. GAAP	2,938,998	2,466,707	1,889,572
Adjustments			
Pensions	3,200	3,111	2,414
Amortization of goodwill	2,342	—	—
Capitalised interest regarding aircraft acquisition programme	17,502	10,289	5,027
Darley Investments Limited	(151)	(239)	(327)
Total assets as adjusted to accord with U.S. GAAP	2,961,891	2,479,868	1,896,686
Shareholders' equity as reported in the consolidated balance sheets and in accordance with Irish and U.K. GAAP	1,455,288	1,241,728	1,002,274
Adjustments			
Pension	3,200	3,111	2,414
Amortization of goodwill	2,342	—	—
Employment grants	—	—	(469)
Capitalised interest regarding aircraft acquisition programme	17,502	10,289	5,027
Darley Investments Limited	(151)	(239)	(327)
Minimum pension liability (net of tax)	(2,631)	(2,656)	—
Unrealized (losses) on derivative financial instruments (net of tax)	(116,681)	(73,371)	12,448
Tax effect of adjustments (excluding pension and derivative adjustments)	(2,588)	(1,675)	(1,760)
Shareholders' equity as adjusted to accord with U.S. GAAP	1,356,281	1,177,187	1,019,607

Source: 2004 and 2003 Ryanair annual reports.

EXHIBIT 9   **Ryanair stock price: January–June 2004**

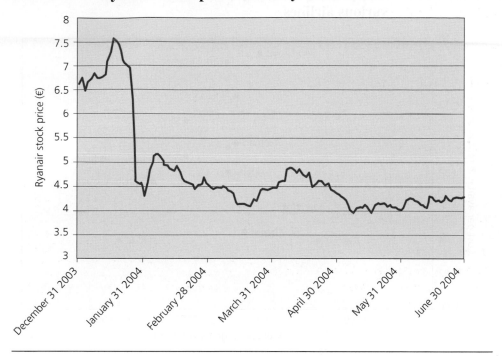

Source: Center for Research on Security Prices database.

EXHIBIT 10   **Ryanair financial performance 1997–2004 (€000)**

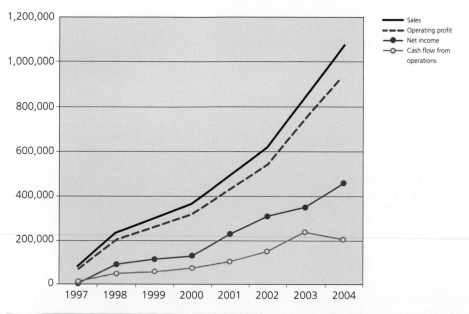

Source: Thomson Financial Datastream.

Ryanair Holdings plc

EXHIBIT 11 **Comparison of costs per available seat kilometer for various airlines**

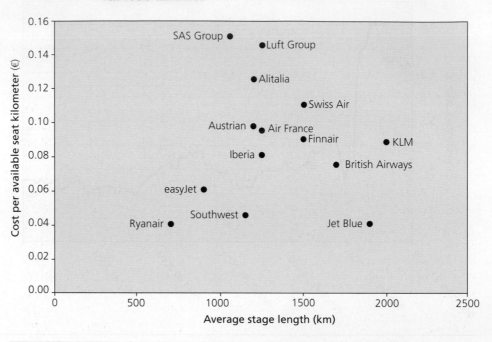

Source: Davy Stockbroker report on Ryanair, February 16, 2004.

EXHIBIT 12 **Financial and operating metrics for selected airlines**

	P/E	Market Value (000 $US)	Average Revenue/ Passenger ($US)	Load Factor	Margin	Turnover	Leverage	ROE
JetBlue Airways	50.5	2420	104	0.83	0.04	0.45	3.70	0.06
Southwest Airlines	40.7	1,2780	89	0.69	0.05	0.58	2.05	0.06
British Airways	24.2	5,501	330	0.73	0.03	0.67	4.60	0.10
Japan Airlines	24.2	6,752	201	0.64	0.01	0.98	11.10	0.15
Ryanair	20.8	4,273	49	0.74	0.20	0.44	1.99	0.17
Lufthansa	13.1	6,564	280	0.74	0.02	0.86	4.55	0.09
easyJet	12.4	917	77	0.85	0.04	0.82	1.68	0.05
Qantas Airways	9.8	4,526	208	0.78	0.06	0.62	3.02	0.11
Singapore Airlines	9.6	8,000	540	0.73	0.12	0.54	1.76	0.11
SAS	n.m.	1,486	137	0.64	−0.03	0.91	5.16	−0.15
American Airlines	n.m.	1,765	185	0.75	−0.04	0.65	n.m.	n.m.
Delta Air Lines	n.m.	1,046	125	0.75	−0.35	0.69	n.m.	n.m.
Northwest Airlines	n.m.	952	152	0.80	−0.08	0.80	n.m.	n.m.
United Airlines	n.m.	151	176	0.79	−0.10	0.79	n.m.	n.m.
US Airways	n.m.	60	151	0.76	−0.09	0.85	n.m.	n.m.

Notes: n.m. = not meaningful.

Load factor = Revenue passenger miles (or kilometers)/Available seat miles (or kilometers).

Margin = Net income/Sales.

Turnover = Sales/Total assets.

Leverage = Total assets/Stockholders' equity.

Source: Jane's World Airlines, company annual reports.

Ryanair Holdings plc

EXHIBIT 13   Ratio analysis, 2002–2004[a]

Decomposing Profitability: Dupont Alternative	2001	2002	2003	2004
NOPAT / Sales	20.1%	23.0%	28.4%	21.2%
X Sales / Net Assets	2.3	1.4	1.3	1.1
= **Operating ROA**	**46.2%**	**31.8%**	**36.3%**	**22.4%**
Financial Spread[b]	43.4%	28.6%	36.1%	32.0%
X Net Financial Leverage[c]	−0.5	−0.3	−0.3	−0.2
= Financial Leverage Gain	−22.6%	−9.4%	−12.4%	−5.7%
ROE (Operating ROA + Financial Spread *Net Financial Leverage)	**23.7%**	**22.4%**	**23.9%**	**16.6%**

Evaluating Operating Management	2001	2002	2003	2004
Key Growth Rates:				
Annual Sales Growth	**31.7%**	**28.0%**	**35.0%**	**27.5%**
Annual Net Income Growth	**44.1%**	**43.9%**	**59.2%**	**−13.7%**
Key Profitability Ratios:				
Sales / Sales	**100.0%**	**100.0%**	**100.0%**	**100.0%**
Cost of Sales / Sales	76.6%	73.9%	68.7%	76.6%
Gross Margin	**23.4%**	**26.1%**	**31.3%**	**23.4%**
SG&A / Sales	0.0%	0.0%	0.0%	0.0%
Other Operating Expense / Sales	0.0%	0.0%	0.0%	0.0%
Investment Income / Sales	0.0%	0.0%	0.0%	0.0%
Other Income, net of Other Expense / Sales	0.3%	0.2%	0.1%	0.1%
Minority Interest / Sales	0.0%	0.0%	0.0%	0.0%
EBIT Margin	**23.7%**	**26.3%**	**31.3%**	**23.5%**
Net Interest Expense (Income) / Sales	−1.6%	−1.3%	−0.1%	2.2%
Pre-Tax Income Margin	25.3%	27.6%	31.4%	21.3%
Taxes / Sales	3.9%	3.5%	3.0%	2.0%
Unusual Gains, Net of Unusual Losses (after tax) / Sales	0.0%	0.0%	0.0%	0.0%
Net Income Margin	**21.4%**	**24.1%**	**28.4%**	**19.2%**
EBITDA Margin	35.9%	35.8%	43.3%	37.1%
NOPAT Margin	20.1%	23.0%	28.4%	21.2%
Recurring NOPAT Margin	19.8%	22.8%	28.3%	21.2%

Ryanair Holdings plc

EXHIBIT 13 **Ratio analysis, 2002–2004[a]** *(continued)*

Evaluating Investment Management	2001	2002	2003	2004
Working Capital Management:				
Operating Working Capital / Sales	−18.0%	−21.2%	−26.8%	−24.1%
Operating Working Capital Turnover	−5.5	−4.7	−3.7	−4.2
Accounts Receivable Turnover	22.2	71.8	81.6	71.8
Inventory Turnover	26.8	28.9	33.8	36.1
Accounts Payable Turnover	16.3	15.4	12.4	13.4
Days' Receivables	16.5	5.1	4.5	5.1
Days' Inventory	13.6	12.6	10.8	10.1
Days' Payables	22.3	23.7	29.5	27.3
Long-Term Asset Management:				
Net Long-Term Assets Turnover	1.6	1.1	1.0	0.8
Net Long-Term Assets / Sales	61.5%	93.5%	105.0%	119.0%
PP&E Turnover	1.5	1.0	0.9	0.8
Depreciation & Amortization / Sales	12.1%	9.5%	11.9%	13.6%

Evaluating Financial Management	2001	2002	2003	2004
Short-Term Liquidity:				
Current Ratio	2.77	3.28	3.04	2.95
Quick Ratio	2.63	3.14	2.95	2.85
Cash Ratio	2.47	3.10	2.92	2.81
Operating Cash Flow Ratio	1.04	1.03	1.13	1.22
Debt and Long-Term Solvency:				
Liabilities-to-Equity	0.61	0.91	0.89	0.99
Debt-to-Equity	0.28	0.61	0.55	0.68
Net-Debt-to-Equity	−0.52	−0.33	−0.34	−0.18
Debt-to-Capital	0.22	0.38	0.36	0.40
Net-Debt-to-Net Capital	−1.08	−0.49	−0.52	−0.22
Interest Coverage Ratio	11.31	9.79	9.57	5.80
Dividend Payout Ratio	n/a	n/a	n/a	n/a
Sustainable Growth Rate:	23.7%	22.4%	23.9%	16.6%

[a]All ratios incorporating balance sheet measures are computed using beginning-of-year values

[b]Operating ROA – effective after-tax interest rate.

[c]Net Debt/Net Equity, where Net Debt = Interest-bearing liabilities – cash and marketable equity securities.

Source: Ryanair annual reports.

Ryanair Holdings plc

EXHIBIT 14 Equity analyst reports on Ryanair, January–June 2004

Ryanair Holdings plc

				(€ per share, except where noted)	
Report date	Equity Research Firm	Report title	Recommendation	Price	Target price
28-Jan-04	ABN Amro	The Emporer Falls Off His Throne	Sell	4.75	5.15
29-Jan-04	UBS	More Questions than Answers	Reduce 2 (Sell)	4.72	6.25
29-Jan-04	BNP/Paribas	Reach for the Alka-Selzer? Buy Instead	Outperform	4.75	6.10
2-Feb-04	UBS	Business Model Under the Microscope	Reduce 2 (Sell)	4.87	4.50
3-Feb-04	Deutsche Bank	Stop Talking and Do Your Business – Upgrade to Buy	Buy	4.66	5.70
3-Feb-04	Smith Barney Citigroup	Talk of Its Demise is Greatly Exaggerated	Hold (2)	4.95	5.50
4-Feb-04	BNP/Paribas	No Lasting Damage (But a Slap on the Wrist!)	Outperform	4.95	6.10
4-Feb-04	ABN Amro	Imperial Lather	Reduce	4.66	4.40
4-Feb-04	Raymond James	EU Decision Announced	Market Perform	$35.75	—
5-Feb-04	NCB Group	Commission Ruling Will Not Derail the Model	Buy	—	6.00
11-Feb-04	CSFB	Profits Shock	Underperform	5.20	4.42
12-Feb-04	Raymond James	Raising Rating to Outperform	Outperform	$37.68	$45.00
3-Mar-04	NCB Group	All to Play For in March	Buy	4.84	6.00
9-Mar-04	Raymond James	February Traffic Results; Establishing FY05 Quarterly Estimates	Outperform 2	$34.28	$40.00
6-Apr-04	ABN Amro	Yields Set to Improve	Add	4.97	5.50
3-May-04	NCB Group	It Isn't Broken – It's Just More Visibly Seasonal	Buy	4.80	6.00
6-May-04	Panmure Gordon	easyJet and Ryanair Passenger Growth and Load Factors	Hold	4.45	5.00
21-May-04	UBS	Full Year Results – June 1st	Reduce 2 (Sell)	4.65	4.40
21-May-04	CSFB	FY Results Preview	Underperform	4.55	4.42
25-May-04	Deutsche Bank	FY 03/04 Results Preview	Buy	4.53	5.70
27-May-04	Smith Barney Citigroup	FY04 Results Expectations – Outlook Uncertain	Hold (2)	4.39	5.50
1-Jun-04	Deutsche Bank	Good Results but Competition Remains Tough	Buy	4.38	5.70
1-Jun-04	Smith Barney Citigroup	Results in Line, Outlook Slightly Better	Hold (2)	4.38	5.50
1-Jun-04	William deBroe	Ryanair Results	Sell	4.45	—
2-Jun-04	ABN Amro	Walking a tightrope	Add	4.38	5.00
2-Jun-04	NCB Group	No Major Surprises – Forecasts Creep Up on Stronger Summer Trading	Buy	4.41	6.00
3-Jun-04	CSFB	Challenging Outlook	Underperform	4.41	4.42

Source: Investext.

BUSINESS ANALYSIS AND VALUATION APPLICATIONS

Equity Security Analysis

Equity **security analysis** is the evaluation of a firm and its prospects from the perspective of a current or potential investor in the firm's shares. Security analysis is one step in a larger investment process that involves:

1 Establishing the objectives of the investor.
2 Forming expectations about the future returns and risks of individual securities.
3 Combining individual securities into portfolios to maximize progress toward the investment objectives.

Security analysis is the foundation for the second step, projecting future returns and assessing risk. Security analysis is typically conducted with an eye toward identification of mispriced securities in hopes of generating returns that more than compensate the investor for risk. However, that need not be the case. For analysts who do not have a comparative advantage in identifying mispriced securities, the focus should be on gaining an appreciation for how a security would affect the risk of a given portfolio, and whether it fits the profile that the portfolio is designed to maintain.

Security analysis is undertaken by individual investors, by analysts at brokerage houses (sell-side analysts), and by analysts that work at the direction of fund managers for various institutions (buy-side analysts). The institutions employing buy-side analysts include collective investment funds, pension funds, insurance companies, universities, and others.

A variety of questions are dealt with in security analysis:

- A sell-side analyst asks: Is the industry I am covering attractive, and if so why? How do different firms within the industry position themselves? What are the implications for my earnings forecasts? Given my expectations for a firm, do its shares appear to be mispriced? Should I recommend this share as a buy, a sell, or a hold?

- A buy-side analyst for a "value share fund" asks: Does this security possess the characteristics we seek in our fund? That is, does it have a relatively low ratio of price to earnings, low price-to-book value, and other fundamental indicators? Do its prospects for earnings improvement suggest good potential for high future returns on the security?

- An individual investor asks: Does this security offer the risk profile that suits my investment objectives? Does it enhance my ability to diversify the risk of my portfolio? Is the firm's dividend payout rate low enough to help shield me from taxes while I continue to hold the security?

As the above questions underscore, there is more to security analysis than estimating the value of equity securities. Nevertheless, for most sell-side and buy-side analysts, the key goal remains the identification of mispriced securities.

INVESTOR OBJECTIVES AND INVESTMENT VEHICLES

The investment objectives of individual savers in the economy are highly idiosyncratic. For any given saver they depend on such factors as income, age, wealth, tolerance for risk, and tax status. For example, savers with many years until retirement are likely to prefer to have a relatively large share of their portfolio invested in equities, which offer a higher expected return than fixed income (or debt) securities and higher short-term variability. Investors in high tax brackets are likely to prefer to have a large share of their portfolio in shares that generate tax-deferred capital gains rather than shares that pay dividends or interest-bearing securities.

Collective investment funds (mutual funds, unit trusts, OEICs, SICAVs, or BEVEKs as they are termed in some countries) have become popular investment vehicles for savers to achieve their investment objectives.[1] Collective investment funds sell shares in professionally managed portfolios that invest in specific types of equity and/or fixed income securities. They therefore provide a low-cost way for savers to invest in a portfolio of securities that reflects their particular appetite for risk.

The major classes of collective investment funds include:

1   Money market funds that invest in commercial paper, certificates of deposit, and treasury bills.

2   Bond funds that invest in debt instruments.

3   Equity funds that invest in equity securities.

4   Balanced funds that hold money market, bond, and equity securities.

5   Real estate funds that invest in commercial real estate.

Within the bond and equities classes of funds, however, there are wide ranges of fund types. For example, bond funds include:

- *Corporate bond funds* that invest in investment-grade rated corporate debt instruments.[2]
- *Government bond funds* that invest in government debt instruments.
- *High yield funds* that invest in non-investment-grade rated corporate debt.
- *Mortgage funds* that invest in mortgage-backed securities.

Equity funds include:

- *Income funds* that invest in equities that are expected to generate dividend income.
- *Growth funds* that invest in equities expected to generate long-term capital gains.
- *Income and growth funds* that invest in equities that provide a balance of dividend income and capital gains.
- *Value funds* that invest in equities that are considered to be undervalued.
- *Short funds* that sell short equity securities that are considered to be overvalued.
- *Index funds* that invest in equities that track a particular market index, such as the MSCI World Index or the DJ Euro Stoxx 50.
- *Sector funds* that invest in equities in a particular industry segment, such as the technology or health sciences sectors.
- *Regional funds* that invest in equities from a particular country or geographic region, such as Japan, the Asia-Pacific region, or the US

Since the 1990s, hedge funds have gained increased prominence and the assets controlled by these funds have grown significantly. While generally open only to institutional investors and certain qualified wealthy individuals, hedge funds are becoming an increasingly important force in the market. Hedge funds employ a variety of investment strategies including:

- *Market neutral funds* that typically invest equal amounts of money in purchasing undervalued securities and shorting overvalued ones to neutralize market risk.

- *Short-selling funds*, which short-sell the securities of companies that they believe are overvalued.

- *Special situation funds* that invest in undervalued securities in anticipation of an increase in value resulting from a favorable turn of events.

These fund types employ very different strategies. But, for many, fundamental analysis of companies is the critical task. This chapter focuses on applying the tools we have developed in Part 2 of the book to analyze equity securities.

EQUITY SECURITY ANALYSIS AND MARKET EFFICIENCY

How a security analyst should invest his or her time depends on how quickly and efficiently information flows through markets and becomes reflected in security prices. In the extreme, information would be reflected in security prices fully and immediately upon its release. This is essentially the condition posited by the *efficient markets hypothesis*. This hypothesis states that security prices reflect all available information, as if such information could be costlessly digested and translated immediately into demands for buys or sells without regard to frictions imposed by transactions costs. Under such conditions, it would be impossible to identify mispriced securities on the basis of public information.

In a world of efficient markets, the expected return on any equity security is just enough to compensate investors for the unavoidable risk the security involves. Unavoidable risk is that which cannot be "diversified away" simply by holding a portfolio of many securities. Given efficient markets, the investor's strategy shifts away from the search for mispriced securities and focuses instead on maintaining a well-diversified portfolio. Aside from this, the investor must arrive at the desired balance between risky securities and risk-free short-term government bonds. The desired balance depends on how much risk the investor is willing to bear for a given increase in expected returns.

The above discussion implies that investors who accept that share prices already reflect available information have no need for analysis involving a search for mispriced securities. If all investors adopted this attitude, of course no such analysis would be conducted, mispricing would go uncorrected, and markets would no longer be efficient![3] This is why the efficient markets hypothesis cannot represent an equilibrium in a strict sense. In equilibrium there must be just enough mispricing to provide incentives for the investment of resources in security analysis.

The existence of some mispricing, even in equilibrium, does not imply that it is sensible for just anyone to engage in security analysis. Instead, it suggests that securities analysis is subject to the same laws of supply and demand faced in all other competitive industries: it will be rewarding only for those with the strongest comparative advantage. How many analysts are in that category depends on a number of factors, including the liquidity of a firm's shares and investor interest in the company.[4] For example, there are about 45 sell-side professional analysts who follow British Petroleum, a company with highly liquid shares and considerable investor interest. There are many other buy-side analysts who track the firm on their own account without issuing any formal reports to outsiders. For the smallest publicly traded firms in Europe, there is typically no formal following by analysts, and would-be investors and their advisors are left to form their own opinions on a security.

Market efficiency and the role of financial statement analysis

The degree of **market efficiency** that arises from competition among analysts and other market agents is an empirical issue addressed by a large body of research spanning the last three decades. Such research has important implications for the role of financial statements in security analysis. Consider for example the implications of an extremely efficient market, where information is fully impounded in prices within minutes of its revelation. In such a market, agents could profit from digesting financial statement information in two ways. First, the information would be useful to the select few who receive newly announced financial data, interpret it quickly, and trade on it within minutes. Second, and probably more important, the information would be useful for gaining an understanding of the firm, so as to place the analyst in a better position to interpret other news (from financial statements as well as other sources) as it arrives.

On the other hand, if securities prices fail to reflect financial statement data fully, even days or months after its public revelation, market agents could profit from such data by creating trading strategies designed to exploit any systematic ways in which the publicly available data are ignored or discounted in the price-setting process.

Market efficiency and managers' financial reporting strategies

The degree to which markets are efficient also has implications for managers' approaches to communicating with their investment communities. The issue becomes most important when the firm pursues an unusual strategy, or when the usual interpretation of financial statements would be misleading in the firm's context. In such a case, the communication avenues managers can successfully pursue depend not only on management's credibility, but also on the degree of understanding present in the investment community. We will return to the issue of management communications in more detail in Chapter 12.

Evidence of market efficiency

There is an abundance of evidence consistent with a high degree of efficiency in securities markets.[5] In fact, during the 1960s and 1970s, the evidence was so one-sided that the efficient markets hypothesis gained widespread acceptance within the academic community and had a major impact on the practicing community as well.

Evidence pointing to very efficient securities markets comes in several forms:

- When information is announced publicly, the markets react *very* quickly.
- It is difficult to identify specific funds or analysts who have consistently generated abnormally high returns.
- A number of studies suggest that share prices reflect a rather sophisticated level of fundamental analysis.

While a large body of evidence consistent with efficiency exists, recent years have witnessed a re-examination of the once widely accepted thinking. A sampling of the research includes the following:

- On the issue of the speed of share price response to news, a number of studies suggest that even though prices react quickly, the initial reaction tends to be incomplete.[6]

- A number of studies point to trading strategies that could have been used to outperform market averages.[7]

- Some related evidence – still subject to ongoing debate about its proper interpretation – suggests that, even though market prices reflect some relatively sophisticated analyses, prices still do not fully reflect all the information that could be garnered from publicly available financial statements.[8]

The controversy over the efficiency of securities markets is unlikely to be resolved soon. However, there are some lessons that are accepted by most researchers. First, securities markets not only reflect publicly available information, but they also anticipate much of it before it is released. The open question is what fraction of the response remains to be impounded in price once the day of the public release comes to a close. Second, even in most studies that suggest inefficiency, the degree of mispricing is relatively small for large firms.

Finally, even if some of the evidence is currently difficult to align with the efficient markets hypothesis, it remains a useful benchmark (at a minimum) for thinking about the behavior of security prices. The hypothesis will continue to play that role unless it can be replaced by a more complete theory. Some researchers are developing theories that encompass the existence of market agents who are forced to trade for unpredictable "liquidity" reasons, and prices that differ from so-called "fundamental values," even in equilibrium. Also, behavioral finance models recognize that cognitive biases can affect investor behavior.[9]

APPROACHES TO FUND MANAGEMENT AND SECURITIES ANALYSIS

Approaches used in practice to manage funds and analyze securities are quite varied. One dimension of variation is the extent to which the investments are actively or passively managed. Another variation is whether a quantitative or a traditional fundamental approach is used. Security analysts also vary considerably in terms of whether they produce formal or informal valuations of the firm.

Active versus passive management

Active portfolio management relies heavily on security analysis to identify mispriced securities. The passive portfolio manager serves as a price taker, avoiding the costs of security analysis and turnover while typically seeking to hold a portfolio designed to match some overall market index or sector performance. Combined approaches are also possible. For example, one may actively manage 20 percent of a fund balance while passively managing the remainder. The growing popularity of passively managed funds in Europe over the past 20 years serves as testimony to the growing belief that it is difficult to consistently earn returns that are superior to broad market indices.

Quantitative versus traditional fundamental analysis

Actively managed funds must depend on some form of security analysis. Some funds employ "technical analysis," which attempts to predict share price movements on the basis of market indicators (prior share price movements, volume, etc.). In contrast, "fundamental analysis," the primary approach to security analysis, attempts to evaluate the current market price relative to projections of the firm's future earnings and cash flow generating potential. Fundamental analysis involves all the steps described in the previous chapters of this book: business strategy analysis, accounting analysis, financial analysis, and prospective analysis (forecasting and valuation). In recent years, some analysts have supplemented traditional fundamental analysis, which involves a substantial amount of subjective judgment, with more quantitative approaches.

The quantitative approaches themselves are quite varied. Some involve simply "screening" shares on the basis of some set of factors, such as trends in analysts' earnings revisions, price-earnings ratios, price-book ratios, and so on. Whether such approaches are useful depends on the degree of market efficiency relative to the screens. Quantitative approaches can also involve implementation of some formal model to predict future stock returns. Longstanding statistical techniques such as regression analysis and probit analysis can be used, as can more recently developed computer-intensive techniques such as neural network analysis. Again, the success of these approaches depends on the degree of market efficiency and whether the analysis can exploit information in ways not otherwise available to market agents as a group.

Quantitative approaches play a more important role in security analysis today than they did a decade or two ago. However, by and large, analysts still rely primarily on the kind of fundamental analysis involving complex human judgments, as outlined in our earlier chapters.

Formal versus informal valuation

Full-scale, formal valuations based on the methods described in Chapter 7 have become more common, especially in recent years. However, less formal approaches are also possible. For example, an analyst can compare his or her long-term earnings projection with the consensus forecast to generate a buy or sell recommendation. Alternatively, an analyst might recommend a share because his or her earnings forecast appears relatively high in comparison to the current price. Another possible approach, that might be labeled "marginalist," involves no attempt to value the firm. The analyst simply assumes that if he or she has unearthed favorable (or unfavorable) information believed not to be recognized by others, the share should be bought (or sold).

Unlike many security analysts, investment bankers produce formal valuations as a matter of course. Investment bankers, who estimate values for purposes of bringing a private firm to the public market, for evaluating a merger or buyout proposal, for issuing a fairness opinion or for making a periodic managerial review, must document their valuation in a way that can readily be communicated to management and, if necessary, to the courts.

THE PROCESS OF A COMPREHENSIVE SECURITY ANALYSIS

Given the variety of approaches practiced in security analysis, it is impossible to summarize all of them here. Instead, we briefly outline **steps to be included in a comprehensive security analysis**. The amount of attention focused on any given step varies among analysts.

Selection of candidates for analysis

No analyst can effectively investigate more than a small fraction of the securities on a major exchange, and thus some approach to narrowing the focus must be employed. Sell-side analysts are often organized within an investment house by industry or sector. Thus they tend to be constrained in their choices of firms to follow. However, from the perspective of a fund manager or an investment firm as a whole, there is usually the freedom to focus on any firm or sector.

As noted earlier, funds typically specialize in investing in shares with certain risk profiles or characteristics (e.g. growth shares, "value" shares, technology shares, cyclical shares). Managers of these types of funds seek to focus the energies of their analysts on identifying shares that fit their fund objective. In addition, individual investors who seek to maintain a well-diversified portfolio without holding many shares also need information about the nature of a firm's risks and how they fit with the risk profile of their overall portfolio.

An alternative approach to security selection is to screen firms on the basis of some potential mispricing followed by a detailed analysis of only those shares that meet the specified criteria. For example, one fund managed by a large insurance company screens shares on the basis of recent "earnings momentum," as reflected in revisions in the earnings projections of sell-side and buy-side analysts. Upward revisions trigger investigations for possible purchase. The fund operates on the belief that earnings momentum is a positive signal of future price movements. Another fund complements the earnings momentum screen with one based on recent short-term share price movements, in the hopes of identifying earnings revisions not yet reflected in share prices.

KEY ANALYSIS QUESTIONS

Depending on whether fund managers follow a strategy of targeting equities with specific types of characteristics, or of screening shares that appear to be mispriced, the following types of questions are likely to be useful:

- What is the risk profile of a firm? How volatile is its earnings stream and share price? What are the key possible bad outcomes in the future? What is the upside potential? How closely linked are the firm's risks to the health of the overall economy? Are the risks largely diversifiable, or are they systematic?

- Does the firm possess the characteristics of a growth share? What is the expected pattern of sales and earnings growth for the coming years? Is the firm reinvesting most or all of its earnings?

- Does the firm match the characteristics desired by "income funds"? Is it a mature or maturing company, prepared to "harvest" profits and distribute them in the form of high dividends?

- Is the firm a candidate for a "value fund"? Does it offer measures of earnings, cash flow, and book value that are high relative to the price? What specific screening rules can be implemented to identify misvalued shares?

Inferring market expectations

If the security analysis is conducted with an eye toward the identification of mispricing, it must ultimately involve a comparison of the analyst's expectations with those of "the market." One possibility is to view the observed share price as the reflection of market expectations and to compare the analyst's own estimate of value with that price. However, a share price is only a "summary statistic." It is useful to have a more detailed idea of the market's expectations about a firm's future performance, expressed in terms of sales, earnings, and other measures. For example, assume that an analyst has developed new insights about a firm's near-term sales. Whether those insights represent new information for the stock market, and whether they indicate that a "buy" recommendation is appropriate, can be easily determined if the analyst knows the market consensus sales forecast.

Around the world a number of agencies summarize analysts' forecasts of sales and earnings. Forecasts for the next year or two are commonly available, and for many firms, a "long-run" earnings growth projection is also available – typically for three to five years. Some agencies provide continuous online updates to such data, so if an analyst revises a forecast,that can be made known to fund managers and other analysts within seconds.

As useful as analysts' forecasts of sales and earnings are, they do not represent a complete description of expectations about future performance, and there is no guarantee that consensus analyst forecasts are the same as those reflected in market prices. Further, financial analysts typically forecast performance for only a few years, so that even if these do reflect market expectations, it is helpful to understand what types of long-term forecasts are reflected in share prices. Armed with the models in Chapters 7 and 8 that express price as a function of future cash flows or earnings, an analyst can draw some educated inferences about the expectations embedded in share prices.

For example, consider the valuation of British Petroleum (BP). On March 31 2006, BP's share price was 661 pence. For the year ended December 31 2005, the company reported that earnings per share increased from 49 pence the prior year to 63 pence, reflecting the increase of crude oil prices to previously unseen levels. BP's book value of equity per share was 226 pence. By the end of March analysts were forecasting that BP would experience a slowdown in earnings growth in 2006, with earnings projected to grow by 5 percent to 66 pence. Modestly higher growth was projected for following years: 9 percent in 2007 (72 pence) and 8 percent per year for 2008 to 2010.[10] Analysts expected BP to pay out approximately 35 percent of its annual earnings in dividends.

How do consensus forecasts by analysts reconcile with the market valuation of BP? What are the market's implicit assumptions about the short-term and long-term earnings growth for the company? By altering the amounts for key value drivers and arriving at combinations that generate an estimated value equal to the observed market price, the analyst can infer what the market might have been expecting for BP in March 2006. Table 9.1 summarizes the combinations of earnings growth, book value growth, and cost of capital that generate prices comparable to the market price of 661 pence.

BP has an equity beta of 1.2. Given long-term UK government bond rates of 4.5 percent and a market risk premium of 5–6 percent, BP's cost of equity capital probably lies between 10.5 and 11.7 percent. In addition, the company's growth in book value has been 4 percent for the last year, which is close to the historical long-term book value growth rate for the economy. Critical questions for judging the market valuation of BP are (1) how quickly will the company's earnings return to the level reported in 2004, and (2) how quickly will earnings growth revert to the same level as average firms in the economy, historically around 4 percent. The analysis reported in Table 9.1 presents three scenarios for BP's earnings growth that are consistent with an observed market price of 661 pence. The three scenarios assume that earnings growth reverts to the economy average after 2010 and that BP's dividend payout ratio between 2006 and 2010 is 35 percent.

Table 9.1 shows the implications for BP's earnings growth between 2008 and 2010 if a reduction in oil prices drives down earnings in 2006 and 2007. This analysis indicates that with an 11.7 percent cost of equity and a rapid return to pre-2005 performance (i.e., 10 percent decline in 2006 and 2007), earnings need to grow by more than 18 percent per year between 2008 and 2010 to justify the 661 pence share price. However, if growth is

TABLE 9.1 Alternative assumptions about value drivers for BP consistent with the observed market price of 661 pence

	2006	2007	2008	2009	2010	Implied earnings per share in 2010
Assumed equity cost of capital of 10.5%						
Earnings growth:						
Scenario 1	5.0%	9.0%	− 0.3%	− 0.3%	− 0.3%	71 pence
Scenario 2	−10.0%	−10.0%	11.9%	11.9%	11.9%	72 pence
Scenario 3	2.5%	2.5%	2.5%	2.5%	2.5%	71 pence
Assumed equity cost of capital of 11.7%						
Earnings growth:						
Scenario 1	5.0%	9.0%	5.4%	5.4%	5.4%	84 pence
Scenario 2	−10.0%	−10.0%	18.4%	18.4%	18.4%	85 pence
Scenario 3	6.0%	6.0%	6.0%	6.0%	6.0%	84 pence

5 and 9 percent in 2006 and 2007 respectively, as the consensus predicts, expected earnings growth is close to the economy average (of 4 percent) for the next three years. The 661 pence share price is also consistent with a scenario that predicts constant earnings growth of 6.0 percent between 2006 and 2010. The value of BP's equity is computed as in Table 9.2. Because one quarter of the fiscal year has passed on March 31, two adjustments must be made in the analysis. First, the present value factor for the first five years equals $(1 - r_e)^{-(t - 0.25)}$. Second, the book value on March 31 is set equal to the book value on January 1 times $(1 + r_e)^{0.25}$.

Unless the analyst has good indications that oil prices will rebound after two years, given BP's 661 pence share price it is unlikely that the market anticipates that earnings will be hit by declining oil prices in 2006 and 2007. BP's share price more likely reflects the expectation that earnings growth will be moderate but stable in future years. This type of scenario analysis provides the analyst with insights about investors' expectations for BP, and is useful for judging whether the share is correctly valued. Security analysis need

TABLE 9.2 Computing the value of BP's equity

Year	Beginning book value	Earnings (6.0% annual growth)	Abnormal earnings (11.7% cost of equity)	PV factor	PV of abnormal earnings
2006	226.0p	66.8p	40.3p	0.9200	37.1p
2007	269.4	70.8	39.3	0.8236	32.3
2008	315.4	75.0	38.1	0.7374	28.1
2009	364.2	79.5	36.9	0.6601	24.4
2010	415.9	84.3	35.7	0.5910	21.1
After 2010			37.1	7.6752	284.6
Cumulative PV of abnormal earnings					427.6
+ Book value on March 31, 2006					232.3
= Equity value per share					659.8p

not involve such a detailed attempt to infer market expectations. However, whether or not an explicit analysis, a good analyst understands what economic scenarios could plausibly be reflected in the observed price.

KEY ANALYSIS QUESTIONS

By using the discounted abnormal earnings/ROE valuation model, analysts can infer the market's expectations for a firm's future performance. This permits analysts to ask whether the market is overvaluing or undervaluing a company. Typical questions that analysts might ask from this analysis include the following:

- What are the market's assumptions about long-term ROE and growth? For example, is the market forecasting that the company can grow its earnings without a corresponding level of expansion in its asset base (and hence equity)? If so, how long can this persist?

- How do changes in the cost of capital affect the market's assessment of the firm's future performance? If the market's expectations seem to be unexpectedly high or low, has the market reassessed the company's risk? If so, is this change plausible?

Developing the analyst's expectations

Ultimately, a security analyst must compare his or her own view of a share with the view embedded in the market price. The analyst's view is generated using the same tools discussed in Chapters 2 through to 8. The final product of this work is, of course, a forecast of the firm's future earnings and cash flows and an estimate of the firm's value. However, that final product is less important than the understanding of the business and its industry that the analysis provides. It is such understanding that enables the analyst to interpret new information as it arrives and to infer its implications.

KEY ANALYSIS QUESTIONS

In developing expectations about the firm's future performance using the financial analysis tools discussed throughout this book, the analyst is likely to ask the following types of questions:

- How profitable is the firm? In light of industry conditions, the firm's corporate strategy, and its barriers to competition, how sustainable is that rate of profitability?

- What are the opportunities for growth for this firm?

- How risky is this firm? How vulnerable are operations to general economic downturns? How highly levered is the firm? What does the riskiness of the firm imply about its cost of capital?

- How do answers to the above questions compare to the expectations embedded in the observed share price?

The final product of security analysis

For financial analysts, the final product of security analysis is a recommendation to buy, sell, or hold the share (or some more refined ranking). The recommendation is supported by a set of forecasts and a report summarizing the foundation for the recommendation. Analysts' reports often delve into significant detail and include an assessment of a firm's business as well as a line-by-line income statement, balance sheet, and cash flow forecasts for one or more years.

In making a recommendation to buy or sell a share, the analyst has to consider the investment time horizon required to capitalize on the recommendation. Are anticipated improvements in performance likely to be confirmed in the near-term, allowing investors to capitalize quickly on the recommendation? Or do expected performance improvements reflect long-term fundamentals that will take several years to play out? Longer investment horizons impose greater risk on investors that the company's performance will be affected by changes in economic conditions that cannot be anticipated by the analyst, reducing the value of the recommendation. Consequently, thorough analysis requires not merely being able to recognize whether a share is misvalued, but being able to anticipate when a price correction is likely to take place.

Because there are additional investment risks from following recommendations that require long-term commitments, security analysts tend to focus on making recommendations that are likely to pay off in the short-term. This potentially explains why so few analysts recommended selling dot-com and technology shares during the late 1990s when their prices would be difficult to justify on the basis of long-term fundamentals. It also explains why analysts recommended Enron's share at its peak, even though the kind of analysis performed in this chapter would have shown that the future growth and ROE performance implied by this price would be extremely difficult to achieve. It also implies that to take advantage of long-term fundamental analysis can often require access to patient, long-term capital.

PERFORMANCE OF SECURITY ANALYSTS AND FUND MANAGERS

There has been extensive research on the performance of security analysts and fund managers during the last three decades. A few of the key findings are summarized below.

Performance of security analysts

Despite the recent failure of security analysts to foresee the dramatic price declines for dot-com and telecommunications shares, and to detect the financial shenanigans and overvaluation of companies such as Ahold, Enron, and Parmalat, research shows that analysts generally add value in the capital market. Analyst earnings forecasts are more accurate than those produced by time-series models that use past earnings to predict future earnings.[11] Of course this should not be too surprising since analysts can update their earnings forecasts between quarters to incorporate new firm and economy information, whereas time-series models cannot. In addition, share prices tend to respond positively to upward revisions in analysts' earnings forecasts and recommendations, and negatively to downward revisions.[12] Finally, recent research finds that analysts play a valuable role in improving market efficiency. For example, share prices for firms with higher analyst following more rapidly incorporate information on accruals and cash flows than prices of less followed firms.[13]

Several factors seem to be important in explaining analysts' earnings forecast accuracy. Not surprisingly, forecasts of near-term earnings are much more accurate than those of long-term performance.[14] This probably explains why analysts typically make detailed forecasts for only one or two years ahead. Studies of differences in earnings forecast accuracy across analysts find that analysts that are more accurate tend to specialize by industry and by country and work for large well-funded firms that employ other analysts who follow the same industry.[15]

Although analysts perform a valuable function in the capital market, research shows that their forecasts and recommendations tend to be biased. Early evidence on bias indicated that analyst earnings forecasts tended to be optimistic and that their recommendations were almost exclusively for buys.[16] Several factors potentially explain this finding. First, security analysts at brokerage houses are typically compensated on the basis of the trading volume that their reports generate. Given the costs of short selling and the restrictions on short selling by many institutions, brokerage analysts have incentives to issue optimistic reports that encourage investors to buy shares rather than to issue negative reports that create selling pressure. Second, analysts that work for investment banks are rewarded for promoting public issues by current clients and for attracting new banking clients, creating incentives for optimistic forecasts and recommendations. Studies show that analysts that work for lead underwriters make more optimistic long-term earnings forecasts and recommendations for firms raising equity capital than unaffiliated analysts.[17]

Evidence indicates that during the late 1990s there was a marked decline in analyst optimism for forecasts of near-term earnings.[18] One explanation offered for this change is that during the late 1990s analysts relied heavily on private discussions with top management to make their earnings forecasts. Management allegedly used these personal connections to manage analysts' short-term expectations downward so that the firm could subsequently report earnings that beat analysts' expectations. In response to concerns about this practice, in October 2000 the US SEC approved Regulation Fair Disclosure, which prohibits management from making selective disclosures of nonpublic information. In Europe, the EU Transparency and Market Abuse Directives, adopted in 2004, may counter such practices, albeit less directly.

There also has been a general decline in sell-side analysts' optimistic recommendations during the past few years. Many large investment banks now require analysts to use a forced curve to rate shares, leading to a greater number of the lower ratings. Factors that underlie this change include a sharp rise in trading by hedge funds, which actively seek shares to short-sell. In contrast, traditional money management firms are typically restricted from short-selling, and are more interested in analysts' buy recommendations than their sells. Second, regulatory changes require tight separation between investment banking and equity research at investment banks.

Performance of fund managers

Measuring whether collective investment and pension fund managers earn superior returns is a difficult task for several reasons. First, there is no agreement about how to estimate benchmark performance for a fund. Studies have used a number of approaches – some have used the capital asset pricing model (CAPM) as a benchmark while others have used multifactor pricing models. For studies using the CAPM, there are questions about what type of market index to use. For example, should it be an equal- or value-weighted index, an exchange-related index or a broader market index? Second, many of the traditional measures of fund performance abstract from market-wide performance, which understates fund abnormal performance if fund managers can time the market by reducing portfolio risk prior to market declines and increasing risks before a market run-up. Third, given the overall volatility of stock returns, statistical power is an issue for measuring fund performance. Finally, tests of fund performance are likely to be highly sensitive to the time period examined. Value or momentum investing could therefore appear to be profitable depending on when the tests are conducted.

Perhaps because of these challenges, there is no consistent evidence that actively managed collective investment funds generate superior returns for investors. While some studies find evidence of positive abnormal returns for the industry, others conclude that returns are generally negative.[19] Of course, even if collective investment fund managers on average can only generate "normal" returns for investors, it is still possible for the best managers to show consistently strong performance. Some studies do in fact document that funds earning positive abnormal returns in one period continue to outperform in subsequent periods. However, more recent evidence suggests that these findings are caused by general momentum in stock returns and fund expenses rather than superior fund manager ability.[20] Researchers have also examined which, if any, investment strategies are most successful. However, no clear consensus appears – several studies have found that momentum and high turnover strategies generate superior returns, whereas others conclude that value strategies are better.[21]

Finally, recent research has examined whether fund managers tend to buy and sell many of the same shares at the same time. They conclude that there is evidence of "herding" behavior, particularly by momentum fund managers.[22] This could arise because managers have access to common information, because they are affected by similar cognitive biases, or because they have incentives to follow the crowd.[23] For example, consider the calculus of a fund manager who holds a share but who, through long-term fundamental analysis, estimates that it is misvalued. If the manager changes the fund's holdings accordingly and the share price returns to its intrinsic value in the next quarter, the fund will show superior relative portfolio performance and will attract new capital. However, if the share continues to be misvalued for several quarters, the informed fund manager will underperform the benchmark and capital will flow to other funds. In contrast, a risk-averse manager who simply follows the crowd will not be rewarded for detecting the misvaluation, but neither will this manager be blamed for a poor investment decision when the share price ultimately corrects, since other funds made the same mistake.

There has been considerably less research on the performance of pension fund managers. Overall, the findings show little consistent evidence that pension fund managers either overperform or underperform traditional benchmarks.[24]

SUMMARY

Equity security analysis is the evaluation of a firm and its prospects from the perspective of a current or potential investor in the firm's shares. Security analysis is one component of a larger investment process that involves:

1 Establishing the objectives of the investor or fund.

2 Forming expectations about the future returns and risks of individual securities.

3 Combining individual securities into portfolios to maximize progress toward the investment objectives.

Some security analysis is devoted primarily to assuring that a share possesses the proper risk profile and other desired characteristics prior to inclusion in an investor's portfolio. However, especially for many professional buy-side and sell-side security analysts, the analysis is also directed toward the identification of mispriced securities. In equilibrium, such activity will be rewarding for those with the strongest comparative advantage. They will be the ones able to identify any mispricing at the lowest cost and exert pressure on the price to correct the mispricing. What kinds of efforts are productive in this domain depends on the degree of market efficiency. A large body of evidence exists that is supportive of a high degree of efficiency in stock markets, but recent evidence has reopened the debate on this issue.

In practice, a wide variety of approaches to fund management and security analysis are employed. However, at the core of the analyses are the same steps outlined in Chapters 2 through to 8 of this book: business strategy analysis, accounting analysis, financial analysis, and prospective analysis (forecasting and valuation). For the professional analyst, the final product of the work is, of course, a forecast of the firm's future earnings and cash flows, and an estimate of the firm's value. But that final product is less important than the understanding of the business and its industry that the analysis provides. It is such understanding that positions the analyst to interpret new information as it arrives and infer its implications.

Finally, the chapter summarizes some key findings of the research on the performance of both sell-side and buy-side security analysts.

CORE CONCEPTS

Active versus passive portfolio management Active portfolio management involves the use of security analysis to identify mispriced securities; passive portfolio management implies holding a portfolio of securities to match the risk and return of a market or sector index.

Collective investment funds Funds selling shares in professionally managed portfolios of securities with similar risk, return and/or style characteristics.

Market efficiency Degree to which security prices reflect all available information. Market inefficiencies can lead to security mispricing and increase opportunities for earning abnormal investment returns through the use of comprehensive security analysis.

Security analysis Projecting future returns and assessing risks of a security with the objective of identifying mispriced securities or understanding how the security affects the risk, return and style characteristics of a portfolio.

Steps of security analysis Comprehensive security analysis consists of the following steps:

1 Selection of candidates for analysis on the basis of risk, return or style characteristics, industry membership or mispricing indicators.

2 Inferring market expectations about the firm's future profitability and growth from the current security price.

3 Developing expectations about the firm's profitability and growth using the four steps of business analysis.

4 Making an investment decision after comparing own expectations with those of the market.

QUESTIONS

1 Despite many years of research, the evidence on market efficiency described in this chapter appears to be inconclusive. Some argue that this is because researchers have been unable to link company fundamentals to share prices precisely. Comment.

2 Geoffrey Henley, a professor of finance, states: "The capital market is efficient. I don't know why anyone would bother devoting their time to following individual shares and doing fundamental analysis. The best approach is to buy and hold a well-diversified portfolio of shares." Do you agree? Why or why not?

3 What is the difference between fundamental and technical analysis? Can you think of any trading strategies that use technical analysis? What are the underlying assumptions made by these strategies?

4 Investment funds follow many different types of investment strategies. Income funds focus on shares with high dividend yields, growth funds invest in shares that are expected to have high capital appreciation, value funds follow shares that are considered to be undervalued, and short funds bet against shares they consider to be overvalued. What types of investors are likely to be attracted to each of these types of funds? Why?

5 Intergalactic Software Plc went public three months ago. You are a sophisticated investor who devotes time to fundamental analysis as a way of identifying mispriced shares. Which of the following characteristics would you focus on in deciding whether to follow this share?

- The market capitalization.
- The average number of shares traded per day.
- The bid–ask spread for the share.
- Whether the underwriter that took the firm public is a Top Five investment banking firm.
- Whether its audit company is a Big Four firm.
- Whether there are analysts from major brokerage firms following the company.
- Whether the share is held mostly by retail or institutional investors.

6 There are two major types of financial analysts: buy-side and sell-side. Buy-side analysts work for investment firms and make recommendations that are available only to the management of funds within that firm. Sell-side analysts work for brokerage firms and make recommendations that are used to sell shares to the brokerage firms' clients, which include individual investors and managers of investment funds. What would be the differences in tasks and motivations of these two types of analysts?

7 Many market participants believe that sell-side analysts are too optimistic in their recommendations to buy shares and too slow to recommend sells. What factors might explain this bias?

8 Joe Klein is an analyst for an investment banking firm that offers both underwriting and brokerage services. Joe sends you a highly favorable report on a share that his firm recently helped go public and for which it currently makes the market. What are the potential advantages and disadvantages in relying on Joe's report in deciding whether to buy the share?

9 Intergalactic Software's shares have a market price of €20 per share and a book value of €12 per share. If its cost of equity capital is 15 percent and its book value is expected to grow at 5 percent per year indefinitely, what is the market's assessment of its steady state return on equity? If the share price increases to €35 and the market does not expect the firm's growth rate to change, what is the revised steady state

ROE? If instead the price increase was due to an increase in the market's assessments about long-term book value growth rather than long-term ROE, what would the price revision imply for the steady state growth rate?

10. Joe states, "I can see how ratio analysis and valuation help me do fundamental analysis, but I don't see the value of doing strategy analysis." Can you explain to him how strategy analysis could be potentially useful?

NOTES

1. OEIC stands for "Open-Ended Investment Company" and is a UK collective investment fund. SICAV stands for "Société d'Investissement à Capital Variable" and is an open-ended collective investment fund in France and Luxembourg. BEVEK stands for "Beleggingsvennootschap met Veranderlijk Kapitaal" and is an open-ended collective investment fund in Belgium.

2. Investment-grade rated bonds have received a credit rating by Moody's of Baa or above and/or a credit rating by Standard & Poor's of BBB or above. We discuss these rating categories in more detail in Chapter 10.

3. P. Healy and K. Palepu, "The Fall of Enron," *Journal of Economic Perspectives* 17, No. 2 (Spring 2003): 3–26, discuss how weak money manager incentives and long-term analysis contributed to the share price run-up and subsequent collapse for Enron. A similar discussion on factors affecting the rise and fall of dot-com shares is provided in "The Role of Capital Market Intermediaries in the Dot-Com Crash of 2000," Harvard Business School Case 9–101–110, 2001.

4. See R. Bhushan, "Firm Characteristics and Analyst Following," *Journal of Accounting and Economics* 11 (2/5), July 1989: 255–275, and P. O'Brien and R. Bhushan, "Analyst Following and Institutional Ownership," *Journal of Accounting Research* 28, Supplement (1990): 55–76.

5. Recent reviews of evidence on market efficiency are provided by E. Fama, "Efficient Capital Markets: II," *Journal of Finance* 46 (December 1991): 1575–1617; S. Kothari, "Capital Markets Research in Accounting," *Journal of Accounting and Economics* 31 (September 2001): 105–231; and C. Lee, "Market Efficiency in Accounting Research," *Journal of Accounting and Economics* 31 (September 2001): 233–253.

6. For example, see V. Bernard and J. Thomas, "Evidence That Stock Prices Do Not Fully Reflect the Implications of Current Earnings for Future Earnings," *Journal of Accounting and Economics* 13 (December 1990): 305–341.

7. Examples of studies that examine a "value share" strategy include J. Lakonishok, A. Shleifer, and R. Vishny, "Contrarian Investment, Extrapolation, and Risk," *Journal of Finance* 49 (December 1994): 1541–1578, and R. Frankel and C. Lee, "Accounting Valuation, Market Expectation, and Cross-Sectional Stock Returns," *Journal of Accounting and Economics* 25 (June 1998): 283–319.

8. For example, see J. Ou and S. Penman, "Financial Statement Analysis and the Prediction of Stock Returns," *Journal of Accounting and Economics* 11 (November 1989): 295–330; R. Holthausen and D. Larcker, "The Prediction of Stock Returns Using Financial Statement Information," *Journal of Accounting and Economics* 15 (June/September 1992): 373–412; and R. Sloan, "Do Stock Prices Fully Reflect Information in Accruals and Cash Flows about Future Earnings?" *The Accounting Review* 71 (July 1996): 298–325.

9. For an overview of research in behavioral finance, see *Advances in Behavioral Finance* by R. Thaler (New York: Russell Sage Foundation, 1993), and *Inefficient Markets: An Introduction to Behavioral Finance* by A. Shleifer (Oxford: Oxford University Press, 2000).

10. These forecasts were taken from multexinvestor.com.

11. Time-series model forecasts of future annual earnings are the most recent annual earnings (with or without some form of annual growth), and forecasts of future quarterly earnings are a function of growth in earnings for the latest quarter relative to both the last quarter and the same quarter one year ago. See L. Brown and M. Rozeff, "The Superiority of Analyst Forecasts as Measures of Expectations: Evidence from Earnings," *Journal of Finance* 33 (1978): 1–16; L. Brown, P. Griffin, R. Hagerman, and M. Zmijewski, "Security Analyst Superiority Relative to Univariate Time-Series Models in Forecasting Quarterly Earnings," *Journal of Accounting and Economics* 9 (1987): 61–87;

and D. Givoly, "Financial Analysts' Forecasts of Earnings: A Better Surrogate for Market Expectations," *Journal of Accounting and Economics* 4, No. 2 (1982): 85–108.

12. See D. Givoly and J. Lakonishok, "The Information Content of Financial Analysts' Forecasts of Earnings: Some Evidence on Semi-Strong Efficiency," *Journal of Accounting and Economics* 2 (1979): 165–186; T. Lys and S. Sohn, "The Association Between Revisions of Financial Analysts' Earnings Forecasts and Security Price Changes," *Journal of Accounting and Economics* 13 (1990): 341–364; and J. Francis and L. Soffer, "The Relative Informativeness of Analysts' Stock Recommendations and Earnings Forecast Revisions," *Journal of Accounting Research* 35, No. 2 (1997): 193–212.

13. See M. Barth and A. Hutton, "Information Intermediaries and the Pricing of Accruals," working paper, Stanford University, 2000.

14. See P. O'Brien, "Forecasts Accuracy of Individual Analysts in Nine Industries," *Journal of Accounting Research* 28 (1990): 286–304.

15. See G. Bolliger, "The Characteristics of Individual Analysts' Forecasts in Europe," *Journal of Banking and Finance* 28 (2004): 2283–2309; M. Clement, "Analyst Forecast Accuracy: Do Ability, Resources, and Portfolio Complexity Matter?" *Journal of Accounting and Economics* 27 (1999): 285–304; J. Jacob, T. Lys, and M. Neale, "Experience in Forecasting Performance of Security Analysts," *Journal of Accounting and Economics* 28 (1999): 51–82; and S. Gilson, P. Healy, C. Noe, and K. Palepu, "Analyst Specialization and Conglomerate Stock Breakups," *Journal of Accounting Research* 39 (December 2001): 565–573.

16. See L. Brown, G. Foster, and E. Noreen, "Security Analyst Multi-Year Earnings Forecasts and the Capital Market," *Studies in Accounting Research*, No. 23, (Sarasota, FL) American Accounting Association, 1985. M. McNichols and P. O'Brien, in "Self-Selection and Analyst Coverage," *Journal of Accounting Research,* Supplement (1997): 167–208, find that analyst bias arises primarily because analysts issue recommendations on firms for which they have favorable information and withhold recommending firms with unfavorable information.

17. See H. Lin and M. McNichols, "Underwriting Relationships, Analysts' Earnings Forecasts and Investment Recommendations," *Journal of Accounting and Economics* 25, No. 1 (1998): 101–128; R. Michaely and K. Womack, "Conflict of Interest and the Credibility of Underwriter Analyst Recommendations," *Review of Financial Studies* 12, No. 4 (1999): 653–686; and P. Dechow, A. Hutton, and R. Sloan, "The Relation Between Analysts' Forecasts of Long-Term Earnings Growth and Stock Price Performance Following Equity Offerings," *Contemporary Accounting Research* 17, No. 1 (2000): 1–32.

18. See L. Brown, "Analyst Forecasting Errors: Additional Evidence," *Financial Analysts' Journal* (November/December 1997): 81–88, and D. Matsumoto, "Management's Incentives to Avoid Negative Earnings Surprises," *The Accounting Review* 77 (July 2002): 483–515.

19. For example, evidence of superior fund performance is reported by M. Grinblatt and S. Titman, "Mutual Fund Performance: An Analysis of Quarterly Holdings," *Journal of Business* 62 (1994), and by D. Hendricks, J. Patel, and R. Zeckhauser, "Hot Hands in Mutual Funds: Short-Run Persistence of Relative Performance," *The Journal of Finance* 48 (1993): 93–130. In contrast, negative fund performance is shown by M. Jensen, "The Performance of Mutual Funds in the Period 1945–64," *The Journal of Finance* 23 (May 1968): 389–416, and B. Malkiel, "Returns from Investing in Equity Mutual Funds from 1971 to 1991," *Journal of Finance* 50 (June 1995): 549–573.

20. M. Grinblatt and S. Titman, "The Persistence of Mutual Fund Performance," *Journal of Finance* 47 (December 1992): 1977–1986, and D. Hendricks, J. Patel, and R. Zeckhauser, "Hot Hands in Mutual Funds: Short-Run Persistence of Relative Performance," *Journal of Finance* 48 (March 1993): 93–130, find evidence of persistence in mutual fund returns. However, M. Carhart, "On Persistence in Mutual Fund Performance," *The Journal of Finance* 52 (March 1997): 57–83, shows that much of this is attributable to momentum in stock returns and to fund expenses; B. Malkiel, "Returns from Investing in Equity Mutual Funds from 1971 to 1991," *The Journal of Finance* 50 (June 1995): 549–573, shows that survivorship bias is also an important consideration.

21. See M. Grinblatt, S. Titman, and R. Wermers, "Momentum Investment Strategies, Portfolio Performance, and Herding: A Study of Mutual Fund Behavior," *The American Economic Review* 85 (December 1995): 1088–1105.

22. For example, J. Lakonishok, A. Shleifer, and R. Vishny, "Contrarian Investment, Extrapolation, and Risk," *Journal of Finance* 49 (December 1994): 1541–1579, find that value funds show superior performance, whereas M. Grinblatt, S. Titman, and R. Wermers, "Momentum Investment Strategies, Portfolio Performance, and Herding: A Study of Mutual Fund Behavior," *The American Economic Review* 85 (December 1995): 1088–1105, find that momentum investing is profitable.

23. See D. Scharfstein and J. Stein, "Herd Behavior and Investment," *The American Economic Review* 80 (June 1990): 465–480, and P. Healy and K. Palepu, "The Fall of Enron," *Journal of Economic Perspectives* 17, no. 2 (Spring 2003): 3–26.

24. For evidence on performance by pension fund managers, see J. Lakonishok, A. Shleifer, and R. Vishny, "The Structure and Performance of the Money Management Industry," *Brookings Papers on Economic Activity*, Washington, DC American Accounting Association (1992): 339–392; T. Coggin, F. Fabozzi, and S. Rahman, "The Investment Performance of U.S. Equity Pension Fund Managers: An Empirical Investigation," *The Journal of Finance* 48 (July 1993): 1039–1056; and W. Ferson and K. Khang, "Conditional Performance Measurement Using Portfolio Weights: Evidence for Pension Funds," *Journal of Financial Economics* 65 (August 2002): 249–282.

Valuation at Novartis

In early 2007, Novartis announced record annual earnings of $7.2 billion for the year ended December 31, 2006, representing a 17% increase over the prior year. The company's return on beginning book equity of 21.7% far exceeded the company's estimate of its cost of equity (8.5%). Further, since 2003, the company had grown earnings by an average of 17% per year, and its return on beginning book equity had increased steadily from 16.8%. Despite this superior performance, the company's stock performance had lagged that of the S&P500 and Swiss Market indexes, growing by an average of 10% per year (see **Exhibit 1**). In addition, its price-to-earnings multiple had declined steadily from 22.9 2003 to 19.4 in 2006 (see **Exhibit 9**).

Several explanations for the gap between the company's earnings and stock performance were plausible. First, given the sustained strong performance of the pharmaceutical industry and the company's past success, market expectations were likely to be high. Merely meeting those heady expectations would generate only normal stock price appreciation. A second explanation was that the market questioned whether Novartis could sustain such strong performance, perhaps because of heightened regulatory oversight and proposed changes in the U.S. medical system, or as a result of concerns about the viability of the company's unique strategy of investing in both branded pharmaceuticals and generics. Finally, it was possible that investors had under-estimated Novartis and the stock was undervalued. For Novartis's management, understanding which of these best explained the company's situation was a necessary first step before deciding on an appropriate course of action.

The pharmaceutical industry

The pharmaceutical industry had an impressive track record of generating strong growth and returns for shareholders over an extended period. From 2003 to 2006, the industry reported revenue and earnings growth of 11% per year, and had an average return on book equity of 17.5%.[1] Two forces had combined to help create this sustained high performance. First, the industry had been remarkably successful in creating new innovative drugs to address patient needs. This was a costly process. Only one in 5,000 to 10,0000 compounds tested in the laboratory reached the market, and of these only 30% were a commercial success.[2] As a result of extensive testing and regulatory approval to ensure drug efficacy and safety, total drug development time lasted around fourteen years and cost more than $800 million per drug. On average, in 2006 pharmaceutical companies spent

Professor Paul Healy prepared this case. This case was developed from published sources. HBS cases are developed solely as the basis for class discussion. Cases are not intended to serve as endorsements, sources of primary data, or illustrations of effective or ineffective management.

[1] Source: Capital IQ.
[2] See "Pharmaceutical Industry Profile 2007," Pharmaceutical Research and Manufacturers of America website, www.phrma.org/publications.

$55.2 billion (17.5% of sales) on research and development.[3] However, patent protection of new compounds prevented competitors from copying successful new innovations and enabled innovators to recover the heavy costs of drug discovery and development. The average effective patent life for branded drugs was 11.5 years.[4]

A second factor behind the industry's performance was its strong sales and marketing capability. On average, pharmaceutical companies spent around 30% of sales on sales and marketing costs. In many markets, drug companies employed an army of sales reps who visited doctors to convince them to prescribe their firms' drugs. However, given the time constraints faced by physicians, sales rep visits were typically short, enabling the reps to drop off promotional materials and free sample drugs. Drug companies therefore frequently organized educational conferences, dinners and other events to enable sales reps to spend time with doctors. Firms also appealed directly to patients by consumer advertizing. By 2005, direct-to-consumer advertising was $4.2 billion.[5]

In early 2007, the pharmaceutical industry faced a number of challenges. Public concern over the cost of medical care and drugs had escalated, particularly in the U.S., the most expensive (and also most profitable) health care market in the world. For the first time in fifteen years politicians had seriously begun debating whether the health care system in the U.S. needed to be changed. Candidates for the 2008 presidential elections from both political parties were in the process of developing new health care initiatives to solve dual problems of a large uninsured population and the increased cost of health care. While increased access to health care could potentially benefit the pharmaceutical industry, there was also a significant risk that changes would increase the power of health care providers (including federal and state governments) which would use their leverage to obtain price cuts of as much as 40%, reducing the industry's profitability and the financial resources available for developing new drugs.

A second challenge had emerged following publication of research showing adverse cardiac risks for patients using Merck's blockbuster Vioxx painkiller. Merck had voluntarily withdrawn Vioxx from the market in September 2004 following the publication. However, research findings from a 2001 study presented to the company also showed cardiac risks, leading critics to allege that the company had over-promoted the drug and underplayed its risks. By early 2007, roughly 22,000 lawsuits in U.S. state and federal courts had been filed against Merck. Analysts estimated that company's legal liabilities could range from $4 billion to more than $25 billion. Merck opted to defend each suit separately on its merits. Of the 17 cases tried as of March 28, 2007, Merck won ten, lost five, and two had ended in mistrials.[6] Merck planned to or had appealed the cases it had lost. However, the problems had increased pressure on the Food and Drug Administration, which regulated drug approvals in the U.S., to be more cautious in approving new drugs and to respond more promptly to drug safety questions.

In addition, it appeared that the industry was becoming less productive in discovering and commercializing new drugs to replace those going off patent. Drug development costs had increased from $54 million per new drug in 1976 to $231 million in 1987 and to $802 million in 2001.[7] A study by Bain & Co. discovered that by 2003, only one in thirteen drugs that reached animal testing actually reached the market, down from one in eight in the late 1990s. Opinions were divided on the causes of this decline. Some argued that it was becoming more difficult to discover breakthrough drugs. Others pointed to increased regulatory oversight to improve drug safety. Despite questions about research productivity, spending on R&D continued to grow, both in dollar terms and as a percent of sales. In

---

[3]Ibid.

[4]Ibid.

[5]Julie M. Donohue, Marisa Cevasco, and Meredith B. Rosenthal, "A Decade of Direct-to-Consumer Advertising of Prescription Drugs," *New England Journal of Medicine*, Vol. 357 (August 16, 2007): 673–681.

[6]Standard & Poor's Healthcare, "Pharmaceuticals Industry Survey," May 10, 2007.

[7]"Pharmaceutical Industry Profile 2007," Pharmaceutical Research and Manufacturers of America website, www.phrma.org/publications.

2006, industry R&D totaled $55.2 billion, a 7.8% increase over the prior year. As a percentage of sales, R&D increased from 12.9% in 1985 to 17.5% in 2006.[8]

Finally, the industry faced increased pricing pressure from generics companies that produced and marketed drugs for which patent protection had expired. Generics drugs sold at 30% to 90% discounts relative to prices of brand-name drugs prior to patent expiration. Analysts estimated that in the first year after patent expiration, a brand-name drug could lose more than 80% of its volume to generics. The generics share of the U.S. prescription drug market had grown from 19% in 1994 to 47% in 2000 and 54% in 2005.[9] This growth was driven by managed care providers, which substituted generics drugs for the brand names to reduce costs. Generics companies followed a very different business model than traditional pharma companies. They spent much less on research and development, and on marketing and sales. Their focus was on aggressively challenging existing brand name drugs about to lose patent protection since the first to market was granted six-month period of market exclusivity. Once this six month period ended, however, other generics firms were free to enter the market, leading to intense competition.

Novartis

Novartis was founded in 1996 through the merger of Ciba-Geigy and Sandoz. Under the leadership of Daniel Vasella, who was appointed CEO in 1999, Novartis grew through a combination of successful new drug discoveries and selected acquisitions. From 1999 to 2006, revenues increased from $20.4 billion to $36 billion, and operating earnings grew from $4.6 to $8.1 billion (see **Exhibit 2** for Novartis's income statement and balance sheet data for the period 1999 to 2006).[10] During this period Novartis was among the industry leaders in introducing new drugs, including Femura (for breast cancer), Excelon (for Alzheimers), Diovan/Co-Diovan (for hypertension), Visudyne (for age-related macular degeneration), Gleevac/Gilvec (for chronic myeloid leukemia), and Zometa (for cancer complications).[11] It also successfully refocused by divesting its agribusiness and made several key acquisitions, including contact lens maker Wesley Jessen for $845 million in 2000, generics companies Lek ($959 million in 2002), Eon and Hexal ($8.4 billion in 2005), and Chiron, a biopharmaceutical, vaccine and diagnostics firm for $6.3 billion in 2006.[12]

By early 2007, Novartis comprised four divisions: Pharmaceuticals, Sandoz (its generics business), Consumer Health, and Vaccines and Diagnostics. The company's strategy was to provide customers with a full complement of the health care products they needed, including branded drugs, generic drugs, vaccines, and over-the-counter medicines.

Pharmaceuticals, the largest division with sales of $26.6 billion, boasted highly successful drugs in the cardiovascular, oncology and neuroscience areas (see **Exhibit 3** for data on the company's top twenty drug sales and **Exhibit 4** for sales by drug maturity). Sales growth at Pharma exceeded 12% for 2006 with profit margins of 28.7%. The unit's strong performance was expected to continue in 2007 and 2008 with approvals pending in the U.S. and Europe for a number of new drugs, including Exforge and Tekturna (hypertension), Galvus (type 2 diabetes), and Lucentis (for blindness). A total of 138 new projects were in progress at the end of 2006, 36% classified as new molecular entities, and the remainder as life cycle management projects. Fifteen projects had been submitted to regulatory authorities, thirteen were in phase III (large clinical trials), and another 76 were in phase II clinical trials.[13] The company's major competitors in this sector included

[8]Ibid.
[9]"Insights 2006, Highlights from the Pharmaceutical Industry Profile," Pharmaceutical Research and Manufacturers of America website, www.phrma.org/publications.
[10]Source: Novartis annual reports, 1999 to 2006.
[11]Ibid.
[12]Source: Capital IQ.
[13]Source: Novartis 2006 annual report.

GlaxoSmithKline, Johnson & Johnson, Merck, and Pfizer (**see Exhibit 5** for data on the performance of these firms).

Sandoz, with sales of $5.6 billion in 2006, was the world's second-largest generics business. In 2003, Novartis consolidated its different generics businesses using the Sandoz brand. It subsequently invested in building the generics business with acquisitions of Lek, Hexal and Eon. Novartis was the only major pharma company with a generics drug business. In commenting on the strategy, CEO Vasella explained that the company viewed "generic medicines as a critical complement to innovative medicines. Large purchasers like Wal-Mart, and private and state-run health care providers want to buy a range of generic and patented products."[14] Also, generic drugs were projected to increase their market share as patents for many large drug companies were scheduled to expire in the U.S. market. However, some analysts expressed doubts about the move, pointing out that "competition is high in the (generics) sector, fueled by the entry of low-cost producers from emerging markets like India which (has) hurt (generic drug) margins and profitability."[15] In 2006, Sandoz sales grew by 27% and operating profit margins increased to 12% as a result of the completion of the Hexal and Eon acquisitions, and rapid growth in the U.S. and Eastern European markets. Key competitors in this sector included Teva Pharmaceutical Industries, Watson Pharmaceuticals, and a range of smaller companies (see **Exhibit 6** for data on the performance of key competitors in the industry).

The Consumer Health division included several businesses, Over-the-Counter (OTC), Animal Health, CIBA Vision, and Gerber. In 2006, the group's Medical Nutrition unit was sold to Nestle for $2.5 billion. Consumer Health sales from continuing operations grew by 8% to $6.5 billion. This was led by strong performance in OTC, which jumped from sixth largest in sales to the fourth largest in the world, and in Animal Health which jumped three positions to number five. The group's other major business units included eye lens firm CIBA Vision and Gerber, the leading baby nutrition company in the U.S. Key competitors in this sector included Johnson & Johnson, Schering-Plough, Reckitt and Benkiser, and Pfizer (see **Exhibit 7** for data on the performance of key competitors).

The Vaccines and Diagnostics unit arose from the acquisition of Chiron. 2006 sales for the post-acquisition eight months were $956 million, up 42% over the comparable period for 2005. This increase was driven by a sharp increase in influenza vaccines in the U.S. market. Novartis reported that given novel new products and innovations in manufacturing technologies it anticipated double digit growth in this segment during the following decade. Key competitors in this sector included Johnson & Johnson, Sanofi-Aventis, Merck, and Abbott Laboratories (see **Exhibit 8** for data on the performance of competitors).

Valuation

The healthcare industry had experienced declining stock multiples from 2003 to 2006. Price-to-earnings multiples during the period had dropped steadily from 47.8 to 33.0, despite strong earnings growth in 2006. Price-to-book multiples had declined from 6.0 to 4.0 during the same period despite sustained strong returns on book equity (see **Exhibit 9**).

In early 2007, Novartis's price to earnings multiple was higher than that of three of its five leading competitors (GlaxoSmithKline, Pfizer and Johnson & Johnson). Yet its price to book multiple was lower than that all but Pfizer (see **Exhibit 10**). Despite continued strong earnings performance, its record of new drug introductions, and its strong pipeline of future new drugs, management was puzzled by the stock's three-year record of merely tracking the S&P index. What assumptions was the market making about Novartis's future performance? How were questions about the future of the industry, and the company's unique strategy affecting its valuation? And what actions if any should the company's management team take to respond to market's assessments?

[14]Tom Wright, "Novartis to become generics leader," *International Herald Tribune*, February 22, 2005.
[15]Ibid.

EXHIBIT 1 **Stock performance for Novartis and indexes for the period 2003 to 2006**

	Novartis	Swiss Market Index	S&P 500 Index	Morgan Stanley World Pharmaceutical Index
2003	13%	21%	26%	3%
2004	4%	5%	9%	−8%
2005	22%	36%	3%	19%
2006	2%	17%	14%	7%
Average	10%	20%	13%	5%

Source: Novartis 2006 annual report for performance of Novartis stock, Swiss market index, and Pharmaceutical Index, and Standard & Poor's for S&P500 Index.

Valuation at Novartis

Valuation at Novartis

EXHIBIT 2 Novartis's income statement for the years ended December 31, 1999 to 2006 in $US millions

	1999	2000	2001	2002	2003	2004	2005	2006
Total Revenue	20,380	21,846	18,762	20,877	24,930	27,277	31,319	36,749
Cost of Goods Sold	6,166	6,321	4,744	4,994	6,457	6,700	8,259	10,299
Gross Profit	**14,214**	**15,525**	**14,018**	**15,883**	**18,473**	**20,577**	**23,060**	**26,450**
Selling General & Administrative Expense	6,939	7,785	7,153	7,883	9,235	9,989	11,078	12,411
R&D Expense	2,665	2,874	2,528	2,843	3,729	4,152	4,493	5,349
Other Operating Expense	—	—	—	65	15	270	350	548
Operating Income	**4,609**	**4,865**	**4,337**	**5,092**	**5,494**	**6,166**	**7,139**	**8,142**
Interest Expense	(340)	(315)	(218)	(194)	(243)	(261)	(294)	(266)
Interest and Invest. Income	725	705	404	484	340	400	408	375
Net Interest Expense	**385**	**391**	**186**	**290**	**97**	**139**	**114**	**109**
Income/(Loss) from Affiliates	240	60	83	(7)	(279)	68	193	264
Currency Exchange Gains (Loss)	(213)	(124)	(152)	69	64	95	115	38
Other Non-Operating Inc. (Expense)	(68)	(77)	(86)	333	272	(66)	(107)	(316)
EBT Excl. Unusual Items	4,953	5,115	4,368	5,777	5,648	6,402	7,454	8,237
EBT Incl. Unusual Items	5,347	5,599	4,692	5,698	5,734	6,410	7,162	8,301
Income Tax Expense	1,151	1,123	844	959	947	1,045	1,090	1,282
Minority Int. in Earnings	(17)	(26)	(12)	(14)	(44)	(15)	(11)	(27)
Earnings from Continuing Operations	**4,180**	**4,450**	**3,836**	**4,725**	**4,743**	**5,350**	**6,061**	**6,992**
Earnings of Discontinued Operations	—	—	—	—	—	15	69	183
Net Income	**4,180**	**4,450**	**3,836**	**4,725**	**4,743**	**5,365**	**6,130**	**7,175**
Per Share Items								
Basic EPS	$1.575	$1.703	$1.492	$1.878	$1.993	$2.278	$2.628	$3.059
Basic EPS Excluding Extra Items	1.575	1.703	1.492	1.878	1.993	2.271	2.598	2.981
Weighted Average Basic Shares Outstanding	2,653.8	2,613.5	2,571.7	2,515.3	2,380.1	2,355.5	2,332.8	2,345.2
Dividends per Share	$0.5	$0.52	$0.54	$0.68	$0.8	$0.86	$0.94	$1.11
Payout Ratio %	29.1%	28.6%	33.1%	28.9%	35.0%	35.3%	34.4%	28.6%

Source: Standard & Poor's Capital IQ data.

EXHIBIT 2   Novartis's balance sheet for the years ended December 31, 1999 to 2006 in $US millions (*continued*)

	1999	2000	2001	2002	2003	2004	2005	2006
ASSETS								
Cash and Short-Term Investments	10,250	12,667	13,346	12,542	13,259	13,358	10,449	7,848
Accounts Receivable	4,420	3,261	3,223	4,982	5,480	6,334	6,663	8,041
Inventory	4,323	2,544	2,477	2,963	3,346	3,558	3,725	4,498
Other Current Assets	2,776	1,858	1,544	328	188	670	606	1,017
Total Current Assets	21,770	20,330	20,590	20,815	22,273	23,920	21,443	21,404
Net Property, Plant & Equipment	7,323	5,573	5,458	6,321	7,597	8,497	8,679	10,945
Long-term Investments	4,967	1,864	5,362	7,789	8,362	9,206	8,996	8,424
Goodwill	963	1,276	1,382	1,704	1,477	1,899	7,279	10,659
Other Intangibles	1,044	2,313	2,563	2,691	3,231	3,430	5,177	8,205
Deferred Charges, Long Term	11	9	—	—	—	300	838	2,366
Other Long-Term Assets	2,896	2,547	2,917	3,527	3,976	3,001	2,757	4,468
Total Assets	41,134	35,919	40,222	45,025	49,317	52,488	57,732	68,008
LIABILITIES								
Accounts Payable	1,237	982	1,090	1,266.	1,665	2,020	1,961	2,487
Short-term Borrowings	4,197	2,287	2,281	2,399	2,235	3,142	5,768	5,220
Current Portion of Long-Term Debt	498	46	776	111	45	680	1,122	1,340
Other Current Liabilities	4,999	3,870	4,407	4,496	5,375	6,007	6,477.	7,187
Total Current Liabilities	10,931	7,184	8,553	8,272	9,320	11,849	15,328	16,234
Long-Term Debt	1,534	1,409	1,506	2,729	3,191	2,736	1,319	656
Minority Interest	139	48	63	66	90	138	174	183
Pension & Other Post-Retirement Benefits	1,543	965	1,084	1,342	1,573	2,706	2,797	2,679
Deferred Tax Liability, Non-Current	2,289	2,153	2,341	2,821	3,138	2,340	3,472	5,290
Other Non-Current Liabilities	1,336	1,408	1,223	1,526	1,576	1,542	1,652	1,855
Total Liabilities	17,772	13,168	14,770	16,756	18,888	21,311	24,742	26,897
Total Common Equity	23,362	22,751	25,452	28,269	30,429	31,177	32,990	41,111
Total Liabilities and Equity	41,134	35,919	40,222	45,025	49,317	52,488	57,732	68,008

Source: Standard & Poor's Capital IQ data.

Valuation at Novartis

Valuation at Novartis

EXHIBIT 3   **Sales for Novartis pharmaceutical division's top 20 drugs in 2006**

Brands	Therapeutic Area	USA USD millions	% change in local currencies	Rest of world USD millions	% change in local currencies	Total USD millions	% change in USD	% change in local currencies
Diovan/Co-Diovan	Hypertension	1858	20	2365	12	4223	15	15
Gleevec/Glivec	Chronic myeloid leukemia	630	20	1924	16	2554	18	17
Lotrel	Hypertension	1352	26			1352	5	4
Zometa	Cancer complications	696	–1	587	12	1283	5	4
Lamisil (group)	Fungal infections	574	7	404	–31	978	–14	–13
Neural/Sandimmun	Transplantation	125	–17	793	–1	918	–4	–4
Sandostatin (incl. LAR)	Acromegaly	367	–2	548	4	915	2	2
Lescol	Cholesterol reduction	256	0	469	–8	725	–5	–5
Trileptal	Epilepsy	549	19	172	11	721	17	17
Femara	Breast cancer	338	40	381	27	719	34	33
Top ten products total		**6745**	**15**	**7643**	**7**	**14388**	**10**	**10**
Voltaren (group)	Inflammation/pain	8	60	682	0	690	0	1
Zelnorm/Zelmac	Irritable bowel syndrome	488	37	73	20	561	34	34
Exelon	Alzheimer's disease	187	9	338	12	525	12	11
Tegretol (incl. CR/XR)	Epilepsy	120	10	271	–5	391	–1	–1
Visudyne	Macular degeneration	70	–62	284	–6	354	–27	–27
Miacalcic	Osteoporosis	199	–13	140	3	339	–7	–7
Comtan/Stalevo Group	Parkinson's disease	157	18	182	24	339	22	21
Foradil	Asthma	14	0	317	–1	331	0	–1
Ritalin/Focalin (group)	Attention deficit/ hyperactive disorder	264	47	66	6	330	37	37
Famvir	Viral infections	166	10	102	–3	268	6	5
Top twenty products total		**8418**	**14**	**10098**	**5**	**18516**	**9**	**9**
Rest of portfolio		1054	43	3006	14	4060	21	21
Total Division net sales		**9472**	**17**	**13104**	**7**	**22576**	**11**	**11**

Source: Novartis 2006 annual report.

EXHIBIT 4   **2006 sales for Novartis pharmaceutical division by drug maturity**

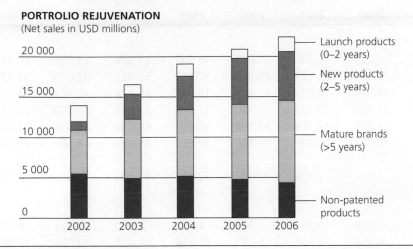

PORTROLIO REJUVENATION
(Net sales in USD millions)

Source: Novartis 2006 annual report.

EXHIBIT 5 Performance of key competitors in the pharmaceutical industry (in $US millions)

	2000	2001	2002	2003	2004	2005	2006
Revenues							
AstraZeneca plc	19,200	16,480	17,841	18,849	21,426	23,950	26,475
GlaxoSmithKline plc	23,074	25,021	28,963	32,439	32,852	32,075	39,334
Johnson & Johnson	11,954	14,851	17,151	19,517	22,128	22,322	23,267
Merck & Co. Inc.	23,320	19,732	20,130	21,038	21,494	20,679	20,375
Novartis	11,202	12,159	15,183	16,020	18,497	20,515	23,000
Pfizer	24,027	26,949	29,843	39,631	46,133	44,284	45,083
Weighted average sales growth		2.1%	12.1%	22.1%	53.6%	6.0%	11.2%
EBIT							
AstraZeneca plc	4,008	3,954	4,356	4,202	4,770	6,502	8,216
GlaxoSmithKline plc	6,455	6,256	8,157	10,348	10,400	10,586	13,958
Johnson & Johnson	4,175	4,928	5,787	5,896	7,376	6,365	6,894
Merck & Co. Inc.	11,564	12,200	12,723	13,250	13,507	13,158	13,649
Novartis	3,334	3,420	4,353	4,423	5,253	6,014	6,703
Pfizer	8,859	10,936	12,920	6,837	21,510	19,594	20,718
Weighted average EBIT margin	34.0%	36.2%	37.4%	30.5%	35.0%	34.2%	34.8%
Net Operating Assets							
AstraZeneca plc	na	na	21,576	23,573	25,616	24,840	29,932
GlaxoSmithKline plc	29,017	26,278	29,950	33,927	36,165	28,242	33,179
Johnson & Johnson	9,209	10,591	11,112	15,351	16,058	16,091	18,799
Merck & Co. Inc.	na	na	na	na	na	na	na
Novartis	10,423	11,225	12,118	13,836	14,914	14,655	20,418
Pfizer	15,854	16,881	18,541	81,522	81,651	74,406	72,497
Weighted average revenues to net operating assets	1.09	1.22	1.17	0.75	0.81	0.90	0.90

Notes: Data are actual reported segment data reported at each year end. Changes in the performance measures therefore include the effect of any acquisitions or divestitures, such as Pfizer's acquisition of Pharmacia in mid-2003. EBIT are earnings before interest and taxes. Net operating assets are operating assets less non-interest-bearing liabilities.
Source: Standard & Poor's Capital IQ data.

EXHIBIT 6   **Performance of key competitors in the generics industry (in $US millions)**

	2000	2001	2002	2003	2004	2005	2006
Revenues							
Novartis	1,973	2,433	2,809	2,906	3,045	4,712	5,983
Teva Pharmaceutical Inds. Ltd.	1,548	1,838	2,240	2,885	4,276	4,703	7,821
Watson Pharmaceuticals Inc.	423	552	650	749	1,239	1,247	1,517
Weighted average sales growth rate		22.3%	18.2%	14.8%	30.9%	24.6%	43.7%
EBIT							
Novartis	242	281	406	473	235	342	736
Teva Pharmaceutical Inds. Ltd.	223	297	427	692	307	981	372
Watson Pharmaceuticals Inc.	na	na	na	na	na	356	321
Weighted average EBIT margin	13.2%	13.5%	16.5%	20.1%	7.4%	15.8%	9.3%
Net Operating Assets							
Novartis	2,575	3,362	4,673	4,321	5,379	14,057	15,009
Teva Pharmaceutical Inds. Ltd.	1,439	1,367	2,521	3,205	5,973	6,094	na
Watson Pharmaceuticals Inc.	na	na	na	na	na	na	na
Weighted average revenues to net operating assets	0.88	0.90	0.70	0.77	0.64	0.47	0.40

Notes: Data are actual reported segment data reported at each year end. Changes in the performance measures therefore include the effect of any acquisitions or divestitures, such as Novartis's acquisition of Hexal and Eon in mid-2005. EBIT are earnings before interest and taxes. Net operating assets are operating assets less non-interest-bearing liabilities.
Source: Standard & Poor's Capital IQ data.

Valuation at Novartis

EXHIBIT 7 **Performance of key competitors in the consumer health industry (in $US millions)**

	2000	2001	2002	2003	2004	2005	2006
Revenues							
GlaxoSmithKline plc	3,963	4,776	5,178	5,817	6,156	5,155	6,165
Johnson & Johnson	6,904	6,320	6,564	7,431	8,333	9,096	9,774
Novartis	4,880	5,098	5,532	5,938	5,595	6,092	6,579
Pfizer Animal Health	5,547	5,310	2,530	4,640	5,469	6,084	2,311
Reckit & Benkiser	na	4,665	5,334	6,279	7,053	6,848	9,262
Schering Plough (Consumer & Animal Health)	na	1,341	1,412	1,662	1,855	1,944	2,033
Average sales growth rate		1.0%	−3.5%	19.6%	8.5%	2.2%	2.6%
EBIT							
GlaxoSmithKline plc	618	628	777	1,056	1,268	1,229	1,338
Johnson & Johnson	867	1,004	1,229	1,393	1,444	1,592	1,374
Novartis	598	659	886	821	919	952	1,068
Pfizer Animal Health	813	787	546	671	1,019	1,103	419
Reckit & Benkiser	na	675	861	1,140	1,358	1,363	1,979
Schering Plough (Consumer & Animal Health)		281	267	195	322	355	348
Weighted average EBIT margin	13.6%	14.7%	17.2%	16.6%	18.4%	18.7%	18.1%
Net Operating Assets							
GlaxoSmithKline plc	3,271	5,596	5,986	8,850	7,095	4,204	5,423
Johnson & Johnson	4,761	4,209	5,056	5,371	6,142	6,275	25,380
Novartis	4,688	4,576	5,136	5,417	6,155	6,863	6,480
Pfizer Animal Health	3,840	3,553	2,105	7,514	7,878	8,158	1,951
Reckit & Benkiser	na	na	na	na	5,737	5,370	10,634
Schering Plough (Consumer & Animal Health)	na	na	na	na	na	na	na
Weighted average revenues to net operating assets	1.29	1.20	1.08	0.88	0.99	1.08	0.68

Notes: Data are actual reported segment data reported at each year end. Changes in the performance measures therefore include the effect of any acquisitions or divestitures, such as Proctor & Gamble's acquisition of Gillette in 2005, Pfizer's acquisition of its animal health business in 2003 and the sale of its consumer health business to Johnson & Johnson in 2006. Net operating assets are operating assets less non-interest-bearing liabilities. EBIT are earnings before interest and taxes.
Source: Standard & Poor's Capital IQ data.

Valuation at Novartis

EXHIBIT 8 **Performance of key competitors in the vaccines and diagnostics industry (in $US millions)**

	2000	2001	2002	2003	2004	2005	2006
Revenues							
Abbot Labs Vaccines	2,924	2,929	2,897	3,040	3,378	3,756	3,979
J&J Medical Devices & Diagnostics	10,281	11,146	12,583	14,914	16,887	19,096	20,283
Merck Vaccines	na	na	na	na	973	984	1,706
Novartis	na	na	na	na	na	na	1,187
Sanofi-Aventis Vaccines	na	na	na	na	925	2,512	3,436
Weighted average sales growth rate	33.2%	6.6%	10.0%	16.0%	12.9%	18.9%	11.6%
EBIT							
Abbot Labs Vaccines	331	357	220	249	378	495	431
J&J Medical Devices & Diagnostics	1,696	2,001	2,489	3,370	3,924	5,240	6,126
Merck Vaccines	na	na	na	na	881	767	893
Novartis	na	na	na	na	na	na	(26)
Sanofi-Aventis Vaccines	na	na	na	na	(1,374)	220	673
Weighted average EBIT margin	15.4%	16.8%	17.5%	20.2%	17.2%	25.5%	26.5%
Net Operating Assets							
Abbot Labs Vaccines	na	na	na	na	3,691	3,742	4,073
J&J Medical Devices & Diagnostics	12,745	13,645	15,052	16,082	15,805	16,540	18,601
Merck Vaccines	na	na	na	na	na	na	na
Novartis	na	na	na	na	na	na	5,609
Sanofi-Aventis Vaccines	na	na	na	na	7,099	8,130	8,582
Weighted average sales to net operating assets	0.81	0.82	0.84	0.93	0.80	0.89	0.78

Notes: Data are actual reported segment data reported at each year end. Changes in the performance measures therefore include the effect of any acquisitions or divestitures, such as Novartis's acquisition of Chiron in 2006, and Sanofi's acquisition of Aventis in 2004. Net operating assets are operating assets less non-interest-bearing liabilities. EBIT are earnings before interest and taxes. Source: Standard & Poor's Capital IQ data.

Valuation at Novartis

EXHIBIT 9 **Healthcare industry and Novartis valuation multiples for the period 2003 to 2006**

	2003	2004	2005	2006
Healthcare Industry				
Price-to-earnings multiple	47.8	40.1	34.4	33.0
Price-to-book multiple	6.0	4.7	4.3	4.0
Return on equity %	13.3%	12.7%	12.7%	13.4%
Revenue growth %	14.4%	13.6%	8.8%	16.0%
Earnings growth	26.5%	19.1%	12.6%	21.7%
Novartis AG				
Price to Earnings Multiple	22.9	21.2	21.0	19.4
Price to Book Multiple	3.4	3.3	3.9	3.3

Note: Multiples are based on year-end financial information and stock price data from March 31 the following year.
Source: Standard & Poor's Capital IQ data.

EXHIBIT 10 Valuation and multiples for leading pharmaceutical companies based on financial statement data for fiscal year-end 2006 and stock price data on March 31, 2007

Company	Stock Price ($US)	Market Equity Capitalization ($US million)	Enterprise Value ($US million)	Book Equity	Price-Book Multiple	Diluted EPS ($US)	PE Multiple	ROE	Beta
Johnson & Johnson	60.26	174,451	176,960	39,318	4.4	3.734	16.1	28.3%	0.33
Pfizer Inc.	25.26	178,761	159,169	71,217	2.5	1.515	16.7	16.1%	0.69
Roche Holding AG	177.64	153,227	146,024	32,590	4.7	7.46	23.8	21.6%	0.16
GlaxoSmithKline plc	27.37	153,337	158,650	18,388	8.3	1.85	14.8	64.6%	0.27
Novartis AG	57.59	135,233	134,780	41,111	3.3	2.962	19.4	17.5%	0.33
Merck & Co. Inc.	44.17	95,848	96,377	17,560	5.5	2.027	21.8	25.0%	0.96
Weighted average					4.7		18.4	24.1%	0.43

Notes: Market capitalization is the stock price multiplied by the number of shares outstanding. Earnings per share are diluted earnings per share excluding extraordinary items. Enterprise value is the market equity capitalization plus the book value of interest-bearing debt and minority interest, less cash and marketable securities and earnings. ROE is net income as a percentage of average book equity. Beta is the systematic risk of the stock, estimated by regressing the firm's stock for the previous 36 months on the S&P 500 index returns. The weighted average price-book and PE multiples are weighted by the market capitalizations of the firms, whereas the weighted ROE is weighted by their relative book equity values. Data for Glaxo-SmithKline plc and Roche Holding AG are translated into $US using exchange rates on March 31, 2007.

Source: Standard & Poor's Capital IQ data.

Valuation at Novartis

Credit Analysis and Distress Prediction

Credit analysis is the evaluation of a firm from the perspective of a holder or potential holder of its debt, including trade payables, loans, and public debt securities. A key element of credit analysis is the prediction of the likelihood a firm will face financial distress. Credit analysis is involved in a wide variety of decision contexts:

- A commercial banker asks: Should we extend a loan to this firm? If so, how should it be structured? How should it be priced?

- If the loan is granted, the banker must later ask: Are we still providing the services, including credit, that this firm needs? Is the firm still in compliance with the loan terms? If not, is there a need to restructure the loan, and if so, how? Is the situation serious enough to call for accelerating the repayment of the loan?

- A potential investor asks: Are these debt securities a sound investment? What is the probability that the firm will face distress and default on the debt? Does the yield provide adequate compensation for the default risk involved?

- An investor contemplating purchase of debt securities in default asks: How likely is it that this firm can be turned around? In light of the high yield on this debt relative to its current price, can I accept the risk that the debt will not be repaid in full?

- A potential supplier asks: Should I sell products or services to this firm? The associated credit will be extended only for a short period, but the amount is large and I should have some assurance that collection risks are manageable.

Finally, there are third parties – those other than borrowers and lenders – who are interested in the general issue of how likely it is that a firm will avoid financial distress:

- An auditor asks: How likely is it that this firm will survive beyond the short run? In evaluating the firm's financials, should I consider it a going concern?

- An actual or potential employee asks: How confident can I be that this firm will be able to offer employment over the long-term?

- A potential customer asks: What assurance is there that this firm will survive to provide warranty services, replacement parts, product updates, and other services?

- A competitor asks: Will this firm survive the current industry shakeout? What are the implications of potential financial distress at this firm for my pricing and market share?

This chapter develops a framework to evaluate a firm's creditworthiness and assess the likelihood of financial distress.

WHY DO FIRMS USE DEBT FINANCING?

Before discussing the credit market and credit analysis, it is worth understanding why firms use debt financing. Debt financing is attractive to firms for two key reasons:

- Corporate interest tax shields. In many countries tax laws provide for the corporate tax deductibility of interest paid on debt. No such corporate tax shield is available for dividend payments or retained earnings. Therefore, corporate tax benefits should encourage firms with high effective tax rates and few forms of tax shields other than interest to favor debt financing.

- Management incentives for value creation. Firms with relatively high leverage face pressures to generate cash flows to meet payments of interest and principal, reducing resources available to fund unjustifiable expenses and investments that do not maximize shareholder value. Debt financing, therefore, focuses management on value creation, reducing conflicts of interest between managers and shareholders.

However, in addition to these **benefits of debt**, there are also **costs of debt** financing. As a firm increases its use of debt financing, it increases the likelihood of financial distress, where it is unable to meet interest or principal repayment obligations to creditors. When a firm is in serious financial distress, its owners' claims are likely to be restructured. This can take place under formal bankruptcy proceedings or out of bankruptcy, depending on the jurisdiction in which the firm operates. Financial distress has multiple negative consequences for the firm:

- Legal costs of financial distress. Restructurings are likely to be costly, since the parties involved have to hire lawyers, bankers, and accountants to represent their interests, and to pay court costs if there are formal legal proceedings. These are often called the direct costs of financial distress.

- Costs of foregone investment opportunities. Distressed firms face significant challenges in raising capital as potential new investors and creditors will be wary of becoming embroiled in the firm's legal disputes. Thus, firms in distress are often unable to finance new investments even though they may be profitable for its owners.

- Costs of conflicts between creditors and shareholders. When faced with financial distress, creditors focus on the firm's ability to service its debt while shareholders worry that their equity will revert to the creditors if the firm defaults. Thus, managers face increased pressure to make decisions that typically serve the interests of the stockholders, and creditors react by increasing the costs of borrowing for the firm's stockholders.

DEBT FINANCING AND FREE CASH FLOW

The debt introduced as a result of leveraged buyouts is viewed by many as an example of debt creating pressure for management to refocus on value creation for shareholders. The increased debt taken with the LBO forces management to eliminate unnecessary perks, to limit diversification into unrelated industries, and to cancel unprofitable projects. For example, in 2004 Italy-based yellow pages publisher Seat Pagine Gialle followed many of its international industry peers, such as Yell, Tele-Media, and Qwest Dex, by being acquired in a leveraged buyout for €5.65 billion. The acquisition, which was one of the largest leveraged buyouts in Europe, was financed for about €3.2 billion with senior debt and €1.15 billion with high yield bonds, which Standard and Poor's had rated at BB. The company's industry, the telephone directories advertising market, was characterized by stable cash flows because the demand for advertising in directories was much less cyclical than the demand for advertising in, for example, daily newspapers. The industry's investment opportunities were, however, limited, which made it attractive for LBOs. The Seat Pagine Gialle LBO was followed by other LBOs in the same industry, such as Dutch VNU's sell-off of its yellow pages business unit.

Financial ratio and prospective analysis can help analysts assess whether there are currently free cash flow inefficiencies at a firm as well as risks of future inefficiencies. Symptoms of excessive management perks and investment in unprofitable projects include the following:

■ *High ratios of general and administrative expenses and overhead to sales.* If a firm's ratios are higher than those for its major competitors, one possibility is that management is wasting money on perks.

■ *Significant new investments in unrelated areas.* If it is difficult to rationalize these new investments, there might be free cash flow problems.

■ *High levels of expected operating cash flows (net of essential capital expenditures and debt retirements) from pro forma income and cash flow statements.*

■ *Poor management incentives to create additional shareholder value*, evidenced by a weak linkage between management compensation and firm performance.

Firms are more likely to fall into financial distress if they have high business risks and their assets are easily destroyed in financial distress. For example, firms with human capital and brand intangibles are particularly sensitive to financial distress since dissatisfied employees and customers can leave or seek alternative suppliers. In contrast, firms with tangible assets can sell their assets if they get into financial distress, providing additional security for lenders and lowering the costs of financial distress. Firms with intangible assets are therefore less likely to be highly leveraged than firms whose assets are mostly tangible.

The above discussion implies that a firm's long-term decisions on the use of debt financing reflects a trade-off between the corporate interest tax shield and incentive benefits of debt against the costs of financial distress. As the firm becomes more highly leveraged, the costs of leverage presumably begin to outweigh the tax and monitoring benefits of debt.

Table 10.1 shows median leverage ratios for all publicly-traded stocks in selected industries for the fiscal years 1992–2008. Median ratios are reported for all listed

TABLE 10.1 Median net interest-bearing debt-to-book equity and net interest-bearing debt-to-market equity for selected European industries in 1992–2008

	Net interest-bearing debt-to-book equity	
Industry	All listed firms	Large listed firms
Computer programming and data processing	−22%	−18%
Pharmaceutical	−7%	14%
Hotels and motels	79%	62%
Heavy construction	70%	75%
Air transportation	95%	97%
Water supply	61%	100%
Electric services	124%	126%

companies and for large companies (with market capitalizations greater than €300 million) only.

Median debt-to-book equity ratios are highest for the water supply and electric services industries, which are typically not highly sensitive to economy risk and whose core assets are primarily physical equipment and property that are readily transferable to debt holders in the event of financial distress. In contrast, the software and pharmaceutical industries' core assets are their research staffs and sales force representatives. These types of assets can easily be lost if the firm gets into financial difficulty as a result of too much leverage. In all likelihood, management would be forced to cut back on R&D and marketing, allowing their most talented researchers and sales representatives to be subject to offers from competitors. To reduce these risks, firms in these industries have relatively conservative capital structures.[1] Construction, air transportation and hotel firms have leverage in between these extremes, reflecting the need to balance the impact of having extensive physical assets and being subject to more volatile revenue streams.

It is also interesting to note that large firms tend to have higher leverage than small firms in the same industries. This probably reflects the fact that larger firms tend to have more product offerings and to be more diversified geographically, reducing their vulnerability to negative events for a single product or market, and enabling them to take on more debt.

THE MARKET FOR CREDIT

An understanding of **credit analysis** requires an appreciation of the various players in the market for credit. We briefly describe below the major **suppliers of debt financing**.

Commercial banks

Commercial banks are very important players in the market for credit. Since banks tend to provide a range of services to a client, and have intimate knowledge of the client and its operations, they have a comparative advantage in extending credit in settings where (1) knowledge gained through close contact with management reduces the perceived riskiness of the credit and (2) credit risk can be contained through careful monitoring of the firm. This is even more so in countries where commercial banks also provide investment banking services to their clients. Examples of investment banking services are asset management, investment advice, and the underwriting of clients' securities. Banks that engage in investment banking sometimes hold substantial equity stakes in other companies, including their clients. The combination of commercial banking and investment banking services, which is called universal banking, therefore not only helps banks to become better informed about their clients' operations but also makes banks more influential over their clients through the equity stakes that they control. Universal banking activities are especially common among the larger banks in Continental European countries such as Germany and Switzerland.[2]

Bank lending operations are constrained by a low tolerance for risk to ensure that the overall loan portfolio will be of acceptably high quality to bank regulators. Because of the importance of maintaining public confidence in the banking sector and the desire to shield government deposit insurance from risk, governments have incentives to constrain banks' exposure to credit risk. Banks also tend to shield themselves from the risk of shifts in interest rates by avoiding fixed-rate loans with long maturities. Because banks' capital mostly comes from short-term deposits, such long-term loans leave them exposed to increases in interest rates, unless the risk can be hedged with derivatives. Thus, banks are less likely to play a role when a firm requires a very long-term commitment to financing. However, in some cases banks place the debt with investors looking for longer-term credit exposure.

Non-bank financial institutions

Banks face competition in the commercial lending market from a variety of sources. Finance companies compete with banks in the market for asset-based lending (i.e., the secured financing of specific assets such as receivables, inventory, or equipment). Insurance companies are also involved in a variety of lending activities. Since life insurance companies face obligations of a long-term nature, they often seek investments of long duration (e.g., long-term bonds or loans to support large, long-term commercial property and development projects). Investment bankers are prepared to place debt securities with private investors or in the public markets (discussed below). Various government agencies are another source of credit.

Public debt markets

Some firms have the size, strength, and credibility necessary to bypass the banking sector and seek financing directly from investors, either through sales of commercial paper or through the issuance of bonds. Such debt issues are facilitated by the assignment of a **public debt rating**, which measures the underlying credit strength of the firm and determines the yield that must be offered to investors.

Banks often provide financing in tandem with a public debt issue or other source of financing. In highly levered transactions, such as leveraged buyouts, banks commonly provide financing along with public debt that has a lower priority in case of bankruptcy. The bank's "senior financing" would typically be scheduled for earlier retirement than the public debt, and it would carry a lower yield. For smaller or start-up firms, banks often provide credit in conjunction with equity financing from venture capitalists. Note that in the case of both the leveraged buyout and the start-up company, the bank helps provide the cash needed to make the deal happen, but it does so in a way that shields it from risks that would be unacceptably high in the banking sector.

Sellers who provide financing

Another sector of the market for credit is manufacturers and other suppliers of goods and services. As a matter of course, such firms tend to finance their customers' purchases on an unsecured basis for periods of 30 to 60 days. Suppliers will, on occasion, also agree to provide more extended financing, usually with the support of a secured note. A supplier may be willing to grant such a loan in the expectation that the creditor will survive a cash shortage and remain an important customer in the future. However the customer would typically seek such an arrangement only if bank financing is unavailable because it could constrain flexibility in selecting among and/or negotiating with suppliers.

COUNTRY DIFFERENCES IN DEBT FINANCING

Country factors and credit types

The above described suppliers of credit are not equally important in every country. One source of differences across countries is the extent to which national bankruptcy laws protect credit providers. A stylized classification of bankruptcy laws involves two groups: laws that provide extensive creditor protection in the case of default versus laws that are oriented toward keeping the company in default a going concern and shielding the company from the influence of creditors. The former types of laws typically offer creditors a first right to repossess collateral and enforce other contractual rights when their borrower is in default. These laws therefore increase the probability that creditors recover their loans but reduce the probability that borrowers survive bankruptcy. The latter types of laws typically impose court-administered bankruptcy procedures on the borrower in default and its creditors as well as an automatic stay on the borrower's assets. An automatic stay on the assets means that creditors cannot repossess their collateral during the period in which the borrower's financial obligations are being restructured. The UK is an example of a European country that has strong creditor protection laws. Examples of European countries that have weak creditor protection laws, or borrower-friendly bankruptcy laws, are France, Italy, and Portugal. Germany takes a position in between these two extremes. In Germany, courts impose bankruptcy procedures on the borrower and its creditors, but there is no automatic stay on the borrower's assets and creditors have considerable influence on the borrower's reorganization process.[3]

The orientation of a country's bankruptcy laws can affect the characteristics of credit provided in various ways. A few examples of how legal differences matter are the following:

- Multiple-bank borrowing. In countries where the legal rights of banks are weakly protected and banks experience difficulties in repossessing collateral when a borrower defaults, they are likely to be hesitant in extending long-term credit. As an alternative, companies may borrow smaller proportions of debt from multiple banks. Because it is more difficult for a company in default to renegotiate its loans with multiple banks than with one bank, multiple-bank borrowing reduces the company's incentive to strategically default. Research has found that multiple-bank borrowing is most common in Belgium, France, Italy, Spain, and Portugal, where banks are indeed weakly protected in case of bankruptcy.[4]

- Supplier financing. Supplier financing is also an efficient alternative form of debt financing when creditor rights are weakly protected.[5] A reason for this is that suppliers are often well informed about their debtors' operations and they have a straightforward way to discipline their debtors. That is, in case of default of payment, suppliers can repossess the delivered goods and withhold future deliveries. In fiscal year 2008, public companies in Belgium, France, Italy, Spain, and Portugal had an average payables-to-sales ratio of 19.3 percent. The ratio ranged from 14.2 percent in Portugal to 26.4 percent in Spain. In contrast, public companies in Denmark, Finland, Germany, the Netherlands, Norway, Sweden, Switzerland, and the UK had an average payables-to-sales ratio of 10.2 percent.

- Off-balance sheet financing. Research has indicated that in countries where companies' access to bank debt is restricted or relatively expensive, companies may also resort to off-balance sheet financing.[6] One example of off-balance sheet financing is the

TABLE 10.2 The importance of public debt markets in the economy (end-2008 data)

Country	Market value of (bank-owned) public corporate debt securities as a percentage of GDP
Belgium	10.1%
Denmark	5.6%
Finland	10.2%
France	22.0%
Germany	10.2%
Italy	18.9%
Netherlands	16.4%
Portugal	24.6%
Spain	41.4%
Sweden	14.0%
Switzerland	4.8%
UK	11.6%

Source: International Banking Statistics of the Bank for International Settlements.

factoring of receivables, where companies sell their customer receivables to a lender at a discount. In the first half of the 2000s, the use of factoring was fastest growing in Eastern Europe, where bankruptcy laws were weak. Further, companies in Italy made relatively more use of factoring than companies in other parts of Europe.

■ Public debt. Public debt markets are also not equally developed in all parts of the world. Table 10.2 shows the value of (bank-owned) public debt securities as a percentage of national gross domestic product (GDP) in 12 European countries at the end of 2008. These percentages show that public debt markets were especially large in France, Italy, Portugal and Spain, suggesting that public debt is used as an alternative to bank debt in countries with borrower-friendly bankruptcy laws.

Country factors and the optimal mix of debt and equity

In summary, the above discussion shows that in countries with borrower-friendly, creditor-unfriendly bankruptcy laws:

■ Creditors extend more short-term debt because this allows them to frequently review the borrower's financial position and adjust the terms of the loan when necessary.

■ Companies make greater use of supplier financing.

■ Companies make greater use of off-balance sheet financing such as the factoring of customer receivables.

■ Public debt markets tend to be more developed.

The net effect of these country differences in loan maturity, off-balance sheet financing, supplier financing, and public debt markets importance on country differences in leverage is unfortunately anything but straightforward. For example, we showed that Belgian, French, and Italian companies have, on average, greater amounts of trade payables on their balance sheets. In these three countries, however, equity markets are still not as well

TABLE 10.3 Median cash and marketable securities holdings and leverage for 13 European countries in 2008

Country	Interest-bearing debt-to-book equity	Cash and marketable securities-to-book equity	Net interest-bearing debt-to-book equity	Net interest-bearing debt-to-market equity
Portugal	208%	15%	187%	121%
Italy	110%	24%	85%	83%
Spain	108%	18%	82%	63%
Belgium	93%	29%	76%	67%
Norway	87%	24%	74%	63%
Netherlands	83%	17%	58%	49%
Finland	80%	19%	56%	39%
France	71%	28%	46%	35%
Germany	67%	28%	42%	28%
Denmark	47%	13%	35%	25%
Switzerland	45%	26%	25%	12%
UK	34%	23%	14%	10%
Sweden	31%	19%	10%	5%

developed as in some other parts of Europe. Thus, supplier financing might just as well serve as a substitute for long-term debt and equity, leaving the net debt to net capital ratio unchanged.

To provide a rough indication of how the mix of debt and equity financing varies across Europe, Table 10.3 shows median debt-to-equity, cash-to-equity, and net debt-to-equity ratios for 13 European countries in 2008. Germany, Sweden, Switzerland, and the UK tend to have the lowest net debt-to-equity ratios. Cash and marketable securities holdings of the median company in these countries tend to be close to the book value of its interest-bearing debt. Maybe surprisingly, the net interest-bearing debt-to-equity ratios are highest in countries with borrower-friendly, creditor-unfriendly bankruptcy laws, such as Italy, Portugal, and Spain. Two reasons may explain this.

First, in countries where bankruptcy laws shield management from its creditors in situations of financial distress, the threat of creditors intervening in the company's operations and repossessing collateral is less severe. Consequently, managers in these countries may feel comfortable with taking on more debt. As argued, despite being weakly protected, creditors are willing to extend debt because they can force borrowers to borrow smaller proportions of debt from multiple banks and can choose to extend loans with short maturities.

Second, the net debt-to-equity ratios are lowest in the countries where equity markets are most developed, such as the UK and Switzerland. Companies from these countries can more easily use equity financing as an alternative to debt financing than companies from countries with weakly developed equity markets, such as Portugal and Italy.

THE CREDIT ANALYSIS PROCESS IN PRIVATE DEBT MARKETS

Credit analysis is more than just establishing the creditworthiness of a firm, that is, its ability to pay its debts at the scheduled times. The decision to extend credit is not a binary one – the firm's exact value, its upside potential, and its distance from the threshold of creditworthiness are all equally important. There are ranges of creditworthiness, and it is important for purposes of pricing and structuring a loan to understand where a firm lies within that range. While downside risk must be the primary consideration in credit analysis, a firm with growth potential offers opportunities for future income-generating financial services from a continuing relationship.

This broader view of credit analysis involves most of the issues already discussed in the prior chapters on business strategy analysis, accounting analysis, financial analysis, and prospective analysis. Perhaps the greatest difference is that credit analysis rarely involves any explicit attempt to estimate the value of the firm's equity. However, the determinants of that value are relevant in credit analysis because a larger equity cushion translates into lower risk for the creditor.

Below we describe a representative but comprehensive series of steps that is used by commercial lenders in credit analysis. However, not all credit providers follow these guidelines. For example, when compared to a banker, manufacturers conduct a less extensive analysis on their customers since the credit is very short-term and the manufacturer is willing to bear some credit risk in the interest of generating a profit on the sale.

We present the steps in a particular order, but they are in fact all interdependent. Thus, analysis at one step may need to be rethought depending on the analysis at some later step.

Step 1: Consider the nature and purpose of the loan

Understanding the purpose of a loan is important not just for deciding whether it should be granted but also for structuring the loan based on duration, purpose, and size. Loans might be required for only a few months, for several years, or even as a permanent part of a firm's capital structure. Loans might be used for replacement of other financing, to support working capital needs, or to finance the acquisition of long-term assets or another firm.

The required amount of the loan must also be established. When bankruptcy laws provide a bank sufficient protection, it would typically prefer to be the sole financier of small and medium-sized companies. This preference is not only to gain an advantage in providing a menu of financial services to the firm but also to maintain a superior interest in case of bankruptcy. If other creditors are willing to subordinate their positions to the bank, that would of course be acceptable so far as the bank is concerned.

Often the commercial lender deals with firms that may have parent-subsidiary relations, posing the question of the appropriate counterparty. In general, the entity that owns the assets that will serve as collateral (or that could serve as such if needed in the future) acts as the borrower. If this entity is the subsidiary and the parent presents some financial strength independent of the subsidiary, a guarantee of the parent could be considered.

National bankruptcy laws in the country where the potential borrower is located also affect the maturity of the loan. When the bankruptcy laws provide weak protection to the credit provider it may decide only to extend a loan with a short maturity. Short-term loans carry the advantage that the lender can frequently review the borrower and make adjustments to the terms of the loan when necessary.[7] Commercial lenders are inclined to shorten loan maturities especially when lending to firms with little collateral, such as intangible-intensive firms.[8]

Step 2: Consider the type of loan and available security

The type of loan is a function of not only its purpose but also the financial strength of the borrower. Thus, to some extent, the loan type will be dictated by the financial analysis described in step 3. Some of the possibilities are as follows:

- Open line of credit. An open line of credit permits the borrower to receive cash up to some specified maximum on an as-needed basis for a specified term, such as one year. To maintain this option, the borrower pays a fee (e.g., 3/8 of 1 percent) on the unused balance in addition to the interest on any used amount. An open line of credit is useful in cases where the borrower's cash needs are difficult to anticipate.

- Revolving line of credit. When it is clear that a firm will need credit beyond the short run, financing may be provided in the form of a "revolver." The terms of a revolver, which is sometimes used to support working capital needs, require the borrower to make payments as the operating cycle proceeds and inventory and receivables are converted to cash. However it is also expected that cash will continue to be advanced so long as the borrower remains in good standing. In addition to interest on amounts outstanding, a fee is charged on the unused line.

- Working capital loan. Such a loan is used to finance inventory and receivables, and it is usually secured. The maximum loan balance may be tied to the balance of the working capital accounts. For example, the loan may be allowed to rise to no more than 80 percent of receivables less than 60 days old.

- Term loan. Term loans are used for long-term needs and are often secured with long-term assets such as plant or equipment. Typically, the loan will be amortized, requiring periodic payments to reduce the loan balance.

- Mortgage loan. Mortgages support the financing of real estate, have long-terms, and require periodic amortization of the loan balance.

- Lease financing. Lease financing can be used to facilitate the acquisition of any asset but is most commonly used for equipment, including vehicles, and buildings. Leases may be structured over periods of 1 to 15 years, depending on the life of the underlying asset.

Much bank lending is done on a secured basis, especially with smaller and more highly leveraged companies. Security will be required unless the loan is short-term and the borrower exposes the bank to minimal default risk. When security is required, an important consideration is whether the amount of available security is sufficient to support the loan. The amount that a bank will lend on given security involves business judgment, and it depends on a variety of factors that affect the liquidity of the security in the context of a situation where the firm is distressed. It also depends on the extent to which creditor protection laws permit banks to quickly repossess collateral in the event of default. In countries where bankruptcy laws provide weak creditor protection, such as France, banks typically require more collateral for a given loan amount.[9] The following are some rules of thumb often applied in commercial lending to various categories of security:

- Receivables. Trade receivables are usually considered the most desirable form of security because they are the most liquid. An average bank allows loans of 50 to 80 percent of the balance of nondelinquent accounts. The percentage applied is lower when:

  1 There are many small accounts that would be costly to collect in case the firm is distressed.

  2 There are a few very large accounts, such that problems with a single customer could be serious.

3 Bankruptcy laws are creditor-unfriendly and preclude the bank claiming and collecting the receivables while the borrower in default is being restructured.

4 The customer's financial health is closely related to that of the borrower, so that collectibility is endangered just when the borrower is in default.

On the latter score, banks often refuse to accept receivables from affiliates as effective security.

■ Inventory. The desirability of inventory as security varies widely. The best-case scenario is inventory consisting of a common commodity that can easily be sold to other parties if the borrower defaults. More specialized inventory, with appeal to only a limited set of buyers, or inventory that is costly to store or transport is less desirable. An average bank typically lends up to 60 percent on raw materials, 50 percent on finished goods, and 20 percent on work in process.

■ Machinery and equipment. Machinery and equipment is less desirable as collateral. It is likely to be used, and it must be stored, insured, and marketed. Keeping the costs of these activities in mind, banks typically will lend only up to 50 percent of the estimated value of such assets in a forced sale such as an auction.

■ Real estate. The value of real estate as collateral varies considerably. Banks will often lend up to 80 percent of the appraised value of readily salable real estate. On the other hand, a factory designed for a unique purpose would be much less desirable.

Even when a loan is not secured initially, a bank can require a "negative pledge" on the firm's assets – a pledge that the firm will not use the assets as security for any other creditor. In that case, if the borrower begins to experience difficulty and defaults on the loan, and if there are no other creditors in the picture, the bank can demand the loan become secured if it is to remain outstanding.

Step 3: Conduct a financial analysis of the potential borrower

This portion of the analysis involves all the steps discussed in our chapters on business strategy analysis, accounting analysis, and financial analysis. The emphasis, however, is on the firm's ability to service the debt at the scheduled rate. All the factors that could impact that ability, such as the presence of off-balance-sheet lease obligations and the sustainability of the firm's operating profit stream, need to be carefully examined. The focus of the analysis depends on the type of financing under consideration. For example, if a short-term loan is considered to support seasonal fluctuations in inventory, the emphasis would be on the ability of the firm to convert the inventory into cash on a timely basis. In contrast, a term loan to support plant and equipment must be made with confidence in the long-run earnings prospects of the firm. This step incorporates both an assessment of the potential borrower's financial status using ratio analysis and a forecast to determine future payment prospects.

Ratio analysis

Ultimately, since the key issue in the financial analysis is the likelihood that cash flows will be sufficient to repay the loan, lenders focus much attention on solvency ratios: the magnitude of various measures of profits and cash flows relative to debt service and other requirements. Therefore, ratio analysis from the perspective of a creditor differs somewhat from that of an owner. There is greater emphasis on cash flows and earnings available to *all* claimants (not just owners) *before* taxes (since interest is tax-deductible and paid out of pretax euros). The *funds flow coverage ratio* illustrates the creditor's perspective:

$$\text{Funds flow coverage} = \frac{\text{EBIT} + \text{Depreciation}}{\text{Interest} + \dfrac{\text{Debt repayment}}{(1 - \text{tax rate})} + \dfrac{\text{Preference dividends}}{(1 - \text{tax rate})}}$$

Earnings before both interest and taxes in the numerator is compared directly to the interest expense in the denominator, because interest expense is paid out of pretax euros. In contrast, any payment of principal scheduled for a given year is nondeductible and must be made out of after-tax profits. In essence, with a 50 percent tax rate, one euro of principal payment is "twice as expensive" as a one-euro interest payment. Scaling the payment of principal by (1 – tax rate) accounts for this. The same idea applies to preference dividends, which are not tax-deductible.

The funds flow coverage ratio provides an indication of how comfortably the funds flow can cover unavoidable expenditures. The ratio excludes payments such as dividend payments to ordinary shareholders and capital expenditures on the premise that they could be reduced to zero to make debt payments if necessary.[10] Clearly, however, if the firm is to survive in the long run, funds flow must be sufficient to not only service debt but also maintain plant assets. Thus, long-run survival requires a funds flow coverage ratio well in excess of 1.[11]

To the extent that the ratio exceeds 1, it indicates the "margin of safety" the lender faces. When such a ratio is combined with an assessment of the variance in its numerator, it provides an indication of the probability of nonpayment. However, it would be overly simplistic to establish any particular threshold above which a ratio indicates a loan is justified. A creditor clearly wants to be in a position to be repaid on schedule, even when the borrower faces a reasonably foreseeable difficulty. That argues for lending only when the funds flow coverage is expected to exceed 1, even in a recession scenario – and higher if some allowance for capital expenditures is prudent.

The financial analysis should produce more than an assessment of the risk of nonpayment. It should also identify the nature of the significant risks. At many commercial banks it is standard operating procedure to summarize the analysis of the firm by listing the key risks that could lead to default and factors that could be used to control those risks if the loan were made. That information can be used in structuring the detailed terms of the loan so as to trigger default when problems arise, at a stage early enough to permit corrective action.

Forecasting

Implicit in the discussion of ratio analysis is a forward-looking view of the firm's ability to service the loan. Good credit analysis should also be supported by explicit forecasts. The basis for such forecasts is usually management, though lenders perform their own tests as well. An essential element of this step is a sensitivity analysis to examine the ability of the borrower to service the debt under a variety of scenarios such as changes in the economy or in the firm's competitive position. Ideally, the firm should be strong enough to withstand the downside risks such as a drop in sales or a decrease in profit margins.

At times it is possible to reconsider the structure of a loan so as to permit it to "cash flow." That is, the term of the loan might be extended or the amortization pattern changed. Often a bank will grant a loan with the expectation that it will be continually renewed, thus becoming a permanent part of the firm's financial structure (labeled an "evergreen" loan). In that case the loan will still be written as if it is due within the short-term, and the bank must assure itself of a viable "exit strategy." However, the firm would be expected to service the loan by simply covering interest payments.

Step 4: Assemble the detailed loan structure, including loan covenants

If the analysis thus far indicates that a loan is in order, the final step is to assemble the detailed structure. Having previously determined the type of loan and repayment schedule, the focus shifts to the loan covenants and pricing.

Writing loan covenants

Loan covenants specify mutual expectations of the borrower and lender by specifying actions the borrower will and will not take. Covenants generally fall into three categories:

1 Those that require certain actions such as regular provision of financial statements.

2 Those that preclude certain actions such as undertaking an acquisition without the permission of the lender.

3 Those that require maintenance of certain financial ratios.

Loan covenants must strike a balance between protecting the interests of the lender and providing the flexibility management needs to run the business. The covenants represent a mechanism for ensuring that the business will remain as strong as the two parties anticipated at the time the loan was granted.

The principal covenants that govern the management of the firm include restrictions on other borrowing, pledging assets to other lenders, selling substantial assets, engaging in mergers or acquisitions, and paying of dividends. The financial covenants should seek to address the significant risks identified in the financial analysis, or to at least provide early warning that such risks are surfacing. Some commonly used financial covenants include:

- Maintenance of minimum net worth. This covenant assures that the firm will maintain an "equity cushion" to protect the lender. Covenants typically require a level of net worth rather than a particular level of profit. In the final analysis, the lender may not care whether that net worth is maintained by generating profit, cutting dividends, or issuing new equity. Tying the covenant to net worth offers the firm the flexibility to use any of these avenues to avoid default.

- Minimum coverage ratio. Especially in the case of a long-term loan, such as a term loan, the lender may want to supplement a net worth covenant with one based on coverage of interest or total debt service. The funds flow coverage ratio presented above would be an example. Maintenance of some minimum coverage helps assure that the ability of the firm to generate funds internally is strong enough to justify the long-term nature of the loan.

- Maximum ratio of total liabilities to net worth. This ratio constrains the risk of high leverage and prevents growth without either retaining earnings or infusing equity.

- Minimum net working capital balance or current ratio. Constraints on this ratio force a firm to maintain its liquidity by using cash generated from operations to retire current liabilities (as opposed to acquiring long-lived assets).

- Maximum ratio of capital expenditures to earnings before depreciation. Constraints on this ratio help prevent the firm from investing in growth (including the illiquid assets necessary to support growth) unless such growth can be financed internally, with some margin remaining for debt service.

Required financial ratios are typically based on the levels that existed at the time that the agreement was executed, perhaps with some allowance for deterioration but often with some expected improvements over time. Violation of a covenant represents an event of default that could cause immediate acceleration of the debt payment, but in most cases the lender uses the default as an opportunity to re-examine the situation and either waive the violation or renegotiate the loan.

Covenants are included not only in private lending agreements but also in public debt agreements. However, public debt agreements tend to have less restrictive covenants for two reasons. First, since negotiations resulting from a violation of public debt covenants are costly (possibly involving not just the trustee, but bondholders as well), the covenants are written to be triggered only in serious circumstances. Second, public debt is usually issued by stronger, more creditworthy firms, though there is a large market for high-yield debt. For the most financially healthy firms with strong debt ratings, very few covenants will be used, generally only those necessary to limit dramatic changes in the firm's operations, such as a major merger or acquisition.

Dividend payout restrictions are not only included in debt contracts, but may also be mandated by law. For example, in several Continental European countries firms are legally obliged to transfer a proportion of their profits to a legal reserve, out of which they cannot distribute dividends. The law then prescribes the minimum legal reserve that a company must maintain.

Loan pricing

A detailed discussion of loan pricing falls outside the scope of this text. The essence of pricing is to assure that the yield on the loan is sufficient to cover:

1 The lender's cost of borrowed funds.

2 The lender's costs of administering and servicing the loan.

3 A premium for exposure to default risk.

4 At least a normal return on the equity capital necessary to support the lending operation.

The price is often stated in terms of a deviation from a bank's base rate – the rate charged to stronger borrowers. For example, a loan might be granted at base rate plus 2 percent. An alternative base is LIBOR, or the London Interbank Offered Rate, the rate at which large banks from various nations lend large blocks of funds to each other.

Banks compete actively for commercial lending business, and it is rare that a yield includes more than 2 percentage points to cover the cost of default risk. If the spread to cover default risk is, say, 1 percent, and the bank recovers only 50 percent of amounts due on loans that turn out bad, then the bank can afford only 2 percent of their loans to fall into that category. This underscores how important it is for banks to conduct a thorough analysis and to contain the riskiness of their loan portfolio.

FINANCIAL STATEMENT ANALYSIS AND PUBLIC DEBT

Fundamentally, the issues involved in analysis of public debt are no different from those of bank loans and other private debt issues. Institutionally, however, the contexts are different. Bankers can maintain very close relations with clients so as to form an initial assessment of their credit risk and monitor their activities during the loan period. In the case of public debt, the investors are distanced from the issuer. To a large extent, they must depend on professional debt analysts, including debt raters, to assess the riskiness of the debt and monitor the firm's ongoing activities. Such analysts and debt raters thus serve an important function in closing the information gap between issuers and investors.

The meaning of debt ratings

A firm's debt rating influences the yield that must be offered to sell the debt instruments. After the debt issue, the rating agencies continue to monitor the firm's financial condition. Changes in the rating are associated with fluctuation in the price of the securities. The three major debt rating agencies in the world are Moody's and Standard and Poor's. Other rating agencies include Fitch Ratings and Dun & Bradstreet.

Using the Standard and Poor's labeling system, the highest possible rating is AAA. Proceeding downward from AAA, the ratings are AA, A, BBB, BB, B, CCC, CC, C, and D, where D indicates debt in default. Table 10.4 presents examples of firms in rating categories AA through CCC, as well as the average interest expense as a percentage of total

TABLE 10.4 Debt ratings: European example firms and average interest expense by category

S&P debt rating	Example firms in 2008	Percentage of European companies given same rating by S&P	Average interest expense to total debt, fiscal 2005–2008 (%)
AA	Aeroports de Paris AstraZeneca Novartis Roche Siemens	3.4	4.83
A	Abertis Infraestructuras BMW Carrefour Groupe Danone Philips Electronics Vodafone	17.6	5.34
BBB	Adecco ArcelorMittal Deutsche Post Fiat InBev Telefonica	42.4	5.95
BB	Alcatel Lucent Cable & Wireless Invensys Pernod Ricard Piaggio TUI	23.9	7.17
B	Escada Thomson Tiscali	11.2	8.56
CCC	Head Waterford Wedgwood	1.5	11.49

Source: Standard and Poor's 2008 and S&P's Global Vantage.

debt across all firms in each category. As of mid-2008, none of the European public non-financial companies rated by Standard & Poor's had the financial strength to merit an AAA rating. Among the few that had an AAA rating but received a downgrade in 2007 or 2008 are the European firms Novartis and Nestlé – both among the largest, most profitable firms in the world. AA firms are also very strong and include Aeroports de Paris, Astra-Zeneca, and Roche. Firms rated AAA and AA have the lowest costs of debt financing; in fiscal year 2008 their average interest expense was roughly 4.8 percent of total debt.

To be considered investment grade, a firm must achieve a rating of BBB or higher. Many funds are precluded by their articles from investing in any bonds below that grade. Even to achieve a grade of BBB is difficult. Fiat, one the largest car manufacturers in the world, was rated as "only" BBB, or barely investment grade in 2008. Pernot Ricard and Alcatel Lucent were in the BB category. Alcatel Lucent, which was the result of the 2006 merger between France-based Alcatel and US-based Lucent Technologies, was the world's largest telecom equipment manufacturer. However, after the merger the company had struggled to integrate the operations of the two units and had to cope with an industry-wide downturn in equipment spending. Consequently, Alcatel Lucent had reported losses in every quarter since the merger. The B category includes Escada, Thomson, and Tiscali, all of which were facing financial difficulty. In Europe, only a few of the industrial companies rated by Standard & Poor's are in a category below the B category. An example of a firm that was rated CCC in 2008 is the Irish china and glass company Waterford Wedgwood plc, which was close to bankruptcy and later acquired by a private equity firm.

Table 10.4 shows that the cost of debt financing rises markedly once firms' debt falls below investment grade. For example, in fiscal 2007/2008 the interest expenses of companies with BBB rated debt were 6.0 percent of total debt, on average; interest rates for BB rated companies were 7.2 percent; and interest rates for firms with B rated debt were 8.6 percent.

Table 10.5 shows median financial ratios for firms by debt rating category. Firms with AAA and AA ratings have very strong earnings and cash flow performance as well as minimal leverage. Firms in the BBB class are only moderately leveraged, with about 35 percent of net capital coming in the form of debt. Earnings tend to be relatively strong, as indicated by a pretax interest coverage (EBIT/interest) of 5.2 percent and a cash flow

TABLE 10.5 Debt ratings: Median financial ratios by category

S&P debt rating	NOPAT to net capital	Pretax interest coverage	Cash flow from operations to total debt	Net debt to net capital
	Median ratios for overall category between July 2005 and July 2008 (European non-financial companies only)			
AAA	18.2%	29.0 times	111.7%	−4.4%
AA	18.9	20.5	91.4	16.8
A	13.7	8.5	45.7	29.8
BBB	11.5	5.2	33.8	34.6
BB	10.1	3.0	22.0	45.9
B	5.0	1.4	8.2	52.5
CCC	−3.8	−0.2	−10.8	60.7

Source: Standard & Poor's Global Vantage.

TABLE 10.8 Debt ratings prediction model estimated on a sample of European companies

Firm or debt characteristic	Variable reflecting characteristic	Coefficients
	Model intercept	2.504
Firm size	Natural logarithm of total assets (in € billions)	0.667
Interest coverage	EBIT to interest expense	0.053
Profitability	NOPAT to net capital (Operating ROA)	2.507
Riskiness of profit stream	Standard deviation of Operating ROA over 5 years	−2.859
Cash flow performance	Cash flow from operations to total debt	−0.214
Leverage	Net debt to net capital	−0.259

The score from the model is converted to a debt rating as follows:

If score > 8.85, predict AAA
   score 8.85–6.88, predict AA
   score 6.88–5.25, predict A
   score 5.25–3.41, predict BBB
   score 3.41–1.93, predict BB
   score 1.93–0.00, predict B
   score < 0.00, predict CCC

companies. The model was off by one category for 41 percent of the companies and off by two categories for 4 percent of the companies. The model was never off by more than two categories.

In the "European" debt ratings prediction model, factors similar to those in the Kaplan-Urwitz model are most significant. That is, Standard and Poor's European debt ratings between 2005 and 2008 were primarily driven by firm size, profitability, riskiness of the profit stream, and leverage (in order of statistical significance). We did not include equity market data in the model to make it usable for privately-held firms, which may be one of the reasons why this model predicts debt ratings slightly less accurately than the Kaplan-Urwitz model.

Given that debt ratings can be explained reasonably well in terms of a handful of financial ratios, one might question whether ratings convey any *news* to investors – anything that could not already have been garnered from publicly available financial data. The answer to the question is yes, at least in the case of debt rating downgrades. That is, downgrades are greeted with drops in both bond and share prices.[13] To be sure, the capital markets anticipate much of the information reflected in rating changes. But that is not surprising, given that the changes often represent reactions to recent known events and that the rating agencies typically indicate in advance that a change is being considered.

PREDICTION OF DISTRESS AND TURNAROUND

The key task in credit analysis is assessing the probability that a firm will face financial distress and fail to repay a loan. A related analysis, relevant once a firm begins to face distress, involves considering whether it can be turned around. In this section we consider evidence on the predictability of these states.

The prediction of either distress or turnaround is a complex, difficult, and subjective task that involves all of the steps of analysis discussed throughout this book: business strategy analysis, accounting analysis, financial analysis, and prospective analysis. Purely quantitative models of the process can rarely serve as substitutes for the hard work the analysis involves. However, research on such models does offer some insight into which financial indicators are most useful in the task. Moreover, there are some settings where extensive credit checks are too costly to justify, and where quantitative distress prediction models are useful. For example, the commercially available "Zeta" model is used by some manufacturers and other firms to assess the creditworthiness of their customers.[14]

Models for distress prediction

Several **financial distress prediction models** have been developed over the years.[15] They are similar to the debt rating models, but instead of predicting ratings, they predict whether a firm will face some state of distress, typically defined as bankruptcy, with a specified period such as one year. One study suggests that the factors most useful (on a stand-alone basis) in predicting bankruptcy one year in advance are the firm's level of profitability, the volatility of that profitability (as measured by the standard deviation of ROE), and its leverage.[16] Interestingly, liquidity measures turn out to be much less important. Current liquidity won't save an unhealthy firm if it is losing money at a fast pace.

A number of more robust, multifactor models have also been designed to predict financial distress. One such model, the Altman Z-score model, weights five variables to compute a bankruptcy score.[17] For public companies the model is as follows:[18]

$$Z = 1.2(X_1) + 1.4(X_2) + 3.3(X_3) + 0.6(X_4) + 1.0(X_5)$$

where X_1 = net working capital/total assets (measure of liquidity)

X_2 = retained earnings/total assets (measure of cumulative profitability)

X_3 = EBIT/total assets (measure of return on assets)

X_4 = market value of equity/book value of total liabilities

      (measure of market leverage)

X_5 = sales/total assets (measure of sales generating potential of assets)

The model predicts bankruptcy when $Z < 1.81$. The range between 1.81 and 2.67 is labeled the "gray area."

The following table presents calculations for two companies, TUI AG and BP plc:

	Model coefficient	TUI AG		BP plc	
		Ratios	Score	Ratios	Score
Net working capital/assets	1.2	0.042	0.05	−0.015	−0.02
Retained earnings/Total assets	1.4	0.002	0.00	0.294	0.41
EBIT/Total assets	3.3	−0.002	−0.01	0.154	0.51
Market value of equity/Book value of total liabilities	0.6	0.140	0.08	1.047	0
Sales/Total assets	1.0	1.120	1.12	1.602	
			1.25		

The table shows a performance gap between the two companies. BP's Z score demonstrates its financial strength. BP has delivered steady sales growth and abnormal profitability over the past five years, and the book value of its liabilities is slightly lower than the market value of its equity. TUI's Z-score, on the other hand, highlights its poor performance. In the past few years, difficult market conditions in TUI's container shipping segment drove down the its margins and eventually made the company decide to (partly) dispose of its container shipping subsidiary and focus more on its tourism divisions. Losses in 2006 and 2008 reduced the company's retained earnings to almost zero. Further, TUI's liabilities are seven times larger than its market capitalization, an indication of its precarious financial state. As a result, TUI's debt was downgraded to B in 2008.

Such models have some ability to predict failing and surviving firms. Altman reports that when the model was applied to a holdout sample containing 33 failed and 33 nonfailed firms (the same proportion used to estimate the model), it correctly predicted the outcome in 63 of 66 cases. However, the performance of the model would degrade substantially if applied to a holdout sample where the proportion of failed and nonfailed firms was not forced to be the same as that used to estimate the model.

The Altman Z-score model was estimated on a sample of US firms. When applying this model to a sample of non-US firms, the following complications must be considered. First, accounting practices may differ from country to country. In particular, under some accounting systems total liabilities may be substantially understated because of firms' use of off-balance sheet financing. When comparing the Altman Z-scores of two firms with different accounting practices, the preferred approach would be to undo these firms' financial statements from accounting distortions and bring all off-balance sheet liabilities on the balance sheet before calculating the scores. Second, although the model may be equally useful across countries in predicting financial distress, the likelihood that financial distress leads to bankruptcy depends on national bankruptcy laws and thus varies from country to country.

One way to overcome the above problems is to use distress prediction models that were estimated in a particular firm's home country. An international survey of distress prediction models suggests that more than 40 variants of such models exist worldwide.[19] A common characteristic of these models is that they all include some measures of profitability and leverage. For example, one model that was developed by Taffler and is commonly used in the UK calculates Z-scores as follows:[20]

$$Z = 3.20 + 12.18(X_1) + 2.50(X_2) - 10.68(X_3) + 0.0289(X_4)$$

where X_1 = profit before tax/current liabilities

X_2 = current assets/total liabilities

X_3 = current liabilities/total assets

X_4 = no-credit interval (in days)

The no-credit interval is defined as immediate assets (current assets excluding inventories and prepaid expenses) minus current liabilities, divided by total operating expenses excluding depreciation and multiplied by 365 days. This variable measures how long the firm can finance its current operations when other sources of short-term finance are unavailable. The model predicts bankruptcy when $Z < 0$. In fiscal year 2008, the Taffler -scores for TUI and AstraZeneca were -0.90 and 6.13, respectively.

While simple distress prediction models like the Altman and the Taffler models cannot as a replacement for in-depth analysis of the kind discussed throughout this book, provide a useful reminder of the power of financial statement data to summarize dimensions of the firm's performance. In addition, they can be useful for screening large numbers of firms prior to more in-depth analysis of corporate strategy, management expertise, market position, and financial ratio performance.

Investment opportunities in distressed companies

The debt securities of firms in financial distress trade at steep discounts to par value. Some hedge fund managers and investment advisors specialize in investing in these securities – even purchasing the debt of firms operating under bankruptcy protection. Investors in these securities can earn attractive returns if the firm recovers from its cash flow difficulties.

Distressed debt investors assess whether the firm is likely to overcome its immediate cash flow problems and whether it has a viable long-run future. Two elements of the framework laid out in Part 2 of this book are particularly relevant to analyzing distressed opportunities. The first is a thorough analysis of the firm's industry and competitive positioning and an assessment of its business risks. This is followed by the construction of well reasoned forecasts of its future cash flow and earnings performance in light of the business analysis.

SUMMARY

Debt financing is attractive to firms with high marginal tax rates and few non-interest tax shields, making interest tax shields from debt valuable. Debt can also help create value by deterring management of firms with high, stable profits/cash flows and few new investment opportunities from over-investing in unprofitable new ventures.

However, debt financing also creates the risk of financial distress, which is likely to be particularly severe for firms with volatile earnings and cash flows, and intangible assets that are easily destroyed by financial distress.

Prospective providers of debt use credit analysis to evaluate the risks of financial distress for a firm. Credit analysis is important to a wide variety of economic agents – not just bankers and other financial intermediaries but also public debt analysts, industrial companies, service companies, and others.

At the heart of credit analysis lie the same techniques described in Chapters 2 through 8: business strategy analysis, accounting analysis, financial analysis, and portions of prospective analysis. The purpose of the analysis is not just to assess the likelihood that a potential borrower will fail to repay the loan. It is also important to identify the nature of the key risks involved, and how the loan might be structured to mitigate or control those risks. A well structured loan provides the lender with a viable "exit strategy," even in the case of default. Properly designed accounting-based covenants are essential to this structure.

Fundamentally, the issues involved in analysis of public debt are no different from those involved in evaluating bank loans or other private debt. Institutionally, however, the contexts are different. Investors in public debt are usually not close to the borrower and must rely on other agents, including debt raters and other analysts, to assess creditworthiness. Debt ratings, which depend heavily on firm size and financial measures of performance, have an important influence on the market yields that must be offered to issue debt.

The key task in credit analysis is the assessment of the probability of default. The task is complex, difficult, and to some extent, subjective. A few financial ratios can help predict financial distress with some accuracy. The most important indicators for this purpose are profitability, volatility of profits, and leverage. While there are a number of models that predict distress based on financial indicators, they cannot replace the in-depth forms of analysis discussed in this book.

CORE CONCEPTS

Benefits of debt Two benefits of debt financing are:

1 The tax deductibility of interest payments creates a corporate tax shield.

2 Debt reduces the free cash flow that is available to management and, consequently, strengthens managerial incentives for value creation.

Costs of debt Three potential costs of debt financing are:

1 Too much debt can lead to financial distress and costly debt restructurings.

2 Financial distress can make a firm forego valuable investment opportunities.

3 Financial distress creates conflicts between creditors, who wish to maximize the value of the firm's assets, and shareholders, who wish to maximize the value of equity.

Country differences in the use of debt The use of debt financing differs across countries because of institutional differences, such as differences in the legal protection of creditors' interests. Institutional differences affect, amongst others, the occurrence of multiple-bank borrowing, the use of supplier financing, the use of off-balance sheet financing (such as factoring of receivables), and the development of public debt markets. The ultimate effect of institutional differences on firms' leverage ratios is complex and uncertain.

Credit analysis Credit analysis includes assessing the creditworthiness of a firm; determining the type of loan, loan structure, and the necessity of security and/or loan covenants; and assessing whether the firm's future growth opportunities can be valuable to the lender. The credit analysis process consists of the following four steps:

1 Understanding why the firm applies for a loan and for what purpose the loan will be used.

2 Determining the type of loan on the basis of the purpose of the loan and the firm's financial strength. This step also includes determining the type of security that will be required to reduce the lender's risk (and thereby the cost of debt).

3 Analyzing the creditworthiness of the firm using ratio analysis and forecasting.

4 Determining the loan structure, including loan covenants and price (interest rate).

Debt rating prediction models Quantitative models explaining firms' public debt ratings on the basis of observable firm and debt characteristics. An example of a debt rating prediction model is the Kaplan-Urwitz model. The primary firm characteristics used to predict debt ratings are: firm size, profitability, leverage, and interest coverage.

Financial distress prediction models Quantitative models predicting the likelihood that a firm will become financially distressed within a period of typically one year (on the basis of observable firm characteristics). An example of a financial distress prediction model is the Altman Z-score model. Some firm characteristics used to predict financial distress are: (cumulative) profitability, leverage, and liquidity.

Public debt ratings Scores assigned to the financial condition of firms issuing public debt by debt rating agencies such as Fitch, Moody's and Standard and Poor's.

Suppliers of debt financing Major suppliers of debt financing are: commercial banks, non-bank financial institutions such as finance and insurance companies, public debt markets, and suppliers of goods and services.

QUESTIONS

1   What are the critical performance dimensions for (a) a retailer and (b) a financial services company that should be considered in credit analysis? What ratios would you
suggest looking at for each of these dimensions?

2   Why would a company pay to have its public debt rated by a major rating agency
(such as Fitch, Moody's or Standard & Poor's)? Why might a firm decide not to have
its debt rated?

3   Some have argued that the market for original-issue junk bonds developed in the US
in the late 1970s as a result of a failure in the rating process. Proponents of this argument suggest that rating agencies rated companies too harshly at the low end of the
rating scale, denying investment-grade status to some deserving companies. What are
proponents of this argument effectively assuming were the incentives of rating agencies? What economic forces could give rise to this incentive?

4   Many debt agreements require borrowers to obtain the permission of the lender before
undertaking a major acquisition or asset sale. Why would the lender want to include
this type of restriction?

5   Betty Li, the Finance Director of a company applying for a new loan, states, "I will
never agree to a debt covenant that restricts my ability to pay dividends to my shareholders because it reduces shareholder wealth." Do you agree with this argument?

6   A bank extends three loans to the following companies: an Italy-based biotech firm; a
France-based car manufacturer; and a UK-based food retailer. How may these three loans
differ from each other in terms of loan maturity, required collateral, and loan amount?

7   Cambridge Construction Plc follows the percentage-of-completion method for reporting long-term contract revenues. The percentage of completion is based on the cost of
materials shipped to the project site as a percentage of total expected material costs.
Cambridge's major debt agreement includes restrictions on net worth, interest coverage, and minimum working capital requirements. A leading analyst claims that "the
company is buying its way out of these covenants by spending cash and buying materials, even when they are not needed." Explain how this may be possible.

8   Can Cambridge improve its Z score by behaving as the analyst claims in Question 7?
Is this change consistent with economic reality?

9   A banker asserts, "I avoid lending to companies with negative cash from operations
because they are too risky." Is this a sensible lending policy?

10 A leading retailer finds itself in a financial bind. It doesn't have sufficient cash flow
from operations to finance its growth, and it is close to violating the maximum debt-
to-assets ratio allowed by its covenants. The Marketing Director suggests, "We can
raise cash for our growth by selling the existing stores and leasing them back. This
source of financing is cheap since it avoids violating either the debt-to-assets or interest coverage ratios in our covenants." Do you agree with his analysis? Why or why
not? As the firm's banker, how would you view this arrangement?

NOTES

1. Rahim Bah and Pascal Dumontier provide empirical evidence that R&D-intensive firms in Europe, Japan, and the US have lower debt and pay out lower dividends than non-R&D firms. See Rahim Bah and Pascal Dumontier, "R&D Intensity and Corporate Financial Policy: Some International Evidence," *Journal of Business Finance and Accounting* 28 (June/July 2001): 671–692.

2. Some arguments that have been raised in other countries against universal banking are the following. First, because of their investment banking activities, universal banks may incur greater risks than other commercial banks and, consequently, jeopardize the stability of a country's financial system. Second, universal banks may become too powerful because of their size and hold back competition in the banking industry. Third, universal banks could potentially misuse inside information about clients that they obtained through their lending activities in securities trading. In the US, these concerns led to ban on universal banking until 1999. For a discussion of the potential advantages and disadvantages of universal banking, see, for example, George J. Benston, "Universal Banking," *Journal of Economic Perspectives* (1994): 121–143.

3. See Sergei A. Davydenko and Julian R. Franks, "Do Bankruptcy Codes Matter? A Study of Defaults in France, Germany and the U.K.," working paper, University of Toronto and London Business School, 2005.

4. See Steven Ongena and David C. Smith, "What Determines the Number of Bank Relationships? Cross-Country Evidence," *Journal of Financial Intermediation* (2000): 26–56.

5. See Asli Demirgüç-Kunt and Vojislav Maksimovic, "Firms as Financial Intermediaries: Evidence from Trade Credit Data," working paper, World Bank and University of Maryland, 2001.

6. See Marie H. R. Bakker, Leonora Klapper, and Gregory F. Udell, "Financing Small and Medium-Sized Enterprises with Factoring: Global Growth and Its Potential In Eastern Europe," working paper, World Bank and Indiana University, 2004.

7. See Asli Demirgüç-Kunt and Vojislav Maksimovic, "Institutions, Financial Markets, and Firm Debt Maturity," *Journal of Financial Economics* 54 (1999): 295–336.

8. See Mariassunta Giannetti, "Do Better Institutions Mitigate Agency Problems? Evidence from Corporate Finance Choices," *Journal of Financial and Quantitative Analysis* 38 (2003): 185–212.

9. Sergei A. Davydenko and Julian R. Franks, op. cit.

10. The same is true of preference dividends. However, when preference shares are cumulative, any dividends missed must be paid later, when and if the firm returns to profitability.

11. Other relevant coverage ratios are discussed in Chapter 5.

12. Robert Kaplan and G. Urwitz, "Statistical Models of Bond Ratings: A Methodological Inquiry," *Journal of Business* (April 1979): 231–261.

13. See Robert Holthausen and Richard Leftwich, "The Effect of Bond Rating Changes on Common Stock Prices," *Journal of Financial Economics* (September 1986): 57–90; and John Hand, Robert Holthausen, and Richard Leftwich, "The Effect of Bond Rating Announcements on Bond and Stock Prices," *Journal of Finance* (June 1992): 733–752.

14. See *Corporate Financial Distress* by Edward Altman (New York: John Wiley, 1993).

15. See Edward Altman, "Financial Ratios, Discriminant Analysis, and the Prediction of Corporate Bankruptcy," *Journal of Finance* (September 1968): 589–609; Altman, *Corporate Financial Distress,* op. cit.; William Beaver, "Financial Ratios as Predictors of Distress," *Journal of Accounting Research,* Supplement (1966): 71–111; James Ohlson, "Financial Ratios and the Probabilistic Prediction of Bankruptcy," *Journal of Accounting Research* (Spring 1980): 109–131; and Mark Zmijewski, "Predicting Corporate Bankruptcy: An Empirical Comparison of the Extant Financial Distress Models," working paper, SUNY at Buffalo, 1983.

16. Zmijewski, op. cit.

17. Altman, *Corporate Financial Distress,* op. cit.

18. For private firms, Altman, ibid., adjusts the public model by changing the numerator for the variable X_4 from the market value of equity to the book value. The revised model follows:

$$Z = .717(X_1) + .847(X_2) + 3.107(X_3) + 0.420(X_4) + .998(X_5)$$

where X_1 = net working capital/total assets

X_2 = retained earnings/total assets

X_3 = EBIT/total assets

X_4 = book value of equity/book value of total liabilities

X_5 = sales/total assets

The model predicts bankruptcy when Z < 1.20. The range between 1.20 and 2.90 is labeled the "gray area."

19. See E. Altman and P. Narayanan, "An International Survey of Business Failure Classification Models," *Financial Markets, Institutions and Instruments* (May 1997): 1–57, for an extensive description of various non-US bankruptcy prediction models.

20. The Taffler model and tests of its predictive accuracy are described in R. Taffler, "The Assessment of Company Solvency and Performance Using a Statistical Model," *Accounting and Business Research* (1983): 295–307 and R. Taffler, "Empirical Models for the Monitoring of UK Corporations," *Journal of Banking and Finance* (1984): 199–227.

Getronics' debt ratings

G etronics N.V. is a Netherlands-based provider of Information and Communication Technology (ICT) services. The company originates from a leveraged management buyout of Geveke Electronics N.V. and was taken public by its privately held owner SHV Holdings N.V. in 1985. Following its initial public offering, the company adopted a strategy of aggressive expansion through internal growth, acquisitions, and strategic investments. Between 1985 and 1999, Getronics managed to double its sales and earnings every three years, on average. In 1999, the company turned from a moderate player in the European ICT industry into one of the world's largest ICT service providers through its acquisition of US-based Wang Global. This acquisition more than doubled Getronics' revenues (from €1.5 billion to €3.7 billion) and almost tripled the company's employee base.

To finance the acquisition of Wang Global, Getronics needed to issue new shares and attract a substantial amount of new debt. Therefore, the company entered into a €500 million syndicated revolving variable-rate credit facility, which would mature on April 2004, and issued €350 million of subordinated convertible bonds. The subordinated convertible bonds bore an annual interest rate of 0.25 percent but would be redeemed at 113.21 percent of their face value if they remained unconverted until the maturity date (April 2004). Hence, the yield to maturity of unconverted bonds was 2.75 percent. The bonds' conversion price was €14.53 per ordinary share, while Getronics' share price on December 31, 1999 had reached €26.40.

At the end of fiscal year 1999, Getronics had 343,724,237 ordinary shares and 21,950,000 cumulative preference shares outstanding. The preference shares earned cumulative dividend, paid annually in arrears, at 5.7 percent and had been issued at €10.75 per share (€236 million in total).

During fiscal year 2000, Getronics issued €500 million of new subordinated convertible bonds (with an annual interest rate of 0.25 percent, a redemption price of 116.01 percent, and a conversion price of €36.98), maturing in March 2005, and reduced its debt under the revolving credit facility by €150 million. Getronics' share price at the end of 2000 was €6.26; by the end of 2001, it had dropped further to €3.64.

During fiscal year 2001, Getronics temporarily lowered the conversion price of its subordinated convertible bonds to persuade its bondholders to convert their bonds into ordinary shares. As a result, convertible debt with a total book value €295 million was converted into equity, increasing the number of outstanding shares with 61,078,827. In 2003, Getronics eventually redeemed its outstanding subordinated convertible bonds by paying the bondholders €325 million in cash and agreeing to repay the remaining €250 million through quarterly installment payments during a five-year period. The interest rate on the new installment bonds equaled 13 percent. To finance the redemption, Getronics issued new unsubordinated convertible bonds, maturing in five years, for an amount of €100 million (with an annual interest rate of 5.5 percent, a redemption price of 100 percent, and a conversion price of €1.58). At the end of 2003, Getronics' share price was €1.66.

In 2004 and 2005, Getronics issued 100 million and 48.5 million new shares. The company used the proceeds of the 2004 issue to redeem its installment bonds early. In

Professor Erik Peek prepared this case. The case is intended solely as the basis for class discussion and is not intended to serve as an endorsement, source of primary data, or illustration of effective or ineffective management.

addition, the company obtained a new €175 credit facility in 2004—which got replaced by a €300 credit facility in 2005—to help finance the redemption as well as replace a €100 credit facility and issued new unsubordinated convertible bonds (with an annual interest rate of 5.5 percent and a redemption price of 100 percent) in 2005. As a consequence of the adoption of IFRS in 2005, Getronics reclassified its cumulative preference shares from equity to debt. The par value and premium reserve of these shares (i.e., the book value of the new debt) amounted to €235 million.

Fiscal year 2006 was another challenging year for Getronics. The company incurred unexpected losses in Italy, had to recognize an impairment charge of €65 million on goodwill relating to the Wang Global acquisition and, consequently, reported a significant net loss. During 2006, Getronics did not change much to its borrowings other than replacing maturing bonds with new unsubordinated convertible bonds. The losses continued in 2007, when competitors started to consider the company as a takeover candidate. On July 31, 2007, Royal KPN N.V. announced its interest in acquiring Getronics. On October 22, 2007, KPN completed its acquisition.

EXHIBIT 1   Getronics N.V.—summary of events

Date	Event/announcement
May 5, 1999	Getronics acquires US-based industry peer Wang Global; the company finances the acquisition through a mixture of new equity (€0.7 billion common and €0.3 billion preferred) and debt (€0.5 billion loans and €0.3 billion convertible bonds). The amount of goodwill that Getronics recognized on the transaction is close to €2.4 billion.
February 9, 2000	Getronics sells its ATM business, realizing a profit on the sale.
March 3, 2000	Annual results 1999 announcement. The acquisition of Wang Global boosts the company's results. Getronics announces ambitious growth plans.
March 16, 2000	Getronics issues €450 million in subordinated convertible debt (to replace maturing debt).
First half 2000	End of the dot-com bubble. Technology shares decline.
August 17, 2000	First half-year report.
November 22, 2000	Getronics announces that this year's earnings will be below expectations. Getronics' share price declines by 42 percent.
February 5, 2001	Getronics signs €75 million contract with Shell.
February 28, 2001	Annual results 2000 announcement
June 1, 2001	Getronics' CEO Cees van Luijk resigns and is succeeded by Peter van Voorst.
August 16, 2001	First half-year report
December 11, 2001	Getronics exchanges €295.3 million of subordinated convertible bonds for equity.
December 18, 2001	Getronics signs €90 million contract with Barclays.
March 5, 2002	Annual results 2001 announcement. Getronics decides to freeze wages of its employees after incurring a record loss.
April 22, 2002	Getronics announces that it plans to repurchase some of its outstanding convertible bonds
August 13, 2002	Getronics' share price drops by close to 40 percent after rumors that the company is close to applying for bankruptcy.
August 15, 2002	First half-year report
December 31, 2002	Getronics repays all its amounts outstanding under the €500 million credit facility.
February 12, 2003	Getronics offers (mostly institutional) subordinated convertible bondholders equity in exchange for their bonds. Convertible bondholders deny the offer, resulting in a conflict between management and bondholders.
February 21, 2003	CEO Peter van Voorst and CFO Jan Docter step down. The new CEO of Getronics is Klaas Wagenaar.
March 4, 2003	Annual results 2002 announcement
March 21, 2003	Getronics announces to reduce debt by selling assets rather than offering bondholders equity.
April 22, 2003	Getronics sells Getronics HR Solutions for €315 million in cash (and realizes a profit on the sale of €270 million).
June 10, 2003	Getronics immediately repays bondholders €325 million (in cash) and agrees for the repayment of the remaining €250 million in installments. The agreement resolves the company's conflict with its convertible bondholders.
July 1, 2003	Getronics obtains a loan of €100 million, which will be used to replace a €200 million credit facility.
August 13, 2003	First half-year report
October 13, 2003	Getronics issues €100 million in convertible debt (to replace maturing debt).
February 4, 2004	Getronics sells 100 million new shares to institutional investors (proceeds: €233 million). The proceeds are used to repay €250 million in subordinated installment bonds on March 30, 2004.

EXHIBIT 1   **Getronics N.V.—summary of events** (*continued*)

Date	Event/announcement
March 2, 2004	Annual results 2003 announcement
April 19, 2004	Getronics obtains a new credit facility of €175 million from a consortium of banks.
August 11, 2004	First half-year report
November 1, 2004	Getronics announces the acquisition of industry peer PinkRoccade N.V for the amount of €350 million. The company will obtain a new credit facility of €125 million that, together with the credit facility obtained in April, will be used to finance the acquisition.
March 3, 2005	Annual results 2004 announcement
April 11, 2005	Getronics issues new shares (proceeds: €388 million).
August 3, 2005	First half-year report.
September 29, 2005	Getronics issues €150 million in unsecured convertible debt (to replace maturing bonds).
March 2, 2006	Annual results 2005 announcement. Getronics also announces that its Italian subsidiary has committed fraud, hiding €15 million in expenses.
April 20, 2006	Getronics receives four bids for its Italian subsidiary.
June 23, 2006	Getronics sells its Italian subsidiary to Eutelia for an estimated amount of €135 million, realizing a loss of €50 million. The sale helps the company to meet its debt covenants again.
August 1, 2006	First half-year report. Disappointing results cause share prices to decline by close to 24 percent. Getronics announces restructuring plans.
November 15, 2006	CFO Theo Janssen resigns unexpectedly. Two other Board Members follow his example.
December 14, 2006	Getronics issues €95 million in convertible bonds (to replace maturing bonds).
February 27, 2007	Annual results 2006 announcement. Getronics announces its annual results early. The company realized an unexpected loss of €145 million.
July 30, 2007	Royal KPN acquires Getronics.

Getronics' debt ratings

Getronics' debt ratings

EXHIBIT 2 Getronics N.V.—financial information (in € millions)

	2007 H2	2007 H1	2006 H2	2006 H1	2005 H2	2005 H1	2004 H2	2004 H1	2003 H2	2003 H1	2002 H2	2002 H1	2001 H2	2001 H1	2000 H2	2000 H1
Revenue	1224	1280	1319	1308	1271	1322	918	1188	1308	1363	1757	1838	2048	2101	2214	1913
Cost of sales	−996	−1051	−1040	−1062	−988	−1079	−740	−981	−1103	−1131	−1463	−1495	−1703	−1723	−1768	−1514
Gross profit	**228**	**229**	**279**	**246**	**283**	**243**	**178**	**207**	**205**	**232**	**294**	**343**	**345**	**378**	**446**	**399**
Selling expenses	−91	−97	−99	−108	−95	−98	−68	−86	−84	−92	−124	−132	−135	−131	−131	−125
General and administrative expenses	−153	−108	−111	−106	−98	−106	−67	−94	−105	−128	−126	−151	−148	−162	−180	−161
Other operating expenses/income	0	−13	−2	−11	−43	−3	−6	6	15	−62	−33	0	3	—	—	—
Amortization/impairment of intangible assets	−13	−88	−65	0	0	0	0	0	−22	−21	−403	−30	−983	−49	−50	−48
Earnings before interest and taxes (EBIT)	**−29**	**−77**	**2**	**21**	**47**	**36**	**37**	**33**	**9**	**−71**	**−392**	**30**	**−918**	**36**	**85**	**65**
Financial income and expenses	−29	−22	−40	−23	−17	−46	−2	−21	−23	−35	−13	−15	−17	−30	−24	−19
Earnings before taxes (EBT)	**−58**	**−99**	**−38**	**−2**	**30**	**−10**	**35**	**12**	**−14**	**−106**	**−405**	**15**	**−935**	**6**	**61**	**46**
Income taxes	6	−9	−38	24	24	0	60	−4	22	74	−9	−11	−12	−14	−26	−22
Income from unconsolidated investments and discontinued operations (net of income taxes)	1	0	−28	−63	−40	0	−47	0	9	261	0	0	−8	−76	−28	31
Net earnings	**−51**	**−108**	**−104**	**−41**	**14**	**−10**	**48**	**8**	**17**	**229**	**−414**	**4**	**−955**	**−84**	**7**	**55**
Intangible fixed assets	517	534	681	896	913	925	530	553	623	—	654	1213	1238	2196	2201	2258
Tangible fixed assets	109	102	95	107	113	143	73	76	83	—	144	177	185	240	223	202
Other non–current assets	322	281	281	352	283	241	147	191	160	—	91	79	88	100	168	161
Total non-current assets	**948**	**917**	**1057**	**1355**	**1309**	**1309**	**750**	**820**	**866**	**833**	**889**	**1469**	**1511**	**2536**	**2592**	**2621**
Total current assets	**701**	**714**	**793**	**841**	**907**	**963**	**889**	**872**	**1087**	**1042**	**1287**	**1564**	**1752**	**1805**	**1882**	**1604**
– of which cash and cash equivalents	134	122	174	144	251	141	236	217	409	214	296	269	387	250	292	150
Assets held for sale	**0**	**161**	**90**	**22**	**181**											
Total assets	**1649**	**1792**	**1940**	**2218**	**2397**	**2272**	**1639**	**1692**	**1953**	**1875**	**2176**	**3033**	**3263**	**4341**	**4474**	**4225**

Shareholders' equity	409	321	408	524	597	602	357	386	299	320	122	522	532	1209	1257	1317
Minority interests	0	0	0	0	0	0	0	2	2	1	2	2	3	3	4	3
Subordinated convertibles	—	—	—	—	—	—	—	—	—	—	520	522	554	849	849	849
Short-term interest bearing debt	67	223	137	85	100	10	6	2	105	38	15	12	24	20	15	15
Long-term debt	347	340	323	551	337	453	197	199	330	301	80	367	427	542	435	395
Provisions	—	—	—	—	—	—	—	—	—	286	337	391	411	413	458	452
Employee benefit plans	95	110	119	155	160	185	202	237	126	—	—	—	—	—	—	—
Provisions for liabilities and charges	27	16	26	51	39	40	22	23	81	—	—	—	—	—	—	—
Deferred income tax liabilities	10	7	6	20	12	72	12	51	50	—	—	—	—	—	—	—
Other non-current liabilities	13	29	24	6	15	0	4	0	0	—	—	—	—	—	—	—
Non-current liabilities and short-term debt	559	725	635	868	663	760	443	512	692	625	432	770	862	975	908	862
Current liabilities (excl. short-term debt)	681	684	862	814	888	910	839	792	960	929	1100	1217	1312	1305	1456	1194
Liabilities from discontinued activities	0	62	35	12	249	—	—	—	—	—	—	—	—	—	—	—
Total equity and liabilities	1649	1792	1940	2218	2397	2272	1639	1692	1953	1875	2176	3033	3263	4341	4474	4225
Cash flow from operations	12	-148	144	-142	95	-160	34	-14	96	-103	175	5	229	-27	-16	-13
Cash flow from capital expenditures	13	-26	65	-81	-28	-344	-19	-1	32	259	150	-17	22	-83	-29	-17
Cash flow from financing activities	-20	115	-203	127	48	403	9	-53	92	-231	-307	-97	-114	68	181	—
Market capitalization at year end		753			1392		846		679	237			1489			
Statutory tax rate	25.50%	25.50%	29.60%	29.60%	31.50%	31.50%	34.50%	34.50%	34.50%	34.50%	34.50%	34.50%	34.50%	34.50%	34.50%	34.50%

Getronics' debt ratings

Source: 2000 – 2007 annual and semiannual reports of Getronics N.V.

11 Mergers and Acquisitions

Mergers and acquisitions have long been a popular form of corporate investment, particularly in countries with Anglo-American forms of capital markets. There is no question that these transactions provide a healthy return to target shareholders. However, their value to acquiring shareholders is less understood. Many skeptics point out that given the hefty premiums paid to target shareholders, acquisitions tend to be negative-valued investments for acquiring shareholders.[1]

A number of questions can be examined using financial analysis for mergers and acquisitions:

■ Securities analysts can ask: Does a proposed acquisition create value for the acquiring firm's shareholders?

■ Risk arbitrageurs can ask: What is the likelihood that a hostile takeover offer will ultimately succeed, and are there other potential acquirers likely to enter the bidding?

■ Acquiring management can ask: Does this target fit our business strategy? If so, what is it worth to us, and how can we make an offer that can be successful?

■ Target management can ask: Is the acquirer's offer a reasonable one for our shareholders? Are there other potential acquirers that would value our company more than the current bidder?

■ Investment bankers can ask: How can we identify potential targets that are likely to be a good match for our clients? And how should we value target firms when we are asked to issue fairness opinions?

In this chapter we focus primarily on the use of financial statement data and analysis directed at evaluating whether a merger creates value for the acquiring firm's shareholders. However, our discussion can also be applied to these other merger contexts. The topic of whether acquisitions create value for acquirers focuses on evaluating:

1 Motivations for acquisitions.

2 The pricing of offers.

3 Forms of payment.

4 The likelihood that an offer will be successful.

Throughout the chapter we use France-based Alcatel's merger with US-based Lucent Technologies in 2006 to illustrate how financial analysis can be used in a merger context.

MOTIVATION FOR MERGER OR ACQUISITION

There are a variety of reasons why firms merge or acquire other firms. Some acquiring managers may want to increase their own power and prestige. Others, however, realize that business combinations provide an opportunity to create new economic value for their shareholders. **Merger or acquisition benefits** include the following:

1. Taking advantage of economies of scale. Mergers are often justified as a means of providing the two participating firms with increased economies of scale. Economies of scale arise when one large firm can perform a function more efficiently than two smaller firms. For example, Alcatel and Lucent are both telecommunications equipment makers and had considerable overlap in management, information technology, sales, and research and development activities. The merger was expected to provide operating synergies from eliminating duplicate functions and excess capacity, and from reducing research, material, general and administrative costs. At the time of the merger, management estimated that it would save €1.4 billion over the first three years following the merger by cutting roughly 9,000 jobs, closing offices, trimming business overlap, and sharing research and development facilities, procurement budgets, and information technology. All told, management stated that it could realize cost savings with a present value of €10 billion through the merger.

2. Improving target management. Another common motivation for acquisition is to improve target management. A firm is likely to be a target if it has systematically underperformed its industry. Historical poor performance could be due to bad luck, but it could also be due to the firm's managers making poor investment and operating decisions, or deliberately pursuing goals that increase their personal power but cost shareholders. Lucent had reported losses and negative operating cash flows in the years 2001 through 2003. The company became profitable again in 2004. However, at the time of the merger announcement, Lucent's price-earnings ratio of 10.5 was substantially below the industry average. For the following fiscal year, analysts reckoned that Lucent's revenues and earnings per share would decline by 4 and 43 percent, respectively. Nonetheless, the merger agreement provided that Patricia F. Russo, who took over as Lucent's CEO in 2002, would also become the CEO of the combined company.

3. Combining complementary resources. Firms may decide that a merger will create value by combining complementary resources of the two partners. For example, a firm with a strong research and development unit could benefit from merging with a firm that has a strong distribution unit. In the Alcatel-Lucent merger, the two firms appeared to have complementary capabilities and resources. Alcatel had a strong market position in IP network transformation and triple play. Lucent was the global leader in building IP multimedia subsystems as well as spread spectrum networks for third-generation mobile communication systems such as UMTS. In addition, both firms had a strong market presence in different geographical areas. Alcatel generated close to 50 percent of its revenues in Europe, whereas 66 percent of Lucent's revenues came from its North American operations. The merger thus increased Alcatel's and Lucent's geographical reach. After the merger, the combined company would generate approximately one-third of its revenues in Europe and one-third of its revenues in North America.

4. Capturing tax benefits. Companies may obtain several tax benefits from mergers and acquisitions. The major benefit is the acquisition of operating tax losses. If a firm does not expect to earn sufficient profits to fully utilize operating loss carryforward benefits, it may decide to buy another firm that is earning profits, provided that these profits are made in the same tax jurisdiction as where the loss carryforwards arose. The operating losses and loss carryforwards of the acquirer can then be offset against the target's

taxable profit. A second tax benefit often attributed to mergers is the tax shield that comes from increasing leverage for the target firm. That is, the interest expense on the additional debt is tax-deductible and lowers the target firm's tax payments. This was particularly relevant for leveraged buyouts in the 1980s.[2]

5. Providing low-cost financing to a financially constrained target. If capital markets are imperfect, perhaps because of information asymmetries between management and outside investors, firms can face capital constraints. Information problems are likely to be especially severe for newly formed, high-growth firms. These firms can be difficult for outside investors to value since they have short track records, and their financial statements provide little insight into the value of their growth opportunities. Further, since they typically have to rely on external funds to finance their growth, capital market constraints for high-growth firms are likely to affect their ability to undertake profitable new projects. Public capital markets are therefore likely to be costly sources of funds for these types of firms. An acquirer that understands the business and is willing to provide a steady source of finance may therefore be able to add value.[3]

6. Creating value through restructuring and break-ups. Acquisitions are often pursued by financial investors such as leveraged buy-out firms that expect to create value by breaking up the firm. The break-up value is expected to be larger than the aggregate worth of the entire firm. Often, a consortium of financial investors will acquire a firm with a view of unlocking value from various components of the firm's asset base.

7. Increasing product-market rents. Firms also can have incentives to merge to increase product-market rents. By merging and becoming a dominant firm in the industry, two smaller firms can collude to restrict their output and raise prices, thereby increasing their profits. This circumvents problems that arise in cartels of independent firms, where firms have incentives to cheat on the cartel and increase their output. At the time of the Alcatel-Lucent merger, telecom service providers such as AT&T, Vodafone, and Telefónica, who were the major buyers of Alcatel's and Lucent's equipment, were also in the midst of consolidation. The merger thus improved the combined company's bargaining power over its increasingly powerful customers.

While product-market rents make sense for firms as a motive for merging, the two partners are unlikely to announce their intentions when they explain the merger to their investors, since most countries have competition (antitrust) laws which regulate mergers between two firms in the same industry. For example, in the EU large mergers must be approved by the European Commission, which examines whether mergers do not impede effective competition by creating a dominant market position. National mergers are generally reviewed by national competition authorities. In the US there are three major antitrust statutes – The Sherman Act of 1890, The Clayton Act of 1914, and The Hart Scott Rodino Act of 1976.

Anti-competitive concerns were significant for the Alcatel-Lucent merger because the merger created the world's largest telecommunications equipment maker. Merger approval was required from both the US Federal Trade Commission (FTC) and the European Commission.

While many of the motivations for acquisitions are likely to create new economic value for shareholders, some are not. Firms that are flush with cash but have few new profitable investment opportunities are particularly prone to using their surplus cash to make acquisitions. Shareholders of these firms would probably prefer that managers pay out any surplus or "free" cash flows as dividends, or use the funds to repurchase their firm's shares. However, these options reduce the size of the firm and the assets under management's control. Management may therefore prefer to invest the free cash flows to buy new companies, even if they are not valued by shareholders. Of course managers will never announce that they are buying a firm because they are reluctant to pay out funds to shareholders.

They may explain the merger using one of the motivations discussed above, or they may argue that they are buying the target at a bargain price.

Another motivation for mergers that is valued by managers but not shareholders is diversification. Diversification was a popular motivation for acquisitions in the 1960s and early 1970s. Acquirers sought to dampen their earnings volatility by buying firms in unrelated businesses. Diversification as a motive for acquisitions has since been widely discredited. Modern finance theorists point out that in a well-functioning capital market, investors can diversify for themselves and do not need managers to do so for them. In addition, diversification has been criticized for leading firms losing sight of their major competitive strengths and expanding into businesses where they do not have expertise.[4] These firms eventually recognize that diversification-motivated acquisitions do not create value, leading to divestitures of business units.

KEY ANALYSIS QUESTIONS

In evaluating a proposed merger, analysts are interested in determining whether the merger creates new wealth for acquiring and target shareholders, or whether it is motivated by managers' desires to increase their own power and prestige. Key questions for financial analysis are likely to include:

- *What is the motivation(s) for an acquisition and any anticipated benefits disclosed by acquirers or targets?*

- *What are the industries of the target and acquirer?* Are the firms related horizontally (the firms are suppliers of similar products) or vertically (one firm is the other firm's supplier)? How close are the business relations between them? If the businesses are unrelated, is the acquirer cash-rich and reluctant to return free cash flows to shareholders?

- *What are the key operational strengths of the target and the acquirer?* Are these strengths complementary? For example, does one firm have a renowned research group and the other a strong distribution network?

- *Is the acquisition a friendly one, supported by target management, or hostile?* A hostile takeover is more likely to occur for targets with poor-performing management who oppose the acquisition to preserve their jobs. However, as discussed below, this typically reduces acquirer management's access to information about the target, increasing the risk of overpayment.

- *What is the premerger performance of the two firms?* Performance metrics are likely to include ROE, gross margins, general and administrative expenses to sales, and working capital management ratios. On the basis of these measures, is the target a poor performer in its industry, implying that there are opportunities for improved management? Is the acquirer in a declining industry and searching for new directions?

- *What is the tax position of both firms?* What are the average and marginal current tax rates for the target and the acquirer? Does the acquirer have operating loss carryforwards and the target taxable profits?

This analysis should help the analyst understand what specific benefits, if any, the merger is likely to generate.

Motivation for the Alcatel-Lucent merger

Several industry factors influenced Alcatel and Lucent to merge. At the time of the merger, the telecommunications services industry, to which Alcatel and Lucent supplied most of their equipment, was going through a wave of consolidation. For example, in 2005 US-based SBC Communications acquired AT&T to become the world's largest telecom service provider. One year later, the company, which was named AT&T after the merger, strengthened its dominant market position even further by acquiring US-based BellSouth. Similarly, in 2005 Spanish Telefónica agreed to acquire British O2. In the same year, Sweden-based Tele2 acquired Netherlands-based Versatel, a specialist in triple play. These mergers substantially impaired telecom equipment makers' bargaining power over their primary customers. The merger between Alcatel and Lucent therefore somewhat restored the balance of power between suppliers and buyers of telecom equipment. Other telecom equipment makers followed a similar strategy. For example, in 2006 Germany-based Siemens and Finland-based Nokia combined their telecom equipment units into a joint venture.

The fixed telecommunications networks market was also in a state of transition. At the end of the first half of the 2000s, fixed network operators started to combine telephone, internet, and video services, under the label "triple play." The great demand from customers for these converged services and networks allowed the fixed networks market to expand for the first time since the burst of the telecom bubble in 2001. The merger between Alcatel and Lucent could strengthen the companies' position in the fixed networks segment and improve the probability that Alcatel-Lucent would benefit from the segment's growth. Lucent's experience in building IP multimedia systems could become complementary to Alcatel's experience with triple play in becoming a leader in converged networks.

The management of Alcatel and Lucent argued that a merger would provide the new company with four significant benefits. First, as noted above, the combined firm would be able to reduce costs by €1.4 billion per year through efficiency improvements such as streamlining administrative overhead, eliminating excess capacity and duplicate facilities, using purchasing power to reduce material costs, and coordinating research and development in areas where the two firms operated separately. These savings were expected to be fully realized by the third year after the merger. Second, the merger increased Alcatel's and Lucent's geographical reach by creating a combined company that operated on a global scale. Third, management noted that the two companies had complementary expertise that would help increase productivity. For example, Alcatel was a leader in IP network transformation and triple play, which complemented Lucent's leadership in building IP multimedia systems and spread spectrum networks. The combined company would be better able to offer its customers telecom solutions that integrated telephone, internet, and video. Fourth, combining the companies' research and development budgets and patents portfolios helped Alcatel-Lucent to increase the scale of its global research and development and could make Alcatel-Lucent an industry leader in innovation.

Analysts and the financial media generally concurred with management's assessments of the economic benefits that potentially would be derived from the merger. Some analysts nevertheless expressed concern that the large size of the two companies might make it difficult for them to actually achieve these synergies. Because the companies' existing customers expected support for years to come, analysts feared that the combined company would not be able to eliminate duplicate products in its product portfolio.[5]

ACQUISITION PRICING

A well thought out economic motivation for a merger or acquisition is a necessary but not sufficient condition for it to create value for acquiring shareholders. The acquirer must be careful to avoid overpaying for the target. Overpayment makes the transaction highly desirable and profitable for target shareholders, but it diminishes the value of the deal to acquiring shareholders. A financial analyst can use the following methods to assess whether the acquiring firm is overpaying for the target.

Analyzing premium offered to target shareholders

One popular way to assess whether the acquirer is overpaying for a target is to compare the premium offered to target shareholders to premiums offered in similar transactions. If the acquirer offers a relatively high **acquisition premium**, the analyst is typically led to conclude that the transaction is less likely to create value for acquiring shareholders.

Premiums differ significantly for friendly and hostile acquisitions. Premiums tend to be about 30 percent higher for hostile deals than for friendly offers, implying that hostile acquirers are more likely to overpay for a target.[6] There are several reasons for this. First, a friendly acquirer has access to the internal records of the target, making it much less likely that it will be surprised by hidden liabilities or problems once it has completed the deal. In contrast, a hostile acquirer does not have this advantage in valuing the target and is forced to make assumptions that may later turn out to be false. Second, the delays that typically accompany a hostile acquisition often provide opportunities for competing bidders to make an offer for the target, leading to a bidding war.

Comparing a target's premium to values for similar types of transactions is straightforward to compute, but it has several practical problems. First, it is not obvious how to define a comparable transaction. European takeover premiums differ on various dimensions. As argued, average premiums are greater in hostile takeovers than in friendly takeovers. Further, takeover premiums vary by means of payment. Equity-financed acquisitions (share-for-share mergers) require lower premiums than cash-financed acquisitions because the former type makes the target firms' shareholders also shareholders of the new company. Target shareholders thereby keep benefiting – through capital gains – from the synergies created by the merger. Takeover premiums may also depend on the target firms' country of domicile. When a target firm is located in a country with strict takeover rules, the target firm's shareholders may have more power to negotiate higher premiums. Recent research has indicated that takeover premiums in the UK, where hostile takeover are more common and takeover rules are stricter, are on average higher than in Continental Europe.[7]

A second problem in using premiums offered to target shareholders to assess whether an acquirer overpaid is that measured premiums can be misleading if an offer is anticipated by investors. The share price run-up for the target will then tend to make estimates of the premium appear relatively low. This limitation can be partially offset by using target share prices one month prior to the acquisition offer as the basis for calculating premiums. However, in some cases offers may have been anticipated for even longer than one month.

Finally, using target premiums to assess whether an acquirer overpaid ignores the value of the target to the acquirer after the acquisition. The acquirer expects to benefit from the merger by improving the target firm's operating performance through a combination of economies of scale, improved management, tax benefits, and spillover effects derived from the acquisition. Clearly, acquirers will be willing to pay higher premiums for targets that are expected to generate higher merger benefits. Thus, examining the premium alone cannot determine whether the acquisition creates value for acquiring shareholder.

Analyzing value of the target to the acquirer

A second and more reliable way of assessing whether the acquirer has overpaid for the target is to compare the offer price to the estimated value of the target to the acquirer. This latter value can be computed using the valuation techniques discussed in Chapters 7 and 8. The most popular methods of valuation used for mergers and acquisitions are earnings multiples and discounted cash flows. Since a comprehensive discussion of these techniques is provided earlier in the book, we focus here on implementation issues that arise for valuing targets in mergers and acquisitions.

We recommend first computing the value of the target as an independent firm. This provides a way of checking whether the valuation assumptions are reasonable, because for publicly listed targets we can compare our estimate with premerger market prices. It also provides a useful benchmark for thinking about how the target's performance, and hence its value, is likely to change once it is acquired.

Earnings multiples

To estimate the value of a target to an acquirer using earnings multiples, we have to forecast earnings for the target and decide on an appropriate earnings multiple, as follows:

- Step 1: Forecasting earnings. Earnings forecasts are usually made by first forecasting next year's net profit for the target assuming no acquisition. Historical sales growth rates, gross margins, and average tax rates are useful in building a pro forma earnings model. Once we have forecasted the profit for the target prior to an acquisition, we can incorporate into the pro forma model any improvements in earnings performance that we expect to result from the acquisition. Performance improvements can be modeled as:

  - Higher operating margins through economies of scale in purchasing, or increased market power.

  - Reductions in expenses as a result of consolidating research and development staffs, sales forces, and/or administration.

  - Lower average tax rates from taking advantage of operating tax loss carryforwards.

- Step 2: Determining the price-earnings multiple. How do we determine the earnings multiple to be applied to our earnings forecasts? If the target firm is listed, it may be tempting to use the preacquisition price-earnings multiple to value postmerger earnings. However, there are several limitations to this approach. First, for many targets earnings growth expectations are likely to change after a merger, implying that there will be a difference between the pre- and postmerger price-earnings multiples. Postmerger earnings should then be valued using a multiple for firms with comparable growth and risk characteristics (see the discussion in Chapter 7). A second problem is that premerger price-earnings multiples are unavailable for unlisted targets. Once again it becomes necessary to decide which types of listed firms are likely to be good comparables. In addition, since the earnings being valued are the projected earnings for the next 12 months or the next full fiscal year, the appropriate benchmark ratio should be a forward price-earnings ratio. Finally, if a premerger price-earnings multiple is appropriate for valuing postmerger earnings, care is required to ensure that the multiple is calculated prior to any acquisition announcement because the price will increase in anticipation of the premium to be paid to target shareholders.

Table 11.1 summarizes how price-earnings multiples are used to value a target firm before an acquisition (assuming it will remain an independent entity), and to estimate the value of a target to a potential acquirer.

Limitations of price-earnings valuation

As explained in Chapter 7, there are serious limitations to using earnings multiples for valuation. In addition to these limitations, the method has two more that are specific to merger valuations:

1. PE multiples assume that merger performance improvements come either from an immediate increase in earnings or from an increase in earnings growth (and hence an

TABLE 11.1 Summary of price-earnings valuation for targets

Value of target as an independent firm	Target earnings forecast for the next year, assuming no change in ownership, multiplied by its *premerger* PE multiple
Value of target to potential acquirer	Target *revised* earnings forecast for the next year, incorporating the effect of any operational changes made by the acquirer, multiplied by its *postmerger* PE multiple

increase in the postmerger PE ratio). In reality, improvements and savings can come in many forms – gradual increases in earnings from implementing new operating policies, elimination of overinvestment, better management of working capital, or paying out excess cash to shareholders. These types of improvements are not naturally reflected in PE multiples.

2. PE models do not easily incorporate any spillover benefits from an acquisition for the acquirer because they focus on valuing the earnings of the target.

Discounted abnormal earnings, abnormal earnings growth, or cash flows

As discussed in Chapters 7 and 8, we can also value a company using the discounted abnormal earnings, discounted abnormal earnings growth, and discounted free cash flow methods. These require us to first forecast the abnormal earnings, abnormal earnings growth, or free cash flows for the firm and then discount them at the cost of capital, as follows.

- Step 1: Forecast abnormal earnings/abnormal earnings growth/free cash flows. A pro forma model of expected future profits and cash flows for the firm provides the basis for forecasting abnormal earnings, abnormal earnings growth, and free cash flows. As a starting point, the model should be constructed under the assumption that the target remains an independent firm. The model should reflect the best estimates of future sales growth, cost structures, working capital needs, investment and research and development needs, and cash requirements for known debt retirements, developed from financial analysis of the target. The abnormal earnings (growth) method requires that we forecast earnings or net operating profit after tax (NOPAT) for as long as the firm expects new investment projects to earn more than their cost of capital. Under the free cash flow approach, the pro forma model will forecast free cash flows to either the firm or to equity, typically for a period of five to ten years. Once we have a model of the abnormal earnings, abnormal earnings growth or free cash flows, we can incorporate any improvements in earnings/free cash flows that we expect to result from the acquisition. These will include the cost savings, cash received from asset sales, benefits from eliminating overinvestment, improved working capital management, and paying out excess cash to shareholders.

- Step 2: Compute the discount rate. If we are valuing the target's postacquisition NOPAT or cash flows to the firm, the appropriate discount rate is the weighted average cost of capital (WACC) for the target, using its expected *postacquisition* capital structure. Alternatively, if the target equity cash flows are being valued directly or if we are valuing abnormal earnings, the appropriate discount rate is the target's *postacquisition cost of equity* rather than its WACC. Two common mistakes are to use the acquirer's cost of capital or the target's *preacquisition* cost of capital to value the postmerger earnings/cash flows from the target.

TABLE 11.2 Summary of discounted abnormal earnings/abnormal earnings growth/cash flow valuation for targets

Value of target without an acquisition	a. Present value of abnormal earnings/abnormal earnings growth/free cash flows to target equity assuming no acquisition, discounted at *premerger* cost of equity; or
	b. present value of abnormal NOPAT/abnormal NOPAT growth/ free cash flows to target debt and equity assuming no acquisition, discounted at *premerger* WACC, less value of debt.
Value of target to potential acquirer	(a) Present value of abnormal earnings/abnormal earnings growth/free cash flows to target equity, *including benefits from merger*, discounted at *postmerger* cost of equity; or
	(b) present value of abnormal abnormal NOPAT/abnormal NOPAT growth/free cash flows to target, *including benefits from merger*, discounted at *postmerger* WACC, less value of debt.

The computation of the target's postacquisition cost of capital can be complicated if the acquirer plans to make a change to the target's capital structure after the acquisition, since the target's costs of debt and equity will change. As discussed in Chapter 8, this involves estimating the asset beta for the target, calculating the new equity and debt betas under the modified capital structure, and finally computing the revised cost of equity capital or weighted cost of capital. As a practical matter, the effect of these changes on the weighted average cost of capital is likely to be quite small unless the revision in leverage has a significant effect on the target's interest tax shields or its likelihood of financial distress.

Table 11.2 summarizes how the discounted abnormal earnings/cash flow methods can be used to value a target before an acquisition (assuming it will remain an independent entity), and to estimate the value of a target firm to a potential acquirer.

- Step 3: Analyze sensitivity. Once we have estimated the expected value of a target, we will want to examine the sensitivity of our estimate to changes in the model assumptions. For example, answering the following questions can help the analyst assess the risks associated with an acquisition:

  - What happens to the value of the target if it takes longer than expected for the benefits of the acquisition to materialize?

  - What happens to the value of the target if the acquisition prompts its primary competitors to respond by also making an acquisition? Will such a response affect our plans and estimates?

KEY ANALYSIS QUESTIONS

To analyze the pricing of an acquisition, the analyst is interested in assessing the value of the acquisition benefits to be generated by the acquirer relative to the price paid to target shareholders. Analysts are therefore likely to be interested in answers to the following questions:

- What is the premium that the acquirer paid for the target's shares? What does this premium imply for the acquirer in terms of future performance improvements to justify the premium?

- What are the likely performance improvements that management expects to generate from the acquisition? For example, are there likely to be increases in the revenues for the merged firm from new products, increased prices, or better distribution of existing products? Alternatively, are there cost savings as a result of taking advantage of economies of scale, improved efficiency, or a lower cost of capital for the target?

- What is the value of any performance improvements? Values can be estimated using multiples or discounted abnormal earnings/cash flow methods.

Alcatel's pricing of lucent

The Alcatel-Lucent merger was structured as a share-for-share exchange. For each share they held, Lucent shareholders would receive almost one-fifth of an Alcatel ADR. ADRs, or American Depository Receipts, are certificates that are issued by US banks and represent foreign shares that are held on deposit by these banks. The Alcatel ADRs were listed on the New York Stock Exchange and provided the former Lucent shareholders with a convenient way to invest in Alcatel. Alcatel's €11.2 ($13.5) billion price for Lucent represented a 7 percent premium to target shareholders over the market value on March 23, 2006, when Alcatel and Lucent disclosed their merger talks.

With average takeover premiums in share-for-share exchanges of 15 percent, the premium that Alcatel offered to Lucent shareholders was relatively low. In terms of traditional multiple forms of valuation, Alcatel's pricing of Lucent also appeared to be on the low side. For example, at the time of the announcement of Alcatel's offer, the average PE value for other firms in the US telecom equipment industry that were comparable to Lucent was close to 30. Alcatel's premerger PE value was 19 and US-based Cisco Systems, which was of similar size to the Alcatel-Lucent combination, traded at around 25 times current earnings. Alcatel's offer valued Lucent at 13 times current earnings and 20 times next year's expected earnings.

The market reaction to the acquisition announcement on April 2, 2006 suggests that analysts believed that the deal created value for Alcatel's shareholders – Alcatel's share price increased by 8.4 percent (adjusted for market-wide changes), or €1.37 billion, during the 11 days prior to the announcement through to the actual announcement day. By the tenth trading day after the announcement, Alcatel's share was up 8.8 percent, or €1.44 billion. Given the €0.73 ($0.88) billion premium that Alcatel paid for Lucent, investors believed that the merger would create value of €2.17 billion.

ACQUISITION FINANCING AND FORM OF PAYMENT

Even if an acquisition is undertaken to create new economic value and is priced judiciously, it may still destroy shareholder value if it is inappropriately financed. Several financing options are available to acquirers, including issuing shares or warrants to target shareholders, or acquiring target shares using surplus cash or proceeds from new debt. The trade-offs between these options from the standpoint of target shareholders usually hinge on their tax and transaction cost implications. For acquirers, they can affect the firm's capital structure and provide new information to investors.

As we discuss below, the financing preferences of target and acquiring shareholders can diverge. Financing arrangements can therefore increase or reduce the attractiveness of an acquisition from the standpoint of acquiring shareholders. As a result, a complete analysis of an acquisition will include an examination of the implications of the financing arrangements for the acquirer.

Effect of form of payment on acquiring shareholders

From the perspective of the acquirer, the form of payment is essentially a financing decision. As discussed in Chapter 10, in the long-term firms choose whether to use debt or equity financing to balance the tax and incentive benefits of debt against the risks of financial distress. For acquiring shareholders the costs and benefits of different financing options usually depend on how the offer affects their firm's capital structure, any information effects associated with different forms of financing.

Capital structure effects of the form of financing

In acquisitions where debt financing or surplus cash are the primary form of consideration for target shares, the acquisition increases the net financial leverage of the acquirer. This increase in leverage may be part of the acquisition strategy, since one way an acquirer can add value to an inefficient firm is to lower its taxes by increasing interest tax shields. However, in many acquisitions an increase in postacquisition leverage is a side effect of the method of financing and not part of a deliberate tax-minimizing strategy. The increase in leverage can then potentially reduce shareholder value for the acquirer by increasing the risk of financial distress.

To assess whether an acquisition leads an acquirer to have too much leverage, financial analysts can assess the acquirer's financial risk following the proposed acquisition by these methods:

- Analyze the business risks and the volatility of the combined, postacquisition cash flows against the level of debt in the new capital structure, and the implications for possible financial distress.

- Assessing the pro forma financial risks for the acquirer under the proposed financing plan. Popular measures of financial risk include debt-to-equity and interest coverage ratios, as well as projections of cash flows available to meet debt repayments. The ratios can be compared to similar performance metrics for the acquiring and target firms' industries to determine whether postmerger ratios indicate that the firm's probability of financial distress has increased significantly.

- Examining whether there are important off-balance sheet liabilities for the target and/or acquirer that are not included in the pro forma ratio and cash flow analysis of post-acquisition financial risk.

- Determining whether the pro forma assets for the acquirer are largely intangible and therefore sensitive to financial distress. Measures of intangible assets include such ratios as market to book equity and tangible assets to the market value of equity.

Information problems and the form of financing

In the short-term, information asymmetries between managers and external investors can make managers reluctant to raise equity to finance new projects. Managers' reluctance arises from their fear that investors will interpret the decision as an indication that the firm's equity is overvalued. In the short-term, this effect can lead managers to deviate from the firm's long-term optimal mix of debt and equity. As a result, acquirers are likely to prefer to use internal funds or debt to finance an acquisition, because these forms of consideration are less likely to be interpreted negatively by investors.[8]

The information effects imply that firms forced to use equity financing are likely to face a share price decline when investors learn of the method of financing.[9] From the viewpoint of financial analysts, the financing announcement may, therefore, provide valuable news about the preacquisition value of the acquirer. On the other hand, it should have no implications for analysis of whether the acquisition creates value for acquiring shareholders, since the news reflected in the financing announcement is about the *preacquisition* value of the acquirer and not about the *postacquisition* value of the target to the acquirer.

A second information problem arises if the acquiring management does not have good information about the target. Equity financing then provides a way for acquiring shareholders to share the information risks with target shareholders. If the acquirer finds out after the acquisition that the value of the target is less than previously anticipated, the accompanying decline in the acquirer's equity price will be partially borne by target shareholders who continue to hold the acquirer's shares. In contrast, if the target's shares were acquired in a cash offer, any postacquisition loss would be fully borne by the acquirer's original shareholders. The risk-sharing benefits from using equity financing appears to be widely recognized for acquisitions of private companies, where public information on the target is largely unavailable.[10] In practice it appears to be considered less important for acquisitions of large public corporations.[11]

Corporate control and the form of payment

There is a significant difference between the use of cash and shares in terms of its impact on the voting control of the combined firm postacquisition. Financing an acquisition with cash allows the acquirer to retain the structure and composition of its equity ownership. On the other hand, depending on the size of the target firm relative to the acquirer, an acquisition financed with shares could have a significant impact on the ownership and control of the firm postacquisition. This could be particularly relevant to a family-controlled acquirer. Therefore, the effects of control need to be balanced against the other costs and benefits when determining the form of payment.

Research has found that European acquirers whose primary shareholder controls between 40 and 60 percent of the equity votes indeed have a preference for cash as the primary form of consideration.[12] For shareholders who hold an equity stake between 40 and 60 percent, the threat of losing control after a share-for-share exchange is most imminent.

Effect of form of payment on target shareholders

The key payment considerations for target shareholders are the tax and transaction cost implications of the acquirer's offer.

Tax effects of different forms of consideration

Target shareholders care about the after-tax value of any offer they receive for their shares. In many countries, whenever target shareholders receive cash for their shares, they are required to pay capital gains tax on the difference between the takeover offer price and their original purchase price. Alternatively, if they receive shares in the acquirer as consideration, they can defer any taxes on the capital gain until they sell the new shares. To qualify for the deferral of capital gains taxes, governments may require additional conditions to be met.[13] In the UK, taxes on capital gains from takeovers can only be deferred when the acquirer and the target firm operate in the same industry. In the US, the acquisition must be undertaken as a tax-free reorganization. Within the EU, not only capital gains on national, within-border share-for-share exchanges can be deferred. The EU Merger

Directive guarantees that the option to defer capital gains taxes, if allowed for national mergers, applies also to cross-border share-for-share exchanges.

Tax laws that allow the deferral of capital gains taxes appear to cause target shareholders to prefer a share offer to a cash one. This is certainly likely to be the case for a target founder who still has a significant stake in the company. If the company's share price has appreciated over its life, the founder will face substantial capital gains tax on a cash offer and will therefore probably prefer to receive shares in the acquiring firm. However, cash and share offers can be tax-neutral for some groups of shareholders. For example, consider the tax implications for risk arbitrageurs, who take a short-term position in a company that is a takeover candidate in the hope that other bidders will emerge and increase the takeover price. They have no intention of holding shares in the acquirer once the takeover is completed and will pay ordinary income tax on any short-term trading gain. Cash and share offers therefore have identical after-tax values for risk arbitrageurs. Similarly, tax-exempt institutions are likely to be indifferent to whether an offer is in cash or shares.

Transaction costs and the form of payment

Transaction costs are another factor related to the form of financing that can be relevant to target shareholders. Transaction costs are incurred when target shareholders sell any shares received as consideration for their shares in the target. These costs will not be faced by target shareholders if the bidder offers them cash. Transaction costs are unlikely to be significant for investors who intend to hold the acquirer's shares following a share acquisition. However they may be relevant for investors who intend to sell, such as risk arbitrageurs.

KEY ANALYSIS QUESTIONS

For an analyst focused on the acquiring firm, it is important to assess how the method of financing affects the acquirer's capital structure and its risks of financial distress by asking the following questions:

- What is the leverage for the newly created firm? How does this compare to leverage for comparable firms in the industry?

- What are the projected future cash flows for the merged firm? Are these sufficient to meet the firm's debt commitments? How much of a cushion does the firm have if future cash flows are lower than expected? Is the firm's debt level so high that it is likely to impair its ability to finance profitable future investments if future cash flows are below expectations?

Alcatel's financing of Lucent

Alcatel offered Lucent shareholders 0.1952 Alcatel ADRs for each Lucent share. Given Lucent's 4,469 million shares outstanding, Alcatel issued 872 million shares, which at €12.85 per share implied a total offer of €11.2 billion. The merger was structured as a "tax-free reorganization" for federal tax purposes. This implied that Lucent shareholders would not recognize any gain or loss for federal tax purposes from exchanging their Lucent shares for Alcatel ADRs in the merger.

By using shares to finance the acquisition, Alcatel reduced its financial leverage. The market reacted positively to the offer, increasing Alcatel's share price by 1.1 percent (adjusting for market-wide returns) on the announcement date (March 23, 2006). This reaction suggests that investors did not interpret Alcatel's share offer as indicating that its equity was overvalued. Also, in the following ten days Alcatel's share price increased, albeit by a mere 0.4 percent.

ACQUISITION OUTCOME

The final question of interest to the analyst evaluating a potential acquisition is whether it will indeed be completed. If an acquisition has a clear value-based motive, the target is priced appropriately, and its proposed financing does not create unnecessary financial risks for the acquirer, it may still fail because the target receives a higher competing bid, there is opposition from entrenched target management, or the transaction fails to receive necessary regulatory approval. Therefore, to evaluate the likelihood that an offer will be accepted, the financial analyst has to understand whether there are potential competing bidders who could pay an even higher premium to target shareholders than is currently offered. They also have to consider whether target managers are entrenched and, to protect their jobs, likely to oppose an offer, as well as the political and regulatory environment in which the target and the acquirer operate.

Other potential acquirers

If there are other potential bidders for a target, especially ones who place a higher value on the target, there is a strong possibility that the bidder in question will be unsuccessful. Target management and shareholders have an incentive to delay accepting the initial offer to give potential competitors time to also submit a bid. From the perspective of the initial bidder, this means that the offer could potentially reduce shareholder value by the cost of making the offer (including substantial investment banking and legal fees). In practice, a losing bidder can usually recoup these losses and sometimes even make healthy profits from selling to the successful acquirer any shares it has accumulated in the target.

KEY ANALYSIS QUESTIONS

The financial analyst can determine whether there are other potential acquirers for a target and how they value the target by asking the following questions:

- Are there other firms that could also implement the initial bidder's acquisition strategy? For example, if this strategy relies on developing benefits from complementary assets, look for potential bidders who also have assets complementary to the target. If the goal of the acquisition is to replace inefficient management, what other firms in the target's industry could provide management expertise?
- Who are the acquirer's major competitors? Could any of these firms provide an even better fit for the target?

Target management entrenchment

If target managers are entrenched and fearful for their jobs, it is likely that they will oppose a bidder's offer. Some firms have implemented "golden parachutes" for top managers to counteract their concerns about job security at the time of an offer. Golden parachutes provide top managers of a target firm with attractive compensation rewards should the firm get taken over. However, many firms do not have such schemes, and opposition to an offer from entrenched management is a very real possibility.

In some European countries the entrenchment of management is facilitated by legal provisions that allow a company to install various takeover defenses. For example, in most countries, firms can limit the number of votes that a shareholder can exercise at a share-holders' meeting. A voting cap effectively reduces the voting power that a potential acquirer can obtain. Another example of a takeover defense mechanism, which is commonly used in the Netherlands, is the issuance of depository receipts by an administrative office that is controlled by the firm whose shares the office holds.[14] Holders of depository receipts have the right to receive dividends but no voting rights. Instead, the administrative office retains and exercises the voting rights. This construction makes it difficult for an acquiring firm to obtain any voting power.

While the existence of takeover defenses for a target indicates that its management is likely to fight a bidding firm's offer, defenses do not often prevent an acquisition from taking place. Instead, they tend to cause delays, which increase the likelihood that there will be competing offers made for the target, including offers by friendly parties solicited by target management, called "white knights." Takeover defenses therefore increase the likelihood that the bidder in question will be outbid for the target, or that it will have to increase its offer significantly to win a bidding contest. These risks may discourage acquirers from embarking on a potentially hostile acquisition. Nonetheless, in recent years hostile takeovers have become more rather than less popular in Europe. For example, in 2006, steel producer Mittal Steel was engaged in a hostile takeover attempt for industry peer Arcelor. Arcelor called in the help of "white knight" Severstal, but eventually was forced by its shareholders to accept Mittal's offer. The takeover battle had caused a delay of five months and had driven up the takeover price by 49 percent, or €8.4 billion.

Takeover regulations have the objectives of preventing management entrenchment and protecting minority shareholders during European takeovers. During the 1990s, national takeover regulations in Europe began converging toward the UK regime model. In 2004 the European Commission issued a heavily debated Takeover Directive, which applies to companies whose shares are traded on a (regulated) public exchange. The most important rules in this Directive (effective since May 2006) are the following:[15]

- The equal-treatment rule and the mandatory-bid rule aim at protecting minority share-holders in takeovers. The mandatory-bid rule prescribes that the acquiring firm makes an offer for all remaining shares, once its equity stake exceeds a predefined threshold. In Denmark, Italy, and the UK, this threshold is, for example, 30 percent. The equal-treatment rule requires that the acquiring firm makes equally favorable offers to the controlling and minority shareholders of the target firm.

- Under the squeeze-out rule, the acquiring firm can force the remaining minority share-holders to sell their shares at the tender offer price, once the firm holds a predefined equity stake of, usually, between 80 and 95 percent. Under the sell-out rule, the remaining shareholders can force the acquiring firm to buy their shares at a fair price.

- The board-neutrality rule requires that during takeovers management will not take actions that may frustrate the takeover.

Another proposed rule, the breakthrough rule, did make it into the final Directive but can be opted out of by individual countries. The breakthrough rule mandates that a firm that has acquired a predefined percentage of shares can exercise votes on its shares *as if* all outstanding shares, including the firm's shares, carry one vote per share. For example, the breakthrough rule guarantees that an acquiring firm that owns 90 percent of the target firm's ordinary shares can exercise exactly 90 percent of the votes during a shareholders' meeting of the target firm, irrespective of the takeover defense mechanisms that are in place.

The rules in the EU Takeover Directive can affect the analysis of a takeover offer. For example, in some jurisdictions the laws prescribe that when the mandatory-bid rule comes into effect, the acquiring firm must offer the remaining shareholders no less than the highest price it has paid to other shareholders. This rule, of course, invites the investor to strategically wait until the last moment before accepting the offer. The board-neutrality rule reduces management entrenchment through postbid takeover defenses and therefore reduces the probability that a target firm will oppose an acquisition. The breakthrough rule, if implemented, can remove firms' prebid takeover defenses, such as voting caps.

KEY ANALYSIS QUESTIONS

To assess whether the target firm's management is entrenched and therefore likely to oppose an acquisition, analysts can ask the following questions:

- Does the target firm have takeover defenses designed to protect management? If so, do national takeover rules reduce the effect of such defenses? Further, do national takeover rules regulate that minority shareholders receive a fair price?

- Has the target been a poor performer relative to other firms in its industry? If so, management's job security is likely to be threatened by a takeover, leading it to oppose any offers.

- Is there a golden parachute plan in place for target management? Golden parachutes provide attractive compensation for management in the event of a takeover to deter opposition to a takeover for job security reasons.

Antitrust and security issues

Regulators such as the European Commission's DG for Competition Analysts and the Federal Trade Commission in the US assess the effects of an acquisition on the competitive dynamics of the industry in which the firms operate. The objective is to ensure that no one firm, through mergers and acquisitions, creates a dominant position that can impede effective competition in specific geographies or product markets.

Analysis of outcome of Alcatel's offer for Lucent

Analysts covering Lucent had little reason to question whether Lucent would be sold to Alcatel. The offer was a friendly one that had received the approval of Lucent's management and board of directors. There probably was some risk of another telecom equipment maker entering the bidding for Lucent. For example, following the merger announcement there were rumors that Sweden-based Ericsson would launch a competing bid to acquire Lucent. However, Ericsson's management explicitly denied that it had any interest in acquiring Lucent after already having acquired one of Lucent's UK competitors, Marconi. Eventually, none of Alcatel's competitors made a bid for Lucent.

SUMMARY

This chapter summarizes how financial statement data and analysis can be used by financial analysts interested in evaluating whether an acquisition creates value for an acquiring firm's shareholders. Obviously, much of this discussion is also likely to be relevant to other merger participants, including target and acquiring management and their investment banks.

For the external analyst, the first task is to identify the acquirer's acquisition strategy. We discuss a number of strategies. Some of these are consistent with maximizing acquirer value, including acquisitions to take advantage of economies of scale, improve target management, combine complementary resources, capture tax benefits, provide low-cost financing to financially constrained targets, and increase product-market rents.

Other strategies appear to benefit managers more than shareholders. For example, some unprofitable acquisitions are made because managers are reluctant to return free cash flows to shareholders, or because managers want to lower the firm's earnings volatility by diversifying into unrelated businesses.

The financial analyst's second task is to assess whether the acquirer is offering a reasonable price for the target. Even if the acquirer's strategy is based on increasing shareholder value, it can overpay for the target. Target shareholders will then be well rewarded but at the expense of acquiring shareholders. We show how the ratio, pro forma, and valuation techniques discussed earlier in the book can all be used to assess the worth of the target to the acquirer.

The method of financing an offer is also relevant to a financial analyst's review of an acquisition proposal. If a proposed acquisition is financed with surplus cash or new debt, it increases the acquirer's financial risk. Financial analysts can use ratio analysis of the acquirer's postacquisition balance sheet and pro forma estimates of cash flow volatility and interest coverage to assess whether demands by target shareholders for consideration in cash lead the acquirer to increase its risk of financial distress.

Finally, the financial analyst is interested in assessing whether a merger is likely to be completed once the initial offer is made, and at what price. This requires the analyst to determine whether there are other potential bidders, and whether target management is entrenched and likely to oppose a bidder's offer.

CORE CONCEPTS

Acquisition financing Methods of acquisition financing are through equity issues, debt issues or the use of surplus cash. The latter two methods increase net financial leverage and potentially increase distress risk. Information problems make acquirers reluctant to use equity to finance the acquisition. Different forms of payment may have different tax effects across countries.

Acquisition premium Premium offered to target shareholders. Acquisition premiums tend to be:

1 Higher for hostile than friendly takeovers.

2 Higher for cash-financed than equity-financed (share-for-share) acquisitions.

3 Higher when the target's country's takeover rules are stricter.

Entrenched target management Target management's use of takeover defense mechanisms to deter the acquisition. The use of takeover defense mechanisms may discourage acquisitions or drive up acquisition premiums.

Merger and acquisition benefits Mergers or acquisitions can create value through:

1 Increasing economies of scale.

2 Improving the target firm's management.

3 Combining complementary resources.

4 Capturing tax benefits such operating tax losses or interest tax shields.

5 Providing a source of finance to the target.

6 Restructuring.

7 Increasing product market rents.

Takeover regulations Rules aimed at preventing target management entrenchment, such as the EU Takeover Directive.

Target value analysis Target value analysis includes estimating the value of a target both as an independent firm and to the potential acquirer, using earnings multiples or using discounted abnormal earnings of cash flow methods. Earnings multiple-based valuations tend to ignore the long-term effects of the acquisition.

QUESTIONS

1   Since the year 2000, there was a noticeable increase in mergers and acquisitions between firms in different countries (termed cross-border acquisitions). What factors could explain this increase? What special issues can arise in executing a cross-border acquisition and in ultimately meeting your objectives for a successful combination?

2   Private equity firms have become an important player in the acquisition market. These private investment groups offer to buy a target firm, often with the cooperation of management, and then take the firm private. Private equity buyers tend to finance a significant portion of the acquisition with debt.

   a   What types of firms would make ideal candidates for a private equity buyout? Why?

   b   How might the acquirer add sufficient value to the target to justify a high buyout premium?

3   Kim Silverman, Finance Director of the First Public Bank, notes: "We are fortunate to have a cost of capital of only 10 percent. We want to leverage this advantage by acquiring other banks that have a higher cost of funds. I believe that we can add significant value to these banks by using our lower cost financing." Do you agree with Silverman's analysis? Why or why not?

4   The Munich Beer Company plans to acquire Liverpool Beer Co. for £60 per share, a 50 percent premium over the current market price. Jan Höppe, the Financial Director of Munich Beer, argues that this valuation can easily be justified, using a price-earnings analysis. "Munich Beer has a price-earnings ratio of 15, and we expect that we will be able to generate long-term earnings for Liverpool Beer of £5 per share. This implies that Liverpool Beer is worth £75 to us, well above our £60 offer price." Do you agree with this analysis? What are Höppe's key assumptions?

5   You have been hired by GS Investment Bank to work in the merger department. The analysis required for all potential acquisitions includes an examination of the target for any off-balance sheet assets or liabilities that have to be factored into the valuation. Prepare a checklist for your examination.

6   A target company is currently valued at €50 in the market. A potential acquirer believes that it can add value in two ways: €15 of value can be added through better working capital management, and an additional €10 of value can be generated by making available a unique technology to expand the target's new product offerings. In a competitive bidding contest, how much of this additional value will the acquirer have to pay out to the target's shareholders to emerge as the winner?

7   A leading oil exploration company decides to acquire an internet company at a 50 percent premium. The acquirer argues that this move creates value for its own shareholders because it can use its excess cash flows from the oil business to help finance growth in the new internet segment. Evaluate the economic merits of this claim.

8   Under current International Financial Reporting Standards, acquirers are required to capitalize goodwill and report any subsequent declines in value as an impairment charge. What performance metrics would you use to judge whether goodwill is impaired?

NOTES

1. In a review of studies of merger returns, Michael Jensen and Richard Ruback, "The Market for Corporate Control: The Scientific Evidence," *Journal of Financial Economics* 11 (April 1983): 5–50, conclude that target shareholders earn positive returns from takeovers, but that acquiring shareholders only break even.
2. See Steven Kaplan, "Management Buyouts: Evidence on Taxes as a Source of Value," *Journal of Finance* 44 (1989): 611–632.
3. Krishna Palepu, "Predicting Takeover Targets: A Methodological and Empirical Analysis," *Journal of Accounting and Economics* 8 (March 1986): 3–36.
4. Chapter 2 discusses the pros and cons of corporate diversification and evidence on its implications for firm performance.
5. See "Alcatel and Lucent: The Urge to Merge," *The Economist,* April 6, 2006.
6. See Paul Healy, Krishna Palepu, and Richard Ruback, "Which Mergers Are Profitable – Strategic or Financial?," *Sloan Management Review* 38, No. 4 (Summer 1997): 45–58. For empirical evidence on European target firms' cumulative stock returns around the takeover announcement, see Martina Martynova and Luc Renneboog, "Mergers and Acquisitions in Europe," Working Paper, Tilburg University, 2006. This study reports that 60 days after a hostile takeover announcement European target firms' share prices have run up by, on average, 45 percent since 60 days prior to the announcement. In contrast, after friendly takeover announcements, share prices have run up by, on average, 10 percent. The average difference in price runup of 35 percent can be interpreted as the average difference in (expected) takeover premiums.
7. See, for example, Martina Martynova and Luc Renneboog, op. cit.
8. See Stewart Myers and Nicholas Majluf, "Corporate Financing and Investment Decisions When Firms Have Information That Investors Do Not," *Journal of Financial Economics* (June 1984): 187–221.
9. For evidence see Nicholas Travlos, "Corporate Takeover Bids, Methods of Payments, and Bidding Firms' Stock Returns," *Journal of Finance* 42 (1987): 943–963.
10. See S. Datar, R. Frankel, and M. Wolfson, "Earnouts: The Effects of Adverse Selection and Agency Costs on Acquisition Techniques," *Journal of Law, Economics, and Organization* 17 (2001): 201–238.
11. See Mara Faccio and Ronald W. Masulis, "The Choice of Payment Method in European Mergers and Acquisitions," *Journal of Finance* 60 (2005): 1345–1388.
12. See Mara Faccio and Ronald W. Masulis, op. cit.
13. In several European countries, such as in Belgium, Denmark, and Germany, individual shareholders pay no or little taxes on the capital gains that they make from selling or exchanging their shares in a takeover, provided that they have held the shares for a defined period, typically being a period of one or two years. For these shareholders the after-tax value of a takeover offer does not depend on whether they receive cash or shares as consideration.
14. See Rezaul Kabir, Dolph Cantrijn, and Andreas Jeunink, "Takeover Defenses, Ownership Structures, and Stock Returns in the Netherlands: An Empirical Analysis," *Strategic Management Journal* 18 (1997): 97–109.
15. Marc Goergen, Marina Martynova, and Luc Renneboog give a complete description of the most important rules in the EU Takeover Directive in their study "Corporate Governance Convergence: Evidence from Takeover Regulation Reforms in Europe," *Oxford Review of Economic Policy* 21 (2005): 243–268.

The Air France–KLM merger

*We have always been convinced of the necessity of consolidation in the airline indus-
try. Today, we announce a combination with KLM that will create the first European
airline group, which is a milestone in our industry. This will bring significant benefits to customers, shareholders and employees. Capitalizing on the two brands and
on the complementary strengths of both companies, we should, within SkyTeam, be
able to capture enhanced growth opportunities.*

—Jean-Cyril Spinetta, Chairman and CEO of Air France

*KLM has been pointing out the need for consolidation in light of the challenges
facing our industry, and we have not made it a secret we were looking for a strong
European partner. Through this innovative partnership with Air France and our
subsequent expected participation in the SkyTeam alliance, we are confident that we
have secured a sustainable future for our company. Our valuable Schiphol hub will
be an integral part of the dual hub strategy of the new airline group, allowing us to
build on what KLM and its staff have achieved over nearly 85 years.*

—Leo van Wijk, President and CEO of KLM

On September 30, 2003, Air France and KLM Royal Dutch Airlines – two European
airlines that provided international passenger and cargo airline services – issued a press
release that announced their planned merger. The merger envisaged the creation of the leading European airline Air France–LM. In 2003, both airlines were the primary national ("flag
carrying") airlines in their home countries, France and the Netherlands. However, poor
industry conditions put pressure on the airlines' growth and operating margins. In the fiscal
year ending on March 31, 2003, Air France, the larger of the two airlines, reported an
increase in total sales of slightly more than one percent to €12,687 million and a net profit
of €120 million (€0.55 per share). KLM performed worse than Air France. In the same fiscal
year, KLM reported a decrease in total sales of slightly less than one percent to €6,485 million and a loss (before extraordinary items) of €186 million (€3.97 per share).

For a number of years, KLM had been searching for a strategic partner, which seemed
to be of essential importance given the deteriorating industry conditions. Initially, KLM
attempted to form an alliance with the Italian flag carrier, Alitalia. However, this alliance
soon appeared to be unsuccessful because of the poor functioning of Milan Malpensa Airport, an unexpected delay in the privatization of Alitalia, and cultural incompatibilities
between the Italians and the Dutch.[1] After breaking with Alitalia, KLM kept on searching
for another partner. In early 2000, talks about joining forces with British Airways
remained unfruitful, as KLM and its main shareholder, the Dutch state, were unwilling to
hand over control to the British flag carrier.[2] In the second half of 2003, Air France came
to the rescue.

Professor Erik Peek prepared this case. The case is intended solely as the basis for class discussion and is not
intended to serve as an endorsement, source of primary data, or illustration of effective or ineffective
management.

[1] "KLM Ends Venture With Alitalia, Imperiling US Airline Alliance," *Wall Street Journal*, May 1, 2000; "Alitalia is Seeking Damages for Breakup with KLM," *Wall Street Journal*, August 2, 2000.

[2] "Europe's Flag Airlines: Going Nowhere," *Business Week*, February 26, 2001.

KLM Royal Dutch Airlines[3]

KLM Royal Dutch Airlines was founded in 1919, which, at the time of the merger, made it the oldest continuously operating airline in the world. Landmarks in the company's history were its very first scheduled flight to London in 1920, its first intercontinental flight to Jakarta (formerly Batavia) in 1924, and its operating scheduled flights to New York from 1946.

Over the years, the core activities of KLM remained very much the same. The airline provided worldwide passenger and cargo transport, engineering and maintenance, and, in a later stage, charter and low-cost scheduled flights. KLM operated its charter and low-cost flights primarily through its subsidiaries Buzz and Transavia. In 1994, KLM served 153 cities in 81 countries on six continents and ranked eighth among the largest international airlines based upon ton-kilometer traffic on international flights. Nine years later, KLM served 350 cities in 73 countries on six continents and ranked fifth among the largest international airlines.

In its prospectus from 1994, which accompanied the issuance of 18.5 million additional ordinary shares, the airline summarized its most important operating risks. First, the airline operated in an industry that was cyclical and highly competitive. The cyclical nature could have a strong adverse effect on KLM's profitability because, as every other airline, it had a high degree of operating leverage (high fixed-to-variable cost ratio). Second, the airline's profitability depended strongly on exchange rate fluctuations as well as on fluctuations in aircraft fuel prices. Third, because in many parts of the world airlines and international air traffic were highly regulated, KLM's operations could be affected by foreign governments' actions of protectionism.

Within this uncertain economic environment, KLM's corporate objective was ". . . to position itself as an airline operating worldwide from a European base that provides quality service for passengers and cargo shippers at competitive cost levels." The strategy that KLM used to attain this objective was to:

- *Increase customer preference.* KLM focused on achieving a high level of customer satisfaction, for example, by closely monitoring customer demand and by expanding its "Flying Dutchman" frequent flyer program.

- *Strengthen its market presence around the world.* KLM strengthened its market presence in the world's major air transportation markets by expanding its hub-and-spoke operations at Schiphol Airport and by creating alliances with other European, American, and Asian airlines. For example, in 1989, KLM had acquired a 20 percent stake in Northwest Airlines, a North American airline having its operations hubs in Boston, Detroit, and Minneapolis. This acquisition helped KLM to gain better access to American destinations. The alliance between KLM and Northwest implied that both airlines operated as a joint venture on transatlantic flights, while KLM did all their marketing in Europe and Northwest in the US.

- *Reduce its costs to at least an internationally competitive level.* During the early 1990s, KLM launched a restructuring program that aimed to reduce its costs and increase its productivity. The program included spinning off noncore business units, network optimization, eliminating the first class section on intercontinental flights, redesigning business processes, and acquiring more efficient aircraft. KLM launched a second restructuring program, Focus 2000, in 1996, and a third one, Baseline, in 2000.

In 2003, KLM's shares were listed on the Amsterdam Euronext Exchange and on the New York Stock Exchange. Since early in KLM's history, the Dutch state had been KLM's primary shareholder. The state's ownership interest in KLM gradually decreased

---

[3]Material in this section is drawn from KLM's 1994 prospectus, its 2002/2003 Annual Report, and its corporate website.

over the years, from 38 percent of the votes in 1994 to 14 percent in 2003. Nonetheless, the state remained able to effectively influence the airline's major (non-operating) decisions through various mechanisms. First, up to the date of the merger, the state had the option to obtain a 50.1 percent voting interest to prevent any undesirable accumulation of share ownership in the hands of others. This option was especially important to prevent a country imposing restrictions on KLM exercising international traffic rights. Because such traffic rights were the result of bilateral treaties between governments and tied to domestically owned airlines, countries could deny these rights to KLM if in their view the airline was no longer in Dutch hands. Second, the articles of association offered the state the right to appoint a majority of the Supervisory Board. Third, the state held the majority of KLM's priority shares, through which it had a veto over important decisions such as the issuance of shares, payments of stock dividends, and changes in the articles of association.

The merger agreement[4]

During 2002, while renewed negotiations between British Airways and KLM reached deadlock, KLM representatives also started to meet with Air France representatives to talk about the possibilities of cooperation. Parallel to these meetings, Air France's North American alliance partners, Continental Airlines and Delta Airlines, discussed possible cooperation with KLM's North American alliance partner, Northwest Airlines. In August 2002, the three North American airlines signed a ten-year agreement to improve schedule connections between the airlines and to share codes, frequent flyer programs, and airport lounges. After the signing of the agreement, the three airlines encouraged Air France and KLM to start similar cooperation in Europe. However, because the French state was planning to privatize Air France (i.e., reduce its shareholdings to a level below 20 percent), Air France and KLM envisaged a closer form of cooperation. Initially, both parties discussed the option of creating a dual listed company structure. Air France and KLM would keep their separate listings but cross-hold 50 percent of the shares of each other's operating subsidiaries. Because Air France had a substantially greater market value than KLM, Air France would also become the direct owner of 52 percent of KLM's shares and certain of its assets would be excluded from the transaction. However, the idea of creating a dual listed company structure appeared too complex and both airlines soon opted for a simpler alternative, which they presented to their shareholders on September 30, 2003.

The alternative proposal implied that the former shareholders of KLM and Air France became shareholders of the publicly listed holding company Air France–KLM, which would hold 100 percent of the shares of two private operating companies, Air France and KLM. Former Air France shareholders would receive one Air France–KLM share for every Air France share that they held. In exchange for 10 KLM shares, former KLM shareholders would receive 11 Air France–KLM shares plus 10 Air France–KLM warrants. The warrants had a strike price of €20.00, were exercisable after 18 months and had an exercise period of 3.5 years. Three warrants gave the warrant holder the right to purchase two Air France–KLM shares.

Based on Air France's closing price on September 29, 2003, the estimated value of one warrant was equal to €1.68 (according to the Air France–KLM merger announcement). This warrant value was based on the following assumptions:

- The September 29 AIR France(–KLM) share price was €13.69.
- The risk-free rate equaled 2.89 percent.
- The estimated future volatility of the AIR France(–KLM) share price was 40 percent.
- Estimated dividends per share were €0.096, €0.144, and €0.188 during the exercise period (based on I/B/E/S estimates).

[4]Material in this section is drawn from the Air France–KLM merger prospectus (April 5, 2004).

The Air France–KLM merger

Based on the AIR France (–KLM) share price of €13.69 and a warrant value of €1.68, the total value of the offer for KLM shareholders equaled €16.74 per share (11/10 × €13.69 + €1.68), which implied a premium of 40 percent over KLM's closing share price on September 29, 2003. After the share exchange, former KLM shareholders would own 19 percent of the ordinary shares (and voting rights) of Air France–KLM. The share exchange offer would commence only after approval from the EU and US competition authorities, and if no third party announced a public offer for either KLM's or Air France's shares.

The transaction between Air France and KLM was not a full-blown merger. The two private operating companies, Air France and KLM, remained separate entities, in particular because it was important to preserve the two established brand names. Further, the Dutch state retained the option to acquire a 50.1 percent voting interest in KLM (the operating company) if necessary to preserve KLM's landing rights.

Motivation for the merger

Airline industry analysts tend to distinguish two phases of evolution in a deregulated airline industry – i.e., the expansion phase and the consolidation phase. To illustrate, in the 1970s, the US government deregulated the US airline industry, which led to a serious expansion of supply from 1978 to 1990. In this expansion phase, US airlines responded by cutting their costs, but their operating margins experienced a secular decline. In the early stages of consolidation, from 1986 onwards, mergers resulted in the elimination of several brands, but did not restrict or reallocate capacity. Since the mergers initially raised costs, profit margins remained under pressure. In the later stages of the consolidation phase, US airlines reallocated their capacity from unprofitable (geographical) areas to profitable (geographical) areas. This significantly improved US airlines' profit margins. In the mid-1990s, the European airline industry was in a different stage of development than the US airline industry. At that time, European airlines had just entered into the earlier stages of consolidation by creating alliances. However, alliances made it difficult to reallocate capacity and improve profitability. Furthermore, government interference hindered efficient allocation of capacity.[5]

During the late 1990s and the early 2000s, the profit potential of the European airline industry changed substantially. At the end of the 1990s, Europe had an increasing number of large and small airlines, many airports close together, and most governments supporting loss-making national airlines. Government support resulted in very few unprofitable companies leaving the market. At the same time, many airlines started downgrading their product by offering low levels of service on short-haul flights to compete on costs. All major airports had capacity constraints, which (in combination with their slot trading system that favored current slot-owners) made access to established airports difficult for new entrants. However, new entrants, such as Ryanair and easyJet were moving to smaller, local airports to avoid the capacity constraints of the major airports. These new entrants further intensified the competition (on costs) in the European airline industry. Finally, the use of web booking systems made the market more transparent. Customers were able to easily compare prices, which substantially reduced switching costs.

After 2000, the profit potential of the European airline industry improved slightly. The European Commission had allowed governments to cover insurance risks and costs faced by airlines after the September 11, 2001 terrorist attacks; however, other forms of government support were no longer allowed. Further, after September 2001, many airlines significantly reduced (fixed) capacity, which reduced competition. Finally, more and more countries signed bilateral "open skies" agreements with the US, implying that European

---

[5]See "Global Airlines: Survival of the Fittest," *Goldman Sachs Global Research*, September 22, 1997.

airlines could fly to any place in the US, at any fare, at any time (but only from their home countries). In early 2004, a European agreement with the US was being negotiated, implying that, for example, the German national airline Lufthansa would be allowed to fly from Milan to New York. Nonetheless, KLM's return on equity during the fiscal years ending in 2001, 2002, and 2003 was 3.7, −7.8, and −24.1 percent respectively.

Exhibit 1 reports KLM's and Air France's motivation for entering into the merger agreement, as it was set out at the merger presentation on September 30, 2003.

Response of the Dutch Investor Association

In early 2004, the Dutch Investor Association (VEB; Vereniging voor Effectenbezitters) began to oppose the merger proposal. The VEB was of the opinion that during the months following the merger, KLM's value had increased substantially due to changed circumstances, which would justify a higher takeover price. KLM shareholders had to decide before May 5, 2004 (just before KLM's publication of its 2003/2004 financial statements) whether or not they wished to offer their shares to Air France. The VEB claimed that KLM shareholders should be able to take these latest financial results into account when making their decision. Air France and KLM refused this, supported by a Dutch court decision on April 29, 2004. **Exhibit 2** sets out the VEB's objections in detail.

On May 6, 2004, KLM announced that net profit, operating profit, and revenues for the fiscal year 2003/2004 were €24 million, €120 million, and €5,870 million, respectively.

Questions

1   Evaluate the motivating factors behind the Air France–KLM merger. Does the merger effectively address the strategic challenges faced by KLM and Air France?

2   Calculate the present value of the synergies. To what extent is the actual market response to the merger announcement consistent with the estimated value of the expected performance improvements?

3   To what extent can the premium be justified by the expected performance improvements (as presented in **Exhibit 1**)?

4   Critically analyze each of the VEB's (Dutch Investor Association) objections to the proposed takeover price (as presented in **Exhibit 2**). Do you have any evidence that Air France shareholders agree with the VEB?

5   If you were a shareholder of KLM, would you support this merger proposal?

The Air France–KLM merger

EXHIBIT 1   Appendix to the offer document

Strategic rationale of the transaction

The airline industry is fragmented and its current competitive structure, with national carriers for each individual country, is an inheritance from a former era. This has contributed to low profitability and lack of value creation for shareholders. The need for structural changes and consolidation in Europe is widely accepted, but has not yet commenced as a consequence of regulatory and political constraints.

The single European market and its current enlargement to some 455 million inhabitants reinforce the need for consolidation.

The evolution of the European regulatory framework highlighted by (i) the November 2002 European Court of Justice ruling and (ii) the mandate given in June 2003 to the European Commission to negotiate the open sky agreement with the US now creates an attractive environment for a value creating combination.

If commercial alliances have contributed over the past years to initiate the first steps towards consolidation, deeper cooperation is now needed to generate significant and sustainable synergies.

The proposed transaction between Air France and KLM is the first significant move in this context and will create a leading airline group in Europe with aggregated revenues of EUR 19.2 billion (2002/03 fiscal year).

The combination with KLM is a major step in Air France's strategy. In parallel, KLM's strategy over the years has consistently been built on two pillars: the strengthening of its own organization, as well as the participation in a global alliance, for which it seeks a strong European partner. The combination with Air France is the achievement of this strategy.

The transaction will benefit from the complementarities of the two airlines' operations:

- Two reputable and strong brands that will be further strengthened.

- Two operational hubs (Paris CDG and Amsterdam Schiphol) which are among the most efficient in Europe and provide significant development potential.

- Two complementary networks both in medium and long haul. In medium haul Air France has a strong position in Southern Europe and KLM has developed a strong position in Northern and North Eastern Europe, and both will be able to expand their positions in Central and Eastern Europe. The long haul networks currently consist of 101 destinations

of which only 31 are common (essentially the world's largest cities with high traffic volumes).

- A combined network of 226 destinations with 93 new destinations for KLM passengers and 48 new destinations for Air France passengers.

- A strong presence in cargo where Air France and KLM are the 4th and 11th largest in the world respectively but with complementary capabilities and expertise.

- A strong combination in the field of aircraft maintenance, creating one of the largest MRO providers worldwide.

- SkyTeam will eventually become the second largest global airline alliance and with its partners being able to offer passengers a more truly worldwide network.

Synergies

Potential synergies arising from the proposed transaction have been thoroughly assessed and quantified by a joint working group of Air France and KLM who has reviewed the feasibility and quantum of the synergies and their build-up over time.

Sales and distribution

By coordinating the two sales organizations the new group will have an improved presence around the world and will be able to offer a wider range of products to passengers. Cost savings could be achieved by coordinating the sales structures of the two companies. A joint negotiation position with catering and ground-handling partners could also lead to additional benefits.

Network/revenue management and fleet

By full code sharing, harmonizing the flight schedules and optimizing common management revenue policy the two airlines will be able to offer more destinations, a larger number and more convenient connections for passengers and to improve sales performance.

Cargo

The offering of an improved product through a more extensive network in combination with coordinated freighter planning, should lead to an increase of revenues. Cost savings should also be possible by more efficient hub handling.

CHAPTER 11 MERGERS AND ACQUISITIONS   **497**

Engineering and maintenance

The two airlines will be able to integrate purchasing of stock, to create centres of excellence in engineering and optimize the use of existing E&M platforms.

IT

Converging the IT applications used by both airlines should generate considerable cost savings in the medium term.

Other

Optimizing and harmonizing other activities such as simulator utilization and joint purchasing of goods should deliver further cost savings.

The identified potential synergies are expected to result in an annual improvement of the combined operating income (earnings before interest and tax) of between EUR 385 million and EUR 495 million, following a gradual implementation over a period of five years, with further upward potential thereafter.

Approximately 60 percent of potential synergies are expected to be derived from cost savings.

This does not include additional expected synergies from marketing cooperation with respective partners. Furthermore, any improvement from the common fleet policy and lower capital expenditure requirements have not yet been determined and have not been taken into account in these estimates.

KLM restructuring plan

The KLM restructuring plan, which was announced in April 2003, with targeted annual operating income improvement of EUR 650 million by April 1, 2005, are additional to the synergies mentioned above. The KLM management remains fully committed to achieving this objective.

Estimated value of the synergies

Synergies by activity (Euro amounts in millions)

Activity	Main actions	Year 3 (2006/2007)	Year 5 (2008/2009)
Sales/Distribution	Coordination of sales structures; Sales cost improvements; Handling and catering.	€40	€100
Network, revenue management, fleet	Network/scheduling management; Revenue management harmonization; optimization of fleet utilization; Coordinated management.	€95–130	€30–195
Cargo	Network optimization; Commercial alignments; support services.	€35	€35
Maintenance	Procurement; Insourcing; pooling (stocks etc.).	€25	€60–€65
IT systems	Progressive convergence of IT systems	€20	€50–€70
Other	Procurement synergies	€5–€10	€10–€30
Total cost savings		€220–€260	€385–€495

Total expected synergies per year (Euro amounts in millions)

	2004/2005	2005/2006	2006/2007	2007/2008	2008/2009	Long-term
Total savings	65–75	110–135	220–260	295–370	385–495	>600

The Air France–KLM merger

EXHIBIT 2   Press release of the Dutch Investor Association (VEB): "Air France shareholders get it on the cheap", April 19, 2004[a]

After two postponements on 22 March and 31 March, KLM and Air France announced they intend to pursue their merger plans unchanged. This means that Air France will make an offer worth €784 million, whereby each KLM share will be worth 1.1 Air France shares plus a warrant. Far too low an offer.

Half a year has gone by since the merger was announced on 30 September 2003. In the intervening 6 months a number of circumstances have emerged that would justify a higher bid. The prospectus and the bid offer show that KLM is worth considerably more than was apparent until now. There are other questions that remain unanswered that would provide a clearer view of KLM's value. Here are ten reasons why the Air France bid is far too low.

Net equity per share is €34

KLM net worth (assets after debt) is €1,501 million, or €34.14 per share. At an Air France share price of €15 the offer amounts to €17.80 per KLM share. The bid is thus equivalent to just over its net equity value. Air France shareholders will obtain half KLM for free.

A further point is that KLM owns significant intangible assets that are not valued on the balance sheet. This includes the KLM brand name and the landing rights owned by KLM which have a definite economic value. Since these important intangibles are not valued at all in the balance sheet, a price in excess of net equity value stands to reason.

The bid is worth a mere 7 times earnings (2004) and 5 times earnings (2005)

Analysts forecast a substantial increase of profit for Fiscal 2004/2005 and the following Fiscal. They predict earnings in the €100–€110 million range in 2004. In the following year they could reach the €150–€170 million range. This equates to €2.50 and €3.60 per share. The bid is thus 7 times expected earnings for 2004 and 5 times expected earnings for 2005. Compared with other listed companies, whose average p/e ratio is 14, this is a very low valuation. Prices paid for other airline companies score are 17 times 2004 earnings and 11 times 2005.

Real estate assets include a surplus value of at least €248 million, or €5.60 per share

The bid documentation (p. F-158) prepared by Air France and KLM reveals significant hidden reserves in KLM's stock of real estate. These are valued in KLM's balance sheet at €331 million. Price at purchase was €728 million, 55% of which has been written off. According to KLM these assets are now worth €248 million more. Put against 44.2 million shares on the market this corresponds to a surplus value of €5.60 per share. Specialists say the surplus value is closer to the €450–€650 million bracket!

Unlike Air France, KLM has accumulated a pension fund surplus of €2.4 billion

According to French GAAP (Generally Accepted Accounting Principles) KLM equity is worth about €3 billion, roughly double the equity according to Dutch GAAP and four times the value of the bid. Some significant modifications have been made to arrive at these figures. On the one hand the pension fund reserve has been added to shareholder equity. This is worth €2.4 billion. Against that a negative adjustment has to be made for contingent tax liabilities falling upon KLM of €811 million. French GAAP values equity per share at €69.

The exchange ratio is partly the result of operating results in 2002/2003 and 2003/2004: These were seriously depressed by the SARS health scare and the crisis in Iraq

KLM has been looking for years for a partner. There were several previous rounds of negotiation with British Airways. In 2001 a merger attempt with Alitalia failed. Processing the consequences of this failure were unpleasant. KLM was obliged to pay Alitalia €275 million, which was equivalent to €6 per KLM share. The media reported that KLM had refused an out of court settlement worth €50 million. The Alitalia costs appear as a charge in the 2002/2003 accounts. Last year operating results came under pressure as a result of the SARS health scare which significantly reduced passenger traffic to and from Asia. The first quarter of calendar 2003 put heavy pressure on both sales and profit

[a]Reprinted with permission from the Vereniging van Effectenbezitters.

as a result of the coming war in Iraq and the danger of terrorist attacks directed at aircraft. It is obvious that these factors depressed the price negotiations which clearly took account of current operational results. KLM would have been far better served by sitting it out until it could enter into negotiations from a more comfortable and more profitable situation.

The last two quarters show results significantly above the estimates of analysts

The merger and the price were announced on 30 September. In the intervening period KLM published its quarterly results, first on 23 October 2003 (Q2) and then on 22 January 2004 (Q3). KLM's results exceeded – even significantly – expectations. This has led to KLM anticipating a slightly positive result for 2003/2004 – despite SARS, Iraq, the low dollar and a poor economy. These improvements alone would have justified an adjustment of the price.

The earnings trend on the French side is less attractive. In the last 9 months Air France net profit has fallen from €143 million to €80 million.

Air France gets control of KLM without paying a premium

Air France will be the masters in the newly merged company. Previous Air France shareholders will hold onto an 81% share in the company. The CEO will be a Frenchman, Jean-Cyrille Spinetta. In both the Executive and the Supervisory Boards the Dutch will be in a minority. Of the eight Executive Board Directors four will be Dutch and four will be French. Although both companies pay lip-service to the mantra of a merger, it is in reality a takeover. Air France pitches a bid priced in its own shares for KLM and gains control. It might be that the changing of the guard will take place in stages to allow landing rights to be preserved, but after three years this formal structure will be dissolved as well. In cases of takeover, a control premium payable in addition to the standard economic valuation is the norm. Air France is not paying it.

KLM has started a cost savings program worth €650 million, but KLM shareholders will get only 19% of the benefit

On 8 May 2003 KLM announced a cost cutting programme designed to yield €650 million in savings. The major share of these cost reductions have still to be carried out. On 22 January KLM announced that €125 millions worth of savings had been achieved. Clearly, successful execution of the programme will lead to better profitability at KLM. If the cost reduction programme is implemented in full and half of the benefits are given back to the customer in the form of reduced fares, operational results will go up by €325 million. Stripping out 35% corporation tax, this leads to a contribution of €211 million to the bottom line. If the transaction goes through, KLM shareholders will own 19% of the joint company, as a result of which only 19% of these benefits will flow to KLM shareholders. But every single percentage point of the improvement will have come from the business they used to own.

Key factors show that KLM should obtain over 30% of the merged airline

On a total passengers carried basis KLM is the world's tenth largest airline and Air France is number three. Taken by sales, Air France with revenues worth €12.7 billion is about twice the size of KLM (revenues of €6.5 billion). A revenue criterion thus leads to a 66:34 ratio: KLM shareholders deserve a one third share in the merged airline. Other measures of size lead to the same ratio. Based on four criteria – sales, number of aircraft, shareholder equity and headcount – an average ratio comes out at 69:31. The figure means that the KLM figure should be 63% higher than the agreed 19%. If there are no signs of structural differences in profitability between Air France and KLM – and nothing has emerged to show this – these yardsticks can be used to make a reliable estimate of what the share swap ratio should be.

Benefits of synergy

The bid prospectus (p. 50) lists significant benefits of synergy the two companies expect to achieve if the merger goes through. Year One factors for €75 million in synergy benefits, rising to €450 million in Year Five. Clearly KLM shareholders should be compensated for these synergies in the form of a proper price offer, or share swap. It is scarcely an adequate response to claim that, because Air France has brought out an offer priced in shares, KLM shareholders will thereby participate in the benefits. For whatever reasons that they may consider relevant – let us say, for issues of control – KLM shareholders may decide to decline the offer to become Air France shareholders. If they accept the merger and do decide to become Air France shareholders they will share in the benefits of synergy to the tune of a mere 19%.

The Air France–KLM merger

The Air France–KLM merger

Key dates

Above are ten reasons why the offer for KLM is far too low. In terms of procedure there are two important dates. On Monday 19 April an Extraordinary General Meeting of Shareholders will be held. Information about the offer will be given, questions will be answered and a proposal to change the Articles of Association – which will permit the merger – will be put to the vote. At 11 a.m. on 3 May the offer will close. Prior to that KLM shareholders will have to decide whether they want to accept or reject the bid. If less than 70% of the shares are tendered the

transaction will be a dead letter. If less than 95% of shares are tendered, KLM's share listing will be maintained.

We have tried to shed light on the true worth of KLM. It is significantly higher than the current bid offer. This will not dispense KLM shareholders from taking their own decision. That can be based on other decisions such as enthusiasm over the prospects of Air France, a need for cash or whatever.

Peter Paul de Vries
Chairman of Vereniging van Effectenbezitters (Dutch Investor Association)

EXHIBIT 3   Abridged merger prospectus

Unaudited condensed pro forma consolidated financial information

The following unaudited condensed pro forma consolidated financial information is being provided to give you a better understanding of what the results of operations and financial position of Air France-KLM might have looked like had the offer of Air France for KLM common shares occurred on an earlier date. The unaudited condensed pro forma financial information is based on the estimates and assumptions set forth in the notes to such information. The unaudited condensed pro forma consolidated financial information is preliminary and is being furnished solely for illustrative purposes and, therefore, is not necessarily indicative of the combined results of operations or financial position of Air France–KLM that might have been achieved for the dates or periods indicated, nor is it necessarily indicative of the results of operations or financial position of Air France–KLM that may, or may be expected to, occur in the future. No account has been taken within the unaudited condensed pro forma consolidated financial statements of any synergy or efficiency that may, or may be expected to, occur following the offer.

For accounting purposes, the combination will be accounted for as Air France's acquisition of KLM using the purchase method of accounting under both French and U.S. GAAP. Under French GAAP, this determination has been based on the assessment of effective control of KLM by Air France, primarily through the ability of Air France to control the significant decisions of KLM as a result of its deciding vote on the strategic management committee. Under U.S. GAAP, Air France believes that its ability to cast the deciding vote for majority matters of the strategic management committee, combined with its ownership of 49% of the voting share capital of KLM, and its ownership of all of the outstanding depositary receipts related to the administered shareholdings which will exist following the completion of the exchange offer, will provide Air France with a controlling financial interest in KLM, and that consolidation of KLM provides the most meaningful presentation of the combined financial position and results of operations of Air France–KLM. We have also concluded that Air France should initially measure all assets, liabilities and non-controlling interests of KLM at their fair values at the date of completion of the exchange offer.

As a result of the above considerations under French GAAP and U.S. GAAP, the accompanying unaudited pro forma financial information includes adjustments to reflect the fair values of KLM's net assets as further described in the accompanying footnotes. The final combination will be accounted for based on the final determination of the transaction value and the fair values of KLM's identifiable assets and liabilities at the date of exchange of control. Therefore, the actual goodwill amount, as well as other balance sheet items, could differ from the preliminary unaudited condensed pro forma consolidated financial information presented herein, and in turn affect items in the preliminary unaudited condensed pro forma consolidated income statements and balance sheet, such as amortization of intangible assets, income of equity affiliates, long-term assets, negative goodwill, pre-paid pension assets and related income taxes.

The following unaudited pro forma consolidated financial information gives pro forma effect to the offer, after giving effect to the pro forma adjustments described in the notes to the unaudited pro forma consolidated financial information. The unaudited condensed pro forma consolidated income statements for the financial year ended March 31, 2003 and for the six months ended September 30, 2003 give effect to the offer and the business combination as if they had occurred on April 1, 2002. The unaudited condensed pro forma consolidated balance sheet as of September 30, 2003 gives effect to the offer and the business combination as if they had occurred on September 30, 2003. The unaudited condensed pro forma consolidated financial information of Air France–KLM is based on the historical consolidated financial statements of Air France, which are included elsewhere in this prospectus, and on the historical consolidated financial statements of KLM, which are included in KLM's Annual Report on Form 20-F for the year ended March 31, 2003, as amended, and in the unaudited interim condensed consolidated financial statements for the six months ended September 30, 2003 filed by KLM on Form 6-K dated December 30, 2003, incorporated by reference in this prospectus. The historical financial statements of Air France and KLM are prepared in accordance with French GAAP and Dutch GAAP, respectively. Dutch GAAP differs in some respects from French GAAP. Accordingly, the historical financial statements of KLM have been adjusted

The Air France–KLM merger

to French GAAP for all periods presented in this unaudited condensed pro forma consolidated financial information.

Air France has presented the unaudited condensed pro forma consolidated financial information in accordance with both French GAAP and U.S. GAAP for the year ended March 31, 2003 and as of September 30, 2003 and for the six-month period then ended in order to fulfill regulatory requirements in the United States. The combined entity will continue to prepare its consolidated financial statements in accordance with

French GAAP until application of IFRS becomes mandatory within the European Union for financial years beginning on or after January 1, 2005. Air France will also provide additional information in accordance with U.S. GAAP in order to fulfill regulatory requirements in the United States.

These unaudited condensed pro forma consolidated financial statements are only a summary and should be read in conjunction with the historical consolidated financial statements and related notes of Air France and KLM.

**UNAUDITED CONDENSED PRO FORMA COMBINED INCOME STATEMENT
FOR THE SIX-MONTH PERIOD ENDED SEPTEMBER 30, 2003**

| (euro amounts in millions) | French GAAP | | |
	Air France	KLM	Pro forma combined
Net sales	€6,193	€3,036	€9,229
Salaries and related costs	(2,025)	(922)	(2,947)
Depreciation and amortization	(618)	(218)	(806)
Aircraft fuel	(657)	(396)	(1,053)
Landing fees and other rents	(654)	(268)	(922)
Aircraft maintenance materials and outside repairs	(186)	(263)	(449)
Aircraft rent	(239)	(133)	(372)
Selling expenses and passenger commissions	(533)	(191)	(724)
Contracted services and passenger revenues	(533)	(286)	(819)
Other operating expenses	(660)	(264)	(924)
Income (loss) from operations	88	95	213
Restructuring costs	(11)	(75)	(86)
Interest expense	(71)	(53)	(124)
Interest income and other financial income, net	65	26	91
Other income (expense), net	0	7	7
Gain on sale of stock subsidiaries	0	12	12
Income of equity affiliates	22	7	32
Income (loss) before taxes and minority interests and goodwill amortization	93	19	145
Income tax	(32)	4	(38)
Minority interest	(1)	0	(1)
Goodwill amortization and impairment	(8)	(2)	115
Income (loss) from continuing operations	€52	€21	€221

The accompanying notes are an integral part of the unaudited condensed pro forma consolidated financial statements.

The Air France–KLM merger

UNAUDITED CONDENSED PRO FORMA COMBINED INCOME STATEMENT
FOR THE YEAR ENDED MARCH 30, 2003

	French GAAP		
(euro amounts in millions)	Air France	KLM	Pro forma combined
Net sales	€12,687	€6,367	€19,054
Salaries and related costs	(3,856)	(1,714)	(5,570)
Depreciation and amortization	(1,310)	(528)	(1,776)
Aircraft fuel	(1,369)	(866)	(2,235)
Landing fees and other rents	(1,362)	(525)	(1,887)
Aircraft maintenance materials and outside repairs	(477)	(642)	(1,119)
Aircraft rent	(521)	(256)	(777)
Selling expenses and passenger commissions	(1,157)	(486)	(1,643)
Contracted services and passenger revenues	(1,086)	(594)	(1,680)
Other operating expenses	(1,357)	(663)	(2,020)
Income (loss) from operations	192	93	347
Restructuring costs	(13)	0	(13)
Interest expense	(161)	(140)	(301)
Interest income and other financial income, net	76	(4)	72
Other income (expense), net	0	(42)	(42)
Gain on sale of stock subsidiaries	4	6	10
Income of equity affiliates	29	(4)	31
Income (loss) before taxes and minority interests and goodwill amortization	127	(91)	104
Income tax	13	30	22
Minority interest	(4)	0	(4)
Goodwill amortization and impairment	(16)	(4)	230
Income (loss) from continuing operations	€120	€(65)	€352

The accompanying notes are an integral part of the unaudited condensed pro forma consolidated financial statements.

The Air France–KLM merger

UNAUDITED CONDENSED PRO FORMA COMBINED BALANCE SHEET, SEPTEMBER 30, 2003

(euro amounts in millions)	French GAAP		
	Air France	KLM	Pro forma combined
Current assets:			
Cash and cash equivalents	€1,202	€55	€1,257
Short-term investments and restricted cash	169	475	644
Accounts receivables	1,574	728	2,302
Inventories	209	145	354
Prepaid expenses and other	559	2,511	1,981
Total current assets	3,713	3,914	6,538
Flight and ground equipment, net	6,353	2,350	8,674
Flight and ground equipment under capital lease, net	1,515	2,592	3,708
Investment in equity affiliates	312	216	484
Investment in securities	103	0	66
Deferred income taxes	76	53	657
Other non-current assets	154	10	164
Intangible assets	159	48	207
Goodwill	103	12	103
Total assets	€12,488	€9,195	€20,705
Current liabilities:			
Current maturities of long-term debt	€223	€16	€239
Short-term obligation (other)	297	148	445
Current obligation under capital leases	113	151	265
Trade payables	1,204	546	1,750
Deferred revenue on ticket sales	807	471	1,278
Taxes payable	4	11	15
Accrued salaries, related benefits and employee-related liabilities	559	236	795
Other current liability	626	329	955
Total current liabilities	3,833	1,908	5,741
Long-term debt	2,349	591	2,940
Non-current obligation under capital leases	1,204	2,453	3,657
Pension liability	601	4	641
Provisions	450	223	1,906
Other non-current liability	0	212	212
Deferred tax liability, non-current	0	747	747
Minority interest	29	0	29
Total stockholders' equity	4,022	3,058	4,833
Total liabilities and stockholders' equity	€12,488	€9,195	€20,705

The accompanying notes are an integral part of the unaudited condensed pro forma consolidated financial statements

The Air France–KLM merger

Excerpts from the notes to the pro forma financial statements – significant differences between Dutch GAAP and French GAAP (euro amounts in millions, except per share data)

KLM prepares its consolidated financial statements in accordance with Dutch GAAP, which differ in certain material respects from French GAAP. For purposes of preparing the unaudited condensed pro forma consolidated financial information, KLM's historical consolidated financial statements have been adjusted to conform to French GAAP as applied by Air France for each period presented. These adjustments have been made based on estimates of the management of Air France and KLM. These adjustments are unaudited, and may not fully reflect the application of French GAAP for the periods presented as if KLM had prepared its financial statements using French GAAP. Upon completion of the exchange offer, Air France and KLM will perform a detailed review of their accounting policies and financial statement classifications, and additional adjustments may be required to conform the KLM financial statements to Air France-KLM's financial statements as presented under French GAAP.

Although Air France and KLM do not expect that this detailed review will result in material changes to accounting policies or classifications other than noted below, no such assurance can be given at this time. The table below summarizes the net effect of French GAAP adjustments on KLM's stockholders' equity as of September 30, 2003:

Note	Differences	Stockholders' equity at September 30, 2003
1	Pension benefits	€2,355
2	Derivative instruments	11
4	Accounting for treasury stock	23
7	Frequent flyer program	(16)
5	Deffered income taxes	(811)
	Stockholders' equity without tax	€1,562

Note 1 Pension benefits

Under Dutch GAAP, pension costs for KLM's defined benefit pension plans are generally expensed on the basis of the actuarially determined contributions that KLM is required to pay under various worldwide pension schemes. Air France accounts for the costs and obligations of its pension plans in accordance with French GAAP, which does not significantly differ from IAS 19.

This French GAAP adjustment provides for the costs and obligations related to KLM's pension plans as if these amounts had been determined using IAS 19 as applied on a historical basis of accounting. This adjustment, reflected in the "French GAAP adjustment" third column of the condensed pro forma income statements resulted in a decrease in Salaries and related costs by €45 million and €170 million for the six months ended September 30, 2003 and for the year ended March 31, 2003, respectively. The KLM balance sheet at September 30, 2003 was adjusted as follows in this respect: an increase in the "Prepaid expenses and other" caption of €2,336 million and a decrease in Provisions by €19 million resulting in an increase in stockholders' equity before tax by €2,355 million.

Note 2 Derivative instruments

Under Dutch GAAP, derivatives are recorded separately on the balance sheet and are accounted for at fair value. Changes in the fair value of derivatives which meet certain criteria for cash flow hedge accounting may be deferred and recognized in other comprehensive income until such time as the hedged transaction is recognized. Ineffective portions of hedges are recognized immediately in earnings. Under French GAAP qualifying hedge instruments are presented on the balance sheet net of the hedged item. For cash flow hedges, changes in values of derivative instruments are deferred, as no separate presentation of other comprehensive income is included under French GAAP.

Certain derivatives do not meet the criteria for hedge accounting under Dutch GAAP, but do meet criteria for hedge accounting under French GAAP. As a result, changes in fair values of certain derivatives have been included in income under Dutch GAAP but would have been deferred under French GAAP. The French GAAP adjustment gives effect to reclassifications to reflect net presentation of qualifying hedges, and reverses the effects of changes in fair values of cash flow hedges that had been included in other comprehensive income under Dutch GAAP. In addition, the impacts on income of some non-qualifying derivatives under Dutch GAAP which meet French GAAP criteria have been reversed. The September 30, 2003 balance sheet impacts are described in the following table (in € millions):

Flight equipment	€(110)
Other non-current assets	(409)
Long-term debt	(291)
Capital lease obligation	(239)
Stockholders' equity before tax	11

Before tax, the income (loss) statement adjustment amounts to €(13) million and €(11) million for the six months ended September 30, 2003 and the year ended March 31, 2003, respectively.

Note 3 Recognition of restructuring costs

Under Dutch GAAP, €75 million (with a €26 million tax effect) arising from decisions made by KLM's Board of Managing Directors have been classified as extraordinary items in the unaudited condensed pro forma consolidated financial information. Under French GAAP, the expense of €49 million relating to the restructuring provision would have been recognized as the actual costs were incurred. The provision balance at March 31, 2003 is reversed in the balance sheet as a Dutch GAAP to French GAAP adjustment. During the six months ended September 30, 2003, the restructuring costs did qualify for French GAAP purposes and consequently were recorded in the Dutch GAAP to French GAAP reconciliation, with an impact of €75 million on restructuring costs with a related tax impact of €26 million.

Note 4 Accounting for treasury stock

Under French GAAP, treasury shares held by Air France to fulfill commitments under employee stock option plans are accounted for as an asset. Provisions are recorded in order to record the shares at the lower of cost or market value, with related gains and losses recognized in the income statement. Under Dutch GAAP, the purchase price of these shares is deducted from stockholders' equity. The French GAAP adjustment reclassifies €23 million of KLM's acquired treasury shares to short-term investments and recognizes a realized income on the sale of those shares for an amount of €13 million for the six month period ended September 30, 2003 and a loss of €(16) million in the income statement for the year ended March 31, 2003.

Note 5 Deferred income taxes

These adjustments reflect the deferred tax impacts of the French GAAP adjustments listed above, except for treasury stock adjustments which are tax exempted in the Netherlands. Income tax effect has been calculated using the KLM current tax rate of 34.5%. The net tax effect of French GAAP adjustments is a decrease in stockholders' equity of KLM of €811 million (an increase by €747 million of the deferred tax liabilities and a decrease by €64 million of the deferred tax assets).

For the year ended March 31, 2003, the deferred income taxes caption also reflects the French GAAP reclassification, from operating income and income tax to extraordinary items, net of tax, of the outcome of the dispute between KLM and Alitalia.

Note 6 Lease deposits

Under Dutch GAAP, lease deposits are either classified as investments in debt securities or other noncurrent assets, or deducted from financial debt, while under French GAAP lease deposits are offset with financial debt (obligation under capital leases). This reclassification leads to the decrease of financial debt and lease deposits by €475 million.

Note 7 Frequent flyer program

Under Dutch GAAP, the liability recorded for the accrued costs related to flight awards earned by members of the frequent flyer program is classified as a long-term liability. Under French GAAP, amounts accrued related to the Fréquence Plus frequent flyer program are included in advance ticket liability in the consolidated balance sheet of Air France and classified as a current liability for purposes of the pro forma financial information. The French GAAP adjustment reclassifies €42 million provision recorded by KLM under Dutch GAAP to unearned revenue in accordance with French GAAP as applied by Air France. This reclassification impacts provision for €26 million, stockholders' equity for €10 million and deferred tax assets for €6 million.

Note 8 Inventory

Under Dutch GAAP, certain rotable and exchangeable parts have been classified in inventories. Under French GAAP, these items are classified as flight equipment. The net book value of these rotable parts and exchangeable components is €66 million at September 30, 2003.

Note 9 Other

Under French GAAP, unrealized foreign exchange gain or loss on working capital elements is classified in financial income or expense. This reclassification amounts to €17 million and €22 million for the six months ended September 30, 2003 and the year ended March 31, 2003, respectively. In addition, as required under French GAAP, the Goodwill amortization or impairment caption has been reclassified to a separate line item below operating income. This reclassification amounts to €2 million and €4 million for the six months ended September 30, 2003 and the year ended March 31, 2003, respectively.

Note 10 Discontinued operation and extraordinary Items

Under French GAAP, KLM would have presented the disposal of its business "Buzz" as a discontinued operation in the income statement. This disposal was consummated during the six months ended September 30, 2003.

In addition, the outcome of the dispute between KLM and Alitalia would have been presented as an extraordinary item net of tax under French GAAP. This results in a reclassification of €(276) million and €95 million from operating income and income tax to extraordinary items, respectively, in the KLM pro forma French GAAP income statement for the year ended March 31, 2003. Discontinued operation net of tax, extraordinary items net of tax and cumulative effect of change in accounting principles are captions below income (loss) from continuing operations and are not presented in the pro forma condensed income statements.

Excerpts from the notes to the pro forma financial statements – pro forma adjustments (euro amounts in millions, except per share data)

Under French GAAP, Air France is the acquirer of KLM and will account for its acquisition of KLM using the purchase method of accounting. Under the purchase method, Air France will allocate the total purchase price of KLM to the acquired assets and liabilities (including previously unrecognized items) based on their relative fair values as determined on the date of the transaction. This unaudited condensed pro forma consolidated financial information has been prepared and presented assuming that Air France will acquire a 100% controlling economic interest in KLM following the completion of the combination and the conditional acquisition of the Cumulative Preference Shares A.

Under French GAAP, the estimated aggregate purchase price has been calculated as follows (in € millions, except number of shares and per share data):

KLM common shares outstanding	46,810,000
Exchange ratio into Air France's shares	1.10
Equivalent number of Air France's shares	51,491,000
Air France's share price	13.34
Estimated fair value of Air France shares issued	686.9
Estimated fair value of Air France warrants issued	73.5
Estimated fair value of preferred and priority shares	35.5
Estimated transaction-related expenses	15.1
Total estimated purchase price consideration	811.0

The preliminary allocation of its purchase price reflected herein presents preliminary estimates of fair values as determined at September 30, 2003. Such estimates are based on an independent appraisal. The actual allocation of the purchase price will be based on the fair values determined at the date of the transaction, which may differ, in some respects, from those presented below. The estimated excess of purchase price consideration over the approximate value of KLM's net assets, the estimated fair value adjustments and the estimated negative goodwill are as follows (in € millions):

Total estimated purchase price consideration	811
Less: KLM's net assets under French GAAP	(3,058)
Consideration of fair values of acquired assets and liabilities:	
Reduction in fair value of aircraft	(675)
Reduction in reported value of intangible assets	(12)
Incremental fair value of buildings and lands	248
Reduction in fair value of equity investment	(44)
Reduction in fair value in pension and post-retirement plans and increase in pension provision	(1,125)
Deferred tax adjustments	528
Other items, net	66
Excess of the fair value of net assets acquired over purchase consideration	(1,233)

Preliminary estimates of fair values and the final purchase price allocation may materially differ from preliminary amounts and allocations provided in this section. This analysis presents a preliminary allocation of purchase price to the assets and liabilities of KLM, based on independent appraisals conducted at September 30, 2003. The final allocation of purchase price will be completed at the latest at the end of the fiscal year following the acquisition fiscal period, and will be based on valuations and appraisals conducted as of the date of the exchange offer closing date, as

The Air France–KLM merger

specified under French GAAP. We have identified aircraft and pension plans valuations as the most significant areas for potential material discrepancies between pro forma and final purchase price allocation.

Aircraft market value references are principally U.S. dollar-based and therefore, the euro-denominated fair value of the KLM fleet may fluctuate significantly based on €/$ exchange rate fluctuations. The exchange rate retained for the purpose of the pro forma purchase price allocation was $1.13 per €1.00. Should this exchange rate fluctuate to $1.18 for €1.00 or $1.24 for €1.00, the downward fair value adjustment to the KLM fleet would increase by €140 million or €270 million, respectively. Should the exchange rate fluctuate oppositely to $1.07 for €1.00, the downward fair value adjustment to the KLM fleet would decrease by €155 million.

The purchase price allocation may also differ significantly from our preliminary estimates, based on market conditions and assumptions prevailing to the pension plans valuation, mainly based on long term discount rates, anticipated inflation, stock market current valuation, overall economic prospects, and changes in agreements applicable to pensions in the Netherlands and to KLM employees. As further discussed below, the purchase price allocation may also need to be revised in case the overfunded pension plan assets recognition would be limited by the asset ceiling rules introduced by IAS 19.

Under French GAAP, in accordance with the accounting rules governing the purchase method of accounting, Air France is not allowed to recognize intangible assets, such as KLM's trademark or certain take-off and landing slots, when a negative residual goodwill amount results from the purchase price allocation.

KLM sponsors a number of pension benefit plans across the various locations where it operates. As of September 30, 2003, total obligations in respect of these plans amount to €7,055 million, and available pension funds assets have been fair valued at €8,260 million. Benefit plans for employees outside the Netherlands account for less than 5% of total obligations. In the Netherlands, pension benefits consist of final or average career salary plans which are funded through separate legal entities to which employees also contribute. Other post-employment benefits consist of sponsored medical coverage for some retirees, resulting in an estimated obligation (''PBO'') for these plans of €67 million with no related assets. The adjustment to the carrying value of the KLM pension plans is based on this preliminary assessment of PBO and current values of plan assets. As of September 30, 2003, some plans have assets in excess of the PBO estimated by external actuaries. Under French GAAP, the amount of net asset which can be recognized is limited by the asset ceiling rules introduced by IAS 19. These rules limit the amount of net asset which can be recognized on the employer's balance sheet to the present value of any economic benefits available in the form of refunds from the plans or reductions in future contributions to the plans. Following the proposed transaction, the asset ceiling limitation will also consider amounts of cumulative unrecognized actuarial losses and past service costs in determining the maximum asset to be recorded by the combined companies. As of September 30, 2003, the amount of net asset recognized is €1,247 million.

Following the completion of the transaction Air France will perform a full valuation of the acquired KLM plans, in order to determine the actual amount of pension assets to be included in the allocation of purchase price to the acquired plans of KLM. This valuation will occur as of the closing date for the proposed transaction. It is not possible to predict at this time what the final value of the pension asset will be or whether the amount of such asset to be recorded by Air France will need to be reduced by a provision as a result of the asset ceiling restrictions. As a result, the final value to be allocated to the acquired plans could be subject to significant change. Furthermore, the amount of net pension asset recorded would be subject to reconsideration of the asset ceiling test, which could result in significant increases or decreases of the provision/non-cash impacts to Air France's results of operations.

For purposes of the presentation of the pro forma condensed consolidated income statements, the adjustments listed above have been presented as if the transaction had occurred on the first day of the first period presented. The impacts of the pro forma allocation of purchase consideration affect the results of operations for the six-month period ended September 30, 2003 and the year ended March 31, 2003 as follows:

- **Note 11 Tangible assets.** Reflects adjustments to the reported depreciation of KLM based on the reduction in the fair value of the fixed assets.

- **Note 12 Investments in equity affiliates.** Reflects adjustments to the carrying value of KLM's investments in affiliates, primarily KLM's 50% investment in Martinair. For purposes of the pro forma income statements, the decrease in the carrying value of Martinair has been attributed to the fleet assets having an estimated remaining useful life of seven years. The amortization of these adjustments results in an increase to the reported income from this equity investee of €3 million and €6 million for the six months ended September 30, 2003 and the year ended March 31, 2003, respectively.

■ **Note 13 Goodwill.** This adjustment reflects the elimination of the amounts of historical goodwill and goodwill amortization of €2 million for the six-month period ended September 30, 2003 and €4 million for the year ended March 31, 2003.

■ **Note 14 Negative goodwill.** For French GAAP purposes, the excess of the purchase consideration over the fair value of the individual assets and liabilities recognized above results in residual negative goodwill of €1,233 million. Under French GAAP, the residual negative goodwill is allocated to the income statement on a straight line method over a period that reflects assumptions made and management plans as of the acquisition date. On a preliminary basis, Air France's management has estimated that a five-year period would satisfy these criteria. Therefore, for pro forma purposes, the negative goodwill amount has been amortized over a five year period which results in a positive adjustment to net income of €246 million per year ended March 31, 2003 and €123 million for the six months ended September 30, 2003.

The above list is not exhaustive, and there may be other assets and liabilities which may have to be adjusted to fair value when both final valuations and allocations are made following the completion of the exchange offer.

Air France will complete the determination of fair values and the allocation of the purchase price after the completion of the exchange offer. French GAAP allows Air France to complete the purchase price allocation no later than the end of the fiscal year subsequent to the fiscal year in which the exchange offer was completed. The determination of fair values will be based on an independent appraisal.

The exchange ratio agreed between Air France and KLM implicitly valued KLM at less than KLM's net asset value. KLM performs an impairment test whenever there is an indication that the carrying amounts of its assets may not be recoverable. KLM has performed impairment tests on its owned and financially leased aircraft in a manner consistent with Statement of Financial Accounting Standards No. 144 (SFAS 144) under U.S. GAAP as well as in accordance with the Guideline of the Council for Annual Reporting No. 121

(RJ 121) under Netherlands GAAP. SFAS 144 requires the recognition of an impairment loss if the carrying amount of a long-lived asset or group of assets is not recoverable and exceeds its fair value. The carrying amount of an asset or group of assets is generally not recoverable if it exceeds the sum of the undiscounted, pre-tax, future cash flows expected to result from the use and eventual disposition of the asset or group of assets. Assets must be grouped at the lowest level for which identifiable cash flows are largely independent of the cash flows of other assets. Under Netherlands GAAP, KLM compared the carrying amount of each asset group (cash generating unit) to its recoverable amount, which is defined as the higher of the net selling price and its value in use.

In conducting its impairment tests, KLM grouped its fleet assets into four groups:

■ KLM's wide body fleet,

■ KLM's 737 fleet,

■ KLM's regional fleet, and

■ Transavia's fleet.

KLM's wide body fleet, which is used for long-haul destinations, consists of a total of five different kinds of aircraft. Impairment tests for KLM's wide body fleet were conducted for each of these kinds of aircraft, because KLM monitors and optimizes its employment of, and revenues from, each of these kinds of aircraft separately. Therefore, KLM considers this the lowest level for which identifiable cash flows are largely independent of the cash flows of other assets. Impairment tests for KLM's 737 fleet, KLM's regional fleet and Transavia's fleet were conducted at the fleet level instead of by aircraft type or subtype level because in KLM's operations the aircraft composing those fleets are generally interchangeable and therefore cash flows of types or subtypes are not meaningfully identifiable. In its impairment tests KLM:

■ calculated total cash flows during the estimated economic life of each type of asset by multiplying the estimated annual cash flows from that asset type by the remaining average economic life of that asset type,

■ estimated future cash flows based on historical cash flows and KLM's business plan for 2004–2005,

■ estimated the residual asset value at the end of each aircraft's estimated economic life by reference to KLM's depreciation calculations, the Aircraft Value Reference Guide (published by the Aircraft Value Reference Company) and KLM's historical sales experience,

The Air France–KLM merger

- considered the estimated residual asset value as a cash inflow at the end of the asset's economic life,
- assumed that KLM would replace each of its aircraft at the end of its economic life, and
- did not take into account expected changes in yields.

Based on undiscounted cash flows, the asset groups described above passed the recoverability test under SFAS 144 and RJ 121. Although KLM assumed that its aircraft would be replaced at the end of their economic life, KLM also considered the potential scenario involving a gradual decline in operations, under which KLM would be unable to invest in replacement aircraft, and concluded that such a scenario would take decades to transpire and is remote within the time-frame covered by KLM's estimated future cash flows.

KLM's management and supervisory boards agreed to accept Air France's offer at a significant discount to KLM's net asset value after they reviewed all of the strategic options available to KLM, including remaining

an independent company, and concluded that at that time there was no superior strategic alternative to the combination. In assessing the offer in light of the fact that the consideration offered by Air France was below KLM's net asset value, the KLM management and supervisory boards considered certain factors, including the benefits that KLM believed may arise from combining certain complementary features of Air France's and KLM's businesses, KLM's expectation that cost savings and revenue-increasing synergies could be realized following completion of the offer, and the benefits associated with KLM's expected admission into the SkyTeam alliance (subject to KLM's fulfilling the admission criteria) following completion of the offer. The factors that the KLM management and supervisory boards considered in arriving at their decisions to approve and recommend the offer to holders of KLM's common shares are described in KLM's Solicitation/Recommendation Statement on Schedule 14D-9, which has been filed with the Securities and Exchange Commission and which is being mailed to KLM's shareholders together with this prospectus.

The Air France–KLM merger

EXHIBIT 4   **KLM–Air France merger announcement,
September 30, 2003**

A: KLM share price from June 30, 2003 to May 5, 2004

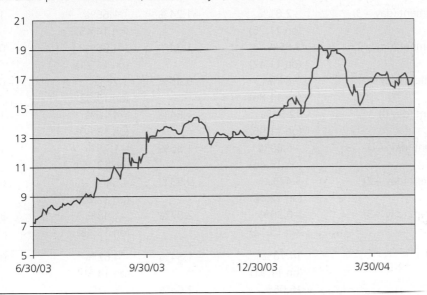

Source: Thomson Datastream.

B: Air France share price from June 30, 2003 to May 5, 2004

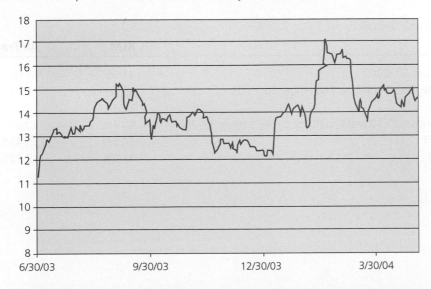

Source: Thomson Datastream.

The Air France–KLM merger

C: Stock returns (and prior day's closing share prices) surrounding the merger announcement

	KLM return (previous closing price)	Dutch AEX Index	Air France return (previous closing price)	French CAC40 Index
3 days before announcement (day −3)	−2.81% (on 11.75)	−1.24%	−1.66% (on 14.45)	−1.02%
2 days before announcement (day −2)	3.85% (on 11.42)	−1.34%	−4.86% (on 14.21)	−0.43%
1 day before announcement (day −1)	0.84% (on 11.86)	−0.46%	1.26% (on 13.52)	−0.87%
Day of the announcement (day 0)	12.54% (on 11.96)	−1.84%	−4.16% (on 13.69)	−1.68%
1 day after announcement (day +1)	−5.69% (on 13.46)	1.56%	−1.75% (on 13.12)	1.79%
2 days after announcement (day +2)	3.47% (on 12.68)	0.93%	4.58% (on 12.89)	0.06%
3 days after announcement (day +3)	−0.30% (on 13.12)	2.87%	−1.48% (on 13.48)	3.24%
From day −10 to day +10	14.78% (on 11.91)	−1.54%	−4.62% (on 14.50)	0.18%
From day −5 to day 5	16.06% (on 11.27)	−2.68%	−5.67% (on 14.64)	−0.35%
From September 30, 2003 to May 5, 2004	45.90% (on 11.96)	10.60%	6.50% (on 13.69)	16.96%

Source: Thomson Datastream.

D: Valuation data and other information

	KLM	Air France
Closing price on September 30, 2003	11.96	13.69
Number of ordinary shares outstanding on September 30, 2003	46,809,699	219,780,887
Beta	1.63	1.36
Yield on government bonds with 10 years' maturity on September 30, 2003	4.14%	4.13%
Statutory tax rate in 2003	34.5%	35.43%
Effective tax rate in 2003	32.0%	13.27%

The Air France–KLM merger

Communication and Governance

Corporate governance has become an increasingly important issue in capital markets throughout the world following financial market meltdowns in the European and US markets at the beginning of the 2000s. These market collapses exposed problems of accounting misstatements and lack of corporate transparency, as well as governance problems and conflicts of interest among the intermediaries charged with monitoring management and corporate disclosures.

The breakdowns have increased the challenge for managers in communicating credibly with skeptical outside investors, making it more difficult than ever for new (and in some cases even established) firms to raise capital. Financial reports, the traditional platform for management to communicate with investors, are viewed with increased skepticism following a number of widely publicized audit failures and the demise of Arthur Andersen.

The market crashes have also raised questions about improving the quality of governance by information and financial intermediaries. New regulations, such as the Eighth Company Law Directive in the EU and the Sarbanes-Oxley Act in the US, attempt to increase accountability and financial competence of audit committees and external auditors, who are charged with reviewing the financial reporting and disclosure process.

This chapter discusses how many of the financial analysis tools developed in Chapters 2 through 8 can be used by managers to develop a coherent disclosure strategy, and by corporate board members and external auditors to improve the quality of their work. The following types of questions are dealt with:

- Managers ask: Is our current communication strategy effective in helping investors understand the firm's business strategy and expected future performance, thereby ensuring that our share price is not seriously overvalued or undervalued?

- Audit committee members ask: What are the firm's key business risks? Are they reflected appropriately in the financial statements? How is management communicating on important risks that cannot be reflected in the financial statements? Is information on the firm's performance presented to the board consistent with that provided to investors in the financial report and firm disclosures?

- External auditors ask: What are the firm's key business risks, and how are they reflected in the financial statements? Where should we focus our audit tests? Is our assessment of the firm's performance consistent with that of external investors and analysts? If not, are we overlooking something, or is management misrepresenting the firm's true performance in disclosures?

Throughout this book we have focused primarily on showing how financial statement data can be helpful for analysts and outside investors in making a variety of decisions. In this chapter we change our emphasis and focus primarily on management and governance agents. Of course an understanding of the management communication process and corporate governance is also important for security analysts and investors. The approach taken here, however, is more germane to insiders because most of the types of analyses we discuss are not available to outsiders.

GOVERNANCE OVERVIEW

As we discuss throughout this book, outside investors require access to reliable information on firm performance, both to value their debt and equity claims and to monitor the performance of management. When investors agree to provide capital to the firm, they require that managers provide information on their company's performance and future plans.

However, left to their own devices, managers are likely to paint a rosy picture of the firm's performance in their disclosures. There are three reasons for manager optimism in reporting. First, most managers are genuinely positive about their firms' prospects, leading them to unwittingly emphasize the positive and downplay the negative.

A second reason for management optimism in reporting arises because firm disclosures play an important role in mitigating "agency" problems between managers and investors.[1] Investors use firm disclosures to judge whether managers have run the firm in investors' best interests or, on the other hand, have abused their authority and control over firm resources. Reporting consistently poor earnings increases the likelihood that top management will be replaced, either by the Board of Directors or by an acquirer who takes over the firm to improve its management.[2] Of course managers are aware of this and have incentives to show positive performance.

Finally, managers are also likely to make optimistic disclosures prior to issuing new equity. Recent evidence indicates that entrepreneurs tend to take their firms public after disclosure of strong reported, but frequently unsustainable, earnings performance. Also, seasoned equity offers typically follow strong, but again unsustainable, share and earnings performance. The strong earnings performance prior to IPOs and seasoned offers appears to be at least partially due to earnings management.[3] Of course rational outside investors recognize management's incentives to manage earnings and downplay any bad news prior to a new issue. They respond by discounting the shares, demanding a hefty new issue discount, and in extreme cases refusing to purchase the new shares. This raises the cost of capital and potentially leaves some of the best new ventures and projects unfunded.[4]

As discussed in Chapter 1, **financial and information intermediaries** help reduce agency and information problems faced by outside investors. The intermediaries evaluate the quality of management representations in the firm's disclosures, providing their own analysis of firms' (and managers') performance and making investment decisions on behalf of investors. As presented in Figure 12.1, these intermediaries include internal governance agents, assurance professionals, information analyzers, and professional investors. The importance of these intermediaries is underscored by the magnitude of the fees that they collectively receive from investors and entrepreneurs.

Internal governance agents are responsible for monitoring a firm's management. In Europe there exist two different governance systems. In a one-tier board system, such as that prevailing in the UK, non-executive directors are members of the same corporate board as firm management (executive directors), whom they monitor. In a two-tier board system, such as that prevailing in Continental Europe, the task of monitoring the Management Board has been delegated to a separate Supervisory Board. In many Continental European countries, the law explicitly requires the members of the Supervisory Board to act in the interests of all stakeholders, not just the shareholders. In large German firms, up to half of the members of the Supervisory Board are representatives of the firm's employees. The

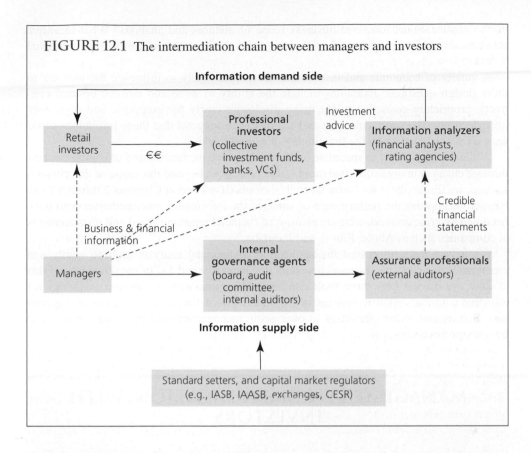

FIGURE 12.1 The intermediation chain between managers and investors

functions of Corporate or Supervisory Boards include reviewing business strategy, evaluating and rewarding top management, and assuring the flow of credible information to external parties.

Assurance professionals, such as external auditors, enhance the **credibility of financial information** prepared by managers. Information analyzers, such as financial analysts and rating agencies, are responsible for gathering and analyzing information to provide performance forecasts and investment recommendations to both professional and retail individual investors. Finally, professional investors (such as banks, collective investment funds, insurance, and venture capital firms) make investment decisions on behalf of dispersed investors. They are therefore responsible for valuing and selecting investment opportunities in the economy.

In this framework, management, internal governance agents, and assurance professionals are charged with supplying information. The demand for information comes from individual and professional investors and information analyzers. Both the supply and demand sides are governed by a variety of regulatory institutions. These include public regulators, such as the European securities and bank regulators, as well as private sector bodies, such as the International Accounting Standards Board, the International Auditing and Assurance Standards Board, and stock exchanges.

The level and quality of information and residual information and agency problems in capital markets are determined by the organizational design of these intermediaries and regulatory institutions. Key organizational design questions include the following: What are the optimal incentive schemes for rewarding top managers? What should be the composition and charter of Corporate Boards? Should auditors assure that financial reports comply with accounting standards or represent a firm's underlying economics? Should there be detailed accounting standards or a few broad accounting principles? What should be the organizational form and business scope of auditors and analysts? What incentive schemes should be used for professional investors to align their interests with individual investors?

A variety of economic and institutional factors are likely to influence the answers to these design questions. Examples include the ability to write and enforce optimal contracts, proprietary costs that might make disclosure costly for investors, and regulatory imperfections. The spectacular rise and fall of Enron suggests that these limitations could have a first-order effect on the functioning of capital markets.

While it is interesting to speculate on how to improve the functioning of capital markets through changes in organizational design, that issue goes beyond the scope of this chapter. Instead, we discuss how the financial analysis tools developed in Chapters 2 through 8 can be used to improve the performance of some of the information intermediaries who have been widely criticized following revelations of financial reporting fraud and misstatements at companies such as Ahold, Enron, and Parmalat.[5]

We have already discussed the application of financial analysis tools to equity and credit analysts and to professional investors in Chapters 9 and 11. In the remainder of this chapter, we discuss how these tools can be used by managers to develop a strategy for effective communication with investors, by members of Boards of Directors or Supervisory Boards and audit committees in overseeing management and the audit process, and by audit professionals.

MANAGEMENT COMMUNICATION WITH INVESTORS

Some managers argue that communication problems are not worth worrying about. They maintain that as long as managers make investment and operating decisions that enhance shareholder value, investors will value their performance and the firm's shares accordingly. While this is true in the long run, since all information is eventually public, it may not hold in the short- or even medium-term. If investors do not have access to the same information as management, they will probably find it difficult to value new and innovative investments. In an efficient capital market, they will not consistently overvalue or undervalue these new investments, but their valuations will tend to be noisy. This can make share prices relatively noisy, leading management at various times to consider their firms to be either seriously overvalued or undervalued.

Does it matter if a firm's shares are overvalued or undervalued for a period? Most managers would prefer to not have their shares undervalued, since it makes it more costly to raise new financing. They may also worry that undervaluation is likely to increase the chance of a takeover by a hostile acquirer, with an accompanying reduction in their job security. Managers of firms that are overvalued may also be concerned about the market's assessment, since they are legally liable for failing to disclose information relevant to investors.[6] They may therefore not wish to see their shares seriously overvalued, even though overvaluation provides opportunities to issue new equity at favorable rates.

A word of caution

As noted above, it is natural that many managers believe that firms are undervalued by the capital market. This frequently occurs because it is difficult for managers to be realistic about their company's future performance. After all, it is part of their job to sell the company to new employees, customers, suppliers, and investors. In addition, forecasting the firm's future performance objectively requires them to judge their own capabilities as managers. Thus many managers may argue that investors are uninformed and that their firm is undervalued. Only some can back that up with solid evidence.

If management decides that the firm does face a genuine information problem, it can begin to consider whether and how this could be redressed. Is the problem potentially serious enough that it is worth doing something to alter investors' perceptions? Or is the problem likely to resolve itself within a short period? Does the firm have plans to raise new equity or to use equity to acquire another company? Is management's job security threatened? As we discuss below, management has a wide range of options in this situation.

KEY ANALYSIS QUESTIONS

We recommend that before jumping to the conclusion that their firms are undervalued, managers should analyze their firms' performance and compare their own forecasts of future performance with those of analysts, using the following approach:

- *Is there a significant difference between internal management forecasts of future earnings and cash flows and those of outside analysts?*

- *Do any differences between managers' and analysts' forecasts arise because of different expectations about economy-wide performance?* Managers may understand their own businesses better than analysts, but they may not be any better at forecasting macro-economic conditions.

- *Can managers identify any factors that might explain a difference between analysts' and managers' forecasts of future performance?* For example, are analysts unaware of positive new R&D results, do they have different information about customer responses to new products and marketing campaigns, etc.? These types of differences could indicate that the firm faces an information problem.

Example: Communication issues for Royal Dutch Shell

Royal Dutch Shell Plc is the world's third largest energy and petrochemical group, operating in 140 countries and employing more than 110,000 people. At the beginning of the 2000s the group had a complicated ownership structure. The service and operating companies of the Royal Dutch Shell group were owned by two holding companies: Shell Petroleum N.V. and the Shell Petroleum Company Ltd. These two companies were, in turn, owned by two exchange-listed companies: Netherlands-based Royal Dutch Petroleum Company, which held a 60 percent equity stake, and UK-based Shell Transport and Trading Company, which held a 40 percent equity stake. Together, Royal Dutch and Shell were named the Royal Dutch Shell group. Royal Dutch and Shell had their shares listed on their domestic exchanges as well as on the New York Stock Exchange. Both exchange-listed companies had their own Management Boards but coordinated many of their decisions and activities by means of explicit arrangements and joint conferences. In the period from 2000 to 2002, the Royal Dutch Shell group reported gradually declining returns on its assets between 19.5 and 14.0 percent. Both exchange-listed holding companies experienced share price declines of about 30 and 20 percent, respectively, reaching a combined market capitalization of €148.6 billion.

By the end of 2002, Royal Dutch Shell had estimated that its "proved reserves" were 10.1 billion barrels of crude oil and natural gas liquids and 53.4 trillion standard cubic feet of natural gas. Proved reserves were the estimated quantities of oil and gas that Royal Dutch Shell expected to recover from its current reservoirs with a reasonable degree of certainty. Following US accounting principles, Royal Dutch Shell had estimated that the present value of these proved reserves was almost €63 billion. The calculation of this present value incorporated the future costs of extraction, production, and distribution activities but was based on current price levels, current tax rates, and a fixed discount rate of 10 percent. The company reported in its financial statements that "oil and gas reserves cannot be measured exactly since estimation of reserves involves subjective judgment and arbitrary determinations. Estimates remain subject to revision." In addition, Royal Dutch Shell assured that "a substantial but unknown proportion of future real cash flows from oil and gas production activities is expected to derive from reserves which have already been discovered but which cannot yet be regarded as proved."

On January 9, 2004, Royal Dutch Shell surprised investors with the announcement that its proved oil and gas reserves were about 20 percent smaller than it had previously disclosed. Specifically, the company reclassified 2.7 billion barrels of oil and natural gas liquids as well as 7.2 trillion standard cubic feet of natural gas as "probable but not proved." The estimated value of the reclassified reserves was close to €6 billion. The market value of Royal Dutch Shell decreased by 7.5 percent, or €10.6 billion, upon the announcement. In February and March, two exchange regulators, the US Securities and Exchange Commission (SEC) and the UK Financial Services Authority (FSA), started their investigations into the matter. On April 30, 2004, the company's market value had decreased by 8.9 percent (adjusted for changes in the FTSE All-World Oil & Gas Price Index), or €12.6 billion since the day before the announcement. By that time, rating agency Standard & Poor had also downgraded Royal Dutch Shell's debt from AAA to AA.

The lasting decline in Royal Dutch Shell's market value exceeded the present value of the change in the company's proved reserves. On April 30, 2004, the company had a price-earnings ratio of 7.6, which was substantially lower than the price-earnings ratios of its competitors, such as British Petroleum (12.1), Exxon Mobil (11.0), and Total (10.4). The market's negative response to the announcement contrasted with management's view on the matter. On April 19, 2004, management reported that they expected to "book nearly all of these volumes as proved over time, some 85 percent within the next decade." The question therefore arises whether the market was further discounting the reserves of Royal Dutch Shell and undervaluing the firm because the firm had lost some of its credibility. Before this can be concluded, a number of questions need to be answered:

- What are the assumptions that analysts made when calculating the present value of Royal Dutch Shell's oil and gas reserves. Did they use lower discount rates? How did analysts value the discovered but unproved oil and gas reserves? Had analysts also revised their value estimates of unproved reserves?

- Did analysts see the unexpected announcement as a confirmation of their concerns that the oil and gas industry experienced severe difficulties in replacing its reserves? Were analysts truly more pessimistic than management about the future profitability and riskiness of the oil and gas industry?

- What was the value that analysts attached to the losses that potentially arose from penalties in lawsuits and settlements with exchange regulators? What was the value loss attributed to Standard & Poor's downgrading the company's debt?

- What other events may explain the company's sudden drop in market value? The primary question for investors was probably the quality of the firm's reserve disclosures. However, management needs to have a deeper understanding of these issues.

- If management believes that the firm is actually undervalued, what options are available to correct the market's view of the company?

COMMUNICATION THROUGH FINANCIAL REPORTING

Financial reports are the most popular format for management communication. Below we discuss the role of financial reporting as a means of investor communication, the institutions that make accounting information credible, and when it is likely to be ineffective.

Accounting as a means of management communication

As we discussed in Chapters 3 and 4, financial reports are an important medium for management communication with external investors. Reports provide investors with an explanation of how their money has been invested, a summary of the performance of those investments, and a discussion of how current performance fits within the firm's overall philosophy and strategy.

Accounting reports not only provide a record of past transactions, they also reflect management estimates and forecasts of the future. For example, they include estimates of bad debts, forecasts of the lives of tangible assets, and implicit forecasts that outlays will generate future cash flow benefits that exceed their cost. Since management is likely to be in a position to make forecasts of these future events that are more accurate than those of external investors, financial reports are a potentially useful way of communicating with investors. However, as discussed, investors are also likely to be skeptical of reports prepared by management. The EU Transparency Directive and the US Sarbanes-Oxley Act require management to certify that financial statements give a true and fair view of the firm's performance and financial position. This requirement increases the accountability of management and mitigates some of the investors' skepticism.

Factors that increase the credibility of accounting communication

A number of mechanisms mitigate conflicts of interest in financial reporting and increase the credibility of accounting information that is communicated to shareholders. These include accounting standards, auditing, monitoring of management by financial analysts, and management reputation.

Accounting standards and auditing

Accounting standards, such as those promulgated by the International Accounting Standards Board (IASB), provide guidelines for managers on how to make accounting decisions and provide outside investors with a way of interpreting these decisions. Uniform accounting standards attempt to reduce managers' ability to record similar economic transactions in different ways, either over time or across firms. Compliance with these standards is enforced by external auditors who attempt to ensure that managers' estimates are reasonable. Auditors therefore reduce the likelihood of earnings management.

Monitoring by financial analysts

Financial intermediaries such as analysts also limit management's ability to manage earnings. Financial analysts specialize in developing firm- and industry-specific knowledge, enabling them to assess the quality of a firm's reported numbers and to make any necessary adjustments. Analysts evaluate the appropriateness of management's forecasts implicit in accounting method choices and reported accruals. This requires a thorough understanding of the firm's business and the relevant accounting rules used in the preparation of its financial reports. Superior analysts adjust reported accrual numbers, if necessary, to reflect economic reality, perhaps by using the cash flow statement and the footnote disclosures.

Analysts' business and technical expertise as well as their legal liability and incentives differ from those of auditors. Consequently, analyst reports can provide information to investors on whether the firm's accounting decisions are appropriate or whether managers are overstating the firm's economic performance to protect their jobs.[7]

Management reputation

A third factor that can counteract external investors' natural skepticism about financial reporting is management reputation. Managers that expect to have an ongoing relationship with external investors and financial intermediaries may be able to build a track record for unbiased financial reporting. By making accounting estimates and judgments that are supported by subsequent performance, managers can demonstrate their competence and reliability to investors and analysts. As a result, managers' future judgments and accounting estimates are more likely to be viewed as credible.

Limitations of financial reporting for investor communication

While accounting standards, auditing, monitoring of management by financial analysts, and management concerns about its reputation increase the credibility and informativeness of financial reports, these mechanisms are far from perfect. Consequently there are times when financial reporting breaks down as a means for management to communicate with external investors. These breakdowns can arise when:

1 There are no accounting rules to guide practice or the existing rules do not distinguish between poor and successful performers.

2 Auditors and analysts do not have the expertise to judge new products or business opportunities.

3 Management faces credibility problems.

Accounting rule limitations

Despite the rapid increase in new accounting standards, accounting rules frequently do not distinguish between good and poor performers. For example, current accounting rules do not permit managers to show on their balance sheets in a timely fashion the benefits of investments in quality improvements, human resource development programs, research and development (with the exception of development expenditures of which the future benefits can be reliably measured), and customer service.

Some of the problems with accounting standards arise because it takes time for standard setters to develop appropriate standards for many new types of economic transactions. Other difficulties arise because standards are the result of compromises between different interest groups (e.g., auditors, investors, corporate managers, and regulators).

Auditor and analyst limitations

While auditors and analysts have access to proprietary information, they do not have the same understanding of the firm's business as managers. The divergence between managers' and auditors'/analysts' business assessments is likely to be most severe for firms with distinctive business strategies, or firms that operate in emerging industries. In addition, auditors' decisions in these circumstances are likely to be dominated by concerns about legal liability, hampering management's ability to use financial reports to communicate effectively with investors.

Finally, conflicts of interest faced by auditors and analysts make their analysis imperfect. Conflicts can potentially induce auditors to side with management to retain the firm as an audit client or to enable the audit firm to sell profitable non-audit services to the client. They can also arise for analysts who provide favorable ratings and research on companies to support investment banking services, or to increase trading volume among less informed investors.

Management credibility problems

There is limited evidence on when management likely to face credibility problems with investors. However, managers of new firms, firms with volatile earnings, firms in financial distress, and firms with poor track records in communicating with investors should expect to find it difficult to be seen as credible reporters.

If management has a credibility problem, financial reports are likely to be viewed with considerable skepticism. Investors will see financial reporting estimates that increase income as evidence that management is padding earnings. This makes it very difficult for management to use financial reports to communicate positive news about current or future performance.

Example: Accounting communication for Royal Dutch Shell

Royal Dutch Shell's key financial reporting estimates are for proved oil and gas reserves. The company makes these estimates using geological information about each reservoir, reservoir production histories, and reservoir pressure histories. The distinction between proved and unproved reserves is important. Accounting standards consider oil and gas reserves to be proved when the company has government and regulatory approval for the extraction of reserves and is able to bring the reserves quickly to the market in a commercially viable manner. Although Royal Dutch Shell discloses the size and present value of its proved reserves outside the financial statements instead of recording the reserves as an on-balance sheet asset, proved reserves estimates can affect net income. First, depreciation, depletion, and amortization of production plants are calculated using the unit-of-production method, where the expected production capacity is derived from the proved reserves. Second, the company capitalizes exploration drilling costs for one year, after which it chooses between continued capitalization and immediate amortization based on whether the exploration has successfully led to the booking of proved reserves. Third, the company recognizes provisions for the decommissioning of production facilities over the life of its proved reserves. Hence, despite the fact that the estimation of proved oil and gas reserves is a fairly subjective exercise, several important accounting choices are unavoidably based on the exercise's results. The inherent uncertainty of establishing proved oil and gas reserves thus also introduces substantial uncertainty into Royal Dutch Shell's income numbers. In addition, any attempt to distinguish proved from unproved reserves is bound to be artificial. Royal Dutch Shell repeatedly indicated that the reclassified reserves had been discovered and remained under the company's control, but only could not be brought to the market quickly enough to be classified as proved.

External auditors did not scrutinize the proved reserve disclosures as part of their annual audit. One reason why external auditors do not audit the reserves estimates is likely to be that they lack the expertise to do so. Some oil companies, especially those from the emerging markets, voluntarily hired outside experts to provide independent verification of reserves. This helped them to signal the accuracy of their estimates to outside investors and reduce potential information problems. In 2004, Royal Dutch Shell also decided to let outside experts certify the quality of its reserves disclosures. However, prior to 2004, this had not been its practice.

The overstatement of proved oil and gas reserves had likely impaired management credibility. To restore credibility, Royal Dutch Shell undertook the following steps:

- In March 2004, the current and the previous Managing Directors of Royal Dutch Shell's exploration and production unit stepped down from their positions. One month later, the company's Finance Director also resigned. These three directors were principally accountable for the overstatements of oil and gas reserves.

- Royal Dutch Shell abandoned its practice of evaluating business unit's performance and calculating managers' bonuses based on reserve bookings. Although the fraction of bonuses related to reserve bookings had been small, investors could have perceived this compensation practice as a potential cause of the reserves overstatements.

- Management concluded that there had been material weaknesses in the company's internal control procedures. To address these weaknesses, the company reviewed its global reserve portfolio, revised its guidelines for booking reserves, established a committee that should oversee the implementation of the reserves guidelines, and increased the independence of the internal auditor who was responsible for auditing the company's reserves. Management announced that "the controls we now have in place will be rigorously enforced and will be subject to far greater levels of scrutiny within Shell. Despite the difficulties of recent months Shell is a sound and profitable business. We are making the changes to our reserves practices to ensure that that remains the case."

- In October 2004, management decided to unify Royal Dutch Petroleum and Shell Transport and Trading under a single parent company, Royal Dutch Shell Plc. The combined company would have a single Board of Management. According to management the simplification of the board and company structure would improve managers' decision-making processes, accountability, and leadership.

KEY ANALYSIS QUESTIONS

For management interested in understanding how effectively the firm's financial reports help it communicate with outside investors, the following questions are likely to provide a useful starting point:

- What are the key business risks that have to be managed effectively? What processes and controls are in place to manage these risks? How are the firm's key business risks reflected in the financial statements? For example, credit risks are reflected in the bad debt allowance, and product quality risks are reflected in allowances for product returns and the method of revenue recognition. For these types of risks, what message is the firm sending on the management of these risks through its estimates or choices of accounting methods? Has the firm been unable to deliver on the forecasts underlying these choices? Alternatively, does the market seem to be ignoring the message underlying the firm's financial reporting choices, indicating a lack of credibility?

- How does the firm communicate about key risks that cannot be reflected in accounting estimates or methods? For example, if technological innovation risk is critical for a company, it is unable to reflect how well it is managing this risk through research and development in its financial statements. But investors will still have questions about this business issue.

COMMUNICATION THROUGH FINANCIAL POLICIES

Managers can also use financing policies to communicate effectively with external investors. One important difference between this type of communication and additional disclosure is that the firm does not provide potentially proprietary information to competitors. **Financial policies** that are useful in this respect include dividend payouts, stock repurchases, financing choices, and hedging strategies.

Dividend payout policies

A firm's dividend payout decisions can provide information to investors on managers' assessments of the firm's future prospects. Dividend payout, defined as cash dividends as a percentage of income available to common shareholders, reflects the extent to which a company pays out profits or retains them for reinvestment. Because paying dividends reduces financial slack and is thus costly, a firm's dividend policy can help management communicate effectively with external investors. Investors recognize that managers will only increase their firm's dividend rate if they anticipate that the payout will not have a serious effect on the firm's future financing options. Thus, the decision to increase dividends can help investors appreciate management's optimism about the firm's future performance and ability to finance growth. This arises because dividend payouts tend to be sticky as managers are reluctant to cut dividend payouts. Managers will only increase dividends when they are confident that they will be able to sustain the increased payout rate in future years. Consequently, investors interpret dividend increases as signals of managers' confidence in the quality of current and future earnings.[8]

As a result, managers in high-growth firms tend to set low dividend payout policies and retain their internally generated funds for reinvestment to minimize any costs from capital market constraints on financing growth options. On the other hand, firms with high and stable operating cash flows and few investment opportunities have high dividend payouts to reduce managers' incentives to reinvest free cash flows in unprofitable ventures.

Share repurchases

In some countries, such as the US and the UK, managers can use share repurchases to communicate with external investors. Under a share repurchase, the firm buys back its own shares, either through a purchase on the open market, through a tender offer, or through a negotiated purchase with a large shareholder. Of course a share repurchase, particularly a tender offer repurchase, is an expensive way for management to communicate with outside investors. Firms typically pay a hefty premium to acquire their shares in tender offer repurchases, potentially diluting the value of the shares that are not tendered or not accepted for tender. In addition, the fees to investment banks, lawyers, and share solicitation fees are not trivial. Given these costs, it is not surprising that research findings indicate that share repurchases are effective signals to investors about the level and risk of future earnings performance.[9] Research findings also suggest that firms that use share repurchases to communicate with investors have accounting assets that reflect less of firm value and have high general information asymmetry.[10]

Financing choices

Firms that have problems communicating with external investors may be able to use financing choices to reduce them. For example, a firm that is unwilling to provide proprietary information to help dispersed public investors value may be willing to provide such information to a knowledgeable private investor – which can become a large shareholder/creditor – or to a bank that agrees to provide the company with a significant new loan. A firm with credibility problems in financial reporting can sell shares or issue debt to an informed private investor such as a large customer who has superior information about the quality of its product or service.

Such changes in financing and ownership can mitigate communication problems in two ways. First, the terms of the new financing arrangement and the credibility of the new lender or shareholder can provide investors with information to reassess the value of the firm. Second, the accompanying increased concentration of ownership and the role of large block holders in corporate governance can have a positive effect on valuation. If investors are concerned about management's incentives to increase shareholder value, the presence of a new block shareholder or significant creditor on the board can be reassuring. This type of monitoring arises in leveraged buyouts, start-ups backed by venture capital firms, and in firms with equity partnership investments. In Japanese and German corporations, it may also arise because large banks own both debt and equity and have close working relationships with firms' managers.

Of course, in the extreme, management can decide that the best option for a firm is to no longer operate as a public company. This can be accomplished by a management buyout, where a buyout group (including management) leverages its own investment (using bank or public debt finance), buys the firm, and takes it private. The buyout group hopes to run the firm for several years and then take the company public again, hopefully with a track record of improved performance that enables investors to value the firm more effectively.

Hedging

An important source of mispricing arises if investors are unable to distinguish between unexpected changes in reported earnings due to management performance and transitory shocks that are beyond managers' control (e.g., foreign currency translation gains and losses). Managers can counteract these effects by hedging such "accounting" risks. Even though hedging is costly, it may be valuable if it reduces information problems that potentially lead to misvaluation.

Example: Share buybacks at Royal Dutch Shell

During the first half of the 2000s, the strong rise in crude oil prices had had a significantly positive impact on oil companies' profits and free cash flows. Because of a lack of investment opportunities and to restrict management from investing in unprofitable projects, oil companies frequently repurchased shares from their investors or paid out special dividends. In fiscal years 2001 and 2002, Royal Dutch Petroleum and Shell Transport and Trading both had repurchased 2.8 percent of their outstanding shares. In 2003, no shares were repurchased. On April 29, 2004, Royal Dutch Shell announced that it would immediately relaunch its share repurchase program. The company would return close to €1.4 billion to its shareholders in 2004 and €3.6 billion in 2005.

KEY ANALYSIS QUESTIONS

For management considering whether to use financing policies to communicate more effectively with investors, the following questions are likely to provide a useful starting point for analysis:

- Have other potentially less costly actions, such as expanded disclosure or accounting communication, been considered? If not, would these alternatives provide a lower cost means of communication? Alternatively, if management is concerned about providing proprietary information to competitors, or has low credibility, these alternatives may not be effective.

- Does the firm have sufficient free cash flow to be able to implement a share repurchase program or to increase dividends? If so, these may be feasible options. If the firm has excess cash available today but expects to be constrained in the future, a share repurchase may be more effective. Alternatively, if management expects to have some excess cash available each year, a dividend increase may be in order.

- Is the firm cash constrained and unable to increase disclosure for proprietary reasons? If so, management may want to consider changing the mix of owners as a way of indicating to investors that another informed outsider is bullish on the company. Of course another possibility is for management itself to increase its stake in the company.

ALTERNATIVE FORMS OF INVESTOR COMMUNICATION

Given the limitations of accounting standards, auditing, and monitoring by financial analysts, as well as the reporting credibility problems faced by management, firms that wish to communicate effectively with external investors are often forced to use alternative media. Below we discuss three alternative ways that managers can communicate with external investors and analysts: meetings with analysts to publicize the firm, expanded voluntary disclosure, and using financing policies to signal management expectations. These forms of communication are typically not mutually exclusive.

Analyst meetings

One popular way for managers to help mitigate communication problems is to meet regularly with financial analysts that follow the firm. At these meetings management will field questions about the firm's current financial performance and discuss its future business plans. In addition to holding analyst meetings, many firms appoint a director of public relations, who provides further regular contact with analysts seeking more information on the firm.

In the last ten years, conference calls have become a popular forum for management to communicate with financial analysts. Recent research finds that firms are more likely to host calls if they are in industries where financial statement data fail to capture key business fundamentals on a timely basis.[11] In addition, conference calls themselves appear to provide new information to analysts about a firm's performance and future prospects.[12] Smaller and less heavily traded firms in particular benefit from initiating investor conference calls.[13]

While firms continue to meet with analysts, rules such as the EU Market Abuse Directive, affect the nature of these interactions. Under these rules, which became effective in 2004, all EU countries must have regulations and institutions in place that prevent unfair disclosure. Specifically, countries must ensure that exchange-listed companies disclose nonpublic private information promptly and simultaneously to all investors. This can reduce the information that managers are willing to disclose in conference calls and private meetings, making these less effective forums for resolving information problems.

Voluntary disclosure

Another way for managers to improve the credibility of their financial reporting is through voluntary disclosure. Accounting rules usually prescribe minimum disclosure requirements, but they do not restrict managers from voluntarily providing additional information. These could include an articulation of the company's long-term strategy, specification of nonfinancial leading indicators that are useful in judging the effectiveness of the strategy implementation, explanation of the relationship between the leading indicators and future profits, and forecasts of future performance. Voluntary disclosures can be reported in the firm's annual report, in brochures created to describe the firm to investors, in management meetings with analysts, or in investor relations responses to information requests.[14]

One constraint on expanded disclosure is the competitive dynamics in product markets. Disclosure of proprietary information on strategies and their expected economic consequences may hurt the firm's competitive position. Managers then face a trade-off between providing information that is useful to investors in assessing the firm's economic performance, and withholding information to maximize the firm's product market advantage.

A second constraint in providing voluntary disclosure is management's legal liability. Forecasts and voluntary disclosures can potentially be used by dissatisfied shareholders to bring civil actions against management for providing misleading information. This seems ironic, since voluntary disclosures should provide investors with additional information. Unfortunately, it can be difficult for courts to decide whether managers' disclosures were good-faith estimates of uncertain future events which later did not materialize, or whether management manipulated the market. Consequently many corporate legal departments recommend against management providing much in the way of voluntary disclosure. One aspect of corporate governance, earnings guidance, has been particularly controversial. There is growing evidence that the guidance provided by management plays an important role in leading analysts' expectations towards achievable earnings targets, and that management guidance is more likely when analysts' initial forecasts are overly optimistic.[15]

Finally, management credibility can limit a firm's incentives to provide voluntary disclosures. If management faces a credibility problem in financial reporting, any voluntary disclosures it provides are also likely to be viewed skeptically. In particular, investors may be concerned about what management is not telling them, particularly since such disclosures are not audited.

THE ROLE OF THE AUDITOR

In Europe, the auditor is responsible for providing investors with assurance that the financial statements are prepared in accordance with an identified set of accounting standards, such as IFRS. This requires the auditor to evaluate whether transactions are recorded in a way that is consistent with the rules produced by regulators (including the IASB and local exchange regulators) and whether management estimates reflected in the financial statements are reasonable. However, audits are required to not only assess whether the financial statements are prepared in accordance with IFRS, but also to judge whether they fairly reflect the client's underlying economic performance. This additional requirement is explicitly mentioned in the Fourth EU Company Law Directive, which regulates firms' financial reporting within the EU, as well as in International Accounting Standard 1.[16] IAS 1 requires "an entity, in extremely rare circumstances in which management concludes that compliance with a requirement in a Standard or an Interpretation would be so misleading that it would conflict with the objective of financial statements . . ., to depart from the requirement unless departure is prohibited by the relevant regulatory framework." This additional assurance requires more judgment on the part of the auditor but also increases the value of the audit to outside investors.

The results of the audit are disclosed in the audit report, which is part of the financial statements. The auditor issues an unqualified report if (a) the firm's financial statements conform to the IFRSs and give a true and fair view of the assets, liabilities, and performance and (b) there is no substantial doubt about the firm's ability to survive. If the financials do not conform to the IFRSs or unfairly present the firm's financial position, the auditor is required to issue a qualified or an adverse report that provides information to investors on the discrepancies. If the auditor is uncertain about whether the firm can survive during the coming year, a going concern report is issued that points out the firm's survival risks.

The key procedures involved in a typical audit include:

1 Understand the client's business and industry to identify key risks for the audit.

2 Evaluate the firm's internal control system to assess whether it is likely to produce reliable information.

3 Perform preliminary analytic procedures to identify unusual events and possible errors.

4 Collect specific evidence on controls, transactions, and account balance details to form the basis for the auditor's opinion.

In most cases client management is willing to respond to issues raised by the audit to ensure that the company receives an unqualified audit opinion. Once the audit is completed, the auditor presents a summary of audit scope and findings to the firm's audit committee.

It is worth noting that the audit is not intended to detect fraud. Of course in some cases it may do so, but that is not its purpose. The detection of fraud is the domain of the internal audit department of the firm itself.

Challenges facing audit industry

During the 1980s and 1990s, the large audit firms in some European countries started to develop more and more consulting services because they decided that the profit margins on regular audits were too thin in a world of standardized audits. This diversification strategy deflected top management energy and partner talent from the audit side of the business to the more profitable consulting part. In addition, the audit firms were sometimes aggressively pursuing a high volume strategy, and so audit partner compensation and promotion became more closely linked to a cordial relationship with top management that attracted new audit clients and retained existing clients. This made it difficult for partners to be effective watchdogs.

In the early 2000s, the accounting debacles of companies like Ahold, Enron, and Parmalat, made regulators and users of financial statements question the independence of auditors from their clients and the quality of the audit. Since then, several regulatory changes have been passed to correct the structural problems facing the industry. In the EU, the revised Eighth Company Law Directive has forced member countries to implement changes in their national regulations to improve auditor independence and audit quality. The Directive has set minimum educational qualifications for admission to the profession and requires European auditors to participate in continuing professional development programs. All audits must be carried out in accordance with the International Auditing Standards (ISA), as promulgated by the International Auditing and Assurance

Standards Board (IAASB) and endorsed by the EU. This requirement should standardize the quality of audits across the EU. Furthermore, the Directive prescribes that the external auditor does not provide any non-audit services to the audited company if this may compromise his independence. To maintain independence, the auditor (the person, not the firm) must also not audit the same company for more than five consecutive years. To enforce these rules, every EU country must install a public oversight system. These requirements are all likely to improve the dynamics of the audit industry.

Role of financial analysis tools for auditing

How can the financial analysis tools discussed in this book be used by audit professionals? The relevance to the audit of the four steps in financial analysis – strategy analysis, accounting analysis, financial analysis, and prospective analysis – is discussed briefly below.

Strategy analysis

Strategy analysis is critical to the first stage of the audit, understanding the client's business and industry. It is important that the auditor develops the expertise to be able to identify the chief risks facing its client. Given the sheer volume of activity, it is impossible to review all transactions of the firm during the audit. Time and attention should be focused on the areas that investors need in order to evaluate the firm's value proposition and how well it is managing its key success factors. These are also likely to be the areas worth further testing and analysis by the auditor, to assess their impact on the financial statements.

Accounting analysis

For the auditor, accounting analysis involves two steps. First, the auditor must understand how the key success factors and risks are reflected in the financial statements. The second step in accounting analysis is for the auditor to evaluate management judgment reflected in the key financial statements items.

Financial analysis

Financial ratios help auditors judge whether there are any unusual performance changes for their client, either relative to past performance or relative to their competitors. Any such changes merit further investigation to ensure that the reasons for the change can be fully explained, and to determine what additional tests are required to satisfy the auditor that the reported changes in performance are justified. Careful ratio analysis can also reveal whether clients are facing business problems that might induce management to conceal losses or keep key obligations off the balance sheet. Such information should alert auditors that extra care and additional detailed tests are likely to be required to reach a conclusion on the client's financial statements.

Prospective analysis

Auditors use prospective analysis to assess whether estimates and forecasts made by management are consistent with the firm's economic position. In addition, the market's perception of a client's future performance provides a useful benchmark for affirming or disconfirming the auditor's assessment of the client's prospects. If the auditor reaches a different conclusion about a client than the market, he or she can determine whether additional disclosure will help investors develop a more realistic view of the company's prospects.

KEY ANALYSIS QUESTIONS

The following questions are likely to provide a useful starting point for auditors in their analysis of a client's financial statements:

- What are the key business risks facing the firm? How well are these risks managed?

- What are the accounting policies and estimates that reflect the firm's key risks? What tests and evidence are required to evaluate management judgment that is reflected in these accounting decisions?

- Do key ratios indicate any unusual changes in client performance? What tests and evidence are required to understand the causes of such changes?

- Has firm performance deteriorated, creating pressure on management to manage earnings or record off-balance sheet transactions? If so, what additional tests and evidence are required to provide assurance that the financial statements are consistent with GAAP and fairly represent the firm's financial position?

- How is the market assessing the client's prospects? If different from the auditor, what is the reason for the difference? If the market is overly optimistic or pessimistic, are there implications for client disclosure or accounting estimates?

Example: Auditing Royal Dutch Shell

For Royal Dutch Shell, how well the company manages its oil and gas reserves is one of its most critical success factors. Surprisingly, in 2004 regulators did not require oil companies to have their oil and gas reserves reviewed by an independent auditor. Some oil companies had their reserves voluntarily reviewed but Royal Dutch Shell only started to do that in 2004, after an internal investigative report advised it to do so.

The auditor most likely lacks the expertise to closely scrutinize the quality of the oil company's reserves estimates. Nonetheless, because the estimates of proved reserves also affect Royal Dutch Shell's accounting numbers, the auditor could at least ask the following questions:

- Are there any unusual changes in the speed with which the company replaces its currently extracted reserves? If so, does the change reflect a change in the scope of the company's exploration or extraction activities?

- Does the change reflect excessive overstatement of reserves by the client in earlier periods? If so, why did the auditors approve this earlier policy? Why did management select this year to revise those estimates?

- Is the change in reserve estimates justifiable, or is management simply responding to pressure to meet unrealistic market expectations?

- What information is available about the size of reserves and which procedures are followed to produce such information? Are geological reports, production histories, and pressure histories for each reservoir produced using reliable procedures? Which internal control procedures are in place to minimize the possibility that reserves estimates are managed?

- Does the company have the necessary regulatory approvals for the extraction of its proved reserves? Is there any reason to question the commercial viability of pending extraction activities?

- If the change in reserves estimates appears to be reasonable, what additional information can the firm provide to investors to address their concerns? Will this information need to be audited?

THE ROLE OF THE AUDIT COMMITTEE

Audit committees are responsible for overseeing the work of the auditor, for ensuring that the financial statements are properly prepared, and for reviewing the internal controls at the company. Audit committees, which are mandated by many stock exchanges as well as the EU Eighth Company Law Directive, typically comprise three to four outside directors or Supervisory Board member who meet regularly before or after their full board meetings.

According to the Eighth Directive, the audit committee monitors the company's reporting process and internal audit and control procedures. Next to overseeing the auditor's work, the audit committee must make sure that the auditor acts with independence from management. Finally, the audit committee makes a selection of auditors at the time that an auditor must be appointed.

In the US, stricter audit committee requirements have been created after the collapse of Enron. In 1999, the SEC, the national stock exchange(s), and the Auditing Standards Board issued new audit committee rules that defined best practices for judging audit committee members' independence and their qualifications. The Sarbanes-Oxley Act of 2002 further required that audit committees take formal responsibility for appointing, overseeing, and negotiating fees with external auditors. Audit committee members are required to be independent directors with no consulting or other potentially compromising relationship to management. It is recommended that at least one member of the committee have financial expertise, such as being a Finance or Managing Director, or being a retired audit partner.

Ideally the audit committee is expected to be independent of management and to take an active role in reviewing the propriety of the firm's financial statements. Committee members are expected to question management and the auditors about the quality of the firm's financial reporting, the scope and findings of the external audit, and the quality of internal controls.

In reality, however, the audit committee has to rely extensively on information from management as well as internal and external auditors. Given the ground that it has to cover, its limited available time, and the technical nature of accounting standards, audit committees are not in a position to catch management fraud or auditors' failures on a timely basis.

How then can the audit committee add value?[17] We believe that many of the financial analysis tools discussed in this book can provide a useful way for audit committees to approach their tasks. Many of the applications of the financial analysis steps discussed for auditors also apply for audit committees.

In its scrutiny of financial statements, the committee should use the 80–20 rule, devoting most of its time to assessing the effectiveness of those *few* policies and decisions that have the *most* impact on investors' perceptions of the company's critical performance indicators. This should not require any additional work for committee members, since they should already have a good understanding of the firm's key success factors and risks from discussions of the full Board.

Audit committee members should also have sufficient financial background to identify where in the financial statements the key risks are reflected. Their discussions with management and external auditors should focus on these risks. How well are they being managed? How are the auditors planning their work to focus on these areas? What evidence have they gathered to judge the adequacy of key financial statement estimates?

The audit committee also receives regular reviews of company performance from management as part of their regular Board duties. Committee members should be especially proactive in requesting information that helps them evaluate how the firm is managing its key risks, since this information can also help them judge the quality of the financial statements. Audit committee members need to ask: Is information on company performance we are receiving in our regular Board meetings consistent with the picture portrayed in the financial statements? If not, what is missing? Are additional disclosures required to ensure that investors are well informed about the firm's operations and performance?

Finally, audit committees need to focus on capital market expectations, not just statutory financial reports. In today's capital markets, the game begins when companies set expectations via analyst meetings, press releases, and other forms of investor communications. Indeed, the pressure to manage earnings is often a direct consequence of investors' unrealistic expectations, either deliberately created by management or sustained by their inaction. Thus it is also important for audit committees to oversee the firm's investor relations strategy and ensure that management sets realistic expectations for both the short and long term.

Example: Royal Dutch Shell's audit committee

Royal Dutch Shell had established an audit committee in 1976. The audit committee advised both the Supervisory Board of Royal Dutch and the Board of Directors of Shell.[18] Royal Dutch Shell reported that its audit committee frequently assessed the effectiveness of the company's internal control procedures and risk management processes. The committee further evaluated internal and external audit reports and assessed the performance of the internal and external audits. The Supervisory Board of Royal Dutch and the Board of Directors of Shell each had three members on the audit committee. In 2004, the audit committee met 23 times, compared with six times in 2003. The substantial increase in the number of meetings highlights the important role that the committee played during Royal Dutch Shell's reporting crisis.

Following the announcement of Royal Dutch Shell on January 9, 2004, the company's audit committee appointed an independent law firm to perform an investigation into the facts that had given rise to the reclassification. One of the recommendations that were made by the report was that in the future, the internal auditor who was responsible for the audit of the oil and gas reserves estimates should report directly to the Internal Audit Department, which, in turn, should report directly to the audit committee. This communication structure ensured that the audit committee gained better and timelier access to crucial information about the company's reserves estimates. In addition, the report recommended that the frequency and depth of internal reserves audits be increased.

KEY ANALYSIS QUESTIONS

The following questions are likely to provide a useful starting point for audit committees in their discussions with management and auditors over the firm's financial statements:

- How are the critical business risks facing the firm managed?
- How are these risks reflected by accounting policies and estimates in the financial statements? What was the basis for the external auditor's assessment of these items?
- Is information on the critical value drivers and firm performance presented to the full Board consistent with the picture of the firm reflected in the financial statements and Management Report?
- What expectations is management creating in the capital market? Are these likely to cause undue pressure to manage earnings?

SUMMARY

This chapter discussed how many of the financial analysis tools developed in Chapters 2 through 8 can be used by managers to develop a coherent disclosure strategy, and by Corporate Board members and external auditors to improve the quality of their work.

By communicating effectively with investors, management can potentially reduce information problems for outside investors, lowering the likelihood that the shares will be mispriced or unnecessarily volatile. This can be important for firms that wish to raise new capital, avoid takeovers, or whose management is concerned that its true job performance is not reflected in the firm's share price.

The typical way for firms to communicate with investors is through financial reporting. Accounting standards and auditing make the reporting process a way for managers to not only provide information about the firm's current performance, but to indicate, through accounting estimates, where they believe the firm is headed in the future. However, financial reports are not always able to convey the types of forward-looking information that investors need. Accounting standards sometimes do not permit firms to capitalize outlays, such as research expenditures, that provide significant future benefits to the firm.

A second way that management can communicate with investors is through nonaccounting means. We discussed several such mechanisms, including meeting with financial analysts to explain the firm's strategy, current performance, and outlook; disclosing additional information, both quantitative and qualitative, to provide investors with similar information as management's; and using financial policies (such as share repurchases, dividend increases, and hedging) to help signal management's optimism about the firm's future performance.

In this chapter we have stressed the importance of communicating effectively with investors. But firms also have to communicate with other stakeholders, including employees, customers, suppliers, and regulatory bodies. Many of the same principles discussed here can also be applied to management communication with these other stakeholders.

Finally, we examined the capital market role of governance agents, such as external auditors and audit committees. Both have faced considerable public scrutiny following a spate of financial reporting meltdowns in Europe and the US Much has been done to improve the governance and independence of these intermediaries. We focus on how the financial analysis tools developed in the book can be used to improve the quality of audit and audit committee work. The tools of strategy analysis, accounting analysis, financial analysis, and prospective analysis can help auditors and audit committee members to identify the key issues in the financial statements to focus on and provide commonsense ways of assessing whether there are potential reporting problems that merit additional testing and analysis.

CORE CONCEPTS

Credibility of financial reporting Factors that help enhance the credibility of financial reporting are:

1 Strictly enforced high-quality accounting and auditing standards.

2 Financial analysts scrutinizing a firm's accounting choices.

3 Management's track record in providing forthcoming and accurate disclosures in a timely manner.

Financial and information intermediaries Financial and information intermediaries that help in reducing agency and information problems faced by outside investors are:

1 Internal governance agents (such as outside directors or Supervisory Board members).
2 Assurance professionals (such as external auditors).
3 Information analyzers (such as financial analysts and rating agencies).
4 Professional investors.

Public regulators and private sector bodies govern the information demand of and supply by these intermediaries.

Financial policies Financial policies that are useful in reducing communication problems are:

1 Stable dividend payout policies that fit the firm's investment opportunities.
2 Share repurchases.
3 Obtaining financing from a private (privately informed) investor.
4 Hedging.

Limitations of financial reporting Factors that reduce the effectiveness of financial reporting as a management communication device are:

1 The rigidness of accounting standards.
2 Lack of auditor independence or expertise.
3 Management credibility problems due to management's short or poor track record in investor communication.

Management communication mechanisms Management can communicate with investors, and hence reduce information problems, through financial reporting, financial policies, analyst meetings and voluntary disclosures.

Role of the audit committee The audit committee, which consists of Supervisory Board members or outside directors, oversees the firm's reporting process and internal audit and control procedures, selects the external auditor and actively communicates with the external auditor about the audit process and outcomes.

Role of the auditor The auditor's role is to provide investors with the assurance that the financial statements comply with the accounting standards and fairly reflect the firm's economic performance.

QUESTIONS

1 In December 2004, Denmark-based Danske Bank experienced a share price decline of 6 percent upon its announcement that it planned to acquire the Irish bank National Europe Holdings. The Danish bank's Finance Director explained that "the market perception of us changed from being a high-yield equity story, because we'd been paying a huge amount of dividends and doing massive share buybacks, to being a growth-oriented, cross-border story." What actions could the Finance Director take to restore investor confidence?

2 a What are likely to be the long-term critical success factors for the following types of firms?
   ■ A high technology company, such as semiconductor equipment maker ASM Lithography.
   ■ A large, low-cost retailer such as Aldi.

b How useful is financial accounting data for evaluating how well these two companies are managing their critical success factors? What other types of information would be useful in your evaluation? What are the costs and benefits to these companies from disclosing this type of information to investors?

3 The International Financial Reporting Standards permit management to revalue fixed assets that have increased in value. Revaluations are typically based on estimates of realizable value made by management or independent valuers. Do you expect that these accounting standards will make earnings and book values more or less useful to investors? Explain why or why not. How can management make these types of disclosures more credible?

4 Under a management buyout, the top management of a firm offers to buy the company from its shareholders, usually at a premium over its current share price. The management team puts up its own capital to finance the acquisition, with additional financing typically coming from a private buyout firm and private debt. If management is interested in making such an offer for its firm in the near future, what are its financial reporting incentives? How do these differ from the incentives of management that are not interested in a buyout? How would you respond to a proposed management buyout if you were the firm's auditor? What about if you were a member of the audit committee?

5 You are approached by the management of a small start-up company that is planning to go public. The founders are unsure about how aggressive they should be in their accounting decisions as they come to the market. The Managing Director, asserts, "We might as well take full advantage of any discretion offered by accounting rules, since the market will be expecting us to do so." What are the pros and cons of this strategy? As the partner of a major audit firm, what type of analysis would you perform before deciding to take on a new start-up that is planning to go public?

6 Two years after a successful public offering, the Managing Director of a biotechnology company is concerned about equity market uncertainty surrounding the potential of new drugs in the development pipeline. In his discussion with you, the Managing Director notes that even though they have recently made significant progress in their internal R&D efforts, the shares have performed poorly. What options does he have to help convince investors of the value of the new products? Which of these options are likely to be feasible?

7 Why might the Managing Director of the biotechnology firm discussed in Question 6 be concerned about the firm being undervalued? Would the Managing Director be equally concerned if the shares were overvalued? Do you believe that the Managing Director would attempt to correct the market's perception in this overvaluation case? How would you react to company concern about market undervaluation or overvaluation if you were the firm's auditor? Or if you were a member of the audit committee?

8 When companies decide to shift from private to public financing by making an initial public offering for their shares, they are likely to face increased costs of investor communications. Given this additional cost, why would firms opt to go public?

9 In some Continental European countries firms are traditionally financed by banks, which have representatives on the companies' Boards. How would communication challenges differ for these firms relative to UK firms, which rely more on public financing?

NOTES

1. M. Jensen and W. Meckling, "Theory of the Firm: Managerial Behavior, Agency Costs, and Capital Structure," *Journal of Financial Economics* 3 (October 1976): 305–360, analyzed agency problems between managers and outside investors. Subsequent work by B. Holmstrom and others examined how contracts between managers and outside investors could mitigate the agency problem.

2. Kevin J. Murphy and Jerold L. Zimmerman, "Financial Performance Surrounding CEO Turnover," *Journal of Accounting and Economics* 16 (January/April/July 1993): 273–315, find a strong relation between CEO turnover and earnings-based performance.

3. See S. Teoh, I. Welch, and T. Wong, "Earnings Management and the Long-Run Market Performance of Initial Public Offerings, *The Journal of Finance* 63 (December 1998): 1935–1974; S. Teoh, I. Welch, and T. Wong, "Earnings Management and the Underperformance of Seasoned Equity Offerings," *Journal of Financial Economics* 50 (October 1998): 63–99; and L. Shivakumar, "Do Firms Mislead Investors by Overstating Earnings Before Seasoned Equity Offerings?," *Journal of Accounting and Economics* 29 (June 2000): 339–371. The latter study explains why managers may overstate earnings prior to seasoned equity offerings despite the possibility that rational investors undo such earnings management.

4. This market imperfection is often referred to as a "lemons" or "information" problem. It was first discussed by G. Akerlof in relation to the used car market (see "The Market for 'Lemons': Quality Uncertainty and the Market Mechanism," *Quarterly Journal of Economics* 90 (1970): 629–650. Akerlof recognized that the seller of a used car knew more about the car's value than the buyer. This meant that the buyer was likely to end up overpaying, since the seller would accept any offer that exceeded the car's true value and reject any lower offer. Car buyers recognized this problem and would respond by only making low-ball offers for used cars, leading sellers with high quality cars to exit the market. As a result, only the lowest quality cars (the "lemons") would remain in the market. Akerlof pointed out that qualified independent mechanics could correct this market breakdown by providing buyers with reliable information on a used car's true value.

5. Of course, improved analysis alone is unlikely to be sufficient to improve market intermediation if the structural reforms implemented by the Eighth EU Directive, the Sarbanes-Oxley Act, and the stock exchanges fail to correct the serious conflicts of interest for intermediaries that we have witnessed in the past few years.

6. Douglas J. Skinner, "Earnings Disclosures and Stockholder Lawsuits," *Journal of Accounting and Economics* (November 1997): 249–283, finds that firms with bad earnings news tend to predisclose this information, perhaps to reduce the cost of litigation that inevitably follows bad news quarters.

7. For example, G. Foster, "Briloff and the Capital Market," *Journal of Accounting Research* 17, No. 1 (Spring 1979): 262–274, finds firms that are criticized for their accounting by Abraham J. Briloff on average suffer an 8 percent decline in their share price.

8. Findings by Paul Healy and Krishna Palepu in "Earnings Information Conveyed by Dividend Initiations and Omissions," *Journal of Financial Economics* 21 (1988): 149–175, indicate that investors interpret announcements of dividend initiations and omissions as managers' forecasts of future earnings performance.

9. See Larry Dann, Ronald Masulis, and David Mayers, "Repurchase Tender Offers and Earnings Information," *Journal of Accounting and Economics* (September 1991): 217–252; and Michael Hertzel and Prem Jain, "Earnings and Risk Changes Around Stock Repurchases," *Journal of Accounting and Economics* (September 1991): 253–276.

10. See Mary Barth and Ron Kasznik, "Share Repurchases and Intangible Assets," *Journal of Accounting and Economics* 28 (December 1999): 211–241.

11. See Sarah Tasker, "Bridging the Information Gap: Quarterly Conference Calls as a Medium for Voluntary Disclosure," *Review of Accounting Studies* 3, No. 1–2 (1998): 137–167.

12. See Richard Frankel, Marilyn Johnson, and Douglas Skinner, "An Empirical Examination of Conference Calls as a Voluntary Disclosure Medium," *Journal of Accounting Research* 37, No. 1 (Spring 1999): 133–150.

13. See M. Kimbrough, "The Effect of Conference Calls on Analyst and Market Underreaction to Earnings Announcements," *The Accounting Review* 80, No. 1 (January 2005): 189–219.

14. Recent research on voluntary disclosure includes Mark Lang and Russell Lundholm, "Cross-Sectional Determinants of Analysts' Ratings of Corporate Disclosures," *Journal of Accounting Research* 31 (Autumn 1993): 246–271; Lang and Lundholm, "Corporate Disclosure Policy and Analysts,"

The Accounting Review 71 (October 1996): 467–492; M. Welker, "Disclosure Policy, Information Asymmetry and Liquidity in Equity Markets," *Contemporary Accounting Research* (Spring 1995); Christine Botosan, "The Impact of Annual Report Disclosure Level on Investor Base and the Cost of Capital," *The Accounting Review* (July 1997): 323–350; and Paul Healy, Amy Hutton, and Krishna Palepu, "Stock Performance and Intermediation Changes Surrounding Sustained Increases in Disclosure," *Contemporary Accounting Research* 16, No. 3 (Fall 1999): 485–521. This research finds that firms are more likely to provide high levels of disclosure if they have strong earnings performance, issue securities, have more analyst following, and have less dispersion in analyst forecasts. In addition, firms with high levels of disclosure policies tend to have a lower cost of capital and bid-ask spread. Finally, firms that increase disclosure have accompanying increases in stock returns, institutional ownership, analyst following, and share liquidity. In "The Role of Supplementary Statements with Management's Earnings Forecasts," working paper, Harvard Business School, 2003, A. Hutton, G. Miller, and D. Skinner examine the market response to management earnings forecasts and find that bad news forecasts are always informative but that good news forecasts are informative only when they are supported by verifiable forward-looking statements.

15. See J. Cotter, I. Tuna, and P. Wysocki, "Expectations Management and Beatable Targets: How do Analysts React to Explicit Earnings Guidance," *Contemporary Accounting Research* 23, No. 3 (Autumn 2006): 593–628.

16. The actual wording of the Fourth EU Directive is that financial statements "shall give a true and fair view of the company's assets, liabilities, financial position and results." This provision in the Fourth Directive has, however, not been equally accepted by all EU member states and has influenced accounting especially in Denmark, the Netherlands, and the UK. For a discussion of the impact of the "true and fair view" provision on European accounting, see the *European Accounting Review*, Volume 6, Issue 4, 1997. The coming years will show whether and how the "true and fair view" provision in IAS 1 will affect European accounting practices.

17. See P. Healy and K. Palepu, "Audit the Audit Committees: After Enron Boards Must Change the Focus and Provide Greater Financial Transparency," *Financial Times,* June 10, 2002, p. 14.

18. Royal Dutch and Shell had different governance structures. Royal Dutch had a two-tier board structure in which the Supervisory Board monitored the Management Board. Shell had a one-tier board structure in which outside directors monitored the inside directors, but in which outside and inside directors were members of one and the same Board of Directors.

Investor relations at Total

Jérôme Schmitt knew not to surprise. As head of Investor Relations (IR) at Total, the world's fourth-largest publicly traded oil and gas company and France's flagship enterprise, he had seen first-hand how fast the financial markets and the company's many other stakeholders could change their views of Total based on unexpected news. It was the fundamental task of the IR-group, though, to maintain long-term relationships with investors and avoid short-term sensibilities.

As an integrated oil and gas company, Total was involved both in exploration and production as well as in refining, shipping, and marketing. Present in over 130 countries, the company produced oil and gas in 27 countries,[1] ran 28 refineries worldwide,[2] and managed over 16,000 gas stations—and the nature and mere size of its operations made Total a natural focal point for many interested parties. Providing pertinent information to such a diverse group—consisting of employees, investors (both institutional and individual), customers, partners, environmentalists, governments, and the general public, especially in the company's home market France—complicated Total's communication approach, especially as the groups all called for different types of information. Still, the communication had to be consistent. "It is the same story we have to tell everyone," said Schmitt.

Total believed it had a successful communication policy based on being consistent and on never over-promising. In September 2005, however, the system was being put to the test. While Total wanted to save money and create buffers against future bad times—against increasing oil prices and to ensure that the French corporate beacon did not become a takeover target—it also showed a €5.8 billion profit for the first half year 2005.[3] Telling the public both about strong earnings and about the need to save made for a complex communication situation—especially within the sociopolitical context in France, where Total employed half of its 110,000 employees. Total received further media attention when France's finance minister announced on September 9 that he would hit the oil majors with extra taxation unless they increased refining capabilities and cut petrol prices in France. The executive management, Schmitt, and his IR team had some communication challenges ahead of them.

Professor Gregory S. Miller, Executive Director of the HBS Europe Research Center Vincent Dessain, and Research Associate Anders Sjöman prepared this case. HBS cases are developed solely as the basis for class discussion. Cases are not intended to serve as endorsements, sources of primary data, or illustrations of effective or ineffective management.

[1] Total Annual Report 2004, p. 58.

[2] From Hoover's, Inc. coverage of Total, http://premium.hoovers.com/subscribe/co/overview.xhtml?ID=12393, accessed September 2005.

[3] Total press release, "Total Second Quarter 2005 results," Paris , 4 August, 2005, available at http://www.total.com/static/en/medias/topic1126/Total_20050804_en_PR_2Q_Results.pdf, accessed 3 October 2005.

Total: The company, its history and its communication

Total was founded in 1924 as Compagnie Française des Pétroles (CFP) on initiative from the French president and in order for France to develop an oil industry. With no domestic oil reserves, CFP immediately ventured abroad, using a stake that the French state had in a Turkish petroleum company. CFP also proceeded to open new oil production fields, starting in 1927 in Iraq, and grew both in scope (adding refining, transporting and marketing) and geographical size (prospecting in places such as Venezuela, Algeria, Indonesia, and the North Sea). The word "Total," which originally was a brand introduced in 1954, became part of the company name in 1985 and the sole moniker in 1991. That year, Total listed ADRs (American Depository Receipts) on the New York Stock Exchange. Said CFO Robert Castaigne:

> *1991 in a way marks the beginning of our financial communication. We were still unknown in the U.S. and U.K. We were a relatively small company, which had to set large targets and sell these to the market. Luckily, we were able to meet our targets and establish a "capital of trust" with the financial community.*

Listed on the French stock exchange since 1929, CFP's main shareholder for many years was the French state. However, the government sold off large parts of its holdings in the mid-1990s to hold less than 1% (and later divested this remaining interest in 1998). Also in the mid-1990s, Total was reorganized by then CEO Serge Tchuruk, who wanted to turn a bureaucratically run company into a world oil major. Said Castaigne, "Tchuruk woke up the company and brought new impetus." Tchuruk was in turn succeeded in 1995 by Thierry Desmarest, who continued Total's revitalization. Described as preferring to let action speak louder than words, Desmarest made a few "loud" decisions early on. For instance, he braved U.S. sanctions and developed two large oil fields in Iran, a country that U.S.-based Conoco Oil had just abandoned for political reasons.[4] The investment in Iran followed Total's involvement in the region for over 70 years. Total under Desmarest was also not shy about investing in other politically charged locations, such as Libya and Myanmar (the former Burma).[5]

In the late 1990s, Total's portfolio of exploration and production operations gave the oil and gas company a decidedly "upstream" look, as industry observers put it. Selling the North American subsidiary had streamlined the company even further by divesting downstream activities such as refineries and gas stations. Total emphasized that it would concentrate on the upstream segment while rationalizing downstream operations in mature markets. Exploration and production were the more profitable parts of the oil business and where Total would continue to focus.

The acquisitions in 1999 and 2000

Investors and industry observers were therefore taken aback when on December 1, 1998, Total announced it would acquire Belgian group Petrofina, a downstream-heavy company with refineries, chemical plants, and gas stations.[6] The sudden downstream move

[4] "France Total CEO/Oil -5: Snapshot," *Dow Jones International News*, 9 January 1998, accessed via Factiva, September 2005.

[5] Stanley Reed in London , with Stan Crock in Washington, "Total loves to go where others fear to tread—The Iran deal is just the latest of Desmarest's shrewd moves," 13 October 1997, *BusinessWeek*, accessed via Factiva, September 2005.

[6] John Tagliabue, "A French Oil Company That Doesn't Act the Part," 13 December 1998, *The New York Times*, accessed via Factiva, September 2005.

surprised analysts, who cringed at the 37% premium[7] over the Petrofina share price that Total would pay. Total's stock price dropped 11% the day after the announcement;[8] several analysts abruptly downgraded Total; and others claimed the merger's benefits added up to only half the premium Total had paid.[9] In the following week, Total shares dropped a total of 22%.[10] Desmarest and his team found themselves having to fly to the financial centers of the world to make their case directly to investors.[11] Said Castaigne, "It was necessary. Our message until then had always been 'Total is upstream, only upstream.' We decided to visit the financial community and investors to explain the strategy. They were very upset." Total could understand the market's reaction, commented Ian Howat, senior vice president of Strategy:

> *We massacred the implicit contract we had with the investors and the analysts. They thought we were one type of animal and now all of a sudden we were another. But sometimes you have to do things you know the markets will not like. There wasn't an alternative. We had about 4% market share in a mature R&M [refining and marketing] market in most European countries. There is no way to grow out of that situation unless you make some acquisitions.*

The message that Desmarest and his team now kept repeating was that Total had to make external acquisitions to grow in a maturing—and also consolidating—market in order to avoid becoming a takeover target or a niche player. The industry was already seeing similar examples: Exxon and Mobil had announced plans to merge, and BP and Amoco Corp. had already joined in the summer.[12] Acquiring Petrofina gave Total downstream assets such as oil refining and marketing in northwest Europe and parts of the U.S.[13] Investors argued that the company did not need the downstream market; they also pointed out that Petrofina's chemical operations almost fully overlapped with Total's.[14] Upstream, however, analysts agreed that the two companies were complementary: Total was strong in the Middle East, Latin America, and Southeast Asia, and Petrofina in the North Sea and North America.[15] Ten days after the announcement, Total's share price was still 17% below its November level.[16] (See **Exhibit 1** for Total's share price between October 1998 and December 1999.) More calculations were presented, showing even larger cost savings due to synergies, but it would be time-consuming to help the financial markets overcome their surprise. Said Castaigne:

> *This is a good example of how you learn as a company to be consistent in your message. [When you present to the financial community,] you are in front of people who take notes of everything you say—and next time, they will of course try to see what is different between what you said before and what you say now. So it is important to be consistent. For us, this surprise change of strategy meant we had to slowly rebuild the trust with the financial markets by visits, visits, and more visits, and also by listening more to our investors. We were helped somewhat in this phase by one*

[7]Marcel Michelson, "Total plugs merger, says profit slip limited," *Reuters News*, 6 January 1999, accessed via Factiva, September 2005.

[8]John Tagliabue, "A French Oil Company That Doesn't Act the Part."

[9]Bhushan Bahree and Martin Du Bois, "Total Will Buy Belgium's Petrofina at Big Premium," 2 December 1998, *The Wall Street Journal Europe*, accessed via Factiva, September 2005.

[10]Casewriter interview with Total CFO Robert Castaigne, August 2005, La Defense, Paris, France.

[11]John Tagliabue, "A French Oil Company That Doesn't Act the Part."

[12]Bhushan Bahree and Martin Du Bois, "Total Will Buy Belgium's Petrofina at Big Premium."

[13]Ibid.

[14]"Upstream Focus," 31 January 1999, accessed via Factiva, September 2005.

[15]"All The Way," 31 January 1999, *International Petroleum Finance*, accessed via Factiva, September 2005.

[16]"A wise move by Total," 6 January 1999, *Petroleum Economist*, accessed via Factiva, September 2005.

financial institution who quickly understood our strategy. They invested when others were selling off their shares in Total.

It took Total seven months to complete the acquisition process and on July 1, 1999, the new company, named TotalFina, was officially formed. "And the following Monday," said Castaigne, "we moved on Elf Aquitaine."

Interestingly, thought Castaigne, the financial markets appreciated this second acquisition more than the first. Going after rival Elf was seen as a sign that Total stood firm by its new aggressive growth strategy. TotalFina was the world's sixth-largest oil company with a market capitalization of $40 billion,[17] but it was still too small to be a "major." Merging Total with Elf made sense to analysts, if Total wanted to end up on equal footing with industry giants. The match also looked good geographically: TotalFina was a west-east company and Elf's focus was north-south.

The move, however, came as a complete surprise to previously state-run Elf Aquitaine (it was privatized in 1995). The hostile takeover bid of €42 billion[18] (15% over Elf's share price)[19] was turned down by an infuriated Elf management. The French government, which held a "golden share" in Elf with veto rights against any takeover,[20] could have blocked the deal. It announced, however, that it would not oppose a merger—which made Elf, led by CEO Philippe Jaffre, make a counteroffer to buy TotalFina for €49 billion.[21] As a response, TotalFina upped its offer by almost 10%, arguably both to appease Elf shareholders and also to serve as a warning to other potential suitors such as Italy's ENI.[22] By September 1999, Desmarest and Jaffre agreed to merge and create the world's fourth-largest oil company after Exxon Mobil, Shell, and BP/Amoco. Desmarest was to lead the new group with Jaffre leaving the group. The new entity, named TotalFinaElf, became the largest company in the Eurozone and on the French stock market, with a market capitalization of €95.47 billion, ahead of telecom group France Telecom and the food retailer Carrefour.[23]

The disasters in 2000 and 2001

The two high-profile acquisitions raised awareness of the Total group both in the industry and for the general public. Said Yves-Marie Dalibard, VP of Corporate Communication, "Unfortunately, though, the Total story with the public and the media since 1999 is more about two serious accidents than these two acquisitions."

The first accident happened as the Elf merger was concluding. On December 12, 1999, the oil tanker Erika, a vessel that Total had chartered to carry heavy fuel oil, broke into two off the coast of Brittany after heavy storms. No lives were lost, but the sinking ship leaked about 15,000 tons of oil. At first, officials predicted that the rough weather would break up the oil slick before reaching land. However, by Christmas Day oil hit the

---

[17]"Petrofina and Total catch merger mania," *Petroleum Review*, 5 January 1999, accessed via Factiva, September 2005.

[18]"TotalFina at stalemate with Elf Acquitaine over merger," 1 September 1999, *Process Engineering*, accessed via Factiva, September 2005.

[19]"Oil Giant Launches Hostile Takeover France's Total Fina Bids For Elf Acquitaine," *Associated Press*, 6 July 1999, accessed via Factiva, September 2005.

[20]Ibid.

[21]"TotalFina at stalemate with Elf Acquitaine over merger," 1 September 1999, *Process Engineering*, accessed via Factiva, September 2005.

[22]Lara Marlowe, "TotalFina, Elf Aquitaine agree terms for merger," 14 September 1999, *Irish Times*, accessed via Factiva, September 2005.

[23]Ibid.

French Biscay coastline. Eventually over 10,000 tons came ashore, killing over 120,000 seabirds.[24] Total was made the media's focal point and journalists hung to the company's first comment that the tanker did not actually belong to Total.[25] Said Dalibard:

> Top management had been working seven days a week for 18 months with our mergers. So when the wreckage happened, it did not receive our full dedication, especially when the maritime department told us that the oil spill would not be that severe. People left for Christmas. Then, two to three days later, we have 10,000 tons on the shores. So yes, our reaction was late. Also, the words we used did not show appropriate compassion. Legally speaking we were not responsible but the public needed someone that could be assigned responsibility. So the public opinion, fueled by our lack of timely response, decided we were the responsible ones.

Eventually, Total agreed to finance all oil removal operations from the wreck. It also helped to clean the coastline, pump out the remaining cargo from the sunken tanker, and process over 230,000 tons of waste.[26] By 2005, the French courts were still a year away from assigning legal responsibility and Total and five employees were still under investigation. Legal repercussions aside, however, Total knew that the oil spill heavily influenced the company in its home market. Said Dalibard:

> When we conduct brand surveys, 44% say that "Erika" or "oil spills" are important parts of the Total story. Surprisingly, they also think that the Total story consists of the Prestige wreckage, when a tanker chartered by a Russian oil company sank off the Spanish coast in 2002. Total was not a party in any shape or form to that oil spill.

While Total handled the Erika-effects and continued to integrate Petrofina and Elf, another disaster occurred: On September 21, 2001, a plant belonging to the group blew up in Toulouse, France. The AZF factory was part of the group's chemical division Grande Paroisse and specialized in nitrogen chemistry, especially for fertilizers. An accident in a stockpile of ammonium nitrate pellets caused an explosion which killed 30 people and injured over 2,500. As the plant was located within the city boundaries, a portion of the city was also significantly damaged.[27] Said Dalibard:

> It was very sad and very dramatic. This is ten days after 9/11, so terrorism is of course on our mind, but it may also have been a pure accident. This time, the company reacted completely different compared to Erika. One hour after the blast, our chairman flew to Toulouse, and two hours after he was on site. He expressed all his sorrow and support to the community and directly took full responsibility on behalf of Total.

Going silent until 2003

Total's quick response positively affected the company image. "In our branding surveys now, there is no sign of people remembering AZF as a disaster for Total," said Dalibard. "Very strange, because for us it was a horrendous event." In fact, the two accidents combined made Total's management take a drastic decision: they stopped all corporate

[24]Presentation from Organization Cetacea's website, www.orcaweb.org.uk/downloads/Erikaoilspill.doc, accessed September 2005.

[25]Peter Gumbel, "Operation Total Makeover," *Time Europe*, December 8, 2003, http://www.time.com/time/europe/magazine/article/0,13005,901031208-552068-2,00.html, accessed September 2005.

[26]Compiled from Total corporate website, information available at http://www.total.com/en/group/corporate_social_responsibility/special_reports/Erika/total_actions, accessed September 2005.

[27]Total Annual Report 2004, p. 176, "Risk Factors." The number of injured (2,500) was taken from company website.

communication to the general public. The "blackout" lasted until 2003, and did not include financial communication. Dalibard explained:

> The executive committee concluded that we had no right to speak. We had to solve the problems of the people suffering from the wreckage and the explosion. Advertising or sponsoring would be completely unsuitable. "We have to be attentive to the people of the area," is what we said—and then be silent for the rest, keep a low profile, just hold our breath.

The decision was not limited to France but was applied worldwide, even in countries where the public opinion hardly knew of Total. Dalibard explained: "I think it reflects the state of mind of the executive committee. It is not totally rational to do this across the board, but it is linked to what happened to these people personally. It was a trauma." The company did continue with standard press relations and financial communication. Limited so-called "commercial communication" was also allowed. Explained Dalibard:

> We separated between a person's relationship to the institution and to the commerce. The commercial relationship was somewhat kept, through for instance our "You know where to turn" campaign for our filling stations. But institutional messages were forbidden. So although the company was successful, we did not tell the public of our growth.

(**Exhibit 2** shows Total's stock price development between 1991 and 2005; **Exhibit 3** compares Total's stock during the first nine months of 2005 with the other oil majors.)

Commented Schmitt, "of course, the IR activities continued: we did tell our shareholders and the financial community about our strategy and objectives." In 2003, Total decided it was time to lift the ban on corporate communication. At the same time, the group was renamed from TotalFinaElf back to just Total and a new visual identity was introduced. The group also launched an advertising campaign to re-establish a relationship with the public. The campaign ran on the motto "Our energy is your energy" (or in French, "Pour vous, notre énergie est inépuisable," literally translated as "For you, our energy is inexhaustible"; see **Exhibit 4** for an ad sample). Said Dalibard:

> The campaign explains the job of an oil group: refine existing resources, find new resources, do this in good conditions while preserving the environment, and all to the benefit of the customer. We run customized campaigns in different regions, but they are all based on the same concept and all try to restore the image and understanding for what an oil group does.

Total in 2005

Total could by 2005 present itself as the world's fourth-largest publicly traded oil and gas integrated company. It operated in more than 130 countries, covering the entire oil and gas chain from exploration to distribution, and also held large operations in chemicals manufacturing. 2004 sales reached €123 billion, up from €104 billion the year before. Ninety-five percent of Total's profit came from outside of France. (**Exhibit 5** shows Total's 2004 financials.) In 2004, Total had over 110,000 employees worldwide with 44% working in France. Employees held 4% of the shares. (See **Exhibit 6** for Total's shareholder and employee base in 2004.)

Total divided its activities into three segments. The first segment, *Upstream*, encompassed exploration and production (E&P) of oil and natural gas, along with some other gas and power activities. Total had E&P activities in 44 countries and produced oil and gas in 27 countries. Europe stood for 32% of the group's production, Africa 31%, North America 2%, South America 9%, Asia-Pacific 9%, and the Middle East 16%. As a country, Norway was the largest contributor with 406 thousand barrels of oil equivalent (kboe) per day in 2004. (**Exhibit 7** shows production by region.) New exploration opportunities were evaluated based on geological, technical, political, and economic factors as well as on projected oil and gas prices.[28]

The second segment, *Downstream*, covered trading and shipping, refining, and the marketing of Total and Elf brand petroleum products, automotive and other fuels, and specialties such as LPG (liquefied petroleum gases), aviation fuel, and lubricants, through both the retail network and other outlets worldwide. In 2004 Total had refinery capacity of 2.7 million barrels per day (b/d) and nearly 17,000 service stations, 2,700 of them in France under the Total and Elf brands.

The third segment, *Chemicals*, included petrochemicals, fertilizers and specialty chemicals. It also housed Arkema, a new legal entity which Total intended to spin off in spring 2006 and which included vinyl products, industrial chemicals, and performance products.[29]

The three operational segments were each built around an organizational pole (**Exhibit 8** shows the organizational chart.) The segments were then supported by functions such as finance, strategy, legal affairs, HR, and corporate communications. An Executive Committee (COMEX) managed the company and answered to its board of directors. COMEX worked with an extended Management Committee (CODIR), which included all COMEX members plus 22 senior managers. (**Exhibit 9** shows all committee members.) The extended board consisted of French and Belgian nationals, with the exception of Howat who was Scottish. He described the company: "Total is basically a bunch of engineers with a few hard-nosed finance people at the top—who by the way also happen to be engineers. Their job is to make sure the ingenuity of the engineers is set to create shareholder value."

In 2001, Total formed an Ethics Committee to coordinate Total's ethics practices, described in the company's 26-page Code of Conduct. The committee organized educational and auditing resources and also handled the procedure for answering employee concerns. This included accepting so-called "whistle blowers" or employees who anonymously reported perceived conduct violations. Richard Lanaud, head of the Ethics Committee, reported directly to the CEO Desmarest. He said:

> *The code of conduct guides our business principles and individual behavior as they link to the environment, to people, to sustainable development. It is a top-driven initiative that the CEO decided to implement. It is also not targeted to one stakeholder group over another. External pressures may play a role in developing an ethics policy, but more important are the rewards it brings for the internal organization: creating a common language of shared values, satisfaction among employees, and growth for the company by protecting its name.*

Lanaud believed that the code of conduct had only a limited impact on persuading investors to invest in Total stock. Personally, he spent 80% of his time on internal activities over external ones.

Organizational units could also use a self-assessment procedure to determine themselves how well they complied with the code.[30] Total further worked with U.K.-based accreditation company GoodCorporation to conduct ethical assessments of subsidiaries. GoodCorporation had turned Total's code into 84 points of control which they used as a checklist when assessing subsidiaries. Lanaud explained:

[28]Total Annual Report 2004, pp. 58–75.
[29]Total corporate website, http://www.total.com/en/group/activities/, accessed September 2005.
[30]Total Corporate Social Responsibility Report 2004, p. 10.

We don't ask GoodCorporation to give our subsidiaries an accreditation although they handle the assessment. You couldn't give an accreditation to Total on a group level and it doesn't make sense on a subsidiary level. Also, we didn't want to create a race between our subsidiaries. We just wanted to find our weaknesses and also our good practices. To use an external party for this was fundamentally easier than doing it ourselves; they had an existing methodology and could also meet our stakeholders to get an outsider's more impartial view. Their job is important: you cannot set an efficient ethics policy without checking.

Financial communication

Financial communication at Total consisted of several formal processes, such as issuing the annual report, preparing the quarterly result publications, managing the conference calls that went with these, organizing investor "road shows," and managing the shareholders' annual general meeting. In addition, financial communication also included the daily activities of keeping the company's stakeholders up-to-date with the strategy, the results, and activities of the company.

The annual report

The most technical piece of communication that Total delivered was its annual report. It was also the document that was the most code-driven since it had to abide by financial rules and regulations. Thierry Reveau de Cyrières, general legal counsel to the board of directors, said, "Our accounts must give an image of the company's financial situation which is true. As a lawyer, I check that nothing significant has been omitted—to the extent I am aware of it, of course." The actual process of drafting the annual report involved some 50 people. Among those, three participants stood out, explained Reveau de Cyrières: "There are three key players: IR, legal function, and the communications group. Of course [we] also involve people in accounting and treasury. Naturally, the people in the divisions make a very significant contribution as well, since they are the major part of the report."

Once the annual report had been put together it went through a detailed release process. It started with the disclosure committee made up of the group's main functional executives, which checked that there were no outstanding issues. It then went to the audit committee, consisting of three independent directors with more time to examine risks more broadly, who made a final report to the board of directors. The board then received the report, which was not made public until the board approved it. With Total's financial year following the calendar year, the annual report was published in early spring. It then formed the discussion basis for the annual shareholders' meeting, thought of as "a true discussion between shareholders and the CEO."

Road shows

Twice a year (once in September and once in February), Total went on "road shows" where a group of senior executives visited around 35 cities[31] and met with institutional investors and analysts. Four teams traveled the world, led by CEO Desmarest, CFO

[31]In 2004, meetings were held in Europe (Paris, Brussels, Amsterdam, the Hague, Rotterdam, London, Dublin, Edinburgh, Frankfurt, Munich, Cologne, Düsseldorf, Zurich, Geneva, Lausanne, Stockholm, Helsinki, Copenhagen, Milan and Madrid); North America (New York, Boston, Philadelphia, Chicago, Denver, Atlanta, Houston, Austin, Des Moines, Miami, San Francisco, Los Angeles, San Diego, Montreal and Toronto); and Asia (Tokyo). (Source: Total Annual Report 2004, p. 47.)

Castaigne, Head of Strategy and Risk Assessment Bruno Weymuller, and Ian Howat, senior vice president of Strategy. Overall, Total had in 2004 organized about 400 investor and analyst meetings.[32] The message that the teams presented during those presentations was crafted throughout the year by the Investor Relations group together with Desmarest and Castaigne, as well as the strategy and planning group and the operational business team. Said Schmitt, "Management has to be deeply involved in crafting the message because they will have to deliver it." The end result was a slide show of some 30–35 slides. Schmitt expanded:

> In an ideal world, IR should not exist. Thierry Desmarest could talk once or twice a year and tell the company's strategy. But it doesn't work that way. We are dealing with an audience that is also tracking a lot of other companies, which means they have time and attention constraints. So we on our end have to be both clear and simple in our message—which we then have to repeat over and over again.

Dalibard emphasized that consistency was key to making sure Total's message was received and taken at face value. He said:

> The most important [issue] here is to use the same criteria and targets between each presentation and between road shows. Otherwise the analysts won't trust you. For four to five years now, we have had the same strategy and criteria to measure our success. We have changed the targets once or twice, based on changes in the external environment, but we have continued to use the same strategy and criteria, which make our presentations very coherent over time.

Schmitt explained further:

> Total doesn't change the broad message that everyone is getting. What might change is how deep you get into certain issues. More and more investors walk in the room and they already know the broad message and want answers to some very specific questions. Obviously Total must be prepared to answer them in a detailed way. But generally speaking, consistency and transparency of the broad message is crucial, because if there were message differences investors would find out quickly as they are bound to talk with each other—and that would hurt the company's credibility.

During the road shows, however, the company did not provide valuation multiples or other calculations of firm value. Said Castaigne: "It is not our job to calculate these numbers. They are for the financial community to create. We give them the information they need, but we let them value the company. In the end, the market sets the share price."

Day-to-day communication

Although Total's main message was formulated once or twice a year, the company issued press releases year-round. Press releases were issued for one of three reasons: material events where the company by law or regulation was obliged to inform; events that were related to the main IR crafted story; or happenings that were in Total's interest to report on but were coincidental to the main message, such as opening a new facility or sponsoring a sports event. All press releases, regardless of their purpose, were reviewed by the investor relations team to make sure they were consistent with the overall message that Total wanted to spread. As a matter of standard, every press release also referred systematically to the geographic location and gave the environmental dimension of the event.

[32]Total Annual Report 2004, p. 38.

Investor Relations at Total

In Schmitt's view, in addition to spreading the corporate message, the IR group also had a function of being receptive to and understanding the expectations of the market participants. He explained:

> *IR must be able to understand a trend even before it becomes apparent. For example, how would the investors react to Total's dividends policy or share buyback strategy? Or about mergers and acquisitions in 2005? Before putting out the story, we need to have an idea of whether it will be valid for our shareholders—and for all stakeholders in general.*

Investors' sentiments toward Total, or their general assessment of a situation, could often be gauged through their ratings of a company or by simply picking up the phone and talking with them. However, the general public's views were harder to assess. To help with this, Total ran frequent market surveys, measuring both the public's awareness of Total as a company and the public's sentiments toward it. Said Dalibard:

> *The surveys show us how quickly views can change. In January [2005], surveys showed overall positive results for Total. Then came February with three different incidents. First, our financial results were very good—which is actually not that accepted by the French public. It is a very specific aspect of this country. Second, we had a small legal problem connected to Erika, which gave our opponents a new chance to emphasize Total's involvement in the story. Finally, we also had a social situation in a subsidiary in the south of France. So from a 68% positive rating in January, we dropped to 48% in February. Only to rebound two months later, back to 63%—which I think shows that the public in France is very sensitive to any event concerning Total.*

Interestingly, the surveys seemed to indicate the French public made a distinction between Total, the company, and Total, the gas stations. The gas stations consistently received higher ratings than the company of the same name; Total interpreted this as the public having a "warmer" relationship with the gas stations and a "colder" relation with the company itself.

Given the impact that any information about the company—financial, corporate or otherwise—seemed to have on the general sentiment towards Total, IR worked closely with the company's internal media group to make sure they all conveyed the same story. Said Dalibard,

> *Press relations link completely with financial communication, since journalists of course will look at how we talk to investors. We have to maintain a strong internal relationship between our media and financial people to "keep the same tempo." Actually, every new press officer we hire has to be trained on the rules of financial communication. For media relations, we have processes and rules—but in terms of financial communication we as a company have legal commitments to be transparent, fair. . . . Our media people have to take all these rules into consideration. Journalists and analysts cross-check what we tell them to get the full presentation. So even if we may differ in the emphasis on pieces between the two audiences, the overall message has to be the same.*

However, working with two types of audiences presented its own problems. Dalibard continued:

> *Most journalists work like analysts: they are their papers' specialists in the oil and gas business. If we have problems, it is not with them but with the general journalists that do not understand our business. But they are just as powerful [in shaping public opinion], probably more so, since few in the general public read the specialist*

section of the newspaper and instead read the front page or main section articles where these generalists write.

Investor relations: Communicating with stakeholders

In 2005 the Financial Communication team at Total consisted in 2005 of about 10 people in Paris, with an additional team in New York of three people. The group's job, as described by its head Schmitt, could be divided into three main areas: communicating with retail investors, with institutional analysts and shareholders, and with ethical or environmental analysts and investors. The last area was newly established in order to match the growing number of specialized analysts on the investor side who looked specifically into the corporate social responsibility (CSR) aspects of a company. (See **Exhibit 10** for the formal mission statement of the Financial Communication group.)

Members of the IR-group attended some executive committee meetings, long-term planning meetings, budget meetings, etc., and also met regularly with the CEO. In order to understand the business issues, the IR team members all had operational backgrounds within Total. The IR group under Jérôme Schmitt reported to the CFO Castaigne. (See **Exhibit 11** for the organization of the IR and Financial Communication group.) Commented Castaigne, "In the financial reports of any company, there are strategic messages that are very important. So the financial communication office is placed at the highest level internally."

Communicating with institutional investors

During the two 2004 road shows, members of the company's management met, as they did every year, with portfolio managers and financial analysts in the leading financial centers of the world. In addition, institutional investors could download material on the Total corporate website, and the CFO conducted three telephone conferences during the year. (**Exhibit 12** shows the 2005 IR calendar.)[33] To Schmitt, the bulk of the IR work was to deal with institutional investors and convey the company's strategy. Howat further commented on the role of IR vis-à-vis institutional investors:

> *Contrary to the popular belief that the financial markets are always short-sighted, we are fortunately in an industry which investors like for its long-term perspectives and development potential. Most of our presentations and most of the market's interest are on the company's long-term plans. Specifically for our E&P [exploration and production] activities we give a five-year indication of production targets. We should not disappoint the market, so our five-year numbers come out of our own planning, but with prudence built into them.*

Not disappointing the market was a recurring theme in internal discussions, said Howat:

> *This was really drummed into us by our previous CEO. Financial communication is an exercise in honesty. Like the old saying, "You can fool some people all of the time, you can fool all of the people some of the time, but you can't fool all the people all the time." You can't fudge. Everything you choose to say should be the truth, the whole truth, and nothing but.*

Communicating with retail investors

As Elf Aquitaine had had many more individuals as shareholders than Total, the merger meant that Total now had to cater to a large number of retail investors, a number that continued to grow. By 2005, Total had 520,000 retail investors, or 9% of the shareholder base.

[33]Total Annual Report 2004, p. 47.

Investor Relations at Total

About 40% of these had fewer than 30 shares; about 40% between 30 and 99; 10% between 100 and 200 shares; and the remaining 10% had more than 200 shares. About 90% of all retail investors were French; about 60% of the shareholders had held their Total shares for more than 10 years and 25% between 5 and 10 years. Valérie Laugier had been head of Retail Investor Service for four years and was responsible for all communication that went to this group. She said:

After the merger, my unit was attached directly to the financial communication group as it had been at Elf. It is not attached to the corporate communication, sustainable development, or general secretary. Instead, since we belong to the financial communication group, we are linked directly to the CFO, which makes it easier for us to all communicate the same message. Even if the message I bring to my retail investors may have been simplified or made more pedagogical—since my audience is not made up of "petrol pros" like the oil analysts—it is the same exact message as the "pros" get. Although I may spend my days thinking about retail needs, I sit next to people that "swim" daily (so to speak) in the main message.

While the basic message and information conveyed were the same as with institutional investors, Laugier pointed out that the approach used to communicate with Total's retail investor was based on very different strategies:

We base our retail investor communication on techniques that come from consumer communication. I was nine years with Total's gas station network, working with consumer services, and it felt natural to use the same approach when talking with our retail investors. These are individuals with whom we have a relationship, just like with our gas station clients. I installed, for instance, a CRM [customer relationship management] system to keep a history of all communication with each shareholder. Before we did not know if someone who wrote or called us had ever been in contact with us—but now the CRM system can tell us that and also provide information about the person, such as how many Total shares they own, etc. Each individual shareholder has a file in our CRM system, to which we link all communication with that person. It allows us to not only trace previous communication but also to personalize it.

Another change Laugier brought was to limit the number of publications created for retail investors, while at the same time increasing the distribution of the remaining printed material. She said, "My argument was that nobody will hear us unless we turn up the volume, regardless of how many times we change the CD. I wanted to reach more retail investors more often." Thus, by 2005, Total communicated with its retail investors in carefully selected diffusion channels. One was the shareholders journal, *Journal des Actionnaires*, which 300,000 shareholders (the ones holding a minimum of 10 shares) received four times a year. Once a year, at the time of the annual report, all 520,000 individual shareholders received the journal.[34] Other channels were the company's website and the toll-free number through which shareholders could obtain information about the company. The toll-free number received 80,000 calls annually and was run by an interactive voice server. The callers who did not find their answer in the preset menu were connected with a staff member (who reported to Laugier), who since early 2004 had been dedicated to answering shareholder questions, whether by telephone, e-mail, fax, or regular letters.

As another channel, Total invited shareholders with more than 30 bearer shares or one registered share to join the "Shareholders' Circle," which organized events such as visits

[34]Total Annual Report 2004, p. 43, and Interview Valérie Laugier, 27 September 2005, Total headquarters, Paris, France.

to industrial or cultural sites. For this group, Total also ran one-day training programs on "Understanding Total Financial Statements," which since its inception in May 2003 had attracted about 700 participants. About 100 shareholders had also attended a new program called "Moving to IFRS Norm Accounting." The training programs had so far been held in Paris (twice), Nice, and Clermont-Ferrand.

Another channel for communication was a schedule of about four annual information sessions for individual shareholders, which were held in Paris and in other regions. CEO Desmarest led the session in Paris; the others were chaired by Schmitt. These sessions were open to all individual shareholders. In addition, Total participated at the annual Actionaria Trade Show held in Paris. In 2004, Desmarest had participated in a question-and-answer session with two journalists in front of 1,200 individual shareholders.[35]

The year's largest retail investor event, however, was the shareholders' meeting or annual general meeting (AGM). The 3.5-hour meeting was prepared by several Total teams: IR, corporate communication, legal, security and logistics. In 2004, the AGM was held on May 15 at the Paris Convention Center at Porte Maillot in central Paris. Personal invitations were sent to all shareholders holding 100 shares or more, about 100,000 people. Said Laugier:

> *A few years ago, we only sent out invitations to people with more than 10,000 shares. This basically meant that nearly no invitations were sent at all. We then changed that to a minimum of 100 shares—and for the next year we will set the limit even lower, at 50 shares.*

In 2002, the AGM had seen 1,900 attendants; by 2005 this number had grown to 2,300 shareholders, with many more attending from outside of the Paris region. Commented Laugier:

> *The shareholders' meeting is one of the most important things we do. But when I discuss this with any Anglo-Saxon colleague, they don't understand the need. In their cultures, especially the American, it is so much more common for individuals to invest in shares. But for us, the French, it is still not established and the people who do invest need the attention.*

Since many retail shareholders were both investors and French citizens, many of the issues with the general public were also of concern for retail shareholders. For example, Laugier commented about the Erika and AZF disaster in Total's past, and about the decision to freeze corporate communication for a while:

> *At the time, people were ashamed to hold Total shares. They told us time after time that we needed to stand up and defend ourselves—but what they were really asking for was for us to defend them and their choice to hold Total shares. They want to be shareholders—but they also want to have a good conscience and even build their personal image by owning Total shares. We also see this reflected in the increasing number of questions on how we behave socially, ethically, and environmentally.*

In order to better understand how retail investors perceived Total both as a company and as an investment opportunity, Total had a 12-person strong Shareholders Advisory Committee (in French, *Comité Consultatif*). The committee was appointed for a specific time and the incoming committee members were chosen by Total in cooperation with an external recruitment agency. Said Laugier:

> *Earlier we could end up with an unrepresentative committee, consisting of too many retirees, too many Parisians, and (in fact) also people who sat on similar boards*

[35]Total Annual Report 2004, p. 44.

almost for a living. So we hired this recruitment agency to help us make a more representative selection—and also find committee members more likely to argue with us on issues they don't agree with.

The committee met four times a year in meetings that Schmitt and Laugier chaired. After a short presentation of the latest financial results by Schmitt, the meetings would quickly turn into a workshop where the members would criticize the latest financial publication or other official communication piece, and would also work with benchmark exercises to come up with suggestions for Total to improve its communication.

Communicating with employee investors

A special category of retail investors were the company's own employees, who owned 4% of Total. Said Dalibard:

Since our staff follows media we have to be attentive to the message coming from the outside. Every press release we issue for investors and media is put on the intranet, with comments added for specific business areas. We need to manage the rhythm of communication to the financial community, to media, and internally. They have to be done at the same time. When the rhythm breaks, you have problems. So internal communication is linked to financial communication, absolutely. Take, for instance, the issue of share buy-back. The shareholders like it since it is a way of increasing the value of each share. However, it means that this money is not distributed to staff or invested back into the company, so employees will argue that "if Total is successful enough to buy back shares, why can't we take part in that success?"

Some employees would try to use the annual shareholders' meeting as a platform for their views, whether they were shareholders or not. For instance, at the 2004 meeting, employees upset with the company's decision to spin off part of its chemical business into a separate company attempted—unsuccessfully—to march onto the meeting stage.

Communicating with ethical investors

As the financial markets had more analysts dedicated to ethical issues, as well as certain funds investing only in "ethical companies," Total had adapted its IR organization. Eve Gautier was now responsible for Corporate Social Responsibility information. Previously in the corporate communication and internal audit departments at Total, she had for the last six months been in charge of Total's relationship with CSR analysts. Schmitt commented on her role within the IR group:

Previously, I'd say that mainstream analysts often ignored these concerns, but the concerns didn't going away. The business of analysts is to pick the stock that will appreciate in the shortest amount of time; their bonus is calculated on that capital gain; so if any corporate social responsibility issues appear, they want them to go away as fast as possible. That is when they contact us directly.

One specific example involved a large Scandinavian investor. Said Gautier:

We got a contact from a Scandinavian investment fund. They said they were considering dropping our stock because of our presence in Myanmar. So for the analyst in that fund to be able to justify keeping our stock, we need to explain to him why we are in Myanmar and why this is in accordance with our ethical charter.

Retail shareholders also took a direct interest in Total's ethical policies, explained Gautier:

For retail shareholders, CSR is important, as is respecting the environment. The fact that we invest in bio diesel and solar energy renewables, for instance, is significant for retail investors. Retail shareholders want to be able to go to a dinner and say that they are proud to have invested in a socially responsible company.

Overall, Total saw how the importance of ethical and social responsibility continued to grow. A recent example came from the kick-off meeting on the 2005 fall road show: The first question from the first analyst did *not* deal with the company financials, as normally was the case, but targeted the company's sustainable development activities.

Presenting a balanced message

Although the IR group at Total could point to a successful track record (they were, for instance, given four awards by IR Magazine in 2004, including the Grand Prize for Best Financial Communication), its corporate communication efforts were growing increasingly complicated. The task of staying with "only one message" was more challenging than ever, especially given the large variety of stakeholders. Commented Schmitt:

How we communicate our financial results is a key issue. We want to be confident with analysts and the financial community and say, "Look how well we have done . . ." but at the same time, we have to be modest and show both them and others that although we did a good job we have to prepare for the future. It is all about semantics: how blunt do you want to be? Everything has to be in the message but the fine tuning happens in the subtleties. It is obvious that with an institutional investor we will spend more time dwelling on dividend policy. In other situations, with other audiences, we don't speak much about the dividend, only a short sentence, and instead we go deeper on different issues.

Continued Dalibard:

For our upcoming September road show, we know people will ask "What do you do with all your money?" We have prepared descriptions of our investments and projects to make both investors and the public understand how difficult, expensive, and time-consuming it is to prepare the future of the company. Also, a number we like to emphasize is that we only represent 14% of the world's oil production, while our share of the oil industry investments is approximately 23%. And by "we" I don't mean Total alone, but all the five biggest oil majors. Most production activity actually lies with national oil companies. Many [people] don't know this.

The topic of share buybacks was also expected to come up at the road-show. In 2004, Total bought back 22.44 million of its own shares at a cost of €3.6 billion. The buybacks involved 3.5% of the company's capital. For 2005, Total had announced that share buybacks would continue, adjusted for the financial environment and asset sales.[36] Commented Schmitt:

There is a real tension here: investment analysts want us to talk about dividend policy, share buybacks, restructuring; but employees and unions prefer to hear that Total is investing more for the future, hiring more people, etc. This is why we spend quite a lot of time detailing our cash allocation policy, which consists first of carefully selected investments projects, then dividends and share buybacks, all of this with a gearing comprised between 25% and 30%.

[36]Total Annual Report 2004, p. 40.

The volatile nature of oil and gas prices complicated both setting the strategy and then communicating it. CFO Castaigne summarized the approach:

> There are really three important factors when it comes to financial communication. The first is that it is a long-term process. You build your reputation over time. Second, be consistent. Third, don't sell your results, sell your performance. Since we are in a business where external conditions affect us heavily, we must distinguish between the impact of the environment and our own performance. If the environment changes drastically and we cannot meet our targets, we have to be clear in our communication about the link between the target and the change. We have to sell to the market that which is under our control—for instance, costs, projects to increase production, the efficiency of our explorations, or the advantage of our technologies. But it is hard for us to guess on, say, oil taxes that countries may or may not introduce.

Castaigne then added:

> You have to remember that in the life of a company, you have good times and bad times. So when reporting in good times, you have to keep in mind that tomorrow might be bad. You have to caution for things that may go wrong—because you know your own weaknesses. So over time, we have managed to sell the evolution of Total compared to our targets. That builds a good capital of trust with the investors, which allows them to plan long-term, and for us this also translates into an increased share price.

Total's emphasis on a message that was consistent over time seemed to be appreciated by the financial analyst community. Wrote one analyst after Total's road show in September 2005: "Total's mid-year review contained no major surprises and represented a continuation and extension of its successful strategy and equity story, in our view." Given that consistency, minor modifications to the overall strategy then appeared to be acceptable, as evidenced by another analyst report: "Small changes in strategic outlook we consider to be the hallmark of a high-quality major running the business for the long-term." (See **Exhibit 13** for a summary of analyst reports after the September 2005 road show.)

The balance in communication between rejoicing in good results while still emphasizing the need to save for future downturns was not an easy one to strike. Desmarest said in a press interview that French critics might "have difficulty understanding the size of the company. They wonder, perhaps it is too big."[37] Expanded Howat:

> In a French political context, vis-à-vis the trade unions and the politicians, this type of message is a bit controversial. First, in France, nobody has ever seen a company that makes a net profit of €1 billion a month—so that immediately gets people's attention. And when they look at our level of dividend and the fact that we have typically been buying back 3%-4% of the company every year and in the context of France's culture and politics . . . it is not that simple.

A surprise windfall tax?

As if to prove Howat's point, the apparent contradiction of Total's message became the focus of a debate that erupted in late 2005. On September 8, French finance minister Thierry Breton told reporters that France might adopt a windfall tax on the "exceptional profits" of the oil companies.[38] The government was worried that high oil prices would

---

[37]Carl Mortished, "Empire builder who plays a waiting game," *The Times*, 21 February 2005.

[38]Several sources: Martin Arnold, "France threatens oil majors with windfall tax," *Financial Times*, 9 September 2005; Martin Arnold, "Threat of French oil windfall tax," *Financial Times*, 16 September 2005; Martin Arnold, "Investors ask Total to move tax domicile," *Financial Times*, 21 September 2005; Frédéric de Moincault, Jacques-Olivier Martin, Philippe Reclus, "Le débat sur la taxe exceptionnelle n'aurait jamais dû avoir lieu," *Le Figaro*, 20 September 2005.

deter consumer spending, so Breton called on "all the actors of the oil sector" to "behave as citizen businesses and make proposals, such as one could imagine them lowering prices at the petrol pump." If not, the French state would put in place new taxation on the oil companies, in addition to the taxes that already accounted for two-thirds of French petrol prices and more than half of diesel prices.[39]

In a meeting with Breton the following week, CEO Desmarest reiterated what he had already announced at Total's "First Half 2005 Financial Results" presentation in early September: that Total would boost investments in French refineries and renewable energy research. Total would also wait about three weeks every time oil prices rose before raising consumer prices, while it would, on the other hand, immediately lower petrol prices if oil prices dropped. Although apparently satisfied with the outcome, Desmarest did tell reporters that some Total shareholders had asked the company to move its tax domicile abroad to avoid similar threats in the future. A spokesperson for the finance ministry emphasized emphatically that oil groups "should not just consider their shareholders but all stakeholders."[40]

Schmitt and the IR group at Total knew this all too well.

Investor Relations at Total

---

[39]Martin Arnold, "Threat of French oil windfall tax," *Financial Times*, 16 September 2005.
[40]Martin Arnold, "France threatens oil majors with windfall tax," *Financial Times*, 9 September 2005.

EXHIBIT 1   **Price development October 1998–December 1999: Total share price (Paris stock exchange) against Dow Jones industrial index and CAC 40 index**

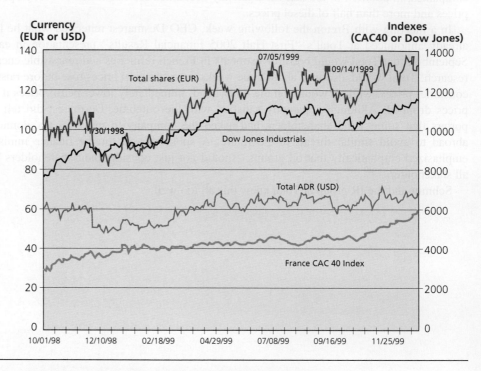

Notes: 11/30/1998: Last day before Total announced acquisition of Petrofina.
07/05/1999: Total announces takeover plans of Elf Acquitaine.
09/14/1999: Press release: TotalFina and Elf Aquitaine reach amicable accord on merger.

In 2005, Total was listed in Paris, Brussels, London and New York. It was included in the French stock index CAC 40 (weight of 13.71%) and the Dow Jones Stoxx 50, Dow Jones Euro Stoxx 50 (weight of 6.24%), and Dow Jones Global Titans 50 Index. (Source: Total Annual Report 2004, p. 38.)

Left Y-axis: USD- or EUR-value of Total stock.
Right Y-axis: Index value.

Source: Thomson Datastream.

EXHIBIT 2 **Price development January 1991–June 2005:**
Total share price and oil barrel

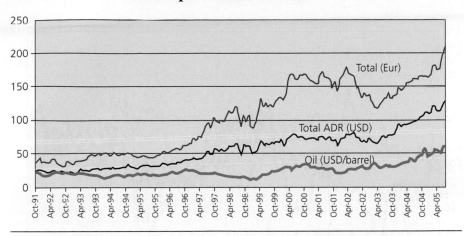

Source: Thomson Datastream for Total share price, Global Financial Data for oil barrel price.

EXHIBIT 3   **Total's stock development vs. the top six oil companies,
1 January–9 September 2005**

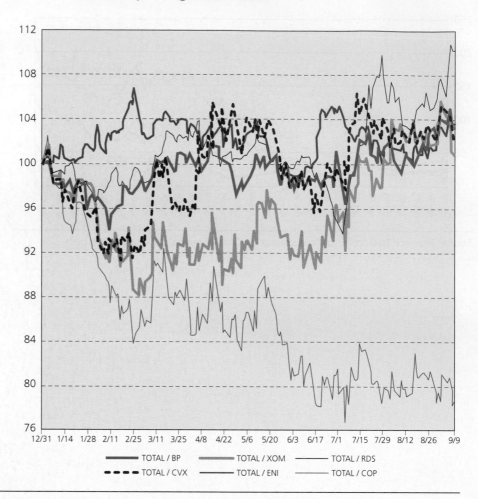

Note: Each line represents Total's share value over the share value of another oil major. The differential is assigned an index value of 100 for January 1, 2005. A downward sloping line then indicates that Total's share value is lower in value relative to the other oil major, compared to the starting date. An upward sloping line indicates that Total's share is appreciating in value vis-à-vis the other stock.

Company abbreviations: BP = British Petroleum (UK)
XOM = Exxon Mobil (USA)
RDS = Royal Dutch Shell (Netherlands)
CVX = Chevron (USA)
ENI = Ente Nazionale Idrocarburi (Italy)
COP = Conoco Philips (USA)

Source: Total.

EXHIBIT 4   **Ad in total's 2005 corporate image campaign "our energy is your energy"**

Source: Company document.

EXHIBIT 5   Total financials 2002–2004

a. Financial Highlights

(in millions of euros, except earnings per share, dividends)	2004	2003	2002
Sales	122,700	104,652	102,540
Operating income from business segments	17,123	13,004	10,995
Net operating income from business segments	8,792	6,973	5,868
Net income (Group share)	9,039	7,344	6,260
Earnings per share (in €)	14.68	11.56	9.4
Dividend per share (in €)	5.4	4.7	4.1
Net debt-to-equity ratio	27%	26%	29%
Return on equity	31%	26%	20%
Cash flow from operating activities	14,429	12,487	11,006
Total expenditures	8,668	7,728	8,657

b. Sales by Segment 2004 and 2003

(in millions of euros)	Upstream	Downstream	Chemicals
For year ended Dec 31, 2004			
Total sales	36,203	83,476	20,741
Operating income adjusted for special items	12,820	3,217	1,086
Net operating income adjusted for special items	5,834	2,302	656
Expenditures	6,170	1,516	905
For year ended Dec 31, 2003			
Total sales	30,250	70,947	17,850
Operating income adjusted for special items	10,476	1,970	558
Net operating income adjusted for special items	5,259	1,460	254
Expenditures	5,302	1,235	1,115

c. Consolidated Statement of Income

(in millions of euros)	2004	2003	2002
Sales	122,700	104,652	102,540
Operating expenses	−101,141	−86,905	−86,622
Depreciation, depletion and amortization of tangible assets	−5,498	−4,977	−5,792
Operating income			
Corporate	−215	−209	−210
Business Segments	16,276	12,979	10,3364
Total operating income	**16,061**	**12,770**	**10,126**
Interest expense, net	−234	−232	−195
Dividend income on non-consolidated companies	164	152	170
Dividends on subsidiaries' redeemable preferred shares	−6	−5	−10
Other income (expense), net	2,174	−1,060	243
Provision for income taxes	−8,316	−5,353	−5,034
Equity in income (loss) of affiliates	337	1,086	866
Income before amortization of acquisition goodwill	**10,180**	**7,358**	**6,166**
Amortization of acquisition goodwill	−308	−139	−212
Consolidated net income	**9,872**	**7,219**	**5,954**
Of which minority interests	260	194	13
Net income	**9,612**	**7,025**	**5,941**
Earnings per share (euros)	**15.61**	**11.06**	**8.92**

d. Consolidated Balance Sheet

(in millions of euros)	2004	2003	2002
Assets			
Non-current assets			
Intangible assets, net	1,908	2,017	2,752
Property, plant and equipment, net	36,422	36,286	38,592
Equity affiliates: investments and loans	9,874	7,833	7,710
Other investments	1,090	1,162	1,221
Other non-current assets	3,239	3,152	3,735
Total non-current assets	**52,533**	**50,450**	**54,010**
Current assets			
Inventories, net	7,053	6,137	6,515
Accounts receivable, net	14,025	12,357	13,087
Prepaid expenses and other current assets	5,363	4,779	5,243
Short-term investments	1,350	1,404	1,508
Cash and cash equivalents	3,837	4,836	4,966
Total current assets	**31,628**	**29,513**	**31,319**
TOTAL ASSETS	**84,161**	**79,963**	**85,329**
Liabilities and shareholders' equity			
Shareholders' equity			
Common shares	6,350	6,491	6,872
Paid-in surplus and retained earnings	33,266	30,408	30,514
Cumulative translation adjustment	−4,653	−3,268	−830
Treasury shares	−3,703	−3,225	−4,410
Total shareholders' equity	**31,260**	**30,406**	**32,146**
Subsidiaries' redeemable preferred shares	**147**	**396**	**477**
Minority interest	**629**	**664**	**724**
Long-term liabilities			
Deferred income taxes	6,063	5,443	6,390
Employee benefits	3,600	3,818	4,103
Other long-term liabilities	6,449	6,344	6,150
Total long-term liabilities	**16,112**	**15,605**	**16,643**
Long-term debt	**9,734**	**9,783**	**10,157**
Current liabilities			
Accounts payable	11,672	10,304	10,236
Other creditors and accrued liabilities	11,084	8,970	9,850
Short-term borrowings and bank overdrafts	3,523	3,835	5,096
Total current liabilities	**26,279**	**23,109**	**25,182**
TOTAL LIABILITIES AND SHAREHOLDERS' EQUITY	**84,161**	**79,963**	**85,329**

Note: Totaling the sales by segment in panel **b** does not match the sales total in panel **a** due to corporate and intercompany sales that are not reported in panel **b**.

Source: All financials taken from Total Annual Report 2004.

Investor Relations at Total

EXHIBIT 6 Total shareholder and employee base 2004

a. Shareholder base		b. Employees	
By Region		**By Region**	
France	33%	France	44%
United Kingdom	18%		
Rest of Europe	24%	Rest of Europe	27%
North America	23%		
Rest of World	2%	Rest of World	29%
By Type		**By Segment**	
Institutional shareholders	87%	Upstream	13%
Group employees	4%	Downstream	31%
Individual shareholders	9%	Chemicals	55%
		Holding	1%

Source: Total Annual Report 2004.

EXHIBIT 7   **Production by geographic area 2004**

Geographic Area	Liquids	Natural Gas	Total
	(kb/d)	(Mcf/d)	(Kboe/d)
Europe	**424**	**2,218**	**832**
France	9	143	35
Norway	263	775	406
Netherlands	1	330	59
United Kingdom	151	970	332
Africa	**693**	**440**	**776**
Algeria	42	160	72
Angola	159	27	164
Cameroon	13		13
Congo	87	21	90
Gabon	99	27	104
Libya	62		62
Nigeria	231	205	271
North America	**16**	**241**	**61**
United States	16	241	61
Asia	**31**	**1,224**	**245**
Brunei	3	58	14
Indonesia	22	854	177
Myanmar		110	14
Thailand	6	202	40
Middle East	**110**	**39**	**117**
Iran	26		26
Qatar	31	1	31
Syria	30	32	36
U.A.E.	16	6	17
Yemen	7		7
South America	**128**	**474**	**213**
Argentina	11	325	70
Bolivia	3	82	18
Colombia	24	32	30
Venezuela	90	35	95
Others	**9**		**9**
Russia	9		9
Total production	**1,411**	**4,636**	**2,253**
Equity and non-consolidated affiliates			
Africa	37	4	37
Middle East	247	254	295
Total equity and non-consolidated affiliates	**284**	**258**	**332**
Worldwide production	1,695	4,894	2,585

Note: kb/d = thousands of barrels per day
      Mcf/d = million cubic feet per day
      Kboe/d = thousands barrel of oil equivalent per day

Source: Total Annual Report 2004, p. 62.

Investor Relations at Total

EXHIBIT 8 Total organizational chart (1 April 2005)

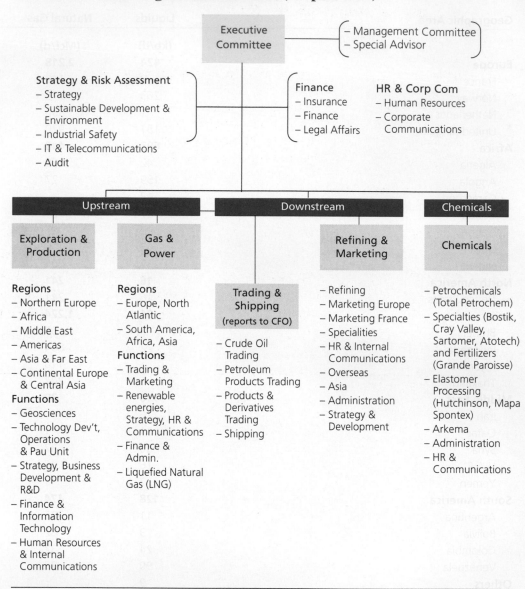

Investor Relations at Total

Source: Adapted by casewriter from Total Annual Report 2004.

EXHIBIT 9 Total executive committee (COMEX) and management committee (CODIR)

Executive Committee (COMEX)

- Thierry Desmarest — Chairman and Chief Executive Officer
- François Cornélis — Vice-Chairman, President of Chemicals
- Robert Castaigne — Chief Financial Officer
- Yves-Louis Darricarrère — President of Gas & Power
- Christophe de Margerie — President of Exploration & Production
- Jean-Paul Vettier — President of Refining & Marketing
- Bruno Weymuller — President of Strategy & Risk Assessment

Management Committee (CODIR)

All Executive Committee members, plus:

Holding Company	Upstream	Downstream	Chemicals
Patrick de la Chevardière	Michel Bénézit	Alain Champeaux	Pierre-Christian Clout
Jean-Pierre Cordier	Philippe Boisseau	Jean-Claude Company	Philippe Goebel
Jean-Marc Jaubert	Jean-Marie Masset	François Groh	Jean-Bernard Lartigue
Jean-Michel Gires	Charles Mattenet	Pierre Klein	Thierry Le Hénaff
Jean-Jacques Guilbaud	Jean Privey	Eric de Menten	Hugues Woestelandt
Ian Howat		André Tricoire	

Source: Total Annual Report 2004.

EXHIBIT 10 Mission statement for total financial communication department

The Financial Communication Department has as its mission to establish, develop, and maintain the Total Group's relationships with both its shareholders and the financial analysts that follow the oil sector. This mission entails, in particular:

- Managing the Group's daily relationship with institutional investors and financial analysts;

- Writing and editing financially related press releases and creating strategic presentation/conference calls made by the management for the financial communication, most notably for results presentations (accounts, strategies for each activity sector, group perspective);

- Organizing and conducting road shows;

- Validating and/or creating (as needed), in close liaison with the Communications and Legal Departments, reference documents (annual report, 20-F);

- Organizing sector presentations, conference participations, and field trips for investors and analysts;

- Managing the relationship with individual shareholders and, in particular, managing the relationship with the Shareholders Advisory Committee and the Shareholders' Circle, including their participation at meetings and shareholder conventions;

- Writing and editing documents with general financial information targeted at the financial community and individual shareholders (fact book, shareholder letter, etc.);

- Managing the Group's relationship with analysts and investors in the CSR (Corporate Social Responsibility) domain;

- More generally, together with the Communication Department, distribute financial information published by the Group.

To carry out its obligations, the Financial Communication Department can turn to all other Group entities and will be associated, when needed, to the work carried out by the operational departments.

The Director of Financial Communication's report to the Chief Financial Officer.

Jérôme Schmitt, Director of Financial Communication
Robert Castaigne, Chief Financial Officer

Source: Total internal document, translated from French by casewriter.

EXHIBIT 11 Investor relations and financial communications group—organizational overview

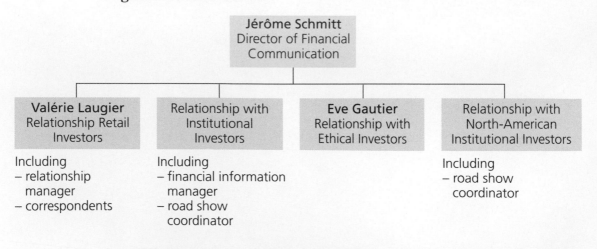

Note: Managers mentioned in case are indicated by name in chart above.

Source: Total.

EXHIBIT 12 Investor relations calendar 2005–2006

Date	Event
2005	
17 Feb	Results for 4th quarter, 2004
13 Apr	Telephone conference on the shift to IFRS standards
14 Apr	Meeting of the shareholders in Strasbourg
4 May	Results for 1st quarter 2005
17 May	Shareholders' Meeting at the Paris Convention Center
24 May	Payment of the cash dividend
20 Jun	Meeting of shareholders in Montpellier
4 Aug	Results for 2nd quarter and 1st half 2005
7 Sep	Presentation of mid-2005 outlook
12 Oct	Meeting of shareholders in Bordeaux
4 Nov	Results for the 3rd quarter 2005
18–19 Nov	Actionaria Trade Show in Paris
2006	
15 Feb	Presentation of 2005 Results
12 May	Shareholders' Meeting in Paris

Source: Total Annual Reports 2005 and 2006, p. 47.

Investor Relations at Total

Investor Relations at Total

EXHIBIT 13 Summary of analyst reports after total's September 2005 road show

	Sector[a]	Total	BP	RD Shell	Exxon Mobil	Chevron Texaco	ENI	Repsol-YPF	Conoco Phillips
Anglo-Saxon Analysts									
Banc of America		2	2	3	3	2			2
Bernstein	3	2	3	3		3	3		3
BBVA	2	2	3	4			4	2	
Bear Stearns	3	2	2	4	2	4			2
BNP Exane	4	3	2	4			2	3	
SCH	2	2	3	3			2	2	
Cazenove	3	3							
Citigroup Smith Barney	3	2	3	3		2	2	3	3
CSFB	2	2	3	3	3	2	2	4	3
Daiwa Securities	3	3	3	2				3	
Deutsche Bank	3	2	2	3	2	2	2	3	2
Dresdner KW		2							
Friedman Billings Ramsey	2	3	3	4	3	2			2
Goldman Sachs	3	2	3	2	2	3		3	3
HSBC	4	2	2	4			3	3	
ING	3	2	2	4			2	3	
JP Morgan	3	3	2	2		2	3	4	2
Lehman Brothers	4	2	4	3	2	2	2	3	2
Merrill Lynch	2	2	3	2	2	2	3	3	2
Morgan Stanley Dean Witter	2	3	3	2	2	3	4	2	2
Simmons	2	2	2	2	2	2	2	3	2
UBS Warburg	4	2	2	3	2	3	3	2	
Williams de Bröe	3	2	2	3			3	3	
Average	2.86	2.26	2.57	3.00	2.29	2.43	2.56	2.88	2.31
French Analysts									
Cheuvreux	3	2	1	4			1	3	
Ixis	2	1	2	2			2	2	
CM – CIC Securities		1	2	3			3	3	
Dexia Securities	3	2		3			2	4	
KBC Securities	2	2	4	3			2	2	
Kepler Equities	2	2		3			2	4	
Natexis	3	2	2	3			3	3	
Société Générale	3	2	2	3			2	3	
Average	2.57	1.75	2.17	3.00			2.13	3.00	
Overall Average	**2.79**	**2.13**	**2.48**	**3.00**	**2.29**	**2.43**	**2.42**	**2.92**	**2.31**

[a]sector grading:

(2) Overweight / Positive
(3) Neutral / Cautious
(4) Underweight / Negative

Company grading
(1) Strong buy, Recommended list, Select list, Buy (ABN Amro)
(2) Buy, Add, Accumulate, Market outperform, Outperform, Overweight
(3) Neutral, Market perform, Hold, Equal weight
(4) Reduce, Underperform, Underweight
(5) Sell

Source: Total's internal compilation of analyst reports.

ADDITIONAL CASES

1 Amazon.com in the year 2000

On June 22, 2000, Ravi Suria, a credit analyst at Lehman Brothers, issued a report sounding an alarm about the convertible debt of Amazon.com. When he looked at the company's financials, he saw a "weak balance sheet, poor working capital management, and massive negative operating cash flow." He regarded the debt as "extremely weak and deteriorating" and strongly advised investors to avoid it.

Amazon.com was, he noted, "the pioneering and best-established brand" among internet retailers. Nevertheless, he was convinced that the company was going to run out of cash in less than a year because of its poor operating performance, reflecting basic weaknesses in its business model. Amazon, he said, had really evolved from a "virtual" retailer to something more like a "real world" retailer, and was encountering the same kinds of cash flow problems and problems related to management of working capital that had spelled disaster for many retailers in the past. In February 1999 the company had issued $1.25 billion in convertible debt. A year later, it completed a second offering of convertible debt, this time for $680 million. As Suria saw things, however, the company was burning cash up fast, and if it was not able to start generating positive free cash flows soon, it would be in dire straits. "The party is over," he said, "and the February round of financing seems to have been the last call."[1]

In response to Suria's report, the price of Amazon's convertible debt dropped 15%, and its stock price dropped 19%, in one day after the report became public.

Background[2]

Jeff Bezos—Amazon's founder, chairman, and CEO—knew a good deal about the worlds of both technology and finance. After earning a degree in computer science and electrical engineering at Princeton, he worked for two years in commercial banking; then four years in investment banking in New York, managing a hedge fund. Then, fascinated by the possibilities of selling consumer goods over the internet, he started Amazon.com. The company was founded in 1994, began selling books online in 1995, and went public in 1997.

Research Associate Jeremy Cott prepared this case under the supervision of Professor Krishna Palepu. This case was developed from published sources. HBS cases are developed solely as the basis for class discussion. Cases are not intended to serve as endorsements, sources of primary data, or illustrations of effective or ineffective management.

[1]Ravi Suria (Lehman Brothers), "Amazon.com, Inc.: Credit Analysis of the Convertible Bonds," June 22, 2000.

[2]For a detailed description of Amazon's business and its competitive strategy during its early years, see "Leadership Online: Barnes & Noble vs. Amazon.com" (HBS No. 798-063).

Bezos initially considered a number of possible retailing businesses for the internet. He regarded book selling as especially attractive for several reasons:

- The number of products that customers might want was far larger than any physical store could carry. There wcre over a million books in print—and many more that were out of print. (The largest physical book stores, so-called "superstores," carried about 150,000 titles. Mall stores and small independent stores carried a small fraction of that.)

- The existing market was large. Annual retail sales of books were about $25 billion in the United States and about $80 billion worldwide.

- The book publishing and retailing industries were relatively fragmented. No book publisher controlled more than 15% of the U.S. market, and the two largest land-based book retailers, Barnes & Noble and Borders, controlled about 25% of the market. (Barnes & Noble and Borders, however, had been expanding significantly in recent years.)

Bezos' decision to locate the company in Seattle, Washington was also deliberate. The Seattle area had a lot of computer-technical talent (e.g., Microsoft was located nearby); it was near one of the largest book wholesalers in the country; and it would provide, he felt, a time-zone advantage in making shipments to customers around the country.[3]

Evolution of corporate strategy

As the company developed, it made two major changes in strategy: (1) it began doing more self-distribution, and (2) it expanded the product line from books to other products.

Self-distribution

During the first few years of its existence, Amazon pursued a "sell all, carry few" strategy. In the fall of 1997, for example, it billed itself as the world's largest bookstore, offering a selection of 2.5 million different titles. It actually stocked, however, only a few thousand. Generally, it ordered books from its suppliers (primarily wholesalers) only after making the sale to a customer. About 95% of Amazon's sales were handled that way.

Competition from Barnes & Noble, the largest land-based book retailer in the country, prompted a change in this approach. When Barnes & Noble opened its online store in May 1997, it said that it would use the distribution strength of its land-based operation to gain a competitive advantage in its online selling. Barnes & Noble operated a large distribution center in New Jersey where it stocked about 400,000 titles and from which it shipped books to its many physical stores around the country. Barnes & Noble said that it would also use this distribution center to fill many of the individual orders that it received from online customers.[4] There were two advantages to this approach:

- First, it reduced the cost of goods. Most of the books that Barnes & Noble stocked in its distribution center were ordered direct from publishers rather than wholesalers. Books ordered from publishers cost less than books ordered from wholesalers. The difference was several additional percentage points in discount, which, in a low-margin business like book retailing, was significant. (The cost of holding inventory was of course an offsetting cost factor.) Amazon had been ordering most of its books from wholesalers because wholesalers delivered books much faster than publishers. In the fall of 1997, however, the Chief Operating Officer of Barnes & Noble, Steve Riggio, said: "The cost advantages of self-distribution are tremendous." He said that 40% of

[3]Ibid.

[4]"Barnes & Noble Drops Names, Disses Amazon.com as website Launches," *Book Publishing Report*, May 19, 1997.

the books it sold were supplied by its own distribution complex, and he planned to get to 50% within a year. Jeff Bezos said: "The logistics of distribution are the iceberg below the waterline of online bookselling."[5]

- Second, having greater control over the order fulfillment process could provide greater assurance of the quality of a key element of customer service. In 1999, for example, Toys "R" Us, in planning to go online to challenge eToys, concluded that it needed to handle the fulfillment operation itself. "The minute you outsource," the CEO of Toys "R" Us said, "it's just something that's out of your hands. What happens at Christmas time when you're using [a certain third-party fulfillment operation]? They're servicing [someone else]. How do you get your service priorities to the top of the list?"[6]

The move to self-distribution changed the competitive landscape. When Barnes & Noble opened its online store in May 1997, it said that it would offer "the lowest everyday prices of any online bookseller."[7] It began by announcing discounts on a lot of books that were greater than what Amazon at that point was offering, and stiffer price competition was thus set in motion.

In response, in the fall of 1997 Amazon announced that it would enlarge its Seattle warehouse by 70%, open a new one on the East Coast, in Delaware, and buy a much larger portion of its books direct from publishers.

Then in 1999 Amazon made a dramatic move. It increased the number of distribution centers it had from two to ten, thus giving it over four million square feet of warehouse and distribution space. In its 1999 10-K it said that it carried "increased levels of inventory in order to be able to meet customer demand and ship products to customers on a timely basis," and that in 1999 it "increased our direct purchasing from manufacturers." It didn't disclose, however, what percentage of customer orders it filled from its own stock.

Selling other products

When Amazon first went online in 1995, it sold only books. When it went public in May 1997 it was selling books and a small number of tapes and CDs related to books.

In 1998, however, Amazon began to significantly expand its product offerings, and by mid-2000 it had established, and was operating on its website, businesses that sold not only books, but also music CDs, video tapes, DVDs, computer games, toys, software, consumer electronics, tools and hardware, lawn and patio products, and kitchen products. All of these products it sold itself: that is, it bought the actual inventory, and it sold it directly to customers. The company also set itself up as a middleman for, or strategic partner to, a number of other businesses that were allowed to use space on Amazon's website to sell their own products to Amazon's customers.

[5]Quotations come from Anthony Bianco, "Virtual Bookstores Start to Get Real," *Business Week*, October 27, 1997. The economics of order-fulfillment in e-tailing could take a few different forms. At one extreme, Buy.-com—a multi-product e-tailer that opened for business in 1997—outsourced almost everything having to do with inventory: it didn't maintain any inventory on its balance sheet, and wholesalers fulfilled all of the orders that it received. Buy.com said that this was the most efficient way of handling things, but it paid the wholesalers' markup on the goods as well as a fee that wholesalers charged for carrying out the fulfillment function. Many e-tailers outsourced some, but not all, of its order fulfillment. When Musicland—the successful, land-based retailer of CDs, tapes, DVDs, and books—went online in 1999, it said that it would do its own order fulfillment. It claimed that, by using its existing distribution infrastructure, it would save 10% of sales compared with e-tailers who outsourced the order fulfillment function. It would save about 5%, it said, by ordering direct from manufacturers, thereby avoiding the wholesaler's markup; and about 5% by using its own distribution system, which was what it said other companies paid third-party distributors. (The source for the information about Musicland is Jim McCartney, "Launching Website Is More Than Defensive Strategy for Some Retailers," *Saint Paul Pioneer Press*, June 16, 1999.)

[6]Abigail Goldman, "E-Commerce Gets an F Without the D Word," *Los Angeles Times*, July 25, 1999.

[7]"Barnes & Noble Drops Names. . .," op. cit.

1 Amazon.com in the Year 2000

Marketplace services

In these arrangements the company provided space on its website to auction businesses and thousands of small, non-auction businesses so that consumers could eventually come to the Amazon website and—as Jeff Bezos put it—"find and discover anything they want to buy. That's anything with a capital 'A.' "[8] He ruled out only animals, porn, and contraband.

One auction business involved the famous art auction house Sothebys. The large assemblage of small, non-auction businesses was named "zShops." As Bezos said when announcing the zShops program in the fall of 1999, the "z" stands for zero. "What we're trying to do is create a shopping environment that has zero risk, zero hassles, and zero products you can't find." For example, he said that Amazon would guarantee up to $1,000 of any customer's purchase from these zShops. That is, the customer would get up to $1,000 of his or her money back if the merchant didn't fulfill the order.[9]

From these small, non-auction businesses Amazon would receive monthly subscription fees ($9.99) and sales commissions (up to 5% of the sale). Amazon wouldn't own or manage any of their inventories. Bezos characterized this as a low-top-line, high-margin business. When asked, however, whether he had any sense of how much of Amazon's revenue would come from this service, Bezos said he didn't.

Strategic partnerships

Amazon was also making minority investments in many e-commerce companies.[10] These companies were given distinct, co-branded sections on the Amazon website where they sold their products or services, and Amazon received advertising revenues from them for allowing them to do so. Thus, for example, the "health and beauty products" section was co-branded with the company Drugstore.com, in which Amazon had made a minority investment; the "pet products" section was co-branded with the company Pets.com, in which Amazon had also made a minority investment. Amazon considered these strategic partnerships (of which there were, in 2000, about a dozen) part of the "Amazon Commerce Network" (ACN). The company had high hopes for them. In a press release in February 2000, the company said that these equity-method partnerships/investments "represent more than $500 million in revenue commitments to Amazon.com over the next five years." In the first quarter of 2000 Amazon recorded $20 million of ACN revenues, and analysts believed that the direct cost of those revenues was negligible.

These strategic partnerships had been attracting both admiration and skepticism from analysts. To some, Amazon was partly adopting the role of a venture capitalist, investing in various early-stage e-commerce companies that it viewed as especially promising. As a principal at Chase Capital Partners said, "If you can lock up the best of breed corporate partners, you can effectively block out the competition."[11] To other analysts, however, there was an illusory quality to these relationships. Amazon had begun to record high-margin advertising revenues from these companies, but the companies as a whole were losing a lot of money.[12] (As **Exhibit 1a** shows, Amazon's share of the losses of its equity-method investees in 1999 was $77 million; in the first quarter of 2000, $88 million.)

---

[8]Helen Jung, "Amazon Opens Site to Other Merchants," *Seattle Times*, September 29, 1999.

[9]Ibid.

[10]Most of these companies were identified in Amazon's financial statements as "equity-method investees." Equity-method accounting applied to investments that gave the investor "significant influence," but not outright control, over an investee. (This was normally assumed to involve ownership of between 20% and 50% of the investee's common stock.) Once the investment was made, the investing company would record in its financial statements its proportional share of the investee's profit or loss.

[11]Stephen Lacey, "Amazon.com: Venture Capital on Steriods," *IPO Reporter*, March 27, 2000.

[12]Gretchen Morgenson, "Bond Market Seems Wary of Amazon," *New York Times*, February 9, 2000; Herb Greenberg, "More on the Bear Case for Amazon," *TheStreet.com*, April 27, 2000.

Rationale

What was the business rationale for this dramatic expansion in product offerings? Bezos said that it would allow the company to leverage its "internet platform." By this he meant the company's growing customer base and brand name, the innovative technology it was developing, and its distribution capabilities. "We believe," the company's Annual Report stated, "that this platform allows us to launch new e-commerce businesses quickly, with a high quality of customer experience, economical incremental cost, and good prospects for success."

Implications of Amazon's strategy

Bezos said repeatedly that he was committed to placing growth ahead of profitability during the first few years of the company's existence. The key to Amazon's appeal, he believed, would be the high level of customer service it provided, involving huge product selection, easy-to-use search and browse features, personalized shopping services, secure payment protection, and reliable and timely delivery.

Amazon's expansion was also geographic. It could ship products almost anywhere, but in 1999 it also established distinct websites and distribution facilities in England and Germany.

Thus in mid-2000 Amazon was the largest internet retailer in the world, with $1.9 billion in trailing twelve-month revenues and 20 million customers in over 150 countries. It claimed to offer for sale 18 million different products (SKUs). And its brand was very well known.

Some observers, however, believed that Amazon was badly over-extending itself. In trying to be all things to all people, some people felt, the company was taking on more than it could handle. Al Ries, the author of a book on internet branding, said: "The most powerful brands in the world stand for something simple. Volvo stands for safety. Dell is a personal computer. Even Microsoft is software. Now Amazon is going to stand for books and charcoal grills. This makes no sense to me."[13]

Since the web was indifferent to distance and place, it was, in the view of some people, better suited to specialist retailers, to "category killers," than to generalists. (For example, eToys specialized in selling toys; CDNow specialized in selling CDs, Outpost.com specialized in selling computers and other electronic products.) Specialist retailers would, in this view, know more about particular categories of products and would be better able to develop the merchandising skills necessary to make their particular businesses successful.

Customer service

In Jeff Bezos' view, however, what Amazon.com "stood for" was high-quality customer service. And part of the reason why it could provide that, he believed, was that people at Amazon knew more about e-commerce than anyone else. In 1998 the chairman of Putnam/Penguin, one of the largest book publishers in the world, said: "When you talk to Amazon, you realize it's a technology company, not a merchant."[14] Such was the sophistication of the company's software, Bezos claimed, that "coming to Amazon will not be like entering the halls of a huge, soulless department store. It will be more like stopping by at a local shop where your every taste and preference is known."[15] The company had in fact been developing many information-rich features for its website—for example, product reviews by both outside experts and other Amazon customers, the customer's own purchasing history, "collaborative filtering" software that aimed to provide a kind of

[13]Quoted in Robert Hof, "Can Amazon Make It?" *Business Week*, July 10, 2000.

[14]David Streitfeld, "Booking the Future," *Washington Post*, July 10, 1998.

[15]"Amazon's Delta," *The Economist*, November 20, 1999.

electronic word-of-mouth among people with similar tastes, e-mails to alert customers to the release of new products they had asked about, an ability given to customers to track the shipment of products they had ordered.

Pricing

An academic study, published in April 2000, seemed to support Bezos' view of things.[16] Amazon often engaged in aggressive pricing in order to attract customers, but the academic study found that pricing differences among internet retail businesses, even for commodity-type products like books and CDs, were as pronounced as they were for conventional retailers and that internet sites with the lowest prices didn't necessarily have the largest market shares. Amazon, for example, was the leader in online book and CD sales but, this study found, didn't necessarily have the lowest prices. The level of customer satisfaction and customer service it provided was evidently key to its ability to attract customers.

Amazon itself, however, regarded the pricing issue as a threat. "New and expanded web technologies," it said in its 1999 10-K, "may increase the competitive pressures on online retailers. For example, 'shopping agent' technologies permit customers to quickly compare our prices with those of our competitors. This increased competition may reduce our operating margins, diminish our market share, or impair the value of our brand."

A professor of operations and information management, Eric Clemons, writing in the *Financial Times* in June 2000 about particular kinds of risk in the e-commerce world, noted that Amazon, like most e-commerce businesses, was continuing to spend significant amounts of money to acquire new customers, but he wasn't at all sure that that made sense:

> *It is too early to determine if consumers will remain loyal to these sites, allowing these retailers time to harvest profits and cover the costs of their acquisition, or whether the web's empowerment of consumer choice will mean that customers constantly migrate to the lowest-cost online seller. If the web is as liberating and empowering as most accounts have led us to believe, all business models based on paying to acquire share are flawed.[17]*

Financing strategy

Amazon had started with private equity financing of about $1 million. It sold $8 million of convertible preferred in 1996 (which was converted to common the following year). The IPO in May 1997 brought in about $50 million. The company had also been receiving cash from employees when they exercised their stock options.

The company had issued debt on three occasions:

- In May 1998 the company sold 10% senior discount notes due in 2008. They were sold for $326 million, but their value at maturity would be $530 million. They accreted interest until 2003 and paid cash interest after that. (During 1999 the company repurchased $266 million principal amount of this issue [representing $178 million accreted value]. Thus as of year-end 1999, the accreted amount outstanding was $191 million.)

- In February 1999 the company sold $1.25 billion par value of 4.75% convertible subordinated notes due in 2009.

- In February 2000 the company sold 690 ($680 million) par value of 6.875% euro-denominated convertible subordinated notes due in 2010.

---

[16]Erik Brynjolfsson, "Frictionless Commerce?" *Management Science*, March 2000.
[17]Eric Clemons, "Managing Risk," *Financial Times*, June 13, 2000.

When this second set of convertibles was issued, observers noted the much-higher interest rate that Amazon had to offer compared to the 4.75% interest rate it offered on the convertibles it had sold just a year earlier. Some observers also suggested that Amazon had taken the offering to Europe because it had been a tough sell in the United States. The company denied this. It said that it sold this second set of convertibles in Europe because it wanted to broaden its market recognition there. It also said that it intended to use some of the proceeds from the issue to support growth in its European operations.

Thus at the end of the first quarter of 2000, Amazon had $2.15 billion in debt outstanding (including some capital leases), of which about $1.9 billion consisted of the convertibles. The convertibles were rated triple C by both Standard & Poor's and Moody's. A summary of the terms of the two convertible issues is provided in **Exhibit 5**. **Exhibit 6** shows the company's cash obligations, for interest and principal, for all of its debt securities over the next ten years.

Financial performance

Exhibits 1a, 1b, and 1c show Amazon.com's Income Statements, Balance Sheets, and Cash Flow Statements for the last few years. **Exhibit 2** shows some data about customers that analysts referred to a fair amount. **Exhibit 3** shows segment information for the company for the last three years and for the first quarter of 2000. **Exhibit 4** provides information about its fixed assets.

Since its inception the company had recorded total sales of about $3 billion and total losses of $1.2 billion (of which about $350 million was amortization of goodwill and other intangibles). Total cash flows from operations had been a negative $380 million. The stock went public in May 1997 at about $2 a share (split adjusted), peaked at $106 in late 1999, and had declined to $42 just before the Lehman analyst issued his critical report.

Some of the components of the Income Statement involved accounting policies or had meanings that were somewhat different from what one would expect in most businesses.

Sales

Most of Amazon's sales were product sales. The sales figures also included, however, revenue that the company had begun to record from its "Amazon Commerce Network" partners. Most of the revenue from these companies wasn't coming in the form of cash, however; it was coming in the form of the companies' stock. (As **Exhibit 1c** shows, $18 million of the $20 million of ACN revenues that Amazon recorded during the first quarter of 2000 was non-cash.) What happened essentially was that Amazon would receive a certain amount of these companies' stock when the partnership agreements were signed. The stock would be valued as of that date, recorded initially as unearned revenue, and then later credited to revenue as Amazon provided the related services (space on its website). If the value of the stock declined, that would be reflected in Amazon's financial statements only when Amazon marked it down as a "permanent impairment."

Marketing and sales expense

This included not only standard kinds of marketing and sales expense (e.g., advertising and promotional expenditures and payroll for those functions) but also fulfillment expense. Fulfillment expense, the company said, represented "those costs incurred in operating and staffing distribution and customer service centers, including costs attributable to receiving, inspecting and warehousing inventories; picking, packaging and preparing customers' orders for shipment; and responding to inquiries from customers." All of the company's distribution centers were leased, and almost all of them were accounted for as operating leases.

Another key component of Amazon's marketing expenses was what it called its "Associates Program." Many companies were agreeing to place on their websites a link to Amazon.com—involving, say, a product recommendation—and for every sale that Amazon made as a result of that link, Amazon would pay a referral fee of between 5% and 15%. Many internet businesses were developing this kind of "associate" or "affiliate" marketing, but Amazon had the largest such program, involving (as of early 2000) 430,000 websites.

Technology and content

Technology and content expenses consisted primarily of payroll and related expenses for the development of computer software and telecommunications systems, as well as for the acquisition of certain editorial content such as freelance reviews. Technology and content costs, it said, "are generally expensed as incurred, except for certain costs relating to the development of internal-use software that are capitalized and depreciated over estimated useful lives."

In Bezos' view, certain expenditures on technology could reduce fulfillment costs. For example, he said that a lot of customers had been calling its customer service department regarding problems that the company had now enabled them to handle themselves by means of an online software tool.[18]

Amortization of goodwill and other intangibles

Amazon had acquired a number of companies; the acquisitions were generally accounted for as "purchases"; and most of the purchase prices had been allocated to goodwill and other intangible assets. Amazon said that it was amortizing those assets over a period of only two to four years.

Stock options

Amazon didn't record the cost of stock options in its income statements—which was acceptable under generally accepted accounting standards. However, it disclosed that, had it recorded the fair value of stock options granted (using the Black-Scholes option pricing model), its net profit in 1999 and 1998 would have been $312 million and $70 lower, respectively.

Business model

Amazon's business plan, of course, was premised on the expectation that it would ultimately perform better than comparable land-based retailers. **Exhibit 7a** shows some key operating data for Barnes & Noble and Borders, the two largest land-based book retailers in the United States. (Both of these companies were involved in online bookselling businesses, but those businesses were structured as separate entities. Therefore the data in **Exhibit 7a** should reasonably represent the performance of their land-based bookselling operations.) Amazon's aggressive pricing resulted in relatively low gross margins, and **Exhibit 7b** shows some key operating data for two very successful, land-based retailers that operated with low gross margins. (Wal-Mart was the largest retailer in the world. Costco was the largest operator of discount warehouse stores in the United States.)

---

[18]"Newsmaker Q&A," *BusinessWeek Online: Daily Briefing*, <http//www.businessweek.com>, June 30, 2000.

Company guidance

In April, when it reported first quarter 2000 results, the company told analysts that it expected to have positive cash flows from operations for the balance of the calendar year. It said it also expected that its cash flows from operations would fully cover its planned capital expenditures of approximately $250-$300 million and that its cash balance at the end of the calendar year would be about $1 billion. It said that it hoped to reduce fulfillment expense as a percentage of sales from 17% in the 1st quarter to the low teens by the fourth quarter. It also said it expected its operating margin loss (excluding amortization, stock-based compensation, and other special charges) to fall from 21% in 1999 to single digits for all of 2000. In addition, Bezos reiterated his intention to continue to invest in new product lines and to expand further in international markets.

Analysts' assessment of Amazon's stock and debt

During the first few years of Amazon's existence, stock analysts had been groping for ways to value the company's stock. Some analysts assumed certain multiples of sales or earnings for a company of this sort, forecasted sales or earnings figures for Amazon a number of years down the road, and then discounted those values back to the present. Some analysts attempted to calculate the present value of each of Amazon's customers (which involved an extraordinary array of assumptions). Most analysts gave very little attention to cash flows.[19]

An equity analyst at Prudential Securities, however, argued in February 1999 that "one of the appeals of Amazon.com's business model is its cash flow." She pointed out that, since its inception, the company had generated positive cash flow from operations of $30 million, had spent $37 million on capital expenditures, and therefore had had cumulative cash outflow of under $10 million. Thus, she said, the company "has essentially built its business with a net cash outlay of less than $10 million."[20]

Lehman Brothers report

When the Lehman Brothers analyst, Ravi Suria, sounded his alarm about the company's debt in June 2000, he focused almost exclusively on cash flows. He was a debt analyst, and although the upside potential of the debt securities he was dealing with was tied to their convertibility into common stock, he focused his analysis on the company's credit risk.[21]

"In a best-case scenario," he said, "we believe that the current cash balances will last the company through the first quarter of 2001." "Despite [the company's] much-touted brand identity, first mover advantage, virtual storefronts, hits and visits," he said he found the company "woefully lacking from an operational aspect."

He noted that the company, since it opened for business, had recorded $1.2 billion in accounting losses. More important from his point of view, however, was the fact that its operating cash flows had been negative almost every quarter. Add its capital expenditures

---

[19]For example, in her first report on Amazon in September 1997, Mary Meeker, the soon-to-be very influential analyst of internet stocks at Morgan Stanley Dean Witter, recommended the stock, but more or less said that it was almost impossible to do a valuation of it. She put together a matrix indicating a whole range of possible valuations based on a variety of assumptions about price-to-sales ratios, net margins, discount rates, and sales figures for the year 2001. She stated: "We have learned that too much focus on valuation can often lead to short-sighted investment errors." (Mary Meeker [Morgan Stanley Dean Witter], "Amazon.com: Initiating Coverage," September 22, 1997.)

[20]Amy Ryan (Prudential Securities), "Amazon.com," February 1, 1999.

[21]Ravi Suria (Lehman Brothers), op. cit.

to that, he said, and total free cash flows from the fourth quarter of 1997 through the first quarter of 2000 had been a minus $718 million. (**Exhibit 8** shows information that he put together.)

So far the company had been supported, in his view, by an extremely forgiving capital market. For every $1 of revenue that the company had generated from the start of 1997 through the first quarter of 2000, he claimed, it had raised $.95 from the capital markets. The total figures he cited were $2.9 billion in revenue during that period and $2.8 billion raised from the capital markets. He defined money raised from the capital markets as consisting of money from the IPO in 1997, cash received from the three debt securities, and cash received from employees' exercise of stock options.

The component of Amazon's financial performance that Suria emphasized more than anything else in his report was what he called "cash flow per unit of product sold." He said: "We believe that the fundamental problem with the operations lies in the fact that Amazon does not generate positive net cash flow per unit of product it sells." The first few times he referred to this he didn't define what he meant, but then later in his report he said: "Our favorite metric for measuring success of a company is to look at its operating cash flow. . . . It is the best measurement of the ability of a retailing business to make money per unit sold." By this measurement, he said, Amazon's performance had been getting worse as time went on. There was, he said, "a clear correlation between [Amazon's] cash outflows and [its] revenues—indicating operational inefficiencies at the unit sales level."

From his point of view, the most important ingredient in Amazon's cash flow was its management of working capital. Thus he focused on accounts receivable, accounts payable, and inventory.

- **Accounts receivable**. Amazon didn't have any (because customers paid with credit cards). This, he said, was the strongest operating characteristic of the company.

- **Accounts payable**. Amazon, he thought, had become fairly savvy in stretching payables. However, payment of accounts payable in the first quarter of 2000 increased cash outflow by $207 million, and he thought that payables flexibility was likely to decrease for the company.

- **Inventory**. Suria thought this was the biggest problem Amazon faced. The critical period for most retailers, he said, was the fourth and first quarters, the periods tied to peak seasonal sales. Suria calculated Amazon's inventory turnover quarter by quarter, and he also used sales in the numerator (rather than cost of goods) because, he said, of the different accounting conventions used by companies to determine expense classifications. **Exhibit 9** shows the inventory turnover figures that he calculated. They had decreased steadily, he said, from 8.5 in the first quarter of 1998 to a low of 2.9 in the first quarter of 2000. More important than the absolute level of inventory turnover, he said, was its steady deterioration. This showed that the company wasn't managing its sales growth well.

Then there were, in his view, other problems on the horizon as well: the fact that the company was now selling greater numbers of toys and electronics, which he said were logistically more difficult to handle than books; the presence of an increasing number of old-world retailers in the e-tailing space; Amazon's intention to continue to establish new businesses; a probable slowdown in the economy.

His pessimistic view of Amazon's prospects had to do largely with its business model:

As the e-tailing model begins to look more and more like standard retailers, the cash flow cycle of the business will track that of an Old Economy retailer. Thus, depending upon the season, working capital either sucks in cash or spins out cash. But, net-net for a successful retailer, the annualized operating cash flow should be consistently positive, especially when the operating costs are not burdened by startup costs that many expanding retailers face in opening new physical locations.[22]

Finally, he pointed out, Amazon had very little financial flexibility. As of the end of the first quarter of 2000, the company's debt to capital ratio was 99%. The ratio of debt to tangible capital, however—that is, netting out the large amount of goodwill and other intangibles—was 141%. "Going into what is arguably its most challenging holiday season," he said, "we believe that the combination of negative cash flow, poor working capital management, and high debt load in a hyper competitive environment will put the company under extremely high risk."

The company, he said, had to do either one of two things—start becoming cash sufficient, or keep raising capital until it became cash sufficient. He was doubtful about the prospects for either of these two things.

Reactions

The financial markets reacted immediately to the Lehman Brothers report. The day after it was issued, the prices of the two convertible debt securities dropped 15%. The common stock dropped 19%, thus losing about $2.8 billion of its market value. **Exhibit 10** shows graphs of the prices of Amazon's two convertible debt issues from their issue date through the end of June 2000. **Exhibit 11** shows, for the period from the beginning of 1999 through the end of June 2000, the return on Amazon's stock compared to the return on the Nasdaq index.

Amazon's reaction

A company spokesperson called the Lehman Brothers report "pure hogwash," although he didn't identify any specific facts or assumptions that were wrong. "We are nowhere near running out of cash," he said, "and anybody who understands the cash flow dynamics of our company understands that."[23]

Bezos said the report was "baloney." When asked why the company, then, wasn't profitable, Bezos said that the books, music, and video segment was now showing an operating profit but that, at the same time, the company was investing in a lot of young businesses. "It would have been easy to make the business profitable at much lower revenue levels," he said, "but we wouldn't have had the opportunity to build an important and lasting company." Bazos said the argument had been made innumerable times that the company was buying products for a dollar and selling them for 90 cents. He said that wasn't the case. He said the company was selling dollar bills for $1.20 but that the reason it wasn't profitable was that it was investing in a lot of new things.[24]

Barron's

Alan Abelson, in his "Up and Down Wall Street" column in *Barron's* on June 26, called the Lehman Brothers report "brilliant, thorough, and very well crafted." He also said it was "miraculously free of the gibberish and webbygook that ooze from virtually all the brokerage stuff churned out on anything tech and everything internet." Abelson noted that "Amazon has inspired comment in [*Barron's*] on a number of occasions in the past few years, and we have been consistently underwhelmed by the company and its prospects. . . . Indeed, the first truly penetrating dissection of Amazon appeared in [*Barron's*] in January 1999."

[22] Ibid.

[23] "Irrational Over-reaction," *Business Line*, July 5, 2000.

[24] "Newsmaker Q&A," *BusinessWeek Online: Daily Briefing*, <http//www.businessweek.com>, June 30, 2000.

(The article was entitled "Bubble Trouble" and the byline for it was "Alan Abelson and Rhonda Brammer.") He said that the thrust of that article was that "the company's fabled business plan had been anticipated by the pig farmer who lost 50 bucks on every pig he sold but was confident of making it up in volume." The article, he said, had essentially argued that "it was a reasonably safe bet that Amazon would never make any money." And he said that that, in a sense, was the core of the Lehman Brothers report.[25]

Business Week

Business Week ran a long article providing a more mixed reaction.[26] It restated the key arguments and figures that the Lehman analyst had presented, said that this was "scary stuff," and noted that timing now was critical. The sharp downturn that had occurred in the stocks of many internet companies "means that Amazon's access to new capital will likely be cut off now, so the clock is ticking." The article also raised questions about Amazon's whole "one-stop shopping mentality" (selling everything from books to charcoal grills) and what some people considered the over-extension of its brand.

On the other hand, it pointed out various positive trends. The company's operating losses (excluding special items like amortization and stock-based compensation) declined from 26% in the fourth quarter of 1999 to 17% in the first quarter of 2000. The company, it said, was evidently able to move customers quickly to new product offerings—for example, the company became the largest seller of CDs after only four months—and both its repeat business as a percentage of total business and the average dollar sale per customer were increasing (see **Exhibit 2**). It also noted the view of some people that the Lehman analyst made the mistake of "focusing on the one year of Amazon's greatest expansion and projecting those costs forward into the future."

Other analysts

Mary Meeker, the influential analyst of internet stocks at Morgan Stanley Dean Witter, reiterated her "buy" recommendation but sounded a note of caution. She said she thought the year-end holiday season could be a make-or-break time for the company.[27] Most stock analysts reiterated their "buy" recommendation. That included the equity analyst at Lehman Brothers.

The analyst at Salomon Smith Barney, Tim Albright, said he thought the concerns about Amazon's running out of cash were way overblown. He projected revenues for the company of $3.0 billion in 2000 and $4.9 billion in 2001. He also expected the company to lose $342 million in cash from March 2000 through March 2001 but to generate $93 million in cash flow from March 2001 through March 2002, thus ending the March 2001 and 2002 quarters with $666 million and $757 million in cash, respectively. He said that even when he stress-tested his cash flow model for lower inventory turnover and higher payables turnover, the company would still have plenty of cash on hand at the end of both periods.[28]

The chief executive of an e-commerce company based in Seattle said in early July that he thought Amazon had the best chance of surviving the e-tailing shakeout but that it might have to drastically revise its business model in the face of competition from real-world retailers like Wal-Mart. "The economics haven't proven their way out yet," he said. "It's a tough issue. I come down on either side of it on any given day. It's going to be a wait and see thing."[29]

[25] Alan Abelson, "Virtual Disaster," *Barron's*, June 26, 2000.

[26] Robert Hof, op. cit.

[27] Frances Katz, "Fear Spurs Amazon Drop," *Atlanta Journal and Constitution*, June 24, 2000.

[28] Tim Albright (Salomon Smith Barney), "Amazon.com," July 13, 2000.

[29] Scott Hillis, "Amazon Turns 5, But Some Doubt It Will Survive," *Toronto Star*, July 17, 2000.

Later developments

Exhibit 12 shows Amazon's income statements, balance sheets, and cash flow statements through the first quarter of 2001. Ravi Suria's claim in June 2000 that "in a best-case scenario . . . the current cash balances will last the company through the first quarter of 2001" didn't pan out. At the end of the first quarter of 2001 Amazon had total cash and marketable securities of $643 million.

In August 2000 Amazon transferred much of the management and risk of its toys business to Toys "R" Us—an established bricks and mortar retailer that had entered the online world the previous year. Amazon sold all of its toys inventory to Toys "R" Us (for $29 million). The website for Toys "R" Us, however, became part of Amazon's website. Per an agreement that the two companies reached, Toys "R" Us would purchase and own all of the inventory for the toys business, and Amazon would provide the necessary customer service, order fulfillment, and warehousing, for which it would receive from Toys "R" Us a combination of fixed payments and variable payments related to sales volume.

In the second half of 2000 two of the online retailers with which Amazon had had "strategic relationships" closed down. One was Living.com, which had been selling furniture and other home products and in which Amazon had invested about $10 million. The other was Pets.com, which had been selling pet supplies and in which Amazon had invested $58 million. Both companies had attempted to raise additional capital to keep going but were unable to do so.

In January 2001 Amazon indicated that although 2000 sales were 68% higher than prior year's sales, they had fallen short of expectations, and it announced the closure of one of its distribution facilities in the United States and the partial closure of another. (Prior to the announcement the company had been operating eight distribution centers in the U.S.) It also announced the streamlining of various departments, which involved laying off about 1,300 employees. (At the end of 2000 it had employed about 9,000 people.) These moves produced restructuring charges in the first quarter of 2001 of $114 million (classified as "Impairment-related and other" in its income statement.)

The company's securities continued to decline. From the end of June 2000 to the end of April 2001, its stock price fell about 58%, and the prices of its convertible debt issues fell about 20% (to about 50% of par). Market analysts were divided on whether Amazon would fall prey to the ongoing internet retailing shakeout, or would be an exception to the trend and emerge as a winner.

Questions

1   What is your assessment of the long-term viability of Amazon's business model?

2   Do you agree with Ravi Suria's analysis of the credit risks associated with Amazon's bonds?

3   Why did the markets (both bond and stock) react so significantly to Suria's report?

1 Amazon.com in the Year 2000

EXHIBIT 1A   Amazon.com: Income statements ($ millions)

	1997	1998	1999	2000
	Full year	Full year	Full year	1st qtr.
Sales[a]	148	610	1,640	574
Cost of sales[b]	(119)	(476)	(1,349)	(446)
Gross profit	29	134	291	128
Operating expenses				
Marketing and sales[c]	(40)	(133)	(413)	(140)
Technology & content	(14)	(46)	(160)	(61)
General & administrative	(7)	(16)	(70)	(26)
Stock-based compensation	(1)	(2)	(31)	(14)
Amortization of goodwill & other intangibles	0	(42)	(215)	(83)
Merger, acquisition, & investment-related costs	0	(4)	(8)	(2)
Operating loss	(33)	(109)	(606)	(198)
Interest expense	—	(27)	(84)	(27)
Interest income	2	14	45	10
Other income (expense), net	0	0	2	(5)
	(31)	(122)	(643)	(220)
Equity in losses of equity-method investees		(3)	(77)	(88)
Net loss	(31)	(125)	(720)	(308)
Average # of shares o/s (millions)	261	296	327	344

[a]Revenues consisted primarily of sales to customers. However, beginning in 2000 a portion represented advertising revenue from the Amazon.com Commerce Network (ACN) ($20 million in the first quarter of 2000).

[b]Cost of sales'' consisted of the cost of merchandise sold, the cost of inbound and outbound shipping charges, and the cost of packaging materials. One special charge was an inventory writedown of $39 million in the 4th quarter of 1999.

[c]The two largest components were advertising and fulfillment expenses. Advertising expense in full-year 1999, 1998, and 1997 was $141 million, $60 million, and $21 million respectively. Fulfillment expense in full-year 1999, 1998, and 1997 was $188 million, $50 million, and $12 million, respectively. During the first quarters of 2000 and 1999 it was $100 million and $34 million, respectively.

Source: Company 10-Ks and 10-Qs.

1 Amazon.com in the Year 2000

EXHIBIT 1B   Amazon.com: Balance sheets ($ millions)

	1997	1998	1999	2000
	31-Dec	**31-Dec**	**31-Dec**	**31-Mar**
Current assets				
Cash & marketable securities	125	373	706	1,009
Inventories	9	30	221	172
Prepaid expenses etc.	3	21	85	90
	137	424	1,012	1,271
Fixed assets	10	30	318	335
Goodwill & other purchased intangibles		179	730	647
Investments		7	371	422
Other	2	8	40	55
Total assets	149	648	2,471	2,730
Current liabilities				
Accounts payble	33	113	463	256
Accrued expenses & other current liabilities	10	48	207	161
Unearned revenue	—	—	55	134
Current portion of long-term debt	1	1	14	16
	44	162	739	567
Long-term debt	77	348	1,466	2,137
Stockholders' equity				
Common stock	66	300	1,148	1,216
Accumulated deficit	(38)	(162)	(882)	(1,190)
	28	138	266	26
Total liabilities & stockholders equity	149	648	2,471	2,730

Source: Company 10-Ks and 10-Qs

EXHIBIT 1C   Amazon.com: Cash flow statements ($ millions)

	1997	1998	1999		2000
	Full year	Full year	4th qtr.	Full year	1st qtr.
Operating activities					
Net loss	(31)	(125)	(324)	(720)	(308)
Depreciation & amortization of fixed assets	3	10		37	18
Amort.of deferred stock-based compensation	2	2		31	14
Equity in losses of equity-method investees	—	3		77	88
Amortization of goodwill & other intangibles	—	43		215	83
Non-cash interest expense	—	24		29	6
Non-cash revenue for advertising & promotional services	—	—		(6)	(18)
Other	—	2		17	(1)
	(26)	(41)	(171)	(320)	(118)
Changes in operating assets & liabilities, net of effects from acquisitions					
Inventories	(8)	(21)	(83)	(172)	48
Prepaid expenses & other current assets	(3)	(17)	(27)	(60)	3
Accounts payable	30	79	208	330	(207)
Accrued expenses & other current liabilities	8	31	90	107	(37)
Interest payable	—	—	15	25	(9)
	27	72	203	230	(202)
Net cash provided (used) in op. activities	1	31	31	(90)	(320)
Investing activities					
Sales of marketable securities	4	332		4,025	1,014
Purchases of marketable securities	(122)	(547)		(4,290)	(1,333)
Purchase of fixed assets	(8)	(28)		(287)	(27)
Acquisitions & investments in businesses, net of cash acquired	—	(19)		(370)	(47)
Net cash used in investing activities	(126)	(262)		(922)	(393)
Financing activities					
Proceeds from long-term debt	75	326		1,264	679
Repayment of long-term debt	—	(78)		(189)	(4)
Financing costs & other	(2)	(8)		(35)	(16)
Proceeds from issuance of capital stock and exercise of stock options[a]	53	14		64	21
Net cash provided by financing activities	126	254		1,104	680
Net increase (decrease) in cash	1	23		92	(33)
Cash at beginning of period	1	2		25	117
Cash at end of period	2	25		117	84
Supplemental cash flow information					
Stock issued in connection with business acquisitions	—	217		774	—
Equity securities for unearned Amazon Commerce Network services	—	—		54	98
Cash paid for interest	—	27		60	—

[a]Proceeds from the exercise of stock options were $68 million and $6 million in 1999 and 1998, respectively. In 1997 the company received approximately $50 million through its IPO.

Source: Company 10-Ks and 10-Qs.

EXHIBIT 2 Amazon.com: Customer data

	1997	1998	1999					2000
	Full year	Full year	1st qtr.	2nd qtr.	3rd qtr.	4th qtr.	Full year	1st qtr.
No. of customer accounts	1,510,000	6,200,000	8,400,000	10,700,000	13,100,000	16,900,000	16,900,000	20,000,000
No. of new customers	1,375,000	4,690,000	2,200,000	2,300,000	2,400,000	3,800,000	10,700,000	3,100,000
Average sale per customer in trailing 12-month period			$108			$116		$121
Orders from repeat customers as % of all orders			66%			73%		76%
Customer acquisition cost[a]			$13	$19	$14	$19	$19	$13

[a] "Customer acquisition cost" was a metric used by a good many analysts of e-commerce businesses. For Amazon, analysts calculated it by dividing total sales and marketing costs (excluding fullfillment costs) by the number of new customers acquired during a given period of time. (This assumes that sales and marketing costs relate solely to new customers.) Studies done by the Boston Consulting Group and Forrester Research concluded that the average "customer acqusition cost" in the e-commerce world in 1999 was about $40.

Source: Company reports; estimates by Morgan Stanley Dean Witter, Merrill Lynch, Robertson Stephens; various press reports.

1 Amazon.com in the Year 2000

EXHIBIT 3 Amazon.com: Segment information ($ millions)

	U.S. books, music, and DVD/video	International	Early-stage businesses & other	Consolidated
2000 (first quarter)				
Revenues from external customers	401	75	97	574
Gross profit (loss)	83	16	29	128
Segment loss	(2)	(27)	(69)	(99)
Other operating expenses	—	—	—	(99)
Net interest expense and other	—	—	—	(22)
Equity in losses of equity-method investees	—	—	—	(88)
Net loss				(308)
1999				
Revenues from external customers	1,308	168	164	1,640
Gross profit (loss)	263	35	(8)	291
Segment loss	(31)	(79)	(242)	(352)
Other operating expenses	—	—	—	(253)
Net interest expense and other	—	—	—	(38)
Equity in losses of equity-method investees	—	—	—	(77)
Net loss				(720)
1998				
Revenues from external customers	588	22	—	610
Gross profit	129	5	—	134
Segment loss	(35)	(25)	—	(61)
Other operating expenses	—	—	—	(48)
Interest expense, net	—	—	—	(12)
Equity in losses of equity-method investees	—	—	—	(3)
Net loss				(125)
1997				
Revenues from external customers	148	—	—	148
Gross profit	29	—	—	29
Segment loss	(31)	—	—	(31)
Other operating expenses	(1)	—	—	(1)
Interest income, net	1	—	—	1
Equity in losses of equity-method investees	—	—	—	—
Net loss				(31)

Notes:
* "Other operating expenses" include amortization of goodwill and other intangibles, acquisition- and investment-related costs, and stock-based compensation.
* "Early-stage businesses" includes electronics, software, video games, toys, home improvement products, "marketplace services," and the "Amazon Commerce Network."

Source: Company 10-K and 10-Q

EXHIBIT 4   Amazon.com: Fixed assets ($ millions)

	Dec. 31	
	1999	1998
Computers, equipment and software[a]	187	36
Leasehold improvements	44	6
Leased assets	52	—
Construction in progress	83	2
	366	44
Less accumulated depreciation and amortization	(49)	(14)
Fixed assets, net	317	30

[a]Consists mostly of servers, storage, and telecom systems.

Source: Company 10-K

EXHIBIT 5   Summary of terms of Amazon's convertible notes

Terms common to both issues

- Rank equally, but are subordinate to all existing and future senior debt, including trade payables of subsidiaries. "As of December 31, 1999, we had approximately $901 million of indebtedness that constituted senior indebtedness."

- Unsecured.

- "The indenture does not contain any financial covenants and does not restrict us from paying dividends, incurring indebtedness, or issuing or repurchasing our other securities. The indenture does not protect you in the event of a highly leveraged transaction or a change in control except in limited circumstances."

- "We may from time to time reduce the conversion price [by any amount] . . . if our board of directors has made a determination that this reduction would be in our best interests."

Terms specific to 4.75% convertible notes

- Pay interest semi-annually.

- Convertible to 12.816 common shares; the conversion price was therefore $78.03.

- Redeemable by the company after 2002 at fairly standard redemption prices, involving small premiums. Prior to 2002 the company could redeem them at par if the company's average stock price

for a certain number of days exceeded 150% of the conversion price. If the company did so, however, it would have to pay a significant penalty (approximately $208 for every $1,000 note).

Terms specific to 6.875% convertible notes

- Pay interest annually.

- Convertible to 9.529 common shares; the conversion price was therefore €104.94. Include a sweetener—reset provisions that would lower the conversion price in February 2001 and February 2002 if the company's stock price fell. (Specifically, the conversion price would be lowered if the euro-equivalent of the average stock price for a certain number of days was below €104.94. The conversion price couldn't, however, be reset below €84.883.)

- Redeemable by the company after 2003 at par. Prior to 2003 the company could withdraw the conversion rights altogether if the company's average stock price for a certain number of days exceeded 160% of the initially stated conversion price (thus €167.92). If the company did so, however, it would have to pay a significant penalty (approximately €200 for every €1,000 note).

- Exchange ratio between the euro and the dollar not fixed.

Source: Form S-3, dated 3/15/99; Form 8-K, dated 2/14/00.

EXHIBIT 6 Cash obligations for debt: Interest plus repayment of principal ($ millions)

Year	10% discount notes due 2008	4.75% convertible notes due 2009	6.875% convertible notes due 2010	Total
2000	0	59	0	59
2001	0	59	47	106
2002	0	59	47	106
2003	26	59	47	132
2004	26	59	47	132
2005	26	59	47	132
2006	26	59	47	132
2007	26	59	47	132
2008	290	59	47	396
2009		1,309	47	1,356
2010			727	727

Note: The 6.875% notes are euro-denominated. Dollar proceeds from the issue in 2000 were $680, and the above interest and repayment amounts assume that the exchange rate between the euro and dollar is unchanged. The indenture of the issue, however, doesn't fix the exchange rate.

Source: 10-K and 10-Qs.

EXHIBIT 7A   **Comparison with the two largest land-based book retailers**

	1999	1998	1997
Barnes & Noble			
Total sales (billions)	$3.5	$3.0	$2.8
Total selling space in retail stores (millions of square feet)	15.1	13.8	
Gross margin	39%	39%	39%
Ordinary overhead exps. as % of sales	33%	33%	33%
ROE	16%	15%	
ROE excluding goodwill	22%	18%	
Inventory turnover	2.1	2.0	
Ratio of inventory to accounts payable (year-end)	1.8	1.9	
Borders			
Total sales (billions)	$3.00	$2.60	$2.3
Total selling space in retail stores (millions of square feet)	11.6	9.5	
Gross margin	39%	39%	39%
Ordinary overhead exps. as % of sales	34%	33%	33%
ROE	12%	14%	
ROE excluding goodwill	14%	16%	
Inventory turnover	1.7	1.7	
Ratio of inventory to accounts payable (year-end)	1.9	1.7	

Notes:
* Inventory turnover is an annualized figure calculated in the customary way: cost of goods sold divided by the average of beginning and ending inventory balances.
* Gross margin, overhead expense, and inventory turnover involve estimates made by the casewriter to make those figures comparable to Amazon. The problem is that Barnes & Noble and Borders include "occupancy costs" (i.e., rent, CAM charges, etc.) with cost of goods sold, and the estimates reassign occupancy costs to ordinary overhead expense.
* In addition to selling space in retail stores, Barnes & Noble and Borders each had about 1 million square feet of space in its distribution centers (from which it shipped merchandise to retail stores).

Source: Company 10-Ks

1 Amazon.com in the Year 2000

EXHIBIT 7B **Comparison with financially successful companies with low gross margins**

	1999	1998	1997
Wal-Mart			
Total sales (billions)	$165	$138	$118
Gross margin	21%	21%	21%
Ordinary overhead exps. as % of sales	16%	16%	16%
ROE	24%	22%	
Inventory turnover	7	6	
Ratio of inventory to accounts payable (year-end)	1.5	1.7	
Costco			
Total sales (billions)	$27	$24	$22
Gross margin	12%	12%	12%
Ordinary overhead exps. as % of sales	9%	9%	9%
ROE	16%	17%	
Inventory turnover	12	12	
Ratio of inventory to accounts payable (year-end)	1.2	1.2	

Notes:

* Inventory turnover is an annualized figure calculated in the customary way: cost of goods sold divided by the average of beginning and ending inventory balances.
* Neither of these companies had any significant amount of goodwill on their balance sheets.

Source: Company 10-Ks

EXHIBIT 8 **Lehman Brothers information: Amazon's cash flows ($ millions)**

Quarter	Operating cash flow	Capital expenditures	Free cash flows
Dec-97	7	(3)	4
Mar-98	(7)	(2)	(9)
Jun-98	2	(6)	(4)
Sep-98	(3)	(11)	(14)
Dec-98	39	(10)	29
Mar-99	(17)	(19)	(36)
Jun-99	(30)	(92)	(122)
Sep-99	(75)	(71)	(146)
Dec-99	31	(105)	(74)
Mar-00	(320)	(27)	(347)
	(373)	(346)	(719)

Source: Ravi Suria (Lehman Brothers), op. cit.

EXHIBIT 9 **Lehman Brothers information: Amazon's inventory turnover**

Quarter	Inventory turnover
Mar-98	8.5
Jun-98	8.1
Sep-98	8.3
Dec-98	10.3
Mar-99	7.9
Jun-99	6.0
Sep-99	4.0
Dec-99	4.0
Mar-00	2.9

Source: Ravi Suria (Lehman Brothers), op. cit.

EXHIBIT 10A **Amazon's 4.75% convertible note**

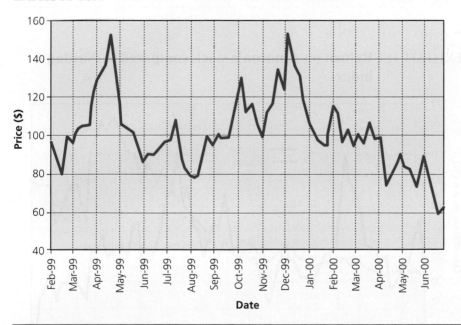

Source: Bloomberg

EXHIBIT 10B   **Amazon's 6.875% convertible note**

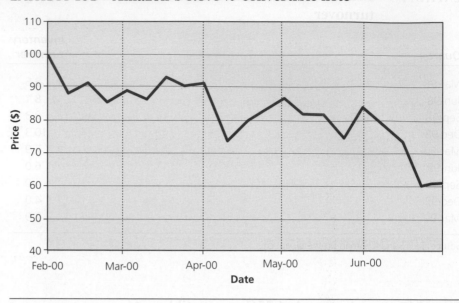

Source: Bloomberg

EXHIBIT 11   **Return on Amazon's stock compared to Nasdaq index**

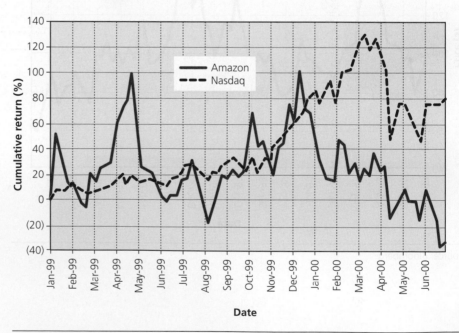

Source: Bloomberg

EXHIBIT 12A   Amazon.com: Income statements ($ millions)

	2000	2001
	Full year	**1st qtr.**
Sales	2,762	700
Cost of sales	(2,106)	(518)
Gross profit	656	182
Operating expenses		
Fulfillment	(415)	(98)
Marketing	(180)	(37)
Technology & content	(269)	(70)
General & administrative	(109)	(26)
Stock-based compensation	(25)	(3)
Amortization of goodwill & other intangibles	(322)	(51)
Impairment-related and other	(200)	(114)
Operating loss	(864)	(217)
Interest expense	(131)	(34)
Interest income	41	10
Other income (expense), net	(10)	(4)
Non-cash gains and losses, net	(142)	34
Net interest expense and other	(242)	6
Loss before equity in losses of equity-method investees	(1,106)	(211)
Equity in losses of equity-method investees	(305)	(13)
Loss before change in accounting	(1,411)	(224)
Cumulative effect of change in accounting principle	—	(10)
Net loss	(1,411)	(234)
Average no. of shares o/s (millions)	351	357

Source: Company 10-Ks and 10-Qs

EXHIBIT 12B Amazon.com: Balance sheets ($ millions)

	2000	2001
	Dec. 31	31-Mar
Current assets		
Cash	823	447
Marketable securities	278	196
Inventories	174	156
Prepaid expenses etc.	86	57
	1,361	856
Fixed assets	367	304
Goodwill & other purchased intangibles	255	204
Investments in equity-method investees	52	23
Other equity investments	40	29
Other	60	54
Total assets	2,135	1,470
Current liabilities		
Accounts payble	485	257
Accrued expenses & other current liabilities	342	234
Unearned revenue	131	94
Current portion of long-term debt	17	19
	975	604
Long-term debt	2,127	2,119
Stockholders' equity		
Common stock	1,326	1,274
Accumulated deficit	(2,293)	(2,527)
	(967)	(1,253)
Total liabilities & stockholders equity	2,135	1,470

Source: Company 10-Ks and 10-Qs

EXHIBIT 12C Amazon.com: Cash flow statements ($ millions)

	2000	2001
	Full year	1st qtr.
Operating activities		
Net loss	(1,411)	(234)
Depreciation & amortization of fixed assets	84	23
Amort. of deferred stock-based compensation	25	3
Equity in losses of equity-method investees	305	13
Amortization of goodwill & other intangibles	322	51
Impairment-related and other	200	62
Amortization of previously unearned revenue	(108)	(33)
Non-cash investment gains and losses, net	143	(34)
Non-cash interest expense and other	25	7
Cumulative effect of change in accounting principle	—	10
	(415)	(132)
Changes in operating assets & liabilities		
Inventories	46	20
Prepaid expenses & other current assets	(9)	27
Accounts payable	22	(230)
Accrued expenses & other current liabilities	94	(58)
Unearned revenue	98	18
Interest payable	34	(52)
	285	(275)
Net cash provided (used) in operating activities	(130)	(407)
Investing activities		
Sales of marketable securities	546	94
Purchases of marketable securities	(184)	(30)
Purchase of fixed assets	(135)	(19)
Investments in equity-method investees and other investments	(63)	—
Net cash used in investing activities	164	45
Financing activities		
Proceeds from long-term debt	681	10
Repayment of long-term debt	(17)	(5)
Financing costs & other	(16)	—
Proceeds from issuance of capital stock and exercise of stock options	45	6
Net cash provided by financing activities	693	11
Effect of exchange-rate changes on cash	(38)	(24)
Net increase (decrease) in cash	689	(375)
Cash at beginning of period	133	822
Cash at end of period	822	447
Supplemental cash flow information		
Stock issued in connection with business acqs.	32	—
Fixed assets acquired under financing agreements	9	2
Equity securities received for commercial agreements	107	—
Cash paid for interest	92	86

Source: Company 10-Ks and 10-Qs.

2 KarstadtQuelle AG

C redit analyst Felix Brüggen glanced through the latest annual and quarterly reports of the German publicly listed company KarstadtQuelle AG. He was given the task to assess the creditworthiness of KarstadtQuelle, determine whether the company could bear the burden of another loan, and, if so, determine the maximum loan amount and set the appropriate interest rate on the new loan. KarstadtQuelle was a German diversified company that operated 90 German department stores and 32 German sport stores, provided European mail order services under the brand names neckermann.de and Quelle, held a 50 percent stake in tour operator Thomas Cook AG, and held investments in real estate through its subsidiary Karstadt Immobilien.[1] The company had been close to bankruptcy in 2004, but had shown a remarkable turnaround in 2005. In March 2006, KarstadtQuelle announced that it was debt-free, which suggested that the company had been able to substantially improve its creditworthiness.

KarstadtQuelle in 2004[2]

In the second half of 2004, KarstadtQuelle was on the verge of bankruptcy. The company did not reach its financial targets for that year and struggled under the debt load it had built up over the years, while lacking access to new long-term financing. The main reasons for the company's problems, which KarstadtQuelle's (new) management outlined in the company's 2005 Annual Report, were mismanagement and difficult market circumstances. The poor financial situation required drastic measures. In 2004, KarstadtQuelle's Management Board changed composition – by replacing the managing and finance directors – and the company reorganized the Management Boards of many of its subsidiaries. In addition, the company negotiated a new three-year credit facility of €1.75 billion with a syndicate of 16 banks, agreed with its current shareholders to issue new shares for an amount of approximately €500 million, and issued €140 million in convertible bonds. These capital increases were supported by the announcement of a new restructuring plan that was to be carried out in fiscal 2005. During 2004, KarstadtQuelle's share price decreased, however, by 61 percent, from €19.70 to €7.60.

KarstadtQuelle in 2005

Fiscal year 2005 was labeled by management "the year of restructuring." KarstadtQuelle's restructuring program had the following components:

■ *Divestments in retail.* The company would strengthen its 88 larger department stores – with sales space above 8,000 square meters and total revenues of €4.5 billion – and divest its 77 smaller department stores – with sales space below 8,000 square meters and total revenues of €0.7 billion. It also planned to divest its specialty store chains,

Professor Erik Peek prepared this case. The case is intended solely as the basis for class discussion and is not intended to serve as an endorsement, source of primary data, or illustration of effective or ineffective management.

[1] Thomas Cook AG has been proportionally consolidated in KarstadtQuelle's financial statements.

[2] This and the following sections are primarily based on material from KarstadtQuelle's 2005 Annual Report, its Interim Reports of March 2006 and June 2006, and its press releases issued during 2004, 2005, and 2006.

such as sports stores RunnersPoint and GolfHouse. These divestments should help KarstadtQuelle to expand its high-margin products in the department store business.

■ *Focus within mail order.* In the mail order business, KarstadtQuelle would focus its efforts on growth in the specialty mail order segment and in the e-commerce segment.[3] The company would further strategically reorient its traditionally strong universal mail order business in Germany.

■ *Cost savings.* KarstadtQuelle expected to be able to achieve €210 million in cost savings in its department store business and €150 million in cost savings in its universal mail order business by the year 2006.

■ *Real estate.* The company considered segregating its real estate business from its department store (retail) business.

■ *Reorientation of the group.* KarstadtQuelle would streamline its portfolio, abandon marginal operations and outsource some of its processes in the retail business.

Although the financial and operational state of the company's mail order business appeared worse than anticipated, KarstadtQuelle's management had been able to make some important changes to the segment in 2005. Mail order companies Quelle and neckermann.de were converted into limited liability companies and started to operate separately under their own management to improve these subsidiaries' decision processes. In the mail order segment the company also positioned Quelle and neckermann.de in the market as two sharply distinct brands and combined several separately operating service units into one to reduce costs.

KarstadtQuelle also sold several specialty stores as well as its small department stores. The divestiture program also resulted in the sale of Karstadt Hypothekenbank AG to the company's pension fund. After the sale, Karstadt Hypothekenbank AG took over from KarstadtQuelle's finance companies the financing of the company's hire purchase business in its mail order segment, thereby helping KarstadtQuelle to derecognize its discounted installment receivables (in accordance with IAS 39). The sale of Karstadt Hypothekenbank reduced KarstadtQuelle's net non-current liabilities by approximately €1 billion. The sale of the company's marginal operations and smaller department stores yielded close to €1.1 million. In addition, Kartstadt Quelle sold and leased back its mail order logistics real estate at a price of over €400 million. As a result of the restructuring, KarstadtQuelle was able to reduce its workforce by roughly one-fifth, or 25,000 employees.

In KarstadtQuelle's 2005 Annual Report, management reported that although performance in the mail order segment was still below plan, the company had reached its targets. In 2005, sales had declined from €17.2 billion to €15.8 billion, but the company had been able to cut its net loss from €1.6 billion to €316 million. During the fiscal year 2005, KarstadtQuelle's share price increased by 68 percent, from €7.60 to €12.74, to imply a market value of €2.69 billion.

KarstadtQuelle in the first half of 2006

After the financial restructuring of the company in 2005, KarstadtQuelle's management considered the company's equity position too vulnerable. To reduce leverage further, the company sold its real estate portfolio – consisting of department stores, car parks, sport stores, and office buildings – for an amount of €4.5 billion. The real estate was sold to and leased back from an entity that was jointly owned by a subsidiary of Goldman Sachs – the

[3]Specialty mail order companies focus on selling one product type, such as baby products or fashion products, whereas universal mail order companies offer a broad assortment of product categories.

Whitehall Fund – and KarstadtQuelle. KarstadtQuelle had a participation of 49 percent in the joint entity but, as it reported, carried no other risks than arising from its equity contribution of €120 million. The operational management of the joint entity was in the hands of the Whitehall Fund. The first payment under the real estate transaction – €2.7 billion – was received on July 3, 2006. The second payment – the remaining €1.8 billion – would be received later in the year 2006.

According to KarstadtQuelle, the real estate transaction had several positive effects. First, it yielded a high short-term cash inflow that helped the company to quickly reduce its financial liabilities. Second, it improved important balance sheet ratios such as the equity-to-assets ratio. Third, it resulted in a high non-recurring income component for fiscal 2006. Fourth and finally, it led to a lasting improvement in pretax profits to the order of €100 million.

The company continued to restructure its business. It repositioned its department stores by distinguishing "Premium" stores that sold high-margin products at prime locations from "Boulevard" stores that focused on selling brands in the middle to higher price segment. Further, KarstadtQuelle increased its purchase volume in Asia and set up local design centers in Europe and Asia to develop fashionable and timely products. To facilitate procurement in Asia, the company signed an agreement to cooperate with the Chinese export company Li & Fung. These actions aimed to reduce purchase expenses and increase inventory turnover, thereby reducing working capital by an estimated €500 million. The proceeds from the real estate transaction further helped KarstadtQuelle to invest another €200 million in restructuring its universal mail order business.

In the first half of 2006, KarstadtQuelle managed to report a net profit of €558.1 million. During this half year, KarstadtQuelle's share price increased by 62 percent, from €12.74 to €20.59, to reach a market value of €4.34 billion.

Questions

1   When preparing a report that summarizes the main factors affecting KarstadtQuelle's creditworthiness, which factors should the credit analyst focus on? How do these factors affect KarstadtQuelle's creditworthiness?

2   Assess whether KarstadtQuelle could bear the burden of another €500 million loan. If so, what would be the appropriate interest rate on this new loan?

EXHIBIT 1 KarstadtQuelle's consolidated financial statements

INCOME STATEMENTS (€ thousands)

	Half year ending June 30, 2006	Year ending December 31, 2005	Half year ending June 30, 2005	Year ending December 31, 2004
Sales	6,474,551	15,845,032	7,166,102	17,199,007
Cost of sales and expenses for tourism services	(3,614,132)	(8,911,823)	(3,911,755)	(9,631,912)
Gross income	2,860,419	6,933,209	3,254,347	7,567,095
Other capitalized own costs	13,987	50,691	22,242	53,519
Operating income	1,315,470	1,102,555	388,286	819,669
Staff costs	(1,180,843)	(2,630,323)	(1,382,563)	(3,109,417)
Operating expenses	(2,321,642)	(5,152,129)	(2,245,903)	(5,575,730)
Other taxes	(10,702)	(29,344)	(13,644)	(30,262)
Earnings before interest, tax and depreciation and amortization (EBITDA)	676,689	274,659	22,765	(275,126)
Depreciation and amortization (not including amortization of goodwill)	(145,297)	(343,329)	(171,828)	(425,115)
Impairment loss	(507)	(48,193)	(57,550)	(101,641)
Earnings before interest, tax and amortization of goodwill (EBITA)	530,885	(116,863)	(206,613)	(801,882)
Amortization of goodwill	0	(8,399)	205	(152,446)
Earnings before interest and tax (EBIT)	530,885	(125,262)	(206,408)	(954,328)
Income from investments	2,740	(9,454)	2,259	1,314
Income from investments in associates	4,259	16,681	8,535	12,481
Net interest income	(192,055)	(292,953)	(153,537)	(326,863)
Other financial results	19,634	15,783	(12,911)	(165,371)
Earnings before tax (EBT)	365,463	(395,205)	(362,062)	(1,432,767)
Taxes on income	194,500	81,180	117,053	178,008
Earnings from continuing operations	559,963	(314,025)	(245,009)	(1,254,759)
Result from discontinued operations	0	(258)	(25,352)	(370,531)
Net profit/loss before minority interests	559,963	(314,283)	(270,361)	(1,625,290)
Profit/loss due to minority interests	(1,847)	(2,199)	(1,515)	(24)
Net loss after minority interests	558,116	(316,482)	(271,876)	(1,625,314)

2 KarstadtQuelle AG

EXHIBIT 1   KarstadtQuelle's consolidated financial statements *(continued)*

BALANCE SHEETS (€ thousands)

	Half year ending June 30, 2006	Year ending December 31, 2005	Half year ending June 30, 2005	Year ending December 31, 2004
Intangible assets	1,087,878	1,104,831	1,117,732	1,100,986
Tangible assets	1,061,660	2,452,839	2,659,840	2,786,185
Shares in associates	86,343	98,398	110,226	105,877
Other financial assets	624,494	535,220	1,032,739	1,405,772
Other non-current assets	96,764	94,167	129,746	116,313
Deferred taxes	220,891	228,249	283,529	164,914
Non-current assets	3,178,030	4,513,704	5,333,812	5,680,047
Inventories	1,547,838	1,621,095	1,700,643	1,823,904
Trade receivables	795,267	844,385	1,400,712	1,295,494
Tax receivables	127,316	50,430	89,381	61,800
Other receivables and other assets	1,011,858	1,139,128	1,046,039	911,201
Purchase price receivable from real estate transaction	2,690,203	0	0	0
Cash and cash equivalents and securities	770,550	707,163	657,504	661,156
Current assets	6,943,032	4,362,201	4,894,279	4,753,555
Assets classified as held for sale	481,506	262,658	1,942,263	1,209,587
Balance sheet total	10,602,568	9,138,563	12,170,354	11,643,189
Subscribed share capital	514,544	510,398	510,398	510,398
Reserves	790,711	(237,068)	(196,053)	58,663
Minority interests	12,192	16,745	31,595	26,783
Equity	1,317,447	290,075	345,940	595,844
Long-term capital of minority interests	0	0	53,203	58,983
Non-current financial liabilities	1,007,146	3,012,793	3,361,517	3,372,376
Other non-current liabilities	485,925	566,606	596,024	549,694
Pension provisions	886,923	906,756	859,101	891,911
Other non-current provisions	368,220	383,784	350,802	365,483
Deferred taxes	18,880	11,673	8,483	12,533
Non-current liabilities	2,767,094	4,881,612	5,229,130	5,250,980
Current financial liabilities	3,062,043	724,776	2,164,105	2,062,517
Trade payables	1,331,760	1,600,870	1,424,662	1,554,497
Current tax liabilities	180,695	201,746	151,775	229,840
Other current liabilities	1,405,913	768,855	1,286,692	799,186
Current provisions	506,277	609,677	564,313	626,136
Current liabilities	6,486,688	3,905,924	5,591,547	5,272,176
Liabilities from assets classified as held for sale	31,339	60,952	1,003,737	524,189
Balance sheet total	10,602,568	9,138,563	12,170,354	11,643,189

EXHIBIT 1 KarstadtQuelle's consolidated financial statements *(continued)*

CASH FLOW STATEMENTS (€ thousands)

	Half year ending June 30, 2006	Year ending December 31, 2005	Half year ending June 30, 2005	Year ending December 31, 2004
EBITDA	676,689	274,659	22,765	(275,126)
Profit/loss from the disposal of fixed assets	(906,419)	(155,154)	(24,278)	(1,304)
Profit/loss from foreign currency	(4,457)	(1,907)	3,038	4,919
Decrease of non-current provisions (not including pension and tax provisions)	(2,178)	(95,099)	(18,760)	(59,880)
Addition to (Utilization of) restructuring provision	(130,367)	255,853	(84,830)	583,809
Other expenses/income not affecting cash flow	146,904	168,307	98,454	146,161
Gross cash flow	(219,828)	446,659	(3,611)	398,579
Changes in working capital	(68,114)	1,006,822	(173,859)	93,576
Changes in other current assets and liabilities	317,002	(231,280)	114,760	165,831
Dividends received	1,165	13,278	2,803	24,958
Payments/refunds of taxes on income	(46,068)	(8,253)	(37,395)	(46,452)
Cash flow from operating activities	(15,843)	1,227,226	(97,302)	636,492
Cash flow from acquisitions/divestments of subsidiaries less cash and cash equivalents disposed of	79,572	250,388	10,080	(3,060)
Purchase of tangible and intangible assets	(81,127)	(258,785)	(84,686)	(331,475)
Purchase of investments in non-current financial assets	(140,295)	(7,953)	(69,020)	(83,283)
Cash receipts from sale of tangible and intangible assets	62,133	703,648	133,560	119,356
Cash receipts from sale of non-current financial assets	8,522	43,723	40,665	32,835
Cash flow from investing activities	(71,195)	731,021	30,599	(265,627)
Interest received	72,957	134,202	62,773	131,533
Interest paid	(185,698)	(377,162)	(190,584)	(331,834)
Pension payments	(54,135)	(62,272)	(90,365)	(95,867)
Cash receipts/payments under mortgage bond program and for (financial) loans	334,309	(1,546,621)	297,971	(192,959)
Payment of liabilities due under finance lease	(9,729)	(47,264)	(16,208)	(39,489)
Cash payments/cash receipts for dividends and capital increase	3,979	(1,520)	(571)	473,006
Cash flow from financing activities	161,683	(1,900,637)	63,016	(55,610)
Changes in cash and cash equivalents affecting cash flow	74,645	57,610	(3,687)	315,255
Changes in cash and cash equivalents due to changes in exchange rates or other changes caused by the consolidated companies	(11,258)	(14,856)	(1,020)	(14,367)
Cash and cash equivalents at the beginning of the period	707,163	653,162	662,211	352,274
Cash and cash equivalents at the end of the period	770,550	695,916	657,504	653,162

2 KarstadtQuelle AG

EXHIBIT 2   Excerpts from the notes to the consolidated financial statements – KarstadtQuelle's annual report 2005

Consolidation

In the year under review the shares In Karstadt Hypothekenbank AG were exchanged for shares held by the II.KarstadtQuelle Pension Trust e.V. In Quelle Neckermann Versand Finanz GmbH & Co. KG and Karstadt Hypothekenbank AG deconsolidated. During the year the company was treated as a disposal group and its assets and liabilities recognized under Assets qualified as held for sale and Liabilities in connection with assets classified as held for sale. Impairment of €51,440 thousand resulting within the year from estimated sales proceeds from company assets has proved to be no longer necessary in connection with this exchange.

Sale of receivables

Individual group companies are selling trade receivables to Karstadt Hypothekenbank AG, which was transferred to the II.KarstadtQuelle Pension Trust e.V. under the CTA program. Karstadt Hypothekenbank AG at the end of the fiscal year took over from the finance companies the purchase of receivables being sold by these companies under the ABS programs. In this connection, the sale of receivables was classified as an actual derecognition under IAS 39. International companies in mail order are continuing to sell under asset-backed securitization (ABS) transactions their receivables to a finance company, which refinances the purchases on the capital market. Under the ABS program the purchasers of these receivables withhold part of the purchase price as security until receipt of the payments. If there is sufficient likelihood of realization, the anticipated payment is shown as a separate financial asset.

The vendors must assume responsibility for collecting the debts. At the balance sheet date adequate provisions are set aside for these commitments. For the assumption of the risks and interim financing the vendors pay a program fee, which, depending on the classification of the sales, is shown as a true sale or a sale which does not qualify for derecognition under other operating expenses or interest.

Operating income

Amounts shown in € thousands	2005	2004
Income from the disposal of assets classified as held for sale	167,613	12,949
Income from advertising cost subsidies	154,738	169,702
Earnings from rental income and commissions	131,155	103,239
Income from charged-on goods and services	57,800	55,283
Income from the disposal of non-current assets	52,080	11,885
Income from the reversal of other liabilities	37,514	27,883
Income from exchange rate differences	28,157	44,121
Income from the reversal of other provisions	27,697	19,851
Income from deconsolidation	20,471	10,659
Income from other services	18,779	21,569
Income from the reversal of allowances	9,783	8,310
Other income	396,768	334,218
	1,102,555	819,669

Operating expenses

Amounts shown in € thousands	2005	2004
Logistics costs	1,431,003	1,459,007
Catalog costs	893,853	861,938
Operating and office/workshop costs	693,058	777,016
Advertising	615,761	648,103
Administrative costs	559,386	479,393
Restructuring costs	269,342	651,455
Allowances on and derecognition of trade receivables	223,506	256,577
Losses from the disposal of assets classified as held for sale	60,050	1,894
Outside staff	32,435	23,632
Expenses due to currency differences and losses	26,250	49,040
Losses from the disposal of fixed assets	4,491	21,636
Other expenses	342,994	346,039
	5,152,129	5,575,730

Net interest income

Amounts shown in € thousands	2005	2004
Interest costs from pension expense	(133,384)	(137,104)
Other interest and similar income	254,790	217,699
Other interest and similar expenses	(414,359)	(407,458)
	(292,953)	(326,863)

The previous year's value included non-recurring charges of €51.9 million from restructuring.

Through application of the new IAS 39 the Group's receivables sales were classified as non-disposal of receivables. Accordingly, the corresponding expenses from prefinancing of receivables (so-called program fees) are recognized under interest expenses. These amount to €55,641 thousand (previous year: €41,165 thousand) for the 2005 financial year. The previous year's amounts were adjusted accordingly for better comparability.

2 KarstadtQuelle AG

Leases

Finance lease agreements have a firmly agreed basic leasing period of between 20 and 25 years and include a purchase option for the lessee after expiry of the basic leasing period. Assets under finance lease agreements have a carrying amount of €237,783 thousand (previous year: €262,686 thousand) at the balance sheet date. These assets relate to buildings, aircraft and reserve engines where the carrying value of the future minimum lease payments covers the material purchase costs. For aircraft financing normally a purchase option for the residual value plus an amount equal to 25% of the amount by which the fair value exceeds the residual value exists after the expiry of the lease period. If the purchase option is not exercised, the aircraft is sold by the lessor. If the proceeds from the sale are lower than the residual value, the lessee must pay the difference to the lessor. The lessee is entitled to up to 75% of the amount by which the sales proceeds exceed the residual value.

The operating lease agreements comprise mainly building leases without purchase option or aircraft leases where the assessment of the criteria of IAS 17 resulted in classification as operating lease.

	Up to 1 year		1 to 5 years		Over 5 years	
Amounts shown in € thousands	**2005**	**2004**	**2005**	**2004**	**2005**	**2004**
Finance lease agreements:						
Lease payments due in future	38,328	65,875	320,653	185,498	138,313	131,161
Discount	(759)	(36,209)	(35,783)	(48,924)	(31,598)	(14,162)
Present value	37,569	29,666	284,870	136,574	106,715	116,999
Lease payments under subleases	1,152	0	4,606	0	5,758	0
Operating lease agreements:						
Lease payments due in future	343,359	311,629	919,291	863,627	1,221,619	842,697
Discount	(11,072)	(16,953)	(124,498)	(131,195)	(600,007)	(364,210)
Present value	332,287	294,676	794,793	732,432	621,612	478,487
Lease payments under subleases	23,847	22,694	63,318	43,098	75,363	15,940

Trade receivables

Breakdown of trade receivables by business segment (Amounts shown in € thousands)	2005	2004
Karstadt	82,441	41,324
Mail order	602,074	1,093,715
Thomas Cook	82,113	73,508
Services	76,626	79,287
Other	1,131	7,660
	844,385	1,295,494

In connection with the application of IAS 39 sales of receivables under ABS programs were not subject to any further disposals at the beginning of the 2005 financial year. Accordingly, the previous year's figures of €622 million have been adjusted to suit the change in recognition. The reorganization of the receivables sale program at home with the sale of receivables amounting to €613 million to Karstadt Hypothekenbank AG at the end of the financial year, however, resulted in an actual disposal and thus to a marked reduction in trade receivables.

To secure claims under a global agreement for the sale of receivables, security was provided to Karstadt Hypothekenbank AG on existing and future trade receivables.

Under the syndicated loan agreement and the second lien financing amounts totaling €243,414 thousand owed by customers to various Group companies were assigned as security for debtors' liabilities.

2 KarstadtQuelle AG

Financial liabilities

Amounts shown in € thousands	Up to 1 year		1 to 5 years		Over 5 years	
	2005	2004	2005	2004	2005	2004
Bank loans and overdrafts	231,438	734,047	797,776	694,086	326,934	469,513
Liabilities under leasing agreements	18,800	33,249	244,719	145,809	68,013	163,177
Other financial liabilities	474,538	1,295,221	200,511	677,130	1,374,840	1,222,661
Total	724,776	2,062,517	1,243,006	1,517,025	1,769,787	1,855,351

Interest-bearing bank loans and overdraft loans are recognized at the amount paid out less directly assignable issue costs. Financing costs, including premiums payable as repayments or redemption, are allocated with effect for income. Liabilities under lease agreements are shown at present value.

The terms and conditions of the facility were adjusted in December 2005 mainly with regard to the conclusion of the secondary loan facility explained below with regard to adherence to financial ratios. €275 million of the loan facility had been utilized at the balance sheet date. The financial ratios to be adhered to relate to adjusted EBITDA, interest coverage, debt coverage and the level of equity. For the mail order segment there is a further financial ratio relating to adjusted EBITDA.

To secure the Group's finances for the long term, in December of the financial year the KarstadtQuelle Group also agreed a further secondary loan facility amounting to nominally €309 million, which had been fully utilized by the balance sheet date. The security provided for the liabilities is for the most part identical with the security underlying the syndicated loan facility, although ranking below the syndicated facility.

The loans secured by mortgage bear interest rates between 2.75% p.a. and 7.24% p.a. at the balance sheet date. The syndicated loan facility taken up the previous year and the recently concluded second-ranking loan facility bear interest on the basis of EURIBOR (or LIBOR, if drawing in currencies other than euros) plus margin and regulatory costs. In the case of the syndicated loan facility the bullet facility is initially subject to a margin of 3.5% p.a., which will rise to 4.5% p.a. in 2006 and to 5.5% p.a. in 2007. For the seasonal facility and the revolving loan facility initially a margin of 3.75% p.a. has been agreed from December 10, 2005, for the period of one year. Thereafter under certain circumstances it will rise to 4.75% p.a. The second-ranking loan facility bears interest with a margin of 12%.

Financial liabilities also include liabilities to customers of the KarstadtQuelle Bank from savings deposits, night money, balances on card accounts, promissory notes and savings certificates amounting to €77,642 thousand.

Of first-ranking financial liabilities €484,675 thousand (previous year: €742,172 thousand) are secured by mortgages and €350,372 thousand by other rights. In addition, there is first-ranking mortgage security amounting to €1,249,465 thousand (previous year: €1,419,737 thousand) under the Karstadt Hypothekenbank AG's (Essen) mortgage bond program. Liabilities of €91,238 thousand proportionate (previous year €74,060 thousand) arising from real estate financing at Thomas Cook are likewise supported by mortgage or similar security.

KarstadtQuelle AG has undertaken a guarantee to the Karstadt Hypothekenbank AG, Essen, for loans of Karstadt Finance B.V., Hulst, Netherlands, amounting to €1.8 billion, which translates to €1.3 billion at the balance sheet date.

Under the agreed syndicated loan facility a partial land charge assignment declaration was agreed with real estate management companies, and the creation of overall land charges and in some cases binding security pledges in respect of land charges was agreed. Furthermore, shares in Thomas Cook AG and various fully consolidated Group companies and amounts due from customers of the various Group companies were assigned. Furthermore, unrecognized brands held by KarstadtQuelle AG, Karstadt Warenhaus GmbH, Quelle GmbH and neckermann.de GmbH were assigned as security for liabilities of KarstadtQuelle AG.

Liabilities of €350,273 thousand (previous year: €391,850 thousand) arising from aircraft financing are secured by aircraft mortgages or are subject to availability limitations resulting from the financing structure.

Leasing liabilities carried as liabilities are effectively secured by the lessor's rights to buildings or aircraft specified in the finance lease.

2 KarstadtQuelle AG

Pension provisions

The recognized amount from pension obligations results as follows:

Amounts shown in € thousands	Commitments financed from funds	Commitments financed from provisions	2005	2004
Present value of future pension commitments (DBO)	1,564,743	1,019,941	2,584,684	2,602,586
Unrecognized actuarial gains/losses	(71,678)	(117,610)	(189,288)	(72,217)
Unrecognized past service costs	(119)	(336)	(455)	(634)
Fair value of plan assets	(1,485,424)	0	(1,485,424)	(1,504,939)
	7,522	901,995	909,517	1,024,796
Pension provisions in connection with disposal groups	0	(2,761)	(2,761)	(132,885)
	7,522	899,234	906,756	891,911

Pension costs are as follows:

Amounts shown in € thousands	Commitments financed from funds	Commitments financed from provisions	2005	2004
Service costs	3,856	8,378	12,234	15,126
Interest costs	70,151	39,009	109,160	141,735
Expected return on plan assets	(84,723)	0	(84,723)	(83,865)
Actuarial gains/losses with effect on income	32	305	337	113,424
Past service costs	1,255	2,386	3,641	99
Income from changes in plans/expenses from deconsolidation	4,987	3,201	8,188	351
	(4,442)	53,279	48,837	186,168

Whereas the cost of pension claims acquired during the financial year is shown under staff costs, the interest and the expected return on plan assets and the actuarial losses affecting plan assets are recorded with effect for income and shown under financial results.

The composition of plan assets is calculated from the following table:

Amounts shown in € thousands	2005	2004
Real estate, incl. dormant holdings	987,966	1,091,060
Corporate investments	351,000	348,674
Financial resources	146,458	65,205
	1,485,424	1,504,939

The Group utilizes parts of real estate assets itself. The lease payments are made on the basis of usual market estimates. Furthermore, under their articles of incorporation the pension trusts may lend up to 10% of their assets back to the Group in the form of cash and cash equivalents. An amount of €72,982 thousand (previous year: €26,971 thousand) results here at the balance sheet date.

2 KarstadtQuelle AG

Other non-current provisions

Amounts shown in € thousands	Staff	Guarantees/ warranties	Contingent losses resulting from pending transactions	Restructuring effects	Other
As at 01.01.2005	31,866	958	298	235,295	34,659
Changes in consolidated companies	(123)	0	0	(626)	(128)
Currency differences	(8)	(2)	0	8	0
Recourse	(705)	(642)	276	(43,444)	(1,804)
Reversal	(13,283)	(23)	(248)	(6,704)	(678)
Appropriation	965	647	0	72,227	11,660
Reclassification acc. to IFRS 5	(285)	(1)	0	8,694	(701)
As at 31.12.2005	18,427	937	326	265,450	43,008

Staff provisions include provisions for severance payments and jubilee payments and death benefits. Other provisions relate mainly to litigation risks and restoration liabilities.

3 Home Depot, Inc. in the new millennium

On October 12, 2000, Home Depot, the largest and fastest growing Do-It-Yourself (DIY) home improvement and building supply retailer, and the third-largest retailer of any sort in the United States, shocked many investors by announcing that earnings in the third and fourth quarters of 2000 would be a good deal lower than expected. In response, the company's stock price experienced its largest one-day drop, falling 28% (to $35), which erased $33 billion from its market value.

Arthur Blank, Home Depot's CEO, said that the earnings shortfall was primarily the result of a slowing economy. In fact, retail stocks generally had been down all year, and when Home Depot made its announcement, other retail stocks fell as well. To many analysts, however, Home Depot had competencies that very few other retailers had. It was one of the most successful retailers in American history. From the fall of 1981, when the company went public, to the end of 1999, its stock had risen at a compound annual rate of 52%. During the decade of the 1990s, its diluted earnings per share had risen at a compound annual rate of 29%. On October 12, however, the company said that it expected earnings for the third quarter (ending at the end of October) to be only $.28 per share, compared with $.25 in the third quarter of 1999. For the fourth quarter (ending in January), it expected earnings to be $.26 or $.25, compared with $.25 in the fourth quarter of the previous year. For the full year, it expected earnings to be $1.16 or $1.17, compared with $1.00 in 1999.

The U.S. economy had experienced uninterrupted growth since 1992. Between June 1999 and May 2000, however, the Federal Reserve had raised interest rates six times—or a total of 1.75 percentage points—in an effort to slow the economy, and economists had been noticing some softening of overall consumer demand.

Because of the nature of Home Depot's business, many observers regarded it as, if not recession proof, fairly protected from the vicissitudes of the economy. It was primarily involved in selling materials that ordinary people used for home improvement projects. The company was undertaking several significant growth initiatives, and it wasn't clear whether the decline in the company's stock price was primarily a function of a slowing economy, a reaction to an overvaluation of the stock, or a reflection of possible problems with the company's strategy for the future. Despite a fourth quarter that was deemed to be the most challenging in the company's history, during which earnings declined 20% compared to the prior year's quarter, by the time Home Depot released financial results for the current fiscal year (fiscal 2000, ended January 31, 2001), the company's stock price had rebounded to $48. **Exhibit 1** provides a graph of Home Depot's stock price from January 1, 2000 through January 31, 2001. **Exhibit 2** compares changes in Home Depot's stock to those of the S&P 500 and the S&P Retail Stores index (a composite of 35 retail stocks) during the same period.

Research Associates Jeremy Cott and Jonathan Barnett prepared this case under the supervision of Professor Krishna Palepu. HBS cases are developed solely as the basis for class discussion. Cases are not intended to serve as endorsements, sources of primary data, or illustrations of effective or ineffective management.

History

Bernard Marcus and Arthur Blank founded Home Depot in 1978 in Atlanta, Georgia. They had been managing a chain of Handy Dan home improvement stores but thought that if they had to compete against a no-frills warehouse, they would be in trouble. So they started such a company themselves.

The company they founded revolutionized the do-it-yourself home improvement market in the United States. They opened stores that contained a huge assortment of building materials and home improvement products and targeted as customers both individual homeowners and small contractors. The stores *were* the warehouses, and they sold large volumes of goods at low prices. The really distinctive feature of Home Depot, however, was that it also provided knowledgeable customer service. Many salespeople had themselves worked in the building trades, and in any case they were all required to attend product knowledge training classes. Thus in 1988, *Fortune* magazine viewed Home Depot as "the only company that has successfully brought off the union of low prices and high service."[1] The company was thus able to make home improvement projects both less expensive and more understandable for many people.

Competitive advantages

Not only did Home Depot introduce the "Big-Box" method of hardware merchandising, but the firm's successful strategic union of low price, high assortment, high service, and a quality guarantee, drew scores of customers from smaller hardware stores and home centers, leaving many competitors with no option but to go out of business. In the face of mounting pressure from the Big-Box model, remaining industry participants sought to adopt a similar format, yet Home Depot's rapid proliferation and operational efficiency was overwhelming, triggering industry-wide consolidation.

As Home Depot grew in size, it garnered significant buying power over its suppliers. For example, Home Depot gained concessions in pricing, exclusive merchandise, and other benefits that were not available to smaller chains, and which contributed further to the retrenchment or dissolution of other home center competitors. The company earned a reputation for pressuring its suppliers who, lured by the opportunity to secure a purchase order commitment from the giant retailer, often went the extra yard to secure the relationship.

Home Depot's low-price, high-service strategy put continuous pressure on management to minimize operating expenses. While management minimized the cost of goods sold through aggressive negotiations with suppliers, the firm's geographic clustering strategy (also referred to as a market saturation strategy) allowed the firm to realize economies of scale in logistics, supply chain management, and advertising. Focused primarily on large metropolitan areas, the store clustering strategy simultaneously prevented smaller would-be competitors from securing premium sites and realizing similar gains in operating efficiency. While other home improvement retailers struggled to identify alternative sources of cost savings in order to compete, economies of scale in Home Depot's aggressive advertising, in turn, further entrenched the firm's positioning in the minds' of consumers.

In addition to the competitive advantages associated with its bargaining power and its store location strategy, Home Depot was also proactive in identifying and implementing best-practices that aided the bottom line. For example, the company has consistently stayed at the forefront of information systems technology. As early as 1990, all stores were connected via a proprietary satellite data communications network that provided for a fast and accurate exchange of information, and which expedited the firm's ability to respond

---

[1] Bill Saporito, "The Fix Is In at Home Depot," *Fortune*, February 29, 1988.

to market changes. A more recent example is Home Depot's Service Performance Improvement (SPI) program introduced in 2000. SPI is a series of programs designed to shift most of the handling of inventory to hours after the store is closed. As a result, the store is easier for customers to shop, products are more readily available, and Home Depot employees can focus all of their time on serving customers. Thus, SPI simultaneously increased sales productivity and customer satisfaction. In fiscal 2000, SPI milestones included a 28% increase in nighttime freight team productivity, and a 98% decrease in pallets left on the floor, creating a better shopping environment for customers.[2] As evidence of its commitment to rollout best practices as quickly as possible, Home Depot planned to implement the program in every store by year-end 2001.[3]

Home Depot's high-service offering was well received by customers and became an added source of competitive advantage. Met with a knowledgeable sales staff that included professional plumbers, electricians, carpenters, painters, and other experienced home improvement tradespeople, Home Depot customers who sought out advice at the start of a project often placed follow-up calls to that same advisor, as the store's policy encouraged, and were apt to make follow-on purchases from the same store. Home Depot's experience showed that high levels of customer satisfaction readily translated into high levels of customer loyalty, making it difficult for competitors to attract Home Depot's customers.

Financial and operating performance

Over the years the company's financial and operating performance had been extraordinary. **Exhibit 3** shows its return on book equity, and the decomposition of that return on equity, from 1986 through 2000. **Exhibit 4** shows various measures of operating performance over the same period.

The company's stock price had risen dramatically over the years. There were, however, significant variations in stock returns from year to year. **Exhibit 5** shows annual changes in returns on the company's stock for the past decade, along with comparable data for the S&P 500. It also shows annual figures for earnings per share figures and the number of common shares outstanding. Finally, **Exhibit 6** provides detailed income statements, balance sheets, and cash flow statements for the past few years. As of the end of 1999 the company was by far the largest home improvement retailer in the country. (The second-largest, Lowe's, was about half Home Depot's size.) It operated 930 stores, almost all of them in the United States and Canada. The company was planning on 21%–22% annual growth in stores over the next several years, so that the number of stores by the end of 2003 would total over 1,900.

Macroeconomic factors

During the period in which Home Depot had existed, the home improvement industry in the United States had grown at an annual rate of about 6%, or slightly slower than the U.S. economy as a whole. In 1998, however, it grew about 10.4% and in 1999 about 7.3%—which exceeded the economy as a whole. In June 2000, with the expectation of some slowing in the economy, the Home Improvement Research Institute projected average nominal growth in the industry of about 4.5% a year over the next several years (see **Exhibit 7**).

The home improvement industry was generally thought to have benefited in recent years from low interest rates, strong housing turnover, rising home ownership, and increases in discretionary income. During the recession of 1990–1991 Home Depot experienced only a small decline in same-store sales, but at that point it occupied a far smaller share of the market. In 1995 macroeconomic factors evidently had a greater impact. Between February

---

[2]Ann F. Dabrowski, *Home Depot*, Lehman Brothers Global Equity Research report, February 20, 2001.

[3]Home Depot 2000 Annual Report, *Letter to Shareholders*, February 19, 2001.

1994 and January 1995, 30-year mortgage interest rates increased from 7.15% to 9.15% (a 20% increase). By contrast, in full-year 1990, 1991, 1992, 1993, 1996, 1997, and 1998, they declined. In October 1998, they reached a 31-year low of 6.5%. In May 2000, however, they had climbed up to 8.6%, before falling a bit below 8% in the fall.

Management changes

Over the years, Bernard Marcus and Arthur Blank had generally worked closely together. To some people they seemed, in terms of the decisions they made, almost interchangeable. In 1997, however, Blank succeeded Marcus as CEO of the company, with Marcus remaining as chairman. (Marcus was 68 years old in 1997; Blank was 13 years younger.) Blank commented in 1999: "My role is certainly very different than Bernie's was in the earlier days of our company. Back then, we were just trying to open the stores. Now the role is much more complex because we're thinking about how to drive deeper into the industry and how to serve customers differently in other segments of the industry."[4]

Fiscal 2000 witnessed yet another management succession. In a somewhat rare move in the retailing industry, Home Depot went outside the business in recruiting Robert Nardelli to succeed Arthur Blank as President and CEO. Nardelli was formerly the President and CEO of GE Power Systems, a division of General Electric. Blank, in turn, joined Marcus as Co-Chairman of the Board.

Style of operating

The company never seemed to regard the way it operated as settled. It spoke fairly often of "reexamining" or "reviewing" certain procedures and practices, and "testing" or "experimenting" with new ones. It would typically try out new products or procedures in a small number of stores, and only after it saw the results there would it extend them to many more stores.

Decision-making regarding the location of new stores also had a distinctive character. Stores existed in almost all states in the United States, as well as in all Canadian provinces. Some of the new stores the company opened were in new markets for the company (new regions or metropolitan areas). However, in recent years about two-thirds of new stores were opened in existing markets. Company management had specific reasons for this:

> In existing markets, we believe a number of Home Depot stores are operating at or above their optimum capacity. To increase customer service levels and enhance long-term market penetration, we often open new stores near the edge of the market areas served by existing stores. While these openings may initially have a negative impact on comparable store-for store sales, we believe this "cannibalization" strategy increases customer satisfaction and overall market share by reducing delays in shopping, increasing utilization by existing customers and attracting new customers to more convenient locations.[5]

The company had for years offered special services in its stores closely related to the products it sold. For example, there were brief courses—"how-to clinics"—to help customers in carrying out projects (e.g., installing tile, organizing closets). There were also longer, four-week courses that were part of what the company called Home Depot University. (About 50,000 customers took these longer courses in 1999.) Through a closely related operation, customers could also rent trucks on an hourly basis if they had bulky

---

[4]Patti Bond, "Executive Pushes New Concepts," *Cox News Service*, August 9, 1999.
[5]1999 10-K.

purchases that they needed to transport. The company also offered proprietary credit cards, which accounted for 17% of all sales. (During 1999 it also began testing a program that would allow customers to apply for unsecured loans to make large purchases in its stores.)

Competition

Among home improvement retailers that sold primarily to do-it-yourself customers, Home Depot's principal competitor was Lowe's, which had annual sales of $18.8 billion. Lowe's operated 650 stores at the end of 2000 and planned to add 115–120 new stores in 2001.[6] Lowe's began in 1946 with small stores in rural towns. In the mid-1990s, however, it began to copy Home Depot's model, opening huge, warehouse-type stores in metropolitan markets, complete with how-to clinics for its customers. Lowe's sold some product lines that Home Depot didn't and also tried to appeal more to women shoppers, with wider aisles and brighter lighting than Home Depot. In certain markets Lowe's and Home Depot went head to head with each other. Some of their stores were virtually within eyesight of each other. (**Exhibit 8** shows summary data for Lowe's for 1997–2000.)

The next largest competitors—Menards and HomeBase—were far smaller, but they were geographically more focused. Menards, which had annual sales of about $4 billion, operated solely in several midwestern states and was said to have a loyal customer base. In the greater Milwaukee area, for instance, Menards' share of the home improvement market in 1998 was 35%; Home Depot's was 15%. HomeBase, which had annual sales of about $1.5 billion, operated solely in several western states. Its stores were as large as Home Depot's—averaging over 100,000 square feet—and 50 of them were located in California (where Home Depot had 122 sites).

When Home Depot began growing in the 1980s its most important competitor was Hechinger, which was considered "the premium home-improvement chain by which Wall Street measured every other chain."[7] Hechinger had historically operated a chain of upscale community hardware and building-supply stores that were known for very good customer service, but when it tried to follow Home Depot into the "big box" warehouse format, it lost out in market after market. In 1999, after years of declining performance, it went out of business. A customer visiting one of its stores during the waning days of the company said: "It's obvious they don't put anything into employee training. There are good people there who are just not prepared. If I needed anything serious I'd go to Home Depot."[8]

Redefinition of the market

Home Depot reports noted that the company's name was "synonymous" with home improvement. Total home improvement product sales in the United States totaled $159 billion in 1999. That would make Home Depot's market share close to 24%.

In 1997, however, the company engaged in what it called a "redefinition" of its industry. Most of its sales came from do-it-yourself customers. Product sales for that market, it said, totaled about $100 billion in the United States in 1997. However, product sales to professional customers (e.g., contractors, electricians, plumbers, landscapers, property maintenance managers) represented an even larger market. It totaled approximately $265 billion in the United States in 1997. Excluding the "heavy industrial" sector, which the company said it didn't serve, the professional market totaled about $215 billion. Of that market, the company said, its share was less than 4%.

[6]Lowe's Companies 2000 Annual Report.

[7]Erica Johnston, "The Region in Review," *Washington Post*, September 12, 1999.

[8]Stephanie Stoughton, "Hechinger Files For Bankruptcy Protection," *Washington Post*, June 12, 1999.

3 Home Depot, Inc. in the New Millennium

Thereafter the company would refer to its relevant market as something a lot broader than the market with which it had historically been associated—residential home repair and remodeling by do-it-yourself customers. It now said its market consisted of "all sales of home improvement and other housing and building-related products for new and existing homes." And it said that it was developing long-term strategies with this view of the market in mind.[9]

At the end of 1998 the company said its total market was $365 billion. This included the "heavy industrial" sector. At the end of 1999 it said that, although it couldn't measure its market share precisely, it estimated it was about 8.9%. It also said that it expected to increase its North American market share to 18% by the end of 2003.[10]

Growth initiatives

The company had a variety of growth initiatives in the works. It was pursuing growth in terms of customer groups, product categories, store formats, store location, and sales channels.

Customer groups

The customer group with which Home Depot had for years been associated was non-professional, do-it-yourself (DIY) customers. In recent years, however, it had shifted to a triple-customer strategy, which also included:

Buy-it-yourself customers

The company was making increased efforts to serve the needs of what it called buy-it-yourself (BIY) customers, people who wanted to select the materials that would go into their homes but who wanted someone else to actually install them. The company already offered a number of installation services and was in the process of adding new services of this sort for roofing, vinyl siding, and replacement windows. (The company arranged for these services through approximately 6,200 third-party contractors, from whom it collected a fee.) "As the population ages," the company said, "we expect more customers will want products installed for them." The total market for installation services in the United States was about $75 billion. The company said that it was about to surpass Sears Roebuck as the largest installer of home improvement products but that it still had less than 2% of the installation market. It therefore regarded this as a terrific opportunity. It expected its installation services to increase at least 40% a year over the next few years.

Professional customers

The company was also working hard on expanding its share of the market for professional customers (e.g., contractors, electricians, plumbers, landscapers, property maintenance managers). The market for professional customers was huge, and it also involved a greater propensity for repeat business. Thus, for example, the company was increasing the availability in its stores of products packaged in "job lot" quantities; it was providing customer service geared specifically to professionals through a "Pro Service Desk" in many of its stores; it was doing mass mailings of catalogues containing over 15,000 products of particular interest to facility maintenance managers and the building trades. In addition, in late 1999 it acquired a company named Apex Supply, which was a wholesaler of plumbing, air conditioning, and related products geared to professional customers. "Through this acquisition," the company said, "we believe we will increase our penetration of the

[9]Home Depot 1998 Annual Report.
[10]Home Depot 1999 Annual Report.

professional plumbing trades and be able to handle special orders for plumbing products more efficiently in Home Depot stores."

Company management recognized that the needs of professional customers were quite different from the needs of its do-it-yourself customers. Thus it claimed that it "experimented" with certain changes geared to professional customers in its stores before fully implementing them in order "to ensure that the do-it-yourself customer is not disadvantaged."[11] National "rollout" of the "pro initiative" was expected to take place over the next three years. At the start of 2000 it was operating in 110 stores.

In 1999 the analyst at Deutsche Banc Alex. Brown, Dan Wewer, thought, "the pro business will probably influence [Home Depot's] sales and profitability more than any of the other initiatives."[12] At the same time, the professional segment of the business was apt to be more cyclical than the DIY segment.

Product categories

The store was always in the process of reviewing and revising its product offerings. Occasionally, however, it made some significant changes. In 1999, for example, the company began selling major appliances (e.g., ovens, refrigerators, dishwashers) at 135 of its stores and said that it expected to be selling them in all of its stores by the end of 2000. (It actually stocked in the stores only "the more popular" items but provided computer kiosks at which customers could special-order many more items.) It said that it regarded appliances as a natural extension of the products and services it was already selling and a way of "extending the trusting relationship" it had with customers.

In 1999 Home Depot acquired a company named Georgia Lighting, a specialty lighting designer, distributor, and retailer. Management believed that the acquisition would "strengthen our sourcing, training, and merchandising in lighting" in its stores.

In an appeal to both do-it-yourself and professional customers, the company was also expanding a tool rental service. It already had 10 different categories of tools that it rented on an hourly, weekly, or monthly basis. Company management believed that this service "increased the sales of related merchandise without reducing the sales of equipment similar to that available for rental." This service was growing fast. At the end of 1998 the tool rental service existed in 46 stores; at the end of 1999, 150 stores; and the company expected the service to be available in 350 stores by the end of 2000. (It expected the service would ultimately exist in 60% of all of its stores.)

Store formats

The store format with which Home Depot was primarily associated was the warehouse-type store that carried a huge assortment of home improvement products. The company was now, however, about to move forward with a very different store format. This was the Expo Design Center stores, which targeted customers interested in carrying out major home decorating projects.

Expo Design stores were often located right next to a warehouse store and were almost as large. Expo Design stores, however, sold higher-end products and services. They carried much less inventory than the warehouse stores. About 80% of the floor space consisted of sample displays of how different rooms (e.g., a kitchen or bedroom or bathroom) might look when remodeled. If a customer was interested in a major home decorating project, he or she would pay a retainer fee to get started, and store employees would work with the customer to handle every aspect of the remodeling process. The goal was for each project to generate $10,000 or more worth of products and services. As a business model,

[11] 1997 Annual Report.

[12] Patti Bond, "Executive Pushes New Concepts," *Cox News Service*, August 9, 1999.

the Expo stores involved—compared with the warehouse stores—less inventory, higher gross margins, higher payroll expense, and probably a greater sensitivity to cyclical changes in discretionary income.

Home Depot opened its first Expo Design store in 1991 and added a few more in the next few years. They were initially treated as a kind of laboratory, and, over the years, the company made many changes in their size and format. By the end of 1998 there were 8 of these stores. Then in 1999 the company added 7 more, and it said it planned to be operating about 200 of them within 5 to 6 years.

The company had also begun testing a much smaller store format, one that was meant to satisfy customers' needs for smaller projects. These stores would be about one-third the size of the big stores, would be in more "convenient" locations, and would operate not under the Home Depot name but under the name Villager's Hardware. (They would compete with neighborhood hardware stores like TrueValue and Ace Hardware.) In 1999 the company opened two of these smaller stores in New Jersey and planned to open two more in 2000. Blank said that this store concept would be in "test mode" for an unspecified period of time.

International growth

The company was beginning to expand internationally. In 1998 it opened two stores in Chile and one in Puerto Rico. In 1999 it added two more in Chile and another in Puerto Rico.[13] (The Chilean stores it operated as a joint venture with a Chilean department store. Home Depot controlled two-thirds of the equity.) Over the next few years it planned to open several additional stores in Chile and Argentina. "Every day," Blank said in March 1999, "we learn more about serving the diverse needs of customers in other areas of the world. We are also learning that the Home Depot culture is, indeed, transferable, and customer service is valued around the world."[14]

How far the company would go with international expansion, however, wasn't clear. In August 1999 Blank said that "international growth is going to be very important in the next 5 to 15 years. We'll be planting seeds in the next 5 years, maybe in the Far East, or it could be in Europe." He noted some potential problems with this, however. "There are challenges in all of our growth initiatives, but the international realm is the most complex because of real estate and the logistics of the supply chain. Obviously, there are language and cultural differences to overcome, too."[15]

Alternative channel

The company was in the process of developing its internet site. The site was meant, in the first place, to provide people with information about home improvement projects (e.g., a calculator to estimate the amount of material a person would need). The company was also going to sell products over the internet, but it was moving into this only gradually, and it regarded the internet not as an alternative sales channel but as a sales channel that would be additional or complementary to its physical stores. So far its e-commerce was in operation only in a few metropolitan markets: orders placed over the internet were being fulfilled from the company's physical stores, and customers could choose to pick them up at the stores or have them delivered. Arthur Blank claimed, however, that the website would eventually be the "world's largest e-commerce site in our industry."[16]

[13]For an extended account of Home Depot's considerations in opening its first stores in Chile, see Clifford Krauss, "Foreign Expansion: Well-Planned or Ill-Timed?" *New York Times*, September 6, 1998.

[14]1998 Annual Report.

[15]Patti Bond, "Executive Pushes New Concepts," *Cox News Service*, August 9, 1999.

[16]Debbie Howell, "Home Depot Touts Pro, E-Tail Initiatives," *National Home Center News*, June 19, 2000.

Potential problems

The company's growth plans involved some risks. The following describes a few of them.

Market saturation

One risk was the possibility of over saturation of certain big-city markets. Home Depot and Lowe's were both planning on opening a lot of new stores in the United States in the next few years, and many of them would be in markets that they were already in. These markets were seen as extremely attractive, but there was a question of how many stores they could support. In the Atlanta, Georgia, area, for example, there were 43 Home Depot, Lowe's, Ace Hardware, and True Value stores within 20 miles of each other. In Portland, Oregon, Home Depot was planning in 2000 to increase the number of stores it had from 7 to 13. Lowe's was in the process of constructing 2 large stores there. HomeBase wasn't planning any additions but already had 4 stores there. In the Dallas/Fort Worth area, Home Depot had 30 stores, while Lowe's had 14. Lowe's had been in the Dallas market for just a few years, and observers noted that when it moved in, prices at home improvement stores fell.

Different customer groups

Home Depot was a "category killer," but there were components of its product mix that other companies addressed in a more focused way. For example, national and regional wholesalers of electrical products, who sold to professional customers, believed that they could offer more than Home Depot—in terms of a broader and deeper inventory, more knowledgeable sales help with technical questions, and reliable delivery. In their view, "Home Depot, for all its high-profile positioning as a source of supply for professional contractors, still focuses primarily on the fastest-moving items." Some of these wholesalers found that "their customers still needed more than that."[17]

The example of one company demonstrated the problems in pursuing a "dual-customer" strategy. A regional seller of home improvement products named National Home Centers opened stores in the late 1970s that were geared primarily to professional contractors. In 1983 it began marketing to both professional contractors and do-it-yourself customers. In 1998, however, it shifted its focus back to professional contractors, saying that it couldn't adequately compete in both markets.

Appliances

Home Depot's chairman, Bernard Marcus, said that the company planned to eventually be number one in the retail market for major appliances. At the moment, Sears had about 30%, or $6 billion, of the market; it offered on its premises a broad product assortment; and it also maintained an extensive service network. Circuit City had recently given up on selling appliances, which freed up about 5% of the market. Wal-Mart, however, had announced that it was entering the market along with Home Depot, and both of those companies intended to sell most appliances through computer kiosks in their stores. (Home Depot's current market share was about 3%.)

Cross-selling

There was also a question of how much cross-selling, or bundling of products and services, Home Depot could successfully handle. Its big stores were already, in a sense, department stores (what people in the past might have bought at the lumber shop, the paint shop, the wallpaper shop, and so on), but the company was now taking this concept much farther (e.g., providing installation services, selling appliances). Huge financial corporations like

[17]Jim Lucy, "The Super Influencials," *Broadcast Engineering*, May 1999.

Citicorp were basing much of their strategy on cross-selling. In order to be successful at cross-selling, however, companies had to be able to truly integrate different products within a given organizational structure. In addition, the increasing availability of information through the internet made it easier for consumers to locate providers of different products and services on their own.

Employees

Home Depot ended 1999 with 201,000 employees. It had long regarded high-quality customer service as one of the keys to its success. The company planned, however, on more than doubling the number of stores over the next four years. It claimed that attracting good "associates" wasn't difficult, but the challenges of maintaining high levels of customer service over a far larger market base could be substantial.

Macroeconomy

Naturally, the macroeconomy was a wild card. The company had historically claimed that its fortunes were relatively insulated from changes in the macroeconomy, but the record suggested that that might not be the case. (See **Exhibit 2**.)

The view of stock analysts

In the previous year or two, sell-side analysts had generally been supportive of Home Depot's various growth initiatives (e.g., going more after professional customers, expanding the Expo Design store format, adding to its product line, opening some sites in other countries, developing internet business). There occasionally were expressions of concern about the possible saturation of certain big-city markets, particularly given the competition from Lowe's. However, large parts of the country weren't remotely near any Home Depot or Lowe's store, and analysts were aware that Home Depot and Lowe's generally took a certain amount of market share away from other businesses and that they helped to actually expand the market (by making home-improvement projects less expensive and more understandable for many people).[18]

In the previous 10 months, however, there had been very different views among analysts about the appropriate valuation of the company's stock. The following provide some examples.

- Raymond James report on 12/29/99, when the stock price had just reached its all-time high of $68. The price was at that point 70 times trailing earnings and 56 times the analyst's estimated earnings for the year 2000. He expected an earnings growth rate of 25% over the next several years. He said that, in his view, Home Depot was the best-managed retailer in the country, if not the world. It continued to have, he believed, great fundamentals. But at the current stock price, he essentially regarded it as overvalued. Interestingly, he also noted that company management had "conditioned the Street to expect it to beat [estimated] numbers."

- Credit Suisse/First Boston report on 2/25/00, when the stock was trading at $54. The analyst noted that the market had just had a "tepid" reaction to the company's announcement of fourth quarter results, even though they exceeded consensus estimates by a bit. He said that this reflected a general concern over interest rates and the Federal Reserve's intent to slow consumer spending, which would hurt most retailers. He thought that Home Depot's ability to continue to gain market share and increase margins would, however, offset some of the slowdown in consumer spending. He had

[18]SalomonSmithBarney's report on Home Depot, dated December 2, 1998, contains a detailed analysis of the possibility of market saturation.

positive comments about all of the company's growth initiatives. He regarded the "pro initiative" (the effort to increase sales to professional customers) as the company's most important growth initiative, thought that it could eventually increase sales by 7% to 10% in each store where it was operating, but also believed that it wasn't yet operating in enough stores to have a material impact on earnings growth. He expected an earnings growth rate of 23% over the next several years, an EPS of $1.25 in 2000, and a 25% increase in the stock price over the next 12 months.

■ Morgan Stanley Dean Witter report on 3/1/00, when the stock was trading at $55. The analyst expected earnings growth rate over the next several years of 22%. Her EPS estimate for 2000 was $1.25. She had positive comments on all of the company's growth initiatives. She thought that rising interest rates would have some impact on the company. Nevertheless, she thought the current P/E of 44 (relative to 2000 estimated earnings) would be maintained, and she expected an 18% increase in the stock price over the next 12 months.

■ CIBC World Markets report on 4/12/00, when the stock was trading at $66. He noted that the stock was at that point trading at 66 times trailing earnings and 53 times his estimated earnings for the year 2000 (which was $1.25). He noted that the latter was twice the multiple for the S&P 500 (which was 26 times estimated earnings). He expected an earnings growth rate of 25% over the next few years—although, given the strength of the company's growth initiatives, he felt that it might exceed that. He noted that the Fed had been raising interest rates in an effort to slow the economy down. He disputed the analogy, however, to the last period of rising interests (1994–1995) and the negative impact that that evidently had on Home Depot's performance. Things were different now, in his view. For example, the company's growth initiatives had a lot of potential; consumer spending remained strong; the company's greater purchasing clout now would help it maintain gross margins; the company's competitive position had improved with the weakening of smaller competitors. Thus he was bullish on the stock, with a 12-month price target roughly 30% higher than its current price.

■ Lehman Brothers report on 5/16/00, when the stock was trading at $56. Like other analysts, he expected an earnings growth rate of 25% over the next few years. He noted that the stock was currently trading at a 45 times his estimated EPS for 2000 (which was $1.25). He noted that the P/E multiple of 45 represented a 79% premium to the S&P 500 and a 81% premium to his long-term estimated growth rate for the company of 25%. He regarded this valuation as "attractive."

■ A.G. Edwards report on 8/22/00, when the stock was trading at $50. This analyst was cautious about the stock, even though he regarded Home Depot as a great company. He noted that the annual growth rate in the company's earnings over the last 10 years had averaged about 30%, and he now expected a more moderate growth rate of about 25% a year. He therefore anticipated a contraction of the then-current P/E multiple of 41 (based on his estimated EPS for 2000, which was $1.25).

■ SalomonSmithBarney report on 8/23/00, when the stock was trading at $50. This analyst was also cautious about the stock, even though he also regarded Home Depot as a great company. He expected a deceleration in the company's earnings growth to about 25% a year. He thought this would occur primarily because of the macroeconomic environment—higher interest rates and a slowing economy. He noted that the stock was currently trading at a P/E multiple of 41 (based on his estimated EPS for 2000, which was $1.25) but that the average multiple for the company during the 1990s had been about 32. He also noted that the company's P/E-to-growth ratio was currently about 1.5 (based on earnings for the next 12 months and assuming a long-term earnings growth rate of 25%) but that, over the last 10 years, the company's P/E-to-growth ratio had averaged about 1.2. The lowest such ratio for the company occurred in late 1995, when it was 0.7. He thought that the current economic environment for housing-oriented businesses like Home Depot was similar to that in 1995 (e.g., a lagging effect from rising mortgage interest rates), and he noted that in 1995 Home Depot experienced a sharp deceleration in same-store sales increases. He was confident that the stock would not move down to the valuation level reached in late 1995. The company's business was, in his view, too outstanding for that. Nevertheless, he was cautious about the stock's near-term prospects. He added that he wasn't downgrading Lowe's stock as well because Lowe's stock didn't have nearly as high a valuation.

Prospects

Several months earlier, in the spring of 2000, Arthur Blank acknowledged that the company's share price had already suffered to some extent because of concerns about rising interest rates, but he said he wasn't concerned about these short-term dips. He continued to expect 23% to 25% growth in earnings per share over the next several years. "At the end of the day," he said, "we feel our prospects are very good. Essentially what we've done for the last 21 years is what we'll continue to do."[19]

Questions

1   What is your estimate of the intrinsic value of Home Depot's stock as of February 1, 2001?

2   What set of assumptions regarding Home Depot's future growth rate, return on equity, and cost of equity consistent with its observed stock price of $48.20 on February 1, 2001?

---

[19]Patti Bond, "Home Depot: Retailer Plans to Stick to Usual Winning Script," *Atlanta Journal and Constitution*, May 21, 2000.

EXHIBIT 1 **Home Depot's stock price**

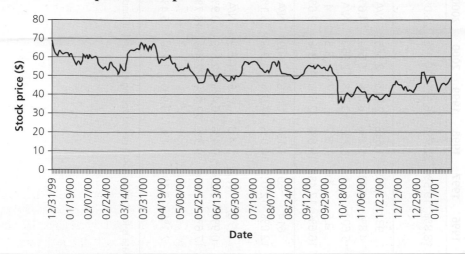

Source: Bloomberg; Federal Reserve; *The Wall Street Journal*. Date as of early October 2000: Home Depot's beta: 1.09 Yields on Treasury securities: 30-day: 6.00%; 90-day: 6.18%; 1-year: 6.13%; 10-year: 5.8%; 30-year: 5.83%.

EXHIBIT 2 **Cumulative return on Home Depot's stock compared to S&P retail index and S&P 500**

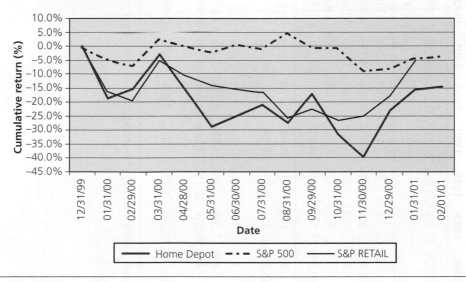

Source: Bloomberg.

3 Home Depot, Inc. in the New Millennium

EXHIBIT 3   Home Depot: Decomposition of ROE, 1986–2000

Average

	1986	1987	1988	1989	1990	1991	1992	1993	1994	1995	1996	1997	1998	1999	2000	1986–2000
ROE	26.8%	33.2%	23.9%	29.2%	31.9%	36.5%	21.5%	19.9%	21.5%	21.3%	18.8%	19.5%	22.7%	26.5%	20.9%	25.0%
Decomposition:																
NOPAT ($ millions)	30	56	77	114	167	240	346	439	609	722	932	1,159	1,618	2,315	2,565	N/A
NOPAT margin	2.9%	3.8%	3.9%	4.1%	4.4%	4.7%	4.8%	4.7%	4.9%	4.7%	4.8%	4.8%	5.4%	6.0%	5.6%	4.6%
Net assets ($ millions)	290	263	347	475	681	1,079	1,568	2,735	3,267	4,390	5,602	6,647	8,235	10,258	12,950	N/A
Operating asset turnover	3.5	5.5	5.8	5.8	5.6	4.8	4.6	3.4	3.8	3.5	3.5	3.6	3.7	3.7	3.5	4.3
Operating ROA	10.2%	21.1%	22.3%	24.0%	24.5%	22.2%	22.1%	16.1%	18.6%	16.4%	16.6%	17.4%	19.6%	22.6%	19.8%	19.6%
Net debt ($ millions)	201	100	27	92	169	395	(123)	431	413	968	614	691	1,137	1,518	609	N/A
Net financial leverage	225.0%	61.0%	8.0%	24.0%	33.0%	58.0%	−7.0%	19.0%	16.0%	28.0%	12.0%	12.0%	16.0%	17.0%	4.9%	35.1%
Net interest expense after tax ($ millions)	5.7	1.5	0.6	1.6	3.7	(9.1)	(16.7)	(18.7)	4.6	(9.5)	(5.8)	(1.2)	4.3	(5.5)	(15.9)	N/A
Net interest rate after tax	2.8%	1.5%	2.2%	1.8%	2.2%	−2.3%	13.6%	−4.3%	1.0%	−1.0%	−0.9%	−0.2%	0.4%	−0.4%	−2.6%	0.9%
Spread	7.4%	19.6%	20.1%	22.2%	22.4%	24.6%	8.4%	20.4%	17.6%	17.4%	17.6%	17.6%	19.3%	22.9%	22.4%	18.7%
Financial leverage effect	16.7%	12.0%	1.7%	5.3%	7.4%	14.3%	−0.6%	3.9%	2.8%	4.9%	2.1%	2.1%	3.1%	3.9%	1.1%	5.4%

Notes: *Explanations of terms appears on following page. *Years indicated end in January of the following year. Thus, 2000 data is for the 12-month period ending at the end of January 2001. N/A, Not applicable.
Source: Compustat and casewriter's calculations.

EXHIBIT 3 Home Depot: Decomposition of ROE, 1986–2000 (*continued*)

Explanation of terms

ROE
= Net income/ Equity
= Operating ROA + Financial leverage effect

NOPAT (net operating profit after taxes) = Net income + Net interest expense after tax
NOPAT margin = NOPAT/Sales
Net assets = Operating working capital + Net long-term assets
          Operating working capital = (Current assets − Cash and marketable securities) − (Current liabilities − Short-term
               debt and current portion of long-term debt)
          Net long-term assets = Total long-term assets − Non-interest-bearing long-term liabilities
Operating asset turnover = Sales/ Net assets
Operating ROA
= NOPAT/ Net assets
= NOPAT margin × Operating asset turnover

Net debt = Total interest-bearing liabilities − Cash and marketable securities
Net financial leverage = Net debt/ Equity
Net interest expense after tax = (Interest expense − Interest income) × (1 − effective tax rate)
Net interest rate after tax = (Net interest expense after tax)/Net debt
Spread = Operating ROA − Net interest rate after tax
Financial leverage effect
= Net financial leverage × Spread

Source: Palepu, Healy, and Bernard, *Business Analysis and Valuation* (2nd edition).

3 Home Depot, Inc. in the New Millennium

EXHIBIT 4   Home Depot: Operational data, 1986–2000

	1986	1987	1988	1989	1990	1991	1992	1993	1994	1995	1996	1997	1998	1999	2000	1986–2000 Average
Sales ($ millions)	$1,011	$1,454	$2,000	$2,758	$3,815	$5,137	$7,148	$9,239	$12,477	$15,470	$19,535	$24,156	$30,219	$38,434	$45,738	N/A
Number of stores	60	75	96	118	145	174	214	264	340	423	512	624	761	930	1,134	N/A
Total square footage at year-end (000)	5,000	6,000	8,000	10,000	13,000	16,000	21,000	26,000	35,000	44,000	54,000	66,000	81,000	100,000	123,000	N/A
Increase in square footage	20.6%	27.6%	33.4%	26.9%	27.4%	24.1%	26.8%	26.3%	33.2%	26.3%	21.6%	23.1%	22.8%	23.5%	22.6%	26%
Average square footage per store (000)	80	82	86	88	92	95	98	100	103	105	105	106	107	108	108	N/A
Sales growth rate		44%	38%	38%	38%	35%	39%	29%	35%	24%	26%	24%	25%	27%	19%	31%
Same-store sales increase	7%	18%	13%	13%	10%	11%	15%	7%	8%	3%	7%	7%	7%	10%	4%	10%
Weekly sales per store (000)	$355	$418	$464	$515	$566	$633	$724	$764	$802	$787	$803	$829	$844	$876	$864	N/A
Sales per square foot	$230	$265	$282	$303	$322	$348	$387	$398	$404	$390	$398	$406	$410	$423	$415	N/A
Number of customer transactions (millions)	34	48	64	84	112	146	189	236	302	370	464	550	665	797	937	N/A
Average sale per transaction	$29.73	$30.24	$31.13	$32.65	$33.92	$35.13	$37.72	$39.13	$41.29	$41.78	$42.09	$43.63	$45.05	$47.87	$48.65	N/A
Working capital/ Sales	10.6%	5.1%	4.3%	4.6%	3.7%	3.2%	3.2%	4.3%	4.5%	5.8%	5.9%	5.4%	6.1%	5.3%	5.7%	5%
Net long-term assets/ Sales	18.1%	13.0%	13.1%	12.6%	14.2%	17.8%	18.7%	25.3%	21.3%	22.7%	22.8%	22.1%	21.2%	21.4%	22.6%	19%
Number of employees at year-end	6,600	9,100	13,000	17,500	21,500	28,000	38,900	50,600	67,300	80,800	98,100	124,400	156,700	201,400	227,300	N/A

Note: *Years indicated end in January of the following year. Thus, 2000 data is for the 12-month period ending at the end of January 2001. *N/A, Not applicable.
Source: Company Annual Reports; Compustat; casewriter's calculations.

EXHIBIT 5 Home Depot: EPS and stock data, 1990–2000

	1990	1991	1992	1993	1994	1995	1996	1997	1998	1999	2000
Diluted EPS	$0.10	$0.13	$0.18	$0.22	$0.29	$0.34	$0.43	$0.55	$0.71	$1.00	$1.10
Diluted EPS increase	43%	30%	38%	22%	32%	17%	26%	28%	29%	41%	10%
Weighted number of shares oustanding assuming dilution (millions)	1,824	1,985	2,096	2,132	2,142	2,151	2,195	2,287	2,320	2,342	2,352
Total return on stock											
Home Depot	54%	167%	48%	−20%	19%	6%	6%	81%	111%	77%	−21%
S&P 500	−5%	32%	8%	10%	2%	38%	22%	34%	28%	21%	−3%

Source: Company Annual Report; Bloomberg.

3 Home Depot, Inc. in the New Millennium

EXHIBIT 6A   Home Depot: Income statements ($ millions, except earnings per share)

	Years Ending January			
	2001	**2000**	**1999**	**1998**
Net Sales	45,738	38,434	30,219	24,156
Cost of Merchandise Sold	32,057	27,023	21,614	17,375
Gross Profit	13,681	11,411	8,605	6,781
Operating Expenses				
Selling and Store Operating	8,513	6,832	5,341	4,303
Pre-Opening	142	113	88	65
General and Administrative	835	671	515	413
Non-Recurring Charge	—	—	—	104
Total Operating Expenses	9,490	7,616	5,944	4,885
Operating Income	4,191	3,795	2,661	1,896
Interest and Investment Income	47	37	30	44
Interest Expense	(21)	(28)	(37)	(42)
Interest, net	26	9	(7)	2
Earnings Before Income Taxes	4,217	3,804	2,654	1,898
Income Taxes	1,636	1,484	1,040	738
Net Earnings	2,581	2,320	1,614	1,160
Basic Earnings Per Share	1.11	1.03	0.73	0.53
Diluted Earnings Per Share	1.10	1.00	0.71	0.52

Note: Cost of merchandise sold includes all of the company's depreciation and amortization expense, which totaled $463 million, $373 million, and $283 million in years ending January 2000, 1999, and 1998, respectively. By contrast, Lowe's does not include depreciation and amortizations in its cost of merchandise sold figures; it has a separate operating expense line for them.
Source: Company 10-K.

3 Home Depot, Inc. in the New Millennium

EXHIBIT 6B   Home Depot: Balance sheets ($ millions)

	Years Ending January		
	2001	**2000**	**1999**
Assets			
Cash and Cash Equivalents	167	168	62
Short-term Investments	10	2	—
Receivables, net	835	587	469
Merchandise Inventories	6,556	5,489	4,293
Other Current Assets	209	144	109
Total Current Assets	7,777	6,390	4,933
Property and Equipment			
Land	4,230	3,248	2,739
Buildings	6,167	4,834	3,757
Furniture, Fixtures and Equipment	2,877	2,279	1,761
Leasehold Improvements	665	493	419
Construction in Progress	1,032	791	540
Capital Leases	261	245	206
	15,232	11,890	9,422
Less Accumulated Depreciation and Amortization	2,164	1,663	1,262
Net Property and Equipment	13,068	10,227	8,160
Cost in Excess of the Fair Value of Net Assets Acquired	314	311	268
Other	226	153	104
Total Assets	21,385	17,081	13,465
Liabilities and Stockholders' Equity			
Accounts Payable	1,976	1,993	1586
Accrued Salaries and Related Expenses	627	541	395
Sales Taxes Payable	298	269	176
Other Accrued Expenses	1,402	763	586
Income Taxes Payable	78	61	100
Current Installments of Long-Term Debt	4	29	14
Total Current Liabilities	4,385	3,656	2,857
Long-term Debt, excluding current installments	1,545	750	1,566
Other Long-Term Liabilities	245	237	208
Deferred Income Taxes	195	87	85
Minority Interest	11	10	9
Stockholders' Equity			
Common Stock	116	115	111
Paid-in Capital	4,810	4,319	2,817
Retained Earnings	10,151	7,941	5,876
Other	(73)	(34)	(64)
Total Stockholders' Equity	15,004	12,341	8,740
Total Liabilities and Stockholders' Equity	21,385	17,081	13,465

Source: Company 10-K.

3 Home Depot, Inc. in the New Millennium

EXHIBIT 6C Home Depot: Cash flow statements ($ millions)

	Years Ending January			
	2001	**2000**	**1999**	**1998**
Cash Flows from Operating Activities				
Net Earnings	2,581	2,320	1,614	1,160
Depreciation and Amortization	601	463	373	283
(Increase) Decrease in Receivables, net	(246)	(85)	85	(166)
Increase in Merchandise Inventories	(1,075)	(1,142)	(698)	(885)
Increase in Accounts Payable and Accrued Expenses	754	820	423	577
Increase in Income Taxes Payable	151	93	59	83
Other	30	(23)	61	(23)
	2,796	2,446	1,917	1,029
Cash Flows from Investing Activities				
Capital Expenditures	(3,558)	(2,581)	(2,053)	(1,420)
Purchase of Remaining Interest in The Home Depot Canada	–	–	(261)	–
Payments for Businesses Acqauired, net	(26)	(101)	(6)	(61)
Proceeds from Sales of Property and Equipment	95	87	45	85
Purchases of Investments	(39)	(32)	(2)	(194)
Proceeds from Maturieties of Investments	30	30	4	599
Advances Secured by Real Estate, net	(32)	(25)	2	20
	(3,530)	(2,622)	(2,271)	(971)
Cash Flows from Financing Activities				
(Repayments) Issuance of Commercial Paper Obligations, net	754	(246)	246	–
Proceeds from Long-Term Borrowings, net	32	522	–	15
Repayments of Long-Term Debt	(29)	(14)	(8)	(40)
Proceeds from Sale of Common Stock, net	351	267	167	122
Cash Dividends Paid to Stockholders	(371)	(255)	(168)	(139)
Minority Interest Congtributions to Partnership	–	7	11	10
	737	281	248	(32)
Effect of Exchange Rate Changes	(4)	1	(4)	–
Increase (Decrease) in Cash and Cash Equivalents	(1)	106	(110)	26
Cash and Cash Equivalents at Beginning of Year	168	62	172	146
Cash and Cash Equivalents at End of Year	167	168	62	172

Note: At the end of 1999, the company said it owned 77% of its stores and leased 23% of them. In recent years it had increased the relative percentage of sores that were owned because it felt that doing so provided greater operating control and flexibility and generally lower occupancy costs. It noted that the cost of new stores to be constructed and owned by the company averaged $13.2 million. The cost to fix up stores to be leased averaged $4.3 million. The cost of inventory for new stores averaged $3.2 million, net of vendor financing.
Source: Company 10-K.

EXHIBIT 7 **Projected growth in U.S. market for home improvement products, as of June 2000**

Year	Percent Change over Previous Year
2000	6.30%
2001	3.20%
2002	4.00%
2003	4.40%
2004	4.60%

Source: Home Improvement Research Institute.

EXHIBIT 8 **Summary data for Lowe's ($ millions)**

	2000	1999	1998	1997
Sales	$18,779	$15,905	$13,330	$11,108
NOPAT	$853	$727	$530	$398
NOPAT margin	4.5%	4.6%	4.0%	3.6%
Net assets	$8,029	$4,961	$3,545	$2,810
Operating ROA (NOPAT/Net assets)	10.6%	14.7%	15.0%	14.2%
Number of stores at year–end	650	576	520	477
Same-store sales increase	1.2%	6.0%	6.0%	4.0%
Sales per square foot	$277	$303	$273	$302

Source: Company Annual Report and 10-K; casewriter's calculations.

3 Home Depot, Inc. in the New Millennium

4 Krispy Kreme Doughnuts

Krispy Kreme is one of a kind phenomena, in our view, boasting a combination of a powerful consumer brand, a multi-channel distribution channel and a business model that produces best-in-class financial returns. . . . Krispy Kreme is still an attractive growth story, in our view, and represents a well-established brand still early in its growth trajectory.

—CIBC World Markets analysts John Glass and Jeffrey Farmer, June 3, 2002

Krispy Kreme Doughnuts completed its initial public offering on April 5, 2000. By the end of the first day of trading, its stock had soared 76% from the $5.50 offering price to $9.25 (adjusted for two 2-for-1 stock splits). In the following two years, Krispy Kreme's stock price reached a high of $45.66 (in late December 2001) and was trading at around $37 in late May 2002. (**Exhibit 1** shows Krispy Kreme's stock performance relative to the S&P 500 from the IPO date to May 30, 2002.)

During the two years following the IPO, Krispy Kreme reported strong growth and financial performance. For example, for the year ended February 3, 2002, revenue growth was 31%, earnings growth was 80%, and the company's return on beginning equity was 21%. (Financial statements for Krispy Kreme for the year ended February 3, 2002 and the first quarter of 2003 are shown in **Exhibit 2**.)

A key challenge for CIBC World Markets' John Glass and Jeffrey Farmer was to forecast the company's financial performance for the next few years. Would Krispy Kreme be able to sustain its recent revenue and earnings growth? What working capital and other resources would the company require? How would it finance its growth? To answer these questions, Glass and Farmer would have to understand Krispy Kreme's growth strategy, the basis for its recent financial performance, and the nature of competition in the doughnut industry.

Krispy Kreme's business[1]

In 1937 Vernon Rudolph purchased a secret recipe for yeast-raised doughnuts from a French chef from New Orleans, rented a building in Winston-Salem, North Carolina, and began selling Krispy Kreme doughnuts to local grocery stores. Within a year, he had knocked a hole in the wall of his production facility and begun selling "hot original glazed" doughnuts to customers directly.

[1]Information on Krispy Kreme's history, operations, and financing strategy are from the company's 10-K statement for the fiscal year ended February 3, 2002.

The company's reputation for making tasty, high-quality doughnuts grew steadily throughout the southeastern United States in the 1960s and 1970s. New stores were added either as company-owned outlets or as franchise operations (known as franchise associates). In the mid-1990s the company's management decided to pursue a strategy of geographic expansion using a new area developer franchise model. Under this model, a developer for a metropolitan region was granted a license to develop a specified number of new Krispy Kreme stores. New area developer stores soon appeared in Washington and Baltimore. In 1996, the first New York City store was opened; in 1999, stores were opened in California; and in 2001, the first international store was added, in Toronto, Canada. In the years ended January 2001 and January 2002, area developer store openings accounted for 72% and 83% of systemwide store growth, respectively.

By April 2002, the Krispy Kreme network comprised 222 factory stores in 34 states and produced 5 million doughnuts a day, or 2 billion doughnuts a year. Systemwide sales were $621.7 million in the year ended February 3, 2002, and $183.1 million for the first quarter of 2002 (a 30.4% increase over the first quarter for the prior year). Comparable store sales grew by 11.7% in the year ended February 3, 2002, and 10.5% in the first quarter of 2002.

Krispy Kreme generated revenues from three sources. First, it owned and operated doughnut stores. Second, it received royalties from franchise associates and area developers. Finally, it received revenues from the sale of doughnut mixes and doughnut-making equipment to franchise associates and area developers.

In April 2002, 75 of the Krispy Kreme network stores were company owned, an increase of 12 over the prior year. These stores baked and sold doughnuts and complementary products on-site. They also sold to grocery stores and supermarkets under either the Krispy Kreme brand or under the retailer's label.

Franchise associates owned and operated 53 of the 222 network stores in April 2002. Associate agreements with Krispy Kreme were typically for 15 years and required franchise owners to pay royalties of 3% for on-premises sales and 1% for all other sales (excluding private-label sales). Associates were not required to contribute to company advertising. Krispy Kreme anticipated that it would not add any further stores under this model, preferring instead to use the new area developer model.

Area developers had opened 94 stores by April 2002. Under the terms of the area developer agreements, Krispy Kreme received a one-time franchise fee between $20,000 and $40,000 for each new store opening, a 4.5% royalty fee on all sales, and a 1% contribution toward company advertising. These agreements had a 15-year term and could be renewed at Krispy Kreme's discretion. Krispy Kreme typically did not provide financing to area developers.

Finally, Krispy Kreme received revenues from the sale of proprietary doughnut mixes and doughnut-making equipment, both produced in Winston-Salem, to franchise associates and area developers. The revenues generated from these sales were attributed to Krispy Kreme Manufacturing and Distribution (KKM&D). (**Exhibit 3** shows the breakdown of revenues and operating expenses for KKM&D as well as for the company store and franchise business segments.)

Competitors

The doughnut industry was highly fragmented. The second-largest retailer after Krispy Kreme, Dunkin Donuts, was owned by the British food and spirits conglomerate Allied Domecq. Dunkin Donuts operated 4,736 franchise stores in 43 states and 20 countries and sold 4.4 million doughnuts a day, or 1.6 billion doughnuts per year.[2] Other competitors

[2]See Allied Domecq financial report for 2002.

4 Krispy Kreme Doughnuts

were regional operators. Winchell's was located primarily on the West Coast and operated 200 stores;[3] Donut Connection had 140 stores in 13 states, primarily in the mid-Atlantic region;[4] and Honeydew Donuts operated 100 stores in New England.[5] Finally, there were hundreds of regional bakeries that sold doughnuts through supermarkets, convenience stores, restaurants, and retail stores.

Growth plans[6]

Krispy Kreme expected to open 62 new stores in 2003, mostly franchise stores. Area developers were contractually obligated to open 200 stores in the period 2003 to 2006. In addition to domestic growth, the company indicated that it was exploring long-term opportunities for growth in Japan, South Korea, Australia, Spain, and the United Kingdom.

On average, the development of a new store required an initial investment of $800,000 for a building of around 4,600 square feet, plus $625,000 for equipment, furniture, and fixtures. In February 2002, company-owned stores generated average weekly sales per store of $72,000 versus $53,000 for franchise stores. This difference reflected significantly lower sales for older associate stores. Area developer franchise stores showed similar sales patterns to those of company-owned stores. (Average weekly sales per store for company-owned and franchise stores in the period 1998 to 2002 are shown in **Exhibit 4**.)

In addition to growth through opening new stores, Krispy Kreme planned to increase the sale of complementary products through existing stores. In February 2001, it acquired Digital Java, a small Chicago-based coffee company, to enable the addition of enhanced espresso and coffee offerings at Krispy Kreme stores.

In fall 2000 Krispy Kreme announced the development of a smaller hot doughnut machine that produced the same quality doughnuts as existing larger machines. The new machine was being tested in three doughnut and coffee shops in 2002 and was to be added to 10 to 12 more stores in 2003. If successful, the smaller machine would enable Krispy Kreme to begin offering hot doughnuts in small coffee shops and malls, allowing it to expand into smaller markets and into dense urban areas that were more costly to reach under the larger factory store model.

The growth in franchise operations required Krispy Kreme to invest heavily in plants, property, and equipment. For example, in the year ended February 2002 the company spent $37 million to construct and equip new company-owned factory stores, to remodel older company stores, to acquire and upgrade equipment-manufacturing facilities, to install coffee-roasting operations in stores, and to construct doughnut and coffee shops. The company's management anticipated that to achieve its planned growth it would have to continue to invest aggressively in both long-term assets and working capital.

Krispy Kreme had historically used a combination of debt and equity to finance its growth. In 2002, it raised funds through a $17.2 million stock offering (for 10.4 million shares), increased its revolving credit facility from $28 million to $40 million, and agreed to a $35 million bank loan to fund the construction of a new mix and distribution facility.[7] Kripsy Kreme's management anticipated that, as of February 2002, the company's capital needs for the next 24 months could be covered by "the proceeds from the initial public offering completed in April 2000 and our follow-on public offering completed in early

---

[3]See Winchell's website.

[4]See Donut Connection's website.

[5]See Honeydew Donuts' website.

[6]Information on Krispy Kreme's growth plans is from the company's 10-K statement for the fiscal year ended February 3, 2002.

[7]Under the terms of the revolving credit agreement, the company would pay interest at the lower of the prime rates less 110 basis points and one-month LIBOR plus 100 basis points.

February 2001, cash flow generated from operations and our borrowing capacity under lines of credit. . . . If additional capital is needed, we may raise such capital through public or private equity or debt financing."

Analyst forecasts

An important function performed by the analysts who followed Krispy Kreme was to forecast the company's financial performance for the coming two years. As shown in **Exhibit 5**, which contains excerpts from their June 2, 2002 report on Krispy Kreme, Glass and Farmer approached this task by first forecasting system-wide revenues (for company-owned stores and stores owned by franchise associates and area developers). These forecasts reflected the company's plans for new store growth and growth in sales from existing stores given the company's business model and competitive pressures. From these forecasts, Glass and Farmer were able to forecast Krispy Kreme's revenues and margins for its three core businesses (store sales, franchise operations, and sales of mix and equipment). Based on this analysis, they predicted that Krispy Kreme would report earnings per share of $0.64 for the year ended January 2003 and $0.83 for the January 2004 year. These forecasts represented projected earnings growth of 42% and 33% for the next two years, respectively, virtually identical to consensus predictions for all analysts covering Krispy Kreme.[8]

Questions

1   Analysts are predicting that Krispy Kreme will be able to perform highly effectively and continue to grow rapidly in the coming two years. Do you agree with their analysis? If so, why? If not, why not?

2   What factors did the CIBC analysts examine to forecast sales growth for KKD in the years ended January 2003 and 2004? What assumptions did they implicitly make about number of new stores and weekly sales per store (for both company and franchise stores)? What are their implicit assumptions about revenue growth from franchise operations and KKM&D? Do you agree with these forecasts?

3   What are the NOPAT margins that the CIBC analysts have forecasted for KKD for the years ended January 2003 and 2004? What assumptions were made about specific expense items (e.g. margins, G&A, D&A, taxes)? Do you agree with these forecasts?

4   The CIBC analysts do not forecast KKD's balance sheet for the following year (ended January 2003). Make your own balance sheet forecasts.

5   In general, do you expect analysts' forecasts for a company like KKD to be optimistic, pessimistic or unbiased? Why?

---

[8]See First Call consensus earnings forecasts at June 1, 2002. A total of eight firms followed Krispy Kreme at the end of May 2002. In addition to CIBC World Markets, they included BB&T Capital Markets (Andrew Wolf), Brean Murray & Co. (Kathleen Heaney), Dain Rauscher Wessels (David Geraty), JP Morgan & Co. (John Ivankoe and David Linsen), Merrill Lynch (Peter Oakes), Thomas Weisel Partners (Skip Carpenter), and Deutsche Banc Alex. Brown. Source: Krispy Kreme Doughnuts Investors Relations Website.

EXHIBIT 1 **Stock performance for Krispy Kreme and the S&P 500, April 2000 to May 2002**

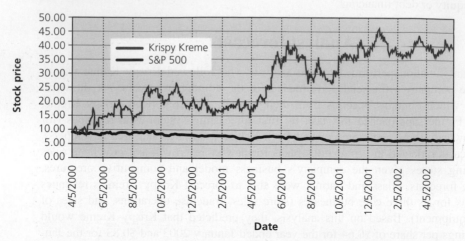

Note: Krispy Kreme's equity beta was 1.4 (source: SmartMoney.com). The long-term government bond rate on May 30, 2002 was 5.79% (source: Federal Reserve Statistical Release).

Source: Chart created from information found on Standard & Poor's Research Insight.

EXHIBIT 2   **Financial statements for Krispy Kreme Doughnuts for the fiscal years ended January 30, 2000 to February 3, 2002, and for the quarters ended April 29, 2001 and May 5, 2002**

CONSOLIDATED BALANCE SHEETS

In Thousands	Year Ended			Quarter Ended	
	Jan. 30, 2000	Jan. 28, 2001	Feb. 3, 2002	Apr. 29, 2001	May 5, 2002
ASSETS					
CURRENT ASSETS:					
Cash and cash equivalents	$3,183	$7,026	$21,904	$21,326	$21,601
Short-term investments	—	18,103	15,292	24,738	22,073
Accounts receivable, net	17,965	19,855	26,894	20,202	29,232
Accounts receivable, affiliates	1,608	2,599	9,017	5,028	8,443
Other receivables	794	2,279	2,771	2,498	1,919
Inventories	9,979	12,031	16,159	11,511	21,118
Prepaid expenses	3,148	1,909	2,591	1,796	2,700
Income taxes refundable	861	—	2,534	34	—
Deferred income taxes	3,500	3,809	4,607	4,775	5,741
Total current assets	41,038	67,611	101,769	91,908	112,827
Property and equipment, net	60,584	78,340	112,577	85,464	151,152
Deferred income taxes	1,398	—	—	—	—
Long-term investments	—	17,877	12,700	11,319	6,058
Investment in unconsolidated joint ventures	—	2,827	3,400	4,921	4,382
Intangible assets	—	—	16,621	—	16,508
Other assets	1,938	4,838	8,309	6,578	7,387
Total assets	$104,958	$171,493	$255,376	$200,190	$298,314
LIABILITIES AND SHAREHOLDERS' EQUITY					
CURRENT LIABILITIES:					
Accounts payable	$13,106	$8,211	$12,095	$15,671	$14,763
Book overdraft		5,147	9,107	—	8,074
Accrued expenses	14,080	21,243	26,729	16,941	20,832
Revolving line of credit	—	3,526	3,871	4,400	4,171
Current maturities of long-term debt	2,400	—	731	—	2,382
Income taxes payable	—	41	—	—	303
Total current liabilities	29,586	38,168	52,533	37,012	50,525
Deferred income taxes	—	579	3,930	2,113	727
Compensation deferred (unpaid)	990	1,106	727	954	35,133
Long-term debt, net of current portion	20,502	—	3,912	—	5,957
Accrued restructuring expenses	4,259	3,109	1,919	2,855	1,653
Other long-term obligations	1,866	1,735	2,197	1,641	2,883
Total long-term liabilities	27,617	6,529	12,685	7,563	46,353
Minority interest	—	1,117	2,491	1,059	2,703

EXHIBIT 2   Financial statements (*continued*)

In Thousands	Year Ended			Quarter Ended	
	Jan. 30, 2000	Jan. 28, 2001	Feb. 3, 2002	Apr. 29, 2001	May 5, 2002
SHAREHOLDERS' EQUITY:					
Common stock, no par value, 100,000 shares authorized; issued and outstanding – 51,832 (2001) and 54,271 (2002)	—	85,060	121,052	108,741	123,777
Common stock, $10 par value, 1,000 shares authorized; issued and outstanding – 467 (2000) and 0 (2001)	15,475	—	—	—	—
Unearned compensation	—	(188)	(186)	(176)	(169)
Notes receivable, employees	(2,547)	(2,349)	(2,580)	(2,958)	(2,556)
Nonqualified employee benefit plan assets	—	(126)	(138)	(126)	(339)
Nonqualified employee benefit plan liability	—	126	138	126	339
Accumulated other comprehensive income	—	609	456	683	(105)
Retained earnings	34,827	42,547	68,925	48,266	77,786
Total shareholders' equity	47,755	125,679	187,667	154,556	198,733
Total liabilities and shareholders' equity	$104,958	$171,493	$255,376	$200,190	$298,314

STATEMENT OF OPERATIONS

In Thousands, Except Per Share Data	Year			Three Months	
	Jan. 30, 2000	Jan. 28, 2001	Feb. 3, 2002	Apr. 29, 2001	May 5, 2002
Total revenues	$220,243	$300,715	$394,354	$87,921	$111,059
Operating expenses	190,003	250,690	316,946	71,195	86,362
General and administrative expenses	14,856	20,061	27,562	6,222	7,623
Depreciation and amortization expenses	4,546	6,457	7,959	1,872	2,546
Income (loss) from operations	10,838	23,507	41,887	8,632	14,528
Interest expense (income), net, and other	1,232	(1,698)	(2,408)	(976)	(495)
Equity loss in joint ventures	—	706	602	(171)	(198)
Minority interest	—	716	1,147	(175)	(533)
Loss on sale of property and equipment	—	—	—	(39)	—
Income (loss) before income taxes	9,606	23,783	42,546	9,223	14,292
Provision (benefit) for income taxes	3,650	9,058	16,168	3,504	5,431
Net income (loss)	$5,956	$14,725	$26,378	$5,719	$8,861
Net income (loss) per share:					
Basic	$0.16	$0.30	$0.49	$0.11	$0.16
Diluted	0.15	0.27	0.45	$0.10	$0.15
Shares used in calculation of net income (loss) per share:					
Basic	37,360	49,184	53,703	51,991	55,381
Diluted	39,280	53,656	58,443	57,190	59,073

EXHIBIT 2 **Financial statements** (*continued*)

CONSOLIDATED STATEMENTS OF CASH FLOWS

In Thousands	Year Ended			Quarter Ended	
	Jan. 30, 2000	Jan. 28, 2001	Feb. 3, 2002	Apr. 29, 2001	May 5, 2002
CASH FLOW FROM OPERATING ACTIVITIES:					
Net income	$5,956	$14,725	$26,378	$5,719	$8,861
Items not requiring (providing) cash:					
Depreciation and amortization	4,546	6,457	7,959	1,872	2,546
Deferred income taxes	258	1,668	2,553	568	893
Loss on disposal of property and equipment, net	—	20	235	39	—
Compensation expense related to restricted stock awards	—	22	52	12	17
Tax benefit from exercise of nonqualified stock options	—	595	9,772	2,944	1,689
Provision for restructuring	(127)	—	—		
Provision for store closings and impairment	1,139	318	—		
Minority interest	—	716	1,147	175	533
Equity loss in joint ventures	—	706	602	171	198
Change in assets and liabilities:					
Receivables	(4,760)	(3,434)	(13,317)	(2,127)	(912)
Inventories	(93)	(2,052)	(3,977)	520	(4,846)
Prepaid expenses	(1,619)	1,239	(682)	113	(109)
Income taxes, net	(2,016)	902	(2,575)	(75)	2,837
Accounts payable	540	2,279	3,884	(450)	2,668
Accrued expenses	4,329	7,966	4,096	(3,165)	(6,255)
Deferred compensation and other long-term obligations	345	(15)	83	(246)	319
Net cash provided by operating activities	8,498	32,112	36,210	6,070	8,439
CASH FLOW FROM INVESTING ACTIVITIES:					
Purchase of property and equipment	(11,335)	(25,655)	(37,310)	(8,956)	(40,954)
Proceeds from disposal of property and equipment	—	1,419	3,196	9	—
Proceeds from disposal of assets held for sale	830	—	—		
Acquisition of associate and area developer markets, net of cash acquired	—	—	(20,571)		
Investments in unconsolidated joint ventures	—	(4,465)	(1,218)	(1,265)	(1,187)
(Increase) decrease in other assets	479	(3,216)	(4,237)	(3,696)	755
(Purchase) sale of investments, net	—	(35,371)	7,877	(3)	(235)
Net cash used for investing activities:	(10,026)	(67,288)	(52,263)	(13,911)	(41,621)

4 Krispy Kreme Doughnuts

EXHIBIT 2 Financial statements *(continued)*

In Thousands	Year Ended			Quarter Ended	
	Jan. 30, 2000	Jan. 28, 2001	Feb. 3, 2002	Apr. 29, 2001	May 5, 2002
CASH FLOW FROM FINANCING ACTIVITIES:					
Repayment of long-term debt	$(2,400)	$(3,600)	$—	$—	$(128)
Net (repayments) borrowings from revolving line of credit	—	(15,775)	345	874	300
Borrowings of long-term debt	4,282	—	4,643	—	33,000
Proceeds from stock offering	—	65,637	17,202	17,202	—
Proceeds from exercise of stock options	—	104	3,906	2,656	1,036
Minority interest	—	401	227	(233)	(321)
Book overdraft	482	(941)	3,960	1,372	(1,033)
Cash dividends paid	(1,518)	(7,005)	—	—	—
Issuance of notes receivable	(674)	—	—	—	—
Collection of notes receivable	226	198	648	270	25
Net cash provided by financing activities:	398	39,019	30,931	22,141	32,879
Net increase (decrease) in cash and cash equivalents	(1,130)	3,843	14,878	14,300	(303)
Cash and cash equivalents at beginning of year	4,313	3,183	7,026	7,026	21,904
Cash and cash equivalents at end of year	$3,183	$7,026	$21,904	$21,326	$21,601
Supplemental schedule of non-cash investing and financing activities					
Issuance of stock to Krispy Kreme Profit-Sharing Stock Ownership Plan	—	$3,039	—	—	—
Issuance of restricted common shares	—	210	50	—	—
Issuance of stock in conjunction with acquisition of associate market	—	—	4,183	—	—
Issuance of stock in exchange for employee notes receivable	—	—	879	—	—
Unrealized gain (loss) on investments	—	609	(111)	74	(94)
Foreign currency translation adjustment	—	—	—	—	(8)
Change in fair value of cash flow hedge	—	—	—	—	459

Source: Krispy Kreme Doughnut's Annual Report for February 3, 2002 and the quarterly report for May 5, 2002.

EXHIBIT 3 Business segment data for Krispy Kreme Doughnuts for the fiscal years ended January 30, 2000 to February 3, 2002

	Year Ended		
In Thousands	**Jan. 30, 2000**	**Jan. 28, 2001**	**Feb. 3, 2002**
REVENUES BY BUSINESS SEGMENT:			
Company Store Operations	$164,230	$213,677	$266,209
Franchise Operations	5,529	9,445	14,008
KKM&D	50,484	77,593	114,137
Total revenues	$220,243	$300,715	$394,354
OPERATING EXPENSES BY BUSINESS SEGMENT:			
Company Store Operations	$142,925	$181,470	$217,419
Franchise Operations	4,012	3,642	1,896
KKM&D	43,066	65,578	94,631
Total operating expenses	$190,003	$250,690	$316,946

Source: Krispy Kreme Doughnut's Annual Report, February 3, 2002.

EXHIBIT 4 Operating data for Krispy Kreme Doughnuts for the fiscal years ended February 1, 1998 to February 3, 2002

	Feb. 1, 1998	**Jan. 31, 1999**	**Jan. 30, 2000**	**Jan. 28, 2001**	**Feb. 3, 2002**
Systemwide sales ($000)	$203,439	$240,316	$318,854	$448,129	$621,665
Number of stores at end of period:					
Company	58	61	58	63	75
Franchised	62	70	86	111	143
Systemwide	120	131	144	174	218
Average weekly sales per store ($000)					
Company	$42	$47	$54	$69	$72
Franchised	23	28	38	43	53
Operating cash flow/store revenues	NA	20.3%	23.2%	26.1%	28.6%

Source: Krispy Kreme Doughnut's 10-K, February 3, 2002.

EXHIBIT 5 **Excerpts from the CIBC world markets equity research report on Krispy Kreme Doughnuts, Inc., prepared by John S. Glass and Jeffery D. Farmer on June 3, 2002**

Company Overview

For both investors and consumers, Krispy Kreme is one of a kind phenomena, in our view, boasting a combination of a powerful consumer brand, a multi-channel distribution channel and a business model that produces best-in-class financial returns. What's more, the company is vertically integrated, not only retailing doughnuts, but also manufacturing and distributing high-margin doughnut mix as well as manufacturing proprietary doughnut-making equipment.

Krispy Kreme is still an attractive growth story, in our view, and represents a well-established brand still early in its growth trajectory. The company is just one-third of the way through the rollout of their large-format factory stores—not including the substantial incremental growth prospects of its prototype smaller-format units.

These prospects have not gone unnoticed. Since its IPO in April 2000 priced at a split-adjusted $5.50, the stock has risen over 600% in the last 26 months, making it the most successful public offering in recent years. That performance has been fueled by substantial sales and earnings outperformance—as well as a fair amount of publicity. The key components to the Krispy Kreme business model follow.

TABLE A
Company-Operated and Systemwide Unit Same Store Sales (1999–2002E)

Company Stores	1999	2000	2001	2002
1Q	7.1%	23.3%	13.1%	10.5%
2Q	9.7%	24.4%	11.9%	10.0%E
3Q	14.0%	23.6%	11.1%	8.0%E
4Q	17.1%	20.6%	10.7%	8.0%E
Year	12.0%	22.9%	11.7%	9.0%E

Systemwide Stores	1999	2000	2001	2002
1Q	9.8%	19.1%	11.4%	12..9%
2Q	13.4%	19.4%	13.1%	10.5%E
3Q	15.9%	15.5%	13.6%	8.5%E
4Q	16.6%	14.9%	13.1%	8.5%E
Year	14.1%	17.1%	12.8%	10.0%E

Source: CIBC World Markets and company information.

Company-owned Retail Stores

Company-owned stores, most of which are in the Deep South, are referred to internally as the 'heritage markets,' representing about 60% of Krispy Kreme's profits. Although the company has focused most of its growth in franchised markets and has owned few new stores of its own, sales and profit trends have nonetheless been healthy due to a combination of strong comp store sales, driven by a combination of retail and wholesale business. While management has designated franchising in new markets as its primary growth driver, there is nonetheless substantial opportunity for growth in the heritage markets to develop underpenetrated markets as well as increase same-store sales through more efficient wholesale distribution and new wholesale accounts.

TABLE B
Systems and Operating Margin Leverage

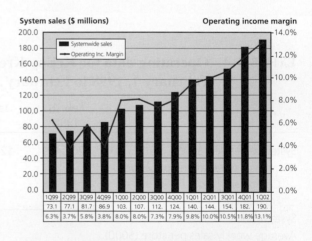

	1Q99	2Q99	3Q99	4Q99	1Q00	2Q00	3Q00	4Q00	1Q01	2Q01	3Q01	4Q01	1Q02
	73.1	77.1	81.7	86.9	103.	107.	112.	124.	140.	144.	154.	182.	190.
	6.3%	3.7%	5.8%	3.8%	8.0%	8.0%	7.3%	7.9%	9.8%	10.0%	10.5%	11.8%	13.1%

Source: CIBC World Markets and company information.

In addition, management has from time to time elected to repurchase older franchised markets—particularly those where there is still significant growth potential. Markets recently acquired include Charleston, SC, Savannah, GA, Cleveland and Akron, OH, and Baltimore, MD. In many cases, the company will resell a stake in these markets but retain the majority.

Margin expansion in the company-owned markets has been substantial, up 500 bp to 16% in 2001 as the company leveraged fixed costs through volume increases and focused on operation, particularly better labor cost management. Best-in-class store margins (including D&A) run into the high teens, particularly given that average weekly sales at company units were $72,000 in 2001, or $3.7 million annualized.

TABLE C
Average Weekly Sales per Store (1999–2001)

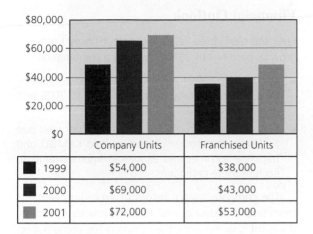

	Company Units	Franchised Units
1999	$54,000	$38,000
2000	$69,000	$43,000
2001	$72,000	$53,000

Source: CIBC World Markets and company information.

Franchise Income

While the company has always had a close-knit group of original franchisees—known as the Associates—its real franchising growth came in the mid-1990s when the company began committing to area developer agreements outside its heritage markets. These new agreements are more profitable—4.5% royalties vs. 3% for Associates—and the income stream is much faster growing as the area developers rapidly roll out new units. In 2001, the area developer store base grew at a 68% clip to 143 units. Franchise income now represents 16% of profits, but given its inherent high-margin nature (current profit flow through is 65% on its way to 75% to 80%) and growth rate (franchise profits grew by nearly 60% in 2001) we expect the franchise income will continue to be a margin and earnings driver over the next several years as area developers continue to grow sales faster than the company-owned units.

In part, the growth in franchise income has been driven by massive new store openings as the company enters new markets. In fact, Krispy Kreme's new store openings follow an inverse store maturation curve, often producing peak volumes in a new store the first few weeks and then slowly settling over the next 12 months to a normalized level. *Typically, new stores retain about 40% of opening week sales. However, given the unusually strong first week sales recently, in some cases the retention rate is likely to be closer to 15% to 25%.* For example, new stores opened recently in Denver, Seattle, and Minneapolis have produced opening week volumes of $400,000 to $480,000. Over time, average weekly volume may settle around $75,000 to $100,000.

TABLE D
Krispy Kreme's Record Opening Week Sales

Date	Location	Opening Week Sales*
May 2002	Minneapolis, MN	$480,693
December 2001	Toronto, ONT	$465,003
November 2001	Seattle, WA	$454,125
April 2001	Denver, CO	$369,000

* Toronto opening in Canadian dollars

Source: CIBC World Markets and company information.

This honeymoon phenomenon could negatively impact systemwide comp store sales. If sales do not stabilize within 18 months (the point when stores enter the comp base), systemwide comp store sales will be negatively impacted—the magnitude depends on the number of units coming into the comp base, but could be as great as a 5% to 10% negative impact in some quarters. *Big-store openings also give rise to another phenomenon: 70% of franchisee sales are not in the comp base, so comp store sales are not yet a key driver of franchise income and KKM&D sales.* Since the company itself is not opening new stores, the above *has no impact* on company-owned comp store sales.

TABLE E
Hypothetical Weekly Sales Trends

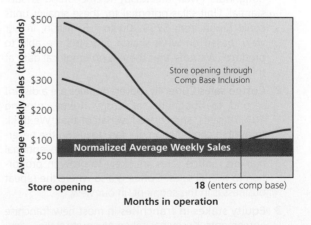

Source: CIBC World Markets and company information.

Krispy Kreme Manufacturing and Distribution (KKM&D)

KKM&D is the company's captive manufacturing and distribution arm. The manufacturing—primarily of doughnut mix which must be purchased by franchisees and machinery—is the higher-margin business, while the distribution margins are cost plus an estimated 2% to 3% markup. Blended margins for KKM&D run 16.6% of sales and are rising at a 100bp clip per year due to greater capacity utilization. The company opened a second distribution facility on the West Coast last year, and will open a second manufacturing facility in Effingham, IL shortly, helping to reduce shipping costs (both in and out) and raising margins. Sales growth for KKM&D should keep lock step with top-line growth of franchises.

Incremental Sales/Earnings Drivers

Embedded in each of these three lines, we think there are at least four incremental earnings drivers beyond the current base business. Those are:

1 **Hot Doughnut Shop** Late in 2001, the company announced it had developed a prototype small-format unit (1,000–1,500 square feet), complete with a much smaller doughnut machine which reheats and glazes doughnuts. The implication on growth and unit potential is profound, in our view, allowing Krispy Kreme to enter urban centers, malls, and a variety of other locations that could not be reached through the factory store model. These small units also facilitate the sale of coffee, which has a much tighter draw radius than a traditional doughnut shop. Data on these new units is scarce as only a handful exist. But, based on the number of Starbucks (4,000) and Dunkin Donuts (3,600) in the U.S., the opportunity for high-quality coffee and doughnuts given the Krispy Kreme brand is substantial. Unit sales potential for these smaller units could range from $750,000 to 1.5 million, in our view, based on what similar concepts are able to produce. We note that there is no empirical data at this time.

2 **Coffee sales** Currently, beverage sales are a distant second to doughnuts at Krispy Kreme, running 10% of sales, and coffee just half of that. We think through a combination of more focus on the beverage program and the smaller more conventional markets, coffee sales are likely to grow in proportion to overall sales. Coffee is also where the repeat business is in this segment, in our view.

3 **Equity stakes in franchises** In most new franchise agreements, Krispy has taken an equity stake—anywhere from 20% to 70%. As franchisees become profitable, these equity stakes will become profit contributors. Currently, they run at a modest loss.

4 **International** We believe the brand has significant international potential and is natural in places such as the U.K., Japan, and potentially other European countries. International expansion is not currently in our forecast.

Financial Outlook

Over the next three years, we expect Krispy Kreme to grow its earnings by 35%, driven by a combination of:

- Top-line growth of 25% to 30%, including system-wide square footage growth of 25% to 30% and mid-single digit comp sales.
- Margin expansion of 75 bp to 100 bp per year due to 1) mix shift toward higher margin KKM&D and franchise income, and 2) margin improvements in each of these categories.

The company's track record of exceeding earnings expectations is strong, with outperformance in each of the eight quarters since the company has come public. Earnings per share grew 65% in 2001. Our current forecast calls for 36% EPS growth in 2002.

An element for continued earnings growth at Krispy Kreme will be margin expansion. As Table F shows, the company now is already at its original long-term operating margin goal of 10%. Given the revenue mix shift toward higher profit income streams, operating efficiency improvements in company stores, and increased capacity utilization and lower shipping costs for the distribution and manufacturing operations, we believe operating profit margins can reach 15% over the next three to five years, well ahead of the original 10% goal.

TABLE F
Upward Revision of Margin Guidance

	CY 1998	CY 2001	Long-Term at IPO	Long-Term Today
Company Stores	9.0%	16.0%	13–14%	16–18%
Franchise Ops	13.5%	65.0%	70–75%	70–75%
Support Ops	13.0%	16.6%	16–17%	17–18%
G & A	6.0%	7.0%	6–7%	6–7%
EBIT	3.0%	10.6%	9–10%	14–16%

Source: CIBC World Markets and company information.

Financial Condition

Given the company's primary focus on the franchising and strong cash flow, to date the company has been able to fund its own expansion internally. In 2001, cash from operations of $30.5 million financed the company's $25.6 million cap-ex budget and $6.3 million in investments in joint ventures. However, Krispy Kreme's financing needs are likely to be greater in the near future given the addition of more manufacturing and distribution assets and more joint venture investment opportunities. In 2002, we expect that cap-ex will be $43 million plus an additional $35 million from the recently canceled synthetic lease program, which is likely now to be funded by debt. We expect cash from operations to be around $35 million to $40 million.

Recent Trends

Business trends for the last three quarters have been very consistent with systemwide comp store sales around 11% to 13% and company stores at about 10%; these results were achieved despite challenging comparisons from 2000 of 17% on a systemwide basis. In the F1Q, EPS grew 51%, driven by 26% top line and over 300 bp of operating margin expansion. Although store development was modest—a net of four units— the company is still committed to operating 62 new units, or 28% systemwide square footage growth.

Our current forecast for 2002 calls for 26% revenue growth, driven by 9% to 10% systemwide comps and 62 new units, as well as 100 bp of operating margin expansion (to 12+%).

Risk and Uncertainties

- **Decelerating comp store sales** Decelerating comp store sales, particularly due to large new store openings entering the comp base, could negatively impact comp store sales—a metric widely used in valuing retail stocks. We note as before that 70% of franchisee revenues are still noncomp, therefore a comp deceleration in the franchise base would not materially impact earnings near term.

- **Increasing capital costs** Given the need for new production and distribution capacity, capital intensity is rising, as described earlier in this report. New unit costs have risen to $1.3 million to $1.5 million from an initial $1 million cost (ex-land) due to increased equipment and building costs. This primarily impacts franchisees as company new unit development has been limited.

- **Limited operating history with small-format units** While we are highly optimistic about the company's new smaller-format units, there is limited operating history to date and no public information on the unit economics.

- **Competition** Although we are less concerned about competition in the doughnut category, Krispy Kreme will encounter competition as it enters the coffee segment. Still, it is our view that its existing brand and customer loyalty will mitigate that risk.

- **Fad risk** Although Krispy Kreme is about 65 years old, its initial reception in many markets is unlikely to be sustained over time. We expect some cannibalization as the brand becomes better established. Offsetting this, we believe, will be the positive impact of the more convenience-oriented small-format units.

4 Krispy Kreme Doughnuts

TABLE G
Krispy Kreme Income Statement (FY01–FY04E)

Fiscal Year Ends: January	FY 2001A	FY 2002A	FY 2003E	FY 2004E
Company Stores	213,677	266,209	303,206	334,624
Franchised Stores	234,452	355,456	533,968	779,888
Systemwide Sales	$448,129	$621,655	$837,174	$1,114,512
Company Stores	213,677	266,209	303,206	334,624
Franchise Operations	9,445	14,963	22,615	32,128
Support Sales	77,516	114,137	169,507	239,445
Net Sales	$300,638	$394,354	$494,818	$606,197
Company Store Expenses	181,469	217,418	245,065	270,026
Franchise Expenses	3,643	4,896	6,771	9,780
Support Operations Expenses	65,512	94,631	138,413	194,058
Operating Expenses	250,624	316,946	390,249	473,864
D & A	6,458	7,959	10,121	12,081
General & Admin. Expense	20,061	27,562	33,959	40,918
Operating Profit	29,953	41,887	60,489	79,334
Interest/Other Expense (Income)	(1,593)	(2,408)	(1,395)	(1,400)
Joint Venture Income (Loss)	(600)	(602)	(198)	450
Minority Interest	(717)	(1,147)	(1,183)	(850)
Earnings Before Taxes	23,771	42,546	60,503	80,334
Income Taxes	9,058	16,168	22,991	30,527
Net Income	14,713	26,378	37,512	49,807
EPS	$0.27	$0.45	$0.63	$0.84
Avg. Shs. Outs. (FD)	53,656	58,434	59,174	59,574
Sales Ratios				
Operating Expenses	83.36%	80.37%	78.87%	78.17%
Contribution Profit (Bef. G & A)	16.64%	19.63%	21.13%	21.83%
D & A	2.15%	2.02%	2.05%	1.99%
General Administrative Exp.	6.67%	6.99%	6.86%	6.75%
Operating Income	9.96%	10.62%	12.22%	13.09%
Tax Rate	38.10%	38.00%	38.00%	38.00%
Net Income	4.89%	6.69%	7.58%	8.22%
Year-Over-Year % Change:				
Systemwide Sales	40.6%	38.7%	34.7%	33.1%
Company Sales	36.5%	31.2%	25.5%	22.5%
Operating Expenses	29.6%	26.5%	23.1%	21.4%
Selling General & Admin. Expense	27.5%	37.4%	23.2%	20.5%
Operating Profit	167.5%	39.8%	44.4%	31.2%
Net Income	147.0%	79.3%	42.2%	32.8%
EPS	81.1%	64.6%	40.4%	31.9%

Source: CIBC World Markets and company information.

4 Krispy Kreme Doughnuts

TABLE H
Krispy Kreme Balance Sheet (FY2000–FY2002)

Fiscal Year Ended: January (dollars in millions)	FY 2000A	FY 2001A	FY 2002A
Assets			
Cash/S-T investments	$3,183	$25,129	$37,196
Receivables (net)	20,367	24,733	38,682
Inventory	9,979	12,031	16,159
Other	7,509	5,718	9,732
Total Current Assets	41,038	67,611	101,769
Net Plant, Property, & Equipment	60,584	78,340	112,577
Other Assets	3,336	25,542	41,030
Total Long-term assets	63,920	103,882	153,607
Total Assets	**$104,958**	**$171,493**	**$255,376**
Liabilities & Stockholders' Equity			
Accounts Payable	$13,106	$14,697	$21,202
Accrued Liabilities	14,080	19,904	26,729
Current Mat. of Debt	2,400	0	0
Other		3,567	4,602
Total current liabilities	29,586	38,168	52,533
Long-term debt	20,502	0	3,912
Other long-term liabilities	7,115	6,529	8,773
Total long-term liabilities	27,617	6,529	12,685
Total liabilities	57,203	44,697	65,218
Minority interest		1,117	2,491
Total Stockholders' Equity	47,755	125,679	187,667
TOTAL LIABILITIES & EQUITY	**$104,958**	**$171,493**	**$255,376**

4 Krispy Kreme Doughnuts

5 Pre-Paid Legal Services, Inc.

Pre-Paid Legal plans are designed to help middle-income Americans have afford-able access to quality legal assistance.

Pre-Paid Legal Services Corporate Vision

Harland C. Stonecipher founded the Pre-Paid Legal Services, Inc. (PPLS) in 1972 after an expensive encounter with lawyers stemming from an automobile accident. PPLS sold legal expense insurance that provided for partial payment of legal fees in connection with the defense of certain civil and criminal actions. The company went public in 1979 and grew rapidly throughout the 1980s as an increasing number of Americans subscribed to legal service insurance (see **Exhibit 1**). In 1998 the company had membership revenues of $110 million, earnings of $30.2 million, and end–of-year book equity of $101.1 million. In May 1999 it began trading on the New York Stock Exchange and in August 1999 its market capitalization reached $738 million, an increase of 101% over the previous year.

Despite its strong financial performance, opinions about the future of Pre-Paid Legal Services (PPLS) varied widely among U.S. equity analysts in the period late-1997 to mid-1999. The company was highly recommended by a number of analysts, but there was also persistent short selling of the stock.[1] Short sellers' primary concern about the company was outlined in a *Fortune* article in late 1997. The business publication alleged that the company was using an inappropriate method of accounting for sales commissions. As a result of this uncertainty, the company's stock price fluctuated widely from a high of $40.50 to a low of $13.50 between late 1997 and mid-1999 (see **Exhibit 2**).

Business description[2]

PPLS offered its customers (termed members) a wide range of legal insurance. The most popular plan, The Family Plan, accounted for 94% of all memberships in 1998. This plan provided reimbursement for a broad range of legal expenses incurred by members and their spouses, including will and testament preparation, document review and letter writing, and some of the legal costs associated with employment-related trial defense, traffic

Professor Paul Healy and Teaching Fellow Jacob Cohen J.D. prepared this case. HBS cases are developed solely as the basis for class discussion. Cases are not intended to serve as endorsements, sources of primary data, or illustrations of effective or ineffective management. This is an abridged version of "Pre-Paid Legal Services, Inc. (A)," HBS No. 100-029 and "Pre-Paid Legal Services, Inc. (B)," HBS No. 100-030, prepared by Professor Paul Healy and Teaching Fellow Jacob Cohen J.D.

[1]Short sellers borrow stock certificates from a brokerage firm and sell the stocks on the open market. If the stock price declines, short sellers can buy back stock, cover their loan from the brokerage firm, and earn a profit. Of course, if the price increases, short sellers make a loss.

[2]The material in this section is from Pre-Paid Legal Services, Inc.'s 1998 10-K Statement.

violations, and Internal Revenue Service audits.[3] The Family Plan specified limits on the number of hours of attorney time that a member was entitled to receive for many of these services. It also provided a 25% discount on attorney rates for the purchase of any legal services over and above those provided under the insurance contract.

PPLS's membership premiums in 1998 averaged $19.08 per month (or $229 per year). Premiums were typically paid on a monthly basis either by automatic charges to the member's credit card or through employee payroll deductions. The premiums were generally guaranteed renewable and non-cancelable except for fraud, nonpayment of premiums, or upon written request by a member. The annual membership persistency rate in 1998 was high; approximately 75% of members at the beginning of the year and new members during the year continued to be enrolled in the program at the end of the year. At March 31 1999, PPLS had 648,475 active members, and membership had been increasing at about 40% per year.

PPLS marketed its memberships through a multi-level program that encouraged buyers to become salespeople. Members that sought to become sales associates paid the company a fee, typically $65, to cover the cost of training materials, training meetings, and home office support services. Registered sales associates sold the company's services to their friends and business associates. The most successful even recruited and developed their own sales force. In 1998 PPLS generated 76% of its annual sales from the roughly 150,000 members registered as sales associates. The remaining 24% of sales were generated through arrangements with insurance and service companies with established sales forces, such as CNA and Primerica Financial Services.

Sales associates were compensated on a commission basis (see **Exhibit 3**). Prior to 1995, associates that signed-up a new member received a commission of 70% of the first year premium, and a 16% commission for subsequent year renewals. First year commissions were paid in advance whereas renewal commissions were paid as premiums were received. For example, if a new member signed up at a premium of $229 per year, the associate responsible for the sale received a first year commission of $160 (0.70 × $229) at sign-up. If the member renewed in subsequent years, the sales associate received a monthly commission of $3.04 (0.16 × $19).

After 1995 PPLS modified its commission formula to a flat 25% commission for both initial year and subsequent renewal memberships. To retain and attract sales associates, PPLS advanced the sales associate three years of commission on every new membership sold. If a membership lapsed before the advances had been recovered, PPLS deducted 50% of any unearned advances from future commissions to the relevant associate. For example, if a new member signed up at a premium of $229, the associate received a commission advance of $171.75 (25% × 3 × $229). If one year later the member cancelled the policy, PPLS sought to recover $57.25, equal to 50% of the second and third year commissions (50% of $229 × 2 × 0.25).

PPLS had historically offered two forms of legal services, each with very different implications for managing legal claim costs. The first form of service, termed open panel, allowed members to use their own attorney to provide legal services available under their policy. Member's attorneys were reimbursed for their services using a payment schedule that reflected "usual, reasonable and customary fees" for a particular service and geographic area.

The second form of service, closed panel memberships, required members to access legal services through a network of independent attorneys that were under contract with PPLS. These provider attorneys were paid a fixed monthly fee on a per capita basis to provide services to plan members living within the state in which the attorney was licensed to practice. PPLS contracted with one large, highly rated legal firm in each of its 36 major

---

[3]Legal services specifically excluded from coverage included domestic matters, bankruptcy, deliberate criminal acts, alcohol or drug-related matters, business matters, and pre-existing conditions.

markets. Provider attorneys are typically rated 'AV' by Martindale-Hubbell, its highest rating. They were selected after a detailed review by PPLS management.

Average costs of membership benefits in 1998 were 33% of membership premiums and management reported that these costs were expected to remain at around 35% in the future.

Financial performance

PPLS reported record financial performance in period 1997 and 1998 (see **Exhibit 4** for summary financial data and **Exhibit 5** for 1998 financial statements and excerpted footnotes.). Membership revenues during this period grew by an average of 59% per year, net income grew by 71% per year, and operating cash flows grew 500% per year. The firm's financial performance for the first six months of 1999 continued to be impressive. Membership revenues grew by 20%, earnings by 54%, and operating cash flows by 138% (from $2.4 million to $5.7 million).

As a result of the company's growth performance, a number of equity analysts that followed the stock recommended it to their clients. For example, David Strasser of Salomon Brothers issued strong buy recommendations for PPLS in August 1997 and commented on the stock as follows:

> We reiterate our Strong Buy recommendation on the shares of Pre-Paid Legal Services, Inc. . . . We have recently increased our one-year price to $34 from $26. We did this for several reasons. First, the company continues to demonstrate consistent earnings growth, in line with Wall Street estimates, which gives us greater visibility of our projected 36% growth rate. . . . We are also encouraged by the company's ability to generate positive operating cash flow while still growing revenues 53%. This positive cash flow is indicative of the seasoned membership base that generates cash in spite of the company's policy of paying commission advances to its associates for new sales. We continue to believe that the company will announce an alliance with a major insurance company to sell the company's products. This would essentially double the size of the company's productive sales force and increase overall visibility of the prepaid legal product.[4]

Accounting dispute

Despite its strong financial performance, in late 1997 PPLS was a target of short selling. On November 24, 1997, *Fortune* published an article titled "Will Pre-Paid Keep Growing?" The article cited short seller Robert Olstein of Olstein's Financial Alert Fund, who explained that his concern arose because "PPLS's accounting for commissions is unrealistic and not in accordance with economic reality."[5] The *Fortune* article noted that:

> Rather than record the commissions as an instant hit to earnings, Pre-Paid spreads them out over a three-year period. Such deferrals, the shorts argue, make today's earnings growth look stronger than it really is. In the first half of this year, for example, if the company had swallowed commissions when they were paid, it would have shown little if any earnings growth—certainly not a level of growth to justify the stock's trading at nearly 40 times earnings.
>
> Plus, trouble could emerge if the company's cancellation rate on its policies increases and it can't somehow recover the commissions it has already paid. Pre-Paid shrugs this off, arguing that its historic cancellation rate is a manageable 24%.

[4]Analyst Report, David Strasser, Salomon Brothers, August 1997.

[5]Herb Greenberg, "Will Pre-Paid Keep Growing? A Company's HMO-Style Approach to Legal Services Has Won It Plenty of Fans—And a Soaring Price. But Shortsellers Say The Numbers Don't Add Up," *Fortune*, November 24, 1997.

And, Harp (PPLS's CEO) boasts, "I can predict this business more precisely than anybody you want to mention."

Maybe so, but the company's own figures, disclosed in SEC filings, show that the rate is on an upward trend. The fillings also state that Pre-Paid's cancellation rate will rise if newly written policies make up a greater portion of its business, and the company warns (deep in its 10-K annual report) that it experienced a "significant increase" in sales of new contracts last year. Unless this shift is offset by "other factors," the 10-K says, financial performance could be severely hurt. In other words, Olstein contends, Pre-Paid may face a big write-off at some point.

Management response

PPLS argued that its policy of accounting for commissions resulted in a commission expense that was more consistent with the collection of the premiums generated by the sale of such contracts. **Exhibit 6** shows management's discussion of commissions and membership persistency in the firm's 10-K statement. In addition, between October 1998 and June 1999 management acquired 1,384,440 of the firm's shares on the open market at an average price of $28 per share.[6]

Nonetheless, concern over the company's accounting persisted. In late June 1999, short sales were 6.5% of outstanding shares, more than four times the level of typical companies.[7] The company's stock traded at $26.63, well off its yearly high of $39.25 and the all-time high of $40.50.

Rick Nelson, an analyst at Furman Selz, summed up the market sentiment this way: "insiders feel they've got a company that's trading well off its high where the operating fundamentals are going gangbusters. But the shorts have caught on the notion that from a cash flow standpoint, the company just can't handle the growth, and that their business model itself will come back to haunt them."[8]

Questions

1   How does PPLS create value for its customers? What are the critical risks that it has to manage well?

2   How did the pre-1995 commission formula work? Why do you think the company changed its policy?

3   Based on the post-1995 commission formula and information in the case on pricing and commission rates, calculate the cash inflows for premiums and cash outflows for commissions for years 1 to 3 that would arise from the sign-up of 1000 new members at the beginning of year 1. Assume that (a) actual member renewal rates are 75 percent for both years 2 and 3 and (b) 25 percent of recoverable commission advances in each of years 2 and 3 prove uncollectable.

4   How does PPLS account for the transactions described in question 3?

5   Do you agree with *Fortune*'s criticism of PPLS's method of reporting for commissions? Why or why not?

6   What actions could PPLS's management take to reduce the unease among key investors about the firm's accounting and its business model?

[6]Quicken.com, Insider Trading in Pre-Paid Legal Services.
[7]"Uncovered Short Positions Rise on Big Board and Amex," *The New York Times*, June 22, 1999.
[8]Ian Mount, "The Long and Short of It," SmartMoney.com, May 25, 1999.

5 Pre-Paid Legal Services, Inc.

EXHIBIT 1   **Number of subscribers to legal service plans in the US in the period 1981 to 1997**

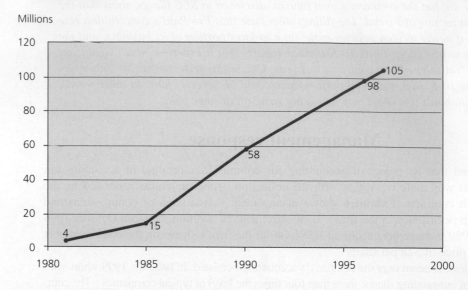

Note: The above estimates were developed by The National Resources Center for Consumer Legal Services (NRC) and reported by PPLS in its 1998 10-K Report. NRC estimates included free member plans sponsored by labor unions, the American Association for Retired Persons, the National Education Association and military services, as well as employer-paid plans. PPLS estimated that 10% of the total legal insurance market was covered by plans comparable to those provided by PPLS. The other major companies servicing this market were Hyatt Legal Services, ARAG Group, LawPhone, National Legal Plan, and the Signature Group. The NRC estimated that in 1997 the market share of these firms (and PPLS) was 79%. The market share of PPLS alone was estimated at 15%.
Source: Prepaid Legal Annual Report, 1998

EXHIBIT 2 **Stock performance for Pre-Paid Legal Services Inc. versus Dow Jones industrial average in the period August 1997 to July 1999.**

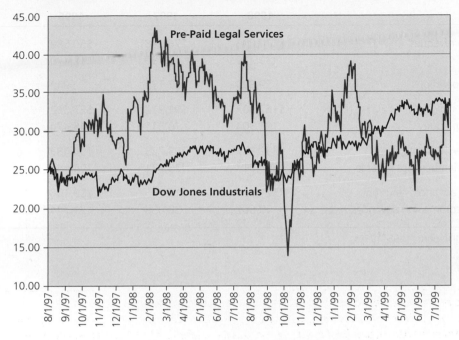

Source. Datastream International

EXHIBIT 3 **Summary of commission rates and timing of payment for PPLS**

Plan	First Year Commission	Subsequent Year Commissions
Pre-1995		
Commission rate	70% of subscription	16% of subscription
Timing of payment	At customer sign-up	Monthly
1995		
Commission rate	25% of subscription	25% of subscription
Timing of payment	Advance of three years' worth of commissions at customer sign-up	None for first three years, then monthly

EXHIBIT 4 **Summary financial information for Pre-Paid Legal Services (for year ended December 31 (in $000)**

	1998	1997	1996	1995
Membership revenues	$110,003	$76,688	$50,582	$31,290
Net Income	30,210	18,790	12,470	7,312
Cash from operations	$9,895	$7,733	$942	$548
Total assets	$167,903	$91,912	$57,532	$35,629
Book value of equity	101,304	70,511	45,474	29,740
New Memberships sold	391,827	283,723	194,483	109,922
Period end Memberships in force	603,017	425,381	294,151	203,535
Commission advances—current	$21,224	$15,705	$9,108	$3,923
Noncurrent commission advances, net	60,661	38,038	21,744	8,548

Source: Annual Reports, 1995–1998

EXHIBIT 5   Financial statements and selected footnotes for Pre-Paid Legal Services, December 31, 1998

Balance Sheet	December 31, 1998	December 31, 1997
In Thousands of Dollars		
ASSETS		
Current assets:		
Cash and cash equivalents	$8,604	$27,722
Available-for-sale investments, at fair value	2,368	0
Held-to-maturity investments	0	4,242
Accrued Membership income	3,595	2,399
Inventories	2,588	2,116
Prepaid product commissions	1,384	2,136
Amount due from coinsurer	12,498	0
Membership commission advances – current portion	21,224	15,705
Total current assets	52,261	54,320
Available-for-sale investments, at fair value	36,207	0
Held-to-maturity investments	0	650
Investments pledged	2,922	2,772
Membership commission advances, net	60,661	38,038
Property and equipment, net	7,678	5,226
Production costs, net	1,373	1,008
Other	6,801	3,702
Total assets	$167,903	$105,716
LIABILITIES AND STOCKHOLDERS' EQUITY		
Current liabilities:		
Membership benefits	$3,808	$2,649
Deferred product sales revenue	3,932	4,737
Accident and health reserves	12,498	0
Life insurance reserves	970	0
Current portion of capital lease obligation	487	142
Accounts payable and accrued expenses	9,386	12,009
Total current liabilities	31,081	19,537
Deferred income taxes	27,148	16,471
Life insurance reserves	7,711	0
Capital lease obligation, net of current portion	659	238
Total liabilities	66,599	36,246
Stockholders' equity:		
Preferred stock, $1 par value; authorized 400 shares; 3 issued and outstanding as follows: $3.00 Cumulative Convertible Preferred Stock, 3 shares authorized, issued and outstanding at December 31, 1998 and 1997, respectively; liquidation value of $55.00 at December 31, 1998.	3	3
Special preferred stock, $1 par value; authorized 500 shares, issued and outstanding in one series designated as follows: $1.00 Non-Cumulative Special Preferred Stock, 18 and 23 shares authorized, issued and outstanding at December 31, 1998 and 1997, respectively; liquidation value of $240 and $304 at December 31, 1998 and 1997, respectively	18	23

EXHIBIT 5 Financial statements *(continued)*

Balance Sheet	December 31, 1998	December 31, 1997
Common stock, $.01 par value; 100,000 shares authorized; 24,321 and 24,151 issued at December 31, 1998 and 1997, respectively	243	242
Capital in excess of par value	55,241	52,051
Retained earnings	49,528	19,328
Accumulated other comprehensive income:		
Unrealized gains (losses) on investments	(24)	0
Less: Treasury stock at cost; 797 and 747 shares held at December 31, 1998 and 1997, respectively	(3,705)	(2,177)
Total stockholders' equity	101,304	69,470
Total liabilities and stockholders' equity	167,903	105,716

Source: This data was extracted from Pre-Paid Legal Services Inc.'s 10-K Statement and downloaded from the SEC's EDGAR database using PricewaterhouseCoopers Global Technology Centre Edgarscan. Please read the on-line disclaimer at <http://edgarscan.pwcglobal.com/EdgarScan/edgarscan_disclaimer.html>.

5 Pre-Paid Legal Services, Inc.

EXHIBIT 5   Financial statements *(continued)*

Income Statement	December 31, 1998	December 31, 1997	December 31, 1996
In Thousands of Dollars except for per share measures			
Revenues:			
Membership premiums	$110,003	$76,688	$50,582
Product sales	27,779	41,070	26,425
Associate services	17,255	12,143	5,646
Interest income	2,576	1,689	1,303
Other	2,840	1,814	1,678
	160,453	133,404	85,634
Costs and expenses:			
Membership benefits	36,103	25,132	16,871
Product costs	17,967	27,017	20,568
Commissions	24,261	16,717	11,476
General and administrative	21,902	20,311	15,150
Associate services and direct marketing	14,738	11,431	4,544
Depreciation	2,944	2,026	533
Premium taxes	1,206	866	372
	119,121	103,500	69,514
Income before income taxes	41,332	29,904	16,120
Provision for income taxes	11,122	12,381	5,857
Net income	30,210	17,523	10,263
Less dividends on preferred shares	10	13	15
Net income applicable to common stockholders.	$30,200	17,510	10,248
Basic earnings per common share	$1.29	$0.76	$0.46
Diluted earnings per common share	$1.26	$0.74	$0.44
Comprehensive Income			
Net income	$30,210	$17,523	$10,263
Other comprehensive income (loss):			
Unrealized gains (losses) on investments:			
Unrealized holding gains (losses) arising during period	(24)	0	0
Other comprehensive income	(24)	0	0
Comprehensive income	$30,186	$17,523	$10,263

5 Pre-Paid Legal Services, Inc.

EXHIBIT 5 Financial statements (*continued*)

Cash Flow Statement	December 31, 1998	December 31, 1997	December 31, 1996
In Thousands of Dollars			
Cash flows from operating activities:			
Net income	$30,210	$17,523	$10,263
Adjustments to reconcile net income to net cash provided by operating activities:			
Provision for stock grant, stock transfer and associate stock options	0	644	1,122
Provision for deferred income taxes	11,122	12,293	5,857
Depreciation and amortization	2,944	2,026	533
Net changes in asset and liability accounts, net of effects of purchase of UFL:			
Increase in accrued Membership income	(1,196)	(689)	(672)
Increase in commission advances	(28,142)	(22,891)	(18,381)
Increase in other assets	(304)	(678)	(1,360)
Increase in inventories	(472)	(489,)	(1,270)
Decrease (increase) in prepaid product commissions	752	(513)	(622)
(Decrease) increase in deferred revenue	(805)	771	1,390
Increase in Membership benefits	1,159	787	315
(Decrease) increase in accounts payable and accrued expenses	(5,373)	5,688	1,914
Net cash provided by (used in) operating activities	9,895	14,472	(911)
Cash flows from investing activities:			
Acquisition of UFL, net of cash acquired	(18,995)	0	0
Additions to property and equipment and production costs	(4,926)	(3,619)	(1,592)
Purchases of held-to-maturity investments	(36,116)	(3,035)	(1,374)
Proceeds from sales of held-to-maturity investments	23,718	0	0
Maturities of held-to-maturity investments	4,892	400	111,000
Net cash used in investing activities	(31,427)	(6,254)	(2,855)
Cash flows from financing activities:			
Proceeds from sale of common and preferred stock	3,186	3,229	4,904
Increase in capital lease obligations	766	248	84
Purchase of treasury stock	(1,528)	0	0
Dividends paid on preferred stock	(10)	(13)	(15)
Net cash provided by financing activities	2,414	3,464	4,973
Net (decrease) increase in cash and cash equivalents	(19,118)	11,682	1,207
Cash and cash equivalents at beginning of year	27,722	16,040	14,833
Cash and cash equivalents at end of year	$8,604	$27,722	$16,040
Supplemental disclosure of cash flow information:			
Cash paid for interest	47	36	28
Purchases of property and equipment under capital leases	1,104	445	63
Assets acquired in acquisition of UFL	44,598		
Liabilities assumed in acquisition of UFL	23,929		

Source: This data was extracted from Pre-Paid Legal Services Inc.'s 10-K Statement and downloaded from the SEC's EDGAR database using PricewaterhouseCoopers Global Technology Centre Edgarscan. Please read the on-line disclaimer at <http://edgarscan.pwcglobal.com/EdgarScan/edgarscan_disclaimer.html>.

EXHIBIT 5 Financial statements *(continued)*

Selected Footnote Information

Note 1 – Nature of Operations and Summary of Significant Accounting Policies

Estimates

The preparation of financial statements in conformity with generally accepted accounting principles requires management to make estimates and assumptions that affect the reported amounts of assets and liabilities and disclosure of contingent assets and liabilities at the date of the financial statements and the reported amounts of revenues and expenses during the reporting period. Actual results could differ from those estimates.

Commissions

Effective March 1, 1995, the Company implemented a level membership commission schedule of approximately 25% of annual premium revenue for all Membership years. This commission schedule results in the Company incurring commission expense related to the sale of its legal expense plans on a basis consistent with the collection of the premiums generated by the sale of such Memberships. The Company currently advances the equivalent of three years of commissions on new Membership sales. In January 1997, the Company implemented a new policy whereby associates receive only earned commissions on the first three Memberships submitted unless the associate successfully completes a training program which includes an intensive one-day training seminar, produces three Memberships and recruits one associate within 15 business days from their training date. Prior to March 1, 1995, first year commissions payable on the sale of a Membership, and earned in the first Membership year, were approximately 70% of annual Membership premiums while renewal commissions (payable as earned after the first Membership year) were approximately 16% of annual premiums.

Revenue Recognition

Membership premiums are recognized in income when due in accordance with Membership terms which generally require the holder of the Membership to remit premiums on a monthly basis. Memberships are canceled for nonpayment of premium after ninety days. Premiums due but not collected at the end of an accounting period are recorded as accrued Membership income; a provision for uncollectible premiums, if any, is recorded currently. Revenues from Associates'

training program fees and sales of marketing supplies are recognized as income when cash is received. Revenues for product sales are recognized when products are shipped or services provided.

Commission Advances

Commission advances represent the unearned portion of commissions advanced to Associates on sales of Memberships. Commissions are earned as premiums are collected, usually on a monthly basis. The Company reduces Commission advances as premiums are paid and commissions earned. Unearned commission advances on lapsed Memberships are recovered through collection of premiums on an associate's active Memberships. At December 31, 1998 and 1997, the Company had an allowance of $4.0 million and $3.7 million, respectively, to provide for estimated uncollectible balances. The Company charges interest at the prime rate on unearned commission advances relating to Memberships that canceled subsequent to the advance being made.

Membership Benefit Liability

The Membership benefit liability represents claims reported but not paid and actuarially estimated claims incurred but not reported on open panel Memberships and per capita amounts due provider attorneys on closed panel Memberships. The Company calculates the benefit liability costs on open panel Memberships based on completion factors that consider historical claims experience based on the dates that claims are incurred, reported to the Company and subsequently paid. Processing costs related to these claims are accrued based on an estimate of expenses to process such claims.

Life Insurance Reserves

Incurred but not reported claim estimates are actuarially estimated based on life insurance in-force and estimated claims occurrences.

5 Pre-Paid Legal Services, Inc.

5 Pre-Paid Legal Services, Inc.

EXHIBIT 6 **Management discussion of commissions and membership persistency, excerpted from management's discussion and analysis of financial condition and results, Pre-Paid Legal Services 10-K, December 31, 1998.**

Commissions

Beginning with new Memberships written after March 1, 1995, the Company implemented a level commission schedule which results in the Company incurring commission expense related to the sale of its legal expense plans on a basis more consistent with the collection of the premiums generated by the sale of such Memberships. Prior to March 1, 1995, the Company had incurred much higher commissions (approximately 70%) during the first year of the Membership with substantially lower commissions (approximately 16%) in all subsequent years. The level commission structure results in the Company incurring commissions at the rate of approximately 25% per year for all Membership years.

Prior to January 1997 the Company advanced commissions at the time of sale of all new Memberships. In January 1997, the Company implemented a policy whereby the associate receives only earned commissions on the first three sales unless the associate has successfully completed the new training program that was implemented at the same time. For all sales beginning with the fourth Membership or all sales made by an associate successfully completing the new training program, the Company currently advances commissions at the time of sale of a new Membership. The amount of cash potentially advanced upon the sale of a new Membership, prior to the recoupment of any charge-backs (described below), represents an amount equal to up to three years commission earnings. Although the average number of marketing associates receiving an advance commission payment on a new Membership is 11, the overall initial advance may be paid to more than twenty different individuals, each at a different level within the overall commission structure. This commission advance immediately increases an associate's account with the Company and represents prepaid commissions on active Memberships.

Should a Membership lapse before the advances have been recovered for each commission level, the Company immediately generates a "charge-back" to the applicable sales associate to recapture 50% of any unearned advance. This charge-back is immediately deducted from any future advances that would otherwise be payable to the associate for additional new Memberships. The Company historically has been able

to immediately recover the majority of such charge-backs. Any remaining unrecovered advance on a Membership that has lapsed represents a receivable from the associate and is reflected as commission advances and is categorized as current or non-current based on the expected recovery period. Additionally, even though a commission advance may have been fully recovered on a particular Membership, no additional commission earnings from any Membership will be paid to an associate until all previous advances on all Memberships, both active and lapsed, have been recovered. During 1998, 22% of all associates submitting new Memberships accounted for 75% of all such new Memberships produced thereby further enhancing the recovery of commission advances.

The Company's commission advance policy exposes the Company to the risk of uncollectible commission advances particularly for associates who do not receive commissions on a large number of Memberships or who experience below average Membership persistency. The Company closely monitors such commission advances to ensure maximum recoverability and maintains a recoverability reserve which at December 31, 1998 and 1997, was $4.0 million and $3.7 million, respectively.

Associates also receive compensation when associates sponsored by them or other associates that they have sponsored in their organization successfully complete the new training program implemented by the Company on January 4, 1997. In order to successfully qualify, the new associate going through the training program must produce 3 new Memberships and recruit 1 new associate within 15 days of receiving the training.

Membership Persistency

One of the major factors affecting the Company's profitability and cash flow is Membership ersistency, which represents the ability of the Company to retain a Membership, and therefore receive premiums, once it has been written. The Company monitors its overall Membership persistency rate, as well as the persistency rates with respect to Memberships sold by individual associates and agents and persistency rates with respect to Membership sales by geographic region and payment method. The Company's Membership persistency rate measures the number of Memberships in force at the end of a year as a percentage of the total of (i) Memberships in force at the beginning of such year, plus (ii) new Memberships sold during such year. From 1981 through the year ended December 31, 1998, the Company's annual Membership persistency rates, using the foregoing method, have averaged approximately 75%. The annual Membership persistency rates were 73.8%, 73.6% and 73.9% for 1998, 1997 and 1996, respectively. The Company's overall Membership persistency rate varies based on, among other factors, the relative age of total Memberships in force. The Company's overall Membership persistency rate could be lower when the Memberships in force include a higher proportion of newer Memberships. During the last three years, the Company has experienced significant increases in new Membership sales and, as a result, the percentage of newer Memberships in its total Memberships in force has

increased. Unless offset by other factors, this increase could result in a decline in the Company's overall Membership persistency rate as determined by the formula described above, but does not necessarily indicate that the new Memberships written are less persistent, only that the ratio of new Memberships to total Memberships is higher than it averaged during the 1981 through 1998 period. The Company's financial condition and results of operations may be materially adversely affected if the persistency rates of existing and new Memberships are materially lower than the Company's historical experience.

Source: This data was extracted from Pre-Paid Legal Services Inc.'s 10-K Statement and downloaded from the SEC's EDGAR database using PricewaterhouseCoopers Global Technology Centre Edgarscan. Please read the on-line disclaimer at <http://edgarscan.pwcglobal.com/EdgarScan/edgarscan_disclaimer.html>.

CASE

6 Spyker Cars N.V.

On March 24, 2006, Spyker Cars N.V. published its financial statements for the fiscal year 2005. The company reported its fifth loss in a row. The company's revenues, however, had almost doubled since 2004 to €8 million and management announced that it expected positive cash flows from operations for the first quarter of 2006. On the financial statements publication date, Spyker's shares traded at about €18.50 per share.

Company background[1]

In May 2004 – 3.5 years after the company's foundation – Netherlands-based Spyker Cars N.V. offered its ordinary shares for public trading on the Amsterdam Stock Exchange. One of the reasons that the company wanted to have its shares publicly traded was that it would signal transparency, reliability, and credibility to its prospective customers. Although the company's brand "Spyker" had a long history, Spyker Cars N.V. still had to build its reputation.

The first Spyker-branded motorcar (with a Benz-engine) had been built in 1898 by the two Dutch brothers Jacobus and Hendrik-Jan Spijker. In 1903, the Spijker brothers built the first car with a six-cylinder engine, four-wheel drive, and four-wheel brakes. They established their reputation for high-quality engineering and production even more when in 1907 the Spyker 14/18HP Tourer arrived second in the famous Peking-to-Paris car rally. After producing aircraft engines and fighter aircrafts during the First World War, Spyker continued its development and production of luxurious cars. The company went bankrupt in 1925. In 2000, Spyker Cars N.V. acquired the rights to the brand name "Spyker".

The strategy of the new company was (quoted from Spyker's 2005 Annual Report):

■ To position the Spyker brand as a premium brand for exclusive and hand-built (sports) cars and related products in the high-end (sports) car market with a high-end distribution network to match.

■ To create a distinctive, custom-made high-end product incorporating aviation and racing styling elements derived from the original Spyker brand in the period 1898–1925 in the form of a high-tech package with state-of-the-art underpinnings.

■ To prove reliability and quality, and to create credibility, brand recognition and business, by engaging in active racing in the international endurance race arena.

During its first five years of operations, Spyker had introduced four different car models: the C8 Spyder (in 2000, approximate selling price €217,000), the C8 Laviolette (in 2001, approximate selling price €235,000), the C8 Double 12R (in 2001, approximate selling price €254,000), and the C12 LaTurbie (in 2005, approximate selling price €276,000).

Professor Erik Peek prepared this case. The case is intended solely as the basis for class discussion and is not intended to serve as an endorsement, source of primary data, or illustration of effective or ineffective management.

[1]Most of the material in this section comes from Spyker's Annual Report for fiscal 2005 and its IPO Prospectus (March 27, 2004).

The C12 LaTurbie would be in production in the course of 2006. These models were all cars that the company labeled "super sports cars" and all part of one product line. In February 2006, Spyker entered a new market segment by starting a second product line. The company introduced a new Super Sports Utility Vehicle (SSUV), the D12 Peking-to-Paris (approximate selling price €230,000). The new car model was named after the 1907 Paris-to-Peking pioneer race. Spyker quickly received 114 orders for this car model from all over the world. Production of the first Spyker D12 Peking-to-Paris was planned for the fourth quarter of 2007. Car models in Spyker's market segment would typically stay in production for at least seven years. Spyker's management expected that the C8 Spyder, the Laviolette, and the Double 12 would remain in production until (at least) the end of 2010.

In 2005, Spyker's production increased to 48 super cars (from 31 in 2004), of which 26 were produced in the fourth quarter. The fourth quarter increase in production was supported by the outsourcing of the "bodies-in-white" production to Germany-based Wilhelm Karmann GmbH. Of the 48 cars that Spyker produced, 26 were sold (compared to 15 cars in 2004), 9 were held in stock (compared to 11 in 2004), and 10 were used for marketing and development activities (compared to 5 in 2004). Spyker's primary geographic segments were the US (39 percent), Europe (27 percent), and China (15 percent). At the end of 2004, Spyker had an order backlog (number of cars ordered but still to be produced) of 99 cars. The order backlog increased to 191 in 2005. This increase was primarily the consequence of obtaining the necessary permissions to sell cars in the US, such as an EPA emission certificate and NHTSA waivers. To meet the increased demand for its super cars, Spyker had purchased a new 12,000 square meter production plant in March 2006. The company further planned to increase its staff from 77 in 2005 to 125 full-time equivalents in 2006. Management expected that Spyker would increase production from 48 super cars in 2005 to more than 100 cars in 2006.

Industry analysts estimated that the size of the market for "super cars" was less than a half percent of the total global car market. The greatest demand for super cars came from the US, followed by western Europe and Japan. Emerging demand, however, came from eastern Europe, Russia, China, and the Far East. In 2005, worldwide super car sales increased – especially sales of "low-priced" super cars such as the Bentley Continental and the Lamborghini Gallardo (approximate selling prices between €200,000 and €250,000). Analysts expected this increase to continue in the following years because the post-war baby boomers would reach the optimum of their purchasing power. Spyker's management expected to benefit from the aging of the population but, at the same time, worked on entering a new market segment with a different type of customer – the luxury Sports Utility Vehicle (SUV) segment.

In its IPO Prospectus of May 27, 2004, Spyker summarized the main business risks that the company was subject to:

- The company had a short operating history during which it had not been able to make a profit and pay out dividends. Spyker further operated in a competitive market that was sensitive to adverse economic conditions or changes in consumer sentiment. The company's results could be substantially influenced by changes in prices for super cars or changes in exchange rates.

- It was uncertain whether in the future Spyker would be able to fund its growth. In addition, because the market demand for Spyker cars exceeded and would likely continue to exceed the company's production capacity, the company ran the risk that it would lose market share to competitors who had no such capacity constraints.

- Spyker relied on third-party suppliers to whom the company had outsourced part of its production and assembly activities.

6 Spyker Cars

- The company's future success would crucially depend on its ability to attract highly skilled personnel, innovate its products, protect its intellectual property rights and trademarks, secure brand recognition, and adequately anticipate changes in consumer preferences.

- Future increases in safety or environmental regulation could increase the company's development and production costs.

- Spyker sold its cars via a network of multibrand dealerships. Because these dealers were not solely dependent on Spyker, it remained uncertain whether the company would be able to expand and maintain its distribution network.

Spyker Cars had several large shareholders. The company's Chief Executive Officer, Victor Muller, held more than 25 percent of its voting capital. Four outside block-holders held more than 10 percent each of the company's shares.

Question

Estimate the value of Spyker's shares on March 28, 2006. Would you invest in the company?

EXHIBIT 1 Spyker Car's income statements, balance sheets and cash flow statements for the fiscal years ending December 31, 2002 to 2005

INCOME STATEMENTS (€ thousands)

	2002 (Dutch GAAP)	2003 (Dutch GAAP)	2004 (IFRS)	2005 (IFRS)
Net sales	215	910	3,697	5,848
Movement in work in process	416	738	169	(589)
Other revenues	557	1,247	337	2,775
Total revenues	**1,188**	**2,895**	**4,203**	**8,034**
Raw materials and consumables	(616)	(1,397)	(2,832)	(2,558)
Subcontracted work and other external costs	(452)	(1,326)	(210)	(1,190)
Employee benefits	(283)	(1,164)	(1,911)	(2,577)
Amortization and depreciation	(462)	(903)	(1,443)	(1,621)
Other operating expenses	(801)	(2,321)	(2,719)	(3,263)
Operating profit	**(1,426)**	**(4,216)**	**(4,912)**	**(3,175)**
Financial income	2	7	0	61
Financial expenses	(477)	(934)	(818)	(530)
Result before taxation	**(1,901)**	**(5,143)**	**(5,730)**	**(3,644)**
Taxation	656	335	633	1,679
Result for the year	**(1,245)**	**(4,808)**	**(5,097)**	**(1,965)**
Attributable to minority interests	0	0	111	35
Net result	**(1,245)**	**(4,808)**	**(4,986)**	**(1,930)**
Number of shares outstanding on December 31			2,491,303	3,667,781
Number of shares outstanding on December 31 (diluted)			2,491,303	3,917,558

6 Spyker Cars

BALANCE SHEETS (€ thousands)

	2002 (Dutch GAAP)	2003 (Dutch GAAP)	2004 (IFRS)	2005 (IFRS)
Property, plant, and equipment	2,596	3,315	3,084	7,036
Development costs	5,794	10,083	15,915	19,715
Patents and licenses	0	0	50	99
Deferred tax assets	1,162	1,440	2,354	4,400
Total fixed assets	**9,552**	**14,838**	**21,403**	**31,250**
Raw materials	417	714	1,318	634
Work in process	416	531	377	686
Finished products	0	0	2,081	946
Trade and other receivables	245	840	3,745	11,129
Receivables from group companies	26	12	0	0
Receivables from participants	0	0	402	467
Taxes and social security contributions	423	624	250	425
Cash and cash equivalents	0	0	243	222
Total current assets	**1,527**	**2,721**	**8,416**	**14,509**
Total assets	**11,079**	**17,559**	**29,819**	**45,759**
Total equity attributable to equity holders of the company	(1,715)	(4,339)	16,453	28,396
Minority interest	0	0	(111)	(146)
Group equity	**(1,715)**	**(4,339)**	**16,342**	**28,250**
Provisions	0	10	52	122
Interest-bearing borrowings	1,499	2,137	1,863	6,902
Loans granted by shareholders	7,040	11,833	0	0
Total non-current liabilities	**8,539**	**13,980**	**1,915**	**7,024**
Credit institutions	2,495	4,699		
Bank overdraft			3,829	1,413
Interest-bearing borrowings			955	2,230
Trade and other payables	953	2,459	6,616	6,755
Loans granted by shareholders	756	0	0	0
Taxes and social security contributions	51	106	162	87
Accrued development costs	0	654	0	0
Total current liabilities	**4,255**	**7,918**	**11,562**	**10,485**
Group equity and liabilities	**11,079**	**17,559**	**29,819**	**45,759**

6 Spyker Cars

CASH FLOW STATEMENTS (€ thousands)

	2002 (Dutch GAAP)	2003 (Dutch GAAP)	2004 (IFRS)	2005 (IFRS)
Operating profit	(1,426)	(4,216)		
Net result for the year			(5,097)	(1,965)
Adjusted for:				
Amortization and depreciation	462	903	1,443	1,621
Addition to provisions	0	10	42	70
Equity-settled share-based expenses			0	75
Income tax effect			(633)	(1,679)
Net financing costs			818	469
Movement in working capital:				
Receivables	(266)	(782)	(2,921)	(7,624)
Inventories	(791)	(412)	(2,531)	1,510
Short-term liabilities	628	1,459	4,025	1,339
Cash flow from interest and taxes				
Interest income / charges	(475)	(927)	(818)	(469)
Corporate income tax paid / received	0	0	0	0
Cash flow from operating activities	**(1,868)**	**(3,965)**	**(5,672)**	**(6,653)**
Investments in non-current assets	(5,928)	(6,178)	(7,851)	(6,683)
Disposal of non-current assets	0	324	476	137
Cash flow from investment activities	**(5,928)**	**(5,854)**	**(7,375)**	**(6,546)**
Increase in loans	5,065	6,058	3,082	3,800
Accrued interest	0	628	366	0
Redemption of long-term liabilities	(117)	(1,255)	(15,555)	(1,529)
Net proceeds from new share issues	360	2,184	25,778	13,323
Cash flow financing activities	**5,308**	**7,615**	**13,671**	**15,594**
Movement in cash and equivalents	**(2,488)**	**(2,204)**	**624**	**2,395**
Balance of cash and bank overdraft as at 1 January	(7)	(2,495)	(4,210)	(3,586)
Balance of cash and bank overdraft as at 31 December	**(2,495)**	**(4,699)**	**(3,586)**	**(1,191)**

6 Spyker Cars

EXHIBIT 2   **Excerpts from the notes to Spyker Car's financial statements for the fiscal year ending on December 31, 2005**

Note 5. Intangible assets

31 December 2005 (€ thousands)	Externally acquired development costs	Internally acquired development costs	Patents and licenses	Total
Costs as at 1 January, net of accumulated amortization and impairment	15,401	514	50	15,965
Investments	3,330	1,120	58	4,508
Amortization	(598)	(52)	(9)	(659)
At 31 December, net of accumulated amortization and impairment	18,133	1,582	99	19,814
At 1 January 2005:				
Cost	14,886	1,577	66	16,529
Accumulated amortization and impairment	(501)	(47)	(16)	(564)
Net carrying amount	14,385	1,530	50	15,965
At 1 January 2005:				
Cost	18,216	2,697	124	21,037
Accumulated amortization and impairment	(1,099)	(99)	(25)	(1,223)
Net carrying amount	17,177	2,598	99	19,814

The development costs in 2005 mainly relate to the following subjects:

■ Start of the development of the Spyker SSUV Peking-to-Paris.

■ Development costs for subsequent expenditure related to increased future economic benefits.

■ Further development and innovation of Spyker Squadron.

■ Certification (LEV-II and other).

Impairment testing did not result in an impairment loss. The impairment test is performed based on expectations regarding future revenues, results, cash flows and investments including amortization cost. The capital development costs are amortized over their estimated useful lives by a fixed amount for each sold car based on expected sales over that period. Patents and licenses are being amortized over their useful lives of 10 years.

Note 6. Deferred tax assets

Recognized deferred tax assets (€ thousands)	2005	2004
Losses carried forward at 1 January	15,687	8,342
Add: costs of IPO and share issues	842	1,873
Add: loss carried forward for the year	3,293	5,472
Total loss carried forward at 31 December	19,822	15,687
Calculated deferred tax	5,867	5,412
Provisions	(1,467)	(3,058)
Recognized deferred tax asset	4,400	2,354
Tax percentage	29.6%	34.5%

The carry-forward tax losses only relate to the Netherlands. Some minor tax losses in foreign countries have not been recognized since future usage depends on, among other things, profit-earning capacity. The deferred tax assets relate to carry-forward losses in corporate income tax. The deferred tax is calculated based on the expected future taxable result of the Company, less a provision for uncertainty in respect of realization. The amount is calculated with the anticipated tax rate in the expected realization period.

Note 21. Amortization and depreciation

The amortization and depreciation of intangible fixed assets and property, plant and equipment can be specified as follows:

(€ thousands)	2005	2004
Amortization development costs	650	425
Amortization intellectual property rights	9	7
Depreciation of property, plant and equipment	962	1,011
	1,621	1,443

Note 22. Other operating expenses

(€ thousands)	2005	2004
Advice costs	345	294
Freight and transportation costs	201	117
Rent and housing costs	260	228
Insurance	239	78
Office costs	226	246
Other	522	456
PR and marketing costs	923	1,031
Travel expenses and costs of company cars	547	269
	3,263	2,719

Note 23. Net financing costs

Net financing income comprises the foreign exchange results for an amount of €61 thousand. Net financing expenses comprises interest payments.

Note 24. Taxation

The Company has recorded an estimated value of carry-forward losses in Dutch corporate income tax. This item has been included as a deferred tax asset under the non-current assets in the balance sheet. The taxation has been calculated as follows:

(€ thousands)	2005	2004
Consolidated result before taxes	(3,644)	(5,730)
Less: result of foreign participations	350	259
Taxable amount	(3,294)	(5,471)
Applied tax rate (29.6% for 2005 and 34.5% for 2004)	975	1,888
Less: provision	(244)	(1,067)
Effective taxation	731	821
Adjustment related to change in applied tax rate and provision	948	(188)
Taxation	1,679	633

The deferred tax assets are calculated based on the expected future taxable result of the Company, less a provision for the uncertainty in respect of realization. The amount is calculated with the anticipated tax rate in the expected realization period and the forecast for the coming five years.

Note 29. Explanation of transition to IFRS

As stated in note 2, these are the Group's first consolidated financial statements prepared in accordance with IFRS. The accounting policies set out in note 2 have been applied in preparing the financial statements for the year ended 31 December 2005, the comparative information presented in these financial statements for the year ended 31 December 2004 and in the preparation of an opening IFRS balance sheet at 1 January 2004 (the Group's date of transition). In preparing its opening IFRS balance sheet, the Group did not have to adjust amounts reported previously in financial statements prepared in accordance with Dutch GAAP. Despite the change in accounting policies the transition from Dutch GAAP to IFRS did not affect the consolidated equity and consolidated result.

7 The Home Depot, Inc.

The difference between a company with a concept and one without is the difference between a stock that sells for 20 times earnings and one that sells for 10 times earnings. The Home Depot is definitely a concept stock, and it has the multiple to prove it—27–28 times likely earnings in the current fiscal year ending this month. On the face of it, The Home Depot might seem like a tough one for the concept-mongers to work with. It's a chain of hardware stores. But, as we noted in our last visit to the company in the spring of '83, these hardware stores are huge warehouse outlets—60,000 to 80,000 feet in space. You can fit an awful lot of saws in these and still have plenty of room left over to knock together a very decent concept.

And in truth, the warehouse notion is the hottest thing in retailing these days. The Home Depot buys in quantum quantities, which means that its suppliers are eager to keep within its good graces and hence provide it with a lot of extra service. The company, as it happens, is masterful in promotion and pricing. The last time we counted, it had 22 stores, all of them located where the sun shines all the time.

Growth has been sizzling. Revenues, a mere $22 million in fiscal '80, shot past the quarter billion mark three years later. As to earnings, they have climbed from two cents in fiscal '80 to an estimated 60 cents in the fiscal year coming to an end [in January 1985].

Its many boosters in the Street, moreover, anticipate more of the same as far as the bullish eye can see. They're confidently estimating 30% growth in the new fiscal year as well. Could be. But while we share their esteem for the company's merchandising skills and imagination, we're as bemused now as we were the first time we looked at The Home Depot by its rich multiple. Maybe a little more now than then.[1]

The above report appeared on January 21, 1985, in "Up & Down Wall Street," a regular column in *Barron's* financial weekly.

Company background

Bernard Marcus and Arthur Blank founded The Home Depot in 1978 to bring the warehouse retailing concept to the home center industry. The company operated retail "do-it-yourself" (DIY) warehouse stores which sold a wide assortment of building materials and home improvement products. Sales, which were on a cash-and-carry basis, were concentrated in the home remodeling market. The company targeted as its customers individual homeowners and small contractors.

[1]Reprinted with permission from *Barron's*, January 21, 1985.

The Home Depot's strategy had several important elements. The company offered low and competitive prices, a feature central to the warehouse retailing concept. The Home Depot's stores, usually in suburbs, were also the warehouses, with inventory stacked over merchandise displayed on industrial racks. The warehouse format of the stores kept the overhead low and allowed the company to pass the savings to customers. Costs were further reduced by emphasizing higher volume and lower margins with a high inventory turnover. While offering low prices, The Home Depot was careful not to sacrifice the depth of merchandise and the quality of products offered for sale.

To ensure that the right products were stocked at all times, each Home Depot store carried approximately $4,500,000 of inventory, at retail, consisting of approximately 25,000 separate stock-keeping units. All these items were kept on the sales floor of the store, thus increasing convenience to the customer and minimizing out-of-stock occurrences. The company also assured its customers that the products sold by it were of the best quality. The Home Depot offered nationally advertised brands as well as lesser known brands carefully chosen by the company's merchandise managers. Every product sold by The Home Depot was guaranteed by either the manufacturer or by the company itself.

The Home Depot complemented the above merchandising strategy with excellent sales assistance. Since the great majority of the company's customers were individual homeowners with no prior experience in their home improvement projects, The Home Depot considered its employees' technical knowledge and service orientation to be very important to its marketing success. The company pursued a number of policies to address this need. Approximately 90% of the company's employees were on a full-time basis. To attract and retain a strong sales force, the company maintained salary and wage levels above those of its competitors. All the floor sales personnel attended special training sessions to gain thorough knowledge of the company's home improvement products and their basic applications. This training enabled them to answer shoppers' questions and help customers in choosing equipment and material appropriate for their projects. Often, the expert advice the sales personnel provided created a bond that resulted in continuous contact with the customer throughout the duration of the customer's project.

Finally, to attract customers, The Home Depot pursued an aggressive advertising program utilizing newspapers, television, radio, and direct mail catalogues. The company's advertising stressed promotional pricing, the broad assortment and depth of its merchandise, and the assistance provided by its sales personnel. The company also sponsored in-store demonstrations of do-it-yourself techniques and product uses. To increase customers' shopping convenience, The Home Depot's stores were open seven days a week, including weekday evenings.

Fortune magazine commented on The Home Depot's strategy as follows:

> *Warehouse stores typically offer shoppers deep discounts with minimal service and back-to-basics ambiance. The Home Depot's outlets have all the charm of a freight yard and predictably low prices. But they also offer unusually helpful customer service. Although warehouse retailing looks simple, it is not: As discounting cuts into gross profit margins, the merchant must carefully control buying, merchandising, and inventory costs. Throwing in service, which is expensive and hard to systematize, makes the job even tougher. In the do-it-yourself (DIY) segment of the industry—which includes old-style hardware stores, building supply warehouses, and the everything-under-one-roof home centers—The Home Depot is the only company that has successfully brought off the union of low prices and high service.[2]*

The Home Depot's strategy was successful in fueling an impressive growth in the company's operations. The first three Home Depot stores, opened in Atlanta in 1979, were a

[2]Reprinted with permission from *Fortune*, February 1988, p. 73.

7 The Home Depot, Inc.

quick success. From this modest beginning, the company grew rapidly and went public in 1981. The company's stock initially traded over-the-counter and was listed on the New York Stock Exchange in April 1984. Several new stores were opened in markets throughout the sunbelt and the number of stores operated by The Home Depot grew from 3 in 1979 to 50 by the end of fiscal 1985. As a result, sales grew from $7 million in 1979 to $700 million in 1985. **Exhibit 1** provides a summary of the growth in the company's operations. The company's stock price performance during 1985 is summarized in **Exhibit 2**.

Industry and competition

The home improvement industry was large and growing during the 1980s. The industry sales totaled approximately $80 billion in 1985 and strong industry growth was expected to continue, especially in the do-it-yourself (DIY) segment, which had grown at a compounded annual rate of 14% over the last 15 years. With the number of two-wage-earner households growing, there was an increase in families' average disposable income, making it possible to increase the frequency and magnitude of home improvement projects. Further, many homeowners were undertaking these projects by themselves rather than hiring a contractor. Research conducted by the Do-It-Yourself Institute, an industry trade group, showed that DIY activities had become America's second most popular leisure-time activity after watching television.

The success of warehouse retailing pioneered by The Home Depot attracted a number of other companies into the industry. Among the store chains currently operating in the industry were Builders Square (a division of K Mart), Mr. HOW (a division of Service Merchandise), The Home Club (a division of Zayre Corp.), Payless Cashways (a division of W.R. Grace), and Hechinger Co. Most of these store chains were relatively new and not yet achieving significant profitability.

Among The Home Depot's competitors, the most successful was Hechinger, which had operated hardware stores for a long time and recently entered the do-it-yourself segment of the industry. Using a strategy quite different from The Home Depot's, Hechinger ran gleaming upscale stores and aimed at high profit margins. As of the end of fiscal 1985, the company operated 55 stores, located primarily in southeastern states. Hechinger announced that it planned to expand its sales by 20 to 25% a year by adding 10 to 14 stores a year. A summary of Hechinger's recent financial performance is presented in **Exhibit 3**.

The Home Depot's future

While The Home Depot had achieved rapid growth every year since its inception, fiscal 1985 was probably the most important in the company's seven-year history. During 1985 the company implemented its most ambitious expansion plan to date by adding 20 new stores in eight new markets. Nine of these stores were acquired from Bowater, a competing store chain which was in financial difficulty. As The Home Depot engaged in major expansion, its revenues rose 62% from $432 million in fiscal 1984 to $700 million in 1985. However, the company's earnings declined in 1985 from the record levels achieved during the previous fiscal year. In fiscal 1985, The Home Depot earned $8.2 million, or $0.33 per share, as compared with $14.1 million or $0.56 per share in fiscal 1984.

Bernard Marcus, The Home Depot's chairman and chief executive officer, commented on the company's performance as follows:

Fiscal 1985 was a year of rapid expansion and continued growth for The Home Depot. Feeling the time was ripe for us to enhance our share of the do-it-yourself market, we seized the opportunity to make a significant investment in our long-term future. At the same time, we recognized that our short-term profit growth would be affected.

The Home Depot's 1985 annual report (**Exhibit 4**) provided more details on the firm's financial performance during the year.

As fiscal 1985 came to a close, The Home Depot faced some critical issues. The competition in the do-it-yourself industry was heating up. The fight for market dominance was expected to result in pressure on margins, and industry analysts expected only the strongest and most capable firms in the industry to survive. Also, The Home Depot had announced plans for further expansion that included the opening of nine new stores in 1986. The company estimated that site acquisition and construction would cost about $6.6 million for each new store, and investment in inventory (net of vendor financing) would require an additional $1.8 million per store. The company needed significant additional financing to implement these plans.

Home Depot relied on external financing—both debt and equity—to fund its growth in 1984 and 1985. However, the significant drop in its stock price in 1985 made further equity financing less attractive. While the company could borrow from its line of credit, it had to make sure that it could satisfy the interest coverage requirements (see Note 3 in **Exhibit 4** for a discussion of debt covenant restrictions). Clearly, generating more cash from its own operations would be the best way for Home Depot to invest in its growth on a sustainable basis.

Questions

1   Evaluate Home Depot's business strategy. Do you think it is a viable strategy in the long run?

2   Analyze Home Depot's financial performance during the fiscal years 1983–1985. Compare Home Depot's performance in this period with Hechinger's performance. (You may use the ratios and the cash flow analysis in Exhibit 3 in this summary.)

3   How productive were Home Depot's stores in the fiscal years 1983–1985? (You may use the statistics in Exhibit 1 in this analysis.)

4   Home Depot's stock price dropped by 23 percent between January 1985 and February 1986, making it difficult for the company to rely on equity capital to finance its growth. Covenants on existing debt (discussed in Note 3 of Exhibit 4) restrict the magnitude of the company's future borrowing. Given these constraints, what specific actions should Home Depot take with respect to its current operations and growth strategy? How can the company improve its operating performance? Should the company change its strategy? If so, how?

7 The Home Depot, Inc.

EXHIBIT 1 Summary of performance during fiscal years 1981–1985

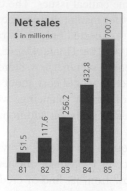

Net sales
$ in millions

81	82	83	84	85
51.5	117.6	256.2	432.8	700.7

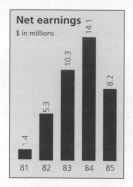

Net earnings
$ in millions

81	82	83	84	85
1.4	5.3	10.3	14.1	8.2

Stockholders' equity
$ in millions

81	82	83	84	85
5.2	18.4	65.3	80.2	89.1

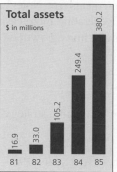

Total assets
$ in millions

81	82	83	84	85
16.9	33.0	105.2	249.4	380.2

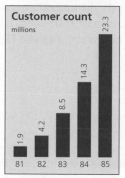

Customer count
millions

81	82	83	84	85
1.9	4.2	8.5	14.3	23.3

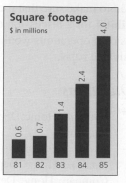

Square footage
$ in millions

81	82	83	84	85
0.6	0.7	1.4	2.4	4.0

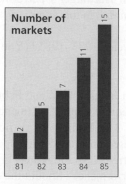

Number of markets

81	82	83	84	85
2	5	7	11	15

Number of stores

81	82	83	84	85
8	10	19	31	50

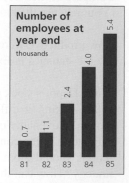

Number of employees at year end
thousands

81	82	83	84	85
0.7	1.1	2.4	4.0	5.4

EXHIBIT 2   **The Home Depot's common stock price and standard
& poor's 500 composite index from January 1985 to
February 1986**

Date	Home Depot Stock Price	S & P 500 Composite Index
1/2/85	$17.125	165.4
2/1/85	16.375	178.6
3/1/85	19.000	183.2
4/1/85	17.000	181.3
5/1/85	18.000	178.4
6/3/85	16.125	189.3
7/1/85	13.000	192.4
8/1/85	12.625	192.1
9/2/85	11.875	197.9
10/1/85	11.375	185.1
11/1/85	10.750	191.5
12/2/85	11.000	200.5
1/2/86	12.625	209.6
2/3/86	13.125	214.0
Cumulative Return:	−23.4%	29.4%

The Home Depot's ß = 1.3 (Value Line estimate).

EXHIBIT 3   Summary of financial performance of Hechinger company

PART I – HECHINGER'S FINANCIAL RATIOS

	Year Ending		
	February 1, 1986	February 2, 1985	January 28, 1984
Profit Before Taxes/Sales (%)	7.80	9.40	9.80
× Sales/Average Assets	1.48	1.72	2.02
× Average Assets/Average Equity	2.21	2.12	1.79
× (1 – Average Tax Rate)	0.62	0.55	0.54
= Return on Equity (%)	15.80	18.90	19.10
× (1 – Dividend Payout Ratio)	0.93	0.95	0.95
= Sustainable Growth Rate (%)	14.70	18.00	18.10
Gross Profit/Sales (%)	29.30	30.10	32.10
Selling, General and Administrative Expenses/Sales (%)	21.60	21.10	22.90
Interest Expenses/Sales (%)	2.10	1.30	0.70
Interest Income/Sales (%)	2.20	1.70	1.30
Inventory Turnover	4.50	4.50	4.40
Average Collection Period* (Days)	32.00	33.00	35.00
Average Accounts Payables Period** (Days)	58.00	61.00	63.00

* Assumed 365 days in the fiscal year.

**Payables also include accrued wages and expenses. Purchases are computed as cost of sales plus increase in inventory during the year. Assumed 365 days in the fiscal year.

7 The Home Depot, Inc.

EXHIBIT 3 Summary of financial performance of Hechinger company *(continued)*

PART II: HECHINGER'S CASH FLOW

(Dollars In Thousands)	February 1, 1986	February 2, 1985	January 28, 1984
Cash Provided from Operations			
Net Earnings	$23,111	$20,923	$16,243
Items not requiring the use of cash or marketable securities			
Depreciation and amortization	6,594	4,622	3,429
Deferred income taxes	1,375	2,040	1,515
Deferred rent expense	2,321	2,064	1,463
	33,401	29,649	22,650
Cash Invested in Operations			
Accounts receivable	4,657	7,905	7,954
Merchandise inventories	17,998	8,045	20,596
Other current assets	4,891	3,760	1,304
Accounts payable and accrued expenses	(6,620)	(12,099)	(9,767)
Taxes on income—current	285	3,031	(575)
	21,211	10,642	19,512
Net Cash Provided from Operations	12,190	19,007	3,138
Cash Used for Investment Activities			
Expenditures for property, furniture and equipment, net of disposals, and other assets	(36,037)	(25,531)	(16,346)
Cash Used to Pay Dividends to Shareholders	(1,550)	(1,091)	(868)
Cash Provided from Financing Activities			
Proceeds from public offering of 8½% Converted Subordinated Debentures, net of expenses	—	85,010	—
Proceeds from public offering of common stock net of expenses	28,969	—	13,439
Proceeds from sale and leaseback transactions under operating leases	—	8,338	6,874
Increase (decrease) in long-term debt	—	(4,750)	6,366
Decrease in short-term debt	—	—	(318)
Exercise of stock options including income tax benefit	180	674	611
Decrease in capital lease obligations	(311)	(280)	(254)
	28,838	88,992	26,718
Increase in Cash and Marketable Securities	$ 3,441	$ 81,377	$ 12,642

7 The Home Depot, Inc.

EXHIBIT 4   Abridged annual report for fiscal year 1985

A Letter to Our Shareholders:

Fiscal 1985 was a year of rapid expansion and continued growth for The Home Depot. Feeling the time was ripe for us to enhance our share of the do-it-yourself market, we seized the opportunity to make a significant investment in our long-term future. At the same time, we recognized that our short-term profit growth would be affected.

The Home Depot intends to be the dominant factor in every market we serve. The key to our success has been that upon entering a new market, we make a substantial commitment—opening multiple stores, providing excellent customer service, creating highly visible promotions, and growing the entire market. We turn the novice into a do-it-yourselfer and enable the expert to do more for less money.

From shortly before the end of fiscal 1984 to the close of fiscal 1985, The Home Depot entered eight new markets—Dallas, Houston, Jacksonville, San Diego, Los Angeles, Shreveport, Baton Rouge and Mobile—in a period of approximately 13 months. In that time, the number of Home Depot stores rose dramatically, from 22 to 50, including 9 stores acquired in the Bowater acquisition which had not been in our original plan. Twenty of these stores were opened during the past fiscal year alone. During this time span, we have become the only national warehouse retailing chain serving markets across the Sunbelt.

This expansion program required a tremendous investment of capital expenditures and inventory, as well as in personnel. As a result, our net earnings declined from record levels achieved during the previous fiscal year. In fiscal 1985, The Home Depot earned $8,219,000, or $.33 per share, as compared with $14,122,000, or $.56 per share, in fiscal 1984. However, as The Home Depot engaged in this major thrust forward, it also increased its market share and market presence as revenues rose 62% from $432,779,000 in fiscal 1984 to $700,729,000 in fiscal 1985.

Despite our significant investments, we still continue to be in a very strong financial condition. In December, The Home Depot replaced a prior $100 million bank credit line with an eight-year decreasing revolving credit agreement of $200 million. In addition, we are pursuing sale-and-leaseback negotiations for an aggregate of approximately $50 million for ten of our stores. These sources of additional funds, along with internally generated cash flow, will provide us with an ample financial foundation to continue to underwrite our growth over the next several years.

We are also quite proud that The Home Depot achieved its substantial gain in sales and market share in what turned out to be a very difficult year for our industry and retailing in general. The do-it-yourself "warehouse" industry, which we pioneered only a few short years ago, has recently attracted many competitors, some of whom have already fallen by the wayside, having mistaken our dramatic success as a path towards easy profits. Now the industry is faced with a situation when only the strongest and most capable will survive. As this process continues, we expect to encounter additional cost competition in the fight for market dominance. However, with our strengths—both financial and our successful ability to develop a loyal customer base—we are confident that The Home Depot will emerge an even stronger company.

We have never doubted The Home Depot's ability to be a leader in our business. We have the market dominance, the superior retailing concepts and the necessary foundation of experienced management. Further, we have the determination to maintain our position.

Looking at some of our markets individually, clearly our most difficult environment has been in Houston, where the oil-related economy is undergoing painful contractions combined with particularly fierce industry competition. This has caused our newly-opened stores to operate at a sub par level. In Dallas/Fort Worth, the stores we acquired at the end of fiscal 1984 have not yet generated the profits we expect. Such difficult market conditions demand a flexible reaction both in merchandising and operations. Recognizing the future potential of both of these markets, our management team is addressing the issues and feels confident that the final outcome will be positive.

In the other markets entered this year, the situation has been considerably more positive. There, our stores are experiencing growth much closer to our historical patterns.

In support of our California and Arizona operations, a west coast division was inaugurated to facilitate a timely response to the demands of that marketplace. With management personnel in place, this division is now responsible for the merchandising and operations of all stores in the western states.

Other highlights of the past year's activities include the progress we have made in expanding our management team, and the computer systems we installed into our operations to enhance our efficiency.

During the year, we completed the store price look-up phase of our management information system. This facilitates tracking individual items' sales through our registers, resulting in a more concise method of inventory reorder and margin management with the information now available.

During the coming year we will be testing a perpetual inventory tie-in with our price look-up system, eliminating pricing of our merchandise at the store level. The latter is being tested in several stores presently and hopefully will be expanded to include all of our stores by year end. This will have a significant effect on labor productivity at the store level.

The Home Depot is always looking for ways in which to do things better, priding ourselves on our flexibility and ability to innovate and to react to changing conditions. Whether it is a matter of developing state-of-the-art computer systems, reevaluating our store layouts or adapting to fast-changing markets and new types of merchandising, flexibility has always been a Home Depot characteristic.

In fiscal 1986, The Home Depot will continue to expand, but at a much more moderate pace. We plan to open nine new stores. These stores will be in existing markets except for the two locations in the new market of San Jose, California.

When we open stores in existing markets, sharing advertising costs and operational expenses, we achieve a faster return than stores in new markets. With this in mind, in January 1986, we withdrew from the Detroit market and delayed the opening of stores in San Francisco. These stores were targeted for a substantial initial loss in earnings that would have been necessary to achieve market dominance. From our standpoint, these new markets would have had the combined effect of diluting our personnel and negatively affecting our earnings.

It has always been Home Depot's philosophy to maintain orderly growth and achieve market dominance as we expand to new markets. Indeed, growth for growth's sake has never been and never will be our objective. We intend to invest prudently and expand aggressively in our business and our markets only when such expenditures meet our criteria for long-term profitability.

We are quite optimistic about our company's future—both for fiscal 1986 and for the years to follow. Essential to this optimism is the fact that The Home Depot has consistently proven that we can grow the market in every geographical area we enter. Simply, this means that we do not have to take business away from hardware stores and other existing home-improvement outlets, but rather, to create new do-it-yourselfers out of those who have never done their own home improvements.

Our philosophy is to educate our customers on how to be do-it-yourselfers. Our customers have come to expect The Home Depot's knowledgeable sales staff to guide them through any project they care to undertake, whether it be installing kitchen cabinets, constructing a deck, or building an entire house. Our sales staff knows how to complete each project, what tools and material to include, and how to sell our customers everything they need.

The Home Depot traditionally holds clinics for its customers in such skills as electrical wiring, carpentry, and plumbing, to name a few. Upon the successful completion of such clinics, our customers are confident in themselves and in The Home Depot. This confidence allows them to attempt increasingly advanced and complex home improvements.

Concerning our facilities, Home Depot's warehouse retailing concept allows us to carry a truly fantastic selection of merchandise and offer it at the lowest possible prices. Each of our stores ranges from about 65,000 to over 100,000 square feet of selling space, with an additional 4,000 to 10,000 square feet of outdoor selling area. In these large stores, we are able to stock all the materials and tools needed to build a house from scratch, and to landscape its grounds. With each store functioning as its own warehouse, with a capacity of over 25,000 different items, we are able to keep our prices at a minimum while providing the greatest selection of building materials and name brand merchandise.

For the majority of Americans, their home is their most valuable asset. It is an asset that consistently appreciates. It is also an asset in need of ongoing care and maintenance. By becoming do-it-yourselfers, homeowners can significantly enhance the value of their homes. We at The Home Depot have found that by successfully delivering this message, we have created loyal and satisfied customers. And by maintaining leadership in our markets, we have established a sound basis on which to build a future of growth with profitability.

The Home Depot management and staff are dedicated to the proposition that we are—and will remain—America's leading do-it-yourself retailer.

Bernard Marcus
Chairman and
Chief Executive Officer

Arthur M. Blank
President and
Chief Operating Officer

7 The Home Depot, Inc.

CONSOLIDATED STATEMENTS OF EARNINGS

	Fiscal Year Ended		
	February 2, 1986 (52 weeks)	February 3, 1985 (53 weeks)	January 29, 1984 (52 weeks)
Net Sales (note 2)	$700,729,000	$432,779,000	$256,184,000
Cost of Merchandise Sold	519,272,000	318,460,000	186,170,000
Gross Profit	181,457,000	114,319,000	70,014,000
Operating Expenses:			
Selling and store operating expenses	134,354,000	74,447,000	43,514,000
Preopening expenses	7,521,000	1,917,000	2,456,000
General and administrative expenses	20,555,000	12,817,000	7,376,000
Total Operating Expenses	162,430,000	89,181,000	53,346,000
Operating Income	19,027,000	25,138,000	16,668,000
Other Income (Expense):			
Net gain on disposition of property and equipment (note 7)	1,317,000	—	—
Interest income	1,481,000	5,236,000	2,422,000
Interest expense (note 3)	(10,206,000)	(4,122,000)	(104,000)
	(7,408,000)	1,114,000	2,318,000
Earnings Before Income Taxes	11,619,000	26,252,000	18,986,000
Income Taxes (note 4)	3,400,000	12,130,000	8,725,000
Net Earnings	$ 8,219,000	$ 14,122,000	$10,261,000
Earnings per Common and Common Equivalent Share (note 5)	$ .33	$ .56	$.41
Weighted Average Number of Common and Common Equivalent Shares	25,247,000	25,302,000	24,834,000

CONSOLIDATED BALANCE SHEETS

	February 2, 1986	February 3, 1985
Assets:		
Current Assets:		
Cash, including time deposits of $43,374,000 in 1985	$ 9,671,000	$ 52,062,000
Accounts receivable, net (note 7)	21,505,000	9,365,000
Refundable income taxes	3,659,000	—
Merchandise inventories	152,700,000	84,046,000
Prepaid expenses	2,526,000	1,939,000
Total current assets	190,061,000	147,412,000
Property and Equipment, at Cost (note 3):		
Land	44,396,000	30,044,000
Buildings	38,005,000	3,728,000
Furniture, fixtures, and equipment	34,786,000	18,162,000
Leasehold improvements	23,748,000	11,743,000
Construction in progress	27,694,000	14,039,000
	168,629,000	77,716,000
Less accumulated depreciation and amortization	7,813,000	4,139,000
Net property and equipment	160,816,000	73,577,000
Cost in Excess of the Fair Value of Net Assets Acquired, net of accumulated amortization of $730,000 in 1985 and $93,000 in 1984 (note 2)	24,561,000	25,198,000
Other	4,755,000	3,177,000
	$380,193,000	$249,364,000
Liabilities and Stockholders' Equity		
Current Liabilities:		
Accounts payable	$53,881,000	$32,356,000
Accrued salaries and related expenses	5,397,000	3,819,000
Other accrued expenses	13,950,000	10,214,000
Income taxes payable (note 4)	—	626,000
Current portion of long-term debt (note 3)	10,382,000	287,000
Total current liabilities	83,610,000	47,302,000
Long-Term Debt, Excluding Current Installments (note 3):		
Convertible subordinated debentures	100,250,000	100,250,000
Other long-term debt	99,693,000	17,692,000
	$199,943,000	$117,942,000
Other Liabilities	861,000	1,320,000
Deferred Income Taxes (note 4)	6,687,000	2,586,000
Stockholders' Equity (note 5)		
Common stock, par value $.05. Authorized: 50,000,000 shares; issued and outstanding—25,150,063 shares at February 2, 1986 and 25,055,188 shares at February 3, 1985	1,258,000	1,253,000
Paid-in capital	48,900,000	48,246,000
Retained earnings	38,934,000	30,715,000
Total stockholders' equity	89,092,000	80,214,000
Commitments and Contingencies (notes 5, 6 and 8)	$380,193,000	$249,364,000

7 The Home Depot, Inc.

7 The Home Depot, Inc.

CONSOLIDATED STATEMENTS OF CHANGES IN FINANCIAL POSITION

	Fiscal Year Ended		
	February 2, 1986	February 3, 1985	January 29, 1984
Sources of Working Capital:			
Net earnings	**$ 8,219,000**	$ 14,122,000	$ 10,261,000
Items which do not use working capital:			
Depreciation and amortization of property and equipment	**4,376,000**	2,275,000	903,000
Deferred income taxes	**3,612,000**	1,508,000	713,000
Amortization of cost in excess of the fair value of net assets required	**637,000**	93,000	
Net gain on disposition of property and equipment	**(1,317,000)**	—	—
Other	**180,000**	77,000	59,000
Working Capital Provided by Operations	**15,707,000**	18,075,000	11,936,000
Proceeds from disposition of property and equipment	**9,469,000**	861,000	3,000
Proceeds from long-term borrowings	**92,400,000**	120,350,000	4,200,000
Proceeds from sale of common stock, net	**659,000**	814,000	36,663,000
	$ 118,235,000	$ 140,100,000	$ 52,802,000
Uses of Working Capital:			
Additions to property and equipment	**$ 99,767,000**	$ 50,769,000	$ 16,081,000
Current installments and repayments of long-term debt	**10,399,000**	6,792,000	52,000
Acquisition of Bowater Home Center, Inc., net of working capital of $9,227,000 (note 2):			
Property and equipment	—	4,815,000	—
Cost in excess of the fair value of net assets acquired	—	25,291,000	—
Other assets, net of liabilities	—	(913,000)	—
Other, net	**1,728,000**	2,554,000	252,000
Increase in working capital	**6,341,000**	50,792,000	36,417,000
	$ 118,235,000	$ 140,100,000	$ 52,802,000
Changes in Components of Working Capital:			
Increase (decrease) in current assets:			
Cash	**(42,391,000)**	$ 29,894,000	$ 13,917,000
Receivables, net	**15,799,000**	7,170,000	1,567,000
Merchandise inventories	**68,654,000**	25,334,000	41,137,000
Prepaid expenses	**587,000**	1,206,000	227,000
	42,649,000	63,604,000	56,848,000
Increase (decrease) in current liabilities:			
Accounts payable	**21,525,000**	10,505,000	17,150,000
Accrued salaries and related expenses	**1,578,000**	(93,000)	2,524,000
Other accrued expenses	**3,736,000**	2,824,000	341,000
Income taxes payable	**(626,000)**	(657,000)	406,000
Current portion of long-term debt	**10,095,000**	233,000	10,000
	36,308,000	12,812,000	20,431,000
Increase in Working Capital	**$ 6,341,000**	$ 50,792,000	$ 36,417,000

SELECTED FINANCIAL DATA

	Fiscal Year Ended				
	February 2, 1985	**February 3, 1985**[1]	**January 29, 1984**	**January 30, 1983**	**January 31, 1982**
Selected Consolidated Statement of Earnings Data:					
Net sales	**$700,729,000**	$432,779,000	$256,184,000	$117,645,000	$51,542,000
Gross Profit	**181,457,000**	114,319,000	70,014,000	33,358,000	14,735,000
Earnings before income taxes and extraordinary item	**11,619,000**	26,252,000	18,986,000	9,870,000	1,963,000
Earnings before extraordinary item	**8,219,000**	14,122,000	10,261,000	5,315,000	1,211,000
Extraordinary item—reduction of income taxes arising from carryforward of prior years operating losses	**—**	—	—	—	234,000
Net earnings	**$8,219,000**	$14,122,000	$10,261,000	$5,315,000	$1,445,000
Per Common and Common Equivalent Share:					
Earnings before extraordinary item	**$.33**	$.56	$.41	$.24	$.06
Extraordinary item	**—**	—	—	—	.01
Net earnings	**$ .33**	$ .56	$ .41	$ .24	$ .07
Weighted average number of common and common equivalent shares	**25,247,000**	25,302,000	24,834,000	22,233,000	21,050,000
Selected Consolidated Balance Sheet Data:					
Working Capital	**$ 106,451,000**	$ 100,110,000	$ 49,318,000	$ 12,901,000	$ 5,502,000
Total assets	**380,193,000**	249,364,000	105,230,000	33,014,000	16,906,000
Long-term debt	**199,943,000**	117,942,000	4,384,000	236,000	3,738,000
Stockholders' equity	**89,092,000**	80,214,000	65,278,000	18,354,000	5,024,000

[1] *53 week fiscal year, all others were 52 week fiscal years.*

7 The Home Depot, Inc.

MANAGEMENT DISCUSSION AND ANALYSIS OF RESULTS OF OPERATIONS AND FINANCIAL CONDITION

The data below reflect the percentage relationship between sales and major categories in the Consolidated Statements of Earnings and selected sales data *of the percentage change in the dollar amounts of each of the items.*

	Fiscal Year[a]			Percentage Increase (Decrease) of Dollar Amounts	
	1985	1984	1983	1985 v 1984	1984 v 1983
Selected Consolidated Statements of Earnings Data:					
Net sales	**100.0%**	100.0%	100.0%	**61.9%**	68.9%
Gross profit	**25.9**	26.4	27.3	**58.7**	63.3
Cost and expenses:					
Selling and store operating	**19.2**	17.2	17.0	**80.5**	71.1
Preopening	**1.1**	.4	.9	**292.3**	(21.9)
General and administrative	**2.9**	3.0	2.9	**60.4**	73.8
Net gain on disposition of property and equipment	**(.2)**	—	—	**—**	—
Interest income	**(.2)**	(1.2)	(.9)	**(71.7)**	116.2
Interest expense	**1.4**	.9	—	**147.6**	3,863.5
	24.2	20.3	19.9	**92.9**	72.6
Earnings before income taxes	**1.7**	6.1	7.4	**(55.7)**	38.3
Income taxes	**.5**	2.8	3.4	**(72.0)**	39.0
Net earnings	**1.2%**	3.3%	4.0%	**(41.8%)**	37.6%
Selected Consolidated Sales Data:					
Number of customer transactions	**23,324,000**	14,256,000	8,479.000	**63.6%**	68.1%
Average amount of sale per transaction	**$ 30.04**	$ 30.36	$ 30.21	**(1.1)**	.5
Weighted average weekly sales per operating store	**$ 342,500**	$ 365,500	$ 360,300	**(6.3)**	1.4

[a]*Fiscal years 1985, 1984 and 1983 refer to the fiscal years ended February 2, 1986, February 3, 1985 and January 29, 1984, respectively. Fiscal 1984 consisted of 53 weeks while 1985 and 1983 each consisted of 52 weeks.*

Results of Operations

For an understanding of the significant factors that influenced the Company's performance during the past three fiscal years, the following discussion should be read in conjunction with the consolidated financial statements appearing elsewhere in this annual report.

Fiscal Year Ended February 2, 1986 Compared to February 3, 1985

Net sales in fiscal year 1985 increased 62% from $432,779,000 to $700,729,000. The growth is attributable to several factors. First, the Company opened 20 new stores during 1985 and closed one store. Second, second-year sales increases were realized from the three new stores opened in 1984 and from the nine former Bowater Home Center stores acquired during 1984. Third, comparable store sales increases of 2.3% were achieved despite comparing the 52-week 1985 fiscal year to the sales of the 53-week 1984 fiscal year, due in part to the number of customer transactions increasing by 64%. Finally, the weighted average weekly sales per operating store declined 6% in 1985 due to the significant increase in the ratio of the number of new stores to total stores in operation—new stores have a lower sales rate than mature stores until they establish market share.

Gross profit in 1985 increased 59% from $114,319,000 to $181,457,000. This increase was due to the increased sales and was partially offset by a reduction in the gross profit margin from 26.4% to 25.9%. The reduction is primarily due to lower margins achieved while establishing market presence in new markets.

Cost and expenses increased 93% during 1985 and, as a percent of sales, increased from 20.3% to 24.2%. The increase in selling and store operating, preopening expenses and net interest expense is due to the opening of 20 new stores, the costs associated with the former Bowater Home Center stores, and the related cost of building market share. The large percentage of new stores which have lower sales but fixed occupancy and certain minimum operating expenses tends to cause the percentage of selling and store operating costs to increase as a percentage of sales. The net gain on disposition of property and equipment is discussed fully in note 7 to the financial statements.

Earnings before income taxes decreased 56% from $26,252,000 to $11,619,000 resulting from the increase in operating expenses to support the Company's expansion program. The Company's effective income tax rate declined from 46.2% to 29.3% resulting from an increase in investment and other tax credits as a percentage of the total tax provision. As a percentage of sales, earnings decreased from 3.3% in 1984 to 1.2% in 1985 due to the increase in operating expenses as discussed above.

Fiscal Year Ended February 3, 1985 Compared to January 29, 1984

Net sales in fiscal 1984 increased 69% from $256,184,000 to $432,779,000. The growth was attributable to several factors. First, the company opened three new stores during fiscal 1984. Second, the Company had sales of $9,755,000 from the nine former Bowater Home Center stores acquired on December 3, 1984. Third, second-year sales increases were realized from the nine stores opened during fiscal 1983. Fourth, comparable store sales increases of 14% were due in part to 53 weeks in fiscal 1984 compared to 52 weeks in fiscal 1983 and in part to the number of customer transactions increasing by 63%. Finally, excluding the sales of the former Bowater Home Center stores, the weighted average weekly sales per operating store increased 6% to $383,500 in fiscal 1984.

Gross profit in fiscal 1984 increased 63% from $70,014,000 to $114,319,000. This net increase was due to the increased sales and was partially offset by a reduction in the gross profit margin from 27.3% to 26.4%. The reduction in the gross profit percentage is largely the result of the purchase of a high proportion of promoted merchandise by customers in the second quarter.

Costs and expenses increased 73% during fiscal 1984. As a percent of sales, costs and expenses increased from 19.9% to 20.3% due to increased selling, store operating, general and administrative expenses. This planned increase was in preparation of the Company's future expansion. Interest expense increased significantly as a result of the issuance of substantial debt during fiscal 1984 to fund the Company's expansion. These increases were partially offset by reduced preopening expenses and increased interest income resulting from temporary investment of the proceeds of the debt financing.

Earnings before income taxes increased 38% from $18,986,000 to $26,252,000 resulting from the factors discussed above. Such pretax earnings, however, were reduced by a loss from the Bowater stores of approximately $1,900,000 from date of acquisition (December 1984) to year end. The Company's effective income tax rate increased slightly from 46.0% to 46.2% resulting principally from less investment and other tax credits as a percentage of the total tax provision. As a percentage of sales, earnings decreased from 4.0% in fiscal 1983 to 3.3% in fiscal 1984. The decline is a result of the company's reduced gross profit percentage and increases in the operating expenses discussed above.

Impact of Inflation and Changing Prices

Although the Company cannot accurately determine the precise effect of inflation on its operations, it does not believe inflation has had a material effect on sales or results of operations. The Company has complied with the reporting requirements of the Financial Accounting Standards Board Statement No. 33 in note 10 to the financial statements. Due to the experimental techniques, subjective estimates and assumptions, and the incomplete presentation required by this accounting pronouncement, the Company questions the value of the required reporting.

Liquidity and Capital Resources

Cash flow generated from existing store operations provided the Company with a significant source of liquidity since sales are on a cash-and-carry basis. In addition, a significant portion of the Company's

7 The Home Depot, Inc.

inventory is financed under vendor credit terms. The Company has supplemented its operating cash flow from time to time with bank credit and equity and debt financing. During fiscal 1985, $88,000,000 of working capital was provided by the revolving bank credit line, $4,400,000 from industrial revenue bonds, and approximately $15,707,000 from operations. In addition, during fiscal 1985, the Company entered into a new credit agreement for a $200,000,000 revolving credit facility with a group of banks.

The Company has announced plans to open nine new stores during fiscal 1986, two in the new market of northern California and the balance in existing markets. The cost of this store expansion program will depend upon, among other factors, the extent to which the Company is able to lease second-use store space as opposed to acquiring leases or sites and having stores constructed to its own specifications. The Company estimates that approximately $6,600,000 per store will be required to acquire sites and construct facilities to the Company's specifications and that approximately $1,700,000 will be required to open a store in leased space plus any additional costs of acquiring the lease. These estimates include costs for site acquisition, construction expenditures, fixtures and equipment, and in-store minicomputers and point-of-sale terminals. In addition, each new store will require approximately $1,800,000 to finance inventories, net of vendor financing. The Company believes it has the ability to finance these expenditures through existing cash resources, current bank lines of credit which include a $200,000,000 eight-year revolving credit agreement, funds generated from operations, and other forms of financing, including but not limited to various forms of real estate financing and unsecured borrowings.

NOTES TO CONSOLIDATED FINANCIAL STATEMENTS

1. Summary of Significant Accounting Policies

Fiscal Year

The Company's fiscal year ends on the Sunday closest to the last day of January and usually consists of 52 weeks. Every five or six years, however, there is a 53-week year. The fiscal year ended February 2, 1986 (1985) consisted of 52 weeks, the year ended February 3, 1985 (1984) consisted of 53 weeks and the year ended January 29, 1984 (1983) consisted of 52 weeks.

Principles of Consolidation

The consolidated financial statements include the accounts of the Company and its wholly owned subsidiary. All significant intercompany transactions have been eliminated in consolidation. Certain reclassifications were made to the 1984 balance sheet to conform to current year presentation.

Merchandise Inventories

Inventories are stated at the lower of cost (first-in, first-out) or market, as determined by the retail inventory method.

Depreciation and Amortization

The Company's buildings, furniture, fixtures, and equipment are depreciated using the straight-line method over the estimated useful lives of the assets. Improvements to leased premises are amortized on the straight-line method over the life of the lease or the useful life of the improvement, whichever is shorter.

Investment Tax Credit

Investment tax credits are recorded as a reduction of Federal income taxes in the year the credits are realized.

Store Preopening Costs

Non-capital expenditures associated with opening new stores are charged to expense as incurred.

Earnings Per Common and Common Equivalent Share

Earnings per common and common equivalent share are based on the weighted average number of shares and equivalents outstanding. Common equivalent shares used in the calculation of earnings per share represent shares granted under the Company's employee stock option plan and employee stock purchase plan.

Shares issuable upon conversion of the 8½% convertible subordinated debentures are also common stock equivalents. Shares issuable upon conversion of the 9% convertible subordinated debentures would only be included in the computation of fully diluted earnings per share. However, neither shares issuable upon conversion of the 8½% nor the 9% convertible debentures were dilutive in any year presented, and thus neither were considered in the earnings per share computations.

2. Acquisition

On December 3, 1984 the Company acquired the outstanding capital stock of Bowater Home Center, Inc. (Bowater) for approximately $38,420,000 including costs incurred in connection with the acquisition. Bowater operated nine retail home center stores primarily in the Dallas, Texas metropolitan area. The acquisition was accounted for by the purchase method and, accordingly, results of operations have been included with those of the Company from the date of acquisition. Cost in excess of the fair value of net assets acquired amounted to approximately $25,291,000, which is being amortized over forty years from date of acquisition using the straight-line method.

The following table summarizes, on a pro forma, unaudited basis, the estimated combined results of operations of the Company and Bowater for the years ended February 3, 1985 and January 29, 1984, as though the acquisition were made at the beginning of fiscal year 1983. This pro forma information does not purport to be indicative of the results of operations which would have actually been obtained if the acquisition had been effective on the dates indicated.

	Fiscal Year ended	
	February 3, 1985	January 29, 1984*
	(Unaudited)	
Net sales	$482,752,000	$274,660,000
Net earnings	9,009,000	6,913,000
Earnings per common and common equivalent share	.36	.28

Includes the operations and pro forma adjustments from the date of inception of Bowater's operations in August, 1983.

7 The Home Depot, Inc.

3. Long-Term Debt and Lines of Credit

Long-Term debt consists of the following: **February 2, 1986**   **February 3, 1985**

	February 2, 1986	February 3, 1985
8½% convertible subordinated debentures, due July 1, 2009, convertible into shares of common stock of the Company at a conversion price of $26.50 per share. The debentures are redeemable by the Company at a premium from July 1, 1986 to July 1, 1995, will retire 70% of the issue prior to maturity. Interest is payable semi-annually.	$ 86,250,000	$ 86,250,000
9% convertible subordinated debentures, due December 15, 1999, convertible into shares of common stock of the Company at a conversion price of $16.90 per share. The debentures are redeemable by the Company at a premium from December 15, 1986 to December 15, 1994. An annual mandatory sinking fund of $2,000,000 per year is required from 1994 to 1998. Interest is payable semi-annually.	14,000,000	14,000,000
Total convertible subordinated debentures	100,250,000	100,250,000
Revolving credit agreement. Interest may be fixed for any portion outstanding for up to 180 days, at the Company's option, based on a CD rate plus 3/4%, the LIBOR rate plus ½% or at the prime rate.	88,000,000	—
*Variable Rate Industrial Revenue Bond (see note 7)	10,100,000	10,100,000
*Variable Rate Industrial Revenue Bond, secured by a letter of credit, payable in sinking fund installments from December 1, 1991 through December 1, 2010	4,400,000	—
9 5/8% Industrial Revenue Bond, secured by a letter of credit, payable on December 1, 1993, with interest payable semi-annually	4,200,000	4,200,000
*Variable Rate Industrial Revenue Bond, secured by land, payable in annual installments of $233,000 with interest payable semi-annually	3,267,000	3,500,000
Other	108,000	179,000
Total long-term debt	210,325,000	118,229,000
Less current portion	10,382,000	287,000
Long-term debt, excluding current portion	**$199,943,000**	**$117,942,000**

The interest rates on the variable rate industrial revenue bonds are related to various short-term municipal money market composite rates.

Maturities of long-term debt are approximately $10,382,000 for fiscal 1986 and $234,000 for each of the next four subsequent years.

During the fiscal year ended February 2, 1986, the Company entered into a new unsecured revolving line of credit for a maximum of $200,000,000, subject to certain limitations, of which $88,000,000 is outstanding at year-end. Commitment amounts under the agreement decrease by $15,000,000 on July 31, 1990, by $20,000,000 each six months from that date through January 31, 1993, by $35,000,000 on July 31, 1993 and with the remaining $50,000,000 commitment expiring on January 31, 1994. Maximum

borrowings outstanding within the commitment limits may not exceed specified percentages of inventories, land and buildings, and fixtures and equipment, all as defined in the Agreement. Under certain conditions, the commitments may be extended and/or increased. An annual commitment fee of ¼% to 3/8% is required to be paid on the unused portion of the revolving line of credit. Interest rates specified may be increased by a maximum of 3/8 of 1% based on specified ratios of interest rate coverage and debt to equity.

Under the revolving credit agreement, the Company is required, among other things, to maintain during fiscal year 1985 a minimum tangible net worth

7 The Home Depot, Inc.

(defined to include the convertible subordinated debentures) of $150,000,000 (increasing annually to $213,165,000 by January 3, 1989), a debt to tangible net worth ratio of no more than 2 to 1, a current ratio of not less than 1.5 to 1, and a ratio of earnings before interest expense and income taxes to interest expense, net, of not less than 2 to 1. The Company was in compliance with all restrictive covenants as of February 2, 1986. The restrictive covenants related to the letter of credit agreements securing the industrial revenue bonds and the convertible subordinated debentures are no more restrictive than those under the revolving line of credit agreement.

Interest expense in the accompanying consolidated statements of earnings is net of interest capitalized of $3,429,000 in fiscal 1985 and $1,462,000 in fiscal 1984.

4. Income Taxes

The provision for income taxes consists of the following:

| | Fiscal Year Ended | | |
	February 1, 1986	February 3, 1985	January 29, 1984
Current:			
Federal	$ (578,000)	$ 9,083,000	$ 6,916,000
State	366,000	1,539,000	1,096,000
	(212,000)	10,622,000	8,012,000
Deferred:			
Federal	3,306,000	1,464,000	713,000
State	306,000	44,000	—
	3,612,000	1,508,000	713,000
Total	$ 3,400,000	$12,130,000	$8,725,000

The effective tax rates for fiscal 1985, 1984, and 1983 were 29.3%, 46.2%, and 46.0%, respectively. A reconciliation of income tax expense at Federal statutory rates to actual tax expense for the applicable fiscal years follows:

| | Fiscal Year Ended | | |
	February 2, 1986	February 3, 1985	January 29, 1984
Income taxes at Federal statutory rate, net of surtax exemption	$5,345,000	$12,076,000	$ 8,734,000
State income taxes, net of Federal income tax benefit	363,000	855,000	592,000
Investment and targeted jobs tax credits	(2,308,000)	(800,000)	(747,000)
Other, net	—	(1,000)	146,000
	$ 3,400,000	$12,130,000	$ 8,725,000

Deferred income taxes arise from differences in the timing of reporting income for financial statement and income tax purposes. The sources of these differences and the tax effect of each are as follows:

| | Fiscal Year Ended | | |
	February 2, 1986	February 3, 1985	January 29, 1984
Accelerated depreciation	$2,526,000	$1,159,000	$713,000
Interest capitalization	855,000	349,000	—
Other, net	231,000	—	—
	$3,612,000	$1,508,000	$713,000

5. Leases

The Company leases certain retail locations, office, and warehouse and distribution space, equipment, and vehicles under operating leases. All leases will expire within the next 25 years; however, it can be expected that in the normal course of business, leases will be renewed or replaced. Total rent expense, net of minor sublease income for the fiscal years ended February 2, 1986, February 3, 1985 and January 29, 1984 amounted to approximately $12,737,000, $6,718,000 and $4,233,000, respectively. Under the building leases, real estate taxes, insurance, maintenance, and operating expenses applicable to the leased property are obligations of the Company. Certain of the store leases provide for contingent rentals based on percentages of sales in excess of specified minimums. Contingent rentals for fiscal years ended February 2, 1986, February 3, 1985 and January 29, 1984 were approximately $650,000, $545,000 and $111,000.

The approximate future minimum lease payments under operating leases at February 2, 1986 are as follows:

Fiscal Year	
1986	$ 16,093,000
1987	16,668,000
1988	16,345,000
1989	16,086,000
1990	16,129,000
Thereafter	171,455,000
	$252,776,000

7. Disposition of Property and Equipment

During the fourth quarter of fiscal year 1985, the Company disposed of certain properties and equipment at a net gain of $1,317,000. The properties represented real estate located in Detroit, Houston and Tucson, and the equipment represented the trade-in of cash registers of current generation point of sale equipment. Under the terms of the Detroit real estate sale, the purchaser will either assume the bond obligations of the Company of $10,100,000 after February 2, 1986 or pay the Company the funds disbursed under the bonds in order for the Company to prepay the total amount outstanding. Included in accounts receivable at February 2, 1986 is $13,800,000 related to these transactions.

8. Commitments and Contingencies

At February 2, 1986, the Company was contingently liable for approximately $5,300,000 under outstanding letters of credit issued in connection with purchase commitments.

The Company has litigation arising from the normal course of business. In management's opinion, this litigation will not materially affect the Company's financial condition.

9. Quarterly Financial Data (Unaudited)

The following is a summary of the unaudited quarterly results of operations for fiscal years ended February 2, 1986 and February 3, 1985:

	Net Sales	Gross Profit	Net Earnings	Net Earnings per Common and Common Equivalent Share
Fiscal year ended February 2, 1986:				
First Quarter	**$145,048,000**	**$ 36,380,000**	**$ 1,945,000**	**$.08**
Second Quarter	**174,239,000**	**45,572,000**	**2,499,000**	**.10**
Third Quarter	**177,718,000**	**46,764,000**	**1,188,000**	**.05**
Fourth Quarter	**203,724,000**	**52,741,000**	**2,587,000**	**.10**
	$ 700,729,000	**$ 181,457,000**	**$ 8,219,000**	**$ .33**
Fiscal year ended February 3, 1985:				
First Quarter	$ 95,872,000	$ 25,026,000	$ 3,437,000	$.14
Second Quarter	119,068,000	29,185,000	3,808,000	.15
Third Quarter	100,459,000	27,658,000	3,280,000	.13
Fourth Quarter	117,380,000	32,450,000	3,597,000	.14
	$ 432,779,000	$ 114,319,000	$ 14,122,000	$ .56

AUDITORS' REPORT

The Board of Directors and Stockholders,
The Home Depot, Inc.:

We have examined the consolidated balance sheets of The Home Depot, Inc. and subsidiary as of February 2, 1986 and February 3, 1985 and the related consolidated statements of earnings, stockholders' equity, and changes in financial position for each of the years in the three-year period ended February 2, 1986. Our examinations were made in accordance with generally accepted auditing standards, and, accordingly, included such tests of the accounting records and such other auditing procedures as we considered necessary in the circumstances.

In our opinion, the aforementioned consolidated financial statements present fairly the financial position of The Home Depot, Inc. and subsidiary at February 2, 1986 and February 3, 1985, and the results of their operations and the changes in their financial position for each of the years in the three-year period ended February 2, 1986, in conformity with generally accepted accounting principles applied on a consistent basis.

PEAT, MARWICK, MITCHELL & CO.
Atlanta, Georgia
March 24, 1986

8 The initial public offering of PartyGaming Plc

O n June 30, 2005, PartyGaming Plc offered 781,629,050 of its ordinary shares for public trading on the London Stock Exchange. The offer price of the shares was 116 pence per ordinary share. The number of shares offered for public trading represented approximately 19.5 percent of PartyGaming's 4 billion shares outstanding.

An investment in PartyGaming's shares was not without risks. In its prospectus, Party-Gaming warned its prospective investors that they

> . . . should be aware that an investment in PartyGaming Plc involves a high degree of risk and that, if certain of the risks described in Part 3 occur, they may lose all or a very substantial part of their investment. Accordingly, an investment in the Shares is only suitable for investors who are particularly knowledgeable in investment matters and who are able to bear the complete loss of their investment.

PartyGaming and its industry[1]

PartyGaming was founded in 1997. Between 1997 and 2005 the company had become one of the largest online gaming suppliers in the world. In 2005, the company generated the largest proportion of its revenues from accommodating online poker games, partly by means of its own website PartyPoker.com – the world's leading online poker site. Specifically, online poker produced 92 percent of the company's revenues; the remaining 8 percent came from online casino and bingo games. The company had achieved its leading position in online poker through a timely entry into the online poker market, supported by effective online and offline sales and marketing, a reliable technology, and high-level customer support.

In 1997, Ruth Parasol started PartyGaming with the launch of the Starluck casino site, which was operated and managed from the Caribbean. Three years later, Anurag Dikshit and Vikrant Bhargava – who would later become the company's Operations and Marketing Directors – became investors in PartyGaming and started to develop the company's poker business. The poker site PartyPoker.com was launched in 2001 from Canada. With the help of famous poker player Mike Sexton, PartyGaming was able to attract a lot of publicity for its new website by organizing the "PartyPoker.com Million" tournament, for which the qualification rounds took place online. In 2002 and 2003, PartyGaming launched PartyBingo.com and moved its operations to Hyderabad (India) and its headquarters to Gibraltar.

The online gaming market had experienced rapid growth in the years just prior to 2005. Primary drivers of this growth were the increasing worldwide popularity of the internet as well as the increasing customer awareness of the sector's existence. Increasing customer awareness had resulted from greater television exposure and intensified marketing activities by the major industry players. In addition, online gaming companies had invested in their growth by developing new products and improving payment processing, transaction services, and customer support. Industry analysts did not expect this growth to stop in the

---

Professor Erik Peek prepared this case. The case is intended solely as the basis for class discussion and is not intended to serve as an endorsement, source of primary data, or illustration of effective or ineffective management.

[1]The material in this and the following sections largely draws from PartyGaming's IPO prospectus (June 14, 2005).

near term. The online sector's share of the global gaming market was expected to increase from 3 to 8 percent between 2004 and 2009.

Industry analysts estimated the size of the global online and offline gaming market to be $243 billion (in revenues) in 2004 and $282 billion in 2009. The online gaming market was estimated to generate revenue of approximately $8.2 billion in 2004 and $22.7 billion in 2009. In 2004, online casino and bingo games accounted for 29 percent of the online gaming revenues, whereas online poker games accounted for 13 percent. Respectively 50 percent, 27 percent, and 15 percent of the global online gaming revenues had been generated from the US, Europe, and Asia. Industry analysts expected the US share of the global online gaming market to decline to 40 percent in 2009 as a result of the above-average market growth in Europe and Asia. The key drivers of such growth would be the increasing number of internet users, the increasing popularity of gaming, increasing marketing investments made by the industry players, and the development of new distribution channels, such as mobile phones.

Poker had become more popular over the years mostly because of the increased television coverage of poker tournaments and the exposure of the game on popular television shows. Because many of the poker players around the world were still playing offline, the online poker market could potentially grow from the migration of offline players to online play. Analysts estimated that this migration, in combination with the attraction of new poker players, could make the online poker market's revenues grow from slightly more than $1 billion in 2004 to close to $6.4 billion in 2009 – representing 28 percent of the global online gaming market. In comparison, analysts estimated that the online casino market would grow from $2,157 million (in revenues) in 2004 to $5,587 million in 2009. According to PartyGaming's management there were a number of barriers to entry to the online poker market, creating a competitive advantage for the company:

- *Player liquidity.* To be able to organize games with a wide range of stakes at all times of players' choosing, online poker providers needed to have a large customer base.

- *Software control.* The leading online poker providers had invested significant amounts in software. Having control over their own software helped them to make the software improvements that were necessary for attracting and retaining customers.

- *Payment processing expertise.* To attract and maintain customers, online poker providers must be able to provide a wide range of payment methods (credit cards, e-checks, online wallets) and must have built a reputation for quick, efficient, and error-free payment processing.

- *Customer support.* Online poker providers must make significant investments in customer service operations.

- *Marketing and global reach.* Online poker providers needed to have significant market resources to penetrate new geographic markets and increase advertising expenditures as competition increased.

Having the mission to be the world's largest gaming company, with the most trusted brands, innovative technology, and high-level customer service, PartyGaming focused its strategy on the following areas: (1) sustain brand value and maintain leadership in its current markets, (2) expand to markets outside the US, first in Europe, later in Asia, (3) continue to provide innovative technology and high-level customer support, (4) stretch the "Party" brand to other games, either acquired or self-developed, and (5) make use of alternative delivery channels, such as mobile phones and interactive television.

In 2004, PartyGaming was the undisputed market leader in the online poker segment. Based on the average ring game rake – the amount of money the provider takes from the pot – the company had a market share of 54 percent. The five next-largest providers of online poker gaming all had market shares between 5 and 8 percent.

The risks

As pointed out, an investment in PartyGaming's ordinary shares involved substantial risks. The following risks were especially high:

■ *Regulatory risks.* One apparent risk affecting the online gaming market in 2005 was that in many countries national gaming laws had been developed to govern offline gaming activities and were not particularly suited to govern online gaming activities. Consequently, in some of PartyGaming's geographical segments there was much uncertainty about whether the supply of online gaming was legal or not. In some countries, foreign suppliers of online gaming were not able to obtain a license and it was uncertain whether and how local regulators would bring actions against foreign suppliers who had no license but were not physically present. PartyGaming ran the risk that regulators would change their laws and take actions that would inhibit the company's ability to process payments and advertise in a particular country. The advantage of these regulatory risks was, however, that they prevented many other companies from entering PartyGaming's industry, thereby reducing competition.

■ *Taxation risks.* PartyGaming and most of its group companies had their domicile in Gibraltar, where they were exempt from paying taxes because they offered no services to Gibraltarians or Gibraltar residents. However, in early 2005 the European Commission and the governments of Gibraltar and the UK had agreed to abolish the Gibraltar exempt company tax regime by the end of 2010. PartyGaming would even lose its tax exempt status – and become subject to a 35 percent tax rate – on December 31, 2007, if it had a change in ownership before June 30, 2006, and immediately lose its tax exempt status if it had a change in ownership after June 30, 2006. At the time of the IPO, it was still unclear what regulators would consider a "change in ownership." Party-Gaming expected that the IPO would not be treated as a change in ownership. The company's principal shareholders had agreed not to dispose of their shares within two years of the IPO. Further, the decision to abolish the exempt company tax regime had been appealed to the European Court. Finally, the government of Gibraltar was seeking alternative ways to provide companies with an attractive tax regime.

■ *Technology risks.* PartyGaming ran the risk that hackers would attempt to gain access to its systems and disrupt its services. Further, the growing demand for the company's online gaming services could lead to a situation in which its technological architecture as well as the technological architecture of its third-party providers was not developed enough to ensure the absence of errors, failures, interruptions, or delays in the provision of its services. Finally, PartyGaming needed to make investments in technology that facilitated the delivery of its online gaming services to customers who were not using personal computers but other devices such as mobile phones or television set-top devices.

■ *Competitive risks.* Other companies in PartyGaming's industry offered formidable competition. At the time of the IPO there were more than 2,000 online gaming sites and more than 200 online poker sites competing for the same customers. An increasing proportion of PartyGaming's revenues came from "third-party skins" – third-party brands that used PartyGaming's platform and shared their revenues. Third-party skins were competition to the company's own operations and brought significant risks of disputes and litigation.

■ *Intellectual property rights.* A substantial part of PartyGaming's technology and know-how was proprietary and any misappropriated or unauthorized disclosure of its technology and know-how could harm the company's competitive advantage. Similarly, the use of "Party" domain names or the "Party" brand by third parties without approval could harm the value of the company's brand. In some countries where PartyGaming operated, national laws did not sufficiently protect the company's intellectual property rights, or actions to enforce its intellectual property rights, were costly. PartyGaming also ran the risk that other technology companies would claim that their intellectual property rights were infringed by PartyGaming, which could result in litigation.

■ *Risks of international expansion.* Because of the legal uncertainties in the US, Party-Gaming planned to expand internationally. Competition outside the US was, however, stronger than within the US. Further, international expansion would bring a number of additional risks, such as legal, political, cultural, and currency risks. Operating on an international scale could also increase the company's transaction costs.

■ *Short operating history.* PartyGaming's short operating history made it difficult to assess the company's prospects. In its prospectus, the company reported that it did not expect that its rapid historic growth would persist in the future. In order to grow, Party-Gaming should innovate new products and services, countering the declining growth of the online poker market. The company also expected that, when growth would decline, the cyclicality and seasonality (lower yields per active player day in the second quarter, higher yields in the first and fourth quarters) of its operations would become more pronounced.

■ *Principal shareholders.* After the IPO, the principal shareholders of PartyGaming would hold close to 73 percent of the company's ordinary shares. Consequently, they could have a decisive influence on the company's financial and operating decisions as well as the success of any takeover offer.

Although PartyGaming had no physical presence in the US, it did not block US customers from signing up to the company's websites. The company generated almost 87 percent of its revenues from the US, where the regulatory risks were significant. It advertised its gaming sites in the US and made use of the services of US payment processors to collect from and pay out funds to its US customers. At the time of the IPO, the US Department of Justice considered the US operations of PartyGaming illegal. Further, at least seven US states had laws that explicitly prohibited online gaming, while many other states prohibited all forms of unlicensed gaming. US federal laws were, however, inconclusive about whether online gaming was indeed illegal and the status of state laws in the matter was unclear. The company had not received an official notification from any US authority that it sought to bring action against the company for its US operations. Any future action by US authorities to issue an injunction, impose fines or imprisonment, or seize gaming proceeds could, however, impose considerable (legal) costs upon the company and reduce the company's revenues and profits.

US law enforcement officials targeted their enforcement activities at US-based companies who provided services such as IT, payment processing, and advertising to PartyGaming. In particular, they alleged the violation of US laws to discourage US banks from processing online gaming transactions and US media from advertising online gaming sites. As a consequence, several banks, such as Citibank, financial service companies, such as PayPal, and media companies, such as Discovery, had decided not to provide any services to PartyGaming. Another threat to PartyGaming's US operations was posed by the proposals of the US Congress to prohibit online gaming or the provision of payment processing services to online gaming companies. Over past years, several proposals were made but did not receive sufficient support to be passed. In 2005, the US Congress would consider the "Kyl Bill", which sought to prohibit the processing of online gaming transactions. At the time of the IPO, this proposal seemed to lack sufficient support from the US Congress.

PartyGaming's governance

In early 2005 PartyGaming's Board of Directors comprised four executive directors and four nonexecutive directors. All nonexecutive directors were denoted as independent. The company's board had established an audit committee, a remuneration committee, a nominations committee, and an ethics committee. The company's CEO was Richard Lawrence Segal, who had joined the company in August 2004, after having been the CEO of cinema operator Odeon Limited for seven years.

Two executive directors were also principal shareholders of PartyGaming. After the IPO, Anurag Dikshit, Operations Director, would own 31.6 percent of the company's shares; Vikrant Bhargava, Marketing Director, would own 16.3 percent. Two other principal shareholders were co-founder Ruth Parasol – owning 16.3 percent – and her husband, Russell DeLeon – owning 9.0 percent. Each of the principal shareholders had agreed not to sell any shares during the 12 months following the IPO. Principal shareholders owning more than 15 percent of the company's shares had the right to nominate one nonexecutive director. However, they also agreed that at any time at least half of the company's board would comprise independent directors.

PartyGaming's performance

At the time of the IPO, PartyGaming's management considered the company's key strengths to be its high-margin business model, its strong marketing program and brand name, its large active player base, its high-quality and innovative technology, its offering of a wide variety of pay-in and withdrawal methods, its high-level 24/7 customer support, its well-developed systems of risk management and fraud detection, and its strong management team.

To sustain brand value and attract active players, PartyGaming made significant investments in marketing. The company made use of a variety of marketing strategies such as television and radio advertising, affiliate marketing (sharing revenues with other sites that market PartyGaming sites), direct mail, sign-up bonuses, and sponsorships. In addition, PartyGaming invested in the retention of customers by organizing the PartyPoker.com Million Tournaments, for which the qualification rounds were held online, introducing player loyalty programs (award schemes), and awarding bonuses to existing players who pay in new funds.

As evidence of PartyGaming's marketing success stands the large increase in the company's registered poker and casino players prior to 2005. **Exhibit 1** shows the number of registered and active poker and casino players by period, as well as the average yield per player day. The number of active players, the average daily active players, active player days (average daily active players times the number of days in a period), and yield per active player day were PartyGaming's key performance indicators. The yield per active player day followed a seasonal pattern. In 2003 (2004), the yield per active poker player day was $21.0 ($19.8), $18.1 ($18.7), $18.8 ($18.9), and $20.0 ($19.1) in the first, second, third, and fourth quarter, respectively. Although PartyGaming had a large player base, the company was reliant on a relatively small number of customers. For example, close to 10 percent of the active poker players contributed 70 percent of the company's revenues from poker games. Similarly, 5 percent of the active casino players contributed 82 percent of the company's revenues from casino games.

Exhibit 2 shows PartyGaming's financial statements for the fiscal years 2003 and 2004, as well as for three fiscal quarters. These figures illustrate PartyGaming's growth in revenues and profits. One apparent development was the strong decline in equity between 2003 and 2004. The reason for this decline was the acquisition of PartyGaming Holdings

Limited by PartyGaming Plc in 2004. PartyGaming acquired its interest in PartyGaming Holdings Limited in a transaction under common control. An acquisition under common control occurs when the acquirer and the target firm are both controlled by the same party. As a result of this transaction, PartyGaming Plc became the group's ultimate parent company. International Accounting Standards did not require acquisitions under common control to be accounted for using the purchase method. Consequently, PartyGaming used the pooling method to account for the acquisition, and the deficit in equity reflected the group's cumulative profits as if the new group structure had always been in place.

Questions

1   The initial offer price of PartyGaming's ordinary shares was 116 pence per share. Which sales growth and net operating profit margin assumptions are consistent with an offer price of 116 pence?

2   Using your own assumptions, estimate the value of PartyGaming's ordinary shares at the time of the IPO. How do the risks that PartyGaming faced affect your value estimate?

EXHIBIT 1 Information about PartyGaming's registered and active players

	Fiscal year ending December 31, 2002	Fiscal year ending December 31, 2003	Fiscal year ending December 31, 2004	Three months ending March 31, 2005
Total registered poker players	105,000	1,283,000	5,225,000	6,603,000
Total registered casino players	535,000	903,000	1,296,000	1,376,000
Registered real-money poker players	20,000	210,000	806,000	1,020,000
Of which active players (in the last month of the period)	6,000	125,000	324,000	411,000
Registered real-money casino and bingo players	282,000	320,000	374,000	388,000
Of which active players (in the last month of the period)	4,000	9,000	13,000	14,000
Average daily active poker players	1,297	17,043	77,094	121,570
Average yield per active poker player day	$20.8	$19.5	$19.1	$18.6
Average daily active casino and bingo players	580	832	1,797	1,875
Average yield per active casino and bingo player day	$90.7	$96.9	$73.9	$73.1

Source: PartyGaming's IPO prospectus (June 14, 2005). The item total registered players includes "play money" players who participate in games for free.

EXHIBIT 2   **PartyGaming's consolidated income statements, balance sheets, cash flow statements, and pro forma income statement and segment information for two fiscal years and three fiscal quarters**

CONSOLIDATED INCOME STATEMENTS ($ MILLIONS)

	Three months ending March 31, 2005	Three months ending December 31, 2004	Three months ending March 31, 2004	Fiscal year ending December 31, 2004	Fiscal year ending December 31, 2003
Revenue – net gaming revenue	222.6	194.0	115.4	601.6	153.1
Other operating revenue/(expenses)	−0.3	0.4	0.0	0.1	0.4
Administrative expenses					
– other administrative expenses	−23.3	−21.6	−15.8	−73.1	−29.4
– share-based payments	−4.6	−2.3	0.0	−3.2	0.0
– strategic review costs	−1.5	0.0	0.0	0.0	0.0
Distribution expenses	−64.6	−48.8	−28.7	−142.2	−34.9
Profit from operating activities	128.3	121.7	70.9	383.2	89.2
Finance income	0.6	0.8	0.2	1.4	0.0
Finance costs	−3.0	−4.4	−0.1	−12.9	0.0
Share of losses of associate	−0.3	0.0	0.0	0.0	0.0
Profit before tax	125.6	118.1	71.0	371.7	89.2
Tax	−8.2	−7.4	−3.9	−21.6	−5.6
Profit after tax	117.4	110.7	67.1	350.1	83.6
Minority interest	0.0	0.0	−1.6	−1.6	−6.6
Profit from ordinary activities attributable to equity holders of the parent	117.4	110.7	65.5	348.5	77.0
Net earnings per share ($ cents)	3.11	2.93	1.73	9.23	2.04
Net earnings per share ($ cents) – diluted	3.09	2.91	1.72	9.16	2.02
Weighted average shares outstanding	3,776	3,776	3,776	3,776	3,776
Weighted average shares outstanding, diluted	3,803	3,803	3,803	3,803	3,803

PRO FORMA INCOME STATEMENT AND SEGMENT INFORMATION ($ Millions)

	Three months ending March 31, 2005	Three months ending December 31, 2004	Three months ending March 31, 2004	Fiscal year ending December 31, 2004	Fiscal year ending December 31, 2003
Revenues					
– Poker	210.3	183.5	102.9	553.0	123.7
– Casino/Bingo	12.3	10.5	12.5	48.6	29.4
– Other	0.0	0.0	0.0	0.0	0.0
Administrative expenses					
– Transaction fees	−10.1	−8.9	−6.2	−29.3	−9.8
– Staff costs	−10.5	−8.0	−4.3	−21.8	−8.3
– Depreciation and amortization	−1.7	−1.4	−0.8	−4.6	−1.1
– Other overheads	−7.1	−5.6	−4.5	−20.6	−10.2
Distribution expenses					
– Affiliate fees	−23.6	−18.8	—	−53.7	−13.3
– Customer acquisition and retention (primarily advertising)	−24.1	−14.5	—	−37.6	−10.6
– Chargebacks (amounts unrecoverable from customers)	−11.6	−10.2	—	−36.7	−8.2
– Customer bonuses	−3.7	−4.1	—	−10.0	−1.6
– Web-hosting	−1.6	−1.2	—	−4.2	−1.2
Profit before tax					
– Poker	128.0	118.0	64.5	360.1	81.2
– Casino/Bingo	6.2	6.0	6.7	28.4	8.2
– Other	−8.6	−5.9	−0.2	−16.8	−0.2
Impairment losses – trade receivables	−11.7	−10.1	−10.3	42.2	−9.9
Impairment losses – other	0.0	0.0	0.0	0.0	−0.4

8 PartyGaming

CONSOLIDATED BALANCE SHEETS ($ Millions)

	Three months ending March 31, 2005	Three months ending December 31, 2004	Three months ending March 31, 2004	Fiscal year ending December 31, 2004	Fiscal year ending December 31, 2003
Intangible assets	7.7	7.7	8.0	7.7	0.0
property, plant, and equipment	25.4	13.3	9.1	13.3	5.7
Investment in associates	1.5	0.0	0.0	0.0	0.0
Total non-current assets	34.6	21.0	17.1	21.0	5.7
Trade and other receivables	132.9	107.8	76.5	107.8	53.2
Cash and cash equivalents	78.3	133.9	131.7	133.9	74.6
Short-term investments	3.5	0.0	0.0	0.0	0.0
Total current assets	214.7	241.7	208.2	241.7	127.8
Total assets	249.3	262.7	225.3	262.7	133.5
Bank overdraft	2.9	1.8	2.3	1.8	0.0
Trade and other payables	46.4	39.5	18.7	39.5	14.4
Shareholder loans	229.3	223.9	0.0	223.9	0.0
Income taxes	36.2	28.0	10.7	28.0	6.7
Client liabilities and progressive prize pools	124.1	104.6	49.1	104.6	35.4
Provisions	7.9	4.7	3.0	4.7	1.9
Total current liabilities	446.8	402.5	83.8	402.5	58.4
Trade and other payables	5.0	6.1	7.5	6.1	0.0
Shareholder loans	80.2	258.9	0.0	258.9	0.0
Total non-current liabilities	85.2	265.0	7.5	265.0	0.0
Share capital	0.1	0.0	0.0	0.0	0.0
Share premium account	0.4	0.4	0.4	0.4	0.4
Retained earnings	534.4	417.0	134.0	417.0	68.6
Other reserve	−825.4	−825.4	−0.4	−825.4	−0.4
Share option reserve	7.8	3.2	0.0	3.2	0.0
Equity attributable to equity holders of the parent	−282.7	−404.8	134.0	−404.8	68.6
Minority interest	0.0	0.0	0.0	0.0	6.5
Total liabilities and shareholders' equity	249.3	262.7	225.3	262.7	133.5

CONSOLIDATED CASH FLOW STATEMENTS ($ Millions)

	Three months ending March 31, 2005	Three months ending December 31, 2004	Three months ending March 31, 2004	Fiscal year ending December 31, 2004	Fiscal year ending December 31, 2003
Profit before tax	125.6	118.1	71.0	371.7	89.2
Adjustment for:					
Amortization of intangibles	0.0	0.1	0.0	0.3	0.2
Interest expense	3.0	4.4	0.1	12.9	0.0
Interest income	−0.6	−0.8	−0.2	−1.4	0.0
Depreciation of property, plant, and equipment	1.7	1.3	0.8	4.3	0.9
Gains on sale of property, plant, and equipment	0.0	0.0	0.0	0.0	0.1
Increase in share-based payments reserve	4.6	2.3	0.0	3.2	0.0
Loss on investment in associate	0.3	0.0	0.0	0.0	0.0
Operating cash flows before movements in working capital and provisions	134.6	125.4	71.7	391.0	90.4
Increase in trade and other receivables	−24.6	−15.3	−23.3	−54.6	−48.1
Increase in trade and other payables	26.5	31.3	15.2	89.9	43.4
Increase in provisions	3.2	−3.5	1.1	2.8	0.4
Income taxes paid	−0.8	0.0	0.0	0.0	0.0
Cash generated/(used) by working capital	4.3	12.5	−7.0	38.1	−4.3
Net cash from operating activities	138.9	137.9	64.7	429.1	86.1
Purchases of property, plant, and equipment	−13.8	−4.0	−4.1	−11.9	−5.9
Purchases of intangible assets	0.0	0.0	0.0	0.0	−0.2
Purchase of minority interest in subsidiary	0.0	0.0	−5.8	−5.8	0.0
Interest received	0.6	0.5	0.2	1.4	0.0
Purchase and cancelation of own shares	0.0	0.0	−0.1	−2.0	−3.1
Investment in associated undertaking	−1.8	0.0	0.0	0.0	0.0
Increase in short-term investments	−3.5	0.0	0.0	0.0	0.0
Net cash used in investing activities	−18.5	−3.5	−9.8	−18.3	−9.2
Issue of shares	0.0	0.0	0.0	0.9	0.0
Interest paid	−3.8	−4.6	−0.1	−11.0	0.0
Equity dividends paid	0.0	0.0	0.0	0.0	−8.1
Payments to shareholders	−173.3	−113.5	0.0	−343.2	0.0
Net cash used in financing activities	−177.1	−118.1	−0.1	−353.3	−8.1

Source: PartyGaming's IPO Prospectus (June 14, 2005). Note that at the time of the IPO, the total number of shares outstanding was 4,000,000,000.

9 Two European hotel groups (A): Equity analysis

Accor[1]

In 2005, France-based Accor S.A. was Europe's largest and the world's fourth largest hotel group (based on the number of rooms). The company employed 168,000 people in 140 countries and operated restaurants, casinos, travel agencies, and 4,065 hotels with 475,433 rooms in 90 countries. Major brand names owned by Accor included Sofitel, Novotel, Mercure, Ibis, Formule 1, Motel 6, and Red Roof Inn. Fifty-two percent of the company's hotel rooms were located in Europe and 29 percent in the U.S. Accor did not own all of its hotels. About 60 percent of its rooms were owned or leased, 20 percent were operated under management contracts, and 20 percent were franchised. In 2005, Accor's hotel business generated €5.2 billion in revenues, whereas its casino, restaurant, travel, and onboard train business generated €1.8 billion in revenues.

Accor generated a smaller proportion of revenues (approximately €0.6 billion) from selling service vouchers. The voucher system worked as follows. Accor's customers – mostly companies and institutions – purchased various types of vouchers from Accor at face value plus a service premium. These customers' beneficiaries, such as their employees, could use the vouchers to purchase services from affiliated service providers. Because the service providers had to pay a refund commission upon redemption, Accor's revenues consisted of the service premiums, the refund commissions, and the interest earned in the period between the issuance and the redemption of the vouchers. Examples of service vouchers were Accor's "Ticket restaurant" vouchers for meals, "Childcare" vouchers for family assistance services, and "Domiphone" vouchers for elderly home-help services.

In its hotel business, Accor served several segments, ranging from the upscale segment with Sofitel to the budget segment with Motel 6 and Formule 1. The company's preferred operating structure depended on the type of segment. For example, Accor preferred to operate its hotels under management contracts in the upscale segment and franchised in the budget segment. Under a management contract structure, Accor typically signed a 25-year agreement to manage a hotel and retained a 25 percent interest in the company that owned the hotel. Accor planned to open another 200,000 new hotel rooms between 2006 and 2010, primarily in the economy segment. In mature markets, which would account for 33 percent of the new openings, the company preferred to grow through low-capital-intensive property development, such as through management contracts and franchises. In total, Accor expected that it would invest €2.5 billion in the expansion of its hotel business between 2006 and 2010. During the same period, the company planned to invest €500 million in its services business.

Exhibit 2 shows Accor's financial statements for the fiscal years ending December 31, 2004 and 2005. Accor applied International Financial Reporting Standards for the first time in its 2005 financial statements. In 2005, Accor's total revenues grew by close to 8.0 percent. Revenues in the hotel segment increased by 4.8 percent, of which 1.2 percent came from the company's expansion of its capacity and 3.6 percent represented growth on a like-for-like basis (e.g., because of increases in occupancy rates or average room

Professor Erik Peek prepared this case. The case is intended solely as the basis for class discussion and is not intended to serve as an endorsement, source of primary data, or illustration of effective or ineffective management.

[1]Most of the material in this section comes from Accor's 2005 Annual Report.

rates). Revenues from Accor's service operations increased from €518 million to €630 million (21.7 percent) and by 14.1 percent on a like-for-like basis. The revenue growth of 12.9 percent in Accor's other operating segments was primarily driven by the creation of Groupe Lucien Barrièrre in the casino segment, where the reported growth was 47.7 percent but like-for-like growth did not exceed 1 percent. Like-for-like revenue growth in the other segments ranged from 3.3 percent in the travel agencies business to 6.9 percent in the restaurants business.

NH Hoteles[2]

Spain-based NH Hoteles S.A. competed with Accor primarily in the midscale segment of the European hotel market. In 2005, NH Hoteles ranked seventh among Europe's largest hotel chains, after brands such as Hilton, Holiday Inn, Novotel, and Mercure. The total number of rooms that NH Hoteles operated was 38,054 at the beginning of 2006. About 47 percent of these rooms were leased, 27 percent were owned, 14 percent were managed, and 12 percent were leased with a purchase option. In 2005, the company's hotel business generated close to €910 million in revenues. Next to investing in hotels, NH Hoteles had invested a smaller proportion of its capital in the development and exploitation of real estate properties. The company's revenues in this segment consisted of revenues from the exploitation of a private and exclusive golf club and revenues from the sale of luxury apartments and villas. The real estate activities were managed by an exchange-listed company, Sotogrande S.A., in which NH Hoteles had an 80 percent stake. By the end of 2005, NH Hoteles had made a public bid for Sotogrande's remaining shares. Sotogrande's real estate business generated €83.4 million in revenues in 2005, largely stemming from the sale of real estate.

NH Hoteles followed a strategy of international expansion. Whereas in 1999, NH Hoteles had operations only in its domestic market (Spain), five years later, the company had developed clear market presence in especially Germany and the Benelux (Belgium and the Netherlands). In early 2006, 34 percent of the company's rooms were located in Spain, 24 percent in Germany, 18 percent in the Benelux, and 14 percent in Latin America. In 2005, NH Hoteles opened 2,329 new rooms. Management expected that by the end of 2008 the number of leased, owned or managed hotel rooms would have increased to 41,509, of which 36 percent would be located in Spain, 22 percent in Germany, 16 percent in the Benelux, and 16 percent in Latin America. NH Hoteles acquired its first hotel in the U.K. in 2005 and planned to open its first hotel in France in 2008.

Exhibit 3 shows NH Hoteles' financial statements for the fiscal years ending December 31, 2004 and 2005. NH Hoteles applied International Financial Reporting Standards for the first time in its 2005 financial statements. In 2005, the company's total revenues grew by close to 1.0 percent. Revenues in the hotel segment increased by 4.5 percent, but revenues from NH Hoteles' real estate operations decreased by 26.8 percent. Operating profits and pretax profits in the hotel business were €58.2 million and €34.1 million, respectively, compared with €53.7 million and €54.2 million, respectively, in the real estate business.

9 Two European hotel groups (A): Equity analysis

---

[2]Most of the material in this section comes from NH Hoteles' 2005 Annual Report.

EXHIBIT 2   Accor's consolidated income statements, balance sheets, and cash flow statements for the fiscal years ending December 31, 2004 and 2005

CONSOLIDATED INCOME STATEMENTS (€ millions)

	Fiscal year ending December 31, 2005	Fiscal year ending December 31, 2004
Revenue	7,562	7,013
Other operating revenue	60	51
Consolidated revenue	**7,622**	**7,064**
Cost of goods sold	(747)	(676)
Employee benefits expense	(2,915)	(2,710)
Energy, maintenance, and repairs	(372)	(346)
Taxes, insurance, and service charges (co-owned properties)	(299)	(279)
Other operating expenses	(1,303)	(1,228)
EBITDAR	**1,986**	**1,825**
Rental expense	(837)	(790)
EBITDA	**1,149**	**1,035**
Depreciation, amortization, and provision expense	(432)	(423)
EBIT	**717**	**612**
Net financial expense	(135)	(123)
Dividend income from non-consolidated companies	6	5
Exchange gains and losses	6	13
Movement in provisions	1	4
Share of profit of associates after tax	8	2
Operating profit before tax and non-recurring items	**603**	**513**
Restructuring costs	(43)	(22)
Impairment losses	(107)	(52)
Gains and losses on management of hotel properties	72	(8)
Gains and losses on management of other assets	(37)	(23)
Profit before tax	**488**	**408**
Income tax expense	(124)	(152)
Net profit	**364**	**256**
Minority interests	(31)	(23)
Net profit, group share	**333**	**233**
Net earnings per share (€)	1.55	1.08
Net earnings per share (€) – diluted	1.55	1.08
Dividend payout per share (€)	1.15	1.30
Net book value per share (€)	20.02	14.56
Net book value per share (€) – diluted	20.02	14.56
Weighted average shares outstanding	214.783	214.783
Weighted average shares outstanding, diluted	214.783	214.783
End-of-year share price (€)	46.46	32.21

CONSOLIDATED BALANCE SHEETS (€ millions)

	Fiscal year ending December 31, 2005	Fiscal year ending December 31, 2004
Goodwill	1,897	1,667
Intangible assets	437	400
Property, plant, and equipment	3,891	3,717
Financial assets	1,212	1,220
Deferred tax assets	387	279
Non-current assets	**7,824**	**7,283**
Inventories	64	69
Trade receivables	1,508	1,272
Other receivables and accruals	770	628
Service vouchers reserve funds	327	346
Receivables on disposals of assets	23	44
Short-term loans	39	45
Current financial assets	600	77
Cash and cash equivalents	1,763	1,589
Current assets	**5,094**	**4,070**
Non-current assets held for sale	260	0
Total assets	**13,178**	**11,353**
Shareholders' equity, group share	4,301	3,128
Minority interests	95	70
Total shareholders' equity and minority interests	**4,396**	**3,198**
Convertible bonds	1,001	950
Other long-term debt	520	2,258
Long-term finance lease liabilities	352	337
Deferred tax	314	312
Long-term provisions	171	147
Non-current liabilities	**2,358**	**4,004**
Trade payables	849	760
Other payables and income tax payable	1,460	1,228
Service vouchers in circulation	1,940	1,561
Current provisions	203	148
Short-term debt and finance lease liabilities	1,915	382
Bank overdrafts	57	72
Current liabilities	**6,424**	**4,151**
Liabilities held for sale	0	0
Total liabilities and shareholders' equity	**13,178**	**11,353**

9 Two European hotel groups (A): Equity analysis

CONSOLIDATED CASH FLOW STATEMENTS (€ millions)

	Fiscal year ending December 31, 2005	Fiscal year ending December 31, 2004
EBITDA	1,149	1,035
Net financial expense	(122)	(101)
Income tax expense	(200)	(144)
Noncash revenue and expense included in EBITDA	0	14
Elimination of provision movements included in net financial expense, income tax expense and non-recurring taxes	102	43
Dividends received from associates	6	6
Funds from operations	**935**	**853**
Cash received (paid) on non-recurring transactions (included in restructuring costs and non-recurring taxes)	(124)	(67)
Decrease (increase) in working capital	271	130
Net cash from operating activities	**1,082**	**916**
Renovation and maintenance expenditure	(449)	(314)
Development expenditure	(479)	(680)
Proceeds from disposals of assets	313	429
Net cash used in investments/divestments	**(615)**	**(565)**
Proceeds from issue of share capital	822	312
Reduction in capital	0	0
Dividends paid	(287)	(284)
Repayments of long-term debt	(702)	(49)
Payment of finance lease liabilities	(52)	(33)
New long-term debt	664	128
Increase (decrease) in short-term debt	(178)	131
Net cash from financing activities	**267**	**205**
Effect of changes in exchange rates	(27)	11
Net change in cash and cash equivalents	**707**	**567**
Cash and cash equivalents at beginning of the period	1,594	1,024
Effect of changes in fair value of cash and cash equivalents	5	3
Cash and cash equivalents at end of period	**2,306**	**1,594**

EXHIBIT 3   **NH Hoteles' consolidated income statements, balance sheets, and cash flow statements for the fiscal years ending December 31, 2004 and 2005**

CONSOLIDATED INCOME STATEMENTS (€ thousands)		
	Fiscal year ending December 31, 2005	Fiscal year ending December 31, 2004
Net turnover	976,543	965,035
Other operating income	17,466	20,997
Net profit/(loss) on disposals of long-term assets	2,689	(2,455)
Raw materials and consumables	(108,533)	(107,203)
Staff costs	(300,802)	(298,438)
Write-down	(68,101)	(62,019)
Net losses due to asset impairment	(799)	(15,288)
Leases	(169,490)	(164,390)
External services	(235,601)	(216,935)
Other operating charges	(1,422)	(2,941)
Operating profit/(loss)	**111,950**	**116,363**
Profit and loss of companies valued using the equity method	(649)	(550)
Financial income	9,961	11,373
Interest expense	(35,188)	(36,832)
Net differences on exchange (income/(expense))	2,152	1,129
Profit before taxation of ongoing activities	**88,226**	**91,483**
Corporation tax	(17,813)	(25,680)
Minority interests	(8,170)	(10,600)
Profit/(loss) for the year	**62,243**	**55,203**
Net earnings per share (€)	0.52	0.46
Net earnings per share (€) – diluted	0.52	0.46
Dividend payout per share (€)	0.26	0.26
Net book value per share (€)	6.46	5.97
Net book value per share (€) – diluted	6.46	5.97
Weighted average shares outstanding	119,318	118,889
Weighted average shares outstanding, diluted	119,318	118,889
End-of-year share price (€)	13.25	9.76

9 Two European hotel groups (A): Equity analysis

CONSOLIDATED BALANCE SHEETS (€ thousands)

	Fiscal year ending December 31, 2005	Fiscal year ending December 31, 2004
Tangible fixed assets	1,408,314	1,357,574
Goodwill	113,586	96,834
Intangible assets	59,397	61,967
Holdings in associated companies	92,728	36,834
Permanent investments – loans and accounts receivable not available for trading	94,481	50,764
Permanent investments – other	22,436	16,193
Advance taxes	35,868	40,877
Other long-term assets	3,998	6,037
Total long-term assets	**1,830,808**	**1,667,080**
Inventories	96,902	83,519
Trade debtors	130,356	81,425
Taxes refundable	13,527	14,119
Other debtors	14,367	19,916
Current-asset investments – financial asset investments at maturity	26,621	64,142
Current-asset investments – traded financial assets	1,223	500
Own shares	0	257
Cash and banks and other cash equivalents	18,039	23,751
Other current assets	10,947	9,409
Total current assets	**311,982**	**297,038**
Total assets	**2,142,790**	**1,964,118**
Net equity attributable to shareholders of the Controlling Company	770,586	709,935
Minority interests	119,682	137,266
Total net worth	**890,268**	**847,201**
Debenture loans and other traded securities	83	108
Bank loans and overdrafts	592,871	563,857
Creditors for finance leases	316	13,568
Other long-term liabilities	81,335	81,589
Provisions for charges and liabilities	42,999	44,696
Deferred taxes	114,254	128,935
Total long-term liabilities	**831,858**	**832,753**
Debenture loans and other traded securities	25	25
Bank loans and overdrafts	136,829	38,461
Creditors for finance leases	399	615
Trade creditors and other accounts payable	169,394	148,767
Other current financial liabilities	1,130	1,094
Taxes and social security contributions	36,971	26,161
Provisions for charges and liabilities	7,892	40,252
Other current liabilities	68,024	28,789
Total current liabilities	**420,664**	**284,164**
Total liabilities and net equity	**2,142,790**	**1,964,118**

CONSOLIDATED CASH FLOW STATEMENTS (€ Thousands)

	Fiscal year ending December 31, 2005	Fiscal year ending December 31, 2004
Consolidated profit/(loss) before taxes	88,226	91,483
Depreciation and amortization of tangible and intangible assets	68,101	62,019
Losses on asset impairment (net)	799	15,288
Provisions (net)	878	392
Profit and loss on sale of tangible and intangible assets	(2,689)	2,455
Profit and loss of companies consolidated using the equity method	649	550
Financial income	(9,961)	(11,373)
Interest expense	35,188	36,832
Adjusted profit/(loss)	**181,191**	**197,646**
(Increase)/decrease in inventories	(13,383)	(3,669)
(Increase)/decrease in trade debtors and other accounts receivable	(42,790)	8,427
(Increase)/decrease in other current assets	(1,538)	1,822
Increase/(decrease) in trade creditors	20,627	(6,920)
Increase/(decrease) in other current liabilities	38,031	(17,379)
Increase/(decrease) in provisions for charges and liabilities	(40,773)	(16,622)
Income taxes paid	(16,573)	(20,680)
Total net cash flows from operating activities	**124,792**	**142,625**
Financial income	9,961	11,373
Group and associated companies and joint ventures	(53,488)	27,922
Tangible and intangible assets and property investments	(128,758)	(90,601)
Permanent investments	(44,979)	(24,403)
Investments and other current financial assets	37,055	(20,935)
Other assets	7,048	(7,779)
Total net cash flows from investing activities	**(173,161)**	**(104,423)**
Dividends paid	(29,882)	(29,882)
Pre-paid interest on debt	(36,388)	(37,564)
Changes in equity instruments – reserves	23,518	(2,304)
Changes in equity instruments – minority interests	(25,754)	(6,401)
Changes in bank loans and overdrafts	128,582	32,244
Changes in leasing	(13,468)	(616)
Changes in debenture loans and other traded securities	(25)	(22)
Other long-term liabilities	(3,926)	(22,603)
Total net cash flow from financing activities	**42,657**	**(67,148)**
Increase/decrease in cash or cash equivalents	**(5,712)**	**(28,946)**
Cash and cash equivalents at the beginning of the year	23,751	52,697
Cash and cash equivalents at the end of the year	**18,039**	**23,751**

9 Two European hotel groups (A): Equity analysis

EXHIBIT 4 Excerpts from the notes to Accor's and NH Hoteles' financial statements for the fiscal year ending December 31, 2005

A. Accor

Note 1. Summary of significant accounting policies

[...] In accordance with the optional exemptions to the retrospective application of IFRSs provided by IFRS 1, the Group has elected:

- Not to restate business combinations that occurred before January 1, 2004.

- To transfer cumulative translation differences at January 1, 2004 to retained earnings.

- To designate, at the date of transition to IFRS, a financial instrument as a financial asset or financial liability at fair value through profit or loss or as available for sale.

The Group has elected not to apply the following optional exemptions:

- Measurement of property, plant and equipment and intangible assets at fair value at the transition date, and use of that fair value as deemed cost.

- Application of IFRS 2 "Share-based Payment" to equity instruments granted on or before November 7, 2002 and to those granted after November 7, 2002 that vested before the date of transition to IFRS.

The other optional exemptions are not applicable to Accor Group.

D.2. Property, plant and equipment

Property, plant and equipment are measured at cost less accumulated depreciation and any accumulated impairment losses, in accordance with IAS 16 "Property, Plant and Equipment". Cost includes borrowing costs directly attributable to the construction of assets. Assets under construction are measured at cost less any accumulated impairment losses. They are depreciated from the date when they are ready for use. Property, plant and equipment are depreciated on a straight-line basis over their estimated useful lives, determined by the components method, from the date when they are put in service. The main depreciation periods applied are as follows:

	Upscale and Midscale hotels	Economy hotels
Buildings and capitalized construction-related costs	50 years	35 years
Building improvements, fixtures and fittings	7 to 25 years	7 to 25 years
Equipment	5 to 10 years	5 to 10 years

Note 6. Rental expense

Rental expense amounted to €837 million in fiscal 2005 compared with €790 million in fiscal 2004. In accordance with the policy described in note 1.D.4, the expense reported on this line only concerns operating leases. [...]

Rental expense is recognized on a straight-line basis over the lease term, even if payments are not made on that basis. Most leases have been signed for periods exceeding the traditional nine-year term of commercial leases in France, primarily to protect Accor against the absence of commercial property rights in certain countries. None of the leases contain any clauses requiring advance payment of rentals in the case of a ratings downgrade or other adverse event affecting Accor, and there are no cross-default clauses or covenants.

The €837 million in rental expense corresponds to 1,510 hotel leases, including 58% with a purchase option. Where applicable, the option price corresponds to either a pre-agreed percentage of the owner's original investment or the property's market value when the option is exercised. The options are generally exercisable after 10 or 12 years. Certain contracts allow for the purchase of the property at the appraised value at the end of the lease.

C. Minimum rental commitments (cash basis)

Minimum future rentals in the following tables only correspond to long-term rental commitments in the Hotels Division. The other divisions' rental commitments are generally for periods of less than three years and are not reflected in the tables below. Undiscounted minimum future rentals in foreign currency have been converted at the closing exchange rate and for the period beyond January 1, 2006, based on latest known rates, are as follows:

Years	€ millions	Years	€ millions
2006	659	2016	542
2007	656	2017	518
2008	656	2018	467
2009	655	2019	436
2010	651	2020	358
2011	643	2021	280
2012	625	2022	240
2013	610	2023	168
2014	594	2024	129
2015	567	> 2025	489
		Total	9,943

Note 18.1 Property, plant and equipment by nature

(in € millions)	2004	2005
Land	522	527
Buildings	2,644	2,544
Fixtures	1,777	1,955
Equipment and furniture	1,525	1,666
Constructions in progress	179	268
Property, plant and equipment, at cost	6,647	6,960
Buildings	(929)	(817)
Fixtures	(949)	(1,021)
Equipment and furniture	(982)	(1,096)
Constructions in progress	(6)	(5)
Total of depreciation	(2,866)	(2,939)
Land	(7)	(7)
Buildings	(56)	(118)
Constructions in progress	0	(5)
Total of impairment	(63)	(130)
Property, plant and equipment, net	3,717	3,891

Changes in the carrying amount of property, plant and equipment during the period were as follows:

(in € millions)	2004	2005
Net carrying amount at beginning of period	3,914	3,717
Property, plant and equipment of newly acquired companies	19	159
Capital expenditure	463	601
Disposals	(205)	(129)
Depreciation for the period	(383)	(392)
Impairment losses for the period	(5)	(86)
Translation adjustment	(72)	198
Reclassifications on non current assets held for sale	0	(260)
Other reclassifications	(14)	83
Net carrying amount at end of period	3,717	3,891

Borrowing costs included in the carrying amount of property, plant and equipment at December 31, 2005 came to €6 million. The capitalization rate used to determine the amount of borrowing costs eligible for capitalization was 4.93% (Group average borrowing cost at December 31, 2004).

Note 22.1 Details of trade receivables

(in € millions)	2004	2005
Gross value	1,342	1,575
Provisions	(70)	67
Net	3,717	3,891

Note 22.2 Details of other receivables and accruals

(in € millions)	2004	2005
Recoverable VAT	208	207
Prepaid payroll taxes	7	9
Other prepaid and recoverable taxes	21	97
Other receivables	264	287
Other prepaid expenses	141	194
Other receivables and accruals	641	794
Provisions	(13)	(24)
Other receivables and accruals, net	628	770

B. NH Hoteles

Note 2.3 Main decisions concerning the first application

In accordance with the standard first applied, the Group has applied the IFRS fully, apart from the following exceptions provided for in said standards:

- Business combinations: IFRS 3 shall not apply retrospectively to any business combinations that took place prior to the changeover date (1 January 2004).

- The Group has decided, on the date of the changeover to the IFRS, to state part of its tangible fixed assets at fair value, deeming this value to be the market cost attributed on said date, in accordance with IFRS 1, based on the assessment made by an independent expert.

- The balance of translation differences as at January 1st 2004 has been cancelled. This cancellation has been recorded as a reduction in the value of the reserves of the consolidated companies where said differences originated.

- Financial instruments: the Group has decided to apply IAS 32 and 39 as from January 1st 2005, as allowed by said Standards. Their application essentially involves:

9 Two European hotel groups (A): Equity analysis

a) Classifying own shares held, the balance of which was 259 thousand euros on that date, as a lower value of net worth.

b) Stating derivative contracts at their market value, recording an increase in net worth of 3,492 thousand euros.

Note 5.1 Accounting policies – tangible fixed assets

Tangible fixed assets are stated at cost, less accumulated depreciation and any recognized loss for impairment, except for those dependent companies whose tangible fixed assets were acquired before 31 December 1983 where the cost price was revalued in accordance with various different legal provisions. Later additions have been stated at cost.

At the time of the changeover to IFRS, the Group has restated at fair value certain pieces of land based on assessments made by an independent expert, by a gross total amount of 217 million euros. The revalued cost of this land has been regarded as cost in the changeover to the IFRS. The Group's policy has been not to revalue any of its tangible fixed assets when closing its accounts for subsequent financial years. Set

out below is the information concerning said revaluation (€ thousands):

Book value at origin	Fair value	Gain	Tax effect	Effect on reserves	Attributable to minority interests
207,972	424,867	217,075	34,796	170,002	12,277

The costs of extensions, modernisations or improvements which represent an increase in productivity, capacity or efficiency, or extend the life of existing assets are recorded as an increase in the cost of the related assets. Expenditure for maintenance and repairs is charged to consolidated expense as incurred.

The Group charges depreciation for its tangible fixed assets on a straight-line basis. The cost of the assets is spread over the years of their useful lives as shown in the following table:

	Estimated useful life in years
Constructions	33–50
Plant and machinery	10–12
Other plant, tools and furniture	5–10
Other investments	4–5

Note 9 Tangible fixed assets

Set out below is an analysis of the movements on the different tangible asset accounts in 2005 (thousand euros):

	Balance as at 31.12.04	Change in the scope of consolidation	Translation differences	Net additions/ disposals	Balance as at 31.12.05
COST					
Land and buildings	1,207,315	755	27,233	4,838	1,240,141
Technical plant and machinery	345,946	(215)	5,027	35,245	386,003
Other plant, tools and furniture	256,025	(249)	3,985	18,249	278,010
Other investments	20,238	(223)	2,017	11,449	33,481
Fixed assets under construction	25,835	32	239	10,418	36,524
	1,855,359	100	38,501		1,974,159
ACCUMULATED DEPRECIATION					
Constructions	(111,860)	275	(7,817)	(11,308)	130,710
Technical plant and machinery	(160,748)	271	(704)	(16,232)	177,413
Other plant, tools and furniture	(145,419)	100	(2,343)	(23,885)	171,547
Other investments	(12,083)	219	(1,924)	(3,524)	17,312
	(430,110)	865	(12,788)	(54,949)	496,982
Provisions	(67,675)		(1,111)	(77)	68,863
Net book value	1,357,574				1,408,314

Note 13 Trade debtors

"Trade debtors" record the different debtor accounts relating to the Group's current activities as well as the Controlling Company's earlier industrial activities. Set out below is an analysis of "Trade debtors" as at 31 December (thousand euros):

(in € thousands)	2005	2004
Trade accounts receivable for services provided	96,042	87,496
Trade debtors for sales of property products	45,542	4,971
	141,584	92,467
Less provision for bad debts	(11,228)	(11,042)
Total	130,356	81,425

Movements of the provision for bad debts during the years ended on 31 December 2005 and 2004 are as follows (thousand euros):

(in € thousands)	2005	2004
Balance as at 1 January	11,042	10,168
Translation differences	96	(56)
Charges	90	2,932
Applications	0	(1,902)
Balance as at 31 December	11,228	11,042

Note 19 Creditors for finance leases

[...] During the year ended on 31 December 2005, the average effective interest rate for the debt was 6.24% (7.20% in 2004). The interest rates were set on the date of the contract. The leases are paid on a fixed basis and no agreement has been made for the contingent rent payments.

Note 27.5 Operating leases

As at 31 December 2005 and 2004, the Group had acquired commitments for future minimum lease payments under operating leases that cannot be cancelled, falling due on the following dates:

(in € thousands)	2005	2004
Less than one year	175,557	169,493
Between two and five years	483,035	520,584
More than five years	743,660	848,720
Total	1,402,252	1,538,797

The table above, records present value of lease payments using an interest rate in line with the weighted cost of capital of the NH Hoteles Group. This table also includes, guarantee fees commitments arising from hotels operated under management contracts. The average life of the operating lease agreements signed by the NH Hoteles Group varies between 15 and 25 years.

Two European hotel groups (B): Debt analysis

At the end of fiscal year 2005, European hotel group Accor S.A. had a substantial amount of publicly traded convertible and nonconvertible bonds outstanding. The company had issued three tranches of convertible bonds in 2002, 2003, and 2005. The first tranche of convertible "OCEANE" bonds, which was issued in May 2002, consisted of 3,415,424 (publicly traded) bonds. The bonds had an issue price of €166.89, an annual interest rate of 1 percent, and a gross yield to maturity of 3.125 percent. One May 2002 OCEANE bond was exchangeable for three new or existing Accor shares before January 1, 2005, exchangeable for two Accor shares between January 1, 2005 and January 1, 2006, and exchangeable for one Accor share between January 1, 2006 and January 1, 2007. If bondholders would not exchange their bonds for shares, Accor would redeem €58.86, €60.14, and €61.47 on January 1, 2005, 2006, and 2007, respectively. The second tranche of convertible OCEANE bonds was issued in October 2003. This tranche consisted of 15,304,348 (publicly traded) bonds due January 2008. These bonds had an issue price of €41.25, an annual interest rate of 1.75 percent and were exchangeable for new or existing Accor shares when Accor's share price would exceed €44.27. The third tranche consisted of 116,279 convertible bonds which were due in May 2010. These convertible bonds had an issue price of €4,300, an annual interest rate of 3.25 percent and were exchangeable for 100 Accor shares.

Early in 2006, 6,383,362 bonds from the second tranche and all bonds from the first and third tranche were still outstanding. In addition to these convertible bonds, Accor had issued senior unsecured public debt for an amount of €400 million (due in December 2006). Two of the world's largest rating agencies, Standard and Poor's and Fitch, had rated Accor and its public debt at BBB.

Accor's competitor NH Hoteles S.A. had almost no public debt outstanding at the end of fiscal year 2005. In 1955 the company had issued bonds for an amount of €450,000. These bonds had a coupon rate of 6.75 percent. At the end of 2005, an amount of €83,000 in public bonds was still outstanding. At that time, the bonds had a yield to maturity of slightly more than 9.5 percent. Because of the small size of NH Hoteles' public debt, the company and its debt were not rated by one of the large rating agencies.

Question

Determine a credit rating for NH Hoteles' debt. Compare the rating to Accor's rating. If NH Hoteles' credit rating differs from Accor's rating, what explains the difference?

Professor Erik Peek prepared this case. The case is intended solely as the basis for class discussion and is not intended to serve as an endorsement, source of primary data, or illustration of effective or ineffective management.

EXHIBIT 1   Selected historical financial information

(in € millions)		2005 (IFRS)	2004 (IFRS)	2003 (local GAAP)	2002 (local GAAP)	2001 (local GAAP)
Net income	Accor	364	256	270	430	474
	NH Hoteles	62	55	51	86	82
After-tax net interest expense	Accor	(88)	(80)	(48)	(43)	(60)
	NH Hoteles	(16)	(17)	(21)	(24)	(16)
Sales	Accor	7,562	7,013	6,774	7,071	7,218
	NH Hoteles	977	965	922	886	762
Total assets	Accor	13,178	11,353	10,956	11,275	12,100
	NH Hoteles	2,143	1,964	1,845	1,977	1,934
Market capitalization	Accor	9,604	6,431	7,153	5,749	8,098
	NH Hoteles	1,584	1,167	1,089	1,250	1,335

EXHIBIT 2 Excerpts from Accor's and NH Hoteles' annual reports for the fiscal year ending December 31, 2005

A. Accor

Note 29. Debt by currency and maturity

Note 29.A. Long and short-term debt
Long and short-term debt at December 31, 2005 breaks down as follows by currency and interest rate after hedging transactions:

(in € millions)	2004	Effective rate in 2004 (%)	2005	Effective rate in 2005 (%)
EUR	2,583	4.59	2,311	4.50
USD	495	6.10	560	5.07
AUD	114	6.41	116	6.62
Other currencies	114	6.18	137	5.37
Long and short-term borrowings	**3,306**	**4.93**	**3,124**	**4.72**
Long and short term finance lease liabilities	370		388	
Purchase commitments	90		119	
Changes in fair value of financial liabilities	37		12	
Liability derivatives	23		13	
Other short-term financial liabilities and bank overdrafts	173		189	
Long and short-term debt	**3,999**		**3,845**	

Note 29.B. Maturities of debt
At December 31, 2005, maturities of debt were as follows:

	2004	2005
Year Y+1	454	1,972
Year Y+2	1,948	462
Year Y+3	287	929
Year Y+4	703	157
Year Y+5	444	57
Year Y+6	33	68
Beyond	130	200
Total long and short-term debt	**3,999**	**3,845**

At December 31, 2005, Accor had several unused confirmed lines of credit with maturities of more than one year, for a total of €2,395 million, expiring between January 2007 and October 2009. As a result, €77 million in short-term facilities that the Group intends to roll over has been reclassified as long-term debt. After reclassifications, long-term unused confirmed lines of credit total €2,318 million.

Note 29.D. Long and short-term debt by interest rate after hedging

(in € millions)	Fixed rate debt		Variable rate debt		Total debt	
	Amount	Rate	Amount	Rate	Amount	Rate
December 31, 2004	1,793	6.01%	1,513	3.61%	3,306	4.93%
December 31, 2005	1,698	4.97%	1,426	4.41%	3,124	4.72%

At December 31, 2005, fixed rate debt was denominated primarily in EUR (86%) and USD (10%), while variable rate debt was denominated mainly in EUR (59%), USD (27%) and AUD (8%). The Group's loan agreements do not contain any rating triggers. Acceleration clauses stipulate that the interest cover ratio (ratio of EBITDA to interest expense plus one-third of annual rental expense) may not exceed $3.8\times$. These clauses apply solely to lines of credit that were not used at December 31, 2005.

None of the €3,124 million in debt carried in the balance sheet at December 31, 2005 is subject to any acceleration clauses. None of the Group's loan agreements contain any cross default clauses. Cross acceleration clauses only concern loans for periods of at least three years and they would be triggered only for similar loans representing a significant amount.

B. NH Hoteles

Note 17 Debenture loans and other traded securities

Set out below is an analysis of bonds and debentures outstanding as at 31 December (thousand euros):

	2005 Long-term	2005 Short-term	2004 Long-term	2004 Short-term
Series B debentures	83	23	108	23
Bond and debenture interest		2		2
Total	83	25	108	25

This 1955 series B bond issue pays interest at 6.75% a year and is being redeemed in increasing payments and shall be fully redeemed by 2009. This issue is secured by a bank guarantee.

Note 18 Bank loans and overdrafts

Set out below is an analysis of bank loans and overdrafts as at 31 December 2005 (thousand euros):

	Drawn down	2006	2007	2008	2009	Remainder
Mortgage loans						
Fixed interest	49,082	11,513	23,771	1,290	1,313	11,195
Variable interest	80,494	13,915	27,460	4,438	3,349	31,331
Long-term unsecured loans						
Fixed interest	1,402	356	534	344	168	0
Variable interest	419,979	43,990	116,791	83,924	84,426	90,848
Credit lines (variable interest)						
Variable interest	181,599	64,980	81,086	28,495	7,038	
Accrued interest	3,113	3,113				
Debt formalisation expense	(5,969)	(1,038)	(1,039)	(1,039)	(1,039)	(1,814)
Debt situation as at 31.12.05	729,700	136,829	248,603	117,452	95,255	131,561

The line "Long term unsecured loans, variable interest", includes a syndicated loan granted to NH Hoteles, S.A. by 25 European banks, on 23rd June 2004, for 350 million euros. As at 31st December 2005, this loan had been drawn down in full. This loan expires on 23rd June 2010 and pays annual interest at one-month Euribor plus a spread that varies between 1.1% and 0.60% depending on the Net financial debt/EBITDA ratio. Repayments are to be made in five instalments. The first will be made in July 2006. This loan requires that certain financial ratios be complied with. As at 31st December 2005, none of these are in a position that is likely to trigger off a declaration of early termination by the lending entities.

Furthermore, the line "Long term unsecured loans, variable interest" includes a syndicated loan through Banco Bilbao Vizcaya Argentaria granted to NH Hoteles, S.A. for a maximum of 42.07 million euros, to be used to finance the acquisition, via a takeover bid, of shares in Promociones Eurobuilding, S.A. (a company merged into NH Hoteles, S.A. in 2002). As at 31st December 2005, 29 million euros were still outstanding. The interest on this loan is charged at a rate equal to Euribor plus a spread and the loan will be repaid gradually starting in 2001 and ending in 2011.

Set out below are the average rates of financing of the Group during 2005 and 2004:

	2005	2004
Mortgage loans		
Fixed interest	5.09%	5.09%
Variable interest	EURIBOR +1.18%	EURIBOR +1.09%
Long-term unsecured loans		
Fixed interest	5.19%	5.19%
Variable interest	EURIBOR +0.74%	EURIBOR +0.80%
Credit lines		
Variable interest	EURIBOR +0.26%	EURIBOR +0.33%

Note 20 Other long-term liabilities

Set out below is an analysis of "Other long-term liabilities" as at 31 December 2005 and 2004 (in thousand euros):

	2005	2004
Preference shares issued by subsidiary companies	28,122	42,307
Right of beneficial use of Hotel Plaza de Armas	11,960	13,455
Residencial Marlin, S.L.	9,000	9,000
Financial instruments	4,089	7,746
Capital grants	3,446	3,645
Purchase minority interests in NH Hoteles Deutschland, GmbH and NH Hoteles Austria, GmbH	15,000	
Other liabilities	9,718	5,436
Total	81,335	81,589

The line "Preference shares issued by subsidiary companies" records the preference shares issued by NH Participaties N.V. outstanding as at 31 December 2005 and 2004 which have, by their nature, been classified as a financial liability. These preference shares earn interest at a fixed annual rate of 5.55% and mature on 1 January 2008. The line "Capital grants" basically records, as at 31 December 2005, a total of 3.45 million euros (3.64 million euros as at 31 December 2004) for the grants received to build the hotels and golf courses of subsidiary company Sotogrande. The amount recorded for "Residencial Marlin, S.L." represents 50% of the participating loan granted to that company by the minority shareholder of Sotogrande, S.A., which has a 50% holding in said company. This participating loan expires on July 2007 (see Note 11.1). As mentioned in Note 2.6.6 of these annual accounts, this year the NH Hoteles Group has acquired the remaining 20% of NH Hoteles Deutschland, GmbH, and NH Hoteles Austria, GmbH, for 45 million euros. As at 31 December 2005, 30 million euros were still outstanding, 15 million of which are recorded as short-term in the caption "Other current liabilities" (see Note 25), and the last instalment is due to be paid in 2007.

10 Two European hotel groups (B): Debt analysis

11 United Parcel Service's IPO

This is an historic step for UPS. We intend to remain the pre-eminent company in our industry and expand our role as an enabler of global commerce. A publicly traded stock will build on our financial strength as a triple-A rated company and give us more flexibility to pursue strategic opportunities around the world. This will allow us to better meet the changing needs of our customers for innovative new products and services.

—James Kelly, UPS Chairman and CEO, July 21, 1999

I n July of 1999, United Parcel Service (UPS) surprised both Wall Street and Main Street with the announcement that, after more than 90 years as a private, employee-owned operation, it was planning an initial public offering that would transform "Big Brown" into a publicly traded company. UPS was a company with $1.7 billion of net income and almost a century-long track record of financial performance, a marked contrast to the internet and technology-related IPOs launched in the late 1990s. Although pricing for the shares had yet to be announced, the offering looked likely to be the largest IPO in U.S. history.

Determining an appropriate price for the new shares was a central concern of the joint Morgan Stanley Dean Witter & Co.–UPS deal team that had been charged with launching the offering. The actual price per share would be set only hours before the first trading day for the new stock. In the weeks before the listing the deal team would be expected to consider a variety of factors in fixing the offer price, including current and future trends in the package delivery industry, UPS's strengths and weaknesses relative to other competitors, UPS's recent financial performance, and the valuation of comparable companies.

The package delivery industry

In 1999, package delivery in the United States was a $43 billion industry serving a broad array of distinct customer segments—individuals sending overnight letters, small-to-medium-sized enterprises demanding affordable shipment of time-critical parcels, and large corporations moving heavy freight between facilities.

The industry offered two basic products—air and ground. Ground traditionally referred to deliveries made within one to six business days using surface transportation such as cars, vans, trucks, and trains. For much of the century, ground was the only reliable option for moving letters and parcels. Air delivery enabled customers to request overnight service, which was expedited using complex air networks. Two- and three-day air products, a segment that rapidly expanded in the 1980s and 1990s given its substantially lower price compared to overnight products and faster delivery time relative to traditional ground

Professor Paul Healy and Brett Laschinger and Ajay Shroff (MBAs 2002) prepared this case. HBS cases are developed solely as the basis for class discussion. Cases are not intended to serve as endorsements, sources of primary data, or illustrations of effective or ineffective management.

services, was often referred to as "time-deferred" or "deferred" service. Although the lines between air express and ground had blurred somewhat as ground networks improved to the point where overnight and "two-day air" deliveries could be made on the ground, industry analysts continued to segment the market in these terms. As of 1999, the domestic air industry (including overnight and deferred) comprised 60% of the market by revenue and 46% by volume, compared with 40% of revenue and 54% of volume for ground.[1] **(See Exhibits 1 to 3** for historical market size and growth data.)

The asset-intensive and highly complex nature of both the domestic air and ground industries had resulted in intense competition among three very large competitors: Atlanta-based UPS (51% share of market by revenue), Memphis-based Federal Express (26%), and the U.S. Postal Service (17%).[2] **See Exhibit 4** for overnight, deferred, and ground market share data. UPS was the market leader in the $17 billion ground segment, with competition coming from FedEx and USPS as well as private delivery fleets of individual companies, courier services, regional delivery services, LTL trucking firms and third-party logistics companies. UPS was the number two player to the USPS in the deferred segment, and number two to FedEx in the overnight express market.

U.S. Postal Service

The U.S. Postal Service (USPS) was a quasi-government entity which moved more than four times as many deliveries each day as UPS and FedEx combined,[3] and operated a delivery network that reached every household and commercial address in the country, six days a week. The USPS offered a number of delivery products that competed directly with UPS's offerings. The most prominent of these was Priority Mail, which offered ground shipment of packages in 1 to 3 business days to any destination in the United States. Priority Mail was generally considered to be less expensive but also less reliable than either UPS's or FedEx's two- and three-day offerings. The USPS also lacked the premier logistics and package tracking information systems that both FedEx and UPS had developed. However, rumor had it that Lockheed Martin had been hired to help the Postal Service create a comparable tracking system to be completed in 2001.[4]

Observers pointed out that with e-mail and other forms of electronic communication cutting deeply into the USPS's traditional regular mail monopoly, the Service was especially eager to allocate resources to other segments of the package delivery market, which would mean more frequent competition with UPS and FedEx.[5]

FedEx

FedEx, a $17 billion global transportation and logistics enterprise, was credited with single-handedly pioneering the concept of overnight delivery in the early 1970s. By the late 1990s, FedEx moved over 3 million packages each day, with the ability to reach virtually every business address in the United States and almost every country around the world within 24 hours. Federal Express, the overnight delivery arm of FedEx Corp., was by far its largest and most important operating unit, accounting for 84% of total revenues and 83% of operating income in 1998. FedEx also controlled a variety of other related businesses. FedEx Custom Critical was a time-critical carrier, FedEx Logistics provided logistics solutions and assistance to other businesses, and Viking Freight operated as a

[1]SJ Consulting estimates.

[2]SJ Consulting estimates.

[3]USPS website. Includes first-class mail in addition to parcel volume. First-class mail represents about 90% of USPS's total shipment volume.

[4]Brian O'Reilly, "UPS vs. FedEx: They've Got Mail,'" *Fortune*, February 7, 2000.

[5]Deutsche Bank Alex. Brown UPS Equity Research Report, December 1, 1999.

less-than-truckload West Coast regional carrier. FedEx's operating philosophy with respect to these various companies was to "operate independently, compete collectively,"[6] and hence each operating company remained a separate operating entity with discrete management and its own trucks, sorting hubs and other assets.

With the 1998 acquisition of Roadway Package System (RPS), the second-largest ground delivery business-to-business small-package shipper in the nation (after UPS), FedEx also developed a presence in the ground business. Prior to the acquisition, RPS employed 22,000 direct and contract employees, operated 365 sorting and other facilities in North America, and reported revenues of $1.3 billion. It was estimated that RPS served 10%–12% of the U.S. B2B ground delivery market in 1998.[7] RPS had achieved its considerable success in part by selectively targeting some of UPS's most valuable accounts—high-volume customers in high-density locations. RPS had also developed the premier package logistics and tracking software in the ground delivery industry. Following the acquisition, FedEx renamed RPS as FedEx Ground to take advantage of its own strong brand.

Other competitors

Smaller players in the U.S. market included Airborne Freight, CNF, and DHL. Airborne Freight, with 1998 revenues of just over $3 billion, was the third-largest U.S. express delivery carrier, and had achieved significant growth over the 1990s by positioning itself as the low-cost overnight delivery alternative for business-to-business customers. CNF focused on ground delivery and heavyweight airfreight. DHL, a European international express-mail carrier, was active in U.S. international shipping. In 1998, the German-government backed Deutsche Post AG acquired a 25% stake in DHL and was expected to compete more aggressively for U.S. domestic business.

Industry outlook

In July 1999, the outlook for the package industry was mixed. Robust GDP growth and ever-increasing demands for faster delivery suggested continued strong growth potential for the air express segment, which had enjoyed double-digit expansion through the 1980s and high single-digit growth in the 1990s. However, the digitization of documents and emergence of electronic signatures threatened the significant overnight letter business. As for the ground industry, which had grown at a rate somewhat in excess of U.S. GDP, the rapid expansion of internet shopping hinted at a potential boost for the B2C ground business, while industry rivalry threatened intense price competition.[8]

In terms of international delivery, the large integrated carriers had constructed global delivery networks that could reach over 90% of the world's population. International revenue was derived from the export needs of U.S.-based customers as well as intra-country operations in other parts of the world. As saturation occurred in the U.S. market, industry observers anticipated that this market would provide an attractive growth opportunity.

United Parcel Service (UPS)

With over 340,000 employees, 149,000 delivery vehicles, 500 planes, and $25 billion in annual revenues, UPS was the largest parcel delivery company in the world. The company delivered nearly 13 million packages each business day (9,000 packages every minute) to

[6]FedEx website.

[7]"RPS Adopts a New Name as Parent FedEx Shifts its Marketing Strategy," *Pittsburgh Business Times Journal*, January 21, 2000.

[8]SJ Consulting estimates.

over 200 countries worldwide. Each year UPS moved some 6% of the United States' Gross Domestic Product (GDP). In addition to air and ground package delivery, UPS helped its customers with supply chain management, logistics, and financial services. The company had daily contact with 1.8 million customers (including every company in the *Fortune* 1000) and made deliveries to 6 million business and residential addresses. In 1999, *Fortune* magazine recognized UPS as the "World's Most Admired Global Mail, Package and Freight Delivery Company" and *Forbes* magazine named UPS "Company of the Year."[9]

History

Using $100 borrowed from a friend, 19-year old James "Jim" Casey founded the American Messenger Company in Seattle, Washington, in 1907. The company provided private messenger and delivery services—such as the transportation of letters, hand-baggage, and trays of food—by bicycle, foot, and streetcar.[10]

In the 1920s, the company, renamed the United Parcel Service, shifted its focus to package delivery for retailers who sought to outsource that function. UPS grew quietly alongside the retail industry for the next three decades, slowly expanding its geographical reach and breadth of services. During this period, the company pioneered the concept of consolidated delivery—combining packages for a particular neighborhood within one delivery vehicle—and developed the first-ever mechanical sorter and conveyor belt system.

Gradual innovation and expansion continued until the 1950s when UPS realized that its growth options would be limited if it remained solely focused on package delivery for retailers. As of 1954, UPS had operations in only 16 cities. To expand its geographic reach and scope of operations, UPS had to petition state and federal authorities for broader business activity rights. Over the next 30 years, UPS fought dozens of legal and regulatory battles to gain the right to operate delivery vehicles within each state, and between any two states—known in the industry as "common carrier" rights. By 1980, UPS achieved national coverage and had become a direct and formidable competitor to the USPS. By the early 1980s, UPS's ground business had grown so rapidly that it quickly surpassed USPS's in terms of parcel (i.e., non-letter) volume. Over the next two decades UPS went on to become the largest player in the ground delivery segment.[11]

UPS grew its air network in parallel with its ground infrastructure. Blue Label Air, a two-day service between major cities, began in 1953 and reached national coverage by 1978. During the 1970s, despite the rapid growth of the overnight express market which newly formed Federal Express pioneered, UPS stuck to 2–3 day air service at a rate one-tenth that of FedEx's overnight service.[12] In August 1982, however, "in response to customer demand," UPS finally announced its entry into the next-day air express arena, nine years after FedEx.[13]

The 1980s and early 1990s were pivotal for UPS as it was forced to play "catch up" to FedEx in the air express segment and respond to market share gains by RPS and the USPS on the ground. The company's responses included a major technology upgrade, changes in pricing, and a change in marketing strategy. Between 1988 and 1999, UPS spent more

---

[9]UPS 1999 Annual Report filed March 30, 2000.

[10]"United Parcel Service (A)," HBS Case No. 488-016 (Boston, MA: Harvard Business School Publishing, 1992), p. 3.

[11]John D. Williams, Staff Reporter for *The Wall Street Journal* (New York, NY), "The Brown Giant: UPS Delivers Profits By Expanding Its Area," August 25, 1980, p. 1.

[12]John D. Williams, Staff Reporter for *The Wall Street Journal* (New York, NY). "The Brown Giant: UPS Delivers Profits By Expanding Its Area," August 25, 1980, p. 1.

[13]Sharen Kindel, "When Elephants Dance," *Financial World*, June 9, 1992, p. 76.

than $1 billion per year upgrading its infrastructure to track packages precisely, deliver electronic proof of delivery, and manage shipments on-line. The new systems included electronic scanners, bar codes on packages, and computerized clipboards for all UPS drivers.[14] In addition, the company hired thousands of programmers and technicians to manage its information needs and develop innovative applications and services for its customers. By 1999, UPS could handle six times as many on-line tracking requests as FedEx,[15] leading *Forbes* magazine to declare, "UPS used to be a trucking company with technology. Now it's a technology company with trucks."[16]

UPS also responded to competitive challenges by changing its pricing and marketing strategies. It began transitioning away from using standard rates to allowing prices to vary across markets and customers based on cost differences. It also introduced a widely aired new ad campaign that touted "We run the tightest ship in the shipping business,"[17] a marked change from its prior policy of shying away from publicity.

Throughout the 1990s UPS steadily captured market share in the express arena, reaching an estimated 32% share by 1998, and its ground business returned to a pace of moderate growth despite cost-cutting and targeted sales efforts by competitors.[18] Reflecting on UPS's transformation during the 1990s, UPS CEO Jim Kelly proclaimed, "Truth is, we're not your father's UPS anymore!"[19]

UPS chose to expand the scope of its business in 1993 with the formation of UPS Logistics Group, which provided supply chain management solutions and consulting services to UPS's customer base. Typical service contracts included back-end fulfillment for Sprint PCS, the timely delivery of fresh ingredients to all Papa John's Pizza locations, and the distribution of vehicles from Ford's manufacturing plants to automobile dealerships nationwide. By 1999, the Logistics Group generated nearly $1 billion in incremental revenue for the company.[20]

Operations

UPS coordinated and managed the pickup of 13 million packages each day from 2 million addresses for delivery to over 6 million commercial and residential addresses worldwide. To do so, it relied on a carefully designed network of vehicles, sorting facilities, and hubs as well as the support of a sophisticated IT system. The system had been developed and refined over the last decade and was continually enhanced to ensure the highest levels of reliability, efficiency, and speed.

Drivers followed precisely defined routes to pickup packages from customers at pre-set times. Those packages were taken to hubs where they were consolidated and sorted at speeds of upwards of hundreds of thousands of packages per hour. Packages for the same zip code or delivery area were loaded onto the appropriate conveyor belt and then onto the familiar brown trucks in the order in which they would be delivered. This allowed drivers to deliver their packages in sequence, "from one address to the next-closest address . . . as quickly and productively as possible."[21]

Unlike FedEx, UPS made no distinction between the operating facilities for air and ground operations. All facilities were shared, including the single fleet of trucks that

[14]Kenneth Labich, "Big Changes at Big Brown," *Fortune*, January 18, 1988, p. 60.

[15]Fedex.com and UPS.com company websites.

[16]From <www.ups.com>. "Speeches," Mike Eskew, March 29, 2000.

[17]Kenneth Labich, "Big Changes at Big Brown," *Fortune*, January 18, 1988, p. 57.

[18]SJ Consulting.

[19]James Kelly, Speech at the Robert C. Goizueta Global Leadership Award Breakfast, December 14, 2001 (available at <www.ups.com>, "Speeches").

[20]1999 UPS Annual Report.

[21]<http://www.pressroom.ups.com/about/history/0,1701,,00.html> or <www.ups.com>, "Company History."

handled the pickup and delivery of all UPS shipments. The integration of its air and ground operations gave UPS the ability to optimize utilization of its assets while still meeting customer service requirements. For example, the same fleet of UPS trucks was used to pick up and deliver ground and air packages. Also, because the operations were integrated, a package marked for "Next Day Air" delivery could be transported by truck if that method of transportation was deemed less expensive and just as reliable (**see Exhibit 5**). UPS's sophisticated IT systems coordinated this process.[22]

Human resource management

Since its inception, UPS enjoyed a loyal workforce with an operational and service-excellence culture. Employees were recruited through part-time positions and educational assistance programs. They were trained in carefully studied work methods and educated about UPS's time-tested policies and procedures at a cost of over $300 million annually.[23] These educational programs, combined with on-the-job training and role modeling, helped UPS command one of the lowest turnover rates in the industry (less than 5% annually) and succeeded in developing a portion of its workforce for management positions each year. UPS took pride in this "promote from within" policy which was epitomized by the fact that James "Jim" Kelly, UPS's chairman and chief executive officer, started his career as a package delivery driver.

The company's unique culture emphasized accountability and efficient execution at every level of the organization. Operating employees adhered to fairly rigid operational guidelines developed by industrial engineers and rooted in time motion studies. Drivers, for example, were instructed on how to best perform their jobs from the moment they started work until the end of their day. A lengthy and detailed guide precisely defined how a driver should start the delivery vehicle's engine, greet customers, scan packages, and even buckle and unbuckle his or her safety belt between stops. Within corporate headquarters, employees faced similar policies that focused on efficiency, "such as no coffee at desks, and two 15-minute breaks during the work day."[24] These and other operating features were captured in the company's *Policy Book,* which had guided the company since 1929.

Since 1919, union issues were a way of life at UPS. Over 200,000 of UPS's 340,000 employees belonged to the International Brotherhood of Teamsters, making UPS the largest single constituency for that union. Labor relations had generally been harmonious. The only exception had arisen during a 15-day work stoppage in 1997 that cost UPS several hundred million in lost revenues and an immeasurable loss of goodwill among certain customers. Management and the unions were able to strike flexible work arrangements when needed to allow UPS to offer customers a greater range of services. In return, UPS drivers and other unionized personnel enjoyed the highest pay in the industry.

Experts believed UPS's combination of "controls, rules, a detailed union contract, and carefully studied work methods . . . helped guarantee the customer reliable, low-cost service."[25]

Valuation benchmarks

The IPO team considered several potential benchmarks for valuing UPS. The first potential benchmark was the trucking industry. Industry analysts typically included package

[22]Ibid.

[23]<http://www.pressroom.ups.com/about/history/0,1701,,00.html> or <www.ups.com>, "Company History."

[24]"United Parcel Service (A)," HBS Case No. 488-016 (Harvard Business School Publishing, Boston, MA: 1992), p. 15.

[25]David E. Bowen and Edward E. Lawler, "The Empowerment of Service Workers: What, Why, How, and When," *Sloan Management Review,* Spring 1992: 32.

delivery firms in the trucking industry, making it a natural comparison. However, the team decided that the fragmented trucking industry, with its low barriers to entry and poor profitability, was of limited value as a benchmark for UPS. Instead, the investment banking members of the team favored using Federal Express as a benchmark, whereas UPS's management argued that UPS was better compared to "best of breed" companies in other industries.

Federal Express

UPS's foremost publicly listed competitor, particularly in the overnight express segment of the market, was Tennessee-based FedEx Corporation. FedEx operated a fleet of 634 aircraft and 41,000 pickup and delivery vehicles, and employed 88,000 permanent full-time and 50,000 permanent part-time employees. On November 1, 1999, FedEx's stock price closed at $41.50, representing a price-earnings multiple of 19.8 and a price-book value of 2.7 **(see Exhibit 6)**.

Although FedEx had been created as an overnight air express carrier and UPS had focused on multi-day ground delivery, over time their business models had converged. This had been accelerated by FedEx's acquisition of RPS. FedEx Chairman Fred Smith noted the newly merged company transformed FedEx into a "global transportation and logistics powerhouse. Customers increasingly demand a complete, seamless solution to supply chain management needs on a global basis, and the [Federal Express] companies will be able to offer it."[26]

In an effort to keep ground delivery operating costs below those of UPS, FedEx was planning to utilize contracted drivers and trucks, which were significantly cheaper than their rival's Teamster-organized delivery workforce. FedEx also planned to invest in RPS's existing ground network to expand its reach and capacity,[27] and to increase RPS's customer service levels through enhancing technology and training.[28]

UPS and FedEx also both looked to the international delivery business as a key source of growth. In 1999, FedEx's international services represented 25% of total revenues and had been growing at an annual rate of almost 10%. For UPS, international operations for the nine months ended September 30, 1999, accounted for $2.56 billion (or 13%) of UPS's revenues and $147 million (or 5%) of operating profits.

However, there were also important differences between the two companies that could be relevant in using FedEx multiples for valuing UPS. UPS's recent financial performance was superior to FedEx's. Over the three years from 1997 to 1999, UPS reported average net profit margins of 6.5% and Return on Equity (ROE) of 25.2%, versus 2.8% and 10.6% respectively for FedEx. Financial statements for UPS and FedEx are shown in **Exhibits 7 and 8**.

The differences in FedEx and UPS's financial and non-financial performance reflected several underlying factors. UPS relied to a greater degree than FedEx on the ground delivery business, which had a different cost structure than the air-express delivery business **(see Exhibits 9 and 10)**. Further, UPS's ground delivery business took advantage of much higher daily package volumes and customer density than FedEx's operations, which meant that UPS drivers would on average pick up and deliver significantly more packages per hour than FedEx drivers could. Finally, some observers believed that UPS's decision to operate their ground and express businesses as one integrated company sharing the same

---

[26]"RPS Greets World with New Parent Federal Express," *Pittsburgh Post-Gazette*, January 29, 1998.

[27]"FedEx Hits the Ground Running," *Modern Materials Handling*, July 2001.

[28]"They've Got Mail," *Fortune*, February 7, 2000.

trucks and sorting centers gave it an operating advantage over FedEx, which maintained separate operating units for each of express and ground delivery.[29]

Superior customer service was one of the distinguishing hallmarks of FedEx, and for this reason FedEx was generally seen as competing most effectively at the higher-end, high-service segment of the package-delivery market. FedEx's commitment to high-customer service was reflected in its best-in-industry on-time reliability record, and the flexibility it offered customers in pickup and delivery times. For example, it had even been known to keep trucks idling outside a customer's business to help deliver an unforeseen order on time.

Finally, there were differences in financial management policies at the two companies. UPS maintained a AAA credit rating, whereas FedEx's rating was BBB.[30] FedEx used operating leases to finance much of its aircraft fleet, whereas UPS financed its fleet with operating cash flow, public debt, or long-term capital leases. **Exhibits 11 and 12** present footnote information on lease obligations for the two companies.

Best of breed industry leaders

UPS's management believed that the company's stock price should be valued at a premium to reflect its superior performance over other firms in the industry. It noted that there was support for this approach in the market, where other companies with comparable dominant positions in their industry commanded significant best-of-breed stock price premiums over their competitors. For example, Coca-Cola's price-to-earnings and market-to-book multiples were 39 and 15 respectively, versus 25 and 8 for PepsiCo. Wal-Mart commanded a price-to-earnings multiple of 46 and a market-to-book multiple of 11.6, versus 27 and 6 for Target. **Exhibit 13** presents a comparison of price premiums and financial performance for selected companies considered "best of breed" industry leaders.

UPS's IPO

Industry trends and opportunities

UPS management had decided by the late 1990s to focus on three emerging trends that they believed would define the package delivery industry of the future, and which would present the company with opportunities for continued growth. These were the emerging trends of globalization, e-commerce, and supply-chain management.

Globalization

By the late 1990s, international trade represented over one-quarter of total U.S. GDP—up from only 11% in 1970. While UPS had not expanded globally as quickly or forcefully as other companies, by 1998 it was generating over $3 billion in global revenues, with 37,000 non-U.S. UPS employees delivering almost 1 million packages a day to, from and within over 200 countries. John Alden, vice-chairman of UPS, noted: "In the package delivery industry, globalization means that we must knit together worldwide distribution networks that match our customers' geographic operations. If we don't, our competitors will."[31] As a result, one of UPS's major strategic growth initiatives was building capacity in non-U.S. markets—first Europe and more recently Asia and Latin America.[32]

---

[29]Bear Stearns UPS Equity Research Report, November 24, 1999.

[30]On August 31, 1999, the yield 20 year US Treasury bonds was 6.5%, the yield for AAA rated debt was 6.9%, and the yield for BBB rated debt was 8.0%. Source: Standard & Poor's Inc.

[31]"What in the World Drives UPS?," *International Business*, March/April 1998.

[32]As of October 1999, UPS, unlike FedEx, had not received rights to fly to China.

E-commerce

UPS projected that by 2003 online B2C sales in the United States would surpass the $100 billion spent annually on catalog sales.[33] Already the preferred shipper for online commerce, UPS was moving to strengthen its position in this new market through a number of initiatives. For instance, it was aggressively pursuing partnerships with online retailers and other e-commerce players like e-Bay, and by 1999 UPS functionality was being offered on over 10,000 business websites.[34] The company was also working on UPS Returns on the Web, a service that, when unveiled, would allow customers to print a return label from their home PC to ease the process of customer returns of online purchases to the retailer of origin.[35]

Supply chain management

UPS managers likened the supply-chain of the future to a moving conveyor belt: "a supply chain in constant motion means minimal inventory, lower costs, and faster time-to-market. The inventory, if you could call it that, is always in transit."[36] Increasingly, UPS was forging partnerships with supplier companies, from auto manufacturer suppliers to electronic component producers, which involved UPS handling the continuous flow of shipments to down-market corporate customers. Additionally, through its UPS Logistics Group, UPS began offering suppliers a portfolio of financial services and logistics technology software applications designed to help them better manage their inventory and shipping logistics.

UPS's management anticipated that the company would be able to fund much of these growth opportunities through operating cash flows. The primary benefit from the IPO would, therefore, not be the funds raised from the stock offering; indeed management committed that it would use the IPO proceeds to repurchase its own stock. Instead, the IPO would provide UPS with publicly traded stock—an attractive tax-efficient medium of exchange—to fund any subsequent acquisitions. In explaining the change in strategy, management noted:

> As we enter the twenty-first century, we face a rapidly changing competitive and operating environment. The package-delivery industry is globalizing and consolidating at an unprecedented rate. We face new competitive challenges from postal monopolies, which have considerable resources and infrastructures. We believe that we should have a publicly traded equity security that we could use when appropriate for strategic alliances and acquisitions in order to maintain our pre-eminent position.[37]

Impact on current owners and UPS culture

In 1999, approximately two-thirds of UPS's equity was held by current and retired employees; the remaining third was owned by founding families and foundations. Under the company's Management Incentive Plan, in place since the mid-1940s, 15% of profits were set aside each year for stock awards to supervisors and managers. Employees that received stock awards were encouraged to hold the stock as long as they remained with the company, and most chose to do so. For those employees that wished to sell, typically after retirement, the company would buy back the stock at a price set each quarter by the board of directors. In mid-1999, the price set by the board was $25.50.

[33]Jim Kelly Speech to the Economic Club of Detroit, January 19, 1999.
[34]Ibid.
[35]UPS 2000 Annual Report.
[36]Jim Kelly Speech to the Houston Forum, October 6, 1999.
[37]UPS Form S-4 Registration Statement, July 21, 1999, p. 63.

UPS's employee ownership had served the company well. It had enabled the company to grow a capital-intensive business without needing to incur the costs of outside financing. Its employees were extremely loyal; many had joined the firm as part-time workers while at college, and then stayed after graduation. It was not uncommon for employees to spend their entire working career at UPS. Virtually all of the seven executives that served on the firm's board began their careers "tossing boxes in the warehouse, driving trucks through the streets or handling paperwork in the back office."[38] As a result, experts on corporate culture and resource management observed that the company succeeded by "promoting a 'we all win together, we all fail together' kind of mentality. . . . The common experience of getting packages delivered creates tremendous loyalty among UPS employees. . . . Senior management understands what it means to be a regular person, because they once were that."[39]

To ensure that the IPO preserved the company's culture and control by employees, the offering created two classes of shares. Class A shares, for existing owners, would carry 10 votes each, whereas Class B shares, to be issued to the public, would carry only one vote each. The funds raised in the IPO would then be used to repurchase shares from Class A shareholders, enabling them to divest up to 10% of their holdings. For the following 18 months, Class A shares would gradually become available to be sold in the market, at which point they would become Class B shares. As a result of this arrangement, it was anticipated that after the IPO, current UPS shareowners would own 90% of the firm's equity and control about 99% of the vote. Considerable time at UPS was devoted to educating management owners about the reasons for becoming a public company, the details of the share changes, and company policy on employee share ownership and trading.

Offer pricing

As the IPO date approached, Morgan Stanley Dean Witter & Co.-UPS deal team considered what price to recommend for the offer. What were UPS's future business and financial prospects, given its positioning in the package delivery industry? Were FedEx multiples reasonable benchmarks for valuing UPS stock? Or, given its consistently strong financial returns, should UPS be benchmarked relative to best-in-breed industry leaders?

Questions

1   What are the key success factors and risks for UPS given its business strategy?

2   How is UPS performing? What factors are driving this performance? Is the current performance likely to be sustained? Why or why not?

3   How is FedEx performing? How, if at all, do its performance and plans affect your assessment of the sustainability of UPS's current performance?

4   Given your assessment of the company's strategy and the sustainability of its performance, forecast the key factors for UPS's stock value.

5   What is your estimate of UPS's value and its multiples?

6   How do your estimates of UPS's PE and PB multiples compare with those for FedEx? How do they compare with those for the "best-of-breed" companies' multiples?

---

[38]Jerry Knight, "Managers Are No Strangers To the Brown-Collar World," *The Washington Post*, August 13, 1997.
[39]Ibid.

EXHIBIT 1   Size of U.S. overnight, deferred, and ground markets, 1990–1999

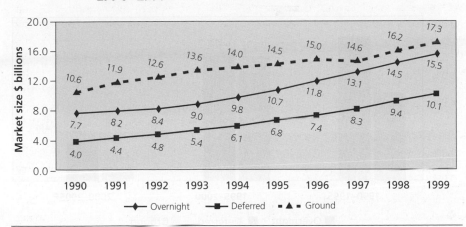

Source: SJ Consulting Group.

EXHIBIT 2   Package volume in U.S. overnight, deferred, and ground markets, 1990–1999

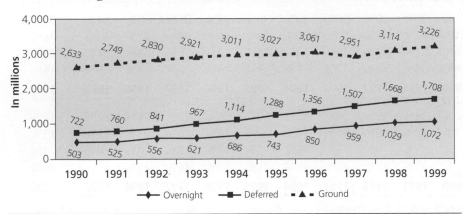

Source: SJ Consulting Group.

11 United Parcel Service's IPO

EXHIBIT 3   Air express and ground market growth rates, 1990–2005E

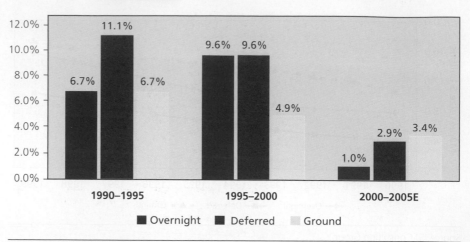

Source: SJ Consulting Group.

EXHIBIT 4   Overnight, deferred, and ground market shares, 1990–1999

Overnight	By Revenue										By Volume
	1990	1991	1992	1993	1994	1995	1996	1997	1998	1999	1999
UPS Next Day Air	31%	30%	30%	30%	30%	30%	32%	31%	32%	34%	25%
FDX Overnight	51%	51%	50%	50%	50%	49%	49%	48%	47%	46%	46%
ABF Next Day	10%	11%	12%	13%	13%	14%	13%	15%	15%	14%	23%
USPS Express Mail	8%	8%	8%	7%	7%	7%	6%	6%	6%	6%	6%
Deferred	**1990**	**1991**	**1992**	**1993**	**1994**	**1995**	**1996**	**1997**	**1998**	**1999**	**1999**
UPS Deferred	40%	38%	35%	34%	32%	30%	30%	28%	26%	27%	13%
FDX Deferred (E2, ES)	16%	17%	16%	18%	18%	19%	18%	20%	23%	22%	13%
ABF Second Day	5%	5%	6%	6%	6%	6%	7%	6%	6%	6%	4%
USPS Priority Mail	39%	40%	43%	42%	44%	45%	45%	46%	45%	45%	70%
Ground	**1990**	**1991**	**1992**	**1993**	**1994**	**1995**	**1996**	**1997**	**1998**	**1999**	**1999**
UPS Ground	87%	87%	85%	85%	83%	82%	82%	81%	80%	80%	79%
FedEx Ground *without* RPS	*0%*	*0%*	*0%*	*0%*	*0%*	*0%*	*0%*	*0%*	*0%*	*0%*	*0%*
With RPS[a]	5%	5%	6%	7%	8%	8%	8%	9%	10%	10%	11%
USPS Parcel Post	8%	8%	9%	8%	9%	10%	10%	10%	10%	10%	10%

[a]*RPS acquired by FedEx in 10/97.*

Note: Ground market shares are based on the revenues and volume of the largest providers in the industry. They do not include data for private delivery fleets of individual companies, courier services, regional delivery services, LTL trucking firms and third-party logistics companies
Source: SJ Consulting Group.

EXHIBIT 5   UPS vs. FedEx process flow diagrams

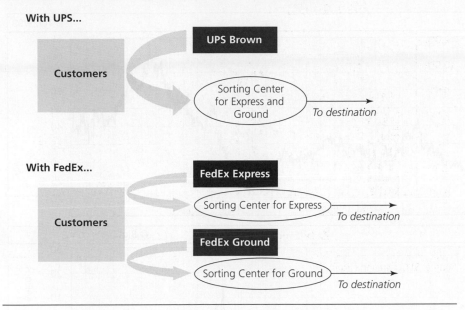

With UPS...

Customers → UPS Brown

Customers → Sorting Center for Express and Ground → *To destination*

With FedEx...

Customers → FedEx Express → Sorting Center for Express → *To destination*

Customers → FedEx Ground → Sorting Center for Ground → *To destination*

Source: Derived by case writers.

EXHIBIT 6   FedEx stock price performance and valuation multiples

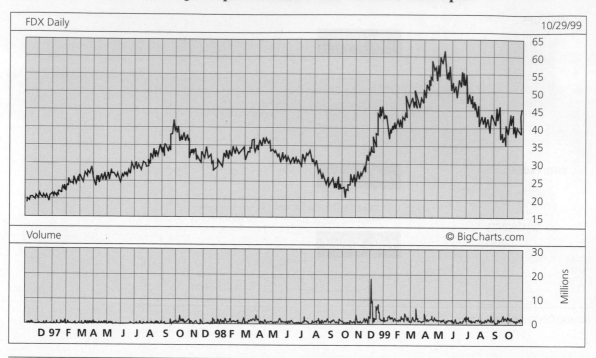

Source: BigCharts.com.

MARKET DATA AND MULTIPLES—(NOVEMBER 1, 1999)

Shares outstanding (weighted average, diluted)	300.6 million
Share price	$41.50
Price/Earnings[a]	19.8
Price/Total revenue[b]	0.74
Market/Book value[c]	2.68
Equity Beta[d]	1.16

[a]Total market capitalization/Net income.
[b]Total market capitalization/Total revenue.
[c]Total market capitalization/Shareholders' equity.
[d]Salomon Smith Barney Equity Research report on FedEx, June 22, 1999.

Source: FedEx company filings.

EXHIBIT 7 UPS financial statements, 1994–1999

STATEMENT OF INCOME (YEAR-ENDED DECEMBER 31)

(Financial data in millions, except per share amounts)	1994	1995	1996	1997	1998	Nine Months Ended September 30, 1998	Nine Months Ended September 30, 1999
REVENUE							
U.S. domestic package	16,943	17,773	18,881	18,868	20,650	15,129	16,239
International package	2,346	2,886	2,989	2,934	3,237	2,342	2,562
Non-package	287	386	498	656	901	653	805
TOTAL REVENUES	19,576	21,045	22,368	22,458	24,788	18,124	19,606
Operating expenses:							
Compensation and benefits	11,727	12,401	13,326	13,289	14,346	10,587	11,226
Other	6,293	6,478	7,013	7,461	7,352	5,315	5,522
Restructuring charge	—	372	—	—	—	—	—
TOTAL OPERATING EXPENSES	18,020	19,251	20,339	20,760	21,698	15,902	16,748
OPERATING PROFIT (LOSS)							
U.S. domestic package	1,821	1,937	2,181	1,654	2,899	2,098	2,522
International package	(390)	(250)	(281)	(67)	56	19	147
Non-package	125	107	129	111	135	105	85
Corporate	—	—	—	—	—	—	104
TOTAL OPERATING PROFIT	1,556	1,794	2,029	1,698	3,090	2,222	2,858
Other income (expense):							
Investment income	13	26	39	70	84	56	115
Interest expense	(29)	(77)	(95)	(187)	(227)	(169)	(170)
Tax assessment	—	—	—	—	—	—	(1,786)
Miscellaneous, net	35	(35)	(63)	(28)	(45)	(3)	(30)
INCOME BEFORE INCOME TAXES	1,575	1,708	1,910	1,553	2,902	2,106	987
Income taxes	632	665	754	644	1,161	847	765
NET INCOME	943	1,043	1,146	909	1,741	1,259	222
Per share amounts:							
Basic earnings per share	0.84	0.93	1.03	0.82	1.59	1.16	0.20
Diluted earnings per share	0.82	0.92	1.01	0.81	1.57	1.14	0.20
Dividends declared per share	0.28	0.32	0.34	0.35	0.43	0.20	0.28
Net income before impact of tax assessment	943	1,043	1,146	909	1,741	1,259	1,664
As a percentage of revenue	4.8%	5.0%	5.1%	4.0%	7.0%	7.0%	8.5%

Source: UPS Company Filings.

11 United Parcel Service's IPO

BALANCE SHEET
United Parcel Service in millions, except where noted.

As of December 31	1997	1998
ASSETS		
CURRENT ASSETS		
Cash and cash equivalents	460	1,240
Marketable securities and short-term investments	—	389
Accounts receivable	2,405	2,713
Prepaid employee benefit costs	669	703
Materials, supplies and other prepaid expenses	417	380
Common stock held for stock plans	526	—
Total Current Assets	4,477	5,425
PROPERTY, PLANT, AND EQUIPMENT		
Vehicles	3,519	3,482
Aircraft (including aircraft under capitalized leases)	6,771	7,739
Land	654	651
Buildings	1,433	1,478
Leasehold improvements	1,734	1,803
Plant equipment	4,063	4,144
Construction-in-progress	328	257
	18,502	19,554
Less accumulated depreciation and amortization	7,495	8,170
Net Property, Plant, and Equipment	11,007	11,384
Other Assets	428	258
TOTAL ASSETS	15,912	17,067
LIABILITIES AND SHAREOWNERS' EQUITY		
CURRENT LIABILITIES		
Accounts payable	1,207	1,322
Accrued wages and withholdings	1,194	1,092
Dividends payable	191	247
Deferred income taxes	140	—
Current maturities of long-term debt	41	410
Other current liabilities	625	646
Total Current Liabilities	3,398	3,717
Long-Term Debt (including capitalized lease obligations)	2,583	2,191
Accumulated Postretirement Benefit Obligation	911	969
Deferred Taxes, Credits and Other Liabilities	2,933	3,017
SHAREOWNERS' EQUITY		
Preferred stock, no par value, authorized 200,000,000 shares, none issued	—	—
Class A common stock, par value $.01 per share, authorized 4,600,000,000 shares, issued 1,101,295,534 and 1,118,000,000 in 1999 and 1998 Class B common stock, par value $.01 per share, authorized 5,600,000,000 shares, issued 109,400,000 and -0- in 1999 and 1998	56	11
Additional paid-in capital	—	325
Retained earnings	6,112	7,325
Accumulated other comprehensive loss	(81)	(63)
Unrealized loss on marketable securities	—	—
	6,087	7,598
Treasury stock, at cost (-0- and 23,211,904 shares in 1997 and 1998)	—	(425)
	6,087	7,173
TOTAL LIABILITIES AND SHAREOWNERS' EQUITY	15,912	17,067

Source: UPS Company Filings.

Financial Data in Millions:		Year Ended December 31				6 Months Ended
Balance Sheet Data (at end of period):	1994	1995	1996	1997	1998	June 30, 1999
Working Capital	$120	$261	$1,097	$1,079	$1,708	$434
Long-term debt	$1,127	$1,729	$2,573	$2,583	$2,191	$2,138
Total assets	$11,182	$12,645	$14,954	$15,912	$17,067	$18,302
Shareowner's equity	$4,647	$5,151	$5,901	$6,087	$7,173	$6,122

Source: UPS Company Filings.

EXCERPTS FROM MANAGEMENT'S DISCUSSION AND ANALYSIS OF FINANCIAL CONDITION AND RESULTS OF OPERATIONS, JUNE 30, 1999

1999 Compared to 1998

Net income for 1999 decreased by $858 million from 1998, resulting in a decrease in diluted earnings per share from $1.57 in 1998 to $0.77 in 1999. These results reflect the charge we recorded during the second quarter of 1999, resulting from an unfavorable ruling of the U.S. Tax Court. Excluding the impact of this one-time charge of $1.442 billion, our net income for 1999 would have been $2.325 billion, with an associated diluted earnings per share of $2.04.

On August 9, 1999, the U.S. Tax Court issued an opinion unfavorable to us regarding a Notice of Deficiency asserting that we are liable for additional tax for the 1983 and 1984 tax years. The Court held that we are liable for tax on income of Overseas Partners Ltd., a Bermuda company, which had reinsured excess value package insurance purchased by our customers beginning in 1984.

The Court held that for the 1984 tax year we are liable for taxes of $31 million on income reported by OPL, penalties and penalty interest of $93 million and interest for a total after-tax exposure estimated at approximately $246 million. In February 2000, the Court entered a decision in accord with its opinion.

In addition, during the first quarter of 1999, the IRS issued two Notices of Deficiency asserting that we are liable for additional tax for the 1985 through 1987 tax years, and the 1988 through 1990 tax years. The primary assertions by the IRS relate to the reinsurance of excess value package insurance, the issue raised for the 1984 tax year. The IRS has based its assertions on the same theories included in the 1983–1984 Notice of Deficiency.

We anticipate that the IRS will take similar positions for tax years subsequent to 1990. Based on the Tax Court opinion, we currently estimate that our total

after-tax exposure for the tax years 1984 through 1999 could be as high as $2.353 billion. We believe that a number of aspects of the Tax Court decision are incorrect, and we intend to appeal the decision to the U.S. Court of Appeals for the Eleventh Circuit.

In the second quarter 1999 financial statements, we recorded a tax assessment charge of $1.786 billion, which included an amount for related state tax liabilities. The charge included taxes of $915 million and interest of $871 million. This assessment resulted in a tax benefit of $344 million related to the interest component of the assessment. As a result, our net charge to net income for the tax assessment was $1.442 billion, increasing our total after-tax reserve at that time with respect to these matters to $1.672 billion. The tax benefit of deductible interest is included in income taxes; however, since none of the income on which this tax assessment is based is our income, we have not classified the tax charge as income taxes.

We determined the size of our reserve with respect to these matters in accordance with generally accepted accounting principles based on our estimate of our most likely liability. In making this determination, we concluded that it was more likely that we would be required to pay taxes on income reported by OPL and interest, but that it was not probable that we would be required to pay any penalties and penalty interest. If penalties and penalty interest ultimately are determined to be payable, we would have to record an additional charge of up to $681 million.

On August 31, 1999, we deposited $1.349 billion with the IRS related to these matters for the 1984 through 1994 tax years. We included the profit of the excess value package insurance program, using the IRS's methodology for calculating these amounts, for both 1998 and 1999 in filings we made with the IRS in the fourth quarter of 1999. In February 2000, we deposited $339 million with the IRS related to these matters for the 1995 through 1997 tax years.

These deposits and filings were made in order to stop the accrual of interest, where applicable, on that amount of the IRS's claim, without conceding the IRS's position or giving up our right to appeal the Tax Court's decision.

1998 Compared to 1997

Net income increased by $832 million in 1998 over 1997. Approximately $496 million of this improvement was due primarily to higher revenue per piece on U.S. domestic products, improved product mix, improved international operating results and the containment of operating expense growth. The remaining increase of $336 million resulted from the change in net income for August 1998 as compared to August 1997, the period in which the Teamsters strike occurred.

Source: UPS Company Filings.

EXHIBIT 8 FedEx financial statements, 1996–1999

CONSOLIDATED STATEMENTS OF INCOME
FDX CORPORATION

Years ended May 31

(in thousands, except Earnings Per Share)	1996	1997*	1998	1999
REVENUES	$10,273,619	$14,237,892	$15,872,810	$16,773,470
OPERATING EXPENSES:				
Salaries and employee benefits	4,619,990	6,150,247	6,647,140	7,087,728
Purchased transportation	370,650	1,252,901	1,481,590	1,537,785
Rentals and landing fees	959,055	1,138,690	1,304,296	1,396,694
Depreciation and amortization	719,609	928,833	963,732	1,035,118
Maintenance and repairs	617,657	773,765	874,400	958,873
Fuel	578,614	734,722	726,776	604,929
Merger expenses	—	—	88,000	—
Restructuring and impairment charges (credits)	—	225,036	(16,000)	—
Other	1,784,220	2,526,696	2,792,216	2,989,257
	9,649,795	13,730,890	14,862,150	15,610,384
OPERATING INCOME	623,824	507,002	1,010,660	1,163,086
OTHER INCOME (EXPENSE):				
Interest, net	(95,599)	(104,195)	(124,413)	(98,191)
Other, net	11,734	23,058	13,271	(3,831)
	(83,865)	(81,137)	(111,142)	(102,022)
INCOME FROM CONTINUING OPERATIONS BEFORE INCOME TAXES	539,959	425,865	899,518	1,061,064
PROVISION FOR INCOME TAXES	232,182	229,761	401,363	429,731
INCOME FROM CONTINUING OPERATIONS	307,777	196,104	498,155	631,333
INCOME FROM DISCONTINUED OPERATIONS, NET OF INCOME TAXES	—	—	4,875	—
NET INCOME	$307,777	$196,104	$503,030	$631,333
EARNINGS PER COMMON SHARE				
Continuing operations	$2.69	$.67	$1.70	$2.13
Discontinued operations		—	.02	—
	$2.69	$.67	$1.72	$2.13
EARNINGS PER COMMON SHARE, ASSUMING DILUTION				
Continuing operations	$2.69	$.67	$1.67	$2.10
Discontinued operations	—	—	.02	—
	$2.69	$.67	$1.69	$2.10

* Financial results for 1997 and subsequent years are consolidated to include the acquisition of Caliber System Inc.
Source: FedEx Company Filings.

11 United Parcel Service's IPO

FEDEX CORPORATION
CONSOLIDATED BALANCE SHEETS
FDX CORPORATION

May 31 (in millions)	1995	1996	1997*	1998	1999
ASSETS					
CURRENT ASSETS					
Cash and cash equivalents	357.6	93.5	160.9	229.6	325.3
Receivables, less allowances	1,130.3	1,271.6	1,878.0	1,943.4	2,153.2
Spare parts, supplies and fuel	193.3	222.1	339.4	364.7	291.9
Deferred income taxes	115.8	92.6	197.0	232.8	290.7
Prepaid expenses and other	72.2	48.5	68.6	109.6	79.9
Total current assets	1,869.1	1,728.3	2,643.7	2,880.1	3,141.0
PROPERTY AND EQUIPMENT, AT COST					
Flight equipment	3,006.7	3,372.6	3,741.4	4,056.5	4,556.7
Package handling and ground support equipment and vehicles	1,841.1	2,148.5	3,131.1	3,425.3	3,858.8
Computer and electronic equipment	1,224.0	1,439.9	1,957.9	2,162.6	2,363.6
Other	1,625.9	1,717.5	2,557.6	2,819.4	2,940.7
	7,697.7	8,678.5	11,387.9	12,463.9	13,719.9
Less accumulated depreciation and amortization	3,982.5	4,561.9	5,917.5	6,528.8	7,160.7
Net property and equipment	3,715.2	4,116.6	5,470.4	5,935.1	6,559.2
OTHER ASSETS					
Goodwill	397.3	380.7	370.3	356.3	344.0
Equipment deposits and other assets	451.8	473.4	559.8	514.6	604.0
Total other assets	849.0	854.1	930.2	870.9	948.0
	6,433.4	6,699.0	9,044.3	9,686.1	10,648.2
LIABILITIES AND STOCKHOLDERS' INVESTMENT					
CURRENT LIABILITIES					
Current portion of long-term debt	255.4	8.0	356.7	257.5	14.9
Accounts payable	618.6	705.5	999.8	1,145.4	1,134.0
Accrued expenses	904.5	904.9	1,223.0	1,400.9	895.4
Other Liabilities	—	—	—	—	740.5
Total current liabilities	1,778.5	1,618.4	2,579.5	2,803.8	2,784.8
LONG-TERM DEBT, LESS CURRENT PORTION	1,324.7	1,325.3	1,598.0	1,385.2	1,359.7
DEFERRED INCOME TAXES	56.0	64.0	181.8	274.1	293.5
OTHER LIABILITIES	1,028.6	1,115.1	1,183.9	1,261.7	1,546.6
COMMITMENTS AND CONTINGENCIES (NOTES 5, 13 and 14)					
COMMON STOCKHOLDERS' INVESTMENT					
Common Stock, $.10 par value	5.6	5.7	14.8	14.7	29.8
Additional paid-in capital	775.3	815.1	938.0	992.8	1,061.3
Retained earnings	1,466.4	1,766.6	2,621.5	2,999.4	3,615.8
Accumulated other comprehensive income	0.0	0.0	0.0	(27.3)	(24.7)
	2,247.3	2,587.4	3,574.3	3,979.6	4,682.2
Less treasury stock, at cost, and deferred compensation	1.7	11.3	73.1	18.4	18.5
Total common stockholders' investment	2,245.6	2,576.1	3,501.2	3,961.2	4,663.7
	6,433.4	6,699.0	9,044.3	9,686.1	10,648.2

* Note: Financial results for 1997 and subsequent years are consolidated to include the acquisition of Caliber System Inc.
Source: FedEx Company Filings.
The accompanying Notes to Consolidated Financial Statements are an integral part of these balance sheets.

11 United Parcel Service's IPO

EXHIBIT 9 Selected UPS operating statistics (financial data in millions)

	Year Ended December 31			
	1995	1996	1997	1998
Operating Data:				
Delivery volume (in millions of packages)	3,094	3,153	3,038	3,137
Average daily package volume (in thousands)				
U.S. domestic:				
Next Day Air	668	760	822	938
Deferred	716	763	771	783
Ground	9,949	10,015	9,521	9,645
Total U.S. domestic	11,333	11,538	11,114	11,366
International				
Domestic	722	683	678	730
Export	175	194	217	256
Total International	897	877	895	986
Total average daily package volume	12,230	12,415	12,009	12,352
Average revenue per piece:				
U.S. domestic:				
Next Day Air	$19.34	$19.34	$19.49	$19.69
Deferred	11.27	11.39	11.86	12.39
Ground	4.95	5.09	5.19	5.51
Total U.S. domestic	6.20	6.44	6.71	7.15
International				
Domestic	6.22	6.10	5.36	5.14
Export	37.18	37.32	35.01	33.46
Total International	12.26	13.01	12.55	12.49
Total average revenue per piece	$6.64	$6.91	$7.15	$7.58
Revenue:				
U.S. domestic:				
Next Day Air	$3,269	$3,734	$4,054	$4,690
Deferred	2,041	2,207	2,314	2,464
Ground	12,463	12,940	12,500	13,496
Total U.S. domestic	17,773	18,881	18,868	20,650
International				
Domestic	1,136	1,058	919	953
Export	1,646	1,839	1,922	2,176
Cargo	176	177	226	270
Total International	2,958	3,074	3,067	3,399
Non-package	314	413	523	739
Total revenue	$21,045	$22,368	$22,458	$24,788
Operating weekdays	253	254	253	254
Capital expenditures (in millions)	$2,096	$2,333	$1,984	$1,645

Source: UPS Prospectus Filing, September 1999.

11 United Parcel Service's IPO

EXHIBIT 10   Summary of FedEx and UPS operating statistics

	UPS	FedEx
Calendar 1998 Average Daily Package Volume (thousands of packages)		
• U.S. Express	938	1,957
• U.S. Deferred	783	894
• U.S. Ground	9,645	1,385
• Total U.S.	11,366	4,236
• Total International	986	282
• Total packages	12,352	4,518
Calendar 1998 Average U.S. Revenue per package[a]		
• Express	$19.69	$14.34
• Deferred	$12.39	$9.93
• Ground	$5.51	$5.36
Number of Employees (full-time and contract positions)	340,000	156,386
Total on-balance sheet assets	$23.0 billion	$10.6 billion
Number of jet and small aircraft owned and leased	536	634
Number of vehicles	149,000	46,000

[a]Revenues per package (yield) is a function of both average package weight and distance.

Source: Derived by case writers using UPS and FedEx Company Filings.

EXHIBIT 11   FedEx note on leases

The company utilizes certain aircraft, land, facilities and equipment under capital and operating leases that expire at various dates through 2027. In addition, supplemental aircraft are leased under agreements that generally provide for cancellation upon 30 days' notice.

The components of property and equipment recorded under capital leases were as follows:

May 31, 1999 ($ thousands)

Package handling and ground support equipment and vehicles	$245,041
Facilities	134,442
Computer and electronic equipment and other	6,496
	385,979
Less accumulated depreciation	268,696
	$117,283

Rent expense under operating leases for the years ended May 31 was as follows:

($ thousands)

Minimum rentals	$1,246,259
Contingent rentals	59,839
	$1,306,098

Contingent rentals are based on hours flown under supplemental aircraft leases.

A summary of future minimum lease payments under capital leases and non-cancelable operating leases (principally aircraft and facilities) with an initial or remaining term in excess of one year at May 31, 1999 is as follows:

($ thousands)	Capital Leases	Operating Leases
2000	$15,023	$1,011,957
2001	15,023	933,339
2002	15,023	876,055
2003	15,023	809,770
2004	14,894	764,550
Thereafter	302,502	8,717,952
	$377,488	$13,113,623

At May 31, 1999, the present value of future minimum lease payments for capital lease obligations including certain tax exempt bonds was $200,077,000.

FedEx makes payments under certain leveraged operating leases that are sufficient to pay principal and interest on certain pass through certificates. The pass through certificates are not direct obligations of, or guaranteed by, the Company or FedEx.

Source: 1999 FedEx Annual Report, Notes to Consolidated Statements.

11 United Parcel Service's IPO

EXHIBIT 12 UPS note on leases

UPS has capitalized lease obligations for certain aircraft, which are included in Property, Plant, and Equipment at December 31 as follows:

1998 ($ millions)

Aircraft	$614
Accumulated amortization	(38)
	$576

UPS leases certain aircraft, facilities, equipment, and vehicles under operating leases, which expire at various dates through 2034. Total aggregate minimum lease payments under capitalized leases and under operating leases are as follows (in millions):

($ millions)	Capitalized Leases	Operating Leases
1999	$67	$211
2000	67	146
2001	67	115
2002	67	94
2003	67	77
After 2003	526	477
Total minimum lease payments	$861	$1,120
Less inputed interest	(263)	
Present value of minimum capitalized lease payments	598	
Less current portion	(39)	
Long-term capitalized lease obligations	$559	

Source: UPS Prospectus Filing, September 1999, Notes to Financial Statements.

EXHIBIT 13   Selected "best of breed" ratios vs. industrial comparables

	Stock Price[a]	Market Cap (billions)	Net Income[b] (millions)	ROE	Price to Earnings	Market to Book
Home Depot	$68.50	100.8	1,979	25%	50.9	12.7
Lowes	$49.31	18.9	556	17%	34.1	5.8
Coca-Cola	$49.94	124.7	3,174	40%	39.3	15.6
PepsiCo	$32.19	48.9	1,921	31%	25.5	7.9
Wal-Mart	$50.81	227.4	4,927	25%	46.1	11.6
Target	$64.31	28.4	1,052	22%	27.0	6.0

[a]As of close of trading October 15, 1999.
[b]Latest 12 months.

Source: Derived by case writers using SEC filings and market data from bigcharts.com. accessed on 06/23/02.

12 Valuation ratios in the airline industry

In mid-2001, the U.S. airline industry appeared to be headed into its first cyclical downturn in ten years. In May, air travel fell in the United States for the first time in a decade and ticket prices softened.[1] In addition, profitability in the industry (as measured by return on equity, "ROE") declined from 25% in 1997 to 12% in 2000. Analysts forecasted that ROE would decline further to 2.3% in 2001.[2]

The downturn also affected industry valuation ratios. For example, price-to-book ratios declined from 2.8 in 1997 to 2.0 in 2000,[3] while price-to-earnings ratios, which were 8.3 in 1997, were not meaningful in mid-2001 since aggregate earnings for the industry were negative.[4] However, these ratios varied widely across firms. For example, in mid-2001, price-to-book ratios ranged from a low of 0.4 to a high of 3.7, and price-to-earnings ratios for firms with positive earnings ranged from 8 to 22.

Industry overview

The deregulation of the U.S. domestic market in 1978 was a turning point for domestic air travel. The 20 years following this event saw real fares decline by 50%, and air traffic triple.[5] The period was also marked by turbulence for many firms that had pioneered air travel in the United States, with Pan Am, Eastern, and TWA being forced into bankruptcy. By mid-2001, the industry was dominated by a relatively small number of long-haul national-international carriers, while dozens of regional and commuter carriers competed for "point-to-point" (or nonstop) short-haul routes.[6]

National carriers

Six national carriers, United Airlines, American Airlines, Delta Air Lines, Northwest Airlines, US Airways, and Continental Airlines provided both long-haul domestic and

Professors Paul Healy and Krishna Palepu and Research Associate Jonathan Barnett prepared this case. This case was developed from published sources. HBS cases are developed solely as the basis for class discussion. Cases are not intended to serve as endorsements, sources of primary data, or illustrations of effective or ineffective management.

[1]Airline traffic growth was predicted to increase 3.5% in 2001, a marked decline from the 4.7% and 5.2% increases in 1999 and 2000. Yield (or average revenue per passenger) was forecast to grow 4% in 2001. Stephen Klein and Richard Stice, *Airlines*, Standard & Poor's (S&P) Industry Surveys, March 29, 2001.

[2]Stephen Sanborn, *The Air Transport Industry*, Value Line Investment Survey, June 15, 2001.

[3]S&P Research Insight.

[4]The airline industry's average beta was 0.89. Given the long-term government bond rate in June 2001 of 5.7% and the long-term risk premium of 7.6%, the average cost of equity for the industry was therefore 12.5%. (S&P Research Insight.)

[5]"Air Travel, Air Trouble," *The Economist*, July 7, 2001.

[6]In 2000, the 10 largest U.S. airlines accounted for 92.3% of total U.S. traffic. (Stephen Klein and Richard Stice, *Airlines*, S&P Industry Surveys, March 29, 2001.)

12 Valuation ratios in the airline industry

international service for U.S.-based passengers. Using "hub-and-spoke" networks, long-haul carriers or their regional "spoke" affiliates shuttled passengers from lightly traveled markets to central hubs where they could connect to longer flight-legs. In addition to enabling long-haul carriers to take advantage of economies of scale on their long flights, the hub-and-spoke system had increased concentration in many of the smaller "hub" cities, where the hub carrier owned a dominant share of the terminal gates.

Long-haul carriers had little control over the pricing of key inputs, including aircraft and jet fuel. Two suppliers, Boeing and Airbus, controlled the development and production of large-scale jet aircraft, and the price of jet fuel was heavily influenced by the impact of OPEC's oil production policies on global supply. Labor costs, the other major airline operating cost, were typically determined through intense and protracted negotiations between each carrier and the more than one dozen unions that represented distinct groups of airline personnel (e.g., pilots, attendants, mechanics, baggage handlers, etc.).

The economics of the airline business made it difficult for operators to pass on production-cost increases to passengers. Given their high fixed costs and low marginal costs, airline carriers had frequently resorted to fare reductions to boost flight capacity and yield (defined as average revenue per passenger). However, competing airlines were quick to match or undercut rivals' fare reductions, resulting in periodic fare wars. Thus, the continual threat of intense price competition dampened the industry's prospects for revenue growth.

Long-haul carriers developed a number of responses to the challenges of price competition and yield management. In the 1980s, frequent flyer programs were introduced to increase customer loyalty and mitigate the effect of fare wars. In the 1990s, the industry was quick to take advantage of the internet to improve the booking and ticketing process. However, the results were mixed: while online reservation systems helped airlines to improve yield management, the broad dissemination of information on competing flight schedules and fares enabled price-sensitive consumers to search for the lowest possible fares.

In response to growth opportunities in international travel in the mid-1990s, long-haul carriers had used alliances to strengthen their international presence. Alliances took advantage of "open skies" treaties between the United States and other governments that permitted code-sharing and partial ownership between international airlines. In mid-2001, there were four global airline alliances involving U.S. carriers.[7] However, allegiance within the alliances had proven weak, with a number of carriers switching alliance memberships.

Regional carriers

U.S regional carriers, such as America West, ComAir, Frontier Airlines, Mesa Air, and SkyWest Airlines, typically provided nonstop short-haul service. Many of these airlines were affiliated with long-haul carriers. Affiliations typically permitted regional carriers to schedule flights under a "code-sharing" arrangement, so that each carrier could sell seats for flights on joint routes. To schedule these trips, regional affiliates, operating under the major carrier's designator code, were granted access to that carrier's computer reservation system.

---

[7]The four major global airline alliances included the Star Alliance (anchored by United Airlines and Lufthansa), the OneWorld alliance (anchored by American Airlines and British Airways), the SkyTeam alliance (anchored by Delta Air Lines and Air France), and Wings (anchored by KLM and Northwest Airlines). Each alliance also included a number of smaller carriers.

Regional carriers were subject to many of the same economic forces as their long-haul counterparts. They, too, had little control over fuel prices and were forced to negotiate with a small number of aircraft manufacturers.[8] However, some of the newer regional carriers did not have a unionized labor force, making it easier to design flexible work arrangements and to manage labor costs.

Recent technological advances in the design of regional jets had opened up new opportunities for regional carriers in under-served domestic markets. Although jet aircraft were first introduced to U.S. passenger service in 1958, they had proved uneconomical for small markets. However, following the 1995 introduction of new low-cost jet aircraft by Brazil's Embraer and Canada's Bombardier, regional jet operations proliferated as the short-haul markets that were previously abandoned by major airlines became viable destinations.[9] In addition to opening new markets, the seating capacity and travel range of regional jets continued to expand. As a result, regional jets were increasingly used not only to feed passengers to hub airports, but also to provide point-to-point competition against carriers employing full-sized jets. Having recognized the value of regional carriers, major airlines had recently taken steps to increase their control over such operators, primarily through acquiring equity positions.

Strategy and performance for four airline carriers

The following brief sketches of two long-haul carriers (American Airlines and Delta Air Lines), one regional carrier (SkyWest Airlines), and one hybrid carrier (Southwest Airlines) illustrate the differences in business strategy and performance experienced by firms in the airline industry. See **Exhibits 1 and 2** for a comparison of the recent financial performance of these carriers.

American Airlines

American Airlines ("American"), the principal operating subsidiary of parent AMR Corporation, traced its roots back to the Embry-Riddle Company in the early 1920s. Later renamed the Aviation Corporation (AVCO), American became one of the first U.S. airline giants through the acquisition of 82 smaller airlines.

In 2000, American was the largest U.S. airline based on revenues. It operated hubs in Dallas-Forth Worth, Chicago O'Hare, Miami, and San Juan (Puerto Rico), and provided service to 169 destinations throughout North America, Europe, the Caribbean, Latin America, and the Pacific Rim.[10] The company owned two regional airlines operating as "American Eagle," American Eagle Airlines and Executive Airlines, which provided connecting service from eight of American's high-traffic hubs to smaller markets in the United States, Canada, the Caribbean and the Bahamas. American was also a member of the global OneWorld alliance, which linked the operations of American, British Airways, Canadian Airlines, Cathay Pacific Airways, Qantas Airways, Finnair, Iberia, and Lan-Chile. In addition to its passenger services, American was one of the largest airfreight

---

[8]While long-haul and regional carriers could not directly influence the price of jet fuel, both types of carriers frequently hedged their fuel-price risk using futures as part of a comprehensive risk-management strategy.

[9]Breakeven capacity for a regional jet was approximately 50%, versus 63% for larger jet aircraft. In 2000 there were an estimated 529 regional jets in service in the United States versus 137 in 1997. (Stephen Klein and Richard Stice, *Airlines*, Standard & Poor's ("S&P") Industry Surveys, March 29, 2001.)

[10]In its 2000 10-K Report, American reported that domestic and foreign operations comprised 71% and 29% of total revenues, respectively.

carriers in the world, providing a full range of freight and mail services to shippers throughout its system.[11]

On most of its nonstop domestic routes, American faced competition from one or more of the other U.S. long-haul carriers, regional airlines, and other cargo-service firms. As many as nine airlines provided service on American's most competitive routes. Its pricing decisions were affected, in part, by competition from other airlines, some of which had cost structures significantly lower than American's and could therefore operate profitably at lower fare levels. On international routes, American competed with state-owned carriers, foreign investor-owned carriers, international cargo service providers, and U.S. airlines that had been granted authority to provide international passenger service.[12]

American touted several sources of competitive advantage. First, its fleet of aircraft, one of the youngest in the United States, was efficient and quiet. Second, in 2000, the company began aggressively deploying its American Eagle regional jet fleet. Third, by operating a comprehensive domestic and international route network anchored by efficient hubs, the company expected to be able to benefit from whatever traffic growth occurred. The firm's chairman, Donald Carty, reported in his 2000 *Letter to Shareholders* that American would continue to expand its domestic and international network in Boston, New York, Los Angeles, San Jose, Paris, and Taipei. Finally, through its AAdvantage frequent flyer program, the largest in the industry, its More Room Throughout Coach program, and its continuing efforts to provide superior service, American sought to enhance its position in the industry.

During 2000, American's revenues increased by 11%. Net income for the year declined by 17%, although profits before special items and discontinued operations rose nearly 19%.[13] Despite 4% revenue growth for the three months ended March 31, 2001, American reported a net loss from continuing operations of $43 million, versus a net gain of $89 million in the same quarter for 2000.[14] These results primarily reflected an increase in fares, offset by higher fuel costs. To mitigate the financial impact of the downturn in air travel in mid-2001, American retired older aircraft, cancelled options to purchase new jets, imposed a management hiring freeze, and deferred spending on capital projects. Despite these changes, analysts predicted that American would show a loss for 2001.[15] For 2002, analysts expected that American would show revenue growth of 8% and return to profitability, with an expected return on equity of 8.5%.[16]

Delta Air Lines

Delta Air Lines ("Delta") was founded as the world's first crop-dusting service in 1924 (then named Huff Daland Dusters). In 1928, the company began to diversify by securing airmail contracts, and in 1929 inaugurated passenger service between Dallas and Jackson, Mississippi. Following World War II and throughout the 1950s and 1960s, Delta prospered as a major regional airline. During the 1970s and 1980s, the company expanded its domestic network, largely by acquiring other regional carriers (including Northeast Airlines and Western Airlines). In 1991 it made a major push into international markets.

In 2001, Delta operated four hubs located in Atlanta, Cincinnati, Dallas-Fort Worth, and Salt Lake City. The company was the largest U.S. airline in terms of aircraft departures and number of passengers served, and the third largest U.S. airline in terms of

---

[11]As reported in American's 2000 10-K Report, American's revenue mix consisted of 90% passenger service and 10% cargo and other.

[12]AMR Corp., December 31, 2000 10-K Report.

[13]AMR Corp., December 31, 2000 10-K Report.

[14]AMR Corp., March 31, 2001 10-Q Report.

[15]Thompson Financial, FirstCall estimates.

[16]Stephen Sanborn, AMR Corp., *Value Line Investment Survey*, June 15, 2001.

operating revenues.[17] Including its wholly owned regional subsidiaries Atlantic Southeast Airlines, Inc. and ComAir, Inc., Delta serviced 201 U.S. cities in 45 states, the District of Columbia, the U.S. Virgin Islands, and Puerto Rico, as well as 50 cities in 32 countries in Europe, Asia, Latin America, the Caribbean and Canada.[18] The company also operated a cargo service.[19]

Delta's services included the Delta Shuttle, Delta Express, the Delta Connection Program, and its international alliances. The Delta Shuttle was a high-frequency service providing hourly nonstop service between New York's La Guardia Airport and both Washington, D.C.'s Ronald Reagan National Airport and Boston's Logan International Airport. Delta Express was a low-fare, leisure-oriented service providing flights from select cities in the Northeast and Midwest to five destinations in Florida. The Delta Connection Program was Delta's regional carrier serving passengers in small and medium-sized cities. Finally, the company's international alliance agreements included code-sharing, frequent flyer benefits, shared or reciprocal access to passenger lounges, joint advertising, and other marketing arrangements with Aeromexico, Aeropostal, Air France, Air Jamaica, CSA Czech Airlines, Korean Air, China Southern, Royal Air Maroc, South African Airways, and Transbrasil.

Despite its prominent industry rankings, Delta sustained several years of heavy losses in the early 1990s, and in 1994 announced a drastic cost-cutting plan dubbed the Leadership 7.5 program.[20] The restructuring initiative, which included a 20% reduction in the company's workforce, a realignment of its domestic route system, and the discontinuation of less profitable European routes, was designed to eliminate $2 billion in operating expenses over a three-year period, and to reduce the cost of flying to 7.5 cents per mile, per seat. Though the company was successful in engineering a quick financial comeback, posting a profit in the fourth quarter of fiscal 1995, the accompanying reduction in the company's customer service team resulted in a significant increase in passenger complaints, and by 1997, Delta dropped to last place in on-time rankings among the ten leading U.S. airlines.[21]

In 2000, Delta also struggled with a number of labor issues. In May, its pilots' contract expired and was followed by months of unproductive negotiations. When the impasse dragged into December, the pilots retaliated by refusing voluntary overtime during one of the airline's busiest seasons, forcing Delta to cancel 3,500 flights over the course of the month and an additional 1,700 flights during the first ten days of 2001.[22] Although Delta reached an agreement with its mainline pilots in April 2001, granting them substantial pay raises, it continued to be negatively impacted by the ComAir pilots' strike announced on March 26, 2001. ComAir was the second largest regional airline in the United States, and some analysts believed that the outcome of these negotiations would be an "industry-defining event . . . likely to affect regional pilot pay scales throughout the industry."[23] By mid-June of 2001, the dispute remained unresolved and was estimated to be costing Delta $3–4 million per day in lost revenues.

During 2000, Delta's revenues increased 12%, yet profits fell by 31%. Excluding extraordinary items and discontinued operations, profits fell 25%.[24] In an effort to improve the bottom line, Delta reduced advertising costs, retired aircraft, released employees,

---

[17]Rankings are based on calendar year-end data. Delta Air Lines, 2000 10-K Report.

[18]Delta acquired Atlantic Southeast Airlines and ComAir in 1999.

[19]In 2000, cargo and other revenues accounted for 6% of total revenues; passenger revenues represented the remaining 94%.

[20]Delta Air Lines Inc., June 30, 1994 Annual Report.

[21]For additional background information, see Thomas Derdack, *The International Directory of Company Histories*, vol. 39 (St. James Press).

[22]Thomas Derdack, *The International Directory of Company Histories*, vol. 39.

[23]Caglar Somek, Delta Air Lines, Credit Suisse First Boston, May 22, 2001.

[24]Delta Air Lines Inc., June 30, 2000 Annual Report.

and implemented a new management structure. The company's Chairman and CEO, Leo F. Mullin, also announced the industry's largest regional jet order ever, designed to "cement [Delta's] competitive advantage in this important market."[25]

Analysts predicted that the current difficult economic climate and the accompanying slowing in demand for air transport would result in a net loss for Delta for 2001, followed by a moderate rebound in 2002. Consensus forecasts called for an 8% return on equity in 2002, growing to 13% between 2004 and 2006.[26]

SkyWest Airlines

In 1972, attorney J. Ralph Atkin founded SkyWest Airlines (then named "Inter American Aviation, Inc.") so that he and four friends could own a plane for fun. That same year, Atkin decided to offer commercial flights. Since then, SkyWest Airlines ("SkyWest"), the principal operating subsidiary of SkyWest Inc., had grown to become one of the larger regional airlines in the United States. The company operated a fleet of 108 aircraft from six hubs located in Los Angeles, Salt Lake City, San Francisco, Portland, and Seattle/Tacoma. It offered passenger and airfreight service with over 1,000 daily departures to 68 destinations in 14 western states and Canada.

Nearly 70% of SkyWest flights were jointly coded with Delta Air Lines and United Airlines flights under long-term revenue code-sharing relationships.[27] Under the terms of these relationships, on SkyWest-controlled flights, SkyWest oversaw scheduling, ticketing, pricing, and seat inventories, and received a prorated portion of passenger fares. On contract routes, where SkyWest's major airline partner handled these functions, SkyWest received negotiated payments per flight departure and incentives based on passenger volumes and levels of customer satisfaction.[28] SkyWest first became a code-sharing partner with Delta Air Lines in Salt Lake City in 1987, and teamed up with United Airlines in Los Angeles in 1997.

SkyWest management attributed the carrier's success in securing these contracts to its delivery of high-quality customer service and argued that these relationships provided important benefits for SkyWest. First, they enabled the carrier to "reduce reliance on any single major airline [designator] code and to enhance and stabilize operating results through a mixture of SkyWest-controlled flying and contract flying."[29] They also provided SkyWest with opportunities to grow the airline. Based on its existing Delta Connection and United Express code-sharing contracts, which were to be in place until 2008 and 2010, SkyWest had committed to acquire an additional 113 regional jets with options on another 119 aircraft. However, this commitment was not without risk, since both Delta and United could terminate the code-sharing arrangements "for any or no reason" with 180 days advance notice.[30]

SkyWest primarily competed with other regional airlines, some of which were owned by or were operated as code-sharing partners of major airlines. On certain routes, SkyWest also competed with low-fare carriers and other major airlines. While SkyWest's joint affiliation with Delta and United distinguished it from the majority of its competitors, so, too, did the carrier's strong relationship with its wholly non-unionized workforce.

[25]Delta Air Lines Inc., June 30, 2000 Annual Report.

[26]Damon Churchwell, Delta Air Lines, *Value Line Investment Survey*, June 15, 2001.

[27]SkyWest operated as the Delta Connection in Salt Lake City and as United Express in Los Angeles, San Francisco, Denver, and the Pacific Northwest. SkyWest's contract business was nearly evenly distributed between United Airlines (55%) and Delta Air Lines (45%). (Caglar Somek, Delta Air Lines, Credit Suisse First Boston, May 22, 2001.)

[28]SkyWest Inc., March 31, 2001 10-K Report.

[29]SkyWest Inc., March 31, 2001 Annual Report.

[30]SkyWest Inc., March 31, 2000 Annual Report.

For the year ended March 31, 2001, SkyWest reported that revenues grew 12%, versus 22% in 2000. Profits were flat due to a nearly 17% increase in operating expenses, primarily from increased fuel costs and, to a lesser extent, from increased salaries and wages as the airline continued to add personnel.[31] Despite the slowdown in revenue growth, analysts forecasted that SkyWest's sales would grow at a compound annual growth rate of more than 30% between 2002 and 2003, while earnings were forecasted to grow 32% in 2002 and 22% in 2003. Based on these forecasts, the company was expected to generate a return on equity of nearly 23% in 2002 and 2003.[32]

Southwest Airlines

Founded in 1971 with three Boeing 737 aircraft serving just three destinations in Texas, Southwest Airlines ("Southwest") rapidly grew to become a major domestic airline. Based on data for the second quarter of 2001, Southwest operated 344 aircraft, provided scheduled service to 57 destinations in 29 states, and was the largest U.S. airline based on domestic departures and the fourth largest based on number of domestic passengers served.[33]

Southwest had achieved its rapid growth by positioning itself as a cost leader in the industry. To accomplish this position, Southwest offered its customers "no-frills" service at a low price. It had elected not to develop the costly hub-and-spoke networks used by United, American, Delta, and the other major domestic carriers. Instead, the company provided frequent flights to conveniently located, but typically less congested, satellite airports such as Dallas Love Field, Chicago Midway, and T.F. Green in Providence, Rhode Island. In so doing, Southwest was able to develop a record for reliable on-time performance and achieved high asset utilization. High asset utilization and tight control over operating expenses were maintained through the operation of a single type of aircraft, the Boeing 737, which simplified scheduling, maintenance, flight operations, and training activities. As a result of these and other activities, Southwest reduced the amount of time an aircraft sat idle at a gate to approximately 25 minutes (less than half of the industry average), which reduced the number of aircraft and gate facilities that would otherwise be required.

There were other notable differences between Southwest and other major U.S. carriers. For example, Southwest did not enter into code-sharing relationships with other airlines, nor did it maintain any commuter feeder relationships. Southwest also eschewed both a ticket reservation system (to avoid paying fees to travel agents), and the commonly used multi-tier pricing strategy, in favor of a simple fare structure that featured low, unrestricted, unlimited, everyday coach fares. Being majority-owned by its employees, Southwest had enjoyed strong relationships with its predominantly non-unionized work force, yielding further cost savings and labor flexibility. Finally, Southwest's frequent flyer program also differed from those of the other major airlines, with travel awards based on the number of trips taken, rather than on the number of miles accrued. All told, management estimated that the company's strategy resulted in its providing approximately 90% of all low-fare airline service in the United States.[34]

Fiscal 2000 was Southwest's twenty-second consecutive year of profitability and ninth consecutive year of increased profits. During 2000, Southwest's revenues and profits increased by 19% and 27%, respectively, and the company earned a 22% return on equity.[35] For the three months ended March 31, 2001, revenues and profits increased

[31]SkyWest Inc., March 31, 2001 10-K Report.

[32]Thompson Financial FirstCall and casewriter estimates.

[33]Southwest Airlines Co., December 31, 2000 10-K Report.

[34]Southwest Airlines Co., December 31, 2000 Annual Report.

[35]Southwest Airlines Co., December 31, 2000 Annual Report.

12 Valuation ratios in the airline industry

15% and 25%, respectively, compared to the same quarter one year earlier.[36] 2001 and 2002 consensus forecasts for revenue and earnings growth were 11% and 19%, and 12% and 24%, respectively. Based on these estimates, analysts predicted a ROE of 17% in 2001 and 17.5% in 2002.[37]

Questions

1 Match the valuation multiples below with each of the four airlines discussed in the case. What is your reasoning for the matches you selected?

VALUATION MULTIPLES[38]

Airline	Price/Earnings	Price/Book Value
A	7.5	0.8
B	6.8	1.2
C	16.8	3.1
D	26.8	4.9

2 What is the general relationship between a company's strategy, its current performance, and price-to-book and price-to-earnings ratios?

[36]Southwest Airlines Co., March 31, 2001 10-Q Report.

[37]Thorpe, Warren, Southwest Airlines, *Value Line Investment Survey*, June 15, 2001.

[38]The ratios were calculated using fiscal 2000 year-end figures. (Source: Case writer estimates.)

EXHIBIT 1 Comparison of financial performance for American Airlines, Delta Airlines, Skywest Airlines, and Southwest Airlines

American Airlines	2000	1999	1998	1997	1996
Net operating profit margin	0.05	0.07	0.08	0.06	0.07
Net operating asset turnover	1.74	1.96	2.34	2.03	2.16
Operating ROA = product of above	0.09	0.13	0.18	0.13	0.16
Spread	0.05	0.05	0.11	0.08	0.10
Net financial leverage	0.65	0.35	0.32	0.58	1.16
Financial leverage gain	0.03	0.02	0.03	0.05	0.12
ROE = Operating ROA + Financial leverage gain	0.12	0.15	0.21	0.17	0.27
5-year compound annual growth rates (CAGR):					
Revenues	3.1				
Assets	6.0				
Equity	14.6				
Beta	1.16				

Delta Air Lines	2000	1999	1998	1997	1996
Net operating profit margin	0.06	0.09	0.08	0.07	0.02
Net operating asset turnover	2.25	3.33	3.46	4.12	4.30
Operating ROA = product of above	0.13	0.29	0.26	0.29	0.09
Spread	0.07	0.01	0.19	0.15	−0.01
Net financial leverage	0.51	0.07	0.29	0.23	0.59
Financial leverage gain	0.04	0.00	0.06	0.03	−0.01
ROE = Operating ROA + Financial leverage gain	0.17	0.29	0.32	0.32	0.09
5-year compound annual growth rates (CAGR):					
Revenues	6.1				
Assets	12.4				
Equity	18.3				
Beta	0.76				

SkyWest Airlines	2000	1999	1998	1997	1996
Net operating profit margin	0.09	0.11	0.11	0.08	0.04
Net operating asset turnover	2.64	2.88	3.75	2.18	1.87
Operating ROA = product of above	0.24	0.32	0.40	0.18	0.07
Spread	0.16	0.28	0.39	0.17	0.09
Net financial leverage	−0.35	−0.35	−0.51	−0.02	0.14
Financial leverage gain	−0.06	−0.10	−0.20	0.00	0.01
ROE = Operating ROA + Financial leverage gain	0.18	0.22	0.20	0.18	0.08
5-year compound annual growth rates (CAGR):					
Revenues	16.1				
Assets	20.1				
Equity	17.2				
Beta	0.70				

Southwest Airlines	2000	1999	1998	1997	1996
Net operating profit margin	0.11	0.10	0.11	0.09	0.07
Net operating asset turnover	1.71	1.78	1.95	2.21	1.91
Operating ROA = product of above	0.19	0.19	0.21	0.19	0.13
Spread	0.15	0.12	0.09	−0.01	0.07
Net financial leverage	0.16	0.11	0.06	0.05	0.25
Financial leverage gain	0.02	0.01	0.01	0.00	0.02
ROE = Operating ROA + Financial leverage gain	0.21	0.20	0.22	0.19	0.15
5-year growth rates (CAGR):					
Revenues	14.5				
Assets	15.4				
Equity	18.5				
Beta	0.72				

Source: OneSource, Dow Jones Interactive, and case writer estimates, August 1, 2001.

12 Valuation ratios in the airline industry

EXHIBIT 2   Definitions of ratios and corresponding accounting items

Definition of Ratios

Ratio	Definition
Net operating profit margin	Net operating profit after taxes (NOPAT) / Sales
Net operating asset turnover	Sales / Net assets
Operating ROA	Net operating profit margin × Net operating asset turnover
Net financial leverage	Net debt / Equity
Spread	Operating ROA − Effective interest rate after tax
Financial leverage gain	Spread × Net financial leverage
ROE	Operating ROA + Spread × Net financial leverage

Source: From *Business Analysis and Valuation: Using Financial Statements, Text and Cases*, 2nd edition, by Krishna Palepu and Paul Healy © 2000, p. 9–5. Reprinted with permission of South-Western, a division of Thomson Learning, www.thomsonrights .com, fax 800-730-2215.

Definitions of Accounting Items used in Ratio Analysis

Item	Definition
Net interest expense after tax	(Interest expense − Interest income) × (1 − Tax rate)
Net operating profit after taxes (NOPAT)	Net income + Net interest expense after tax
Operating working capital	(Current assets − Cash and marketable securities) − (Current liabilities − Short-term debt and current portion of long-term debt)
Net long-term assets	Total long-term assets − Non-interest-bearing long-term liabilities
Net debt	Total interest bearing liabilities − Cash and marketable securities
Net assets	Operating working capital + Net long-term assets
Net capital	Net debt + Shareholders' equity

INDEX

AUTHOR INDEX